MANAGERIAL
ECONOMICS

What Went Right/What Went Wrong: Big Box U.S. Retailers in China 200

What Went Right/What Went Wrong: GM, Toyota, and the Celica GT-S Coupe 203

Example: Big Mac Index of Purchasing Power Parity 204

Example: Are Dirty Dishes Mobile? Dixan, Joy, Dawn, and Generic Patti Scala from Scala S.p.A. 206

Example: President Bush's 2002 Steel Tariffs and President Obama's 2009 Tire Tariffs: Justified Sanctions or Hypocritical Protectionism? 214

Example: Intel's Chip Market Access Improves in Japan 216

Example: Microsoft and Apple: A Role for Protective Tariffs? 217

Example: If Europe, What about One Currency for NAFTA? 220

Example: Household Iron Manufacturer in Mexico Becomes Major Engine Block Supplier to Detroit: Cifunsa SA 221

Example: EU Ban on Some Parallel Imports Pleases European but Not U.S. and Japanese Manufacturers 223

What Went Right/What Went Wrong: Ford Motor Co. and Exide Batteries: Are Country Managers Here to Stay? 224

Case Exercise: Predicting the Long-Term Trends in Value of the U.S. Dollar and the Euro 229

Case Exercise: Elaborate the Debate on NAFTA 229

Appendix 6A: Foreign Exchange Risk Management 230

Example: Internal Hedge from BMW Operations on I-85 in South Carolina 230

Toyota and Honda Buy U.S. Assembly Capacity 231

Example: Cummins Engine Goes Short 231

PART III: PRODUCTION AND COST 233

Chapter 7: Production Economics 234

Managerial Challenge: Green Power Initiatives Examined: What Went Wrong in California's Deregulation of Electricity? 234

Example: An Illustrative Production Function: Deep Creek Mining Company 237

What Went Right/What Went Wrong: Factory Bottlenecks at a Boeing Assembly Plant 241

Example: Increasing Returns at Sony Blu-ray and Microsoft Windows 242

Example: Three Stages of Production on the Malibu Assembly Line 245

Example: Just What Exactly Is a Refinery, and Why Won't Anyone Build One? 249

Example: Isocost Determination: Deep Creek Mining Company 253

Example: Cost Minimization: Deep Creek Mining Company 256

Example: GM's A-Frame Supplier Achieves 99.998 Percent Technical Efficiency 258

Example: Technical and Allocative Efficiency in Commercial Banks at BB&T 259

Example: Moneyball: A Production Function for Major League Baseball 262

Case Exercise: The Production Function for Wilson Company 268

Appendix 7A: Production Economics of Renewable and Exhaustible Natural Resources, Advanced Material 270

Example: Oyster Seedbed Replenishment on Chesapeake Bay 273

Example: Saudi Arabian Oil Minister Plays a Waiting Game 276

Chapter 8: Cost Analysis 280

Managerial Challenge: Can a Leaner General Motors Compete Effectively? 280

Example: Opportunity Costs at Bentley Clothing Store 283

Example: Inventory Valuation at Westside Plumbing and Heating 284

Example: Short-Run Cost Functions: Deep Creek Mining Company 286

Example: The Average Cost per Kilowatt-Hour in Underutilized Power Plants 292

Example: Mass Customization and the Learning Curve 293

Example: Percentage of Learning: Emerson Corporation 294

Example: IBM and Intel Fabricate Monster Silicon Wafers 295

Example: Refuse Collection and Disposal in Orange County 295

Example: Flexibility and Operating Efficiency: Ford Motor Company's Flat Rock Plant 296

How Japanese Companies Deal with the Problems of Size 297

Example: Aluminum-Intensive Vehicle Lowers the MES at Ford 298

Case Exercise: Cost Analysis of Patio Furniture 302

Case Exercise: Profit Margins on the Amazon Kindle 304

Chapter 9: Applications of Cost Theory 305

Managerial Challenge: How Exactly Have Computerization and Information Technology Lowered Costs at Chevron, Timken, and Merck? 305

What Went Right/What Went Wrong: Boeing: The Rising Marginal Cost of Wide-Bodies 309

Example: Short-Run Cost Function for Multi-Product Food Processing 310

Example: Short Run Cost Functions: Electricity Generation 310

Example: Long-Run Cost Functions: Electricity Generation 312

Example: Scale Economies in the Satellite and Traditional Cable TV Industry: Dish Network and Time-Warner 313

Example: Economies of Scope in the Banking Industry 315

Example: Boeing 777 Exceeds Break-Even Sales Volume 317

Example: Break-Even Analysis: Allegan Manufacturing Company 320

Example: Fixed Costs and Production Capacity at General Motors 320

Example: Taco Bell Chihuahua Drives Sales 322

Example: Operating Leverage: Allegan Manufacturing Company 324

Case Exercise: Cost Functions 327

Case Exercise: Charter Airline Operating Decisions 328

PART IV: PRICING AND OUTPUT DECISIONS: STRATEGY AND TACTICS 331

Chapter 10: Prices, Output, and Strategy: Pure and Monopolistic Competition 332

Managerial Challenge: Resurrecting Apple in the Tablet World 332

What Went Right/What Went Wrong: Xerox 335

Example: Rawlings Sporting Goods Waves Off the Swoosh Sign 336

Example: Think Small to Grow Big: Southwest Airlines 337

Example: The E-Commerce of Lunch at 7-Elevens in Japan 338

Example: What Went Right What Went Wrong at Fuji and Kodak? 339

Example: The Relevant Market for Web Browsers: Microsoft's Internet Explorer 342

Example: Potential Entry at Office Depot/Staples 343

Example: Eli Lilly Poses a Threat of Potential Entry for AstraZeneca 343

Example: Objective versus Perceived Product Differentiation: Xerox 344

MANAGERIAL
ECONOMICS
APPLICATIONS, STRATEGY, and TACTICS

13e

JAMES R. McGUIGAN
JRM Investments

R. CHARLES MOYER
University of Louisville

FREDERICK H. deB. HARRIS
School of Business
Wake Forest University

CENGAGE
Learning

Australia • Brazil • Mexico • Singapore • United Kingdom • United States

Managerial Economics: Applications, Strategy, and Tactics, 13th Edition
James R. McGuigan, R. Charles Moyer, and Frederick H. deB. Harris

Senior Vice President, LRS/Acquisitions & Solutions Planning: Jack W. Calhoun

Editorial Director, Business & Economics: Erin Joyner

Editor-in-Chief: Joe Sabatino

Senior Acquisition Editor: Steven Scoble

Developmental Editor: Ted Knight

Editorial Assistant: Elizabeth Beiting-Lipps

Brand Manager: Robin Lefevre

Brand Management Director: Jason Sakos

Marketing Development Manager: John Carey

Marketing Development Director: Lisa Lysne

Art and Cover Direction, Production Management, and Composition: PreMediaGlobal

Media Editor: Anita Verma

Rights Acquisition Director: Audrey Pettengill

Rights Acquisition Specialist, Text and Image: John Hill

Senior Manufacturing Planner: Kevin Kluck

Cover Image(s):

Airplane: © iStockphoto/Maciej Noskowski

GEnx Jet Engine (Turbofan): © Olga Besnard/Shutterstock.com

Equipment, Cables and Piping as Found Inside of Industrial Power Plant: © nostal6ie/Shutterstock

New Gas Pipelines: © CDuschinger/Shutterstock

Three Legged Oil and Gas Production Platform: © James Jones Jr/Shutterstock.com

Oil Rig: © Dariush M./Shutterstock.com

Car Production Line: © iStockphoto/Rainer Plendl

Lexus ES300h Hybrid: © Ritu Manoj Jethani/Shutterstock.com

Internal Image(s):

Part Opener: © Nostal6ie/Shutterstock.com

Chapter Opener: © CDuschinger/Shutterstock.com

2 Abstract Backgrounds with Arrows: © Anastasiya Zalevska/Shutterstock.com

Cover Design with Copy Space: © Vladfoto/Shutterstock.com

Recycled and Reflective Icon: © Russelltatedotcom/iStockphotos.com

For product information and technology assistance, contact us at **Cengage Learning Customer & Sales Support, 1-800-354-9706.**

For permission to use material from this text or product, submit all requests online at **www.cengage.com/permissions**
Further permissions questions can be emailed to **permissionrequest@cengage.com**

Library of Congress Control Number: 2013935706

ISBN-13: 978-1-285-42092-9

ISBN-10: 1-285-42092-6

Cengage Learning
200 First Stamford Place, 4th Floor
Stamford, CT 06902
USA

Cengage Learning is a leading provider of customized learning solutions with office locations around the globe, including Singapore, the United Kingdom, Australia, Mexico, Brazil, and Japan. Locate your local office at: **www.cengage.com/global**

Cengage Learning products are represented in Canada by Nelson Education, Ltd.

To learn more about Cengage Learning Solutions, visit **www.cengage.com**

Purchase any of our products at your local college store or at our preferred online store **www.cengagebrain.com**

Printed in the United States of America
1 2 3 4 5 6 7 17 16 15 14 13

To my family
J.R.M.

To Sally, Laura, and Craig
R.C.M.

To my family and Ken Elzinga
F.H.B.II.

Brief
Table of Contents

Preface xix
About the Authors xxiii

PART I

INTRODUCTION 1

1 Introduction and Goals of the Firm 2
2 Fundamental Economic Concepts 28

PART ii

DEMAND AND FORECASTING 63

3 Demand Analysis 64
4 Estimating Demand 99
4A Problems in Applying the Linear Regression Model 127
5 Business and Economic Forecasting 139
6 Managing in the Global Economy 176
6A Foreign Exchange Risk Management 230

PART III

PRODUCTION AND COST 233

7 Production Economics 234
7A Production Economics of Renewable and Exhaustible Natural Resources, Advanced Material 270
8 Cost Analysis 280
9 Applications of Cost Theory 305

PART IV

PRICING AND OUTPUT DECISIONS: STRATEGY AND TACTICS 331

10 Prices, Output, and Strategy: Pure and Monopolistic Competition 332
11 Price and Output Determination: Monopoly and Dominant Firms 382
12 Price and Output Determination: Oligopoly 409

13 Best-Practice Tactics: Game Theory 444
13A Entry Deterrence and Accommodation Games 489
14 Pricing Techniques and Analysis 500
14A The Practice of Revenue Management 535

PART V

ORGANIZATIONAL ARCHITECTURE AND REGULATION 547

15 Contracting, Governance, and Organizational Form 548
15A Auction Design and Information Economics 583
16 Government Regulation 611
17 Long-Term Investment Analysis 648

APPENDICES

A The Time Value of Money A-1
B Differential Calculus Techniques in Management B-1
C Tables C-1
D Check Answers to Selected End-of-Chapter Exercises D-1
  Glossary G-1
  Index I-1
  Notes

WEB APPENDICES

A Consumer Choice Using Indifference Curve Analysis
B International Parity Conditions
C Linear-Programming Applications
D Capacity Planning and Pricing against a Low-Cost Competitor: A Case Study of Piedmont Airlines and People Express
E Pricing of Joint Products and Transfer Pricing
F Decisions under Risk and Uncertainty
G Maximization of Production Output Subject to a Cost Constraint, Advanced Material
H Long-Run Costs with a Cobb-Douglas Production Function, Advanced Material

Contents

Preface xix
About the Authors xxiii

PART I

INTRODUCTION 1

1 Introduction and Goals of the Firm 2
Chapter Preview 2

**Managerial Challenge: How to Achieve
Sustainability: Southern Company
Electric Power Generation 2**
What Is Managerial Economics? 4
The Decision-Making Model 5
The Responsibilities of Management 5

**What Went Right/What Went Wrong:
Saturn Corporation 6**
Moral Hazard in Teams 6
The Role of Profits 8
Risk-Bearing Theory of Profit 8
Temporary Disequilibrium Theory of Profit 9
Monopoly Theory of Profit 9
Innovation Theory of Profit 9
Managerial Efficiency Theory of Profit 9
Objective of the Firm 9
The Shareholder Wealth-Maximization
Model of the Firm 10
Separation of Ownership and Control:
The Principal-Agent Problem 11
Divergent Objectives and Agency Conflict 11
Agency Problem 13
Implications of Shareholder Wealth
Maximization 15

**What Went Right/What Went Wrong:
Eli Lilly Depressed by Loss of Prozac
Patent 15**
Caveats to Maximizing Shareholder Value 17
Residual Claimants 19
Goals in the Public Sector and Not-for-Profit
Enterprises 19
Not-for-Profit Objectives 20
The Efficiency Objective in Not-for-Profit
Organizations 20

Summary 21
Exercises 22
Case Exercise: Designing a Managerial
Incentives Contract 23
Case Exercise: Shareholder Value of Renewable
Energy from Wind Power at Hydro Co.:
Is RE < C? 24

2 Fundamental Economic Concepts 28
Chapter Preview 28

**Managerial Challenge: Why Charge
$25 per Bag on Airline Flights? 28**
Demand and Supply: A Review 29
The Diamond-Water Paradox and the
Marginal Revolution 31
Marginal Utility and Incremental Cost
Simultaneously Determine Equilibrium
Market Price 32
Individual and Market Demand Curves 33
The Demand Function 34
Import-Export Traded Goods 36
Individual and Market Supply Curves 37
Equilibrium Market Price of Gasoline 38
Marginal Analysis 43
Total, Marginal, and Average Relationships 44
The Net Present Value Concept 48
Determining the Net Present Value of an
Investment 48
Sources of Positive Net Present Value Projects 50
Risk and the NPV Rule 51
Meaning and Measurement of Risk 52
Probability Distributions 52
Expected Values 53
Standard Deviation: An Absolute Measure
of Risk 54
Normal Probability Distribution 54
Coefficient of Variation: A Relative Measure
of Risk 56

**What Went Right/What Went Wrong:
Long-Term Capital Management (LTCM) 56**
Risk and Required Return 57
Summary 59
Exercises 59
Case Exercise: Revenue Management at
American Airlines 61

PART II

DEMAND AND FORECASTING   63

3   Demand Analysis   64
Chapter Preview   64

**Managerial Challenge: Health Care
   Reform and Cigarette Taxes   64**
Demand Relationships   66
   The Demand Schedule Defined   66
   Constrained Utility Maximization and
      Consumer Behavior   67

**What Went Right/What Went Wrong:
   Chevy Volt   71**
The Price Elasticity of Demand   72
   Price Elasticity Defined   73
   Interpreting the Price Elasticity: The Relationship
      between the Price Elasticity and Sales Revenue   76
   The Importance of Elasticity-Revenue
      Relationships   82
   Factors Affecting the Price Elasticity of Demand   84

**International Perspectives: Free Trade
   and the Price Elasticity of Demand:
   Nestlé Yogurt   86**
The Income Elasticity of Demand   87
   Income Elasticity Defined   87
Cross Elasticity of Demand   90
   Cross Price Elasticity Defined   90
   Interpreting the Cross Price Elasticity   90
   Antitrust and Cross Price Elasticities   90
   An Empirical Illustration of Price, Income,
      and Cross Elasticities   92
The Combined Effect of Demand Elasticities   92
   Summary   93
   Exercises   94
   Case Exercise: Polo Golf Shirt Pricing   97

4   Estimating Demand   99
Chapter Preview   99

**Managerial Challenge: Demand for
   Whitman's Chocolate Samplers   99**
Statistical Estimation of the Demand Function   100
   Specification of the Model   101
A Simple Linear Regression Model   103
   Assumptions Underlying the Simple Linear
      Regression Model   104
   Estimating the Population Regression
      Coefficients   105
Using the Regression Equation to Make
   Predictions   108
   Inferences about the Population Regression
      Coefficients   110
   Correlation Coefficient   113

The Analysis of Variance   114
Multiple Linear Regression Model   116
   Use of Computer Programs   116
   Estimating the Population Regression
      Coefficients   116
   Using the Regression Model to Make Forecasts   116
   Inferences about the Population Regression
      Coefficients   117
   The Analysis of Variance   119
   Summary   120
   Exercises   120
   Case Exercise: Soft Drink Demand Estimation   124

**4A   Problems in Applying the Linear
   Regression Model   127**
Introduction   127
   Autocorrelation   127
   Heteroscedasticity   129
   Specification and Measurement Errors   130
   Multicollinearity   131
   Simultaneous Equation Relationships and
      the Identification Problem   131
Nonlinear Regression Models   134
   Semilogarithmic Transformation   134
   Double-Log Transformation   134
   Reciprocal Transformation   135
   Polynomial Transformation   135
   Summary   136
   Exercises   136

5   Business and Economic Forecasting   139
Chapter Preview   139

**Managerial Challenge: Excess Fiber Optic
   Capacity at Global Crossing Inc.   139**
The Significance of Forecasting   141
Selecting a Forecasting Technique   141
   Hierarchy of Forecasts   141
   Criteria Used to Select a Forecasting
      Technique   142
   Evaluating the Accuracy of Forecasting Models   142

**What Went Right/What Went Wrong:
   Crocs Shoes   142**
Alternative Forecasting Techniques   143
Deterministic Trend Analysis   143
   Components of a Time Series   143
   Some Elementary Time-Series Models   144
   Secular Trends   145
   Seasonal Variations   148
Smoothing Techniques   150
   Moving Averages   151
   First-Order Exponential Smoothing   153
Barometric Techniques   156
   Leading, Lagging, and Coincident Indicators   156
Survey and Opinion-Polling Techniques   157
   Forecasting Macroeconomic Activity   158

Sales Forecasting 159
Econometric Models 159
Advantages of Econometric Forecasting
Techniques 159
Single-Equation Models 159
Multi-Equation Models 161
Consensus Forecasts: Livingston and
Blue Chip Forecaster Surveys 162
Stochastic Time-Series Analysis 163
Forecasting with Input-Output Tables 166

**International Perspectives: Long-Term
Sales Forecasting by General Motors
in Overseas Markets** **166**
Summary 167
Exercises 167
Case Exercise: Cruise Ship Arrivals in Alaska 171
Case Exercise: Lumber Price Forecast 172
Case Exercise: Forecasting in the Global
Financial Crisis 173

6 **Managing in the Global Economy** **176**
Chapter Preview 176

**Managerial Challenge: Financial Crisis
Slows U.S. Household Consumption
and Crushes Business Investment: Can
Exports to China Provide a Recovery?** **176**
Introduction 179

**What Went Right/What Went Wrong:
Export Market Pricing at Toyota** **180**
Import-Export Sales and Exchange Rates 180
Foreign Exchange Risk 180

**International Perspectives: Collapse
of Export and Domestic Sales
at Cummins Engine** **182**
Outsourcing 184
China Trade Blossoms 186
China Today 188
The Market for U.S. Dollars as Foreign
Exchange 190
Import-Export Flows and Transaction
Demand for a Currency 190
The Equilibrium Price of the U.S. Dollar 192
Speculative Demand, Government Transfers,
and Coordinated Intervention 192
Short-Term Exchange Rate Fluctuations 193
Determinants of Long-Run Trends in
Exchange Rates 193
The Role of Real Growth Rates 194
The Role of Real Interest Rates 196
The Role of Expected Inflation 197
Purchasing Power Parity 198
PPP Offers a Better Yardstick of
Comparative Size of Business Activity 199

**What Went Right/What Went Wrong:
Big Box U.S. Retailers in China** **200**
Relative Purchasing Power Parity 201
Qualifications of PPP 202
The Appropriate Use of PPP: An Overview 202

**What Went Right/What Went Wrong: GM,
Toyota, and the Celica GT-S Coupe** **203**
Trade-Weighted Exchange Rate Index 204
International Trade: A Managerial Perspective 207
Shares of World Trade and Regional Trading
Blocs 207
Comparative Advantage and Free Trade 210
Import Controls and Protective Tariffs 212
The Case for Strategic Trade Policy 214
Increasing Returns 216
Network Externalities 216
Free Trade Areas: The European Union
and NAFTA 217
Optimal Currency Areas 218
Intraregional Trade 219
Mobility of Labor 219
Correlated Macroeconomic Shocks 219
Largest U.S. Trading Partners: The Role
of NAFTA 220
A Comparison of the EU and NAFTA 222
Gray Markets, Knockoffs, and Parallel
Importing 223

**What Went Right/What Went Wrong:
Ford Motor Co. and Exide Batteries:
Are Country Managers Here to Stay?** **224**
Perspectives on the U.S. Trade Deficit 225
Summary 227
Exercises 228
Case Exercise: Predicting the Long-Term
Trends in Value of the U.S. Dollar and
the Euro 229
Case Exercise: Elaborate the Debate on
NAFTA 229

6A **Foreign Exchange Risk Management** **230**

**International Perspectives: Toyota and
Honda Buy U.S. Assembly Capacity** **231**

PART III

PRODUCTION AND COST **233**

7 **Production Economics** **234**
Chapter Preview 234

**Managerial Challenge: Green Power
Initiatives Examined: What Went
Wrong in California's Deregulation
of Electricity?** **234**

The Production Function | 236
Fixed and Variable Inputs | 237
Production Functions with One Variable
Input | 239
Marginal and Average Product Functions | 239
The Law of Diminishing Marginal
Returns | 240

**What Went Right/What Went Wrong:
Factory Bottlenecks at a Boeing
Assembly Plant** | **241**
Increasing Returns with Network Effects | 241
Producing Information Services under
Increasing Returns | 243
The Relationship between Total, Marginal,
and Average Product | 244
Determining the Optimal Use of the
Variable Input | 246
Marginal Revenue Product | 247
Marginal Factor Cost | 247
Optimal Input Level | 247
Production with Multiple Variable Inputs | 248
Production (Output Constant) Isoquants | 248
The Marginal Rate of Technical
Substitution | 250
Determining the Optimal Combination of
Inputs | 252
Isocost Lines | 253
Minimizing Cost Subject to an Output
Constraint | 254
A Fixed Proportions Optimal Production
Process | 255
Production Processes and Process Rays | 256
Measuring the Efficiency of a Production
Process | 257
Returns to Scale | 258
Measuring Returns to Scale | 259
Increasing and Decreasing Returns to Scale | 260
The Cobb-Douglas Production Function | 260
Empirical Studies of the Cobb-Douglas
Production Function in Manufacturing | 261
A Cross-Sectional Analysis of U.S.
Manufacturing Industries | 261
Summary | 264
Exercises | 265
Case Exercise: The Production Function
for Wilson Company | 268

**7A Production Economics of Renewable and
Exhaustible Natural Resources, Advanced
Material** | **270**
Renewable Resources | 270
Exhaustible Natural Resources | 274
Exercises | 279

8 Cost Analysis | **280**
Chapter Preview | 280

**Managerial Challenge: Can a Leaner
General Motors Compete Effectively?** | **280**
The Meaning and Measurement of Cost | 281
Accounting versus Economic Costs | 281
Three Contrasts between Accounting
and Economic Costs | 282
Short-Run Cost and Product Functions | 286
Average and Marginal Cost Functions | 286
Long-Run Cost Functions | 291
Optimal Capacity Utilization: Three
Concepts | 291
Economies and Diseconomies of Scale | 292
The Percentage of Learning | 293
Diseconomies of Scale | 296
The Overall Effects of Scale Economies and
Diseconomies | 296

**International Perspectives: How Japanese
Companies Deal with the Problems
of Size** | **297**
Summary | 299
Exercises | 300
Case Exercise: Cost Analysis of Patio Furniture | 302
Case Exercise: Profit Margins on the
Amazon Kindle | 304

9 Applications of Cost Theory | **305**
Chapter Preview | 305

**Managerial Challenge: How Exactly Have
Computerization and Information
Technology Lowered Costs at Chevron,
Timken, and Merck?** | **305**
Estimating Cost Functions | 306
Issues in Cost Definition and Measurement | 307
Controlling for Other Variables | 307
The Form of the Empirical Cost-Output
Relationship | 308

**What Went Right/What Went Wrong:
Boeing: The Rising Marginal Cost
of Wide-Bodies** | **309**
Statistical Estimation of Short-Run Cost
Functions | 310
Statistical Estimation of Long-Run Cost
Functions | 311
Determining the Optimal Scale of an Operation | 311
Economies of Scale versus Economies of Scope | 314
Engineering Cost Techniques | 314
The Survivor Technique | 316
A Cautionary Tale | 317
Break-Even Analysis | 317
Graphical Method | 318

Algebraic Method   318
Some Limitations of Break-Even Analysis   321
Doing a Break-Even versus a Contribution
    Analysis   321
A Limitation of Contribution Analysis   323
Operating Leverage   323
Inherent Business Risk   325
Summary   325
Exercises   326
Case Exercise: Cost Functions   327
Case Exercise: Charter Airline Operating
    Decisions   328

PART IV

PRICING AND OUTPUT DECISIONS: STRATEGY AND TACTICS   331

**10   Prices, Output, and Strategy: Pure and
      Monopolistic Competition   332**
Chapter Preview   332

**Managerial Challenge: Resurrecting
    Apple in the Tablet World   332**
Introduction   333
Competitive Strategy   334

**What Went Right/What Went Wrong:
    Xerox   335**
Generic Types of Strategies   336
Product Differentiation Strategy   336
Cost-Based Strategy   336
Information Technology Strategy   337
The Relevant Market Concept   339
Porter's Five Forces Strategic Framework   339
The Threat of Substitutes   340
The Threat of Entry   341
The Power of Buyers and Suppliers   344
The Intensity of Rivalrous Tactics   345
The Myth of Market Share   349
A Continuum of Market Structures   349
Pure Competition   350
Monopoly   351
Monopolistic Competition   352
Oligopoly   352
Price-Output Determination under Pure
    Competition   353
Short Run   353
Profit Maximization under Pure Competition
    (Short Run): Adobe Corporation   356
Long Run   357
Price-Output Determination under
    Monopolistic Competition   360

**What Went Right/What Went Wrong:
    The Dynamics of Competition at
    Amazon.com   361**
Short Run   361
Long Run   361
Selling and Promotional Expenses   363
Determining the Optimal Level of Selling
    and Promotional Outlays   364
Optimal Advertising Intensity   365
The Net Value of Advertising   366
Competitive Markets under Asymmetric
    Information   367
Incomplete versus Asymmetric Information   367
Search Goods versus Experience Goods   368
Adverse Selection and the Notorious Firm   368
Insuring and Lending under Asymmetric
    Information: Another Lemons Market   370
Solutions to the Adverse Selection Problem   371
Mutual Reliance: Hostage Mechanisms Support
    Asymmetric Information Exchange   371
Brand-Name Reputations as Hostages   372
Price Premiums with Non-Redeployable Assets   374
Summary   376
Exercises   377
Case Exercise: Netflix and Redbox Compete
    for Movie Rentals   379
Case Exercise: Saving Sony Music   380

**11   Price and Output Determination:
      Monopoly and Dominant Firms   382**
Chapter Preview   382

**Managerial Challenge: Dominant
    Microprocessor Company Intel
    Adapts to Next Trend   382**
Monopoly Defined   383
Sources of Market Power for a Monopolist   383
Increasing Returns from Network Effects   384

**What Went Right/What Went Wrong:
    Pilot Error at Palm   387**
Price and Output Determination for a
    Monopolist   388
Spreadsheet Approach: Profit versus Revenue
    Maximization for Polo Golf Shirts   388
Graphical Approach   389
Algebraic Approach   390
The Importance of the Price Elasticity of
    Demand   391
The Optimal Markup, Contribution Margin,
    and Contribution Margin Percentage   393
Gross Profit Margins   395
Components of the Margin   395
Monopolists and Capacity Investments   396

Limit Pricing 397
Using Limit Pricing to Hamper the Sales
of Generic Drugs 398
Regulated Monopolies 399
Electric Power Companies 400

**What Went Right/What Went Wrong:
The Public Service Company of
New Mexico** 400
Natural Gas Companies 401
The Economic Rationale for Regulation 401
Natural Monopoly Argument 401
Summary 403
Exercises 403
Case Exercise: Differential Pricing of
Pharmaceuticals: The HIV/AIDS Crisis 407

**12 Price and Output Determination:
Oligopoly** 409
Chapter Preview 409

**Managerial Challenge: Google's Android
and Apple's iPhone Displace Nokia in
Smart phones?** 409
Oligopolistic Market Structures 411
Oligopoly in the United States: Relative
Market Shares 411
Interdependencies in Oligopolistic Industries 416
The Cournot Model 416
Cartels and Other Forms of Collusion 418
Factors Affecting the Likelihood of Successful
Collusion 420
Cartel Profit Maximization and the Allocation
of Restricted Output 421

**International Perspectives: The OPEC
Cartel** 423
Cartel Analysis: Algebraic Approach 428
Price Leadership 430
Barometric Price Leadership 430
Dominant Firm Price Leadership 431
The Kinked Demand Curve Model 434
Avoiding Price Wars 435

**What Went Right/What Went Wrong:
Good-Better-Best Product Strategy at
Marriott Corporation and Kodak** 438
Summary 440
Exercises 441
Case Exercise: Web-Based Satellite Phones
Displace Motorola's Mobile Phone 443

13 Best-Practice Tactics: Game Theory 444
Chapter Preview 444

**Managerial Challenge: Large-Scale Entry
Deterrence of Low-Cost Discounters:
Southwest Airline/AirTran** 444

Oligopolistic Rivalry and Game Theory 446

**What Went Right/What Went Wrong:
Nintendo's Wii U** 446
A Conceptual Framework for Game Theory
Analysis 447
Components of a Game 448
Cooperative and Noncooperative Games 450
Other Types of Games 450
Analyzing Simultaneous Games 451
The Prisoner's Dilemma 451
Dominant Strategy and Nash Equilibrium
Strategy Defined 453
The Escape from Prisoner's Dilemma 456
Multiperiod Punishment and Reward
Schemes in Repeated Play Games 456
Unraveling and the Chain Store Paradox 457
Mutual Forbearance and Cooperation in
Repeated Prisoner's Dilemma Games 459
Bayesian Reputation Effects 460
Winning Strategies in Evolutionary Computer
Tournaments: Tit for Tat 460
Price-Matching Guarantees 462
Industry Standards as Coordination
Devices 464
Analyzing Sequential Games 465
A Sequential Coordination Game 466
Subgame Perfect Equilibrium in
Sequential Games 468
Business Rivalry as a Self-Enforcing
Sequential Game 469
First-Mover and Fast-Second Advantages 470
Credible Threats and Commitments 472
Mechanisms for Establishing Credibility 473
Replacement Guarantees 475
Hostages Support the Credibility of
Commitments 476
Credible Commitments of Durable Goods
Monopolists 477
Planned Obsolescence 478
Post-Purchase Discounting Risk 479
Lease Prices Reflect Anticipated Risks 481
Summary 481
Exercises 482
Case Exercise: International Perspectives:
The Superjumbo Dilemma 487

**13A Entry Deterrence and Accommodation
Games** 489
Excess Capacity as a Credible
Threat 489
Precommitments Using Non-Redeployable
Assets 489
Customer Sorting Rules 492
A Role for Sunk Costs in Decision Making 493

Perfectly Contestable Markets   494
Brinkmanship and Wars of Attrition   495
Tactical Insights about Slippery
    Slopes   497
    Summary   498
    Exercises   499

14   Pricing Techniques and Analysis   500
Chapter Preview   500

**Managerial Challenge: Pricing the
    Chevy Volt   500**
A Conceptual Framework for Proactive,
    Systematic-Analytical, Value-Based
    Pricing   501
Optimal Differential Price Levels   504
    Graphical Approach   505
    Algebraic Approach   506
    Multiple-Product Pricing Decision   507
    Differential Pricing and the Price Elasticity
        of Demand   508
Differential Pricing in Target Market
    Segments   513
    Direct Segmentation with "Fences"   514
    Optimal Two-Part Tariffs   516

**What Went Right/What Went Wrong:
    Unlimited Data at Verizon Wireless   516**
Couponing   518

**What Went Right/What Went Wrong:
    Two-Part Pricing at Disney World   518**

**What Went Right/What Went Wrong:
    Price-Sensitive Customers Redeem   519**
Bundling   519
Price Discrimination   522
Pricing in Practice   524
    Product Life Cycle Framework   524
    Full-Cost Pricing versus Incremental
        Contribution Analysis   526
    Pricing on the Internet   528
    Summary   531
    Exercises   532

14A The Practice of Revenue Management   535
A Cross-Functional Systems Management
    Process   536
Sources of Sustainable Price Premiums   538
Revenue Management Decisions, Advanced
    Material   538
    Proactive Price Discrimination   539
    Capacity Reallocation   540
    Optimal Overbooking   543
    Summary   546
    Exercises   546

PART V

**ORGANIZATIONAL ARCHITECTURE
AND REGULATION   547**

**15   Contracting, Governance, and
    Organizational Form   548**
Chapter Preview   548

**Managerial Challenge: Controlling the
    Vertical: Ultimate TV versus
    Google TV   548**
Introduction   549
The Role of Contracting in Cooperative
    Games   549
    Vertical Requirements Contracts   551
    The Function of Commercial Contracts   552
    Incomplete Information, Incomplete Contracting,
        and Post-Contractual Opportunism   555
Corporate Governance and the Problem
    of Moral Hazard   555

**What Went Right/What Went Wrong:
    Forecasting the Great Recession with
    Workouts and Rollovers   557**
    The Need for Governance Mechanisms   558

**What Went Right/What Went Wrong:
    Moral Hazard and Holdup at Enron
    and WorldCom   559**
The Principal-Agent Model   559
    The Efficiency of Alternative Hiring
        Arrangements   559
    Creative Ingenuity and the Moral Hazard
        Problem in Managerial Contracting   561
    Formalizing the Principal-Agent Problem 563
    Screening and Sorting Managerial Talent
        with Optimal Incentives Contracts   564

**What Went Right/What Went Wrong:
    Why Have Restricted Stock Grants
    Replaced Executive Stock Options at
    Microsoft?   565**
Choosing the Efficient Organizational Form   567

**What Went Right/What Went Wrong:
    Cable Allies Refuse to Adopt Microsoft's
    WebTV as an Industry Standard   570**

**International Perspectives: Economies
    of Scale and International Joint
    Ventures in Chip Making   571**
    Prospect Theory Motivates Full-Line Forcing 572
Vertical Integration   574

**What Went Right/What Went Wrong:
    Dell Replaces Vertical Integration
    with Virtual Integration   577**

The Dissolution of Assets in a Partnership 577
Summary 579
Exercises 580
Case Exercise: Borders Books and
    Amazon.com Decide to Do Business
    Together 581
Case Exercise: Designing a Managerial
    Incentive Contract 582
Case Exercise: The Division of Investment
    Banking Fees in a Syndicate 582

**15A Auction Design and Information
        Economics** **583**
Optimal Mechanism Design 583
    Queue Service Rules 583
First-Come, First-Served versus Last-Come,
    First-Served 584
    Stratified Lotteries for Concerts 585
Auctions 586
    Types of Auctions 586
    Winner's Curse in Asymmetric Information
        Bidding Games 587
    Information Revelation in Common-Value
        Auctions 589
    Bayesian Strategy with Open Bidding Design 590
    Strategic Underbidding in Private-Value
        Auctions 592
    Second-Highest Sealed-Bid Auctions:
        A Revelation Mechanism 594
    Revenue Equivalence of Alternative Auction
        Types 596
    Contractual Approaches to Asymmetric
        Information in Online Auctions 598
Incentive-Compatible Revelation
    Mechanisms 600
    Cost Revelation in Joint Ventures and
        Partnerships 600
    Cost Overruns with Simple Profit-Sharing
        Partnerships 601
    Clarke-Groves Incentive-Compatible
        Revelation Mechanism 603
    An Optimal Incentives Contract 603

**International Perspectives: Joint Venture
in Memory Chips: IBM, Siemens, and
Toshiba** **604**
    Implementation of IC Contracts 605

**International Perspectives: Whirlpool's
Joint Venture in Appliances Improves
upon Maytag's Outright Purchase of
Hoover** **606**
    Summary 607
    Exercises 608
    Case Exercise: Spectrum Auction 609
    Case Exercise: Debugging Computer
        Software: Versioning at Intel 610

16 Government Regulation **611**
Chapter Preview 611
**Managerial Challenge: Cap and Trade,
    Deregulation, and the Coase
    Theorem** **611**
The Regulation of Market Structure and
    Conduct 612
    Market Performance 613
    Market Conduct 613
    Contestable Markets 614
Antitrust Statutes and Their Regulatory
    Enforcement 615
    The Sherman Act (1890) 615
    The Clayton Act (1914) 615
    The Robinson-Patman Act (1936) 616
    The Hart-Scott-Rodino Antitrust
        Improvement Act (1976) 617
Antitrust Prohibition of Selected Business
    Decisions 618
    Collusion: Price Fixing 618
    Mergers That Substantially Lessen
        Competition 620
    Merger Guidelines (2010) 621
    Monopolization 621
    Wholesale Price Discrimination 623
    Refusals to Deal 624
    Resale Price Maintenance Agreements 624
Command and Control Regulatory
    Constraints: An Economic Analysis 625
    The Deregulation Movement 627
**What Went Right/What Went Wrong:
    The Need for a Regulated
    Clearinghouse to Control Counterparty
    Risk at AIG** **627**
Regulation of Externalities 628
    Coasian Bargaining for Reciprocal
        Externalities 629
    Qualifications of the Coase Theorem 630
    Impediments to Bargaining 631
    Resolution of Externalities by Regulatory
        Directive 632
    Resolution of Externalities by Taxes and
        Subsidies 633
    Resolution of Externalities by Sale of Pollution
        Rights: Cap and Trade 635
Governmental Protection of Business 635
    Licensing and Permitting 635
    Patents 636
The Optimal Deployment Decision:
    To License or Not 636
    Pros and Cons of Patent Protection and
        Licensure of Trade Secrets 637
**What Went Right/What Went Wrong:
    Delayed Release at Aventis** **638**

What Went Right/What Went Wrong: Technology Licenses Cost Palm Its Lead in PDAs   **640**

What Went Right/What Went Wrong: Motorola: What They Didn't Know Hurt Them   **641**
Conclusion on Licensing   641
Summary   642
Exercises   643
Case Exercise: Do Luxury Good Manufacturers Have a Legitimate Interest in Minimum Resale Price Maintenance: *Leegin v. Kay's Kloset*?   645
Case Exercise: Microsoft Tying Arrangements   646
Case Exercise: Music Recording Industry Blocked from Consolidating   647

17 Long-Term Investment Analysis   **648**
Chapter Preview   648

Managerial Challenge: Industrial Renaissance in America: Insourcing of GE Appliances   **648**
The Nature of Capital Expenditure Decisions   649
A Basic Framework for Capital Budgeting   650
The Capital Budgeting Process   650
Generating Capital Investment Projects   651
Estimating Cash Flows   651
Evaluating and Choosing the Investment Projects to Implement   653
Estimating the Firm's Cost of Capital   656
Cost of Debt Capital   657
Cost of Internal Equity Capital   657
Cost of External Equity Capital   659
Weighted Cost of Capital   659
Cost-Benefit Analysis   660
Accept-Reject Decisions   661
Program-Level Analysis   662
Steps in Cost-Benefit Analysis   662
Objectives and Constraints in Cost-Benefit Analysis   664

Analysis and Valuation of Benefits and Costs   665
Direct Benefits   665
Direct Costs   665
Indirect Costs or Benefits and Intangibles   665
The Appropriate Rate of Discount   666
Cost-Effectiveness Analysis   667
Least-Cost Studies   667
Objective-Level Studies   668
Summary   668
Exercises   669
Case Exercise: Industrial Development Tax Relief and Incentives   672
Case Exercise: Multigenerational Effects of Ozone Depletion and Greenhouse Gases   673

APPENDICES

A   The Time Value of Money   A-1
B   Differential Calculus Techniques in Management   B-1
C   Tables   C-1
D   Check Answers to Selected End-of-Chapter Exercises   D-1
Glossary   G-1
Index   I-1
Notes

WEB APPENDICES

A   Consumer Choice Using Indifference Curve Analysis
B   International Parity Conditions
C   Linear-Programming Applications
D   Capacity Planning and Pricing against a Low-Cost Competitor: A Case Study of Piedmont Airlines and People Express
E   Pricing of Joint Products and Transfer Pricing Decisions under Risk and Uncertainty
F   Decisions under Risk and Uncertainty
G   Maximization of Production Output Subject to a Cost Constraint, Advanced Material
H   Long-Run Costs with a Cobb-Douglas Production Function, Advanced Material

Preface

ORGANIZATION OF THE TEXT

The 13th edition has been thoroughly updated with 45 new applications and dozens of new figures and tables. Responding to user request, we continue to expand the review of microeconomic fundamentals in Chapter 2, employing a wide-ranging discussion of the equilibrium price of crude oil and gasoline as well as the marginal analysis of long-lasting lightbulbs and driving a Mini-Cooper. A wind vane symbol highlights discussion of environmental effects and sustainability spread throughout the text. Another special feature is the extensive treatment in Chapter 6 of managing global businesses, import-export trade, exchange rates, currency unions and free trade areas, trade policy, and an expanded new section on China.

Several major new analyses appear in the 13th edition (and the chapter in which they appear): moral hazard in teams (1), demand for a branded candy product (4), forecasting in the global financial crisis (5), geographic distribution of value-added for an iPad (6), GM's cost structure post-bailout (8), $80 operating loss on flat screen TVs (10), Chrome takes share (12), pricing the Chevy Volt and ebook pricing (14), luxury goods and RPMs (16), and insourcing of appliance manufacturing at GE (17).

There is more comprehensive material on applied game theory in Chapters 13, 13A, 15, 15A, and Web Appendix D than in any other managerial economics textbook, and a unique treatment of revenue (yield) management appears in Chapter 14A. Part V includes the hot topics of corporate governance, information economics, auction design, and the choice of organizational form. Chapter 16 on economic regulation includes a broad discussion of cap and trade policy, pollution taxes, and the optimal abatement of externalities. Chapter 17 now leads off with a capital budgeting decision by GE to return appliance manufacturing to the United States.

By far the most distinctive feature of the book is its 300 boxed examples, Managerial Challenges, What Went Right/What Went Wrong explorations of corporate practice, and mini-case examples on every other page demonstrating what each analytical concept is used for in practice. This list of concept applications is highlighted on the inside front and back covers.

STUDENT PREPARATION

The text is designed for use by upper-level undergraduates and first-year graduate students in business schools, departments of economics, and professional schools of management, public policy, and information science as well as in executive training programs. Students are presumed to have a background in the basic principles of microeconomics, although Chapter 2 offers an extensive review of those topics. No prior work in statistics is assumed; development of all the quantitative concepts employed is self-contained. The book makes occasional use of elementary concepts of differential calculus. In all cases where calculus is employed, at least one alternative approach, such as graphical, algebraic, or tabular analysis, is also presented. Spreadsheet applications have become so prominent in the practice of managerial economics that we now address optimization in that context.

PEDAGOGICAL FEATURES OF THE 13TH EDITION

The 13th edition of *Managerial Economics* makes extensive use of pedagogical aids to enhance individualized student learning. The key features of the book are:

1. **Managerial Challenges.** Each chapter opens with a Managerial Challenge (MC) illuminating a real-life problem faced by managers that is closely related to the topics covered in the chapter. Instructors can use the new discussion questions following each MC to "hook" student interest at the start of the class or in preclass preparation assignments.

2. **What Went Right/What Went Wrong.** This feature allows students to relate business mistakes and triumphs to what they have just learned, and helps build that elusive goal of managerial insight.

3. **Extensive Use of Boxed Examples.** More than 300 real-world applications and examples derived from actual corporate practice are highlighted throughout the text. These applications help the analytical tools and concepts to come alive and thereby enhance student learning. They are listed on the inside front and back covers to highlight the prominence of this feature of the book.

4. **Environmental Effects Symbol.** A wind vane symbol highlights numerous passages that address environmental effects and sustainability throughout the book.

5. **Exercises.** Each chapter contains a large problem analysis set. Check answers to selected problems color-coded in blue type are provided in Appendix D at the end of the book. Problems that can be solved using Excel are highlighted with an Excel icon. The book's Web site (www.cengage.com/economics/mcguigan) has answers to all the other textbook problems.

6. **Case Exercises.** Most chapters include mini-cases that extend the concepts and tools developed into a deep fact situation context of a real-world company.

7. **Chapter Glossaries.** In the margins of the text, new terms are defined as they are introduced. The placement of the glossary terms next to the location where the term is first used reinforces the importance of these new concepts and aids in later studying.

8. **International Perspectives.** Throughout the book, special International Perspectives sections that illustrate the application of managerial economics concepts to an increasingly global economy are provided. A globe symbol highlights this internationally relevant material.

9. **Point-by-Point Summaries.** Each chapter ends with a detailed, point-by-point summary of important concepts from the chapter.

10. **Diversity of Presentation Approaches.** Important analytical concepts are presented in several different ways, including tabular, spreadsheet, graphical, and algebraic analysis to individualize the learning process.

ANCILLARY MATERIALS

A complete set of ancillary materials is available to adopters to supplement the text, including the following:

Instructor's Manual and Test Bank

The instructor's manual and test bank that accompany the book contain suggested answers to the end-of-chapter exercises and cases. The authors have taken great care to provide an error-free manual for instructors to use. The manual is available to instructors on the book's Web site as well as on the Instructor's Resource CD-ROM (IRCD).

The test bank, containing a large collection of true-false, multiple-choice, and numerical problems, is available to adopters and is also available on the Web site in Word format, as well as on the IRCD.

Exam *View*

Simplifying the preparation of quizzes and exams, this easy-to-use test creation software includes all of the questions in the printed test bank and is compatible with Microsoft Windows. Instructors select questions by previewing them on the screen, choosing them randomly, or picking them by number. They can easily add or edit questions, instructions, and answers. Quizzes can also be created and administered online, whether over the Internet, a local area network (LAN), or a wide area network (WAN).

Textbook Support Web Site

When you adopt *Managerial Economics: Applications, Strategy, and Tactics*, 13e, you and your students will have access to a rich array of teaching and learning resources that you won't find anywhere else. Located at www.CengageBrain.com, this outstanding site features additional Web Appendices including appendices on indifference curve analysis of consumer choice, international parity conditions, linear programming applications, a capacity planning entry deterrence case study, joint product pricing and transfer prices, decision making under uncertainty, and production optimization subject to cost constraints. It also provides links to additional instructor and student resources.

Accessing CengageBrain

1. Use your browser to go to www.CengageBrain.com.
2. The first time you go to the site, you will need to register. It's free. Click on "Sign Up" in the top right corner of the page and fill out the registration information. (After you have signed in once, whenever you return to CengageBrain, you will enter the user name and password you have chosen and you will be taken directly to the companion site for your book.)
3. Once you have registered and logged in for the first time, go to the "Search for Books or Materials" bar and enter the author or ISBN for your textbook. When the title of your text appears, click on it and you will be taken to the companion site. There you can choose among the various folders provided on the Student side of the site. NOTE: If you are currently using more than one Cengage textbook, the same user name and password will give you access to all the companion sites for your Cengage titles. After you have entered the information for each title, all the titles you are using will appear listed in the pull-down menu in the "Search for Books or Materials" bar. Whenever you return to CengageBrain, you can click on the title of the site you wish to visit and go directly there.

PowerPoint Presentation

Available on the product companion Web site, this comprehensive package provides an excellent lecture aid for instructors. Prepared by Richard D. Marcus at the University of Wisconsin–Milwaukee, these slides cover many of the most important topics from the text, and they can be customized by instructors to meet specific course needs.

CourseMate

Interested in a simple way to complement your text and course content with study and practice materials? Cengage Learning's Economics CourseMate brings course concepts to life with interactive learning, study, and exam preparation tools that support the printed textbook. Watch student comprehension soar as your class works with the printed textbook and the textbook-specific Web site. Economics CourseMate goes beyond the book to deliver what you need! You and your students will have access to ABC/BBC videos, Cengage's EconApps (such as EconNews and EconDebate), unique study guide content specific to the text, and much more.

ACKNOWLEDGMENTS

A number of reviewers, users, and colleagues have been particularly helpful in providing us with many worthwhile comments and suggestions at various stages in the development of this and earlier editions of the book. Included among these individuals are:

William Beranek, J. Walter Elliott, William J. Kretlow, William Gunther, J. William Hanlon, Robert Knapp, Robert S. Main, Edward Sussna, Bruce T. Allen, Allen Moran, Edward Oppermann, Dwight Porter, Robert L. Conn, Allen Parkman, Daniel Slate, Richard L. Pfister, J. P. Magaddino, Richard A. Stanford, Donald Bumpass, Barry P. Keating, John Wittman, Sisay Asefa, James R. Ashley, David Bunting, Amy H. Dalton, Richard D. Evans, Gordon V. Karels, Richard S. Bower, Massoud M. Saghafi, John C. Callahan, Frank Falero, Ramon Rabinovitch, D. Steinnes, Jay Damon Hobson, Clifford Fry, John Crockett, Marvin Frankel, James T. Peach, Paul Kozlowski, Dennis Fixler, Steven Crane, Scott L. Smith, Edward Miller, Fred Kolb, Bill Carson, Jack W. Thornton, Changhee Chae, Robert B. Dallin, Christopher J. Zappe, Anthony V. Popp, Phillip M. Sisneros, George Brower, Carlos Sevilla, Dean Baim, Charles Callahan, Phillip Robins, Bruce Jaffee, Alwyn du Plessis, Darly Winn, Gary Shoesmith, Richard J. Ward, William H. Hoyt, Irvin Grossack, William Simeone, Satyajit Ghosh, David Levy, Simon Hakim, Patricia Sanderson, David P. Ely, Albert A. O'Kunade, Doug Sharp, Arne Dag Sti, Walker Davidson, David Buschena, George M. Radakovic, Harpal S. Grewal, Stephen J. Silver, Michael J. O'Hara, Luke M. Froeb, Dean Waters, Jake Vogelsang, Lynda Y. de la Viña, Audie R. Brewton, Paul M. Hayashi, Lawrence B. Pulley, Tim Mages, Robert Brooker, Carl Emomoto, Charles Leathers, Marshall Medoff, Gary Brester, Stephan Gohmann, L. Joe Moffitt, Christopher Erickson, Antoine El Khoury, Steven Rock, Rajeev K. Goel, Lee S. Redding, Paul J. Hoyt, Bijan Vasigh, Cheryl A. Casper, Semoon Chang, Kwang Soo Cheong, Barbara M. Fischer, John A. Karikari, Francis D. Mummery, Lucjan T. Orlowski, Dennis Proffitt, and Steven S. Shwiff.

People who were especially helpful in the preparation of the 13th edition include Robert F. Brooker, Kristen E. Collett-Schmitt, Simon Medcalfe, Dr. Paul Stock, Shahab Dabirian, James Leady, Stephen Onyeiwu, and Karl W. Einoff. A special thanks to B. Ramy Elitzur of Tel Aviv University for suggesting the exercise on designing a managerial incentive contract and to Bob Hebert, Business Librarian at Wake Forest School of Business, for his tireless pursuit of reference material.

We are also indebted to Wake Forest University and the University of Louisville for the support they provided and owe thanks to our faculty colleagues for the encouragement and assistance provided on a continuing basis during the preparation of the manuscript. We wish to express our appreciation to the members of the Cengage Learning staff for their help in the preparation and promotion of this book. We are grateful to the Literary Executor of the late Sir Ronald A. Fisher, F.R.S.; to Dr. Frank Yates, F.R.S.; and to Longman Group, Ltd., London, for permission to reprint Table III from their book *Statistical Tables for Biological, Agricultural, and Medical Research* (6th ed., 1974).

James R. McGuigan
R. Charles Moyer
Frederick H. deB. Harris

About the Authors

James R. McGuigan

James R. McGuigan owns and operates his own numismatic investment firm. Prior to this business, he was Associate Professor of Finance and Business Economics in the School of Business Administration at Wayne State University. He also taught at the University of Pittsburgh and Point Park College. McGuigan received his undergraduate degree from Carnegie Mellon University. He earned an M.B.A. at the Graduate School of Business at the University of Chicago and his Ph.D. from the University of Pittsburgh. In addition to his interests in economics, he has coauthored books on financial management. His research articles on options have been published in the *Journal of Financial and Quantitative Analysis*.

R. Charles Moyer

R. Charles Moyer earned his B.A. in Economics from Howard University and his M.B.A. and Ph.D. in Finance and Managerial Economics from the University of Pittsburgh. Professor Moyer is Dean of the College of Business at the University of Louisville. He is Dean Emeritus and former holder of the GMAC Insurance Chair in Finance at the Babcock Graduate School of Management, Wake Forest University. Previously, he was Professor of Finance and Chairman of the Department of Finance at Texas Tech University. Professor Moyer also has taught at the University of Houston, Lehigh University, and the University of New Mexico, and spent a year at the Federal Reserve Bank of Cleveland. Professor Moyer has taught extensively abroad in Germany, France, and Russia. In addition to this text, Moyer has coauthored two other financial management texts. He has been published in many leading journals, including *Financial Management, Journal of Financial and Quantitative Analysis, Journal of Finance, Financial Review, Journal of Financial Research, International Journal of Forecasting, Strategic Management Journal,* and *Journal of Economics and Business*. Professor Moyer is a member of the Board of Directors of King Pharmaceuticals, Inc., Capital South Partners, and the Kentucky Seed Capital Fund.

Frederick H. deB. Harris

Frederick H. deB. Harris is the John B. McKinnon Professor of Managerial Economics and Finance at the School of Business, Wake Forest University. His specialties are pricing tactics and capacity planning. Professor Harris has taught integrative managerial economics core courses and B.A., B.S., M.S., M.B.A., and Ph.D. electives in business schools and economics departments in the United States, Germany, France, Italy, and Australia. He has won two school-wide Professor of the Year teaching awards and two Researcher of the Year awards. Other recognitions include Outstanding Faculty by *Inc.* magazine (1998), Most Popular Courses by *Business Week Online* 2000–2001, and Outstanding Faculty by *BusinessWeek's Guide to the Best Business Schools*, 5th to 9th eds., 1997–2004.

Professor Harris has published widely in economics, marketing, operations, and finance journals, including the *Review of Economics and Statistics, Journal of Financial and Quantitative Analysis, Journal of Operations Management, Journal of Industrial Economics,* and *Journal of Financial Markets*. From 1988 through 1993, Professor Harris served on the Board of Associate Editors of the *Journal of Industrial Economics*.

His path breaking work on price discovery has been frequently cited in leading academic journals, and several articles with practitioners have been published in the *Journal of Trading*. In addition, he often benchmarks the pricing, order processing, and capacity planning functions of large companies against state-of-the-art techniques in revenue management and writes about his findings in journals like *Marketing Management* and INFORMS's *Journal of Revenue and Pricing Management*.

PART I

Introduction

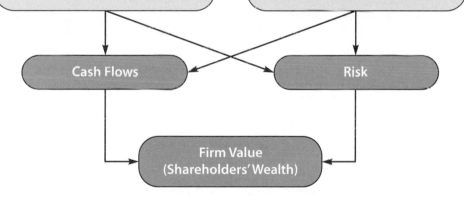

ECONOMIC ANALYSIS AND DECISIONS

1. Demand Analysis
2. Production and Cost Analysis
3. Product, Pricing, and Output Decisions
4. Capital Expenditure Analysis

ECONOMIC, POLITICAL, AND SOCIAL ENVIRONMENT

1. Business Conditions (Trends, Cycles, and Seasonal Effects)
2. Factor Market Conditions (Capital, Labor, and Raw Materials)
3. Competitors' Reactions and Tactical Response
4. Organizational Architecture and Regulatory Constraints

Cash Flows

Risk

Firm Value (Shareholders' Wealth)

Introduction and Goals of the Firm

CHAPTER PREVIEW

Managerial economics is the application of microeconomics to problems faced by decision makers in the private, public, and not-for-profit sectors. Managerial economics assists managers in efficiently allocating scarce resources, planning corporate strategy, and executing effective tactics. In this chapter, the responsibilities of management are explored. Economic profit is defined, and the role of profits in allocating resources in a free enterprise system is examined. The primary goal of the firm, namely, shareholder wealth maximization, is developed along with a discussion of how managerial decisions influence shareholder wealth. The problems associated with the separation of ownership and control, moral hazard in teams, and principal-agent relationships in large corporations are explored.

MANAGERIAL CHALLENGE

How to Achieve Sustainability: Southern Company Electric Power Generation[1]

In the second decade of the twenty-first century, companies all across the industrial landscape are seeking to achieve sustainability. Sustainability is a powerful metaphor but an elusive goal. It means much more than aligning oneself with environmental sensitivity, though that commitment itself tests higher in opinion polling of the latent preferences of Americans and Europeans than any other response. Sustainability also implies renewability and longevity of business plans that are adaptable to changing circumstances. But what exactly should management pursue as a set of objectives to achieve this goal?

Management response to pollution abatement illustrates one type of sustainability challenge. At the insistence of the prime minister of Canada during the Reagan Administration, the U.S. Congress enacted a bipartisan cap-and-trade bill to address smokestack emissions. Sulfur dioxide and nitrous oxide (SOX and NOX) emissions precipitate as acid rain, mist, and ice, imposing damage downwind hundreds of miles away to trees, painted and stone surfaces, and asthmatics. The Clean Air Act (CAA) of 1990, amended in 1997 and 2003, granted tradable pollution allowances (TPAs) to known polluters. The CAA also authorized an auction market for these TPA assets. The Environmental Protection Agency Web site (www.epa.gov) displays on a daily basis the equilibrium, market-clearing price of these new assets on the balance sheet (e.g., $250 per ton of soot). The cap-and-trade system literally identified for the first time a price for the use of what had previously been unpriced common property resources—namely, acid-free air and rainwater. As a result, large point-source polluters like power plants and steel mills now incur an actual cost per ton for the SOX and NOX–laden soot by-products of burning lots of high sulfur coal. These amounts were promptly placed in spreadsheets designed to find ways of minimizing operating costs.[2] No less importantly, each polluter felt

Cont.

MANAGERIAL CHALLENGE *Continued*

© AP Photo/Stephen Morton

(see Figure 1.1). Although this approach "grandfathered" a substantial amount of pollution, the gradual transition cap-and-trade legislation was pivotally important to its widespread success. Industries such as steel and electric power were given five years to comply with the regulated emissions requirements, and then in 1997, the initial allowances were cut in half. Duke Power initially bought 19,146 allowances for Belews Creek at prices ranging from $131 to $480 per ton and then in 2003 built two 30-story smokestack scrubbers that reduced the NOX emissions by 75 percent.

Another major electric utility, Southern Company, analyzed three compliance choices on a least-cost cash flow basis: (1) buying allowances, (2) installing smokestack scrubbers, or (3) adopting fuel-switching technology to burn low-sulfur coal or even cleaner natural gas. In a widely studied case, the Southern Company found its huge Bowen plant in North Georgia would require a $657 million scrubber that after tax deductions for capital equipment depreciation and further offsets from excess allowance revenue cost $476 million. Alternatively, continuing to burn high-sulfur coal from the

powerful incremental incentives to reduce compliance cost by abating pollution. And an entire industry devoted to developing pollution abatement technology sprang up.

The TPAs granted were set at approximately 80 percent of the known pollution taking place at each plant in 1990. For example, Duke Power's Belews Creek power plant, generating 120,085 tons of nitrous oxide acidic soot annually from burning 400 train carloads of coal per day, was granted 96,068 tons of allowances

---

FIGURE 1.1   Nitrous Oxide from Coal-Fired Power Plants (Daily Emissions in Tons, pre Clean Air Act)

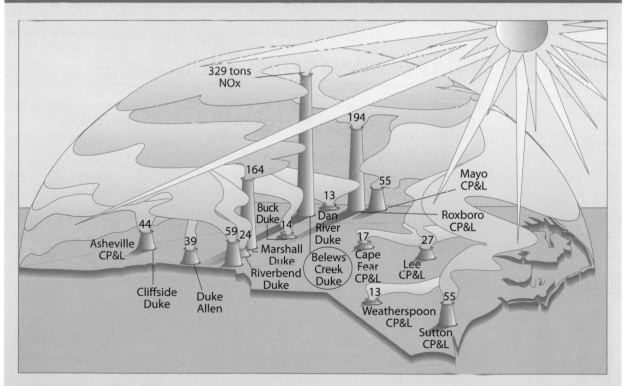

Source: NC Division of Air Quality.

MANAGERIAL CHALLENGE *Continued*

nearby Appalachian Mountain region and purchasing the requisite allowances in the cap-and-trade market was projected to cost $266 million. And finally, switching to low-sulfur coal while adopting fuel-switching technology was found to cost $176 million. All these analyses were performed on a present value basis with cost projections over 25 years. Chapter 2 offers a quick primer on the net present value concept.

Southern Company's decision to switch to low-sulfur coal was hailed far and wide as environmentally sensitive and sustainable. Many electric utilities support cap-and-trade policies and actively pursue the mandate of the states in which they operate to derive 15 percent of their power from renewable energy (RE). In a Case Study at the end of the chapter, we analyze several wind power RE alternatives for generating electricity.

The choice of fuel-switching technology to abate smokestack emissions was a shareholder value-maximizing choice for Southern Company for two reasons. First, switching to low-sulfur coal minimized their projected cash flow compliance costs under the CAA but, in addition, the fuel-switching technology created a strategic flexibility (a "real option") and that in itself created additional shareholder value. In this chapter, we will see what maximizing capitalized value of equity (shareholder value) is and what it is not.

Discussion Questions

■ What is the basic externality problem with acid rain? What objectives should management serve in responding to the acid rain problem?

■ How does the Clean Air Act's cap-and-trade approach to air pollution affect the Southern Company's analysis of the previously unpriced common property air and water resources damaged by smokestack emissions?

■ How should management comply with the Clean Air Act, or should the Southern Company just pay the EPA's fines? Why? How would you decide?

■ Which among Southern Company's three alternatives for compliance offered the most strategic flexibility? Explain.

---

[1]Based on Frederick Harris, Alternative Energy Symposium, Wake Forest Schools of Business (September 2008); and "Acid Rain: The Southern Company," Harvard Business School Publishing, HBS: 9-792-060.

[2]EPA fines for noncompliance of $2,000 per ton have always far exceeded the auction market cost of allowances ($131–$473 in recent years).

WHAT IS MANAGERIAL ECONOMICS?

Managerial economics extracts from microeconomic theory those concepts and techniques that enable managers to select strategic direction, to allocate efficiently the resources available to the organization, and to respond effectively to tactical issues. All such managerial decision making seeks to do the following:

1. identify the alternatives,
2. select the choice that accomplishes the objective(s) in the most efficient manner,
3. taking into account the constraints,
4. and the likely actions and reactions of rival decision makers.

For example, consider the following stylized decision problem:

Example

Capacity Expansion at Honda, N.A., and Toyota Motors, N.A.

Honda and Toyota are attempting to expand their already substantial assembly operations in North America. Both companies face increasing demand for their U.S.-manufactured vehicles, especially Toyota Camrys and Honda Accords. Camrys and Accords rate extremely highly in consumer reports of durability and reliability.

(continued)

The demand for used Accords is so strong that they depreciate only 45 percent in their first four years. Other competing vehicles may depreciate as much as 65 percent in the same period. Toyota and Honda have identified two possible strategies (S1NEW and S2USED) to meet the growing demand for Camrys and Accords. Strategy S1NEW involves an internal expansion of capacity at Toyota's $700 million Princeton, Indiana, plant and Honda's Marysville, Ohio, plant. Strategy S2USED involves the purchase and renovation of assembly plants now owned by General Motors. The new plants will likely receive substantial public subsidies through reduced property taxes. The older plants already possess an enormous infrastructure of local suppliers and regulatory relief.

The objective of Toyota's managers is to maximize the value today (present value) of the expected future profit from the expansion. This problem can be summarized as follows:

Objective function: Maximize the present value (P.V.) of profit (S1NEW, S2USED)

Decision rule: Choose strategy S1NEW if P.V. (Profit S1NEW)
> P.V. (Profit S2USED)
Choose strategy S2USED if the reverse.

This simple illustration shows how resource-allocation decisions of managers attempt to maximize the value of their firms across forward-looking dynamic strategies for growth while respecting all ethical, legal, and regulatory constraints.

THE DECISION-MAKING MODEL

The ability to make good decisions is the key to successful managerial performance. All decision making shares several common elements. First, the decision maker must *establish the objectives*. Next, the decision maker must *identify the problem*. For example, the CEO of electronics retailer Best Buy may note that the profit margin on sales has been decreasing. This could be caused by pricing errors, declining labor productivity, or the use of outdated retailing concepts. Once the source or sources of the problem are identified, the manager can move to an *examination of potential solutions*. The choice between these alternatives depends on an *analysis of the relative costs and benefits*, as well as other organizational and societal constraints that may make one alternative preferable to another.

The final step in the decision-making process, after all alternatives have been evaluated, is to analyze the best available alternative under a variety of changes in the assumptions before making a recommendation. This crucial final step is referred to as a *sensitivity analysis*. Knowing the limitations of the planned course of action as the decision environment changes, the manager can then proceed to an *implementation of the decision*, monitoring carefully any unintended consequences or unanticipated changes in the market. The case problem at the end of the chapter highlights the role of sensitivity analysis in analyzing wind turbines as a renewable energy source of electricity.

The Responsibilities of Management

In a free enterprise system, managers are responsible for a number of goals. Managers are responsible for proactively solving problems in the current business model before

WHAT WENT RIGHT • WHAT WENT WRONG

Saturn Corporation[3]

When General Motors (GM) rolled out their "different kind of car company," J.D. Powers rated product quality 8 percent ahead of Honda, and customers liked the no-haggle selling process. Saturn achieved the 200,000 unit sales enjoyed by the Honda Civic and the Toyota Corolla in two short years and caught the 285,000 volume of the Ford Escort in Saturn's fourth year. Making interpersonal aspects of customer service the number-one priority and possessing superior inventory and MIS systems, Saturn dealerships proved very profitable and quickly developed a reputation for some of the highest customer loyalty in the industry.

However, with pricing of the base Saturn model $1,200 below the $12,050 rival Japanese compact cars, the GM parent earned only a $400 gross profit margin per vehicle. In a typical year, this meant GM was recovering only about $100 million of its $3 billion capital investment, a paltry 3 percent return. Netting out GM's 11 percent cost of capital, each Saturn was losing approximately $1,000. These figures compare to a $3,300 gross profit margin per vehicle in some of GM's other divisions. Consequently, cash flow was not reinvested in the Saturn division, products were not updated, and the models stagnated. By 1997, sales were slumping at −9 percent and in 1998 they fell an additional 20 percent. In 2009, GM announced it was permanently closing the Saturn division.

GM managers had not established the next Saturn business model which would have transferred young childless couples to more profitable GM divisions as their lifecycle called for bigger sedans, minivans, and SUVs. Rather than trading up to Buick and Pontiac, middle-aged loyal Saturn owners sought to trade up within Saturn, and finding no sporty larger models available, they switched to larger Japanese imports like the Honda Accord and Toyota Camry. After almost collapsing, Saturn introduced a sport wagon, an efficient SUV, and a high-profile sports coupe. GM ultimately abandoned the brand in 2009.

[3]Based on M. Cohen, "Saturn's Supply-Chain Innovation," *Sloan Management Review* (Summer 2000), pp. 93–96; "Small Car Sales Are Back" and "Why Didn't GM Do More for Saturn?" *BusinessWeek*, September 22, 1997, pp. 40–42, and March 16, 1998, p. 62.

they become crises and for selecting strategies to assure the more likely success of the next business model. Research In Motion built the world's best international cell phone (the Blackberry) but missed the market as customer demand evolved to web-enabled smart phones with 500,000 and then millions of apps. Managers create organizational structure and culture based on the organization's mission. Senior management especially is responsible for establishing a vision of new business directions and setting stretch goals to get there. In addition, managers coordinate the integration of marketing, operations, and finance functions. If plant managers don't know the realized margins from particular segments targeted by the sales team, then they will often expedite and fulfill orders to the wrong customers. Finally, managers undertake the critical responsibility of motivating and monitoring teamwork.

Moral Hazard in Teams

Teamwork skills and the ability to motivate teams is widely acknowledged as the single most critical trait of effective managers. This applies equally to Navy Seal teams, factory work cell teams, brand management teams, or consulting teams. Why is that? Why is teamwork so important, and why is attaining good teamwork so hard? The essence of teamwork is synergistic value creation in excess of the sum of the parts. As individuals on a team, we can each "pull our own weight" or contribute more than that and compound our extra effort with the extraordinary efforts of those around us. Just as in sports, 110 percent effort on company teams often defeats more skilled opponents and sometimes even those with better resources. But how does a manager attain the commitment from a team to put forth 110 percent effort when doing less would not impose as much personal sacrifice, and when individual shirking on one's effort may not be transparently obvious? This constitutes the so-called moral hazard problem in team-making.

If penalties and sanctions are few and far between, only a sense of moral duty induces full-effort teamwork rather than the reduced effort associated with free-riding.

Consider the following example of the teamwork involved in bringing a product to market. Mack and Myer are collaborating on a product launch. Each has specialized skills that are required to achieve the maximum output and a gross profit of $100 if they each "Pull Hard," devoting their best effort to the project. In that event, $25 personal cost for each leaves $25 net profit available to each of them. If either shirks and reduces effort unilaterally, the output is reduced and gross profit declines by 30 percent to $70 to be divided between them, but the shirker reduces his or her personal cost to $0, thereby yielding a $35 net profit to the free rider and only $10 to the dutiful teammate who Pulled Hard. If both shirk and fail to provide best effort, then output collapses, gross profit falls to $30, yielding each just $15 net profit. These payoffs are depicted in the normal form game matrix Figure 1.2, Panel A.

What if this is a one-time-only situation, and each player must decide simultaneously without knowing the choice of his or her teammate? One of the insights of game theory is that in the absence of repeated games involving the same teammates, rational players in such situations will ignore reputation effects and select the action whose payoff dominates all others. In this case, that means each player will choose to Shirk since the $35 outcome exceeds $25, and the $15 outcome exceeds $10. In short, the outcomes from the action Shirk in the right-hand column dominate those in the Pull Hard column (and so too in the rows of the payoff matrix). Each team member therefore prefers to defect (by choosing Shirk), whatever the choice of his or her teammate; Shirk is said to be a dominant strategy. Therefore, {Shirk, Shirk} emerges as a dominant strategy outcome with great predictability.

But if they both do so, a tragic dilemma arises. In the southeast {Shirk, Shirk} cell, the payoff to each player is just $15, and total value added is only $30. Both teammates

---

FIGURE 1.2   Payoffs from Team Production with and without a Supervisor

Panel A   No Supervisor

		Mack	
		Pull Hard	**Shirk**
Meyer	**Pull Hard**	$25 / $25	$10 / $35
	Shirk	$35 / $10	$15 / $15

Panel B   Supervisor Present. A $10 Manager is Hired as a Monitor of Shirking for which A $15 Penalty is Imposed.

		Mack	
		Pull Hard	**Shirk**
Meyer	**Pull Hard**	$20 / $20	$5 / $15
	Shirk	$15 / $5	$-5 / $-5

© Cengage Learning

realize, however, that if they had just found a way to elicit cooperation from one another, $50 net profit would have been available in the northwest {Pull Hard, Pull Hard} cell. Their individually optimal decision-making (reflected by the dominant strategy to defect from cooperative arrangements) leaves −$20 foregone profits until the players themselves organize their team-making differently. As a result, we might well expect that the players would evolve mechanisms for contracting around the moral hazard problem in order to capture the foregone value. How can this be accomplished?

What if the team hired a manager as project supervisor to monitor the teamwork and punish shirking? Splitting the cost of paying a manager $10 leaves $40 gross profit in the {Pull Hard, Pull Hard} cell, to be divided evenly between Mack and Meyer. In the diagonal cells, the manager now penalizes whichever teammate shirks their duty −$15. The payoff for this unilateral defector now becomes ($70/2 = $35) − $15 − $5 = $15, less than the ($100/2 = $50) − $25 − $5 = $20 associated with the cooperative decision to Pull Hard. And this is a symmetric payoff game, so both players now conclude the same thing—that is, it pays to adopt mutually cooperative teamwork and deliver full effort. Since each player will receive only ($30/2 = $15) − $15 − $5 = −$5 in the event they both shirk their duties, and ($70/2 = $35) − $25 − $5 = $5 in the event their Hard Pull is unilaterally defected upon, each decides to Pull Hard. Indeed, examining the new payoff matrix in Figure 1.2, Panel B the choice pair {Pull Hard, Pull Hard} has now become the dominant strategy. So, in conclusion, moral hazard in teams can be avoided. What is needed is a manager as supervisor who imposes sanctions for the shirking behavior of teammates that decide to free ride.

Managers in a capitalist economy are motivated to monitor teamwork ultimately because of their overarching goal to maximize returns to the owners of the business—that is, economic profits.

Economic profit is the difference between total sales revenue (price times units sold) and total economic cost. The *economic cost* of any activity may be thought of as the highest valued alternative opportunity that is forgone. To attract labor, capital, intellectual property, land, and matériel, the firm must offer to pay a price that is sufficient to convince the owners of these resources to forego other alternative activities and commit their resources to this use. Thus, economic costs should always be thought of as *opportunity costs*—that is, the costs of attracting a resource such as investment capital from its next best alternative use.

economic profit The difference between total revenue and total economic cost. Economic cost includes a "normal" rate of return on the capital contributions of the firm's partners.

THE ROLE OF PROFITS

In a free enterprise system, economic profits play an important role in guiding the decisions made by the thousands of competing independent resource owners. The existence of profits determines the type and quantity of goods and services that are produced and sold, as well as the resulting derived demand for resources. Several theories of profit indicate how this works.

Risk-Bearing Theory of Profit

Economic profits arise in part to compensate the owners of the firm for the risk they assume when making their investments. Because a firm's shareholders are not entitled to a fixed rate of return on their investment—that is, they are claimants to the firm's residual cash flows after all other contractual payments have been made—they need to be compensated for this risk in the form of a higher rate of return.

The risk-bearing theory of profits is explained in the context of normal profits, where *normal* is defined in terms of the relative risk of alternative investments. Normal profits for a high-risk firm, such as Las Vegas hotels and casinos, a biotech pharmaceutical company, or an oil field exploration well operator, should be higher than normal profits for firms of lesser risk, such as water utilities. For example, in 2005, the industry average return on net worth for the casino hotel/gaming industry was 12.6 percent, compared to 9 percent for the water utility industry.

Temporary Disequilibrium Theory of Profit

Although there exists a long-run equilibrium normal rate of profit (adjusted for risk) that all firms should tend to earn, at any point in time, firms may find themselves earning a rate of return above or below this long-run normal return level. This can occur because of temporary dislocations (shocks) in various sectors of the economy. Rates of return in the oil industry rose substantially when the price of crude oil doubled from $75 in mid-2007 to $146 in July 2008. However, those high returns declined sharply by late 2008, when oil market conditions led to excess supplies and the price of crude oil fell to $45.

Monopoly Theory of Profit

In some industries, one firm is effectively able to dominate the market and persistently earn above-normal rates of return. This ability to dominate the market may arise from economies of scale (a situation in which one large firm, such as Boeing, can produce additional units of 747 aircraft at a lower cost than can smaller firms), control of essential natural resources (crude oil), control of critical patents (biotech pharmaceutical firms), or governmental restrictions that prohibit competition (cable franchise owners). The conditions under which a monopolist can earn above-normal profits are discussed in greater depth in Chapter 11.

Innovation Theory of Profit

The innovation theory of profit suggests that above-normal profits are the reward for successful innovations. Firms that develop high-quality products (such as Porsche) or successfully identify unique market opportunities (such as Apple) are rewarded with the potential for above-normal profits. Indeed, the U.S. patent system is designed to ensure that these above-normal return opportunities furnish strong incentives for continued innovation.

Managerial Efficiency Theory of Profit

Closely related to the innovation theory is the managerial efficiency theory of profit. Above-normal profits can arise because of the exceptional managerial skills of well-managed firms. No single theory of profit can explain the observed profit rates in each industry, nor are these theories necessarily mutually exclusive. Profit performance is invariably the result of many factors, including differential risk, innovation, managerial skills, the existence of monopoly power, and chance occurrences.

OBJECTIVE OF THE FIRM

These theories of simple profit maximization as an objective of management are insightful, but they ignore the timing and risk of profit streams. Shareholder wealth maximization as an objective overcomes both these limitations.

Shareholder Wealth Maximization at Berkshire Hathaway

Warren E. Buffett, chairman and CEO of Berkshire Hathaway, Inc., has described the long-term economic goal of Berkshire Hathaway as follows: "to maximize the average annual rate of gain in intrinsic business value on a per-share basis."[4] Berkshire's book value per share has increased from $19.46 in 1964, when Buffett acquired the firm, to $141,537 in 2013, a compound annual rate of growth of 20.3 percent. The Standard and Poor's 500 companies experienced 9.6 percent growth over this same time period.

Berkshire's directors are all major stockholders. In addition, at least four of the directors have over 50 percent of their family's net worth invested in Berkshire. Managers and directors own over 47 percent of the firm's stock. As a result, Buffett's firm has always placed a high priority on the goal of maximizing shareholder wealth.

[4]*Annual Report*, Berkshire Hathaway, Inc. (2005).

The Shareholder Wealth-Maximization Model of the Firm

shareholder wealth A measure of the value of a firm. Shareholder wealth is equal to the value of a firm's common stock, which, in turn, is equal to the present value of all future cash returns expected to be generated by the firm for the benefit of its owners.

Shareholder wealth is measured by the market value of a firm's common stock, which is equal to the present value of all expected future cash flows to equity owners discounted at the shareholders' required rate of return, plus a value for the firm's embedded real options:

$$V_0 \cdot (\text{Shares Outstanding}) = \frac{\pi_1}{(1 + k_e)^1} + \frac{\pi_2}{(1 + k_e)^2} + \frac{\pi_3}{(1 + k_e)^3} + \cdots + \frac{\pi_\infty}{(1 + k_e)^\infty}$$
$$+ \text{Real Option Value}$$

$$V_0 \cdot (\text{Shares Outstanding}) = \sum_{t=1}^{\infty} \frac{\pi_t}{(1 + k_e)^t} + \text{Real Option Value} \qquad [1.1]$$

where V_0 is the current value of a share of stock (the stock price), π_t represents the economic profits expected in each of the future periods (from period 1 to ∞), and k_e equals the required rate of return.

A number of different factors (like interest rates and economy-wide business cycles) influence the firm's stock price in ways that are beyond the manager's control, but many factors (like innovation and cost control) are not. Real option value represents the cost savings or revenue expansions that arise from preserving flexibility in the business plans the managers adopt. For example, the Southern Company saved $90 million in complying with the Clean Air Act by adopting fuel-switching technology that allowed burning of alternative fuels (coal, fuel oil or natural gas) whenever the full cost of one input became cheaper than another.

Note that Equation 1.1 does take into account the timing of future profits. By discounting all future profits at the required rate of return, k_e, Equation 1.1 shows that a dollar received in the future is worth less than a dollar received immediately. (The techniques of discounting to present value are explained in more detail in Chapter 2 and Appendix A at the end of the book.) Equation 1.1 also provides a way to evaluate different levels of risk since the higher the risk the higher the required rate of return k_e used to discount the future cash flows, and the lower the present value. In short, shareholder value is determined by the amount, timing, and risk of the firm's expected future profits.

Resource-Allocation Decisions and Shareholder Wealth: Apple Computer[5]

In distributing its stylish iPad personal computers and high tech iPhone smart phones, Apple has considered three distribution channels. On the one hand, copying Dell's direct-to-the-consumer approach would entail buying components from Motorola, AMD, Intel, and so forth and then hiring third-party manufacturers to assemble what each customer ordered just-in-time to fulfill Internet or telephone sales. Inventories and capital equipment costs would be very low indeed; almost all costs would be variable. Alternatively, Apple could enter into distribution agreements with an independent electronics retailer like ComputerTree. Finally, Apple could retail its own products in Apple Stores. This third approach entails enormous capital investment and a higher proportion of fixed cost, especially if the retail chain sought high visibility locations and needed lots of space.

When Apple opened its 147th retail store on Fifth Avenue in New York City. The location left little doubt as to the allocation of company resources to this new distribution strategy. Apple occupies a sprawling subterranean space topped by a glass cube that Steve Jobs himself designed, across from Central Park, opposite the famed Plaza Hotel. Apple's profits in this most heavily trafficked tourist and retail corridor will rely on several initiatives: (1) in-store theatres for workshop training on iMac programs to record music or edit home movies, (2) numerous technical experts available for troubleshooting with no waiting time, and (3) continuing investment in one of the world's most valuable brands. Shortly after opening, Apple made $151 million in operating profits on $2.35 billion in sales at these Apple Stores, a 6.4 percent profit margin relative to approximately a 2 percent profit margin company wide.

[5]Based on Nick Wingfield, "How Apple's Store Strategy Beat the Odds," *Wall Street Journal* (May 17, 2006), p. B1.

SEPARATION OF OWNERSHIP AND CONTROL: THE PRINCIPAL-AGENT PROBLEM

Profit maximization and shareholder wealth maximization are very useful concepts when alternative choices can be easily identified and when the associated costs and revenues can be readily estimated. Examples include scheduling capacity for optimal production runs, determining an optimal inventory policy given sales patterns and available production facilities, introducing an established product in a new geographic market, and choosing whether to buy or lease a machine. In other cases, however, where the alternatives are harder to identify and the costs and benefits less clear, the goals of owners and managers are seldom aligned.

Divergent Objectives and Agency Conflict

As sole proprietorships and closely held businesses grow into limited liability corporations, the owners (the principals) frequently delegate decision-making authority to professional managers (the agents). Because the manager-agents usually have much less to lose than the owner-principals, the agents often seek acceptable levels (rather than a maximum) of profit and shareholder wealth while pursuing their own self-interests. This is known as a principal-agent problem or "agency conflict."

For example, as crude oil prices fluctuated wildly by 30 to 50 percent, Exxon-Mobil's managers once diversified the company into product lines like computer software development—an area where Exxon-Mobil had little or no expertise or competitive advantage. The managers were hoping that diversification would smooth out their executive bonuses tied to quarterly earnings, and it did. However, the decision to diversify ended up causing an extended decline in the value of Exxon-Mobil's stock.

Pursuing their own self-interests can also lead managers to focus on their own long-term job security. In some instances this can motivate them to limit the amount of risk taken by the firm because an unfavorable outcome resulting from the risk could lead to their dismissal. Kodak is a good example. In the early 2000s, Kodak's executives didn't want to risk developing immature digital photography products. When the demand for digital camera products subsequently soared, Kodak was left with too few markets for its traditional film products. In 2012, Kodak filed for bankruptcy.

Finally, the cash flow to owners erodes when the firm's resources are diverted from their most productive uses to perks for managers. In 1988, RJR Nabisco was a firm that had become bloated with corporate retreats in Florida, an extensive fleet of corporate airplanes and hangars, and an executive fixation on an awful-tasting new product (the "smokeless" cigarette Premier). This left RJR Nabisco with substantially less value in the marketplace than would have been possible with better resource allocation decisions. Recognizing the value enhancement potential, Kohlberg Kravis Roberts & Co. (KKR) initiated a hostile takeover bid and acquired RJR Nabisco for $25 billion in early 1989. The purchase price offered to common stockholders by KKR was $109 per share, much better than the $55 pre-takeover price. The new owners moved quickly to sell many of RJR's poorly performing assets, slash operating expenses, and cancel the Premier project. Although the deal was heavily leveraged with a large amount of debt borrowed at high interest rates, a much-improved cash flow allowed KKR to pay down the debt within seven years, substantially ahead of schedule.

To forge a closer alliance between the interests of shareholders and managers, some companies structure a larger proportion of the manager's compensation in the form of performance-based payments. For example, in 2011, CEO of Exxon-Mobil, Rex Tillotson received $17.9 million in restricted stock as long-term incentive pay (in addition to his $1.8 million salary and $2.3 million bonus for current performance). If Mr. Tillotson succeeds in raising shareholder value, he will profit handsomely in 2016 when his deferred compensation in the form of stock can be sold and converted to cash. Other firms like Hershey Foods, CSX, Union Carbide, and Berkshire Hathaway require senior managers and directors to own a substantial amount of company stock in order to align the pocketbook interests of managers directly with those of stockholders. In sum, how motivated a manager will be to act in the interests of the firm's stockholders depends on the structure of his or her compensation package, the threat of dismissal, and the threat of takeover by a new group of owners.

Example

Agency Costs and Corporate Restructuring: O.M. Scott & Sons[6]

The existence of high agency costs sometimes prompts firms to financially restructure themselves to achieve higher operating efficiencies. For example, the lawn products firm, O.M. Scott & Sons, was purchased by the Scott managers in a highly leveraged

(continued)

buyout (an MBO). Faced with large interest and principal payments and having the potential to profit directly from more efficient operation of the firm, the new owner-managers quickly put in place accounting controls and operating procedures designed to improve Scott's performance. By monitoring inventory levels more closely and negotiating more aggressively with suppliers, the firm was able to reduce its average monthly working capital investment from an initial level of $75 million to $35 million. At the same time, new incentive pay for the sales force caused revenue to increase from $160 million to a record $200 million.

---

[6]A more complete discussion of the Scott experience can be found in Brett Duval Fromson, "Life after Debt: How LBOs Do It," *Fortune* (March 13, 1989), pp. 91–92.

Agency Problem

Principal-agent problems arise from the inherent unobservability of managerial effort combined with the presence of random disturbances in team production. The job performance of piecework garment workers is easily monitored, but the work effort of managers may not be observable at less-than-prohibitive cost. The creative ingenuity in anticipating and then proactively solving problems before they arise is inherently unobservable. Yet, this is what senior managers do. Owners know it when they see it, but often do not recognize when it is missing because a manager's creative ingenuity is often inseparable from good and bad luck. Owners therefore find it difficult to know when to reward managers for upturns and when to blame them for poor performance.

Separation of ownership (shareholders) and control (management) in large corporations permits managers to pursue goals, such as maximization of their own personal welfare, that are not always in the long-term interests of shareholders. As a result of pressure from large institutional shareholders, such as Fidelity Funds, from statutes such as Sarbanes-Oxley mandating stronger corporate governance, and from federal tax laws severely limiting the deductibility of executive pay, a growing number of corporations are seeking to assure that a larger proportion of the manager's pay occurs in the form of performance-based bonuses. They are doing so by (1) tying executive bonuses to the performance of comparably situated competitor companies, (2) by raising the performance hurdles that trigger executive bonuses, and (3) by eliminating severance packages that provide windfalls for executives whose poor performance leads to a takeover or their own dismissal.

Just prior to the Financial Crisis, CEOs of the 350 largest U.S. corporations were paid $6 million in 2005 in median total direct compensation. The 10 companies with the highest shareholder returns the previous five years paid $10.6 million in salary, bonus, and long-term incentives. The 10 companies with the lowest shareholder returns paid $1.6 million. Figure 1.3 shows that across these 350 companies, CEO total compensation has mirrored corporate profitability, spiking when profits grow and collapsing when profits decline. In the global economic crisis of 2008–2009, CEO salaries declined in 63 percent of NYSE Euronext companies, and bonuses and raises were frozen, cut, or eliminated in 47 percent and 52 percent, respectively.[7]

---

[7]"NYSE Euronext 2010 CEO Report," NYSEMagazine.com (September 2009), p. 27.

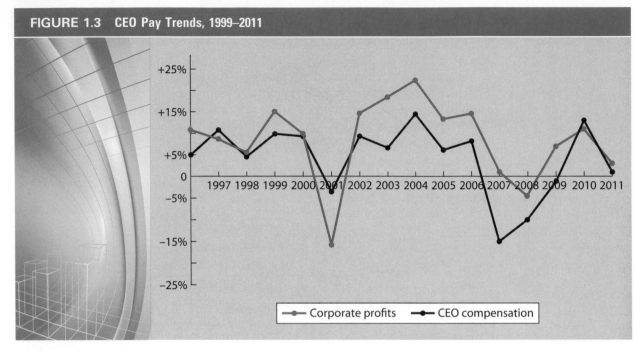

FIGURE 1.3   CEO Pay Trends, 1999–2011

Source: Mercer Human Resource Consulting and The Hay Group.

Executive Performance Pay: General Electric[8]

As a representative example of a performance-based pay package, General Electric CEO Jeff Immelt had in 2006 a salary of $3.2 million, a cash bonus of $5.9 million, and gains on long-term incentives that converted to stock options of $3.8 million. GE distributes stock options to 45,000 of its 300,000 employees, but decided that one-half of CEO Jeff Immelt's 250,000 "performance share units" should only convert to stock options if GE cash flow grew at an average of 10 percent or more for five years, and the other one-half should convert only if GE shareholder return exceeded the five-year cumulative total return on the S&P 500 index.

Basing these executive pay packages on demonstrated performance relative to industry and sector benchmarks has become something of a cause célèbre in the United States. The reason is that by 2011 median CEO total compensation of $10.6 million had grown to 258 times the $41,000 salary of the average U.S. worker. In Europe, the comparable figure is 38 times the median worker salary of $35,000, and similar multipliers to those in Europe apply in Asia. So, what U.S. CEOs get paid was the focus of much public policy discussion even before the pay scandals at AIG and Merrill Lynch/Bank of America.

[8]Based on http://people.forbes.com/rankings/jeffrey-r-immelt/36126.

agency costs Costs associated with resolving conflicts of interest among shareholders, managers, and lenders.

In an attempt to mitigate these agency problems, firms incur several **agency costs**, which include the following:

1. Grants of restricted stock or deferred stock options to structure executive compensation in such a way as to align the incentives for management with shareholder interests.
2. Internal audits and accounting oversight boards to monitor management's actions. In addition, many large creditors, especially banks, now monitor financial ratios and investment decisions of large debtor companies on a monthly or even biweekly basis. These initiatives strengthen the firm's *corporate governance*.
3. Bonding expenditures and fraud liability insurance to protect the shareholders from managerial dishonesty.
4. Complex internal approval processes designed to limit managerial discretion, but which prevent timely responses to opportunities.

IMPLICATIONS OF SHAREHOLDER WEALTH MAXIMIZATION

Critics of those who want to align the interests of managers with equity owners often allege that maximizing shareholder wealth focuses on short-term payoffs—sometimes to the detriment of long-term profits. However, the evidence suggests just the opposite. Short-term cash flows reflect only a small fraction of the firm's share price; the first 5 years of expected dividend payouts explain only 18 percent, and the first 10 years only 35 percent of the share prices of NYSE stocks.[9] The goal of shareholder wealth maximization requires a long-term focus.

WHAT WENT RIGHT • WHAT WENT WRONG

Eli Lilly Depressed by Loss of Prozac Patent[10]

Pharmaceutical giants like GlaxoSmithKline, Merck, Pfizer, and Eli Lilly expend an average of $802 million to develop a new drug. It takes 12.3 years to research and test for efficacy and side effects, conduct clinical trials, and then produce and market a new drug. Only 4 in 100 candidate molecules or screening compounds lead to investigational new drugs (INDs). Only 5 in 200 of these INDs display sufficient efficacy in animal testing to warrant human trials. Clinical failure occurs in 6 of 10 human trials, and only half of the FDA-proposed drugs are ultimately approved. In sum, the joint probability of successful drug discovery and development is just $0.04 \times 0.025 \times 0.4 \times 0.5 = 0.0002$, two hundredths of 1 percent. Those few patented drugs that do make it to the pharmacy shelves, especially the blockbusters with several billion dollars in sales, must contribute enough operating profit to recover the cost of all these R & D failures.

In 2000, one of the key extension patents for Eli Lilly's blockbuster drug for the treatment of depression, Prozac, was overturned by a regulator and a U.S. federal judge. Within one month, Eli Lilly lost 70 percent of Prozac's sales to the generic equivalents. Although this company has several other blockbusters, Eli Lilly's share price plummeted 32 percent. CEO Sidney Taurel said he had made a mistake in not rolling out Prozac's successor replacement drug when the patent extension for Prozac was first challenged. Taurel then moved quickly to establish a new management concept throughout the company. Now, each new Eli Lilly drug is assigned a team of scientists, marketers, and regulatory experts who oversee the entire life cycle of the product from research inception to patent expiration. The key function of these cross-functionally integrated teams is contingency analysis and scenario planning to deal with the unexpected.

[10]C. Kennedy, F. Harris, and M. Lord, "Integrating Public Policy and Public Affairs into Pharmaceutical Marketing: Differential Pricing and the AIDS Pandemic," *Journal of Public Policy and Marketing* (Fall 2004), pp. 1–23; and "Eli Lilly: Bloom and Blight," *The Economist* (October 26, 2002), p. 60.

[9]J. R. Woolridge, "Competitive Decline: Is a Myopic Stock Market to Blame?" *Journal of Applied Corporate Finance* (Spring 1988), pp. 26–36.

Admittedly, value-maximizing managers must manage change—sometimes radical changes in competition (free-wheeling electric power), in technology (Internet signal compression), in revenue collection (music), and in regulation (cigarettes)—but they must do so with an eye to the long-run sustainable profitability of the business. In short, value-maximizing managers must anticipate change and make contingency plans.

Shareholder wealth maximization also reflects dynamic changes in the information available to the public about a company's expected future cash flows and foreseeable risks. An accounting scandal at Krispy Kreme caused the stock price to plummet from $41 to $20 per share in one month. Stock price also reflects not only the firm's preexisting positive net present value investments, but also the firm's strategic investment opportunities (the "embedded real options") a management team develops. Amgen, a biotechnology company, had shareholder value of $42 million in 1983 despite no sales, no cash flow, no capital assets, no patents, and poorly protected trade secrets. By 1993, Amgen had sales of over $1.4 billion and cash flow of $408 million annually. Amgen had developed and exercised enormously valuable strategic opportunities.

Example

Amgen's Potential Profitability Is Realized

Amgen, Inc. uses state-of-the-art biotechnology to develop human pharmaceutical and diagnostic products. After a period of early losses during their start-up phase, profits increased steadily from $19 million in 1989 to $355 million in 1993 to $670 million in 1996. On the strength of royalty income from the sale of its Epogen product, a stimulator of red blood cell production, profits jumped to $900 million per year by 1999. In 2009, Amgen was valued at $60 billion with revenues and cash flows having continued to grow throughout the previous 10 years at 19 percent annually.

In general, only about 85 percent of shareholder value can be explained by even 30 years of cash flows.[11] The remainder reflects the capitalized value of strategic flexibility to expand some profitable lines of business, to abandon others, and to retain but delay investment in still others until more information becomes available. These additional sources of equity value are referred to as *embedded real options*.

We need to address why NPV and option value are additive concepts. NPV was invented to value bonds where all the cash flows are known and guaranteed by contract. As a result, the NPV analysis adjusts for timing and for risk but ignores the value of flexibility present in some capital budgeting projects but not others. These so-called embedded options present the opportunity but not the obligation to take actions to maximize the upside or minimize the downside of a capital investment. For example, investing in a fuel-switching technology in power plants allows Southern Company to burn fuel oil when that input is cheap and burn natural gas when it is cheaper. Similarly, building two smaller assembly plants, one in Japan and another in the United States, allows Honda Camry production to be shifted as currency fluctuations cause costs to fall in one plant location relative to the other. In general, a company can create flexibility in their capital budgeting by: (1) facilitating follow-on projects through growth options, (2) exiting early without penalty through abandonment options, or (3) staging

---

[11]Woolridge, *op. cit.*

investment over a learning period until better information is available through deferral options. The scenario planning that comes from such financial thinking compares the value of expanding, leaving, or waiting to the opportunity loss from shrinking, staying, or immediate investment. Strategic flexibility of this sort expands upon the NPV from discounted cash flow alone.

Example

Real Option Value Attributable to Fuel-Switching Technology at Southern Company

Ninety-six percent of all companies employ NPV analysis.[12] Eighty-five percent employ sensitivity analysis to better understand their capital investments. Only 67 percent of companies pursue the scenario planning and contingency analysis that underlies real option valuation. A tiny 11 percent of companies formally calculate the value of their embedded real options. That suggests an opportunity for recently trained managers to introduce these new techniques of capital budgeting to improve stockholder value. Southern Company recently calculated that its embedded real option from fuel-switching technology was worth more than $45 million on a capital budgeting proposal of approximately one-half billion dollars—so, the strategic flexibility of a real option reduced cost approximately by almost 10 percent.

[12]Based on P. Ryan and G. Ryan, "Capital Budgeting Practices of the Fortune 1000: How Have Things Changed?" *Journal of Business and Management* (Fall 2002). pp. 355–364

Value-maximizing behavior on the part of managers is also distinguishable from satisficing behavior. Satisficers strive to "hit their targets" (e.g., on sales growth, return on investment, or safety ratings). Not value maximizers. Rather than trying to meet a standard like 97 percent, 99 percent, or 99.9 percent error-free takeoffs and landings at O'Hare field in Chicago, or deliver a 9, 11, or 12.1 percent return on shareholders' equity, the value-maximizing manager will commit himself or herself to continuous incremental improvements. Any time the marginal benefits of an action exceed its marginal costs, the value-maximizing manager will respond "Just do it!"

Caveats to Maximizing Shareholder Value

Managers should concentrate on maximizing shareholder value alone only if three conditions are met. These conditions require: (1) complete markets, (2) no significant asymmetric information, and (3) known recontracting costs. We now discuss how a violation of any of these conditions necessitates a much larger view of management's role in firm decision making.

Complete Markets   To directly influence a company's cash flows, forward or futures markets as well as spot markets must be available for the firm's inputs, outputs, and by-products. For example, forward and futures markets for crude oil and coffee bean inputs allow Texaco-Chevron and Starbucks coffeehouses to plan their costs with more accurate cash flow projections. For a small 3 to 5 percent fee known in advance, value-maximizing managers can lock in their input expense using the commodity futures markets and avoid unexpected cost increases. This completeness of the markets allows a reduction in the cost-covering prices of gasoline and cappuccino.

Tradable Pollution Permits at Duke Power[13]

By establishing a market for tradable air pollution permits, the Clean Air Act set a price on the sulfur dioxide (SO_2) by-product from burning high-sulfur coal. Uncontrolled SO_2 emissions from coal-fired power plants in the Midwest raised the acidity of rain and mist in eastern forests from Maine to Georgia to levels almost 100 times higher than the natural acidity of rainfall. Dead trees, peeling paint, increased asthma, and stone decomposition on buildings and monuments were the result.

To elicit substantial pollution abatement at the least cost, the Clean Air Act of 1990 authorized the Environmental Protection Agency to issue tradable pollution allowances (TPAs) to 467 known SO_2 polluters for approximately 70 percent of the previous year's emissions. The utility companies doing the polluting then began to trade the allowances. Companies that were able to abate their emissions at a low cost sold their allowances to plants that couldn't abate their emissions as cost effectively. In other words, the low-cost abaters who were able to cut their emissions cheaply could then sell their permits they didn't need to higher-cost abaters. The result was that the nation's air got 30 percent cleaner at the least possible cost.

As a result of the growing completeness of this market, electric utilities like Duke Power now know what expense line to incorporate in their cash flow projections for the SO_2 by-products of operating with high-sulfur coal. TPAs can sell for more than $100 per ton, and a single utility plant operation may require 15,000 tons of permits or more. The continuous trade-off between installing $450 million pollution abatement equipment, utilizing higher-cost alternative fuels like low-sulfur coal and natural gas, or paying the current market price of these EPA-issued pollution permits can now be explicitly analyzed and the least-cost solutions found.

[13]Based on "Acid Rain: The Southern Company," Harvard Business School Publishing, HBS: 9-792-060; "Cornering the Market," *Wall Street Journal* (June 5, 1995), p. B1; and *Economic Report of the President*, February 2000 (Washington, DC: U.S.G.P.O., 2000), pp. 240–264.

No Asymmetric Information   Monitoring and coordination problems within the corporation and contracting problems between sellers and buyers often arise because of asymmetric information. Line managers and employees can misunderstand what senior executives want when they challenge employees to find a thousand different ways to save 1 percent. At Food Lion such miscommunications elicited undesirable shortcuts in food preparation and storage. Diane Sawyer of ABC News then secretly recorded seafood-counter employees spraying old salmon with a light concentration of ammonia to restore the red appearance of fresh fish. Clearly, this was not what the senior executives at Food Lion intended.

Building a good reputation with customers, workers, and the surrounding tax jurisdiction is one way companies deal with the problem of asymmetric information, and managers must attend to these reputational effects on shareholder value. We discuss the implications of asymmetric information further in Chapter 10.

Known Recontracting Costs   Finally, to focus exclusively on the discounted present value of future cash flows necessitates that managers obtain not only sales revenue and expense estimates but also forecasts of future *recontracting costs* for pivotal inputs. Owners of professional sports teams are acutely aware of how unknown recontracting costs with star players can affect the value of their franchises. The same thing can occur with an indispensable one corporate executive. A CFO, COO, CMO, or CIO can often "hold up" the firm's owners when the time comes for contract renewals. In another arena, Westinghouse entered into long-term supply contracts to provide fuel rods to nuclear power plants across the country. Thereafter, when the market price of uranium quadrupled, Westinghouse refused to deliver the promised fuel rods, and recontracting costs skyrocketed. Value-maximizing managers must anticipate and mitigate these recontracting problems.

To the extent markets are incomplete, information is asymmetric, or recontracting costs are unknown, managers must attend to these matters in order to maximize shareholder wealth rather than simply focus myopically on maximizing profits.

Residual Claimants

Why is it that the primary duty of management and the board of directors of a company is to the shareholders themselves? Shareholders have a residual claim on the firm's net cash flows after all expected contractual returns have been paid. All the other stakeholders (employees, customers, bondholders, banks, suppliers, the surrounding tax jurisdictions, the community in which plants are located, etc.) have *contractual* expected returns. If expectations created by those contracts are not met, any of these stakeholders has access to the full force of the contract law in securing what they are due. Shareholders have contractual rights, too, but those rights simply entitle them to whatever is left over, that is, to the residual. As a consequence, when shareholder owners hire a CEO and a board, they create a fiduciary duty to allocate the company's resources in such a way as to maximize the net present value of these residual claims. This is what constitutes the objective of shareholder wealth maximization.

Be very clear, however, that the value of any company's stock is quite dependent on reputation effects. Underfunding a pension plan or polluting the environment results in massive losses of capitalized value because the financial markets anticipate (correctly) that such a company will have reduced future cash flows to owners. Labor costs to attract new employees will rise; tax jurisdictions will reduce the tax preferences offered in new plant locations; customers may boycott; and the public relations, lobbying, and legal costs of such a company will surely rise. All this implies that wealth-maximizing managers must be very carefully attuned to stakeholder interests precisely because it is in their shareholders' best interests to do so.

Goals in the Public Sector and Not-for-Profit Enterprises[14]

The value-maximization objective developed for private sector firms is not an appropriate objective in the public sector or in not-for-profit (NFP) organizations. These organizations pursue a different set of objectives because of the nature of the goods and services they supply and the manner in which they are funded.

There are three characteristics of NFP organizations that distinguish them from for-profit enterprises and influence their decision making. First, no one possesses a right to receive profit or surpluses in an NFP enterprise. This absence of a profit motive can have a serious impact on the incentive to be efficient. Second, NFP enterprises are exempt from taxes on corporate income. Finally, donations to NFPs are tax deductible, which gives NFP enterprises an advantage when competing for capital.

Not-for-profit organizations include performing arts groups, museums, libraries, hospitals, churches, volunteer organizations, cooperatives, credit unions, labor unions, professional societies, foundations, and fraternal organizations. Some of these organizations

---

[14]This section draws heavily on Burton A. Weisbrod, *The Nonprofit Economy* (Cambridge, MA: Harvard University Press, 1988).

offer services to a group of clients, such as the patients of a hospital. Others provide services primarily to their members such as tennis clubs or credit unions. Finally, some NFP organizations produce products to benefit the general public. Local symphony and theater companies are examples.

NFPs as well as government agencies tend to provide services that have significant public-good characteristics. In contrast to private goods, like a bite-sized candy bar, a public good can be consumed by more than one person. Moreover, excluding those who do not pay can only be done at a prohibitively high cost. Examples of **public goods** include national defense and flood control. If an antiballistic missile system or a flood control levy is constructed, no one can be excluded from its protection even those that refuse to contribute to the cost. Therefore, even if exclusion were feasible, the indivisibility of missile defense or flood control makes the incremental cost (and therefore the efficient price) of adding another participant quite low.

Some goods, such as recreational facilities and the performing arts, have both private-good and public-good characteristics. For example, concerts and parks may be shared (within limits) and are partially non-excludable in the sense that they convey prestige and quality-of-life benefits to the entire community.[15] The more costly the exclusion, the more likely the good or service will be provided by the public sector rather than the private sector. Portrait artists and personal fitness trainers offer pay-as-you-go private fee arrangements. Chamber music fans and tennis court users often organize in consumption-sharing and cost-sharing clubs. At the end of the spectrum, open-air symphony concerts and large parks usually necessitate some public financing.

public goods Goods that may be consumed by more than one person at the same time with little or no extra cost, and for which it is expensive or impossible to exclude those who do not pay.

Not-for-Profit Objectives

Several organizational objectives have been suggested for the NFP enterprise. These include the following:

1. Maximizing the quantity and quality of output subject to a break-even budget constraint.
2. Maximizing the outcomes preferred by the NFP's contributors.
3. Maximizing the longevity of the NFP's administrators.

The Efficiency Objective in Not-for-Profit Organizations

cost-benefit analysis A resource-allocation model that can be used by public sector and not-for-profit organizations to evaluate programs or investments on the basis of the magnitude of the discounted costs and benefits.

Cost-benefit analysis has been developed to more efficiently allocate public and NFP resources among competing uses. Because government and NFP spending is normally constrained by a budget ceiling, the goals actually used in practice can be any one of the following:

1. Maximize the benefits for given costs.
2. Minimize the costs while achieving a fixed level of benefits.
3. Maximize the net benefits (benefits minus costs).

Cost-benefit analysis is only one factor in the final decision, however. It does not incorporate many of the more subjective considerations or less easily quantifiable objectives, like how fair it might be. Such matters must be introduced at a later stage in the analysis, generally through the political process.

---

[15]William J. Baumol and W. G. Bowen, *Performing Arts: The Economic Dilemma* (Brookfield, VT: Ashgate Publishing Co., 1993).

SUMMARY

- Managers are responsible for proactively solving problems in the current business model, for setting stretch goals, establishing the vision, and setting strategy for future business, for monitoring teamwork, and integrating the operations, marketing, and finance functions.

- Teamwork is subject to moral hazard because shirking one's duty is a dominant strategy in one time only prisoners' dilemmas. Hiring managers as monitors of teamwork may mitigate the moral hazard problem and elicit mutually cooperative best efforts from all members of a team.

- *Economic profit* is defined as the difference between *total revenues* and *total economic costs*. Economic costs include a normal rate of return on the capital contributed by the firm's owners. Economic profits exist to compensate investors for the risk they assume, because of temporary disequilibrium conditions, because of the existence of monopoly power, and as a reward to firms that are especially innovative or highly efficient.

- As an overall objective of the firm, the *shareholder wealth-maximization* model is flexible enough to account for differential levels of risk and timing differences in the receipt of benefits and the incurring of future costs. Shareholder wealth captures the net present value of future cash flows to owners from positive NPV projects plus the value of embedded real options. The latter place a dollar value on strategic flexibility.

- Managers may not always behave in a manner consistent with the shareholder wealth-maximization objective. The agency costs associated with preventing or at least mitigating these deviations from the owner-principal's objective are substantial.

- Random changes in company performance, perhaps unrelated to a manager's effort, combined with the unobservable nature of their task—to apply creative ingenuity in proactive problem solving—presents a difficult *principal-agent problem* to resolve. Owner-principals seldom know when to blame manager-agents for weak company performances or give them credit for strong performances either of which may have resulted from chance.

- *Governance mechanisms* (including internal monitoring by subcommittees appointed by boards of directors and large creditors, internal/external monitoring by large block shareholders, auditing and variance analysis) can be used to limit managerial discretion and thereby mitigate agency problems.

- Shareholder wealth maximization implies a firm should be forward-looking, dynamic, and have a long-term outlook; anticipate and manage change; acquire strategic investment opportunities; and maximize the present value of expected cash flows to owners within the boundaries of the statutory law, administrative law, and ethical standards of conduct.

- Shareholder wealth maximization will be difficult to achieve when firms suffer from problems related to incomplete markets, asymmetric information, and unknown recontracting costs. In the absence of these complications, managers should maximize the present value of the discounted future net cash flows to residual claimants—namely, equity owners. If any of the complicating factors is present, managers must first attend to those issues before attempting to maximize shareholder wealth.

- Not-for-profit enterprises exist to supply a good or service desired by their primary contributors.

- Public sector organizations often provide services having significant public-good characteristics. Public goods are goods that can be consumed by more than one person at a time with little additional cost, and for which excluding those who do not pay for the goods is exceptionally difficult or prohibitively expensive.

- Regardless of their specific objectives, both public and private institutions should seek to furnish their goods or services in the most efficient way, that is, at the least cost possible.

Exercises

Answers to the exercises in blue can be found in Appendix D at the back of the book.

1. One of the approaches for the Southern Company to comply with the Clean Air Act is to adopt fuel-switching technology. Do you think this strategic flexibility would have value to Southern Company's shareholders? Why?

2. Explain several dimensions of the shareholder-principal conflict with manager-agents known as the principal-agent problem. To mitigate agency problems between senior executives and shareholders, should the compensation committee of the board devote more to executive salary and bonus (cash compensation) or more to long-term incentives? Why? What role does each type of pay play in motivating managers?

3. Corporate profitability declined by 20 percent from 2008 to 2009. What performance percentage would you use to trigger executive bonuses for that year? Why? What issues would arise with hiring and retaining the best managers?

4. In the Southern Company Managerial Challenge, which alternative for complying with the Clean Air Act creates the greatest real option value? How exactly does that alternative save money? Why? Explain why installing a scrubber "burns" this option.

5. Firms in the patented pharmaceutical industry earned an average return on net worth of 22 percent in 2006, compared with an average return of 14 percent earned by over 1,400 firms followed by *Value Line*. Which theory or theories of profit do you think best explain(s) the performance of the drug industry?

6. In the context of the shareholder wealth-maximization model of a firm, what is the expected impact of each of the following events on the value of the firm? Explain why.
   a. New foreign competitors enter the market.
   b. Strict pollution control requirements are enacted.
   c. A previously nonunion workforce votes to unionize.
   d. The rate of inflation increases substantially.
   e. A major technological breakthrough is achieved by the firm, reducing its costs of production.

7. In 2008–2009, the price of jet and diesel fuel used by air freight companies decreased dramatically. As the CEO of FedEx, you have been presented with the following proposals to deal with the situation:
   a. Reduce shipping rates to reflect the expense reduction.
   b. Increase the number of deliveries per day in some markets.
   c. Make long-term contracts to buy jet fuel and diesel at a fixed price for the next two years and set shipping rates to a level that will cover these costs.
   Evaluate these alternatives in the context of the decision-making model presented in the text.

8. How would each of the following actions be expected to affect shareholder wealth?
   a. Southern Company adopts fuel-switching technology at its largest power plants.
   b. Ford Motor Company pays $2.5 billion for Jaguar.
   c. General Motors offers large rebates to stimulate sales of its automobiles.
   d. Rising interest rates cause the required returns of shareholders to increase.
   e. Import restrictions are placed on the French competitors of Napa wineries.
   f. There is a sudden drop in the expected future rate of inflation.
   g. A new, labor-saving machine is purchased by Wonder Bread and results in the layoff of 300 employees.

Case Exercises

Designing a Managerial Incentives Contract

Specific Electric Co. asks you to implement a pay-for-performance incentive contract for its new CEO and four EVPs on the Executive Committee. The five managers can either work really hard with 70 hour weeks at a personal opportunity cost of $200,000 in reduced personal entrepreneurship and increased stress-related health care costs or they can reduce effort, thereby avoiding the personal costs. The CEO and EVPs face three possible random outcomes: the probability of the company experiencing good luck is 30 percent, medium luck is 40 percent, and bad luck is 30 percent. Although the senior management team can distinguish the three "states" of luck as the quarter unfolds, the Compensation Committee of the Board of Directors (and the shareholders) cannot do so. Once the board designs an incentive contract, soon thereafter the good, medium, or bad luck occurs, and thereafter the senior managers decide to expend high or reduced work effort. One of the observable shareholder values listed below then results.

	SHAREHOLDER VALUE		
	GOOD LUCK (30%)	MEDIUM LUCK (40%)	BAD LUCK (30%)
High Effort	$1,000,000,000	$800,000,000	$500,000,000
Reduced Effort	$ 800,000,000	$500,000,000	$300,000,000

Assume the company has 10 million shares outstanding offered at a $65 initial share price, implying a $650,000,000 initial shareholder value. Since the EVPs and CEOs effort and the company's luck are unobservable to the owners and company directors, it is not possible when the company's share price falls to $50 and the company's value to $500,000,000 to distinguish whether the company experienced reduced effort and medium luck or high effort and bad luck. Similarly, it is not possible to distinguish reduced effort and good luck from high effort and medium luck.

Answer the following questions from the perspective of a member of the Compensation Committee of the board of directors who is aligned with shareholders' interests and is deciding on a performance-based pay plan (an "incentive contract") for the CEO and EVPs.

Questions

1. What is the maximum amount it would be worth to shareholders to elicit high effort all of the time rather than reduced effort all of the time?

2. If you decide to pay 1 percent of this amount (in Question 1) as a cash bonus, what performance level (what share price or shareholder value) in the table should trigger the bonus? Suppose you decide to elicit high effort by paying a bonus should the company's value rise to $800,000,000. What two criticisms can you see of this incentive contract plan?

3. Suppose you decide to elicit high effort by paying a bonus only for an increase in the company's value to $1,000,000,000. When, and if, good luck occurs, what two criticisms can you see of this incentive contract plan?

4. Suppose you decide to elicit high effort by paying the bonus when the company's value falls to $500,000,000. When, and if, bad luck occurs, what two criticisms can you see of this incentive contract plan?

5. If the bonus compensation scheme must be announced in advance, and if you must pick one of the three choices in questions 2, 3 and 4, which one would you pick and

why? In other words, under incomplete information, what is the optimal decision by the Board's Compensation Committee dedicated to act in the shareholders' interest?

6. Audits are basically sampling procedures to verify with a predetermined accuracy the sources and uses of the company receipts and expenditures; the larger the sample, the higher the accuracy. In an effort to identify the share price that should trigger a bonus, how much would you, the Compensation Committee, be willing to pay an auditing consultant who could sample the expense and revenue flows in real time and deliver perfect forecasting information about the "luck" the firm's sales force is experiencing? Compare shareholder value with this perfect forecast information relative to the best choice among the bonus plans you selected in Question 5. Define the difference as the Potential Value of Perfect Forecast Information.

7. Design a stock option-based incentive plan to elicit high effort. Show that one million stock options at a $70 exercise price improve shareholder value relative to the best of the cash bonus plans chosen in Question 5.

8. Design an incentive plan that seeks to elicit high effort by granting restricted stock. Show that one-half million shares granted at $70 improves shareholder value relative to all prior alternatives.

9. Sketch the game tree for designing this optimal managerial incentive contract among the alternatives in question 2, 3, and 4. Who makes the first choice? Who the second? What role does randomness play? Which bonus pay contract represents a best reply response in each endgame? Which bonus pay contract should the Compensation Committee of the Board select to maximize expected value? How does that compare with your selection based on the contingent claims analysis in Questions 1–8?

Shareholder Value of Renewable Energy from Wind Power at Hydro Co.:[16] Is RE < C?

Despite a decade of subsidies and considerable success in Denmark, Germany, and Britain, renewable energy in the U.S. accounts for only 7 to 8 percent of total energy consumption. Hydroelectric power remains the most successful source of renewable energy in the United States where it accounts for 2.8 percent at a cost of $0.89/kwh (see Figure 1.4). Ethanol and other biofuels account for 1.6 percent, and surprisingly wind power and solar power are good for only 0.7 percent and 0.1 percent, respectively. Part of the explanation is that the EU is more ambitious, setting a stretch goal of 20 percent of energy consumption from renewable by 2020.

Electricity from renewables in the United States must compete against conventional fossil fuels averaging approximately $.11/kwh costs nationwide. Land-based wind turbines, for example, have now become as inexpensive as conventional coal and natural gas at $.096/kwh and $.098/kwh, respectively, accounting for plant construction, fuel, maintenance, and other operating costs (again see Figure 1.4). Of course with carbon capture and storage, coal becomes much more expensive at $.141/kwh. The extensive shale gas discoveries in the U.S. have made combined-cycle natural gas-fired power plants cheaper than coal at $.092/kwh.

Solar energy remains a huge disappointment. Photovoltaic technology and storage has progressed but remains in its infancy such that the ratio of yield onto the electric grid relative to 24-day potential capacity is only 25 percent. Steam-generating solar farms have an even lower *energy conversion factor* of 20 percent. Consequently even though solar capacity can be dispersed to individual rooftop installations and transmission costs are therefore much lower than wind or geothermal power, solar energy remains the most expensive source of renewable energy at $.153/kwh. With much better technology, geothermal and biomass are major RE successes at $.098/kwh and $.115/kwh, respectively.

---

[16]Based on Frederick Harris, Alternative Energy Symposium, Wake Forest University (September 19, 2008).

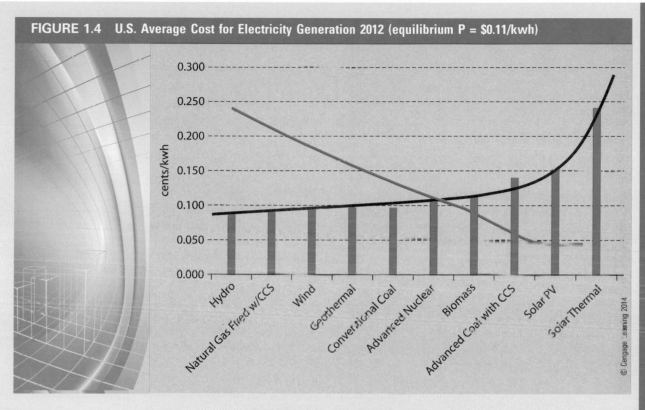

FIGURE 1.4   U.S. Average Cost for Electricity Generation 2012 (equilibrium P = $0.11/kwh)

Wind farms and massive solar collector arrays already provide 20 percent of the electric power generation in Denmark and 15 percent in Germany. Hydro, a Norwegian aluminum company, has established wind turbine pilot projects where entire communities are electricity self-sufficient. At 80 meters of elevation, class 3 wind energy (steady 22 kph breeze) is available almost everywhere on the planet, implying wind power potential worldwide of 72 million megawatts. Harvesting just the best 5 percent of this wind energy (3.6 million megawatts) would make it possible to retire *several thousand* coal-fired power plants, 617 of which operate in the United States today.[17]

So-called alternative energy is: (1) renewable, (2) in abundant local supply, and (3) generates a low carbon footprint. Renewables are naturally replenishing sources including wind, solar, hydro, biofuel, biomass, geothermal, tidal, ocean current, and wave energy. Nuclear energy is not renewable because of the waste disposal issues. To date, by far the most successful renewables are hydroelectric power plants and ethanol-based biofuels, each accounting for about 2 percent of energy worldwide. New sources of renewable energy such as wind and solar power are often judged against fuel oil at $15, natural gas at $6, and coal at $4 per million BTUs (see Figure 1.5). One ton of plentiful high-sulfur-content coal generates approximately a megawatt of electricity and a ton of carbon dioxide (CO_2). In 2008, the European Union's cap-and-trade legislation to reduce carbon emissions imposed a $.023 per ton additional CO_2 emissions charge atop the $.085 purchase price of coal. Finding renewable energy sources that have full costs lower than coal's $.023 + $.085 = $.108 for a megawatt hour (RE < C) is a reasonable objective of energy policy.

---

[17]Older, smaller 500-megawatt coal-fired plants have adopted little pollution abatement technology. Nuclear power plants are much larger, generating typically 2,000 megawatts of electricity. Duke Power's Belews Creek plant at 2,200 megawatts is one of the largest coal-fired power plants in the United States (see Figure 1.1). Following the installation of a $450 million smokestack scrubber, it is also one of the cleanest.

FIGURE 1.5 RE < C? Can Renewable Energy Cost Less Than Coal?, 1999–2011

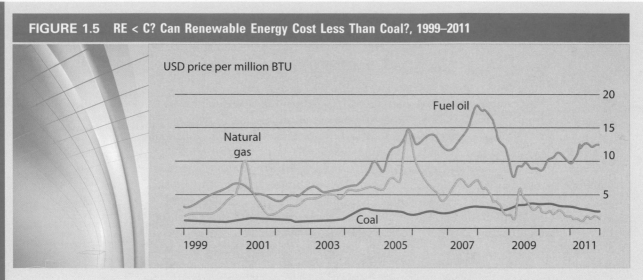

Source: Thomson Datastream; U.S. Energy Information Administration.

Why pursue wind and solar power rather than other alternative energy sources? Nuclear energy has a decades-long timeline for construction and permitting especially of nuclear waste disposal sites. Corn-based ethanol runs up the cost of animal feedstocks and raises food prices. In addition, corn contains only one-eighth the BTUs of sugarcane, which is in abundant supply in the Caribbean and Brazil. Unfortunately, the U.S. Congress has placed a $0.54 per gallon tariff on sugarcane-based ethanol. Natural gas is 80 percent cleaner than coal and extraordinarily abundant in the United States, the world's biggest energy user at 21 million barrels per day (mbd), 13 mbd being imported. The United States contains almost 30 percent of the known deposits worldwide of natural gas (and coal) but only 3 percent of the proven reserves of crude oil.

A 0.6 megawatt wind turbine that costs $1.2 million today will generate $4.4 million in discounted net present value of electricity over a 15-year period, sufficient to power 440 Western European or American households with 100 percent capacity utilization and continuous 15 mph wind.[18] Mechanical energy in the turbine is converted directly into electrical potential energy with a magnetic coil generator. When the wind does not blow, Hydro has demonstrated and patented a load-shifting technology that consists of a hydrolysis electrolyzer splitting water into oxygen and hydrogen, a hydrogen storage container, and a fuel cell to convert the hydrogen chemical energy back to electrical current (see Figure 1.6). With the three extra pieces of equipment, the capital investment rises from $1.2 million to $2.7 million. Even so, wind power can be quite profitable with full cost recovery periods as short as seven years under ideal operating conditions.

Of course, frequently the operating conditions with wind power are far less than ideal. Despite the presence of wind at elevation across the globe, few communities want 80+ meter wind turbines as tall as a football field in their backyard sight lines. Lower installations result in less wind and therefore less electricity. In addition, the conversion of one form of energy to another always burns energy. In Hydro's load-shifting process of converting mechanical energy from the turbine to chemical energy in the electrolyzer and then to electrical energy in the hydrogen fuel cell, about 30 percent of the maximum energy coming

---

[18]600,000 kilowatt hours × $0.11 average electricity rates × 24 hours × 365 days equals $578,160 per year for 15 years of expected working life of the turbine. Based on "Hydro: From Utsira to Future Energy Solutions," Ivey School of Business, Case #906M44, 2006.

FIGURE 1.6   Continuous Electricity from Wind Power

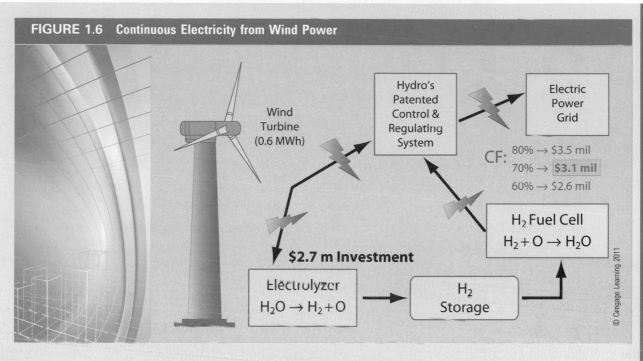

directly to the electrical grid from the turbine's generator when the wind is blowing hard and steady is lost. Experiments in many wind conditions at the Utsira site suggest that baseline output of Hydro's pilot project in Norway has a maximum energy conversion factor (CF) of 70 percent with 60 percent more typical. Even lower 45 percent CFs are expected in typical operating conditions elsewhere. Seventy percent CF realizes $3.1 million of electricity.

Questions

1. As a value-maximizing aluminum company, should Hydro invest in wind power in light of the Utsira pilot project? Why or why not?

2. Larger-scale turbines increase the electricity more than proportionately to the increase in costs. A 1 megawatt turbine costs $2.6 million, with the remaining equipment costs unchanged, for a total required investment of $4.1 million to power approximately 760 households. Electricity revenue over 15 years rises to $7.2 million in discounted present value. What conversion factor allows cost recovery of this larger-scale turbine?

3. If the net present value of the Utsira project is negative, yet Hydro goes ahead and funds the investment anyway, what ethical obligations does Hydro have to its shareholders? Discuss the role of corporate social responsibility and of back-up plans to address the possible full costing of coal, as in the European Union where carbon permits for a ton of coal have at times increased coal resource costs by 25 percent.

4. On what basis could shareholder value possibly rise if Hydro invests in negative NPV wind power projects?

5. Electric power generation is responsible for 43 percent of all energy consumption in the United States. Coal provides the preponderant fuel (38 percent), with nuclear power (19 percent) and natural gas (30 percent) providing most of the rest. Renewable energy provides only 12 percent. Recently, T. Boone Pickens proposed converting the trucking fleet in the United States to liquefied natural gas (LNG) and using wind power to replace the missing LNG in electric power production. What infrastructure issues do you see that must be resolved before the Pickens plan could be adopted?

CHAPTER 2

Fundamental Economic Concepts

CHAPTER PREVIEW

A few fundamental microeconomic concepts provide cornerstones for all of the analysis in managerial economics. Four of the most important are demand and supply, marginal analysis, net present value, and the meaning and measurement of risk. We will first review how the determinants of demand and supply establish a market equilibrium price for gasoline, crude oil, and hybrid electric cars. Marginal analysis tools are central when a decision maker is seeking to optimize some objective, such as maximizing cost savings from changing a lightbulb (e.g., from normal incandescent to compact fluorescent lights [CFL] or light-emitting diodes [LED]). The net present value concept makes alternative cash flows occurring at different points in time directly comparable. In so doing, it provides the linkage between the timing and risk of a firm's projected profits and the shareholder wealth-maximization objective. Risk-return analysis is important to an understanding of the many trade-offs that managers must consider as they introduce new products, expand capacity, or outsource overseas in order to increase expected profits at the risk of greater variation in profits.

Two appendices elaborate these topics for those who want to know more analytical details and seek exposure to additional application tools. Appendix C develops the relationship between marginal analysis and differential calculus. Web Appendix F shows how managers incorporate explicit probability information about the risk of various outcomes into individual choice models, decision trees, risk-adjusted discount rates, simulation analysis, and scenario planning.

MANAGERIAL CHALLENGE
Why Charge $25 per Bag on Airline Flights?

In May 2008, American Airlines (AA) announced that it would immediately begin charging $25 per bag on all AA flights, not for extra luggage but for the first bag! Crude oil had nearly doubled from $70 to $130 per barrel in the previous 12 months, and jet fuel prices had accelerated even faster. AA's new baggage policy applied to all ticketed passengers except first class and business class. On top of incremental airline charges for sandwiches and snacks introduced the previous year, this

new announcement stunned the travel public. Previously, only a few deep discount U.S. carriers with very limited route structures such as People Express had charged separately for both food and baggage service. Since American Airlines and many other major carriers had belittled that policy as part of their overall marketing campaign against deep discounters, AA executives faced a dilemma.

Jet fuel surcharges had recovered the year-over-year average variable cost increase for jet fuel expenses, but

MANAGERIAL CHALLENGE *Continued*

incremental variable costs (the marginal cost) remained uncovered. A quick back-of-the-envelope calculation outlines the problem. If total variable costs for a 500-mile flight on a 180-seat 737-800 rise from $22,000 in 2007 Q2 to $36,000 in 2008 Q2 because of $14,000 of additional fuel costs, then competitively priced carriers would seek to recover $14,000/180 = $78 per seat in jet fuel surcharges. The average variable cost rise of $78 would be added to the price for each fare class. For example, the $188 Super Saver airfare, restricted to 14-day advance purchase and Saturday night stayovers, would go up to $266. Class M airfares, requiring 7-day advance purchase but no Saturday stayovers, would rise from $289 to $367. Full coach economy airfares without purchase restrictions would rise from $419 to $497, and so on.

The problem was that by 2008 Q2, the marginal cost for jet fuel had risen to approximately $1 for each pound transported 500 miles. Carrying an additional 170-pound passenger in 2007 had resulted in $45 of additional fuel costs. By May 2008, the marginal fuel cost was $170 − $45 = $125 higher! So although the $78 fuel surcharge was offsetting the accounting expense increase when one averaged in cheaper earlier fuel purchases, additional current purchases were much more expensive. Managers realized they should focus on this much higher $170 marginal cost when deciding on incremental seat sales and deeply discounted prices.

And similarly, this marginal $1 per pound for 500 miles became the focus of attention in analyzing baggage cost. A first suitcase was traveling free under the prior baggage policy, as long as it weighed less than 42 pounds. But that maximum allowed suitcase imposed $42 of marginal cost in May 2008. Therefore, in mid-2008, American Airlines (and now other major

carriers) announced a $25 baggage fee for the first bag in order to cover the marginal cost of the representative suitcase on AA, which weighs 25.4 pounds.

Discussion Questions

■ How should the airline respond when presented with an overweight bag (more than 42 pounds)?

■ Explain whether or not each of the following should be considered a variable cost that increases with each additional airline seat sale: baggage costs, crew costs, commissions on ticket sales, airport parking costs, food costs, and additional fuel costs from passenger weight.

■ If jet fuel prices reverse their upward trend and begin to decline, fuel surcharges based on average variable cost will catch up with and surpass marginal costs. How should the airlines respond then?

DEMAND AND SUPPLY: A REVIEW

Demand and supply simultaneously determine equilibrium market price (P_{eq}). P_{eq} equates the desired rate of purchase Q_d/t with the planned rate of sale Q_s/t. Both concepts address intentions—that is, purchase intentions and supply intentions. Demand is therefore a potential concept often distinguished from the transactional event of "units sold." In that sense, demand is more like the potential sales concept of customer traffic than it is the accounting receivables concept of revenue from completing an actual sale. Analogously, supply is more like scenario planning for operations than it is like actual production, distribution, and delivery. In addition, supply and demand are explicitly rates per unit time period (e.g., autos per week at a Chevy dealership and the aggregate purchase intentions of the households in the surrounding target market). Hence, P_{eq} is a market-clearing equilibrium concept, a price that equates the flow rates of intended purchase and planned sale.

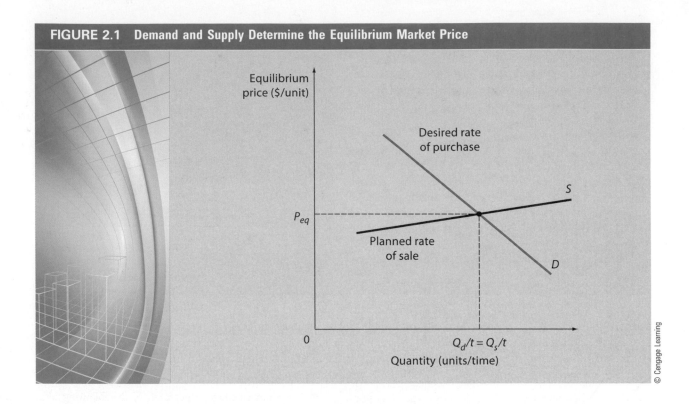

FIGURE 2.1 Demand and Supply Determine the Equilibrium Market Price

When the order flow to buy at a given price (Q_d/t) in Figure 2.1 just balances against the order flow to sell at that price (Q_s/t), P_{eq} has emerged, but what ultimately determines this metric of "value" in a marketplace? Among the earliest answers can be found in the Aristotelian concept of intrinsic use value. Because diamonds secure marriage covenants and peace pacts between nations, they provide enormous use value and should therefore exhibit high market value. The problem with this theory of value taken alone arises when one considers cubic zirconium diamonds. No one other than a jewel merchant can distinguish the artificial cubic zirconium from the real thing, and therefore the intrinsic uses of both types are identical. Yet, cubic zirconium diamonds sell for many times less than natural stones of like grade and color. Why? One clue arose at the end of the Middle Ages, when Catholic monasteries produced beautiful hand-copied Bibles and sold them for huge sums (i.e., $22,400 in 2012 dollars) to other monasteries and the nobility. In 1455, Johannes Gutenberg offered a "mass produced" printed facsimile that could be put to exactly the same intrinsic use, and yet the market value fell almost one-hundredfold to $250 in 2010 dollars. Why?

Equilibrium market price results from the interaction of demanders and suppliers involved in an exchange. In addition to the use value demanders anticipate from a product, a supplier's variable cost will also influence the market price observed. Ultimately, therefore, what minimum asking price suppliers require to cover their variable costs is just as pivotal in determining value in exchange as what maximum offer price buyers are willing to pay. Gutenberg Bibles and cubic zirconium diamonds exchange in a marketplace at lower "value" not because they are intrinsically less useful than prior copies of the Bible or natural diamonds, but simply because the bargain struck between buyers and sellers of these products will likely be negotiated down to a level that just covers their lower variable cost plus a small profit. Otherwise, preexisting competitors are likely to win the business by asking less.

Even when the cost of production is nearly identical and intrinsic use value is nearly identical, equilibrium market prices can still differ markedly. One additional determinant of value helps to explain why. Market value depends upon the relative scarcity of resources. Hardwoods are scarce in Japan, but plentiful in Sweden. Even though the cost of timber cutting and sawmill planing is the same in both locations, hardwood trees have scarcity value as raw material in Japan that they do not have in Sweden where they are plentiful. To take another example, whale oil for use in lamps throughout the nineteenth and early twentieth centuries stayed at a nearly constant price until whale species began to be harvested at rates beyond their sustainable yield. As whale resources became scarcer, the whalers who expended no additional cost on better equipment or longer voyages came home with less oil from reduced catches. With less raw material on the market, the input price of whale oil rose quickly. Consequently, despite unchanged other costs of production, the scarcer input led to a higher final product price. Similar results occur in the commodity market for coffee beans or orange juice when climate changes or insect infestations in the tropics cause crop projections to decline and scarcity value to rise.

Example

Discovery of Jojoba Bean Causes a Collapse of Whale Oil Lubricant Prices[1]

Until the last decade of the twentieth century, the best-known lubricant for high friction machinery with repeated temperature extremes like fan blades in aircraft jet engines, contact surfaces in metal cutting tools, and gearboxes in auto transmissions was a naturally occurring substance—sperm whale oil. In the early 1970s, the United States placed sperm whales on the endangered species list and banned their harvest. With the increasing scarcity of whales, the world market price of whale oil lubricant approached $200 per quart. Research and development for synthetic oil substitutes tried again and again but failed to find a replacement. Finally, a California scientist suggested the extract of the jojoba bean as a natural, environmentally friendly lubricant. The jojoba bean grows like a weed throughout the desert of the southwestern United States on wild trees that can be domesticated and cultivated to yield beans for up to 150 years.

After production ramped up from 150 tons in 1986 to 700 tons in 1995, solvent-extracted jojoba sold for $10 per quart. When tested in the laboratory, jojoba bean extract exhibits some lubrication properties that exceed those of whale oil (e.g., thermal stability over 400°F). Although 85 to 90 percent of jojoba bean output is used in the production of cosmetics, the confirmation of this plentiful substitute for high-friction lubricants caused a collapse in whale lubricant prices. Sperm whale lubricant has the same cost of production and the same use value as before the discovery of jojoba beans, but the scarcity value of the raw material input has declined tenfold. Consequently, a quart of sperm whale lubricant now sells for under $20 per quart.

[1]Based on "Jojoba Producers Form a Marketing Coop," *Chemical Marketing Reporter* (January 8, 1995), p. 10.

The Diamond-Water Paradox and the Marginal Revolution

So equilibrium price in a marketplace is related to (1) intrinsic use value, (2) production cost, and (3) input scarcity. In addition, however, most products and services have more than one use and more than one method of production. And often these differences relate to how much or how often the product has already been consumed or produced. For example, the initial access to e-mail servers or the Internet for several hours per day is often essential to maintaining good communication with colleagues and business associates. Additional access makes it possible to employ search engines such as Google for information related to a work assignment. Still more access affords an opportunity to meet friends in a chat room. Finally, some households might purchase even more hours of access on the chance that a desire to surf the Web would arise unexpectedly. Each of these uses has its own distinct value along a continuum starting with necessities and ending with frivolous nonessentials. Accordingly, what a customer will pay for another hour of Internet access depends on the incremental hour in question. For any given item or service, the greater the utilization already, the lower the use value remaining.

marginal use value The additional value of the consumption of one more unit; the greater the utilization already, the lower the use value remaining.

This concept of a **marginal use value** that declines as the rate of consumption increases leads to a powerful insight about consumer behavior. The question was posed: "Why should something as essential to human life as water sell for low market prices while something as frivolous as cosmetic diamonds sell for high market prices?" The initial answer was that water is inexpensive to produce in most parts of the world while diamonds require difficult search and discovery, expensive mining, and extensive transportation and security expenses. In other words, diamonds cost more than water, so minimum asking prices of suppliers dictate the higher market value observed for diamonds. However, recall that supply is only one of what Alfred Marshall famously called "two blades of the scissors" representing demand and supply. You can stab with one blade but you can't cut paper, and using supply alone, you can't fully explain equilibrium market price.

The diamond-water paradox was therefore restated more narrowly: "Why should consumers bid low offer prices for something as essential as water while bidding high offer prices for something as frivolous as diamonds?" The resolution of this narrower paradox hinges on distinguishing marginal use value (**marginal utility**) from total use value (total utility). Clearly, in some circumstances and locales, the use value of water is enormous. At an oasis in the desert, water does prevent you from thirsting to death. And even in the typical city, the first couple of ounces of some liquid serve this same function, but that's the first couple of ounces. The next couple of dozen gallons per day remain at high use value for drinking, flushing indoor plumbing, cooking, body washing, and so forth. Thereafter, water is used for clothes washing, landscape watering, car washing, and sundry lesser purposes. Indeed, if one asks the typical American household (which consumes 80–100 gallons per person per day) to identify its least valuable use of water each day, the answer may come back truly frivolous—perhaps something like the water that runs down the sink drain while brushing teeth. In other words, the *marginal use value* of water in most developed countries is the water that saves the consumer the inconvenience of turning the water taps (on and off) twice rather than just once. And it is this marginal use value at the relevant margin, not the total utility across all uses, that determines a typical water consumer's meager willingness to pay.

marginal utility The use value obtained from the last unit consumed.

Marginal Utility and Incremental Cost Simultaneously Determine Equilibrium Market Price

Alfred Marshall had it right: demand and supply do simultaneously determine market equilibrium price. On the one hand, marginal utility determines the maximum offer price consumers are willing to pay for each additional unit of consumption on the demand side of the market. On the other hand, variable cost at the margin (an incremental cost concept sometimes referred to as "marginal cost") determines the minimum asking price producers are willing to accept for each additional unit supplied. Water is

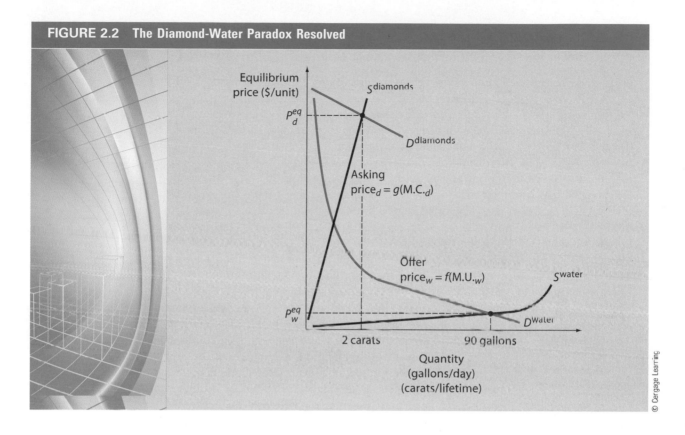

FIGURE 2.2 The Diamond-Water Paradox Resolved

both cheaper to produce and more frivolous than diamonds *at the relevant margin*, and hence water's market equilibrium price is lower than that of diamonds. Figure 2.2 illustrates this concept of marginal use value for water varying from the absolutely essential first few ounces to the frivolous water left running while brushing one's teeth.

At the same time, the marginal cost of producing water remains low throughout the 90-gallon range of a typical household's daily consumption. In contrast, diamonds exhibit steeply rising marginal cost even at relatively small volume, and customers continue to employ cosmetic diamonds for highly valuable uses even out to the relevant margin (one to three carats) where typical households find their purchases occurring. Therefore, diamonds *should* trade for equilibrium market prices that exceed the equilibrium market price of water.

Individual and Market Demand Curves

We have seen that the market-clearing equilibrium price (P_{eq}) that sets the desired rate of purchase (Q_d/t) equal to the planned rate of sale (Q_s/t) is simultaneously both the maximum offer price demanders are willing to pay (the "offer") and the minimum asking price sellers are willing to accept (the "ask"). But what determines the desired rate of purchase Q_d/t and planned rate of sales Q_s/t? The demand schedule (sometimes called the "demand curve") is the simplest form of the demand relationship. It is merely a list of prices and corresponding quantities of a commodity that would be demanded by some individual or group of individuals at uniform prices. Table 2.1 shows the demand schedule for regular-size pizzas at a Pizza Hut restaurant. This demand schedule indicates that if the price were $9.00, customers would purchase 60 per night. Note that the lower the price, the greater the quantity that will be demanded. This is the strongest

TABLE 2.1 SIMPLIFIED DEMAND SCHEDULE: PIZZA HUT RESTAURANT	
PRICE OF PIZZA ($/UNIT)	QUANTITY OF PIZZAS SOLD (UNITS PER TIME PERIOD)
10	50
9	60
8	70
7	80
6	90
5	100

© Cengage Learning

form of the law of demand—if a product or service is income superior, a household will always purchase more as the relative price declines.

The Demand Function

The demand schedule (or curve) specifies the relationship between prices and quantity demanded, *holding constant the influence of all other factors*. A **demand function** specifies all these other factors that management will often consider, including the design and packaging of products, the amount and distribution of the firm's advertising budget, the size of the sales force, promotional expenditures, the time period of adjustment for any price changes, and taxes or subsidies. As detailed in Table 2.2, the demand function for hybrid-electric or all-electric autos can be represented as

$$Q_D = f(P, P_S, P_C, Y, A, A_C, N, C_P, P_E, T_A, T/S \ldots) \qquad [2.1]$$

where Q_D = quantity demanded of (e.g., Toyota Prius or Chevy Volt)

P = price of the good or service (the auto)

P_S = price of **substitute goods** or services (e.g., the popular gasoline-powered Honda Accord or Chevy Cruze)

P_C = price of **complementary goods** or services (replacement batteries)

Y = income of consumers

A = advertising and promotion expenditures by Toyota or General Motors (GM)

A_C = competitors' advertising and promotion expenditures (e.g., Honda)

N = size of the potential target market (demographic factors)

C_P = consumer tastes and preferences for a "greener" form of transportation

P_E = expected future price appreciation or depreciation of hybrid autos

T_A = purchase adjustment time period

T/S = taxes or subsidies on hybrid autos

The demand schedule or demand curve merely deals with the price-quantity relationship itself. Changes in the price (P) of the good or service will result only in movement along the demand curve, whereas changes in any of the other demand determinants in the demand function (P_S, P_C, Y, A, A_C, N, C_P, P_E, and so on) shift the demand curve. This is illustrated graphically in Figure 2.3. The initial demand relationship is line DD'. If the original price were P_1, quantity Q_1 would be demanded. If the price declined to P_2, the quantity demanded would increase to Q_2. If, however, changes occurred in the other determinants of demand, we would expect to have a shift in the entire demand curve. If, for example, a subsidy to hybrids were enacted, the new demand curve might become

demand function A relationship between quantity demanded per unit of time and all the determinants of demand.

substitute goods Alternative products whose demand increases when the price of the focal product rises.

complementary goods Complements in consumption whose demand decreases when the price of the focal product rises.

TABLE 2.2 PARTIAL LIST OF FACTORS AFFECTING DEMAND

DEMAND FACTOR	EXPECTED EFFECT
Increase (decrease) in price of substitute goods[a] (P_S)	Increase (decrease) in demand (Q_D)
Increase (decrease) in price of complementary goods[b] (P_C)	Decrease (increase) in Q_D
Increase (decrease) in consumer income levels[c] (Y)	Increase (decrease) in Q_D
Increase (decrease) in the amount of advertising and marketing expenditures (A)	Increase (decrease) in Q_D
Increase (decrease) in level of advertising and marketing by competitors (A_C)	Decrease (increase) in Q_D
Increase (decrease) in population (N)	Increase (decrease) in Q_D
Increase (decrease) in consumer preferences for the good or service (C_P)	Increase (decrease) in Q_D
Expected future price increases (decreases) for the good (P_E)	Increase (decrease) in Q_D
Time period of adjustment increases (decreases) (T_A)	Increase (decrease) in Q_D
Taxes (subsidies) on the good increase (decrease) (T/S)	Decrease (increase) in Q_D

[a]Two goods are substitutes if an increase (decrease) in the price of Good 1 results in an increase (decrease) in the quantity demanded of Good 2, holding other factors constant, such as the price of Good 2, other prices, income, and so on, or vice versa. For example, margarine may be viewed as a rather good substitute for butter. As the price of butter increases, more people will decrease their consumption of butter and increase their consumption of margarine.

[b]Goods that are used in conjunction with each other, either in production or consumption, are called *complementary goods*. For example, DVDs are used in conjunction with DVD players. An increase in the price of DVD players would have the effect of decreasing the demand for DVDs, *ceteris paribus*. In other words, two goods are complementary if a decrease in the price of Good 1 results in an increase in the quantity demanded of Good 2, *ceteris paribus*. Similarly, two goods are complements if an increase in the price of Good 1 results in a decrease in the quantity demanded of Good 2.

[c]The case of inferior goods—that is, those goods that are purchased in smaller total quantities as income levels rise—will be discussed in Chapter 3.

FIGURE 2.3 Shifts in Demand

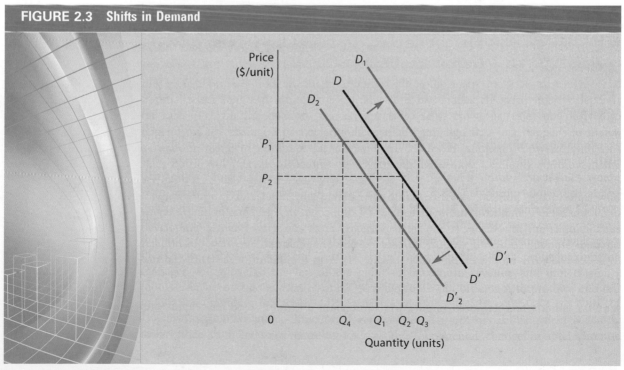

$D_1 D'_1$. At any price, P_1, along $D_1 D'_1$, a greater quantity, Q_3, will be demanded than at the same price before the subsidy on the original curve DD'. Similarly, if the prices of substitute products such as the Honda Civic or Chevy Cruze were to decline sharply, the demand curve would shift downward and to the left. At any price, P_1, along the new curve $D'_2 D_2$, a smaller quantity, Q_4, would be demanded than at the same price on either DD' or $D_1 D'_1$.

In summary, movement along a demand curve is often referred to as *a change in the quantity demanded*, while holding constant the effects of factors other than price that determine demand. In contrast, a shift of the entire demand curve is often referred to as a *change in demand* and is always caused by some demand determinant other than price.

Import-Export Traded Goods

In addition to the previous determinants of demand, the demand for goods traded in foreign markets is also influenced by external factors such as exchange rate fluctuations. When Microsoft sells computer software overseas, it prefers to be paid in U.S. dollars. This is because a company like Microsoft incurs few offshore expenses beyond advertising and therefore cannot simply match payables and receivables in a foreign currency. To accept euros, Japanese yen, or Australian dollars in payment for software purchase orders would introduce an exchange rate risk exposure for which Microsoft would want to be compensated in the form of higher prices on its software. Consequently, the foreign exports of Microsoft are typically transacted in U.S. dollars and are therefore tied inextricably to the price of the dollar against other currencies. As the value of the dollar rises, offshore buyers must pay a larger amount of their own currency to obtain the U.S. dollars required to complete a purchase order for Microsoft's software, and this decreases the export demand. Even in a large domestic market like the United States, companies often find that these export demand considerations are key determinants of their overall demand.

Example

Exchange Rate Impacts on Demand: Cummins Engine Company

Cummins Engine Company of Columbus, Indiana, is the largest independent manufacturer of new and replacement diesel engines for heavy trucks and for construction, mining, and agricultural machinery. Volvo and Daimler-Benz are their major competitors, and 53 percent of sales occur offshore. The Cummins and Daimler-Benz large diesel truck engines sell for approximately $40,000 and €35,000, respectively. In the 2002 recession, Cummins *suffered* substantial declines in cash flow. One reason was obvious: diesel replacement engines are not needed when fewer goods are being delivered, and therefore fewer diesels are wearing out.

In addition, however, between 1999 and 2002, the value of the U.S. dollar (€ per $) increased by 30 percent from €.85/$ to €1.12/$. This meant that a $40,000 Cummins diesel engine that had sold for €34,000 in Munich in 1999 became €44,800, whereas the €35,000 Mercedes diesel alternative that had been selling for $41,176 in Detroit declined to $31,250 because of the stronger U.S. dollar. Cummins faced two unattractive options, either of which would reduce its cash flow. It could either cut its profit

(continued)

margins and maintain unit sales, or maintain margins but have both offshore and domestic sales collapse. The company chose to cut margins and maintain sales. By 2005, the dollar's value had eroded, returning to €.85/$, and Cummins' sales performance markedly improved. In the interim, demand for Cummins engines was adversely affected by the temporary appreciation of the U.S. dollar.

In 2009, with the U.S. dollar at a still lower value of €.64/$, the Cummins Engine Co. could barely keep up with export demand since diesels to Europe were priced at €25,600 versus Mercedes' €32,000. Similarly, in Cleveland, St. Louis, and Atlanta, Cummins $40,000 diesels were up against $54,688 Mercedes substitutes. What a great time to be an American company competing against European manufacturers.

Individual and Market Supply Curves

What determines the planned rate of sale Q_s/t? Like the demand schedule, the supply schedule is a list of prices and corresponding quantities that an individual or group of sellers desires to sell at uniform prices, *holding constant the influence of all other factors.* A number of these other determinants of supply that management will often need to consider are detailed in Table 2.3. The **supply function** can be represented as

supply function
A relationship between quantity supplied and all the determinants of supply.

$$Q_S = f(P, P_I, P_{UI}, T, EE, F, RC, P_E, T_A, T/S \dots)$$ [2.2]

where Q_s = quantity supplied (e.g., of domestic autos)
P = price of the autos
P_I = price of inputs (e.g., sheet metal)
P_{UI} = price of unused substitute inputs (e.g., fiberglass)
T = technological improvements (e.g., robotic welding)
EE = entry or exit of other auto sellers
F = accidental supply interruptions from fires, floods, etc.
RC = costs of regulatory compliance
P_E = expected (future) changes in price
T_A = adjustment time period
T/S = taxes or subsidies

TABLE 2.3 PARTIAL LIST OF FACTORS AFFECTING SUPPLY

SUPPLY FACTOR	EXPECTED EFFECT AT EVERY PRICE
Increase (decrease) in the price of inputs (P_I)	Decrease (increase) in supply
Increase (decrease) in the price of unused substitute inputs (P_{UI})	Decrease (increase) in supply
Technological improvements (T)	Increase in supply
Entry (Exit) of other sellers (EE)	Increase (decrease) in supply
Supply disruptions (F)	Decrease in supply
Increase (decrease) in regulatory costs (RC)	Decrease (increase) in supply
Expected future price increases (decreases) (P_E)	Decrease (increase) in supply
Time period of adjustment lengthens (shortens) (T_A)	Increase (decrease) in supply
Taxes (subsidies) (T/S)	Decrease (increase) in supply

Example

NAFTA and the Reduced Labor Costs of Ford Assembly Plants in Detroit

The North American Free Trade Agreement (NAFTA) made it possible to buy sub-assemblies like axles and engine blocks from Mexican suppliers like Cifunsa, S.A., without paying any import tariff when the parts arrived in the United States. United Auto Worker (UAW) labor in a Detroit auto assembly plants making axle subassemblies can be thought about as an unused substitute input from the point of view of Ford Motor Company. NAFTA in effect lowered the input cost of substitute inputs for Ford. This means fewer employers would pursue labor contracts with the UAW and instead shift some of their production south across the Mexican border. Less demand implies lower equilibrium wages. Hence, the indirect effect of NAFTA was a reduction in the input costs for UAW labor that the Ford Motor Co. did utilize. As usual, lower input cost implies a shift of the supply curve down and to the right, an increase in supply.

supply curve
A relationship between price and quantity supplied per unit time, holding other determinants of supply constant.

Again, changes in the price (P) of the good or service will result only in movement along the given **supply curve**, whereas changes in any of the other independent variables (P_I, P_{UI}, T, EE, F, RC, P_E, T_A, and so on) in the function shift the supply curve. As with demand, a movement *along* a supply curve is referred to as *a change in the quantity supplied*, while holding constant other determinants of supply. A shift of the entire supply curve is often referred to as a change *in supply* and is always caused by some supply determinant other than price.

Equilibrium Market Price of Gasoline

In April–July 2008, Americans woke up to a new reality about gasoline that markedly affected their driving habits as well as U.S. energy policy. The price of a gallon of regular octane gasoline skyrocketed from $3.00 per gallon to $4.10 (see Figure 2.4). The previous summer, when gas prices had hovered around $3 per gallon, Americans had cut back

FIGURE 2.4 Average Gas Prices in the United States, 2005–2011

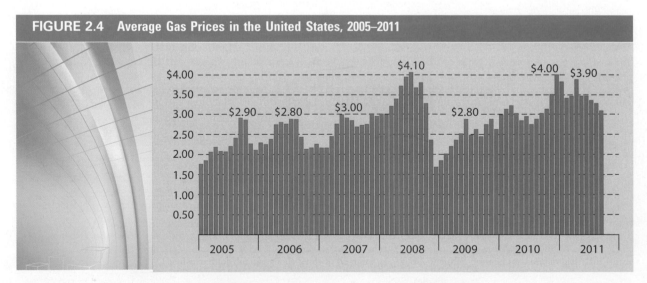

Source: AAA Carolinas.

only slightly on nonessential driving. In the summer of 2008, however, not only summer vacations but urban commuting itself changed in extraordinary ways. Overall, customer demand by the typical two-person urban household shrank from 16 gallons per week to 11.5 gallons as the price rose. As a result, for the first time in U.S. history, gasoline expenditure by U.S. households declined despite a rising price at the pump—that is, 16 gallons/week at $3 in 2007 (Q3) = $48 > 11.5 gallons per week at $4.10 in 2008 (Q3) = $47.15.

Several determinants of demand and supply were identified as possible explanations for the spike in gasoline's equilibrium market price. First, much was written about the fact that no new refinery had been built in the United States in more than 30 years, suggesting that refinery capacity shortages or pipeline bottlenecks might be responsible. Declining capacity does shift the supply curve in Figure 2.2 to the left, which would imply a higher equilibrium price. But no refinery closings or pipeline disruptions could be identified that summer. And the U.S. Department of Energy found refineries command only $0.36 per gallon of the final product price of gasoline in order to achieve cost recovery plus earn a profit. Therefore, refineries could not be responsible for the $1.10 increase in the equilibrium price between July 2007 and July 2008.

Second, retail gas station owners were accused of gouging the driving public. Higher markups at retail also would shift the supply curve for gasoline back to the left, raising the equilibrium market price. But again, retail markup and indeed all gasoline marketing were found to add only $0.28 per gallon to the $4.10 price, much less than could be responsible for the $1.10 run-up that summer in gasoline's equilibrium market price. Third, excise taxes on gasoline (earmarked for bridge building and road maintenance) are levied by both the federal and state governments. Gasoline taxes constitute $0.41 per gallon on average across the United States. Any new excise taxes would have shifted the supply curve leftward, resulting in a higher equilibrium market price for gasoline. President George W. Bush's Council of Economic Advisors in 2007 did explore levying an additional $1 per gallon tax on gasoline to reduce the dependence of the United States on foreign oil, but no tax increase was ever initiated. So what was responsible for the upward spike in gasoline prices?

As we have seen, the variables in the demand and supply functions in Equations 2.1 and 2.2 determining equilibrium market price may be grouped into three broad sets of factors affecting use value, cost of production, and resource scarcity.[2] Since crude oil inputs account for $2.96 of the $4.10 final product price of gasoline, resource scarcity was a likely candidate to explain the increase in gasoline prices from $3 to $4.10. Higher crude oil input prices shift the supply curve leftward, leading to higher final product prices for gasoline. Figure 2.5 shows that the previous three times crude oil input prices shot up, supply disruptions in the crude oil input market were involved (i.e., during the first Gulf War in Kuwait in 1991, during an especially effective era for the OPEC cartel 1999–2001, and during the Iraq War in 2004).

In contrast, the extraordinary price rise of crude oil from $40 to $80 per barrel in 2006–2007 reflected demand-side increased usage especially by India and China. Together India and China represent only 9 percent of the 85 million barrels per day (mbd) worldwide, but these two countries have been growing very quickly. Just 2 to 3 percent additional demand can significantly raise equilibrium prices for crude oil resources because at any point in time there is a very thin inventory (8–10 days supply) working its way through the distribution network from wells to pumps to terminals to tankers to refineries. By late 2007, as gasoline headed toward $4.10 per gallon in the United States, $9.16 per gallon in Germany, and $8.80 per gallon in Great Britain, Western drivers substantially cut back consumption.

---

[2]Two additional factors are speculation and government intervention in the form of taxes, subsidies, and regulations.

FIGURE 2.5 Supply Disruptions and Developing Country Demand Cause Crude Oil Price Spikes

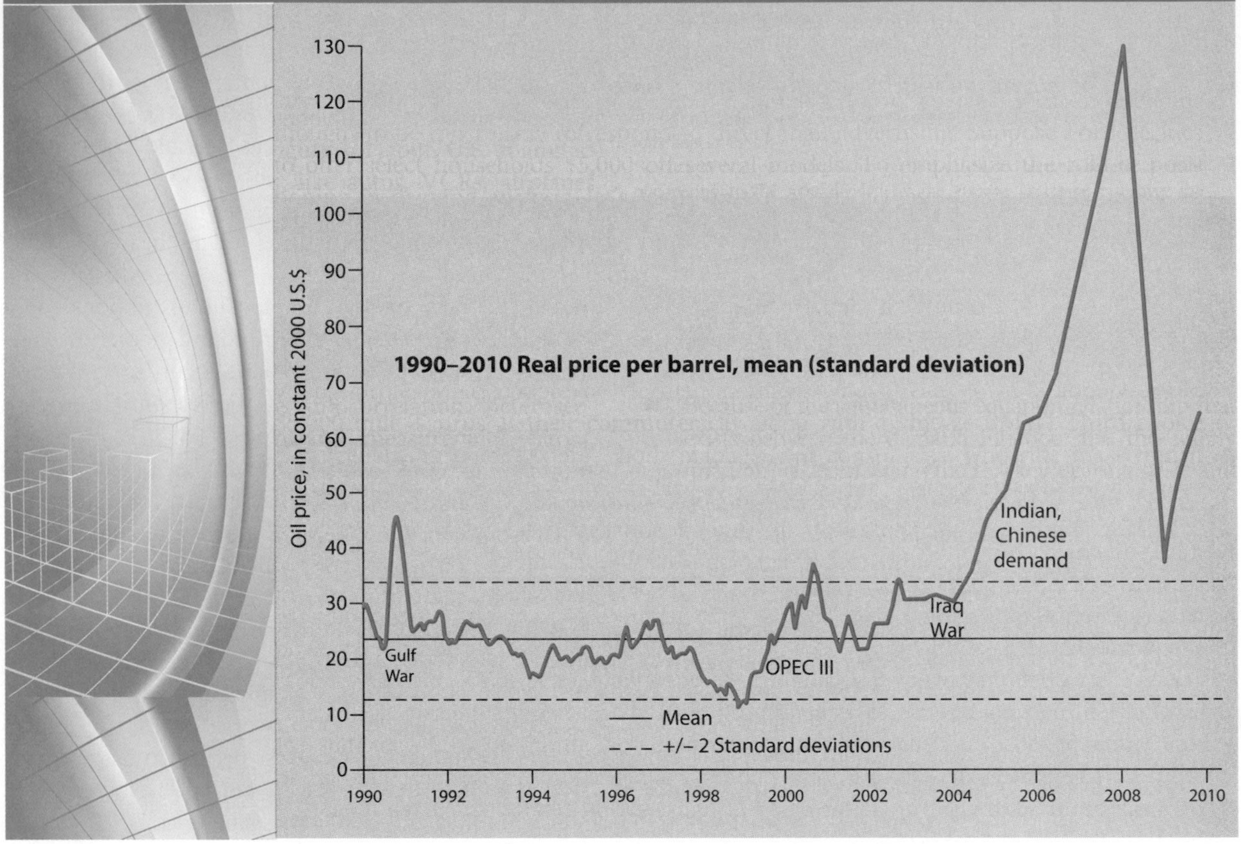

Source: Federal Reserve Bank, St. Louis, *National Economics Trends*, September 2000; FedDallas, Regional Economic Data, 2006.

Was the $80 crude price in late 2007 the highest price ever in the crude oil input market prior to that time? The answer is "no." In 1981, the equilibrium crude oil price reached $36 per barrel. Using the U.S. consumer price index (CPI), since crude oil transactions worldwide are denominated in U.S. dollars, cumulative price increases between 1981 and 2007 total 228.8 percent, so $36 × a 2.288 inflation-adjustment multiplier equals $82 in 2007, and $80/2.288 equals $35 in 1981. Consequently, the $80 crude oil price in late 2007 was in fact lower than the inflation-adjusted $36 crude price in 1981 at the height of the influence of the OPEC II oil cartel.

However, in early 2008, the equilibrium price of crude continued to spike upward.

When the crude price climbed above $100, large numbers of speculators acquired long positions in the crude oil futures market betting on a further price rise. Speculative demand (supply) is always motivated by the anticipation of equilibrium market prices being higher (lower) tomorrow. Those who "go long" and buy futures contracts to take delivery at prices agreed on today are betting the price will go up, and those who "sell short" and write futures contracts promising to deliver in the future at prices agreed on today are betting the other way. The net long direction of speculative trading in the first half of 2008 added to the growing market demand from India and China and drove the crude oil equilibrium price still higher, eventually reaching $147 per barrel in July 2008.

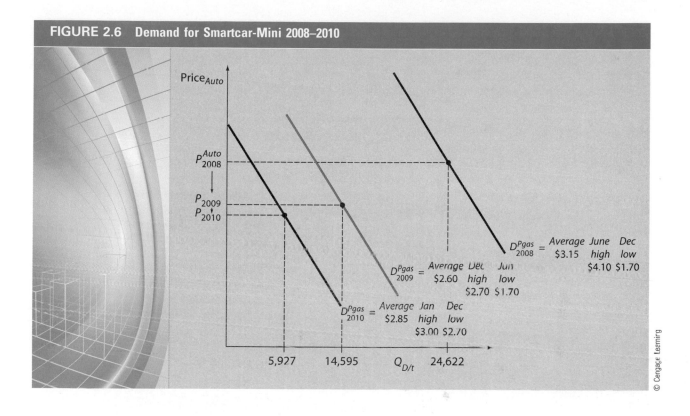

FIGURE 2.6   Demand for Smartcar-Mini 2008–2010

Faced with the need to recover their extraordinary input costs for crude, ExxonMobil, Shell, and other gasoline retailers raised regular prices to $4.10 per gallon. American consumers decided to vacate their SUVs, join carpools, and ride the buses and trains to work. Urban mass transit system ridership shot up 20 percent in a matter of months. Other Americans purchased fuel-efficient hybrids like the Toyota Prius. Figure 2.6 shows 24,622 Smartcar-Mini subcompacts were sold in 2008.

Then, legendary promoter T. Boone Pickens proposed to convert the federal trucking fleet from petroleum-derived fuel oil to natural gas. Fearing an onslaught of feasible substitutes like hybrid electric cars and natural gas-powered trucks, the Saudis decided the equilibrium price of crude had to be driven lower, so they ramped up crude oil production from their average 8.5 mbd 1990–2006. By 2007 and 2008, the Saudi's production capacity rose all the way to 10.5 and 10.9 mbd, respectively (see Figure 2.7).

With U.S. demand for gasoline declining and the capacity to extract and refine expanding, the equilibrium price of crude finally began to reverse course. The late 2008 crude oil price collapse by more than $100 per barrel depicted in Figure 2.8 was caused by a combination of increasing supply fundamentals (shifting the supply curve to the right), slowing demand growth, and a speculative expectation that in the near term crude prices would next be lower (not higher). Saudi capacity eventually grew to 12.5 mbd. Both Saudi Arabia and Kuwait also broke ground on two giant new refining facilities. Over the last two years oil has average about $80/barrel.[3]

---

[3]Appendix 7B explains why a Saudi Arabian oil executive would have preferred the dotted price path in Figure 2.8, with crude oil remaining below $100 a barrel whereas a Texan was delighted to receive all the extra revenue from the price spike to $147.

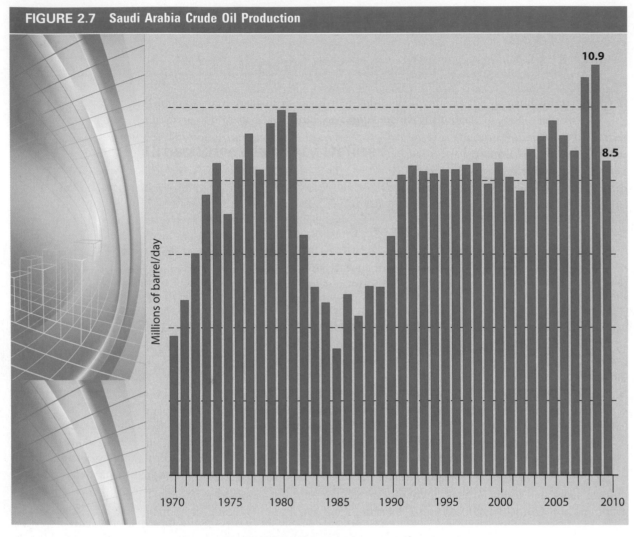

FIGURE 2.7   Saudi Arabia Crude Oil Production

Millions of barrel/day

10.9

8.5

1970   1975   1980   1985   1990   1995   2000   2005   2010

Source: U.S. Energy Information Administration.

Example

Speculation Sends Crude Oil Input Price on a Roller-Coaster Ride at ExxonMobil and Shell

With reversed expectations of lower crude prices in the near term, the speculative bubble in crude oil quickly burst. Despite 5 percent *higher* market demand over the last four months of 2008 (again primarily from China and India), the equilibrium price of crude oil plummeted $107 a barrel from $146 in September 2008 to a low of $39 by January 2009 (see Figure 2.8). By 2009 (Q3), the crude price stood again at $75 per barrel, and regular gasoline was selling for $2.74 per gallon. Figure 2.6 shows Smartcar-Mini demand fell off 10,000 cars to 14,595 in 2009 and another 10,000 to 5,927 in 2010. Over a three-year period, rising Asian demand, massive capacity expansions, a worldwide financial boom, then collapse, and speculative buying followed by speculative selling had taken oil companies and gasoline buyers on quite a roller-coaster ride.

(continued)

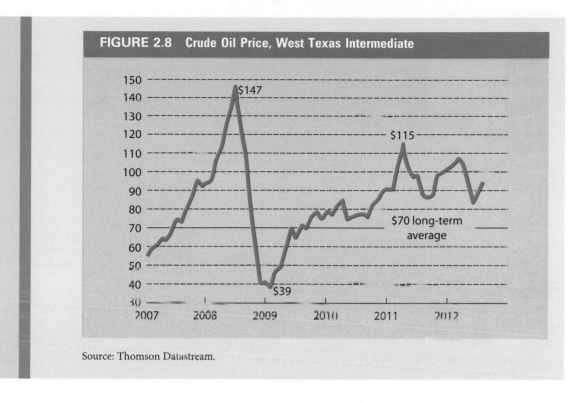

FIGURE 2.8   Crude Oil Price, West Texas Intermediate

Source: Thomson Datastream.

MARGINAL ANALYSIS

Marginal analysis is one of the most useful concepts in microeconomics. Resource-allocation decisions typically are expressed in terms of the marginal equilibrium conditions that must be satisfied to attain an optimal solution. The familiar profit-maximization rule for the firm of setting output at the point where "marginal cost equals marginal revenue" is one such example. Long-term investment decisions (capital expenditures) also are made using marginal analysis decision rules. Only if the expected return from an investment project (i.e., the *marginal return* to the firm) exceeds the cost of funds that must be acquired to finance the project (the *marginal cost* of capital), should the project be undertaken. Following this important marginal decision rule leads to the maximization of shareholder wealth.

Example

Tenneco Shipyard Marginal Analysis

Resource-allocation decisions should be made by comparing the marginal (or incremental) benefits of a change in the level of an activity with the incremental costs of the change. For example, the marginal revenue benefit derived from producing and selling one more supertanker is equal to the difference between total revenue, assuming the additional unit is not sold, and total revenue including the additional sale. Similarly, *marginal cost* is defined as the change in total costs that occurs from undertaking some economic activity, such as the production of an additional ship design including the opportunity costs, and therefore may not necessarily always be equal to the cash outlays alone. Perhaps the Tenneco design team has an opportunity for higher net profit as subcontractors on Boeing projects. If so, Tenneco's routine ship-design work should be contracted out to other shipbuilding design firms who can become a trusted subcontractor to Tenneco.

More generally, a change in the level of an economic activity is desirable if the marginal benefits exceed the marginal (i.e., the incremental) costs. If we define *net marginal return* as the *difference* between marginal benefits and marginal costs, then an equivalent optimality condition is that the level of the activity should be increased to the point where the net marginal return is zero.

In summary, marginal analysis instructs decision makers to determine the additional (marginal) costs and additional (marginal) benefits associated with a proposed action. *Only if the marginal benefits exceed the marginal costs* (i.e., if net marginal benefits are positive) should the action be taken.

Total, Marginal, and Average Relationships

Revenue, cost, profit, and many other economic relationships can be presented using tabular, graphic, and algebraic frameworks. Let us first use a tabular presentation. Suppose that the total profit π_T of a firm is a function of the number of units of output produced Q, as shown in columns 1 and 2 of Table 2.4.

TABLE 2.4   TOTAL, MARGINAL, AND AVERAGE PROFIT RELATIONSHIPS

(1) NUMBER OF UNITS OF OUTPUT PER UNIT OF TIME Q	(2) TOTAL PROFIT $\pi_r(Q)$ ($)	(3) MARGINAL PROFIT $\Delta\pi(Q) = \pi_r(Q) - \pi_r(Q-1)$ ($/UNIT)	(4) AVERAGE PROFIT $\pi_A(Q) = \pi_r(Q)/Q$ ($/UNIT)
0	−200	0	—
1	−150	50	−150.00
2	−25	125	−12.50
3	200	225	66.67
4	475	275	118.75
5	775	300	155.00
6	1,075	300	179.17
7	1,325	250	189.29
8	1,475	150	184.38
9	1,500	25	166.67
10	1,350	−150	135.00

© Cengage Learning

Example

Marginal Analysis and Capital Budgeting Decisions: Sara Lee Corporation

The capital budgeting decision problem facing a typical firm, such as Sara Lee Corporation, can be used to illustrate the application of marginal analysis decision rules. Sara Lee has the following schedule of potential investment projects (all assumed to be of equal risk) available to it:

PROJECT	INVESTMENT REQUIRED ($ MILLION)	EXPECTED RATE OF RETURN	CUMULATIVE INVESTMENT ($ MILLION)
A	$25.0	27.0%	$ 25.0
B	15.0	24.0	40.0

(continued)

PROJECT	INVESTMENT REQUIRED ($ MILLION)	EXPECTED RATE OF RETURN	CUMULATIVE INVESTMENT ($ MILLION)
C	40.0	21.0	80.0
D	35.0	18.0	115.0
E	12.0	15.0	127.0
F	20.0	14.0	147.0
G	18.0	13.0	165.0
H	13.0	11.0	178.0
I	7.0	8.0	185.0

Sara Lee has estimated the cost of acquiring the funds needed to finance these investment projects as follows:

BLOCK OF FUNDS ($ MILLION)	COST OF CAPITAL (%)	CUMULATIVE FUNDS RAISED ($ MILLION)
First 50.0	10.0	50.0
Next 25.0	10.5	75.0
Next 40.0	11.0	115.0
Next 50.0	12.2	165.0
Next 20.0	14.5	185.0

The expected rate of return on the projects listed above can be thought of as the marginal (or incremental) return available to Sara Lee as it undertakes each additional investment project. Similarly, the cost-of-capital schedule may be thought of as the incremental cost of acquiring the needed funds. Following the marginal analysis rules means that Sara Lee should invest in additional projects as long as the expected rate of return on the project exceeds the marginal cost of capital funds needed to finance the project.

Project A, which offers an expected return of 27 percent and requires an outlay of $25 million, is acceptable because the marginal return exceeds the marginal cost of capital (10.0 percent for the first $50 million of funds raised by Sara Lee). In fact, an examination of the tables indicates that projects A through G all meet the marginal analysis test because the marginal return from each of these projects exceeds the marginal cost of capital funds needed to finance these projects. In contrast, projects H and I should not be undertaken because they offer returns of 11 percent and 8 percent, respectively, compared with a marginal cost of capital of 14.5 percent for the $20 million in funds needed to finance those projects.

Example

Marginal Analysis of Driving a Mini Cooper versus a Chevy Volt

Urban sprawl and flight to the suburbs have now resulted in the mean commuter trip in the United States rising to 33 miles one way. With the housing density in most American cities well below what would be required to support extensive light rail

(continued)

and subway lines, the typical household must find economical ways to get at least one worker from a suburban home to the central business district and back each day. A fuel-efficient, small commuter car like the Mini Cooper is one alternative. Others have recently been introduced—the Chevy Volt and Nissan Leaf, both all-electric vehicles that are recharged at the end of each 40-mile commuting trip. Technically, the Leaf and the Volt are e-REVs, extended-range electric vehicles. Each contains a small gasoline-driven internal combustion engine that runs an electric generator, but unlike hybrids such as the Ford Fusion and Toyota Prius, these e-REVs have no mechanical connection between the gasoline engine and the drivetrain. Instead, the Chevy Volt goes 40 miles on the charge contained in 220 lithium ion (L-ion) batteries which are plugged in for a recharging cycle of 8 hours at 110 volts (or 3 hours at 220 volts) at work and at home. When the battery pack falls to a 30 percent state of charge (SOC), the gasoline engine comes on to turn the generator and maintain battery power.

Automotive engineers calculate that each mile traveled in the Chevy Volt's all-electric mode "burns" 0.26 kilowatt hours of electricity. So, the mean commuter trip of 33 miles requires 8.58 kwh of electricity. The price of electricity in the United States varies from a peak period in the midday and evening to a much cheaper off-peak period late at night, and from a low of $0.07 per kwh in Washington state to $0.12 in Rhode Island. On average, a representative nighttime rate is $0.10, and a representative daytime rate is $0.13. This means that each nighttime charge of a Chevy Volt will cost the household $0.86, and the comparable daytime charge downtown at work will be $1.12 for a total operating cost per day of just under $2 per day. For 300 days of work, that's $600 per year. In contrast, the gasoline-powered Mini Cooper gets 32 mpg, so at $3.00 per gallon, the Mini's operating cost is approximately $6 per day or $1,800 per year. The typical commuter use of e-Rev vehicles will save $4 per day or $1,200 per year relative to popular fuel-efficient gasoline-powered commuter cars.

At an EPA-measured 41 mpg throughout a range of driving conditions, the hybrid-electric Ford Fusion qualifies for a federal tax credit of $3,400. In contrast, at an EPA-measured 238 mpg, the Chevy Volt qualifies for a $7,500 tax credit to offset the $12,000 additional cost of the L-ion battery pack over the cost of a conventional battery. Because the Chevy Volt's battery pack is expected to last 10 years, the $1,200 annual capital cost for the battery pack is equal to the $1,200 energy cost savings even without the federal tax credit. To date, sales volumes have been quite low in part because fleet purchasers (especially rental car companies) are waiting to see if the battery packs are durable, which will determine the Volt's resale value.

Marginal profit, which represents the change in total profit resulting from a one-unit increase in output, is shown in column 3 of the table. (A Δ is used to represent a "change" in some variable.) The marginal profit $\Delta\pi(Q)$ of any level of output Q is calculated by taking the difference between the total profit at this level $\pi_T(Q)$ and at one unit below this level $\pi_T(Q - 1)$.[4] In comparing the marginal and total profit functions, we note that for increasing output levels, the marginal profit values remain positive as long as the total profit function is increasing. Only when the total profit function begins decreasing—that is, at $Q = 10$ units—does the marginal profit become negative. The average profit function values $\pi_A(Q)$, shown in column 4 of Table 2.4, are obtained by

---

[4]Web Appendix A expands upon the idea that the total profit function can be maximized by identifying the level of activity at which the marginal profit function goes to zero.

dividing the total profit figure $\pi_T(Q)$ by the output level Q. In comparing the marginal and the average profit function values, we see that the average profit function $\pi_A(Q)$ is increasing as long as the marginal profit is greater than the average profit—that is, up to Q = 7 units. Beyond an output level of Q = 7 units, the marginal profit is less than the average profit and the average profit function values are decreasing.

By examining the total profit function $\pi_T(Q)$ in Table 2.4, we see that profit is maximized at an output level of Q = 9 units. Given that the objective is to maximize total profit, then the optimal output decision would be to produce and sell 9 units. If the marginal analysis decision rule discussed earlier in this section is used, the same (optimal) decision is obtained. Applying the rule to this problem, the firm would expand production as long as the net marginal return—that is, marginal revenue minus marginal cost (marginal profit)—is positive. From column 3 of Table 2.4, we can see that the marginal profit is positive for output levels up to Q = 9. Therefore, the marginal profit decision rule would indicate that 9 units should be produced—the same decision that was obtained from the total profit function.

The relationships among the total, marginal, and average profit functions and the optimal output decision also can be represented graphically. A set of *continuous* profit functions, analogous to those presented in Table 2.4 for discrete integer values of output (Q), is shown in Figure 2.9. At the break-even output level Q_1, both total profits and

FIGURE 2.9   Total, Average, and Marginal Profit Functions

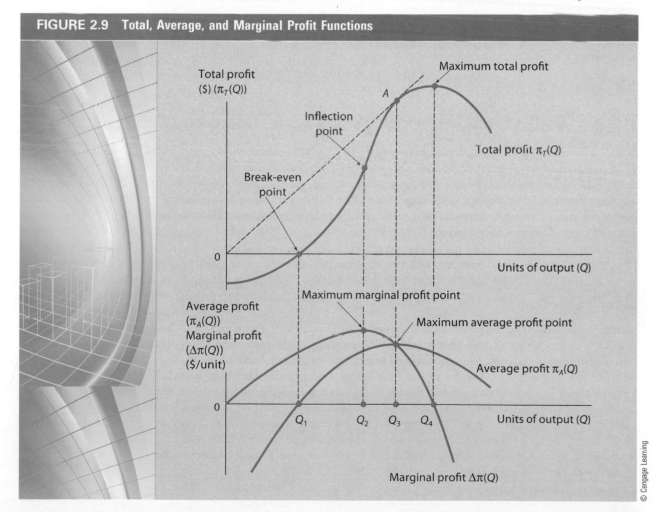

average profits are zero. The marginal profit function, which equals the slope of the total profit function, takes on its maximum value at an output of Q_2 units. This point corresponds to the *inflection point*. Below the inflection point, total profits are increasing at an increasing rate, and hence marginal profits are increasing. Above the inflection point, up to an output level Q_4, total profits are increasing at a decreasing rate, and consequently marginal profits are decreasing. The average profit function, which represents the slope of a straight line drawn from the origin 0 to each point on the total profit function, takes on its maximum value at an output of Q_3 units. The average profit necessarily equals the marginal profit at this point. This follows because the slope of the 0*A* line, which defines the average profit, is also equal to the slope of the total profit function at point *A*, which defines the marginal profit. Finally, total profit is maximized at an output of Q_4 units where marginal profit equals 0. Beyond Q_4 the total profit function is decreasing, and consequently the marginal profit function takes on negative values.

THE NET PRESENT VALUE CONCEPT

When costs and benefits occur at approximately the same time, the marginal decision rule (proceed with the action if marginal benefit exceeds marginal cost) applies. But, many economic decisions require that costs be incurred immediately to capture a stream of benefits over several future time periods. In these cases, the *net present value* (NPV) *rule* replaces the marginal decision rule and provides appropriate guidance for longer-term decision makers. The NPV of an investment represents the contribution of that investment to the value of the firm and, accordingly, to shareholder wealth maximization.

Determining the Net Present Value of an Investment

To understand the NPV rule, consider the following situation. You are responsible for investing $1 million to support the retirement of several family members. Your financial advisor has suggested that you use these funds to purchase a piece of land near a proposed new highway interchange. A trustworthy state road commissioner is certain that the interchange will be built and that in one year the value of this land will increase to $1.2 million. Hence, you believe initially that this is a riskless investment. At the end of one year you plan to sell the land. You are being asked to invest $1 million today in the anticipation of receiving $1.2 million a year from today, or a profit of $200,000. You wonder whether this profit represents a sufficient return on your investment.

You feel it is important to recognize that a return of $1.2 million received one year from today must be worth less than $1.2 million today because you could invest your $1 million today to earn interest over the coming year. Therefore, to compare a dollar received in the future with a dollar in hand today, it is necessary to multiply the future dollar by a *discount factor* that reflects the alternative investment opportunities that are available.

Instead of investing $1 million in the land venture, you are aware that you could also invest in a one-year U.S. government bond that currently offers a return of 3 percent. The 3 percent return represents the return (the opportunity cost) forgone by investing in the land project. The 3 percent rate also can be thought of as the compensation to an investor who agrees to postpone receiving a cash return for one year. The discount factor, also called a *present value interest factor* (PVIF), is equal to

$$PVIF = \frac{1}{1+i}$$

where i is the compensation for postponing receipt of a cash return for one year. The **present value** (PV_0) of an amount received one year in the future (FV_1) is equal to that amount times the discount factor, or

$$PV_0 = FV_1 \times (PVIF)$$ [2.3]

In the case of the land project, the present value of the promised $1.2 million expected to be received in one year is equal to

$$PV_0 = \$1.2 \text{ million} \left(\frac{1}{1 + 0.03} \right) = \$1,165,049$$

If you invested $1,165,049 today to earn 3 percent for the coming year, you would have $1.2 million at the end of the year. You are clearly better off with the proposed land investment (assuming that it really is riskless like the U.S. government bond investment). How much better off are you?

The answer to this question is at the heart of NPV calculations. The land investment project is worth $1,165,049 today to an investor who demands a 3 percent return on this type of investment. You, however, have been able to acquire this investment for only $1,000,000. Thus, your wealth has increased by undertaking this investment by $165,049 ($1,165,049 present value of the projected investment opportunity payoffs minus the required initial investment of $1,000,000). The NPV of this investment is $165,049. In general, the NPV of an investment is equal to

$$NPV = \text{Present value of future returns} - \text{Initial outlay}$$ [2.4]

This example was simplified by assuming that the returns from the investment were received exactly one year from the date of the initial outlay. If the payoff from the land investment had been not one but two years away, the PVIF would have been $1/(1.03)^2 = 0.942596$, and the NPV would have been $1.2 million (.942596) – $1.0 million = $131,115. The NPV rule can be generalized to cover returns received over any number of future time periods with projected growth or decay and terminal values as salvage or disposal costs. In Appendix A at the end of the book, the present value concept is developed in more detail so that it can be applied in these more complex investment settings.

Example

Changing a Lightbulb Saves $30 and May Save the Planet[5]

Incandescent lightbulbs replaced oil lamps for interior lighting more than 100 years ago. Thomas Edison himself improved on some basic designs running electric current through a carbonized filament in an oxygen-free vacuum tube, producing less combustion and more light. General Electric had its origins selling long-lasting tungsten filament incandescent bulbs. Still, 12 percent of the typical household's electric bill goes for lighting 30 lightbulbs, and the standard incandescent bulb loses more than 90 percent of its electrical energy in the form of heat created by the white *hot* filament. Today, the new compact fluorescent light (CFL) bulb uses 75 percent less electricity to heat an argon vapor that emits ultraviolet (UV) light. The UV light excites a fluorescent phosphor coating on the inside of the tube, which then emits visible light. The U.S. Department of Energy estimates that if all 105 million U.S. households replaced just 10 heavily used incandescent bulbs with a CFL bulb yielding comparable light, the electricity saved could light 30 million homes. In addition, the energy saved would remove from the environment an amount of greenhouse gases from

(continued)

coal-burning power plants equal to the CO_2 emitted by 8,000,000 cars. The U.K. Department of Business, Enterprise, and Regulatory Reform estimates that replacing the three most frequently used lightbulbs in U.K. households would save the electricity used by all the streetlamps in Britain.

The magnitude of these energy savings is certainly staggering, but at what cost? Bought for $0.50 per bulb, 1,000-hour incandescent 60-watt bulbs cost much less than CFL bulbs that create the same 1,050 lumens of light, last 8,000 hours, burn only 15 watts of electricity (versus 60), but cost $4.99.[6] So, the lifetime cost comparison hinges on whether the extra $4.49 acquisition cost of the CFL bulb is worth the extended lifetime of energy savings. Net present value techniques are designed to answer just such questions of the time value of money (savings) that are delayed.

Table 2.5 shows the initial net investments of $4.49 and $0.50 per bulb in time period zero, the 45 kilowatt hours (kwh) of power saved on average 2¾ hours per day by the CFL bulb, the $0.11 per kwh representative cost of the electricity,[7] and the additional $0.50 incandescent bulb replacement every year (the typical U.S. household's annual usage). Assuming a 6 percent discount rate, the net present value of the $4.96 annual energy savings plus the $0.50 replacement cost for incandescent bulbs avoided each year for seven years yields a net present value cost savings of $33.59, which exceeds the differential $3.99 acquisition cost for the CFL bulb by $29.60. The European Union has found this $30 net present value of the cost savings from switching to CFL bulbs (plus their CO_2 abatement) so compelling that incandescent bulbs are no longer approved for manufacture or import into the EU. The more gradual U.S. phaseout of incandescent bulbs began in 2012. The average American household has 30 lightbulbs, ten of which are used this heavily, a potential savings of $49.60 + $5.00 as a cash flow each year and a net present value savings of $296 over eight years.

---

[5]Based on "Stores Stock New Bulbs for the Light Switch," *Wall Street Journal*, June 1, 2011, p. D3, www.energy.gov and www.energystar.gov.

[6]Philips has discussed charging $50 for the still higher tech LED bulbs that last roughly 25 times as long as incandescent bulbs.

[7]Electric rates for incremental power vary by region from $.07 per kwh in the state of Washington to $.08 in the Carolinas, to $.12 in California, New York, and across New England. Electricity is much more expensive in Europe because of the carbon credits required to burn coal or fuel oil (the principal source of energy for power plants). For example, in Denmark, electricity costs $0.36 per kwh.

Sources of Positive Net Present Value Projects

What causes some projects to have a positive NPV and others to have a negative NPV? When product and factor markets are other than perfectly competitive, it is possible for a firm to earn above-normal profits (economic rents) that result in positive net present value projects. The reasons why these above-normal profits may be available arise from conditions that define each type of product and factor market and distinguish it from a perfectly competitive market. These reasons include the following barriers to entry and other factors:

1. Buyer preferences for established brand names
2. Ownership or control of favored distribution systems (such as exclusive auto dealerships or airline hubs)
3. Patent control of superior product designs or production techniques
4. Exclusive ownership of superior natural resource deposits

TABLE 2.5 LIFETIME COST SAVINGS OF COMPACT FLUORESCENT LIGHT (CFL) BULBS									
	t = 0	t = 1	t = 2	t = 3	t = 4	t = 5	t = 6	t = 7	t = 8
									(END OF PERIOD VALUES)
Incandescent	−$0.50	−$0.50	−$0.50	−$0.50	−$0.50	−$0.50	−$0.50	−$0.50	0
CFL	−$4.49	2 ¾ hrs × 365 × 45 kwh × $0.11 = $4.96	$4.96	$4.96	$4.96	$4.96	$4.96	$4.96	$4.96
Initial Cost difference	−$3.99	NPV (8 years of $4.96 energy savings at d = 6%) = $30.80							
		NPV (7 years of $0.50 incandescent replacement cost at d = 6%) = $2.79							
		NPV (Lifetime cost savings) − Cost difference ($30.80 + $2.79) = $33.59 − $3.99 = $29.60 per bulb							

5. Inability of new firms to acquire necessary factors of production (management, labor, equipment)
6. Superior access to financial resources at lower costs (economies of scale in attracting capital)
7. Economies of large-scale production and distribution arising from
    a. Capital-intensive production processes
    b. High initial start-up costs

These factors can permit a firm to identify positive net present value projects for internal investment. If the barriers to entry are sufficiently high (such as a patent on key technology) so as to prevent any new competition, or if the start-up period for competitive ventures is sufficiently long, then it is possible that a project may have a positive net present value. However, in assessing the viability of such a project, the manager or analyst must consider the likely period of time when above-normal returns can be earned before new competitors emerge and force cash flows back to a more normal level. It is generally unrealistic to expect to be able to earn above-normal returns over the entire life of an investment project.

Risk and the NPV Rule

The previous land investment example assumed that the investment was riskless. Therefore, the rate of return used to compute the discount factor and the net present value was the riskless rate of return available on a U.S. government bond having a one-year maturity. What if you do not believe that the construction of the new interchange is a certainty, or you are not confident about of the value of the land in one year? To compensate for the perceived risk of this investment, you decide that you require a 15 percent rate of return on your investment. Using a 15 percent required rate of return in calculating the discount factor, the present value of the expected $1.2 million sales price of the land is $1,043,478 ($1.2 million times [1/1.15]). Thus, the NPV of this investment declines to $43,478. The increase in the perceived risk of the investment results in a dramatic $121,571 decline from $165,049 in the NPV on a $1 million investment.

A primary problem facing managers is the difficulty of evaluating the risk associated with investments and then translating that risk into a discount rate that reflects an adequate level of risk compensation. In the next section of this chapter, we discuss the risk concept and the factors that affect investment risk and influence the required rate of return on an investment.

MEANING AND MEASUREMENT OF RISK

risk A decision-making situation in which there is variability in the possible outcomes, and the probabilities of these outcomes can be specified by the decision maker.

Risk implies a chance for some unfavorable outcome to occur—for example, the *possibility that actual cash flows will be less than* the expected outcome. When a range of potential outcomes is associated with a decision and the decision maker is able to assign probabilities to each of these possible outcomes, risk is said to exist. A decision is said to be *risk free* if the cash flow outcomes are known with certainty. A good example of a risk-free investment is U.S. Treasury securities. There is virtually no chance that the Treasury will fail to redeem these securities at maturity or that the Treasury will default on any interest payments owed. In contrast, US Airways bonds constitute a *risky* investment because it is possible that US Airways will default on one or more interest payments and will lack sufficient funds at maturity to redeem the bonds at face value. In summary, *risk* refers to the potential variability of outcomes from a decision. The more variable these outcomes are, the greater the risk.

Probability Distributions

probability The percentage chance that a particular outcome will occur.

The **probability** that a particular outcome will occur is defined as the relative frequency or *percentage chance* of its occurrence. Probabilities may be either objectively or subjectively determined. An objective determination is based on past outcomes of similar events, whereas a subjective determination is merely an opinion made by an individual about the likelihood that a given event will occur. In the case of decisions that are frequently repeated, such as the drilling of developmental oil wells in an established oil field, reasonably good objective estimates can be made about the success of a new well. In contrast, for totally new decisions or one-of-a-kind investments, subjective estimates about the likelihood of various outcomes are necessary. The fact that many probability estimates in business are at least partially subjective does not diminish their usefulness.

Using either objective or subjective methods, the decision maker can develop a probability distribution for the possible outcomes. Table 2.6 shows the probability distribution of net cash flows for two sample investments. The lowest estimated annual net cash flow (NCF) for each investment—$200 for Investment I and $100 for Investment II—represents pessimistic forecasts about the investments' performance; the middle values—$300 and $300—could be considered normal performance levels; and the highest values—$400 and $500—are optimistic estimates.

TABLE 2.6	PROBABILITY DISTRIBUTIONS OF THE ANNUAL NET CASH FLOWS (NCF) FROM TWO INVESTMENTS			
	INVESTMENT I		INVESTMENT II	
POSSIBLE NCF ($)	PROBABILITY		POSSIBLE NCF ($)	PROBABILITY
200	0.2		100	0.2
300	0.6		300	0.6
400	0.2		500	0.2
	1.0			1.0

© Cengage Learning

Example

Probability Distributions and Risk: US Airways Bonds[8]

Consider an investor who is contemplating the purchase of US Airways bonds. That investor might assign the probabilities associated with the three possible outcomes from this investment, as shown in Table 2.7. These probabilities are interpreted to mean that a 30 percent chance exists that the bonds will not be in default over their life and will be redeemed at maturity, a 65 percent chance of interest default during the life of the bonds, and a 5 percent chance that the bonds will not be redeemed at maturity. In this example, no other outcomes are deemed possible.

TABLE 2.7   POSSIBLE OUTCOMES FROM INVESTING IN US AIRWAYS BONDS

OUTCOME	PROBABILITY
No default, bonds redeemed at maturity	0.30
Default on interest for one or more periods	0.65
No interest default, but bonds not redeemed at maturity	0.05
	1.00

© Cengage Learning

[8]The annual report for the US Airways Corporation can be found at http://investor.usairways.com

Expected Values

expected value The weighted average of the possible outcomes where the weights are the probabilities of the respective outcomes.

From this information, the expected value of each decision alternative can be calculated. The **expected value** is defined as the weighted average of the possible outcomes. It is the value that is expected to occur on average if the decision (such as an investment) were repeated a large number of times.

Algebraically, the expected value may be defined as

$$\bar{r} = \sum_{j=1}^{n} r_j p_j \qquad [2.5]$$

where $\bar{r}$ is the expected value; r_j is the outcome for the jth case, where there are n possible outcomes; and p_j is the probability that the jth outcome will occur. The expected cash flows for Investments I and II are calculated in Table 2.8 using Equation 2.5. In this example, both investments have expected values of annual net cash flows equaling $300.

TABLE 2.8   COMPUTATION OF THE EXPECTED RETURNS FROM TWO INVESTMENTS

INVESTMENT I			INVESTMENT II		
r_j	p_j	$r_j \times p_j$	r_j	p_j	$r_j \times p_j$
$200	0.2	$ 40	$100	0.2	$ 20
300	0.6	180	300	0.6	180
400	0.2	80	500	0.2	100
	Expected value: $\bar{r} = \$300$				$\bar{r} = \$300$

© Cengage Learning

Standard Deviation: An Absolute Measure of Risk

standard deviation A statistical measure of the dispersion or variability of possible outcomes.

The **standard deviation** is a statistical measure of the dispersion of a variable about its mean. It is defined as the square root of the weighted average squared deviations of individual outcomes from the mean:

$$\sigma = \sqrt{\sum_{j=1}^{n} (r_j - \bar{r}_j)^2 p_j} \qquad [2.6]$$

where σ is the standard deviation.

The standard deviation can be used to measure the variability of a decision alternative. As such, it gives an indication of the risk involved in the alternative. The larger the standard deviation, the more variable the possible outcomes and the riskier the decision alternative. A standard deviation of zero indicates no variability and thus no risk.

Table 2.9 shows the calculation of the standard deviations for Investments I and II. These calculations show that Investment II appears to be *riskier* than Investment I because the expected cash flows from Investment II are *more variable*.

Normal Probability Distribution

The possible outcomes from most investment decisions are much more numerous than in Table 2.6 but their effects can be estimated by assuming a continuous probability distribution. Assuming a *normal* probability distribution is often correct or nearly correct, and it greatly simplifies the analysis. The normal probability distribution is characterized by a symmetrical, bell-like curve. A table of the *standard normal probability function* (Table 1 in Appendix B at the end of this book) can be used to compute the probability of occurrence of any particular outcome. From this table, for example, it is apparent that the actual outcome should be between plus and minus 1 standard deviation from the

	j	r_j	$\bar{r}$	$r_j - \bar{r}$	$(r_j - \bar{r})^2$	p_j	$(r_j - \bar{r})^2 p_j$
TABLE 2.9 COMPUTATION OF THE STANDARD DEVIATIONS FOR TWO INVESTMENTS							
Investment I	1	$200	$300	−$100	$10,000	0.2	$2,000
	2	300	300	0	0	0.6	0
	3	400	300	100	10,000	0.2	2,000
							$\sum_{j=1}^{3} (r_j - \bar{r})^2 p_j = \$4{,}000$
$\sigma = \sqrt{\sum_{j=1}^{n} (r_j - \bar{r}_j)^2 p_j} = \sqrt{4{,}000} = \$63.25$							
Investment II	1	$100	$300	−$200	$40,000	0.2	$8,000
	2	300	300	0	0	0.6	0
	3	500	300	200	40,000	0.2	8,000
							$\sum_{j=1}^{3} (r_j - \bar{r})^2 p_j = \$16{,}000$
$\sigma = \sqrt{\sum_{j=1}^{n} (r_j - \bar{r}_j)^2 p_j} = \sqrt{16{,}000} = \$126.49$							

© Cengage Learning

FIGURE 2.10   A Sample Illustration of Areas under the Normal Probability Distribution Curve

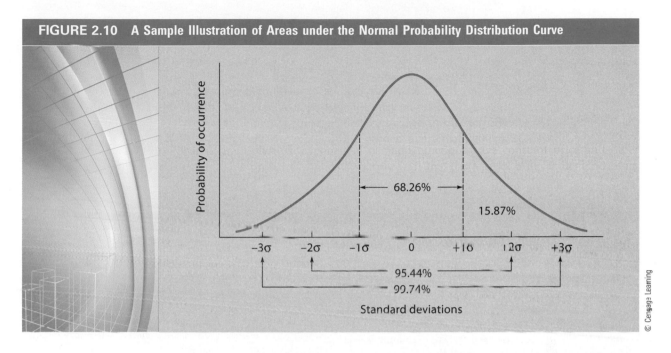

expected value 68.26 percent of the time,[9] between plus and minus 2 standard deviations 95.44 percent of the time, and between plus and minus 3 standard deviations 99.74 percent of the time (see Figure 2.10). So a "3 sigma event" occurs less than 1 percent of the time with a relative frequency 0.0026 (i.e., 1.0 − 0.9974), and a "9 sigma event" occurs almost never, with a relative frequency less than 0.0001. Nevertheless, such extraordinary events can and do happen (see following box on LTCM).

The number of standard deviations z that a particular value of r is from the mean $\bar{r}$ can be computed as

$$z = \frac{r - \bar{r}}{\sigma} \qquad [2.7]$$

Table 1 in Appendix B and Equation 2.7 can be used to compute the probability of an annual net cash flow for Investment I being less than some value r—for example, $205. First, the number of standard deviations that $205 is from the mean must be calculated. Substituting the mean and the standard deviation from Tables 2.8 and 2.9 into Equation 2.7 yields

$$z = \frac{\$205 - \$300}{\$63.25}$$

$$= -1.50$$

In other words, the annual cash flow value of $205 is 1.5 standard deviations below the mean. Reading from the 1.5 row in Table 1 gives a value of 0.0668, or 6.68 percent. Thus, a 6.68 percent probability exists that Investment I will have annual net cash flows less than $205. Conversely, there is a 93.32 percent probability (1 − 0.0668) that the investment will have a cash flow greater than $205.

---

[9]For example, Table 1 indicates a probability of 0.1587 of a value occurring that is greater than +1σ from the mean and a probability of 0.1587 of a value occurring that is less than −1σ from the mean. Hence the probability of a value between +1σ and −1σ is 68.26 percent—that is, 1.00 − (2 × 0.1587).

Coefficient of Variation: A Relative Measure of Risk

coefficient of variation The ratio of the standard deviation to the expected value. A relative measure of risk.

The standard deviation is an appropriate measure of risk when the decision alternatives being compared are approximately equal in size (i.e., have similar expected values of the outcomes) and the outcomes are estimated to have symmetrical probability distributions. Because the standard deviation is an *absolute* measure of variability, however, it is generally not suitable for comparing alternatives of differing size. In these cases the **coefficient of variation** provides a better measure of risk.

WHAT WENT RIGHT • WHAT WENT WRONG

Long-Term Capital Management (LTCM)[10]

LTCM operated from June 1993–September 1998 as a hedge fund that invested highly leveraged private capital in arbitrage trading strategies on the financial derivative markets. LTCM's principal activity was examining interest rate derivative contracts throughout the world for evidence of very minor mispricing and then betting enormous sums on the subsequent convergence of those contracts to predictable equilibrium prices. Since the mispricing might be only several cents per thousand dollars invested, LTCM often needed to risk millions or even billions on each bet to secure a nontrivial absolute dollar return. With sometimes as many as 100 independent bets spread across dozens of different government bond markets, LTCM appeared globally diversified.

In a typical month, 60 such convergence strategies with positions in several thousand counterparty contracts would make money and another 40 strategies with a similar number of counterparties would lose money. Steadily, the profits mounted. From approximately $1 billion net asset value (equity) in February 1994, LTCM reached $7 billion of net asset value in January 1998. LTCM then paid out $2.4 billion in a one-time distribution to non-partners, which equaled a 40 percent annual compound return on their investment (ROI). Shortly thereafter, in August 1998, the remaining $4.6 billion equity shrank by 45 percent, and then one month later shrank by another 82 percent to less than $600 million. In September 1998, the hedge fund was taken over by 14 Wall Street banks who, in exchange for inserting $3.6 billion to cover the firm's debts, acquired 90 percent of the equity ownership. What went wrong?

One potential explanation is that such events are fully expected in an enterprise so risky that it returns a 40 percent ROI. Anticipated risk and expected return are highly positively correlated across different types of investments. However, LTCM's annual return had a standard deviation

from June 1993 to June 1998 of only 11.5 percent per year as compared to 10 percent as the average for all S&P 500 stocks. In this respect, LTCM's return volatility was quite ordinary. Another potential explanation is that LTCM's $129 billion on the June 1998 balance sheet was overwhelmed by excessive off-balance sheet assets and liabilities. Although the absolute size of the numbers is staggering (e.g., $1.2 trillion in interest rate swaps, $28 billion in foreign exchange derivatives, and $36 billion in equity derivatives), LTCM's 9 percent ratio of on-balance sheet to off-balance sheet assets was similar to that of a typical securities firm (about 12 percent). Even LTCM's high financial leverage ($129 billion assets to $4.7 billion equity = 26 to 1) was customary practice for hedge funds.

What appears to have gone wrong for LTCM was that a default of the Russian government on debt obligations in August 1998 set in motion a truly extraordinary "flight to quality." General turmoil in the bond markets caused interest rate volatility to rise to a standard deviation of 36 percent when 3 percent would have been typical. LTCM was caught on the wrong side of many interest rate derivative positions for which no trade was available at any price. Although LTCM had "stress tested" their trading positions against so-called 3 sigma events (a one-day loss of $35 million), this August–September 1998 volatility proved to be a 9 sigma event (i.e., a one day loss of $553 million).

With massive investments highly leveraged and exposed to a 9 sigma event, LTCM hemorrhaged $2 billion in one month. Because liquidity risk exposure of an otherwise fully diversified portfolio was to blame, many investment houses have concluded that leverage should be substantially reduced as a result of the events at LTCM.

[10]R. Lowenstein, *When Genius Failed* (New York: Random House, 2000); remarks by Dave Modest, NBER Conference, May 1999; and "Case Study: LTCM," *eRisk*, (2000).

The coefficient of variation (v) considers relative variation and thus is well suited for use when a comparison is being made between two unequally sized decision alternatives. It is defined as the ratio of the standard deviation σ to the expected value $\bar{r}$, or

$$v = \frac{\sigma}{\bar{r}}$$

[2.8]

Relative Risk Measurement: Arrow Tool Company

Arrow Tool Company is considering two investments, T and S. Investment T has expected annual net cash flows of $100,000 and a standard deviation of $20,000, whereas Investment S has expected annual net cash flows of $4,000 and a $2,000 standard deviation. Intuition tells us that Investment T is less risky because its *relative* variation is smaller. As the coefficient of variation increases, so does the relative risk of the decision alternative. The coefficients of variation for Investments T and S are computed as

Investment T:

$$v = \frac{\sigma}{\bar{r}}$$
$$= \frac{\$20,000}{\$100,000}$$
$$= 0.20$$

Investment S:

$$v = \frac{\sigma}{\bar{r}}$$
$$= \frac{\$2,000}{\$4,000}$$
$$= 0.50$$

Cash flows of Investment S have a larger coefficient of variation (0.50) than do cash flows of Investment T (0.20); therefore, even though the standard deviation is smaller, Investment S is the *more* risky of the two alternatives.

RISK AND REQUIRED RETURN

The relationship between risk and required return on an investment can be defined as

Required return = Risk-free return + Risk premium

[2.9]

The risk-free rate of return refers to the return available on an investment with no risk of default. For debt securities, no default risk means that promised interest and principal payments are guaranteed to be made. The best example of risk-free debt securities are short-term government securities, such as U.S. Treasury bills. The buyer of a U.S. government debt security always is assured of receiving the promised *principal* and *interest* payments because the U.S. government always can print more money. The risk-free return on T-bills equals the real rate of interest plus the expected rate of inflation. The second term in Equation 2.9 is a potential "reward" that an investor can expect to receive from providing capital for a risky investment. This *risk premium* may arise for any number of reasons. The borrower firm may default on its contractual repayment obligations (a default risk premium). The investor may have little seniority in presenting claims against a bankrupt borrower (a seniority risk premium). The investor may be unable to sell his security interest (a liquidity risk premium as we saw in the case of LTCM), or debt repayment may occur early (a maturity risk premium). Finally, the return the investor receives may simply be highly volatile, exceeding expectations during one period and plummeting below expectations during the next period. Investors generally are considered to be *risk averse*; that is, they expect, on average, to be compensated for any and all of these risks they assume when making an investment.

Example

Risk-Return Trade-Offs in Stocks, Bonds, Farmland, and Diamonds

Investors require higher rates of return on debt securities based primarily on their default risk. Bond-rating agencies, such as Moody's, Standard and Poor's, and Fitch, provide evaluations of the default risk of many corporate bonds. Moody's, for example, rates bonds on a 9-point scale from Aaa through C, where Aaa-rated bonds have the lowest expected default risk. As can be seen in Table 2.10, the yields on bonds increase as the risk of default increases, again reflecting the positive relationship between risk and required returns.

TABLE 2.10 RELATIONSHIP BETWEEN RISK AND REQUIRED RETURNS	
DEBT SECURITY	**YIELD (%)**
U.S. Treasury bill	3.8
U.S. Treasury bonds (25 year +)	5.06
Aaa-rated corporate bonds	6.49
Aa-rated bonds	6.93
A-rated bonds	7.18
Baa-rated corporate bonds	7.80
Other investments	
Diamonds	3.0
Farmland	6.5
Stocks	
All U.S. stocks	10.1
Biotech stocks	12.6
Emerging market stocks	16.0

Source: Board of Governors of the Federal Reserve System, *Federal Reserve Bulletin*.

Table 2.10 also shows investment in diamonds has returned 3 percent whereas farmland has returned 6.5 percent, U.S. stocks have returned 10 percent, biotech stocks have returned 12.6 percent, and emerging market stocks have returned 16 percent compounded annually from 1970 to 2010. These compound annual returns mirror the return variance of diamonds (lowest), farmland, U.S. stocks, biotech stocks, and emerging market stocks (highest).

SUMMARY

- Demand and supply simultaneously determine equilibrium market price. The determinants of demand (supply) other than price shift the demand (supply) curve. A change in price alone leads to a change in quantity demanded (supplied) without any shift in demand (supply).

- The offer price demanders are willing to pay is determined by the marginal use value of the purchase being considered. The asking price suppliers are willing to accept is determined by the variable cost of the product or service being supplied.

- The equilibrium price of gasoline fluctuates primarily because of spikes and collapses in crude oil input prices caused at various times by supply disruptions and gluts, increasing demand in developing countries, and speculation.

- Changes in price result in *movement* along the demand curve, whereas changes in any of the other variables in the demand function result in *shifts* of the entire demand curve. Thus "changes in quantity demanded along" a particular demand curve result from price changes. In contrast, when one speaks of "changes in demand," one is referring to shifts in the entire demand curve.

- Some of the factors that cause a shift in the entire demand curve are changes in the income level of consumers, the price of substitute and complementary goods, the level of advertising, competitors' advertising expenditures, population, consumer preferences, time period of adjustment, taxes or subsidies, and price expectations.

- The *marginal analysis* concept requires that a decision maker determine the additional (marginal) costs and additional (marginal) benefits associated with a proposed action. If the marginal benefits exceed the marginal costs (i.e., if the net marginal benefits are positive), the action should be taken.

- The *net present value* of an investment is equal to the present value of expected future returns (cash flows) minus the initial outlay.

- The net present value of an investment equals the contribution of that investment to the value of the firm and, accordingly, to the wealth of shareholders. The net present value of an investment depends on the return required by investors (the firm), which, in turn, is a function of the perceived risk of the investment.

- *Risk* refers to the potential variability of outcomes from a decision alternative. It can be measured either by the *standard deviation* (an absolute measure of risk) or *coefficient of variation* (a relative measure of risk).

- A positive relationship exists between risk and required rates of return. Investments involving greater risks must offer higher expected returns.

Exercises

Answers to the exercises in blue can be found in Appendix D at the back of the book.

1. For each of the determinants of demand in Equation 2.1, identify an example illustrating the effect on the demand for hybrid gasoline-electric vehicles such as the Toyota Prius. Then do the same for each of the determinants of supply in Equation 2.2. In each instance, would equilibrium market price increase or decrease? Consider substitutes such as plug-in hybrids, the Nissan Leaf and Chevy Volt, and complements such as gasoline and lithium ion laptop computer batteries.

2. Gasoline prices above $3 per gallon have affected what Enterprise Rental Car Co. can charge for various models of rental cars. SUVs are $37 with one-day return and subcompacts are $41 with one-day return. Why would the equilibrium price of SUVs be lower than the equilibrium price of subcompacts?

3. The Ajax Corporation has the following set of projects available to it:

cumulitave investment required.

PROJECT*	INVESTMENT REQUIRED ($ MILLION)		EXPECTED RATE OF RETURN (%)
A	500	500	23.0
B	75	575	18.0
C	50	€	21.0
D	125		16.0
E	300		14.0
F	150		13.0
G	250		19.0

*Note: All projects have equal risk.

1st: Put in order

Ajax can raise funds with the following marginal costs:

First $250 million	14.0%
Next 250 million	15.5
Next 100 million	16.0
Next 250 million	16.5
Next 200 million	18.0
Next 200 million	21.0

Use the marginal cost and marginal revenue concepts developed in this chapter to derive an optimal capital budget for Ajax.

4. ESPN currently pays the NFL $1.1 billion per year for eight years for the right to exclusively televise Monday Night Football. What is the net present value of this investment if the parent Disney Company has an opportunity interest rate equal to its cost of capital of 9 percent. Fox and CBS agreed to pay $712 million and $622 million respectively for six years to televise Sunday afternoon NFC games. What was that worth?

5. The demand for MICHTEC's products is related to the state of the economy. If the economy is expanding next year (an above-normal growth in GNP), the company expects sales to be $90 million. If there is a recession next year (a decline in GNP), sales are expected to be $75 million. If next year is normal (a moderate growth in GNP), sales are expected to be $85 million. MICHTEC's economists have estimated the chances that the economy will be either expanding, normal, or in a recession next year at 0.2, 0.5, and 0.3, respectively.
   a. Compute expected annual sales.
   b. Compute the standard deviation of annual sales.
   c. Compute the coefficient of variation of annual sales.

6. Two investments have the following expected returns (net present values) and standard deviation of returns:

PROJECT	EXPECTED RETURNS ($)	STANDARD DEVIATION ($)
A	50,000	40,000
B	250,000	125,000

Which one is riskier? Why?

7. The manager of the aerospace division of General Aeronautics has estimated the price it can charge for providing satellite launch services to commercial firms. Her most optimistic estimate (a price not expected to be exceeded more than 10 percent of the time) is $2 million. Her most pessimistic estimate (a lower price than this one is not expected more than 10 percent of the time) is $1 million. The expected value estimate is $1.5 million. The price distribution is believed to be approximately normal.

   a. What is the expected price?

   b. What is the standard deviation of the launch price?

   c. What is the probability of receiving a price less than $1.2 million?

Case Exercise

Revenue Management at American Airlines[11]

Airlines face highly cyclical demand; American reported profitability in the strong expansion of 2006–2007 but massive losses in the severe recession of 2008–2009. Demand also fluctuates day to day. One of the ways American copes with random demand is through marginal analysis using revenue management techniques. Revenue or "yield" management (RM) is an integrated demand-management, order-booking, and capacity-planning process.

To win orders in a service industry *without slashing prices* requires that companies create perceived value for segmented classes of customers. Business travelers on airlines, for example, will pay substantial premiums for last-minute responsiveness to their flight change requests. Other business travelers demand exceptional delivery reliability and on-time performance. In contrast, most vacation excursion travelers want commodity-like service at rock-bottom prices. Although only 15–20 percent of most airlines' seats are in the business segment, 65–75 percent of the profit contribution on a typical flight comes from this group.

The management problem is that airline capacity must be planned and allocated well in advance of customer arrivals, often before demand is fully known, yet unsold inventory perishes at the moment of departure. This same issue faces hospitals, consulting firms, TV stations, and printing businesses, all of whom must acquire and schedule capacity before the demands for elective surgeries, a crisis management team, TV ads, or the next week's press run are fully known.

One approach to minimizing unsold inventory and yet capturing all last-minute high-profit business is to auction off capacity to the highest bidder. The auction for free-wheeling electricity works just that way: power companies bid at quarter 'til the hour for excess supplies that other utilities agree to deliver on the hour. However, in airlines, prices cannot be adjusted quickly as the moment of departure approaches. Instead, revenue managers employ large historical databases to predict segmented customer demand in light of current arrivals on the reservation system. They then analyze the expected marginal profit from holding in reserve another seat in business class in anticipation of additional "last-minute" demand and compare that seat by seat to the alternative expected marginal profit from accepting one more advance reservation request from a discount traveler.

---

[11]Based on Robert Cross, *Revenue Management* (New York: Broadway Books, 1995); and Frederick Harris and Peter Peacock, "Hold My Place Please: Yield Management Improves Capacity Allocation Guesswork," *Marketing Management* (Fall 1995), pp. 34–46.

Suppose on the 9:00 A.M. Dallas to Chicago flight next Monday, 63 of American's 170 seats have been "protected" for first class, business class, and full coach fares but only 50 have been sold; the remaining 107 seats have been authorized for sale at a discount. Three days before departure, another advance reservation request arrives in the discount class, which is presently full. Should American reallocate capacity and take on the new discount passenger? The answer depends on the marginal profit from each class and the predicted probability of excess demand (beyond 63 seats) next Monday in the business classes.

If the $721 full coach fare has a $500 marginal profit and the $155 discount fare has a $100 marginal profit, the seat in question should not be reallocated from business to discount customers unless the probability of "stocking out" in business is less than 0.20 (accounting for the likely incidence of cancellations and no-shows). Therefore, if the probability of stocking out is 0.25, the expected marginal profit from holding an empty seat for another potential business customer is $125, whereas the marginal profit from selling that seat to the discount customer is only $100 with certainty. Even a pay-in-advance no-refund seat request from the discount class should be refused. Every company has some viable orders that should be refused because additional capacity held in reserve for the anticipated arrival of higher profit customers is not "idle capacity" but rather a predictable revenue opportunity waiting to happen.

In this chapter, we developed the marginal analysis approach used in solving American's seat allocation decision problem. The Appendix to Chapter 14 discusses further the application of revenue management to baseball, theatre ticketing, and hotels.

Questions

1. Make a list of some of the issues that will need to be resolved if American Airlines decides to routinely charge different prices to customers in the same class of service.

2. Would you expect these revenue management techniques of charging differential prices based on the target customers' willingness to pay for change order responsiveness, delivery reliability, schedule frequency, and so forth to be more effective in the trucking industry, the outpatient health care industry, or the hotel industry? Why or why not?

3. Sometimes when reservation requests by deep discount travelers are refused, demanders take their business elsewhere; they "balk." At other times, such demanders negotiate and can be "sold up" to higher fare service like United's Economy Plus. If United experiences fewer customers balking when reservation requests for the cheapest seats are refused, should they allocate preexisting capacity to protect fewer seats (or more) for late-arriving full-fare passengers?

PART II

Demand and Forecasting

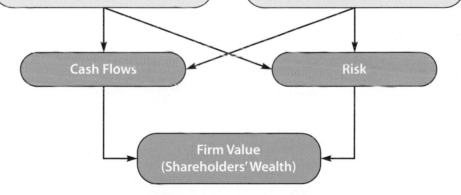

ECONOMIC ANALYSIS AND DECISIONS

1. Demand Analysis and Forecasting
2. Production and Cost Analysis
3. Pricing Analysis
4. Capital Expenditure Analysis

POLITICAL AND SOCIAL ENVIRONMENT

1. Business Conditions (Trends, Cycles, and Seasonal Effects)
2. Factor Market Conditions (Capital, Labor, Land, and Raw Materials)
3. Competitors' Responses
4. External, Legal, and Regulatory Constraints
5. Organizational (Internal) Constraints

Cash Flows

Risk

Firm Value (Shareholders' Wealth)

© Cengage Learning

Demand Analysis

The NFL should end the lockout and rehire the professional referees; NFL owners face inelastic demand.

Steve Young, sportscaster, former San Francisco 49ers quarterback, and winner of the 1994 Super Bowl

CHAPTER PREVIEW

Demand analysis serves three major managerial objectives. First, it provides the insights necessary for marketing teams to effectively manage demand. Second, it helps forecast unit sales to inform operations decisions, and third it projects the revenue portion of a firm's cash flow stream for financial planning. This chapter develops the theory of demand and introduces the elasticity properties of the demand function. The price elasticity of demand is a measure of the sensitivity of quantity demanded to a change in one of the factors influencing demand, such as price, advertising, promotions, packaging, or income levels. We analyze consumer behavior in selecting hotels and auto rentals subject to a reimbursements budget constraint on a business trip. The household demand for gasoline over the past several years is extensively discussed. A Case Study on direct mail couponing by a Chevrolet dealership examines the determinants of price elasticity for various target markets. Web Appendix A develops the relationship between cost-of-living price indices and new product introductions.

MANAGERIAL CHALLENGE
Health Care Reform and Cigarette Taxes[1]

When the Canadian government raised cigarette taxes enough to push the price per pack over $4, adult smoking declined by 38 percent and teenage smoking declined even more, by 61 percent. In 1997, a similar U.S. excise tax increase funded the "Tobacco settlement." In exchange for immunity from civil liability in class action lawsuits by injured smokers, Philip Morris, Reynolds Tobacco, Liggett, and other cigarette manufacturers agreed to pay $368 billion over 25 years. The state attorneys general had sued the cigarette manufacturers to recover the additional Medicare and Medicaid costs of smoking-related illnesses. Under the settlement, the average U.S. price of $1.43 per pack rose by 62 cents to $2.05 (by 35 percent).[2] Some critics of the proposal insisted at the time that the tobacco tax should be higher (perhaps as much as $1.50 higher) to deter young smokers from acquiring the habit. The stated objective for reducing teenage smoking was 30 percent in five years and 50 percent in seven years.

One important element of the debate regarding the "optimal" cigarette tax increase depends on how sensitive consumption is to changes in price. An excellent measure of this sensitivity is the price elasticity of demand, defined as the percentage change in quantity demanded per time period that occurs as a result of some percentage change in price. Economists have estimated the price elasticity of adult cigarette demand to be −0.4, indicating that for a 10 percent increase in

Cont.

MANAGERIAL CHALLENGE *Continued*

price, quantity demanded can be expected to decline by 4 percent. For teenagers, however, the price elasticity is thought to be much higher—namely, −0.6—indicating that for a 10 percent increase in price, quantity demanded can be expected to decline by 6 percent. So, using price elasticity as a guide, the 35 percent increase in price should result in a 21 percent decline in teen smoking.

Because a 21 percent reduction is far below the stated goal of a 30 percent reduction in teenage smoking, the U.S. Congress decided in 1999 to raise the federal excise

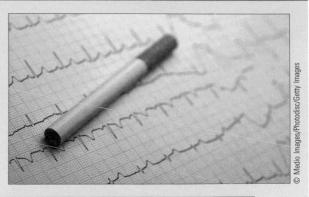

© Medio Images/Photodisc/Getty Images

STATE EXCISE TAX RATES ON CIGARETTES (JULY 1, 2009)					
STATE	TAX RATE (¢ PER PACK)	RANK	STATE	TAX RATE (¢ PER PACK)	RANK
Alabama	42	45	Nebraska	64	38
Alaska	200	9	Nevada	80	34
Arizona	200	10	New Hampshire	178	15
Arkansas	115	27	New Jersey	270	3
California	87	32	New Mexico	91	31
Colorado	84	33	New York	275	2
Connecticut	200	11	North Carolina	35	48
Delaware	115	25	North Dakota	44	44
Florida	133	22	Ohio	125	23
Georgia	37	46	Oklahoma	103	28
Hawaii	260	4	Oregon	118	26
Idaho	57	42	Pennsylvania	135	21
Illinois	98	29	Rhode Island	346	1
Indiana	95	30	South Carolina	7	51
Iowa	136	19	South Dakota	153	17
Kansas	79	35	Tennessee	62	39
Kentucky	60	40	Texas	141	20
Louisiana	36	47	Utah	69	36
Maine	200	14	Vermont	224	7
Maryland	200	12	Virginia	30	49
Massachusetts	251	6	Washington	202	8
Michigan	200	4	West Virginia	55	43
Minnesota	150	18	Wisconsin	252	5
Mississippi	68	37	Wyoming	60	41
Missouri	17	50	Dist. of Columbia	200	13
Montana	170	16	U.S. Median	115	

Source: Tax Foundation.

Cont.

MANAGERIAL CHALLENGE *Continued*

tax another 60 cents. State legislatures got involved as well, such that by 2009 the price is approaching $4.00 and much higher in some states. In the past three years, states from Florida to New Hampshire and out to Texas and South Dakota have added $1.00 to their cigarette excise taxes. New Jersey, New York, Wisconsin, Washington, Hawaii, Rhode Island, Massachusetts, Vermont, and Arizona, for example, have imposed more than $2 a pack in state excise taxes alone, making the price of a pack $5.

In the ongoing debate over the amount of cigarette tax required for health care cost recovery, policy makers face a difficult set of trade-offs. On the one hand, if the primary objective is to generate income to fund health care costs, the tax should be set such that it will maximize tax revenue. On the other hand, if the primary objective is to discourage smoking, a much higher tax could be justified. In either case, however, knowledge of the true price elasticity of demand is an essential element of this important policy decision. In this chapter, we

investigate how to calculate and use such price elasticity metrics.

Discussion Questions

■ Think back to when you were a teenager. Were you more or less price sensitive than you are now in making gasoline consumption decisions when you encounter an unexpected discount or price increase? Brainstorm about why.

■ What about pizza consumption decisions? Again, why?

---

[1]Based in part on "Add $2 to the Cost of a Pack of Cigarettes" and "And Even Teen Smokers May Kick the Habit," *BusinessWeek* (March 15, 1993), p. 18; "Critics Question Tobacco Pact's Effect on Teen Smoking," *Wall Street Journal* (August 19, 1997), p. A20; "Major Makers of Cigarettes Raise Prices," *Wall Street Journal* (August 31, 1999), p. A3; and "Politicians Are Hooked on Cigarette Taxes," *Wall Street Journal* (February 20, 2002), p. A2.

[2]The 35 percent price increase in the United States is calculated by dividing the $0.62 tax increase by the average of the original $1.43 and the post-tax $2.05 price.

DEMAND RELATIONSHIPS

The Demand Schedule Defined

The demand schedule is the simplest form of the demand relationship. It is merely a list of prices and corresponding quantities of a product or service that would be demanded over a particular time period by some individual or group of individuals at uniform prices. Table 3.1 shows the *demand schedule* for gasoline. This demand schedule indicates that *when* the price per gallon is $2.50, U.S. urban households purchase 18 gallons per week. At a price of $3.50, the target households purchase just 14 gallons per week. Note that the lower the price, the greater the quantity demanded. This inverse or negative relationship between price and the desired rate of purchase is generally referred to as the "law of demand" and refers to the *movement* down a single demand schedule.

A *shift* of demand schedules as illustrated in Figure 3.1 is quite different. Demand schedules shift when one of the determinants of demand discussed in Chapter 2 and listed in Equation 2.1 changes. For example, the demand schedule for gas-guzzling SUVs in 1999 reflected low gasoline prices, an important complement in the consumption of heavy fuel-inefficient cars and trucks. In 1999 at $2.00 per gallon gasoline, Ford Motor Co. sold 428,000 Ford Explorers for $22,000 at $4,000 profit each. By 2007, with $3.50 per gallon gasoline, Ford Motor could only sell 127,000 Explorers despite deep discounts to $19,000 that sacrificed essentially all the profit.[3] What had changed? Tastes and preferences were running in favor of "greener," more sustainable transportation (like the gasoline-electric hybrid Toyota Prius). But the main difference from the earlier

---

[3]"Oil's Rise to $100," *Wall Street Journal* (January 3, 2008), p. A6.

TABLE 3.1   U.S. HOUSEHOLD DEMAND FOR GASOLINE

PRICE ($/GALLON)	QUANTITY PURCHASED (GALLONS/WEEK)
4.10	11.5
3.50	14
3.00	16
2.50	18
2.00	20
1.50	22
1.00	24

Source: *Household Vehicles Energy Use: Latest and Trends, Energy Information Administration*, U.S. Department of Energy, various issues.

period was that gasoline prices had risen to $3.50 per gallon. As a result, demand for gas-guzzler SUVs like the Ford Explorer shifted down to the left. By 2008, with gasoline prices rising to over $4.00 for the first time ever in the United States, the Ford Explorer sold fewer than 30,000 units and was withdrawn from the marketplace.

Constrained Utility Maximization and Consumer Behavior

The concept of demand is based on the theory of consumer choice. Each consumer faces a constrained optimization problem, where the objective is to choose among the combinations of goods and services that maximize satisfaction or utility, subject to a constraint on the amount of funds (i.e., the household budget) available. Think of a food and housing budget allowance from your employer while you are traveling on a business trip or, alternatively, a set of friends who share these expenses while rooming together. In this constrained utility-maximizing framework, economists have identified two basic reasons

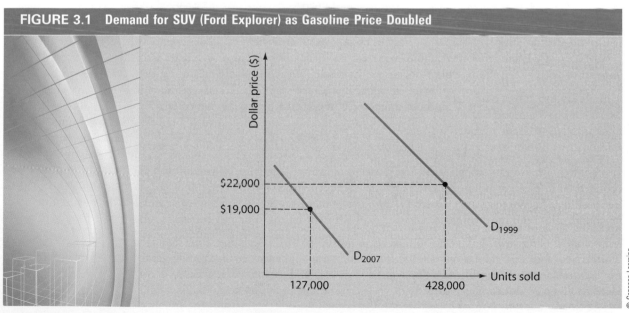

FIGURE 3.1   Demand for SUV (Ford Explorer) as Gasoline Price Doubled

© Cengage Learning

for the increase in quantity demanded as the result of a price reduction. These factors are known as *purchasing power* and *substitution effects*.

Purchasing Power Effect   When the price of a good—for example, apartment housing rent—declines, the effect of this decline is that the purchasing power of the consumer has increased. This is known as the *purchasing power effect of the price change*. For example, if an individual normally purchases 600 square feet at $1,000 per month, a price decline to $800 per month would enable the consumer to purchase the same amount of housing for $200 less per month. This savings of $200 represents an increase in purchasing power, which may be used to purchase greater quantities of housing (as well as other income-superior goods).

Sometimes the purchasing power effect of a price reduction is minuscule because so little of the household's budget is expended on the good (like a salt canister purchased once every other year), but at other times the change in purchasing power is enormous. Consider a young family who spends 40 percent of their disposable income on apartment housing. In general, the sign and magnitude of the purchasing power effect of a price change has much to do with the positioning and targeting decisions in the firm's marketing plan—that is, whether the product is upscale or down market positioned and at whom the product is targeted. French-American families, for example, spend almost twice as much of their disposable income on food (22 percent) as does the representative American family (12 percent). As a result, the quantity demanded of income-superior food items like veal or wines we would expect to be much more price sensitive among French-American families.

Substitution Effect   When the price of a good such as movies declines, it becomes less expensive in relation to other substitute entertainment outings—for example, restaurant meals. As a result of the price decline, the rational consumer can increase his or her satisfaction or utility by purchasing more of the good whose price has declined and less of the substitutes. This is known as the *substitution effect of the price change*.

For example, suppose that the prices of movie admission and snacks versus a restaurant meal are $20 and $30, respectively. Furthermore, assume that initially a household purchases one movie outing and two restaurant meals per week for a total entertainment expenditure of $80 per week. If the price of movies declines to $16.67, some households will decide to increase their consumption to three movies per week and decrease their consumption of restaurant meal outings to one per week—which requires the same total expenditure of $80. Each such household now realizes that they must forego almost two movies per week to fund a restaurant meal outing, so they cut back on restaurant meals. Thus, we see that a decrease in the relative price of movies versus restaurant meals leads to an increase in the quantity demanded of movies.

In summary, because of the combined impact of the purchasing power and substitution effects, a decline in the price will always have a positive impact on the quantity demanded for income-superior goods and services (for which more consumption is preferred to less as purchasing power rises). In this case, both the purchasing power and substitution effects push the consumer toward an increase in quantity demanded as price falls.[4] This *law of demand for goods positioned as income superior* is almost never violated.

---

[4]For income-*inferior* goods and services, like efficiency apartments (for which less is preferred to more as purchasing power rises), the real income and substitution effects have opposite and partially offsetting impacts on the quantity demanded. Nevertheless, the net effect, even in the case of inferior goods, is usually that again more goods and services will be demanded as the price declines. So, the law of demand holds for most inferior goods as well.

Consumption Choices on a Business Trip to San Francisco

On a two-week business trip to San Francisco, your employer has authorized a $1,000 travel budget for your lodging and auto rentals against which you can submit receipts for reimbursement. The price of executive lodging is $100 per 100 sq. ft. for the 10 weekdays, and the price of a mid-size auto rental with parking and gas runs $100 per day. You plan to allocate $700 for housing and use the rest to rent a car for the three-day intervening weekend from Friday noon to Monday noon in order to see Yosemite National Park. While flying to San Francisco, however, you notice in the airline's in-flight magazine a $30 per day Hertz discount coupon good throughout the two weeks you are traveling.

Figure 3.2 illustrates how this Hertz discount coupon expands your purchasing power substantially. Most obviously, now that you face a budget constraint reflecting $70 discount prices for auto rentals (the starred line in the figure), a specialist in consumption who plans to spend the entire $1,000 on auto rentals (and sleep in the car) could rent an auto each of the 14 days in San Francisco whereas earlier only 10 days were available with the initial (the solid line) budget constraint. Whether this increase in your purchasing power from Hertz's $30 price reduction *will*, in fact, trigger several additional auto rental days (say, from three to five) allowing you perhaps to drive across the Golden Gate Bridge or up to the Napa Valley some weekday evening, depends on a number of factors.

FIGURE 3.2   Consumption Choice on a Business Trip

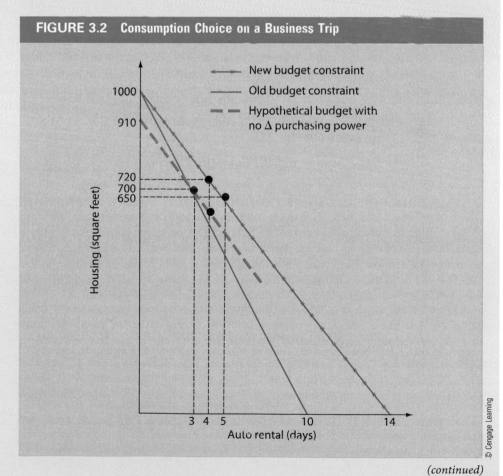

(continued)

First, is the Hertz discount offer for "$30 off" available on all of Hertz's vehicles, or is it just available on subcompacts like the Ford Focus? If the latter, you might decide to spend your increased purchasing power on a nicer, bigger hotel room and actually consume fewer rental days of what you perceive to be the inferior auto. On the other hand, if the discount coupon is only good for luxury car rentals, that choice may be well beyond your budget.

The second factor that determines whether the Hertz price discount stimulates more demand is whether switching costs are high or low. That is, are you a member of the Avis #1 Club, a loyalty program that earns points for free gifts from Avis auto rentals? Or has your employer already prepaid on a nonreimbursable contract with Avis based on your three-day weekend rental plan? Or is a smaller hotel room really unusable because you require the 700 sq. ft. room's seating area separate from your bedroom in which to conduct business meetings? If so, your switching costs are too high for the Hertz price discount to have much of a positive effect on your quantity demanded.

At lower levels of switching costs, however, we would expect you to substitute somewhat toward Hertz rental cars and away from housing as the relative price of auto rentals falls from 100 sq. ft. per rental car day to 70 sq. ft. per day. Conceptually, the magnitude of the substitution effect away from housing space toward more rental car days (say, from your originally planned three to four days) depends upon the perceived closeness of the substitutes, as well as the magnitude of the switching costs. The feasible choices within your original budget are displayed on the dotted hypothetical budget constraint in Figure 3.2 illustrating the lower $70 relative price of rental cars.

Third and finally, the size of the purchasing power effect (up or down from the choice of four rental car days) as spending power rises from the dotted hypothetical budget constraint (at $910 and $70 rental car prices) to the new actual outside budget constraint (at $1,000 and $70 rental car prices) depends upon the positioning of the eligible Hertz vehicles. Are they positioned like the inferior subcompact Ford Focus, like the midsize Ford Taurus you presently drive, or like the income-superior Ford Mustang convertible? If Ford Mustang convertibles are eligible for the discount, perhaps your quantity demanded rises from three to five days. The total effect of the $30 price discount coupon would then be +2 days, the sum of the ever positive substitution effect as relative price declines (from three to four days) and a reinforcing positive purchasing power effect (from four to five days).

On the other hand, if the Hertz coupon is applicable only to subcompacts that you perceive as income inferior, maybe you do business with Hertz but actually decrease auto rental consumption from three days before the price change to two days afterward and spend your increased purchasing power on a better hotel costing $860 for the 10-day stay. The total effect of the $30 price discount coupon in this unusual case would be −1 days, the sum of a positive substitution effect (from three to four days) since relative price has declined plus an offsetting negative purchasing power effect (from four back to two days) in light of the inferior nature of the product positioning. In that event, Hertz should have targeted some economy-class airline customers who will perceive the Ford Focus as income superior.

durable goods Goods that yield benefits to the owner over a number of future time periods.

Up to this point we have been considering the demand for goods and services purchased on a short-term basis. **Durable goods** such as clothes, furniture, autos, appliances, and computers may be stored and repaired rather than replaced after each use. For example, an electric furnace can be fixed again and again at considerably less cost

WHAT WENT RIGHT • WHAT WENT WRONG

Chevy Volt[5]

The hybrid gasoline-electric Toyota Prius at $24,000 proved to be an aspirant good for 20-somethings, but Yuppies revealed a preference for the Toyota Camry, Honda Accord, Chevy Malibu, and BMW 3 series at $28,000 to $38,000. Chevrolet hoped to capture the more green-conscious young professionals with their plug-in hybrid, the Chevy Volt, at a planned price point of $33,000. But the 1,300 lithium ion batteries needed to power the Volt proved to be $8,000 more expensive than Chevrolet had anticipated.

The problem is that the Volt's original target market will likely have insufficient disposable income to purchase at $41,000 ($33,000 + $8,000). Green consumers with more money to spend will also likely reject the Chevy Volt in favor of the $52,000 plug-in hybrid Tesla compact that out-accelerates a Ferrari and is doing very well among Silicon Valley entrepreneurs. The positioning of the Chevy Volt appears problematic for attracting any sizeable customer base.

[5]Based on "Briefing: The Electrification of Motoring," *The Economist* (September 5, 2009), p. 75.

than buying a new heating system. Obsolescence in style, convenience, and prestige plays a large role in affecting the replacement demand of durables. Also, customers may question whether their income will be sufficient and steady enough to make installment loan payments or whether adequate repair services will be available over the economic working life of a discontinued model. Because these expectational factors come into play, demand for durable goods is more volatile, and its analysis is more complex than a similar analysis for nondurables.

Targeting, Switching Costs, and Positioning   The customer's desired rate of purchase can be markedly affected not only by pricing but also by several other marketing decisions such as targeting the most likely customers, establishing loyalty programs, and carefully positioning the product. Expanding Equation 2.1 to include these marketing decisions, we have an implicit demand function such as

$$Q_D = f(P, P_S, P_C, Y, A, A_C, N, C_P, P_E, T_A, T/S, \text{Target, Switching Cost, Positioning})$$

[3.1]

Let's discuss each of these in turn. *Targeting* is often the subject of extensive marketing research using surveys, focus groups, and statistical analysis. Companies want to know the subtle latent inclinations and declinations of potential target customer groups before designing their promotions and ad campaigns. "Knowing thy customer" sufficiently well to pick the right target for a promising product is the first priority in marketing.

Customer loyalty programs that reward more frequent higher profit margin buyers will often attempt to secure repeat purchase customers who perceive substantial *switching costs*. The reason is that selling a larger amount or with greater frequency to a regular customer economizes on selling expenses. One rule of thumb of relevance notes that it costs five times as much to attract a new customer as it does to sell more to a regular customer. "Share of wallet" for a firm's regular customer is more important to sustaining profitability than the more traditional metrics of market share—that is, the firm's share of the relevant market.

For example, Chrysler sold a sequence of minivans to the baby boom generation by offering perfectly positioned cars promoted with exaggerated trade-ins (above market value) for frequent buyers enrolled in an owner loyalty program. The Dodge Caravan and Plymouth Voyager minivans earned $6,100 profit margins on a $19,000 car, and $30,000 Chrysler Town and Country minivans earned almost $10,000. These were extraordinary profit margins in the cutthroat competitive mass market domestic auto industry of the 1990s. At the peak of the baby boom generation's child-rearing years, Chrysler Corporation minivans were the highest volume vehicle sold in the United States (569,449 in 1993).[6]

Correctly *positioning* of a product in the target customer's perception from upscale to "down market" is quite important. As purchasing power rises, any goods and services that the target households perceive as inferior to some preferable substitute will likely experience declining unit sales. Marketers often therefore go to extraordinary lengths to create product images and customer associations to which the target households aspire. But this objective presents quite a challenge because aspirant good perceptions are very sensitive to culture and socio-demographic complexities. In short, positioning involves the attributes, relationships, and images designed to establish the target customer's perception of your product relative to competing products or services. That must be done carefully and done well.

THE PRICE ELASTICITY OF DEMAND

From a decision-making perspective, any firm needs to know not only the direction but also the magnitude effects of changes in the determinants of demand. Some of these factors are under the control of management, such as price, advertising, product quality, and customer service. Other demand determinants, including disposable income and the prices of competitors' products, are outside the direct control of the firm. Nevertheless, effective demand management still requires that a manager be able to measure the magnitude of the impact of changes in these other variables on quantity demanded.

Example

Olive Garden and Ford Dealers Respond to Deficient Demand

Olive Garden anticipates a purchase frequency of 60 servings of lasagna per night at a price of $11.99 and plans their operations accordingly. When fewer than 60 customers arrive on a given evening, the Olive Garden restauranteur does something very different than a Ford auto dealer might in similar circumstances. The restaurant slashes orders; fewer trays of preprepared lasagna are put into the oven and baked. Instead of slashing prices in the face of deficient demand, restaurants order less production and increase the size of their servings. Why is that?

One insight hinges on the lack of customer traffic in a restaurant that might be attracted on short notice by a given discount. The demand by Olive Garden customers, in other words, is not very price sensitive while the final preparation stages of any restaurant's supply are quite flexible and can be adjusted easily. In contrast, in the auto business, customer demand can be stimulated on short notice by sharp price discounts, while the supply schedule at the end of the model year is very inflexible. Ford Motor assembles and ships a number of cars in response to firm orders by their retail dealers and then insists on a no-returns policy. Thereafter, in the face of deficient demand (below the planned rate of sale), Ford dealerships tend to slash their asking prices to clear excess inventory.

(continued)

---

[6]"Iacocca's Minivan: How Chrysler Succeeded in Creating One of the Most Profitable Products of the Decade," *Fortune* (May 30, 1994), p. 112.

In sum, auto dealerships adopt price discounts as their primary adjustment mechanism, while restaurants slash orders. Fundamentally, what causes the difference in these two businesses? In the one case, quantity demanded is very price sensitive and quantity supplied is not (retail autos at the end of the model year). In the other case, demand is price insensitive, and supply is quite flexible (restaurants). This difference is characterized by the price elasticity of demand and supply.

Price Elasticity Defined

ceteris paribus Latin for "all other things held constant."

The most commonly used measure of the responsiveness of quantity demanded or supplied to changes in any of the variables that influence the demand and supply functions is *elasticity*. In general, *elasticity* should be thought of as a ratio of the percentage change in quantity to the percentage change in a determinant, **ceteris paribus** (all other things remaining unchanged). **Price elasticity of demand** (E_D) is therefore defined as:

$$E_D = \frac{\%\Delta Q}{\%\Delta P} = \frac{\Delta Q}{\Delta P} \times \frac{Base\ P}{Base\ Q},\ ceteris\ paribus \qquad [3.2]$$

where

price elasticity of demand The ratio of the percentage change in quantity demanded to the percentage change in price, assuming that all other factors influencing demand remain unchanged.

$$\Delta Q = change\ in\ quantity\ demanded$$
$$\Delta P = change\ in\ price$$

The final terms in Equation 3.2 show that own price elasticity depends on the inverse of the *slope* of the demand curve $\Delta Q/\Delta P$ (i.e., the partial sensitivity of demand in the target market to price changes, *holding all other determinants of demand unchanged*) times the price point *positioning P* where elasticity is calculated for Q unit sales on the demand curve. Because of the law of demand (i.e., the inverse relationship between price and quantity demanded), the sign of the own price elasticity will always be negative.

When the percentage change in price (the denominator in the first term of Equation 3.2) exceeds the percentage change in Q (the numerator), own price elasticity calculates as a fraction, less than one in absolute value. This lack of demand responsiveness is described as "inelastic demand." When the reverse holds,

$$|\%\Delta Q| > |\%\Delta P| \rightarrow |\varepsilon_p| > 1$$

demand is described as "elastic." Because higher price points (and lower baseline Q) result in higher and higher elasticity, eventually, at high enough prices, all linear demand curves become elastic.

Example

Price Elasticity at Various Price Points along Linear Demand Curves for Gasoline and Christmas Trees

To illustrate, the demand for gasoline in Table 3.1 and Figure 3.3 is estimated from U.S. Consumer Expenditure Survey data and varies markedly by the type of household. For two-person urban households with no children, demand is very price inelastic, measuring −0.56 at lower price points like $2.50 per gallon. This means, using

(continued)

Equation 3.1, that if price rises by 40 percent (say, from $2.00 to $3.00), gallons consumed per week will fall by 22 percent (20 to 16 gallons):

$$\frac{-4 \text{ gallons}/18 \text{ gallons}}{+\$1.00/\$2.50} = \frac{-22\%}{+40\%} = -0.56$$

At still higher prices, like $3.00, elasticity has been measured at –0.75. The reason is that even though the incremental decline in the desired rate of purchase remains approximately 4 gallons for each $1 price increase, the base quantity will have fallen from 16 to approximately 12 gallons, so the percentage change in Q will now increase substantially. Similarly, the percentage change in price from another $1 increase will decline substantially because the price base is much bigger at $3.50 than at $2.50.

From January 2008 to July 2008 gasoline prices spiked upward from $3.00 per gallon to $4.10 in many cities across the United States. Despite the peak driving season, quantity demanded collapsed from 14 gallons per week the previous summer (at $3 prices per gallon) to 11.5. Mass transit ridership skyrocketed, growing by 20 percent in that one summer in several U.S. cities. Long Sunday drives in the country ended, and Americans decided to car pool, cutting out essentially all discretionary driving. The price elasticity calculated for this $3.00 to $4.10 price range was:

$$\frac{-4.5 \text{ gallons}/13.75}{+\$1.10/\$3.55} = \frac{-33\%}{+31\%} = -1.06$$

For the first time in U.S. transportation history, the demand for gasoline was price elastic![7] What in previous summers had been a weekly expenditure by urban households of $48 ($3 × 16 gallons) fell to $47.15 ($4.10 × 11.5 gallons). With $|\%\Delta Q| = |-32.7\%| > |\%\Delta P| = +30.9\%$, consumer expenditure on gasoline and the total retail revenue from gasoline sales actually declined (by –1.8%) as prices shot up.

Elsewhere around the world, higher fuel taxes and the resulting higher retail price of gasoline has already induced much less driving than in the United Kingdom Figure 3.4 shows that the typical $6 to $8 retail prices in Europe and the United Kingdom have reduced the fuel consumption of the typical two-person urban household to 7 gallons per week. Of course, urban rail and other mass transit are more prevalent across Europe than in the United States, so without that infrastructure the U.S. urban household has fewer substitutes. Consequently, the peak $4.10 price in July 2008 increased price-sensitivity (from $E_D = -0.56$ at $2.50 to –1.06) and reduced 16 gallon consumption by –32.7 percent but only to 11.5 gallons per week.

---

[7]The above procedures for calculating price elasticity yield an *arc elasticity*. It indicates the effect of a discrete change in price, from P_1 to P_2, on the quantity demanded. The following formula is used to compute this elasticity measure:

$$E_D = \frac{\dfrac{Q_2 - Q_1}{\left(\dfrac{Q_2 + Q_1}{2}\right)}}{\dfrac{P_2 - P_1}{\left(\dfrac{P_2 + P_1}{2}\right)}} = \frac{Q_2 - Q_1}{P_2 - P_1} \times \frac{P_2 + P_1}{Q_2 + Q_1} = \frac{\Delta Q}{\Delta P} \times \frac{P_2 + P_1}{Q_2 + Q_1}$$

where

Q_1 = quantity sold before a price change
Q_2 = quantity sold after a price change
P_1 = original price
P_2 = price after a price change

The fraction $(Q_2 + Q_1)/2$ represents average quantity demanded in the range over which the price elasticity is being calculated. $(P_2 + P_1)/2$ also represents the average price over this range. Because the slope remains constant over the

(continued)

entire schedule of linear demand but the value of $(P_2 + P_1)/(Q_2 + Q_1)$ changes, price elasticity at higher prices and smaller volume is therefore larger (in absolute value) than price elasticity for the same product and same demanders at lower price points and larger volume. And elasticity can be used to compute a price that would have to be charged to achieve a particular level of sales. Consider the NBA Corporation, which had monthly basketball shoe sales of 10,000 pairs (at $100 per pair) before a price cut by its major competitor. After this competitor's price reduction, NBA's sales declined to 8,000 pairs a month. From past experience, NBA has estimated the price elasticity of demand to be about −2.0 in this price-quantity range. If the NBA wishes to restore its sales to 10,000 pairs a month, determine the price that must be charged. Letting $Q_2 = 10,000$, $Q_1 = 8,000$, $P_1 = \$100$, and $E_D = -2.0$, the required price, P_2:

$$-2.0 = \frac{\dfrac{10,000 - 8,000}{(10,000 + 8,000)/2}}{\dfrac{P_2 - \$100}{(P_2 + \$100)/2}}$$

$$P_2 = \$89.50$$

A price cut to $89.50 would be required to restore sales to 10,000 pairs a month.

By employing some elementary calculus, the elasticity of demand at any *price point* along the curve may also be calculated with the following expression:

$$E_D = \frac{\partial Q_D}{\partial P} \cdot \frac{P}{Q_D}$$

where

$\dfrac{\partial Q_D}{\partial P}$ = the partial derivative of quantity with respect to price (the inverse of the slope of the demand curve)

Q_D = the quantity demanded at price P

P = the price at some specific point on the demand curve

This equation consists of two magnitudes: (1) a partial derivative effect of own price changes on the desired rate of purchase ($Q_D/_t$), and (2) a price point that (along with a baseline Q_D) determines the percentage change.

The daily demand function for Christmas trees at sidewalk lots in mid-December can be used to illustrate the calculation of the point price elasticity. Suppose that demand can be written algebraically as quantity demanded per day:

$$Q_D = 45,000 - 2,500P + 2.5Y$$

If one is interested in determining the point price elasticity when the price (P) is equal to $40 and per capita disposable personal income (Y) is equal to $30,000, taking the partial derivative of with respect to P yields:

$$\frac{\partial Q_D}{\partial P} = -2,500 \text{ trees per dollar}$$

Substituting for the relevant values of P and Y gives

$$Q_D = 45,000 - 2,500(40) + 2.50(30,000) = 20,000$$

from which one obtains

$$E_D = -2,500 \frac{\text{trees}}{\$} \left(\frac{\$40}{20,000 \text{ trees}} \right) = -5.0$$

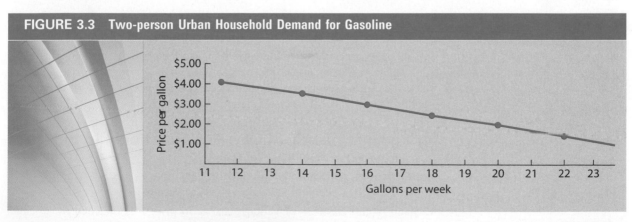

FIGURE 3.3   Two-person Urban Household Demand for Gasoline

Source: Federal Energy Administration.

Taking the total derivative of sales revenue ($P \times Q(P)$) with respect to a small price reduction from P_0 to P_1 necessary to trigger a single additional unit sale beyond Q_0, we obtain

$$\Delta TR / single\ unit\ \Delta Q = (\Delta P \times Q_0) + (\Delta Q \times P_1) \qquad [3.3]$$

Then dividing by $P_1 \times Q_0$ yields the very useful expression,

$$\%\Delta TR = (\Delta P/P_1) + (\Delta Q/Q_0) \qquad [3.4]$$

$$\%\Delta TR = \%\Delta P + \%\Delta Q \qquad [3.5]$$

That is, the percentage effect on sales revenue is the *signed* summation of the percentage change in price and the percentage change in unit sales.

For example, if Johnson & Johnson lowers the price on BAND-AID bandages by 10 percent and sales revenue goes up 24 percent, we can conclude that unit sales must have risen 34 percent, because applying Equation 3.5

$$24\% = -10\% + 34\%$$

Or in our earlier gasoline demand example, if prices are raised \$3.00 to \$4.10 (by 30.9 percent) and revenue declines by –1.8 percent, we may conclude sales fell by –32.7 percent.

That is, since price elasticity of demand is defined as $\%\Delta Q$ divided by $\%\Delta P$, when $|E_D| > 1$ and demand is not very price sensitive (like the –1.06 demand for gasoline in the United States at \$3 to \$4.10 prices), then $\%\Delta Q$ must exceed the $\%\Delta P$. Otherwise, the $|E_D|$ would not be greater than 1.0. In such circumstances, price increases will lead to a small decline in revenue. Again, by Equation 3.5,

$$-1.8\% = +30.9\% - 32.7\%.$$

Steve Young on Demand for NFL Games

Thus, what Steve Young quoted at the start of this chapter meant to say was that the demand facing NFL team owners for attendance at well-officiated professional football games is "relatively price insensitive but still elastic." Therefore, revenue will decline if the owners raise prices but not by very much. So, reasoned Mr. Young, the NFL should meet the demands of the professional referees, knowing that the ticket price increase is necessary to recover their modestly higher salary and pension costs would only slightly reduce the owner's revenues and profits.

So, the smaller/the larger the absolute value of the price elasticity of demand (in the elastic range), the smaller/the larger the revenue decline/rise from a price increase/ decrease. As we shall now see, this relationship between changes in total revenue when prices rise/fall and the calculated price elasticity is not coincidental.

Interpreting the Price Elasticity: The Relationship between the Price Elasticity and Sales Revenue

Price elasticity may take on values over the range from 0 to $-\infty$ (infinity) as indicated in Table 3.2.

When demand is *unit* elastic, a percentage change in price P is matched by an *equal* percentage change in quantity demanded Q_D. When demand is *elastic*, a percentage

FIGURE 3.4   Two-person Urban Household Gasoline Demand, Worldwide 2010 (Fuel tax per gallon)

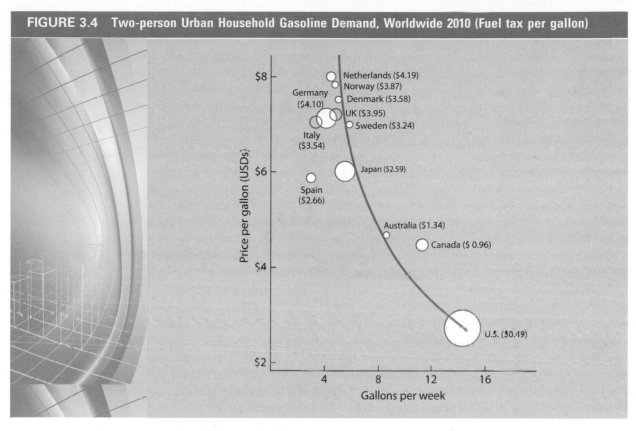

Note: Size of circle is proportional to population.

Source: Worldbank.org and C. Knittel, "Reducing Petroleum Consumption from Transportation," *Journal of Economic Perspectives*, 26 (Winter 2012).

change in P is exceeded by the percentage change in Q_D. For *inelastic* demand, a percentage change in P results in a smaller percentage change in Q_D. The theoretical extremes of perfect elasticity and perfect inelasticity are illustrated in Figure 3.5. AAA-grade January wheat sells on the Kansas City spot market with perfectly elastic demand facing any particular grain dealer; Panel A illustrates this case. Addicted smokers have almost perfectly inelastic demand; their quantity demanded is very inflexible no matter what the price, as indicated in Panel B.

The price elasticity of demand indicates immediately the effect a change in price will have on the total revenue (TR) = total consumer expenditure. Table 3.3 and Figure 3.5 illustrate this connection.

TABLE 3.2   PRICE ELASTICITY OF DEMAND IN ABSOLUTE VALUES

RANGE	DESCRIPTION
$E_D = 0$	Perfectly inelastic
$0 < |E_D| < 1$	Inelastic
$|E_D| = 1$	Unit elastic
$1 < |E_D| < \infty$	Elastic
$|E_D| = \infty$	Perfectly elastic

© Cengage Learning

FIGURE 3.5 Perfectly Elastic and Inelastic Demand Curves

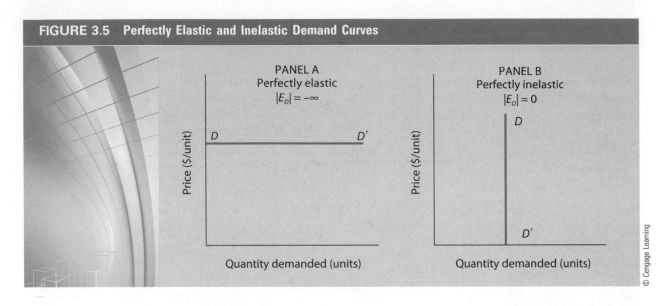

When demand elasticity is less than 1 in absolute value (i.e., inelastic), an increase (decrease) in price will result in an increase (decrease) in $(P \cdot Q_D)$. This occurs because an inelastic demand indicates that a given percentage increase in price results in a smaller percentage decrease in quantity sold, the net effect being an increase in the total expenditures of customers and therefore of sales revenue, $P \cdot Q_D$. When demand is *inelastic*—that is, $|E_D| < 1$—an increase in price from \$2 to \$3, for example, results in an increase in total revenue from \$18 to \$24.

In contrast, when demand is *elastic*—that is, $|E_D| > 1$—a given percentage increase (decrease) in price is more than offset by a larger percentage decrease (increase) in quantity sold. An increase in price from \$9 to \$10 results in that case in a reduction in total consumer expenditure and sales revenue from \$18 to \$10 (again, see Table 3.3).

When demand is *unit elastic*, a given percentage change in price is exactly offset by the same percentage change in quantity demanded, the net result being a constant total consumer expenditure. If the price is increased from \$5 to \$6, total revenue would remain constant at \$30, because the decrease in quantity demanded at the new

TABLE 3.3 THE RELATIONSHIP BETWEEN ELASTICITY AND MARGINAL REVENUE

PRICE, P (\$/UNIT)	QUANTITY, Q_D (UNITS)	ELASTICITY E_D	TOTAL REVENUE $P \cdot Q_D$ (\$)	MARGINAL REVENUE (\$/UNIT)
10	1		10	
9	2	−6.33	18	8
8	3	−3.40	24	6
7	4	−2.14	28	4
6	5	−1.44	30	2
5	6	−1.00	30	0
4	7	−0.69	28	−2
3	8	−0.46	24	−4
2	9	−0.29	18	−6
1	10	−0.15	10	−8

Handwritten margin notes:

if price ↓ 1% then Qty demand is ↑ 6.33

$\dfrac{+1}{1.5}$

$\dfrac{-\$1}{9.50}$ $|-6.33|$ abs. val

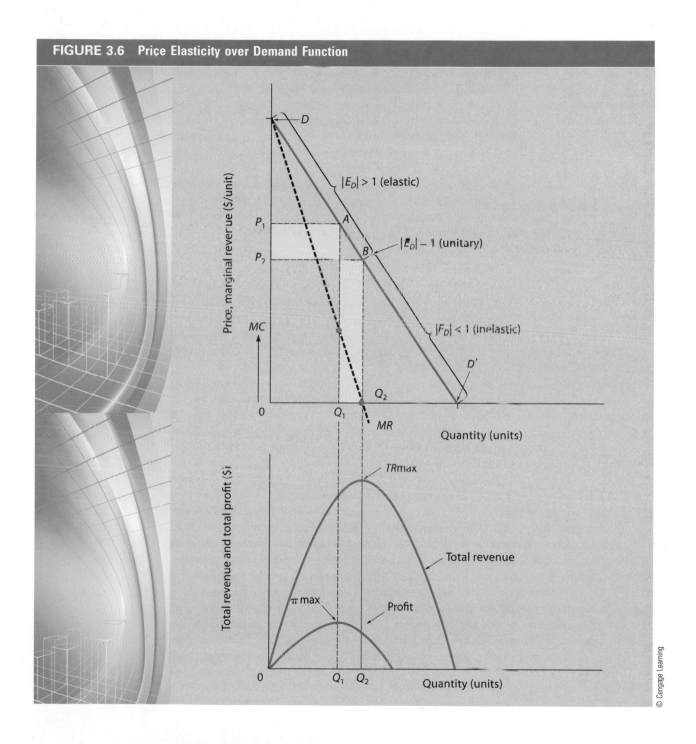

FIGURE 3.6 Price Elasticity over Demand Function

price just offsets the price increase (see Table 3.3). When the price elasticity of demand $|E_D|$ is equal to 1, the total revenue function is maximized and the marginal revenue from lowering price any more to sell an additional unit is zero. In the example, total revenue equals $30 when price P equals either $5 or $6 and quantity demanded Q_D equals either 6 or 5.

As shown in Figure 3.6, when marginal revenue equals zero, any price higher than P_2 results in the demand function being elastic. And at lower prices, demand is increasingly inelastic. Again, then, price P_2 is a pivot point for which total revenue is maximized where marginal revenue equals zero.

This relationship can be derived graphically as well by analyzing the change in revenue resulting from a price change.

marginal revenue The change in total revenue that results from a one-unit change in quantity demanded.

To start, **marginal revenue** is defined as the change in total revenue resulting from lowering price to make an additional unit sale. Lowering price from P_1 to P_2 in Figure 3.6 to increase quantity demanded from Q_1 to Q_2 results in a change in the bottom half of the initial revenue P_1AQ_10 to P_2BQ_20. The difference in these two areas is illustrated in Figure 3.6 as the two shaded rectangles. The horizontal shaded rectangle is the loss of revenue caused by the price reduction $(P_2 - P_1)$ over the previous units sold Q_1. The vertical shaded rectangle is the gain in revenue from selling $(Q_2 - Q_1)$ additional units at the new price P_2. That is, the change in total revenue from lowering the price to sell another unit can always be written as follows:

$$MR = \frac{\Delta TR}{\Delta Q} = \frac{P_2(Q_2 - Q_1) + (P_2 - P_1)Q_1}{(Q_2 - Q_1)} \qquad [3.6]$$

where $P_2(Q_2 - Q_1)$ is the vertical shaded rectangle and $(P_1 - P_2)Q_1$ is the horizontal shaded rectangle. Rearranging, we have:

$$MR = P_2 + \frac{(P_2 - P_1)Q_1}{(Q_2 - Q_1)}$$

$$= P_2\left(1 + \frac{(P_2 - P_1)Q_1}{(Q_2 - Q_1)P_2}\right)$$

$$MR = P_2\left(1 + \frac{\Delta P Q_1}{\Delta Q P_2}\right)$$

The ratio term is the inverse of the price elasticity at the price point P_2 using the quantity Q_1. For small price and quantity changes, this number closely approximates the arc price elasticity between P_1 and P_2. Therefore, the relationship between marginal revenue and price elasticity can be expressed algebraically as follows:

$$MR = P\left(1 + \frac{1}{E_D}\right) \qquad [3.7]$$

For example, at $34 pair of Lee jeans with a $E_D = -1.33$ would have a marginal revenue from lowering price to achieve one more unit sale equal to $8.50:

$$MR = \$34(1 + 1/-1.33) = \$34(1 - 0.75) = \$8.50.$$

Using this equation, one can demonstrate that when demand is unit elastic, marginal revenue is equal to zero. Substituting $E_D = -1$ into Equation 3.7 yields:

$$MR = P\left(1 + \frac{1}{-1}\right)$$

$$= P(0)$$

$$= 0$$

Example

Content Providers Press Music Producers and Recording Companies to Lower Prices

Music producers and recording companies pay songwriters and composers, a fixed percentage of realized sales revenue as a royalty. The two groups often differ as to the preferred price and unit sales. Referring to Figure 3.6, total revenue can be increased by lowering the price any time the quantity sold is less than Q_2. That is, at any price above P_2 (where marginal revenue remains positive), the total revenue will continue to climb only if prices are lowered and additional units sold. Songwriters and composers often therefore press their licensing agents and publishers to lower prices whenever marginal revenue remains positive—that is, to the point where demand is unit elastic. The music publisher, on the other hand, will wish to charge higher prices and sell less quantity because operating profits arise only from marginal revenue in excess of variable cost per unit. Unless variable cost is zero, the publisher always wants a positive marginal revenue and therefore a price greater than P_2 (e.g., P_1). When the innovation of digital music sales on Apple iTunes forced down the price to license a song as a digital download under $1 for the first time, composers and songwriters were pleased even if music producers and recording companies were not. Recent research suggests that a much lower price than iTunes $0.99, as low as $0.60 to $0.70 price per music download, would maximize revenue.[8]

---

[8]Based on "Higher Profits for the Major Record Labels," *Knowledge Wharton* (January 20, 2010).

A commission-based sales force and the management team have this same conflict; salespeople often develop ingenious hidden discounts to try to circumvent a company's list pricing policies. Lowering the price from P_1 to P_2 to set $|E_D| = 1$ will always maximize sales revenue (and therefore, maximize total commissions).

The fact that total revenue is maximized (and marginal revenue is equal to zero) when $|E_D| = 1$ can be shown algebraically with the following example: Custom-Tees, Inc., operates a kiosk in Hanes Mall where it sells custom-printed T-shirts. The demand function for the shirts is

$$Q_D = 150 - 10P \qquad [3.8]$$

where P is the price in dollars per unit and Q_D is the quantity demanded in units per period.

The inverse demand curve can be rewritten in terms of P as a function of Q_D:

$$P = 15 - \frac{Q_D}{10} \qquad [3.9]$$

Total revenue (TR) is equal to price times quantity sold:

$$TR = P \cdot Q_D$$

$$= \left(15 - \frac{Q_D}{10}\right) Q_D$$

$$= 15Q_D - \frac{Q_D^2}{10}$$

Marginal revenue (*MR*) is equal to the first derivative of total revenue with respect to Q_D:

$$MR = \frac{d(TR)}{dQ_D}$$

$$= 15 - \frac{Q_D}{5}$$

To find the value of Q_D where total revenue is maximized, set marginal revenue equal to zero:[9]

$$MR = 0$$

$$15 - \frac{Q_D}{5} = 0$$

$$Q_D^* = 75 \text{ units}$$

Substituting this value into Equation 3.9 yields:

$$P^* = 15 - \frac{75}{10} = \$7.50 \text{ per unit}$$

Thus, total revenue is maximized at $Q_D^* = 75$ and $P^* = \$7.50$. Checking:

$$E_D = \frac{\partial Q_D}{\partial P} \cdot \frac{P}{Q_D} = (-10)\frac{(7.5)}{75} = -1$$
$$|E_D| = 1$$

The Importance of Elasticity-Revenue Relationships

Elasticity is often the key to marketing plans. A product-line manager will attempt to increase sales revenue by allocating a marketing expense budget among price promotions, advertising, retail displays, trade allowances, packaging, and direct mail, as well as in-store coupons. Knowing whether and at what magnitude demand is responsive to each of these marketing initiatives depends on careful estimates of the various demand elasticities of price, advertising, packaging, promotional displays, and so forth.

Example

VW's Invasion of North America

Today the Volkswagen (VW) Beetle is a stylish 200 hp $24,000 sports coupe targeted at the same 20-something Yuppies to whom BMW will later try to sell their 3-series cars. It was not always so. When VW first entered the U.S. market with its no-frills automobile, the original Beetle, European excess inventory during the Marshall Plan in the decade following World War II, had stockpiled at ports and road terminals awaiting export to a new market like the United States. Consequently, VW focused for a time on any demand stimulus that would increase revenue. In the U.S. market, VW had no dealer network and initially provided sales and service only at the docks

(continued)

---

[9]To be certain one has found values for P and Q_D, where total revenue is maximized rather than minimized, check the second derivative of TR to see that it is negative. In this case $d^2TR/dQ_D^2 = -1/5$, so the total revenue function is maximized.

in Bayonne, New Jersey; Charleston, South Carolina; Los Angeles, California; and Houston, Texas. Since General Motors and Ford were beginning to develop compact cars as well, VW decided to enter the market at what appeared to be a ridiculously low promotional price of $5,120 (in 2012 U.S. dollars). As expected, GM and Ford were convinced that nothing that cheap would be perceived as a real car. Yet, the advertising and positioning were an overnight success, and its first full year VW sold well over 400,000 Beetles.

Two years later, a 25 percent price increase was introduced. Although VW lost some potential customers at $6,400, the extra $1,280 per car on all the 384,000 cars they continued to sell easily offset the revenue loss from 16,000 lost sales that could have been made at the original $5,120 price. Compare the long horizontal shaded area in Figure 3.7 that represents increased revenue to the vertical shaded area of lost revenue. The price elasticity of demand was in the inelastic range of demand. By the fourth year, VW had raised the price another 20 percent to $8,000, and again revenue rose.

Finally, at $9,600, the extra receipts from the price increase across all remaining sales were just sufficient to offset the loss in revenue from the lost sales. At $9,600, price elasticity had reached the unit elastic price point. Volkswagen then proceeded to build a U.S. dealer network. These changes increased the potential size of the market in the United States and shifted the demand for Volkswagen products to the right. At the same price of $9,600, with a dealer network and a larger quantity base, the price elasticity then declined (again into the inelastic range), and Volkswagen was again in a position to raise price.

In 1968, 562,000 Beetles were sold at a price of $1,500 (about $10,000 today), and revenue again increased (to $843 million in 1968 dollars). Although the product remained very inexpensive for a new car, the Highway Safety Act of 1966, plus Ralph Nader's safety crusade against the rear-engined Chevy Corvair and the VW Beetle, plus low $1 to $2 per gallon gasoline prices caused consumers to begin losing interest. Instead, they started buying large numbers of Ford Mustangs and Chevy Camaros. In 1969, revenue and price of the Beetle increased one last time. At $1,800 (about $11,500 today), revenue was $968 million ($1,800 × 538,000 units sold). That is, demand remained just inside the inelastic range since a price increase from $1,500 to $1,800 had resulted in higher total revenue.

One managerial insight that this VW example illustrates is that firms should always seek to raise prices for products discovered occupying the inelastic range of their demand. To lower prices in such a range would be "double-dumb." Such sales would both *increase* costs (of producing and distributing additional output demanded at the lower prices) and also *decrease* revenue. It is far better to approach unit elasticity from below, raising prices, thereby increasing revenue while at the same time saving the production and distribution costs. In fact, astute profit-maximizing managers will carry these price increases right on into the elastic range. Specifically, a profit-maximizing manager will move to the left of the point of maximum revenue and unit elasticity (above and beyond point B at P_2 and Q_2 in Figure 3.6) in order not to produce and sell units at an operating loss where MR < variable cost.

Starting from the other direction at zero output, a profit-maximizing firm will only lower price to increase revenue as long as the incremental change in total revenue

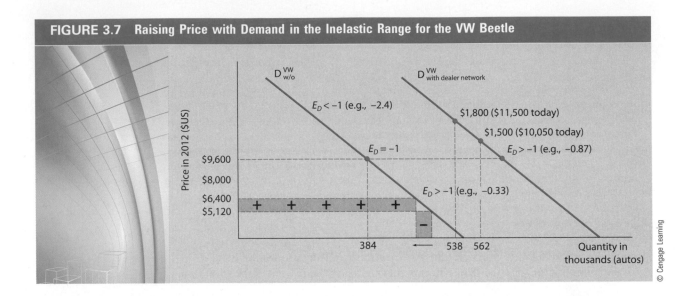

FIGURE 3.7   Raising Price with Demand in the Inelastic Range for the VW Beetle

(the *MR* in Figure 3.6) exceeds the increase in total variable cost (labeled height *MC*). That is, the profit-maximizing output will always occur in the elastic region of the firm's demand at a price above the unit elastic price point.

Example

Price Elasticity Estimate for Coffee Varies by Price[10]

A study on the demand for coffee confirms the relationship between price levels and the price elasticity of demand shown in Figure 3.6. They found that the price elasticity of demand ranged from −0.16 for off-peak up to −0.89 for the peak price level. Thus, coffee users are nearly nine times more sensitive to price changes at high prices than at low price levels. Because these are market-level, not firm-level, elasticity estimates, observing price elasticities less than 1.0 in absolute value does not contradict the managerial insight that is conveyed by Figure 3.7. That is, *firms* will always increase price until demand is no longer in the inelastic region, but the sum of several firm-level demands may well result in an inelastic *market demand* elasticity.

[10]Cliff J. Huang, J. J. Siegfried, and Farangis Zardoshty, "The Demand for Coffee in the United States, 1963–1977," *Quarterly Review of Economics and Business* 20, no. 2 (Summer 1980), pp. 36–50. Another more recent estimate of the demand elasticity for coffee can be found in Albert A. Okunade, "Functional Forms and Habits Effects in the U.S. Demand for Coffee," *Applied Economics* (November 1992).

Factors Affecting the Price Elasticity of Demand

The market demand for bedroom furnishings is extremely price elastic (−3.04), whereas the market demand for coffee (−0.16) is extremely price inelastic. As shown in Table 3.4,

TABLE 3.4 EMPIRICAL PRICE ELASTICITIES

COMMODITY (GOOD/SERVICE)	PRICE ELASTICITY OF MARKET DEMAND	COMMODITY (GOOD/SERVICE)	PRICE ELASTICITY OF MARKET DEMAND
Alcoholic beverages		Bedroom furniture	-3.04^a
Beer	-0.84^b	Glassware/China	-1.20^c
Wine	-0.55^b	Household appliances	-0.64^c
Liquor	-0.50^b	International air transportation	
Apparel		United States/Europe	-1.25^d
Market	-1.1^a	Canada/Europe	-0.82^d
Firms	-4.1^c	Outdoor recreation	-0.56^e
Coffee		School lunches	-0.47^f
Regular	-0.16^g	Shoes	-0.73^c
Instant	-0.36^g	Soybean meal	-1.65^h
Credit charges on bank cards	-2.44^i	Telephones	-0.10^j
Dental visits		Textiles	
Adult males	-0.65^k	Market	-1.5^a
Adult females	-0.78^k	Firms	-4.7^c
Children	-1.40^k	Tires	-0.60^c
Food		Tobacco products	-0.46^c
Market	-1.0^l	Tomatoes	-2.22^m
Firms	-3.8^l	Wool	-1.32^n

© Cengage Learning

[a]Richard D. Stone and D.A. Rowe, "The Durability of Consumers' Durable Goods," *Econometrica* 28 (1960), pp. 407–416.

[b]Dale Heien and Greg Pompelli, "The Demand for Alcoholic Beverages: Economic and Demographic Effects," *Southern Economic Journal* (January 1989), pp. 759–769.

[c]H. S. Houthakker and Lester D. Taylor, *Consumer Demand in the United States*, 2nd ed. (Cambridge, MA: Harvard University Press, 1970).

[d]J.M. Cigliano, "Price and Income Elasticities for Airline Travel: The North Atlantic Market," *Business Economics* (September 1980), pp. 17–21.

[e]Russel L. Gum and W.E. Martin, "Problems and Solutions in Estimating the Demand for and Value of Rural Outdoor Recreation," *American Journal of Agricultural Economics* (November 1975), pp. 558–566.

[f]George A. Braley and P.E. Nelson Jr., "Effect of a Controlled Price Increase on School Lunch Participation: Pittsburgh, 1973," *American Journal of Agricultural Economics* (February 1975), pp. 90–96.

[g]Cliff J. Huang, John J. Siegfried, and Farangis Zardoshty, "The Demand for Coffee in the United States, 1963–1977," *Quarterly Review of Economics and Business* 20, no. 2 (Summer 1980), pp. 36–50.

[h]H. Knipscheer, L. Hill, and B. Dixon, "Demand Elasticities for Soybean Meal in the European Community," *American Journal of Agricultural Economics* (May 1982), pp. 249–253.

[i]J. Starvins, "Can Demand Elasticity Explain Sticky Credit Card Rates?" *New England Economic Review* (July/August 1996), pp. 43–54.

[j]D. Cracknell and M. Knott, "The Measurement of Price Elasticities—The BT Experience," *International Journal of Forecasting* 11 (1995), pp. 321–329.

[k]Willard G. Manning Jr. and Charles E. Phelps, "The Demand for Dental Care," *The Bell Journal of Economics* 10, no. 2 (Autumn 1979), pp. 503–525.

[l]M.D. Shapiro, "Measuring Market Power in U.S. Industry," NBER Working Paper, No. 2212 (1987).

[m]Daniel B. Suits, "Agriculture," in *Structure of American Industry*, 7th ed., ed. W. Adams (New York: Macmillan, 1986).

[n]C.E. Ferguson and M. Polasek, "The Elasticity of Import Demand for Raw Apparel Wool in the United States," *Econometrica* 30 (1962), pp. 670–699.

price elasticities vary greatly among different products and services.[11] Some of the factors that account for the differing responsiveness of consumers to price changes are examined next.

---

[11]RTi is one of a number of consulting firms that estimate price elasticities; access at www.rtiresearch.com

INTERNATIONAL PERSPECTIVES

Free Trade and the Price Elasticity of Demand: Nestlé Yogurt

The 27 Europe Community nations have virtually eliminated trade barriers, and goods flow freely and without tariffs from one European country to another. Increasing standardization of products in these markets further reduced trading barriers. The North American Free Trade Agreement (NAFTA) ratified by the United States, Canada, and Mexico has had the same effects. And the General Agreement on Tariffs and Trade (GATT) has led to a worldwide reduction in tariffs and other trade barriers. What are the implications for estimates of price elasticity of demand?

Free trade results in an effective increase in the number of substitute goods that are available to consumers and businesses in any country. Consequently, as barriers to free trade come down, demand will become more price elastic for goods that historically have not been able to flow easily between countries. Nestlé's yogurt and custard products now travel from manufacturing sites in the British Midlands to Milan, Italy, in 17 hours, whereas the customs processing and transportation bottlenecks once required 38 hours. Similarly, iron forging of crankshafts and engine blocks for U.S. autos now occurs primarily in Mexico, and transmissions for Detroit are often constructed as subassemblies in Japan. The winners in this globalization process should be consumers, who will have a wider variety of products to choose from at ever more competitive prices. The losers will be those firms that cannot compete in a global market on the basis of cost, quality, and service.

The Availability and Closeness of Substitutes   The most important determinant of the price elasticity of demand is the availability and perceived closeness of substitutes. The greater the number of substitute goods within the relevant market, the more price elastic is the demand for a product because a customer can easily shift from one good to a close substitute good if the price rises.[12] The price elasticity of demand for Johnson & Johnson's BAND-AID bandages is high because numerous companies offer a nearly identical product. The closeness of substitutes is a related but different concept. Intravenous feeding systems offer distant substitutes for hospital patients in shock or otherwise unable to digest food, so the price elasticity of demand for that product is low. Sunbeam white bread, however, has very close substitutes from in-store bakeries and from numerous competitors in branded breads. So, in that case, price elasticity of demand is high.

Percentage of the Consumer's Budget   The demand for relatively high-priced goods tends to be more price elastic than the demand for inexpensive items because expensive items account for a greater proportion of a person's budget. Consequently, we would expect the demand for apartment housing to be more price elastic than the demand for children's toys. The greater the percentage of the budget spent on a good, the larger the purchasing power released by any given price reduction or absorbed by any given price increase. And the larger this "purchasing power effect," the greater the price elasticity for income-superior goods.

---

[12]The demand for durable goods tends to be more price elastic than the demand for nondurables. This is true because of the ready availability of a relatively inexpensive substitute in many cases—that is, the repair of a used television, car, or refrigerator, rather than buying a new one.

Positioning as Income Superior How a product is positioned to the target customers has much to do with whether the release in purchasing power associated with a price discount will result in a substantial, moderate, or trivial increase (or possibly even a decrease) in unit sales. In the "Cash for Clunkers" federal subsidy program in 2009, some but not all replacement vehicles were eligible for a $5,000 discount if the customer turned in an older car and bought a more fuel-efficient one. Since the program made no distinction between high-value used cars and almost-worthless junk cars, most participants turned in clunkers and received a $4,000 to near $5,000 increase in their purchasing power. The new automobiles whose demand increased substantially were income-superior full-size family sedans and hybrid SUVs, not the mid-size and economy cars that would have significantly improved fuel efficiency. This should have come as no surprise because many of the fuel-efficient cars like the Ford Fiesta, Ford Focus, and Chevy Geo are seen as income-inferior products.

Time Period of Adjustment To respond to a price decrease, potential customers must first learn about the discount and then incur the cost of adjusting their own schedules to complete a purchase during the sale period. Because both search and adjustment costs for consumers are higher if sale prices last only a few minutes, the demand response to price changes is diminished the shorter the time period of adjustment. Predictable end-of-model-year promotions in the auto industry lasting throughout the month of August stimulate much more elastic demand than unannounced "Midnight Madness" sales that last only a few hours.

The long-run demand for many products also tends to be more elastic than short-run demand because of the increase in the number of effective substitutes that become available over time. For example, the only available alternatives for gasoline consumption in the short run are not taking a trip or using some form of public transportation. Over time, as consumers replace their cars, they find another excellent substitute for gasoline—namely, more fuel-efficient vehicles.

THE INCOME ELASTICITY OF DEMAND

Among the variables that affect demand, disposable income of the target customers is often one of the most important. Business analysts compute an **income elasticity** of demand analogous to the price elasticity of demand.

Income Elasticity Defined

income elasticity
The ratio of the percentage change in quantity demanded to the percentage change in income, assuming that all other factors influencing demand remain unchanged.

Income elasticity of demand can be expressed as

$$E_y = \frac{\%\Delta Q_D}{\%\Delta Y}, \text{ ceteris paribus} \tag{3.10}$$

where

$$\Delta Q_D = \text{change in quantity demanded}$$
$$\Delta Y = \text{change in income}$$

Various measures of income can be used in the analysis. One commonly used measure is consumer disposable income, calculated on an aggregate, household, or per capita basis.

Example

Targeting a Direct Mail Coupon at a Ford Dealership

One of the key steps for successful auto dealerships is to develop an extensive database on prospective and repeat purchase customers. These databases are often used to target promotional material from the manufacturer to specific local households thought to be most likely to respond to direct mail advertising. Suppose Ford decides to offer select households $5,000 off several models. To emphasize the role of positioning in demand analysis, let's focus on the effect of these direct mail coupons on the sporty Ford Taurus four-door sedan. Suppose Taurus is currently experiencing inventory overhang with production runs that have exceeded recent sales.

To whom in the local dealer's database should we target a "$5,000 off" coupon? One choice is a newly married couple attending community college who recently shopped at our dealership for a subcompact Ford Focus. The second choice is a young professional couple of German heritage who already own a four-year-old 85,000 mile Taurus as their commuter car along with a vintage BMW. Third choice is a French immigrant couple, both management consultants, who ride mass transit but recently test-drove a Volvo sedan. The final choice is a retired couple who once owned a Taurus and recently purchased their third Ford Crown Vic, a full-size sedan.

In selecting a target customer for the direct mail coupon, the dealership's marketing team assesses switching costs, positioning, and likely spending power. Although the newlyweds would aspire to a sporty midsize sedan like the Taurus, their anticipated uses and spending power do not match those of typical Taurus customers. The young French immigrant couple aspires already to a Volvo, implying Taurus positioning is perceived as inferior. The retired couple has substantial brand loyalty to Ford but high switching cost, given their full-size uses and needs. Not so with the Germanic yuppies who already spend large amounts of disposable income on autos and may continue to see Taurus as an aspirant good.

The projected demand of the German-heritage couple is likely to be most elastic to the price change on offer. Their switching costs are low because they presently consume an almost identical substitute. They will likely find the new model Taurus an aspirant good. And the percentage of their budget spent on automobiles is largest of the four potential target households.

The income elasticity metric is calculated as an arc elasticity or a point elasticity in the same manner as price elasticity calculations,

$$E_y = \frac{Y}{Q_D} \times \frac{\partial Q_D}{\partial Y}$$

depending on whether the income change is a discrete change (e.g., by several thousand dollars or a substantial percentage of income) versus an incremental change at a particular income level. (Reread footnote 7 for an elaboration of how to calculate arc elasticity versus point elasticity.)

Interpreting the Income Elasticity   For most products, income elasticity is expected to be positive; that is, $E_y > 0$. Such goods are referred to as *income-superior goods*.

Those goods having a calculated income elasticity that is negative are called *inferior goods*. Inferior goods are purchased in smaller absolute quantities as the income of the consumer increases. Subcompact autos and such food items as canned mackerel or dried beans are frequently cited as examples of inferior goods.

Knowledge of the magnitude of the income elasticity of demand for a particular product is especially useful in forecasting unit sales of economic activity. In industries that produce goods having high income elasticities (such as new furniture), a major increase or decrease in economic activity will have a significant impact on demand. Knowledge of income elasticities is also useful in developing marketing strategies for highly divergent products. For example, products having a high income elasticity can be promoted as being luxurious and stylish, whereas goods having a low income elasticity can be promoted as being economical.

Example

Income Elasticities: Empirical Estimates

Estimates of the income elasticity of demand have been made for a wide variety of goods and services, as shown in Table 3.5. Note that the income elasticities for goods that are often perceived as necessities (e.g., many food items and housing) are less than 1.0, whereas the income elasticities for items that are usually viewed as luxuries (e.g., European travel) are greater than 1.0.

TABLE 3.5 EMPIRICAL INCOME ELASTICITIES

COMMODITY (GOOD/SERVICE)	INCOME ELASTICITY
European travel	1.91[a]
Apples	1.32[b]
Beef	1.05[b]
Chicken	0.28[b]
Dental visits	
Adult males	0.61[c]
Adult females	0.55[c]
Children	0.87[c]
Housing (low-income renters)	0.22[d]
Milk	0.50[a]
Oranges	0.83[a]
Potatoes	0.15[a]
Tomatoes	0.24[a]

© Cengage Learning

[a]J.M. Cigliano, "Price and Income Elasticities for Airline Travel: The North Atlantic Market," *Business Economics* (September 1980), pp. 17–21.

[b]Daniel B. Suits, "Agriculture," in *Structure of American Industry*, 7th ed., ed. W. Adams (New York: Macmillan, 1986).

[c]Willand G. Manning Jr. and Charles E. Phelps, "The Demand for Dental Care," *Bell Journal of Economics* 10, no. 2 (Autumn 1979), pp. 503–525.

[d]Elizabeth A. Roistacher, "Short-Run Housing Responses to Changes in Income," *American Economic Review* (February 1977), pp. 381–386.

Advertising Elasticity   Advertising elasticity measures the responsiveness of sales to changes in advertising expenditures as measured by the ratio of the percentage change in sales to the percentage change in advertising expenditures.

$$E_{adv} = \frac{\%\Delta Q_D}{\%\Delta ADV}, \; ceteris\; paribus$$

The higher the advertising elasticity coefficient E_A, the more responsive sales are to changes in the advertising budget. An awareness of this elasticity measure may assist advertising or marketing managers in their determination of appropriate levels of advertising outlays relative to price promotions or packaging expenditures.

CROSS ELASTICITY OF DEMAND

Another determinant of demand that substantially affects the demand for a product is the price of a related (substitute or complementary) product.

Cross Price Elasticity Defined

cross price elasticity The ratio of the percentage change in the quantity demanded of Good A to the percentage change in the price of Good B, assuming that all other factors influencing demand remain unchanged.

The **cross price elasticity** of demand, E_{cross}, is a measure of the responsiveness of changes in the quantity demanded (Q_{DA}) of Product A to price changes for Product B (P_B).

$$E_{cross} = \frac{\%\Delta Q_{DA}}{\%\Delta P_B}, ceteris\ paribus \qquad [3.11]$$

where

$$\Delta Q_{DA} = \text{change in quantity demanded of Product } A$$
$$\Delta P_B = \text{change in price of Product } B$$

Interpreting the Cross Price Elasticity

If the cross price elasticity measured between Products A and B is *positive* (as might be expected in our butter/margarine example or between such products as plastic wrap and aluminum foil), the two products are referred to as *substitutes* for each other. The higher the cross price elasticity, the closer the substitute relationship. A *negative* cross price elasticity, on the other hand, indicates that two products are *complementary*. For example, a significant decrease in the price of DVD players would probably result in a substantial increase in the demand for DVDs.

Antitrust and Cross Price Elasticities

The number of close substitutes may be an important determinant of the degree of competition in a market. The fewer the number of close substitutes that exist for a product, the greater the amount of market power that is possessed by the producing or selling firm. An important issue in antitrust cases involves the appropriate definition of the relevant product market to be used in computing statistics of market control (e.g., market share). A case involving DuPont's production of cellophane was concerned with this issue. Does the relevant product market include just the product cellophane or does it include the much broader flexible packaging materials market?

The Supreme Court found the cross price elasticity of demand between cellophane and other flexible packaging materials to be sufficiently high so as to exonerate DuPont from a charge of monopolizing the market. Had the relevant product been considered to be cellophane alone, DuPont would have clearly lost, because it produced 75 percent of all cellophane output and its only licensee, Sylvania, produced the rest. But when other flexible packaging materials were included in the product market definition, DuPont's share dropped to an acceptable 18 percent level. The importance of the definition of the relevant product market and the determination of the cross price elasticity of demand among close substitute products has often been emphasized by the courts.[13]

[13]See, for example, *U.S. v. Alcoa*, 148 F.2d 416, 424; *Times Picayune Publishing Co. v. U.S.* 345 U.S. 594; *Continental Can Co. v. U.S.*, 378 U.S. 441, 489. See John E. Kwoka and Lawrence J. White, *The Antitrust Revolution: Economics, Competition, and Policy* (New York: Oxford University Press, 1999) for a further discussion of some of the economic issues involved in antitrust laws.

Why Pay More for Fax Paper and Staples at Staples?[14]

Just what constitutes an available substitute has as much to do with the cross price elasticity of rival firm supply as it does with the cross price elasticity of demand. In a hotly contested recent merger proposal, the Federal Trade Commission (FTC) has argued that office superstores like OfficeMax, Office Depot, and Staples are a separate relevant market from other smaller office supply retailers. Office Depot had 46 percent of the $13.22 billion in superstore sales of office supplies, Staples had 30 percent, and OfficeMax had the remaining 24 percent. Office Depot and Staples proposed to merge, thereby creating a combined firm with 76 percent of the market. Such mergers have been disallowed many times under the Sherman Antitrust Act's prohibition of monopolization.

The two companies insisted, however, that their competitors included not only OfficeMax but all office supply distribution channels, including small paper goods specialty stores, department stores, discount stores like Target, warehouse clubs like Sam's Club, office supply catalogs, and some computer retailers. This larger office supply industry is very fragmented, easy to enter (or exit), and huge, topping $185 billion. By this latter standard, the proposed merger involved admittedly the largest players in the industry, but companies with only 3 to 5 percent market shares. Under this alternative interpretation of the relevant market, Office Depot and Staples should have been allowed to proceed with their merger.

Have superstores like Home Depot and Lowes in do-it-yourself building supplies, PetSmart in pet supplies, and Office Depot, OfficeMax, and Staples created a new time-saving customer shopping experience and demand pattern in towns where they are clustered? Office supply products are search goods for which customers *can* detect quality prior to purchase and locate just the quality-price combination they desire. Brand name reputations should therefore have little effect on repeat purchase shopping patterns at Office Depot and Staples. Is this case devoid of a rationale for antitrust action? Have successful entrepreneurs simply created a new segment within the traditional relevant market for office products?

The FTC undertook two sets of experiments to advise the commissioners who voted to deny the proposed merger. Prices for everything from paper clips to fax paper were sampled in 40 cities and towns where Office Depot and Staples competed and in other similar locations where only one of the superstores was present. The prices were significantly higher in the single superstore markets. Apparently, despite an enormous rival supply of traditional office product retailers, target customers (like secretaries responsible for securing resupply) are willing to pay more for staples at Staples.

As Walmart has demonstrated in other search good categories, shoppers will flock to a superstore despite numerous small retailers closer to the customer. So, despite the enormous preexisting supply of traditional rivals and the exceptional ease of entry (and exit) at small scale, competition for superstore retailers comes only from other superstore retailers. As a result, the Sherman Act warrants denying the proposed merger in office supply superstores. Although stores like Walmart are entitled to become "category killers" on their own sales growth, the FTC has decided to bar superstore mergers as a route to obtaining near-monopoly status.

---

[14]Based on "FTC Votes to Bar Staples' Bid for Rival," *Wall Street Journal* (March 11, 1997), p. A3.

TABLE 3.6 ELECTRICITY-USE ELASTICITIES			
	PRICE ELASTICITY	**INCOME ELASTICITY**	**CROSS ELASTICITY (GAS)**
Residential market	−1.3	0.3	0.15
Commercial market	−1.5	0.9	0.15
Industrial market	−1.7	1.1	0.15

© Cengage Learning

An Empirical Illustration of Price, Income, and Cross Elasticities

A study by Chapman, Tyrrell, and Mount examined the elasticity of energy use by residential, commercial, and industrial users.[15] They hypothesized that the demand for electricity was determined by the price of electricity, income levels, and the price of a substitute good—natural gas.

Table 3.6 summarizes the electricity-use elasticities with respect to price, income, and the substitute product (here, natural gas) prices. As shown in the table, the price elasticity of demand for electricity was relatively elastic in all markets, with the highest price elasticity being in the industrial market. This is consistent with the observation that many assembly plants, foundries, and other heavy industrial users switch to self-generated power with natural gas-fired turbines when electricity prices spike. The positive cross elasticity shows that electricity and natural gas are, indeed, substitute goods.

THE COMBINED EFFECT OF DEMAND ELASTICITIES

When two or more of the factors that affect demand change simultaneously, one is often interested in determining their combined impact on quantity demanded. For example, suppose that a firm plans to increase the price of its product next period and anticipates that consumers' disposable incomes will also increase next period. Other factors affecting demand, such as advertising expenditures and competitors' prices, are expected to remain the same in the next period. From the formula for the price elasticity (Equation 3.1), the effect on quantity demanded of a price increase would be equal to

$$\%\Delta Q_D = E_D(\%\Delta P)$$

Similarly, from the formula for the income elasticity (Equation 3.11), the effect on quantity demanded of an increase in consumers' incomes would be equal to

$$\%\Delta Q_D = E_y(\%\Delta Y)$$

Each of these percentage changes (divided by 100 to put them in a decimal form) would be multiplied by current period demand (Q_1) to get the respective changes in quantity demanded caused by the price and income increases. Assuming that the price and income effects are *independent* and *additive*, the quantity demanded next period

---

[15]D. Chapman, T. Tyrrell, and T. Mount, "Electricity Demand Growth and the Energy Crisis," *Science* (November 17, 1972), p. 705.

(Q_2) would be equal to current period demand (Q_1) plus the changes caused by the price and income increases:

$$Q_2 = Q_1 + Q_1[E_D(\%\Delta P)] + Q_1[E_y(\%\Delta Y)]$$

or

$$Q_2 = Q_1[1 + E_D(\%\Delta P) + E_y(\%\Delta Y)] \qquad [3.12]$$

The combined use of income and price elasticities, illustrated here for forecasting demand, can be generalized to include any of the elasticity concepts that were developed in the preceding sections of this chapter.

Example

Price and Income Effects: The Seiko Company

Suppose Seiko is planning to increase the price of its watches by 10 percent in the coming year. Economic forecasters expect real disposable personal income to increase by 6 percent during the same period. From past experience, the price elasticity of demand has been estimated to be approximately −1.3 and the income elasticity has been estimated at 2.0. These elasticities are assumed to remain constant over the range of price and income changes anticipated. Seiko currently sells 2 million watches per year. Determine the forecasted demand for next year (assuming that the percentage price and income effects are independent and additive). Substituting the relevant data into Equation 3.12 yields

$$Q_2 = 2,000,000\,[1 + (-1.3)(.10) + (2.0)(.06)]$$
$$= 1,980,000 \text{ units}$$

The forecasted demand for next year is 1.98 million watches assuming that other factors that influence demand, such as advertising and competitors' prices, remain unchanged. In this case, the positive impact of the projected increase in household income is more than offset by the decline in quantity demanded associated with a price increase.

SUMMARY

- Demand relationships can be represented in the form of a schedule (table), graph, or algebraic function.
- The demand curve is downward sloping, indicating that consumers are willing to purchase more units of a good or service at lower prices (iron law of demand).
- The total effect of a price reduction is the sum of an ever present positive substitution effect and a sometimes positive, sometimes negative, and possibly zero purchasing power (or real income) effect.
- The magnitude of the substitution effect depends upon switching costs—that is, the perceived closeness of substitutes. The magnitude of the purchasing power effect depends upon positioning of the product and the targeting of particular customers who are likely to find the product offering an aspirant good rather than an inferior good.

- Elasticity refers to the responsiveness of quantity demanded (or supplied) to changes in price or another related variable. Thus *price elasticity* of demand refers to the percentage change in quantity demanded associated with a percentage change in price, holding constant the effects of other determinants of demand. Demand is said to be relatively price *elastic* (*inelastic*) if a given percentage change in price results in a greater (smaller) percentage change in quantity demanded.
- When demand is unit elastic, marginal revenue equals zero and total revenue is maximized. When demand is elastic, an increase (decrease) in price will result in a decrease (increase) in total revenue. When demand is inelastic, an increase (decrease) in price will result in an increase (decrease) in total revenue.
- Prices should always be increased in the inelastic region of the firm's demand because lower price points would result in reduced revenue, despite increased unit sales.
- *Income elasticity* of demand refers to the percentage change in quantity demanded associated with a percentage change in income, holding constant the effects of determinants of demand.
- *Cross elasticity* of demand refers to the percentage change in quantity demanded of Good *A* associated with a percentage change in the price of Good *B*.
- The magnitude of price elasticity varies a great deal across target customers and across products because of differences in (1) the number and perceived closeness of substitutes (also known as switching costs), (2) the percentage of the budget expended on the product, (3) the positioning of the product as income superior to that target market, and (4) the time period of adjustment.

Exercises

Answers to the exercises in blue can be found in Appendix D at the back of the book.

1. The Potomac Range Corporation manufactures a line of microwave ovens costing $500 each. Its sales have averaged about 6,000 units per month during the past year. In August, Potomac's closest competitor, Spring City Stove Works, cut its price for a closely competitive model from $600 to $450. Potomac noticed that its sales volume declined to 4,500 units per month after Spring City announced its price cut.
   a. What is the arc cross elasticity of demand between Potomac's oven and the competitive Spring City model?
   b. Would you say that these two firms are very close competitors? What other factors could have influenced the observed relationship?
   c. If Potomac knows that the arc price elasticity of demand for its ovens is −3.0, what price would Potomac have to charge to sell the same number of units it did before the Spring City price cut?
2. The price elasticity of demand for personal computers is estimated to be −2.2. If the price of personal computers declines by 20 percent, what will be the expected percentage increase in the quantity of computers sold?
3. The Olde Yogurt Factory has reduced the price of its popular Mmmm Sundae from $2.25 to $1.75. As a result, the firm's daily sales of these sundaes have increased from 1,500 per day to 1,800 per day. Compute the arc price elasticity of demand over this price and consumption quantity range.
4. The subway fare in your town has just been increased from a current level of 50 cents to $1.00 per ride. As a result, the transit authority notes a decline in ridership of 30 percent.
   Compute the price elasticity of demand for subway rides.
   a. If the transit authority reduces the fare back to 50 cents, what impact would you expect on the ridership? Why?
5. If the marginal revenue from a product is $15 and the price elasticity of demand is −1.2, what is the price of the product?

6. The demand function for bicycles in Holland has been estimated to be

$$Q = 2,000 + 15Y - 5.5P$$

where Y is income in *thousands* of euros, Q is the quantity demanded in units, and P is the price per unit. When $P = 150$ euros and $Y = 15(000)$ euros, determine the following:
   a. Price elasticity of demand
   b. Income elasticity of demand

7. In an attempt to increase revenues and profits, a firm is considering a 4 percent increase in price and an 11 percent increase in advertising. If the price elasticity of demand is −1.5 and the advertising elasticity of demand is +0.6, would you expect an increase or decrease in total revenues?

8. The Stopdecay Company sells an electric toothbrush for $25. Its sales have averaged 8,000 units per month over the past year. Recently, its closest competitor, Decayfighter, reduced the price of its electric toothbrush from $35 to $30. As a result, Stopdecay's sales declined by 1,500 units per month.
   a. What is the arc cross elasticity of demand between Stopdecay's toothbrush and Decayfighter's toothbrush? What does this indicate about the relationship between the two products?
   b. If Stopdecay knows that the arc price elasticity of demand for its toothbrush is −1.5, what price would Stopdecay have to charge to sell the same number of units as it did before the Decayfighter price cut? Assume that Decayfighter holds the price of its toothbrush constant at $30.
   c. What is Stopdecay's average monthly total revenue from the sale of electric toothbrushes before and after the price change determined in part (b)?
   d. Is the result in part (c) necessarily desirable? What other factors would have to be taken into consideration?

9. The Sydney Transportation Company operates an urban bus system in New South Wales, Australia. Economic analysis performed by the firm indicates that two major factors influence the demand for its services: fare levels and downtown parking rates. Table 1 presents information available from 2005 operations. Forecasts of future fares and hourly parking rates are presented in Table 2.

TABLE 1

AVERAGE DAILY TRANSIT RIDERS (2005)	AVERAGE DOWN-TOWN ROUND-TRIP FARE ($)	PARKING RATE ($)
5,000	1.00	1.50

TABLE 2

YEAR	ROUND-TRIP FARE ($)	AVERAGE PARKING RATES ($)
2006	1.00	2.50
2007	1.25	2.50

Sydney's economists supplied the following information so that the firm can estimate ridership. Based on past experience, the coefficient of cross elasticity between bus ridership and downtown parking rates is estimated at 0.2, given a fare of $1.00 per round trip. This is not expected to change for a fare increase to $1.25. The price elasticity of demand is currently estimated at −1.1, given hourly parking rates of $1.50. It is estimated, however, that the price elasticity will change to −1.2 when parking rates increase to $2.50. Using these data, estimate the average daily ridership for 2006 and 2007.

10. The Reliable Aircraft Company manufactures small, pleasure-use aircraft. Based on past experience, sales volume appears to be affected by changes in the price of the planes and by the state of the economy as measured by consumers' disposable personal income. The following data pertaining to Reliable's aircraft sales, selling prices, and consumers' personal income were collected:

YEAR	AIRCRAFT SALES	AVERAGE PRICE ($)	DISPOSABLE PERSONAL INCOME (IN CONSTANT 2006 DOLLARS— BILLIONS)
2006	525	17,200	610
2007	450	8,000	610
2008	400	8,000	590

a. Estimate the arc price elasticity of demand using the 2006 and 2007 data.
b. Estimate the arc income elasticity of demand using the 2007 and 2008 data.
c. Assume that these estimates are expected to remain stable during 2009. Forecast 2009 sales for Reliable assuming that its aircraft prices remain constant at 2007 levels and that disposable personal income will increase by $40 billion. Also assume that arc income elasticity computed in (b) above is the best available estimate of income elasticity.
d. Forecast 2009 sales for Reliable given that its aircraft prices will increase by $500 from 2008 levels and that disposable personal income will increase by $40 billion. Assume that the price and income effects are *independent* and *additive* and that the arc income and price elasticities computed in parts (a) and (b) are the best available estimates of these elasticities to be used in making the forecast.

11. Federal excise taxes on gasoline vary widely across the developed world. The United States has the lowest taxes at USD $0.40 per gallon (or £0.07 per liter), Canada has taxes of $0.60 per gallon, Japan and much of Europe is $2.00 per gallon, while Britain has the highest tax at $2.83 a gallon or £0.5 per liter. If gasoline taxes are intended to reduce the time losses from road congestion in urban environments and gasoline pre-tax costs about £0.40 per liter, why might the optimal tax in Canada be 50 percent higher than in the United States? What would be an explanation for why adjacent countries would have such different estimates of the price elasticity of demand for auto driving?[16]

12. What conceptual determinant of auto demand price elasticity is most closely associated with the differences in switching cost across the target customers in the "Direct Mail Coupon at a Ford Dealership" example—low switching cost for the German couple who commute in an old Taurus and high switching cost for the older couple who drive Crown Vics?

13. Illustrate the relationship between product positioning and customer targeting using the facts of the Ford dealership direct mail coupon example. Which customer is least likely and second least likely to buy a Taurus for this reason?

---

[16]Based on "Fueling Discontent," *The Economist* (May 19, 2001), p. 69.

Case Exercises   ## Polo Golf Shirt Pricing

The setting is a Ralph Lauren outlet store, and the product line is Polo golf shirts. A product manager and the General Manager for Outlet Sales are analyzing the discounted price to be offered at the outlet stores. Let's work through the decision at the level of one color of golf shirts sold per outlet store per day. The decision being made is how low a price to select at the start of any given day to generate sales at that price throughout the day. The demand, revenue, and variable cost information is collected on the following spreadsheet:

QUANTITY SOLD	UNIFORM PRICE ($)	TOTAL REVENUE ($)	MARGINAL REVENUE ($)	VARIABLE COST ($)
0	50.00	0	0	28
1	48.00	48	48	28
2	46.00	92	44	28
3	45.00	135	43	28
4	44.00	176	41	28
5	42.00	210	34	28
6	40.00	240	30	28
7	38.31	268	28	28
8	36.50	292	24	28
9	34.50	311	19	28
10	—	—	16	28
11	—	—	13	28
12	—	—	10	28
13	—	—	7	28
14	—	—	4	28
15	—	—	0	28
16	—	—	(1)	28
17	—	—	(4)	28
18	—	—	(7)	

see pg 80

Questions

1. Identify the change in total revenue (the marginal revenue) from the fourth shirt per day. What price reduction was necessary to sell four rather than three shirts?
2. Does this fourth shirt earn an operating profit or impose an operating loss? How large is it?
3. What is the change in total revenue from lowering the price to sell seven rather than six shirts in each color each day? In what sense is the decision to sell this seventh shirt a "break point"?
4. Decompose the components of the $28 marginal revenue from the seventh unit sale at $38.31—that is, how much revenue is lost per unit sale relative to the price that would sell six shirts per color per day?
5. Calculate the total revenue for selling the 10th through the 16th shirt per day. Calculate the reduced prices necessary to achieve each of these sales rates.

6. How many unit sales per day most pleases a sales clerk with sales-commission-based bonuses?

7. Would you recommend lowering price to the level required to generate 15 unit sales per day? Why or why not? What does it mean to "sell at a negative margin"?

8. At 14 shirts per day, the margin is positive. But what is the operating profit or loss on the 14th? The 12th? The 10th shirt?

9. How many shirts do you recommend selling per color per day? What then is your recommended dollar markup and markup percentage? What dollar margin and percentage margin is that?

Estimating Demand

CHAPTER PREVIEW

The preceding chapter developed the theory of demand, including the concepts of price elasticity, income elasticity, and cross price elasticity of demand. A manager who is contemplating an increase in the price of one of the firm's products needs to know the quantitative magnitude of the impact of this increase on quantity demanded, total revenue, and profits. Is the demand elastic, inelastic, or unit elastic with respect to price over the range of the contemplated price increase? What growth of unit sales can be expected if consumer incomes increase as a result of a recovery from a severe recession?

Governments and not-for-profit institutions are also faced with similar questions. What will be the impact of an increase in mass transit fares or bridge tolls? Will automobile commuting decrease by 5, 10, or 20 percent? Will a sales tax increase boost revenue enough to cover a projected budget shortfall? This chapter discusses some of the techniques and problems associated with estimating demand.

MANAGERIAL CHALLENGE
Demand for Whitman's Chocolate Samplers

Whitman's Sampler is a mid-priced gift box of assorted better quality chocolates sold through the drug store distribution channel. Whitman is a 170-year-old firm now owned by Nestle who also owns Russell Stover Candies, Lindor and Ferrero Rocher, with which the Sampler is often displayed on Rite-Aid or CVS endcaps. The target market is "men in trouble" who wish to pick up something unexpected for wives and girlfriends. The 1-pound Sampler is one-fifth as expensive as the four-piece Godiva's chocolatier assortment but much better chocolate than in candy bars or bagged chocolates at the grocery store. At Christmas and Valentine's Day, the candy aisle at the drugstore expands with seasonal and private label boxed chocolates at a steep discount. Whitman's has $9.99 and $11.99 traditional and sugar-free 12 oz boxes, and these prices are stable throughout the year.

Fifty-four bimonthly observations have been collected on Whitman's marketing mix including price, advertising, promotional expenditures on displays, and packaging choices, as well as two seasonal dummy variables for Christmas (November/December) and Valentine's Day (January/February). You are charged with estimating the dollar sales response of each of these variables. The best-fit regression model is log-linear:

$$\log\$Sales = 13.23 - 0.86\log Price$$
$$- 0.02\log Adver + 0.24\log Promo$$
$$- 0.17Packaging - 0.25N/D - 0.14J/F$$

where the *R*-squared is 0.54, and the *t*-scores for each variable are as follows:[1]

Price 4.30, Adver 0.51, Promo 1.52, Packaging –3.82, N/D –4.74, J/F –1.75. The General Manger asks you how to interpret each factor and what decision recommendation, if any, is warranted.

Cont.

MANAGERIAL CHALLENGE *Continued*

Later, you discover that the 0/1 Packaging dummy variable (signifying a change for 14 bi-months of the traditional royal gold color of the Sampler box to crimson red) interacts strongly with the promotional expenditure variable Promo. Reestimating the model to include this interaction effect, you obtain

$$\log\$Sales = 11.65 - 0.90\log Price - 0.03\log Adver$$
$$+ 1.37\log Promo + 1.59\ Pack - 0.24 N/D$$
$$- 0.14 J/F - 0.13 Packaging * Promo.$$

where R-squared is now 0.60, and the *t*-scores for each variable are as follows: Price 4.53, Adver 0.65, Promo 2.35, Packaging 2.26, N/D −4.83, J/F −2.80, Packaging * Promo −2.67. Interpret any changes, and again make recommendations.

After sorting out the role of Whitman's in seasonal candy sales, you find the General Manager of the Sampler product is not surprised by your findings. She responds to your presentation and recommendation to continue to maintain $9.99 and $11.99 prices throughout the year and not match discount private label prices at Christmas and Valentine's as a "No brainer."

Discussion Questions

- What is initially curious about the negative and statistically significant seasonal dummy variables for Christmas and Valentine's Day?
- Now that you understand the competitive supply of private label seasonal product, provide a explanation of the negative signs on the seasonal dummies in the demand function that matches Whitman's desire to maintain stable prices?
- Why would Whitman's prefer stable prices in this year-round heavily branded boxed candies market?
- What role should Whitman's volunteer to play in the private label candy business of their channel partners CVS and Rite-Aid at Christmas and Valentine's Day?

---

[1]*T*-scores are a hypothesis test statistic obtained by dividing the estimated coefficients by their standard errors. With 54 observations and seven r.h.s. variables, a *t*-score of 2.0 or higher confirms statistically significant effects.

STATISTICAL ESTIMATION OF THE DEMAND FUNCTION

Effective decision making eventually requires the quantitative measurement of economic relationships. *Econometrics* is a collection of statistical techniques available for estimating such relationships. The principal econometric techniques used in measuring demand relationships are *regression* and *correlation analysis*. The simple (two-variable) linear regression model and the more complex cases of multiple linear regression models are presented here. Nonlinear models are presented in Appendix 4A.

Example

Variable Identification and Data Collection: Sherwin-Williams Company

Sherwin-Williams Company is attempting to develop a demand model for its line of exterior house paints. The company's chief economist feels that the most important variables affecting paint sales (*Y*) (measured in gallons) are:

1. Promotional expenditures (*A*) (measured in dollars). These include expenditures on advertising (radio, TV, and newspapers), in-store displays and literature, and customer rebate programs.

(continued)

2. Selling price (P) (measured in dollars per gallon).

3. Disposable income per household (M) (measured in dollars).

The chief economist decides to collect data on the variables in a sample of 10 company sales regions that are roughly equal in population.[2] Data on paint sales, promotional expenditures, and selling prices were obtained from the company's marketing department. Data on disposable income (per capita) were obtained from the Bureau of Labor Statistics. The data are shown in Table 4.1.

---

[2]A sample size of 10 observations was chosen to keep the arithmetic simple. Much larger samples are used in actual applications. The desired accuracy and the cost of sampling must be weighed in determining the optimal sample size.

Specification of the Model

The next step is to specify the form of the equation, or regression relation that indicates the relationship between the independent variables and the dependent variable(s). Normally the specific functional form of the regression relation to be estimated is chosen to depict the true demand relationships as closely as possible. Graphing such relationships often will tell whether a linear equation is most appropriate or whether logarithmic, exponential, or other transformations are more appropriate. See Appendix 4A for a discussion of these transformations.

Linear Model   A linear demand model for Sherwin-Williams paint would be specified as follows:

$$Q = \alpha + \beta_1 A + \beta_2 P + \beta_3 M + \varepsilon \qquad [4.1]$$

where α, β_1, β_2, and β_3 are the parameters of the model and ε is the error term to reflect the fact that the observed demand value will seldom equal the exact value predicted by the model. The values of the parameters are estimated using the regression techniques described later in the chapter. Demand theory implies that price (P) would have a negative effect on gallons of paint sold (Q) (i.e., as the price rises, quantity demanded

TABLE 4.1	SHERWIN-WILLIAMS COMPANY DATA			
SALES REGION	SALES (Y) ($\times 1,000$ GALLONS)	PROMOTIONAL EXPENDITURES (A) ($\times \$1,000$)	SELLING PRICE (P) ($\$$/GALLON)	DISPOSABLE INCOME (M) ($\times \$1,000$)
1	160	150	15.00	19.0
2	220	160	13.50	17.5
3	140	50	16.50	14.0
4	190	190	14.50	21.0
5	130	90	17.00	15.5
6	160	60	16.00	14.5
7	200	140	13.00	21.5
8	150	110	18.00	18.0
9	210	200	12.00	18.5
10	190	100	15.50	20.0

declines, holding constant all other variables) and that promotional expenditures (*A*) and income (*M*) would have a positive effect on paint sales.

The parameter estimates may be interpreted in the following manner. If we rearrange Equation 4.1 to solve for price (*P*), the intercept of the resulting *inverse demand function* identifies the maximum price that can be charged. The value of each β coefficient provides an estimate of the change in quantity demanded associated with a *one-unit* change in the given independent variable, holding constant all other independent variables. The β coefficients are equivalent to the partial derivatives of the demand function:

$$\beta_1 = \frac{\partial Q}{\partial A}, \quad \beta_2 = \frac{\partial Q}{\partial P}, \quad \beta_3 = \frac{\partial Q}{\partial M} \qquad [4.2]$$

Recall that the elasticity of linear demand with respect to price is defined as

$$E_D = \frac{\partial Q}{\partial P} \cdot \frac{P}{Q} \qquad [4.3]$$

Now substitute Equation 4.2 into this expression to yield

$$E_D = \beta_2 \cdot \frac{P}{Q} \qquad [4.4]$$

Equations 4.3 and 4.4 show that price elasticity of linear demand depends upon the target market's price sensitivity ($\partial Q/\partial P$), as well as the price point positioning of the product per unit sale (*P/Q*).

Multiplicative Exponential Model   Another commonly used demand relationship is the multiplicative exponential model. In the Sherwin-Williams example, such a model would be specified as follows:

$$Q = \alpha A^{\beta_1} P^{\beta_2} M^{\beta_3} \qquad [4.5]$$

This model is also popular because of its ease of estimation. For instance, Equation 4.5 may be transformed into a simple linear relationship in logarithms (adding an error term) as follows:

$$\log Q = \log \alpha + \beta_1 \log A + \beta_2 \log P + \beta_3 \log M + \varepsilon \qquad [4.6]$$

and the parameters log α, β_1, β_2, and β_3 can be easily estimated by any regression package. The intuitive appeal of this multiplicative exponential functional form is based on the fact that the marginal impact of a change in price on quantity demanded is dependent not only on the price change, but also on all the other determinants of demand too—that is, all the elements in the marketing mix and the target consumer's household income, and so forth.

Demand functions in the multiplicative exponential form possess the convenient feature that the *elasticities are constant* over the range of data used in estimating the parameters and are equal to the estimated values of the respective parameters. In the Sherwin-Williams data, for example, the price elasticity of demand is defined as

$$E_D = \frac{\partial Q}{\partial P} \cdot \frac{P}{Q} \qquad [4.7]$$

Differentiating Equation 4.5 with respect to price results in

$$\frac{\partial Q}{\partial P} = \beta_2 \alpha A^{\beta_1} P^{\beta_2 - 1} M^{\beta_3} \qquad [4.8]$$

So, using Equation 4.7,

$$E_D = \beta_2 \alpha A^{\beta_1} P^{\beta_2 - 1} M^{\beta_3} \left(\frac{P}{Q} \right) \qquad [4.9]$$

Substituting Equation 4.5 for Q in Equation 4.9, and canceling and then combining terms, yields

$$E_D = \beta_2$$

That is, multiplicative exponential demand functions have constant price and other elasticities. This property contrasts sharply with the elasticity of a linear demand function that changes continuously over the entire price or income range of the demand curve. However, pricing analysts at Sherwin-Williams may be able to tell us that the percentage change in quantity demanded for either a 10 percent price increase or a 10 percent price cut is a constant 15 percent. And the same answer may apply at rather different price points when clearance sales occur. If so, a multiplicative exponential demand model is appropriate.

A SIMPLE LINEAR REGRESSION MODEL

The analysis in this section is limited to the simplest case of one independent and one dependent variable, where the form of the relationship between the two variables is *linear*:

$$Y = \alpha + \beta X + \varepsilon \qquad [4.10]$$

X is used to represent the independent variable and Y the dependent variable.[3]

Example

Linear, Not Exponential, Sales at Global Crossing Inc.[4]

In 2002, telecom network providers like Global Crossing and WorldCom were wildly optimistic about the growth of telecom traffic, because of the projected growth of the Internet. Much like the adoption of color television, the penetration of the Internet into the American household has exhibited a classic S-shaped pattern of exponential growth fueled by the early adopters (1994–1996), followed by a long period of much slower, approximately linear growth in demand. Purchasing and installing fiber optic cable networks as though the exponential demand growth were continuing unabated led to a quick saturation of a market that would have been better specified with a linear time trend,

$$Q = \alpha + \beta_1 A + \beta_2 P + \beta_3 M + \beta_4 T + \varepsilon$$

where T is time (2006 = 0, 2007 = 1, 2008 = 2, etc.). The effect of these demand projections on Global Crossing is examined in the Managerial Challenge at the beginning of Chapter 5.

[4]Based on "Adoption Rate of Internet by Consumers Is Slowing," Wall Street Journal (July 16, 2001), p. B1.

---

[3]Capitalized letters X and Y represent the *name* of the random variables. Lowercase x and y represent *specific values* of the random variables.

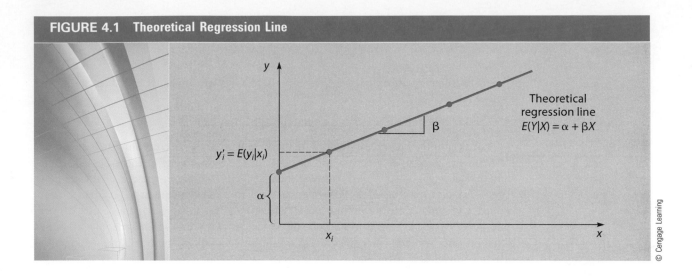

FIGURE 4.1 Theoretical Regression Line

Assumptions Underlying the Simple Linear Regression Model

Assumption 1   The value of the dependent variable Y is postulated to be a random variable, which is dependent on deterministic (i.e., nonrandom) values of the independent variable X.[5]

Assumption 2   A theoretical straight-line relationship (see Figure 4.1) exists between X and the expected value of Y for each of the possible values of X. This theoretical regression line

$$E(Y|X) = \alpha + \beta X \qquad [4.11]$$

has a slope of β and an intercept of α. The regression coefficients α and β constitute population parameters whose values are unknown, and we desire to estimate them.

Assumption 3   Associated with each value of X is a probability distribution, $p(y|x)$, of the possible values of the random variable Y. When X is set equal to some value x_i, the value of Y that is observed will be drawn from the $p(y|x_i)$ probability distribution and will not necessarily lie on the theoretical regression line. As illustrated in Figure 4.2, some values of $y|x_i$ are more likely than others, and the mean $E(y|x_i)$ lies on the theoretical regression line. If ε_i is defined as the *deviation* of the *observed* y_i value from its theoretical value y'_i, then

$$y_i = y'_i + \varepsilon_i$$
$$y_i = \alpha + \beta x_i + \varepsilon_i \qquad [4.12]$$

or, in general, the *linear regression relation* becomes (as illustrated in Figure 4.3)

$$Y = \alpha + \beta X = \varepsilon \qquad [4.13]$$

where ε is a zero mean stochastic disturbance (or error) term.

The disturbance term (ε_i) is assumed to be an independent random variable [i.e., $E(\varepsilon_i \varepsilon_j) = 0$ for $i \neq j$] that is normally distributed with an expected value equal to zero [i.e., $E(\varepsilon_i) = 0$] and with a constant variance equal to σ_ε^2 [i.e., $E(\varepsilon_i^2) = \sigma_\varepsilon^2$ for all i].

---

[5]Stochastic (i.e., random) values of the right-hand-side independent variable are addressed in Appendix 4A under simultaneous equations relationships.

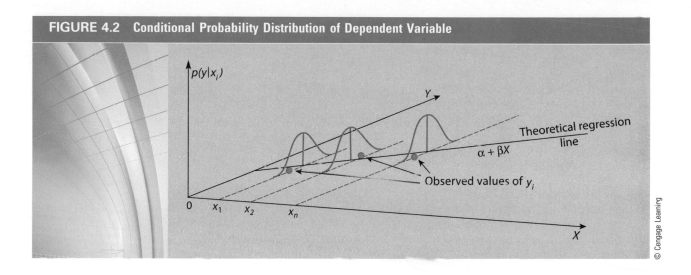

FIGURE 4.2   Conditional Probability Distribution of Dependent Variable

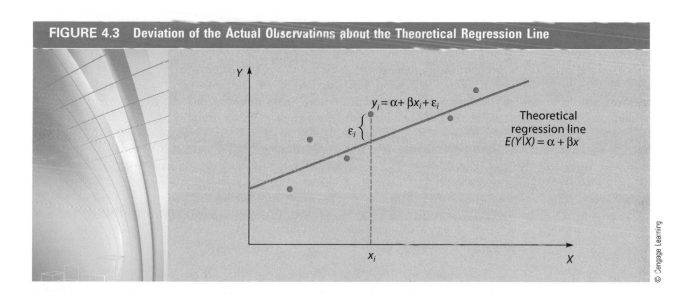

FIGURE 4.3   Deviation of the Actual Observations about the Theoretical Regression Line

Together, Assumptions 1 and 3 imply that the $N(0, \sigma_\varepsilon^2)$ disturbance term is expected to be uncorrelated with the independent variables in the regression model.

Estimating the Population Regression Coefficients

Once the regression model is specified, the unknown values of the population regression coefficients α and β are estimated by using the n pairs of sample observations (x_1, y_1), $(x_2, y_2), \ldots, (x_n, y_n)$. This process involves finding a *sample regression line* that best fits the sample of observations the analyst has gathered.

The sample estimates of α and β can be designated by a and b, respectively. The estimated or predicted value of Y, $\hat{y}_i$, for a given value of X (see Figure 4.4) is

$$\hat{y}_i = a + bx_i \qquad [4.14]$$

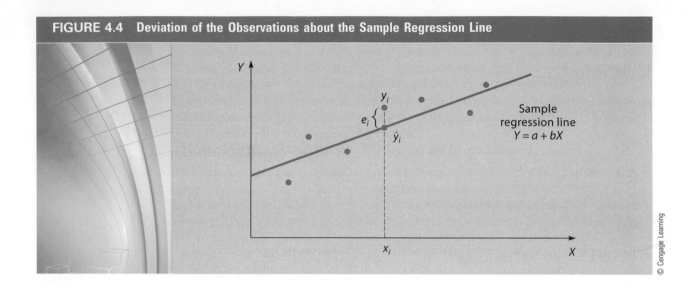

FIGURE 4.4 Deviation of the Observations about the Sample Regression Line

Letting e_i be the *deviation* of the *observed* y_i value from the *estimated value* $\hat{y}_i$, then

$$
\begin{aligned}
y_i &= \hat{y}_i + e_i \\
&= a + bx_i + e_i
\end{aligned}
$$
[4.15]

or, in general, the *sample regression equation* becomes

$$Y = a + bX + e$$
[4.16]

Although there are several methods for determining the values of a and b (i.e., finding the regression equation that provides the best fit to the series of observations), the best known and most widely used is the method of *least squares*. The objective of least-squares analysis is to find values of a and b that *minimize* the sum of the squares of the e_i deviations. (By squaring the errors, positive and negative errors cumulate without canceling each other.) From Equation 4.15, the value of e_i is given by

$$e_i = y_i - a - bx_i$$
[4.17]

Squaring this term and summing over all n pairs of sample observations, one obtains

$$\sum_{i=1}^{n} e_i^2 = \sum_{i=1}^{n} (y_i - a - bx_i)^2$$
[4.18]

Using calculus, the values of a and b that minimize this sum of squared deviations expression are given by

$$b = \frac{n\Sigma x_i y_i - \Sigma x_i \Sigma y_i}{n\Sigma x^2 - (\Sigma x_i)^2}$$
[4.19]

$$a = \bar{y} - b\bar{x}$$
[4.20]

where $\bar{x}$ and $\bar{y}$ are the arithmetic means of X and Y, respectively (i.e., $\bar{x} = \Sigma x/n$ and $\bar{y} = \Sigma y/n$) and where the summations range over all the observations ($i = 1$, $2, \ldots , n$).

Example

Estimating Regression Parameters: Sherwin-Williams Company (continued)

Returning to the Sherwin-Williams Company example, suppose that only promotional expenditures are used to predict paint sales. The regression model can be calculated from the sample data presented earlier in Table 4.1. These data are reproduced here in columns 1–3 of Table 4.2 and shown graphically in Figure 4.5.

The estimated slope of the regression line is calculated as follows using Equation 4.19:

$$b = \frac{10(229,100) - (1,250)(1,750)}{10(180,100) - (1,250)^2}$$

$$= 0.433962$$

Similarly, using Equation 4.20, the intercept is estimated as

$$a = 175 - 0.433962(125)$$
$$= 120.75475$$

Therefore, the equation for estimating paint sales (in thousands of gallons) based on promotional expenditures (in thousands of dollars) is

$$Y = 120.755 + 0.434X \qquad [4.21]$$

and is graphed in Figure 4.5. The coefficient of X (0.434) indicates that for a one-unit increase in X ($1,000 in additional promotional expenditures), expected sales (Y) will increase by 0.434 ($\times$ 1,000) = 434 gallons in a given sales region.

TABLE 4.2   WORKSHEET FOR ESTIMATION OF THE SIMPLE REGRESSION EQUATION: SHERWIN-WILLIAMS COMPANY

SALES REGION	PROMOTIONAL EXPENDITURES ($\times$ $1,000)	SALES ($\times$ 1,000 GAL)			
(1)	(2)	(3)	(4)	(5)	(6)
i	x_i	y_i	$x_i y_i$	x_i^2	y_i^2
1	150	160	24,000	22,500	25,600
2	160	220	35,200	25,600	48,400
3	50	140	7,000	2,500	19,600
4	190	190	36,100	36,100	36,100
5	90	130	11,700	8,100	16,900
6	60	160	9,600	3,600	25,600
7	140	200	28,000	19,600	40,000
8	110	150	16,500	12,100	22,500
9	200	210	42,000	40,000	44,100
10	100	190	19,000	10,000	36,100
Total	1,250	1,750	229,100	180,100	314,900
	Σx_i	Σy_i	$\Sigma x_i y_i$	Σx_i^2	Σy_i^2
	$\bar{x} = \Sigma x_i/n = 1,250/10 = 125$				
	$\bar{y} = \Sigma y_i/n = 1,750/10 = 175$				

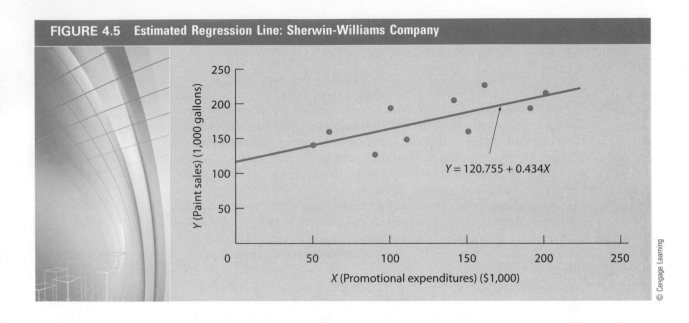

FIGURE 4.5   Estimated Regression Line: Sherwin-Williams Company

$Y = 120.755 + 0.434X$

Y (Paint sales) (1,000 gallons)

X (Promotional expenditures) ($1,000)

© Cengage Learning

USING THE REGRESSION EQUATION TO MAKE PREDICTIONS

A regression equation can be used to make predictions concerning the value of Y, given any particular value of X. This is done by substituting the particular value of X, namely, x_p, into the sample regression equation (Equation 4.14):

$$\hat{y} = a + bx_p$$

where, as you recall, $\hat{y}$ is the hypothesized expected value for the dependent variable from the probability distribution $p(Y|X)$.[6]

Suppose one is interested in predicting Sherwin-Williams's paint sales for a metropolitan area with promotional expenditures equal to $185,000 (i.e., $x_p = 185$). Substituting $x_p = 185$ into the estimated regression equation (Equation 4.21) yields

$$\hat{y} = 120.755 + 0.434(185)$$
$$= 201.045$$

or 201,045 gallons.

Caution must be exercised in using regression models for prediction when the value of the independent variable lies *outside* the range of observations from which the model was estimated. For example, here we cannot be certain that the prediction of paint sales based on the linear regression model would be reasonable for promotional expenditures of $300,000 since $200,000 was our largest sample value. Such factors as diminishing returns and the existence of saturation levels can cause relationships between economic variables to be nonlinear.

A measure of the accuracy of estimation with the regression equation can be obtained by calculating the standard deviation of the errors of prediction (also known as the **standard error of the estimate**). The error term e_i was defined earlier in Equation 4.17 to be the difference between the observed and predicted values of the dependent variable.

standard error of the estimate The standard deviation of the error term in a regression model.

---

[6]The expected value of the error term (e) is zero, as indicated earlier in Assumption 3.

The standard deviation of the e_i term is based on the summed squared error (SSE) Σe_i^2 normalized by the number of observations minus two:

$$s_e = \sqrt{\frac{\Sigma e_i^2}{n-2}} = \sqrt{\frac{\Sigma(y_i - a - bx_i)^2}{n-2}}$$

or, when this expression is simplified,[7]

$$s_e = \sqrt{\frac{\Sigma y_i^2 - a\Sigma y_i - b\Sigma x_i y_i}{n-2}} \qquad [4.22]$$

If the observations are tightly clustered about the regression line, the value of s_e will be small and prediction errors will tend to be small. Conversely, if the deviations e_i between the observed and predicted values of Y are fairly large, both s_e and the prediction errors will be large.

In the Sherwin-Williams Company example, substituting the relevant data from Table 4.2 into Equation 4.22 yields

$$s_e = \sqrt{\frac{314,900 - 120.75475(1,750) - 0.433962(229,100)}{10 - 2}}$$
$$= 22.799$$

or a standard error of 22,799 gallons.

The standard error of the estimate (s_e) can be used to construct prediction *intervals* for y.[8] An *approximate* 95 percent prediction interval is equal to[9]

$$\hat{y} \pm 2s_e \qquad [4.23]$$

Returning to the Sherwin-Williams Company example, suppose we want to construct an approximate 95 percent prediction interval for paint sales in a sales region with promotional expenditures equal to $185,000 (i.e., $x_p = 185$). Substituting $\hat{y} = 201.045$ and $s_e = 22.799$ into Equation 4.23 yields

$$201.045 \pm 2(22.799)$$

or a prediction interval from 155.447 to 246.643 (i.e., from 155,447 gallons to 246,643 gallons) for promotions over the range $50,000 to $200,000.

---

[7]This formula applies to the case of simple regression in Equation 4.16. As additional variables are added to the linear regression model, the degrees of freedom in the denominator of Equation 4.22 becomes smaller and smaller: $n - 3$, $n - 4$, $n - 5$, and so forth.

[8]An *exact* 5 percent prediction interval is a function of both the sample size (n) and how close x_p is to $\bar{x}$ and is given by the following expression:

$$\hat{y} \pm t_{k/2, n-s} s_e \sqrt{1 + \frac{1}{n} + \frac{(x_p - \bar{x})^2}{\Sigma(x_i - \bar{x})^2}}$$

where $t_{k/2, n-2}$ is the value from the t-distribution (with $n - 2$ degrees of freedom) in Table 2 of the Statistical Tables (Appendix B) in the back of the book.

[9]For large n ($n > 30$), the t-distribution approximates a normal distribution, and the t-value for a 95 percent prediction interval approaches 1.96 or approximately 2. For most applications, the approximation methods give satisfactory results.

Inferences about the Population Regression Coefficients

For repeated samples of size n, the sample estimates of α and β—that is, a and b—will tend to vary from sample to sample. In addition to prediction, often one of the purposes of regression analysis is testing whether the slope parameter β is equal to some particular value β_0. One standard hypothesis is to test whether β is equal to zero.[10] In such a test the concern is with determining whether X has a significant effect on Y. If β is either zero or close to zero, then the independent variable X will be of no practical benefit in predicting or explaining the value of the dependent variable Y. When $\beta = 0$, a one-unit change in X causes Y to change by zero units, and hence X has no effect on Y.

To test hypotheses about the value of β, the sampling distribution of the statistic b must be known.[11] It can be shown that b has a t-distribution with $n - 2$ degrees of freedom.[12,13] The mean of this distribution is equal to the true underlying regression coefficient β, and an estimate of the standard deviation can be calculated as

$$s_b = \sqrt{\frac{s_e^2}{\Sigma x_i^2 - (\Sigma x_i)^2/n}} \qquad [4.24]$$

where s_e is the standard deviation of the error terms from Equation 4.22.

Suppose that we want to test the null hypothesis:

$$H_0 : \beta = \beta_0$$

against the alternative hypothesis:

$$H_a : \beta \neq \beta_0$$

at the $k = 5$ percent level of significance.[14] We calculate the statistic

---

[10]The intercept parameter, α, is of less interest in most economic studies and will be excluded from further analysis.

[11]In addition to testing hypotheses about β, one can also calculate confidence intervals for β in a manner similar to Equation 4.23 using the sampling distribution of β.

[12]A t-test is usually used to test for the significance of individual regression parameters when the sample size is relatively small (30 or less). For larger samples, tests of statistical significance may be made using the standard normal probability distribution, which the t-distribution approaches in the limit.

[13]*Degrees of freedom* are the number of observations beyond the minimum necessary to calculate a given regression coefficient or statistic. In a regression model, the number of degrees of freedom is equal to the number of observations less the number of parameters (α's and β's) being estimated. For example, in a simple (two-variable) regression model, a minimum of two observations is needed to calculate the slope (β) and intercept (α) parameters—hence the number of degrees of freedom is equal to the number of observations $n - 2$. Three parameters to be estimated necessitate $n - 3$, and so on.

[14]The *level of significance* (k) used in testing hypotheses indicates the probability of making an incorrect decision with the decision rule—that is rejecting the null hypothesis when it is true. For example, with $H_0 : \beta \geq 0$, setting k equal to 0.05 (i.e., 5 percent) indicates that there is one chance in 20 that we will conclude that an effect exists when no effect is present—that is, a 5 percent chance of "false positive" outcomes.

Medical researchers trying to identify statistically significant therapies that could save lives, and research and development (R&D) researchers trying to identify potential blockbuster products, worry more about reducing the risk of "false negatives"—that is, of concluding they have discovered nothing when their research could save a life or a company. Medical and R&D researchers therefore often perform hypothesis tests with $k = 0.35$ (i.e., with 65 percent confidence that the null hypothesis $\beta = 0$ should be rejected). They are willing to increase from 5 to 35 percent the probability of false positives (i.e., that they will conclude that β is positive for a treatment or therapy and can help the patient when in fact $\beta = 0$). This level of significance is preferred not because they wish to engender false hope but rather because a higher tolerance for false positives reduces the probability of "false negative" decisions that would arise if they conclude that $\beta = 0$ when in fact β is positive. Ultimately, the question of what significance level to choose must be decided by the relative cost of false positives and false negatives in a given situation.

$$t = \frac{b - \beta_0}{s_b} \qquad\qquad [4.25]$$

and the decision is to reject the null hypothesis, if t is either less than $-t_{0.25,n-2}$ or greater than $+t_{0.25,n-2}$ where the $t_{0.25,n-2}$ value is obtained from the t-distribution (with $n-2$ degrees of freedom) in Table 2 (Appendix B).[15] Business applications of hypothesis testing are well advised to keep the level of significance small (i.e., no larger than 1 percent or 5 percent). One cannot justify building a marketing plan around advertising and retail displays incurring millions of dollars of promotional expense unless the demand estimation yields a very high degree of confidence that promotional expenditures actually "drive" sales (i.e., $\beta \neq 0$). There are simply too many other potentially more effective ways to spend marketing dollars.

In the Sherwin-Williams Company example, suppose that we want to test (at the $k = 0.05$ level of significance) whether promotional expenditures are a useful variable in predicting paint sales. In effect, we wish to perform a statistical test to determine whether the sample value—that is, $b = 0.433962$—is significantly different from zero. The null and alternative hypotheses are

H_0: $\beta = 0$ (no relationship between X and Y)
H_a: $\beta \neq 0$ (linear relationship between X and Y)

Because there were 10 observations in the sample used to compute the regression equation, the sample statistic b will have a t-distribution with $8(= n - 2)$ degrees of freedom. From the t-distribution (Table 2 of Appendix B), we obtain a value of 2.306 for $t_{.025,8}$. Therefore, the decision rule is to reject H_0—in other words, to conclude that $\beta \neq 0$ and that a statistically significant relationship exists between promotional expenditures and paint sales—if the calculated value of t is either less than -2.306 or greater than $+2.306$.

Using Equation 4.24, s_b is calculated as

$$s_b = \sqrt{\frac{(22.799)^2}{180,100 - (1,250)^2/10}}$$

$$= 0.14763$$

The calculated value of t from Equation 4.25 becomes

$$t = \frac{0.433962 - 0}{0.14763}$$

$$= 2.939$$

Because this value is greater than $+2.306$, we reject H_0. Therefore, based on the sample evidence, we conclude that at the 5 percent level of significance a linear, positive relationship exists between promotional expenditures and paint sales.

---

[15]*One-tail* tests can also be performed. To test H_0: $\beta \leq \beta_0$ against H_a: $\beta > \beta_0$, one calculates t using Equation 4.25 and rejects H_0 at the k level of significance of $t > t_{k,n-2}$, where $t_{k,n-2}$ is obtained from the t-distribution (Table 2 of Appendix B) with $n - 2$ degrees of freedom. Similarly, to test H_0: $\beta \geq \beta_0$ against H_a: $\beta < \beta_0$, one calculates t using Equation 4.25 and rejects H_0 at the k level of significance if $t < -t_{k,n-2}$.

Example

Are Designer Jeans and Lee Jeans Complements or Substitutes?

To trigger retail sales, merchants often find that promotion, display, and assortment are almost as important as the right price point. VF Corporation, the parent company owning Lee jeans, is considering whether to add to their portfolio a new upscale brand of jeanswear, 7 for All Mankind. One question they hope to answer with demand estimation is whether their Lee jeans are purchased alone or whether the typical customer buying Lee also buys a dress pair of designer jeans such as Guess or 7 for All Mankind. Alternatively, would 7 for All Mankind jeans cannibalize the sales of Lee jeans? In short, are these two products perceived as complements or substitutes? The company collected sales, price, and socioeconomic data on the target market for 48 quarters; the current values of the variables are $Q_{LEE} = 50{,}000$, $P_{LEE} = \$20$, $P_{LEVI} = \$20$, $P_{GUESS} = \$35$, Disposable Income $= \$80{,}000$, Local Target Market Population $= 100{,}000$. Listed below are the results from the demand estimation (t-statistics are in parentheses):

$$Q_{LEE} = 133{,}500 - 1{,}250\ P_{LEE} + 450\ P_{LEVI} - 571.43\ P_{GUESS} - 1.25\ INC + 0.50\ POP$$
$$\phantom{Q_{LEE} = }(3.0)(-9.1)(4.3)(-1.5)(-16.4)(4.97)$$

$$R^2 = 0.92 \qquad SSE = 184{,}000{,}000$$

As one can readily see, price elasticity of demand is statistically significant since the absolute value of the t-score -9.1 is larger than the 99-percent critical value of 3.55. This price elasticity is calculated as $-1250 \times$ current price/current unit sales $= -1{,}250 \times \$20/50{,}000 = -0.5$. This inelastic numerical price elasticity suggests Lee has introduced some effective switching costs and established a brand identity that builds customer loyalty and has desensitized its customers to price increases. Income elasticity is also statistically significant at $-1.25 \times \$80{,}000/50{,}000 = -2.0$, suggesting that VF should not place its product in upscale department stores in suburban malls like Macy's and Neiman Marcus but rather should market its jeans through Dillard's and JCPenney. As expected, the sign on the price of Levi jeans is positive and statistically significant, suggesting that Lee and Levi jeans are substitutes.

What about the designer jeans? If the two products go out of stores together, VF may want to display and promote them together. If not, perhaps 7 for All Mankind jeans should be sold through Internet distribution channels or specialty retail stores like Barney's of New York so as not to cannibalize Lee jeans sales at Dillard's and JCPenney. The marketing team also collects data on the potential size (POP) of the target customer market quarter by quarter and controls for its size. Proxying the effects of changes in the price of designer jeans with historical data on Guess jeans, the demand estimate is -571.43. Multiplying this coefficient estimate times the mean price of \$35 and dividing by 50,000 yields a cross price elasticity estimate of -0.40. But the t-score of -1.5 reveals that the cross price elasticity estimate is statistically significantly different from zero with a confidence level of only 84 percent. This finding implies that indeed Lee jeans and designer jeans are not substitutes, and VF Corporation can stop worrying about the one product cannibalizing sales of the other.

Correlation Coefficient

A first measure of the degree of association between two variables is called the *correlation coefficient*. Given n pairs of observations from the population, $(x_1, y_1), (x_2, y_2), \ldots , (x_n, y_n)$, the sample correlation coefficient is defined as

$$r = \frac{\Sigma(x_i - \bar{x})(y_i - \bar{y})}{\sqrt{\Sigma(x_i - \bar{x})^2\ \Sigma(y_i - \bar{y})^2}}$$

and, when this expression is simplified, it is calculated as

$$r = \frac{n\Sigma x_i y_i - \Sigma x_i\ \Sigma y_i)}{\sqrt{[n\Sigma x_i^2 - (\Sigma x_i)^2][n\Sigma y_i^2 - (\Sigma y_i)^2]}} \tag{4.26}$$

The value of the correlation coefficient (r) ranges from +1 for two variables with perfect positive correlation to −1 for two variables with perfect negative correlation. In Figure 4.6, Panels (a) and (b) illustrate two variables that exhibit perfect positive and negative correlation, respectively. A positive correlation coefficient indicates that high values of one variable tend to be associated with high values of the other variable, whereas a negative correlation coefficient indicates just the opposite: high values of one variable tend to be associated with low values of the other variable. Very few, if any, relationships between economic variables exhibit perfect correlation. Figure 4.6 Panel (c) illustrates zero correlation—no discernible relationship exists between the observed values of the two variables.

The Sherwin-Williams Company example discussed earlier can be used to illustrate the calculation of the sample correlation coefficient. Substituting the relevant quantities from Table 4.2 into Equation 4.26, we obtain a value of

$$r = \frac{10(229,100) - (1,250)(1,750)}{\sqrt{[10(180,100) - (1,250)^2][10(314,900) - (1,750)^2]}}$$

$$= 0.72059 \text{ or } 0.721$$

for the correlation between the sample observations of promotional expenditures and paint sales.

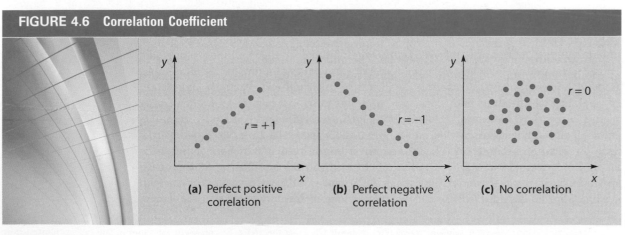

FIGURE 4.6   **Correlation Coefficient**

(a) Perfect positive correlation

(b) Perfect negative correlation

(c) No correlation

The Analysis of Variance

Another convenient measure of the overall "fit" of the regression model to the sample of observations is the r-squared.

We begin by examining a typical observation (y_i) in Figure 4.7. Suppose we want to predict the value of Y for a value of X equal to x_i. While ignoring the regression line for the moment, what error is incurred if we use the average value of Y (i.e., $\bar{y}$) as the best estimate of Y? The graph shows that the error involved, labeled the "total deviation," is the difference between the observed value (y_i) and $\bar{y}$. Suppose we now use the sample regression line to estimate Y. The best estimate of Y, given $X = x_i$, is $\hat{y}_i$. As a result of using the regression line to estimate Y, the estimation error has been reduced to the difference between the observed value (y_i) and $\hat{y}_i$. In the graph, the total deviation ($y_i - \bar{y}$) has been partitioned into two parts—the unexplained portion of the total deviation ($y_i - \hat{y}_i$) and that portion of the total deviation explained by the regression line ($\hat{y}_i - \bar{y}$); that is,

$$\text{Total deviation} = \text{Unexplained error} + \text{Explained error}$$
$$(y_i - \bar{y}) = (y_i - \hat{y}_i) + (\hat{y}_i - \bar{y})$$

If we decompose the total error of each observation in the sample using this procedure and then sum the squares of both sides of the equation, we obtain (after some algebraic simplification):[16]

$$\text{Total SS} = \text{Unexplained SS} + \text{Explained SS}$$
$$\text{SST} = \Sigma e_i^2 + \text{SSR} = \text{SSE} + \text{SSR} \qquad [4.27]$$
$$\Sigma(y_i - \bar{y})^2 = \Sigma(y_i - \hat{y}_i)^2 + \Sigma(\hat{y}_i - \bar{y})^2$$

coefficient of determination A measure of the proportion of total variation in the dependent variable that is explained by the independent variable(s).

We can now use this sum-of-squares analysis to illustrate a measure of the fit of the regression line to the sample observations. The sample **coefficient of determination** or r-squared (r^2) is equal to the ratio of the Explained SS to the Total SS:

$$r^2 = \frac{\Sigma(\hat{y}_i - \bar{y})^2}{\Sigma(y_i - \bar{y})^2} = \frac{\text{SSR}}{\text{SST}} \qquad [4.28]$$

FIGURE 4.7   Partitioning the Total Deviation

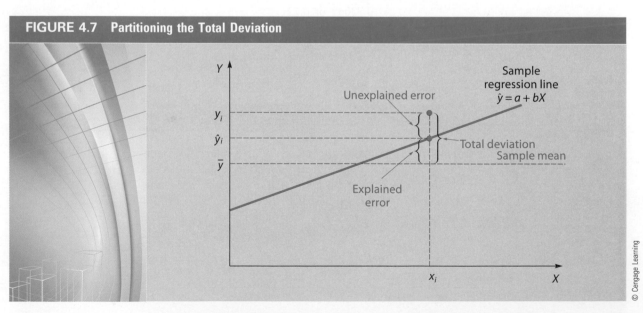

© Cengage Learning

---

[16]A standard convention in statistics is to let the prefix "SS" represent the "Sum of Squares" as illustrated by SSE, the sum of squared errors.

			$\hat{y}=120.75475+$	EXPLAINED	UNEXPLAINED	TOTAL
i	x_i	y_i	$0.433962\,x_i$	SS $(\hat{y}_i - \bar{y})^2$	SS $(y_i - \hat{y}_i)^2$	SS $(y_i - \bar{y})^2$
1	150	160	185.849	117.702	668.171	225.000
2	160	220	190.189	230.696	888.696	2,025.000
3	50	140	142.453	1,059.317	6.017	1,225.000
4	190	190	203.208	795.665	174.451	225.000
5	90	130	159.811	230.696	888.696	2,025.000
6	60	160	146.792	795.665	174.451	225.000
7	140	200	181.509	42.373	341.917	625.000
8	110	150	168.491	42.373	341.917	625.000
9	200	210	207.547	1,059.317	6.017	1,225.000
10	100	190	164.151	117.702	668.171	225.000
				4,491.496	**4,158.504**	**8,650.000**[1]
				$\Sigma(y_i - \bar{y})^2$	$\Sigma(y_i - \hat{y}_i)^2$	$\Sigma(y_i - \bar{y})^2$

TABLE 4.3   CALCULATION OF THE EXPLAINED, UNEXPLAINED, AND TOTAL SS FOR THE SHERWIN-WILLIAMS COMPANY

© Cengage Learning

[1]"Total SS" differs slightly from the sum of "Explained SS" and "Unexplained SS" because of rounding.

This r^2 ratio measures the proportion of the variation in the dependent variable that is explained by the regression line (the independent variable) and ranges in value from 0—when none of the variation in Y is explained by the regression—to 1—when all the variation in Y is explained by regression.

Table 4.3 shows the calculation of the Explained, Unexplained, and Total SS for the Sherwin-Williams Company example that was introduced earlier. The Explained SS is 4,491.506 and the Total SS is 8,650.000, and therefore, by Equation 4.28 the coefficient of determination is

$$r^2 = \frac{4,491.506}{8,650.000}$$

$$= 0.519$$

In sum, the regression model, with promotional expenditures as the sole independent variable, explains about 52 percent of the variation in paint sales in the sample. Note also that this r^2 is equal to the square of the correlation coefficient, that is, $r^2 = 0.519 = (r)^2 = (0.72059)^2$. For the multiple linear regression model, the F-test is used to test the hypothesis that *all* the regression coefficients are zero.

The components of the r^2 can be reconfigured into an F-ratio

$$F = \frac{\text{SSR}}{\text{SSE}/d.f.} \qquad [4.29]$$

to test whether the estimated regression equation explains a significant proportion of the variation in the dependent variable. The decision is to reject the null hypothesis of no relationship between X and Y (i.e., no explanatory power) at the $k = 5$ percent level of significance if the calculated F-ratio is greater than the $F_{.05,1,n-2}$ value obtained from the F-distribution in Table 3 of the Statistical Tables (Appendix B). Thus, forming the F-ratio we obtain

$$F = \frac{4,491.506}{4,158.5/8}$$

$$= 8.641$$

The critical value of $F_{.05,1,8}$ from the F-distribution (Table 3 of Appendix B) is 5.32. Therefore, we reject, at the 5 percent level of significance, the null hypothesis that there is no relationship between promotion expenditures and paint sales. In other words, we conclude that the regression model *does* explain a significant proportion of the variation in paint sales in the sample.

MULTIPLE LINEAR REGRESSION MODEL

A linear relationship containing two or more independent variables is known as a *multiple linear regression model*. In the (completely) general multiple linear regression model, the dependent variable Y is hypothesized to be a function of m independent variables X_1, X_2, ... , X_m, and to be of the form

$$Y = \alpha + \beta_1 X_1 + \beta_2 X_2 + \cdots + \beta_m X_m + \varepsilon \qquad [4.30]$$

In the Sherwin-Williams Company example, paint sales (Y) were hypothesized to be a function of three variables—promotional expenditures (A), price (P), and household disposable income (M) (see Equation 4.1):

$$Q = \alpha + \beta_1 A + \beta_2 P + \beta_3 M + \varepsilon$$

Use of Computer Programs

Using matrix algebra, procedures similar to those explained for the simple linear regression model can be employed for calculating the estimated regression coefficients (α's and β's). A variety of computer programs can be used to perform these procedures.

The output of these programs is fairly standardized to include the estimated regression coefficients, t-statistics of the individual coefficients, R^2, analysis of variance, and F-test of overall significance.

Estimating the Population Regression Coefficients

From the computer output in Figure 4.8, the following regression equation is obtained:

$$Y = 310.245 + 0.008A - 12.202P + 2.677M \qquad [4.31]$$

The coefficient of the P variable (-12.202) indicates that, *all other things being equal*, a \$1.00 price increase will reduce expected sales by $-12.202 \times 1,000 = -12,202$ gallons in a given sales region.

Using the Regression Model to Make Forecasts

As in the simple linear regression model, the multiple linear regression model can be used to make point or interval predictions. Point forecasts can be made by substituting the particular values of the independent variables into the estimated regression equation.

In the Sherwin-Williams example, suppose we are interested in estimating sales in a sales region where promotional expenditures are \$185,000 (i.e., $A = 185$), selling price is \$15.00 (P), and disposable income per household is \$19,500 (i.e., $M = 19.5$). Substituting these values into Equation 4.31 yields

$$\hat{y} = 310.245 + 0.008(185) - 12.202(15.00) + 2.677(19.5) = 180.897 \text{ thousand gallons}$$

Whether to include one, two, or all three independent variables in predicting $\hat{y}$ depends on the mean prediction error (e.g., here $185,000 - 180,897 = 4,103$) in this and subsequent out-of-sample forecasts.

FIGURE 4.8   Computer Output: Sherwin-Williams Company

Dep var: SALES (Y)	**N:**	10	Multiple R: 0.889		Multiple R^2:	0.790

Adjusted multiple R^2 :   0.684   Standard error of estimate: 17.417

Variable	Coefficient	Std error	Std coef	Tolerance	T	P(2 tail)
CONSTANT	310.245	95.075	0.000		3.263	0.017
PROMEXP (X_1)	0.008	0.204	0.013	0.3054426	0.038	0.971
SELLPR (X_2)	−12.202	4.582	−0.741	0.4529372	−2.663	0.037
DISPINC (X_3)	2.677	3.160	0.225	0.4961686	0.847	0.429

Analysis of Variance

Source	Sum-of-squares	DF	Mean square	**F**-ratio	P
Regression	6829.866	3	2276.622	7.505	0.019
Residual	1820.134	6	303.356		

© Cengage Learning

The standard error of the estimate (s_e) from the output in Figure 4.8 can be used to construct prediction intervals for Y. An *approximate* 95 percent prediction interval is equal to

$$\hat{y} \pm 2s_e$$

For a sales region with the characteristics cited in the previous paragraph (i.e., $A = 185$, $P = \$15.00$, and $M = 19.5$), an *approximate* 95 percent prediction interval for paint sales is equal to

$$180.897 \pm 2(17.417)$$

or from 146,063 to 215,731 gallons.

Inferences about the Population Regression Coefficients

Most regression programs test whether *each* of the independent variables (X_s) is statistically significant in explaining the dependent variable (Y). This tests the null hypothesis:

$$H_0: \beta_i = 0$$

against the alternative hypothesis:

$$H_a: \beta_i \neq 0$$

The decision rule is to reject the null hypothesis of no relationship between paint sales (Y) and each of the independent variables at the 0.05 significance level, if the respective *t*-value for each variable is less than $-t_{.025,6} = -2.447$ or greater than $t_{.025,6} = +2.447$. As shown in Figure 4.8, only the calculated *t*-value for the P variable is less than −2.447. Hence, we can conclude that only selling price (P) is statistically significant (at the 0.05 level) in explaining paint sales. This inference might determine that marketing plans for this type of paint should focus on price and not on the effects of promotional expenditures or the disposable income of the target households.

The Estimated Demand for New Automobiles

New car registrations of recently purchased autos vary over time in predictable ways. This economic theory reasoning can identify explanatory variables to include in the empirical model of new car demand. First, any consumer durable demand increases with rising population of the target customer group. Therefore, one must either control for population size as an explanatory variable or, alternatively, divide registrations by population, thereby creating a dependent variable of new car demand per capita, as in Table 4.4. Second, many new car purchases are financed, so minimum cash deposit requirements (Minimum Deposit) and auto financing rates (Interest Rate) are as important as the sale price (Price) in triggering a decision to purchase during one month rather than another. Third, one would expect changes in disposable income (Income) to affect a household's decision to replace its prior car. Higher household income would be associated with increased demand for superior models. Geopolitical events like the first Gulf War with its attendant gas price spikes should also affect demand for autos since gasoline is the primary complement in consumption of automobiles. Finally, as with other fad items, the introduction of popular new models enhances subsequent purchase decisions, so higher auto sales last period should have a positive effect on additional auto sales this period. These positive lagged effects of past sales should dampen as one gets further away from the product introductions that triggered the initial surge in sales.

Table 4.4 reports the empirical results. These are multiplicative exponential models, like Equations 4.5 and 4.6. Thus, the dependent variable and each of the explanatory variables are in logarithms, and therefore the parameter estimates themselves can be interpreted as elasticities—price elasticity of demand, income elasticity of demand, interest rate elasticity of demand, minimum deposit elasticity of demand, and so forth.

TABLE 4.4 OLS ESTIMATES OF THE DETERMINANTS OF THE U.K. PER CAPITA DEMAND FOR NEW AUTOS

EXPLANATORY VARIABLES	COEFFICIENT (t-SCORE)
Constant	$-15.217(-5.66)$[a]
log Price	$-0.341(-2.25)$[b]
log Minimum Deposit	$-0.105(-1.78)$
log Interest Rate	$-0.436(-5.31)$[a]
log Income	$1.947(10.94)$[a]
Oil Crisis Dummy	$-0.146(-4.45)$[a]
log New Car$_{t-1}$	$0.404(3.24)$[a]
Adjusted R^2	0.965
Durbin-Watson	2.11
F	91.62
N	20

Notes: t-statistics in parentheses. Hypotheses tests are one-tailed.

[a,b]Statistical significance at the 1 percent and 5 percent levels, respectively.

Source: Based on *Managerial and Decision Economics* 17 (January 1996), pp. 19–23.

The researchers who performed this study found, first of all, that market demand for new car registrations per capita was price inelastic (-0.341), suggesting some

(continued)

substantial pricing power for many models. Next, a minimum deposit elasticity of −0.105 means that a 20 percent increase in cash deposit leads to a 2.1 percent decrease in demand (i.e., $0.2 \times -0.105 = -0.021$). As expected, a 50 percent increase in auto financing rates from, say, 6 percent to 10 percent, leads to a 22 percent decline in auto demand (i.e., $0.5 \times -0.436 = -0.22$). Autos appear to be income elastic (1.947) such that a 10 percent increase in disposable income results in a 19.5 percent rise in auto demand. Gas shortages and time waiting in queues to buy the complement gasoline led to a 14 percent reduction in auto demand.[17] Finally, one period lagged demand; New Auto$_{t-1}$ had a significant positive effect on current purchases with the coefficient being between 0 and 1, as expected.[18] Overall, this model explained 96 percent of the time-series variation in new car sales per capita.

---

[17]The one exception is that the 0/1 Oil Crisis Dummy variable is added to the regression model directly, without taking logs, since the logarithm of zero is equal to negative infinity and is therefore an undefined value in the regression programs. As a consequence, the elasticity of demand with respect to the 0/1 event is $e^{\beta} - 1$ (or in this case, $e^{-0.146} - 1 = 0.864 - 1 = -13.6\%$). Hence, we conclude −14 percent.

[18]In contrast, a coefficient greater than 1 (or less than −1) on the lagged dependent variable would imply inherently unstable dynamics of exponentially accelerating demand growth (or decay).

The Analysis of Variance

Techniques similar to those described for the simple linear regression model are used to evaluate the *overall* explanatory power of the multiple linear regression model.

The multiple coefficient of determination (r^2) is a measure of the overall "fit" of the regression model. The squared multiple R value of 0.790 in Figure 4.8 indicates that the three-variable regression equation explains 79 percent of the total variation in the dependent variable (paint sales).

The F-ratio in the computer output of Figure 4.8 is used to test the hypothesis that all the independent variables $(X_1, X_2, \dots, X_m)$ together explain a significant proportion of the variation in the dependent variable (Y). One is using the F-value to test the null hypothesis:

$$H_0: \text{All } \beta_i = 0$$

against the alternative hypothesis:

$$H_a: \text{At least one } \beta_i \neq 0$$

In other words, we are testing whether at least one of the explanatory variables contributes information for the prediction of Y. The decision is to reject the null hypothesis at the k level of significance if the F-value from the computer output is *greater* than the $F_{k,m,n-m-1}$ value from the F-distribution (with m and $n - m - 1$ degrees of freedom). Table 3 (Appendix B) provides F-values.

In the Sherwin-Williams example, suppose we want to test whether the three independent variables explain a significant (at the 0.05 level) proportion of the variation in income. The decision rule is to reject the null hypothesis (no relationship) if the calculated F-value is greater than $F_{0.05,3,6} = 4.76$. Because $F = 7.505$, we reject the null hypotheses and conclude that the independent variables *are* useful in explaining paint sales with $(1 - 0.019) = 98.1$ percent confidence.

SUMMARY

- Empirical estimates of the demand relationships are essential if the firm is to achieve its goal of shareholder wealth maximization. Without good estimates of the demand function facing a firm, it is impossible for that firm to make profit-maximizing price and output decisions.

- Statistical techniques are often found to be of great value and relatively inexpensive as a means to make empirical demand function estimates. Regression analysis is often used to estimate statistically the demand function for a good or service.

- The linear model and the multiplicative exponential model are the two most commonly used functional relationships in demand studies.

- In a *linear* demand model, the coefficient of each independent variable provides an estimate of the change in quantity demanded associated with a one-unit change in the given independent variable, holding constant all other variables. This marginal impact is constant at all points on the demand curve. The elasticity of a linear demand model with respect to each independent variable (e.g., price elasticity and income elasticity) is not constant, but instead varies over the entire range of the demand curve.

- In a multiplicative exponential demand model, the marginal impact of each independent variable on quantity demanded is not constant, but instead varies over the entire range of the demand curve. However, the elasticity of a multiplicative exponential demand model with respect to each independent variable is constant and is equal to the estimated value of the respective parameter.

- The objective of *regression analysis* is to develop a functional relationship between the dependent and independent (explanatory) variable(s). Once a functional relationship (i.e., regression equation) is developed, the equation can be used to make forecasts or predictions concerning the value of the dependent variable.

- The *least-squares* technique is used to estimate the regression coefficients. Least-squares minimize the sum of the squares of the differences between the observed and estimated values of the dependent variable over the sample of observations.

- The *t*-test is used to test the hypothesis that a specific independent variable is useful in explaining variation in the dependent variable.

- The *F*-test is used to test the hypothesis that *all* the independent variables (X_1, X_2, ... , X_m) in the regression equation explain a significant proportion of the variation in the dependent variable.

- The *coefficient of determination* (r^2) measures the proportion of the variation in the dependent variable that is explained by the regression equation (i.e., the entire set of independent variables).

- The presence of association does not necessarily imply causation. Statistical tests can only establish whether or not an association exists between variables. The existence of a cause-and-effect economic relationship should be inferred from economic reasoning.

Exercises

Answers to the exercises in blue can be found in Appendix D at the back of the book.

1. Consider the Sherwin-Williams Company example discussed in this chapter (see Table 4.1). Suppose one is interested in developing a simple regression model with paint sales (*Y*) as the dependent variable and selling price (*P*) as the independent variable.
   a. Determine the estimated regression line.
   b. Give an economic interpretation of the estimated intercept (*a*) and slope (*b*) coefficients.
   c. Test the hypothesis (at the 0.05 level of significance) that there is no relationship (i.e., $\beta = 0$) between the variables.
   d. Calculate the coefficient of determination.
   e. Perform an analysis of variance on the regression, including an *F*-test of the overall significance of the results (at the 0.05 level).

f. Based on the regression model, determine the best estimate of paint sales in a sales region where the selling price is $14.50. Construct an *approximate* 95 percent prediction interval.

g. Determine the price elasticity of demand at a selling price of $14.50.

2. The Pilot Pen Company has decided to use 15 test markets to examine the sensitivity of demand for its new product to various prices, as shown in the following table. Advertising effort was identical in each market. Each market had approximately the same level of business activity and population.

a. Using a linear regression model, estimate the demand function for Pilot's new pen.

b. Evaluate this model by computing the coefficient of determination and by performing a *t*-test of the significance of the price variable.

c. What is the price elasticity of demand at a price of 50 cents?

TEST MARKET	PRICE CHARGED (¢)	QUANTITY SOLD (THOUSANDS OF PENS)
1	50	20.0
2	50	21.0
3	55	19.0
4	55	19.5
5	60	20.5
6	60	19.0
7	65	16.0
8	65	15.0
9	70	14.5
10	70¢	15.5
11	80	13.0
12	80	14.0
13	90¢	11.5
14	90	11.0
15	40	17.0

3. In a study of housing demand, the county assessor is interested in developing a regression model to estimate the market value (i.e., selling price) of residential property within his jurisdiction. The assessor feels that the most important variable affecting selling price (measured in thousands of dollars) is the size of house (measured in hundreds of square feet). He randomly selected 15 houses and measured both the selling price and size, as shown in the following table.

OBSERVATION i	SELLING PRICE (× $1,000) Y	SIZE (× 100 ft²) X
1	265.2	12.0
2	279.6	20.2
3	311.2	27.0
4	328.0	30.0
5	352.0	30.0
6	281.2	21.4
7	288.4	21.6

OBSERVATION i	SELLING PRICE ($\times$ \$1,000) Y	SIZE ($\times$ 100 ft^2) X
8	292.8	25.2
9	356.0	37.2
10	263.2	14.4
11	272.4	15.0
12	291.2	22.4
13	299.6	23.9
14	307.6	26.6
15	320.4	30.7

a. Plot the data.
b. Determine the estimated regression line. Give an economic interpretation of the estimated slope (b) coefficient.
c. Determine if size is a statistically significant variable in estimating selling price.
d. Calculate the coefficient of determination.
e. Perform an F-test of the overall significance of the results.
f. Construct an *approximate* 95 percent prediction interval for the selling price of a house having an area (size) of 15 (hundred) square feet.

4. Cascade Pharmaceuticals Company developed the following regression model, using time-series data from the past 33 quarters, for one of its nonprescription cold remedies:

$$Y = -1.04 + 0.24X_1 - 0.27X_2$$

where Y = quarterly sales (in thousands of cases) of the cold remedy
X_1 = Cascade's quarterly advertising ($\times$ \$1,000) for the cold remedy
X_2 = competitors' advertising for similar products ($\times$ \$10,000)

Here is additional information concerning the regression model:

$$s_{b1} = 0.032 \quad s_{b2} = 0.070$$
$$R^2 = 0.64 \quad s_e = 1.63 \quad F\text{-statistic} = 31.402$$

Durbin-Watson (d) statistic = 0.4995
a. Which of the independent variables (if any) appears to be statistically significant (at the 0.05 level) in explaining sales of the cold remedy?
b. What proportion of the total variation in sales is explained by the regression equation?
c. Perform an F-test (at the 0.05 level) of the overall explanatory power of the model.
d. What additional statistical information (if any) would you find useful in the evaluation of this model?

5. General Cereals is using a regression model to estimate the demand for Tweetie Sweeties, a whistle-shaped, sugar-coated breakfast cereal for children. The following (multiplicative exponential) demand function is being used:

$$Q_D = 6,280 P^{-2.15} A^{1.05} N^{3.70}$$

where Q_D = quantity demanded, in 10 oz boxes
P = price per box, in dollars
A = advertising expenditures on daytime television, in dollars
N = proportion of the population under 12 years old

a. Determine the point price elasticity of demand for Tweetie Sweeties.

b. Determine the advertising elasticity of demand.

c. What interpretation would you give to the exponent of N?

6. The demand for haddock has been estimated as

$$\log Q = a + b \log P + c \log I + d \log P_m$$

where Q = quantity of haddock sold in New England

$\qquad P$ = price per pound of haddock

$\qquad I$ = a measure of personal income in the New England region

$\qquad P_m$ = an index of the price of meat and poultry

If $b = -2.174$, $c = 0.461$, and $d = 1.909$,

a. Determine the price elasticity of demand.

b. Determine the income elasticity of demand.

c. Determine the cross price elasticity of demand.

d. How would you characterize the demand for haddock?

e. Suppose disposable income is expected to increase by 5 percent next year. Assuming all other factors remain constant, forecast the percentage change in the quantity of haddock demanded next year.

7. An estimate of the demand function for household furniture produced the following results:

$$F = 0.0036Y^{1.08}R^{0.16}P^{-0.48} \qquad r^2 = 0.996$$

where F = furniture expenditures per household

$\qquad Y$ = disposable personal income per household

$\qquad R$ = value of private residential construction per household

$\qquad P$ = ratio of the furniture price index to the consumer price index

a. Determine the point price and income elasticities for household furniture.

b. What interpretation would you give to the exponent for R? Why do you suppose R was included in the equation as a variable?

c. If you were a supplier to the furniture manufacturer, would you have preferred to see the analysis performed in physical sales units rather than dollars of revenue? How would this change alter the interpretation of the price coefficient, presently estimated as −0.48?

8. Consider again the Sherwin-Williams Company example discussed in this chapter (see Table 4.1). Suppose one is interested in developing a multiple regression model with paint sales (Y) as the dependent variable and promotional expenditures (A) and selling price (P) as the independent variables.

a. Determine the estimated regression line.

b. Give an economic interpretation of the estimated slope (b_s) coefficients.

c. Test the hypothesis (at the 5 percent level of significance) that there is no relationship between the dependent variable and each of the independent variables.

d. Determine the coefficient of determination.

e. Perform an analysis of variance on the regression, including an F-test of the overall significance of the results (at the 5 percent level).

f. Based on the regression model, determine the best estimate of paint sales in a sales region where promotional expenditures are $80(000) and the selling price is $12.50.

g. Determine the point promotional and price elasticities at the values of promotional expenditures and selling price given in part (f).

9. The county assessor (see Exercise 4) feels that the use of more independent variables in the regression equation might improve the overall explanatory power of the model.

   In addition to size, the assessor feels that the total number of rooms, age, and whether or not the house has an attached garage might be important variables affecting selling price. The data for the 15 randomly selected dwellings are shown in the following table.

   a. Using a computer regression program, determine the estimated regression equation with the four explanatory variables shown in the following table.
   b. Give an economic interpretation of each of the estimated regression coefficients.
   c. Which of the independent variables (if any) is statistically significant (at the 0.05 level) in explaining selling price?
   d. What proportion of the total variation in selling price is explained by the regression model?
   e. Perform an F-test (at the 5 percent significance level) of the overall explanatory power of the model.
   f. Construct an *approximate* 95 percent prediction interval for the selling price of a 15-year-old house having 1,800 sq. ft., 7 rooms, and an attached garage.

OBSERVATION	SELLING PRICE ($\times$ \$1,000)	SIZE ($\times$100 ft^2)	TOTAL NO. OF ROOMS	AGE	ATTACHED GARAGE (NO=0, YES=1)
i	Y	X_1	X_2	X_3	X_4
1	265.2	12.0	6	17	0
2	279.6	20.2	7	18	0
3	311.2	27.0	7	17	1
4	328.0	30.0	8	18	1
5	352.0	30.0	8	15	1
6	281.2	21.4	8	20	1
7	288.4	21.6	7	8	0
8	292.8	25.2	7	15	1
9	356.0	37.2	9	31	1
10	263.2	14.4	7	8	0
11	272.4	15.0	7	17	0
12	291.2	22.4	6	9	0
13	299.6	23.9	7	20	1
14	307.6	26.6	6	23	1
15	320.4	30.7	7	23	1

Case Exercises ## Soft Drink Demand Estimation

Demand can be estimated with experimental data, time-series data, or cross-section data. Sara Lee Corporation generates experimental data in test stores where the effect of an NFL-licensed Carolina Panthers logo on Champion sweatshirt sales can be carefully examined. Demand forecasts usually rely on time-series data. In contrast, cross-section data appear in Table 1. Soft drink consumption in cans per capita per year is related to six-pack price, income per capita, and mean temperature across the 48 contiguous states in the United States.

Questions

1. Estimate the demand for soft drinks using a multiple regression program available on your computer.
2. Interpret the coefficients and calculate the price elasticity of soft drink demand.
3. Omit price from the regression equation and observe the bias introduced into the parameter estimate for income.
4. Now omit both price and temperature from the regression equation. Should a marketing plan for soft drinks be designed that relocates most canned drink machines into low-income neighborhoods? Why or why not?

TABLE 1 SOFT DRINK DEMAND DATA (AVAILABLE AS AN EXCEL FILE ON THIS BOOK'S WEB SITE)

	CANS/CAPITA/YR	6-PACK $ PRICE	INCOME $/CAPITA	MEAN TEMP. °F
Alabama	200	2.19	13	66
Arizona	150	1.99	17	62
Arkansas	237	1.93	11	63
California	135	2.59	25	56
Colorado	121	2.29	19	52
Connecticut	118	2.49	27	50
Delaware	217	1.99	28	52
Florida	242	2.29	18	72
Georgia	295	1.89	14	64
Idaho	85	2.39	16	46
Illinois	114	2.35	24	52
Indiana	184	2.19	20	52
Iowa	104	2.21	16	50
Kansas	143	2.17	17	56
Kentucky	230	2.05	13	56
Louisiana	269	1.97	15	69
Maine	111	2.19	16	41
Maryland	217	2.11	21	54
Massachusetts	114	2.29	22	47
Michigan	108	2.25	21	47
Minnesota	108	2.31	18	41
Mississippi	248	1.98	10	65
Missouri	203	1.94	19	57
Montana	77	2.31	19	44
Nebraska	97	2.28	16	49
Nevada	166	2.19	24	48
New Hampshire	177	2.27	18	35
New Jersey	143	2.31	24	54

(continued)

	CANS/CAPITA/YR	6-PACK $ PRICE	INCOME $/CAPITA	MEAN TEMP. °F
New Mexico	157	2.17	15	56
New York	111	2.43	25	48
North Carolina	330	1.89	13	59
North Dakota	63	2.33	14	39
Ohio	165	2.21	22	51
Oklahoma	184	2.19	16	82
Oregon	68	2.25	19	51
Pennsylvania	121	2.31	20	50
Rhode Island	138	2.23	20	50
South Carolina	237	1.93	12	65
South Dakota	95	2.34	13	45
Tennessee	236	2.19	13	60
Texas	222	2.08	17	69
Utah	100	2.37	16	50
Vermont	64	2.36	16	44
Virginia	270	2.04	16	58
Washington	77	2.19	20	49
West Virginia	144	2.11	15	55
Wisconsin	97	2.38	19	46
Wyoming	102	2.31	19	46

Problems in Applying the Linear Regression Model

INTRODUCTION

When the simple linear and multiple linear regression models were discussed in Chapter 4, several assumptions were made about the nature of the relationships among the variables. How can we determine if the assumptions are being violated in a given situation? How does the violation of the assumptions affect the parameter estimates and prediction accuracy of the model? What methods (if any) exist for overcoming the difficulties caused by the inapplicability of the assumptions in a given situation?

Econometrics provides answers to some, but not all, of these questions. Some of the problems that may invalidate the simple regression results and require further analysis include the following:

1. Autocorrelation
2. Heteroscedasticity
3. Specification and measurement errors
4. Multicollinearity
5. Simultaneous equation relationships and the identification problem
6. Nonlinearities

Each of these problems is discussed in this appendix.

Autocorrelation

In many economic modeling and prediction problems, empirical data are in the form of a time series—a series of observations taken on the variables at different points in time. For example, we may be interested in predicting total domestic television sales by using U.S. disposable income as the independent variable over a period of 10 to 15 years. In working with time-series data, a problem known as autocorrelation can arise.

Recall that one of the assumptions underlying the regression model (specifically, Assumption 3) is that the disturbance term e_t must be an independent random variable. In other words, we assume that each successive error, e_t, is independent of earlier and later errors so that the regression equation produces no predictable pattern in the successive values of the disturbance term. The existence of a significant pattern in the successive values of the error term constitutes **autocorrelation**. Successive values of the disturbance term can exhibit either positive or negative autocorrelation. Positive or negative autocorrelation, as shown in Figure 4A.1 (a) and (b), is inferred whenever successive disturbances tend to be followed by disturbances of the same sign and opposite sign, respectively.

Negative autocorrelation reflects an undershooting and overshooting process like purchases of storable consumer goods. If a household buys too much breakfast cereal one week, that household will probably buy less than average the next week, and again more than average the following week. Positive autocorrelation can result from cyclical

autocorrelation An econometric problem characterized by the existence of a significant pattern in the successive values of the error terms in a linear regression model.

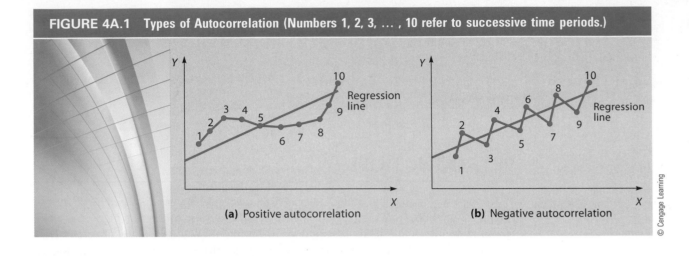

FIGURE 4A.1 Types of Autocorrelation (Numbers 1, 2, 3, ... , 10 refer to successive time periods.)

(a) Positive autocorrelation

(b) Negative autocorrelation

© Cengage Learning

and seasonal variation in economic variables. Another cause of positive autocorrelation is self-reinforcing trends in consumer purchase patterns, for example, in fashion retailing. If Hermes scarves are in fashion, each successive week of sales data will be further above trend than the previous week until the fad slows and the Hermes look goes out of fashion. Either positive or negative autocorrelation may also result if significant explanatory variables are omitted from the regression equation or if nonlinear relationships exist.

As a safeguard when working with time-series data, the disturbances (e_t values) should be examined for randomness. Statistical tests are available to check for autocorrelation. One commonly used technique is the Durbin-Watson statistic. It is calculated as follows:

$$d = \frac{\sum_{t=2}^{n} (e_t - e_{t-1})^2}{\sum_{t=1}^{n} e_t^2}$$ [4A.1]

where e_t is the estimated error term in period t and e_{t-1} is the error term in period $t - 1$. The Durbin-Watson statistic tests for first-order autocorrelation, that is, whether the error in period t is dependent on the error in the preceding period $t - 1$. The value of d ranges from 0 to 4. If there is no first-order autocorrelation, the expected value of d is 2. Values of d less than 2 indicate the possible presence of positive autocorrelation, whereas values of d greater than 2 indicate the possible presence of negative autocorrelation.

The presence of autocorrelation leads to several undesirable consequences in the regression results. First, although the estimates of α and β will be unbiased, the least squares procedure will misestimate the sampling variances of these estimates. (An estimator is unbiased if its expected value is identical to the population parameter being estimated. The computed a and b values are unbiased estimators of α and β, respectively, because $E(a)=\alpha$ and $E(b)=\beta$.) In particular, the standard error (s_e in Equation 4.22) will either be inflated or deflated depending on whether we have positive or negative autocorrelation. As a result, the use of the t-statistic to test hypotheses about these parameters may yield incorrect conclusions about the importance of the individual predictor (i.e., independent) variables. In addition, the r^2 and F tests are invalid under autocorrelation.

Several procedures are available for dealing with autocorrelation.[1] If one can determine the functional form of the dependence relationship in the successive values of the residuals, then the original variables can be transformed by a lag structure to remove this pattern. Another technique that may help to reduce autocorrelation is to include a new linear trend or time variable in the regression equation. A third procedure is to calculate the first differences in the time series of each of the variables (i.e., $Y_{t+1} - Y_t$, $X_{1,t+1} - X_{1,t}$, $X_{2,t+1} - X_{2,t}$, etc.) and then calculate the regression equation using these transformed variables. A fourth method is to include additional variables of the form X_1^2 or $X_1 X_2$ in the regression equation. Usually one of these procedures will yield satisfactory results consistent with the independent errors assumption.

Heteroscedasticity

heteroscedasticity An econometric problem characterized by the lack of a uniform variance of the error terms surrounding the regression line.

In developing the ordinary least-squares regression model, another of the assumptions (Assumption 3) is that the error terms have a constant variance. Departure from this assumption is known as **heteroscedasticity**, which is indicated whenever there is a systematic relationship between the absolute magnitude of the error term and the magnitude of one (or more) of the independent variables.

One form of heteroscedasticity is illustrated in Figure 4A.2. Savings by households is postulated to be a function of household income. In this case, it is likely that more variability will be found in the savings of high-income households compared with low-income households simply because high-income households have more money available for potential savings. Another example arising frequently with cross-sectional sales data is that the error variance with large-size retail stores, divisions, or firms exceeds the error variance for smaller entities.

In many cases, this form of heteroscedasticity can be reduced or eliminated by dividing all the variables in the regression equation by the independent variable that is thought to be causing the heteroscedasticity. Another method for dealing with heteroscedasticity is to take logarithms of the data. Again, this transformation alters the form of the hypothesized relationship among the variables. More advanced, generalized least-squares techniques can account for the nonuniform error variance and preserve the original, hypothesized relationship.

FIGURE 4A.2 Illustration of Heteroscedasticity

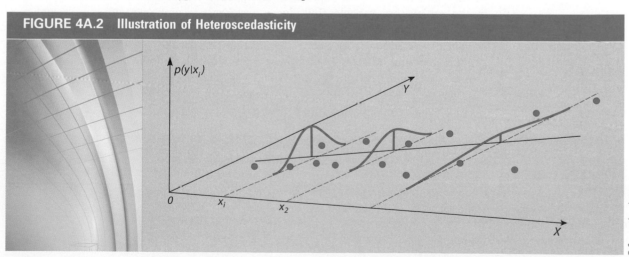

© Cengage Learning

---

[1]See D. Gujarati, *Basic Econometrics* (New York: McGraw-Hill, Inc., 2007), Chapter 12, for a much more detailed discussion of procedures for dealing with autocorrelation.

Specification and Measurement Errors

Specification errors can result whenever one or more significant explanatory variables are omitted from the regression equation. If the omitted variable is moderately or highly correlated with one of the explanatory variables included in the regression equation, then the affected regressor will be estimated with bias. Omitted variable bias may lead to overestimating or underestimating the true regression coefficients.

The direction of bias in the estimated parameters should always be diagnosed. The misestimated parameter for $X_1(b_1)$ may be written as the sum of the true parameter (β_1) plus the effect of the omitted variable j, which depends on β_j and the correlation coefficient $r_{1,j}$

$$b_1 = \beta_1 + \beta_j r_{1,j} \qquad [4A.2]$$

If one knows that the likely sign of the correlation coefficient between the omitted variable and the included explanatory variable ($r_{1,j}$) is positive, and if the hypothesized effect of the omitted variable on the dependent variable (β_j) is positive, the estimated parameter will be positively biased. For example, omitting household income from a demand estimation of luxury car rentals is likely to result in a positive bias on the price parameter, since higher income and the price paid for a luxury car for a week are probably positively correlated and since household income itself is hypothesized to be a positive determinant of luxury car rentals. On the other hand, in the Sherwin-Williams paint demand data, the correlation coefficient between disposable income and price is −0.514 (see Figure 4A.3). Omitting DISPINC from the demand estimation in Figure 4.8 would lead to a negative bias in the estimated effect of price on sales. Although these diagnoses of the omitted variable bias can never replace a fully and correctly specified model, they do allow much more informed decision making based on incomplete data.

Sometimes a close proxy variable is available and should be substituted for the omitted variable. The closer the proxy, the better the estimation because proxy variables always introduce some measurement error. Measurement errors in the dependent variable do not affect the validity of the assumptions underlying the regression model or the parameter estimates obtained by the least-squares procedure because these errors become part of the overall residual or unexplained error. However, measurement error in the explanatory variables introduces a stochastic component in the Xs and may cause the values of the error term e_i to be correlated with the observed values of these explanatory variables. Consequently, the assumption that the disturbance terms are independent random variables (Assumption 3) is violated, and the resulting least-squares estimates of the regression coefficients (α, β) are biased.

FIGURE 4A.3 Correlation Coefficients: Sherwin-Williams Company

	SALES Y	PROMEXP X_1	SELLPR X_2	DISPINC X_3
SALES Y	1.000			
PROMEXP X_1	0.721	1.000		
SELLPR X_2	−0.866	−0.739	1.000	
DISPINC X_3	0.615	0.710	−0.514	1.000

© Cengage Learning

Simultaneous equation estimation techniques discussed in a later section are one method of dealing with stochastic explanatory variables. Measurement error can also be modeled, if the form of the error in the X variables can be specified.

Multicollinearity

Whenever a high degree of intercorrelation exists among some or all of the explanatory variables in the regression equation, it becomes difficult to determine the separate influences of each of the explanatory variables on the dependent variable because the standard deviations (s_b) of their respective regression coefficients become biased upward. Whenever two or more explanatory variables are highly correlated (or collinear), the t-test is therefore no longer a reliable indicator of the statistical significance of the individual explanatory variables. Under such a condition, the least-squares procedure tends to yield highly unstable estimates of the regression coefficients from one sample to the next. The presence of **multicollinearity**, however, does not necessarily invalidate the use of the regression equation for prediction purposes. Provided that the intercorrelation pattern among the explanatory variables persists into the future, the equation can produce reliable forecasts of the value of the dependent variable.

A number of techniques exist for dealing with multicollinearity: taking larger samples, detrending variables, or taking logs. In the end, however, the most important point is to diagnose the presence of multicollinearity so that insignificant hypothesis tests will not be wrongly attributed to weak cause-effect relationships. For example, consider the variables that were used to explain paint sales in the Sherwin-Williams example discussed earlier. The correlation coefficients between each of the variables are shown in Figure 4A.3. Note the high degree of intercorrelation (in absolute value terms) between promotional expenditures and selling price and between promotional expenditures and disposable income, indicating that the standard deviations of the estimates of these three regression coefficients may be inflated.

multicollinearity An econometric problem characterized by a high degree of intercorrelation among explanatory variables in a regression equation.

Simultaneous Equation Relationships and the Identification Problem

Many economic relationships are characterized by simultaneous interactions. For example, recognition of simultaneous relationships is at the heart of marketing plans. The optimal advertising expenditure for a product line like Hanes Her Way hosiery depends on sales (i.e., on the quantity Hanes expects to sell). However, sales obviously also depend on advertising; a particularly effective ad campaign that just happens to match a random swing in customer fashion will drive sales substantially upward. And this sales boost will increase spending on advertising. Sales (i.e., demand) and advertising are simultaneously determined.

In attempting to estimate the parameters of simultaneous equation relationships with single equation models, one encounters the **identification problem**. For example, in developing demand functions from empirical data, one is faced with the simultaneous relationship between the demand function and the supply function. Suppose demand can be written as a function of price (P), income (M), and a random error ε_1,

$$Q_d = \beta_1 + \beta_2 P + \beta_3 M + \varepsilon_1 \qquad [4A.3]$$

and supply can be written as a function of price, input costs (I), and another random error ε_2

identification problem A difficulty encountered in empirically estimating a demand function by regression analysis. This problem arises from the simultaneous relationship between two functions, such as supply and demand.

$$Q_s = \alpha_1 + \alpha_2 P + \alpha_3 I + \varepsilon_2 \qquad\qquad [4A.4]$$

or, rearranging, supply is

$$P = \frac{-\alpha_1}{\alpha_2} + \frac{1}{\alpha_2}(Q_s - \varepsilon_2) - \frac{\alpha_3}{\alpha_2} I \qquad\qquad [4A.5]$$

Because quantity demanded will equal quantity supplied in market-clearing equilibrium (i.e., $Q_d = Q_s$), we can substitute Equation 4A.3 for Q_s in 4A.5 to obtain

$$P = \frac{-\alpha_1}{\alpha_2} + \frac{1}{\alpha_2}(\beta_1 + \beta_2 P + \beta_3 M + \varepsilon_1 - \varepsilon_2) - \frac{\alpha_3}{\alpha_2} I \qquad\qquad [4A.6]$$

$$P = \frac{1}{\alpha_2 - \beta_2}(-\alpha_1 + \beta_1 + \beta_3 M + \varepsilon_1 - \varepsilon_2 - \alpha_3 I) \qquad\qquad [4A.7]$$

Observed values of P in Equation 4A.7 are quite obviously a stochastic explanatory variable because they are correlated with the disturbance term in the demand function ε_1. An ordinary least-squares regression of Equation 4A.3 (the demand function) therefore violates Assumption 3 that disturbance terms must be independent of the Xs—that is, $E(P_i \varepsilon_i)=0$. As a result, the price coefficient in Equation 4A.3 β_2 will be biased.

To see why this poses a problem, recall that the price-output combinations actually observed result from an interaction of the supply and demand curves at a point in time. This is illustrated in Figure 4A.4. If D_1, D_2, D_3, and D_4 represent the true demand curves at four different points in time and S_1, S_2, S_3, and S_4 the corresponding supply curves, one would have been seriously misled to conclude that the true demand relationship was depicted by DD' and was generally inelastic, when in fact demand was quite elastic and shifting. During the four successive time periods in which price-output combinations were observed, both the demand and supply curves had shifted. Recall from Chapter 3 that to obtain a true estimate of the actual demand curve, one must hold constant the effects of all other variables in the demand functions, allowing only price and quantity demanded to vary.

Under what circumstances may valid empirical estimates of the demand curve be made? If the supply curve shifts but the demand curve remains constant, observed price-output combinations will trace out the true demand curve. This is illustrated in Figure 4A.5. If, for example, technological advances were being introduced in the production of computer memory chips during Periods 1, 2, 3, and 4, then the supply curve would shift downward and to the right, from S_1 to S_4, tracing out the actual demand curve.

If both curves have shifted during the time period under consideration, identifying the demand curve requires that more than just price-output data be available. In other words, other variables, such as income and advertising, which may cause a shift in the demand function, must also be included in the model. Alternative statistical estimation techniques, such as two-stage least-squares (2SLS), may be used to separate supply curve shifts from shifts in the demand curve.[2]

---

[2] A discussion of these alternative estimation procedures is beyond the scope of this book. The reader is referred to Gujarati, op. cit., Chapter 18.

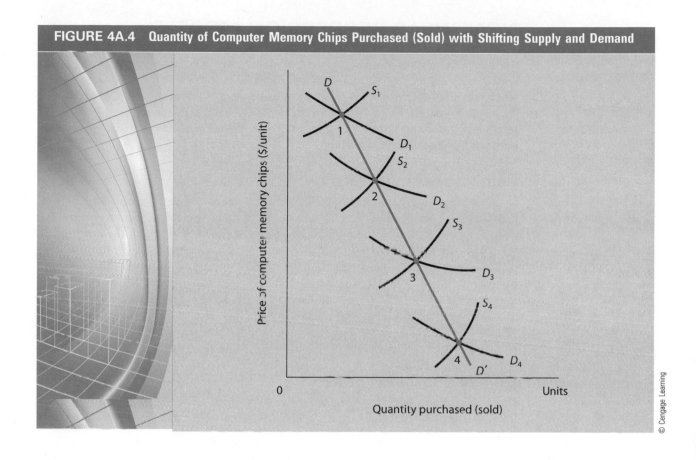

FIGURE 4A.4   Quantity of Computer Memory Chips Purchased (Sold) with Shifting Supply and Demand

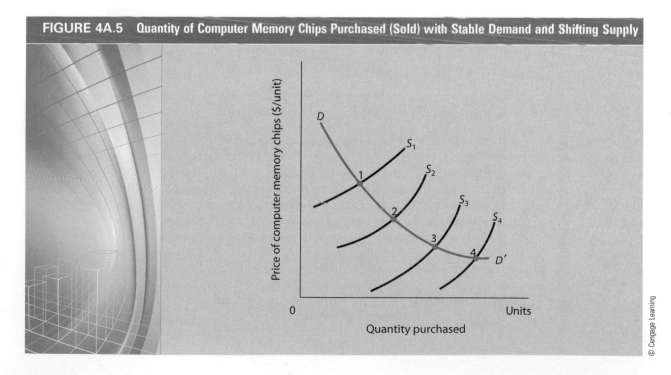

FIGURE 4A.5   Quantity of Computer Memory Chips Purchased (Sold) with Stable Demand and Shifting Supply

NONLINEAR REGRESSION MODELS

Although the relationships among many economic variables can be satisfactorily represented using a linear regression model, situations do occur in which a nonlinear model is clearly required to portray adequately the relationship. Various models are available to deal with these situations. The transformations that are discussed here include the semi-logarithmic transformation, the double-log transformation, reciprocal transformation, and polynomial transformations.

Semilogarithmic Transformation

Sometimes, when heteroscedasticity is suspected, the dependent variable can be estimated best by taking the logarithm of one or more of the independent variables. For example, cross-section regression models, which use firm size as one of the independent variables, often take the log of firm size because of the potential problems caused by including in the same equation firms of $10 million in assets with firms of $10 billion in assets.

A semilog transformation of the form

$$Y = a + b \log Assets + cX + Dz \qquad [4A.8]$$

is then estimated with standard least-squares techniques.

Double-Log Transformation

In Chapter 4, we saw that a multiplicative exponential model (see Equation 4.5 and Table 4.4) is often used in demand studies. A three-variable exponential regression function can be represented as

$$Z = A V^{\beta_1} W^{\beta_2} \qquad [4A.9]$$

Multiplicative exponential functions such as these can be transformed to linear relationships by taking logarithms of both sides of the equation to yield

$$\log Z = \log A + \beta_1 \log V + \beta_2 \log W$$

Example

Constant Elasticity Demand: Pepsi

If the data on soft drinks in the Case Exercise at the end of Chapter 4 (see Table 1) represent firm-level unit sales, marketing analysts in the company (PepsiCo, Inc.) may confirm that price elasticity coefficients have been very similar at several price points in recent years. If the same results of nearly constant elasticity estimates have arisen from detailed studies of income elasticity in upper- and lower-income neighborhoods, then a demand specification like Equation 4A.9 and a double-log estimation of the data in Table 1 would be indicated. Results of such an estimation are listed next:

$$\text{Log } Q = 1.050 \quad - \ 3.196 \text{ LogPrice} \ + \ 0.221 \text{ LogIncome} \ + \ 1.119 \text{ LogTemp}$$
$$(1.72) \qquad (-4.92) \qquad\qquad (1.19) \qquad\qquad\quad (4.23)$$
$$SSE = 0.111 \quad R^2 = 0.671$$

Numbers in parentheses are *t*-score statistics.

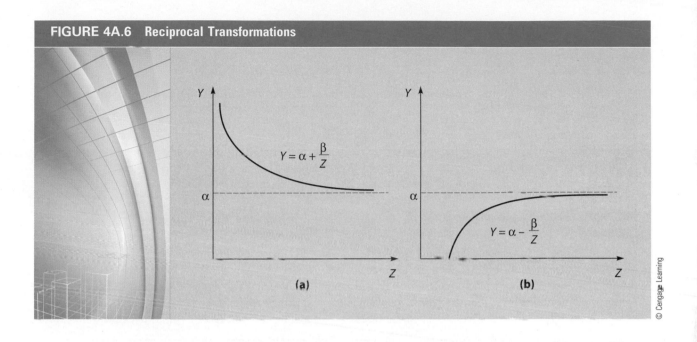

FIGURE 4A.6   **Reciprocal Transformations**

Reciprocal Transformation

Another transformation, which is useful in relationships that exhibit an asymptotic behavior, is the reciprocal transformation. The two possible cases are shown in Figure 4A.1. In Figure 4A.6 (a) the relationship is of the form,

$$Y = \alpha + \frac{\beta}{Z} \qquad\qquad [4A.10]$$

and in Figure 4A.6 (b) it is of the form

$$Y = \alpha - \frac{\beta}{Z} \qquad\qquad [4A.11]$$

Defining the transformation $X = 1/Z$, Equations 4A.10 and 4A.11 yield the following respective simple linear regression models:

$$Y = \alpha + \beta X + \varepsilon$$

and

$$Y = \alpha - \beta X + \varepsilon$$

whose parameters can be estimated by the usual least-squares procedures.

Polynomial Transformation

As will be seen in Chapter 8, the cost-output function for a firm is often postulated to follow a quadratic or cubic pattern. This type of relationship can be represented by means of a polynomial function. For example, a third-degree (i.e., cubic) polynomial function can be represented as

$$Y = \alpha + \beta_1 Z + \beta_2 Z^2 + \beta_3 Z^3 \qquad\qquad [4A.12]$$

Letting $X_1 = Z$, $X_2 = Z_2$, $X_3 = Z_3$, Equation 4A.12 can be transformed into the following multiple linear regression model:

$$Y = \alpha + \beta_1 X_1 + \beta_2 X_2 + \beta_3 X_3$$

Standard least-squares procedures can be used in estimating the parameters of this model.

SUMMARY

- Various methodological problems can occur when applying the single-equation linear regression model. These include autocorrelation, heteroscedasticity, specification and measurement errors, multicollinearity, simultaneous equation relationships, and nonlinearities. Many of these problems can invalidate the regression results. In most cases,

methods are available for detecting and overcoming these problems.
- Because of the simultaneous equation relationship that exists between the demand function and the supply function in determining the market-clearing price and quantity, analysts must exercise great care when estimating and interpreting empirical demand functions.

Exercises

1. Suppose an appliance manufacturer is doing a regression analysis, using quarterly *time-series* data, of the factors affecting its sales of appliances. A regression equation was estimated between appliance sales (in dollars) as the dependent variable and disposable personal income and new housing starts as the independent variables. The statistical tests of the model showed large *t*-values for both independent variables, along with a high r^2 value. However, analysis of the residuals indicated that substantial autocorrelation was present.
   a. What are some of the possible causes of this autocorrelation?
   b. How does this autocorrelation affect the conclusions concerning the significance of the individual explanatory variables and the overall explanatory power of the regression model?
   c. Given that a person uses the model for forecasting future appliance sales, how does this autocorrelation affect the accuracy of these forecasts?
   d. What techniques might be used to remove this autocorrelation from the model?
2. A product manager has been reviewing selling expenses (i.e., advertising, sales commissions, etc.) associated with marketing a line of household cleaning products. The manager suspects that there may be some sort of diminishing marginal returns relationship between selling expenses and the resulting sales generated by these expenditures. After examining the selling expense and sales data for various regions (all regions are similar in sales potential) shown in the following table, however, the manager is uncertain about the nature of the relationship.

REGION	SELLING EXPENSE ($000)	SALES (100,000 UNITS)	LOG (SELLING EXPENSE)	LOG (SALES)
A	5	1	3.6990	5.0000
B	30	4.25	4.4771	5.6284
C	25	4	4.3979	5.6021
D	10	2	4.0000	5.3010
E	55	5.5	4.7404	5.7404
F	40	5	4.6021	5.6990

REGION	SELLING EXPENSE ($000)	SALES (100,000 UNITS)	LOG (SELLING EXPENSE)	LOG (SALES)
G	10	1.75	4.0000	5.2430
H	45	5	4.6532	5.6990
I	20	3	4.3010	5.4771
J	60	5.75	4.7782	5.7597

a. Using the linear regression model

$$Y = \alpha + \beta X$$

where Y is sales and X is selling expenses, estimate α, β, and the r^2 statistic by the least-squares technique.

b. Using the exponential function model

$$Y = \alpha X^{\beta}$$

apply the double-logarithmic transformation to obtain a linear relationship that can be estimated by the least-squares technique.

c. Applying the least-squares technique, estimate α, β, and the r^2 statistic for the transformed (linear) model in part (b). (Note that the logarithms of the X and Y variables needed in the calculations are given in the table.)

d. Based on the r^2 statistics calculated in parts (a) and (c), which model appears to give a better fit of the data?

e. What implications does the result in part (d) have for the possible existence of a diminishing marginal returns relationship between sales and selling expenses as suggested by the manager?

f. What other transformations of the variables might we try to give a better fit to the data?

3. a. Using the data in Table 4.1 for the Sherwin-Williams Company, estimate a multiplicative exponential demand model (see Equation 4.5) for paint sales.

b. Compare the results in part (a) (i.e., parameter estimates, standard errors, statistical significance) with the linear model developed in the chapter.

4. The following table presents data on sales (S), advertising (A), and price (P):

OBSERVATION	SALES (S)	ADVERTISING (A)	PRICE (P)
1	495	900	150
2	555	1,200	180
3	465	750	135
4	675	1,350	135
5	360	600	120
6	405	600	120
7	735	1,500	150
8	435	750	150
9	570	1,050	165
10	600	1,200	150

a. Estimate the following demand models:
  (i) $S = \alpha + \beta_1 A + \beta_2 P$

  (ii) $S = \alpha A^{\beta_1} P^{\beta_2}$

b. Determine whether the estimated values of β_1 and β_2 are statistically significant (at the 0.05 level).

c. Based on the value of R^2 and the F-ratio, which model gives the best fit?

5. The county assessor (see Exercise 9 of Chapter 4) is concerned about possible multicollinearity between the size (X_1) and total number of rooms (X_2) variables. Calculate the correlation coefficient between these two variables and diagnose the magnitude of the collinearity problem.

Business and Economic Forecasting

With over 50 domestic models of cars already on sale in the United States, the Japanese auto industry isn't likely to carve out a big slice of the U.S. auto market.

BusinessWeek, 1958 [In 2012, Toyota and Honda are No. 2 and No. 4 in U.S. car sales.]

CHAPTER PREVIEW

Forecasting demand or input costs is often quite difficult. But it is one of the pivotal concerns of all managers because the shareholder value of a firm depends on accurately forecasting these components of the expected future cash flows. Forecasts at the firm level depend not only on prices and advertising and rival response tactics but also on the growth rate of the macro economy, the level of interest rates, the rate of unemployment, the value of the dollar in foreign exchange markets, and the rate of inflation. In this chapter we discuss the strengths and weaknesses of several classes of forecasting techniques including trend analysis, smoothing techniques, barometric indicators, survey and opinion polling, and time-series econometric methods.

MANAGERIAL CHALLENGE

Excess Fiber Optic Capacity at Global Crossing Inc.[1]

The capacity of U.S. fiber optic networks to transmit high-speed data and voice signals once outstripped telecom demand so much that 97 percent of the installed capacity in the United States was idle "silent fiber." Indeed, if all telecom network traffic in the United States were routed through Chicago, only one-quarter of that city's fiber optic capacity would be in use. With all this excess capacity in the market, fiber optic network providers like Global Crossing Inc. saw their pricing power collapse. A 1-megabyte data connection between New York and Los Angeles that in 1995 had sold for as much as $12,000 per year declined by 2001 to $3,000 and by 2002 to $1,200. As their sales revenue plummeted,

over 50 telecom network companies sought bankruptcy protection from their creditors.

How did this extreme excess capacity situation develop? First, an innovation in signal compression technology caused capacity to outpace the growth of the market. Between 1995 and 2003, dense wave divisional multiplexing (DWDM) expanded the transmission capacity of a single strand of fiber optic cable from 25,000 one-page e-mails per second to 25 million per second, a thousandfold increase. In addition, however, telecom network providers like Global Crossing and WorldCom were wildly optimistic about the growth of telecom traffic, fueled by the projected growth of the

MANAGERIAL CHALLENGE *Continued*

© Don Farrall/Digital Vision/Getty Images

Internet, so they continued to lay additional cable. UUNet, a subsidiary of WorldCom, forecasted that Internet use would continue to double every 100 days. This exponential, more than tenfold growth per year (1,333 percent) was an extrapolation of the sales growth UUNet actually experienced in 1995–1996.

When the U.S. Department of Commerce and the Federal Communications Commission repeated this forecast, network providers continued to buy and bury

redundant fiber optic cable. Between 2001 and 2002, U.S. fiber optic total capacity grew from 8,000 gigabytes per second to 80,000; but by 2003, the growth rate of demand had slowed (from 1,333 percent) to only 40 percent per year. Global Crossing's failure to forecast this demand slowdown proved disastrous.

As we saw in Chapter 4, the penetration of the Internet into the American household has followed a classic S-shaped pattern. Initially, the Internet experienced exponential growth by the early adopters, then linear growth, and eventually fractional growth. This S-shaped penetration curve is drawn in Figure 5.1. It took both color television and the Internet only eight years (1947–1955 for color TVs and 1993–2001 for direct Internet access) to reach approximately 60 percent of U.S. households. However, color television adoptions then hit a wall, requiring another 30 years (1955–1985) to achieve 98 percent penetration. Similarly with the Internet, customers who did not adopt high-speed broadband connections early are resistant to adopt now. Consequently, demand growth will likely remain low in Europe and the United States.

FIGURE 5.1 **Market Penetration Curves of the Color Television and the Internet**

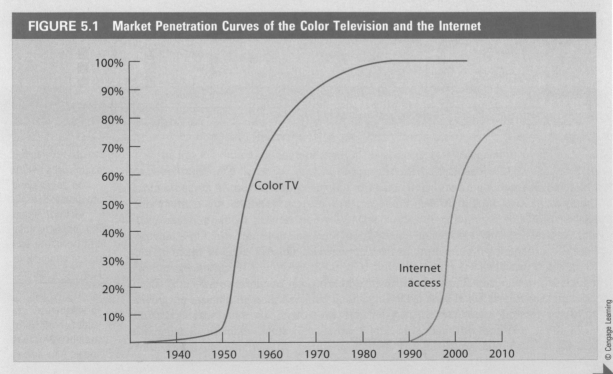

© Cengage Learning

Cont.

MANAGERIAL CHALLENGE *Continued*

Discussion Questions

■ Forecasting provides very useful projections for established products and services, but newly introduced offerings have wildly different success results. Name a few products that have exploded with exponentially increasing demand shortly after their introduction. How about products that have largely been ignored?

■ Do you see any common features among established and new products that might prove useful to an economic forecaster?

---

[1]Based on "Adoption Rate of Internet by Consumers Is Slowing," *Wall Street Journal* (July 16, 2001), p. B1; "Has Growth of the Net Flattened?" *Wall Street Journal* (July 16, 2001), p. B8; "Behind the Fiber Glut," *Wall Street Journal* (July 26, 2001), p. B1; and "Innovation Outpaced the Marketplace," *Wall Street Journal* (September 26, 2002), p. B1.

THE SIGNIFICANCE OF FORECASTING

Accurately forecasting future business prospects is one of the most important functions of management. Sales forecasts are necessary for operations managers to plan the proper future levels of production. The financial managers require estimates of not only future sales revenue but also disbursements and capital expenditures. Forecasts of credit conditions must also be made so that the cash needs of the firm may be met at the lowest possible cost.

Public administrators and managers of not-for-profit institutions must also forecast. City government officials, for example, forecast the level of services that will be required of their various departments during a budget period. How many police officers will be needed to handle the public-safety problems of the community? How many streets will require repair next year, and how much will this cost? What will next year's school enrollment be at each grade level? The hospital administrator must forecast the health care needs of the community and the amount and cost of charity patient care.

SELECTING A FORECASTING TECHNIQUE

The forecasting technique used in any particular situation depends on a number of factors.

Hierarchy of Forecasts

The highest level of economic aggregation that is normally forecast is that of the national economy. The usual measure of overall economic activity is gross domestic product (GDP); however, a firm may be more interested in forecasting some of the specific components of GDP. For example, a machine tool firm may be concerned about plant and equipment expenditure requirements. Retail establishments are concerned about future levels and changes in disposable personal income rather than the overall GDP estimate.

The next levels in the hierarchy of economic forecasts are the industry sales forecast, followed by individual firm sales forecasts. A simple, single firm forecast might take the industry sales estimate and relate this to the expected market share of the individual firm. Future market share might be estimated on the basis of historical market shares as well as on changes that are anticipated in marketing strategies, new products and model changes, and relative prices.

Within the firm, a hierarchy of forecasts also exists. Managers often estimate company-wide or regional dollar sales and unit sales by product line. These forecasts are used by operations managers in planning orders for raw materials, employee-hiring needs, shipment schedules, and release-to-production decisions. In addition, marketing managers use sales forecasts to determine optimal sales force allocations, to set sales goals, and to plan promotions. The sales forecast also constitutes a crucial part of the financial manager's forecast of the cash needs of the firm. Long-term forecasts for the economy, the industry, and the firm are used in planning long-term capital expenditures for plant and equipment and for charting the general direction of the firm.

Criteria Used to Select a Forecasting Technique

Some forecasting techniques are quite simple, inexpensive to develop and use, and best suited for short-term projections, whereas others are extremely complex, require significant amounts of time to develop, and may be quite expensive. The technique used in any specific instance depends on a number of factors, including the following:

1. The cost associated with developing the forecasting model,
2. The complexity of the relationships that are being forecast,
3. The time period of the forecast (long-term or short-term),
4. The lead time needed to make decisions based on the forecast, and
5. The accuracy required of the forecasting model.

Evaluating the Accuracy of Forecasting Models

In determining the accuracy, or reliability, of a forecasting model, one is concerned with the magnitude of the differences between the observed (actual) (Y) and the forecasted values ($\hat{Y}$). Various measures of model accuracy are available. For example, in the discussion of regression analysis in Chapter 4, the coefficient of determination, or R^2, was used as a measure of the "goodness of fit" of the predicted values from the model to the patterns in the actual data. In addition, the mean prediction error, or root mean square error (RMSE),

$$\text{RMSE} = \sqrt{\frac{1}{n}\Sigma(Y_t - \hat{Y}_t)^2} \qquad [5.1]$$

is often used to evaluate the accuracy of a forecasting model (where n is the number of observations). The smaller the value of the RMSE, the greater the accuracy.

WHAT WENT RIGHT • WHAT WENT WRONG

Crocs Shoes[2]

In 2002, a colorful foam clog that was lightweight and nearly indestructible appeared on the market. Crocs were an overnight sensation, and 100 million pairs were sold in seven years. The company forecasted double-digit sales growth for the next five years, and then did a very successful initial public offering that raised $200 million. The new capital was reinvested to ramp up Crocs' manufacturing capacity. Then the severe worldwide recession of 2008–2009 hit, and the bottom fell out of the market. No one needed replacements for a nearly indestructible fashion fad that couldn't help you look for a job. In one year (2007–2008), the company swung from a profit of $168 million to a loss of $185 million. After several years of retrenchment, Crocs are again profitable at less than one-tenth of the previous production capacity.

_____
[2]Based on "Once-Trendy Crocs Could Be on Their Last Legs," *Washington Post* (July 16, 2009), p. C2.

ALTERNATIVE FORECASTING TECHNIQUES

The managerial economist may choose from a wide range of forecasting techniques. These can be classified in the following general categories:

1. Deterministic trend analysis
2. Smoothing techniques
3. Barometric indicators
4. Survey and opinion-polling techniques
5. Macroeconometric models
6. Stochastic time-series analysis
7. Forecasting with input-output tables

DETERMINISTIC TREND ANALYSIS

time-series data A series of observations taken on an economic variable at various points in time.

Data collected for use in forecasting the value of a particular variable may be classified into two major categories—time-series or cross-sectional data. **Time-series data** are defined as a sequence of the values of an economic variable at different points in time. **Cross-sectional data** are an array of the values of an economic variable observed at the same time, like the data collected in a census across many individuals in the population. No matter what type of forecasting model is being used, one must decide whether time-series or cross-sectional data are most appropriate.

cross-sectional data Series of observations taken on different observation units (e.g., households, states, or countries) at the same point in time.

Components of a Time Series

In the analysis of time-series data, time in years, months, or weeks is represented on the horizontal axis, and the values of the dependent variable are on the vertical axis. The variations that are evident in the time series in Figure 5.2 can be decomposed into four components:

secular trends Long-run changes (growth or decline) in an economic time-series variable.

(a) *Secular trends*. These are long-run trends that cause changes in an economic data series [*solid line* in Panel (a) of Figure 5.2]. For example, in empirical demand analyses, such factors as increasing population size or evolving consumer tastes may result in trend increases or decreases of a demand series over time.

cyclical variations Major expansions and contractions in an economic series that usually are longer than a year in duration.

(b) *Cyclical variations*. These are major expansions and contractions in an economic series that are usually greater than a year in duration [*broken line* in Panel (a) of Figure 5.2]. For example, the housing industry appears to experience regular expansions following contractions in demand. When cyclical variations are present, regression estimates using the raw data will be distorted due to the presence of positive autocorrelation. Care must then be taken to specify an appropriate lag structure to remove the autocorrelation.

seasonal effects Variations in a time series during a year that tend to appear regularly from year to year.

(c) *Seasonal effects*. Seasonal variations during a year tend to be more or less consistent from year to year. The data in Panel (b) of Figure 5.2 (*broken line*) show significant seasonal variation. For example, two-thirds of Hickory Farms' (a retailer of holiday food gifts) annual sales occur between November and January.

(d) *Random fluctuations*. Finally, an economic series may be influenced by random factors that are unpredictable [*solid line* in Panel (b) of Figure 5.2], such as hurricanes, floods, and tornados, as well as extraordinary government actions like a wage-price freeze or a declaration of war.

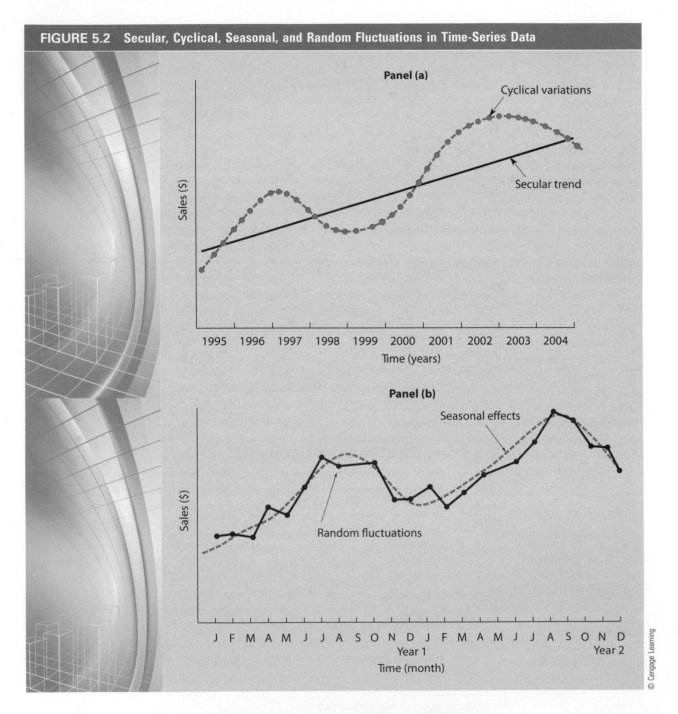

FIGURE 5.2 Secular, Cyclical, Seasonal, and Random Fluctuations in Time-Series Data

Some Elementary Time-Series Models

The simplest time-series model states that the forecast value of the variable for the next period will be the same as the value of that variable for the present period:

$$\hat{Y}_{t+1} = Y_t \qquad [5.2]$$

For example, consider the sales data shown in Table 5.1 for the Buckeye Brewing Company. To forecast monthly sales, the model uses *actual* beer sales for March 2007 of 2,738 (000) barrels as the forecast value for April.

TABLE 5.1	BUCKEYE BREWING COMPANY'S MONTHLY BEER SALES (THOUSANDS OF BARRELS)		
	YEAR		
MONTH	2012	2013	2014
January	2,370	2,446	2,585
February	2,100	2,520	2,693
March	2,412	2,598	2,738
April	2,376	2,533	
May	3,074	3,250	
June	3,695	3,446	
July	3,550	3,986	
August	4,172	4,222	
September	3,880	3,798	
October	2,931	2,941	
November	2,377	2,488	
December	2,983	2,878	

© Cengage Learning

Where changes occur slowly and the forecast is being made for a relatively short period in the future, such a model may be quite useful. However, because Equation 5.2 requires knowledge of this month's sales, the forecaster may be faced with the task of speeding up the collection of actual data. Another problem with this model is that it makes no provision for incorporating special promotions by the firm (or its competitors) that could cause large sales deviations.

Further examination of the Buckeye beer sales data in Table 5.1 indicates a slight upward trend in sales—beer sales in most months are higher than in the same month of the previous year. Second, we note that sales are somewhat seasonal—beer sales are high during the summer months and low during the winter. The tendency for recent increases to trigger further increases in beer sales may be incorporated by slightly adjusting Equation 5.2 to yield this equation:

$$\hat{Y}_{t+1} = Y_t + (Y_t - Y_{t-1})$$ [5.3]

For example, Buckeye's sales forecast for April 2014 using this model would be

$$\hat{Y}_{t+1} = 2{,}738 + (2{,}738 - 2{,}693)$$

$$= 2{,}783(000) \text{ barrels}$$

Other forecasting models that incorporate trends and seasonal effects such as these are discussed in the next two sections.

Secular Trends

Long-run changes in an economic time series can follow a number of different types of trends. Three possible cases are shown in Figure 5.3. A *linear* trend is shown in Panel (a), Panel (b), and Panel (c) depict *nonlinear* trends. In Panel (b), the economic time series follows a *constant rate of growth* pattern. The earnings of many corporations follow this type of trend. Panel (c) shows an economic time series that exhibits a declining rate of growth. Sales of a new product may follow this pattern. As market saturation occurs, the rate of growth will decline over time.

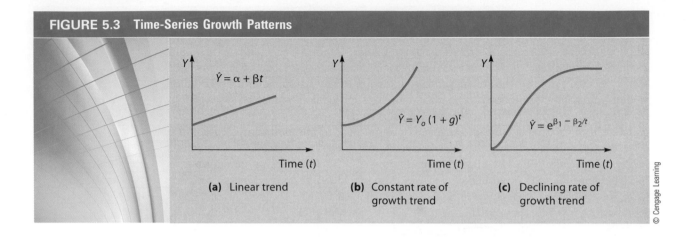

FIGURE 5.3 Time-Series Growth Patterns

(a) Linear trend — $\hat{Y} = \alpha + \beta t$

(b) Constant rate of growth trend — $\hat{Y} = Y_o(1 + g)^t$

(c) Declining rate of growth trend — $\hat{Y} = e^{\beta_1 - \beta_2/t}$

© Cengage Learning

Linear Trends   A linear time trend may be estimated by using *least-squares* regression analysis to provide an equation of a straight line of "best fit." (See Chapter 4 for a further discussion of the least-squares technique.) The equation of a linear time trend is given in the general form

$$\hat{Y} = \alpha + \beta t \qquad [5.4]$$

where $\hat{Y}_t$ is the forecast or predicted value for period t, α is the Y intercept or constant term, t is a unit of time, and β is an estimate of this trend factor.

Example

Linear Trend Forecasting: Prizer Creamery

Suppose one is interested in forecasting monthly ice cream sales of the Prizer Creamery for 2007. A least-squares trend line could be estimated from the ice cream sales data for the past four years (48 monthly observations), as shown in Figure 5.4. Assume that the equation of this line is calculated to be

$$\hat{Y}_t = 30{,}464 + 121.3t$$

where $\hat{Y}_t$ = predicted monthly ice cream sales in gallons in month t

$30{,}464$ = number of gallons sold when $t = 0$

t = time period (months) (where December 2002 = 0, January 2003 = 1, February 2003 = 2, March 2003 = 3, ...)

The coefficient (121.3) of t indicates that sales may be expected to increase by 121.3 gallons on the average each month. Based on this trend line and ignoring any seasonal effects, forecasted ice cream sales for August 2007 ($t = 56$) would be

$$Y_{56} = 30{,}464 + 121.3(56)$$
$$= 37{,}257 \text{ gallons}$$

This *seasonally unadjusted* forecast is given by the August 2007 point (⊙) on the trend line in Figure 5.4. As can be seen in the graph, ice cream sales are subject to seasonal variations. Later in this section we will show how this seasonal effect can be incorporated into the forecast.

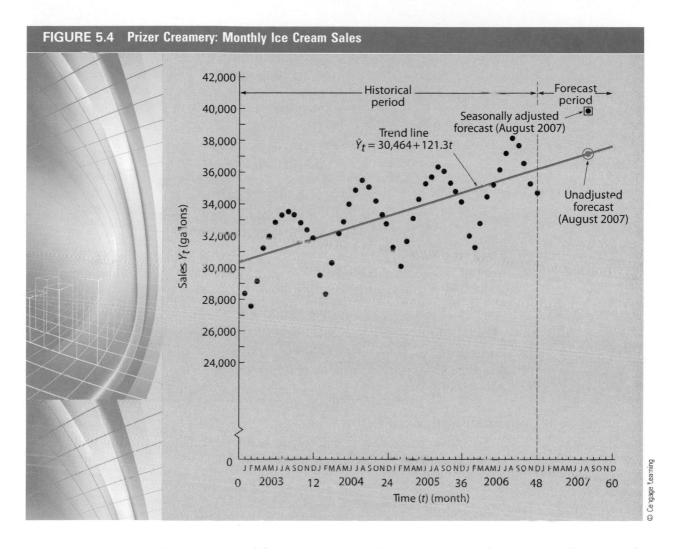

FIGURE 5.4   Prizer Creamery: Monthly Ice Cream Sales

Linear time trend forecasting is easy and inexpensive to do, but it is generally too simple and inflexible to be used in many forecasting circumstances. Constant rate of growth time trends is one alternative.

Constant Rate of Growth Trends   The formula for the constant rate of growth forecasting model is

$$\hat{Y}_t = Y_0(1 + g)^t \tag{5.5}$$

where $\hat{Y}_t$ is the forecasted value for period t, Y_0 is the initial ($t = 0$) value of the time series, g is the constant growth rate per period, and t is a unit of time. The predicted value of the time series in period t, ($\hat{Y}_t$), is equal to the initial value of the series (Y_0) compounded at the growth rate (g) for t periods. Because Equation 5.5 is a nonlinear relationship, the parameters cannot be estimated directly with the ordinary least-squares method. However, taking logarithms of both sides of the equation gives

$$\log\hat{Y}_t = \log Y_0 + \log(1 + g) \cdot t$$

or

$$\hat{Y}_t' = \alpha + \beta t \tag{5.6}$$

where $\hat{Y}_t' = \log \hat{Y}_t$, $\alpha = \log Y_0$; and $\beta = \log(1 + g)$. Equation 5.6 is a linear relationship whose parameters can be estimated using standard linear regression techniques.

For example, suppose that annual earnings data for the Fitzgerald Company for the past 10 years have been collected and that Equation 5.6 was fitted to the data using least-squares techniques. The annual rate of growth of company earnings was estimated to be 6 percent. If the company's earnings this year ($t = 0$) are \$600,000, then next year's ($t = 1$) forecasted earnings would be

$$\hat{Y}_1 = 600,000(1 + 0.06)^1$$
$$= \$636,000$$

Similarly, forecasted earnings for the year after next ($t = 2$) would be

$$\hat{Y}_2 = 600,000(1 + 0.06)^2$$
$$= \$674,160$$

Declining Rate of Growth Trends   The curve depicted in Figure 5.3, panel (c) is particularly useful for representing sales penetration curves in marketing applications. Using linear regression techniques, one can specify a semilog estimating equation,

$$\log \hat{Y}_t = \beta_1 - \beta_2(1/t)$$

and recover the β_1 and β_2 parameters of this nonlinear diffusion process as a new product spreads across a target population. β_1 and β_2 measure how quickly a new product or new technology or brand extension penetrates and then slowly (ever more slowly) saturates a market.

Seasonal Variations

When *seasonal variations* are introduced into a forecasting model, its short-run predictive power may be improved significantly. Seasonal variations may be estimated in a number of ways.

Ratio-to-Trend Method   One approach is the *ratio to trend method*. This method assumes that the trend value is *multiplied by* the seasonal effect.

Example

Seasonally Adjusted Forecasts: Prizer Creamery (continued)

Recall in the Prizer Creamery example discussed earlier that a linear trend analysis (Equation 5.4) yielded a sales forecast for August 2007 of 37,257 gallons. This estimate can be adjusted for seasonal effects in the following manner. Assume that over a four-year period (2003–2006) the trend model predicted the August sales patterns shown in Table 5.2 and that actual sales are as indicated. These data indicate that, on the average, August sales have been 7.0 percent higher than the trend value. Hence, the August 2007 sales forecast should be seasonally adjusted *upward* by 7.0 percent to 39,865. The seasonally adjusted forecast is shown by the point (□) above the trend line in Figure 5.4. If, however, the model predicted February 2007 ($t = 50$) sales to be 36,529, but similar data indicated February sales to be 10.8 percent below trend on the average, the forecast would be adjusted *downward* to $36,529(1 - 0.108) =$ 32,584 gallons.

(continued)

TABLE 5.2 PRIZER CREAMERY'S AUGUST ICE CREAM SALES			
(AUGUST)	**FORECAST**	**ACTUAL**	**ACTUAL/FORECAST**
2002	31,434	33,600	1.0689
2003	32,890	35,600	1.0824
2004	34,346	36,400	1.0598
2005	35,801	38,200	1.0670
2006	37,257	—	—
			Sum = 4.2781
Adjustment factor = 4.2781/4 = 1.0695 (i.e., 1.07)			

© Cengage Learning

Dummy Variables   Another approach for incorporating seasonal effects into the linear trend analysis model is the use of *dummy variables*. A dummy variable is a variable that normally takes on one of two values—either 0 or 1. Dummy variables, in general, are used to capture the impact of certain qualitative factors in an econometric relationship, such as sex—male-0 and female-1. This method assumes that the seasonal effects are added to the trend value. If a time series consists of quarterly data, then the following model could be used to adjust for seasonal effects:

$$\hat{Y}_t = \alpha + \beta_1 t + \beta_2 D_{1t} + \beta_3 D_{2t} + \beta_4 D_{3t} \qquad [5.7]$$

where $D_{1t} = 1$ for first-quarter observations and 0 otherwise, $D_{2t} = 1$ for second-quarter observations and 0 otherwise, $D_{3t} = 1$ for third-quarter observations and 0 otherwise, and α and β are parameters to be estimated using least-squares techniques. In this model the values of the dummy variables (D_{1t}, D_{2t}, D_{3t}) for observations in the fourth quarter of each year (base period) would be equal to zero. In the estimated model, the value $\beta_2 D_{1t}$ represents the impact of a first-quarter observation (D_1) on values of the forecast, Y_t, relative to the forecast from the omitted class (fourth quarter), when D_{2t} and D_{3t} take values of 0.

The introduction of these trend and seasonality factors into a forecasting model should significantly improve the model's ability to predict short-run turning points in the data series, provided the historical causal factors have not changed significantly.[3]

The models of time-series trend forecasting discussed in this section may have substantial value in many areas of business. However, such models do not seek to relate changes in a data series to the causes underlying observed values in the series. For example, the nation's money supply series has at times proved very useful for forecasting inflationary pressure in the economy. But narrow definitions of the nation's money supply have gradually broadened to include bank-card lines of credit, which may have become a more important measure of household purchasing power. Inflation forecasts based on narrow money supply measures today would yield large errors between the actual and predicted inflation (see Figure 5.5).

---

[3]See more extensive discussion of these issues in F. Diebold, *Elements of Forecasting*, 4th ed. (Cincinnati: South-Western College Publishing, 2007).

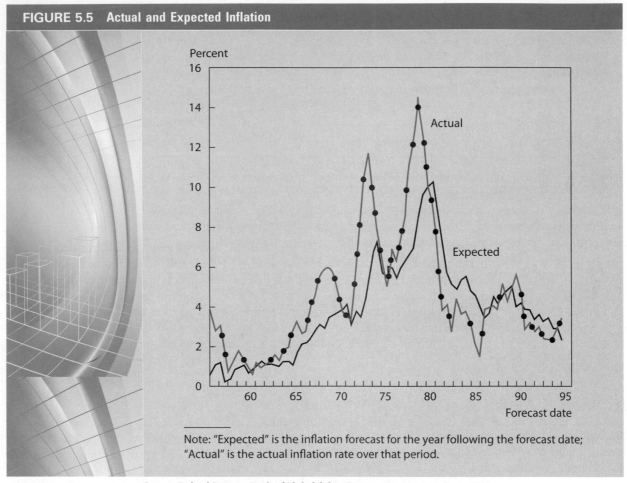

FIGURE 5.5   Actual and Expected Inflation

Note: "Expected" is the inflation forecast for the year following the forecast date; "Actual" is the actual inflation rate over that period.

Source: Federal Reserve Bank of Philadelphia, Business Review, May/June 1996.

SMOOTHING TECHNIQUES

Smoothing techniques are another type of forecasting model, which assumes that a repetitive underlying pattern can be found in the historical values of a variable that is being forecast. By taking an average of past observations, smoothing techniques attempt to eliminate the distortions arising from random variation in the series. As such, smoothing techniques work best when a data series tends to change slowly from one period to the next with few turning points. Housing price forecasts would be a good application for smoothing techniques. Gasoline price forecasts would not. Smoothing techniques are cheap to develop and inexpensive to operate.

Example

Dummy Variables and Seasonal Adjustments: Value-Mart Company

The Value-Mart Company (a small chain of discount department stores) is interested in forecasting quarterly sales for next year (2008) based on Equation 5.7. Using

(continued)

quarterly sales data for the past eight years (2000–2007), the following model was estimated:

$$\hat{Y}_t = 22.5 + 0.25t - 4.5D_{1t} - 3.2D_{2t} - 2.1D_{3t} \qquad [5.8]$$

where $\hat{Y}_t$ = predicted sales ($ million) in quarter t
    22.5 = quarterly sales ($ million) when $t = 0$
        t = time period (quarter) (where the fourth quarter of 1999 = 0;
            first quarter of 2000 = 1, second quarter of 2000 = 2, ...)

The coefficient of t (0.25) indicates that sales may be expected to increase by $0.25 million on the average each quarter. The coefficients of the three dummy variables (−4.5, −3.2, and −2.1) indicate the change (i.e., reduction because the coefficients are negative) in sales in Quarters 1, 2, and 3, respectively, because of seasonal effects. Based on Equation 5.8, Value-Mart's quarterly sales forecasts for 2008 are shown in Table 5.3. On just this basis, Value-Mart would have ordered inventory for what proved to be a disastrous 2008–2009.

TABLE 5.3 VALUE-MART'S QUARTERLY SALES FORECAST (2008)

QUARTER	TIME PERIOD t	DUMMY VARIABLE D_{1t}	D_{2t}	D_{3t}	SALES FORECAST ($ MILLION) $\hat{Y} = 22.5 + 0.25t - 4.5D_{1t} - 3.2D_{2t} - 2.1D_{3t}$
1	33	1	0	0	26.25
2	34	0	1	0	27.80
3	35	0	0	1	29.15
4	36	0	0	0	31.50

© Cengage Learning

Moving Averages

Moving averages are one of the simplest of the smoothing techniques. If a data series possesses a large random factor, a trend analysis forecast like those discussed in the previous section will tend to generate forecasts having large errors from period to period. In an effort to minimize the effects of this randomness, a series of recent observations can be averaged to arrive at a forecast. This is the moving average method. A number of observed values are chosen, their average is computed, and this average serves as a forecast for the next period. In general, a moving average may be defined as

$$\hat{Y}_{t+1} = \frac{Y_t + Y_{t-1} + \cdots + Y_{t-N+1}}{N} \qquad [5.9]$$

where $\hat{Y}_{t+1}$ = forecast value of Y for one period in the future
Y_t, Y_{t-1}, Y_{t-N+1} = observed values of Y in periods $t, t - 1, ..., t - N + 1$, respectively
N = number of observations in the moving average

The greater the number of observations N used in the moving average, the greater the smoothing effect because each new observation receives less weight (1/N) as N increases. Hence, generally, the greater the randomness in the data series and the slower the turning point events in the data, the more preferable it is to use a relatively large number of past observations in developing the forecast. The most appropriate moving average period is the choice of N that minimizes the root mean square error (Equation 5.1).

Moving Average Forecasts: Walker Corporation

The Walker Corporation is examining the use of various smoothing techniques to forecast monthly sales. The company collected sales data for 12 months (2006) as shown in Table 5.4 and Figure 5.6. One technique under consideration is a three-month moving average. Equation 5.9 can be used to generate the forecasts. The forecast for Period 4 is computed by averaging the observed values for Periods 1, 2, and 3.

$$\hat{Y}_4 = \frac{Y_3 + Y_2 + Y_1}{N}$$
$$= \frac{1,925 + 1,400 + 1,950}{3} \qquad [5.10]$$
$$= 1,758$$

Similarly, the forecast for Period 5 is computed as

$$\hat{Y}_5 = \frac{Y_4 + Y_3 + Y_2}{N}$$
$$= \frac{1,960 + 1,925 + 1,400}{3} \qquad [5.11]$$
$$= 1,762$$

TABLE 5.4 WALKER CORPORATION'S THREE-MONTH MOVING AVERAGE SALES FORECAST TABLE

		SALES ($1,000)		ERROR	
t	MONTH	ACTUAL Y_t	FORECAST $\hat{Y}_t$	$(Y_t - \hat{Y}_t)$	$(Y_t - \hat{Y}_t)^2$
1	January 2006	1,950	—	—	—
2	February	1,400	—	—	—
3	March	1,925	—	—	—
4	April	1,960	1,758	202	40,804
5	May	2,800	1,762	1,038	1,077,444
6	June	1,800	2,228	−428	183,184
7	July	1,600	2,187	−587	344,569
8	August	1,450	2,067	−617	380,689
9	September	2,000	1,617	383	146,689
10	October	2,250	1,683	567	321,489
11	November	1,950	1,900	50	2,500
12	December	2,650	2,067	583	339,889
13	January 2007	—	2,283	—	—
					Sum = 2,837,257

© Cengage Learning

$$\text{RMSE} = \sqrt{2,837,257/9} = \$561(000)$$

Note that if one subtracts $\hat{Y}_4$ from $\hat{Y}_5$, the result is the change in the forecast from $\hat{Y}_4$, or

$$\Delta\hat{Y}_4 = \hat{Y}_5 - \hat{Y}_4$$
$$= \frac{Y_4 + Y_3 + Y_2}{N} - \frac{Y_3 + Y_2 + Y_1}{N} \qquad [5.12]$$
$$= \frac{Y_4}{N} - \frac{Y_1}{N}$$

(continued)

Adding this change to $\hat{Y}_4$, the following alternative expression for $\hat{Y}_5$ can be derived:

$$\hat{Y}_5 = \hat{Y}_4 + \frac{Y_4}{N} - \frac{Y_1}{N} \qquad [5.13]$$

or, in general,

$$\hat{Y}_{t+1} = \hat{Y}_t + \frac{Y_t}{N} - \frac{Y_{t-N}}{N} \qquad [5.14]$$

which indicates that each moving average forecast is equal to the past forecast, $\hat{Y}_t$, plus the weighted effect of the most recent observation, Y_t/N, minus the weighted effect of the oldest observation that has been dropped, Y_{t-N}/N. As N becomes larger, the smoothing effect increases because the new observation, Y_t, has a small impact on the moving average.

As shown in Table 5.4, Walker's forecast for January 2007 ($t = 13$) is $2,283 (000). Note also that the root mean square error (RMSE) of the three-month (N) moving average period is $561(000).

First-Order Exponential Smoothing

One criticism of moving averages as smoothing techniques is that they normally give equal weight (a weight of $1/N$) to all observations used in preparing the forecast, even though intuition often indicates that the most recent observation probably contains

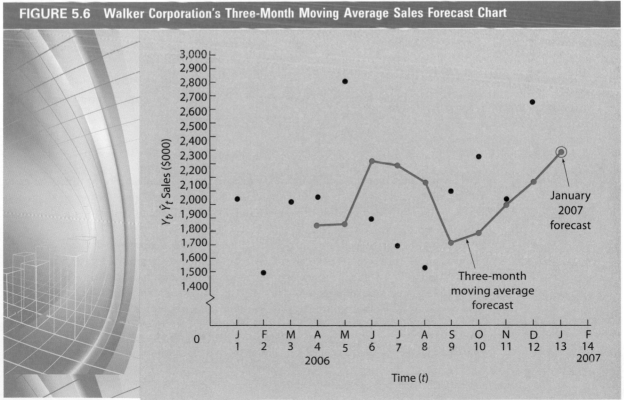

FIGURE 5.6   Walker Corporation's Three-Month Moving Average Sales Forecast Chart

more immediately useful information than more distant observations. Exponential smoothing is designed to overcome this objection.[4]

Consider the following alternative forecasting model:

$$\hat{Y}_{t+1} = wY_t + (1 - w)\hat{Y}_t \qquad [5.15]$$

This model weights the most recent observation by w (some value between 0 and 1 inclusive), and the past forecast by $(1 - w)$. A large w indicates that a heavy weight is being placed on the most recent observation.[5]

Using Equation 5.15, a forecast for $\hat{Y}_t$ may also be written as

$$\hat{Y}_t = wY_{t-1} + (1 - w)(\hat{Y}_{t-1}) \qquad [5.16]$$

By substituting Equation 5.16 into 5.15, we get

$$\hat{Y}_{t+1} = wY_t + w(1 - w)Y_{t-1} + (1 - w)^2\hat{Y}_{t-1} \qquad [5.17]$$

By continuing this process of substitution for past forecasts, we obtain the general equation

$$\hat{Y}_{t+1} = wY_t + w(1 - w)Y_{t-1} + w(1 - w)^2Y_{t-2} + w(1 - w)^3Y_{t-3} + \cdots \qquad [5.18]$$

Equation 5.18 shows that the general formula (Equation 5.15) for an exponentially weighted moving average is a weighted average of all past observations, with the weights defined by the geometric progression:

$$w, (1 - w)w, (1 - w)^2w, (1 - w)^3w, (1 - w)^4w, (1 - w)^5w, \ldots \qquad [5.19]$$

For example, a w of 2/3 would produce the following series of weights:

$$
\begin{aligned}
w &= 0.667 \\
(1 - w)w &= 0.222 \\
(1 - w)^2w &= 0.074 \\
(1 - w)^3w &= 0.024 \\
(1 - w)^4w &= 0.0082 \\
(1 - w)^5w &= 0.0027
\end{aligned}
$$

With a high initial value of w, heavy weight is placed on the most recent observation, and rapidly declining weights are placed on older values.

Another way of writing Equation 5.15 is

$$\hat{Y}_{t+1} = \hat{Y}_t + w(Y_t - \hat{Y}_t) \qquad [5.20]$$

This indicates that the new forecast is equal to the old forecast plus w times the error in the most recent forecast. A w that is close to 1 indicates a quick adjustment process for any error in the preceding forecast. Similarly, a w closer to 0 suggests a slow error correction process.

It should be apparent from Equations 5.15 and 5.20 that exponential forecasting techniques can be very easy to use. All that is required is last period's forecast, last period's observation, plus a value for the weighting factor, w. The optimal weighting factor is normally determined by making successive forecasts using past data with various values of w and choosing the w that minimizes the RMSE given in Equation 5.1.

---

[4]More complex double exponential smoothing models generally give more satisfactory results than first-order exponential smoothing models when the data possess a linear trend over time. See Diebold, *op. cit.*

[5]The greater the amount of serial correlation (correlation of values from period to period), the larger will be the optimal value of w.

Example

Exponential Smoothing: Walker Corporation (continued)

Consider again the Walker Corporation example discussed earlier. Suppose that the company is interested in generating sales forecasts using the first-order exponential smoothing technique. The results are shown in Table 5.5. To illustrate the approach, an exponential weight w of 0.5 will be used. To get the process started, one needs to make an initial forecast of the variable. This forecast might be a weighted average or some simple forecast, such as Equation 5.2:

$$\hat{Y}_{t+1} = Y_t$$

The latter approach will be used. Hence the forecast for Month 2 made in Month 1 would be \$1,950(000) ($\hat{Y}_{t+1} = 1,950$). The Month 3 forecast value is (using Equation 5.20)

$$\hat{Y}_3 = 1,950 + 0.5(1,400 - 1,950)$$
$$= 1,950 - 275 = \$1,675(000)$$

Similarly, the Month 4 forecast equals

$$\hat{Y}_4 = 1,675 + 0.5(1,925 - 1,675)$$
$$= \$1,800(000)$$

The remaining forecasts are calculated in a similar manner.

As can be seen in Table 5.5, Walker's sales forecast for January 2007 using the first-order exponential smoothing technique is \$2,322(000). Also, the root mean square error of this forecasting method (with $w = 0.50$) is \$491(000).

		SALES (\$1,000)		ERROR	
TABLE 5.5	**WALKER CORPORATION: FIRST-ORDER EXPONENTIAL SMOOTHING SALES FORECAST**				
t	MONTH	ACTUAL Y_t	FORECAST $\hat{Y}_t$	$(Y_t - \hat{Y}_t)$	$(Y_t - \hat{Y}_t)^2$
1	January 2006	1,950	—	—	—
2	February	1,400	1,950	−550	302,500
3	March	1,925	1,675	250	62,500
4	April	1,960	1,800	160	25,600
5	May	2,800	1,880	920	846,400
6	June	1,800	2,340	−540	291,600
7	July	1,600	2,070	−470	220,900
8	August	1,450	1,835	−385	148,225
9	September	2,000	1,642	358	128,164
10	October	2,250	1,821	429	184,041
11	November	1,950	2,036	−86	7,396
12	December	2,650	1,993	657	431,649
13	January 2007	—	2,322	—	—
					Sum = 2,648,975

$$\text{RMSE} = \sqrt{2,648,975/11} = \$491(000)$$

BAROMETRIC TECHNIQUES

The time-series forecasting models discussed earlier assume that future patterns in an economic time series may be predicted by projecting a repeat of past patterns, but very few economic time series exhibit consistent enough cyclical variations to make simple projection forecasting reliable. For example, Table 5.6 conveys why the prediction of a business cycle's turning point proves to be so difficult. Although the duration of postwar U.S. business cycles averages 70 months (from peak to peak), three cycles have lasted 100 months or more, while others have been as short as 32 and even 18 months. Economists, however, have long recognized that if it were possible to isolate sets of time series that exhibited a close correlation, and if one or more of these time series normally *led* (in a consistent manner) the time series in which the forecaster had interest, then this leading series could be used as a predictor or barometer.

Although the concept of leading or barometric forecasting is not new,[6] current barometric forecasting is based largely on the work done at the National Bureau of Economic Research (http://www.nber.org). The barometric forecasting model developed there is used primarily to identify potential future changes in *general business conditions*, rather than conditions for a specific industry or firm.

Leading, Lagging, and Coincident Indicators

Economic indicators may be classified as leading, coincident, or lagging indicators, depending on their timing relative to business cycle peaks and troughs (see Figure 5.7).

TABLE 5.6 DURATION OF U.S. BUSINESS CYCLES (IN MONTHS)				
		CONTRACTION*	EXPANSION†	BUSINESS CYCLE‡
October 1945	November 1948	8	37	88	45
October 1949	July 1953	11	45	48	56
May 1954	August 1957	10	39	55	49
April 1958	April 1960	8	24	47	32
February 1961	December 1969	10	106	34	116
November 1970	November 1973	11	36	117	47
March 1975	January 1980	16	58	52	74
July 1980	July 1981	6	12	64	18
November 1982	July 1990	16	92	28	108
March 1991	March 2001	8	120	100	128
November 2001	December 2007	8	73	128	89
July 2009		19		92	
Average postwar cycle		11	59	69	69

[1]*Months from trough to next peak.
†Months from previous peak to trough.
‡Months from previous trough to next trough and months from previous peak to next peak.
Source: "U.S. Business Cycle Expansions and Contractions," National Bureau of Economic Research at www.nber.org.

---

[6]Andrew Carnegie used to count the number of smoke-belching chimneys in Pittsburgh to forecast the level of business activity and consequently the demand for steel.

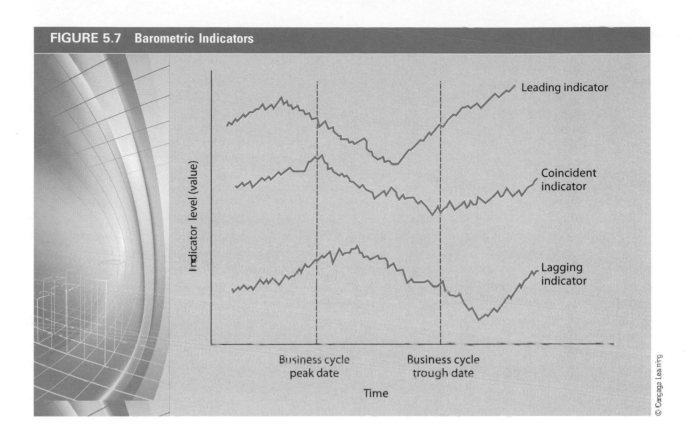

FIGURE 5.7   Barometric Indicators

The Conference Board, a private not-for-profit research institute in New York, has identified 11 series that tend to lead the peaks and troughs of business cycles, 4 series of roughly coincident indicators of economic activity, and 7 series that tend to lag the peaks and troughs of economic activity. The Conference Board calculates for each series and the mean lead or lag of the series in relation to peaks and troughs of economic activity.

The rationale for the use of many of the series listed in this table is obvious. Many of these series represent commitments to future levels of economic activity. Building permits precede housing starts, and orders for durable goods precede their actual production. The value of any one of these indicators depends on the variability in the length of the lead (lag). Leading and lagging indicators predict the *direction* of future change in economic activity; they reveal little or nothing about the *magnitude* of the changes.

SURVEY AND OPINION-POLLING TECHNIQUES

Survey and opinion-polling are other forecasting tools that may be helpful in making short-period forecasts. Business firms normally plan additions to plant and equipment well in advance of the actual expenditures; consumers plan expenditures for autos, vacations, and education in advance of the actual purchase; and governments at all levels prepare budgets in advance of the spending.

The greatest value of survey and opinion-polling techniques is that they may help to uncover if consumer tastes are changing or if business executives begin to lose confidence in the economy; survey techniques may be able to uncover these trends before their impact is felt.

| Example | ## Leading Indicators Change[7] |

The Index of Leading Economic Indicators, which can be accessed at http://www .conference-board.org,[8] is constantly under scrutiny by both private and public fore- casting agencies. When any series appears outdated or begins to generate misleading signals, a replacement can often emerge from a consensus of best practices in business forecasting. Manufacturers' unfilled orders for durables was recently removed from the Index and replaced by the interest rate spread between 10-year Treasury bond yields and 3-month Treasury bill yields.

The interest rate spread is an attempt to capture the effects of monetary policy on the business cycle. A long-bond yield at least 1.21 percent higher than the T-bill yield implies less than a 0.05 probability of recession four quarters ahead. If the Federal Reserve tightens credit, however, such that short-term interest rates rise 0.82 percent above long-term rates, the probability of recession increases to 50 percent and more. At an interest rate spread of 2.40 percent, the probability of recession four quarters ahead rises to 90 percent. This new indicator of credit conditions should effectively supplement the generally poor third predictor, the M2 measure of the nation's money supply.

[7]Based on "Makeup of Leading Indicators May Shift," *Wall Street Journal* (August 11, 1996), p. A2.

[8]The Conference Board is a prominent trade association of major corporations that collects, analyzes, and distributes business cycle data.

Forecasting Macroeconomic Activity

Some of the best-known surveys available from private and governmental sources include the following:

1. *Plant and equipment expenditure plans*—Surveys of business intentions regarding plant and equipment expenditures are conducted by McGraw-Hill, the National Industrial Conference Board, the U.S. Department of Commerce, *Fortune* magazine, the Securities and Exchange Commission, and a number of individual trade associa- tions. The McGraw-Hill survey, for example, is conducted twice yearly and covers all large corporations and many medium-sized firms. The survey reports plans for expenditures on fixed assets, as well as for expenditures on research and develop- ment. More than 50 percent of all new investment is accounted for by the McGraw-Hill survey.

   The Department of Commerce–Bureau of Economic Analysis plant and equip- ment expenditures survey is conducted quarterly and published regularly in the *Sur- vey of Current Business*. The sample is larger and more comprehensive than that used by McGraw-Hill.

   The National Industrial Conference Board surveys capital appropriations commit- ments made by the board of directors of 1,000 manufacturing firms. The survey picks up capital expenditure plans that are to be made sometime in the future and for which funds have been appropriated. It is especially useful to firms that sell heavily to manufacturers and may aid in picking turning points in plant and equipment expenditures. This survey is published in the *Survey of Current Business*. You can access the *Survey of Current Business* on the Internet at http://www.bea. doc.gov.

2. *Plans for inventory changes and sales expectations*—Business executives' expectations about future sales and their intentions about changes in inventory levels are reported in surveys conducted by the U.S. Department of Commerce, McGraw-Hill, Dun & Bradstreet, and the National Association of Purchasing Agents. The National Association of Purchasing Agents survey, for example, is conducted monthly, using a large sample of purchasing executives from a broad range of geographical locations and industrial activities in manufacturing firms.

3. *Consumer expenditure plans*—Consumer intentions to purchase specific products—including household appliances, automobiles, and homes—are reported by the Survey Research Center at the University of Michigan (http://www.isr.umich.edu/src/) and by the Census Bureau. The Census Bureau survey, for example, is aimed at uncovering varying aspects of consumer expenditure plans, including income, holdings of liquid and nonliquid assets, the likelihood of making future durable goods purchases, and consumer indebtedness.

Sales Forecasting

Opinion polling and survey techniques are also used on a micro level within the firm for forecasting sales. Some of the variations of opinion polling that are used include the following:

- *Sales force polling*—Some firms survey their own salespeople in the field about their expectations for future sales by specific geographical area and product line. The idea is that the employees who are closest to the ultimate customers may have significant insights to the state of the future market.
- *Surveys of consumer intentions*—Some firms (especially in durable goods industries) conduct their own surveys of specific consumer purchases. Consider an auto dealer who pursues a "customer for life" relationship with his or her target market. Such a dealer or a furniture company may conduct a mail survey to estimate target households' intentions of purchasing replacement autos or furniture.

ECONOMETRIC MODELS

Another forecasting tool that is available to the managerial economist is econometric modeling. Econometrics is a combination of theory, statistical analysis, and mathematical model building to explain economic relationships. Econometric models may vary in their level of sophistication from the simple to the extremely complex. Econometric techniques for demand estimation were discussed in Chapter 4.

Advantages of Econometric Forecasting Techniques

Forecasting models based on econometric methodology possess a number of significant advantages over time-series trend analysis, barometric models, and survey or opinion poll-based techniques. The most significant advantage is that they identify independent variables (such as price or advertising expenditures in a demand model) that the manager may be able to manipulate.

Another advantage of econometric models is that they predict not only the direction of change in an economic series, but also the magnitude of that change. This represents a substantial improvement over the trend projection models, which failed to identify turning points, and the barometric models, which do not forecast the magnitudes of expected changes.

Single-Equation Models

The simplest form of an econometric model is the single-equation model, as was developed for explaining the demand for Sherwin-Williams house paint in Chapter 4. Once the parameters of the demand equation are estimated, the model can be used to make forecasts of demand for house paint in a given region.

Example

Single-Equation Forecasts: The Demand for Game-Day Attendance in the NFL[9]

Welki and Zlatoper report a model that explains the major determinants of the demand for game-day attendance at National Football League games. A forecasting model such as this might be used by a team to plan the most opportune times for special promotions and to predict demand for items sold at the stadium concession outlets. The following variables were used to estimate the model:

ATTENDANCE	game attendance
PRICE	average ticket price
INCOME	real per capita income
COMPCOST	price of parking at one game
HMTMRECORD	season's winning proportion of the home team prior to game day
VSTMRECORD	season's winning proportion of the visiting team prior to game day
GAME	number of regular season games played by the home team
TEMP	high temperature on game day
RAIN	dummy variable 1 = rain, 0 = no rain
DOME	dummy variable 1 = indoors, 0 = outdoors
DIVRIVAL	dummy variable 1 = teams are in same division, 0 = teams are not in same division
CONRIVAL	dummy variable 1 = conference game, 0 = nonconference game
NONSUNDAY	dummy variable 1 = game day is not Sunday, 0 = game day is Sunday
SUNNIGHT	dummy variable 1 = game moved to Sunday night for coverage on ESPN, 0 otherwise
BLACKOUT	dummy variable = 1 if game is blacked out for local TV, 0 otherwise

INDEPENDENT VARIABLE	EXPECTED SIGN	ESTIMATED COEFFICIENT	*T*-STATISTIC
INTERCEPT	?	98053.00	11.49
PRICE	−	−642.02	−3.08
INCOME	?	−1.14	−3.12
COMPCOST	−	574.94	1.34
HMTMRECORD	+	16535.00	6.38
VSTMRECORD	?	2588.70	1.05
GAME	?	−718.65	−3.64
TEMP	?	−66.17	−1.27
RAIN	−	−2184.40	−1.23
DOME	?	−3171.70	−1.66
DIVRIVAL	+	−1198.00	−0.70
CONRIVAL	?	−1160.00	−0.58
NONSUNDAY	+	4114.80	1.74
SUNNIGHT	+	804.60	0.28
BLACKOUT	−	−5261.00	−3.15

(continued)

These results indicate that weather conditions have little impact on the attendance at games. Fans appear to favor games played outdoors rather than in domed stadiums. Conference and divisional rivalries do not appear to impact demand greatly. Higher prices negatively impact attendance, but demand appears to be inelastic at current price levels. The quality of the team, as measured by its winning percentage, has a significant positive impact on attendance. A model similar to this could be used as the basis for forecasting demand for any type of athletic event.

[9]Based on A.M. Welki and T.J. Zlatoper, "U.S. Professional Football: The Demand for Game-Day Attendance in 1991," *Managerial and Decision Economics* (September–October 1994), pp. 489–495.

Multi-Equation Models

Although in many cases single-equation models may accurately specify the relationship that is being examined, frequently the interrelationships may be so complex that a system of several equations becomes necessary. This can be illustrated by examining a simple model of the national economy:

$$C = \alpha_1 + \beta_1 Y + \varepsilon_1 \qquad [5.21]$$

$$I = \alpha_2 + \beta_2 P_{t-1} + \varepsilon_2 \qquad [5.22]$$

$$T = \beta_3 GDP + \varepsilon_3 \qquad [5.23]$$

$$GDP = C + I + G \qquad [5.24]$$

$$Y = GDP - T \qquad [5.25]$$

where C = consumption expenditures
I = Investment
P_{t-1} = profits; lagged one period
GDP = gross domestic product
T = Taxes
Y = national income
G = government expenditures

Equations 5.21, 5.22, and 5.23 are behavioral or structural equations, whereas Equations 5.24 and 5.25 are identities or definitional equations. Once parameters of a system of equations have been estimated,[10] forecasts may be generated by substituting known or estimated values for the independent variables into the system and solving for a forecast.

Complex Models of the U.S. Economy   A number of complex multiple-equation econometric models of the U.S. economy have been developed and are used to forecast business activity. Information on three of these models and the forecasting techniques they employ is summarized in Table 5.7. As can be seen, some of the large econometric models still rely heavily on the judgment of their staffs of economists.

[10]See Gujarati, *op. cit.*

TABLE 5.7	CHARACTERISTICS OF THREE ECONOMETRIC MODELS OF THE U.S. ECONOMY		
	MODEL		
CHARACTERISTIC	WHARTON ECONOMETRIC FORECASTING ASSOCIATES	CHASE ECONOMETRIC ASSOCIATES	TOWNSEND-GREENSPAN
Approximate number of variables forecasted	10,000	700	800
Forecast horizon (quarters)	2	10–12	6–10
Frequency of model updates (times per year)	12	12	4
Date model forecast first regularly issued	1963	1970	1965
Forecasting techniques			
(a) Econometric model	60%	70%	45%
(b) Judgment	30%	20%	45%
(c) Time-series methods	—	5%	—
(d) Current data analysis	10%	5%	10%

Source: S.K. McNees, "The Record of Thirteen Forecasters," *New England Economic Review* (September–October 1981), pp. 5–21; and A. Bauer et al., "Transparency, Expectations, and Forecasts," *Federal Reserve Bank St. Louis Review* (September–October 2003), pp. 1–25.

Consensus Forecasts: Livingston and Blue Chip Forecaster Surveys

The Federal Reserve Bank of Philadelphia (Livingston surveys) and Blue Chip Economic Indicators in Aspen, Colorado, conduct semiannual surveys of leading U.S. economists regarding their forecasts of unemployment, inflation, stock prices, and economic growth. The 50 to 60 economists who are regularly surveyed represent a cross section from large corporations and banks, labor unions, government, investment banking firms, and universities. The Livingston and Blue Chip Forecaster surveys have been used by federal and state budget offices and many corporations to gauge the expectation of businesses regarding future economic growth and inflation.

As a broad-based consensus forecast, the Livingston and Blue Chip survey data tend to be more stable over time than any individual forecast. Referring again to Figure 5.5, there is evidence that economists have tended to underestimate both increases and decreases in the inflation rate.[11] Figure 5.8 indicates the record of the Livingston and Blue Chip forecasts in predicting major expansions and recessions. As can be seen, economists have tended to predict well the relatively moderate recessions and expansions but have not predicted sharp short recessions like those that occurred in 1974–1975, 2001, and the severe recession in 2008–2009.[12]

---

[11]Based on H. Taylor, "The Livingston Surveys: A History of Hopes and Fears," *Business Review*, Federal Reserve Bank of Philadelphia (May–June 1996), pp. 15–25.

[12]Based on K. Kliesen, "The 2001 Recession," *Federal Reserve Bank St. Louis Review* (September–October 2007), pp. 45–67.

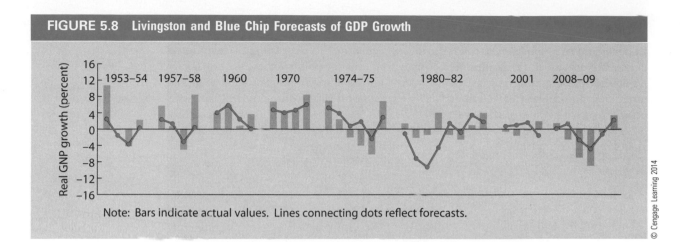

FIGURE 5.8 Livingston and Blue Chip Forecasts of GDP Growth

Note: Bars indicate actual values. Lines connecting dots reflect forecasts.

STOCHASTIC TIME-SERIES ANALYSIS

Finally, consider two forecasting approaches that capitalize on the interdependencies in business data: stochastic time-series analysis and input-output analysis. Deterministic trend analysis, discussed earlier, was concerned with extrapolating deterministic past trends in the data (e.g., seasonal effects and population growth time trends). In contrast, stochastic time-series analysis attempts to remove deterministic time trends and instead model, estimate, and hopefully replicate the stochastic process generating any remaining patterns in the data across successive time periods—that is, any remaining autocorrelation patterns. Autocorrelation was discussed in Appendix 4A.

Consider a simple autoregressive first-order process with positive drift α,

$$y_t = \alpha + \beta y_{t-1} + \varepsilon_t \qquad \overset{iid}{\varepsilon} \sim N(0, \sigma_\varepsilon^2) \qquad [5.26]$$

where $\beta = 1$ by hypothesis and where ε_t is a pure white noise disturbance drawn independently each period from a zero-mean, constant-variance normal probability distribution (an iid, independent and identically distributed, disturbance). As illustrated in Figure 5.9 Panel (a), when α equals zero, such a series has no tendency to revert to any particular value (no "mean reversion"). In contrast, such series wander, and are inherently not forecastable, and therefore the last realization of y_t is the best prediction of the next realization of the series. Similarly, when α is non-zero, the level of y_t has no tendency to mean revert to any particular trend line; each innovation can result in a new trend line as illustrated in Figure 5.9 Panel (b). This is the famous "random walk" model applicable to the level of stock prices. Under the efficient markets hypothesis, a stock price like y_t in Equation 5.26 is "fully informative" in the sense that it incorporates all publicly available information that could possibly be useful in forecasting next period's stock price. For business forecasters, the difficulty is that commodity prices, exchange rates, interest rates, and possibly other macroeconomic variables like real GDP and the overall price index may also exhibit these random walk properties.

Random walk variables pose several problems if one tries to make a forecast based on ordinary least-squares (OLS) regression analysis. For one thing, two random walk variables with positive (negative) drift will almost certainly exhibit spurious correlation. Because each series is trending upward (downward) and not reverting to its mean, an OLS estimation on two variables generated by the process in Equation 5.26 will indicate a significant positive relationship between the variables when no causal link between the

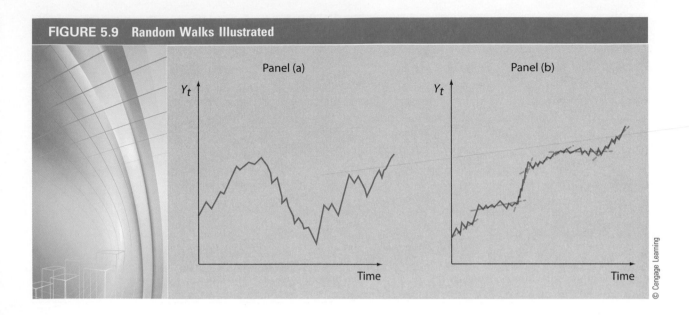

FIGURE 5.9 Random Walks Illustrated

Panel (a)

Y_t

Time

Panel (b)

Y_t

Time

© Cengage Learning

two exists. For example, even though real GDP and the overall price index of the economy (the GDP price deflator) have random shocks that may be totally unrelated, and even though real growth and inflation may have unrelated structural determinants (e.g., population growth versus monetary expansions), the *t*-score in a simple OLS regression of real GDP on the price index can easily be as high as 12.0 (i.e., 99 percent confidence in a positive relationship). This can be very misleading to the forecaster seeking leading indicators for use in a business plan; imagine selling your firm's senior officers on the idea that because inflation is up, the firm can expect substantial real growth in demand next period. You might well be sent on an extended unpaid leave or even fired.

Of course, not all business time series exhibit these random walk properties. For example, a firm's profitability and earnings *do* mean revert in response to competitive entry and exit whenever they move substantially above or below the risk-adjusted mean for the industry, and therefore profits and earnings are not a random walk.[13] Hence, it is crucial to know whether the data one is working with are, or are not, generated by a random walk process.

The second problem posed by random walks is that the level of y_T after a number of periods T is

$$y_T = y_0 + \sum_{i=0}^{T}(\alpha + \varepsilon_{T-i}) \qquad [5.27]$$

$$= y_0 + T\alpha + \Sigma\varepsilon_t \qquad [5.28]$$

the cumulative sum of the drift parameter plus all the white noise errors up to period T. Another way of describing this phenomenon is to say that all innovations to random walk variables result in *permanent* effects; the shocks just continue to cumulate and don't wash out as the time series lengthens. Therefore, "trends" in business data have two meanings. Some trends are deterministic like the upward and downward sales trends for bathing suits in the spring and summer versus the fall and winter buying seasons. Other trends, however, are stochastic; stochastic trends are the permanent effects of

---

[13]See E. Fama and K. French, "Forecasting Profitability and Earnings," *Journal of Business* (April 2000), pp. 164–175.

innovations in a random walk process like Equation 5.28 Since these $\Sigma\varepsilon_t$ do not cancel out, it is appropriate to think of them as trends too. The problem is that the variance of y_t as the time series lengthens is equal to $T\sigma_\varepsilon^2$—that is, the variance of the stock price or interest rate has no limit! This makes it quite difficult to reduce RMSE with the forecasting techniques we have seen so far. For example, even long lag structures in OLS regression models of stock price changes often have R^2 as low as 0.02 to 0.05 and very large RMSEs. Again, such series have enormous variance as T grows.

Although many advanced techniques beyond the scope of this text are motivated by the random walk stochastic process,[14] two simple methods we have already introduced at least partially address both of the previous complications. First, all random walk-like processes have very long, slowly decaying autocorrelation functions. The first-order autoregressive AR(1) random walk process with drift α in Equation 5.26 is said to be *integrated of order one*—written I(1)—because the coefficient on the first autoregressive lag is by hypothesis $\beta - 1$. Indeed, this particular first-order autocorrelation function never decays. Consequently, the Durbin-Watson statistic introduced in Equation 4A.1 and Figure 4A.1 can be used to detect the presence of severe autocorrelation in such variables. The Durbin-Watson statistic will definitely fall well below 2.0 for data generated by Equation 5.26—that is, below d_L for positively autocorrelated series and above $(4\text{-}d_L)$ for negatively autocorrelated series generated by a process like Equation 5.26 with $\beta = -1$. So, one can use the Durbin-Watson statistic as a diagnostic instrument to detect the possibility of a non-mean-reverting, random walk process.

Moreover, the I(1) property of an AR(1) random walk implies that taking the first difference of the price or interest rate series in Equation 5.26,

$$\Delta y_t = \alpha + (\beta - 1)y_{t-1} + \varepsilon_t \qquad [5.29]$$

would leave us with a process that did mean revert—that is, a process that reverted to the drift parameter α—if in fact $\beta = 1$. It is straightforward to estimate the first difference of the time series in Equation 5.29 or, more generally, to estimate a vector autoregression in first differences,

$$\Delta y_t = \alpha + (\beta - 1)y_{t-1} + \sum_{t=1}^{\infty} \Delta y_{t-1} + \varepsilon_t \qquad [5.30]$$

cointegrated Stochastic series with a common order of integration and exhibiting an equilibrium relationship such that they do not permanently wander away from one another.

and test whether the null hypothesis $\beta = 1$ is true or false.[15] If true, any series with these properties should be differenced and incorporated into the forecasting regressions as first differences, not as levels.[16]

If the situation as described in Equations 5.27, 5.28, and 5.29 pertains to both the dependent and an explanatory variable, the entire forecasting model should be specified in first differences. In that case, these two series are said to be **cointegrated** and will exhibit a nonspurious co-movement with one another, the presence of which could prove quite important to achieving the standard forecasting objective of low RMSE.

---

[14]One useful introduction to additional techniques in stochastic time-series analysis is F. Diebold, *Elements of Forecasting*, op cit. For a more advanced treatment, consult W. Enders, *Applied Econometric Time-Series*, 3rd ed (New York: John Wiley and Sons, 2009).

[15]These tests can be performed with the t-statistic on the $(\beta - 1)$ parameter on y_{t-1} but require using a modified set of Dickey-Fuller critical values. See Appendix B, Table 7.

[16]If $\beta = 1$ is rejected, each series in question should be differenced again, and the second differences tested in exactly the same fashion. If in that case $\beta = 1$, second differences would be incorporated rather than first differences. If neither first nor second differences indicate an I(1) or I(2) series, the forecaster proceeds using the levels of the original data.

FORECASTING WITH INPUT-OUTPUT TABLES

Another forecasting approach that capitalizes on the cross-sectional interdependence between various intermediate product and final product industries is *input-output analysis*. Input-output analysis enables the forecaster to trace the effects of an increase in demand for one product to other industries. An increase in the demand for automobiles will first lead to an increase in the output of the auto industry. This in turn will lead to an increase in the demand for steel, glass, plastics, tires, and upholstery fabric. In addition, secondary impacts will occur as the increase in the demand for upholstery fabric, for example, requires an increase in the production of fibers used to make the fabric. The demand for machinery may also increase as a result of the fabric demand, and so the pattern continues. Input-output analysis permits the forecaster to trace through all these inter-industry effects that occur as a result of the initial increase in the demand for automobiles. The Bureau of Economic Analysis of the U.S. Department of Commerce produces a complicated set of tables specifying the interdependence among the various industries in the economy.[17]

INTERNATIONAL PERSPECTIVES

Long-Term Sales Forecasting by General Motors in Overseas Markets

General Motors has an extensive forecasting system for both its North American and its overseas operations that is implemented by the Corporate Product Planning and Economics Staff. The process generates short- and long-term forecasts of the U.S. vehicle market and long-term forecasts for overseas markets. A discussion of the overseas forecasting process follows.

General Motors produces forecasts for motor vehicle sales in nearly 60 countries. These countries vary in the number of cars per 1,000 people (car density), from less than 10 to over 500. The primary factor used to explain the growth in car density is the level of and changes in income in each country. In the first step of the forecasting process, the macroeconomic relationship between key economic variables, including income levels and motor vehicle sales, is estimated. Specifically, estimates are made of the income elasticity of demand in each country. The second step attempts to monitor changes over time in the relationships established in Step 1.

The third step consists of consultations between the Product Planning and Economics Staff and the Marketing Staff of each GM overseas operation. The objective of this phase is to identify any special fac-

tors in each country that might require a significant modification in the forecasts generated from the econometric models. For example, in the early and mid-1980s, it was felt that certain voluntary restraint policies that had been adopted by the Japanese government would hold down demand by up to 50 percent, relative to the forecasts from the econometric model. When these policy barriers were removed, Japanese car sales skyrocketed up to levels predicted by the econometric model. More recently, the entry of China into the World Trade Organization has caused a shift upward in the future projected net exports (exports minus imports) of cars to China.

The final step provides models of alternative future scenarios that reflect the impact of major changes in the economic environment for which full information is unavailable. For example, GM developed a scenario plan for the opening of the Chinese market where the Buick is a very successful luxury brand. As predicted, by 2011 GM sales in the fast-growing market of China exceeded GM sales in the U.S. To derive cash flow forecasts from foreign sales, GM must model (and manage) its exchange rate risk exposure, which is discussed in chapter 6 on managing exports.

---

[17]The most recent input-output tables may be found for 16 industry groups and 432 detailed industries in "Input-Output Tables" on the U.S. Bureau of Economic Analysis Web site at www.bea.gov.

SUMMARY

- A forecast is a prediction concerning the future value of some economic time series.
- The choice of a forecasting technique depends on the cost of developing the forecasting model, the complexity of the relationship being forecast, the time period for the forecast, the accuracy required of the model, and the lead time required to make decisions based on the forecasting model.
- Data used in forecasting may be in the form of a time series—that is, a series of observations of a variable over a number of past time periods— or they may be cross-sectional— that is, observations are taken at a single point in time for a sample of individuals, firms, geographic regions, communities, or some other set of observable units.
- Deterministic trend-forecasting models are based on an extrapolation of past values into the future. Time-series forecasting models may be adjusted for seasonal, secular, and cyclical trends in the data. Stochastic time-series forecasting models investigate the randomness-generating process in the underlying data.
- When a data series possesses a great deal of randomness, *smoothing techniques*, such as moving averages and exponential smoothing, may improve the forecast accuracy.

- Neither trend analysis models nor smoothing techniques are capable of identifying major future changes in the direction of an economic data series.
- *Barometric techniques*, which employ leading, lagging, and coincident indicators, are designed to forecast changes in the direction of a data series but are poorly suited for forecasting the magnitude of the change.
- *Survey and opinion-polling techniques* are often useful in forecasting such variables as business capital spending and major consumer expenditure plans and for generating product-specific or regional sales forecasts for a firm.
- *Econometric methods* seek to explain the reasons for a change in an economic data series and to use this quantitative, explanatory model to make future forecasts. Econometric models are one of the most useful business forecasting tools, but they tend to be expensive to develop and maintain. Their net benefit hinges on their success in reducing root mean forecast error in out-of-sample forecasting environments.
- Trends in business data are either deterministic or stochastic. Stochastic trends introduced by random walk variables like stock prices require careful diagnosis and special methods.

Exercises

Answers to the exercises in blue can be found in Appendix D at the back of the book.

1. The forecasting staff for the Prizer Corporation has developed a model to predict sales of its air-cushioned-ride snowmobiles. The model specifies that sales S vary jointly with disposable personal income Y and the population between ages 15 and 40, Z, and *inversely* with the price of the snowmobiles P. Based on past data, the best estimate of this relationship is

$$S = k\frac{YZ}{P}$$

   where k has been estimated (with past data) to equal 100.
   a. If $Y = \$11,000$, $Z = \$1,200$, and $P = \$20,000$, what value would you predict for S?
   b. What happens if P is reduced to $\$17,500$?
   c. How would you go about developing a value for k?
   d. What are the potential weaknesses of this model?
2. a. Fred's Hardware and Hobby House expects its sales to increase at a constant rate of 8 percent per year over the next three years. Current sales are $\$100,000$. Forecast sales for each of the next three years.
   b. If sales in 2003 were $\$60,000$ and they grew to $\$100,000$ by 2007 (a four-year period), what was the actual annual compound growth rate?

c. What are some of the hazards of employing a constant rate of growth forecasting model?

3. Metropolitan Hospital has estimated its average monthly bed needs as

$$N = 1,000 + 9X$$

where X = time period (months); January 2002 = 0
  N = monthly bed needs

Assume that no new hospital additions are expected in the area in the foreseeable future. The following monthly seasonal adjustment factors have been estimated, using data from the past five years:

MONTH	ADJUSTMENT FACTOR (%)
January	+5
April	−15
July	+4
November	−5
December	−25

a. Forecast Metropolitan's bed demand for January, April, July, November, and December 2007.
b. If the following actual and forecast values for June bed demands have been recorded, what seasonal adjustment factor would you recommend be used in making future June forecasts?

YEAR	FORECAST	ACTUAL
2007	1,045	1,096
2006	937	993
2005	829	897
2004	721	751
2003	613	628
2002	505	560

4. Stowe Automotive is considering an offer from Indula to build a plant making automotive parts for use in that country. In preparation for a final decision, Stowe's economists have been hard at work constructing a basic econometric model for Indula to aid the company in predicting future levels of economic activity. Because of the cyclical nature of the automotive parts industry, forecasts of future economic activity are quite important in Stowe's decision process.

Corporate profits (P_{t-1}) for all firms in Indula were about $100 billion. *GDP* for the nation is composed of consumption C, investment I, and government spending G. It is anticipated that Indula's federal, state, and local governments will spend in the range of $200 billion next year. On the basis of an analysis of recent economic activity in Indula, consumption expenditures are assumed to be $100 billion plus 80 percent of national income. National income is equal to *GDP* minus taxes T. Taxes are estimated to be at a rate of about 30 percent of *GDP*. Finally, corporate investments have historically equaled $30 billion plus 90 percent of last year's corporate profits (P_{t-1}).

a. Construct a five-equation econometric model of the state of Indula. There will be a consumption equation, an investment equation, a tax receipt equation, an equation representing the *GDP* identity, and a national income equation.

b. Assuming that all random disturbances average to zero, solve the system of equations to arrive at next year's forecast values for *C*, *I*, *T*, *GDP*, and *Y*. (*Hint*: It is easiest to start by solving the investment equation and then working through the appropriate substitutions in the other equations.)

5. A firm experienced the demand shown in the following table.

YEAR	ACTUAL DEMAND	5-YEAR MOVING AVERAGE	3-YEAR MOVING AVERAGE	EXPONENTIAL SMOOTHING ($W = 0.9$)	EXPONENTIAL SMOOTHING ($W = 0.3$)
2000	800	xxxxx	xxxxx	xxxxx	xxxxx
2001	925	xxxxx	xxxxx	—	—
2002	900	xxxxx	xxxxx	—	—
2003	1025	xxxxx	—	—	—
2004	1150	xxxxx	—	—	—
2005	1160	—	—	—	—
2006	1200	—	—	—	—
2007	1150	—	—	—	—
2008	1270	—	—	—	—
2009	1290	—	—	—	—
2010	*	—	—	—	—

*Unknown future value to be forecast.

a. Fill in the table by preparing forecasts based on a five-year moving average, a three-year moving average, and exponential smoothing (with a $w = 0.9$ and a $w = 0.3$). *Note*: The exponential smoothing forecasts may be begun by assuming $\hat{Y}_{t+1} = Y_t$.

b. Using the forecasts from 2005 through 2009, compare the accuracy of each of the forecasting methods based on the RMSE criterion.

c. Which forecast would you have used for 2010? Why?

6. The economic analysis division of Mapco Enterprises has estimated the demand function for its line of weed trimmers as

$$Q_D = 18,000 + 0.4N - 350P_M + 90P_s$$

where N = number of new homes completed in the primary market area

$\quad P_M$ = price of the Mapco trimmer

$\quad P_S$ = price of its competitor's Surefire trimmer

In 2010, 15,000 new homes are expected to be completed in the primary market area. Mapco plans to charge $50 for its trimmer. The Surefire trimmer is expected to sell for $55.

a. What sales are forecasted for 2010 under these conditions?

b. If its competitor cuts the price of the Surefire trimmer to $50, what effect will this have on Mapco's sales?

c. What effect would a 30 percent reduction in the number of new homes completed have on Mapco's sales (ignore the impact of the price cut of the Surefire trimmer)?

7. The Questor Corporation has experienced the following sales pattern over a 10-year period:

YEAR	SALES ($000)
2004	121
2005	130
2006	145
2007	160
2008	155
2009	179
2010	215
2011	208
2012	235
2013	262
2014	*

*Unknown future value to be forecast.

a. Compute the equation of a trend line (similar to Equation 5.4) for these sales data to forecast sales for the next year. (Let 2004 = 0, 2005 = 1, etc., for the time variable.) What does this equation forecast for sales in the year 2014?
b. Use a first-order exponential smoothing model with a w of 0.9 to forecast sales for the year 2014.

8. Bell Greenhouses has estimated its monthly demand for potting soil to be the following:

$$N = 400 + 4X$$

where N = monthly demand for bags of potting soil
X = time periods in months (March 2006 = 0)

Assume this trend factor is expected to remain stable in the foreseeable future. The following table contains the monthly seasonal adjustment factors, which have been estimated using actual sales data from the past five years:

MONTH	ADJUSTMENT FACTOR (%)
March	+2
June	+15
August	+10
December	−12

a. Forecast Bell Greenhouses' demand for potting soil in March, June, August, and December 2007.
b. If the following table shows the forecasted and actual potting soil sales by Bell Greenhouses for April in five different years, determine the seasonal adjustment factor to be used in making an April 2008 forecast.

YEAR	FORECAST	ACTUAL
2007	500	515
2006	452	438
2005	404	420
2004	356	380
2003	308	320

9. Savings-Mart (a chain of discount department stores) sells patio and lawn furniture. Sales are seasonal, with higher sales during the spring and summer quarters and lower sales during the fall and winter quarters. The company developed the following quarterly sales forecasting model:

$$\hat{Y}_t = 8.25 + 0.125t - 2.75D_{1t} + 0.25D_{2t} + 3.50D_{3t}$$

where $\hat{Y}_t$ = predicted sales ($million) in quarter t
   8.25 = quarterly sales ($million) when $t = 0$
   t = time period (quarter) where the fourth quarter of 2002 = 0,
       first quarter of 2003 = 1, second quarter of 2003 = 2, ...

$$D_{1t} = \begin{cases} 1 \text{ for first-quarter observations} \\ 0 \text{ otherwise} \end{cases}$$

$$D_{2t} = \begin{cases} 1 \text{ for second-quarter observations} \\ 0 \text{ otherwise} \end{cases}$$

$$D_{3t} = \begin{cases} 1 \text{ for third-quarter observations} \\ 0 \text{ otherwise} \end{cases}$$

Forecast Savings-Mart's sales of patio and lawn furniture for each quarter of 2010.

10. Use the monthly series on the Consumer Price Index (all items) from the previous two years to produce a forecast of the CPI for each of the next three years. Is the precision of your forecast greater or less at 36 months ahead than at 12 months ahead? Why? Compare your answer to that of Moody's online U.S. Macro Model at http://www.economy.com/.

Case Exercises

Cruise Ship Arrivals in Alaska

The summer months bring warm weather, mega fauna (bears), and tourists to the coastal towns of Alaska. Skagway at the top of the Inland Passage was, in the nineteenth century, the entrance to the Yukon. Today this town attracts multiple cruise ships per day; literally thousands of passengers disembark into a town of 800 for a taste of the Alaskan frontier experience between 10 A.M. and 5 P.M. Some ride steam trains into the mountains while others wander the town spending money in galleries, restaurants, and souvenir shops. The Skagway Chamber of Commerce is trying to decide which transportation mode in the table of visitor arrival statistics should receive the highest priority in the tourist promotions for next season.

Questions

1. Plot the raw data on arrivals for each transportation mode against time, all on the same graph. Which mode is growing the fastest? Which the slowest?

2. Plot the logarithm of arrivals for each transportation mode against time, all on the same graph. Which now appears to be growing the fastest?

3. Logarithms are especially useful for comparing series with two divergent scales since 10 percent growth always looks the same, regardless of the starting level. When absolute levels matter, the raw data are more appropriate, but when growth rates are what's important, log scales are better.

4. Now create an index number to represent the growth of arrivals in each transportation mode by dividing the first (smallest) number in each column into the remaining numbers in the column. Plot these index numbers for each transportation mode against time, all in the same graph. Which is growing the fastest?

5. In attempting to formulate a model of the passenger arrival data on cruise ships over time, would a nonlinear (perhaps a multiplicative exponential) model be preferable to a linear model of cruise ship arrivals against time? What about in the case of the passenger arrivals by ferry against time?

6. Estimate the double-log (log linear) time trend model for log cruise ship arrivals against log time. Estimate a linear time trend model of cruise ship arrivals against time. Calculate the root mean square error between the predicted and actual value of cruise ship arrivals. Is the root mean square error greater for the double log time trend model or for the linear time trend model?

Skagway Visitor Arrival Statistics

YEAR	CRUISE	FERRY	HIGHWAY	AIR
1983	48,066	25,288	72,384	3,500
1984	54,907	25,196	79,215	3,750
1985	77,623	31,522	89,542	4,000
1986	100,695	30,981	91,908	4,250
1987	119,279	30,905	70,993	4,953
1988	115,505	31,481	74,614	5,957
1989	112,692	29,997	63,789	7,233
1990	136,512	33,234	63,237	4,799
1991	141,284	33,630	64,610	4,853
1992	145,973	37,216	79,946	7,947
1993	192,549	33,650	80,709	10,092
1994	204,387	34,270	81,172	10,000
1995	256,788	33,961	87,977	17,000
1996	299,651	35,760	86,536	20,721
1997	438,305	27,659	91,849	11,466
1998	494,961	31,324	100,784	20,679
1999	525,507	31,467	92,291	15,963

Data are available as an Excel file on the book's Web site.

Source: *The Skagway News*, November 16, 1999.

Lumber Price Forecast

Questions

1. One of the most important variables that must be forecasted accurately to project the cost of single-family home construction is the price of Southern pine framing

lumber. Use the following data to forecast two- and four-year-ahead lumber prices. Compare the forecast accuracy of at least two alternative forecasting methods.

Lumber Price Index

2012	244.5	1985	100.0
2011	200.6	1984	101.3
2010	190.0	1983	101.2
2009	177.1	1982	93.8
2008	196.8	1981	96.4
2007	205.1	1980	95.2
2006	192.5	1979	99.0
2005	173.2	1978	90.9
2004	160.0	1977	77.9
2003	137.1	1976	67.7
2002	134.5	1975	58.3
2001	140.2	1974	60.5
2000	146.4	1973	58.3
1999	176.3	1972	47.6
1998	168.4	1971	41.9
1997	182.7	1970	37.4
1996	168.7	1969	41.3
1995	162.7	1968	37.3
1994	168.9	1967	32.9
1993	163.2	1966	33.0
1992	137.5	1965	31.6
1991	123.9	1964	31.4
1990	121.7		
1989	118.9		
1988	111.5		
1987	105.8		
1986	100.7		

Data are available as an Excel file on the book's Web site.
Source: *Forest Product Market Prices and Statistics, Annual Yearbooks* (Random Length Productions), various issues.

Forecasting in the Global Financial Crisis

The causes and consequences of the global financial crisis (GFC) are numerous and remain hotly debated.[18] One catalyst was clearly the collapse of the U.S. housing market in 2007–2008. The Federal Reserve played a role by overstimulating the economy during 2004–2007 when the housing asset bubble was forming. Later the Fed tightened credit conditions throughout late 2007 and early 2008 even though the Banker's Roundtable reported that loan demand had "fallen off a cliff." Congress played a role in writing

---

[18]See "Getting Up to Speed on the Financial Crisis," *Journal of Economic Literature*, 50, no. 1 (2012), pp. 128–150.

legislation that encouraged home ownership by those with no real prospect of repaying a mortgage loan. Subprime mortgage loans were even granted to borrowers with no income, no job, and no assets (so-called NINJA loans). Middle-income borrowers played a role by seeking mortgages for much larger houses than they could afford. Mortgage brokers earned fat commissions facilitating these transactions which bankers approved, while bank regulators looked the other way.

In the end, the GFC was a massive failure of the capital markets that triggered what has been called the Great Contraction. U.S. GDP fell at magnitudes unseen since the –20 percent of the Great Depression of 1929–1932. In the last quarter of George W. Bush's presidency (2008Q4), real GDP fell by an astonishing –9 percent. Business confidence and private investment collapsed in 2007–2009 by –37 percent, whilst consumption declined by –2 percent. Cumulatively, four years of potential output growth approaching $1.7 trillion were lost, such that real GDP in the U.S. returned in 2011Q4 to $13.3 trillion for the first time since 2007Q4. What caused this cataclysmic event? Was a lack of corporate governance or a failure of business integrity to blame?

In one sense, fraudulent conveyance underlies the global financial crisis. Mortgage-backed securities that combined prime and subprime mortgages (with subprime containing too little down payment and too much default risk) were packaged and sold as highly rated A-level debt securities. Even worse, the debt buyers then stripped out the bottom tranches, repackaged these riskiest mortgage loans, and sold them worldwide also as A-rated securities. Some would argue this constitutes a fraudulent conveyance, but at a minimum, such transactions violate market integrity, for which senior executives in the banks and brokerage houses were ultimately responsible.

Market integrity is always defined relative to the expectations for fair and orderly markets of the market participants. In equity markets, for example, Aitken and Harris (2011) argue market participants expect regulators to prohibit market manipulation, insider trading, and front running conflicts of interest by broker-dealers serving as both principal and agent.[19] In debt markets, however, partial disclosure, rampant conflicts of interest, and some intentional manipulation and misrepresentation are expected by the market participants. Insiders regularly get on the phones and disclose unaudited financial information that is not publicly available in order to sharpen their bargaining position over a negotiated bond price. But these negotiations about the "haircut" warranted by the bond's perceived risks take place between sophisticated professionals with powerful reputation effects in repeat purchase bilateral agreements.

The contrast between stock and bond markets could hardly be greater. In stock markets, retail buyers and sellers with access to no more nor any less publicly disclosed information meet anonymous sophisticated traders in highly regulated exchange transactions. These on-exchange trades are backed by settlement clearinghouses to mitigate the counterparty risk. Posted prices are available for immediate execution by broker–agents whose duties avoid egregious conflicts of interest. And the trading prices are informationally efficient in part because the dislocations of price attributable to market manipulation are surveilled, detected, and often prevented. So, what is fair and efficient in the equity markets reflect the higher integrity expectations of equity market participants.

But just the opposite permeates the bond markets, and that is where the subprime mortgage problem arose. Highly experienced buyers of mortgage-backed securities knew that sellers were packaging mixed tranche securities with higher default rates than their A-minus ratings should convey. Normally less than 1 percent of prime mortgage

---

[19]M. Aitken and F.H.deB. Harris, "Evidence-Based Policy-Making for Financial Markets," *Journal of Trading* 6, no. 3 (Summer 2011), pp. 22–31 and F. Harris, "Panel Discussion of a Proposed Framework for Assessing Market Quality," 6, no. 3 (Summer 2011), pp. 69–89.

borrowers default on their payments. Normally, subprime mortgage loans default in only 4 percent of all cases.

As housing prices declined 27 percent nationwide in 2007–2009 and the typical house became worth only 73 percent of its 2007 purchase price, these default percentages became 3.5 percent for prime mortgages and 13 percent for subprime mortgages. It was cheaper to walk away from a house worth less than its 80 percent mortgage, allowing the bank to foreclose, rather than to continue to make payments and hope the housing market would improve.

More foreclosures led to more distress sales, and more distress sales caused some states such as California and Florida and some municipalities such as Phoenix and Las Vegas to suffer –45 percent housing price declines. Consequently, as the GFC deepened, and the default rates worsened, everyone involved in mortgage-backed securities knew to apply deeper haircuts to the mixed tranche securities being fraudulently conveyed. The 7 percent haircut on mortgage-backed securities in November 2007 became 45 percent by November 2008. Still, that recognition did little to slow the destruction of household wealth associated with housing assets. And with negative wealth effects came a massive loss in both consumer and business confidence. The typical household became unwilling to buy consumer durables, not even a toaster, and the economy spiralled downward in something of a freefall.

Questions

1. Could stronger corporate governance and greater business integrity have made any difference? The answer to counterfactuals is always uncertain, but brainstorm about how events might have unfolded differently. Suppose more senior executives had refused to sign off on fraudulent conveyance of mis-rated bonds?

2. Suppose more monitoring by corporate-level officers had prevented field-agent mortgage brokers from filing mortgage applications that were clearly fraudulent?

3. Suppose senior risk managers had asked who would be the counterparties that would need to step forward to buy mortgage-backed securities when it became clear their default rates were grossly underestimated. All markets, especially financial markets, do clear with enough price adjustment. But suppose senior executives in the banks had pressed for straight answers to just how much of a haircut such fraudulently conveyed securities would require. Is it possible at least some of what has transpired could have been avoided?

Managing in the Global Economy

CHAPTER PREVIEW

Business plans today involve foreign supply chains, offshore manufacturing, and targeted marketing on several continents. Many U.S., German, Japanese, Taiwanese, and Korean companies engage in foreign direct investment and manufacture through subsidiaries abroad. Other companies outsource to low-wage high-quality contract manufacturing partners in places like China, Mexico, Portugal, Brazil, Indonesia, and the Caribbean. Still others buy parts and supplies or preassembled components from foreign firms. And almost all companies face competition from imports and produce an export product to sell abroad. Indeed, export markets are increasingly the primary source of sales growth for many U.S. manufacturers. The United States is the world's largest import-export trader with 32 percent of U.S. GDP involved in import-export transactions. China and Germany represent the second and third largest shares of world trade. Careful analysis and accurate forecasting of these international purchases and sales provide pivotal information for capacity planning, for production scheduling, and for pricing, promotion, and distribution plans in many companies.

In this chapter, we show how managers incorporate the analysis of exchange rate cycles into their three to five–year business plans. We investigate how international trade in merchandise and services plus international capital flows determine long-term trends in exchange rates. Purchasing power parity provides another way to assess these foreign exchange (FX) trends and incorporate cash flow from net export sales in business scenario planning. We then explore the reasons for and patterns of trade in the world's economy with special attention to regional trading blocs and emergent economies, such as the European Union, NAFTA, China, and India. The chapter closes with perspectives on the U.S. trade deficit. Our attention throughout is focused on a management approach to international trade and policy.

MANAGERIAL CHALLENGE

Financial Crisis Slows U.S. Household Consumption and Crushes Business Investment: Can Exports to China Provide a Recovery?

The gross domestic product (GDP) in the United States, one measure of aggregate business activity, is $15.7 trillion. To understand this figure, one can look from three perspectives: (1) at the comparative size of other big economies like China, Japan, and Germany; (2) at the relative size of the components of U.S. GDP; and (3) at the sheer size of a trillion. The number one trillion (1,000,000,000,000) is 1,000 times larger than the one billion adults in mainland China. And 3,000 times larger than the annual budget of a typical college ($333 million). So, 15.7 trillion is a very large number indeed.

Cont.

MANAGERIAL CHALLENGE *Continued*

AP Photo/Imaginechina

China has the second highest GDP in the world in 2012 at $7.5 trillion U.S. dollars (USD) using the nominal foreign exchange rate of CNY6.34/USD in mid-2012. Japan, Germany, France, Brazil, and the United Kingdom are the world's next five largest economies at $5.9 trillion, $3.6 trillion, and $2.8 trillion, $2.5 trillion, and $2.4 trillion, respectively. The Chinese case is especially interesting because the Chinese currency does not trade on freely fluctuating currency markets. Instead, the Chinese government has insisted on an officially sanctioned rate of exchange (CNY6.37/USD) that is allowed to vary within a daily range of a half of 1 percent—a so-called managed float.

Dividing the $15.7 trillion U.S. GDP in 2011 by the U.S. population of 314 million, U.S. per capita income is $50,000 whereas 2011 Chinese per capita income is $5,539 ($7.5T/1.354 billion population). However, it is estimated by the International Monetary Fund (IMF) that if Chinese output were valued at prices prevailing in the United States, China would be a $11.4 trillion economy. This adjusted figure conveys the comparable amount of business activity taking place in China, albeit at much lower incomes and therefore at much lower mark-ups, margins, and prices than in the United States.

How the $15.7 trillion U.S. GDP divides among its various components of C + I + G + Net X is also insightful for thinking about managing exports. Consumption (C) is by far the largest component of U.S. GDP, accounting for over $11 trillion—of the total $15.7 trillion in recent years:

$$GDP = (C + I + G) + Net X$$
$$2012 \quad (11.1T + 2.1T + 3.1T) + (-0.5T)$$
$$\text{Exports} - \text{Imports}$$
$$(2.2T - 2.7T)$$
$$= 16.242T \qquad + (-561T)$$
$$= \$15.7T$$

These U.S. proportions of GDP (71 percent consumption, 13 percent investment, 20 percent government, 14 percent exports, and 18 percent imports) would not characterize the fast-developing emerging economies such as China and India where investment (I) as a proportion of GDP is much higher (47 percent and 35 percent, respectively) nor the export-driven economies like Germany, South Korea, and the Netherlands where exports constitute 35 percent, 43 percent, and 65 percent of GDP, respectively. But at 32 percent of GDP, import plus export activity does employ lots of Americans, and this fact was crucial in escaping the 2008–2009 severe recession. The U.S. Federal Reserve has kept real interest rates close to zero throughout 2009–2012 not only to stimulate business borrowing and investment but also to keep the U.S. dollar's value low, thereby stimulating U.S. exports. Cummins Inc. of Columbus, Indiana, illustrates a U.S. diesel engine manufacturer whose 59 percent overseas sales is very sensitive to fluctuations in the FX rate.

In recent years, export growth contributed the majority of real U.S. GDP growth: +3.8 percent of +0.4 percent growth in 2010, +1.5 percent of the −2 percent growth in 2009, +0.88 percent of the +1.07 percent growth in 2008. As a result, export growth offered one of the only escape routes from the severe 2008–2009 recession. Remember that domestic consumption (C) had gone down by $220 billion, and investment had collapsed by $400 billion. As a result, in the near term, export growth along with deficit spending through aggressive government fiscal policy (G) was chosen by the Obama administration to stem job losses and jumpstart a recovery.

What were the symptoms of recession in the United States in 2009 and what challenges did managers face as a result? First, U.S. GDP contracted for four quarters in a row [−2.7 percent in 2008 (Q3), −9 percent in 2008 (Q4), −6.7 percent in 2009 (Q1), and −1 percent in 2009 (Q2)]. That has never happened since these national income statistics started being collected at the end of World War II. So, the downturn was severe and persistent. Secondly, unemployment skyrocketed above 10 percent by 2009 (Q3) when 4 to 5 percent constitutes "natural" unemployment in a fully employed U.S. economy. That too has happened only rarely, just once since 1947 (at the depths of the 1982 recession). Finally, industrial production declined for 17 of 18 months.

A first challenge was to understand the sources of these downturns in consumption, investment, and industrial production. Durable goods consumption collapsed because the majority of American households are now mutual fund stockholders, and American mutual fund

Cont.

MANAGERIAL CHALLENGE *Continued*

assets lost $2.4 trillion in value during 2008. So, U.S. households suffered a massive reduction in wealth equivalent to the size of the entire economy of the United Kingdom. Not surprisingly, U.S. consumption of home appliances, furniture, autos, and other durables went down by −5 percent in 2009 after plummeting −40 percent in 2008. Nondurable consumption also declined −3 percent after falling by −11 percent in 2008.

Business investment collapsed as well, by another −20 percent in mid-2009 after declining by −51 percent in 2009 (Q1) and −41 percent in 2008. Inventory purchases particularly were slashed. Why? (1) Demand traffic declined to a trickle suggesting that unit sales forecasts should be drastically cut, (2) energy costs spiked in mid-2008, raising the producer price index by 10 percent, (3) export demand from Japan and the European Union declined by half, reflecting a worldwide recession of −2 percent.

The only bright spot was China, where rapid growth continued. Chinese GNP grew at 9 percent in 2009, at 10.1 percent in 2010, and at 9.2 percent in 2011. Chinese retail sales grew at 17 percent over this three-year period when much of the rest of the world was slowing to a near stop.

In an important sense, China is not an export machine like South Korea or the Netherlands. Exports total 27 percent of Chinese GDP, but for the first time in 2011, China ran a trade deficit with exports

$110 billion less than imports. Over the last 10 years, net exports have represented only one-tenth of Chinese economic growth. Household demand is just starting to accelerate as China changes from developing to developed-country living standards. As a result, U.S. exports to China have continued to grow 2008–2011 from $60 billion to $80 billion, $98 billion, and $107 billion, right through the severe U.S. recession and its aftermath.

Expanding exports has been complemented by massive federal spending on infrastructure and productivity-enhancing training and facilities. Federal tax rebates in 2007 led households to pay down credit card debt rather than go out and replace an appliance. Ironically, credit card companies then flagged those households as greater credit risks and promptly cut their credit limits which induced still more cautious consumption. John Maynard Keynes described this situation as a classic liquidity trap where consumption and investment spiral downward despite tax policy and monetary policy designed to improve household liquidity.

Lower borrowing costs can also enhance the ability of businesses to fund their working capital requirements. Unfortunately for the United States and Japan, short-term interest rates are already near zero (0.1 to 0.4 percent), so traditional monetary policy really has no room left to stimulate these two largest economies. The Federal Reserve has therefore adopted **quantitative easing** that buys longer-term instruments like 10-year

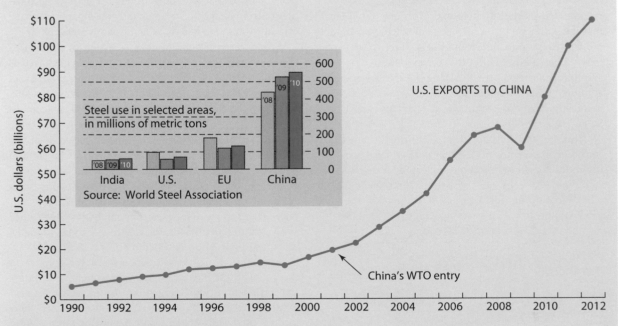

Source: World Trade Organization.

MANAGERIAL CHALLENGE *Continued*

T-bonds in order to reduce mortgage financing costs and stabilize the housing market.

Ingenious *credit policy* initiatives have been tried but are proving largely unsuccessful in breaking loose more bank lending. Bankers have proven stubborn about extending credit to small and medium-sized businesses that survive on such loans from one stage of the business cycles to the next. Having been burned by overextending credit 2004–2007, bankers and bank regulators are overreacting by under-lending. As a result, business credit conditions have tightened precisely when companies need to begin to build inventories to trigger new sales from returning customers.

In this scenario, only deficit federal spending on the Government component of GDP (G) and greater exports especially to India and China hold the prospect of restarting an economic expansion. For the first time ever in 2010 and 2011, U.S. exports to the emerging markets exceeded exports to developed markets.

Discussion Questions

- Identify several reasons why the export sector remains so crucial to the recovery from the 2008–2009 Great Contraction in the United States?
- Why in 2009 were U.S. households not even buying a toaster when it wore out?
- What U.S. companies are likely to profit first from increased exports?
- Does a strong US$ hurt U.S. exports? Why?

INTRODUCTION

quantitative easing Expansionary monetary policy focused on longer-term bonds and mortgage-backed securities.

Around the globe, the reduction of trade barriers and the opening of markets to foreign imports have increased the competitive pressure on manufacturers who once dominated their domestic industries. Tennis shoes and dress footwear once produced in large factories in Britain and the United States now come from South Korea, China, and Italy. Auto and auto parts manufacturing once dominated by Ford, General Motors, and American parts suppliers like Magna now occur largely in Japan and China. In addition, Toyota owns 15 assembly and parts plants in North America, 4 in South America, 6 in Europe, 4 in India and Pakistan, and 28 across Asia. In retailing, McDonald's operates in over 100 foreign countries, Walmart sells $217 billion overseas, and international sales at Coca-Cola, Kellogg, Gillette, and Pampers exceed those in the United States. Boeing and Microsoft are the two largest U.S. exporters but other key U.S. exports include movies, electrical equipment, heavy machinery, accounting and consulting services, and franchise retailers.

Similarly, outsourcing numerous components and subassemblies to foreign companies has become a standard supply chain management practice for U.S. manufacturers. Every three days, the wings for a new long-haul 300-seat Boeing 787 arrive from Japan at Everett, Washington, near Seattle for final assembly by Boeing. For its minivans, Chrysler may decide to cast engine blocks in Mexico, acquire electronics from Taiwan, perform machine tooling of ball bearings in Germany, and locate final assembly in Canada. Wooden furniture "made in the U.S.A." now includes foreign components from Canada, Mexico, and the Far East equal to 38 percent of the total value added. So, when 32 percent of Canadian output and 25 percent of Mexican or Malaysian output flows into the United States as imports, much of that final product flow contains preassembled components owned by U.S. companies. This explains in large measure why fully one-third of U.S. corporate profits come from overseas operations. The world of business truly necessitates managing in the global economy.

WHAT WENT RIGHT • WHAT WENT WRONG

Export Market Pricing at Toyota[1]

In February 2002, 1 U.S. dollar (USD) exchanged for ¥135. A popular performance sports car, the Toyota Celica GT-S Coupe, made in Japan and shipped to U.S. dealers, sold for $21,165, meaning that each sale realized almost ¥3 million (i.e., ¥2,857,275) in sales revenue. Two years later in 2004, the dollar exchanged for only ¥104. This 25 percent depreciation of the USD made Japanese exports to the United States potentially much less profitable. To recover costs and earn the same profit margin back home in Japan, Toyota needed to price the 2004 GT-S Coupe at $27,474 in order to again realize ¥2,857,275.

Rather than steeply raising the sticker price of their sporty performance coupe and trying to limit the erosion of market share by emphasizing horsepower, styling, or manufacturing quality, Toyota opted instead to slash profit margins. Specifically, a tiny $390 price increase to $21,555 for the 2004 Celica GT-S earned just ¥2,241,720 in revenue back at headquarters in Tokyo (¥615,555,000 less than in 2002). Toyota's minimalist approach to price increases lowered profit margins but preserved the Celica's foreign market share.

Different companies react in different ways to the challenges presented by such severe currency fluctuations. General Motors and Ford tend to maintain margins and sacrifice market share whereas Toyota tends to slash margins to grow market share. In part, because of these pricing decisions, between 1985 and 2012 Toyota's share of the North American car market rose from 5 to 16 percent while General Motors' share fell from 45 to 19 percent.

Might one approach have been right for Toyota with 60 percent of its revenue from exports and the opposite approach right for GM? If you were advising Toyota today, would you recommend they emphasize high margins and current profitability or reduced margins and further growth of market share? What role does scale of production and selling cost savings based on market penetration play?

[1]Based on *Ward's Automotive World*, various issues.

IMPORT-EXPORT SALES AND EXCHANGE RATES

As illustrated in the previous example, import-export sales and profit margins are very sensitive to changes in exchange rates. Over the period 1980–2012, FX rates were 4 times more volatile than interest rates and 10 times more volatile than inflation rates. Figure 6.1 shows that the £/$ and DM/$ FX rates in the 1980s, the ¥/$ FX rate in the 1990s, and the €/$ FX rate in the 2000s were particularly volatile. Analyzing and forecasting the cash flow effects of such massive FX rate changes (sometimes called "FX risk") provides crucial information for the marketing, operations, and financial plans of companies like Boeing, Microsoft, and IBM as well as ChemChina, Toyota, and Volkswagen.

Foreign Exchange Risk

Foreign exchange risk exposures are of three types: transaction risk exposure, translation risk exposure, and operating risk exposure.

transaction risk exposure A change in cash flows resulting from contractual commitments to pay in or receive foreign currency.

Transaction risk exposure occurs when a fixed price purchase agreement or sales contract (a specific "transaction") commits the company to make future payables or accept future receivables in a foreign currency. Over the time period between executing the contract and actually making or receiving the payments, the company has FX transaction risk exposure. Many financial derivatives like FX forward, swap, and option contracts have emerged to assist corporate treasurers in constructing hedges that lay off these transaction risk exposures for a modest cost (perhaps 5 percent) known and fixed in advance. Appendix 6A explains the mechanics of these *financial hedges*.

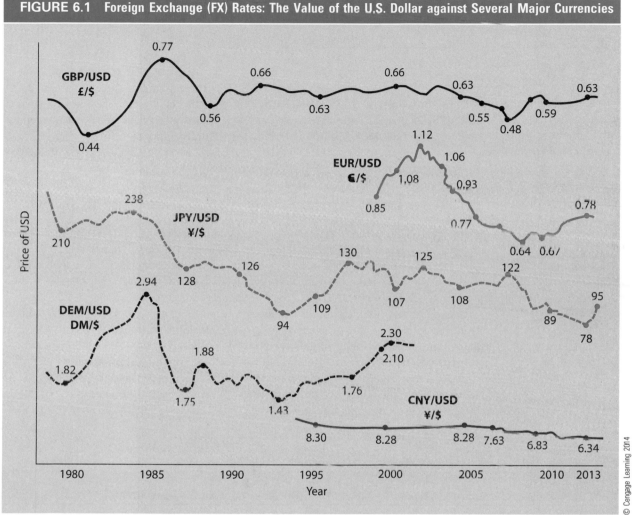

FIGURE 6.1 Foreign Exchange (FX) Rates: The Value of the U.S. Dollar against Several Major Currencies

© Cengage Learning 2014

translation risk exposure An accounting adjustment in the home currency value of foreign assets or liabilities.

Secondly, **translation risk exposure** occurs when a company's foreign assets (or liabilities) are affected by persistent exchange rate trends. Accordingly, the accounting books in the home country must be adjusted. A $100 million assembly plant owned by Volkswagen and located in the United States will need to be written down on the company's German balance sheet when the U.S. dollar falls from 1.12 €/$ in 2001 to 0.64 €/$ in 2008 (again, see Figure 6.1). This €48 million translation risk exposure, [(€1.12 − €0.64)/$] × $100 million, is easily offset with a *balance sheet hedge*. A balance sheet hedge would match the magnitude of Volkswagen's asset loss in the euro value of its American plant to an equivalent reduction in the euro cost of VW's liabilities in the United States (say, a decline from €112 million to €64 million cost of $100 million in pension plan commitments to American workers). The intent is to leave the net asset position of the U.S. division of Volkswagen unchanged. In general, unless the parent company becomes financially distressed such that the foreign asset write-downs threaten important collateral pledged for business loans, such balance sheet adjustments in foreign subsidiaries due to FX risk are often just ignored.

Example

GM Subsidiaries Suffer Currency Loss

In 2011–2012, GM's partner Greely Auto had the top three selling models in the Chinese market. However, the price of the USD was rising steeply. The European debt crisis had set in motion a "flight to quality" wherein foreign investors moved large sums of investment capital to the United States. These financial flows drove up the price of the USD in FX markets by as much as 15 percent. Overseas earnings of GM's foreign subsidiaries were restated at lower dollar value in the income statements and balance sheets of U.S.-headquartered parent companies. Even though their models were market leaders, GM reported that profits on overseas subsidiaries declined from $550 million to $395 million "due to currency losses."

operating risk exposure A change in cash flows from foreign or domestic sales resulting from currency fluctuations.

Finally, FX fluctuations that result in substantial changes in the operating cash flow of foreign subsidiaries, like those befalling Toyota for the Celica GT-S, are examples of FX **operating risk exposure**. Operating risk exposures are more difficult to hedge than transaction risk exposures and more difficult to forecast than translation risk exposures. As a result, operating risk exposures necessitate more managerial attention and extensive analysis.

For one thing, the deterioration of export revenues from sales in foreign subsidiaries is just one side of the problem that a rising domestic currency poses. In addition, depending on the viability of global competition, operating risk exposures may entail a substantial deterioration of domestic sales as well. When a home currency becomes more valuable (appreciates), competing import products become cheaper in the currency of the home market. These relationships are well illustrated by the export and domestic business of the Cummins Engine Co.

INTERNATIONAL PERSPECTIVES

Collapse of Export and Domestic Sales at Cummins Engine[2]

U.S. manufacturer Cummins Engine Co. is the world's leading producer of replacement diesel engines for trucks. Like all durable equipment makers, Cummins's revenues are highly cyclical, declining steeply in economic downturns. If households buy fewer appliances, clothing, and furniture, less shipping by truck is required to deliver inventories from warehouses to restock retail shelves. Less shipping means less truck mileage, and less truck mileage means a slower replacement demand for diesel engines. For example, in the severe recession of 2008–2009, Cummins's sales fell off 29 percent, operating margins collapsed from 9.6 to 4.5 percent, and cash flow plummeted by 49 percent from $5.54 to $2.85 per share. As the U.S. economy improved during late 2009 and 2010, Cummins's sales and cash flow rose quickly (see Figure 6.2). This period exhibited one of Cummins's normal cyclical sales

and profit patterns. But not so during 1999–2001 when Cummins's sales declined 15 percent, margins collapsed from 9.4 to 4.3 percent, and cash flow plunged from $2.58 to $0.82 per share. There was no U.S. recession during this period. What factors were responsible for this earlier collapse of Cummins's sales, margins, and cash flows?

With a 70 percent market share, Cummins Engine competes domestically against Number 2 Caterpillar (20 percent) and Detroit Diesel (10 percent). But Cummins also sells 53 percent of its replacement diesel engines in the *export* market competing primarily against Mercedes-Benz diesels. The euro price that a Cummins Engine can sell for in Munich or Rotterdam (and still recover its cost plus a small profit) is as important to Cummins's cash flow as metal input costs or wage bargains with the United Machinists Union. A $44,750 835 cubic inch

FIGURE 6.2   Cummins Engine Cash Flow and Operating Margins

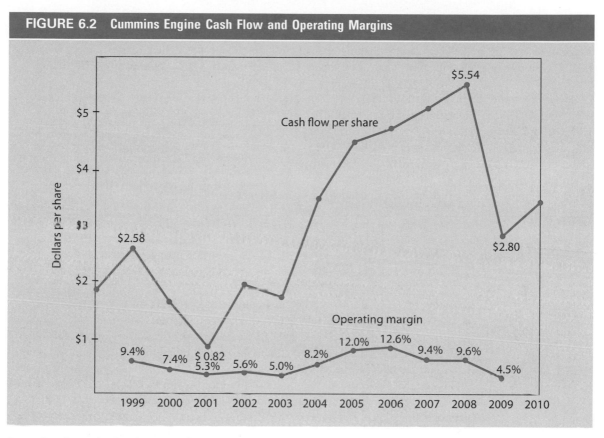

Source: Based on *Value Line Investment Survey, Ratings and Reports*, October 23, 2009.

Cummins Series N diesel sold for approximately €38,000 in 1999 and again in 2004 across Europe. In each of those years, the exchange rate between the euro and the U.S. dollar stood at approximately 0.85—that is, €0.85 per USD. In the intervening time period, however, the U.S. dollar appreciated substantially. By 2001, the value of the dollar had soared 27 percent from €0.85 to €1.12 (again see Figure 6.1).[3]

The effect of the 1999–2001 dollar appreciation on Cummins's export sales was catastrophic. For Lufthansa Airfreight, a German trucking company, to buy a Cummins diesel engine at the dollar's peak in 2001 required €1.12/$ × $44,750 = €50,120! No feature of the equipment had changed. No service offering had changed. No warranty had changed. The export diesels from the United States to Germany (once priced at €38,037) had simply become 12,083 euros more expensive solely because the euro currency of those European buyers had become much less valuable relative to the steeply appreciating U.S. dollar. Such enormous price

increases of the Cummins export product made substitute products, such as a €40,000 Mercedes-Benz diesel, substantially more attractive to European buyers than before the change in the exchange rate.

Moreover, in 2001, Mercedes-Benz perceived a huge opportunity to sell its own replacement diesels into Cummins's home territory in the United States. An import diesel made by Mercedes-Benz (which had sold in Boston, Cleveland, and Chicago for €40,000/0.85 = $47,059 in 1999 and would do so again in 2004) could cover cost and a small profit while selling for just $35,714 (€40,000/1.12) at the peak of the dollar in 2001. Not surprisingly, Mercedes-Benz diesels sold very well that year throughout the United States. Cummins was forced to bargain with its most loyal domestic customers much more than usual and shave its margins. Therefore, in response to the 27 percent steep appreciation of the dollar, not only did Cummins's export sales collapse, but so did Cummins's domestic sales (and margins). These operating risk exposures from

(continued)

fluctuations in the FX rates require substantial management attention because they are of uncertain magnitude and unpredictable timing making them much more difficult to hedge away than transaction risks.

The consistently depreciating U.S. dollar between 2001 and 2008 (see Figure 6.1) put U.S. manufacturers of traded goods, like autos, VCRs, airplanes, and diesel engines, at an advantage. At €0.64/USD, Cummins diesels sold for €28,640 in Germany whereas Mercedes sold in the United States for $62,344. When the dollar strengthened against the euro during 2010–2012 to €0.80/USD, U.S. exports sharply declined, U.S. imports sharply increased, and the U.S. trade deficit (exports minus imports) ballooned from −$350 billion to −$620 billion.

[2]Based on *Value Line Investment Survey, Part III: Ratings and Reports*, various issues.

[3]Exchange rate percentage changes are calculated as the difference from one period to the next divided by the average exchange rate over the period. The reason for this midpoint procedure is that when the EUR/USD exchange rate returns in 2001–2004 to very nearly its original level (i.e., €0.85/$ at 1999 and 2004 in), the midpoint calculation yields a downward adjustment of −27 percent, equal and opposite to the +27 percent rise in 1999–2001.

OUTSOURCING

A lasting effect of all the international competitive pressure on U.S. manufacturers in the strong dollar years of the mid-2000s was a laser-like dedication to cost cutting. With just-in-time delivery of component subassemblies, production to order, and other lean manufacturing techniques, U.S. companies sliced inventory costs, reduced scrap, and cut manufacturing cycle times enough to boost productivity 25 percent from 2001 to 2005.[4] That is, the ratio of merchandise produced to input cost rose at firms like Cummins, Caterpillar, General Electric, and Boeing. One reason was better operations management techniques but another was the outsourcing of IT, less complex assembly, and raw materials handling tasks to places like Mexico, South Korea, Malaysia, and now India and China.

A Hewlett-Packard laptop computer is 95 percent outsourced, with components from eight countries delivered just-in-time each day for assembly in a Shanghai factory and then air freighted overnight to Memphis by FedEx for shipment directly to customers the next day (see Figure 6.3). Outsourcing is not new. U.S. companies like Merck, DuPont, and IBM have outsourced for decades to Germany, France, Ireland, and now India in order to access skilled people for analytical jobs in R & D. In addition, basic manufacturing of low-skill, low-wage jobs has always moved offshore, first from Europe to America in the late nineteenth century and then in the mid-twentieth century to Canada, Mexico, Brazil, and Portugal, and more recently to Malaysia, Thailand, India, and now China.

One reason is that shipping costs from Shanghai to New York for a 40-foot container filled with 6,000 garments runs just $8,000 ($1.35 per garment) for the 30-day ocean voyage through the Panama Canal (see Figure 6.3), and only $10,000 ($1.70 per garment) for the 20-day intermodal service through Long Beach harbor and then onto U.S. trucks. Given their high value/weight ratio, Hewlett-Packard laptops warrant the $50,000 cost for a Boeing 747 air freighter from Shanghai to the FedEx hub in Memphis, Tennessee, adding approximately $2 cost per laptop (see Figure 6.3). Across all types of cargo, ocean shipping adds only 3 to 4 percent to the delivered price of a product—as little as 2.5 cents to the price of T-shirt moving from China to Europe.

[4]Based on "Lean and Unseen," *The Economist* (July 1, 2006), pp. 55–56; and Murray Weidenbaum, "Outsourcing: Pros and Cons," *Business Horizons* (2005), pp. 311–315.

FIGURE 6.3 Outsourcing Shipping Costs and Component Sources for HP Personal Computer

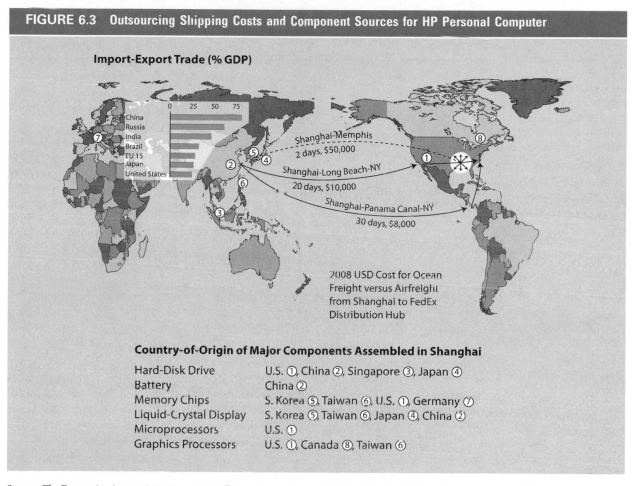

Source: *The Economist*, August 9, 2008, p. 64; *Wall Street Journal*, June 9, 2005, p. B1; World Trade Organization; and Thomson Datastream.

Offshoring does necessitate some additional cost, however. Full costs offshore include costs for careful vendor selection, intellectual property protection, and compensation for expatriate managers. Hewitt Associate LLC estimates that to transfer a director-level U.S. employee to Beijing or Shanghai requires $190,000 additional compensation and a $60,000 housing allowance relative to U.S. job sites. By one estimate, $5 per hour call-center jobs in India or $2 per hour factory jobs in China require another $12 per hour to cover these additional expatriate costs of outsourcing. A pivotal question then is whether domestic factory workers in the United States are available for $14 to $17 per hour. On average, the answer is "no"; the full labor cost of production workers in 2008 U.S. manufacturing totals $24.59 per hour. So, outsourcing to reduce manufacturing cost is going to continue unless two-tiered wage agreements allow lower starting wages.[5]

Outsourcing to foreign contract manufacturers is, however, as much about importing competitiveness as it is about exporting jobs. Time-to-market and the capacity to innovate quickly have become more important in auto manufacturing, for example, than the assembly cost of the next shipment of three-speed transmissions. If Toyota, Nokia, and Advanced Micro Devices (AMD) introduce major product innovations on two-year,

[5]U.S. Department of Labor, Bureau of Labor Statistics, *International Comparisons of Hourly Compensation Costs in Manufacturing, 2008* (March 26, 2009), p. 6.

six-month, and three-week timetables, respectively, and if those cycles have become the key to customer acceptance, then GM, Motorola, and Intel have no choice but to access the people and processes that can match that capability. If those people are Indian software engineers, Mexican foundry employees, and Chinese assembly workers, then the best hope for American workers is to sell to those developing economies in Asia and Europe the International Harvester tractors, GE appliances, Boeing aircraft, Cisco network servers, as well as the management consulting, banking, and legal services those lower-wage economies require at this stage of their development.

As the U.S. dollar weakened persistently against the euro throughout 2003–2009 (again see Figure 6.1), American exporters experienced a turnaround and profited from booming European sales. Seven percent of IBM's reported 11 percent sales growth in 2003–2004 was attributed to currency fluctuations. Similarly, Colgate-Palmolive and Microsoft, respectively, reported two-thirds of a 20 percent sales increase in Europe and nine-tenths of a 12 percent sales increase in Europe, the Middle East, and Africa were attributable to the lower in-country prices emergent from a weaker U.S. dollar.[6]

CHINA TRADE BLOSSOMS

An amazing story is unfolding in the People's Republic of China (PRC) along the Yellow, Yangtze, and Pearl River systems and in the port megacities of Shanghai, Guangzhou, Dalian, and Zhuhai. Three decades ago, China accounted for an insignificant 0.6 percent of world trade despite a highly educated workforce and an immense population of one billion. The Chinese economy has been widely recognized as the fastest growing worldwide throughout the first decade of the new millennium (10 to 15 percent annually from 2000 to 2010), and 7.5 to 9 percent since then.

China contributed 42 percent to global GDP growth in recent years. Chinese steel production reached 627 million tons in 2010 while the United States, Japan, India, and Germany produced 181, 107, 68, and 43 million tons, respectively. China's retail sales to domestic consumers grew at 14 percent per annum from 2004 to 2007 and at a 17 percent pace from 2008 to 2009 when the rest of the world's consumer economy was slowing abruptly.

China generated over 9 percent real GDP growth per annum, 1995–2011 and China's share of world trade has increased more than tenfold in recent decades. Import and export trade worldwide has grown to $4 trillion, equivalent to 54 percent of China's $7.3 trillion economy. The trade share (imports + exports) of China with the United States has risen from 14 percent of all U.S. trade in 2003 to 25 percent in 2011, only marginally less than the United States' largest trading partners—Mexico and Canada with 26 percent and 33 percent, respectively.[7] China's economic real growth is unprecedented both in its longevity and its double digit magnitude.

China's largest trading partners are Japan, Taiwan, the United States, South Korea, and Hong Kong. The principal categories of exports are clothing to Hong Kong; machinery, toys, furniture, shoes, and clothing to the United States; textiles to Japan; and telecommunications equipment to Germany. Indeed, 80 percent of all U.S. shoe imports and 60 percent of all furniture imports now come from China. But in the furniture case, those imports amount to just $15 billion of the $70 billion in U.S. furniture consumption; the great majority of furniture consumed in the U.S. continues to be made in

---

[6]"Dollar's Dive Helps U.S. Companies," *Wall Street Journal* (April 21, 2003), p. A2.

[7]Federal Reserve Bank of St. Louis, *National Economic Trends* (July 2, 2012), p. 18.

the U.S. and elsewhere. In many cases Chinese factories are assembling components in facilities that have emerged as joint venture investments of the PRC's China International Trust and Investment Corp. with Taiwanese, Japanese, European, and U.S. multinationals.

A good example is HP's laptop computer assembled in Shanghai by Quanta Computer, a Taiwanese partner in HP's supply chain (see Figure 6.3). Disk drive components from Japan, memory chips from Germany, liquid crystal displays from Korea, microprocessors from the United States, and graphics processors from Taiwan are flown into China the night after HP confirms an assemble-to-order transaction. All these items count in trade statistics as Chinese imports. When the laptop arrives at the customer's doorstep, its total delivered price is counted as a Chinese export and an American import.

In a similar operation for Apple iPads, it is estimated that only $10 of the $275 final product price represents value-added in China.[8] South Korean firms Samsung and LG providing the display screen and memory chips contribute $20 value-added. Apple's engineering, product design, software, and marketing contribute $110 value added plus an $82 profit earned. Again, upon delivery in the United States, the entire $275 is counted as an American import even though Apple owned all the components at all the stages of production worldwide.

With wage rates of $2 per hour for assembly line work, China has quickly become the world's largest producer of televisions, computers, toys, bicycles, steel, and wood furniture. In the last decade, U.S. multinationals have employed 1.1 million British workers (an 8 percent increase), 1 million Canadian workers (a 6 percent increase), 904,300 Mexican workers (a 17 percent increase), 505,300 Brazilian workers (a 47 percent increase), 943,900 Chinese workers (a 262 percent increase), and 453,300 Indian workers (a 642 percent increase).[9] Chinese import flows reflect the goods and services needed to sustain such astounding growth—that is, electrical machinery and aircraft from the United States, steel from South Korea, autos and chemicals from Japan, rubber, iron ore, ships, and cement from Australia.

From joint ventures in auto parts with Ford Motor to aircraft construction with McDonnell Douglas, foreign companies historically practiced caution in staging their co-investment in China.[10] An unbridled enthusiasm warranted by the growth opportunity of a lifetime was balanced against threats to their intellectual property. Two events in 2000 and 2001 set a different story in motion. In 2001, China joined the World Trade Organization (WTO) and agreed to drop some restrictions on foreign investment and to abide by the WTO standards for protecting patents and copyright. The year before, the U.S. Congress normalized trade relations by extending to China permanent most-favored-nation status, which removed numerous U.S. tariffs.

As a direct result, 57,000 Chinese investment projects have been started with the United States and other foreign direct investment partners since then. Chinese auto parts output has grown the past five years from a ¥315 billion to a ¥960 billion yuan business, about 35 percent of which is exported (to Ford Motor and other partners).[11] Overall, Chinese exports in 2008–2011 grew by 47 percent, and Chinese imports grew by 60 percent. Only the United States imported more merchandise.

---

[8]"Trade Statistics: iPadded," *The Economist* (January 21, 2012), p. 84.

[9]"U.S. Firms Eager to Add Foreign Jobs," *Wall Street Journal* (November 22, 2011), p B1.

[10]See James McGregor, *One Billion Customers: Lessons from the Front Lines of Doing Business in China* (New York: Wall Street Journal Books, 2005).

[11]"Chinese Car-Parts Makers Expand," *Wall Street Journal* (June 12, 2009), p. B2.

FIGURE 6.4 **Map of China (GDP per Capita by Province)**

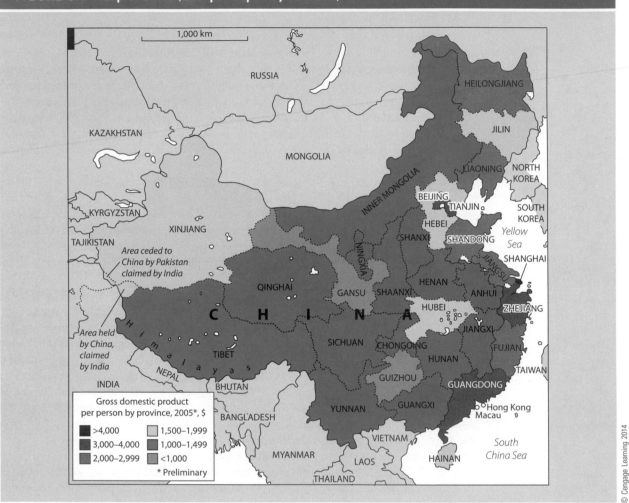

Gross domestic product per person by province, 2005*, $

- >4,000
- 3,000–4,000
- 2,000–2,999
- 1,500–1,999
- 1,000–1,499
- <1,000

* Preliminary

© Cengage Learning 2014

China Today

China today is a study in contrasts not unlike other fast-growing nations throughout history. With GDP doubling every five to six years and population growth of less than 1 percent (about 10 million per year), the standard of living in the Eastern coastal provinces of China is advancing very rapidly (see Figure 6.4). What accelerated Chinese development to make possible this spectacular and almost unprecedented record of economic growth?

If China were simply an export platform for multinational corporations seeking cost savings in assembling manufactured goods, the WTO answer would suffice. And our discussion in the previous section on Hewlett-Packard's laptop computer assembly in Shanghai is instructive. But considering China an export machine like South Korea is misleading. Over the past 10 years, net exports accounted for only about 10 percent of Chinese real GDP growth.[12] Instead, a recent Booz Allen survey found that China was being relied upon for product development as well as procurement, more so than

---

[12]"Rebalancing the World Economy: China," *The Economist* (August 1, 2009), pp. 65–66.

Canada, Europe, Latin America, or India.[13] In addition, some of China's giant state-owned companies like ChemChina are globalizing and competing like private-sector firms against other multinationals.[14] And in 2008 some of China's state-owned enterprises (SOEs) like PetroChina, State Grid Corporation, and China Mobile bid successfully to run offshore utilities in the Philippines and acquired Paktel mobile operations in Pakistan.

In addition, another important part of the answer to the unprecedented Chinese growth is the liberalization of property rights. Starting in 1978, China's enterprising owners of start-ups were granted entitlement to residual cash flows from their small businesses. In 1980, residents near urban areas were given 99-year use rights and residual appropriation rights to three acres. Ownership rights remained with the State but these "resource holders" became entitled to long-term leasing of their land assets to small business (especially small factory) owners. By 1998, still more extensive ownership rights were extended to urban property.[15] The Chinese can now buy and sell and develop for investment not only resident houses and apartments but attached commercial spaces.

The middle class created by these new property rights arrangements is expanding rapidly. One can drive in eastern coastal regions of China along the motorway southwest of Shanghai and see nothing but brick McMansions kilometer after kilometer all the way to Hangzhou 150 km away. The pattern repeats itself in an eerily repetitive way. Each farmer with three acres leases an acre to an aspiring small factory owner. One-half acre contains the factory owner's brick McMansion house; the other half acre contains the factory. Another half acre is the farmer's McMansion, and perhaps a third McMansion and small factory all sit on 2.5 of the 3 acres. A few garden plots survive on the remainder. Next door exactly the same pattern unfolds. The three-story homes are all brick and concrete as building materials and construction labor are very cheap. Take any exit off the motorway and more such three-acre enclaves unfold in every direction. Occasionally these densely packed McMansion patterns are punctuated by a large 10-acre factory complex or a new town development with office buildings, shops, and schools.

The Shanghai region is clearly the most developed in China. Several eastern coastal China provinces have always profited from expanded trade relative to inland provinces. And the Special Economic Zones of Xiamen in Fujian Province across the Taiwan Straits and Guangzhou in Guangdong Province across from Hong Kong have similar geographic, cultural, and government-mandated economic advantages. Nevertheless, Shanghai City in Jiangsu Province and adjacent Hangzhou, capital of Zhejiang Province, are something special. On the approaches to Shanghai or Hangzhou, one can find planned communities with living standards equivalent to the outlying suburban "new towns" like Reston near Washington, DC, and Sun City near Phoenix, Arizona. The Shanghai region looks like this in many directions while more rural provinces in western China remain largely untouched by modern life.

Shanghai and Hangzhou are at the northern and southern reaches of the Yangtze River delta. Hangzhou, the capital of Zhejiang province below Shanghai was the largest city in the world in the thirteenth and first half of the fourteenth centuries. The Lower Song dynasty made the city its capital from 1123 up to the Mongol invasion in 1276. Hangzhou was connected to Beijing 1,260 km away in northeast China by a Grand Canal of China completed in 609. Today Hangzhou is a thriving metropolis of green spaces and light industry the size of Atlanta with four million residents in the

---

[13]Based on Booz Allen Offshoring Business Network Survey, *Forbes* (September 3, 2007), p. 56.

[14]"Special Report: China's Business Landscape," *The McKinsey Quarterly 2008*, no. 3, pp. 1–6.

[15]See "A Survey of China," *The Economist* (March 25, 2006), pp. 1–41.

metropolitan area. It ranks as China's 18th largest city, much smaller than Shanghai (19 million), Beijing in central China (12 million), Guangzhou (10 million), and Shenzhen (9 million).

Massive infrastructure investment is another striking impression in the Shanghai–Hangzhou corridor. Train stations, airports, bridges, and tunnels appear to have been built anew in the past five years. Central planning decisions by Party officials streamline the creation of large infrastructure right-of-ways. For example, the avenue from downtown to the Hangzhou airport is lined with high-tech companies like HP, Sony, and Siemens. Clearing previous land uses and accumulating parcels for such infrastructure developments happen with a speed and certainty in China that belies the difficulty of reaching agreement on such projects in Germany, Japan, or the United States. Constitutional challenge to publicly mandated land use decisions is unknown in China.

THE MARKET FOR U.S. DOLLARS AS FOREIGN EXCHANGE

To understand better the managed float in many developing countries, we first explain the determination of FX rates in countries with freely fluctuating exchange rates. Demand, supply, and market equilibrium in the currency markets is predicated on the fact that manufacturers, such as Cummins Engine, incur many of their expenses at domestic manufacturing sites. American manufacturers therefore tend to require that export purchase orders be made payable in U.S. dollars. This receivables policy requires that Munich buyers of Cummins diesels transact simultaneously in the foreign currency and diesel markets.

To buy a Cummins diesel, Munich customers (or their financial intermediaries) will supply euros and demand dollars to secure the currency required for the dollar-denominated purchase order and payment draft awaited by the Cummins Engine shipping department. This additional demand for the dollar and the concurrent additional supply of euros drive the price of the dollar higher than it otherwise would have been. Thus, the equilibrium price of the dollar as foreign exchange (in euros per dollar on the vertical axis in Figure 6.5) rises. In general, any such unanticipated increase in export sales results in just such an appreciation of the domestic currency (here the USD).

Similarly, any unanticipated decrease in export sales results in a depreciation of the domestic currency. For example, in 2001–2005, collapse of Boeing Aircraft export sales in competition with Europe's Airbus contributed to the dollar's collapse against the euro over that same period (again see Figure 6.1). But this downward FX trend of the dollar assisted Cummins Engine as well as Boeing in stabilizing its sales and cash flows both at home and abroad. With the dollar worth fewer euros, the dollar cost of American imports from Mercedes-Benz and Airbus became more expensive, while American exports priced in euros by Cummins and Boeing sales reps across Europe became cheaper. This automatic self-correcting adjustment of flexible exchange rates in response to trade flow imbalances is one of the primary arguments for adopting a freely fluctuating exchange rate policy.

Import-Export Flows and Transaction Demand for a Currency

To examine these effects more closely, let's turn the argument around and trace the currency flows when Americans demand imported goods. The BMW dealers would have

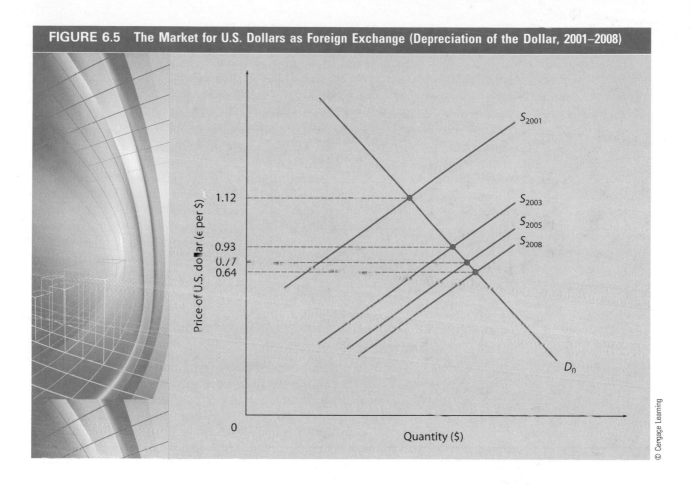

FIGURE 6.5   The Market for U.S. Dollars as Foreign Exchange (Depreciation of the Dollar, 2001–2008)

© Cengage Learning

some inventory stock on hand, but suppose an unexpectedly large number of baby boomers wish to recapture their youth by purchasing sporty BMW convertibles. Just as Cummins Engine prefers to be paid in U.S. dollars, so too BMW wishes to be paid in euros. Therefore, BMW purchase orders must be accompanied by euro cash payments. How is that accomplished? First, the local BMW dealer in Charlotte, North Carolina, requests a wire transfer from Bank of America (BOA). BOA debits the dollar account of the dealer, and then it authorizes payment from the euro cash balances of BOA and presents a wire transfer for an equivalent sum to the Munich branch of Deutsche Bank for deposit in the BMW account. Both import buyer and foreign seller have done business in their home currencies and exchanged a handsome new car. And the merchandise trade account of the U.S. balance of payments would show one additional import transaction valued at the BMW convertible's purchase price.

If BOA failed to anticipate the import transaction and euro wire transfer request, BOA's foreign currency portfolio would now be out of balance. Euro balances must be restored to support future anticipated import-export transactions. BOA therefore goes (electronically) into the interbank foreign currency markets and demands euros. Although the American bank might pay with any currency in excess supply in its foreign currency portfolio that day, it would normally pay in U.S. dollars. In particular, if no other unanticipated import or export flows (and no unanticipated capital flows) have occurred, BOA would pay in U.S. dollars. Therefore, unanticipated demand by Americans for German imports both raises the demand for euros and (as the flip side of that same transaction) *increases* the supply of U.S. dollars in the foreign currency markets.

The Equilibrium Price of the U.S. Dollar

In particular, in the market for U.S. dollars as foreign exchange (see Figure 6.5), the supply curve shifts to the right. This shift of market supply represents BOA and many other correspondent banks supporting import transactions by selling dollars to acquire other foreign currencies. The equilibrium price on the y-axis of Figure 6.5 is the price of the dollar expressed in amounts of foreign currency—for example, British pounds per USD, Chinese yuan per USD, Japanese yen per USD, or euros per USD. As the supply of U.S. dollars increased S_{2001} to S_{2008}, the equilibrium price of the dollar declined continuously from €1.12 to €0.93, €0.77 and €0.64.

For example, in order for the American imports of Airbus airplanes to increase for 2002–2005, the supply of U.S. dollars in the foreign currency market had to increase. Thus, the spectacular dollar appreciation of the previous three years (1999–2001) slowed and the dollar began to depreciate (see Figure 6.1). Again, American consumers and companies needed to acquire euros to purchase Franco-German imports. U.S. financial intermediaries supplied dollars in the market for dollars as foreign exchange to acquire the foreign currencies their local American customers (Delta, United, and Continental) requested in support of these foreign import transactions.

Speculative Demand, Government Transfers, and Coordinated Intervention

The U.S. dollar depreciation of 2001–2010 reflects several factors besides transaction demand. FX rates also depend upon speculative demand, government transfers, and central bank interventions. Speculative demand is very volatile. Transfers can involve either debt repayment (reducing the supply of a currency as a debtor nation takes money out of circulation and returns it to the lender nation's treasury) or foreign aid (increasing the supply of a currency). Government interventions can be coordinated across several central banks or uncoordinated and can be sterilized or unsterilized. **Sterilized interventions** involve offsetting transactions in the relevant government bond market. For example, the Federal Reserve might sell dollars in the foreign currency markets, but then turn around and acquire dollars by selling an equal dollar volume of T-bonds to Japanese or Chinese investors, leaving the supply of dollars in international exchange essentially unchanged.

What is the proportionate weight of each of these factors in determining the equilibrium value of a currency? An important first perspective is that only one out of five foreign exchange transactions supports an import or export trade flow; the other four support international capital flows. In 2011, for example, the average *daily* volume of foreign currency transactions in the 43 largest foreign currency spot markets had a dollar value of $4 trillion. The average *daily* volume of world exports was $50 billion. So the dollar volume of foreign currency flows outstrips the dollar volume of foreign trade flows by 80 to 1. *Daily* FX rate fluctuations therefore reflect not import-export trade flows but rather international capital flows, much of which is speculative and transitory.

Because of the sheer volume of transaction, intervention in the foreign currency markets by any one central bank therefore has almost no chance of affecting the equilibrium value of a currency. Take the Bank of Japan, for instance. In June 2012, the central bank of Japan had official reserves of foreign currencies equal (at existing exchange rates) to $1.3 trillion.[16] By comparison, China had $3.2 trillion, the European Central Bank had $813 billion, while the U.S. Federal Reserve had $148 billion in foreign currency reserves.

sterilized interventions Central bank transactions in the foreign exchange market accompanied by equal offsetting transactions in the government bond market, in an attempt to alter short-term interest rates without affecting the exchange rate.

[16]International Monetary Fund, *International Reserves and Foreign Liquidity*, various issues.

Suppose the Bank of Japan decided to try to initiate a depreciation of the Japanese yen (JPY) to improve the competitiveness of their export sector. Investing one third of their entire reserves or $400 billion, the Bank of Japan's intervention would be easily overwhelmed by the sheer enormity of the $4 trillion mobile capital awash daily in the international currency markets. Indeed, the official reserves of all the central banks *total* only approximately $8 trillion, equal to only *two day's worth* of foreign currency transactions.

It therefore takes a *coordinated intervention* by several large central banks with deep reserves to have any real chance of permanently affecting a currency's value. One such coordinated intervention took place as a result of the Plaza Accords in 1985 when the G-7 nations (the United States, Britain, Japan, Germany, France, Italy, and Canada) all agreed to a sustained sale of U.S. dollars over 1986 and 1987. Figure 6.1 shows that this coordinated intervention was effective in lowering dollar FX rates against the Great Britain Pound (GBP), Japanese Yen (JPY), and the German Deutsche Mark (DEM).

Short-Term Exchange Rate Fluctuations

The transaction demand determinants of long-term quarterly or annual trends in exchange rates are fundamentally different from the determinants of day-to-day exchange rate fluctuations. Short-term exchange rate movements from week to week, day to day, or even hour to hour are determined by arbitrage activity in the international capital markets and by speculative demand. Sometimes current events set speculators off in support of demanding and holding a currency (a long position), and sometimes the reverse (a short position). Behaviorally, each speculator tries to guess what the others will do, and much herd-like stampeding behavior based on volatile investor expectations often ensues.

arbitrage Buying cheap and selling elsewhere for an immediate profit.

Arbitrage is the act of buying real assets, commodities, stocks, bonds, loans, or even televisions, iPods, and sandals cheaply and selling them at higher prices elsewhere. Arbitrage activity is triggered by temporary violations of arbitrage equilibrium conditions, which equalize, for example, real rates of return on 90-day government bonds (adjusted for any differences in default risk). When such conditions do not hold, opportunities for arbitrage profits exist, and arbitrage activity will appear quickly, proceed at huge volume, and continue until the relevant arbitrage equilibrium conditions are reestablished. Again, the sheer magnitude of the flood tide of $4 trillion per day of international currency flows quickly closes (within hours or even minutes) the window of arbitrage profit opportunity in FX trading. If the buying and selling prices and terms of delivery can be arranged simultaneously, then the transaction is one of pure arbitrage. If the second transaction is delayed, we often call the activity **speculation**.

speculation Buying cheap and selling later for a delayed profit (or loss).

DETERMINANTS OF LONG-RUN TRENDS IN EXCHANGE RATES

Long-run trends in FX rates are quite different. Understanding the forces that set in motion the exchange-rate-induced swings in sales and profit margins that constitute operating risk exposure is crucial for effectively managing export business. And since domestic business today is almost universally subject to effective and intense import competition, the same holds true for largely domestic businesses. The quarter-to-quarter or year-to-year trends in FX rates depend on three factors: real growth rates, real interest rates, and anticipated cost inflation rates. We now discuss each of these determinants in turn.

The Role of Real Growth Rates

As we have seen, a primary determinant of the year-to-year exchange rate fluctuations in Figure 6.1 is the net direction of trade flows. Unanticipated increases in imports lower a local currency's value, whereas unanticipated increases in exports raise a local currency's value. The stimulus underlying such trade flow imbalances may be either business cycle-based or productivity-based. In an expansion, domestic consumption (including import consumption) increases, causing exports from a country's trading partners to increase; in a domestic contraction, import consumption decreases, causing exports from the trading partners to decline.

During the years 2002–2006, U.S. gross domestic product (GDP) grew at 1.8 percent, 2.5 percent, 3.6 percent, 3.1 percent, and 2.7 percent in real terms (i.e., adjusted for inflation) (see Table 6.1). The United States had an accelerating economy. In those same years, euro area real GDP, on the other hand, exhibited anemic growth at 1 percent, 0.8 percent, 1.9 percent, 1.8 percent, and finally 3.2 percent. Although Canadian growth rates were comparable to the United States, Mexico and Japan also had slower growth than the United States (again see Table 6.1). Among the five largest U.S. export trading partners, only China was growing faster than the United States (at 9.1 percent, 10 percent, 10.1 percent, 11.3 percent, and 12.7 percent). These growth-rate trends led to increased import flows into the United States of goods like autos, textiles, furniture, and

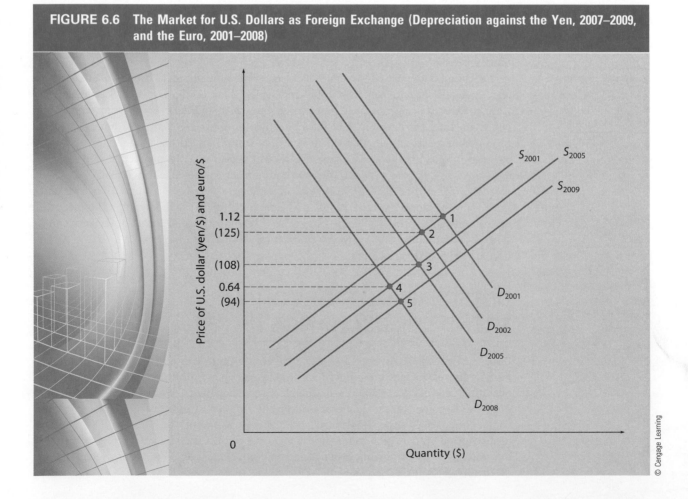

FIGURE 6.6   The Market for U.S. Dollars as Foreign Exchange (Depreciation against the Yen, 2007–2009, and the Euro, 2001–2008)

consumer electronics, while causing decreased exports from the United States of goods like computer software, PCs, grains, films, aircraft, professional services, medical devices, and diesel engines to everywhere except China.

As U.S. net exports fell (declining exports minus rising imports) in 2002–2007, the dollar depreciated, so year after year throughout this period, foreign buyers had to acquire *fewer* dollars to complete purchase transactions with U.S. companies like Microsoft, IBM, Archer Daniels Midland, Boeing, McKinsey, and Cummins Engine. In the market for USDs as foreign exchange depicted in Figure 6.6, the decline of net exports from the United States decreased the demand for dollars; D_{2001} shifted down to D_{2002} and on to D_{2005} and D_{2008}. At the same time, increased purchases of foreign imports by Americans increased the supply of dollars. That is, in the market for dollars as foreign exchange, S_{2001} shifted right to S_{2005} and on to S_{2009}. These shifts led to a depreciation of the U.S. dollar over the period 2001–2008. In sum, the decrease in exports and increase in imports led to a fall in the price of the dollar against the euro from €1.12 per dollar in 2001 to €0.64 per dollar in 2008 and against the yen from ¥125 per dollar in 2002 to ¥94 per dollar in 2009. The collapse of these €/$ and ¥/$ FX rates are depicted at the far right of Figure 6.1.

Example

European Slowdown Decreases DuPont Exports

"Beggar thy neighbor" became the rallying cry for trade policy in the Mercantilist period from 1500 to 1750, during which punitive tariffs and other forms of trade protectionism isolated city and provincial economies. Today, however, rather than attempting self-sufficiency, most nations are better off recognizing mutual interdependence, encouraging both import and export activities, and specializing in accordance with comparative advantage. In that freer trade environment, growing neighbors are the best neighbors.

An economic slowdown in Europe undercuts the export sales of American manufacturers and U.S. multinationals. Not only Cummins Engine with 28 percent, but also Sun Microsystems (36 percent), and DuPont (39 percent), and even Wrigley Chewing Gum (41 percent) and McDonald's (37 percent) realize a large proportion of their revenue in Europe. Across all S&P 500 U.S. companies, 20 percent of sales revenue arises from European sales. DuPont chemicals shipments from the United States to Europe, for example, decline by 20 percent on a year-to-year basis in European recessions like 2002–2003 and 2008–2009.

Continuing decay in the dollar's value threatens to derail the competitiveness of Chinese and Japanese exports and depreciate a massive balance sheet asset held by the central banks of China and Japan. In particular, in 2009 the Chinese (at $1.6 trillion) and Japanese (at $550 billion) alone held over $2 trillion in official U.S. dollar reserves. As a result, in 2008–2009 these two and a few other developing country central banks in Asia regularly purchased hundreds of billions of U.S. Treasury securities in an attempt to bolster the USD's value.[17]

---

[17]By accepting U.S. T-bill promissory notes and T-bonds in exchange for official dollar reserves, the Chinese, Japanese, and Singaporean central banks effectively reduce the supply of U.S. dollars in circulation. Reduced supply of USDs implies a higher equilibrium price.

TABLE 6.1 TRANSACTION DETERMINANTS OF LONG-TERM EXCHANGE RATE TRENDS

	UNITED STATES			GERMANY/EURO AREA			JAPAN			CHINA		
	REAL GDP	REAL r	PPI	REAL GDP	REAL r	PPI	REAL GDP	REAL r	PPI	REAL GDP	REAL r	PPI
1995	2.7	3.1	1.9	2.0	3.2	2.0	1.9	1.3	−0.6	10.5	−6.7	14.1
1996	3.7	2.5	2.7	1.0	1.4	1.0	2.6	0.5	−1.4	9.6	0.7	6.8
1997	4.5	3.3	0.4	1.9	1.4	1.8	1.4	−1.1	0.2	8.8	5.8	2.0
1998	4.4	4.0	−0.8	2.7	2.5	0.5	−2.2	0.0	0.3	7.8	5.5	−0.9
1999	4.8	3.1	1.8	2.9	1.9	3.9	0.0	0.5	−0.9	7.6	4.6	−0.8
2000	4.1	3.1	3.8	4.0	2.3	7.1	2.8	0.9	−0.2	8.4	2.9	2.4
2001	1.1	0.9	1.9	1.9	1.9	2.0	0.2	0.8	−0.7	8.3	2.7	2.8
2002	1.8	0.1	−1.3	1.0	1.0	−0.1	0.3	1.0	−0.9	9.1	3.5	1.3
2003	2.5	−1.1	3.2	0.8	0.3	1.4	1.5	0.34	−0.5	10.0	1.5	3.1
2004	3.6	−1.1	3.6	1.9	0.0	2.3	2.7	0.03	1.4	10.1	−0.7	7.5
2005	3.1	0.1	4.9	1.8	0.0	4.1	1.9	0.33	2.0	11.3	1.5	4.6
2006	2.9	3.0	3.2	3.2	0.9	2.0	2.0	0.0	−0.9	12.7	−1.8	3.6
2007	1.9	3.4	2.7	2.8	1.2	2.3	2.3	0.6	−0.7	14.2	−1.5	4.2
2008	0.0	−0.8	2.2	0.3	1.3	2.3	−1.2	−0.7	−0.9	9.6	−3.1	4.9
2009	−2.6	0.9	−2.5	−4.1	0.9	−3.7	−6.3	1.7	−4.3	9.2	3.5	−3.3
2010	2.9	−1.3	1.7	1.7	−0.8	2.5	4.0	0.9	−0.9	10.3	0.0	4.6
2011	1.8	−2.7	5.5	2.0	−1.5	5.6	−2.4	0.5	−0.2	9.1	−1.1	4.3

Notes: Real GDP refers to the growth rate of gross domestic product adjusted for price changes by the GDP deflator. Real r refers to the short-term interest rate on government debt minus the annual percentage change in consumer prices. PPI is the annual percentage change in producer prices.

Source: Federal Reserve Bank of St. Louis, *International Economic Trends*, August 2012.

The Role of Real Interest Rates

The second factor determining long-run trends in exchange rates is comparable interest rates adjusted for inflation. The higher the real rate of interest in an economy, the greater the demand for the financial assets offered by that economy. If a Japanese, German, or Swiss investor can earn higher returns (for equivalent risk) from U.S. Treasury bills than from Euromoney or Japanese government bills, foreign owners of capital will move quickly to rebalance their portfolios to incorporate more U.S. assets. Since the New York Federal Reserve Bank auctioning off new T-bills; J.P. Morgan underwriting a new issue of DuPont bonds; Merrill-Lynch selling T-bills, T-bonds, and DuPont bonds in the secondary (resale) market; and the New York Stock Exchange settlements department all require payment in U.S. dollars, the foreign investor who desires U.S. financial assets must first acquire U.S. dollars to complete his or her purchase transactions. So, a higher real interest rate in the United States (relative to European, Japanese, and British rates) implies international capital inflow into the United States and an increased demand for and appreciation of U.S. dollars.

What really matters in triggering these international capital flows is an investor's expectation of their own *domestic* value of the foreign interest earned when capital invested overseas is redeemed and the interest paid is converted back to the investor's home currency. Any differences between nominal interest rates minus consumer inflation rates in the foreign country versus the home country approximate this post-redemption return (see the column labeled real r in Table 6.1). In mid-1999, U.S.

three-month and six-month T-bills yielded on average 5.3 percent with a 2.2 percent inflation forecast, returned therefore 3.1 percent after adjusting for inflation. A year later in mid-2000, the real rate of return remained 3.1 percent in the United States (i.e., 6.5 percent − 3.4 percent). In the euro area, short-term interest rates also rose over this period from 3.0 percent to 4.4 percent, but so did anticipated inflation, growing from 1.1 percent in mid-1999 to 2.1 percent in mid-2000. Consequently, the real rate of short-term interest across Europe increased from 1.9 percent to 2.3 percent.

With 120 basis points favoring investment in U.S. assets in 1999 ([0.031 − 0.019] × 100), 150 basis points in 1998, and 190 basis points in 1997, foreign capital literally flooded into T-bills and other U.S. short-term money instruments. For example, between 1996 and 2000, European companies and investment funds like British Petroleum Amoco, British Telecom, BASF, Bayer, and UBS-Warburg invested $650 billion in foreign direct investment (FDI) in the United States. This four-year figure exceeds by half the entire FDI by Europe in the United States over the past 50 years. To reflect such an enormous international capital flow, the demand for the dollar in Figure 6.6 increases, causing the steep dollar appreciation of 1999, 2000, and 2001 shown in the FX rate charts in Figure 6.1.

In 2002, however, following the attack of September 11, 2001, in the midst of a three-quarter U.S. recession, real interest rates in the United States fell to 0.1 percent, the lowest rate in 40 years, and then continued lower to −1.07 percent in 2003 and −1.11 percent in 2004. Predictably, based on this real interest rate factor, the dollar then collapsed against the euro (see Figure 6.1). In 2008-2009 real interest rates in the United States again went negative (see Table 6.1), and the dollar sank to its lowest level ever against the euro—€0.64 per USD (again, see Figure 6.1).

The Role of Expected Inflation

Inflationary expectations provide an important third determinant of long-term trends in exchange rates. Suppose you were entering into a long-term contract to replace the diesel engines installed in a fleet of trucks over the next three to five years. Would you be inclined to approach and enter into negotiation with Cummins Engine, where recent material costs have been low, cost-saving productivity increases have been substantial, and union bargaining pressure may be declining? Or would you approach a substitute supplier such as Daimler's Mercedes-Benz, where all those factors are reversed, suggesting the strong possibility of an upsurging inflationary trend in input costs that underlies the price you could negotiate for a German diesel engine over the next several years?

Cost inflation is usually compared across economies by examining an index of producer prices. From 2003 to 2008, the percentage change in producer prices in the United States was 3.2, 3.6, 4.9, 3.7, 2.7, and 2.2 percent (as shown in Table 6.1) whereas in the euro area, producer prices increased by less—that is, 1.4, 2.3, 4.1, 2.0, 2.0, and 2.3 percent. Clearly, the lower price in a long-term fixed price contract for replacement diesels would not be available from Cummins, the company in a country experiencing higher cost-push inflation. Consequently, export sales on U.S. traded goods like Cummins diesels would decrease.[18]

In Figure 6.6, the D_{2002}, D_{2005}, and D_{2008} demands for the U.S. dollar all shift downward, and the dollar depreciates still further. Indeed, the relative purchasing power parity (PPP) hypothesis (discussed in the next section) holds that goods arbitrage on products

---

[18]Eventually, if producer cost inflation differentials between the United States and Germany persist, import-export companies that specialize in capital equipment transactions between the United States and Germany will join the surging demand for American products and buy replacement diesels cheaply in the United States for resale at a profit in Germany. This goods arbitrage activity, discussed in the next section, limits the extent to which such cost differentials can persist for long periods of time.

like diesel engines will continue until the €/$ exchange rate adjusts downward sufficiently to reflect entirely the inflation differential. That is, the cost inflation between the United States and Europe in 2003 of 1.8 percent (3.2 percent − 1.4 percent) differential in the producer price index favoring Europe should, according to PPP, depreciate the value of the dollar by approximately 1.8 percent. And this is exactly what happened for five years thereafter, until finally in 2008, the two inflation rates were approximately equal.

PURCHASING POWER PARITY

When there are no significant transportation costs, legal impediments, or cultural barriers associated with moving goods or services between markets, then the price of traded goods and services should be the same from one international market to another. This conclusion is known as the *law of one price*. When the different markets represent different countries, the law of one price says that prices will be the same in each country after making the appropriate conversion from one currency to another. Alternatively, one can say that exchange rates between two currencies will equal the ratio of the price indexes between the countries. In international trade and finance, this relationship is known as the absolute version of purchasing power parity.

Absolute purchasing power parity implies that differentially higher core price inflation in one location than another (which results, for example, in a doubling of U.S. prices for traded goods like autos, aircraft, and iPods) will ultimately result in a 50 percent depreciation of the U.S. currency. For example, if after a sustained period of U.S. price inflation, one needs $200 to buy a book that before the inflation cost $100, and if Japanese publishers will continue to print and sell that same book (in English) for an unchanged price of ¥10,000, the book will be produced in Japan and exported to the United States, driving down the dollar. How so? Such imports by Americans will necessitate a demand for Japanese yen to accomplish the purchase, and the supply of dollars to support these import transactions will continue to grow until the exchange rate reflecting the price of the U.S. dollar declines from ¥10,000/$100 = ¥100/$1 all the way down to ¥10,000/$200 = ¥50/$. At that point, the two prices for acquiring the book will again be the same in the two economies, divided by the new FX rate. In short, goods arbitragers in global supply chains will prevent the delivered prices in the United States and Asia from remaining different for very long.

Example

Birkenstocks for Sale Cheap!

Birkenstock sandals provide a good illustration of a traded good for which purchasing power parity should apply. In August 2008, Birkenstocks sold for €57 in Rome and €60 in Paris. Similarly, using the nominal exchange rate of £0.6/$, London and New York prices were nearly identical at £40 and $70. Both differences were too small to cover the shipping and generate an arbitrage profit. Were this not the case, enterprising arbitragers would buy cheap in one location and sell at a discount in the other, causing prices to converge. Birkenstock has authorized dealers in many parts of the world, and sells at a variety of price points through those dealers. Preventing counterfeit knockoffs from being purchased in Hong Kong, where the pricing is equivalent to USD58, for resale in Sydney, where the pricing is equivalent to USD98, presents a constant struggle. Nevertheless, PPP predicts arbitrage activity would emerge between Hong Kong and Australia until these prices are equated.

PPP Offers a Better Yardstick of Comparative Size of Business Activity

Purchasing power parity helps managers answer the difficult question of just how big foreign business opportunities really are. For example, the Chinese economy has become enormous relative to Japan, until recently the world's second biggest economy. To relate the ¥470 trillion Japanese economy to the U.S. economy, one simply divides by the nominal market-based exchange rate—JPY78 per USD. So, in 2011 the Japanese economy was equivalent to a $6 trillion economy. But the same procedure is not available for China because the CNY's "managed float" is far from a market-based equilibrium FX rate.

To address this issue of finding a commensurate yardstick to use in measuring Chinese GDP, one alternative is the FX rate implied by purchasing power parity (PPP). Absolute purchasing power parity hypothesizes that given sufficient time for adjustment, traded goods such as tires, sandals, motorbikes, laptops, iPods, and iron ore will have after-tax prices for which

$$\text{Price}_{\text{local currency A}} = \text{Price}_{\text{local currency B}} \times \text{PPP Implied FX}_{\text{A for B}}.$$

For example, at an FX rate implied by PPP, Apple iPods should sell for identical after-tax prices in the United States and United Kingdom. So, an Apple iPod Silver Classic with 120 gigabytes of memory selling on Amazon in the United States for $225 and on Amazon United Kingdom for £164 implies a PPP FX rate of $1.37/£:

$$\$225_{\text{US}} = £164 \times \text{PPP Implied FX}_{\$ \text{ for } £}$$
$$\$225_{\text{US}} = £164 \times \$1.37/£.$$

Again, $1.37/£ is not a market-based FX rate (i.e., the British pound is commanding $1.60 as this is written in New York trading). Nor is an Apple iPod the perfect traded good. Apple strives with great diligence to segment its market across countries, as do other branded product manufacturers. Moreover, foreign customer preferences (e.g., raw eel in Japan) and foreign retail competition (e.g., McDonald's fast food at Les Halles in downtown Paris) may not be typical. Nevertheless, averaging a thousand such calculations of FX rates implied by purchasing power parity for U.S.-China trade, the International Monetary Fund (IMF) calculates an implied PPP FX rate for China of 4.18 Chinese yuan to the U.S. dollar, or analogously a USD0.239 per CNY value of the yuan.[19] In other words, by the standard of PPP, the official "managed float" exchange rate of CNY6.34 per USD or USD.158 per CNY undervalues the yuan by 41 percent.

The PPP implied size of the Chinese economy today is therefore much bigger than $7.3 trillion; it is closer to $11.3 trillion. This represents 14 percent of the entire world economy relative to the U.S. economy's 19 percent.

Table 6.2 shows the PPP adjustments to the estimated size of various other economies. Where the cost of living (COL) is lower as in China, South Korea, Mexico, Turkey, and Poland, PPP adjustments raise the GDP estimates. Where the COL is higher as in Japan, Germany, and the United Kingdom, PPP adjustments lower the estimated GDP. For example, at prices prevailing in the United States, the business activity in the Australian economy is not USD1.5 trillion but rather just USD0.9 trillion.

How did China grow so fast during the Great Contraction 2008–2009 and its aftermath? One reason was that China introduced the largest fiscal stimulus worldwide (13 percent of GDP) and sharply relaxed credit conditions in late 2008 and early 2009.[20] But another reason is that the Chinese economy is on the brink of developed-country

---

[19]International Monetary Fund, *World Economic Outlook Database* (July 2012).

[20]"Rebalancing the World Economy: China," *The Economist* (August 1, 2009), pp. 65–66.

TABLE 6.2 PPP-ADJUSTED 2011 GDP BY COUNTRY			
	GDP NOMINAL (USD $ TRILLION)	COST OF LIVING % OF U.S. CPI-U(%)	GDP PPP-ADJUSTED (USD $ TRILLION)
U.S.	15.1	100	15.1
China	7.3	71	11.3
Japan	5.9	149	4.4
Germany	3.6	107	3.1
U.K.	2.4	132	2.2
Australia	1.5	157	0.9
S. Korea	1.1	80	1.5
Mexico	1.1	64	1.6
Turkey	0.8	56	1.1
Poland	0.5	59	0.8

© Cengage Learning 2014

living standards as an expectation for perhaps half the population located in the eastern, coastal provinces. That would not be so significant but for the fact that China contains 1.34 billion potential customers. Perhaps as many as 170 million people (equal to half the population of the United States) have recently become "middle class" with PPP-adjusted Chinese incomes over $20,000. These Chinese households are pursuing consumption, both domestic and imported, 10-fold greater than a decade ago. In aggregate, Chinese consumption is presently 35 percent of GDP compared to 50 to 60 percent in most other Asian countries and 70 percent in North America and Western Europe. As this gap narrows, the sales opportunities for Western products adapted to the Chinese market are going to be extraordinary.

 WHAT WENT RIGHT • WHAT WENT WRONG

Big Box U.S. Retailers in China[21]

Although some aspects of doing successful business overseas are obvious; other are more subtle. The Japanese have very small living spaces, whilst the growing middle class in China has more similar square footage relative to Americans to fill with furniture, appliances, and household gadgets in two and a half story suburban brick homes along the motorways. Nevertheless, Home Depot, Best Buy, and Mattel all closed their failing retail operations in China in 2011–2012 after five years of losses.

The reasons are instructive. Home Depot misunderstood that Chinese suburbanites would want to do weekend home improvement projects. But wage rates for a skilled tradesman in China, though rising, are still only $2 per hour, much less than the $5 per hour in Mexico, and far below the $29 per hour in the United States. So, Chinese potential customers of the do-it-yourself (DIY) industry see little reason not to hire patio masons or carpenters whenever they are needed, and therefore do not even consider performing such tasks themselves.

Similarly, after shipping to its nine Chinese stores its normal inventory of espresso makers, computers, televisions, and surround sound stereo equipment, Best Buy found customers wanted more choices in washing machines and window air conditioners to include color choices and load sizes unfamiliar to North Americans. All retail is "local." Foreign buyers may aspire to emulate the North American and European lifestyle but they want product variants that fit their own stage of development and their own culture.

This is especially true in India where a much smaller segment of the urban population has yet to reach middle-class incomes, and even poorer rural Indians have massive cultural differences with the West. As a result, in 2010–2011, even very small commuter autos from Tata Motors, part of the giant Indian conglomerate surrounding Tata Steel, have not fared well relative to traditional three-wheel motorized carts and motorbikes.

[21]Based on "Home Depot: Chinese Prefer 'Do-It-For-Me'" (September 15, 2012), p. B1.

Relative Purchasing Power Parity

relative purchasing power parity A relationship between differential inflation rates and long-term trends in exchange rates.

A less restrictive form of the law of one price is known as **relative purchasing power parity**. The relative PPP hypothesis states that in comparison to a period when exchange rates between two countries are in equilibrium, changes in the differential rates of inflation between two countries will be offset by equal, but opposite, changes in the future spot exchange rate.

The exact relative purchasing power parity relationship is

$$\text{Relative PPP} : \left(\frac{S_1}{S_0}\right) = \left(\frac{1+\pi_h}{1+\pi_f}\right) \qquad [6.1]$$

where S_1 is the expected future spot rate at time period 1, S_0 is the current spot rate, π_h is the expected home country (United States) inflation rate, and π_f is the expected foreign inflation rate.

If U.S. prices are expected to rise by 2 percent over the coming year, whereas prices in Europe are expected to rise by 3 percent, and if the current spot exchange rate (S_0) is \$1.30/€, then relative purchasing power parity implies the expected spot rate for the euro in one year (S_1) will be

$$S_1/\$1.30 = (1 + 0.02)/(1 + 0.03)$$
$$S_1 = \$1.30(0.990291)$$
$$= \$1.2874$$

The 1 percent higher European inflation rate can be expected to result in a decline in the future spot value of the euro relative to the dollar by approximately 1 percent.[22]

The dashed lines in Figure 6.7 indicate purchasing power parity between the strongest European currency that formed the euro and the U.S. dollar, accounting for cumulative inflation in the United States and Germany from 1973 to 2000. Over this period, the consumer price index in Europe rose from 67.1 to 137.2 (a 104 percent increase), and

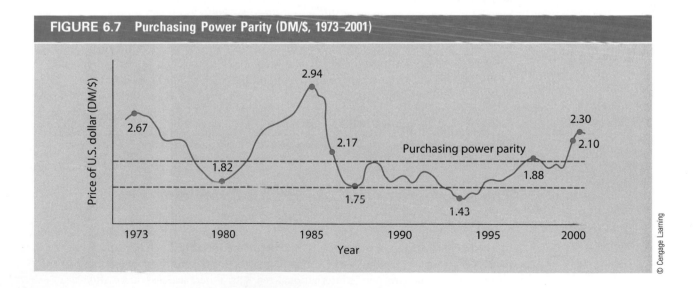

FIGURE 6.7   Purchasing Power Parity (DM/\$, 1973–2001)

Price of U.S. dollar (DM/\$)

2.94
2.67
2.30
2.17
2.10
1.82
Purchasing power parity
1.88
1.75
1.43

1973   1980   1985   1990   1995   2000
Year

© Cengage Learning

---

[22]Several other parity conditions in international finance are discussed in R.C. Moyer, J. McGuigan, R. Rao, and W. Kretlow, *Contemporary Financial Management*, 12th ed. (Cincinnati: Cengage/South-Western, 2012), Chapter 22.

the consumer price index in the United States rose from 49.3 to 166.7 (a 238 percent increase). Therefore, referring again to Figure 6.7, the dollar was substantially above its purchasing power parity level in 1984–1986 and again in 1999–2003. In each case, a subsequent sharp decline in value against European currencies ensued. Between 2001 and 2009, for example, the dollar lost 54 percent of its value against the euro (see Figures 6.1 and 6.7). Since then, the USD has regained almost 20 percent of its former value, reapproaching again purchasing power parity.

Qualifications of PPP

Purchasing power parity calculations can be very sensitive to the starting point for the analysis. In 2000, the ¥/$ exchange rate averaged ¥107/$, whereas in 2002 the average value of the dollar fell to ¥130/$ (see Figure 6.1). Between 2002 and 2009, the United States inflated by 22 percent, and Japan deflated by 2 percent. The 2000 starting point for a relative PPP calculation implies a 2009 exchange rate predicted by PPP of ¥86/$ (quite close to the actual value of ¥89/$), while the 2002 starting point implies a predicted 2009 exchange rate of ¥110/$. Clearly, the difference is nontrivial, and many such applications of the PPP hypothesis will hinge on which year the analyst chooses to start. Figure 6.7 highlights this qualification by displaying a rather wide band of exchange rates implied by the PPP hypothesis.

In addition, cross-cultural preference differences (e.g., the Islamic aversion to Western clothing for women or the proclivity for American football) can short-circuit PPP adjustments. Dissimilar trade policies can also cause violations of the law of one price on which PPP depends. If Europe has much higher agricultural subsidies and trade barriers to foreign crops than the United States, that policy may prevent the trade flows and subsequent exchange rate adjustments hypothesized by PPP.

No one would ever execute a currency arbitrage trade based on the predictions of the purchasing power parity hypothesis alone. Currency arbitrage is triggered by unanticipated events that generate very temporary profit opportunities lasting only several hours or a few days. The arbitrage-motivated trade flows in goods and services predicted by PPP in response to inflation differentials, on the other hand, are a much longer-term process requiring several quarters or even years. Companies with a substantial proportion of their sales abroad must assess these longer-term trends in exchange rates. For example, a realization that the dollar was well above purchasing power parity levels in 1999–2003 should have influenced production and pricing policies at Cummins Engine at the start of the twenty-first century. In the past six years 2004 to 2009, Cummins sales and cash flows have tripled because of the decade-long decline in the USD. Managers can and often do use PPP exchange rates to assess the current strength or weakness of a foreign currency and use that knowledge as an input into their three to five year business plans.

The Appropriate Use of PPP: An Overview

Being attuned to the international business environment of exchange rate trends does not allow fine tuning, but it does allow better medium-term planning of production volume, proactive pricing, target markets, and segmented distribution channels, all of which may offer profit advantages. Some companies make these considerations a focus of their business plans and prosper in international markets; others are less successful.

Arbitrage in goods requires logistical infrastructure like freight terminals, distribution networks, reliable retail relationships, and effective transnational marketing campaigns. Without all these pieces in place, international markets can remain somewhat segmented, thereby preventing the complete convergence of prices of identical products

WHAT WENT RIGHT • WHAT WENT WRONG

GM, Toyota, and the Celica GT-S Coupe[23]

As we saw at the start of the chapter, Toyota tends to preserve unit sales by slicing yen profit margins when their domestic currency strengthens. In contrast, GM often raises export list prices when the dollar strengthens in order to preserve the dollar value of their earnings from overseas subsidiaries when booked on the corporate income statement and balance sheet back in the United States. From 1980 to 1984, for example, GM raised Opel prices 48 percent as the dollar strengthened 47 percent. The depreciated revenue from foreign currency sales transactions in Europe was almost perfectly offset by the list price increases. Of course, this implied a skyrocketing 95 percent (48 percent + 47 percent) higher asking price in Frankfurt, Munich, and Köln. The Opel Division of General Motors found it difficult to explain to potential German customers why asking prices should essentially double in so short a period.

Why do GM and Toyota have such different pricing and markup policies? One might suspect Toyota sought greater sales volume to realize scale economies or take advantage of learning curve reductions in unit cost as cumulative volume increased. Nissan's plant in Smyrna, Tennessee, for example, is heralded as the most efficient assembly line in America, with worker productivity almost 35 percent higher than the average GM plant. In addition, Japanese total quality manufacturing (TQM) initiatives have realized much-heralded cost savings on the assembly plant floor as more vehicles pass quality inspections without requiring rework. Finally, Toyota, Honda, and Nissan certainly are export-driven companies. Nissan often generates 60 percent of its sales abroad (fully 45 percent in the United States alone).

General Motors, in contrast, has 72 percent domestic sales, 12 percent export sales, and 16 percent sales from overseas production divisions such as Opel in Europe and Holden in Australia. Consequently, GM does not focus marketing and operations planning on exports or overseas sales. Nevertheless, every company should always analyze its import market competition. By offsetting approximately half of any unfavorable exchange rate moves (involving an appreciation of the yen) by reducing export margins, all the Japanese auto manufacturers have grown their market share at GM's expense. From a high of 45 percent market share in the mid 1980s, GM has shrunk to 19 percent, and a still growing Toyota at 19 percent became the world's largest car company for several quarters in 2009. By 2011, market shares stood at GM 19 percent, Ford 17 percent, Toyota 15 percent, Honda 11 percent, Chrysler (now a division of Fiat) 9 percent, and Nissan 8 percent.

[23]Based on "General Motors and the Price of the Dollar," Harvard Business School Publishing, 1987.

© Cengage Learning

---

between the United States and Japan, between EU countries, between the United States and the United Kingdom, and even between the United States and Canada. Unlike arbitrage in financial markets, the goods arbitrage underlying PPP may take months, years, or even decades. As a result, the variance of prices for like goods across countries is larger (often 10 times larger) than the variance of prices through time within an economy.[24]

In the short run, therefore, price stickiness in traded goods combined with the lemming-like behavior of herds of FX speculators causes nominal exchange rates to overshoot or undershoot their equilibrium levels in adjusting to demand or monetary shocks. To avoid this problem, many analysts perform cross-border comparisons of price levels or trade statistics using purchasing power parity estimates for the prior 15-year period.

For example, if one observes that in June 2004, 10 feet of 0.019-gauge gutter pipe sells in DIY stores in the United States for $3.36 and that the value of the British pound is $1.80/£ (i.e., £0.55/$), it might be very misleading to calculate that identically priced gutter pipe should sell for £1.84 in the United Kingdom (i.e., $3.36 × £0.55/$). Even if the British are paying £2.10, the apparent arbitrage profit of (£2.10 − £1.84) × $1.80/£ = $0.47 per 10 feet may not be available. Consequently, rushing out to organize the distribution and export of U.S. gutter pipe for sale in United Kingdom every time the

---

[24]C. Engel and J.H. Rogers, "How Wide Is the Border?" *American Economic Review* 86 (1996), pp. 1112–1125; and "Goods Prices and Exchange Rates," *Journal of Economic Literature* 35 (1997), pp. 1243–1272.

exchange rate overshoots or undershoots does not make sense. Instead, one should multiply the $3.36 U.S. price by a £0.63/$ purchasing power parity value of the pound over 1990–2004 (see Figure 6.1). This would imply that gutter pipe in British stores selling for as much as £2.12 would not be overpriced relative to the United States. And, in light of the confidence bounds around PPP conditions, one might consider a British price of £2.12 + or − 10 percent (£1.91 − £2.33) consistent with the absence of arbitrage opportunities in gutter pipe.

Example

Big Mac Index of Purchasing Power Parity[25]

Big Mac hamburgers sold in 120 countries around the world are as close to identical as the McDonald's parent corporation can make them, yet individual country managers have complete discretion in setting the price. When the Big Mac index of PPP for a hamburger in Atlanta and Paris suburbs (i.e., $4.25/€3.33) just equals the actual exchange rate of $1.30/€ in 2012, neither currency is said to be overvalued. However, with a suburban McDonald's beyond the Périphérique in Paris selling the Big Mac for €2.73, the Big Mac PPP hypothesis implies that the euro is substantially overvalued (by 22 percent)—€3.33/€2.73 = 122 percent.

The Big Mac relationships are not a perfect application of the relative PPP hypothesis for several reasons: (1) because the 17 percent European Union VAT tax exceeds the 6 to 10 percent sales tax typical of most states in the U.S., (2) because land rents and utilities in Paris substantially exceed those in Atlanta, and (3) because the degree of fast food industry competition may not be equivalent. Despite these qualifications, the sustained depreciation of the euro against the USD in the first half of 2012 from $1.34/€ to $1.20/€ suggests burger economics has some merit.

[25]Based on "The Big Mac Index" *The Economist* (July 28, 2012), p. 66.

Trade-Weighted Exchange Rate Index

Figure 6.8 shows the value of the U.S. dollar against the currencies of the United States' largest trading partners from 1981 to 2012. This trade-weighted exchange rate, sometimes called the effective exchange rate (EER), calculates the weighted average value of the dollar against 19 currencies, where the weights are determined by the volume of import plus export trade between the United States and each of its trading partners. The EER for the United States is therefore defined as

$$\text{EER}_t^\$ = \sum_i \text{eI}_{it}^\$ \text{w}_{it} \qquad [6.2]$$

where w_{it} is the relative proportion of total import and export trade from and to country i in time period t.

From 1995 to 2001, the trade-weighted U.S. dollar appreciated substantially. All three factors determining long-run trends in exchange rates were involved. Real growth rates in the United States declined over this period relative to several of the United States' largest trading partners so imports declined. Real interest rates on U.S. T-bills were high and rising relative to those same trading partners. And finally, cost inflation in the U.S. producer price index was at a post-World War II low relative to the United States' largest trading partners. So capital flowed into the United States, and U.S. export trade rose dramatically.

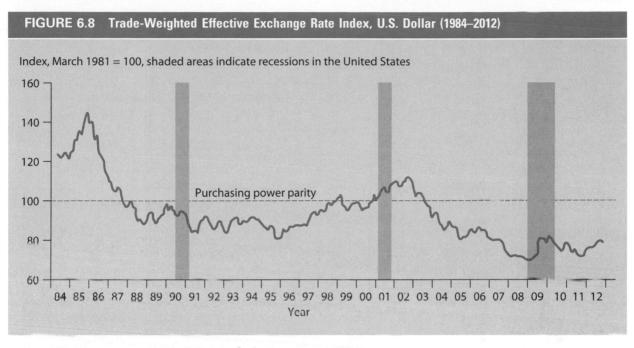

FIGURE 6.8   Trade-Weighted Effective Exchange Rate Index, U.S. Dollar (1984–2012)

Index, March 1981 = 100, shaded areas indicate recessions in the United States

Source: *National Economic Trends*, Federal Reserve Bank of St. Louis, quarterly

As it had been for their Japanese and European competitors in the 1980s, export trade provided the engine of growth for many U.S. companies in the 1990s and in 2005–2008. Panel (a) of Figure 6.9 shows that from the 1970s to the late 2000s, the share of exports relative to U.S. GDP grew from 5 to 18 percent. By 1997, one-third of real U.S. GDP

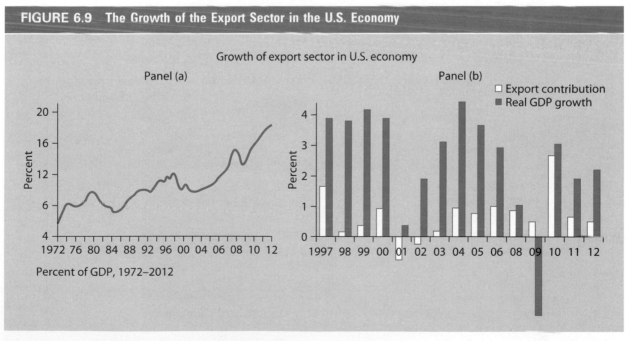

FIGURE 6.9   The Growth of the Export Sector in the U.S. Economy

Source: U.S. Department of Commerce, Bureau of Economic Analysis.

growth was attributable to exports. Between 1994 and 1997, that contribution of exports to GDP growth doubled. Between 1998 and 2002, the U.S. export sector decayed [see Figure 6.9, Panel (b)], primarily because the value of the dollar had appreciated above purchasing power parity (see Figure 6.7). However, at its highest recent peak values of ¥134 in mid-1998, DM2.30 in mid-2000, and €1.12 in 2001, the U.S. dollar was still well below its spectacular 1985 peak of ¥238 and DM2.94. This historical perspective can prove useful, because it took only a 34 percent depreciation of the dollar in 2001–2004 to restart the U.S. export sector. Figure 6.9, Panel (b) shows that with the exception of 2009 at the height of the global recession, exports have steadily increased during 2004–2011 to exceed 14 percent of GDP and are again contributing the majority of U.S. real GDP growth.

Example

Are Dirty Dishes Mobile? Dixan, Joy, Dawn, and Generic Patti Scala from Scala S.p.A.

Sometimes purchasing power parity (PPP) fails to characterize the price of identical items for sale in different currencies because some complementary factors in consumption or production are immobile. Unique real estate is one immobile factor; dirty dishes are another. In July 2001, after a 35 percent two-year appreciation of the U.S. dollar to 2,275 lire and 1.18 euros, Tuscan villagers found themselves serving mountains of *primi piatti* (first dishes) of various pastas to throngs of U.S. tourists. As a result, dirty dishes piled up high in many Italian sinks.

As elsewhere, dirty dishes in Italy eventually require *patti scala* (dish soap), and Scala S.p.A. from Castrocielo, France, supplies lemon-scented generic Patti Scala throughout the grocery stores of Tuscany. Generic Patti Scala at 1,900 lire competes directly against Dixan, a popular branded dish soap at 2,600 lire, both in regular size 750-ml plastic containers. What is extraordinary at first glance about these Italian prices is that in July 2001, the 1,900 lire and 2,600 lire equated to $0.84 and $1.14, respectively, much less than the price of equivalent dish soaps in U.S. stores (e.g., Harris Teeter sold generic dish soap for $1.80, and Joy, Palmolive, and Dawn sold for $1.99, $2.49, and $2.79 in comparable sizes (see Table 6.3). Does this imply that Joy, Palmolive, and Dawn should anticipate massive erosion of their U.S. market share because of an invasion of lower-priced Dixan imports from Italy?

TABLE 6.3   COMPETING DISH SOAP PRODUCTS IN THE UNITED STATES AND ITALY

BRANDED PRODUCTS	JUNE 2001 PRICE ($)	UNIT VOLUME (ml)
Joy	1.99	740
Palmolive	2.49	739
Dawn	2.79	740
Dixan (June 2001)	1.14 (2,600 lire) + 30% shipping = $1.45	750
Dixan (June 1999)	1.56 (2,600 lire) + 30% shipping = $2.03	750
GENERIC PRODUCTS		
Harris Teeter Dish Soap	1.80	828
Patti Scala (June 2001)	0.84 (1,900 lire) + 30% shipping = 1.09	750
Patti Scala (June 1999)	1.15 (1,900 lire) + 30% shipping = 1.48	750

© Cengage Learning

(continued)

The answer is definitely no, for three reasons. First, of course, customers of Joy, Palmolive, and Dawn in the United States do not recognize the Dixan brand. A massive advertising and promotional campaign by Dixan would be necessary to overcome the brand name barriers to entry in the U.S. market. International arbitrage in goods and full attainment of PPP is partially prevented by the customer-switching costs imposed by these brand name investments.

Second, even in the absence of branded products, PPP may fail to hold in the generic dish soap market because dirty dishes are immobile. Although the chemical ingredients, lemon scents, and hand softeners in Scala S.p.A.'s Patti Scala are virtually identical to those in Harris Teeter Dish Soap, and despite the availability of surplus Patti Scala at 1,900 lire in Italy, one must incorporate a transportation cost into these price comparisons. A delivered price of Patti Scala in the United States would be 1,900/2,275 lire = $0.84, plus perhaps 30 percent shipping cost—that is, $1.09. Still, one might reasonably ask why do the prices of generic dish soap products differ by as much as $1.09 to $1.80 across countries?

The answer lies in recognizing that purchasing power parity is a hypothesis about long-term price dynamics. Exchange rates often overshoot/undershoot their equilibrium levels, and consequently the ratio of retail prices in one economy to the exchange rate-adjusted retail prices in another economy should be computed over several years. For example, two years earlier the Italian lira was much stronger than in the summer of 2001; specifically, in June 1999, the U.S. dollar exchanged for just 1,665 lire, versus 2,275 lire in June 2001. With the suggested retail prices of Patti Scala and Dixan the same in 1999 as in 2001, Patti Scala at (1,900/1,665 lire =) $1.14 + 30 percent transportation cost = $1.47. This unit price in Italy is much closer to Harris Teeter's unit price of $1.80. Furthermore, Dixan at (2,600/1,665 lire =) $1.56 + 30 percent transportation cost = $2.03 is nearly identical to Joy's $1.99 price of branded dish soap.

In conclusion, successful brand name campaigns, the immobility of complements, and temporary exchange rate overshooting/undershooting may create significant gaps between the final product prices of like products sold in different currencies.

INTERNATIONAL TRADE: A MANAGERIAL PERSPECTIVE

Shares of World Trade and Regional Trading Blocs

Figure 6.10 shows that over the past two decades the import and export trade flows to and from the United States have grown to 32 percent of GDP; American exports are 14 percent of GDP or about $2 trillion worth of goods and services, of which 59 percent now goes to emerging markets. Some nations are much more export driven. In 2011, Germany and China both exported nearly $1.5 trillion but that represents a whopping 35 percent of German and 28 percent of Chinese GDP. British exports are 27 percent, Mexican exports are 35 percent, Canadian exports are 43 percent, South Korean exports are 43 percent, Malaysian exports are 93 percent, and Netherlands exports are 177 percent of GDP!

The United States is both the second largest exporter and the largest importer in the world's economy. Thus, the United States generates the largest share of the $35.8 trillion

FIGURE 6.10   U.S. Imports and Exports as a Percentage of GDP

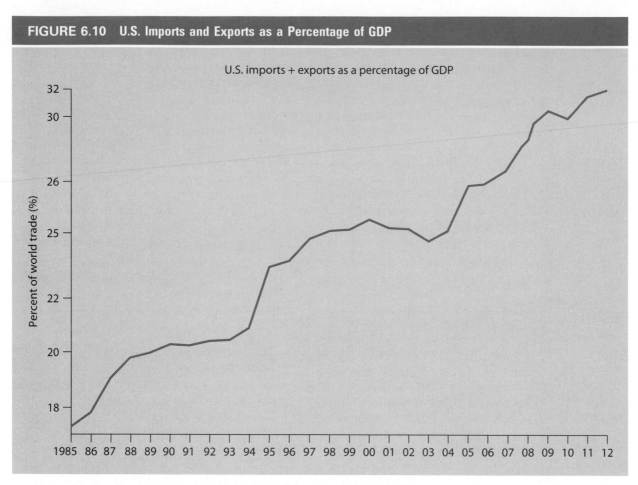

Source: U.S. Department of Commerce, Bureau of Economic Analysis.

in bilateral world trade (10.4 percent), comprising 8 percent of all exports and 13 percent of all imports. Figure 6.11 shows that the next nine countries with the largest shares of world trade in 2011 were China (10.2 percent), Germany (6.4 percent), Japan (4.7 percent), France (4 percent), the Netherlands (4 percent), Italy (3 percent), United Kingdom (3 percent), Belgium (3 percent), and Canada (2.5 percent). Although these largest trading nations are predominantly Western-developed economies, the next five largest trading nations are predominantly rapidly developing Asian economies: South Korea (2.6 percent), Hong Kong (2.3 percent), Russia (2.3 percent), Spain (2 percent), Singapore (2 percent), Mexico (1.9 percent), Taiwan (1.5 percent), and India (1.4 percent). Altogether, the World Trade Organization (WTO) includes 154 nations who have agreed to share trade statistics, coordinate the liberalization of trade policy (i.e., the opening of markets), and cooperatively resolve their trade disputes in accordance with WTO rules and procedures.

Today, the United States, the European Union (EU), and Canada have some of the lowest tariffs equivalent to 3 to 4 percent on imports. Mexico and India have some of the highest, equivalent to 12 to 15 percent. Fortunately, regional trading blocs like the EU and the North American Free Trade Agreement (NAFTA) have been highly successful in removing trade barriers, negotiating multilateral reductions in tariffs, and promoting free trade as a mechanism of peaceful competition between nations.

FIGURE 6.11   Gross Domestic Product, Exports as a Percentage of GDP, and Average Import Tariffs for MERCOSUR Countries

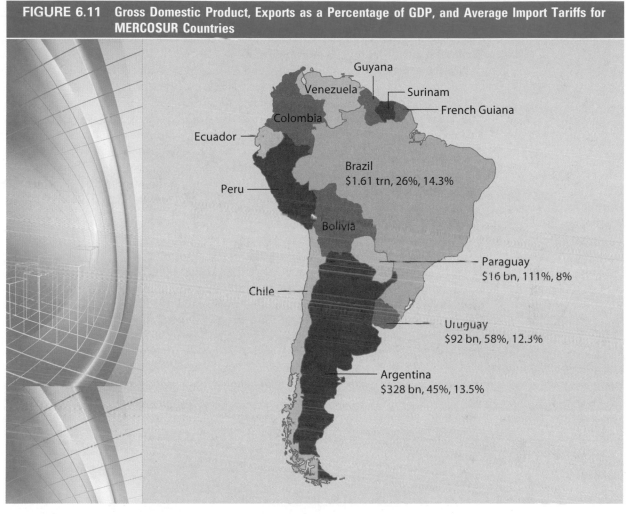

Source: World Trade Organization.

Across the world economy, six such regional trading blocs have emerged. In South America, Argentina, Brazil, Paraguay, and Uruguay have formed one trading block (MERCOSUR) whose import-export merchandise trade doubled from 1996 to 2006 and is now approaching $1 trillion, 80 percent of which is between the member countries. The Andean group (Peru, Colombia, Bolivia, and Ecuador) has formed another trading bloc; both are attempts to mirror the NAFTA free trade area of Canada, the United States, and Mexico.[26] The Brazilian ($1.8 trillion), Canadian ($1.6 trillion) and Mexican ($1.4 trillion) economies are comparable in size, about one-tenth the size of the U.S. economy. Brazil and Argentina have large industrial bases protected by 14 to 16 percent import tariffs, whereas Paraguay, Bolivia, and Guatemala are commodity-based economies employing 6 to 8 percent import tariffs, and Mexico has reduced its tariffs to 8 percent from 14 percent five years ago.

Trade disputes between Brazil and the United States have arisen over Brazilian steel, sugar, frozen orange juice, and ethanol exports. In 2009, Brazil achieved oil independence

---

[26]Seven Southeast Asian (ASEAN) and 16 trans-Pacific economies including Japan and Mexico (APEC) have also formed trading blocs.

through an extensive sugarcane-based ethanol industry producing over five billion gallons a year. Despite being the largest ethanol producer in the world with 6.5 billion gallons produced, the United States has effectively barred competition by imposing a protective ("infant industry") tariff on Brazilian ethanol.

Elsewhere, preferential trading agreements lowering tariffs, as well as capital and labor migration barriers within a regional trading block have been hugely successful. The EU-27 with 39 percent of world trade (equivalent to $8.5 trillion) has long surpassed North America with 13 percent of exports and 16 percent of imports in 2011 (see Figure 6.12). Asia accounts for another 30 percent of world exports, running a deficit with the rest of the world by importing 32 percent, much of these foreign-owned components inbound for final assembly. The fastest growing regions of the world exports in merchandise and services are South and Central America at 32 percent and the Middle East at 34 percent (again, see Figure 6.12). The Commonwealth of Independent States (Russia and its neighbors) is the fastest growing importer at 28 percent.

Comparative Advantage and Free Trade

Within a regional trading bloc like EU, NAFTA, MERCOSUR, or the Asian-Pacific Economic Cooperation (APEC), each member can improve its economic growth by specializing in accordance with comparative advantage and then engaging in free trade. Intuitively, low-wage countries like Spain, Mexico, Puerto Rico, China, and Thailand enjoy a cost advantage in the manufacture of labor-intensive goods such as clothes and the provision of labor-intensive services like sewing or coupon claims processing.

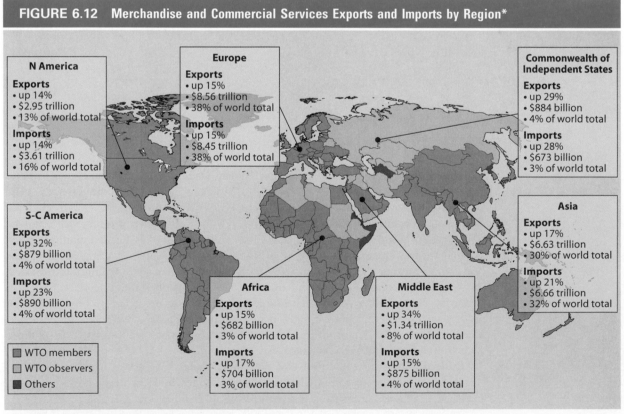

FIGURE 6.12 Merchandise and Commercial Services Exports and Imports by Region*

N America

Exports
• up 14%
• $2.95 trillion
• 13% of world total

Imports
• up 14%
• $3.61 trillion
• 16% of world total

Europe

Exports
• up 15%
• $8.56 trillion
• 38% of world total

Imports
• up 15%
• $8.45 trillion
• 38% of world total

Commonwealth of Independent States

Exports
• up 29%
• $884 billion
• 4% of world total

Imports
• up 28%
• $673 billion
• 3% of world total

S-C America

Exports
• up 32%
• $879 billion
• 4% of world total

Imports
• up 23%
• $890 billion
• 4% of world total

Asia

Exports
• up 17%
• $6.63 trillion
• 30% of world total

Imports
• up 21%
• $6.66 trillion
• 32% of world total

Africa

Exports
• up 15%
• $682 billion
• 3% of world total

Imports
• up 17%
• $704 billion
• 3% of world total

Middle East

Exports
• up 34%
• $1.34 trillion
• 8% of world total

Imports
• up 15%
• $875 billion
• 4% of world total

☐ WTO members
☐ WTO observers
■ Others

*Values and shares include intra-EU trade.

Source: World Trade Organization.

Suppose one of these economies also enjoys a cost advantage in more capital-intensive manufacturing like auto assembly. One of the powerful insights of international microeconomics is that in such circumstances, the low-cost economy should not produce both goods, but rather it should specialize in that production for which it has the lower relative cost, while buying the other product from its higher-cost trading partner. Let's see how this **law of comparative advantage** in bilateral trade reaches such an apparently odd conclusion.

Consider the bilateral trade between the United States and Japan in automobile carburetors and computer memory chips. Suppose the cost of production of carburetors in Japan is ¥10,000 compared to $120 in the United States. At an exchange rate of ¥100/$, the Japanese cost-covering price of $100 is lower than the U.S. cost-covering price of $120. Suppose, in addition, that memory chips cost ¥8,000 in Japan compared to $300 in the United States. Again, the price of the Japanese product (i.e., $80) is lower than the price of the U.S. product. Japan is said to enjoy an **absolute cost advantage** in the manufacture of both products. However, Japan is 83 percent (i.e., $100/$120) as expensive in producing carburetors as the United States while being only 27 percent (i.e., $80/$300) as expensive in producing memory chips. Japan is said to have a comparative advantage in memory chips and should specialize in the manufacture of that product.

The gains from specialization in accordance with comparative advantage and subsequent trade are best demonstrated using the real terms of trade. **Real terms of trade** identify what amounts of labor effort, material, and other resources are required to produce a product in one economy relative to another. In Japan, the manufacture of memory chips requires the sacrifice of resources capable of manufacturing 0.8 carburetors (see Table 6.4), whereas in the United States the manufacture of a memory chip requires the sacrifice of 2.5 carburetors. That is, Japan's relative cost of memory chips (in terms of carburetor production that must be forgone) is less than a third as great as the relative cost of memory chips in the United States. On the other hand, U.S. carburetor production requires the resources associated with only 0.4 U.S. memory chips, while Japanese carburetor production requires the sacrifice of 1.25 Japanese memory chips. The U.S.

law of comparative advantage A principle defending free trade and specialization in accordance with lower relative cost.

absolute cost advantage A comparison of nominal costs in two locations, companies, or economies.

real terms of trade Comparison of relative costs of production across economies.

*Terms of trade
1 chip for 1.5 carb*

TABLE 6.4 REAL TERMS OF TRADE AND COMPARATIVE ADVANTAGE

	ABSOLUTE COST, U.S. ($)	ABSOLUTE COST, JAPAN (¥)
Automobile carburetors	120	10,000
Computer memory chips	300	8,000

	RELATIVE COST, U.S.	RELATIVE COST, JAPAN
Automobile carburetors	120/300 = 0.4 Chips	10K/8K = 1.25 Chips — *for 1 carb.*
Computer memory chips	300/120 = 2.5 Carbs	8K/10K = 0.8 Carbs

	GAINS FROM TRADE, U.S.	GAINS FROM TRADE, JAPAN
Initial goods	1.0 Carb + 1.0 Chip	1.0 Carb + 1.0 Chip
After specialization:		
Carburetors produced	(1.0 + 2.5) Carbs	0
Memory chips produced	0	(1.0 + 1.25) Chips
Trade	+1.0 Chip	+1.5 Carb
	−1.5 Carb	−1.0 Chip
Net goods	2.0 Carbs + 1.0 Chip	1.5 Carbs + 1.25 Chips

specialize in carbs   *spec. in chips*

© Cengage Learning

relative cost of carburetors is much lower than that of the Japanese. Said another way, the Japanese are particularly productive in using resources to manufacture memory chips, and the United States is particularly productive in using similar resources to produce carburetors. Each country has a comparative advantage: the Japanese in producing memory chips and the United States in producing carburetors.

Assess what happens to the total goods produced if each economy specializes in production in accordance with comparative advantage and then trades to diversify its consumption. Assume that the United States and Japan produced one unit of each product initially, that labor is immobile, that no scale economies are present, and that the quality of both carburetors and memory chips is identical. If the Japanese cease production of carburetors and specialize in the production of memory chips, they increase memory chip production to 2.25 chips (see Table 6.4). Similarly, if the United States ceases production of memory chips and specializes in the production of carburetors, it increases carburetor production to 3.5 carburetors. In these circumstances, the United States could offer Japan 1.5 carburetors for a memory chip, and both parties would end up unambiguously better off. The United States would enjoy a residual domestic production after trade of 2.0 carburetors plus the import of one memory chip. And the Japanese would enjoy a residual domestic production after trade of 1.25 memory chips plus the import of 1.5 carburetors. As demonstrated in Table 6.4, each economy would have replaced all the products they initially produced, plus each would thereafter enjoy additional amounts of both goods—that is, unambiguous gains from trade.

Import Controls and Protective Tariffs

Some nations reject free-trade policies and instead attempt to restrain the purchase of foreign imports in order to expand the production of their domestic industries by artificially raising the price of substitute foreign products using *protective tariffs*. Figure 6.13 shows that Hong Kong, the United States, and Australia have some of the lowest protective tariffs while China, South Korea, Brazil, and India have some of the highest. To further bar imports, some nations also impose *direct import controls* like a maximum allowable quota of a specific type of foreign import. Once in the 1990s, to preserve American manufacturing jobs, the U.S. Congress imposed so-called voluntary import restraints (VIRs) on Japanese autos. In response, Toyota and Honda built assembly plants all over the United States, and many laid-off GM, Ford, and Chrysler workers went to work building Camrys and Accords in these U.S.-based Japanese plants. The same U.S. policy has now been proposed against Chinese-manufactured textiles.

National income is typically reduced by countries which impose such import barriers. One reason is because as Japanese and Chinese exports decelerate lower incomes cause Japanese and Chinese households to decrease their import consumption of Buick LeSabres or Cadillacs and of fashion jean merchandise from VF's 7 for Mankind. A second reason is that import controls lead inevitably to an appreciation of a nation's currency in the foreign exchange market. For example, when some American households are prohibited from completing import purchases of Japanese-manufactured Toyotas and Hondas they would otherwise have bought, those households fail to request the Japanese yen they would have needed to accomplish the import purchases. This results in a higher FX value of the USD against the JPY, which in turn retards the U.S. export sector, worsening the trade imbalance the import controls were designed to address.

In short, free trade and open markets offer the prospect of higher national income. The World Bank estimates that developing countries with open economies grow by

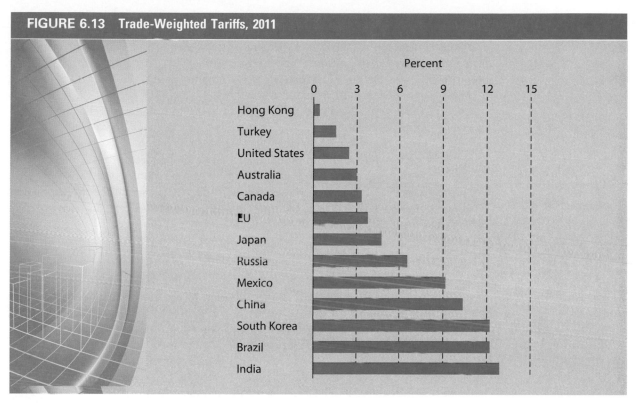

FIGURE 6.13   Trade-Weighted Tariffs, 2011

Source: WTO database, 2011.

4.5 percent per year, whereas those with import controls and protective tariffs grow by only 0.7 percent per year. Rich country comparisons also favored free trade: 2.3 percent to, again, 0.7 percent. In the 1990s, this gap widened still further. Those developing countries whose import plus export trade as a percentage of GDP ranked in the top 50 percentiles of developing countries had GDP growth per person of 5 percent. Those in the bottom 50 percentiles saw GDP growth per person actually shrink by 1 percent.[27] Clearly, globalization and trade enhance prosperity, even in the lesser developed countries.

There *are* several valid arguments against unilateral free trade (and in favor import quotas or tariffs): (1) to protect *infant industries* until they reach minimum efficient scale, (2) to offset government subsidies provided to foreign competitors with one's own *countervailing duties*, and (3) to impose *antidumping sanctions* for foreign goods sold below their domestic cost. Chilean salmon, Argentine honey, Chinese tires, and Brazilian frozen orange juice concentrate, and slab steel have all been subject to U.S. antidumping duties in recent years. The Brazilians, in particular, claim that their export prices are an attempt to offset the enormous $30 billion in farm subsidies that the United States makes available to its agricultural sector. The United States does spend $20,000 per full-time farmer to subsidize agricultural products (third behind Switzerland's $27,000 and Japan's $23,000).

The WTO has undertaken as part of its Doha round of trade talks to begin sorting out these claims and counterclaims on agricultural and industrial subsidies and the

---

[27]"Globalization, Growth and Poverty," *World Bank Report* (December 2001).

countervailing duties they precipitate. For example, the WTO ruled in 2011 that both Boeing and Airbus had received improper government subsidies to their aircraft loan and R&D programs 1984–2001. A settlement between the EU and U.S. disputants is predicted. Brazilian ethanol continues, however, to be effectively barred by a steep American import tariff protecting the corn-based domestic ethanol plants even though sugarcane is three times more energy efficient than Iowa corn.

The WTO also refereed a dispute in 2010 over the Information Technology Agreement (ITA) by which the EU, Japan, Taiwan, the United States and 70 other nations agreed to lower tariffs on $1.5 trillion of high-tech goods like flat-panel computer screens, scanning printers, and so on. HP and Canon joined forces to have the U.S. and Japanese governments file a WTO case seeking the prohibition of the EU's protective tariffs against television converter boxes. The WTO has so ruled, and the threat of countervailing duties on BMWs, Glaxo pharmaceuticals, and French cheese has succeeded in having the offending European tariff removed.

The Case for Strategic Trade Policy

Although the logic of free trade has dominated academic debate since 1750, and the twentieth century saw the repeal of many import controls and tariffs, a few exceptions are worth noting. The WTO has very effectively spearheaded the negotiation of *mutual* trade liberalization policies. However, *unilateral* reduction of tariffs when trading partners stubbornly refuse to relax import controls or open their domestic markets seldom makes sense. The United States has found it necessary to threaten tariffs on Japanese consumer electronics, for example, in order to negotiate successfully the opening of Japanese markets to U.S. cellular phones and computer chips. This threat bargaining and negotiated mutual reduction of trade barriers illustrates the concept of "strategic trade policy."

In the spring of 1999, continued EU import controls on U.S.-based Dole and Chiquita bananas from Central America led the United States to impose WTO-sanctioned duties on $180 million of European products from Louis Vuitton plastic handbags and British cashmere sweaters to French Roquefort cheese and foie gras. The British and French former colonies in the Caribbean such as Saint Lucia enjoy approximately $150 million in banana farm profits as a result of the EU's quota limiting the importing of U.S. bananas into Europe. But the cost to EU consumers has been estimated at $2 billion in higher-priced fruit. Despite this apparently lopsided cost-benefit analysis, it took strategic trade policy by the United States to induce the EU to relax its banana import controls.

internal hedge
A balance sheet offset or foreign payables offset to fluctuations in foreign receipts attributable to exchange rate risk.

Example

President Bush's 2002 Steel Tariffs and President Obama's 2009 Tire Tariffs: Justified Sanctions or Hypocritical Protectionism?[28]

Despite its heavyweight and high transportation cost, steel is sourced from factories around the globe. At $350 per ton, sheet steel from Brazil and South Korea can be transported to the United States for $70 per ton shipping cost and still sell $55 below the $475 per ton cost of the big integrated hot-rolled steel producers in the United States like Bethlehem and Republic Steel (see Table 6.5). As a result, 15 of 17 such integrated U.S. producers who convert iron ore in blast furnaces using 160,000

(continued)

United Steel Workers (USW) are operating under bankruptcy protection from their creditors.

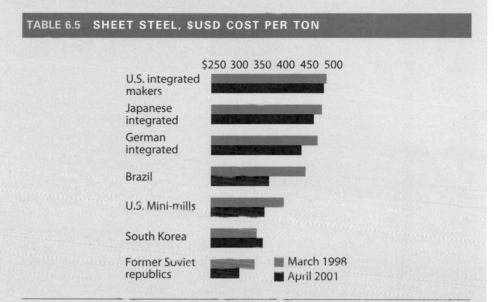

| TABLE 6.5 | SHEET STEEL, $USD COST PER TON |

Source: *World Steel Dynamics*, 2002.

Only AK Steel, U.S. Steel, Nucor, and other mini-mill producers are profitable. Nucor employs one-third as many workers as the integrated mills, using less expensive electric arc furnaces. In addition, because Nucor starts with scrap metal, not iron ore, their principal input cost is highly correlated with final steel sheet and steel slab prices, a highly effective **internal hedge**. For example, when slab steel prices sank from $300 to $200 recently, the price of Nucor's scrap steel input plummeted to all-time low as well.

Yet, the USW is a powerful political lobby, and U.S. International Trade Commission hearings plus WTO antidumping rules and dispute resolution procedures provided the vehicle for President Ford and President George W. Bush to consider imposing tariff sanctions to protect the domestic steel industry. In March 2002, Bush decided to impose quotas on Brazilian steel and 30 percent tariffs on steel slab and steel sheet from several other nations for three years. Citing credit, land, and energy subsidies, President Obama imposed a similar punitive tariff of 35 percent on Chinese light-truck and auto tires in 2009 and 26 percent on Chinese wind turbines in 2012. Section 421 of the U.S. Trade Act allows the President to act before the antidumping or prohibited subsidies case is proved at the WTO. Predictably, such trade restrictions increase the cost of commercial construction and of replacement auto parts in the United States. For example, Precision Technologies of Houston, Texas, estimated it raises its costs by $3 million on $57 million in annual sales of high-stress steel tubing for the drilling industry.

---

[28]Based on "Rust Never Sleeps," *The Economist* (March 9, 2002), p. 61; "U.S. Companies Cry Foul," *Wall Street Journal* (March 19, 2002), p. A2; "U.S. Protectionism Imperils Free Trade Talks with Latins," *Wall Street Journal* (March 20, 2002), p. A15; "Brazil Claims Victory over E.U.," *Wall Street Journal* (August 20, 2004), p. A1; and "Airbus Ruling Fuels Critics," *Wall Street Journal* (September 8, 2009), p. B4.

Example

Intel's Chip Market Access Improves in Japan[29]

In the mid-1980s, Japanese semiconductor producers grabbed much of the world market in the dynamic random access memory (DRAM) chips used in personal computers. Through a combination of very aggressive pricing and an almost closed domestic market, Japanese semiconductors achieved massive economies of scale and unit costs far below those in the United States. When the retail price of PCs declined steeply in 1986, the American and European manufacturers like Intel ceased production of basic memory chips.

That same year, an international dumping complaint filed at the WTO proved that many Japanese chips had been sold in the United States and Europe below cost. The U.S. Department of Commerce then imposed punitive tariffs on Japanese chips, laptop computers, and televisions. To avoid these higher tariffs, the Japanese agreed to open access to their domestic market and set a 20 percent target for foreign memory chip sales in Japan. Intel Corp., Siemens, and other producers expanded, and the Japanese producers Sharp and Toshiba cut production. When the chip access accords expired in 1995, the Japanese, U.S., and German semiconductor manufacturers formed joint ventures to codesign and jointly manufacture subsequent generations of flash memory chips. In this instance, strategic trade policy opened markets and expanded the national income of all the participating nations.

[29]Based on "America Chips Away at Japan," *The Economist* (March 27, 1993); and "Foreign Chip Sales Up in Japan," *Financial Times* (December 16, 1994).

Increasing Returns

The final motivation for strategic trade policy arises in markets where domestic producers encounter increasing returns. Suppose the Boeing Corp. and Airbus find that learning curve advantages in airframe manufacturing offer a 1 percent reduction in *variable* cost for every market share point above 30 percent. A firm with a 40 percent (or 50 percent) market share of the world output of smaller wide-body aircraft (like the Boeing 737s) will experience variable costs only 90 percent (or 80 percent) as great as smaller competitors. These circumstances are very rare indeed in the industrial sector of the economy, since they imply that diminishing returns in production at higher output rates are more than offset by the learning curve advantages. However, where such circumstances exist, the United States, Europe, Japan, and now China continue to use industrial policies to jump-start the preemptive development of dominant companies using public subsidies for research and development.

Network Externalities

The information economy has a higher incidence than the industrial economy of these increasing returns phenomena. Frequently, in the information economy context, cost reductions at larger market share are associated with externalities in the installation of a network or the adoption of a technical standard. As the installed base of Windows software expands, Microsoft finds it increasingly less difficult to convince new customers to adopt their product. Computer users find it much easier to exchange documents and explain new applications if their coworkers and customers employ the same operating system. As a result, the marketing cost to secure the next adoption from a marginal buyer actually declines, the larger the market share that Windows attains. The same thing holds for Apple's operating system. The greater the installed base, the more software the independent programmers will write for use on an iPad or iPhone. The more software or apps available for use, the lower the variable cost to Apple of successfully marketing the next Apple laptop or phone.

Example

Microsoft and Apple: A Role for Protective Tariffs?

Should strategic trade policy in the United States protect a company with the possibility of achieving increasing returns? Microsoft and Apple pose a good case in point. *Without* import controls and protective tariffs, Microsoft successfully achieved a larger dollar volume of export trade than any other American company. Now Apple has achieved similar success without import controls and protective tariffs.

Is it an appropriate role of the government to pursue such cost advantages for one domestic company or an alliance of domestic companies? Or should government pursue the consumer interest of lowest prices wherever that product is produced? These are the questions hotly debated in strategic trade policy today. The case exercise on reciprocal protectionism at the end of Chapter 13 looks at these strategic trade policy questions in the context of tactical choices of Boeing and Airbus.

FREE TRADE AREAS: THE EUROPEAN UNION AND NAFTA

Free trade and increased specialization in accordance with comparative advantage has the relatively low-wage Spaniards and Portuguese assembling high value-added German components for BMWs and Blaupunkt radios. Hungarian factories turn out components for Polish plants assembling school buses. Similarly, reduced trade barriers at borders have cut transportation time within the EU. The English Channel ferry now unloads in 15 minutes rather than the previous 1.5 hours, and yogurt from Nestlé's subsidiary in Birmingham, England, now speeds across Europe to target customers in Milan, Italy, in 11 hours rather than the previous 38 hours. Reduced intra-European tariffs on foodstuffs, beer, wine, and autos have markedly reduced the cost of living. Although employee-paid social security taxes continue to differ widely from 22 percent of earnings in France and Italy, to 14 percent in Germany, and just 6 percent in the United Kingdom, once wide differences in value-added taxes have been reconciled at uniform 17 percent rates.

Few pan-European marketing plans exist. The Spanish consider packaged pet food a luxury and purchase yogurt through the pharmacy. The peak penetration of TV into Spanish households (20 percent viewership) occurs at 2:00 P.M. to 4:00 P.M. Only 8 percent of Spanish households are tuned in from 6:00 P.M. to 8:00 P.M. when the 22 percent peak British audience is "watching the telly." Milanese brag about overpaying for a Sony television, while Munich shoppers search for days to find 5 percent discounts on fashion clothing or appliances. In short, segmented markets characterize the European free trade area.

This is no more easily demonstrated than by examining the price variation for standard goods across the EU-15 enlarged by 12 new members in 2004–2007. In Table 6.6, at the origin of the Common Market in 1992, Coca-Cola and Heinz Ketchup were

TABLE 6.6	PRICE DIFFERENTIALS IN EUROPE		
LARGEST MEAN DIFFERENCE BY COUNTRY		**HIGH**	**LOW**
1992	Coca-Cola (1.5 L)	Ecu 0.69 (Belgium)	Ecu 1.45 (Denmark)
	Heinz Ketchup	Ecu 0.86 (UK)	Ecu 1.92 (Spain)
	Clothes Washer	Ecu 407 (UK)	Ecu 565 (Italy)
	Portable TV	DM434 (Germany)	DM560 (Italy)
	VCR	DM1383 (Germany)	DM1873 (Spain)
1998	Big Mac	Ecu 1.75 (Spain)	Ecu 2.10 (Belgium)
	Ford Mondeo	DM32,000 (Spain)	DM48,000 (Germany)
2004	Compact Disk	€13.50 (France)	€21.80 (Ireland)
	Pampers	€6.75 (Hungary)	€21.00 (Denmark)
	Big Mac Meal	€2.80 (Estonia)	€8.80 (Norway)
	Coca-Cola	€0.65 (Lithuania)	€2.50 (France)
	Movie Ticket	€4.00 (Lithuania)	€15.00 (Britain)
	Milk (1 G)	€2.20 (Czech Rep.)	€4.86 (Norway)

% STANDARD DEVIATION ACROSS EUROPE, EURO-11 PRICE INDEX, PRETAX		
	Household Insurance	51%
	Coca-Cola by the glass	29%
	Local Phone Service	25%
	Yogurt	20%
	Gasoline	14%
	Levi 501 Jeans	10%
	VW Golf	5%

Source: *Financial Times, The Economist,* various issues.

approximately twice as expensive in Denmark and Spain as in Belgium and the United Kingdom. Twelve years later in 2004, food products like Coca-Cola and milk remained 100 percent more expensive in Norway than in Hungary or the Czech Republic. Appliances and consumer electronics can be more easily bought in one location and sold in another. Hence, clothes washers and portable TVs differed in price less than 20 percent. Similarly, the standard deviation of prices across Europe is lowest for highly mobile VW Golf autos and Levi jeans and highest for services like household insurance and soft drinks by the glass.

Optimal Currency Areas

In 1999, 11 European currencies were replaced by the euro in a single currency union. But one of the original E-12 (Britain) decided to opt out, as have Sweden and Denmark subsequently. Today, 10 new Eastern European members of the much enlarged E-27 **free trade area** have been invited to join the euro's currency union of now 17 nations, the E-17. Why is that?

How far and wide a single currency should be adopted as the official monetary unit across a free trade area depends on a complex mix of economic, social, and political factors. The benefits of a single currency are the avoidance of exchange rate risk on intraregional trade and the associated hedging costs plus a massive reduction in FX conversion costs. Companies such as the German pharmaceutical firm Hoechst AG estimates that it saves over €6 million annually in covered forward contract costs by not needing to lay off risk exposure on European currencies. Hedging does cost on average 5 percent of the

free trade area
A group of nations that have agreed to reduce tariffs and other trade barriers.

value at risk
The notional value of a transaction exposed to appreciation or depreciation because of exchange rate risk.

value at risk, and the total value of world trade equals $36 trillion per year, so conceivably $1.8 trillion in hedging costs are at issue worldwide. In addition, just the mere act of exchanging foreign currency, which once required 1 in every 200 full-time employees in Europe, is now totally avoided.

The boundary of an optimal currency area hinges on three factors: the magnitude of intraregional trade, the mobility of labor, and the correlation of macroeconomic shocks between countries within the proposed currency union.

Intraregional Trade

Every nation of the European Union trades more with other EU members than with the rest of the world, and in Belgium, the Netherlands, and Ireland trade makes up a majority of their GDP. Italy, Germany, and France do 55 to 60 percent of their total trade with other European countries, and Spain does 70 percent. Ireland, Portugal, and Benelux do close to 80 percent. Even Britain trades more with their regional trading bloc partners than with the rest of the world combined.

Mobility of Labor

With monetary policy constrained by the need for credibility in fighting inflation, and with fiscal policy constrained by more or less effective debt/GDP guidelines for membership in the currency union, only labor mobility is available to stabilize swings in unemployment caused by localized market conditions. For example, if Italy is in a slump, Germany and France are booming, and Ireland and Portugal plus Eastern Europe are growing slowly, a common monetary policy combined with little fiscal autonomy requires that labor move quickly from the fringes of the EU to Western Europe. Although such mobility occurs easily in the United States where a family can find schools, houses, and language in one state very similar to a state they leave, the same cannot be said in Europe. Relocation costs in the United States of $25,000 compare to an estimated $75,000 in Europe.

In addition, cultural differences are enormous from one corner of the EU to another. While European professionals have trained in foreign capitals and accepted diversity in mannerisms and cultural practices for centuries, working-class Europeans tend to be more culturally prejudicial. Thus, even those who would take the initiative to cross national and cultural borders in pursuit of transitory jobs typically will experience less than full acceptance as "guest workers." Expansion of the EU free trade area into Eastern Europe has compounded this problem of the labor mobility required to justify a currency union.

Correlated Macroeconomic Shocks

European countries differ in the strength of their unions, payroll taxes, minimum wages, layoff restrictions, and unemployment insurance. Europe's many separate labor markets cause common macroeconomic shocks to result in a growing dispersion of natural rates of unemployment from 4 percent in Ireland to 20 percent in Spain. Output per capita differs by 100 percent between wealthy Milan, Munich, and the Rhineland versus poor Greece, Southern Italy, Portugal, and Eastern Europe. Poland is about half as wealthy as the EU-17. Manufacturing labor compensation varies spectacularly from €34 per hour in France and €31 in Germany, falling by 50 percent to €21 in Spain and €20 in the United Kingdom, and then halving again to €8 per hour in Portugal, Hungary, the Czech Republic, and Poland. The breadth of these labor market rates suggests not only an extraordinary immobility of labor but also a heterogeneity of macroeconomic forces that gives rise to uncorrelated shocks.

Example

If Europe, What about One Currency for NAFTA?

Should the Mexican peso, the Canadian dollar, and the U.S. dollar be replaced by a single currency for NAFTA? Seventy-nine percent of Canadian trade and 88 percent of Mexican trade involves the United States, and exports plus imports account for 70 percent of GDP in Canada and 58 percent in Mexico. Nevertheless, a one-size-fits-all monetary policy and little fiscal autonomy may well be as inappropriate for North America as it is for the E-27. Although Canadian macroeconomic shocks and responses are highly correlated with the United States, Mexico is a petroleum exporter with business cycles more similar to Venezuela than to the United States. For the same reason that Britain opted out of a common currency, so should Mexico. And the immigration and labor mobility issues between the United States and Mexico echo similar issues in Europe.

LARGEST U.S. TRADING PARTNERS: THE ROLE OF NAFTA

Canada, not Japan, is by far the largest trading partner of the United States with almost twice the share (18.8 percent) of American goods exported there than anywhere else in the world's economy (see Figure 6.14). U.S. exports to Canada include everything from merchandise, such as Microsoft's software and transmissions, carburetors, and axles for assembly at automated Chrysler minivan plants in Ontario, to professional services such as strategic management consulting by McKinsey & Co. Canada is also the second largest source for U.S. imports (14 percent), with natural resources (oil, gas, and timber) and finished goods manufacturing such as Chrysler minivans leading the list. Only slightly less, China provides 17.9 percent of U.S. imports—especially computers and their parts, telecom equipment, toys and video games, clothing, furniture, iron and steel, shoes—and purchases 6.9 percent of U.S. exports—especially electrical machinery, power turbines, passenger aircraft, and scrap metal. Mexico consumes and assembles a 13.3 percent share of U.S. exports (up 65 percent since 1996) and provides 11.8 percent of U.S. imports. Mexico supplies large quantities of auto parts, iron, steel, and oil to the United States. Following the passage of NAFTA, Mexican tariffs declined from 40 to 16 percent, and exports to the United States increased from 67 to 88 percent of total Mexican exports.

NAFTA also reduced the non-tariff trade barriers for American companies like General Motors and Walmart to sell in Mexico. Walmart now operates 520 retail stores across Mexico. U.S.-owned manufacturing and processing plants have long employed semiskilled labor at $3 per hour in Mexico. This trade activity mirrors the labor-intensive assembly that German manufacturing companies perform in Portugal, Hungary, and the Czech Republic at $8 per hour and Poland and Brazil at $6 per hour. For example, with nontariffed import of subassemblies, NAFTA lowered Mexican production costs for heavy equipment assembler Freightliner by $2,500 per truck between 1992 and 1998, enough to warrant opening a second **maquiladora** assembly plant in Mexico.

NAFTA's million and a half new Mexican jobs have caused wage rates to begin to rise from $1.60 to $3.22 per hour in the past eight years. Consequently, some of the assembly

maquiladora
A foreign-owned assembly plant in Mexico that imports and assembles duty-free components for export and allows owners to pay duty only on the "value added."

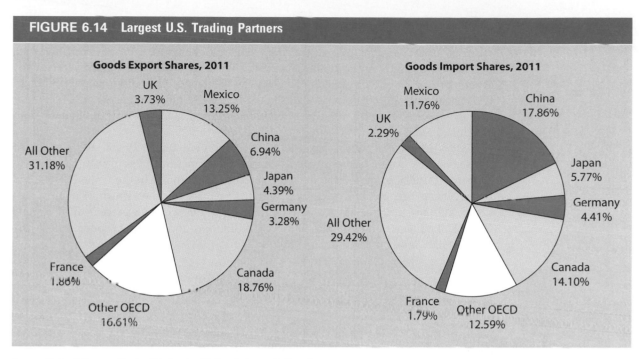

FIGURE 6.14   Largest U.S. Trading Partners

Goods Export Shares, 2011

UK 3.73%
Mexico 13.25%
China 6.94%
Japan 4.39%
Germany 3.28%
Canada 18.76%
Other OECD 16.61%
France 1.86%
All Other 31.18%

Goods Import Shares, 2011

Mexico 11.76%
China 17.86%
UK 2.29%
Japan 5.77%
Germany 4.41%
Canada 14.10%
Other OECD 12.59%
France 1.79%
All Other 29.42%

Source: Federal Reserve Bank of St. Louis, *National Economic Trends.*

line, call center, and data processing jobs have now moved to still lower wage areas in India and China, where manufacturing labor costs are $2 per hour. Recall that manufacturing labor costs in the United States and Canada are $34 and $35 per hour, respectively.

Example

Household Iron Manufacturer in Mexico Becomes Major Engine Block Supplier to Detroit: Cifunsa SA[30]

Since its passage in 1994, NAFTA has made Mexico into a leading outsourcing location for the worldwide auto parts industry. Duty-free access to the United States for auto subassemblies like transmissions and wiring harnesses, plus a growing sector of skilled nonunionized workers, induced GM, Ford, DaimlerChrysler, and Volkswagen, as well as Mexican firms like San Luis Corp. and Grupo Industrial Saltillo SA, to invest $18 billion in auto plants and equipment between 1994 and 2000.

Cifunsa SA is a Grupo subsidiary that specialized immediately after World War II in the manufacture of metal castings for household appliances, especially hand irons. Today, Cifunsa has converted its aluminum and steel casting expertise to the production of engine blocks. Indeed, Cifunsa has the dominant position as a supplier of engine monoblocks to the North American car companies. Other Mexican metal casters play a major role in supplying heavy axles and coil springs for trucks and SUVs. Many windshields installed on U.S.-assembled cars and trucks also come from Mexico. Although some of this import-export trade is motivated by lower wage rates at Mexican than at comparable U.S. parts suppliers, another factor is the desire of the American and European car companies to decrease their dependence on unionized plants. A 2009 strike at GM's Delphi subsidiary lasted almost six weeks.

[30]Based on "Mexico Is Becoming Auto-Making Hot Spot," *Wall Street Journal* (June 23, 1998); and "Mexico Becomes a Leader in Car Parts," *Wall Street Journal* (March 30, 1999), p. A21.

Japanese goods like Toyota and Honda autos, Sony consumer electronics, Canon copiers, and Fuji film constitute 6 percent of total U.S. imports, and the Japanese absorb 4 percent of U.S. exports, primarily aircraft, chemicals, computers, timber, corn, and coal. Germany is the fifth largest trading partner of the United States at 4 percent. Germany exports principally motor vehicles and parts (e.g., Mercedes-Benz diesel engines), specialized machinery, and chemicals to the United States; Germany imports aircraft, computers, motor vehicles and parts (e.g., Cummins Engines), and scientific equipment from the United States.

Besides China, the much-discussed BRIC economies, Brazil, Russia and India each provide approximately half as much as Germany in American import-export trade, 2 to 2.5 percent. India, in particular, sends 11 percent of its exports to the United States, and 18 percent to Europe, and its exports sum 13.7 percent of GDP, much of it in professional and para-professional services. In contrast, China sends 18 percent of its exports to the United States and another 18 percent to Europe, and Chinese exports are 27 percent of GDP, most of it in merchandise.

A Comparison of the EU and NAFTA

Between the EU and NAFTA regional trading blocs, the EU has the larger share of world trade (38 percent compared to 21 percent for the NAFTA in 2011). Recall, however, much of the EU trade (even prior to 1992) was always with other Western European countries *inside* the regional trading bloc. Table 6.7 shows this was also true of U.S.-Canada trade, but not true for trade with Mexico. Twenty years pre-NAFTA, Mexico purchased only 4.4 percent of U.S. exports. After the reduction in trade barriers associated with NAFTA, Mexican growth boomed, and only then in 1998–2003 did Mexico become the second largest purchaser of U.S. exports (with a 12.5 percent share today).

Another important contrast between the EU and NAFTA is that social security programs impose a heavy burden on manufacturing competitiveness in Europe. French, Swedish, Italian, and Czech social security contributions now add over 20 percent to wage costs relative to 5 to 10 percent in Japan, Korea, Canada, and the United States. Five weeks of paid vacation in Germany is standard, and the Germans spend 8.4 percent of GDP on pension payments. Compare two weeks of paid vacation in the United States and the 5 percent of GDP Americans spend on pension payments.

TABLE 6.7 DESTINATION OF U.S. GOODS EXPORTS					
1970–1975		**1998–2003**		**2011**	
COUNTRY	SHARE (%)	COUNTRY	SHARE (%)	COUNTRY	SHARE (%)
Canada	21.4	Canada	24.0	Canada	18.8
Japan	10.2	Mexico	13.5	Mexico	13.3
Germany	5.4	Japan	9.4	China	6.9
United Kingdom	4.9	United Kingdom	5.2	Japan	4.4
Mexico	4.4	Germany	3.9	United Kingdom	3.8
Netherlands	3.9	South Korea	3.8	Germany	3.7
France	3.1	Taiwan	3.2	South Korea	2.9
Italy	2.9	Netherlands	2.9	Brazil	2.7
Brazil	2.7	France	2.8	Netherlands	2.6
Belgium-Luxembourg	2.3	China	2.4	Singapore	2.2

Source: Federal Reserve Bank of St. Louis, U.S. Department of Commerce.

Opting out of these EU social programs has allowed the British economy to match U.S. total labor costs. As a consequence, although wages for time worked in the British, U.S., and German manufacturing sectors are very similar ($22, $23, and $26 per hour, respectively), labor costs for holiday and leave pay plus other benefits add $9 an hour in Germany and only $3 an hour in the United States. When pensions, social security, and health care coverage are included, the total labor cost in Germany in 2011 rises to $46 per hour versus $34 per hour in the United States and $32 in Britain. In addition, some European labor law (especially in France) makes it hard to lay off and furlough workers. Consequently, few entrepreneurial businesses proceed beyond very small sole proprietor-ships in Europe, and the corporate industrial sector dominates the business landscape.

What all this demonstrates is that the institutional arrangements in the country sur-rounding a company are as important to its ultimate competitive success as the business plan, the quality of management decisions, and the commitment of dedicated employees. The enhanced competitive pressure arising from free trade and the opening of markets has served to accentuate the disadvantages of inefficient institutional arrangements. Rather than struggle against regulations that raise costs, global supply chain managers just take their business elsewhere.

Gray Markets, Knockoffs, and Parallel Importing

The prices charged for identical goods varied widely across Europe both before and after the formation of the Common Market (again, see Table 6.6). In 1998, a Ford Mondeo cost 50 percent more in Germany than in Spain. To lower overall consumer prices and to improve competitiveness throughout the Union, the European Commission (EC) adopted policies to encourage price competition. Goods arbitragers who want to buy Black and Decker power tools in Spain and sell them in Germany, or buy Kawasaki motorcycles in the Netherlands and sell them in Britain, are encouraged to do so. Volks-wagen was fined €15 million for refusing to supply Northern Italian VW dealers who sold cars to large numbers of Munich weekenders traveling across the Alps for the Verona opera (at the inexpensive German car prices available in Italy). The EC also has eliminated any contractual link between product sales and after-market service; any government-certified repair shop can purchase parts to perform VW, Nikon, or Sony maintenance and service. The problem, of course, is that such gray markets may lead to counterfeit sales and substandard service passed off as branded sales and authorized service.

As the world's largest exporter in the $182 billion movie industry and the $90 billion computer software industry, the United States has threatened retaliation unless major trading partners aggressively punish violators of international copyright and trademark protection. Japan has agreed by prohibiting Microsoft computer software sales in viola-tion of the manufacturer-authorized distribution agreements. However, at the very same time, Japan's high court allowed the parallel importing of gray-market Steinway pianos and some copyrighted music.

Example

EU Ban on Some Parallel Imports Pleases European but Not U.S. and Japanese Manufacturers[31]

Manufacturers often seek to maintain different prices in different franchise territories for identical branded goods like Levi jeans, Nike shoes, Microsoft Windows, or Sony DVDs. The European Court of Justice (ECJ) has ruled that copyright and trademark protection for Silhouette sunglasses, an Austrian export product, was infringed by an Austrian retailer who purchased the sunglasses at deep discount in Bulgaria and

(continued)

reimported the product for sale in Austria at prices below those suggested for the domestic market authorized distributors. Sourcing a product cheaply wherever it can be purchased around the world and then back-shipping at discounted prices into the high-valued markets is a commonplace occurrence for many trading companies. The policy question is whether the discounted product can be effectively distinguished by customers from knockoff counterfeit products and whether the brand name reputation of the manufacturer is thereby diminished.

Prior EU rulings had allowed such **parallel imports**, which occur any time a foreign export product is purchased in one EU country for resale in another EU country. For example, Tesco, a British retailer, purchases Levi jeans and Nike shoes overseas and offers them for sale at a discount in Britain where the Levi- and Nike-authorized distribution channels have much higher price points. Similarly, American pharmaceuticals produced in Germany for Merck and sold at substantial discount in Spain are shipped back into Germany by discount German retailers without prohibition (*Merck v. Primecrown* and *Beecham v. Europharm*, 1995).

What was new about the Silhouette case was that Silhouette was itself an EU manufacturer. The ECJ decided to extend to *European* brand-name products (such as Silhouette sunglasses) intellectual property protection not extended to *foreign* brand-name products. The purchase in Bulgaria for resale in Austria of an Austrian-manufactured product at prices well below the authorized retail price in Austria was prohibited. So, parallel importing in Europe has been somewhat limited by the Silhouette ruling.

---

[31]Based on "Set-Back for Parallel Imports," *BBC World Service* (July 16, 1998); "Parallel Imports," *Financial Times* (May 20, 1996); "Music Market Indicators," *The Economist* (May 15, 1999); D. Wilkinson, "Breaking the Chain: Parallel Imports and the Missing Link," *European Intellectual Property Review* (1997); and "Prozac's Maker Confronts China over Knock-offs," *Wall Street Journal* (March 25, 1998), p. B9.

WHAT WENT RIGHT • WHAT WENT WRONG

Ford Motor Co. and Exide Batteries: Are Country Managers Here to Stay?[32]

As export market policies on parallel importing change, companies like Ford Motor, Procter and Gamble, and Exide Batteries wrestle with the question of whether to organize worldwide operations by product line or by country. That is, should operations and marketing decisions be controlled by global business units for Tide detergent, Pampers diapers, and Crest toothpaste, or should country managers in Spain, Germany, and China call the shots on input contracts, manufacturing standards, assembly location, and the all-important pricing and promotion decisions?

By developing global product lines, Ford Motor claimed $5 billion in savings when it eliminated overlapping plants, standardized suppliers, realized volume discounts on components, and brought new products to market faster. A consolidated worldwide design team and centralized manufacturing authority saved money. However, Ford Europe's market share slipped from 13 percent to 8.8 percent because untargeted marketing and inflexible pricing became divorced from local market conditions.

Exide pursued the same path by organizing global business units around its automotive, industrial, and network telecom batteries. Major plants were spread out as far apart as China, Brazil, and Germany because subassembly components from these far-flung sources often cut labor costs tenfold and shortened lead times from three months to five weeks. Yet, Exide found that some regional sales teams continued to excel in ways global sales teams could not, and so the North American industrial battery operation has again become a separate division with pricing and promotion authority. As a result, relationship marketing between Exide–North America and Ford headquarters in Detroit secured a major new account for Exide.

---

[32]"Place vs. Product: It's Tough to Choose a Management Model," *Wall Street Journal* (June 21, 2001), p. A1; and "The World as a Single Machine," *The Economist* (June 20, 1998), pp. 3–18.

parallel imports The purchase of a foreign export product in one country to resell as an unauthorized import in another country.

The price impact of a policy prohibiting parallel imports can be enormous, however. In the early 2000s, Australia carefully protected intellectual property by aggressively prosecuting gray-market sellers of music CDs. Cheap imitations and counterfeit substitutes were rare in Sydney or Melbourne, but the result was that popular music CDs sold for $6.33 more in Australia than in other Far Eastern economies. The United Kingdom and China have, on that basis, chosen the opposite policy for selected products. China permits the copying of patented medicines. Eli Lilly's Prozac, an antidepressant, sells for $1.73 per capsule, but a chemically identical knockoff from Shanghai Zhong Qi Pharmaceutical and Jiangsu Changzhou Pharmaceutical sells for $1.02 per capsule under the brand name You Ke. Similarly, the British obtain almost 10 percent of their pharmaceuticals and over 30 percent of their wine, liquor, and beer through parallel importing of products not authorized for retail sale in the United Kingdom.

PERSPECTIVES ON THE U.S. TRADE DEFICIT

Figure 6.15 shows that the U.S. international trade deficit shrank by half during 2006–2009 from −$758 billion ($252 billion of which was with China itself) to −$336 billion (3 percent of GDP in 2009). And well it should. U.S. exports have surged and imports have become prohibitively expensive as the U.S. dollar decayed by fully 43 percent in 2001–2008 (see Figure 6.8). In addition of course, 2007–2008 represented the worst recession in the U.S. in 80 years.

International trade outflow is just one component of a country's balance of payments with the rest of the world. Persistent U.S. trade deficits are offset by massive capital inflows including asset sales (such as British Petroleum's $55 billion purchase of Amoco) and debt issuance of U.S. Treasury bonds and bills to foreign lenders, especially the Japanese and Chinese. Figure 6.15 shows that only once in the past 25 years has the United States generated a trade surplus. Instead, the *services* trade surplus (e.g., McKinsey & Co. exporting management consulting and Halliburton exporting oil field development services) is typically overwhelmed by a massive deficit in merchandise

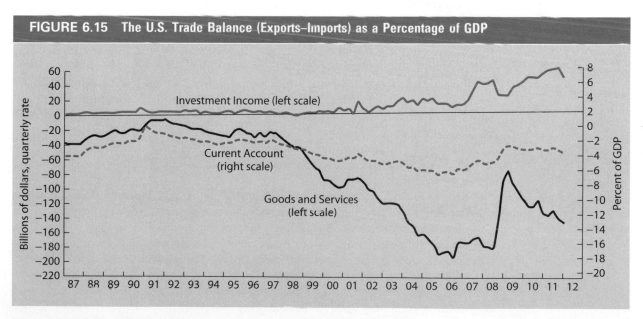

FIGURE 6.15   The U.S. Trade Balance (Exports–Imports) as a Percentage of GDP

Source: Federal Reserve Bank of St. Louis Review, *National Economic Trends* (July 2012), p. 18.

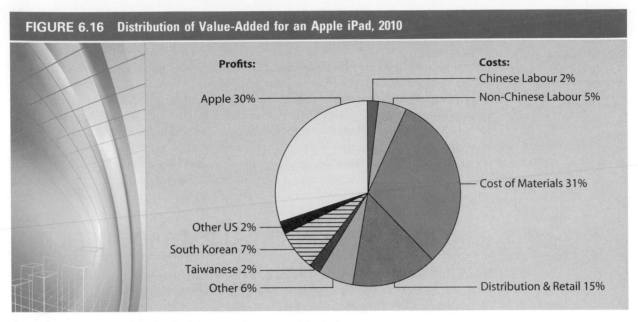

FIGURE 6.16   Distribution of Value-Added for an Apple iPad, 2010

Profits:
- Apple 30%
- Other US 2%
- South Korean 7%
- Taiwanese 2%
- Other 6%

Costs:
- Chinese Labour 2%
- Non-Chinese Labour 5%
- Cost of Materials 31%
- Distribution & Retail 15%

Source: Personal Computing Industry Centre.

trade. In recent years, the trade deficit has accumulated to −10 to −13 percent of GDP. Overseas investment income of Americans then offsets most of the trade deficit to make a current account in the balance of payments equal to −2 to −4 percent of GDP.

Several factors contributed to the persistent U.S. trade deficit. First, the price of crude oil has skyrocketed several times recently. For example, in July 2008, the price of imported crude went to $147 per barrel, three times its normal level. As a consequence, for several months in 2008 the United States was importing from OPEC nations approximately $2 billion per day in crude oil. Just crude oil imports themselves amounted to −5 percent of GDP that year. Second, U.S. manufacturers of merchandise such as Bali bras and capital equipment such as Ford autos increasingly outsource the production of components and subassemblies to lower-wage Caribbean, Mexican, and Chinese partners and subsidiaries. Yet, these intermediate goods show up in the trade statistics as imports when they return for final assembly to the United States, even if they are produced by foreign subsidiaries that are owned by U.S. firms.

Similarly, when Apple purchases components across its worldwide supply chain and has them all flown into Shanghai for final assembly of an iPad, those components all count as exports of the origin countries and imports of China. Moreover, the entire $275 wholesale price of the iPad when assembled and flown to the United States counts in the trade statistics as an import of the United States and an export of China even though only $7 of the iPad's wholesale value is attributable to labor and inputs of China (see Figure 6.16).

With the USD depreciating 43 percent since 2001 and pushing well below purchasing power parity (again see Figure 6.7), U.S. exports were bound to recover. One example is Cummins Engine, which experienced a 26 percent increase in sales in 2006–2008. When combined with the experience of other export power-houses across U.S. manufacturing, a merchandise trade deficit of only −$464 billion ($270 billion with China alone) added to a +$128 billion trade surplus in services to yield to a much reduced −$336 billion trade deficit in 2009 (just 3 percent of U.S. GDP). Since then, as the U.S. economy slowly recovered, imports have again swollen, and the trade deficit is back up to $620 billion.

SUMMARY

- Export sales are very sensitive to changes in exchange rates. Exports become more expensive (cheaper) in the foreign currencies of the importing countries when the domestic (i.e., home) currency of the manufacturer strengthens (weakens).

- Outsourcing to lower-wage manufacturing plants is a centuries-old phenomenon. Outsourcing often imports innovation and access to highly skilled analytical capabilities in testing and design as well as exporting lower-skilled jobs. Containerized ocean shipping is cheap, and yet, outsourcing costs must include increased costs of vendor selection, quality control, intellectual property insurance, and expatriate management compensation.

- The Chinese $7.3 trillion economy is understated by nominal exchange rates. A purchasing power parity measure would be $11.3 trillion.

- For more than a decade, China has grown at 9 to 15 percent with liberalized private property rights, assembly plants for multinational outsourcing, and a booming retail domestic sector. In the aftermath of the global financial crisis, China is the engine for growth worldwide as major trading partners export to its burgeoning middle class.

- Major currencies are traded in the foreign exchange markets; there are markets for U.S. dollars as foreign exchange, British pounds as foreign exchange, euros as foreign exchange, and so forth. Demand and supply in these markets reflect the speculative and transactions demands of investors, import–export dealers, corporations, financial institutions, the International Monetary Fund, central bankers, and governments throughout the global economy.

- Companies often demand payment and offer their best fixed-price quotes in their domestic currency because of transaction risk exposure and operating risk exposure to exchange rate fluctuations. Alternatively, such companies can manage the risk of exchange rate fluctuations themselves by setting up internal or natural hedges involving foreign dual plants as well as financial hedges involving forward, option, or currency swap contracts.

- Internal hedges may be either balance sheet hedges addressing translation risk or operating hedges matching anticipated foreign sales receipts with anticipated expenses in that same foreign currency.

- Financial hedges often address transaction risk exposure by using financial derivative contracts to offset cash flow losses from currency fluctuations. On average, such hedging costs about 5 percent of the value at risk.

- Foreign buyers (or their financial intermediaries) usually must acquire euros to execute a purchase from Mercedes-Benz, U.S. dollars to execute a purchase from General Motors, or yen to execute a purchase from Toyota. Each buyer in these international sales transactions usually supplies its own domestic currency. Additional imports by Americans of Japanese automobiles would normally therefore result in an increased demand for the yen and an increased supply of dollars in the foreign currency markets, that is, a dollar depreciation.

- Long-term trends in exchange rates are determined by transaction demand, government transfer payments, and central bank or IMF interventions.

- Three transaction demand factors are real (inflation-adjusted) growth rates, real (inflation-adjusted) interest rates, and expected cost inflation. The lower the expected cost inflation, the lower the real growth rate, and the higher the real rate of interest in one economy relative to another, the higher the exports, the lower the import demand, and the higher the demand for financial instruments from that economy. All three determinants imply an increased demand or decreased supply of the domestic currency, that is, a currency appreciation.

- Consumer price inflation serves as a good predictor of the combined effect of all three transaction demand factors on post-redemption returns to foreign asset holders. Projected changes in consumer inflation therefore directly affect international capital flows that can easily overwhelm the effect of trade flows on exchange rates.

- The relative strength of a currency is often measured as an effective exchange rate index, a weighted average of the exchange rates against major trading partners, with the weights determined by the volume of import plus export trade.

- Free trade increases the economic growth of both industrialized and developing nations. Tariffs, duties, and import quotas sometimes play a role in strategic trade policy to force multilateral reduction of tariffs, open markets, or secure increasing returns.

- Trade restrictions (quotas or tariffs) may be warranted under special circumstances to protect infant industries, to offset foreign government subsidies with countervailing duties, or to impose anti-dumping sanctions on foreign imports sold at a price point below their domestic cost.

- Speculative demand especially influences short-term changes in exchange rates. Since the total dollar volume of foreign currency trading worldwide is $4 trillion *per day*, these short-term fluctuations can be quite volatile.

- International capital flows and the flow of tradable goods across nations respond to arbitrage opportunities. Arbitrage trading ceases when parity conditions are met. One such condition is relative purchasing power parity.

- Relative purchasing power parity (PPP) hypothesizes that a doubling of consumer prices in one economy will lead to trade flows that cut in half the value of the currency. Over long periods of time and on an approximate basis, exchange rates do appear related to differential rates of inflation across economies. PPP serves a useful benchmark role in assessing long-term trends in exchange rates.

- The European Union (EU) and the North American Free Trade Agreement (NAFTA) are two of several large trading blocs that have organized to open markets to free trade. The EU is the largest producer of world output with very dissimilar economies that have reduced trade barriers and specialized in accordance with comparative advantage. Marketing across the EU must address clusters of very different consumers.

- Whether a nation should join a (single) currency union depends on: (1) the magnitude of intraregional trade, (2) the mobility of labor, and (3) the correlation of macroeconomic shocks.

- The United States is both the largest single-nation exporter and the largest importer in the world economy. The largest trading partner of the United States is Canada followed by, Mexico, China, Japan, and Germany. The United States' share of world export trade (9 percent) has grown in recent years, along with that of Germany and China.

- The trade flows of the United States are often in deficit (i.e., imports exceed exports); the last time there was a trade surplus in the United States was during the recession of 1981–1982. The balance-of-trade deficit of the United States is offset by international capital flows into the United States. The balance-of-payments accounts reflect this accounting identity.

- The U.S. 2011 trade deficit of $560 billion was generated by $738 billion more merchandise imported into the United States than exported. Services generated a $178 billion trade surplus. In recent years, these trade deficits have been approximately 4 percent of a $15 trillion gross domestic product in the United States.

Exercises

Answers to the exercises in blue can be found in Appendix D at the back of the book.

1. If the U.S. dollar depreciates 20 percent, how does this affect the export and domestic sales of a U.S. manufacturer? Explain.

2. If the U.S. dollar were to appreciate substantially, what steps could a domestic manufacturer such as Cummins Engine Co. of Columbus, Indiana, take in advance to reduce the effect of the exchange rate fluctuation on company profitability?

3. After an unanticipated dollar appreciation has occurred, what would you recommend a company such as Cummins Engine do with its strong domestic currency?

4. What is the difference between transaction demand, speculative demand, and autonomous transactions by central banks? Which of these factors determines the long-term quarterly trends in exchange rates?

5. Would increased cost inflation in the United States relative to its major trading partners likely increase or decrease the value of the U.S. dollar? Why?

6. If the domestic prices for traded goods rose 40 percent over 10 years in China and 25 percent over those same 10 years in the United States, what would happen to a freely floating Chinese yuan/U.S. dollar exchange rate? Why?

7. If Boeing's dollar aircraft prices increase 20 percent and the yen/dollar exchange rate declines 15 percent, what effective price increase is facing Japan Air Lines for the purchase of a Boeing 747? Would Boeing's margin likely rise or fall if the yen then depreciated and competitor prices were unchanged? Why?
8. Unit labor costs in Germany approach $30 per hour, whereas in Britain unit labor costs are only $20 per hour. Why would such a large difference persist between two members of the EU free trade area?
9. If unit labor costs in Spain and Portugal rise, but unit labor costs in Germany decline and other producer prices remain unchanged, what effect should these factors, by themselves, have on export trade, and why?
10. What three factors determine whether two economies with separate fiscal and monetary authorities should form a currency union? Give an illustration of each factor using NAFTA economies.
11. Would cappuccino by the cup or Prada handbags have wider price variation in a free trade area like the European Union? Why?
12. If core price inflation has grown at a compound growth rate of 2 percent per annum in the United States and 0.06 percent in Japan for the past eight years, what exchange rate represents PPP today if the two currencies eight years ago in 2005 were in parity and exchanged at the rate of ¥109/$?

Case Exercises

Predicting the Long-Term Trends in Value of the U.S. Dollar and the Euro

Analyze the data on inflation rates, interest rates, and growth rate forecasts in Table 6.1 to determine what the likely near-term trend movement of the U.S. dollar will be. Analyze how each of the previously mentioned factors will affect the euro–dollar rate.

Elaborate the Debate on NAFTA

PROS:

1. trade between Mexico, Canada, and the United States has tripled to $1 trillion,
2. food exports to Mexico have grown at 8 percent annually,
3. Mexico has increased its exports and foreign direct investment,
4. U.S. manufacturing has become more cost competitive using components and subassemblies from Canada and Mexico.

CONS:

1. Hundreds of thousands of U.S. jobs have shifted below the border,
2. wage concessions have been forced upon those U.S. workers who remain employed in industries that outsource to Mexico,
3. the United States has run a persistent trade deficit with Mexico and Canada.

APPENDIX 6A

Foreign Exchange Risk Management

To reduce the potentially wide swings in cash flows and net assets resulting from currency fluctuations, companies either set up *internal hedges* or employ financial derivatives to create *financial hedges*. Internal hedges may be either *operating hedges* or *balance sheet hedges*. Operating hedges reduce operating cash flow risk exposure by matching anticipated foreign sales receipts against projected foreign operating expenses in that same currency. A few companies like Nestlé and Unilever have so many foreign operations and so many global brands (Nestlé Crunch, Carnation, Perrier, Kit Kat, Lipton Tea, Dove Soap, Wishbone, Bird's Eye, Obsession) that their operating hedges circumvent the need for further risk management.

Example

Internal Hedge from BMW Operations on I-85 in South Carolina

The North American subsidiary of BMW now accepts purchase orders accompanied by payment in U.S. dollars and uses those same dollar receipts to cover BMW marketing and plant expenses in the United States. BMW has built a plant in Spartanburg, South Carolina, to assemble its popular Z4 model sports car. This massive facility along the major East Coast Interstate I-85 has tens of millions of dollars of labor and local material expenses. Such offsetting expense flows payable in U.S. dollars is a way of hedging the operating risk exposure of BMW receivables in U.S. dollars. With an internal hedge provided by a German ball-bearing plant, Cummins Engine could accomplish the same thing.

In contrast, balance sheet hedges address primarily translation risk exposure by matching assets and liabilities in various countries and their respective currencies. Fewer than 25 percent of all U.S., Asian, and U.K. companies consider translation risk important.

Financial hedges in a manufacturing or service company reduce transaction risk exposure by setting up positions in financial derivative contracts to offset cash flow losses from currency fluctuations. Over 93 percent of U.S., Asian, and U.K. companies employ forward contracts to manage transaction risk exposure. Goldman Sachs estimates that a financial hedge for $100 million of risk exposure costs about $5.2 million, approximately 5 percent of the value at risk. As the dollar appreciated steeply against the euro in 2000, Coca-Cola established a covered hedge for their euro net cash flow risk exposure that year. Goodyear, in contrast, decided that these hedging costs were prohibitive and ended up earning just $68 million profit on their European operations rather than the $92 million ($97 million gross profit − $5 million hedging cost) that they would have earned with a fully hedged position.

By establishing a short position in the foreign currency forward or options markets, a company can hedge the domestic cash flow from their export sales receipts. For example, suppose Cummins Engine had September sales contracts with their German dealers for

INTERNATIONAL PERSPECTIVES

Toyota and Honda Buy U.S. Assembly Capacity[1]

To exempt their cars and trucks from U.S. tariffs, and to improve the delivery time and reliability for their most popular models, Toyota and Honda have each purchased four assembly plants in North America. When a manufacturer's home currency is strong, foreign direct investment in overseas plant and equipment is especially attractive. From 1985 to 1993, the yen rocketed from ¥238 per U.S. dollar to ¥94 per U.S. dollar (see Figure 6.1), as Honda and Toyota employed the strengthening yen to acquire their U.S. manufacturing capacity. A $1 billion U.S. assembly plant that drew down balance sheet cash by ¥94 billion in 1993 would

have drawn down fully ¥238 billion cash 10 years earlier (or would have introduced a ¥238 billion debt liability on the balance sheet). These reduced liabilities in acquiring new fixed assets provided a balance sheet hedge offsetting the ever lower yen receipts in 1980–1995 from the U.S. sale of another Camry or Accord. Nevertheless, the U.S. assembly plants were clearly a response to U.S. protectionist trade policy and not motivated by the *balance sheet hedges*.

[1]Based on "Japanese Carmakers Plan Major Expansion of American Capacity," *Wall Street Journal* (September 24, 1997), p. A1; and "Detroit Is Getting Sideswiped by the Yen," *BusinessWeek* (November 11, 1996), p. 54.

future delivery in December 2012 of €5 million of diesel engines. Cummins has risk exposure to a decline in the value of these export sales receipts. So, to lay off this exchange rate risk, in September 2012 Cummins *sells* a euro forward contract in the foreign exchange derivative markets to establish a hedge. Cummins's transaction is described as a covered hedge because Cummins anticipates euro receivables (from their German dealers) just equal to the amount of their short forward position. That is, their contract sales receipts "cover" their obligation to deliver as a seller of a euro forward contracts.

Besides setting up internal hedges or short forward positions to achieve a perfect financial hedge, Cummins Engine and BMW could also have entered into a currency-swap contract to exchange their anticipated future streams of dollar and euro cash flows from export sales. Cummins would swap a prespecified amount of Cummins's anticipated euro sales receipts in Germany for a prespecified amount of their anticipated dollar receipts from auto sales in North America. However, these swap contract alternatives to demanding payment in their domestic (home) currency impose some transaction fees on BMW and Cummins Engine. Therefore, BMW generally will offer its best fixed price for an export transaction on a purchase order payable in euros. And for the same reason, the best fixed price from Cummins Engine generally will be available only on a purchase order payable only in U.S. dollars.

Example

Cummins Engine Goes Short

Selling forward contracts in 2009 at a prespecified forward price (say, $1.50/€) that agreed to deliver €5 million at a future settlement date in 2010 would make money for Cummins Engine if the dollar appreciated and the euro receipts from foreign sales declined in dollar value. For example, at $1.30/€ in 2010, Cummins is entitled to receive $1.50/€ for European currency that it could purchase in the spot market in 2010 for $1.30/€. Therefore, Cummins "cancels" its forward position and can collect from the futures market settlements process a gain of $0.20/€ × €5 million = $1,000,000. This cash flow would be just sufficient to cover their $0.20 per euro loss in value on the €5 million in 2010 sales receipts from their German dealers. As intended, these two cash flows from a covered hedge just offset each other; the perfect hedge lays off the foreign exchange (FX) risk.

PART III

Production and Cost

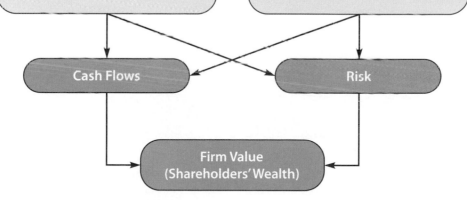

ECONOMIC ANALYSIS AND DECISIONS

1. Demand Analysis
2. Production and Cost Analysis
3. Product, Pricing, and Output Decisions
4. Capital Expenditure Analysis

ECONOMIC, POLITICAL, AND SOCIAL ENVIRONMENT

1. Business Conditions (Trends, Cycles, and Seasonal Effects)
2. Factor Market Conditions (Capital, Labor, Land, and Raw Materials)
3. Competitors' Reactions and Tactical Response
4. Organizational Architecture and Regulatory Constraints

Cash Flows

Risk

Firm Value
(Shareholders' Wealth)

© Cengage Learning

CHAPTER PREVIEW

Managers are required to make resource allocation decisions about production operations, marketing, financing, and personnel. Although these decisions are interrelated, it is useful to discuss each of them separately. Production decisions determine the types and amounts of inputs—such as land, labor, raw and processed materials, factories, machinery, equipment, and managerial talent—to be used in the production of a desired quantity of output. The production manager's objective is to minimize cost for a given output or, in other circumstances, to maximize output for a given input budget. First, we analyze the choice of a single variable input with fixed input prices. Later, we analyze the optimal multi-input combination and introduce the concept of returns to scale. Appendix 7A examines the production economics of renewable and exhaustible natural resources.

The economic theory of production offers a conceptual framework to assist managers in deciding how to combine most efficiently the various inputs needed to produce the desired output (product or service), given the existing technology. Technology consists of available production processes, equipment, labor and management skills, as well as information-processing capabilities. Least-cost production analysis is often applied by managers and plant engineers in deciding the operations plans of the company.

MANAGERIAL CHALLENGE

Green Power Initiatives Examined: What Went Wrong in California's Deregulation of Electricity?[1]

Electric power plants entail huge capital investments. Pollution abatement technology in large coal-fired plants and redundant safety devices in nuclear power plants requires almost a billion dollars of extra capital. Pacific Gas and Electric's (PG&E) Diablo Canyon nuclear power plant near Santa Barbara, California, cost $5.8 billion. The British are installing 5,000 offshore wind turbines at a price of $20 billion to replace half of the 58 gigawatts of power (77 percent of total capacity) the United Kingdom obtains today from natural gas and coal. Why spend so much to secure these greener technologies?

One prominent reason is the €14 ($20) pollution allowance per ton of coal that has emerged from the carbon dioxide emissions trading scheme introduced in 2005 by the European Union to combat the damaging effects of global warming. A second reason to pursue greener power is the $5 per megawatt hour (MWh) carbon tax on electricity enacted in 1991 by Sweden, Finland, Denmark, Norway, the Netherlands, and more recently by Ireland, France, British Columbia, and Boulder, Colorado. The carbon tax on conventional sources of electricity in Boulder is $21 per year for the average residence, $94 for the average commercial site, and $9,600 for the average industrial site.

Cont.

MANAGERIAL CHALLENGE *Continued*

Finally, greener power technologies have much lower variable costs than smaller-scale natural gas–powered and fuel oil–powered electricity-generating plants. The operating cost for coal itself is only $25/Mwh versus $35/Mwh for natural gas and fuel oil–fired power plants or $65/Mwh for diesel-fired plants (see the step function graph in the exhibit below). The operating cost for nuclear and hydro power is even lower—only $4/Mwh. A trade-off between investing in high-fixed-cost plants with lower and stable variable costs versus low-fixed-cost plants requiring higher variable costs came into focus during the electricity deregulation crisis in California.

California implemented legislation to decouple electricity generation and distribution, allowing large retail and industrial customers to purchase electricity from long-distance suppliers in places like the state of Washington where the lowest cost production by hydropower is plentiful. As a result, two California utilities,

© Don Farrall/Photodisc/Getty Images

PG&E and Southern Cal Edison, scaled back their generating plant expansion plans and began to meet peak demand by purchasing 25 percent of their power in wholesale spot markets. A problem arose, however, because peak-hour wholesale prices are determined by the small-scale diesel-fired independent generating

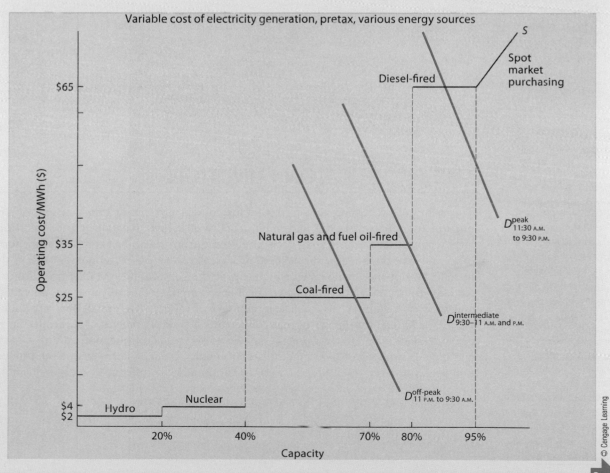

© Cengage Learning

Cont.

MANAGERIAL CHALLENGE *Continued*

plants that come on line to meet the last 5 percent of peak demand (see the graph). As a result, the average wholesale price of electricity in California shot up from $25 to $50/Mwh in the 1990s to $200+/Mwh in the 2000s. When California Edison and PG&E were restrained by the California Public Utility Commission from passing through to their retail customers almost $11 billion in higher whole-sale costs, the companies had little choice in the short run but to institute rolling blackouts and brownouts.

One possible longer-term solution is to charge electricity customers a dynamic price, as the variable cost of electricity rises and falls throughout the day along the supply schedule in the exhibit. France has long applied such time-of-day pricing to electricity. A second approach is to deploy extremely small-scale diesel generators or natural gas–fired microturbine generators in factories and commercial establishments. Operating costs of the microturbines are $70–$120/Mwh, much higher than the utility-supplied electricity in the exhibit. Yet, the capital cost that must be recovered is less than 1/1,000th of the capital cost of a traditional power plant. La Quinta Motels, for example, saved $20,000 in one year with a microturbine at one of its Dallas properties. In this chapter,

we will study the dilemma of whether to substitute higher cost variable inputs for fixed inputs entailing substantial capital investment.

Discussion Questions

- ■ What are the full cost tradeoff issues between coal and natural gas as a source of fuel for electricity?
- ■ Hybrid electric automobiles could massively increase the demand for electricity, driving prices well up the supply schedule. Does this make it more or less likely that the United States will develop trucks that run on natural gas? Explain.
- ■ If you were asked to pay three times as much for electricity use in the early evening as at dawn, would you get up early to do laundry before going to work or school?

[1]Based on "The Lessons Learned" and "Think Small," *Wall Street Journal* (September 17, 2001), pp. R4, R13, R15, and R17; "Are Californians Starved for Energy?" *Wall Street Journal* (September 16, 2002), p. A1; "How to Do Deregulation Right," *BusinessWeek* (March 26, 2001), p. 112; and "The Looming Energy Crunch," *The Economist* (August 8, 2009), p. 49.

THE PRODUCTION FUNCTION

production function
A mathematical model, a spreadsheet, or a graph that relates the maximum feasible quantity of output that can be produced from given amounts of various inputs.

inputs A resource or factor of production, such as a raw material, labor skill, or a piece of equipment that is employed in a production process.

The theory of production centers around the concept of a production function. A **production function** relates the maximum quantity of output that can be produced from given amounts of various inputs for a given technology. It can be expressed in the form of a mathematical model, a spreadsheet, or a graph. A change in technology, such as the introduction of more automated equipment or the substitution of skilled for unskilled workers, results in a new production function. The production of most outputs (goods and services) requires the use of large numbers of **inputs**. The production of gasoline, for example, requires the use of many different labor skills (roughnecks, chemical engineers, refinery maintenance workers), raw materials (crude oil, chemical additives, heat), and types of equipment (boilers, distillation columns, cracking chambers). Also, production processes often result in joint outputs. For example, petroleum refining results in jet fuel, propane, butane, gasoline, kerosene, lubricant oil, tar, and asphalt.

Letting L and K represent the quantities of two inputs (labor L and capital K) used in producing a quantity Q of output, a production function can be represented in the form of a mathematical model, such as

$$Q = \alpha L^{\beta_1} K^{\beta_2} \qquad\qquad [7.1]$$

where α, β_1, and β_2 are constants. This particular multiplicative exponential model is known as the **Cobb-Douglas production function** and is examined in more detail later in the chapter. Production functions also can be expressed in the form of a spreadsheet table, as illustrated in the following ore-mining example.

Example

An Illustrative Production Function: Deep Creek Mining Company

The Deep Creek Mining Company uses capital (mining equipment) and labor (workers) to mine uranium ore. Various sizes of ore-mining equipment, as measured by its brake horsepower (bhp) rating, are available to the company. The amount of ore mined during a given period (Q) is a function only of the number of workers assigned to the crew (L) operating a given type of equipment (K). The data in Table 7.1 show the amount of ore produced (measured in tons) when various sizes of crews are used to operate the equipment.

TABLE 7.1 TOTAL OUTPUT TABLE—DEEP CREEK MINING COMPANY

		CAPITAL INPUT K (BHP, BRAKE HORSEPOWER)							
		250	500	750	1,000	1,250	1,500	1,750	2,000
LABOR INPUT L (NUMBER OF WORKERS)	1	1	3	6	10	16	16	16	13
	2	2	6	16	24	29	29	44	11
	3	4	16	29	44	55	55	55	50
	4	6	29	44	55	58	60	60	55
	5	16	43	55	60	61	62	62	60
	6	29	55	60	62	63	63	63	62
	7	44	58	62	63	64	64	64	64
	8	50	60	62	63	64	65	65	65
	9	55	59	61	63	64	65	66	66
	10	52	56	59	62	64	65	66	67

© Cengage Learning

A two-input, one-output production function at Deep Creek Mining can also be represented *graphically* as a three-dimensional production surface, where the height of the square column associated with each input combination in Figure 7.1 indicates the amount of iron ore output produced.

Cobb-Douglas production function
A particular type of mathematical model, known as a multiplicative exponential function, used to represent the relationship between the inputs and the output.

Fixed and Variable Inputs

In deciding how to combine the various inputs (L and K) to produce the desired output, inputs are usually classified as being either fixed or variable. A *fixed* input is defined as one required in the production process but whose quantity employed in the process is constant over a given period of time regardless of the quantity of output produced. The costs of a fixed input must be incurred regardless of whether the production process is operated at a high or a low rate of output. A *variable* input is defined as one whose quantity employed in the process changes, depending on the desired quantity of output to be produced.

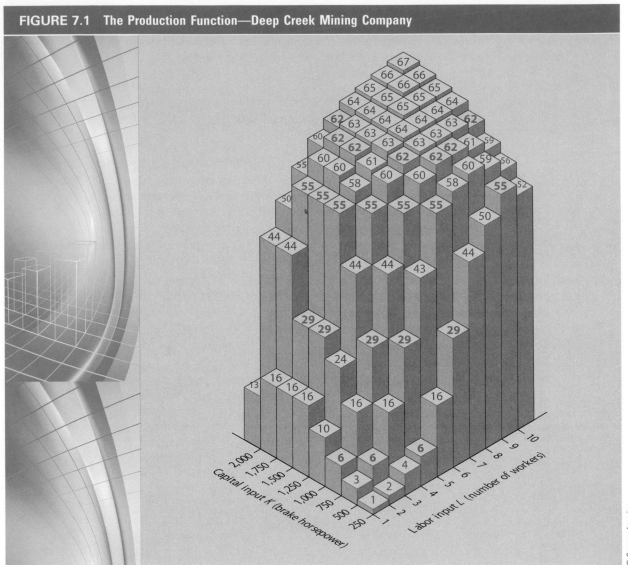

FIGURE 7.1 The Production Function—Deep Creek Mining Company

short run The period of time in which one (or more) of the resources employed in a production process is fixed or incapable of being varied.

long run The period of time in which all the resources employed in a production process can be varied.

The **short run** corresponds to the period of time in which one (or more) of the inputs is fixed. To increase output, then, the firm must employ more of the variable input(s) with the given quantity of fixed input(s). Thus, for example, with an auto assembly plant of fixed size and capacity, the firm can increase output only by employing more labor, such as by scheduling additional shifts.

As the time period under consideration (the planning horizon) is lengthened, however, more of the fixed inputs become variable. Over a planning horizon of about six months, most firms can acquire or build additional plant capacity and order more manufacturing equipment. In lengthening the planning horizon, a point is eventually reached where all inputs are variable. This period of time is called the **long run**.

In the short run, because some of the inputs are fixed, only a subset of the total possible input combinations is available to the firm. By contrast, in the long run, all possible input combinations are available.

TABLE 7.2	TOTAL PRODUCT, MARGINAL PRODUCT, AVERAGE PRODUCT, AND ELASTICITY—DEEP CREEK MINING COMPANY (CAPITAL INPUT, BHP = 750) LABOR INPUT			
LABOR INPUT (NUMBER OF WORKERS)	TOTAL PRODUCT TP_L (=Q) (TONS OF ORE)	MARGINAL PRODUCT OF LABOR, MP_L ($\Delta Q \div \Delta L$)	AVERAGE PRODUCT OF LABOR, AP_L ($Q \div L$)	PRODUCTION ELASTICITY, E_L ($MP_L \div AP_L$)
0	0	—	—	—
1	6	+6	6	1.0
2	16	+10	8	1.25
3	29	+13	9.67	1.34
4	44	+15	11	1.36
5	55	+11	11	1.0
6	60	+5	10	0.50
7	62	+2	8.86	0.23
8	62	0	7.75	0.0
9	61	−1	6.78	−0.15
10	59	−2	5.90	−0.34

PRODUCTION FUNCTIONS WITH ONE VARIABLE INPUT

Suppose, in the Deep Creek Mining Company example of the previous section, that the amount of capital input K (the size of mining equipment) employed in the production process is a fixed factor. Specifically, suppose that the firm owns or leases a piece of mining equipment having a 750-bhp rating. Depending on the amount of labor input L used to operate the 750-bhp equipment, varying quantities of output will be obtained, as shown in the *750* column of Table 7.1 and again in the Q column of Table 7.2.

Marginal and Average Product Functions

marginal product The incremental change in total output that can be obtained from the use of one more unit of an input in the production process (while holding constant all other inputs).

Once the total product function is given (in tabular, graphic, or algebraic form), the marginal and average product functions can be derived. The **marginal product** is defined as the incremental change in total output ΔQ that can be produced by the use of one more unit of the variable input ΔL, while K remains fixed. The marginal product is defined as[2]

$$MP_L = \frac{\Delta Q}{\Delta L} \text{ or } \frac{\partial Q}{\partial L} \qquad [7.2]$$

for discrete and continuous changes, respectively.

The marginal product of labor in the ore-mining example is shown in the third column of Table 7.2 and as MP_L in Figure 7.2.

[2]Strictly speaking, the ratio $\Delta Q/\Delta L$ represents the *incremental* product rather than the *marginal* product. For simplicity, we continue to use the term *marginal* throughout the text, even though this and similar ratios are calculated on an incremental basis.

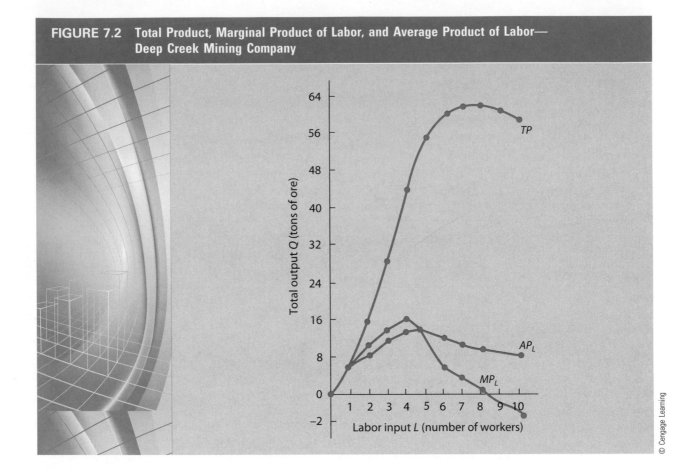

FIGURE 7.2 Total Product, Marginal Product of Labor, and Average Product of Labor—Deep Creek Mining Company

average product The ratio of total output to the amount of the variable input used in producing the output.

The **average product** is defined as the ratio of total output to the amount of the variable input used in producing the output. The average product of labor is

$$AP_L = \frac{Q}{L} \qquad [7.3]$$

The average product of labor for the Deep Creek ore-mining example is shown in the fourth column of Table 7.2 and as AP_L in Figure 7.2.

The Law of Diminishing Marginal Returns

The tabular production function just discussed illustrates the production law of diminishing marginal returns. Initially, the assignment of more workers to the crew operating the mining equipment allows greater labor specialization in the use of the equipment. As a result, the marginal output of each worker added to the crew at first increases, and total output increases at an increasing rate. Thus, as listed in Table 7.2 and graphed in Figure 7.2, the addition of a second worker to the crew results in 10 additional tons of output; the addition of a third worker results in 13 additional tons of output; and the addition of a fourth worker yields 15 additional tons.

A point is eventually reached, however, where the marginal increase in output for each worker added begins to decline. This decrease in output occurs because only a

WHAT WENT RIGHT • WHAT WENT WRONG

Factory Bottlenecks at a Boeing Assembly Plant[3]

The Boeing Company assembles wide-body aircraft (747s, 757, 767s, and 777s) at its 4.3-million-square-foot Everett, Washington, assembly plant, the largest building in the world. Fifteen railcars a day deliver parts that are directed to five assembly lines by overhead cranes cruising on 31 miles of networked track. The variable inputs in this production process are millions of parts and thousands of skilled assembly workers.

As Boeing ramped up production from 244 aircraft deliveries in 1995 to 560 in 1999, the Everett plant went to three shifts of 6,000, 4,000, and 1,500 workers, and twice as many parts poured in. But crowding effects descended on the Everett plant. Although final assembly of an aircraft body continued to take its normal 21 workdays, overtime was required to maintain this roll-out schedule, in large part because of lost, defective, and reworked parts. At

times, piles of redundant parts would appear on the shop floor, while at other times, shortages of seats and electronic gear caused delays. As a result, work-in-progress inventory skyrocketed and work orders got out of sequence. By late 1997, overtime was running almost a billion dollars over budget, and the production operations at Everett were "hopelessly snarled."

To resolve this problem, in 1999 Boeing scrapped its antiquated parts-tracking system and adopted lean production techniques. It cut parts order sizes and outsourced subassembly work away from bottlenecked points on the final assembly line. By 2001, a continuous stream of fewer parts arrived at autonomous worker cells just in time (JIT), as required to complete a smoothly flowing assembly process for an intentionally reduced 527 aircraft deliveries.

---

[3] "Boeing's Secret," *BusinessWeek* (May 20, 2002), pp. 113–116; "Gaining Altitude," *Barron's* (April 29, 2002), pp. 21–25; and Everett plant tours.

---

limited number of ways exist to achieve greater labor specialization and because each additional worker introduces crowding effects. Thus, the addition of a fifth worker to the crew yields a marginal increase in output of 11 additional tons, compared with the marginal increase of 15 additional tons for the fourth worker. Similarly, the additions of the sixth and seventh workers yield successively smaller increases of 5 and 2 tons, respectively. With enough additional workers, the marginal product of labor may become zero or even negative. Some work is just more difficult to accomplish when superfluous personnel are present.

Increasing Returns with Network Effects

The law of diminishing marginal returns is *not* a mathematical theorem, but rather an empirical assertion that has been observed in almost every production process as the amount of the variable input increases. A noteworthy exception occurs, however, with **network effects**. The greater the installed base of a network product, such as Facebook or LinkedIn, the larger the number of compatible network connections and therefore the more possible value for a new customer. Similarly, Microsoft experienced increasing returns when Microsoft Office became an industry standard. Consequently, as the installed base increased, Microsoft's promotions and other selling efforts to acquire new customers became increasingly more productive since independent software vendors (ISV) developed complementary software that increased value for Microsoft's customers. Apple's iPhone has experienced the same thing with its hundreds of thousands of apps from ISVs.

A manufacturer's product line costs usually now include marketing and distribution activities as well as the labor and material direct costs of standard production and assembly. The reason is that, like service firms, many manufacturers today compete on customer inquiry systems, change order responsiveness, delivery reliability, and

network effects An exception to the law of diminishing marginal returns that occurs when the installed base of a network product makes the efforts to acquire new customers increasingly more productive.

technological updates, not just on delivery times and warranty repairs. Qualifying for and actually winning a customer order often requires quality characteristics and support services beyond the physical unit of production. For example, Ford Motor wants all its manufacturing suppliers to meet the ISO 9000 manufacturing quality standards for continuous improvement processes. Walmart requires that its fashion clothing suppliers deliver shipments JIT for planned departure from Walmart distribution centers. Disney World gift shops choose manufacturers who can alter their production schedules on short notice in order to provide much greater change-order responsiveness than traditional make-to-order manufacturing of Mickey Mouse coffee mugs.

Example

Increasing Returns at Sony Blu-ray and Microsoft Windows[4]

At times, increasing returns and declining marginal costs can be secured by the adoption of an industry standard favorable to one's own product. Sony's high-definition Blu-ray digital video standard involves promotional and other selling efforts, which grow *more productive* the more widely the product is adopted by consumers. The more Blu-ray DVDs there are, the more TV networks and independent studios produce programs and movies with this technology. And the more Blu-ray programs and movies that become available, the easier and cheaper it was for Sony in 2006–2007 to sell Blu-ray players initially priced from $800 to $497 to even more customers. In February 2008, when Warner Brothers withdrew their support for the competing Toshiba high-definition DVD standard, Sony and partner Matsushita Electric had the $24 billion home high-definition market to themselves. Blu-ray players were priced at $388. In late 2009, Time-Warner also adopted Blu-ray as its exclusive DVD format, and accentuated still further the increasing returns to Sony's technology.

A similar reason for increasing returns at Microsoft is that the more adoptions Microsoft Windows secures, the more Windows-compatible applications will be introduced by independent software vendors, thereby enhancing the value-added of Microsoft's product. Just as Sony's increasing returns in marketing its Blu-ray player introduced a disruptive technology that displaced Toshiba and Samsung's competing technologies, Netscape's once-dominant Internet search engine experienced exactly this sort of displacement by Microsoft's Windows, which bundled Internet Explorer (IE) for no additional charge. IE then grew to a 92 percent market share in Internet browsers.

[4]Based on "Toshiba Exits HD DVD Business," *Wall Street Journal* (February 19, 2008).

These network-based relationships are depicted in Figure 7.3. From 0 to 30 percent market share, the selling efforts required to achieve each additional share point have a diminishing returns effect on the probability of adoption by the next potential user (note the reduced slope of the sales penetration curve). Consequently, additional share points are increasingly more and more expensive over this range. But once the number of other users of a network-based device reaches a 30 to 40 percent share, the next 40 to 50 share points are cheaper and cheaper to promote.

Beyond the 30 percent *inflection point*, each additional share point of users leads to an increasing probability of adoption by another user, hence a decrease in the marketing expense required to secure another unit sale (note the increased slope of the sales penetration curve in this middle range). So, further share points were cheaper, not more

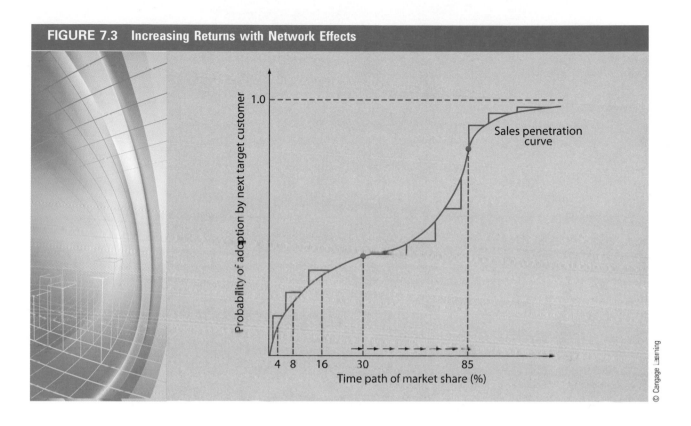

FIGURE 7.3 Increasing Returns with Network Effects

expensive. Eventually, beyond a market share of 80 to 90 percent, securing the final adopters becomes increasingly expensive because selling efforts have again become subject to diminishing returns.

Producing Information Services under Increasing Returns

It is insightful to compare the production economics of old-economy companies that produce *things* to new-economy companies that produce *information*. Things, when sold, the seller ceases to own. Information, when sold, the seller can sell again. Things are replicated through expensive manufacturing processes, whereas information is replicable at almost zero incremental cost. Things exist in one location. Information can exist simultaneously in many locations. The production and marketing of things are subject to eventually diminishing returns. The marketing (and maybe the production) of information is subject to increasing returns. That is, the more people who use my information, the more likely it is that another person will want to acquire it (for any given marketing cost), or, said another way, the cheaper it is to secure another sale. Things often involve economies of massive scale in production. Information is often produced by small companies at comparably low costs in part because of network effects. Things focus a business on supply-side thinking and the high costs of distribution. Information products focus a business on demand-side thinking and have almost no costs of distribution. By getting the next customer to adopt, one can set in motion a "virtuous circle" of higher customer value, lower overhead costs, and lower prices and costs for the next customer. Chapter 11 discusses increasing returns as a source of dominant firm market power to Sony and Microsoft tempered today by streaming video and Google search.

FIGURE 7.4 The Relationships between Total, Average, and Marginal Product Curves

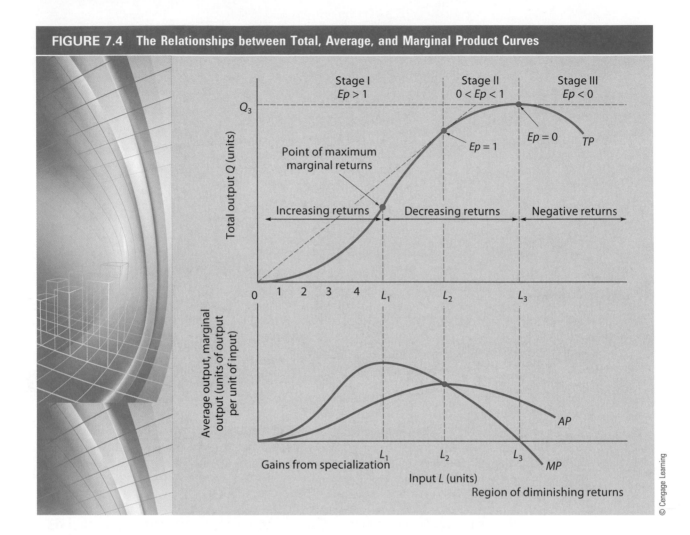

© Cengage Learning

The Relationship between Total, Marginal, and Average Product

Figure 7.4 illustrates a production function total value added or total product (*TP*) with a single variable input to highlight the relationships among the *TP*, *AP*, and *MP* concepts. In the first region labeled "Increasing returns," the *TP* function is increasing at an *increasing rate*. Because the marginal value added or marginal product (*MP*) curve measures the slope of the *TP* curve ($MP = \partial Q/\partial L$), the *MP* curve is increasing up to L_1. In the region labeled "Decreasing returns," the *TP* function is increasing at a *decreasing rate*, and the *MP* curve is decreasing up to L_3. In the region labeled "Negative returns," the *TP* function is *decreasing*, and the *MP* curve continues decreasing, becoming negative beyond L_3. An inflection point occurs at L_1. Next, if a line is drawn from the origin 0 to any point on the *TP* curve, the slope of this line, Q/L, measures the average value added or average product (*AP*). Hence, we see that the *AP* curve reaches a maximum at a point where the average and the marginal products are equated.[5]

---

[5]Note also that the marginal product *MP* equals the average product *AP* at L_2, because the marginal product *MP* is equal to the slope of the *TP* curve ($MP = \partial Q/\partial L$), and at L_2 the average product *AP* is also equal to the slope of the *TP* curve.

Consider, for example, the following analogies: A baseball player's batting *average* for the season is 0.250 or a college student's grade point average is 3.0. If that player has an excellent night at bat (his *marginal* performance) and goes 4 for 4 (1.000), or the student achieves a 4.0 in the current semester, then his season average or GPA will be pulled up. On the other hand, if he goes hitless or the student fails everything, this poor *marginal* performance will pull down his season average. But when the batter goes 1 for 4 (or the student makes 3.0 in semester grades), this marginal performance will have no impact on his average (marginal performance equals average performance). Hence, the *MP* curve will always intersect with the *AP* curve when it is at a maximum. As we will see in Chapter 8, a firm's marginal cost curve always intersects the average cost curve at its minimum point, for the same reason.

Example

Three Stages of Production on the Malibu Assembly Line

In analyzing the production function, economists have identified three different stages of production based on the relationships among the *TP*, *AP*, and *MP* functions. Stage I is defined as the range of L over which the average product (*AP*) is increasing; it occurs from the origin (0) up to L_2 (perhaps from 0 up to 3 auto assembly line workers plus a substitute at job station 44 on the Malibu assembly line, see Figure 7.5) and represents the region of net gains from specialization. Because there are multiple tasks at this job station, specializing allows the second experienced worker to contribute $40 per hour in value added and the third to contribute $50 per hour. Stage II corresponds to the range of L from the point at which the average product is at a maximum (L_2) to the point where the marginal product (*MP*) declines to zero (L_4). At JS 44, Stage II refers to the hiring of a substitute or various apprentices. Note the end point of Stage II thus corresponds to the point of maximum output on the *TP* curve. Stage III encompasses the range of L to the right of L_3 over which the total product is declining or, equivalently, the marginal product is negative. Stage III assembly line labor could refer to "gofers" who secure parts that are running low or soft drinks and candy for the crew. At one time these employees were critical but given JIT operations; they now impose crowding effects that overwhelm any output attributable to the additional workers.

To determine the optimal quantity of labor input L to employ, first note even if the variable input were free, the rational producer would not wish to proceed into Stage III. By the same token, no manager whose average productivity per worker is rising from $38.33 to $38.75 per hour due to the gains from specialization (i.e., *AP* increasing in Stage I) should fail to add the substitute worker. One should always therefore proceed beyond the point of diminishing returns. Further the firm should add apprentice workers as long as the entry-level $25 per hour incremental cost remains below the marginal value added. If labor costs are high, as in a United Auto Workers' unionized assembly plant, production may proceed just a short distance into Stage II in hiring labor. If labor costs are lower in a nonunionized plant, labor hiring may proceed well across Stage II to include relatively low-level-productivity workers, like the second apprentice. In Figure 7.5, however, this would occur only if input costs are subsidized (e.g., with government-sponsored job training programs to reduce the second apprentice's net wage from $25 to $10 per hour).

(continued)

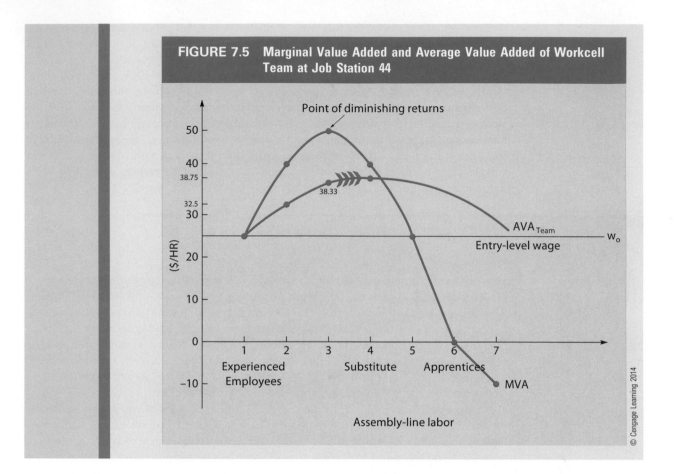

FIGURE 7.5 Marginal Value Added and Average Value Added of Workcell Team at Job Station 44

These same ideas apply to materiel inputs as well. In order to ensure that dredge spoil once removed does not flow back into harbors and navigable waterways, the U.S. Army Corps of Engineers pays concrete block manufacturers for every cubic yard of the muddy slurry that manufacturers will actually use in their production process. Too much dredge spoil, in combination with concrete mix and sand, results in more cracked blocks leaving the kilns in an unsalable condition. However, with a *negative* price on the input, manufacturers employ dredge spoil into the range of Stage III production. Such exceptions prove the general rule that optimal production with a single variable input and positive input prices necessitates restricting input choices to Stage II.

DETERMINING THE OPTIMAL USE OF THE VARIABLE INPUT

With one of the inputs (K) fixed in the short run, let's formalize how the producer determines the optimal quantity of the variable input (L) to employ in the production process. Such a determination requires the introduction into the analysis of output prices and labor costs. Therefore, the analysis begins by defining marginal revenue product and marginal factor cost.

Marginal Revenue Product

Marginal revenue product (MRP_L) is defined as the value of the output that an additional unit of the variable input adds to total revenue, or

$$MRP_L = \frac{\Delta TR}{\Delta L} \tag{7.4}$$

where ΔTR is the change in total revenue associated with the given change (ΔL) in the variable input, and MRP_L is equal to the marginal product of L (MP_L) times the marginal revenue (MR_Q) resulting from the increase in output obtained:

$$MRP_L = MP_L \cdot MR_Q \tag{7.5}$$

Consider again the Deep Creek Mining Company example (Table 7.2) of the previous section where K (capital) is fixed at 750 bhp. Suppose that the firm can sell all the ore it can produce at a price of $10 per ton; for example, in a perfectly competitive market, the firm would realize a constant marginal revenue equal to the going market equilibrium price. The marginal revenue product of labor (MRP_L) is computed using Equation 7.5 and is shown in Table 7.3.[6]

Sometimes in practice this concept is referred to as the **marginal value added**—that is, the amount by which potential sales revenue is increased as a result of employing an additional unit of variable input to increase output. In Europe, for example, rather than taxing the final retail sales value of goods, each level of production from raw material to finished goods distribution is taxed on its marginal value added at each stage of production.

Marginal Factor Cost

Marginal factor cost (MFC_L) is defined as the amount that an additional unit of the variable input adds to total cost, or

$$MFC_L = \frac{\Delta TC}{\Delta L} \tag{7.6}$$

where ΔTC is the change in cost associated with the given change (ΔL) in the variable input.

In the ore-mining example, suppose that the firm can employ as much labor (L) as it needs by paying the workers $50 per shift ($C_L$). In other words, the labor market is assumed to be *perfectly competitive*. Under these conditions, the marginal factor cost (MFC_L) is equal to C_L, or $50 per worker. It is constant regardless of the level of operation of the mine (see the last column of Table 7.3).

Optimal Input Level

Given the marginal revenue product and marginal factor cost, we can compute the optimal amount of the variable input to use in the production process. Recall from the discussion of marginal analysis in Chapter 2 that an economic activity should be expanded as long as the marginal benefits exceed the marginal costs. For the short-run production decision, the optimal level of the variable input occurs where

$$MRP_L = MFC_L \tag{7.7}$$

As can be seen in Table 7.3, the optimal input is $L = 6$ workers (signified with a starred 6) because $MRP_L = MFC_L = 50 at this point. At fewer than six workers,

[6]Input levels in Stage III ($MP_L < 0$) have been eliminated from consideration.

TABLE 7.3   MARGINAL REVENUE PRODUCT AND MARGINAL FACTOR COST—DEEP CREEK MINING COMPANY

LABOR INPUT L (NUMBER OF WORKERS)	TOTAL PRODUCT $Q = (TP_L)$ (TONS OF ORE)	MARGINAL PRODUCT OF LABOR MP_L (TONS PER WORKER)	TOTAL REVENUE $TR = P \cdot Q$ ($)	MARGINAL REVENUE $MR_Q = \dfrac{\Delta TR}{\Delta Q}$ ($/TON)	MARGINAL REVENUE PRODUCT $MRP_L = MP_L \cdot MR_Q$ ($/WORKER)	MARGINAL FACTOR COST MFC_L ($/WORKER)
0	0	—	0	—	—	—
1	6	6	60	10	60	50
2	16	10	160	10	100	50
3	29	13	290	10	130	50
4	44	15	440	10	150	50
5	55	11	550	10	110	50
6*	60	5	600	10	50	50
7	62	2	620	10	20	50
8	62	0	620	10	0	50

$MRP_L > MFC_L$ and the addition of more labor (workers) to the production process will increase revenues more than it will increase costs. Beyond six workers, the opposite is true—costs will increase more than revenues.

PRODUCTION WITH MULTIPLE VARIABLE INPUTS

Using the Deep Creek Mining Company example, suppose now that both capital (measured by the maximum bhp rating of the equipment) and labor (measured by the number of workers) are variable inputs to the ore-mining process. The firm can choose to operate the production process using any of the capital–labor combinations shown previously in Table 7.1.

Production (Output Constant) Isoquants

production isoquant An algebraic function or a geometric curve representing all the various combinations of two inputs that can be used in producing a given level of output.

The industrial engineering of production with two variable inputs can be represented graphically by a set of two-dimensional production isoquants. A **production isoquant** is either a geometric curve or an algebraic function representing all the various combinations of the two inputs that can be used in producing a given quantity (quant) of output. In the Deep Creek example, a production isoquant shows all the alternative ways in which the number of workers and various sizes of mining equipment can be combined to produce any desired level of output (tons of ore). Several of the production isoquants for the ore-mining example are shown in Figure 7.6. For example, an output of 6 tons can be produced using any of three different labor–capital combinations: one worker and 750-bhp equipment, two workers and 500-bhp equipment, or four workers and 250-bhp equipment. Similarly, as seen in the graph, an output of 62 tons can be produced using any one of five different labor–capital combinations.

Although each isoquant indicates how quantities of the two inputs may be *substituted* for one another, these choices are normally limited for two reasons: first, some input combinations in Figure 7.6 employ an excessive quantity of one input. Just as more

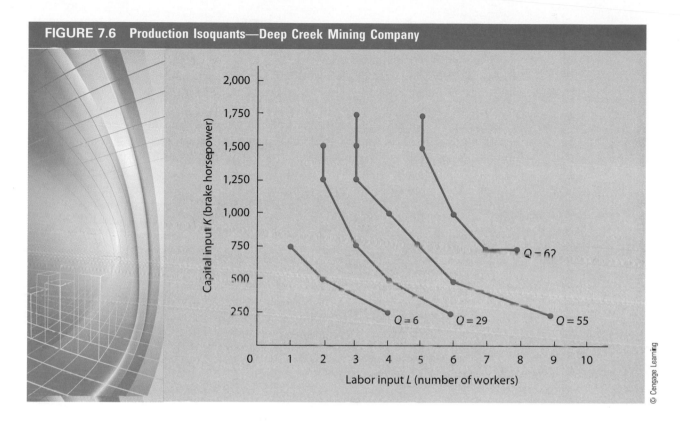

FIGURE 7.6 Production Isoquants—Deep Creek Mining Company

than eight workers result in negative marginal returns in choosing a single variable input for Deep Creek Mining (see Figure 7.2), so too here with 750-bhp machinery crowding effects introduced by the presence of an eighth worker would actually reduce output. Similarly, more than 1,500-bhp machinery would result in negative marginal returns to capital equipment with only five workers. Because all such inefficient mixes of capital and labor increase the input requirements (and therefore costs) without increasing output, they should be eliminated from consideration in making input substitution choices.

Second, input substitution choices are also limited by the technology of production, which often involves machinery that is not divisible. Although one can find smaller and larger mining equipment, not every bhp machine listed on the Y axis of Figure 7.6 will be available. The industrial engineering of mining operations often requires that we select from three or four possible fixed proportions production processes involving a particular size drilling machine and a requisite size labor force to run it.

Example

Just What Exactly Is a Refinery, and Why Won't Anyone Build One?[7]

In essence, refineries are enormous chemical plants that begin by superheating various grades of crude oil in large vessels and then pass the vapors that boil off through fractional distillation columns where they phase change back into various liquids as the distillates cool (see Figure 7.7). Crude oil contains literally hundreds of hydrocarbons, and the distillates run the gamut from propane that boils off at the top to lubricants and grease that "cool" to a liquid at a whopping 450°C near the bottom of the

(continued)

distillation column. Jet fuel and diesel liquefy at 250°C with the help of a catalytic cracking process in a separate converter, and farther up the column naphtha distillate yields gasoline after passing through a reformer. Kerosene, butane, and polyethylene (the basic building block for plastic) also distill out.

Refining is a classic variable proportions production process. The chemical "cracking" process of breaking the long chains of hydrocarbons can use more or less pressure, more or less heat, more or less high-quality but expensive light sweet crude or sulfurous heavy crude. From one 42-gallon barrel of crude, the input mix can be optimized to achieve about 20 gallons of gasoline and 10 gallons of diesel and fuel oil. Much of the equipment involved is 10 stories high and expensive. The fixed-cost investment today for a major refinery totals $2 billion. This cost must be recovered from just 22 percent of the final product price of gasoline, whereas crude itself commands 54 percent of the final product price. Profit margins in refining come to just a few cents per gallon, much like the thin margins in gasoline retailing. Oil exploration and development activites are much more profitable than refining in part to compensate for the extraordinary capital investment risks involved.

**PERCENTAGE OF FINAL PRODUCT PRICE OF GASOLINE
BY STAGE OF PRODUCTION (2006)**

Exploration and development and extraction of crude oil	54%
Federal and state excise taxes	16%
Refining	22%
Distribution and retail	8%

[7]Based on "Working Knowledge: Oil Refineries," *Scientific American* (June 2006), pp. 88–89.

The Marginal Rate of Technical Substitution

In addition to indicating the quantity of output that can be produced with any of the various input combinations that lie on the isoquant curve, the isoquant also indicates the *rate* at which one input may be substituted for another input in producing the given quantity of output. Suppose one considers the meaning of a shift from point A to point B on the isoquant labeled "$Q = 29$" in Figure 7.8. At point A, three workers and a 750-bhp machine are being used to produce 29 tons of output, whereas at point B, four workers and a 500-bhp machine are being used to produce the same amount of output. The first input mix is capital intensive like Chrysler's highly robotic Ontario minivan plant; the second is more labor intensive, like hand-tooled auto assembly. In moving from input mix A to input mix B, we substituted one additional unit of labor for 250 units of capital. The rate at which capital has been replaced with labor in producing the given output is equal to $250/L$ or 250 units of capital per unit of labor. The rate at which one input may be substituted for another input in the production process, while total output remains constant, is known as the **marginal rate of technical substitution (MRTS)**.

MRTS is given by the slope of the curve relating K to L—that is, the slope of the isoquant. The slope of the AB segment of the isoquant in Figure 7.8 is equal to the ratio of AC to CB. Algebraically, $AC = K_1 - K_2$ and $CB = L_1 - L_2$; therefore, the slope is equal

marginal rate of technical substitution (MRTS) The rate at which one input may be substituted for another input in producing a given quantity of output.

FIGURE 7.7   Crude Oil Is Made into Different Fuels from Distillation/Cracking/Reformer Processes

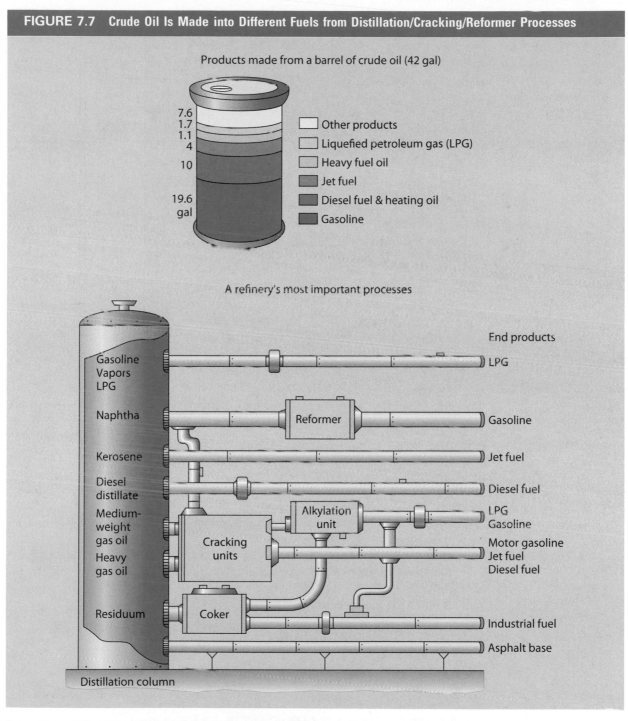

Source: Energy Information Administration, U.S. Department of Energy.

to $(K_1 - K_2) \div (L_1 - L_2)$. Because the slope is negative and one wishes to express the substitution rate as a positive quantity, a negative sign is attached to the slope:

$$MRTS = -\frac{K_1 - K_2}{L_1 - L_2} = \frac{\Delta K}{\Delta L} \qquad [7.8]$$

FIGURE 7.8   The Production Isoquant Curve—Deep Creek Mining Company

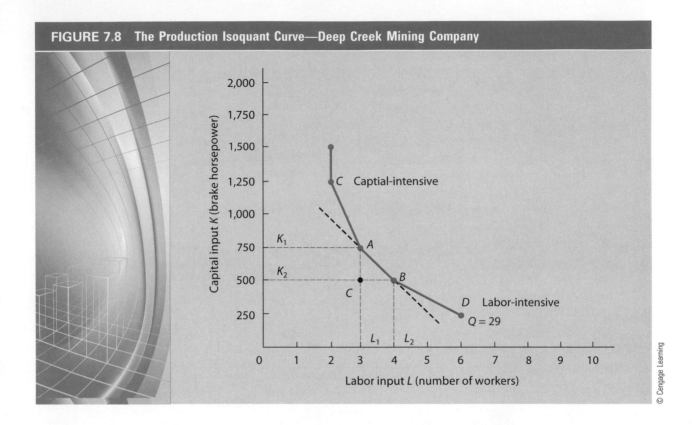

In the Deep Creek Mining Company example, $\Delta L = 3 - 4 = -1$, $\Delta K = 750 - 500 = 250$. Substituting these values into Equation 7.8 yields

$$MRTS = -\frac{250}{-1} = 250$$

Therefore, along $Q = 29$ between input combinations A and B, 250 bhp substituted for one worker.

It can be shown that the $MRTS$ is equal to the ratio of the marginal products of L and K by using the definition of the marginal product (Equation 7.2). This definition yields $\Delta L = \Delta Q/MP_L$ and $\Delta K = \Delta Q/MP_K$. Substituting these expressions into Equation 7.8 (and dropping the minus sign) yields

$$MRTS = \frac{\Delta Q/MP_K}{\Delta Q/MP_L}$$

$$MRTS = \frac{MP_L}{MP_K}$$

[7.9]

DETERMINING THE OPTIMAL COMBINATION OF INPUTS

As shown in the previous section, a given level of output can be produced using any of a large number of possible combinations of two inputs. The firm needs to determine which combination will minimize the total costs for producing the desired output.

Isocost Lines

The total cost of each possible input combination is a function of the market prices of these inputs. Assuming that the inputs are supplied in perfectly elastic fashion in competitive markets, the per-unit price of each input will be constant, regardless of the amount of the input that is purchased. Letting C_L and C_K be the per-unit prices of inputs L and K, respectively, the total cost (C) of any given input combination is

$$C = C_L L + C_K K \qquad [7.10]$$

Example

Isocost Determination: Deep Creek Mining Company (continued)

In the Deep Creek Mining Company example discussed earlier, suppose that the cost per worker is $50 per period (C_L) and that mining equipment can be leased at a price of $0.20 per bhp per period (C_K). The total cost per period of using L workers and equipment having K bhp to produce a given amount of output is

$$C = 50L + 0.20K \qquad [7.11]$$

From this relationship, it can be seen that the mining of 55 tons of ore per period using five workers and equipment having 750 bhp would cost $50(5) + 0.20(750) = \$400$. However, this combination is not the only mixture of workers and equipment that costs $400. Any combination of inputs satisfying the equation

$$\$400 = 50L + 0.20K$$

would cost $400. Solving this equation for K yields

$$
\begin{aligned}
K &= \frac{\$400}{0.20} - \frac{50}{0.20}L \\
&= \$2,000 - 250L
\end{aligned}
$$

Thus, the combinations $L = 1$ and $K = 1,750$; $L = 2$ and $K = 1,500$; $L = 3$ and $K = 1,250$ (plus many other combinations) all cost $400.

The combinations of inputs costing $400 can be represented as the *isocost line* in Figure 7.9 labeled "$C = \$400$." An isocost line exists for every possible total cost C. Solving Equation 7.11 for K gives the equation of each isocost line in Figure 7.8. Note that only the y-intercept $C/0.20$ changes as one moves from one isocost line to another.

$$K = \frac{C}{0.20} - 250L \qquad [7.12]$$

That is, all the isocost lines are parallel, each one having a slope of -250.

Once the isoquants and isocosts are specified, it is possible to solve for the optimum combination of inputs. The production decision problem can be formulated in two different ways, depending on the manner in which the production objective or goal is stated. Operations managers can solve for the combination of inputs that either

1. Minimizes total cost subject to a given constraint on output
2. Maximizes output subject to a given total cost constraint

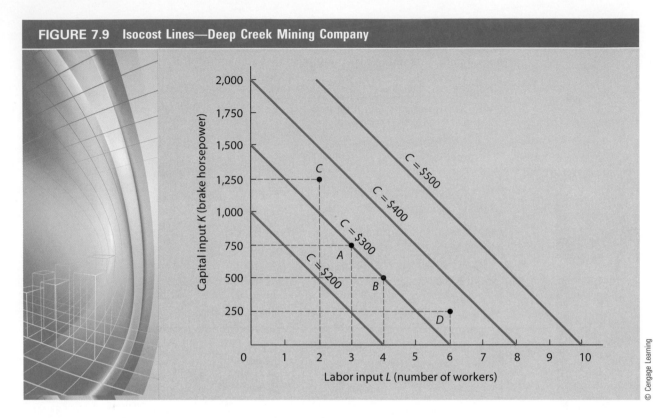

FIGURE 7.9 Isocost Lines—Deep Creek Mining Company

© Cengage Learning

Constrained cost minimization in Option 1 is the dual problem to the constrained output maximization problem in Option 2.

Minimizing Cost Subject to an Output Constraint

Consider first the problem in which a managing director of operations desires to release to production a number of orders for at least $Q^{(2)}$ units of output. As shown in Figure 7.10, this constraint requires that the solution be in the feasible region containing the input combinations that lie either on the $Q^{(2)}$ isoquant or on isoquants that fall above and to the right having larger output values (the shaded area). The total cost of producing the required output is minimized by finding the input combinations within this region that lie on the lowest cost isocost line. Combination D on the $C^{(2)}$ isocost line satisfies this condition. Combinations E and F, which also lie on the $Q^{(2)}$ isoquant, yield higher total costs because they fall on the $C^{(3)}$ isocost line. Thus, the use of L_1 units of input L and K_1 units of input K will yield a (constrained) minimum cost solution of $C^{(2)}$ dollars.

At the optimal input combination, the slope of the given isoquant must equal the slope of the $C^{(2)}$ lowest isocost line. As in the previous section, the slope of an isoquant is equal to dK/dL and

$$-\frac{dK}{dL} = MRTS = \frac{MP_L}{MP_k}$$

[7.13]

Taking the derivative of the isocost equation (Equation 7.12), the slope of the isocost line is given by

$$\frac{dK}{dL} = -\frac{C_L}{C_K}$$

[7.14]

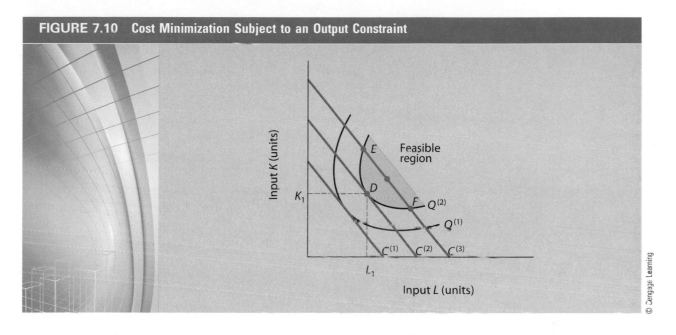

FIGURE 7.10   Cost Minimization Subject to an Output Constraint

Multiplying Equation 7.14 by (-1) and setting the result equal to Equation 7.13 yields

$$-\frac{dK}{dL} = -\left(-\frac{C_L}{C_K}\right)$$

$$= \frac{MP_L}{MP_K}$$

Thus, the following equilibrium condition, the "equimarginal criterion,"

$$\frac{MP_L}{MP_K} = \frac{C_L}{C_K}$$

or, equivalently,

$$\frac{MP_L}{C_L} = \frac{MP_K}{C_K} \qquad\qquad [7.15]$$

must be satisfied in order for an input combination to be an optimal solution to the problem of minimizing cost subject to an output constraint. Equation 7.15 indicates that the marginal product per dollar input cost of one factor must be equal to the marginal product per dollar input cost of the other factor.

Note in Figure 7.11 that maximizing output subject to a feasible region demarcated by the $Q^{(2)}$ cost constraint yields exactly the same (L_1, K_1) optimal input combination that satisfies the equimarginal criterion.

A FIXED PROPORTIONS OPTIMAL PRODUCTION PROCESS

The previous section analyzed the least-cost combination of divisible inputs in variable proportions production, where one input substituted continuously for another. However, Deep Creek Mining's production choices involve indivisible capital equipment, such as one small or one large mining drill and a predetermined number of workers to run the

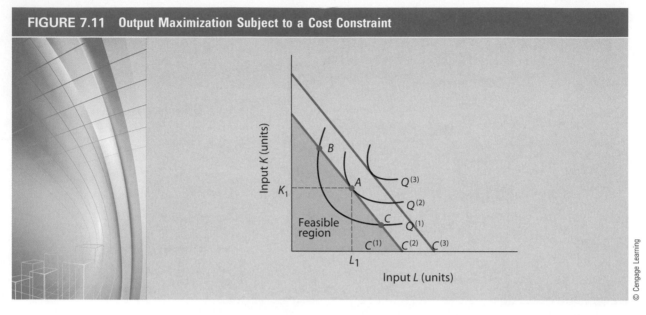

FIGURE 7.11 Output Maximization Subject to a Cost Constraint

chosen equipment. Similarly, an auto fender stamping machine in an assembly plant must be used in fixed proportion to labor and sheet metal supplies. And 3 hours of setup, maintenance, and cleaning may be required to support a 5-hour printing press run. Three additional hours of work by maintenance personnel would be required for a second press run, and a third shift of maintenance workers would be required for 24-hour printing operations. Although a higher output rate can be achieved by scaling up all the inputs, each of these production processes is one of fixed, not variable, proportions.

Although calculus is not applicable under these circumstances, linear programming techniques are available to determine the least-cost process for fixed proportions production. The Deep Creek Mining Company example can be used to illustrate the graphical approach to finding such a solution.

Example

Cost Minimization: Deep Creek Mining Company (continued)

Suppose one is interested in finding the combination of labor input and capital equipment that minimizes the cost of producing at least 29 tons of ore. Assume that the isocost lines are the ones defined by Equation 7.11 and graphed in Figure 7.8 earlier in this section. Figure 7.12 combines several isoquants and isocost lines for the ore-mining problem. The shaded area in the graph represents the set of feasible input combinations, that is, those labor and capital production processes that yield at least $Q = 29$ tons of output. Processes M_2 and M_3 minimize the cost of producing 29 tons at $300. M_1 imposes higher costs of $350.

production process
A fixed proportions production relationship.

Production Processes and Process Rays

A **production process** can be defined as one in which the inputs are combined in fixed proportion to obtain the output. By this definition, a production process can be represented graphically as a ray through the origin having a slope equal to the ratio of the

FIGURE 7.12   A Fixed Proportions Production Decision—Deep Creek Mining Company

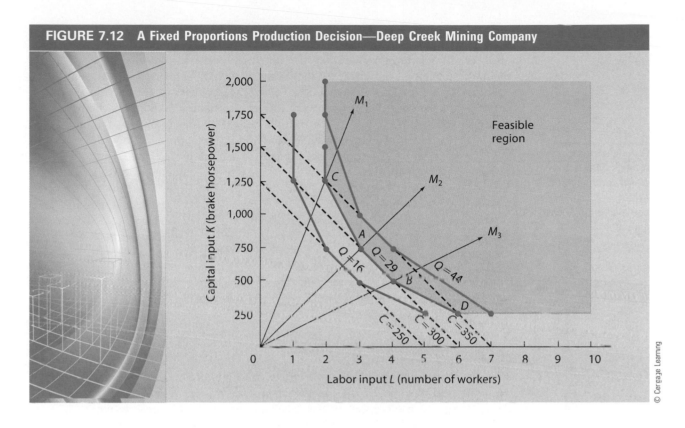

number of units of the respective resources required to produce one unit of output. Three production process rays for Deep Creek Mining are shown in Figure 7.12. Along Process Ray M_1, the inputs are combined in the ratio of two workers to a 1,250-bhp drilling machine. Hence, Ray M_1 has a slope of 625 bhp per mine worker.

Acquiring the strategic flexibility to operate multiple production processes like M_1, M_2, and M_3 can offer a firm flexibility in dealing with unusual orders, interruptions in the availability of resources, or binding resource constraints. However, not all fixed proportions production processes are equally efficient. The firm will prefer to use one or two production processes exclusively if they offer the advantage of substantial cost savings. Mine 1 employs process M_1 to produce 29 tons with two workers and a 1,250-bhp drilling machine at a total cost of $50(2) + 0.20(1,250) = \$350$ or $\$350/29 = \$12.07$ per ton. Mine 2 uses a more labor-intensive process (M_2) with three workers and a smaller 750-bhp machine and incurs a lower total cost of $300. Mine 2 is the benchmark operation for Deep Creek, in that this M_2 process produces 29 tons at minimum cost—specifically, $\$300/29 = \$10.34$ per ton.

MEASURING THE EFFICIENCY OF A PRODUCTION PROCESS

allocative efficiency A measure of how closely production achieves the least-cost input mix or process, given the desired level of output.

Mine 1 with production process M_1 is said to be allocatively inefficient because it has chosen the wrong input mix; the mine has allocated its input budget incorrectly. Its 1,250-bhp machine is too large for the number of workers hired and the output desired. By producing 29 tons of output for $350 relative to the lowest cost benchmark at $300, process M_1 exhibits only $\$300/\$350 = 85.7$ percent **allocative efficiency**.

In addition to allocative inefficiency involving the incorrect input mix, a production operation can exhibit technical inefficiency. For example, the industrial engineering indicated by the production isoquants in Figure 7.13 suggests that the process M_3 also should be capable of producing 29 tons. The "$C = \$300$" isocost line is tangent to the boundary of the feasible region (i.e., the "$Q = 29$" isoquant) at not only three workers and a 750-bhp machine (M_2) but also at four workers and a 500-bhp machine (M_3). In principle, both production processes yield the desired 29 tons of ore at a minimum total cost of $300 and will thereby satisfy the condition in Equation 7.15.

However, suppose Mine 3 has been unable to achieve more than 27 tons of output. Although it has adopted a least-cost process, Mine 3 would then be characterized as *technically inefficient*. In particular, Mine 3 exhibits only 27 tons/29 tons = 93 percent **technical efficiency** by comparison to the benchmark plant. Despite adopting the least-cost process, Mine 3's 93 percent technical efficiency may be inadequate. Benchmark plants often do substantially better, with many processes meeting 98 or 99 percent of their production goals.

technical efficiency A measure of how closely production achieves maximum potential output given the input mix or process.

Example

GM's A-Frame Supplier Achieves 99.998 Percent Technical Efficiency

Continuous quality improvement initiatives frequently raise the standard of excellence for which technically inefficient plants must strive. Just-in-time delivery systems, for example, accentuate the need for high reliability to produce on time as promised with near zero defects. One A-frame supplier to General Motors assembly plants reduced defective parts to five per million (i.e., 0.002 of 1 percent) and agreed to pay a $4,000 *per minute* "chargeback" for any late deliveries or defective parts that cause GM assembly line delays. That figure represents the $80,000 per hour direct cost of the 2,000 manufacturing employees on side-by-side assembly lines, plus $120,000 for the time-and-a-half overtime labor to catch up the 70 vehicles of production lost in an hour, plus $26,000 shipping delay costs, plus $14,000 for utilities—a grand total of $240,000 per hour. Under such enormous penalty costs, this auto component supplier to GM must constantly monitor and proactively solve production problems before they arise in order to ensure near 100 percent technical efficiency.

overall production efficiency A measure of technical and allocative efficiency.

Overall production efficiency is defined as the product of technical, scale, and allocative efficiency. If a 100 percent scale-efficient plant has 93 percent technical efficiency and 85.7 percent allocative efficiency, then its overall production efficiency is $1.00 \times 0.93 \times 0.857 = 0.797$, or 79.7 percent. Your job as an operations manager might be to decide which least-cost process Mine 1 in Figure 7.12 should now adopt. Because M_2 and M_3 are both allocatively efficient for 29 tons of output, but process M_3 experienced technical inefficiency problems resulting in an inability to realize its maximum potential output, Process M_2 would be preferred.

returns to scale The proportionate increase in output that results from a given proportionate increase in *all* the inputs employed in the production process.

RETURNS TO SCALE

An increase in the scale of production consists of a proportionate increase in all inputs simultaneously. The proportionate increase in output that results from the given proportionate increase in all the inputs is defined as the physical **returns to scale**. Suppose, in the Deep Creek Mining Company example, one is interested in determining the effect on the number of tons of ore produced (output) of a 1.50 factor increase in the scale of production from a given labor–capital combination of four workers and equipment having 500 bhp. A 1.50 factor increase in the scale of production would constitute a labor–capital combination of $4 \times 1.5 = 6$ workers and equipment having $500 \times 1.5 = 750$ bhp. From Table 7.1, note that the labor–capital combination of four workers and 500 bhp yields 29 tons of output, whereas the combination of six workers and 750 bhp yields 60 tons of output. Output increased by the ratio of $60/29 = 2.07$. Thus, a 1.50 factor increase in input use has resulted in more than a 1.50 factor output increase (specifically, 2.07).

Example

Technical and Allocative Efficiency in Commercial Banks at BB&T[8]

Wave after wave of bank merger activity may be motivated by the potential for substantial improvements in operating efficiency. Combining loan officers, facilities, and deposits of various kinds, the representative commercial bank in the United States "produces" only 63 percent of the loan value not in default (so-called current-status loans or performing loans) that the most efficient benchmark banks produce. In contrast, natural gas–fired power plants average 93 percent overall efficiency. The problem (and opportunity for improvement) in commercial banks is twofold. First, some banks adopt inefficient processes such as allowing the borrower to pick one senior loan officer who will review and approve or disapprove the loan application versus an anonymous loan officer assigned by the bank. Linear programming studies show that allocative efficiency in U.S. commercial banking averages only 81 percent, meaning that the least-cost process is 19 percent cheaper. Using best practices benchmarking, one bank may need to imitate another bank's borrower-screening or loan-monitoring processes.

When several banks do manage to adopt identical least-cost processes, yet one produces more current-status loans or larger performing loans than the others, the maximum feasible potential output in that type of institution can be identified. Technical efficiency then measures the observed bank output divided by the maximum potential output of the benchmark bank with identical processes. The smaller a bank's loan value not in default, the lower the technical efficiency. The representative commercial bank in the United States is only 78 percent technically efficient.

If the effort to improve allocative and technical efficiency is successful, the so-called bank [in]efficiency ratio of non-interest operating expenses (e.g., headcount) to net interest plus fee income often declines substantially. As a result, capitalized value often then rises enough to allow an acquirer like Branch Banking and Trust (BB&T) to recover the merger premium of up to 20 to 30 percent they would have to pay for Pittsburgh National in excess of the takeover target bank's pre-merger equity value.

[8]Based on D. Wheelock and P. Wilson, "Evaluating the Efficiency of Commercial Banks," *St. Louis Federal Reserve Review* (July/August 1995), pp. 39–52; and A. Kleit and D. Terrell, "Measuring Potential Efficiency Gains from Deregulation of Electricity Generation," *Review of Economics and Statistics* (August 2001), pp. 523–550.

Measuring Returns to Scale

An increase in the scale of production can be represented graphically in a two-dimensional isoquant map, as is shown in Figure 7.13. Increasing the scale of production by a factor of $\lambda = 2$ from the combination of 10 units of input L and 100 units of input K to 20 units of input L and 200 units of K results in an increase in the quantity of

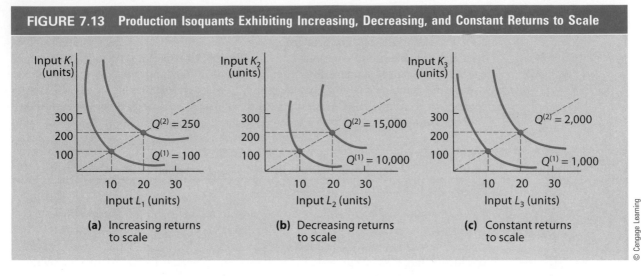

FIGURE 7.13 Production Isoquants Exhibiting Increasing, Decreasing, and Constant Returns to Scale

(a) Increasing returns to scale

(b) Decreasing returns to scale

(c) Constant returns to scale

© Cengage Learning

output from $Q^{(1)}$ to $Q^{(2)}$. Three possible relationships that can exist between the increase in inputs and the increase in outputs are as follows:

1. *Increasing* returns to scale: Output increases by *more than* λ; that is, $Q^{(2)} > \lambda Q^{(1)}$.
2. *Decreasing* returns to scale: Output increases by *less than* λ; that is, $Q^{(2)} < \lambda Q^{(1)}$.
3. *Constant* returns to scale: Output increases by *exactly* λ; that is, $Q^{(2)} = \lambda Q^{(1)}$.

Figure 7.13 illustrates three different production functions that exhibit these three types of returns to scale. In Panel (a), showing increasing returns to scale, doubling input L from 10 to 20 units and input K from 100 to 200 units yields more than double the amount of output (i.e., an increase from 100 to 250). In Panel (b), showing decreasing returns to scale, a similar doubling of two inputs, L and K, yields less than double the amount of output (i.e., an increase from 10,000 to 15,000). Finally, in Panel (c), showing constant returns to scale, a similar doubling of inputs L and K yields exactly double the amount of output (i.e., an increase from 1,000 to 2,000).

Increasing and Decreasing Returns to Scale

Many firm-level production functions are characterized by first increasing and then decreasing returns to scale. A number of industrial engineering arguments have been presented to justify this inconsistency. One major argument given for initially increasing returns is the opportunity for *specialization in the use of capital and labor*. Equipment that is more efficient in performing a limited set of tasks can be substituted for less efficient all-purpose equipment. Similarly, the efficiency of workers in performing a small number of related tasks is greater than that of less highly skilled, but more versatile, workers. Decreasing returns to scale thereafter often arises from the increasingly complex *problems of coordination and control* faced by management as the scale of production is increased. For example, managers may be limited in their ability to transmit and receive status reports over a wider and wider span of control.

The Cobb-Douglas Production Function

A somewhat simpler case is the Cobb-Douglas production function that has returns to scale determined by the sum of the parameters $(\beta_1 + \beta_2)$ in the equation:

$$Q = \alpha L^{\beta_1} K^{\beta_2} \qquad [7.16]$$

If $\beta_1 + \beta_2$ is less than, equal to, or greater than 1, the Cobb-Douglas production function will exhibit decreasing, constant, or increasing returns, respectively.

The multiplicative exponential Cobb-Douglas function can be estimated as a linear regression relation by taking the logarithm of Equation 7.16 to obtain

$$\log Q = \log \alpha + \beta_1 \log L + \beta_2 \log K \qquad [7.17]$$

Thus, once the parameters of the Cobb-Douglas model are estimated, the sum of the exponents of the labor (β_1) and capital (β_2) variables can be used to test for the presence of increasing, constant, or decreasing returns to scale.

Empirical Studies of the Cobb-Douglas Production Function in Manufacturing

In their original study, Cobb-Douglas fitted a production function of the form in Equation 7.16 to indices of production Q, labor L, and capital K over time in the U.S. manufacturing sector. Q was an index of physical volume of manufacturing; L was an index of the average number of employed wage earners only (i.e., salaried employees, officials, and working proprietors were excluded); and K was an index of the value of plants, buildings, tools, and machinery reduced to dollars of constant purchasing power. With the sum of the exponents restricted to one (constant returns to scale), the following function was obtained:

$$Q = 1.01 L^{.75} K^{.25} \qquad [7.18]$$

In later studies, Cobb-Douglas made several modifications that altered their results somewhat. These modifications included revising the output and labor indices, removing the secular trend from each index by expressing each yearly index value as a percentage of its overall trend value, and dropping the assumption of constant returns to scale. With these modifications, the estimated production function for the manufacturing sector was

$$Q = 0.84 L^{.63} K^{.30} \qquad [7.19]$$

A 10 percent increase in labor input results in about a 6 percent increase in output, and a 10 percent increase in capital input results in approximately a 3 percent increase in output. Also, the resulting sum of the exponents of the labor and capital variables is slightly less than 1, which indicates the presence of decreasing returns to scale in the broadly defined manufacturing sector.

A Cross-Sectional Analysis of U.S. Manufacturing Industries

Cross-sectional data have also been used to estimate Cobb-Douglas production functions for 18 U.S. manufacturing industries. Using aggregate data on plants located within each state, John Moroney estimated the following three-variable model:

$$Q = \alpha L_p^{\beta_1} L_n^{\beta_2} K^{\beta_3} \qquad [7.20]$$

where Q is the value added by the production plants, L_p is production worker work hours, L_n is nonproduction work years,[9] and K is gross book values of depreciable and depletable assets.[10] The results for several of the industries are shown in Table 7.4. The

---

[9]Nonproduction workers are management and other staff personnel.

[10]*Book values* of assets are the *historic* values of these assets as they appear on the balance sheet of the firm. Book values may differ significantly from current replacement values and hence may overstate or understate the actual amount of capital employed in the firm.

TABLE 7.4	PRODUCTION ELASTICITIES FOR SEVERAL INDUSTRIES			
INDUSTRY	CAPITAL ELASTICITY* β_1	PRODUCTION WORKER ELASTICITY β_2	NONPRODUCTION WORKER ELASTICITY β_3	SUM OF ELASTICITIES $\beta_1 + \beta_2 + \beta_3$
Food and beverages	.555	.439	.076	1.070*
	(.121)	(.128)	(.037)	(.021)
Textiles	.121	.549	.335	1.004
	(.173)	(.216)	(.086)	(.024)
Furniture	.205	.802	.103	1.109*
	(.153)	(.186)	(.079)	(.051)
Petroleum	.308	.546	.093	.947
	(.112)	(.222)	(.168)	(.045)
Stone, clay, and so on	.632	.032	.366	1.029
	(.105)	(.224)	(.201)	(.045)
Primary metals	.371	.077	.509	.958
	(.103)	(.188)	(.164)	(.035)

Number in parentheses below each elasticity coefficient is the standard error.

*Significantly greater than 1.0 at the 0.05 level (one-tailed test).

Source: From John R. Moroney, "Cobb-Douglas Production Functions and Returns to Scale in U.S. Manufacturing Industry," *Western Economic Journal* 6, no. 1 (December 1967), Table 1, p. 46. Reprinted with permission.

sum of the exponents ($\beta_1 + \beta_2 + \beta_3$) ranged from a low of 0.947 for petroleum to a high of 1.109 for furniture. In 13 of the 18 industries studied, the statistical tests showed that the sum of the exponents was not significantly different from 1.0. This evidence supports the hypothesis that most manufacturing industries exhibit constant returns to scale.

Example

Moneyball: A Production Function for Major League Baseball[11]

Team sports such as major league baseball are similar to other enterprises in that they attempt to provide a product (team victories) by employing various skills of team members. In acquiring team members through trades, the free agent market, and minor leagues/colleges, the owner is faced with various input mix trade-offs. For example, a baseball team owner may have to decide whether to trade a starting pitcher to obtain a power hitter or whether to sign a free agent relief pitcher in exchange for a frequent base stealer. These decisions are all made in the context of a baseball production function, subject to various constraints (e.g., budgetary limits and penalties, league rules on recruiting and transfers). Michael Lewis's 2004 book *Moneyball* argued that most major league baseball teams in the United States were not implementing the most efficient production mix of players, and then explained how the Oakland Athletics had uncovered this production inefficiency and subsequently outperformed their competitors using only a minimal salary budget.

In an attempt to quantify the factors that contribute to winning, a Cobb-Douglas production function for baseball was developed using data from 26 major league

(continued)

baseball teams. Output (Q) was measured by team victories. Inputs (X_1, X_2, X_3, etc.) from five different categories were included in the model:

- *Hitting*. This factor involves two different subskills: hitting frequency, as measured by the team *batting average*, and hitting with power, as measured by the team's *home runs*. *Slugging percentage*, which accounts for the additional contribution of doubles and triples to runs scored, has proven even more effective in predicting wins. *Moneyball* showed that the role of walks was being ignored and argued for an *on-base percentage* rather than slugging percentage. The A's led the American League in walks in 1999 and 2001 and were second or third in 2000, 2002, and 2004.
- *Running*. One measure of speed is a team's *stolen base total*. Oakland's Ricky Henderson had a record-setting 130 stolen bases in one season!
- *Defense*. This factor also involves two subskills: catching those chances that the player is able to reach, as measured by *fielding percentage*, and catching difficult chances that many players would not be able to reach, as measured by *total chances accepted*. Because these two variables are highly correlated with each other (i.e., multicollinear), separate regressions were run with each variable.
- *Pitching*. The most obvious measure of the pitching factor is the team's earned run average (ERA). However, ERA depends not only on pitching skill but also on the team's defensive skills. A better measure of pure pitching skills is the *strikeouts-to-walks* ratio for the pitching staff.
- *Coaching*. Teams often change managers when they are performing unsatisfactorily, so this factor is thought to be important. However, the ability of a manager (coach) is difficult to measure. Two different measures are used in this study—the manager's *lifetime won–lost percentage* and *number of years spent managing in the major leagues*. Separate regressions are run with each variable.

Finally, a dummy variable ($NL = 0$, $AL = 1$) was used to control for any differences between leagues, such as the designated hitter rule.

The results of four regressions are shown in Table 7.5. Several conclusions can be drawn from these results:

TABLE 7.5 EMPIRICAL ESTIMATES OF BASEBALL PRODUCTION FUNCTIONS

VARIABLE	EQUATION 1	EQUATION 2	EQUATION 3	EQUATION 4
Constant	.017	.018	.010	.008
League dummy	−.002	−.003	.004	.003
Batting average	2.017*	1.986*	1.969*	1.927*
Home runs	.229*	.299*	.208*	.215*
Stolen bases	.119*	.120*	.110*	.112*
Strikeouts/walks	.343*	.355*	.324*	.334*
Total fielding chances	1.235	1.200		
Fielding percentage			5.62	5.96
Manager *W/L* percentage		−.003		−.004
Manager years	−.004		−.002	
$\overline{R}^2$ (coef. of determination)	.789	.790	.773	.774

*Statistically significant at the 0.05 level.

© Cengage Learning

(continued)

1. Hitting average contributes almost six times as much as pitching to a team's success. This finding tends to contradict conventional wisdom, which says that pitching and defense win championships.
2. Home runs contribute about twice as much as stolen bases to a team's success.
3. Coaching skills are not significant in any of the regression equations.
4. Defensive skills are not significant in any of the regression equations.
5. Finally, the sums of the statistically significant variables in each of the four equations range from 2.588 to 2.709. Because these are all much greater than 1.0, the baseball production functions examined all exhibit *increasing returns to scale*. Better hitting and on-base and running skills yield more than proportional increases in games won. Because of the link between winning and attendance, ballplayers with these characteristics also yield greater revenues, especially to teams that contend for division and league championships.

[11]Based on Charles E. Zech, "An Empirical Estimation of a Production Function: The Case of Major League Baseball," *The American Economist* 25, no. 2 (Fall 1981), pp. 19–23; Michael Lewis, *Moneyball* (New York: Norton, 2004); John Hakes and Ray Sauer, "An Economic Evaluation of the Moneyball Hypothesis," *Journal of Economic Perspectives* (Summer 2006), pp. 173–185; and "The Real Most Valuable Players," *Wall Street Journal Online* (2007).

SUMMARY

- A *production function* is a schedule, a graph, or a mathematical model relating the maximum quantity of output that can be produced from various quantities of inputs.

- For a production function with one variable input, the *marginal product* is defined as the incremental change in total output that can be produced by the use of one more unit of the variable input in the production process.

- For a production function with one variable input, the *average product* is defined as the ratio of total output to the amount of the variable input used in producing the output.

- The *law of diminishing marginal returns* states that, with all other productive factors held constant, the use of increasing amounts of the variable factor in the production process beyond some point will result in diminishing marginal increases in total output. *Increasing returns* can arise with *network effects*, especially involving information economy goods and industry standards.

- In the short run, with one of the productive factors fixed, the optimal output level (and optimal level of the variable input) occurs where marginal revenue product equals marginal factor cost. *Marginal revenue product* is defined as the amount that an additional unit of the variable input adds to total revenue. *Marginal factor cost* is defined as the amount that an additional unit of the variable input adds to total cost.

- A *production isoquant* is either a geometric curve or an algebraic function representing all the various combinations of inputs that can be used in producing a given level of output.

- The *marginal rate of technical substitution* is the rate at which one input may be substituted for another input in the production process, while total output remains constant. It is equal to the ratio of the marginal products of the two inputs.

- In the long run, with both inputs being variable, minimizing cost subject to an output constraint (or maximizing output subject to a cost constraint) requires that the production process be operated at the point where the marginal product per dollar input cost of each factor is equal.

- The degree of *technical efficiency* of a production process is the ratio of observed output to the maximum potentially feasible output for that process, given the same inputs.

- The degree of *allocative efficiency* of a production process is the ratio of total cost for producing a given output level with the least-cost process to the observed total cost of producing that output.
- Physical *returns to scale* is defined as the proportionate increase in the output of a production

process that results from a given proportionate increase in all the inputs.

- The Cobb-Douglas production function, which is used extensively in empirical studies, is a multiplicative exponential function in which output is a (nonlinear) increasing function of each of the inputs, with the sum of the exponential parameters indicating the returns to scale.

Exercises

Answers to the exercises in blue can be found in Appendix D at the back of the book.

1. In the Deep Creek Mining Company example described in this chapter (Table 7.1), suppose again that labor is the variable input and capital is the fixed input. Specifically, assume that the firm owns a piece of equipment having a 500-bhp rating.
   a. Complete the following table: *w=500*

LABOR INPUT L (NO. OF WORKERS)	TOTAL PRODUCT $TP_L (= Q)$	MARGINAL PRODUCT MP_L	AVERAGE PRODUCT AP_L
1	3	3	3
2	6	3	3
3	16	10	5.33
4	29	13	7.25
5	43	14	8.6
6	55	12	9.17
7	58	3	8.29
8	60	2	7.5
9	59	-1	6.56
10	56	-3	5.6

(handwritten annotations: MP/AP_L, E_p; stage 1; diminishing returns; stage 2; stage 3; $E_p > 1$; $0 \le E_p < 1$; $E_p < 0$)

   b. Plot the (i) total product, (ii) marginal product, and (iii) average product functions.
   c. Determine the boundaries of the three stages of production. *stage 1, 2 & 3*

2. From your knowledge of the relationships among the various production functions, complete the following table:

VARIABLE INPUT L	TOTAL PRODUCT $TP_L (= Q)$	AVERAGE PRODUCT AP_L	MARGINAL PRODUCT MP_L
0	0	—	—
1	—	—	8
2	28	—	—
3	—	18	—
4	—	—	26
5	—	20	—
6	108	—	—
7	—	—	-10

3. The amount of fish caught per week on a trawler is a function of the crew size assigned to operate the boat. Based on past data, the following production schedule was developed:

CREW SIZE (NUMBER OF WORKERS)	AMOUNT OF FISH CAUGHT PER WEEK (HUNDREDS OF LBS)
2	3
3	6
4	11
5	19
6	24
7	28
8	31
9	33
10	34
11	34
12	33

a. Over what ranges of workers are there (i) increasing, (ii) constant, (iii) decreasing, and (iv) negative returns?

b. How large a crew should be used if the trawler owner is interested in maximizing the total amount of fish caught?

c. How large a crew should be used if the trawler owner is interested in maximizing the average amount of fish caught per worker?

4. Consider Exercise 3 again. Suppose the owner of the trawler can sell all the fish caught for $75 per 100 pounds and can hire as many crew members as desired by paying them $150 per week. Assuming that the owner of the trawler is interested in maximizing profits, determine the optimal crew size.

5. Consider the following short-run production function (where L = variable input, Q = output):

$$Q = 6L^2 - 0.4L^3$$

a. Determine the marginal product function (MP_L).

b. Determine the average product function (AP_L).

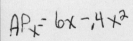
$AP_x = 6x - .4x^2$

c. Find the value of L that maximizes Q.

d. Find the value of L at which the marginal product function takes on its maximum value. *set a to zero d solve.*

e. Find the value of L at which the average product function takes on its maximum value.

6. Consider the following short-run production function (where L = variable input, Q = output):

$$Q = 10L - 0.5L^2$$

Suppose that output can be sold for $10 per unit. Also assume that the firm can obtain as much of the variable input (L) as it needs at $20 per unit.

a. Determine the marginal revenue product function.

b. Determine the marginal factor cost function.

c. Determine the optimal value of L, given that the objective is to maximize profits.

7. Suppose that a firm's production function is given by the following relationship:

$$Q = 2.5\sqrt{LK} \quad (\text{i.e.}, Q = 2.5L^{.5}K^{.5})$$

where

Q = output
L = labor input
K = capital input

a. Determine the percentage increase in output if labor input is increased by 10 percent (assuming that capital input is held constant).
b. Determine the percentage increase in output if capital input is increased by 25 percent (assuming that labor input is held constant).
c. Determine the percentage increase in output if *both* labor and capital are increased by 20 percent.

8. Based on the production function parameter estimates reported in Table 7.4:
a. Which industry (or industries) appears to exhibit decreasing returns to scale? (Ignore the issue of statistical significance.)
b. Which industry comes closest to exhibiting constant returns to scale?
c. In which industry will a given percentage increase in capital result in the largest percentage increase in output?
d. In which industry will a given percentage increase in production workers result in the largest percentage increase in output?

9. Consider the following Cobb-Douglas production function for the bus transportation system in a particular city:

$$Q = \alpha L^{\beta_1} F^{\beta_2} K^{\beta_3}$$

where L = labor input in worker hours
F = fuel input in gallons
K = capital input in number of buses
Q = output measured in millions of bus miles

Suppose that the parameters (α, β_1, β_2, and β_3) of this model were estimated using annual data for the past 25 years. The following results were obtained:

$$\alpha = 0.0012 \quad \beta_1 = 0.45 \quad \beta_2 = 0.20 \quad \beta_3 = 0.30$$

a. Determine the (i) labor, (ii) fuel, and (iii) capital input production elasticities.
b. Suppose that labor input (worker hours) is increased by 2 percent next year (with the other inputs held constant). Determine the approximate percentage change in output.
c. Suppose that capital input (number of buses) is decreased by 3 percent next year (when certain older buses are taken out of service). Assuming that the other inputs are held constant, determine the approximate percentage change in output.
d. What type of returns to scale appears to characterize this bus transportation system? (Ignore the issue of statistical significance.)
e. Discuss some of the methodological and measurement problems one might encounter in using time-series data to estimate the parameters of this model.

10. *Extension of the Cobb-Douglas Production Function*—The Cobb-Douglas production function (Equation 7.16) can be shown to be a special case of a larger class of linear homogeneous production functions having the following mathematical form:[12]

$$Q = \gamma[\partial K^{-\rho} + (1 - \partial)L^{-\rho}]^{-\nu/\rho}$$

---

[12]See R. G. Chambers, *Applied Production Analysis* (Cambridge: Cambridge University Press, 1988).

where γ is an efficiency parameter that shows the output resulting from given quantities of inputs; ∂ is a distribution parameter ($0 \le \partial \le 1$) that indicates the division of factor income between capital and labor; ρ is a substitution parameter that is a measure of substitutability of capital for labor (or vice versa) in the production process; and v is a scale parameter ($v > 0$) that indicates the type of returns to scale (increasing, constant, or decreasing). Show that when $v = 1$, this function exhibits constant returns to scale. (*Hint:* Increase capital K and labor L each by a factor of λ, or $K^* = (\lambda)K$ and $L^* = (\lambda)L$, and show that output Q also increases by a factor of λ, or $Q^* = (\lambda)(Q)$.)

11. Lobo Lighting Corporation currently employs 100 unskilled laborers, 80 factory technicians, 30 skilled machinists, and 40 skilled electricians. Lobo feels that the marginal product of the last unskilled laborer is 400 lights per week, the marginal product of the last factory technician is 450 lights per week, the marginal product of the last skilled machinist is 550 lights per week, and the marginal product of the last skilled electrician is 600 lights per week. Unskilled laborers earn $400 per week, factory technicians earn $500 per week, machinists earn $700 per week, and electricians earn $750 per week.

Is Lobo using the lowest cost combination of workers to produce its targeted output? If not, what recommendations can you make to assist the company?

Case Exercise ## The Production Function for Wilson Company

Economists at the Wilson Company are interested in developing a production function for fertilizer plants. They collected data on 15 different plants that produce fertilizer (see the following table).

Questions

1. Estimate the Cobb-Douglas production function $Q = \alpha L^{\beta_1} K^{\beta_2}$, where Q = output; L = labor input; K = capital input; and α, β_1, and β_2 are the parameters to be estimated.
2. Test whether the coefficients of capital and labor are statistically significant.
3. Determine the percentage of the variation in output that is explained by the regression equation.
4. Determine the labor and capital estimated parameters, and give an economic interpretation of each value.
5. Determine whether this production function exhibits increasing, decreasing, or constant returns to scale. (Ignore the issue of statistical significance.)

PLANT	OUTPUT (000 TONS)	CAPITAL ($000)	LABOR (000 WORKER HOURS)
1	605.3	18,891	700.2
2	566.1	19,201	651.8
3	647.1	20,655	822.9
4	523.7	15,082	650.3
5	712.3	20,300	859.0
6	487.5	16,079	613.0
7	761.6	24,194	851.3
8	442.5	11,504	655.4
9	821.1	25,970	900.6
10	397.8	10,127	550.4
11	896.7	25,622	842.2
12	359.3	12,477	540.5
13	979.1	24,002	949.4
14	331.7	8,042	575.7
15	1064.9	23,972	925.8

Production Economics of Renewable and Exhaustible Natural Resources, Advanced Material

Natural resource inputs pivotally affect the success of major industries in both developed and developing economies. Timber used for home construction, coal and natural gas converted to electric power, and petroleum converted to gasoline are examples where a company's profitability hinges on natural resource inputs. Natural resources are often subdivided into two categories: renewable and exhaustible resources. Renewable resources like clean air, clean water, grazing land, timber, and fisheries often present common property and externality problems that must be analyzed and managed differently from the frequently immobile and therefore usually privatized exhaustible resources such as seabed manganese, coal fields, crude oil pools, and subterranean natural gas deposits. Public regulation is therefore very involved in decision making about renewables. For example, migratory ocean fisheries of bluefin tuna are being overharvested such that their catch is declining at an alarming rate (see Figure 7A.1). Several bilateral trade negotiations and the United Nations have focused on this problem and proposed regulatory solutions.

RENEWABLE RESOURCES[1]

Fundamentally, all renewable resources are capital assets that must be analyzed with a dynamic stock-flow model where time (time to harvest and time to extinction) plays an explicit role. The optimal decision-making question with renewables is when to produce (i.e., when to harvest an oyster, net a fish, or cut down a tree) and when to let the resource grow another year to yield an even greater harvest later. In the following equation, the flow of harvested resources, h, is determined by harvesting effort, E, and by the remaining resource stock (capital stock), S—for example, the population size of the fishery or the cumulative board feet of the still growing forest that remains unharvested:

$$h = f(E, S) \qquad [7A.1]$$

where diminishing positive marginal returns to harvesting effort are assumed $(\partial f/\partial E) > 0$, $\partial^2 f/\partial^2 E < 0$. Larger stocks left in the fishery, the forest, or the oyster bed imply a higher flow rate from harvesting later for any given effort $(\partial f/\partial S > 0)$ and therefore a lower harvesting cost per unit output.

---

[1]This section relies upon the excellent survey by Gardner Brown, "Renewable Resource Management and Use with and without Markets," *Journal of Economic Literature* 38 (December 2000), pp. 875–914.

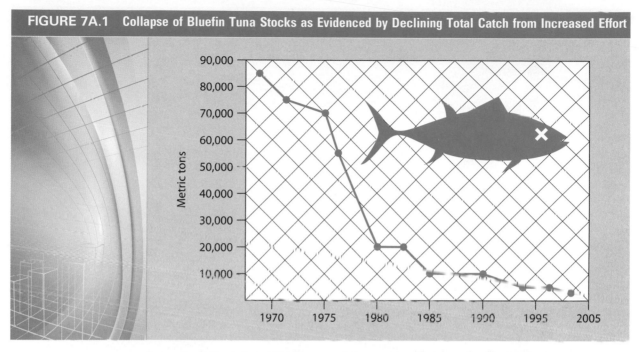

FIGURE 7A.1   Collapse of Bluefin Tuna Stocks as Evidenced by Declining Total Catch from Increased Effort

Source: From Hemispheres, United.com in-flight Magazine, October 2009, p. 24. Reprinted by permission of Ink Publishing.

So, one way to grow a renewable resource is just to do less harvesting. More generally, the net rate of growth of a resource stock per unit of $\Delta S/\Delta t$ is the difference between the planned flow rate of harvest h and the biological growth function $g(S)$.

$$\frac{\Delta S}{\Delta t} = -h + g(S) \qquad [7A.2]$$

Just as it is quite natural to assume diminishing returns relative to harvesting effort, so, too, limitations of habitat, space, or nutrients introduce diminishing returns as a species grows—that is, $\partial^2 g/\partial^2 S < 0$. The eventually diminishing slope of this growth function $\Delta S/\Delta t$ measures the amount of additional fish caught or, analogously, the lumber that comes from waiting a unit of time Δt rather than harvesting the resource immediately. This non-linear law of nature is also reflected by the accelerating decay as a specie collapses. See Figure 7A.1 on the sharply declining tonnage of bluefish tuna caught or, in the extreme, consider the miniscule cumulative board feet of growing lumber in a timber stand that has been essentially clear-cut.

The potential revenue from waiting to harvest and selling the extra resources later, expressed as a percentage growth rate on the value of the timber or fishery stock ($P\Delta S/\Delta t)/PS$, has a pivotal relation to the resource owner's inflation-adjusted, risk-adjusted discount rate, r. The discount rate is the opportunity cost of waiting—that is, the interest that could be earned on the owner's funds if they were invested at comparable risk. In the following Equation 7A.3 and in the lower panel of Figure 7A.2, we express this percentage as a rate of return on investment (ROI) in harvesting. In particular, when the percentage growth of the resource stock is greater than the owner's discount rate (at, for example, Point A in Figure 7A.2), the owner should harvest more (moving down along ROI toward D and up the yield hill in the top panel of Figure 7A.2 toward $h^*_{W/O}$). When the percentage growth of the resource stock is less than the discount rate,

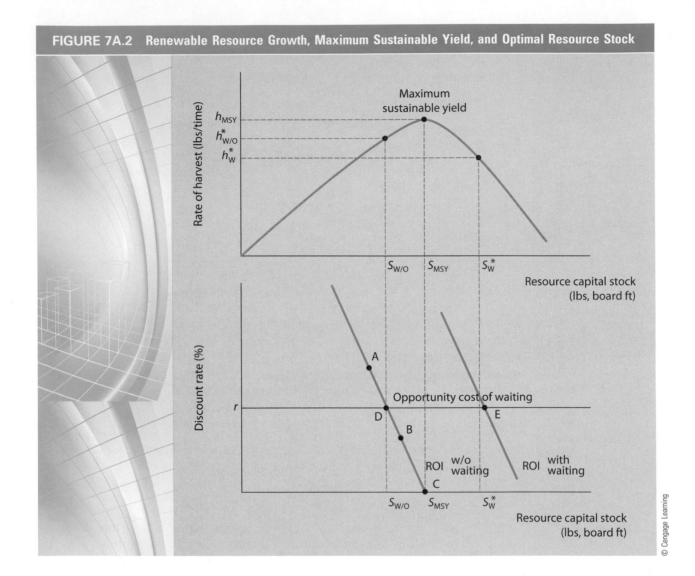

FIGURE 7A.2 Renewable Resource Growth, Maximum Sustainable Yield, and Optimal Resource Stock

the rate of harvest should be decreased as at point B in Figure 7A.2. The optimal capital stock equates the two at $h_{W/O}^*$ and point D:

$$\left[\text{ROI} = \frac{P\Delta S/t}{PS} = \frac{\Delta S/\Delta t}{S}\right] = r \qquad [7A.3]$$

In general, a positive discount rate (reflecting the unassailable fact that there is a cost of waiting) implies that the optimal resource stock (the species population size) is *smaller* than it would be otherwise. Specifically, the optimal population size is always smaller than the maximum sustainable harvest, sometimes called the **maximum sustainable yield (MSY)** (at the peak of the top panel in Figure 7A.2). The reason is that the capital stock S_{MSY} that yields a maximum harvest h_{MSY} drives the ROI in harvesting to zero (at point C). Any positive discount rate would exceed ROI at C and thereby imply that the resource owner should reduce the timber or fishery stock. For example, Figure 7A.2 illustrates that $S_{W/O}$, which equates ROI and r, is smaller than S_{MSY}.

However, it is important to reiterate that the rate of growth of S—that is, $g(S)$—may not be a constant but rather may be a positive function of S itself. Because of this faster

maximum sustainable yield (MSY) The largest production harvest that can be produced by the resource stock as a perpetuity.

biological replenishment of a fishery as its overall size increases, the ROI from harvesting would then become larger than it would otherwise be. That is, $ROI_{W/O}$, which represents the biological process without this extra boost from increasing size, would then shift to the right to ROI_W. Consequently, the optimal capital stock increases to S_W^{*2}. Although these optimal rate of harvest decisions are complex, a thorough understanding of their analysis by environmental economists at the National Oceanic and Atmospheric Administration (NOAA) has allowed several depleted species such as New England scallops, Mid-Atlantic bluefish and flounder, and Pacific lingcod to be restored to full health at S_W^*. This environmental success is important to many seaside economies throughout the Unites States as the commercial and recreational fishing industry generates $183 billion a year and employs 1.5 million.

Example

Oyster Seedbed Replenishment on Chesapeake Bay[3]

Under the NOAA fisheries statutes enacted in 1976, 1996 and 2006, eight regional regulatory bodies manage all offshore fisheries in the United States using science-based harvesting quotas and 10-year recovery programs for depleted fish stocks like the bluefin tuna. After three decades of collaboration between commercial fisherman and NOAA, 86 percent of the 230 federally monitored commercial fisheries in the United States are no longer subject to overfishing. Between 2000 and 2012, a sustainability index for U.S. fisheries has nearly doubled from 350 to 600 where the maximum possible score is 920. Thirteen of the 35 remaining depleted fish populations in the United States are New England cod species whose former status as a mainstay of the Massachusetts economy is memorialized by a "Sacred Cod" carving that hangs over the legislative chamber in Boston.

As a ground fish rather than an offshore migratory fishery, cod are subject to state not federal regulation. State fishery regulators have smaller less efficient harvesters and less funding to work with, but still they manage quite well. Take, for example, the oyster seedbed program in Chesapeake Bay. Oysters in the larval stage (called "spat") grow and multiply quickly under the right conditions but require shell-like surfaces (cultch) on which to attach. One excellent alternative is the clean shell generated as a by-product from oyster packing plants. Unfortunately, overharvesting on common property destroys the private incentive to replenish the oyster beds with clean cultch. Since oyster beds are typically beyond shoreline riparian rights, no individual harvester can fully appropriate the returns from replenishing the deep-water beds with clean cultch. Instead, each harvester has an incentive to reap the maximum yield in a downward spiraling race to exhaustion of the common property resource. This is the so-called "tragedy of the commons."

To prevent overharvesting and inadequate replenishment from destroying the oyster industry, Virginia and Maryland have regulated catch sizes and methods, and both states have provided a public subsidy to replenish the beds with clean shell cultch. Maine lobstermen abide by similar catch restrictions and adopt maintenance quotas largely through a voluntary association—an economic club—that co-manages the renewable natural resources in the Maine lobster fishery.

(continued)

---

[2]Note that, as Figure 7A.2 illustrates, the optimal rate of harvest h_W^* could then be *smaller* than the optimal rate of harvest $h_{W/O}^*$ without this effect. This result is consistent with the intuition that waiting to harvest later will generate a larger and larger resource base from which to harvest (depending upon the particulars of the biological regeneration of the renewable population).

In other cases, like timber stands and wildlife management, the seedling and maturation process can be enhanced by replenishing in a different manner. Thinning the forest by harvesting large older trees and periodically removing the undergrowth allows the best immature trees and seedlings room and sunlight to grow. The same thing is true in many larger game animal species. Winnowing the herd of long-horn deer or bison actually causes its growth rate to increase. Hence, the optimal rate of harvest can actually increase with more proactive forestry and game management.

[3]"Fish Stocks: Plenty More Fish in the Sea," *The Economist*, (May 26, 2012), p. 78.

EXHAUSTIBLE NATURAL RESOURCES

Some natural resources like coal, crude oil, natural gas, and manganese are formed over tens of thousands of years. Although limited and fixed in this geological sense, more intense exploration and development triggered by a spiking resource price can often locate additional resources before exhaustion nears. Nevertheless, eventually the supply of low-sulfur coal or sweet light crude oil or high-quality natural gas will be exhausted. Long before this happens, we usually discover the possibility of a replacement natural resource or a synthetic substitute. As we pointed out in Chapter 2, jojoba bean oil turned out to be a good natural substitute for sperm whale lubricant used with high-friction machinery like jet aircraft engines. Similarly, synthetic diamonds have substituted for natural diamonds in many industrial applications. Today, directional drilling three kilometers down and then arcing as much as 10 kilometers away from an oil rig (see Figure 7A.3) as well as fracking technology to release natural gas from rock formations 10 kilometers deep has led to booming expansions of both the oil and natural gas industries. Both developments occurred within three years of the extraordinary spike of crude oil prices to $147 per barrel in July 2008 (again see Figure 7A.3).

The analysis of exhaustible natural resources can be distinguished from renewable resources in two important ways: First, the net growth rate in Equation 7A.2 for renewable resources reduces to simply $-h$ in the case of exhaustible resources, because the growth rate of the stock itself is exactly zero. Second, the optimal capital stock of a renewable resource does not vary when its price changes. This is easily seen in Equation 7A.3 where the prices, P, in both the numerator and denominator of the return on investment from waiting cancel each other out. Recall that any price change that is unrelated to the size of the capital stock has no effect—none whatsoever—on the efficient rate of harvest or the optimal capital stock of *renewable* natural resources. In contrast, just the opposite is true for an exhaustible resource.

Since there is no way for the exhaustible resource to regenerate itself, the only reason to hold onto and not harvest coal or crude oil or natural gas today is if you, the owner, believe that the price is going to rise in the near future. Price changes and price change expectations are therefore the key to exhaustible resource decisions.

Let's begin an analysis of this exhaustible resource extraction problem by defining consensus expectations for future prices in time period $T(P_T)$ as

$$P_T = P_0(1 + r)^T \qquad [7A.4]$$

where r is the real rate of interest (more precisely, the inflation-adjusted, risk-adjusted discount rate for our exhaustible resource extraction decision). Dividing each unit of

FIGURE 7A.3 Oil Price 1970–2012 and Drilling Rig with Horizontal Drilling

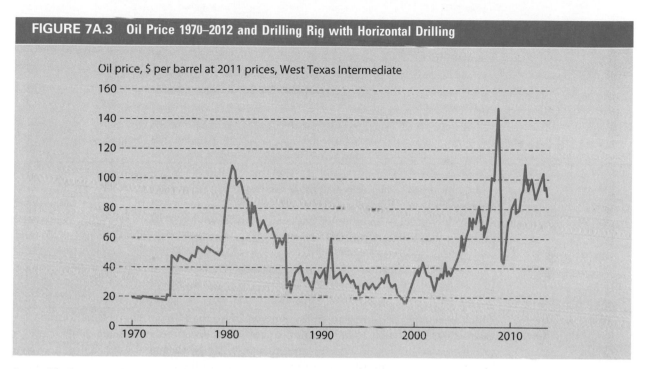

Oil price, $ per barrel at 2011 prices, West Texas Intermediate

Source: *The Economist*, Thomson Reuters.

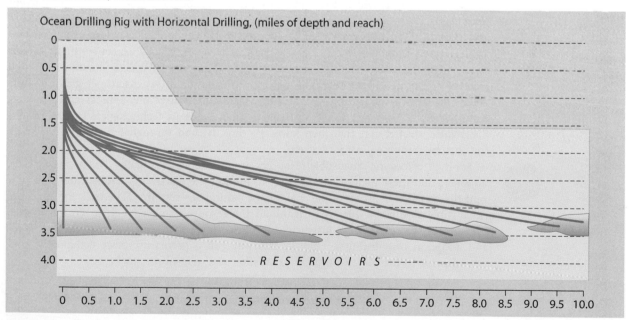

Source: Schlumberger.

time t into n subperiods, the compound growth version of these consensus price expectations may be written as[4]

$$P_T = P_0[\lim_{n \to \infty}(1 + r/n)^{nT}] = P_0 e^{rT} \qquad [7A.5]$$

---

[4]The number e is 2.7183..., the base of the natural logarithms.

As before, we can express the harvest-now-or-wait decision in terms of the opportunity cost of waiting (the real rate of interest r) relative to the percentage rate of growth of resource prices:[5]

$$\frac{\Delta P_T / \Delta T}{P_T} = \frac{r P_0 e^{rT}}{P_T} \qquad \text{[7A.6]}$$

which reduces, using Equation 7A.5, to

$$\frac{\Delta P_T / \Delta T}{P_T} = r \qquad \text{[7A.7]}$$

Equation 7A.7 states that as long as the expected rate of price increase (say, 8 percent) exceeds the rate of interest (say, 4 percent), one should leave the coal, oil, or natural gas in the ground and harvest it later. If interest rates rise above this percentage growth rate of the exhaustible resource prices, the resource should be extracted and sold now.

Rearranging Equation 7A.5 to solve for the current resource price we obtain

$$P_0 = P_T / e^{-rT} \qquad \text{[7A.8]}$$

which has some interesting interpretations as more than a continuous time formula for calculating the present value of future prices. First, T can be interpreted as the time to exhaustion of the resource at the current rate of use (see Figure 7A.4). Hence, new coal field or oil field discoveries that lead to an increase in the proven reserves of coal, oil, or natural gas raise T, which according to Equation 7A.8, must result in a lower current market price P_0. Similarly, more energy dependence and a faster rate of use lowers T and raises the current market price P_0. Finally, since optimal use leads to persistent appreciation of the coal or oil or gas at the rate r, we eventually expect synthetic substitutes to emerge as these natural resources near exhaustion. That is, at a sufficiently high price of crude oil and the resulting high price for gasoline (say, $4.10 per gallon in July 2008), the return for R&D investment to develop alternative fuel sources and products climbs steeply. Sufficient R&D investment often leads to technological breakthroughs like hybrid electric cars that then lower P_T directly, and through Equation 7A.8, lower the current resource price P_0 as well.

So, high prices for exhaustible resources are inevitable, eventually. The goods news is, however, that these high prices often set in motion the discovery of substitutes that prevent the actual exhaustion of the coal, oil, or natural gas resource. The trick for an astute exhaustible resource owner is to withhold the resource long enough to create upward pressure on prices that are just below the price level that would set off the discovery and adoption of substitutes. Only in this way can a premature price collapse be prevented prior to the planned time of exhaustion of the resource stock.

Example

Saudi Arabian Oil Minister Plays a Waiting Game[6]

No resource owner on Earth has more natural resources than the Royal Kingdom of Saud. The proven oil reserves in Saudi Arabia are extensive enough to last, at the current rates of extraction, for almost another 65 years (see Figure 7A.4, A). In particular,

(continued)

---

[5]This expression is based on the calculus result that $\frac{de^{rT}}{dT} = re^{rT}$.

Saudi Arabia extracts about 11 million barrels per day, or 4 billion barrels per year against proven reserves of 265 billion barrels, roughly 18 percent of the entire world's supply. In contrast, the United States, which extracts about 8 million barrels per day, has proven reserves only one-tenth as big—just 31 billion barrels. This is less than 2 percent of the world's supply. Without additional exploration and development, the United States will run out of oil in a scant 11 years.

Saudi Arabia therefore has an objective shared with American consumers: both want the rate of price increase of crude oil (and of gasoline) to remain smaller than the rate preferred by an Oklahoma or Texas oilman. U.S. oil interests are continuously exploring and developing new deposits of crude oil and natural gas, but that doesn't alter the fact that their exhaustible resources will run out sooner rather than later. Therefore, their incentive is to urge policies that will raise the price quickly.

As a result, President Ronald Reagan sent Vice President George H.W. Bush to Saudi Arabia in 1986 to urge the Saudis to raise the price of crude oil. What the Saudis wanted was the opposite: to discourage substitutes by holding down the OPEC cartel's price increases. The U.S. administrators had to relieve the Saudis anxiety in some credible fashion. For 12 years the Reagan and Bush Sr. presidencies never developed synthetic oil from abundant U.S. reserves of shale oil, as proposed by President Jimmy Carter. In addition, the subsequent Clinton and George W. Bush presidencies never adopted a national energy policy that would support replacing gasoline internal combustion engines with hydrogen fuel cell-powered or all-electric vehicles. As a result, the United States lacks the required infrastructure of hydrogen refill stations.

By massively increasing crude oil production from approximately 8 million to 11 million barrels per day (mbd) from 2004 to 2008 (compare Figure 7A.4, A and B), the Saudis have kept gasoline about half as expensive as the full cost of producing and distributing hydrogen fuel for powering cars. Now, the same policy issues revolve around natural gas as a plentiful alternative fuel in North America for powering heavy trucks. Indeed, the United States is estimated to have more natural gas resources than the Saudis have crude oil. Predictably, the Saudis are again investing in massive new extraction projects, pipelines, and shipping terminals to reduce the price of crude oil. Their capacity now extends to 12 mbd in mid-2012. The second most capacity worldwide is in Iran with 4 mbd and the next five are all OPEC members with only 2.4 to 2.7 mbd in Iraq, UAE, Kuwait, Venezuela, and Nigeria.

This was as true in the distant past as in the current decade. Saudi Arabia's initial share of OPEC's output at the formation of the cartel in 1973 was 32 percent. Saudi Arabia continuously increased its rate of extraction until, at peak crude oil prices in 1981, it was producing almost 47 percent of OPEC's total output—9.6 million of the industry's 20 million barrels of oil per day. Again, these policies were designed to discourage the development of substitutes by slowing down the rate of price increases of crude. Any other exhaustible resource owner with a 76-year supply of proven reserves would do the same thing.

---

[6]Based on estimates from the International Energy Agency; OPEC, *Annual Statistical Bulletin* (2002–2012); and "Why the U.S. Is Still Hooked on Oil Imports," *Wall Street Journal* (March 18, 2003), p. A1, "OPEC Nations Spar over Output," *Wall Street Journal* (June 8, 2011), p. A6.

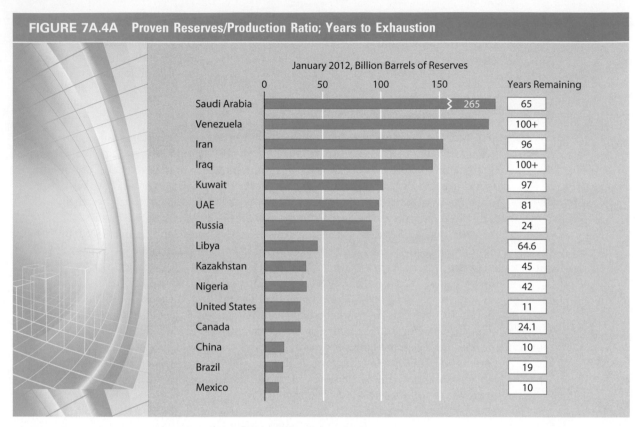

FIGURE 7A.4A   Proven Reserves/Production Ratio; Years to Exhaustion

January 2012, Billion Barrels of Reserves

Country	Years Remaining
Saudi Arabia	65
Venezuela	100+
Iran	96
Iraq	100+
Kuwait	97
UAE	81
Russia	24
Libya	64.6
Kazakhstan	45
Nigeria	42
United States	11
Canada	24.1
China	10
Brazil	19
Mexico	10

Source: *BP Statistical Review of World Energy*, 2012.

FIGURE 7A.4B

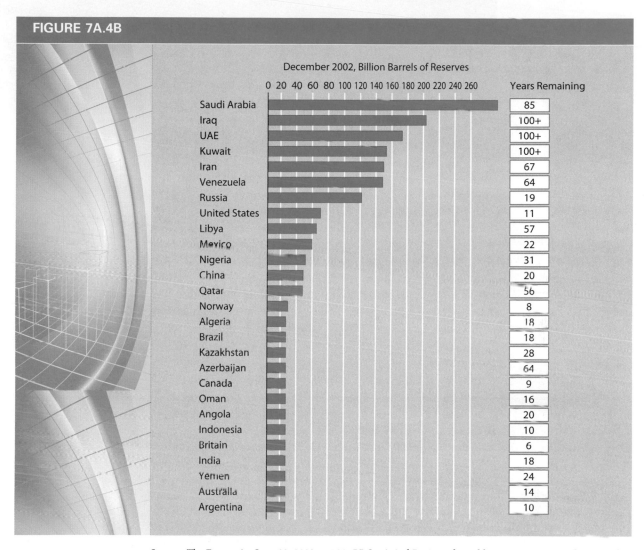

December 2002, Billion Barrels of Reserves

	Years Remaining
Saudi Arabia	85
Iraq	100+
UAE	100+
Kuwait	100+
Iran	67
Venezuela	64
Russia	19
United States	11
Libya	57
Mexico	22
Nigeria	31
China	20
Qatar	56
Norway	8
Algeria	18
Brazil	18
Kazakhstan	28
Azerbaijan	64
Canada	9
Oman	16
Angola	20
Indonesia	10
Britain	6
India	18
Yemen	24
Australia	14
Argentina	10

Source: *The Economist*, June 29, 2002, p. 102; *BP Statistical Review of World Energy*, 2002, U.S. Energy Information Administration; *The Economist*, January 21, 2012, p. 6.

Exercises

1. Figure 7A.3, shows the annual rate of crude oil extraction of the United States was basically unchanged 2002–2012. Not so for Saudi Arabia whose production increased 33%. Explain why with special attention to the price spike in mid-2008.
2. With interest rates at historic lows in the United States, what is the effect on the optimal rate of extraction for a Texas oilfield owner? Explain the intuition that supports your answer.
3. Explain the concept of maximum sustainable yield for a fishery. Is maximum sustainable yield the most efficient rate of harvest for a renewable natural resource? Is it required to preserve biological diversity?

CHAPTER

8

Cost Analysis

CHAPTER PREVIEW

Economic cost refers to the cost of attracting a resource from its next best alternative use (the opportunity cost concept). Managers seeking to make the most efficient use of resources to maximize value must be concerned with both short-run and long-run opportunity costs. Short-run cost-output relationships help managers plan for the most profitable level of output given the capital resources that are immediately available. Long-run cost-output relationships involve attracting additional capital to expand or contract the plant size and change the scale of operations. Achieving minimum efficient scale is often the key to a successful operations strategy.

MANAGERIAL CHALLENGE

Can a Leaner General Motors Compete Effectively?[1]

In 2009, Toyota with 1,556,174 cars became the top-selling brand of auto in North America. Ford was second with 1,445,742 cars sold. Chevrolet fell to third. The 1,344,829 Chevies when combined with 259,779 GMCs, 178,300 Pontiacs, 109,092 Cadillacs, 102,306 Buicks, and 72,660 Saturns still made GM the world's largest car company, but not by much. GM products were largely stale, labor rates were sky high, and investment capital was more interested in Silicon Valley than the Rust Belt. Moreover, Goldman Sachs had estimated that GM, more so than any other car company, was destroying share-holder value. At a price point quite similar to VW, Nissan, Honda and Toyota, GM was earning for investors a lower return than its risk-adjusted cost of capital.

As in other businesses subjected to highly effective low-cost foreign competition (such as textiles and furniture), GM had to find massive cost savings somewhere, and it needed to do so quickly. The Great Contraction had deepened in the fourth quarter of 2008 to –9 percent of GDP. Automobiles were one of the first consumer durable industries to plummet downward. With

American households finding it hard to justify buying even a small appliance such as a toaster, car sales fell off the cliff. In just one year, North American light vehicle sales declined by fully one-third from over 15 million to 10 million, jettisoning all the sales gains of the previous decade.

The Big-3 American automakers could depend at one time upon scale economies to provide a cost advantage over rivals. Massive multimillion-dollar pieces of auto assembly equipment such as the body-stamping machine were responsible. A stamping press uses hydraulic pressure to force sheet metal into the desired shape of fenders, floorpans, hoods, and trunks. Since annual style change required such a machine and since it could not be retooled from one model year to the next, wearing out such an expensive piece of equipment was the only way to reach minimum unit cost. Otherwise, a large write-down of factory assets had to be taken every year and that expense passed along to the customer. To wear out a body-stamping machine necessitates producing and selling at least 250,000 units per model year,

Cont.

MANAGERIAL CHALLENGE *Continued*

20,000 per month, 1,000 per day—at the normal assembly line rate of one per minute rolling off a double-shift 16-hour-per-day plant. Most of the GM and Ford models sold in the 1960s and 1970s reached these minimum efficient scale rates in long production runs that offered further learning curve cost advantages.

But the North American auto market has fragmented across seven firms with at least a 5 percent market share. As a result, only five models—the F-series and Chevy Silverado pick-ups, the Honda Accord, Toyota Camry, and Nissan Altima— sell at least 20,000 units a month. All 172 other models in U.S. showrooms fail to achieve minimum efficient scale.

A further problem for the Big 3 was labor rates and fringe benefits that in 2007 had reached $77 per hour for experienced United Auto Workers (UAW) employees in unionized plants. Workers in competing foreign transplant plants in Tennessee, Ohio, and Mississippi made $55 per hour at Toyota, $45 per hour at Hyundai, and $38 per hour at Volkswagen. With higher costs and many models that customers found undeserving of brand premiums, GM, Ford, and Chrysler were all "destroyers of substantial value," which McKinsey management consultants define as a company whose return on invested capital falls well below its cost of capital.

By 2010 Ford's North American auto sales had rebounded 20 percent, and with redesigned models Chevrolet picked up two share points to 20.4 percent from Toyota, whose share fell to 17 percent. Small fuel-efficient cars such as the Chevy Cruze, the Ford Fiesta, and the Chrysler-Fiat 500 swept into the market. Hybrids like Ford's very successful Fusion competed head to head with the category-defining Toyota Prius. Most importantly, rather than being loss leaders, all these models were profitable.

After a government-assisted bailout to recover from bankruptcy, GM won a collective bargaining right to hire "tier two" employees who receive half the pay of the longer-term UAW workers. This blend of labor rates has driven GM's wages and fringe benefits down to $56/hour, almost identical to Toyota's. Consequently, even GM and Ford pick-ups as well as several popular larger sedans became money-makers. In addition, growth of overseas sales of Buicks and Cadillacs exploded, especially in China. By 2011, GM reported a company-wide return to profitability and began repaying its government-funded debt.

Discussion Questions

- In light of the successful turn around, do you think the federal bailout of GM was warranted? What are the pros and cons after the fact?
- Which factors that were pivotal to the sales rebound at GM were unknown in 2009 when the U.S. government acted?
- Consolidation mergers such as Chrysler-Fiat and phenomenal sales growth in China have restored what type of cost advantage for the Big 3?
- Drawing parallels to the trade debate over Boeing-Airbus subsidies, do you think GM exports to China sold through Greely, its Chinese partner, will be saddled with countervailing duties or other tariffs? Why or why not?

[1]"A Survey of the Car Industry: Driving Change," *The Economist* (September 4, 2004), pp. 21–22; "U.S. Car Business in Major Shift," *Wall Street Journal* (January 5, 2011), pp. B1–B2; "Car Making in America," *The Economist* (September 24, 2011), pp. 75–76.

THE MEANING AND MEASUREMENT OF COST

In its most elementary form, cost simply refers to the sacrifice incurred whenever an exchange or transformation of resources takes place. This association between forgone opportunities and economic cost applies in all circumstances. However, the appropriate manner to measure costs is a function of the purpose for which the cost information is to be used.

Accounting versus Economic Costs

Accountants have been primarily concerned with identifying highly stable and predictable costs for *financial reporting purposes*. As a result, they define and measure cost by the known certain *historical outlay of funds.* Thus, the *price* paid for commodity or service inputs, expressed in dollars, is one measure of the accounting cost. Similarly, the *interest* paid to bondholders or lending institutions is used to measure the accounting cost of funds to the borrower.

Economists, on the other hand, have been mainly concerned with measuring costs for *decision-making purposes.* That objective is somewhat different—namely, to determine the present and future costs of resources associated with various alternative courses of action. Such an objective requires a consideration of the opportunities forgone (or sacrificed) whenever a resource is used in one way rather than another. So, although both the accounting cost and the economic cost of a product will include such *explicit* costs as labor, raw materials, supplies, rent, interest, and utilities, economists will also include the implicit **opportunity costs** of time and capital that the owner-manager has invested in the enterprise. The opportunity cost of the owner's time is measured by the most attractive salary offer that the owner could have received by applying his or her talents, skills, and experience in the management of a similar (but second-best) business owned by someone else. Similarly, the opportunity cost of the capital is measured by the profit or return that could have been received if the owner had chosen to employ capital in his or her second-best (alternative) investment of comparable risk.

Opportunity cost represents the return or compensation that must be forgone as the result of the decision to employ the resource in a given economic activity.

Economic profit is defined as the difference between total revenues and these total economic costs, implicit opportunity costs as well as explicit outlays:

$$\text{Economic profit} = \text{Total revenues} - \text{Explicit costs} - \text{Implicit costs} \qquad [8.1]$$

When one recognizes that such first-best and second-best uses change over time, it becomes clear that the historical outlay of funds to obtain a resource at an earlier date (the accounting cost basis) may not be the appropriate measure of opportunity cost in a decision problem today. For example, consider the following three cases of a substantive distinction between economic cost and accounting cost.

Three Contrasts between Accounting and Economic Costs

Depreciation Cost Measurement The production of a good or service typically requires the use of plant and equipment. As these **capital assets** are used, their service life is expended, and the assets wear out or become obsolete. Depreciation is a loss of asset value. If the Phillips Tool Company owns a machine that has a current market value of $8,000 and is expected with some considerable certainty to have a value of $6,800 after one more year of use, then the opportunity cost of continuing to own and use the machine for one more year (the economist's measure of depreciation cost) is $8,000 − $6,800 = $1,200. Assuming that 2,000 units of output were produced during the year, the depreciation cost per unit would be $1,200 ÷ 2,000 units = $0.60 per unit.

Unfortunately, it is often difficult, if not impossible, to determine the exact service life of a capital asset and the future changes in its market value.[2] Some assets are unique (patents); others are not traded in liquid resale markets (plants); and still others are rendered obsolete with little predictability (computers). To overcome these measurement problems with economic depreciation, accountants have adopted standard allocation procedures for assigning a portion of the acquisition cost of an asset to each accounting time period, and in turn to each unit of output that is produced within that time period. This allocation is typically done by assigning a portion of the historical cost to each year

opportunity costs The value of a resource in its next-best alternative use.

capital assets A durable input that depreciates with use, time, and obsolescence.

---

[2]This concept of the future cost of the partially consumed asset is termed the *replacement cost* of the asset rather than the *historical acquisition cost* of the asset.

of the service life. If the machine is purchased by Phillips for $10,000 and is expected to have a 10-year life and no salvage value, the straight-line method of accounting depreciation ($10,000 ÷ 10 = $1,000) would calculate the depreciation cost of this asset each year. Assuming that 2,000 units of output are produced in a given year, then $1,000 ÷ 2,000 = $0.50 would be allocated to the cost of each unit produced by Phillips. Note from this example that the calculated accounting depreciation cost does not equal the economic depreciation cost of $0.60 actually incurred if in fact the market value of the machine drops to $6,800 after one additional year.

Example

Opportunity Costs at Bentley Clothing Store

Robert Bentley owns and operates the Bentley Clothing Store. A traditional income statement for the business is shown in Panel (a) of Table 8.1. The mortgage on the store has been paid, and therefore no interest expenses are shown on the income statement. Also, the building has been fully depreciated, and thus no depreciation charges are shown. From an *accounting* standpoint and from the perspective of the Internal Revenue Service, Bentley is earning a *positive accounting profit* of $190,000 (before taxes).

TABLE 8.1 PROFITABILITY OF BENTLEY CLOTHING STORE

(a) ACCOUNTING INCOME STATEMENT

Net sales		$650,000
Less: Cost of goods sold		250,000
Gross profit		400,000
Less: Expenses		
Employee compensation*	150,000	
Advertising	30,000	
Utilities and maintenance	20,000	
Miscellaneous	10,000	
Total		210,000
Net profit before taxes		$190,000

(b) ECONOMIC PROFIT STATEMENT

Total revenues		$650,000
Less: Explicit costs		
Cost of goods sold	250,000	
Employee compensation*	150,000	
Advertising	30,000	
Utilities and maintenance	20,000	
Miscellaneous	10,000	
Total		460,000
Accounting profit before taxes		190,000
Less: Implicit costs		
Salary (manager)	130,000	
Rent on building	88,000	
Total		218,000
Economic profit (or loss) before taxes		($28,000)

*Employee compensation does not include any salary to Robert Bentley.

© Cengage Learning

(continued)

However, consider the store's profitability from an *economic* standpoint. As indicated earlier in this chapter, implicit costs include the opportunity costs of time and capital that the entrepreneur has invested in the firm. Suppose that Bentley could go to work as a clothing department manager for a large department or specialty store chain and receive a salary of $130,000 per year. Also assume that Bentley could rent his building to another merchant for $88,000 (net) per year. Under these conditions, as shown in Panel (b) of Table 8.1, Bentley is earning a *negative economic profit* ($28,000 before taxes). By renting his store to another merchant and going to work as manager of a different store, he could make $28,000 more than he is currently earning from his clothing store business. Thus, accounting profits, which do not include opportunity costs, are not always a valid indication of the economic profitability (or loss) of an enterprise.

Inventory Valuation Whenever materials are stored in inventory for a period of time before being used in the production process, the accounting and economic costs may differ if the market price of these materials has changed from the original purchase price. The accounting cost is equal to the actual *acquisition* cost, whereas the economic cost is equal to the current *replacement* cost. As the following example illustrates, the use of the acquisition cost can lead to incorrect production decisions.

Example

Inventory Valuation at Westside Plumbing and Heating

Westside Plumbing and Heating Company is offered a contract for $100,000 to provide the plumbing for a new building. The labor and equipment costs are calculated to be $60,000 for fulfilling the contract. Westside has the materials in inventory to complete the job. The materials originally cost the firm $50,000; however, prices have since declined, and the materials could now be purchased for $37,500. Material prices are not expected to increase in the near future, and hence no gains can be anticipated from holding the materials in inventory. The question is: Should Westside accept the contract? An analysis of the contract under both methods for measuring the cost of the materials is shown in Table 8.2. Assuming that the materials are valued at the acquisition cost, the firm should not accept the contract because an apparent loss of $10,000 would result. By using the replacement cost as the value of the materials, however, the contract should be accepted because a profit of $2,500 would result.

TABLE 8.2 EFFECT OF INVENTORY VALUATION METHODS ON MEASURED PROFIT—WESTSIDE PLUMBING AND HEATING COMPANY

	ACQUISITION COST	REPLACEMENT COST
Value of contract	$100,000	$100,000
Costs		
Labor, equipment	60,000	60,000
Materials	50,000	37,500
	110,000	97,500
Profit (or loss)	($10,000)	$2,500

© Cengage Learning

(continued)

To see which method is correct, examine the income statement of Westside at the end of the accounting period. If the contract *is not* accepted, then at the end of the accounting period the firm will have to reduce the cost of its inventory by $12,500 ($50,000 − $37,500) to reflect the lower market value of this unused inventory. The firm will thus incur a loss of $12,500. If the contract *is* accepted, then the company will make a profit of $2,500 on the contract, but will also incur a loss of $12,500 on the materials used in completing the contract. The firm will thus incur a *net* loss of only $10,000. Hence, acceptance of the contract results in a smaller overall loss to Westside than does rejection of the contract. For decision-making purposes, replacement cost is the appropriate measure of the cost of materials in inventory, and Westside should accept the contract.

Sunk Cost of Underutilized Facilities   The Dunbar Manufacturing Company recently discontinued a product line and was left with 50,000 square feet of unneeded warehouse space. The company rents the entire warehouse (200,000 square feet) from the owner for $1 million per year (i.e., $5 per square foot) under a long-term (10-year) lease agreement. A nearby company that is expanding its operations offered to rent the 50,000 square feet of unneeded space for one year for $125,000 (i.e., $2.50 per square foot). Should Dunbar accept the offer to rent the unused space, assuming that no other higher offers for the warehouse space are expected?

One could argue that Dunbar should reject the offer because the additional rent (revenue) of $2.50 per square foot is less than the lease payment (cost) of $5 per square foot. Such reasoning, however, will lead to an incorrect decision. The lease payment ($5 per square foot) represents a **sunk cost** that must be paid regardless of whether the other company rents the unneeded warehouse space. As shown in Table 8.3, renting the unneeded warehouse space *reduces* the net cost of the warehouse from $1 million to $875,000, a savings of $125,000 per year to Dunbar. The relevant comparison is between the incremental revenue ($125,000) and the incremental costs ($0 in this case). Thus, sunk costs (such as the lease payment of $5 per square foot in this example) should not be considered relevant costs because such costs are unavoidable, independent of the course of action chosen.

sunk cost A cost incurred regardless of the alternative action chosen in a decision-making problem.

Conclusions

1. Costs can be measured in different ways, depending on the purpose for which the cost figures are to be used.
2. The costs appropriate for financial reporting purposes are not always appropriate for decision-making purposes. The *relevant cost* in economic decision making is the opportunity cost of the resources rather than the historical outlay of funds required to obtain the resources.

TABLE 8.3   WAREHOUSE RENTAL DECISION—DUNBAR MANUFACTURING COMPANY

	DECISION	
	DO NOT RENT	**RENT**
Total lease payment	$1,000,000	$1,000,000
Less: Rent received on unused space	—	125,000
Net cost of warehouse to Dunbar Manufacturing Company	$1,000,000	$ 875,000

© Cengage Learning

3. Sunk costs, which are incurred regardless of the alternative action chosen, should seldom be considered in making operating decisions.

SHORT-RUN COST AND PRODUCT FUNCTIONS

In addition to measuring the costs of producing a given quantity of output, economists like accountants are concerned with determining the *behavior of costs* when output is varied over a range of possible values. The relationship between cost and output is expressed in terms of a **cost function**: a schedule, graph, or mathematical relationship showing the minimum achievable cost of producing various quantities of output.

The discussion in Chapter 7 concerning the inputs used in the production process distinguished between fixed and variable inputs. A fixed input was defined as an input that is required in the production process but whose quantity used in the process is constant over a given period of time regardless of the level of output produced. Short-run questions relate to a situation in which one or more of the inputs to the production process are fixed. Long-run questions relate to a situation in which *all* inputs are variable; that is, no restrictions are imposed on the amount of a resource that can be employed in the production process. The length of time required to vary all the inputs can be as long as seven years (e.g., in Tenneco's ship-building business). In other cases, the long run may be just a few weeks (in the 7-Eleven convenience store business).

The total cost of producing a given quantity of output is equal to the sum of the costs of each of the inputs used in the production process. In discussing short-run cost functions, it is useful to classify costs as either *fixed* or *variable costs.* **Fixed costs** represent the costs of all the inputs to the production process that are fixed or constant over the short run. **Variable input costs** consist of the costs of all the variable inputs to the production process.

fixed costs The costs of inputs to the production process that are constant over the short run.

variable input costs The costs of the variable inputs to the production process.

Average and Marginal Cost Functions

Once the total cost function is determined, one can then derive the average and marginal cost functions. The average fixed cost AFC, average variable cost AVC, and average total cost ATC are equal to the respective fixed, variable input, and total costs divided by the quantity of output produced:

$$AFC = \frac{FC}{Q}$$

[8.2]

$$AVC = \frac{VC}{Q}$$

[8.3]

$$ATC = \frac{TTC}{Q}$$

[8.4]

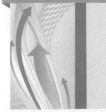

Example

Short-Run Cost Functions: Deep Creek Mining Company

To illustrate the nature of short-run costs and show how the short-run cost function can be derived from the production function for the firm, consider again the Deep Creek Mining Company example that was discussed in Chapter 7. It was assumed

(continued)

that two inputs, capital and labor, are required to produce or mine ore. Various-sized pieces of capital equipment, as measured by their brake horsepower rating K, are available to mine the ore. Each of these pieces of equipment can be operated with various-sized labor crews L. The amount of output (tons of ore) that can be produced in a given period with each capital–labor input combination is shown again in Table 8.4. It was also assumed that the rental cost of using the mining equipment per period is $0.20 per brake horsepower and that the wage plus fringe benefit cost of each worker (labor) employed per period is $50. This yielded the following total cost equation for any given combination of labor L and capital K (Equation 7.21):

$$C = 50L + 0.20K$$

Suppose that Deep Creek has signed a lease agreeing to rent, for the next year, a 750-brake-horsepower piece of mining equipment (capital). During the ensuing year (the short run), the amount of capital that the company can employ in the ore-mining process is fixed at 750 brake horsepower. Therefore, for each period a fixed cost of $0.20 × 750 = $150 will be incurred, regardless of the quantity of ore that is produced. The firm must operate the production process at one of the capital–labor combinations shown in the fourth column of Table 8.4. Output can be increased (decreased) by employing more (less) labor in combination with the given and temporarily unalterable 750-brake-horsepower capital equipment. Labor is thus the only variable input to this production process.

The short-run cost functions for Deep Creek are shown in Table 8.5. The various possible output levels Q and the associated capital–labor input combinations L and K are obtained from Table 8.4. The short-run total variable cost VC is equal to $50 times the number of workers (L) employed in the mining process. The short-run total fixed cost FC is equal to the rental cost of the 750-brake-horsepower equipment ($150). The total cost in the short run is the sum of the fixed and variable costs:

$$TTC = TFC + TVC \qquad [8.5]$$

In Figure 8.1 the three curves from the data given in Table 8.5 are plotted. Note that the TTC curve has an identical shape to that of TVC, being shifted upward by the TFC of $150.

TABLE 8.4 PRODUCTION FUNCTION—DEEP CREEK MINING COMPANY

		CAPITAL INPUT K (BRAKE HORSEPOWER)							
		250	500	750	1,000	1,250	1,500	1,750	2,000
	1	1	3	6	10	16	16	16	13
	2	2	6	16	24	29	29	44	44
	3	4	16	29	44	55	55	55	50
	4	6	29	44	55	58	60	60	55
LABOR INPUT L	5	16	43	55	60	61	62	62	60
(NUMBER OF	6	29	55	60	62	63	63	63	62
WORKERS)	7	44	58	62	63	64	64	64	64
	8	50	60	62	63	64	65	65	65
	9	55	59	61	63	64	65	66	66
	10	52	56	59	62	64	65	66	67

© Cengage Learning

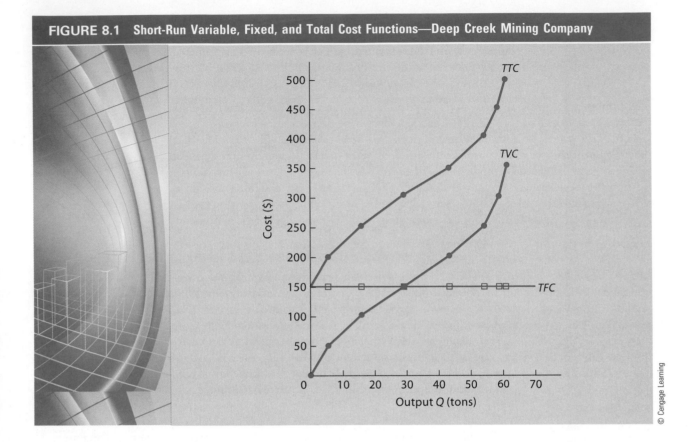

FIGURE 8.1 Short-Run Variable, Fixed, and Total Cost Functions—Deep Creek Mining Company

© Cengage Learning

Also

$$ATC = AFC + AVC \qquad [8.6]$$

marginal cost The incremental increase in total variable cost that results from a one-unit increase in output.

Marginal cost is defined as the incremental increase in total variable cost that results from a one-unit increase in output and is calculated as

$$MC = \frac{\Delta TTC}{\Delta Q}$$

$$= \frac{\Delta TVC}{\Delta Q} \qquad [8.7]$$

or, in the case of a continuous *TTC* or *TVC* function, as

$$MC = \frac{d(TTC)}{dQ} \qquad [8.8]$$

$$= \frac{d(TVC)}{dQ} \qquad [8.9]$$

The average and marginal costs for Deep Creek that were calculated in Table 8.5 are plotted in the graph shown in Figure 8.2. Except for the *AFC* curve, which is continually declining, note that all other average and marginal cost curves are U-shaped. Do you recall why from Chapter 7? Gains from specialization in the use of the variable input are inevitably followed by diminishing returns.

Consider another example where the cost information is represented in the form of an algebraic function. Suppose total fixed costs for the Manchester Company are equal

TABLE 8.5 SHORT-RUN COST FUNCTIONS—DEEP CREEK MINING COMPANY

OUTPUT	VARIABLE COST		FIXED COST		TOTAL COST	AVERAGE FIXED COST	AVERAGE VARIABLE COST	AVERAGE TOTAL COST	MARGINAL COST
Q	LABOR INPUT L	$TVC = \$50 \cdot L$	CAPITAL INPUT K	$TFC = \$150$	$TTC = TFC + TVC$	$AFC = \dfrac{TFC}{Q}$	$AVC = \dfrac{TVC}{Q}$	$ATC = \dfrac{TTC}{Q}$	$MC = \dfrac{\Delta TTC}{\Delta Q}$
0	0	$0	750	$150	$150	—	—	—	—
6	1	50	750	150	200	$25.00	$8.33	$33.33	$\dfrac{50}{6} = \$8.33$
16	2	100	750	150	250	9.38	6.25	15.63	$\dfrac{50}{10} = 5.00$
29	3	150	750	150	300	5.17	5.17	10.34	$\dfrac{50}{13} = 3.85$
44	4	200	750	150	350	3.41	4.55	7.95	$\dfrac{50}{15} = 3.33$
55	5	250	750	150	400	2.73	4.55	7.27	$\dfrac{50}{11} = 4.55$
60	6	300	750	150	450	2.50	5.00	7.50	$\dfrac{50}{5} = 10.00$
62	7	350	750	150	500	2.42	5.65	8.06	$\dfrac{50}{2} = 25.00$

© Cengage Learning

to \$100, and the company's total variable costs are given by the following relationship (where Q = output):

$$TVC = 60Q - 3Q^2 + 0.10Q^3 \qquad [8.10]$$

Given this information, one can derive the total cost function using Equation 8.2:

$$TTC = 100 + 60Q - 3Q^2 + 0.10Q^3$$

Next, AFC, AVC, and ATC can be found using Equations 8.3, 8.4, and 8.5, respectively, as follows:

$$AFC = \frac{100}{Q}$$

$$AVC = 60 - 3Q + 0.10Q^2$$

$$ATC = \frac{100}{Q} + 60 - 3Q + 0.10Q^2$$

Finally, Manchester's marginal cost function can be obtained by differentiating the total variable cost function (Equation 8.10) with respect to Q:

$$MC = \frac{d(TVC)}{dQ} = 60 - 6Q + 0.30Q^2$$

The average total cost curve in Figure 8.2, which is equal to the sum of the vertical heights of the average fixed and average variable cost curves, initially declines and subsequently begins rising beyond a particular level of output. At $Q = 55$ the average total cost curve is at its minimum value. As discussed in Chapter 7, specialization in the use of the variable inputs initially results in increasing returns and declining marginal costs

FIGURE 8.2 Short-Run Average and Marginal Cost Functions—Deep Creek Mining Company

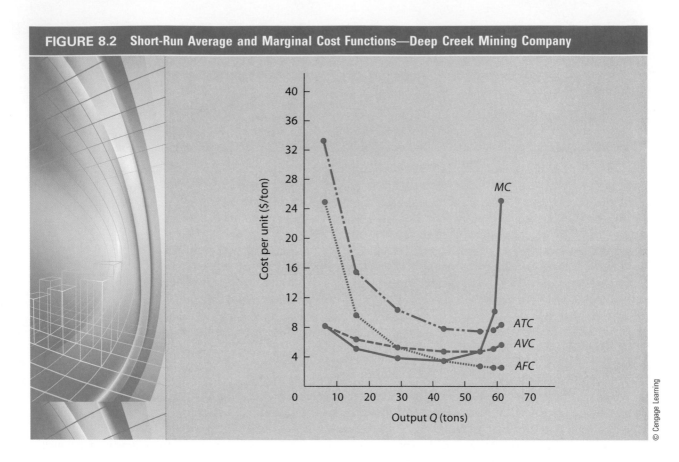

© Cengage Learning

and average variable costs. Eventually, however, the gains from specialization are over-whelmed by crowding effects, diminishing marginal returns set in, and then marginal and average variable costs begin increasing as shown in Figure 8.2. This reasoning is used to explain the U-shaped pattern of the short-run *ATC*, *AVC*, and *MC* curves in Figures 8.2 and 8.3 and indeed in all short-run average cost structures.

FIGURE 8.3 Long-Run and Short-Run Average Cost Functions

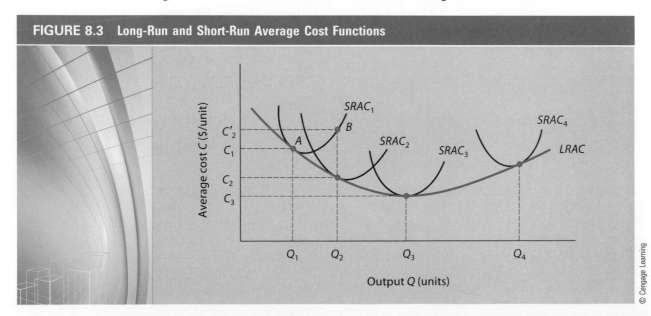

© Cengage Learning

LONG-RUN COST FUNCTIONS

Over the long-run planning horizon, using the available production methods and technology, the firm can choose the plant size, types and sizes of equipment, labor skills, and raw materials that, when combined, yield the lowest cost of producing the desired amount of output. Once the optimum combination of inputs is chosen to produce the desired level of output (at least cost), some of these inputs (plant and equipment) become fixed in the short run. If demand increases unexpectedly and the firm wishes to produce not Q_1, as planned, but rather Q_2 as shown in Figure 8.3, it may have little choice but to add additional variable inputs such as overtime labor and expedite the rush-order delivery of supplies to meet its production goals. Not surprisingly, such arrangements are expensive, and short-run average total cost will temporarily rise from A to B at C_2'.

Should this demand persist, a larger fixed input investment in plant and equipment is warranted. Then, unit cost can be reduced from C_2' to C_2. Associated with the larger fixed input investment is another short-run average total cost function $SRATC_2$. Several of these other short-run average total cost functions ($SRATC_3$, $SRATC_4$) are shown in Figure 8.3. The long-run average cost function consists of the *lower boundary* or *envelope* of all these short-run curves. No other combination of inputs exists for producing each level of output Q at an average cost below the cost that is indicated by the $LRATC$ curve.

Optimal Capacity Utilization: Three Concepts

To assess capacity utilization, assume the firm has been producing Q_1 units of output using a plant of size "1," having a short-run average total cost curve of $SRATC_1$. The average cost of producing Q_1 units is therefore C_1, and Q_1 is the optimal output for the plant size represented by $SRATC_1$. **Optimal output for a given plant size** is one of three short-run concepts of capacity utilization.

Suppose that the firm now wishes to expand output to Q_2. What will the average cost be of producing this higher volume of output? In the short run, as we saw earlier, the average cost would be C_2'. However, in the long run, it would be possible for the firm to build a plant of size "2," having a short-run average total cost curve of $SATC_2$. With this larger plant, the average cost of producing Q_2 units of output would be only C_2. Thus, because the firm has more options available to it in the long run, average total cost of any given output generally can be reduced. $SATC_2$ represents the **optimal plant size for a given output rate** Q_2.

Should demand then collapse, even a company like Toyota may be stuck with excess manufacturing capacity and find it wishes to cut output back to the original level Q_1, despite the much higher unit costs at point A. This is exactly what happened in 2009 after the gasoline price spike to \$4.10 per gallon. U.S. Toyota sales fell by one-third on average, but some models like the gas-hogging Toyota Tundra plunged by 61 percent. For a time, it was reasonable to just fill up storage depots and distribution center parking lots with excess inventory, but eventually it was necessary to slash throughput rates even in very big plants and produce at a point like A

However, as the business cycle recovers, if the firm can execute a marketing plan to sell still more output, expanding capacity by building a still larger plant size may be a more efficient allocation of resources.. Only when optimal output increases to Q_3, where the firm will build the universally least-cost **optimal plant size** represented by $SATC_3$, will further opportunities for cost reduction cease. This concept of optimal capacity utilization applies to the long run, given the technology in place at this plant. Short-run average total cost with underutilization of capacity at Point A or

optimal output for a given plant size
Output rate that results in lowest average total cost for a given plant size.

optimal plant size for a given output rate
Plant size that results in lowest average total cost for a given output.

optimal plant size
Plant size that achieves minimum long-run average total cost.

overutilization of capacity at Point *B* in Figure 8.3 is always higher than the minimum average total cost in the long run (*LRATC*) fundamentally because the production manager can vary plant and equipment in the long run, matching capacity as well as variable inputs like labor to his or her output requirements.

Example

The Average Cost per Kilowatt-Hour in Underutilized Power Plants

Under pressure from regulators, the electric power industry opened its customer distribution systems to freewheeling electricity. A factory in Ohio can now choose to buy contract electricity from Michigan, New York, or Virginia power companies. With the new competition, the price of electricity has declined from $0.11 to $0.095. Higher-cost electric utilities have found themselves priced out of the market. As more efficient power plants are constructed, customers are experiencing an $18 to $30 reduction per month in their residential electricity bills.

ECONOMIES AND DISECONOMIES OF SCALE

The long-run average total cost *LRATC* function is hypothesized to decline as the flow rate of throughput rises over the lower range of operations scale and is hypothesized to remain flat or rise over the higher range. *Declining* long-run average total cost reflects **internal economies of scale** at one of three levels: the product level, the multi-product plant level, or the firm level of operations.

internal economies of scale Declining long-run average costs as the rate of output for a product, plant, or firm is increased.

Product-Level Internal Economies of Scale   A number of different sources of declining cost are associated with producing one product (say, PCs) at a higher rate of throughput per day. Special-purpose equipment, which is more efficient in performing a limited set of operations, can be substituted for less efficient general-purpose equipment. Likewise, the production process can be broken down into a series of smaller tasks, and workers can be assigned to the tasks for which they are most qualified. Workers are then able to acquire additional proficiency through higher repetition of the tasks to which they are assigned.

learning curve effect Declining unit cost attributable to greater cumulative from longer production runs.

In manufacturing, a related phenomenon called the **learning curve effect** has often been observed whereby the amount of labor input required to produce another unit of output decreases as the *cumulative volume* of output rises (e.g., during long production runs of 787 airframes at Boeing with several years of back orders). The learning curve principle was first applied in airframe manufacturing, shipbuilding, and appliance manufacturing. Learning curve effects and **volume discounts** in purchasing inputs (so-called external economies of scale) are easily distinguished from internal economies of scale for two reasons: First, volume discounts on inputs and learning curves lower average variable costs, whereas internal economies of scale lower average fixed costs. Second, volume discounts and learning curves depend upon cumulative volume of output no matter how small the production throughput rate per time period. As such, they may well be associated with no change in the scale of operations whatsoever; the firm simply buys large volumes of input at one time because they anticipate a very long production run or because they have consolidated common component platforms on which they

volume discount Reduced variable cost attributable to larger purchase orders.

produce various product lines. For example, Daimler-Chrysler bought a common transmission for the Mercedes C-class and the Chrysler 300.

The learning curve relationship is usually expressed as a constant percentage by which the amount of an input (or cost) per unit of output is reduced each time production is doubled. For example, consider a production process in which labor input and costs follow an 80 percent learning curve. Assume that the *first* unit requires labor costs of $1,000 to produce. Based on the learning curve relationship, the *second* unit costs $1,000 × 0.80 = $800, the *fourth* unit costs $800 × 0.80 = $640, the *eighth* unit costs $640 × 0.80 = $512, the *sixteenth* unit costs $512 × 0.80 = $409.60, and so on.

This learning curve relationship plotted in Figure 8.4 can be expressed algebraically as follows:

$$C = aQ^b \qquad [8.11]$$

where C is the input cost of the Qth unit of output, Q is consecutive units of output produced, a is the theoretical (or actual) input cost of the first unit of output, and b is the rate of reduction in input cost per unit of output. Because the learning curve is downward sloping, the value of b is normally negative. Taking logarithms of both sides of Equation 8.11 yields

$$\log C = \log a + b \log Q \qquad [8.12]$$

Example

Mass Customization and the Learning Curve[3]

Mass customization is designed to standardize at least some of the production processes associated with fulfilling custom orders. Lee Jeans's customers can choose their own back-pocket stitching and the number of prior stone washings at a mall kiosk, but then Lee actually assembles the custom order from stockpiles of subassemblies in order to preserve long production runs. This operations management decision facilitates a learning curve effect from increased familiarization with the tasks by workers and supervisors, improvements in work methods and the flow of work, and the need for fewer skilled workers as the tasks become more repetitive. Raw material costs per unit may also be subject to the learning curve effect if less scrap and waste occur as workers make suggestions to refine the production process.

[3]An excellent survey on mass customization is found in M. Agrawal, T. V. Kumaresh, and G. A. Mercer, "The False Promise of Mass Customization," *McKinsey Quarterly* (November 3, 2001). See also "A Long March," *The Economist*, (July 14, 2001), pp. 63–65.

Regression analysis can then be used to estimate the parameters b and $\log a$ in order to forecast costs at various cumulative volumes.

The Percentage of Learning

The percentage of learning, which is defined as the proportion by which an input (or its associated cost) is reduced when output is doubled, can be estimated as follows:

$$L = \frac{C_2}{C_1} \times 100\% \qquad [8.13]$$

where C_1 is the input (or cost) for the Q_1 unit of output and C_2 is the cost for the $Q_2 = 2Q_1$ unit of output.

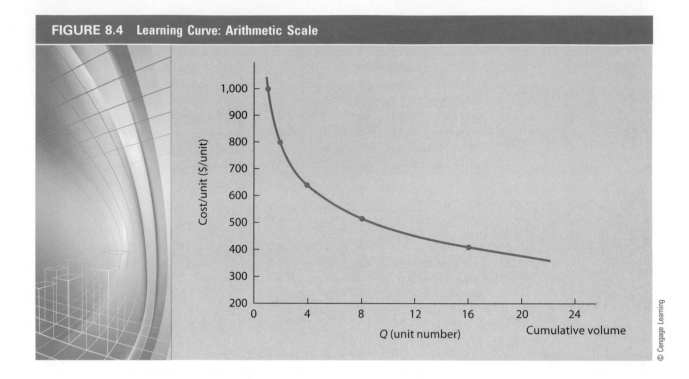

FIGURE 8.4   Learning Curve: Arithmetic Scale

© Cengage Learning

Example

Percentage of Learning: Emerson Corporation

Emerson Corporation makes landing gear for commercial aircraft. To illustrate the calculation of the percentage of learning, suppose Emerson's labor costs for the $Q_1 = 50$th unit of output are $C_1 = \$659.98$, and labor costs for the $2Q_1 = 100$th unit of output are $C_2 = \$540.84$. Substituting these values into Equation 8.13 yields

$$L = \frac{\$540.84}{\$659.98} \times 100\%$$
$$= 81.9\%$$

The percentage of learning for labor costs in the production of these landing gear units is thus approximately 82 percent—indicating that labor costs decline by about 18 percent each time output is doubled.

Plant-Level Internal Economies of Scale   Sources of scale economies at the plant level include capital investment, overhead, and required reserves of maintenance parts and personnel. With respect to *capital investment*, capital costs tend to increase less than proportionately with the productive capacity of a plant, particularly in process-type industries. For example, consider oil pipeline operations. A pipeline with twice the radius of a smaller pipeline can be constructed for perhaps as little as twice the capital investment yet have four times the capacity (i.e., $\pi(2r)^2 = 4\pi r^2$ versus πr^2). Similarly, in the next example we describe a 12-inch silicon wafer that costs 45 percent more than a standard 8-inch silicon wafer yet yields 140 percent more chips, , thereby lowering unit cost.

Example

IBM and Intel Fabricate Monster Silicon Wafers[4]

The semiconductor industry produces thin wafers of silicon and then in super-clean "wafer fab" factories etches them with electrical circuit lines 1/1,000 the width of a human hair. Such intermediate products are then sliced and diced into the tiny memory chips in our PCs, tablets, and PDAs. One 12-inch wafer yields enough memory chips to store 5,000 sets of the *Encyclopedia Britannica*. Until recently, the standard wafer measured about 8 inches across and cost $5,500 to produce in a $1.4 billion wafer fab. New monster wafers are almost 12 inches across and cost $8,000 to produce in $2 billion wafer fabs, but their 125 percent greater surface area yields 575 chips per wafer as opposed to only 240 chips from the standard 8-inch wafer. That is, for a 45 percent increase in cost, the monster wafers yield 140 percent more chips than the standard wafer. As a result, the unit cost of a chip has fallen to $14 from $23.

[4]Based on "Chips on Monster Wafers," *BusinessWeek* (November 4, 2002), pp. 112–126.

Another source of plant-level scale economies is *overhead costs*, which include such administrative costs as management salaries and paperwork documentation associated with regulatory compliance. Overhead costs can be spread over a higher volume of throughput in a larger plant or facility, thus reducing average costs per unit.

Example

Refuse Collection and Disposal in Orange County

Private for-profit trash collectors in California have demonstrated the scale economies of landfills. The environmental safety issues at a landfill require enormous investment in environmental impact studies, lining the site, monitoring for seepage and leeching of toxins, and conducting scientific follow-up studies. Spreading these overhead costs across a larger output volume has led an Orange County company to seek refuse as far away as the northern suburbs of San Diego, almost an hour down the California coast. The trucks from Orange County pass right by several municipal landfills en route. However, the fees charged for dumping at these intermediate sites are much higher. Apparently, the variable transportation costs of hauling a ton of trash prove to be less than the higher start-up costs and environmental monitoring costs per ton at smaller-scale landfills. By state law, all of these municipalities must charge a dumping fee that covers their fully allocated cost, so reduced long-run average total cost provides a substantial price advantage for the large-scale Orange County site.

Firm-Level Internal Economies of Scale   In addition to product-level and plant-level economies of scale, other scale economies are associated with the overall size of the multiplant firm. One possible source of firm-level scale economies is in *distribution*. For example, multiplant operations may permit a larger firm to maintain geographically dispersed plants. Delivery costs are often lower for a geographically dispersed operation compared with a single (larger) plant.

Another possible source of scale economies to the firm is in *raising capital funds*. Because flotation costs increase less than proportionately with the size of the security (stock or bond) issue, average flotation costs per dollar of funds raised is smaller for larger firms. Similar scale economies also exist in *marketing and sales promotion*. These scale economies can take such forms as (1) quantity discounts in securing advertising media space and time or (2) the ability of the large firm to spread the fixed costs of advertising each period over greater thruput.

Diseconomies of Scale

diseconomies of scale Rising long-run average total costs as the level of output is increased.

Rising long-run average total costs at very high throughput rates are often attributed to **diseconomies of scale**. A primary source of diseconomies of scale associated with an individual production plant is *transportation costs*. Another possible source of plant diseconomies is inflexible operations designed for long production runs of one product, based often on highly imperfect forecasts of what the target market wants a year or two ahead.

Diseconomies of scale at the firm level result from problems of coordination and control encountered by management as the scale of operations is increased. These problems often arise from delayed or faulty decisions and weakened or distorted managerial incentives.

Example

Flexibility and Operating Efficiency: Ford Motor Company's Flat Rock Plant[5]

Ford Motor Company spent an estimated $200 million to construct a massive plant in Flat Rock, Michigan, to build cast iron engine blocks. The plant produced exclusively V8 blocks on five ultra-high-speed assembly lines at the rate of 8,000 engine blocks per day or 2 million per year. Ford executives then decided to close the Flat Rock plant and move production to an older Cleveland engine block plant. Ford's Cleveland plant had 10 smaller and slower production lines; the Cleveland plant was clearly the less efficient of the two factories. However, Ford executives realized it would cost less to convert Cleveland's smaller production lines to the new high-performance six- and four-cylinder engines that had become popular.

When Flat Rock was designed, Ford could count on long V8 production runs of perhaps 1 million units of its most popular Ford Mustang model. But then variety in the product line became the key business strategy. By 1998, Ford's top-selling Explorer (383,852 units), Taurus (357,162 units), and Escort (283,898 units) reflected the fragmented auto marketplace. Only the F-series pickup (746,111 units) warranted Flat Rock's massive scale, but even that most popular model required only about one-third of Flat Rock's 2 million engine capacity. As George Booth, iron-operations manager for the casting division at Ford, explained, "Flat Rock was built to make a few parts at very high volumes. But the plant turned out to be very inflexible for conversion to making new types and different sizes of engine blocks. Sometimes you really can be too big."

[5]Based on articles in *The Economist* (January 11, 2001), p. 58; *AI* (February 1998); and *Wall Street Journal* (September 16, 1981, and February 12, 2007).

The Overall Effects of Scale Economies and Diseconomies

For some industries, such as textile and furniture manufacturing, long-run average total costs for the firm remain constant over a wide range of output once scale economies are exhausted. In such cases, many plant sizes are consistent with least-cost production, as

INTERNATIONAL PERSPECTIVES

How Japanese Companies Deal with the Problems of Size[6]

Many large, successful U.S. corporations, such as General Electric, Hewlett-Packard, Sara Lee, and Johnson & Johnson, are attempting to deal with the problems of excessive size by decentralizing their operations. These companies do so by setting up independent business units, each with its own profit-and-loss responsibility, thereby giving managers more flexibility and freedom in decision making.

Like their counterparts in the United States, Japanese corporations are often collections of hundreds of individual companies. For example, Matsushita Electrical Industrial Company consists

of 161 consolidated units. Hitachi, Ltd., consists of 660 companies, with the stock of 27 of these companies being publicly traded. James Abegglen, an expert on Japanese management, has observed that "as something new comes along ... it gets moved out to a subsidiary so the elephant does not roll over and smother it. If all goes well, it becomes a successful company on its own. If not, it gets pulled back in."

_____

[6]Based on an article entitled "Is Your Company Too Big?" *BusinessWeek* (March 17, 1989), pp. 84–94.

minimum efficient scale (MES) The smallest scale at which minimum costs per unit are attained.

shown in Figure 8.5. In other industries (e.g., engine block casting), long-run average total costs rise at large scale. The possible presence of both economies and diseconomies of scale leads to the hypothesized long-run average cost function for a typical manufacturing firm being U-shaped with a flat middle area. Up to some **minimum efficient scale (MES)**, that is, the smallest scale at which minimum long-run average total costs are attained, economies of scale are present. In most industries, it is possible to increase the size of the firm beyond this MES without incurring diseconomies of scale. Over this extended middle-scale range, average costs per unit are relatively constant. However, expansion beyond the maximum efficient scale eventually will result in problems of inflexibility, lack of managerial coordination, and rising long-run average total costs.

FIGURE 8.5   Long-Run Average Cost Function and Scale Economies

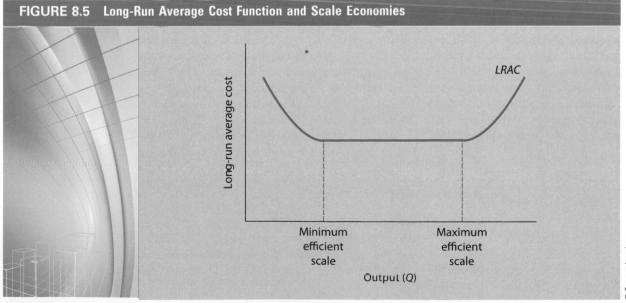

Example

Aluminum-Intensive Vehicle Lowers the MES at Ford[7]

For decades, the largest fixed cost on the auto assembly line has been a $30 million body-stamping machine. This massive piece of capital equipment bends sheet metal into hoods, trunks, and fenders and hydraulically presses steel plate into floor-pan and door-pillar shapes. Because a body-stamping machine has a physical working life of 600,000 vehicles, it has been the source of substantial scale economies in the production of most auto models. Only the top-selling Ford Focus (902,008), F-series pickup (869,001), VW Golf (795,835), Opel Astra (770,003), and Chevy pickup (644,084) had sufficient sales volume in 1999 to fully depreciate a body-stamping machine within the model year. Most moderately successful auto models sell fewer than 100,000 units per year. Therefore, a six-year period is required to physically "wear out" a body-stamping machine as it makes repetitive presses for a typical model.

Should Ford change body shapes and structural components every two to three years to keep its model "current"? Or should it forgo the body style changes and fully depreciate its body-stamping machines over a six-year period or longer? The former decision necessitates scrapping a machine with substantial physical working life remaining and recovering the capital equipment investment with a much higher unit cost per vehicle.

One common approach to achieving sufficient scale to wear out a stamping machine has been to export the product beyond limited domestic markets and sell the same model under different names in different countries (e.g., Ford Focus/Fiesta and VW Golf/Bora/Vento). Another approach has been to consolidate companies across several continents (DaimlerChrysler-Mitsubishi, Ford-Volvo-Mazda, GM-Opel-Isuzu-Suzuki, and Renault-Nissan) to get access for domestic models into foreign markets.

A third approach has been to avoid this classic economy-of-scale issue with aluminum space-frame production or with a greater use of thermoplastics. The aluminum space-frame automobile Ford is designing (or the A2 that Audi has already brought to market) is not even half as heavy as conventional steel-and-sheet-metal cars of today. In addition to phenomenal increases in gas mileage and markedly reduced CO_2 emissions, aluminum-intensive vehicles will change the scale economies of auto assembly dramatically. Aluminum space-frame and thermoplastic components are cast, forged, and extruded into different thicknesses depending upon where strength is needed. Neither requires a body-stamping machine.

Although an aluminum space-frame vehicle is 10 percent more costly on average than the typical steel-and-sheet-metal vehicle, the minimum efficient scale of an aluminum-intensive auto assembly process is only 50,000 cars. As illustrated in Figure 8.6, a marketing plan for smaller volume niche products such as the Ford Fusion, Chevy Volt, and Audi A2 can achieve MES at Point *A* with these new aluminum production techniques. Previously with steel-and-sheet-metal automobiles, production runs at this reduced scale would have resulted in unit costs at Point *B*, more than twice as high as those of a 300,000-unit vehicle such as the VW Passat; compare Point *C* in Figure 8.6. Cost discrepancies this great can seldom be overcome no matter how popular the design. But, by moving to thermoplastic and aluminum components, niche vehicles can achieve cost competitiveness.

---

[7]Based on "Aluminum Cars," *The Economist* (April 15, 2000), p. 89; *Consumer Reports* (April 1997), p. 26; "The Global Gambles of GM," *The Economist* (June 24, 2000), p. 67; and "Daimler-Chrysler Merger," *Wall Street Journal* (May 8, 1998), p. A10.

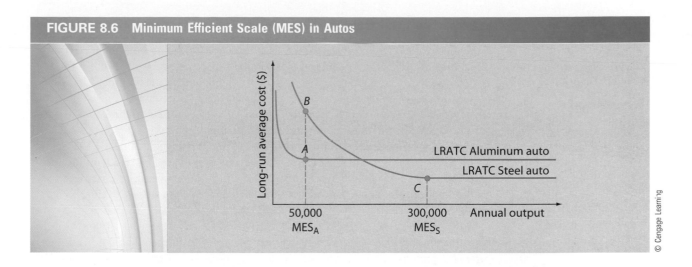

FIGURE 8.6   Minimum Efficient Scale (MES) in Autos

© Cengage Learning

SUMMARY

- *Cost* is defined as the sacrifice incurred whenever an exchange or transformation of resources takes place.

- Different approaches are used in measuring costs, depending on the purposes for which the information is to be used. For financial reporting purposes, the historical outlay of funds is usually the appropriate measure of cost, whereas for decision-making purposes, it is often appropriate to measure cost in terms of the opportunities forgone or sacrificed.

- A *cost function* is a schedule, graph, or mathematical relationship showing the minimum achievable cost (such as total, average, or marginal cost) of producing various quantities of output.

- Short-run total costs are equal to the sum of total fixed and total variable costs.

- *Marginal cost* is defined as the incremental increase in total variable cost that results from a one-unit increase in output.

- The short-run average variable and marginal cost functions of economic theory are hypothesized to be U-shaped, first falling and then rising as output is increased. Falling short-run unit costs are attributed to the gains available from specialization in the use of capital and labor. Rising short-run unit costs are attributed to diminishing returns in production.

- Capacity utilizations refers to three different production concepts depending on the context:

optimal rate of throughput for a given plant size, optimal plant size for a given rate of throughput, and the optimal plant size that achieves minimum efficient scale.

- The theoretical long-run average cost function is often found to be L-shaped due to the frequent presence of scale economies followed by an absence of scale diseconomies. *Economies of scale* are attributed primarily to spreading massive fixed costs over higher rates of throughput, whereas *diseconomies of scale* are attributed primarily to problems of coordination and inflexibility in large-scale organizations.

- Volume discounts in purchasing inputs and learning curve effects, both of which result from a larger cumulative volume of output, can be distinguished from scale effects, which depend on the firm's throughput rate of production. Learning curve advantages often arise in small-scale plants able to make long production runs.

- Both *volume discounts on inputs* and *learning curve cost advantages* lower average variable cost, whereas scale economies lowers average fixed cost.

- *Minimum efficient scale* is achieved by a rate of throughput sufficient to reduce long-run average total cost to the minimum possible level. Smaller rates of throughput imply smaller plant sizes will reduce unit cost, albeit to higher levels than would be possible if a firm's business plan could support minimum efficient scale production.

Exercises

Answers to the exercises in blue can be found in Appendix D at the back of the book.

1. US Airways owns a piece of land near the Pittsburgh International Airport. The land originally cost US Airways $375,000. The airline is considering building a new training center on this land. US Airways determined that the proposal to build the new facility is acceptable if the original cost of the land is used in the analysis, but the proposal does not meet the airline's project acceptance criteria if the land cost is above $850,000. A developer recently offered US Airways $2.5 million for the land. Should US Airways build the training facility at this location?

2. Howard Bowen is a large-scale cotton farmer. The land and machinery he owns has a current market value of $4 million. Bowen owes his local bank $3 million. Last year Bowen sold $5 million worth of cotton. His variable operating costs were $4.5 million; accounting depreciation was $40,000, although the actual decline in value of Bowen's machinery was $60,000 last year. Bowen paid himself a salary of $50,000, which is not considered part of his variable operating costs. Interest on his bank loan was $400,000. If Bowen worked for another farmer or a local manufacturer, his annual income would be about $30,000. Bowen can invest any funds that would be derived if the farm were sold to earn 10 percent annually. (Ignore taxes.)
   a. Compute Bowen's accounting profits.
   b. Compute Bowen's economic profits.

3. Mary Graham worked as a real estate agent for Piedmont Properties for 15 years. Her annual income is approximately $100,000 per year. Mary is considering establishing her own real estate agency. She expects to generate revenues during the first year of $2 million. Salaries paid to her employees are expected to total $1.5 million. Operating expenses (i.e., rent, supplies, utility services) are expected to total $250,000. To begin the business, Mary must borrow $500,000 from her bank at an interest rate of 15 percent. Equipment will cost Mary $50,000. At the end of one year, the value of this equipment will be $30,000, even though the depreciation expense for tax purposes is only $5,000 during the first year.
   a. Determine the (pre-tax) accounting profit for this venture.
   b. Determine the (pre-tax) economic profit for this venture.
   c. Which of the costs for this firm are explicit and which are implicit?

4. From your knowledge of the relationships among the various cost functions, complete the following table.

Q	TTC	TFC	TVC	ATC	AFC	AVC	MC
0	125	125	0	0	0	0	0
10	175	125	50	17.50	12.50	5	5
20	210	125	85	10.50	6.25	4.25	3.50
30	235	125	110	7.83	4.17	3.67	2.50
40	255	125	130	6.38	3.13	3.25	2
50	275	125	150	5.50	2.50	3	2
60	305	125	180	5.08	2.08	3	3
70	350	125	225	5	1.79	3.21	4.50
80	420	125	295	5.25	1.56	3.69	7

5. A manufacturing plant has a potential production capacity of 1,000 units per month (capacity can be increased by 10 percent if subcontractors are employed). The plant is normally operated at about 80 percent of capacity. Operating the plant above this

level significantly increases variable costs per unit because of the need to pay the skilled workers higher overtime wage rates. For output levels up to 80 percent of capacity, variable cost per unit is $100. Above 80 percent and up to 90 percent, variable costs on this additional output increase by 10 percent. When output is above 90 percent and up to 100 percent of capacity, the additional units cost an additional 25 percent over the unit variable costs for outputs up to 80 percent of capacity. For production above 100 percent and up to 110 percent of capacity, extensive subcontracting work is used and the unit variable costs of these additional units are 50 percent above those at output levels up to 80 percent of capacity. At 80 percent of capacity, the plant's fixed costs per unit are $50. Total fixed costs are not expected to change within the production range under consideration. Based on the preceding information, complete the following table.

Q	TTC	TFC	TVC	ATC	AFC	AVC	MC
500	—	—	—	—	—	—	—
600	—	—	—	—	—	—	—
700	—	—	—	—	—	—	—
800	—	—	—	—	—	—	—
900	—	—	—	—	—	—	—
1,000	—	—	—	—	—	—	—
1,100	—	—	—	—	—	—	—

6. The Blair Company's three assembly plants are located in California, Georgia, and New Jersey. Previously, the company purchased a major subassembly, which becomes part of the final product, from an outside firm. Blair has decided to manufacture the subassemblies within the company and must now consider whether to rent one centrally located facility (e.g., in Missouri, where all the subassemblies would be manufactured) or to rent three separate facilities, each located near one of the assembly plants, where each facility would manufacture only the subassemblies needed for the nearby assembly plant. A single, centrally located facility, with a production capacity of 18,000 units per year, would have fixed costs of $900,000 per year and a variable cost of $250 per unit. Three separate decentralized facilities, with production capacities of 8,000, 6,000, and 4,000 units per year, would have fixed costs of $475,000, $425,000, and $400,000, respectively, and variable costs per unit of only $225 per unit, owing primarily to the reduction in shipping costs. The current production rates at the three assembly plants are 6,000, 4,500, and 3,000 units, respectively.

   a. Assuming that the current production rates are maintained at the three assembly plants, which alternative should management select?

   b. If demand for the final product were to increase to production capacity, which alternative would be more attractive?

   c. What additional information would be useful before making a decision?

7. Kitchen Helper Company decides to produce and sell food blenders and is considering three different types of production facilities ("plants"). Plant A is a labor-intensive facility, employing relatively little specialized capital equipment. Plant B is a semiautomated facility that would employ less labor than A but would also have higher capital equipment costs. Plant C is a completely automated facility using much more high-cost, high-technology capital equipment and even less labor

than B. Information about the operating costs and production capacities of these three different types of plants is shown in the following table.

	PLANT TYPE		
	A	B	C
Unit variable costs			
Materials	$3.50	$3.25	$3.00
Labor	4.50	3.25	2.00
Overhead	1.00	1.50	2.00
Total	$9.00	$8.00	$7.00
Annual fixed costs			
Depreciation	$ 60,000	$100,000	$200,000
Capital	30,000	50,000	100,000
Overhead	60,000	100,000	150,000
Total	$150,000	$250,000	$450,000
Annual capacity	75,000	150,000	350,000

a. Determine the average total cost schedules for each plant type for annual outputs of 25,000, 50,000, 75,000, …, 350,000. For output levels beyond the capacity of a given plant, assume that multiple plants of the same type are built. For example, to produce 200,000 units with Plant A, three of these plants would be built.

b. Based on the cost schedules calculated in part (a), construct the long-run average total cost schedule for the production of blenders.

8. The ARA Railroad owns a piece of land along one of its right-of-ways. The land originally cost ARA $100,000. ARA is considering building a new maintenance facility on this land. ARA determined that the proposal to build the new facility is acceptable if the original cost of the land is used in the analysis, but the proposal does not meet the railroad's project acceptance criteria if the land cost is above $500,000. An investor has recently offered ARA $1 million for the land. Should ARA build the maintenance facility at this location?

9. The Emerson Corporation, a manufacturer of airplane landing gear equipment, is trying to develop a learning curve model to help forecast labor costs for successive units of one of its products. From past data, the firm knows that labor costs of the 25th, 75th, and 125th units were $800, $600, and $500, respectively. Using the learning curve equation for these labor costs, $\log C = 3.30755 - 0.28724 \log Q$, calculate the estimated cost of the 200th unit of output. What is the percentage of learning at Emerson?

Case Exercise

Cost Analysis of Patio Furniture

The Leisure Products (LP) Company manufactures lawn and patio furniture. Most of its output is sold to do-it-yourself warehouse stores (e.g., Lowe's Home Improvement) and to retail hardware and department store chains (e.g., Ace Hardware and JCPenney), who then distribute the products under their respective brand names. LP is not involved in direct retail sales. Last year the firm had sales of $35 million.

One of LP's divisions manufactures folding (aluminum and vinyl) chairs. Sales of the chairs are highly seasonal, with 80 percent of the sales volume concentrated in the January–June period. Production is normally concentrated in the September–May period. Approximately 75 percent of the hourly workforce (unskilled and semiskilled workers) is laid off (or takes paid vacation time) during the June–August period of reduced output. The remainder of the workforce, consisting of salaried plant management (line managers and supervisors), maintenance, and clerical staff, are retained during this slow period. Maintenance personnel, for example, perform major overhauls of the machinery during the slow summer period.

LP planned to produce and sell 500,000 of these chairs during the coming year at a projected selling price of $7.15 per chair. The cost per unit was estimated as follows:

Direct labor	$2.25
Materials	2.30
Plant overhead*	1.15
Administrative and selling expense	0.80
TOTAL	$6.50

*These costs are allocated to each unit of output based on the projected annual production of 500,000 chairs.

A 10 percent markup ($0.65) was added to the cost per unit in arriving at the firm's selling price of $7.15 (plus shipping).

In May, LP received an inquiry from Southeast Department Stores concerning the possible purchase of folding chairs for delivery in August. Southeast indicated that they would place an order for 30,000 chairs if the price did not exceed $5.50 each (plus shipping). The chairs could be produced during the slow period using the firm's existing equipment and workforce. No overtime wages would have to be paid to the workforce in fulfilling the order. Adequate materials were on hand (or could be purchased at prevailing market prices) to complete the order.

LP management was considering whether to accept the order. The firm's chief accountant felt that the firm should *not* accept the order because the price per chair was less than the total cost and contributed nothing to the firm's profits. The firm's chief economist argued that the firm should accept the order *if* the incremental revenue would exceed the incremental cost.

The following cost accounting definitions may be helpful in making this decision:

- Direct labor: Labor costs incurred in converting the raw material into the finished product.
- Material: Raw materials that enter into and become part of the final product.
- Plant overhead: All costs other than direct labor and materials that are associated with the product, including wages and salaries paid to employees who do not work directly on the product but whose services are related to the production process (line managers, maintenance, and janitorial personnel), heat, light, power, supplies, depreciation, taxes, and insurance on the assets employed in the production process.
- Selling and distribution costs: Costs incurred in making sales (e.g., billing and salespeople's compensation), storing the product, and shipping the product to the customer. (In this case the customer pays all shipping costs.)
- Administrative costs: Items not listed in the preceding categories, including general and executive office costs, research, development, engineering costs, and miscellaneous items.

Questions

1. Calculate the incremental variable, or marginal, cost per chair to LP of accepting the order from Southeast.
2. What assumptions did you make in calculating the incremental variable cost in Question 1? What additional information would be helpful in making these calculations?
3. Based on your answers to Questions 1 and 2, should LP accept the Southeast order?
4. What additional considerations might lead LP to reject the order?

Profit Margins on the Amazon Kindle[8]

Amazon's new tablet computer, the Kindle Fire, has slim margins at its $199 retail price. Admittedly, this product is trying to change the way we read books. It is therefore positioned so as to penetrate a revolutionary new target market, the twentysomethings who are comfortable never actually holding hard copies of their textbooks, novels, newspapers, or magazines.

Listed here is data on hardware components, software licensing, and other costs: display screen $35, touchscreen $25, assembly labor $11, battery $12, processor chip $18, advertising campaign $7, DRAM memory chip $5, software licenses $37, 8 GB memory module $8, wireless WiFi/Bluetooth $6, hardcase and other materials $34, R&D expense $12, overhead $14.

Questions

1. Categorize the listed costs as variable or fixed and calculate a contribution margin percentage defined as the net price minus variable costs as a proportion of the net sales price.
2. Would you expect the Kindle tablet contribution margin percentage to exceed handset margins of 13 percent to 17 percent at Samsung, RIM, and Nokia? Why or why not?
3. What about Apple iPads? Why would their margins be higher? Be specific.

---

[8]"Slim Profit for Amazon Kindle," *Wall Street Journal* (November 18, 2011), p. B4.

Applications of Cost Theory

CHAPTER 9

CHAPTER PREVIEW

This chapter examines some of the techniques that have been developed for estimating the cost functions of production processes in actual firms. In the short run, knowledge of the firm's cost function is essential when deciding whether to accept an additional order, perhaps at less than "full cost"; whether to schedule overtime for workers; or whether to temporarily suspend operations and shut down but not close the plant or store. In the long run, knowledge of cost-function relationships will determine the capital investments to make, the production technology to adopt, the markets to enter, and the new products to introduce. The first part of this chapter examines various techniques for empirically estimating short-run and long-run cost functions. The second part of this chapter deals with break-even and contribution analysis—perhaps the single most useful application of cost theory for examining the profitability of a firm's operations.

Computerization and robotics have made output per worker higher and therefore lowered unit labor cost when it comes to processing insurance claims, redeeming coupons, or screening job résumés. Personal computers have decreased manyfold the time and talent required to perform routine work done previously with paper forms and time-consuming, repetitive human tasks. However, not every business uses large numbers of PCs. How have computerization and information technology raised productivity and lowered cost so widely across other industries?

One key seems to be enhanced analytical and research and development (R&D) capability provided by computers and information technology (IT) systems. Chevron Corporation once spent anywhere from $2 million to $4 million each to drill 10 to 12 exploratory wells before finding oil. Today, Chevron finds oil

once in every five wells. The reason for the cost savings is a new technology that allows Chevron to display three-dimensional graphs of the likely oil and gas deposits in potential oil fields. New fast parallel processors allow more calculation-intensive 3D simulation modeling. Using only seismic data as inputs, Chevron can now model how the oil and gas deposits will shift and flow as a known field is pumped out. This allows a much more accurate location of secondary wells. As a result, overall production costs have declined 16 percent industry-wide despite second- and third-choice locations for exploration and development.

Timken, a $4 billion ball-bearing manufacturer, has also used digital 3D modeling to reconfigure production processes and implement small production runs of high-profit-margin products. Timken's newest facility in North Carolina is a so-called *flexible manufacturing*

Cont.

MANAGERIAL CHALLENGE *Continued*

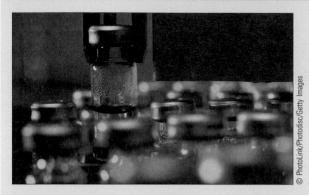

system (FMS) where order taking, limited customization of design, production scheduling, and the actual factory itself are all IT enabled and networked. Networked machine tools make it possible to *build to order* (BTO) against precise specifications deliverable within four hours rather than stockpile inventories of subassemblies or insist that customers wait six to eight weeks, as was the practice before IT. Nissan recently estimated that $3,600 in the final price of an auto is tied up in inventory expense that can be avoided by a BTO system. For the auto industry as a whole, savings could total as much as $50 billion per year out of its $80 billion inventory cost.

Pharmaceutical R&D has experienced a similar benefit from computerization. Drug industry basic research always starts with biochemical or biogenetic modeling of the disease mechanism. In the past, once a mechanism for Hodgkin's disease or pancreatic cancer became well understood, researchers at Merck or Pfizer experimented

on known active compounds one by one in time-consuming chemical trials. Successful therapies emerged only after human trials on the promising compounds showed efficacy with few side effects. Total time to introduction of a new pharmaceutical was often longer than a decade and entailed $1.5 billion in investments.

Today, the first stage of the basic research process remains much the same, but the second stage of dribbling chemicals into a petri dish has ended. Instead, machines controlled and automated by microchips perform thousands of reactions at once and tally the results. Human researchers then take the most likely reagents and perform much more promising experiments that culminate in human trials. The total time to discovery has been cut by more than two-thirds, and all attendant costs have declined sharply.

Discussion Questions

■ Name a business that you believe has experienced declining costs attributable to computerization. Were variable costs reduced? What fixed costs increase was involved? Does it seem clear that average total cost (ATC) went down? Explain.

[1]Based on "The Innovators: The Rocket under the High-Tech Boom," *Wall Street Journal* (March 30, 1999); "Mass Customization," *The Economist* (July 14, 2001), pp. 64–67; and "The Flexible Factory," *BusinessWeek* (May 5, 2003), pp. 90–101.

ESTIMATING COST FUNCTIONS

To make optimal pricing and production decisions, the firm must have knowledge of the shape and characteristics of its short-run cost function. A *cost function* is a schedule, graph, or mathematical relationship showing the total, average, or marginal cost of producing various quantities of output. To decide whether to accept or refuse an order offered at some particular price, the firm must exactly identify what variable costs and direct fixed costs the order entails. A capability to estimate the short-run cost function is therefore crucial. In contrast, the long-run cost function is associated with the longer-term planning period in which all the inputs to the production process are variable and no restrictions are placed on the amount of an input that can be employed in the production process. Consequently, all costs, including indirect fixed costs such as headquarters facility costs, are avoidable and therefore relevant to cost estimates.

Issues in Cost Definition and Measurement

Recall that economic cost is represented by the value of opportunities forgone, whereas accounting cost is measured by the outlays that are incurred. Some companies record the cost of their own output (the coal, uranium, crude oil, or natural gas) shipped downstream to their refining-and-processing operations as expenses at the world market price on the day of shipment (i.e., at their opportunity cost).

Other companies account for these same resources as their out-of-pocket expenses. If actual extraction costs of the company being studied are low (e.g., with Kentucky coal or Persian Gulf oil), these two cost methods will diverge. The reason is because the equilibrium market price of coal, oil, or natural gas is always determined by the considerably higher cost of the most expensive marginal producer presently on line (e.g., a strip mine with mandated reclamation, an oil platform in the North Sea, or natural gas extraction with fracking technology at 5,000 feet depths).

Similar problems arise in measuring variable costs (i.e., costs that vary with output). Some companies employ only direct accounting costs, including materials, supplies, direct labor costs, and any direct fixed costs avoidable by refusing the batch order in question. Direct costs exclude all overhead and any other fixed cost that must be allocated (so-called indirect fixed costs). For batch decisions about whether to accept or refuse an order for a proposed charter air flight, a special production run, or a customer's proposed change order, these estimates of variable plus direct fixed costs are needed. For other questions, such as offering a customized design, however, some indirect accounting cost for the IT system that allows customized design would be an appropriate inclusion in the cost data.

Several other cost measurement issues arise with depreciation. Conceptually, depreciation can be divided into two components: *time depreciation* represents the decline in value of an asset associated with the passage of *time*, and *use depreciation* represents the decline in value of an asset associated with *use*. For example, unneeded aircraft temporarily mothballed in the desert suffer only time depreciation. Note that such time depreciation is completely independent of the rate of output at which the asset is actually operated. Because only use depreciation varies with the rate of output, only use depreciation is relevant in determining the shape of the cost-output relationship. However, accounting data on depreciation seldom break out use depreciation costs separately. Instead, the accounting depreciation of the value of an asset over its life cycle is usually determined by arbitrary tax regulations.

Finally, capital asset values (and their associated depreciation costs) are often stated in terms of historical costs rather than in terms of replacement costs. In periods of rapidly increasing price levels, this approach will tend to understate true economic depreciation costs. Similarly, in industries with sometimes rapid and sometimes slow obsolescence such as computer chips, depreciation schedules applied to historical cost will tend to misstate the loss of asset value for inventories. These limitations need to be kept in mind when interpreting the cost-output relationship for capital-intensive firms like Delta and Intel.

Controlling for Other Variables

In addition to being a function of the output level of the firm, cost is a function of other factors, such as output mix, the length of production runs, employee absenteeism and turnover, production methods, input costs, and managerial efficiency.

To isolate the cost-output relationship itself, one must control for these other influences by:

- *Deflating or detrending the cost data.* Whenever wage rates or raw material prices change significantly over the period of analysis, one can deflate the cost data to reflect these changes in factor prices. Provided suitable price indices are available or can be constructed, costs incurred at different points in time can be restated as inflation-adjusted real costs.[2]

- *Using multiple regression analysis.* Suppose a firm believes that costs should decline gradually over time as a result of innovative worker suggestions. One way to incorporate this effect into the cost equation would be to include a time trend t as an additional explanatory variable.
- *Economies of scope.* Other possible control variables to address economies of scope include the number of product lines, the number of customer segments, and the number of distribution channels.

The Form of the Empirical Cost-Output Relationship

The total cost function in the short run ($SRTC$), as hypothesized in economic theory, is an S-shaped curve that can be represented by a cubic relationship:

$$SRTC = a + bQ + cQ^2 + dQ^3 \qquad [9.1]$$

The familiar U-shaped marginal and average cost functions then can be derived from this relationship. The associated marginal cost function is

$$MC = \frac{d(SRTC)}{dQ} = b + 2cQ + 3dQ^2 \qquad [9.2]$$

The ATC function is

$$ATC = \frac{SRTC}{Q} = \frac{a}{Q} + b + cQ + dQ^2 \qquad [9.3]$$

The cubic total cost function and its associated marginal and ATC functions are shown in Figure 9.1(a). If the results of a regression analysis indicate that the cubic term (Q^3) is not statistically significant, then short-run total cost can be represented by a quadratic relationship:

$$SRTC = a + bQ + cQ^2 \qquad [9.4]$$

as illustrated in Figure 9.1(b). In this quadratic case, total costs increase at an increasing rate throughout the typical operating range of output levels. The associated marginal and average cost functions are

$$MC = \frac{d(SRTC)}{dQ} = b + 2cQ \qquad [9.5]$$

$$ATC = \frac{SRTC}{Q} = \frac{a}{Q} + b + cQ \qquad [9.6]$$

As can be seen from Equation 9.5, this quadratic total cost relationship implies that marginal costs increase linearly as the output level is increased. Rising marginal

---

[2]Two assumptions are implicit in this approach: No substitution takes place between the inputs as prices change, and changes in the output level have no influence on the prices of the inputs. For more automated plants that incorporate only maintenance personnel, plant engineers, and material supplies, these assumptions fit the reality of the production process quite well.

FIGURE 9.1 Polynomial Cost-Output Relationships

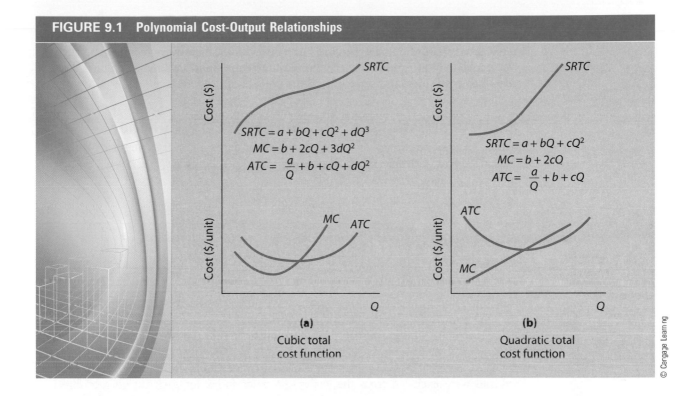

$$SRTC = a + bQ + cQ^2 + dQ^3$$
$$MC = b + 2cQ + 3dQ^2$$
$$ATC = \frac{a}{Q} + b + cQ + dQ^2$$

$$SRTC = a + bQ + cQ^2$$
$$MC = b + 2cQ$$
$$ATC = \frac{a}{Q} + b + cQ$$

(a)
Cubic total
cost function

(b)
Quadratic total
cost function

© Cengage Learning

WHAT WENT RIGHT • WHAT WENT WRONG

Boeing: The Rising Marginal Cost of Wide-Bodies[3]

Boeing and Airbus provide all the wide-bodied jets the world needs. Boeing 747s, 767s, and 777s typically have a 70 percent share of the worldwide market, but Airbus accepted a majority of the new orders in 1994–1995 and doubled its output rate, especially on smaller planes, from 126 to 232 planes per year. Some analysts think Boeing should have given up even more of the order flow. Why?

One reason is that until recently, incremental orders at Boeing necessitated redrawing and duplicating the thousands of engineering diagrams that determine how 200,000 employees assemble any particular customer's plane. Rather than doing mass customization from common platforms, Boeing assembles one plane at a time with new drawings for each $150 million wide-body ordered. Eventually, incremental variable costs must rise as designers and shop floors get congested with new instructions and diagrams.

With backorders running to almost 1,000 planes companywide in the mid-1990s, Boeing boosted production from 180 to 560 commercial jets per year. At the final assembly plant for Boeing wide-bodies, throughput was

increased from 15 planes per month to 21 planes per month (i.e., by 40 percent). To increase production rates, Boeing split bottlenecked assembly stations into parallel processes, which entailed the hiring of additional assembly workers and the authorization of massive overtime. Boeing also contracted out more subassemblies. Splitting bottlenecked assembly stations and contracting out subassemblies substantially increased Boeing's variable costs.

Wide-body prices did not rise because of intense competitive pressure from Airbus, but Boeing's marginal costs certainly did. As a result, for a while in the late 1990s, every wide-body plane delivered had a price less than its incremental variable cost (i.e., a negative operating profit margin). Of course, eventually such orders must be refused. In 2000, Boeing did slow the production throughput rate back to 15 wide-bodies per month in order to return to profitability. Today, a well-equipped 747-400 aircraft earns as much as $45 million in operating profits above its variable cost.

---

[3]Based on "Boeing's Trouble," *Wall Street Journal* (December 16, 1998), p. A23; and an Everett, Washington, site visit to Boeing's final assembly plant for wide-bodied aircraft.

cost ($c > 0$) is characteristic of many manufacturing environments because ultimately that reflects diminishing returns. On the other hand, some information services companies, such as IBM Global Services, or network-based software companies, such as Microsoft, may at times experience increasing returns and declining marginal costs of customer acquisition and service ($c < 0$).

Statistical Estimation of Short-Run Cost Functions

Short-run cost functions have been estimated for firms in a large number of different industries—for example, food processing, furniture, railways, gas, coal, electricity, hosiery, steel, and cement.

Example

Short-Run Cost Function for Multi-Product Food Processing

In a study of a British food processing firm, Johnston constructed individual cost functions for 14 different products and an overall cost function for the firm.[4] Weekly data for nine months were obtained on the physical production of each type of product and total direct costs of each product (subdivided into the four categories of materials, labor, packing, and freight). Indirect costs (e.g., salaries, indirect labor, factory charges, and laboratory expenses) remained fairly constant over the time period studied and were excluded from the analysis. A price index for each category of direct costs for each product was obtained from government sources and used to deflate all four sets of input costs, yielding a weekly deflated direct cost for each product. For the individual products, output was measured by physical production (quantity). For the firm as a whole, an index of aggregate output was constructed by weighing the quantities of each product by its selling price and summing over all products produced each period.

For the 14 different products and for the overall firm, the linear cost function gave an excellent fit between direct cost and output. Therefore, Johnston concluded that total direct costs were a linear function of output, and marginal costs were constant over the observed ranges of output.

[4]See Jack Johnston, *Statistical Cost Analysis* (New York: McGraw-Hill, 1960).

Example

Short-Run Cost Functions: Electricity Generation[5]

Another study by Johnston of the costs of electric power generation in Great Britain developed short-run cost functions for a sample of 17 different firms from annual cost-output data on each firm. To satisfy the basic conditions underlying the short-run cost function, only those firms whose capital equipment remained constant in size over the period were included in the sample. The output variable was measured in kilowatt-hours (kWh). The cost variable included (1) fuel; (2) salaries and wages; and (3) repairs and maintenance,[6] oil, water, and stores. Each of the three cost categories was deflated using an appropriate price index. A cubic polynomial function

(continued)

with an additional linear time trend variable was fitted to each of 17 sets of cost-output observations.

The results of this study did *not* support the existence of a nonlinear cubic or quadratic cost function. The cubic term, Q^3, was not statistically significant in any of the regressions, and the quadratic term, Q^2, was statistically significant in only 5 of the 17 cost equations. A typical linear total cost function is given by

$$C = 18.3 + 0.889Q - 0.639T$$

where C = variable costs of generation, Q = annual output (millions of kilowatt-hours), and T = time (years). The equation "explained" 97.4 percent of the variation in the cost variable.

The results of the two Johnston studies are similar to those found in many other cost studies—namely, that short-run total costs tend to increase *linearly* over the ranges of output for which cost-output data are available. In other words, short-run average costs tend to decline and marginal costs tend to be constant over the "typical" or "normal" operating range of the firm. At higher rates of output, we would expect to see rising marginal cost, but, of course, this circumstance is exactly what firms try to avoid. Recall Boeing's experience in producing too many 747s per month.

---

[5]Ibid., pp. 11–63.

[6]Maintenance cost does not correspond exactly with variable costs unless maintenance is unscheduled and occurs so as to just offset wear and tear from use. Scheduled maintenance like a quarterly safety inspection of an assembly plant or an FAA airworthiness certification for an airplane is an indirect fixed cost not traceable to individual product lines.

Statistical Estimation of Long-Run Cost Functions

Long-run costs can be estimated over a substantial period of time in a single plant (time-series data) or with multiple plants operating at different rates of output (cross-sectional data). The use of cross-sectional data assumes that each firm is using its fixed plant and equipment and variable inputs to accomplish minimum *LRAC* production for that plant size along the envelope of *SRAC* curves we studied in Chapter 8.

The use of time-series data assumes that input prices, the production technology, and the products offered for sale remain unchanged. Both methods, therefore, require heroic assumptions, but cross-sectional data are more prevalent in estimating long-run cost functions.

Determining the Optimal Scale of an Operation

The size at which a company should attempt to establish its operations depends on the extent of the scale economies and the extent of the market. Some firms can operate at minimum unit cost using a small scale. Consider a licensed street vendor of leather coats. Each additional sale entails variable costs for the coat, a few minutes of direct labor effort to answer potential customers' questions, and some small allocated cost associated with the step-van or other vehicle where the inventory is stored and hauled from one street sale location to another. Ninety-nine percent of the operating cost is the variable cost of an additional leather coat per additional sale. Long-run average cost will be essentially flat, constant at approximately the wholesale cost of a leather coat. As a result, in street vending, a small-scale operation will be just as efficient as a large-scale operation.

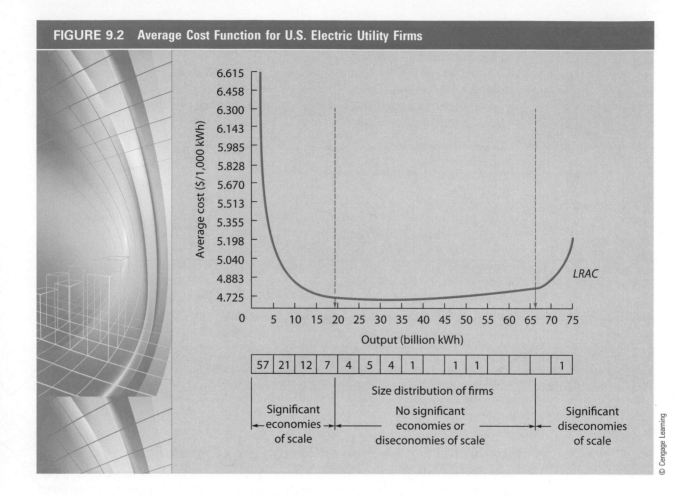

FIGURE 9.2   Average Cost Function for U.S. Electric Utility Firms

© Cengage Learning

Example

Long-Run Cost Functions: Electricity Generation[7]

In a cross-sectional study of U.S. electric utility companies, Christensen and Greene used a logarithmic model to test for the presence of economies and diseconomies of scale. The long-run average cost (*LRAC*) curve using data on 114 firms is shown in Figure 9.2. The bar following the graph indicates the number of firms in each interval. Below 19.8 billion kWh (left arrow in graph), significant economies of scale were found to exist. The 97 firms in this range accounted for 48.7 percent of the total output. Between 19.8 and 67.1 billion kWh (right arrow in the graph), no significant economies of scale were present. The 16 firms in this range accounted for 44.6 percent of the total output. Above 67.1 billion kWh, diseconomies of scale (one firm and 6.7 percent of total output) were found.

[7]Based on L. R. Christensen and W. H. Greene, "Economies of Scale in U.S. Electric Power Generation," *Journal of Political Economy* 84, no. 4 (August 1976).

Scale Economies in the Satellite and Traditional Cable TV Industry: Dish Network and Time-Warner[8]

Satellite and cable TV businesses have cost characteristics similar to electric utilities. Once the satellite or cable wires have been put in place, the incremental cost of extending service to another household is small. The extent of the scale economies in such industries may warrant licensing only one satellite or cable provider. In fact, municipalities have historically issued an exclusive service contract to such public utilities. The rationale was that one firm could service the whole market at much lower cost than several firms dividing the market and failing therefore to realize all of the available scale economies.

However, remember that the optimal scale of operation of any facility, even a declining cost facility, is limited by the extent of the market. The expansion of the satellite and cable TV market has always been limited by the availability of DVD players and movie rental services such as NetFlix and Redbox because they are inexpensive, convenient entertainment substitutes. As a result, the potential scale economies suggested by industrial engineering studies of satellite and cable TV operations have never been fully realized.

In addition, both satellite and cable TV companies are now facing new wireless alternative technologies. Smart phones and web-enabled television have cut deeply into the market once reserved exclusively for satellite and cable companies. As a result, the average unit cost in these businesses increased from B to A as volume declined (see Figure 9.3). Consequently, the price required to break even has necessarily risen. Of course, that sets in motion a vicious circle; the higher the cost-covering price, the more customers the satellite and cable companies lose to wireless alternatives.

[8]See W. Emmons and R. Prager, "The Effects of Market Structure in the U.S. Cable Television Industry," *Rand Journal of Economics* 28, no. 4 (Winter 1997), pp. 732–750.

In contrast, hydroelectric power plants have few variable costs of any kind. Instead, essentially all the costs are fixed costs associated with buying the land that will be flooded, constructing the dam, and purchasing the huge electrical generator equipment. Thereafter, the only variable inputs required are lubricants and a few maintenance workers. Consequently, a hydroelectric power plant has long-run ATCs that decline continuously as the company spreads its enormous fixed cost over additional unit sales by supplying power to more and more households. Similarly, electric distribution lines (the high-tension power grids and neighborhood electrical conduits) are a high-fixed-cost and low-variable-cost operation. In the electrical utility industry, large-scale operations therefore incur lower unit cost than small-scale operations, as demonstrated in Figure 9.2.

"Freewheeling" in the electrical utility industry has similar effects to the wireless access to television signals. When industrial and commercial electricity buyers (e.g., a large assembly plant or hospital) were allowed in January 2003 to contract freely with low-cost power suppliers elsewhere in the state or even several states away, the local public utility experienced "stranded costs." That is, the high initial fixed costs of constructing dams, power plants, and distribution lines were left behind as sales

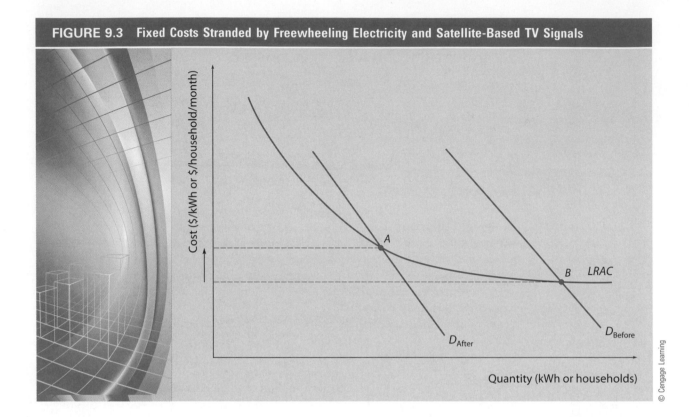

FIGURE 9.3   Fixed Costs Stranded by Freewheeling Electricity and Satellite-Based TV Signals

---

economies of scope Economies that exist whenever the cost of producing two (or more) products jointly by one plant or firm is less than the cost of producing these products separately in separate plants or firms.

engineering cost techniques A method of estimating cost functions by deriving the least-cost combination of labor, capital equipment, and raw materials required to produce various levels of output, using only industrial engineering information.

volume declined and local customers opted out. If the costs involved had been mostly variable, the local power utilities could have simply cut costs and operated profitably at smaller scale. Unfortunately, however, the costs are mostly fixed and unavoidable, so unit costs will unavoidably rise as the number of customers served declines.

Economies of Scale versus Economies of Scope

Economies of scope occur whenever inputs can be shared in the production of different products. For example, in the airline industry, the cost of transporting both passengers and freight on a single airplane is less than the cost of using two airplanes to transport passengers and freight separately. Similarly, commercial banks that manage both credit card–based unsecured consumer loans and deeded property-secured mortgage loans can provide each activity at lower cost than they could be offered separately. These cost savings occur independent of the throughput rate of flying hours per day or loans processed, approved, and in good standing and are therefore independent of the scale of operations in airlines and banking; hence they are distinguished from economies of scale.

Engineering Cost Techniques

Engineering cost techniques provide an alternative way to estimate long-run cost functions without using accounting cost data. Using production data instead, the engineering approach attempts to determine the least-cost combination of labor, capital equipment, and raw materials required to produce various levels of output. Engineering methods offer a number of advantages over statistical methods in examining economies of scale. First, it is generally much easier with the engineering approach to hold constant such factors as input prices, product mix, and product efficiency, allowing one to isolate the effects on costs of changes in output. Second, use of the engineering method avoids some of the cost-allocation and depreciation problems encountered when using accounting data.

Example

Economies of Scope in the Banking Industry

A number of empirical studies have attempted to estimate economies of scale and scope in the banking industry, which includes commercial banks, savings and loan associations, and credit unions. Possible sources of production economies in financial institutions include the following:

- *Specialized labor.* A larger depository institution may be able to employ more specialized labor (e.g., cash managers, financial advisors, risk managers, and specialized loan officers). If the expertise of these workers results in the processing of a higher volume of deposit and performing loan accounts per unit of labor, then larger institutions will experience lower per-unit labor costs compared with smaller institutions.
- *Computer and telecommunications technology.* Once the large setup, or fixed, costs are incurred, computer and electronic funds transfer systems can be used to process additional transactions at small additional costs per transaction. Spreading the fixed costs over a higher volume of transactions may permit the larger firm to achieve lower ATCs.
- *Business credit information.* Credit information, once gathered, can be reused, usually at little additional cost, in making other decisions about lending to the institution's customers. For example, credit information gathered in making commercial space rental loans can also be used in making commercial lending against receivables. Thus, larger financial institutions, which offer a wide array of different types of commercial credit, may realize economies of scope in information gathering. That is, the cost of commercial real estate lending and working capital lending done jointly is lower than the total cost of both when each is done by separate lending institutions.

The following conclusions were derived from logarithmic cost-function studies of banking:

- Some evidence indicates economies of scope between consumer installment credit lending and residential mortgage lending.
- Significant overall (i.e., firm-specific) economies of scale occur only at relatively low levels of output (less than $100 million in deposits). Larger banks exhibit L-shaped *LRAC* where ATC falls steeply at low levels of output and then flattens out and becomes horizontal. In this respect, banking *LRAC* closely mirrors the shape of the *LRAC* in representative manufacturing.

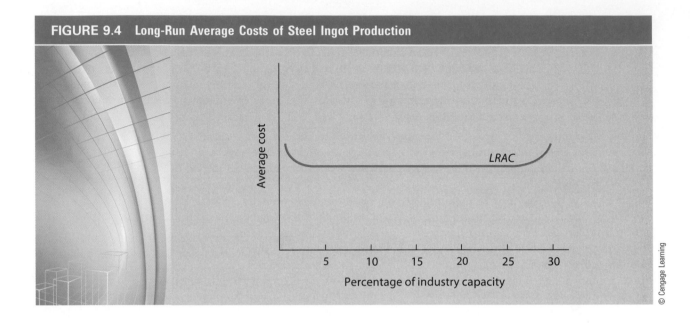

FIGURE 9.4   Long-Run Average Costs of Steel Ingot Production

© Cengage Learning

The Survivor Technique

survivor technique A method of estimating cost functions from the shares of industry output coming from each size class over time. Size classes whose shares of industry output are increasing (decreasing) over time are presumed to be relatively efficient (inefficient) and have lower (higher) average costs.

It is also possible to detect the presence of scale economies or diseconomies without having access to any cost data. The **survivor technique** involves classifying the firms in an industry by size and calculating the share of industry output coming from each size class over time.[9] If the share decreases over time, then this size class is presumed to be relatively inefficient and to have higher average costs. Conversely, an increasing share indicates that the size class is relatively efficient and has lower average costs. The rationale for this approach is that competition will tend to eliminate those firms whose size is relatively inefficient, allowing only those size firms with lower average costs to survive.

The survivor technique has been used to examine the long-run cost functions in steel ingot production by open-hearth or Bessemer processes. Based on over two decades of data on which firms with what capacities survived, Nobel prize-winner George Stigler developed the sleigh-shaped long-run average cost function for steel ingot production shown in Figure 9.4. Because of the declining percentages at the lowest levels of output and at extremely high levels of output, Stigler concluded that both were relatively inefficient size classes. The intermediate size classes (from 2.5 to 27.5 percent of industry capacity) represented the range of optimum size because these size classes grew or held their shares of capacity. Stigler also applied the survivor technique to the automobile industry and found an L-shaped average cost curve, indicating no evidence of diseconomies of scale at large levels of output.

In a study designed to isolate the various sources of scale economies within a plant, Haldi and Whitcomb collected data on the cost of individual units of equipment, on the

---

[9]G. J. Stigler, *The Organization of Industry* (Homewood, IL: Richard D. Irwin 1968), Chapter 7. For other examples of the use of the survivor technique, see H. E. Ted Frech and Paul B. Ginsburg, "Optimal Scale in Medical Practice: A Survivor Analysis," *Journal of Business* (January 1974), pp. 23–26.

initial investment in plant and equipment, and on operating costs. They noted that "in many basic industries such as petroleum refining, primary metals, and electric power, economies of scale are found in very large plant sizes (often the largest built or contemplated)."[10] Few (if any) firms were observed operating beyond these MES plant sizes.

A Cautionary Tale

One final note of caution: the concept of ATC per unit of output (i.e., so-called unit costs), so prominent in our recent discussion of scale economies, is seldom useful for managerial decision making. Indeed, making output or pricing decisions based on ATC is dead wrong. Average variable cost and marginal cost determine optimal shutdown, optimal output, and optimal price decisions. Managers in prominent companies like British Telephone have been fired over this mistake when they included headquarters expense and other corporate overhead in a pricing decision for an incremental new account. So, get in the habit of avoiding the use of unit costs in your decision problem reasoning. Reserve unit costs for one purpose only—describing, debating, and planning issues related to scale and scope economies and diseconomies alone.

BREAK-EVEN ANALYSIS

break-even analysis A calculation of the output level at which total contributions cover direct plus indirect fixed costs.

Long-run planning activities that take place within a firm are based on anticipated levels of output. The study of the interrelationships among a firm's sales, total costs, and operating profit at various anticipated output levels is known as **break-even analysis**.

Break-even analysis is based on the revenue–output and cost-output functions of microeconomic theory. These functions are shown together in Figure 9.5. Total revenue is equal to the number of units of output sold multiplied by the price per unit. Assuming that the firm can sell additional units of output only by lowering the price, the total revenue curve TR will be concave (inverted U-shaped), as indicated in Figure 9.5.

The difference between total revenue and total cost at any level of output represents the total profit that will be obtained. In Figure 9.5, total profit TP at any output level is given by the vertical distance between the total revenue TR and total cost TC curves. A break-even situation (zero profit) occurs whenever total revenue equals total cost. Below an output level of Q_1, losses will be incurred because $TR < TC$. Between Q_1 and Q_3, profits will be obtained because $TR > TC$. At output levels above Q_3, losses will occur again because $TR < TC$. Total profits are maximized within the range of Q_1 to Q_3; the vertical distance between the TR and TC curves is greatest at an output level of Q_2.

Example

Boeing 777 Exceeds Break-Even Sales Volume[11]

Boeing and Airbus, for example, are constantly calculating and recalculating their break-even sales volumes as unanticipated development costs, unknown at the inception of the project, arise on their new planes. The new double-decked jumbo jet, the Airbus 380, has $11.7 billion in development cost, requiring that 259 planes be sold at undiscounted prices in order to break even. Advance orders have only secured 160, much less than the break-even amount. Although Airbus has sold more total planes

(continued)

---

[10]J. Haldi and D. Whitcomb, "Economies of Scale in Industrial Plants," *Journal of Political Economy* 75, no. 1 (August 1967), pp. 373–385.

than Boeing in recent years, Boeing has dominated the wide-bodied submarket for larger jets with a 70 percent market share. For example, by 2006 Boeing had secured 155 orders for its 777 long-haul jet, whereas Airbus had orders for only 15 of its competing Airbus 340s. Break-even appears far off on the 340s as well.

[11]Based on "Testing Times," *The Economist* (April 1, 2006), p. 56.

FIGURE 9.5 Generalized Break-Even Analysis

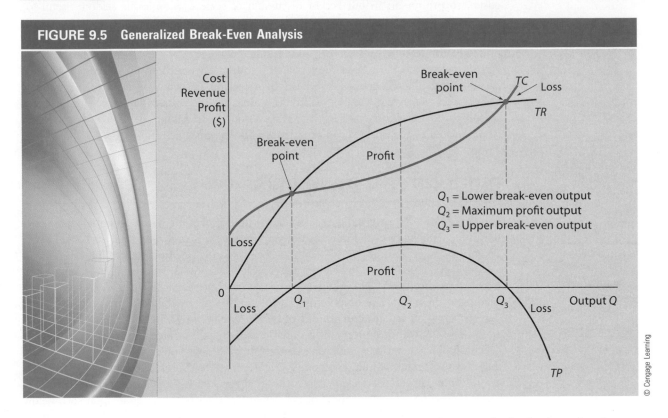

Q_1 = Lower break-even output
Q_2 = Maximum profit output
Q_3 = Upper break-even output

© Cengage Learning

We now discuss both a graphical and an algebraic method of solving break-even problems.

Graphical Method

Constant selling price per unit and a constant variable cost per unit yield the linear *TR* and *TC* functions illustrated in Figure 9.6, which shows a basic linear break-even chart. Total cost is computed as the sum of the firm's fixed costs *F*, which are independent of the output level, and the variable costs, which increase at a constant rate of *VC* per unit of output. Operating profit is equal to the difference between total revenues (*TR*) and total (operating) costs (*TC*).

The break-even point occurs at point Q_b in Figure 9.6, where the total revenue and the total cost functions intersect. If a firm's output level is below this break-even point (i.e., if *TR* < *TC*), it incurs *operating losses*. If the firm's output level is above this break-even point (if *TR* > *TC*), it realizes *operating profits*.

Algebraic Method

To determine a firm's break-even point algebraically, one must set the total revenue and total (operating) cost functions equal to each other and solve the resulting equation for

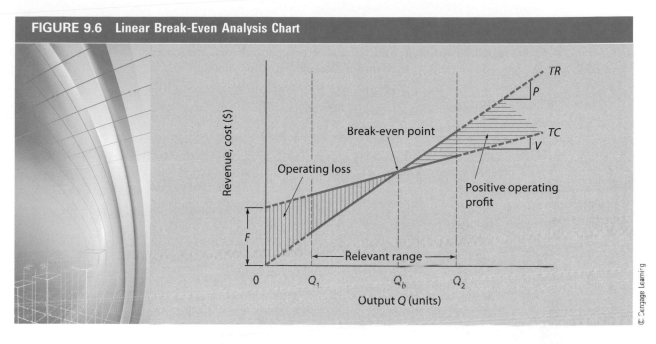

FIGURE 9.6   Linear Break-Even Analysis Chart

the break-even volume. Total revenue is equal to the selling price per unit times the output quantity:

$$TR = P \times Q \tag{9.7}$$

Total (operating) cost is equal to fixed plus variable costs, where the variable cost is the product of the variable cost per unit times the output quantity:

$$TTC = TFC + (VC \times Q) \tag{9.8}$$

Setting the total revenue and total cost expressions equal to each other and substituting the break-even output Q_b for Q results in

$$TR = TTC$$

or

$$PQ_b = TFC + VC \times Q_b \tag{9.9}$$

Finally, solving Equation 9.9 for the break-even output Q_b yields[12]

$$PQ_b - VCQ_b = TFC$$
$$(P - VC)\, Q_b = TFC$$
$$Q_b = \frac{TFC}{(P - VC)} \tag{9.10}$$

The *difference* between the selling price per unit and the variable cost per unit, $P - VC$, is referred to as the **contribution margin**. It measures how much each unit of output contributes to meeting fixed costs and operating profits. Thus, the break-even output is equal to the total fixed cost divided by the contribution margin.

contribution margin The difference between price and variable cost per unit.

---

[12]Break-even analysis also can be performed in terms of dollar *sales* rather than *units* of output. The break-even dollar sales volume S_b can be determined by the following expression:

$$S_b = \frac{TFC}{1 - VC/P}$$

where VC/P is the variable cost ratio (calculated as variable cost per dollar of sales).

Because a firm's break-even output is dependent on a number of variables—in particular, the price per unit, variable (operating) costs per unit, and fixed costs—the firm may wish to analyze the effects of changes in any of these variables on the break-even output. For example, it may wish to consider either of the following:

1. Changing the selling price.
2. Substituting fixed costs for variable costs.

Example

Break-Even Analysis: Allegan Manufacturing Company

Assume that Allegan manufactures one product, which it sells for $250 per unit ($P$). Variable costs ($VC$) are $150 per unit. The firm's fixed costs (TFC) are $1 million. Substituting these figures into Equation 9.10 yields the following break-even output:

$$Q_b = \frac{\$1,000,000}{\$250 - \$150}$$
$$= 10,000 \text{ units}$$

Now assume that Allegan increased the selling price per unit P' by $25 to $275. Substituting this figure into Equation 9.10 gives a new break-even output:

$$Q'_b = \frac{\$1,000,000}{\$275 - \$150}$$
$$= 8,000 \text{ units}$$

An increase in the price per unit reduces the break-even output.

Rather than increasing the selling price per unit, Allegan's management may decide to substitute fixed costs for variable costs in some aspect of the company's operations. For example, as labor wage rates increase over time, many firms seek to reduce operating costs through automation, which in effect represents the substitution of fixed-cost capital equipment for variable-cost labor. Suppose Allegan determines that it can reduce labor costs by $25 per unit by leasing $100,000 of additional equipment. Under these conditions, the firm's new level of total fixed costs TFC' would be $1,000,000 + $100,000 = $1,100,000. Variable costs VC' would be $150 − $25 = $125. Substituting P = $250 per unit, VC' = $125 per unit, and TFC' = $1,100,000 into Equation 9.10 yields a new break-even output:

$$Q'_b = \frac{\$1,100,000}{\$250 - \$125}$$
$$= 8,800 \text{ units}$$

Counterintuitively, this increase in cost fixity of the operations reduces the break-even output. The reason is the more-than-offsetting reduction in variable cost, which substantially increases contribution margins.

Example

Fixed Costs and Production Capacity at General Motors[13]

In an industry with 17 million unit sales annually, GM admitted in March 2002 that it needed to reduce automobile production capacity by 1 million cars per year to match its current sales of 5 million cars. For only the second time in its 100-year history

(continued)

(1988 being the earlier event), the company had significantly shrunk its capacity. As part of its decision to reduce its size, GM planned to close 10 of its U.S. automobile assembly lines.

In the past, GM alternated between (1) building all the cars it could produce and then using costly clearance sales to attract buyers, and (2) reducing output by running plants below capacity through a slowdown in the pace of the assembly line or elimination of an entire shift. The new strategy called for the company to use 100 percent of its American automobile production capacity five days a week with two shifts per day. If automobile demand increased above this capacity level, third-shift operations would be used to boost production. Ford had been following this strategy for some time.

In effect, GM and Ford were trading off lower fixed costs over the entire business cycle against (the possibility of) having to incur higher variable costs (e.g., use of higher cost overtime and third-shift operations) during periods of strong demand. As a consequence, GM's break-even output point declined sharply.

[13]Jacob M. Schlesinger, "GM to Reduce Capacity to Match Its Sales," *Wall Street Journal* (April 25, 1988), p. 2; Lawrence Ingrassia and Joseph B. White, "GM Plans to Close 21 More Factories, Cut 74,000 Jobs, Slash Capital Spending," *Wall Street Journal* (December 19, 1991), p. A3; and "A Duo of Dunces," *The Economist* (March 9, 2002), p. 63.

Some Limitations of Break-Even Analysis

Break-even analysis has a number of limitations that arise from the *assumptions* made in constructing the model and developing the relevant data.

Multiple Products   The break-even model assumes that a firm is producing and selling either a *single* product or a *constant mix* of different products. In many cases the product mix changes over time, and problems can arise in allocating fixed costs among the various products.

Uncertainty   Still another assumption of break-even analysis is that the selling price and variable cost per unit, as well as fixed costs, are known at each level of output. In practice, these parameters are subject to uncertainty. Thus, the usefulness of the results of break-even analysis depends on the accuracy of the estimates of the future selling price and variable cost.

Inconsistency of Planning Horizon   Finally, break-even analysis is normally performed for a planning period of one year or less; however, the benefits received from some costs may not be realized until subsequent periods. For example, research and development costs incurred during a specific period may not result in new products for several years. For break-even analysis to be a dependable decision-making tool, a firm's operating costs must be matched with resulting revenues for the planning period under consideration.

Doing a Break-Even versus a Contribution Analysis

A break-even analysis assumes that all types of costs except the narrowly defined incremental variable cost (VC) of additional unit sales are avoidable and asks the question of whether sufficient unit sales are available at the contribution margin ($P - VC$) to cover all these relevant costs. If so, they allow the firm to earn a net profit. These questions normally arise at entry and exit decision points where a firm can avoid essentially all its fixed costs if the firm decides to stay out or get out of a business. Contribution analysis, in contrast, applies to questions such as whether to adopt an advertising campaign, introduce a new product, shut down a plant temporarily, or close a division. What distinguishes these contribution analysis questions is that many fixed costs remain unavoidable and are therefore irrelevant to the decision (indirect fixed costs), while other fixed costs will be newly committed as a result of the decision (direct fixed costs) and therefore could be avoided by refusing to go ahead with the proposal.

More generally, contribution analysis always asks whether enough additional revenue arises from the ad campaign, the new product, or the projected sales of the plant or division to cover the direct fixed plus variable costs. That is, **contribution analysis** calculates whether sufficient gross operating profits result from the incremental sales (ΔQ) attributable to the ad, the new product, or the promotion to offset the proposed increase in fixed cost. In other words, are the total contributions to cover fixed cost increased by an amount greater than the increase in direct fixed cost avoidable by the decision?

contribution analysis A comparison of margins earned to the direct fixed costs attributable to a decision.

$$
\begin{aligned}
(P - VC)\,\Delta Q &> \Delta \text{ Total Fixed Cost} \\
&> \Delta \text{ Total Indirect Fixed Cost} + \Delta \text{ Total Direct Fixed Cost} \qquad [9.11] \\
&> 0 + \Delta \text{ Total Direct Fixed Cost}
\end{aligned}
$$

An illustration would be to use contribution analysis to approve or reject a new trade promotion. Suppose a $1 million payment to the retail partner elicits a better shelf location for Allegan's product. If marketing research estimates that the effect of this trade promotion is additional sales of 9,000 units, which is less than required to keep total contributions unchanged, the change in contributions from the additional sales will fall below the $1 million increase in direct fixed cost. Applying Equation 9.11,

$$(\$250 - \$150) \times 9{,}000 < \$1{,}000{,}000.$$

Therefore, this trade promotion plan should be rejected.

Such decisions are not break-even decisions because they ignore (abstract from) the indirect fixed costs that, by definition, cannot be avoided by rejecting the ad campaign or new product introduction proposal or by closing the plant temporarily. For example, headquarters facility cost and other corporate overhead are indirect fixed costs that cannot be avoided by any of these decisions. So, corporate overhead is not a relevant cost in making these decisions and is therefore ignored in the contribution analysis done to support making such decisions.

In contrast, corporate overhead is prominent in the preceding examples of break-even analysis done to decide how or whether to enter a new business in the first place. Business certification, licensing, or franchise fees would be a good example of this concept of corporate overhead. The case exercise on charter airline operating decisions at the end of this chapter illustrates the use of contribution analysis as distinguished from break-even analysis.

Example

Taco Bell Chihuahua Drives Sales

Consider the Taco Bell ad campaign with the cute little dog that was designed to pulse twenty-five 15-second spot commercials over several weeks. The ad agency quoted a cost of $750,000 per spot to secure prime-time network television reaching 176 million households. To decide whether to buy this ad campaign, Taco Bell needed to know just two things: (1) the incremental sales that demand analysis suggests will be stimulated by this campaign and (2) the contribution margin in dollars. Suppose the incremental sales are estimated at 2,100 Taco Bell meals per day for 90 days across 48 states, totaling 9,072,000 meals. If $7.99 is the average price per realized unit sale and

(continued)

variable costs are $5.00, should Taco Bell go ahead with the ad? The answer is yes, because when we apply Equation 9.11,

$$(\$7.99 - \$5.00)9{,}072{,}200 > 0 + (25 \times \$750{,}000)$$
$$\$27{,}125{,}280 > \$18{,}750{,}000$$

We see that Taco Bell would increase its operating profit by $8.4 million and make further contributions toward covering fixed cost and profit if it authorized the proposed ad campaign.

A Limitation of Contribution Analysis

Stepwise Operating Costs   Some fixed costs increase in a stepwise manner as output is increased; they are *semivariable*. For example, unscheduled maintenance is needed on aircraft engines after 10 hours of use. These direct fixed costs must be considered avoidable and therefore relevant if a batch production decision entails that much use. Otherwise, like other direct fixed costs these unscheduled maintenace expenses are not incurred (and therefore are avoidable) until the triggering output level is reached.

Operating Leverage

operating leverage The use of assets having fixed costs in an effort to increase expected returns.

Operating leverage involves the use of more fixed-cost assets in exchange for lower variable cost and higher margins. A firm uses operating leverage in the hope of earning higher returns for owners. A firm's **degree of operating leverage (DOL)** is defined as the *percentage change* in earnings before interest and taxes (EBIT) resulting from a given *percentage change* in sales (output):

$$\text{DOL at } Q = \frac{\text{Percentage change in EBIT}}{\text{Percentage change in Sales}}$$

This relationship can be rewritten as follows:

degree of operating leverage (DOL) The percentage change in a firm's earnings before interest and taxes (EBIT) resulting from a given percentage change in sales or output.

$$\text{DOL at } Q = \frac{\dfrac{\Delta \text{EBIT}}{\text{EBIT}}}{\dfrac{\Delta \text{Sales}}{\text{Sales}}} \qquad [9.12]$$

where ΔEBIT and ΔSales are the changes in the firm's EBIT and sales, respectively.

Because a firm's DOL differs at each sales level, it is necessary to indicate the sales point, Q, at which operating leverage is measured. The DOL is algebraically analogous to the elasticity of demand concept because it relates percentage changes in one variable (EBIT) to percentage changes in another variable (sales). Rewriting Equation 9.12 to compute a firm's DOL more easily yields

$$\text{DOL at } Q = \frac{\text{Sales} - \text{Variable costs}}{\text{EBIT}} \qquad [9.13]$$

Replacing sales with $(P \times Q)$, variable cost with $VC \times Q$, and EBIT with $(P \times Q)$ less total (operating) cost, or $(P \times Q) - TFC - (VC \times Q)$, these values can be substituted into Equation 9.13 to obtain the following:

$$\text{DOL at } Q = \frac{(P \times Q) - (VC \times Q)}{(P \times Q) - TFC - (VC \times Q)}$$

or

$$\text{DOL at } Q = \frac{(P - VC)Q}{(P - VC)Q - TFC}$$ [9.14]

Example

Operating Leverage: Allegan Manufacturing Company (continued)

In the earlier discussion of break-even analysis for the Allegan Manufacturing Company, the parameters of the break-even model were determined as $P = \$250$/unit, $VC = \$150$/unit, and $TFC = \$1,000,000$. Substituting these values into Equation 9.14 along with the respective output (Q) values yields the DOL values shown in Table 9.1. For example, a DOL of 6.00 at an output level of 12,000 units indicates that from a base output level of 12,000 units EBIT will increase by 6.00 percent for each 1 percent increase in output.

Note that Allegan's DOL is largest (in absolute value terms) when the firm is operating near the break-even point (where $Q = Q_b = 10,000$ units). Note also that the firm's DOL is negative below the break-even output level. A negative DOL indicates the percentage *reduction* in operating *losses* that occurs as the result of a 1 percent *increase* in output. For example, the DOL of −1.50 at an output level of 6,000 units indicates that from a base output level of 6,000 units the firm's operating *losses* will be *reduced* by 1.5 percent for each 1 percent *increase* in output.

DOL is a reflection of the variance of the firm's operating profits through the business cycle. If the firm employs large amounts of equipment in its operations, it tends to have a relatively high proportion of fixed operating costs and a relatively low proportion of variable costs. Such a cost structure yields a high DOL, which results in large operating profits (positive EBIT) if sales are high and large operating losses (negative EBIT) if sales are depressed.

TABLE 9.1 DOL AT VARIOUS OUTPUT LEVELS FOR ALLEGAN MANUFACTURING COMPANY

OUTPUT Q	DEGREE OF OPERATING LEVERAGE (DOL)
0	0
2,000	−0.25
4,000	−0.67
6,000	−1.50
8,000	−4.00
10,000	(undefined) Break-even level
12,000	+6.00
14,000	+3.50
16,000	+2.67
18,000	+2.25
20,000	+2.00

Inherent Business Risk

Inherent business risk refers to the inherent variability of a firm's EBIT. It is a function of several factors, one of which is the firm's DOL. The DOL is a measure of how sensitive a firm's EBIT is to changes in sales. The greater a firm's DOL, the larger the change in EBIT will be for a given change in sales. Thus, *all other things being equal*, the higher a firm's DOL, the greater the inherent degree of business risk.

Other factors can also affect a firm's inherent business risk, including the variability or uncertainty of sales. A firm with high fixed costs and stable sales will have a high DOL, but it will also have stable EBIT and, therefore, low business risk. Public utilities and pipeline transportation companies are examples of firms having these operating characteristics. In contrast, a firm with unstable sales such as the fad toy maker Hasbro will in the presence of high fixed costs have high inherent business risk.

Another factor that may affect a firm's business risk is uncertainty concerning selling prices and variable costs. A firm having a low DOL can still have high inherent business risk if selling prices and variable costs are subject to considerable variability over time. A cattle feedlot illustrates these characteristics of low DOL but high business risk because both grain costs and the selling price of beef at times fluctuate wildly.

In summary, a firm's DOL is only one of several factors that determine the firm's inherent business risk.

Inherent business risk The inherent variability or uncertainty of a firm's operating earnings (earnings before interest and taxes).

SUMMARY

- In estimating the behavior of short-run and long-run cost functions for firms, the primary methodological problems are (1) differences in the manner in which economists and accountants define and measure costs and (2) accounting for other variables (in addition to the output level) that influence costs.

- Many statistical studies of *short-run* cost-output relationships suggest that total costs increase linearly (or quadratically) with output, implying constant (or rising) marginal costs over the observed ranges of output.

- Many statistical studies of *long-run* cost-output relationships indicate that long-run cost functions are L-shaped. Economies of scale (declining ATC) occur at low levels of output. Thereafter, long-run ATCs remain relatively constant over large ranges of output. Diseconomies of scale are observed in only a few cases, probably because few firms can survive with costs attributable to excessive scale.

- *Engineering cost techniques* are an alternative approach to statistical methods in estimating long-run cost functions. With this approach, knowledge of production facilities and technology is used to determine the least-cost combination of labor, capital equipment, and raw materials required to produce various levels of output.

- The *survivor technique* is a method of determining the optimum size of firms within an industry by classifying them by size and then calculating the share of industry output coming from each size class over time. Size classes whose share of industry output is increasing over time are considered to be more efficient and to have lower ATC.

- *Break-even analysis* is used to examine the relationship among a firm's revenues, costs, and operating profits (EBIT) at various output levels. Frequently the analyst constructs a break-even chart based on linear cost-output and revenue-output relationships to determine the operating characteristics of a firm over a limited output range.

- The *break-even point* is defined as the output level at which total revenues equal total costs of operations. In the linear break-even model, the break-even point is found by dividing total fixed costs by the difference between price and variable cost per unit, the *contribution margin*.

- *Contribution analysis* is used to examine operating profitability when some fixed costs (indirect fixed costs) cannot be avoided and other direct fixed costs can be avoided by a decision. Decisions on advertising, new product introduction, shutdown, and downsizing are made by doing a contribution analysis.

■ *Operating leverage* occurs when a firm uses assets having fixed operating costs. The DOL measures the percentage change in a firm's EBIT resulting from a 1 percent change in sales (or units of output). As a firm's fixed operating costs rise, its DOL increases.

■ *Inherent business risk* refers to the variability of a firm's EBIT. It is a function of several factors, including the firm's DOL and the variability of sales. All other things being equal, the higher a firm's DOL, the greater is its inherent business risk.

Exercises

Answers to the exercises in blue can be found in Appendix D at the back of the book.

1. A study of 86 savings and loan associations in six northwestern states yielded the following cost function

$$C = \underset{(2.84)}{2.38} - \underset{(2.37)}{0.006153Q} + \underset{(2.63)}{0.000005359Q^2} + \underset{(2.69)}{19.2X_1}$$

where C = average operating expense ratio, expressed as a percentage and defined as total operating expense ($million) divided by total assets ($million) times 100 percent.

Q = output; measured by total assets ($million)

X_1 = ratio of the number of branches to total assets ($million)

Note: The number in parentheses below each coefficient is its respective t-statistic.
   a. Which variable(s) is (are) statistically significant in explaining variations in the average operating expense ratio?
   b. What type of cost-output relationship (e.g., linear, quadratic, or cubic) is suggested by these statistical results?
   c. Based on these results, what can we conclude about the existence of economies or diseconomies of scale in savings and loan associations in the Northwest?

2. Referring to Exercise 1 again:
   a. Holding constant the effects of bank branching (X_1), determine the level of total assets that minimizes the average operating expense ratio.
   b. Determine the average operating expense ratio for a savings and loan association with the level of total assets determined in Part (a) and 1 branch. Solve the same question for 10 branches.

3. A study of the costs of electricity generation for a sample of 56 British firms in 1946–1947 yielded the following long-run cost function:[14]

$$AVC = 1.24 + 0.0033Q + 0.0000029Q^2 - 0.000046QZ - 0.026Z + 0.00018Z^2$$

where AVC = average variable cost (i.e., working costs of generation), measured in pence per kilowatt-hour (kWh). (A pence was a British monetary unit equal, at that time, to 2 cents U.S.)

Q = output; measured in millions of kWh per year
Z = plant size; measured in thousands of kilowatts

   a. Determine the long-run average variable cost function for electricity generation.
   b. Determine the long-run marginal cost function for electricity generation.

---

[14]Johnston, *Statistical Cost Analysis*, Chapter 4, *op. cit.*

    c. Holding plant size constant at 150,000 kilowatts, determine the short-run average variable cost and marginal cost functions for electricity generation.

    d. For a plant size equal to 150,000 kilowatts, determine the output level that minimizes short-run average variable costs.

    e. Determine the short-run average variable cost and marginal cost at the output level obtained in part (d).

4. Assuming that all other factors remain unchanged, determine how a firm's break-even point is affected by each of the following:

    a. The firm finds it necessary to reduce the price per unit because of increased foreign competition.

    b. The firm's direct labor costs are increased as the result of a new labor contract.

    c. The Occupational Safety and Health Administration (OSHA) requires the firm to install new ventilating equipment in its plant. (Assume that this action has no effect on worker productivity.)

5. McKee Corporation has annual fixed costs of $12 million. Its variable cost ratio is 0.60.

    a. Determine the company's break-even dollar sales volume.

    b. Determine the dollar sales volume required to earn a target profit of $3 million.

Case Exercises

Cost Functions

The following cost-output data were obtained as part of a study of the economies of scale in operating a charter high school in Wisconsin:[15]

STUDENTS IN AVERAGE DAILY ATTENDANCE	MIDPOINT OF VALUES IN COLUMN A	OPERATING EXPENDITURE PER STUDENT	NUMBER OF SCHOOLS IN SAMPLE
(A)	(B)	(C)	(D)
143–200	171	$531.9	6
201–300	250	480.8	12
301–400	350	446.3	19
401–500	450	426.9	17
501–600	550	442.6	14
601–700	650	413.1	13
701–900	800	374.3	9
901–1,100	1,000	433.2	6
1,101–1,600	1,350	407.3	6
1,601–2,400	2,000	405.6	7

Questions

1. Plot the data in columns B and C in an output (enrollment) cost graph and sketch a smooth curve that would appear to provide a good fit to the data.

---

[15]John Riew, "Economies of Scale in High School Operation," *Review of Economics and Statistics* 48, no. 3 (August 1966), pp. 280–287.

2. Based on the scatter diagram in Question 1, what kind of mathematical relationship would appear to exist between enrollment and operating expenditures per student? In other words, do operating expenditures per student appear to (1) be constant (and independent of enrollment), (2) follow a linear relationship as enrollment increases, or (3) follow some sort of nonlinear U-shaped (possibly quadratic) relationship as enrollment increases?

As part of this study, the following cost function was developed:

$$C = f(Q, X_1, X_2, X_3, X_4, X_5)$$

where C = operating expenditures per student in average daily attendance (measured in dollars)

Q = enrollment (number of students in average daily attendance)

X_1 = average teacher salary

X_2 = number of credit units ("courses") offered

X_3 = average number of courses taught per teacher

X_4 = change in enrollment between 1957 and 1960

X_5 = percentage of classrooms built after 1950

Variables X_1, X_2, and X_3 were considered measures of teacher qualifications, breadth of curriculum, and the degree of specialization in instruction, respectively. Variable X_4 measured changes in demand for school services that could cause some lagging adjustments in cost. Variable X_5 was used to reflect any differentials in the costs of maintenance and operation due to the varying ages of school properties. Statistical data on 109 selected high schools yielded the following regression equation:

$$C = 10.31 - 0.402Q + 0.00012Q^2 + 0.107X_1 + 0.985X_2 + 15.62X_3 + 0.613X_4 - 0.102X_5$$
$$\quad\quad (6.4)^* \quad\quad (5.2)^* \quad\quad (8.2)^* \quad\quad (0.15) \quad\quad (1.3) \quad\quad (3.2)^* \quad\quad (0.93)$$
$$r^2 = .557$$

Notes: The numbers in parentheses are the t-scores of each of the respective (b) coefficients. An asterisk (*) indicates that the result is statistically significant at the 0.01 level.

3. What type of cost-output relationship (linear, quadratic, cubic) is suggested by these statistical results?

4. What variables (other than enrollment) would appear to be most important in explaining variations in operating expenditures per student?

5. Holding constant the effects of the other variables (X_1 through X_5), determine the enrollment level (Q) at which average operating expenditures per student are minimized. (*Hint:* Find the value of Q that minimizes the ($\partial C/\partial Q$ function.)

6. Again, holding constant the effects of the other variables, use the $\partial C/\partial Q$ function to determine, for a school with 500 students, the reduction in per-student operating expenditures that will occur as the result of adding one more student.

7. Again, holding the other variables constant, what would be the saving in per-student operating expenditures of an increase in enrollment from 500 to 1,000?

8. Based on the results of this study, what can we conclude about the existence of scale and scope economies or diseconomies in operating a public high school?

Charter Airline Operating Decisions

Firm-specific demand in the *scheduled airline industry* is segmented by customer class and is highly uncertain so that an order may not lead to realized revenue and a unit sale. Airlines respond to this dynamic, highly competitive environment by tracking reservations at preannounced fares and reassigning capacity to the various market segments ("buckets") as business travelers, vacationers, and convention groups book the flights above or below expected levels several days and even weeks before scheduled departure. This systems management process combining marketing, operations, and finance is referred to as revenue management or yield management and is discussed in Chapter 14.

The *charter airline business*, on the other hand, is much less complicated because capacity requirements are known far in advance, and all confirmed orders lead to realized revenue. We consider the following three decisions for a charter airline: (1) the entry/exit break-even decision, (2) the operate/shut down decision to fly/not fly a charter that has been proposed, and (3) the output decision as to how many incremental seats to sell if the airline decides to operate the charter flight.

Suppose the following costs for a 10-hour round-trip flight apply to the time frame and expenses of an unscheduled 5-hour charter flight from Baltimore to Las Vegas (and return the next day) on a seven-year-old Boeing 737-800 with 120 occupied seats.[16] Some costs listed in the table have been aggregated up to the flight level from a seat-level decision where they are incurred. Others have been allocated down to the flight level from an entry/exit or maintain-ownership company-level decision. Still other costs vary with the go/no go flight-level decision itself. Your job is to analyze each cost item and figure out the "behavior of cost"—that is, with which decision each cost varies.

Fuel and landing fees	$5,200
Quarterly airframe maintenance re: FAA certificate	1,000
Unscheduled engine maintenance per 10 flight hours	1,200
Pro rata time depreciation for seventh year of airframe	7,200
Flight pay for pilots per round-trip flight	4,200
Long-term hangar facility lease	6,600
Annual aircraft engine operating lease	7,100
Base salaries of headquarters personnel	2,000
Food service with seat-by-seat purchase and JIT delivery at each departure	2,400
Airport ground crew baggage handling for two flight arrivals	450

Questions

1. What are the variable costs for the decision to send one more person aboard a charter flight that is already 80 percent booked?
2. In making an entry/exit decision, if competitive pressure is projected to force the price down to $300, what is the break-even unit sales volume this company should have projected as part of its business plan before entering this market and should reconsider each time it considers leaving (exiting) this business altogether?
3. Identify the indirect fixed costs of the charter service for a particular one of many such charters this month.
4. If one were trying to decide whether to operate (fly) or not fly an unscheduled round-trip charter flight, what would be the total direct fixed costs and variable costs of the flight?

---

[16]The aerodynamics of the plane and its fuel efficiency do change as the number of seats occupied falls below 180, but you may ignore this effect.

5. Charter contracts are negotiable, and charter carriers receive many contract offers that do not promise $300 prices or 80-percent-full planes. Should the airline accept a charter flight proposal from a group that offers to guarantee the sale of 90 seats at $250? Why or why not?

6. What are the total contributions of the charter flight with 90 seats at $250 per seat?

7. What are the net income losses for this two-day period if the airline refuses the 90-seat charter, stays in business, but temporarily shuts down? What are the net income losses if it decides to operate and fly the charter that has been proposed?

8. What is the segment-level contribution of a separate group that is willing to join the 90-seat-at-$250-per-seat charter on the same plane and same departure but only wishes to pay $50 per seat for 10 seats?

9. Should you accept their offer? What problems do you anticipate if both charter groups are placed on the 737?

PART IV

Pricing and Output Decisions: Strategy and Tactics

I n the previous chapters, we developed the theories and modeling techniques useful in analyzing demand, production, and cost relationships in a firm. In this part of the book, we consider profit-maximizing price-output decisions, especially as they relate to the firm's strategic choices in competitive markets (Chapter 10). Asymmetric information conditions in a so-called lemons market as well as ideal full information exchanges are discussed. Chapters 11 and 12 consider price and output determination in dominant-firm monopoly and oligopoly markets. Chapter 13 presents a game-theory framework for analyzing rival response tactics.

The final chapter in Part IV, Chapter 14, examines value-based differential pricing in theory and practice, and Appendix 14A presents the concepts of revenue management. Web Appendix E addresses specialized pricing problems including pricing for the multiproduct firm, pricing of joint products, and transfer pricing.

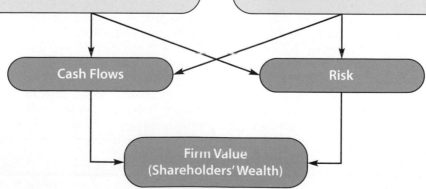

ECONOMIC ANALYSIS AND DECISIONS

1. Demand Analysis and Forecasting
2. Production and Cost Analysis
3. Pricing Analysis
4. Capital Expenditure Analysis

ECONOMIC, POLITICAL, AND SOCIAL ENVIRONMENT

1. Business Conditions (Trends, Cycles, and Seasonal Effects)
2. Factor Market Conditions (Capital, Labor, Land, and Raw Materials)
3. Competitors' Responses
4. External, Legal, and Regulatory Constraints
5. Organizational (Internal) Constraints

Cash Flows

Risk

Firm Value (Shareholders' Wealth)

© Cengage Learning

CHAPTER 10

Prices, Output, and Strategy: Pure and Monopolistic Competition

CHAPTER PREVIEW

Stockholder wealth-maximizing managers seek a pricing and output strategy that will maximize the present value of the future profit stream to the firm. The determination of the wealth-maximizing strategy depends on the production capacity, cost levels, demand characteristics, and the potential for immediate and longer-term competition. In this chapter, we provide an introduction to competitive strategic analysis and discuss Michael Porter's Five Forces strategic framework. Thereafter, we distinguish pure competition with detailed analyses of the home contractor industry from monopolistic competition with detailed analyses of advertising expenditures in ready-to-eat (RTE) cereals. With asymmetrically informed sellers, the rational hesitation of buyers to pay full price and the resulting problem of adverse selection in a "lemons market" are also discussed.

MANAGERIAL CHALLENGE

Resurrecting Apple in the Tablet World[1]

Apple Computer revolutionized personal computing by adapting Xerox's point and click graphical user interface (GUI) into its 1983 Macintosh 3. The GUI was quickly reverse engineered and imitated by Microsoft, whose point and click Windows operating system (OS) captured a 90 percent plus market share by 1997. IBM and then Compaq, Dell, and Hewlett-Packard (HP) personal computers (PCs) equipped with Windows and Intel computer chips then dominated the PC business for more than 15 years (1997–2012).

But recently, PC sales declined by 8.6 percent. Personal computing is now taking place on the fly. Not just telecommunications and web searches, but document preparation and spreadsheet analysis are increasingly occurring in an on-demand mobile environment wherever the user finds herself. In addition, touchscreen tiles are replacing mice and keypads. Microsoft's Windows 8 release in November 2012 confirms this paradigm shift. Tablet-based mobile computing has displaced the desk-top computer and laptop. Apple recently sold its 100 millionth 8-inch screen, 11-ounce, 16–64 gigabyte memory, dual camera–laden tablet.

Today, the assembly of personal computers and tablets is outsourced to a wide variety of supply chain partners operating at massive scale worldwide. With fewer outsourced components, more product features, and extensive R&D costs, Apple's PCs sell for $1,100 and up, whereas HP, Dell, and Toshiba's PCs are priced as low as $600. In tablets, Amazon's Kindle Fire and Google's Nexus 7 both at $199 to $249, and Microsoft's Surface sell well against Apple's newest $499 basic iPad and new iPad Mini at $329 to $659. Like the PC market before it, the tablet market has quickly become very competitive. Apple initially sold primarily through retail outlets like Computer Tree, but to target the consumer sector, Apple has launched dozens of company-owned Apple stores. Apple's closed (proprietary, unlicensable) OS (operating system) architecture sacrificed network effects. In contrast, Google's Android telecom

MANAGERIAL CHALLENGE *Continued*

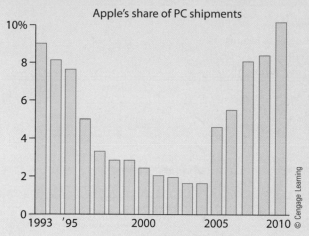

Apple's share of PC shipments

movies. Amazon places a distant third in digital movie sales at 8.5 percent. Microsoft's Surface tablet is projected to garner 20 percent market share by 2016.

system and Microsoft's huge installed base attracted third-party independent software vendors who wrote numerous applications programs. Without compatibility to this Wintel-installed base, Apple's offering stagnated.

Apple PCs retained market leadership only in the education, graphic design, and publishing sectors. Because 55 percent of all PC and OS sales are in corporations, 33 percent are in the home, 7 percent are in government, and only 5 percent are in education, Apple's market share of U.S. PC sales slipped badly from 10 to 3 percent in the late 1990s. In 1999, Steve Jobs oversaw Apple's effort to reinvent itself by introducing the futuristic iMac and the iPod digital music player, merging that technology with the Apple iPad and later the Apple iPhone.

This time, Apple was ready with layer upon layer of enhanced capabilities for each new generation of its resurgent products.[2] The competitive advantages of the iPod and iPad tablet are process-based, rather than product-based. They rely upon cumulative capabilities with its iTunes Music Store, its partnerships with Disney Inc., Paramount, and various record labels. Almost overnight, Apple garnered a 73 percent share of the $9 billion digital music industry and a 56 percent share of digital movie sales. Walmart, the largest seller of DVDs, has achieved a 26 percent market share in head-to-head competition with Apple for digital movies using its Vudu Web site for downloading music and

Discussion Questions

■ In the thrid quarter of 2012 Apple tablet sales of iPads equal to $7.5 billion exceeded Apple personal computer sales of $6.6 billion. Has your use for a PC waned to the point where you would consider owning just a tablet?

■ Have you visited an Apple Store? Did the in-store experience enhance your perceived value for an Apple product?

■ What prices to charge for iMacs, iPods, and iPads remains a central issue for Apple management. On what basis would you justify paying a price premium for an Apple iMac? What about an Apple iPad?

[1]Based on *Apple Inc.*, 2008, Harvard Business School Case Publishing; "Wal-Mart Stores Tries to Play Apple's Game," *Wall Street Journal* (March 19, 2012), p. C8; "iPhone Shines but iPad Dimms," *Wall Street Journal* (October 26, 2012), p. B1; "Tablets on High," *The Economist* (October 27, 2012), p. 63; and "Apple Drops an iPad Mini on Rivals," *Wall Street Journal* (October 24, 2012), p. B1.

[2]In smart phones, Apple has adopted licensable open software architecture to attract apps vendors. It was estimated in 2012 that the iPhone5 incorporated over a quarter million apps, few of which Apple itself had to pay to develop. With 2012 (3Q) sales of $17.1 billion, the iPhone emerged as Apple's most popular product ever.

INTRODUCTION

To remain competitive, many companies today commit themselves to continuous improvement processes and episodes of strategic planning. Competitive strategic analysis provides a framework for thinking proactively about threats to a firm's business model,

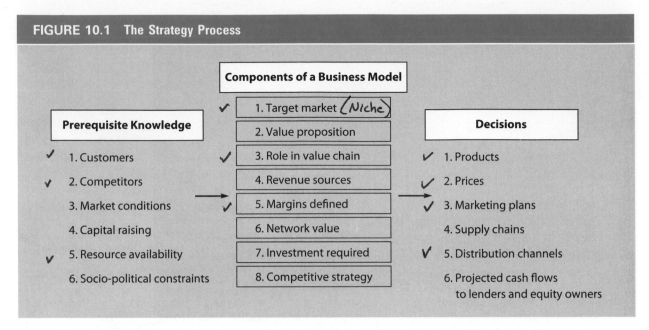

FIGURE 10.1 The Strategy Process

Components of a Business Model

Prerequisite Knowledge	Components of a Business Model	Decisions
1. Customers	✓ 1. Target market *(Niche)*	✓ 1. Products
2. Competitors	2. Value proposition	2. Prices
3. Market conditions	✓ 3. Role in value chain	✓ 3. Marketing plans
4. Capital raising	4. Revenue sources	4. Supply chains
5. Resource availability	✓ 5. Margins defined	✓ 5. Distribution channels
6. Socio-political constraints	6. Network value	6. Projected cash flows to lenders and equity owners
	7. Investment required	
	8. Competitive strategy	

Source: Adapted from H. Chesbrough, *Open Innovation* (Cambridge, MA: Harvard University Press, 2003). Reprinted by permission.

core competencies
Technology-based expertise or knowledge on which a company can focus its strategy.

about new business opportunities, and about the future reconfigurations of the firm's resources, capabilities, and **core competencies**.

Figure 10.1 displays the components of a business model in the context of a firm's prerequisite knowledge and strategic decisions. All successful business models begin by identifying *target markets*—that is, what businesses one wants to enter and stay in. Physical assets, human resources, and intellectual property (like patents and licenses) sometimes limit the firm's capabilities, but business models are as unbounded as the ingenuity of entrepreneurial managers in finding ways to identify new opportunities. Next, all successful business models lay out a value proposition grounded in customer expectations of perceived value and then identify what part of the *value chain* leading to end products the firm plans to create. Business models always must clarify *how and when revenue will be realized* and analyze the sensitivity of *gross and net margins* to various possible changes in the firm's cost structure. In specifying the *required investments*, business models also assess the potential for creating *value in network relationships* with complementary businesses and in joint ventures and alliances. Finally, all successful business models develop a *competitive strategy*.

COMPETITIVE STRATEGY

The essence of competitive strategy is threefold: resource-based capabilities, business processes, and adaptive innovation.[3] First, competitive strategy analyzes how the firm can secure differential access to key resources like patents or distribution channels. From humble beginnings as an Internet bookseller that contracted out its warehousing and book delivery service, Amazon managed to become the preferred fulfillment agent

[3]This section is based on H. Chesbrough, *Open Innovation* (Boston: Harvard Business School Press, 2003), pp. 73–83.

WHAT WENT RIGHT • WHAT WENT WRONG

Xerox[4]

Xerox invented the chemical paper copier and thereafter realized phenomenal 15 percent compound growth rates for almost two decades. When its initial patents expired, Xerox was ready with a plain paper copier that established a first-mover technology advantage, but ultimately the company failed to receive any broad patent extension. Xerox's target market was large corporations and government installations that valued high-quality, high-volume leased machines with an enormous variety of capabilities and full-service maintenance contracts, even though supplies and usage fees were expensive.

Unable to compete on product capabilities, Japanese competitors Canon and Ricoh realized that tremendous market potential lay in smaller businesses where affordability per copy was a major value proposition. Installation and service were outsourced to highly competitive independent dealer networks, and the smaller-volume Japanese copy machine itself was sold at very low initial cost, with self-service replacement cartridges being the principal source of profitability.

As with later events at Apple, Xerox insisted on closed architecture software and built all of its copier components in-house rather than pursuing partnerships that could reduce cost by realizing scale economies and thereby trigger a larger installed base of Xerox machines. Ricoh and Canon pursued just the opposite open architecture and partnership strategy to achieve network effects and drive down costs.

Both became $2 billion firms in a copier business that Xerox had totally dominated only 15 years earlier.

[4]Based on Chesbrough, op. cit.; and on C. Bartlett and S. Ghoshal, *Transnational Management* (Boston, MA: Irwin-McGraw-Hill, 1995), Case 4–1.

for web-based sales in general. That is, the bookseller Amazon acquired enough regular customers searching for CDs, office products, tools, and toys that companies like Toys "R" Us adopted Amazon as their channel partner. In Japan, 7-Eleven stores won that same role for neighborhood pick-up and delivery of web-based purchases. Second, competitive strategy designs business processes that are difficult to imitate and capable of creating unique value for the target customers. For example, the high-frequency point-to-point streamlined operations processes of Southwest Airlines prove very difficult for hub-and-spoke airlines to imitate, and, as a result, the market capitalization of Southwest often exceeds that of all the other major U.S. carriers combined.

Similarly, both Dell and Compaq at one point in their respective corporate histories, had $12 billion in net sales and approximately $1 billion in net income in 1998. But Compaq's business model required $6 billion in net operating assets (i.e., inventories plus net plant and equipment plus working capital) to earn $1 billion, while Dell's required only $2 billion. How could Dell produce the same net income with one-third as much plant and equipment, inventories, and working capital as Compaq? The answer is that Dell created a direct-to-the-customer sales process; Dell builds to order, with subassembly components bought just in time from outside contractors, and it realizes cash from a sale within 48 hours. These value-creating business processes generated 50 percent ($1B/$2B) return on investment (ROI) at Dell, whereas the comparable ROI at Compaq was just 16 percent ($1B/$6B).[5]

Finally, competitive strategy provides a road map for sustaining a firm's profitability, principally through innovation. Think of Polaroid to digital cameras, calculators to spreadsheets, and mobile radios to handheld smart phones: As such industries emerge, evolve, and morph into other product spaces, firms must anticipate these changes and plan how they will sustain their positioning in the industry, and ultimately migrate their business to new industries. IBM, the dominant mainframe leasing company in the 1970s, has reinvented itself

[5]Return on invested capital is defined as net income divided by net operating assets (i.e., net plant and equipment plus inventories plus net accounts receivable).

twice—first in the 1980s as a PC manufacturer, and a second time in the 1990s and 2000s as a systems solution provider for a "smarter planet." In contrast, some firms like Xerox or Kodak became entrenched in outdated competitive strategic positions.

Generic Types of Strategies[6]

industry analysis Assessment of the strengths and weaknesses of a set of competitors or line of businesses.

Strategic thinking initially focuses on **industry analysis**—that is, identifying industries in which it would be attractive to do business. Michael Porter's Five Forces model (discussed later) illustrates this approach. Soon thereafter, however, business strategists want to conduct *competitor analysis* to learn more about how firms can sustain their relative profitability in a *strategic group* of related firms. Efforts to answer these questions are often described as *strategic positioning*. Finally, strategists try to isolate what *core competencies* any particular firm possesses as a result of its *resource-based capabilities* in order to identify **sustainable competitive advantages** vis-à-vis their competitors in a relevant market.

sustainable competitive advantages Difficult-to-imitate features of a company's processes or products.

Product Differentiation Strategy

product differentiation strategy A business-level strategy that relies upon differences in products or processes affecting perceived customer value.

Any one of three generic types of strategies may suffice. A firm may establish a product differentiation strategy, a lowest-delivered-cost strategy, or an information technology (IT) strategy. **Product differentiation strategy** usually involves competing on capabilities, brand names, or product endorsements. Boeing competes on product capabilities. Coca-Cola is by far the world's most widely recognized brand. Gillette, P&G's Pampers, Nestlé, Nescafé, and Kellogg's each has nearly 50 percent market shares. All of these branded products command a price premium worldwide simply because of the product image and lifestyle associated with their successful branding.

Example

Rawlings Sporting Goods Waves Off the Swoosh Sign[7]

Even though $200 million Rawlings competes against heavily branded Nike with annual sales of $14 billion, Rawlings baseball gloves are extremely profitable. The key is that the gloves receive product endorsements by more than 50 percent of major leaguers, such as the California Angles' Pujols and Yankees shortstop Derek Jeter. These superstars receive $20,000 for licensing their autographs to Rawlings for engraving on Little League gloves. But players can talk about a feature of Rawlings' equipment that keeps them coming back year after year. Rawlings is very attentive to this feedback and will lengthen the webbing or stiffen the fingers on a new model in just a few weeks to please its celebrity endorsers. Quick adaptation to the vagaries of the consumer marketplace is a requisite part of any product differentiation strategy.

[7]Based on "I've Got It," *Wall Street Journal* (April 1, 2002), p. A1.

Cost-Based Strategy

cost-based strategy A business-level strategy that relies upon low-cost operations, marketing, or distribution.

Competitive scope decisions are especially pivotal for **cost-based strategy**. For example, a firm like Southwest Airlines with a *focused cost strategy* must limit its business plan to focus narrowly on point-to-point, medium-distance, nonstop routes.

[6]This section is based in part on C. De Kluyver and J. Pearce, *Strategy: A View from the Top* (Upper Saddle River, NJ: Prentice-Hall, 2003).

Think Small to Grow Big: Southwest Airlines

Southwest adopted operations processes for ticket sales, boarding procedures, plane turnarounds, crew scheduling, flight frequency, maintenance, and jet fuel hedging that deliver exceptionally reduced operating costs to target customers in a price-sensitive market niche. Anything that works against this cost-based strategy must be jettisoned from the business plan. Southwest has clearly accomplished its goal. As air travel plummeted in the months following the September 11, 2001, attacks on the World Trade Center, only Southwest had a break-even volume that was low enough to continue to make money. Southwest can cover all of its costs at 64 percent load factors (unit sales/seat capacity), whereas American Airlines, United, Delta, and US Airways often operate well below their break-even points of 75 to 84 percent.

Much has been made of the fact that Southwest has labor costs covered by 36 percent of sales dollars, while United, American, and US Airways have labor costs covered by 48 percent of sales dollars. But the $0.07 gap between United's $0.12 cost per revenue passenger mile (rpm) and Jet Blue's $0.05 and Southwest's $0.07 cost per rpm reflects not just labor costs but hard-to-imitate process differences. Booz, Allen, Hamilton found that only 15 percent of the operating cost difference between full-service and low-cost carriers was labor cost. But the largest source of cost difference between Southwest's $0.07 cost per revenue passenger mile and United's $0.12 is process differences in check-in, boarding, reservations, crew scheduling, and maintenance. These processes make possible the famed 15-minute turnaround time at Southwest.

In contrast, Dell Computers' *cost leadership strategy* allows it to address a wide scope of PC product lines at prices that make its competitors wish to exit the market, as IBM did in 1999. Gateway was also unable to keep pace with Dell's cost-cutting and by 2006 found itself at 5.3 percent market share versus a 10.6 percent peak in 1999. Shortly thereafter Gateway sold off its PC business.

Information Technology Strategy

information technology strategy A business-level strategy that relies on IT capabilities.

Finally, firms can seek their sustainable competitive advantage among relevant market rivals by pursuing an **information technology strategy**. In addition to assisting in the recovery of stolen vehicles, satellite-based GPS has allowed Allstate Insurance to confirm that certain cars on a family policy are not being driven to work, while other less expensive cars are being exposed to the driving hazards of commuting. This allows Allstate to cut some insurance rates and win more business from their competitors. The e-commerce strategy of Southland Corporation's 7-Eleven convenience stores in 6,000 locations across Japan provides another good example.

In conclusion, a company's strategy can result in higher profits if the company configures its resource-based capabilities, business processes, and adaptive innovations in such a way as to obtain a sustainable competitive advantage. Whether cost-based strategy, product differentiation strategy, or IT strategy provides the most effective route to competitive advantage depends in large part on the firm's strategic focus. IT-based strategy is especially conducive to broad target market initiatives. In addition to using IT for merchandizing lunch items, 7-Eleven Japan "drives" customer traffic to its convenience stores by allowing Internet buyers to pick up their web purchases and pay at the 7-Eleven counter. Is 7-Eleven Japan a convenience store, an Internet fulfillment agent like Amazon, or a warehouse and distribution company? In some sense, 7-Eleven Japan is all of these. Unlike Southwest Airlines' cost-focused strategy, 7-Eleven Japan has a much broader IT-based strategy that conveys a competitive advantage across several relevant markets.

Example

The E-Commerce of Lunch at 7-Elevens in Japan[8]

Japanese office workers put in very long hours, often arriving at 8:00 A.M. and staying well into the evening. In the midst of this long day, most take an hour and a quarter break to go out on the street and pick up lunch. Boxed lunches, rice balls, and sandwiches are the routine offerings, but the fashion-conscious Japanese want to be seen eating what's "in." This situation makes an excellent opportunity for Southland Corporation's 7-Eleven stores, which is the biggest retailer in Japan and twice as profitable as the country's second-largest retailer, the clothing outlet Fast Retailing.

7-Eleven Japan collects sales information by proprietary satellite communication networks from its 8,500 locations three times a day. The data are used to improve product packaging and shelf placements with laboratory-like experiments in matched-pair stores throughout the country. But there is more, much more. 7-Eleven Japan has built systems to analyze the entire data inflow in just 20 minutes. Specifically, 7-Eleven forecasts what to prepare for the lunch crowd downtown today based on what sells this morning and what sold yesterday evening in suburban locations. As customers become more fickle, product fashion cycles in sandwiches are shortening from seven weeks to, in some cases, as little time as 10 days. 7-Eleven Japan forecasts the demand daily on an item-by-item, store-by-store basis.

Of course, such short-term demand forecasting would be useless if food preparation were a production-to-stock process with many weeks of lead time required. Instead, supply chain management practices are closely monitored and adapted continuously with electronic commerce tools. Delivery trucks carry bar code readers that upload instantaneously to headquarters databases. Orders for a particular sandwich at a particular store are placed before 10:00 A.M., processed through the supply chain to all component input companies in less than 7 minutes, and delivered by 4:00 P.M. for the next day's sales. Most customers praise the extraordinary freshness, quality ingredients, and minimal incidence of out-of-stock items. All this competitive advantage over rival grocers and noodle shops has led to consistent price premiums for 7-Eleven's in-house brand.

[8]Based on "Over the Counter Commerce," *The Economist* (May 26, 2001), pp. 77–78.

Which of the three generic types of strategies (differentiation, cost savings, or IT) will be most effective for a particular company depends in part on a firm's choice of *competitive scope*—that is, on the number and type of product lines and market segments, the number of geographic locations, and the network of horizontally and vertically integrated businesses in which the company decides to invest. For example, the most profitable clothing retailer in the United States, The Gap, once undertook to expand its competitive scope by opening a new chain of retail clothing stores. Unfortunately, Old Navy's bargain-priced khakis, jeans, and sweaters immediately began cannibalizing sales at its mid-priced parent. Even fashion-conscious teens could see little reason to pay $16.50 for a Gap-emblazoned T-shirt when Old Navy's branding offered style and a nearly identical product for $12.50. The configuration of a firm's resource capabilities, its business opportunities relative to its rivals, and a detailed knowledge of its customers intertwine to determine the preferred competitive scope.

The Relevant Market Concept

relevant market A group of firms belonging to the same strategic group of competitors.

A **relevant market** *is a group of firms that interact with each other in a buyer-seller relationship*. Relevant markets often have both spatial and product characteristics. For example, the market for large, prime-rate commercial loans includes large banks and corporations from all areas of the United States, whereas the market for bagged cement is confined to a 250-mile radius around the plant.

concentrated market A relevant market with a majority of total sales occurring in the largest four firms.

The *market structure* within these relevant markets varies tremendously. The four largest producers of breakfast cereals control 86 percent of the total U.S. output—a **concentrated market**. In contrast, the market for brick and concrete block is **fragmented**, with the largest four firms accounting for only 8 percent of the total U.S. output. Recently, the share of the total U.S. output produced by the largest four firms in the women's hosiery industry has **consolidated**, growing from 32 to 58 percent. These differences in market structures and changes in market structure over time have important implications for the determination of price levels, price stability, and the likelihood of sustained profitability in these relevant markets.

fragmented A relevant market whose market shares are uniformly small.

consolidated A relevant market whose number of firms has declined through acquisition, merger, and buyouts.

PORTER'S FIVE FORCES STRATEGIC FRAMEWORK

Michael Porter[9] developed a conceptual framework for industry analysis, identifying the threats to profitability from five forces of competition in a relevant market. Figure 10.2 displays Porter's Five Forces: the threat of substitutes, the threat of entry, the power of buyers, the power of suppliers, and the intensity of rivalry. Today, a sixth force is often added—the threat of a disruptive technology—such as digital file sharing for the recorded music industry, streaming video on demand for the video rental industry, or digital photography for the film industry.

Example

What Went Right What Went Wrong at Fuji and Kodak?

Eastman Kodak of Rochester, New York, once dominated both the camera and the photographic film industries. Founded in 1888, Kodak had a 90 and 85 percent market shares in North American film and disposable camera sales as late as 1976. Similarly, Fuji Film dominated the film and disposable camera markets in Japan. But digital photography and camera-laden smart phones changed all that. Both firms saw their primary products rendered obsolete by the force of disruptive technology. Kodak

(continued)

---

[9]Michael Porter, *Competitive Strategy* (Cambridge, MA: The Free Press, 1998). See also Cynthia Porter and Michael Porter, eds., *Strategy: Seeking and Securing Competitive Advantage* (Cambridge, MA: Harvard Business School Publishing, 1992).

was persuaded to ignore the inevitable and has shuttered its operations with equity value of only $220 million, whereas Fuji reinvented itself and enjoys a market capitalization of $12.6 billion in 2012. Why such a stark difference?

Rather than pressing a head start in digital cameras, Kodak chose to stay with 70 percent margin traditional chemical film development in light of the comparatively tiny 5 percent margins associated with digital photography services. Fuji, in contrast, shifted its antioxidant chemical compounds to cosmetic use and invested heavily in optical films for liquid crystal display (LCD) flat panel screens. In addition, electronic components for the copier industry proved another profitable Fuji business line. Despite a portfolio of 1,100 highly valuable patents, failing to adapt to a disruptive technology led eventually to Kodak's bankruptcy.

The Threat of Substitutes

First, an incumbent's profitability is determined by the threat of substitutes. Is the product generic, like AAA-grade January wheat, two-bedroom apartments, and office

FIGURE 10.2   Six Forces Strategic Model

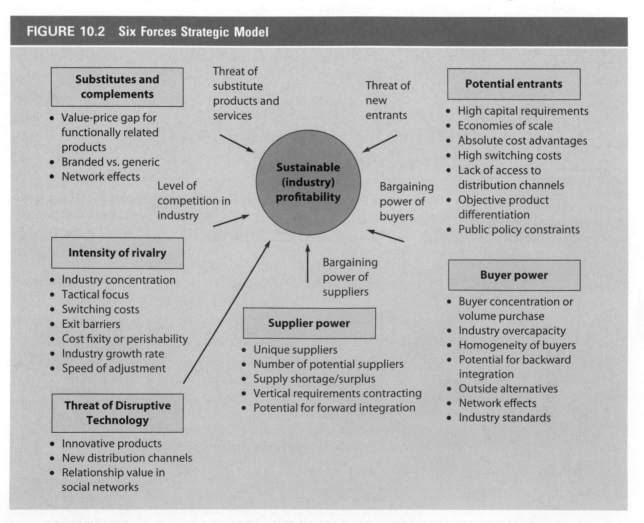

Source: Adapted from M. Porter, *Competitive Strategy* (New York, NA: The Free Press, 1998); and J. Bain, *Industrial Organization* (New York, NY: John Wiley, 1959).

supplies, or is it branded, like Gillette razors, Pepsi-Cola, and Campbell's soup? The more brand loyalty, the less the threat of substitutes and the higher the incumbent's sustainable profitability will be. Also, the more distant the substitutes outside the relevant market, the less price responsive will be demand, and the larger will be the optimal markups and profit margins. As videoconferencing equipment improves, the margins in business air travel will decline. A videoconferencing projector and sound system now leases for just $279 *per month*. Similarly, flavored and unflavored bottled water and other noncarbonated beverages such as juice, tea, and sports drinks are growing as much as eight times faster than U.S. soda sales. This trend will tend to erode the loyalty of Pepsi and Coke drinkers. If so, profitability will decline.

complementors
Independent firms that enhance the focal firm's value proposition.

Network effects are available to enhance profitability if companies can find **complementors**—that is, independent firms that enhance the customer value associated with using the primary firm's product, thereby raising profitability. For example, Microsoft Windows has obtained such a lock-in on PC customers that independent software providers (ISPs) write highly valued applications for Windows for which Microsoft pays nothing. Similarly, Apple's iPad attracts ISPs who enhance the customer value, and thereby support the high price point, and alter the positioning of iPad.

The closeness or distance of substitutes often hinges not only on consumer perceptions created by advertising but also on segmentation of the customers into separate distribution channels. Pantyhose distributed through convenience stores have few substitutes at 9:00 P.M. the night before a business trip, many fewer than pantyhose sold through department store distribution channels. Consequently, the threat of substitutes is reduced, and the sustainable profit margin on convenience store pantyhose is higher. Similarly, one-stop service and nonstop service in airlines are different products with different functionality. United's one-stop service from Chicago provides a distant substitute for Minneapolis-origin air travelers. Consequently, Northwest Airlines (now Delta) enjoys high margins on nonstop service from Minneapolis.

The Threat of Entry

A second force determining the likely profitability of an industry or product line is the threat of potential entrants. The higher the barriers to entry, the more profitable an incumbent will be. Barriers to entry can arise from several factors. First, consider high capital costs. The bottling and distribution business in the soft drink industry necessitates a $50 million investment. Although a good business plan with secure collateral will always attract loanable funds, unsecured loans become difficult to finance at this size. Fewer potential entrants with the necessary capital imply a lesser threat of entry and higher incumbent profitability.

Second, economies of scale and absolute cost advantages can provide another barrier to entry. An absolute cost advantage arises with proprietary IT that lowers a company's cost (e.g., at 7-Eleven Japan). In the traditional cable TV industry, the huge infrastructure cost of laying wire throughout the community deterred multiple entrants. The first mover had a tremendous scale economy in spreading fixed cost across a large customer base. Of course, wireless technology for satellite-based TV may soon lower this barrier, and then numerous suppliers of TV content will exhibit similar unit cost. These new threats of entry imply lower industry profitability in cable TV.

Third, if customers are brand loyal, the costs of inducing a customer to switch to a new entrant's product may pose a substantial barrier to entry. Year after year, hundreds of millions of dollars of cumulative advertising in the cereal industry maintains the pulling power of the Tony the Tiger Frosted Flakes brand. Unadvertised cereals go unnoticed. To take another example, hotel corporations raise the switching costs for their regular customers when they issue frequent-stayer giveaways. Committing room capacity to promotional giveaways raises barriers to entry. A new entrant therefore has a higher cost associated with becoming an effective entry threat in these markets.

Example

The Relevant Market for Web Browsers: Microsoft's Internet Explorer[10]

One of the recurring antitrust policy questions is the definition of the relevant market for computer software. In 1996, Netscape's user-friendly and pioneering product Navigator had an 82 percent share of the Internet browser market. But during 1996–1999, Microsoft's Internet Explorer made swift inroads. Bundling Explorer with its widely adopted Windows OS, Microsoft marketed an integrated software package preinstalled on PCs. Microsoft quoted higher prices for Windows alone than for Windows with Internet Explorer and threatened PC assemblers like Compaq and Gateway with removal of their Windows license unless they mounted Explorer as a desktop icon. Because most PC customers do want Windows preinstalled on their machines, Explorer penetrated deep into the browser market very quickly. By the start of 2000, some estimates showed Explorer's market share as high as 59 percent.

If the relevant market for these products is an integrated PC OS, then Microsoft has simply incorporated new web browser and media player technology into an already dominant Windows OS product. An analogy might be the interlock between an automobile's ignition and steering system to deter auto theft. If, on the other hand, Internet browsers (or, more recently, media players) are a separate relevant market, like stereo equipment for automobiles, then Microsoft should not be entitled to employ anticompetitive practices like refusals to deal to extend their dominance of PC OS into this new software market.

Microsoft's spectacular growth in sales of Windows 98 was not the issue. Winning a near monopoly of 85 percent market share in the previously fragmented OS software industry indicated a superior product, a great business plan, and good management. But allowing Microsoft to extend that market power into a new line of business using tactics that would be ineffective and self-defeating in the absence of the dominant market share in the original business is just what the antitrust laws were intended to prevent. Twenty state attorneys general in the United States and the European antitrust authorities have pursued a case against Microsoft using this line of reasoning. The European Union insisted on multiple versions of Windows with (and without) Media Player stripped out and fined Microsoft $624 million in March 2004. Appeals were exhausted in 2009, and Microsoft paid the fine plus interest.

[10]Based on "U.S. Sues Microsoft over PC Browser" and "Personal Technology," *Wall Street Journal* (October 21 and 30, 1997); "Microsoft's Browser: A Bundle of Trouble," *The Economist* (October 25, 1997); and *U.S. News and World Report*, Business and Technology (December 15, 1997).

Access to distribution channels is another potential barrier that has implications for the profitability of incumbents. The shelf space in grocery stores is very limited; all the slots are filled. A new entrant would therefore have to offer huge trade promotions (i.e., free display racks or slot-in allowances) to induce grocery store chains to displace one of their current suppliers. A related barrier to entry has emerged in the satellite television industry where Direct TV and EchoStar control essentially all the channel slots on satellites capable of reaching the entire U.S. audience. Government regulatory agencies also can approve or deny access to distribution channels. For example, the Food and Drug Administration (FDA) approves prescription drugs for certain therapeutic uses but not for others. The FDA also approves or denies exceptions to the Orphan Drug Act that gives firms patent-like exclusive selling rights when public policy pressure warrants doing so. Biogen's highest sales product, Avonex (a weekly injection for multiple sclerosis patients), received a license under the Orphan Drug Act. Other similarly situated firms have been denied approval; such a barrier to entry may prove insurmountable.

Example

Potential Entry at Office Depot/Staples[11]

Office Depot (a $6 billion company) and Staples (a $4 billion company) proposed to merge. Their combined sales in the $13 billion office supply superstore industry totaled 76 percent. From another perspective, their potential competitors included not only OfficeMax but all small paper goods specialty stores, department stores, discount stores such as Kmart, warehouse clubs like Sam's Club, office supply catalogs, and some computer retailers. This much larger office supply industry is very fragmented, easy to enter, and huge ($185 billion). Using this latter standard, the combined market share of Staples and Office Depot was only 6 percent.

The profit margins of Office Depot, OfficeMax, and Staples are significantly higher when only one office supply superstore locates in a town. This would suggest that the small-scale office suppliers offer little threat of entry into the superstore market. The exceptional ease of entry (and exit) at a small scale moderates the markups and profit margins of incumbent specialty retailers like stationery stores, but not office supply superstores. High capital requirement and scale economies in warehousing and distribution appear responsible for the barriers to entry in the office supply superstore market.

[11]Based on "FTC Rejects Staples' Settlement Offer," *Wall Street Journal* (April 7, 1997), p. A3; and J. Baker, "Econometric Analysis in *FTC* v. *Staples*," *Journal of Public Policy and Marketing* 18, no. 1 (Spring 1999), pp. 11–21.

Preexisting competitors in related product lines provide a substantial threat of entry as well; see the following example.

Example

Eli Lilly Poses a Threat of Potential Entry for AstraZeneca[12]

In 2000, AstraZeneca's cancer treatment Nolvadex became the first drug ever approved for reducing the risk of breast cancer in currently healthy women. Eli Lilly markets a pharmaceutical product, Evista, long approved by the FDA for the treatment of osteoporosis. Preliminary tests have suggested a therapeutic potential for Evista in the prevention of breast cancer. Lilly promptly released an Evista study in which the incidence of developing cancer over a three-year period was reduced 55 percent in 10,575 women with high-risk factors for developing breast cancer. AstraZeneca sued to stop and undoubtedly slowed Lilly's marketing efforts, but the real barrier to entry would come if the FDA denies the use of Evista for breast cancer treatment. Without such a denial, AstraZeneca's Nolvadex faces a formidable direct competitor from a preexisting supplier in an adjacent relevant market.

[12]Zeneca Sues Eli Lilly Over Promotion of Evista for Preventing Breast Cancer, *Wall Street Journal* (February 26, 1999), p. B6.

Finally, a barrier to entry may be posed by product differentiation. Objective product differentiation is subject to reverse engineering, violations of intellectual property, and offshore imitation even of patented technology like the shutter in a Kodak digital camera. In contrast, subjective perceived product differentiation based on customer perceptions of lifestyle images and product positioning (e.g., Pepsi-Cola) can erect effective barriers to entry that allow incumbent firms to better survive competitive attack. In sum, the higher any of these barriers to entry, the lower the threat of potential entrants and the higher the sustainable industry profitability will be.

Example

Objective versus Perceived Product Differentiation: Xerox

Shielded from competition by patents on its landmark dry paper copier, Xerox enjoyed a virtual monopoly and 15 percent compound earnings growth through the 1960s and early 1970s. During this period, its research lab in Palo Alto, California, spun off one breakthrough device after another. One year it was the graphical user interface that Apple later brought to market as a user-friendly PC. Xerox scientists and engineers also developed the Ethernet, the first local area network for connecting computers and printers. Yet, Xerox was able to commercialize almost none of these R & D successes. As a result, Japanese copier companies like Canon and Ikon reverse engineered the Xerox product, imitated its processes, and ultimately developed better and cheaper copiers.

The Power of Buyers and Suppliers

The profitability of incumbents is determined in part by the bargaining power of buyers and suppliers. Buyers may be highly concentrated, like Boeing and Airbus in the purchase of large aircraft engines, or extremely fragmented, like the restaurants that are customers of wholesale grocery companies. If industry capacity approximately equals or exceeds demand, concentrated buyers can force price concessions that reduce an incumbent's profitability. On the other hand, fragmented buyers have little bargaining power unless excess capacity and inventory overhang persist.

Unique suppliers may also reduce industry profitability. The Coca-Cola Co. establishes exclusive franchise arrangements with independent bottlers. No other supplier can provide the secret ingredients in the concentrate syrup. Bottler profitability is therefore rather low. In contrast, Coke's own suppliers are numerous; many potential sugar and flavoring manufacturers would like to win the Coca-Cola account, and the syrup inputs are non-unique commodities. These factors raise the likely profitability of the concentrate manufacturers such as Coca-Cola because of the lack of power among their suppliers.

Supply shortages, stockouts, and a backorder production environment can alter the relative power of buyers and suppliers in the value chain. One of the few levers a supplier has against huge category-killer retailers like Toys "R" Us to prevent their expropriating all the net value is to refuse to guarantee on-time delivery for triple orders of popular products. A deeply discounted wholesale price should never receive 100 percent delivery reliability.

Finally, buyers and suppliers will have more bargaining power and reduce firm profitability when they possess more outside alternatives and can credibly threaten to vertically integrate into the industry. HMOs (health maintenance organizations) can negotiate very low fees from primary care physicians precisely because the HMO has so many outside alternatives. Buyers who control the setting of industry standards can also negotiate substantial reductions in pricing and profitability from manufacturers who may then be in a position to capture network effects. Companies favored by having their product specs adopted as an industry standard often experience increasing returns to their marketing expenditures.

The Intensity of Rivalrous Tactics

In the global economy, few companies can establish and maintain dominance in anything beyond niche markets. Reverse engineering of products, imitation of advertising images, and offshore production at low cost imply that General Motors (GM) cannot hope to rid itself of Ford, and Coca-Cola cannot hope truly to defeat Pepsi. Instead, to sustain profitability in such a setting, companies must avoid intense rivalries and elicit passive, more cooperative responses from close competitors. The intensity of the rivalry in an industry depends on several factors: industry concentration, the tactical focus of competition, switching costs, the presence of exit barriers, the industry growth rate, and the ratio of fixed to total cost (termed the **cost fixity**) in the typical cost structure.

cost fixity A measure of fixed to total cost that is correlated with gross profit margins.

Exactly what firms and what products offer close substitutes for potential customers in the relevant market determine the degree of industry concentration. One measure of industry concentration is the sum of the market shares of the four largest or eight largest firms in an industry. The larger the market shares and the smaller the number of competitors, the more interdependence each firm will perceive, and the less intense the rivalry. The ready-to-eat cereal industry has more intense rivalry than the soft drink industry, in part because Kellogg's (37 percent), General Mills (25 percent), Post (15 percent), and Quaker Oats (8 percent) together comprise 85 percent of the market. When two firms enjoy 60 to 90 percent of industry shipments (e.g., Pepsi and Coke), their transparent interdependence can lead to reduced intensity of rivalry if the firms tacitly collude. Similarly, because Titleist and Spalding dominate the golf ball market, the rivalrous intensity is less than in the fragmented golf club business.

Sustainable profitability is increased by tactics that focus on non-price rather than price competition. Airlines are more profitable when they can avoid price wars and focus their competition for passengers on service quality—for example, delivery reliability, change-order responsiveness, and schedule convenience. But trunk route airlines between major U.S. cities provide generic transportation with nearly identical service quality and departure frequency. Consequently, fare wars are frequent, and the resulting profitability of trunk airline routes is very low. In contrast, long-standing rivals Coca-Cola and Pepsi have never discounted their cola concentrates. This absence of "gain-share discounting" and a diminished focus on price competition tactics in general increases the profitability of the concentrate business. Airlines tried to control gain-share discounting by introducing "frequent flyer" programs to increase the customers' *switching cost* from one competitor to another. This idea to reduce the intensity of rivalry worked well for a time, until business travelers joined essentially all the rival frequent flyer programs.

Example

Price Competition at the Soda Fountain: PepsiCo Inc.[13]

Soft drinks are marketed through several distribution channels at different prices. The channels of distribution include independent beverage resellers, vending machine companies, and company-owned bottlers supplying supermarkets, convenience stores, and vending machines, which account for 31, 12, and 11 percent, respectively, of all

(continued)

soft drink sales. Shelf slots in the store channels are full, and bottlers compete on stocking services and retailer rebates for prime shelf space and vending machine locations in an attempt to grow their brands. With roughly the same percent market shares in the stores, the Coca-Cola- and PepsiCo-owned bottlers attempt to avoid head-to-head price competition, which would simply lower profits for both firms, and instead seek predictable patterns of company-sponsored once-every-other-week discounts. Where independent beverage resellers have established a practice of persistent gain-share discounting, the Coca-Cola Company and PepsiCo have often attempted to purchase the franchises and replace them with company-owned bottlers. Vending operations are very high-margin businesses, and PepsiCo and Coca-Cola increasingly service vending machines directly from their company-owned bottlers. To date, little price competition has emerged in the vending channel, in part because independents must purchase from exclusive franchise bottlers in their areas.

Price competition is heating up, however, in the fountain drink side of the business. As more and more families eat more and more meals outside the household, the fountain drink channel accounted for 37 percent of total sales. Coca-Cola has long dominated the fountain drink business. At restaurants and soda shops in 2000, Coke enjoyed a 59 percent share to Pepsi's 23 percent. Recently, PepsiCo declared an intent to vigorously pursue fountain drink sales through discount pricing tactics if necessary. This development threatens continuing profitability in this important channel of the soft drink industry.

[13]Based on "Cola Wars Continue," Harvard Business School Case Publishing (1994); "Pepsi Hopes to Tap Coke's Fountain Sales," *USA Today* (November 6, 1997), p. 3B; and "Antitrust Suit Focuses on Bottlers' Pricing and Sales Practices," *Wall Street Journal* (January 20, 1999), p. B7.

Sometimes price versus non-price competition simply reflects the lack of product differentiation available in commodity-like markets (e.g., in selling cement). However, the incidence of price competition is also determined in part by the cost structure prevalent in the industry. Where fixed costs as a percentage of total costs are high, margins will tend to be larger. If so, firms are tempted to fight tooth and nail for incremental customers because every additional unit sale represents a substantial contribution to covering the fixed costs. All other things being the same, gain-share discounting will therefore tend to increase the greater the fixed cost is. For example, gross margins in the airline industry reflect the enormous fixed costs for aircraft leases and terminal facilities, often reaching 80 percent. Consider the following **break-even sales change analysis** for an airline that seeks to increase its total contributions by lowering its prices 10 percent:

break-even sales change analysis A calculation of the percentage increase in unit sales required to justify a price discount, given the contribution margin.

$$(P_0 - MC)Q_0 < (0.9\, P_0 - MC)Q_1$$
$$< (0.9\, P_0 - MC)(Q_0 + \Delta Q)$$

[10.1]

where revenue minus variable cost (MC times Q) is the *total contribution*. If discounting is to succeed in raising total contributions, the change in sales ΔQ must be great enough to more than offset the 10 percent decline in revenue per unit sale. Rearranging Equation 10.1 and dividing by P_0 yields

$$\frac{(P_0 - MC)Q_0}{P_0} < \left[\frac{(P_0 - MC)}{P_0} - 0.1\frac{P_0}{P_0}\right](Q_0 + \Delta Q)$$
$$(PCM)Q_0 < (PCM - 0.1)(Q_0 + \Delta Q)$$

where PCM is the price-cost margin, often referred to as the contribution margin. That is,

$$\frac{PCM}{(PCM - 0.1)} < \frac{(Q_0 + \Delta Q)}{Q_0}$$

$$\frac{PCM}{(PCM - 0.1)} < 1 + \frac{\Delta Q}{Q_0} \qquad [10.2]$$

Using Equation 10.2, an 80 percent price-cost margin implies that a sales increase of only 15 percent is all that one requires to warrant cutting prices by 10 percent. Here's how one reaches that conclusion:

$$\frac{0.8}{[0.8 - 0.1]} < 1 + \frac{\Delta Q}{Q_0}$$

$$1.14 < 1 + \frac{\Delta Q}{Q_0}$$

$$1.14 < 1 + 0.15$$

In contrast, in paperback book publishing, a price-cost margin of 12 percent implies sales must increase by better than 500 percent in order to warrant a 10 percent price cut—that is, $0.12/0.02 < 1 + 5.0^{+}$. Because a marketing plan that creates a 15 percent sales increase from a 10 percent price cut is much more feasible than one that creates a 500 percent sales increase from a 10 percent price cut, the airline industry is more likely to focus on pricing competition than the paperback book publishing industry.

barriers to exit
Economic losses resulting from non-redeployable assets or contractual constraints upon business termination.

Contribution Margins at Hanes Discourage Discounting

First-quality white cotton T-shirts and briefs have long been the mainstay of the Hanes Corporation. Selling these "blanks" to other companies that perform value-added finishing, dyeing, embroidering, or custom stitching, Hanes captures only the initial stages in the value chain. At a wholesale price of $1.25 and with $0.85 direct cost of goods sold, the gross margin for Hanes briefs of $0.40 must recover the fixed costs plus the distribution-and-selling expenses to earn a profit. With a $0.15 commission per unit sale as a selling expense, the contribution margin (CM) in dollars is $0.25, and the percentage contribution margin (PCM) is $0.25/$1.25 = 20%.

Because of very price-elastic demand, price discounted by as little as 15 percent can double unit sales. However, with contribution margins (PCM) as low as 20 percent, the additional sales triggered by the discount are much less attractive than one might think. Break-even sales change analysis using Equation 10.2 confirms that a doubling of sales volume is less than the incremental sales change required to restore total contributions to the levels earned before the price cut:

$$PCM/(PCM - \%\Delta P) = 0.20/(0.20 - 0.15) = 4.0 = 1 + 3.0^{+}$$

The interpretation here is that unit sales must increase by 300 percent $(1 + 300\%\Delta Q)$ in order to restore total contributions to their preexisting level. That is, the price reduction must more than *quadruple* unit sales in order to raise total contributions (operating profit). The data displayed in Table 10.1 demonstrate this conclusion in a spreadsheet format.

Barriers to exit increase the intensity of rivalry in a tight oligopoly. If remote plants specific to a particular line of products (e.g., aluminum smelting plants) are

TABLE 10.1	HANES SALES VOLUME REQUIRED TO MAINTAIN OPERATING PROFIT WITH A 15 PERCENT PRICE CUT				
	GIVEN DATA	WITH 15% PRICE CUT	DOUBLE SALES VOLUME	TRIPLE SALES VOLUME	QUADRUPLE SALES VOLUME
Price	1.25	1.0625	2.125	3.1875	4.25
DCGS (VC only)	−0.85	−0.85	−1.70	−2.55	−3.40
Commission	−0.15	−0.15	−0.30	−0.45	−0.60
CM	0.25	0.0625	0.125	0.1875	0.25

© Cengage Learning

non-redeployable, the tactics will be more aggressive because no competitor can fully recover its sunk cost should margins collapse. In addition to capital equipment, non-redeployable assets can include product-specific display racks (L'eggs); product-specific showrooms (Ethan Allen); and intangible assets that prove difficult to carve up and package for resale (unpatented trade secrets and basic research). Trucking companies, on the other hand, own very redeployable assets—that is, trucks and warehouses. If a trucking company attacks its rivals, encounters aggressive retaliation, and then fails and must liquidate its assets, the owners can hope to receive nearly the full value of the economic working life remaining in their trucks and warehouses. As a result, competitive tactics in the trucking industry are not as effective in threatening rivals, so competitive rivalrous intensity is lower and profitability is higher.

Finally, industry demand growth can influence the intensity of rivalry. When sales to established customers are increasing and new customers are appearing in the market, rival firms are often content to maintain market share and realize high profitability. When demand growth declines, competitive tactics sharpen in many industries, especially if capacity planning has failed to anticipate the decline. Furniture companies discount steeply when housing demand slows. Airline prices and profits declined sharply when demand for air travel leveled off unexpectedly after the Gulf War. Similarly, when soft drink sales in the United States flattened out at a gallon per week, Porter's model predicts that flat soft drink demand would lead to more intense rivalry and lower profitability at PepsiCo Inc. and Coca-Cola Co. Coca-Cola has deflected many competitive initiatives to its fast-growing international division in an attempt to reduce the growing likelihood of intense rivalry with PepsiCo here in the United States.

Example

Intensity of Rivalry at US Airways[14]

The Charlotte hub of US Airways is a very concentrated terminal facility; US Airways has over 92 percent of the flights. Thus, US Airways' market share is comparable to Microsoft's dominance of the OS business with Windows. However, high indirect fixed costs for aircraft leases and facilities imply high margins that make it very tempting for airlines to attract incremental customers through price discounting. In contrast, Windows is seldom, if ever, discounted. Also, exit barriers are high in airlines but rather low in computer software, where massive sunk-cost expenses for research and development create largely patentable trade secrets that can be easily resold. Finally, industry demand growth is low in airlines but extremely high in computer software. Consequently, in one-stop flights from Charlotte, US Airways is subject to intense rivalry but Microsoft Windows is not.

(continued)

Frequent price competition, high exit barriers, and flat growth all imply tremendous rivalrous intensity in the airline industry and downward competitive pressure on US Airways' profit margins. The opposite is true in Microsoft's OS software business. Windows software is seldom discounted and remains extremely profitable. In short, airlines have industry characteristics that force nearly competitive performance on even dominant firms, whereas a dominant firm in computer OS faces less intense rivalry.

[14]Based on "Flying to Charlotte Is Easy," *Wall Street Journal* (June 14, 1995), p. S1.

Finally, the speed of adjustment of rivalrous actions and reactions matters. Recall that if incumbents are slow to respond to tactical initiatives of hit-and-run entrants, then profitability may be driven down to the break-even levels in so-called contestable markets. In contrast, if incumbents are easily provoked and exhibit fast adjustment speeds, then profitability is often more sustainable.

The Myth of Market Share

In summary, the key to profitability in many businesses is to design a strategy that reduces the threat of substitutes, the power of buyers and suppliers, and the threat of entry. Then, firms must adopt tactics and elicit tactical responses from their rivals so that the profit potential in their effective business strategy is not eroded away. This often means forsaking gain-share discounting and other aggressive tactics that would spiral the industry into price wars. Price premiums reflecting true customer value are very difficult to win back once buyers have grown accustomed to a pattern of deep discount rivalry between the competitors or predictably timed clearance sales. Airlines and department store retailers are painfully aware of these tactical mistakes.

More generally, discounting and excessive promotions designed to grab market share are seldom a source of long-term profitability and often result in lower capitalized value. The soft-drink bottler 7-Up once doubled and tripled its market share largely through discounting. But profits declined, and the company was eventually acquired by Cadbury Schweppes. Hon Industries makes twice the ROI of Steelcase in the office equipment market even though Hon is one-third of Steelcase's size. Boeing was much more profitable allowing a slight majority of wide-bodied orders to go to government-subsidized Airbus rather than tie up their own assembly-line operations with hundreds of additional orders triggered by the low prices.

After the initial penetration of a new product or new technology into a relevant market, market share should never become an end in itself. Increasing market share is the means to achieve scale economies and learning-curve-based cost advantages. But additional share points at any cost almost always mean a reduction in profits, not the reverse.

A CONTINUUM OF MARKET STRUCTURES

The relationship between individual firms and the relevant market as a whole is referred to as the industry's *market structure* and depends upon:

1. The number and relative size of firms in the industry.
2. The similarity of the products sold by the firms of the industry; that is, the degree of product differentiation.

3. The extent to which decision making by individual firms is independent, not inter-dependent or collusive.

4. The conditions of entry and exit.

Four specific market structures are often distinguished: pure competition, monopoly, monopolistic competition, and oligopoly. We discuss each in turn.

| Pure Competition | Monopolistic Competition | Oligopoly | Monopoly |

Pure Competition

The **pure competition** industry model has the following characteristics:

1. A large number of buyers and sellers, each of which buys or sells such a small proportion of the total industry output that a single buyer's or seller's actions cannot have a perceptible impact on the market price.

2. A homogeneous product produced by each firm; that is, no product differentiation, as with licensed taxi cab services or AAA-grade January wheat.

3. Complete knowledge of all relevant market information by all firms, each of which acts totally independently, such as the 117 home builders of standardized two-bedroom subdivision homes in a large city.

4. Free entry and exit from the market—that is, minimal barriers to entry and exit.

The single firm in a purely competitive industry is, in essence, a price taker. Because the products of each producer are almost perfect substitutes for the products of every other producer, the single firm in pure competition can do nothing but offer its entire output at the going market price. As a result, the individual firm's demand curve approaches perfect elasticity at the market price. It can sell nothing at a higher price because all buyers will rationally shift to other sellers. If the firm sells at a price slightly below the long-run market price, it will lose money.

For example, Figure 10.3 indicates the nature of the industry and firm demand curves under pure competition in tract home building. Line DD' represents the total industry or market demand curve for tract houses and $S'S$ is the market supply curve. At price $175,000, the market price, a total of Q_{DI} houses will be demanded by the sum of all firms in the industry. Line dd' represents the demand curve facing each individual firm. The individual firm sells its entire output, Q_{DF}, at the market price $175,000. By definition, the quantity Q_{DF} represents only a small fraction of the total industry demand of Q_{DI}.

Why get involved in industries where revenues per sale ($175,000 in Figure 10.3) are just sufficient to cover fully allocated unit costs of $175,000? The reason is that these sales at a "razor-thin margin" are the ticket to the occasional windfalls when demand increases and price rises enough to generate excess profits (for a few months in the tract home business, a few weeks in the wildcatter oil business, a few hours in the AAA Kansas City corn business, or a few minutes in the T-bond resale market). Note that the timing and magnitude of these windfalls are not predictable. Otherwise the real estate development land, oil leases, T-bills, and grain silos would rise in value, and the expected excess profit would again reduce to a razor-thin margin above break-even conditions. Also, remember that at competitive equilibrium the business owner-manager is getting a salary or other return as great as could be received in his or her next best activity. In short, this is not the business environment where venture capital

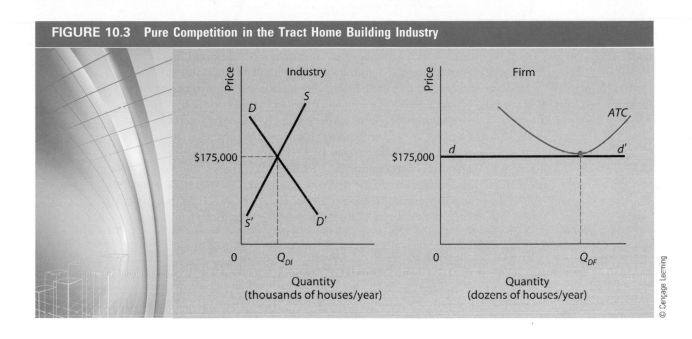

FIGURE 10.3   Pure Competition in the Tract Home Building Industry

and entrepreneurial returns of 40 percent on invested capital occur regularly, but it does provide perhaps a 12 percent return with good managerial skills and cost controls. More importantly, these razor-thin margins are interrupted occasionally when windfall profits of as much as $25,000 on a tract home, $20 per barrel on crude oil, $1.50 per bushel on corn, or $5,000 per $1 million T-bill erupt for a short time.

Contestable Markets   A contestable market is an extreme case of purely competitive markets. In this market structure, break-even performance often occurs with just a handful of firms, perhaps only one. The reason is that entry and exit are free and costless. Consequently, the mere threat of "hit-and-run" entry is sufficient to drive prices down to the zero-profit, full cost-covering level. Incumbents in such markets are often slower to react than the hit-and-run firms that impose all this competitive pressure. An example is the bond markets where financial arbitrage by hedge funds triggers enormous bets (perhaps tens of billions of dollars) that any out-of-line government bond or bill prices will converge back to their equilibrium levels. Similarly, airlines might seem to be a contestable market; aircraft would seem to be the ultimate mobile asset, but landing slots are not, and incumbents react quickly and aggressively to hit-and-run entrants in these markets.

Monopoly

monopoly A market structure characterized by one firm producing a highly differentiated product in a market with significant barriers to entry.

The **monopoly** model at the other extreme of the market structure spectrum from pure competition is characterized as follows:

1. Only one firm producing some specific product line (in a specified market area), like an exclusive cable TV franchise.

2. Low cross-price elasticity of demand between the monopolist's product and any other product, that is, no close substitute products.

3. No interdependence with other competitors because the firm is a monopolist in its relevant market.

4. Substantial barriers to entry that prevent competition from entering the industry. These barriers may include any of the following:
   a. Absolute cost advantages of the established firm, resulting from economies in securing inputs or from patented production techniques.
   b. Product differentiation advantages, resulting from consumer loyalty to established products.
   c. Scale economies, which increase the difficulty for potential entrant firms of financing an efficient-sized plant or building up a sufficient sales volume to achieve lowest unit costs in such a plant.
   d. Large capital requirements, exceeding the financial resources of potential entrants.
   e. Legal exclusion of potential competitors, as is the case for public utilities, and for those companies with patents and exclusive licensing arrangements.
   f. Trade secrets not available to potential competitors.

By definition, the demand curve of the individual monopoly firm is identical with the industry demand curve, because the firm is the entire relevant market. As we will see in Chapter 11, the identity between the firm and industry demand curves allows decision making for the monopolist to be a relatively simple matter, compared to the complexity of rivalrous tactics with few close competitors in tight oligopoly groups, discussed in Chapter 12.

Monopolistic Competition

monopolistic competition A market structure very much like pure competition, with the major distinction being the existence of a differentiated product.

E. H. Chamberlin and Joan Robinson coined the term **monopolistic competition** to describe industries with characteristics both of competitive markets (i.e., many firms) and of monopoly (i.e., product differentiation). The market structure of monopolistic competition is characterized as follows:

1. A few dominant firms and a large number of competitive fringe firms.
2. Dominant firms selling products that are differentiated in some manner: real, perceived, or just imagined.
3. Independent decision making by individual firms.
4. Ease of entry and exit from the market as a whole but very substantial barriers to effective entry among the leading brands.

By far the most important distinguishing characteristic of monopolistic competition is that the outputs of each firm are starkly differentiated in some way from those of every other firm. In other words, the cross-price elasticity of demand between the products of individual firms is much lower than in purely competitive markets—that is, among tract home builders, oil wildcatters, AAA January wheat suppliers, or T-bill resellers. Product differentiation may be based on exclusive features (Disney World), trademarks (Nike's swoosh), trade names (BlackBerry), packaging (L'eggs hosiery), quality (Coach handbags), design (Apple iMacs), color and style (Swatch watches), or the conditions of sale (Dooney & Bourke). These conditions may include such factors as credit terms, location of the seller, congeniality of sales personnel, after-sale service, and warranties.

oligopoly A market structure in which the number of firms is so small that the actions of any one firm are likely to have noticeable impacts on the performance of other firms in the industry.

Because each firm produces a differentiated product, it is difficult to define an industry demand curve in monopolistic competition. Thus, rather than well-defined industries, one tends to get something of a continuum of products. Generally, it is rather easy to identify groups of differentiated products that fall in the same industry, like light beers, after-shave colognes, or perfumes.

Oligopoly

The **oligopoly** market structure describes a market having a few closely related firms. The number of firms is so small that actions by an individual firm in the industry with respect to price, output, product style or quality, terms of sale, and so on, have a perceptible impact on the sales of other firms in the industry. In other words, oligopoly is distinguished by a noticeable degree of *interdependence* among firms in the industry. The products or services that are produced by oligopolists may be homogeneous—as in the cases of air travel, 40-foot steel I-beams, aluminum, and cement—or they may be partially differentiated—as in the cases of soft drinks, luxury automobiles, and cruise ships.

Although the lack of product differentiation is an important factor in shaping an oligopolist's demand curve, the degree of interdependence of firms in the industry is of even greater significance. Primarily because of this interdependence, defining a single firm's demand curve is complicated. The relationship between price and output is determined not only by consumer preferences, product substitutability, and level of advertising, *but also by the responses that other competitors may make to a price change by the focal firm*. A full discussion of rival response expectations and their game-theoretic modeling will be deferred until Chapter 12.

PRICE-OUTPUT DETERMINATION UNDER PURE COMPETITION

As discussed in Chapter 2, the individual firm in a purely competitive industry is effectively a price taker because the products of every producer are perfect substitutes for the products of every other producer. This leads to the familiar horizontal or perfectly elastic demand curve of the purely competitive firm. Although we rarely find instances where all the conditions for pure competition are met, tract home real estate, securities exchanges, and the commodity markets approach these conditions. For instance, the individual tract home seller, wheat farmer, or T-bill reseller has little choice but to accept the going market price. In pure competition, the firm must sell at the market price (p_1 or p_2), and its demand curve is represented by a horizontal line (D_1 or D_2) at the market price, as shown in Figure 10.4.

Short Run

A firm in a purely competitive industry may break-even against all economic costs, make transitory profits (in excess of normal returns to capital and entrepreneurial labor), or operate at a temporary loss in the short run. In the purely competitive case, marginal revenue MR is equal to price P, because the sale of each additional unit increases total revenue by the price of that unit (which remains constant at all levels of output). For instance, if

$$P = \$8/\text{unit}$$

then

$$\text{Total revenue} = TR = P \cdot Q$$
$$= 8Q$$

Marginal revenue is defined as the change in total revenue resulting from the sale of one additional unit of output, or the derivative of total revenue with respect to Q:

$$MR = \frac{dTR}{dQ} = \$8/\text{unit}$$

and in competitive markets marginal revenue equals price.

The profit-maximizing firm will produce all those units of output where marginal revenue exceeds or equals marginal cost (the variable cost of the next unit to be produced). Beyond that point, the production and sale of one additional unit would add more to

FIGURE 10.4   The Firm in Pure Competition: The Short Run

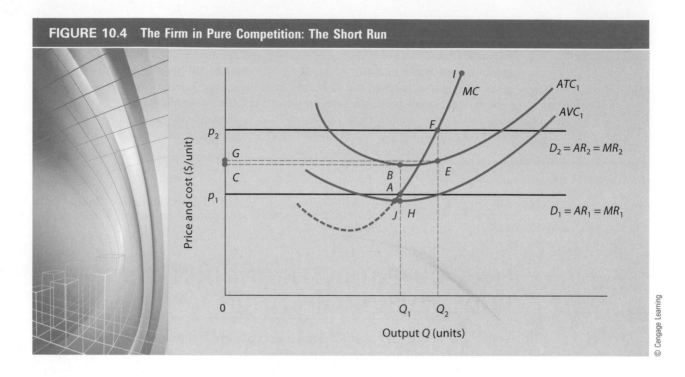

total cost than to total revenue ($MC > MR$), and hence total profit ($TR - TC$) would decline. Up to the point where $MC = MR$, the production and sale of one more unit would increase total revenue more than total cost ($MR > MC$), and total profit would increase as an additional unit is produced and sold. *Producing at the point where marginal revenue* MR *equals marginal cost* MC *maximizes the total profit function.*[15]

The individual firm's supply function in Figure 10.4 is equal to that portion of the MC curve from point J to point I. At any price level below point J, the firm would shut down because it would not even be covering its variable costs (i.e., $P < AVC$). Temporary shutdown would result in limiting the losses to fixed costs alone.

Returning to Figure 10.4, if price $P = p_1$, the firm would produce the level of output Q_1, where $MC = MR$ (profits are maximized or losses minimized). In this case the firm would incur a loss per unit equal to the difference between average total cost ATC and average revenue or price. This is represented by the height BA in Figure 10.4. The total loss incurred by the firm at Q_1 level of output and price p_1 equals the rectangle p_1CBA. This may be conceptually thought of as the loss per unit (BA) times the number of units produced and sold (Q_1).

At price p_1 losses are minimized, because average variable costs AVC have been covered and a contribution remains to cover part of the fixed costs (AH per unit times Q_1 units). If the firm did not produce, it would incur losses equal to the entire amount of fixed costs (BH per unit times Q_1 units). Hence we may conclude that in the short run a

---

[15]This can be proven as follows:

$$\pi = TR - TC$$

$$\frac{d\pi}{dQ} = \frac{dTR}{dQ} - \frac{dTC}{dQ} = MR - MC = 0$$

or $MR = MC$ when profits are maximized.

Check for profit maximization by taking the second derivative of π with respect to Q, or $\frac{d^2\pi}{dQ^2}$. If it is less than zero, then π is maximized.

firm will produce and sell at that level of output where $MR = MC$, as long as the variable costs and direct fixed costs of production (i.e., the avoidable costs from the point of view of the shutdown/operate decision) are being covered $(P > AVC)$.[16]

Example

Flat Screen Televisions Lose $126 per Unit Sold: Sony Corporation[17]

Most of the cost of a flat screen TV involves the LCD panel. Globally, 220 million flat screen TVs were sold in 2011 for $115 billion. Although scale economies in massive factories and volume discounts on electronic input components have driven the cost of LCDs down from $2,400 to $500 the last decade, the price has fallen even faster. In 2001, the average selling price of a large LCD panel was over $4,000. By 2011, this price had fallen below $600 (see Figure 10.5). Sony Corporation finds its flat screen TVs now fail to cover the full cost of the LCD panels and instead impose an $126 ($500 − $374) loss per TV sold. Nevertheless, the indirect fixed costs of the LCD factories Korean Samsung, Japanese Sharp, Panasonic, and Sony constructed are partially covered by operating. Losses would be greater in the short run if they shut down.

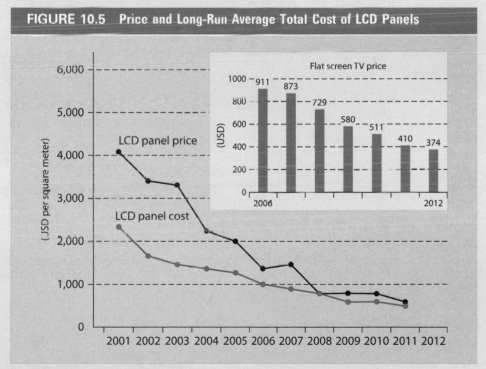

FIGURE 10.5   Price and Long-Run Average Total Cost of LCD Panels

Source: New York Times (December 12, 2008), *CNN Money* (September 9, 2010), *The Economist* (January 21, 2012), p. 47.

[17]Based on "Television-Making: Cracking Up," *The Economist* (January 21, 2012), p. 72.

[16]Variable costs are defined narrowly by accountants to identify the avoidable costs incurred by the smallest unit sale in the company's business plan. In addition, some other costs that are batch costs (like utilities for the third shift on the factory floor) or direct fixed costs traceable to the decision to operate (like unscheduled maintenance to offset wear and tear on the machinery) are avoidable by the decision in question. Therefore, these costs could be varied (avoided) by the decision to shutdown and should therefore be included in the AVC that must be exceeded in order to decide to operate.

If price were p_2, the firm would produce Q_2 units and make a profit per unit of EF, or a total profit represented by the rectangle $FEGp_2$. The supply curve of the competitive firm is therefore often identified as the marginal cost schedule above minimum AVC. Industry supply is the horizontal summation of these firm supply curves.

Profit Maximization under Pure Competition (Short Run): Adobe Corporation

Assume Adobe Corporation faces the following total revenue and total cost functions:

$$\text{Total revenue: } TR = 8Q$$

$$\text{Total cost: } TC = Q^2 + 4Q + 2$$

Marginal revenue and marginal cost are defined as the first derivative of total revenue and total cost, or

$$\text{Marginal revenue: } MR = \frac{dTR}{dQ} = \$8/\text{unit}$$

$$\text{Marginal cost: } MC = \frac{dTR}{dQ} = 2Q + 4$$

Total profit equals total revenue minus total cost:

$$\text{Total profit: } (\pi) = TR - TC$$

$$= 8Q - (Q^2 + 4Q + 2)$$

$$= -Q^2 + 4Q - 2$$

To maximize total profit, we take the derivative of π with respect to quantity, set it equal to zero, and solve for the profit-maximizing level of Q. (It is also necessary to check the second derivative to be certain we have found a maximum, not a minimum!)[18]

$$\frac{d\pi}{dQ} = -2Q + 4 = 0$$

$$Q^* = 2 \text{ units}$$

Because $MR = \$8/\text{unit}$ and $MC = 2Q + 4 = [2(2) + 4] = \$8/\text{unit}$, when total profit is maximized, note that we are merely setting $MC = MR$.

Example

Gasoline Price Rises to Record Levels Reflecting a Spike in Crude Oil Input Costs[19]

Throughout 2006, 2007, and early 2008, the price of gasoline in the United States galloped upward to reach $4 per gallon. Why did it happen? Competitive pressure at retail prevents gas station gouging of retail customers. Excise taxes average only $0.40 across the United States and have been largely unchanged for two decades. Refinery and pipeline bottlenecks were partially to blame after Gulf Coast hurricanes Katrina and Rita but not in July 2008. Instead, the principal source of the run-up in gasoline prices was a spectacular increase in crude oil input prices.

(continued)

---

[18]The check for profit maximization goes as follows:

$$\frac{d^2\pi}{dQ^2} = -2$$

Because the second derivative is negative, we know we have found a maximum value for the profit function.

Figure 10.6(a), shows that six times in the past 30 years, crude oil prices have risen steeply. In each prior case, supply disruptions due to armed conflicts in the Middle East or cartel restrictions of output were responsible. In 1973 and 1999–2000, the OPEC I and OPEC III oil cartels successfully enforced reduced output quotas on members, thereby restraining supply and driving the market price of crude oil higher. In 1978, 1980, and 1990, three military conflicts massively restricted the supply of crude oil leaving the Persian Gulf. In 2004–2008, however, not supply but demand factors were involved. Demand growth in India, China, and the United States in 2004–2008 drove scarce input prices right up the rising marginal cost schedule for crude oil supply exhibited in Figure 10.6(b).

Oil in the Persian Gulf region is cheapest to find, develop, and extract at a marginal cost of $3 per barrel. In contrast, Venezuelan and Russian oil recovers its marginal cost at $9 per barrel, West Texas oil at $13 per barrel, and the North Sea fields necessitate offshore rigs and expensive extraction technology that generate $20 per barrel marginal cost. The delivered costs of incremental oil output from the North Slope of Alaska run $30 per barrel. These oil field production firms and their associated output trace out a traditional upward-sloping long-run supply curve (here a step function) for the crude oil industry—again see Figure 10.6(b).

By mid-year 2006, as crude oil input prices passed through $70 and $80 and headed higher, Missouri and Iowa farmers joined co-ops created to build and operate $65 million corn-fed ethanol plants. The marginal cost at which the booming demand for petroleum products was causing crude oil to be brought to market exceeded the marginal cost of ethanol for the first time ever. For decades, Brazil had been hugely successful with sugarcane-fed ethanol plants—so successful that in 2008 Brazil declared energy independence from foreign oil. But sugarcane has a much higher chemical energy content than corn, so sugarcane-based ethanol is profitable at $40, much lower than the $60 needed to induce suppliers to bring corn-based ethanol to market.

[19]Based on "Special Report: The Oil Industry," *The Economist* (April 22, 2006), pp. 55–73.

Long Run

In the long run, all inputs are free to vary. Hence, no conceptual distinction exists between fixed and variable costs. Under long-run conditions in purely competitive markets, average cost will tend to be just equal to price, and all excessive profits will be eliminated (see Point A where $p_1 = AC_1$ in Figure 10.7). If not, and if, for example, a price above p_1 exceeds average total costs, like p_1' generating temporary quasi-profits, then more firms will enter, the industry supply will increase (as illustrated by the parallel shift outward to the right of the $\Sigma_{SR}S_{FIRM}$ along market demand D^2_{MKT} in Figure 10.7), and market price will again be driven down toward the equilibrium, zero-profit level p_1.

In addition, as more firms bid for the available factors of production (say, skilled carpentry labor or lumber during a housing boom), the cost of these factors will tend to rise. In that event, the entire cost structure of MC_1 and AC_1 will rise to reflect the higher input costs along an upward-sloping input supply schedule like that for crude oil in Figure 10.6(b). This higher input cost results in a shift up of the firm's cost structure to AC_2 (see Figure 10.7) and imposes a two-way squeeze on excess profit. Such a scenario is referred to as an **external diseconomy of scale**. External scale diseconomies

external diseconomy of scale An increase in unit costs reflecting higher input prices.

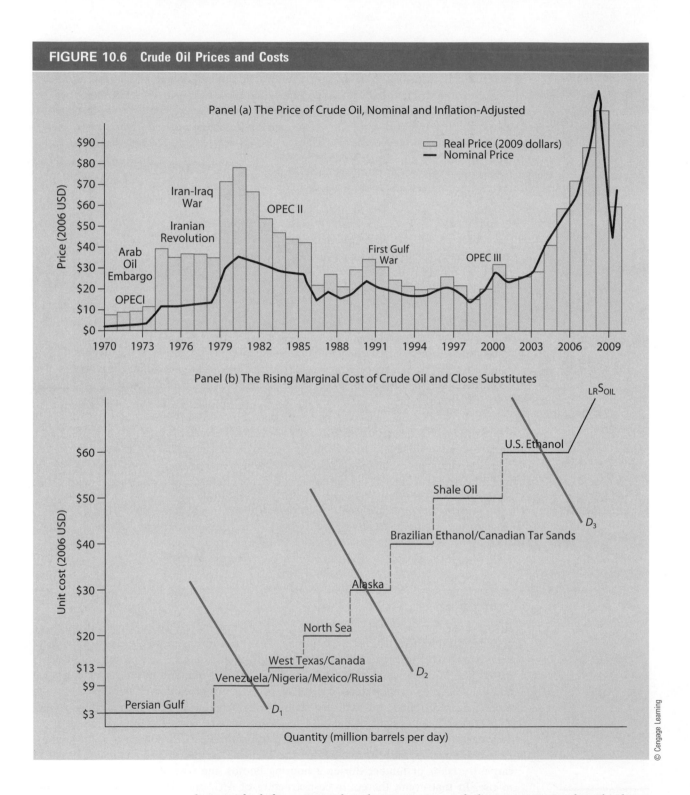

FIGURE 10.6 Crude Oil Prices and Costs

Panel (a) The Price of Crude Oil, Nominal and Inflation-Adjusted

Panel (b) The Rising Marginal Cost of Crude Oil and Close Substitutes

© Cengage Learning

are distinguished from internal scale economies and diseconomies in that the latter reflect unit cost changes as the rate of output increases, *assuming no change in input prices*, whereas the former reflect the bidding up of input prices as the industry expands in response to an increase in market demand.

FIGURE 10.7   Long-Run Equilibrium under Pure Competition (in an Increasing Cost Industry)

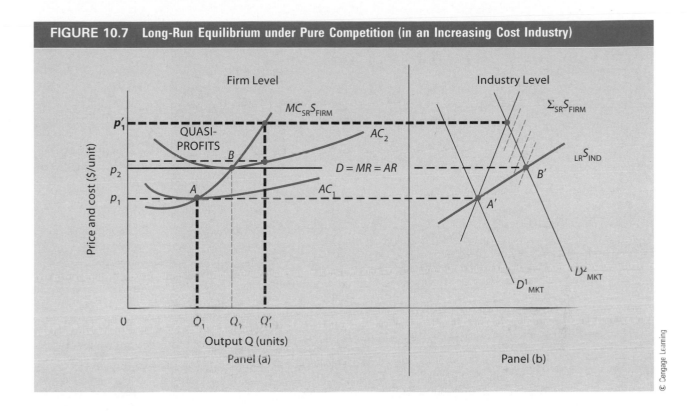

Example

Copper Price Rise by 400 Percent Contributes to Housing Bubble

Home prices across the United States rose to unsustainable heights in 2006–2008. Part of the reason was demand-pull bid price pressure from lower interest rates on mortgages than ever seen in post-war U.S. markets. But another reason was cost-push asking price pressure from spiking commodity prices. A 2,100-square-foot home incorporates 440 pounds of copper plumbing, sheathing, and wiring. Between 2003 and 2007, copper rose in price 400 percent. Lumber prices have responded the same way in the fall of 2012 in the immediate aftermath of Hurricane Sandy.

Under a constant input price assumption, the long-run industry supply curve $_{LR}S_{IND}$ in Figure 10.7 would be flat, a so-called *constant-cost industry* like coal harvesting. However, with the rising input prices for crude oil depicted in Figure 10.6(b), the long-run supply curve $_{LR}S_{IND}$ for the downstream final product gasoline rises to the right, signifying an *increasing-cost industry*, as depicted in Figure 10.7. (It is also quite possible to have downward-sloping long-run supply curves.) A decreasing-cost industry occurred in the 1980s in calculators and in the 1990s in PCs because computer chip inputs became less expensive as the personal computer market expanded, as shown in Figure 10.8.

The net result is that in the long-run equilibrium, all purely competitive firms will tend to have identical costs, and prices will tend to equal average total costs (i.e., the average total cost curve *AC* will be tangent to the horizontal price line p_2). Thus, we

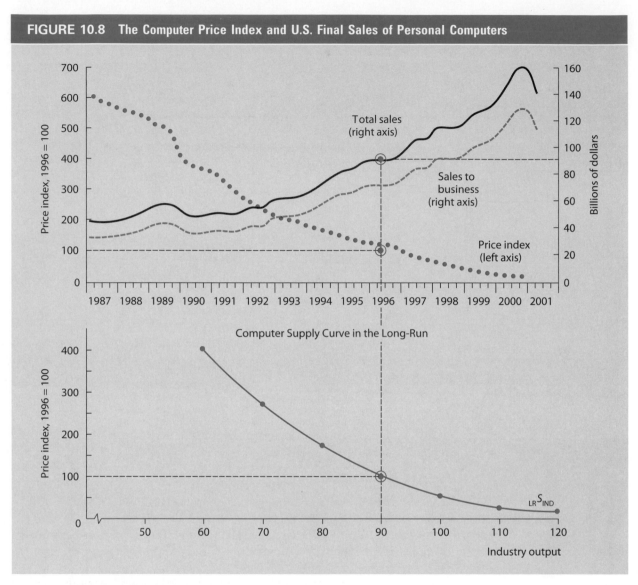

FIGURE 10.8 The Computer Price Index and U.S. Final Sales of Personal Computers

Source: St. Louis Federal Reserve Bank, *National Economic Trends* (May 2001).

may say that at the long-run profit-maximizing level of output under pure competition, equilibrium will be achieved at a point where $P = MR = MC = AC$. In long-run equilibrium, each competitive firm is producing at its most efficient (i.e., its lowest unit cost) level of output and just breaking even.

PRICE-OUTPUT DETERMINATION UNDER MONOPOLISTIC COMPETITION

Monopolistic competition is a market structure with a relatively large number of firms, each selling a product that is differentiated in some manner from the products of its fringe competitors, and with substantial barriers to entry into the group of leading firms.

WHAT WENT RIGHT • WHAT WENT WRONG

The Dynamics of Competition at Amazon.com[20]

Online retailing started very slowly in clothing and other search goods that buyers want to "touch and feel," but it has excelled in one experience good—namely, books. Amazon stocks less than 1,000 bestsellers but displays and provides reviews on 2.5 million popular titles. Using Ingram Book Group, the world's largest book wholesaler, Amazon is able to ship most selections in one to three days. Even though sales have doubled each half year, Amazon.com shares have declined in value.

One difficulty for Amazon.com is that Internet retailing is a classic example of a business with low barriers to entry and exit. As soon as Amazon's business systems for display, order taking, shipping, and payments stabilized, since profits were present, substantial entry activity occurred. For example, Barnes and Noble entered into an exclusive contract with America Online to pitch electronic book sales to AOL's 8.5 million subscribers. And many specialist booksellers of Civil War books, jet plane books, history books, auto books, and so forth have flooded onto the Internet search engines. Even Amazon's wholesale supplier Ingram Book Group has entered the fray; for

$2,500, Ingram support services will set up a Web site on behalf of any new book retailer.

Amazon.com responded by offering customized notification and book discussion services to provide value added for readers with special interests. The information revolution has made relationship marketing to established customers a pivotal element in securing repeat purchases. Nevertheless, the numerous open opportunities for fast, easy, and cheap entry likely will erode the profits in electronic book retailing. The imperfect consumer information, limited time for comparison shopping, and brand loyalty that retailers have depended upon are disappearing with Internet search engines. As a result, retailing's traditionally slim profit margins are quickly becoming hairline thin or nonexistent just like tract home building. A competitive rate of return on time, talent, and investment in online retailing might today amount to only 5 percent.

[20]Based on "Web Browsing," *The Economist* (March 29, 1997), p. 71; "In Search of the Perfect Market: A Survey of Electronic Commerce," *The Economist* (May 10, 1997); "The Net: A Market Too Perfect for Profits," *BusinessWeek* (May 11, 1998), p. 20; "Comparison Shopping Is the Web's Virtue—Unless You're a Seller," *Wall Street Journal* (July 23, 1998), p. A1; and *Value Line, Ratings and Reports*, various issues.

Product differentiation may be based on special product characteristics, trademarks, packaging, quality perceptions, distinctive product design, or conditions surrounding the sale, such as location of the seller, warranties, and credit terms. The demand curve for any one firm is expected to have a negative slope and be extremely elastic because of the large number of close substitutes. The firm in monopolistic competition has some limited discretion over price (as distinguished from the firm in pure competition) because of customer loyalties arising from real or perceived product differences. Profit maximization (or loss minimization) again occurs when the firm produces at that level of output and charges that price at which marginal revenue equals marginal cost.

Short Run

Just as in the case of pure competition, a monopolistically competitive firm may or may not generate a profit in the short run. For example, consider a demand curve such as $D'D'$ in Figure 10.9, with marginal revenue equal to MR'. Such a firm will set its prices where $MR' = MC$, resulting in price P_3 and output Q_3. The firm will earn a profit of EC dollars per unit of output. However, the low barriers to entry in a monopolistically competitive industry will not permit these short-run profits to be earned for long. As new firms enter the industry, industry supply will increase, causing the equilibrium price to fall. This is reflected in a downward movement in the demand curve facing any individual firm.

Long Run

With relatively free entry and exit into the competitive fringe, average costs and a firm's demand function will be driven *toward* tangency at a point such as A in Figure 10.9.

FIGURE 10.9   Long-Run Equilibrium in Monopolistic Competition

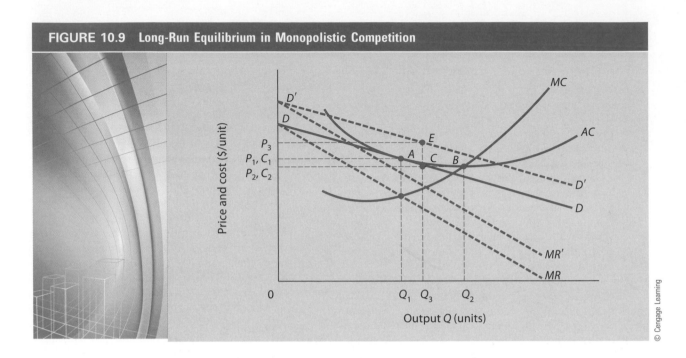

At this price, P_1, and output, Q_1, marginal cost is equal to marginal revenue. Hence a firm selling perfume or beer is producing at its optimal level of output. Any price lower or higher than P_1 will result in a loss to the firm because average costs will exceed price.

Because the monopolistic competitor produces at a level of output where average costs are still declining (between Points A and B in Figure 10.9), monopolistically competitive firms produce with excess capacity. Of course, this argument overlooks the extent to which idle capacity may be a source of product differentiation. Idle capacity means a firm such as Singapore Airlines can operate with high delivery reliability and change-order responsiveness, which can be very important to business travelers and that warrants a price premium relative to competitive fringe airlines.

Example

Long-Run Price and Output Determination: Blockbuster, Inc.

The market for DVD rentals in Charlotte, North Carolina, can best be described as monopolistically competitive. The demand for DVD rentals is estimated to be

$$P = 10 - 0.004Q$$

where Q is the number of weekly DVD rentals. The long-run average cost function for Blockbuster (now owned by Dish Network) is estimated to be

$$LRAC = 8 - 0.006Q + 0.000002Q^2$$

Blockbuster's managers want to know the profit-maximizing price and output levels, and the level of expected total profits at these price and output levels.

First, compute total revenue (TR) as

$$TR = P \cdot Q = 10Q - 0.004Q^2$$

(continued)

Next, compute marginal revenue (MR) by taking the first derivative of TR:

$$MR = \frac{dTR}{dQ} = 10 - 0.008Q$$

Compute total cost (TC) by multiplying $LRAC$ by Q:

$$TC = LRAC \cdot Q = 8Q - 0.006Q^2 + 0.000002Q^3$$

Compute marginal cost (MC) by taking the first derivative of TC:

$$MC = \frac{dTC}{dQ} = 8 - 0.012Q + 0.000006Q^2$$

Next, set $MR = MC$

$$10 - 0.008Q = 8 - 0.012Q + 0.000006Q^2$$

$$0.000006Q^2 - 0.004Q - 2 = 0$$

Use the quadratic formula to solve for Q. Q^* is equal to 1,000.[21] At this quantity, price is equal to

$$P^* = 10 - 0.004(1,000)$$
$$= 10 - 4$$
$$= \$6$$

Total profit is equal to the difference between TR and TC, or

$$\pi = TR - TC$$
$$= 10Q - 0.004Q^2 - [8Q - 0.006Q^2 + 0.000002Q^3]$$
$$= 10(1,000) - 0.004(1,000)^2 - [8(1,000) - 0.006(1,000)^2 + 0.000002(1,000)^3]$$
$$= \$2,000$$

The MR and MC at these price and output levels are \$2.

The fact that Blockbuster expects to earn a profit of \$2,000 suggests that the firm can anticipate additional competition, resulting in price cutting that will ultimately eliminate this profit amount.[22]

---

[21]The solution of the quadratic formula, $aQ^2 + bQ + c = 0$, is

$$Q = \frac{-b \pm \sqrt{b^2 - 4ac}}{2a} = \frac{-(-0.004) \pm \sqrt{(-0.004)^2 - 4(0.000006)(1-2)}}{2(0.000006)}$$

$$= 1,000 \text{ or } -333.33$$

Only the positive solution is feasible.

[22]Recall that the TC function includes a "normal" level of profit. Hence, this \$2,000 represents an economic *rent* above a normal profit level.

SELLING AND PROMOTIONAL EXPENSES

In addition to varying price and quality characteristics of their products, firms may also vary the amount of their advertising and other promotional expenses in their search for profits. This selling and promotional activity generates two distinct types of benefits. First, demand for the general product group may be shifted upward to the right.

The second, more widespread incentive for advertising is the desire to shift the demand function of a particular firm at the expense of other firms offering similar products. This strategy will be pursued both by oligopolists like Philip Morris and General Mills and by firms in more monopolistically competitive industries such as beer—e.g., Anheuser-Busch, Miller, and Coors.

Determining the Optimal Level of Selling and Promotional Outlays

To illustrate the effects of advertising expenditures and to determine the optimal selling expenses of a firm, consider the case where price and product characteristics already have been determined, and all retailers are selling at the manufacturer's suggested retail price.

The determination of the optimal advertising outlay is a straightforward application of the marginal decision-making rules followed by profit-maximizing firms. Define MR to be the change in total revenue received from a one-unit increase in output (and the sale of that output). For fixed-price settings, MR just equals the price, P. Define MC to be the change in total costs of producing and distributing (but not of advertising) an additional unit of output. The marginal profit or contribution margin from an additional unit of output is (from Chapter 9):

$$\text{Contribution Margin } (PCM) = P - MC \qquad [10.3]$$

The marginal cost of advertising (MCA) associated with the sale of an additional unit of output is defined as the change in advertising expenditures (ΔAk) where k is the unit cost of an advertising message, A, or

$$MCA = \frac{\Delta Ak}{\Delta Q} \qquad [10.4]$$

The optimal level of advertising outlays is the level of advertising where the marginal profit contribution (PCM) is equal to the MCA, or

$$PCM = MCA \qquad [10.5]$$

As long as a firm receives a greater contribution margin than the MCA it incurs to sell an additional unit of output, the advertising outlay should be made. If PCM is less than MCA, the advertising outlay should not be made and the level of advertising should be reduced until $PCM = MCA$. This marginal analysis also applies to other types of non-price competition like after-sale service and product replacement guarantees.

Example

Optimal Advertising at Parkway Ford

The marginal profit contribution from selling Ford automobiles at Parkway Ford averages $1,000 across the various models it sells. Parkway estimates that it will have to incur $550 of additional promotional expenses per vehicle to increase its sales by 1 unit per day. Should the outlay for promotions be made?

Because $PCM > MCA$ (i.e., $1,000 > $550), Parkway's operating profit will be increased by $450 if it incurs an additional $550 of promotional expenses. Parkway should continue to make additional promotional outlays (which are likely to be less

(continued)

and less effective at triggering additional sales per day) up to the point where the *MCA* equals the expected (marginal profit) contribution margin.

If Parkway were then to find that *MCA* was greater than *PCM*, it should cut back on promotional outlays until the contribution margin rose enough to again equate *PCM* = *MCA*.

Optimal Advertising Intensity

Optimal expenditure on demand-increasing costs like promotions, couponing, direct mail, and media advertising can be compared across firms. For example, the total contributions from incremental sales relative to the advertising cost of beer ads can be compared to the total contributions relative to the advertising cost of cereal ads. Advertising is often placed in five media (network TV, local TV, radio, newspapers, and magazines). The reach of a TV ad is measured as audience thousands per minute of advertising message; reach is directly related to the advertising message's cost (k). Consider the following contribution analysis of the decision to purchase an ad. A manager should fully fund in her marketing budget any ad campaign for which

$$(P - MC)(\Delta Q / \Delta A) > k \qquad [10.6]$$

where ($P - MC$) is the contribution margin and ($\Delta Q / \Delta A$) is the incremental increase in demand (i.e., a shift outward in demand) attributable to the advertising.[23]

Ford and P&G Tie Ad Agency Pay to Sales

Historically, ad agencies have earned more income each time their clients buy another expensive 30-second slot on network TV (or other media), whatever the performance of the ad in generating incremental sales. More recently, Ford and Procter & Gamble, two of the world's biggest advertisers, announced that henceforth all agency billings would need to be performance based. These incentive payment plans include a fixed fee for designing ad campaigns plus incentive pay based on the incremental sales traceable to the ad. The idea is to encourage agencies to search for database marketing, Internet, and event sponsorships that far exceed the marginal media buy-in advertising productivity, $\Delta Q / \Delta A$.

Expanding Equation 10.6, by multiplying both sides by A and dividing both sides by PQ, identifies the two determinants of the optimal advertising expenditure per dollar sales or "advertising intensity." Ak/PQ is determined by the contribution margin percentage ($P - MC$)/P and by the advertising elasticity of demand E_a:

$$\frac{Ak}{PQ} = \frac{(P - MC)}{P} \frac{A}{Q} (\Delta Q / \Delta A) \qquad [10.7]$$

$$\frac{Ak}{PQ} = \frac{(P - MC)}{P} E_a \qquad [10.8]$$

---

[23]Sometimes the price points at which the product can be sold change after a successful ad campaign. If so, the appropriate valuation of the incremental sales in Equation 10.6 is the new contribution margin.

Both factors are important. With high margins (near 70 percent) and very effective ads, Kellogg's spends almost 30 percent of every dollar of sales revenue on cereal advertising (e.g., $0.294 = 0.70 \times 0.42$, where 0.42 is the estimated E_a). In contrast, the jewelry industry has 92 percent margins, the highest of all four-digit industries, but Zales's advertising inserts in the weekend paper simply do not trigger many jewelry sales. Because the advertising elasticity in jewelry is so low (only 0.11), a company like Zales spends only 10 percent of its sales revenue on advertising (i.e., $0.92 \times 0.11 = 0.10$). Campbell's Soup has relatively high advertising elasticity of demand (0.32) given its strong brand name, but the margins on canned goods are very low (less than 10 percent); consequently, Campbell's Soup spends just one-tenth of what Kellogg's spends on advertising as a percentage of sales revenue—just 3 percent of sales revenue.

Example

Optimal Advertising Intensity at Kellogg's and General Mills[24]

The ready-to-eat (RTE) cereal industry spends 55 percent of its sales revenue on marketing and promotion—30 percent on advertising alone. In part, this resource allocation decision reflects the fact that cereal demand is very sensitive to successful ad campaigns like Kellogg's Tony the Tiger or General Mills' Wheaties, the Breakfast of Champions. In addition, however, RTE cereal margins are among the highest of any four-digit industry. Kellogg's Raisin Bran sells for $4.49 and has a direct fixed plus variable manufacturing cost of $1.63. That calculates as a $(4.49 - 1.63)/4.49 =$ 70 percent gross margin. Frosted Flakes' margin is 72 percent, and Fruit Loops' margin is 68 percent. These margins reflect brand loyalties built up over many years of advertising investments. In the highly concentrated RTE cereal industry, Quaker Oats (8 percent), Post (15 percent), General Mills (25 percent), and Kellogg's (37 percent) control 85 percent of the market.

Until recently, advertising and retail displays were the predominant forms of competition in cereals. Like Coca-Cola and PepsiCo, the dominant RTE cereal companies had concluded that price discounting would be mutually ruinous and ultimately ineffective. Therefore, each company decided independently to refrain from discounting prices in attempting to gain market share. However, in June 1996, 20 percent price cuts swept through the industry, in part in response to the growth of private-label cereals (e.g., Target Corn Flakes) that had collectively grabbed close to 10 percent of the market. Margins on some leading brand-name products fell from 70 to 50 percent, with licensing (15 percent), packaging (10 percent), wages (10 percent), and distribution (15 percent) accounting for the rest of the selling price.

[24]Based on "Cereals," *Winston-Salem Journal* (March 8, 1995), p. A1; and "Denial in Battle Creek," *Forbes* (October 7, 1996), pp. 44–46.

The Net Value of Advertising

Although advertising can raise entry barriers and maintain market power of dominant firms, the economics of information argues that by giving consumers information, advertising can reduce the prices paid. The discovery of price information may be costly and time consuming in the absence of price advertising. For example, Benham[25] found the

[25]Lee Benham, "The Effect of Advertising on the Price of Eyeglasses," *Journal of Law and Economics* (October 1972), pp. 337–352.

price of eyeglasses to be substantially lower in states that permitted price advertising than in those that prohibited such advertising. Also, because advertising creates brand awareness (both for good and inferior brands), advertisers who misrepresent their product will not be successful in generating repeat business.

COMPETITIVE MARKETS UNDER ASYMMETRIC INFORMATION

lemons markets
Asymmetric information exchange leads to the low-quality products and services driving out the higher-quality products and services.

In competitive markets for T-shirts, crude oil, auto rentals, and delivered pizza, both buyers and sellers have full knowledge of the capabilities and after-sale performance of the standard products. Equilibrium price just covers the supplier's cost of production for a product of known reliable quality. If suppliers were to charge more, rival offers and entry would quickly erode their sales. If suppliers were to charge less, they could not afford to stay in business. This has been the message so far of this chapter—in competitive markets under ideal information conditions, you get what you pay for. Such markets differ enormously from competitive markets under asymmetric information, which are sometimes called **lemons markets** One prominent example of asymmetric information in a lemons market is used automobiles, in which the true quality of mechanical repairs, or other features, often is known only to the seller. Other goods sold under asymmetric information include house paint, mail-order computer components, and common cold remedies.

In a lemons market, the buyers discount all unverifiable claims by the sellers, who market only lower-quality products at the reduced prices buyers are willing to offer. This disappearance of higher-quality products from the marketplace illustrates the concept of adverse selection—that is, the lower-quality products are selected in and the higher-quality products are adversely selected out. To resolve the marketing problems posed by adverse selection requires credible commitment mechanisms such as warranties, brand-name reputations, collateral, or price premiums for reliable repeat-purchase transactions.

Incomplete versus Asymmetric Information

incomplete information Uncertain knowledge of payoffs, choices, and so forth.

One distinction that can sharpen our understanding of these complicating factors in competitive exchange is that between asymmetric information and **incomplete information**. Incomplete information is associated with uncertainty, and uncertainty is pervasive. Practically all exchanges, whether for products, financial claims, or labor services, are conducted under conditions of uncertainty. On the one hand, decision makers often face uncertainty as to the effect of random disturbances on the outcome of their actions. This uncertainty typically leads to insurance markets. On the other hand, decision makers are sometimes uncertain as to the payoffs or even types of choices they face. This condition typically leads to intentionally incomplete contracting.

asymmetric information Unequal, dissimilar knowledge.

Asymmetric information exchange, in contrast, refers to situations in which either the buyer or the seller possesses information that the other party cannot verify or to which the other party does not have access. For example, mail-order suppliers of computer components or personal sellers of used cars often have an informationally advantaged position relative to the buyers. The sellers know the machine's capabilities, deficiencies, and most probable failure rate, but these are difficult matters for the buyer to assess from reading magazine ads or kicking the tires. And the typical 90-day warranty does nothing to alter this information asymmetry. Both buyer and seller face uncertainty against which they may choose to insure, but one has more information or better information than the other.

Search Goods versus Experience Goods

In services, retailing, and many manufacturing industries, buyers generally search the market to identify low-price suppliers. Sometimes this search is accomplished by asking for recommendations from recent purchasers, by scouring the catalogs and ads, or by visiting showrooms and sales floors. In selecting a supplier, many customers are also intensely interested in multiple dimensions of product and service quality, including product design, durability, image, conformance to specifications, order delay, delivery reliability, change-order responsiveness, and after-sale service. Customers often spend as much time and effort searching the market for the desired quality mix as they do searching for lowest price. Retailers and service providers understand this and often offer many quality combinations at various prices to trigger a purchase of these **search goods**. Consider, for example, the many price-quality alternatives available in clothing, sporting goods, and furniture stores as well as across hotel chains.

> **search goods**
> Products and services whose quality can be detected through market search.

On the other hand, some products and services have important quality dimensions that *cannot* be observed at the point of purchase. Consider, again, used cars and other resale machinery, nonprescription remedies for the common cold, house paint, and mail-order computer components. The quality of these items can be detected only through experience in using the products. Hence, products and services of this type are termed **experience goods** and are distinguished from search goods.

> **experience goods** Products and services whose quality is undetectable when purchased.

Ultimately, the problem with experience goods in competitive market exchange is the unverifiability of asymmetric information. The seller knows how to detect the difference between high-quality and low-quality products (e.g., between lemons and cream puffs in the used-car market), but cannot credibly relay this information to buyers, at least not in chance encounters between strangers. Fraudulent sellers will claim high quality when it is absent, and realizing this, buyers rationally discount all such information. Because of the private, impacted nature of the product quality information, the seller's claims and omissions can never be verified without experiencing for oneself the reliability of the auto, the efficacy of the common cold remedy, the durability of the house paint, or the capability of the computer component.

All of this is not to say that the buyers of experience goods are without recourse or that the sellers are without ingenuity as to how to market their products. Warranties and investments in reputations provide mechanisms whereby the sellers of house paint and computer components can credibly commit to delivering a high-quality product. The essential point is that in the absence of these bonding or hostage mechanisms, the experience-good buyer will rationally disbelieve the seller's claims. Consequently, the honest seller of truly high-quality experience goods will find little market for his or her higher-cost, higher-priced product. The "bad apples drive out the good" in many experience-good markets.

Adverse Selection and the Notorious Firm

Suppose customers recognize that unverifiable private information about experience-good quality is present, yet knowledge of any fraudulent high-price sale of low-quality products spreads almost instantaneously throughout the marketplace. Is this extreme reputational effect sufficient to restore the exchange of high-quality/high-price experience goods? Or, can the notorious firm continue to defraud customers here and elsewhere? The answer depends on the conditions of entry and exit discussed earlier in this chapter, but not in the way you might expect.

Consider the cost structure and profits of such a notorious firm, depicted in Figure 10.10. If offered the low price P_b, the firm operates in competitive equilibrium at Q_1, where the price just covers the marginal cost and average total cost ($SAC_{low\ quality}$) for

FIGURE 10.10 **Low-Quality Experience Goods Emerge from Competitive Markets**

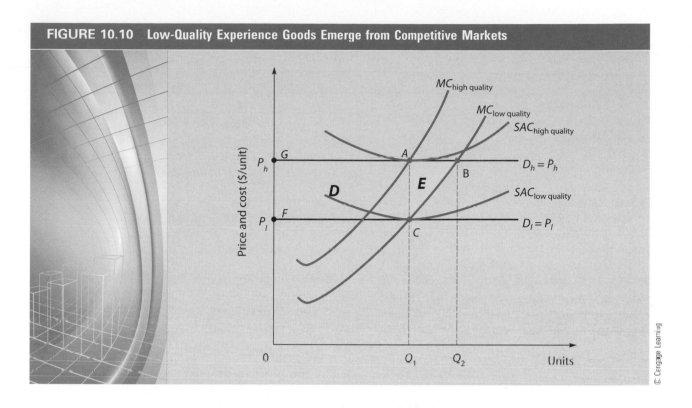

Q_1 units of the low-quality product. Alternatively, if offered the high price P_h, either the firm can competitively supply Q_1 of the high-quality experience good and again just break even against the higher costs of $SAC_{\text{high quality}}$,[26] or the firm can deliver a low-quality experience good at Q_2 and continue to incur the lower costs of $SAC_{\text{low quality}}$. The third alternative entails an expansion of output along $MC_{\text{low quality}}$ in response to the price rise and generates profits. That is, the incremental output $(Q_2 - Q_1)$ earns incremental profit equal to the difference between P_h and $MC_{\text{low quality}}$—namely, the shaded area ABC (labeled bold E)—and in addition, the original output Q_1 earns a fraudulent rent of area $GACF$ (labeled bold D). Although the supplier observes his own cost directly and therefore detects the availability of $D + E$, the problem for the experience-good buyer is that in terms of point-of-sale information, high-price transactions at Point B on $MC_{\text{low quality}}$ and at Point A on $MC_{\text{high quality}}$ are indistinguishable. Both types of products have an asking price of P_h, and only the seller observes the output rate Q_1 versus Q_2.

Of course, the supplier is not indifferent between the two alternatives. The high-quality transaction offers a cash flow from operations just sufficient to cover capital costs and break even at Point A, whereas the fraudulent transaction (a low-quality product at a high price at Point B) offers a net profit for at least one period. Table 10.2 depicts this interaction between experience-good buyers and a potentially fraudulent firm as a payoff matrix. The seller can produce either low or high quality, and the buyer can offer either low or high prices. The row player (the seller) gets the below-diagonal payoffs in each cell, and the column player (the buyer) gets the above-diagonal payoffs in each cell. The buyer prefers to cover the high cost of high-quality

---

[26]The minimum cost output for the plant configuration and cost structure associated with high quality could shift right or left, but to simplify, assume that the SAC just increases vertically from Point C to Point A.

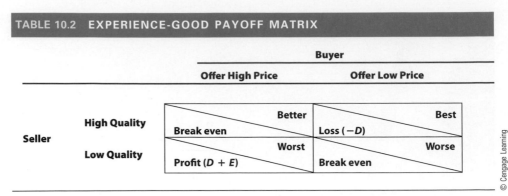

TABLE 10.2 EXPERIENCE-GOOD PAYOFF MATRIX

		Buyer	
		Offer High Price	**Offer Low Price**
Seller	**High Quality**	Better / Break even	Best / Loss ($-D$)
	Low Quality	Worst / Profit ($D + E$)	Worse / Break even

Note: Column-player payoffs are above diagonal. Row-player payoffs are below diagonal.

products (in the northwest cell) rather than pay less and only cover the lower cost of low-quality products (in the southeast cell). However, the buyer is worst off when the seller fails to deliver a high-quality product for which the buyer has paid a high price (in the southwest cell). The buyer also recognizes that getting more than she pays for (in the northeast cell) would impose losses on the seller who would prefer to break even with a low-price/low-quality transaction in the southeast cell.

Each player in this business game attempts to predict the other's behavior and respond accordingly. Knowing that the seller prefers profits to breaking even at high prices and that the seller prefers breaking even to losses at low prices, the buyer predicts that low-quality product will be forthcoming irrespective of the price offered. Therefore, the buyer makes only low-price offers. Only those who wish to be repeatedly defrauded offer to pay high prices for one-shot transactions with strangers offering experience goods.

adverse selection A limited choice of lower-quality alternatives attributable to asymmetric information.

This reasoning motivates **adverse selection** by the rational seller in an experience-good market. Because sellers can anticipate only low-price offers from buyers, the sellers never produce high-quality products—that is, the market for experience goods will be incomplete in that not all product qualities will be available for sale. Anticipating that buyers will radically discount their unverifiable high-quality "cream puffs," individual sellers of used cars choose to place only low-quality "lemons" on the market. The "cream puffs" often are given away to relatives. Similarly, jewelers in vacation locations, anticipating that out-of-town buyers will suspect uncertified spectacular gemstones are fakes, choose to sell only lower-quality gemstones. And unbranded mail-order computer components are inevitably of lower quality. Adverse selection always causes competitive markets with asymmetric information to be incomplete. Again, the bad apples drive out the good.

Insuring and Lending under Asymmetric Information: Another Lemons Market

This same adverse selection reasoning applies beyond experience-good product markets whenever asymmetric information is prominent. Consider the transaction between a bank loan officer and a new commercial borrower, or between an insurance company and a new auto insurance policyholder. Through an application and interview process and with access to various databases and credit references, the lender or insurer attempts to uncover the private, impacted information about the applicant's credit or driving history. Nevertheless, just as in the case of claims made by the itinerant seller of an experience good, verification remains a problem. The applicant has an incentive to omit facts that would tend to result in loan or insurance denial (e.g., prior business failures or unreported accidents), and knowing this, the lender may offer only higher-rate loans and the insurer higher-rate policies.

The problem is that higher-rate loans and expensive insurance policies tend to affect the composition of the applicant pool, resulting in adverse selection. Some honest, well-intentioned borrowers and good-risk insurance applicants will now drop out of the applicant pool because of concern about their inability to pay principal and interest and insurance premiums on time as promised. But other applicants who never intended to repay (or drive carefully), or more problematically, those who will try less hard to avoid default or accidents, are undeterred by the higher rates. The asymmetric information and higher rates have adversely selected out precisely those borrowers and drivers the lender and auto insurance company wanted to attract to their loan portfolio and insurance risk pool. Recognizing this problem, the creditors and insurers offer a restricted and incomplete set of loan and insurance contracts. Credit rationing that excludes large segments of the population of potential borrowers and state-mandated protection against uninsured motorists are reflections of the adverse selection problem resulting from asymmetric information in these commercial lending and auto insurance markets.

SOLUTIONS TO THE ADVERSE SELECTION PROBLEM

In both theory and practice, there are two approaches to eliciting the exchange of high-quality experience goods, commercial loans to new borrowers, or auto insurance policies to new residents. The first involves regulatory agencies such as the Federal Trade Commission, the Food and Drug Administration, and the Consumer Product Safety Commission. These agencies can attempt to set quotas (e.g., on minimum product durability, on minimum lending in "red-lined" underprivileged communities, or on minimum auto liability insurance coverage). They may also impose restrictions (e.g., on the sale of untested pharmaceuticals), enforce product safety standards (e.g., on the flammability of children's sleepwear), and monitor truth-in-advertising laws. We discuss public regulation at greater length in Chapter 16.

Mutual Reliance: Hostage Mechanisms Support Asymmetric Information Exchange

reliance relationships Long-term, mutually beneficial agreements, often informal.

A second, quite different approach involves self-enforcing private solution mechanisms where each party relies on the other. Such **reliance relationships** often involve the exchange of some sort of hostage, such as a reputational asset, an escrow account, or a surety bond. In general, **hostage or bonding mechanisms** are necessary to induce unregulated asymmetric information exchange. For this second approach to the adverse selection problem to succeed, buyers must be convinced that fraud is more costly to the seller than the cost of delivering the promised product quality. Then, and only then, will the customers pay for the seller's additional expected costs attributable to the higher-quality products.

bonding mechanism A procedure for establishing trust by pledging valuable property contingent on your nonperformance of an agreement.

One simple illustration of the use of a hostage mechanism to support asymmetric information exchange is a product warranty, perhaps for an auto tire. Tires are an experience good in that blowout protection and tread wear life are product qualities not detectable at the point of purchase. Only by driving many thousands of miles and randomly encountering many road hazards can the buyer ascertain these tire qualities directly. However, if a tread wear replacement warranty and a tire blowout warranty make the sellers conspicuously worse off should they fail to deliver high-quality tires, then buyers can rely on that manufacturer's product claims. As a consequence, buyers will be willing to offer higher prices for the unverifiably higher-quality product.

Hostage mechanisms can be either self-enforcing or enforced by third parties. Like warranties, a seller's representations about after-sale service and product replacement guarantees are ultimately contractual agreements that will be enforced by the courts. However, other hostage mechanisms require no third-party enforcement. Suppose Du-Pont's industrial chemicals division reveals to potential new customers the names and addresses of several satisfied current customers. This practice of providing references is not only to assist potential buyers in gauging the quality of the product or service for sale but also to deliver an irretrievable hostage. Once new customers have the easy ability to contact regular customers and blow the whistle on product malfunctions or misrepresentations, the seller has an enhanced incentive to deliver high quality to both sets of buyers. Connecting all suppliers and customers in a real-time information system is a natural extension of this familiar practice of providing references. The total quality management's (TQM's) ISO 9000 standards recommend that companies insist on just such information links to their suppliers' other customers.

Example

Credible Product Replacement Claims: Dooney & Bourke

The women's handbag market has a wide selection of brand names, prices, and qualities. Leather products have several search-good characteristics in that one can touch and feel the material in order to assess the fineness or coarseness of the grain, the evenness of the tanning process, the suppleness of the leather, and so forth. In these respects, one can search for just that quality for which one is willing to pay. However, the susceptibility to discoloring with age or exposure to the elements and the quality of the stitching are much harder to detect at the point of purchase. As a result, some aspects of handbag purchase are an experience-good exchange. Therefore, one wonders how the wide variety of prices and qualities can be sustained.

Dooney & Bourke resolved this question by offering an almost preposterous replacement guarantee. Like Revo sunglasses, Dooney & Bourke offered to replace any handbag for the life of the customer. Because each state attorney general will assist any customer in enforcing this promise, the commitment was credible, and the replacement guarantee provides a hostage that supports high-price, high-quality exchanges. In particular, customers can easily discern that Dooney & Bourke is better off producing an exceptionally high-quality handbag to deliver at the first transaction rather than an unlimited series of replacements.

Brand-Name Reputations as Hostages

A marketing mechanism that supports asymmetric information exchange is a brand-name reputation such as Sony Trinitron Wega digital televisions, Apple Macintosh computers, Pepperidge Farm snacks, and Toyota Lexus automobiles. Branding requires a substantial investment over extended periods of time. Moreover, brand names are capital assets that provide future net cash flows from repeat-purchase customers as long as the brand reputation holds up. Defrauding customers by delivering less quality than the brand reputation promised would destroy the capitalized market value of the brand name. Buyers anticipate that value-maximizing managers will not intentionally destroy brand-name capital. Brand names therefore deliver a hostage, providing assurances to buyers that the seller will not misrepresent the quality of an experience good.

Ultimately, brand-name capital provides such a hostage because the disreputation effects on the brand name that result from delivering fraudulent product quality cannot be separated from the salable brand asset. Successful brands can be extended to sell other products; Nestlé's original hot chocolate brand can be extended to sell cereal-based candy bars, and Oreo cookies can be extended to sell ice cream. But the product failure of Texas Instruments (TI) personal computers means that now the TI brand name cannot be easily extended to other consumer electronic products. All the potential buyers have to figure out is whether the seller would be worse off sacrificing the value of the brand name but economizing on production expenses rather than simply incurring the extra expense to produce a high-quality product while retaining the brand value. A brand-name asset such as Pepperidge Farm may suggest one answer, whereas Joe's Garage suggests another.

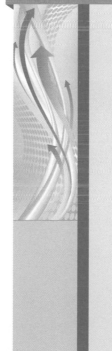

Example

Customers for Life at Sewell Cadillac[27]

The most profitable luxury automobile dealership in the United States is operated in Dallas, Texas, by Carl Sewell. Several decades ago, Mr. Sewell realized that the critical success factor in his business was establishing repeat-purchase transactions with regular customers. Many potential buyers shop for lowest price in the new automobile market, sometimes with no more inconvenience than fingertip browsing of the Internet. And because the alternatives are many, and the information on posted prices is great, many dealerships spend several hundred dollars per car on personal selling costs with little prospect of repeat business.

Carl Sewell decided instead to expend similarly large amounts attracting "customers for life." He began by making the apparently preposterous claim that he would dispatch Sewell Cadillac emergency roadside service to any Sewell Cadillac customer experiencing car trouble anywhere in the state of Texas. Texas is geographically quite a large state. To economize on the need for such trips, Sewell developed an extensive dealer-based maintenance schedule and instituted in his service department one of the first total quality management (TQM) programs in the auto industry.

Because TQM introduced new process-based competitive advantages, they were difficult for other dealers to imitate. These process innovations cost plenty, but the word-of-mouth reputation effects every time the dealership delivered on its promise spread the name and quality image of Sewell Cadillac across North Texas. Soon customers were driving in from surrounding cities for the privilege of doing high-margin business with Carl Sewell. And even more importantly, these same customers came back time and time again with very little additional selling cost to the dealership.

[27]See Carl Sewell and Paul B. Brown, *Customers for Life* (New York: Simon & Schuster, 1992).

If brand-name assets could be sold independently of their reputations (or disreputations), then this hostage mechanism would cease to support experience-good exchange. Assets that can be redeployed at the grantor's wish are not hostages in this reliance contracting sense. The implication is that easy entry and exit, which works to ensure break-even prices just sufficient to cover costs in the normal competitive markets, may have undesirable consequences in markets with asymmetric information experience goods.

Price Premiums with Non-Redeployable Assets[28]

Recall that if sellers are offered prices that just cover high-quality cost, sellers of experience goods prefer the profit from defrauding customers by delivering low-quality products. But suppose buyers offered reliable sellers a continuing price premium above the cost of high-quality products. At P_{hh} in Figure 10.11, the non-notorious firm produces Q'_1 high-quality product and earns a continuous stream of profits ($IJAG + JKA$), labeled $T + U$. This perpetuity may now exceed (in present value) the notorious firm's onetime-only fraudulent rent from production at Q'_2—namely, $D + T$, plus incremental profit $E + U + V$. That is,

$$(T + U)/d > [(D + T) + (E + U + V)]/(1 + d) \qquad [10.9]$$

where d is an appropriate discount rate (e.g., the firm's weighted average cost of capital, perhaps 12 percent). By Equation 10.9, lower discount rates or faster rising marginal cost (i.e., a smaller incremental profit from the expansion of output, shaded area V in Figure 10.11) decreases the likelihood of fraudulent behavior. If reliable delivery of a high-quality product does in fact earn long-term net profit in excess of the one-time-only profit from fraud, sellers will offer both low- and high-quality products at P_l and P_{hh}, respectively, and some buyers will purchase in each market.

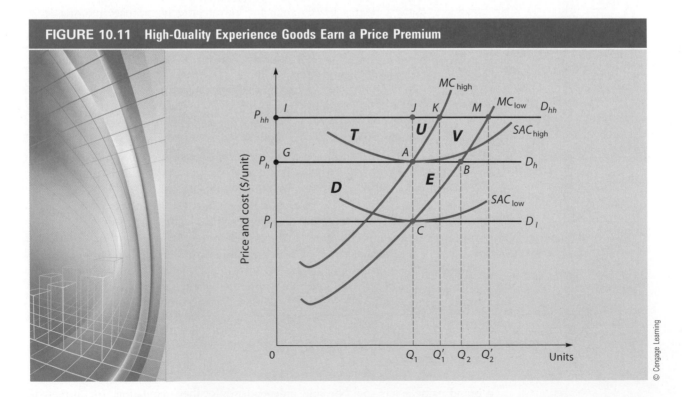

FIGURE 10.11 High-Quality Experience Goods Earn a Price Premium

© Cengage Learning

[28]See B. Klein and K. Leffler, "The Role of Market Forces in Assuring Contractual Performance," *Journal of Political Economy* 89, no. 4 (1981), pp. 615–641.

However, transitory profits alone do not allow an escape from adverse selection. Because profits attract entry in competitive markets, the price premiums will erode, and notorious firm behavior will then return. What is missing is a mechanism to dissipate the rent from the price premiums. If the sellers invest the high-quality price premiums in firm-specific assets, such as Sewell Cadillac's TQM program, L'eggs retail displays for convenience stores, or Ethan Allen's interiors for its showrooms, then new entrants will encounter a higher entry barrier than previously. Such barriers cause potential entrants to perceive much lower potential net profit unless one is planning to deliver a very expensive high-quality product. They therefore deter entry. Sewell Cadillac's, L'eggs, or Ethan Allen's operating profits in excess of production cost can then persist, and high-quality, high-price experience goods can then survive in the marketplace.

The rent-dissipating investments must not be in generic retail sites easily redeployable to the next tenant or capital equipment easily redeployable to the next manufacturer (e.g., corporate jet aircraft). If that were the case, hit-and-run entry would recur each time high-quality prices rose above cost. New entrants would just move in on the business for a short time period and then sell off their assets in thick resale markets when profits eroded. In that event, competitive equilibrium would again induce adverse selection in experience-good markets. Instead, the investment that dissipates the operating profit from high-quality products must be sunk-cost investment in non-redeployable assets.

Example

Hostage Exchange with Efficient Uncut Diamond Sorting at De Beers[29]

Another illustration of experience-good exchange is block booking by the De Beers diamond cartel, which controls over 80 percent of the uncut wholesale diamond business. De Beers offers groupings of diamonds of various grades to approved wholesale buyers. Because buyers are not allowed to cull the less-valuable stones, the quality of the diamonds in any given grouping is unverifiable at the point of purchase, hence the term *sights*. If these arrangements were one time only, no buyer would purchase high-price sights or agree to the culling restrictions. But because block booking economizes on the duplicatory assessments of rejected stones that would otherwise result, De Beers can consistently offer its sights at net costs below the value at which the diamonds grade out. Buyers therefore have a reason for purchasing high-quality experience goods from De Beers.

If a competitor offered no culling restrictions and lower prices, the diamond merchants would carefully weigh the additional cost of sorting the diamonds themselves against the price premiums at De Beers and might well decide to continue doing business with De Beers. Knowing this, very few potential competitors ever enter the uncut diamond wholesale business to challenge De Beers despite its high markups and margins. De Beers' reputation for passing on its cost savings in diamond sorting to buyers is the hostage that brings buyers back time and time again.

[29]Based on R. Kenney and B. Klein, "The Economics of Block Booking," *Journal of Law and Economics* 26 (1983), pp. 497–540.

non-redeployable assets Assets whose value in second-best use is near zero.

Non-redeployable assets are assets whose liquidation value in second-best use is low. Usually this occurs when the assets depend on a firm-specific input such as a Sewell Cadillac, L'eggs, or Ethan Allen brand name. Without the brand name, no firm has a use for the egg-shaped retail racks designed for L'eggs original packaging or the lavish

asset specificity The difference in value between first-best and second-best use.

Ethan Allen showrooms. Non-redeployable assets have high value in their first best use. The difference between value in first best use and liquidation value is a measure of the **asset specificity**. Highly specific assets make the best hostages to convince customers that asymmetric information transactions will be nonfraudulent.

In summary, asymmetric information causes competitive markets for experience goods to differ rather markedly from the competitive markets for search goods. Long-run equilibrium for high-quality experience goods requires revenues in excess of total unit cost. These profits are invested by reliable sellers of experience goods in highly specific assets. Potentially notorious firms with redeployable assets attract only customers seeking low-price/low-quality experience goods. In experience-good markets, you get what you pay for when reputations matter or when other hostage mechanisms establish the seller's credibility.

SUMMARY

- Competitive strategy entails an analysis of the firm's resource-based capabilities, the design of business processes that can secure sustainable competitive advantage, and the development of a road map for innovation.
- Types of strategic thinking include industry analysis, competitor analysis, strategic positioning, and identification of core competencies derived from resource-based capabilities.
- Sustainable competitive advantage may arise from product differentiation strategy (product capabilities, branding, and endorsements), from focused cost or cost leadership strategy, or from information technology strategy.
- The choice of competitive strategy should be congruent with the breadth or narrowness of the firm's strategic focus.
- A successful competitive strategy includes an ongoing process of reinvention and reconfiguration of capabilities and business models.
- A relevant market is a group of economic agents that interact with each other in a buyer-seller relationship. Relevant markets often have both spatial and product characteristics.
- The Five Forces model of business strategy identifies threat of substitutes, threat of entry, power of buyers, power of suppliers, and the intensity of rivalry as the determinants of sustainable incumbent profitability in a particular industry. Such industry analyses are often complemented by an assessment of threats from disruptive technology.

- The threat of substitutes depends upon the number and closeness of substitutes as determined by the product development, advertising, brand-naming, and segmentation strategies of preexisting competitors. Complements in consumption can be an enormous source of network effects, raising sustainable profitability.
- The threat of entry depends upon the height of barriers to potential entrants including capital requirements, economies of scale, absolute cost advantages, switching costs, access to distribution channels, and trade secrets and other difficult-to-imitate forms of product differentiation.
- The bargaining power of buyers and suppliers depends upon their number, their size distribution, the relationship between industry capacity and industry demand, the uniqueness of the inputs, the potential for forward and backward integration, the ability of the buyers to influence the setting of an industry standard, and the extent to which each party to the bargain has outside alternatives.
- The intensity of rivalry depends upon the number and size distribution of sellers in the relevant market, the relative frequency of price versus non-price competition, switching costs, the proportion of fixed to total cost, the barriers to exit, the growth rate of industry demand, and the incumbent's speed of adjustment.
- The *demand* for a good or service is defined as the various quantities of that good or service that consumers are willing and able to purchase during a

particular period of time at all possible prices. The *supply* of a good or service is defined as the quantities that sellers are willing to make available to purchasers at all possible prices during a particular period of time.

- In general, a profit-maximizing firm will desire to operate at that level of output where marginal cost equals marginal revenue.

- In a purely competitive market structure, the firm will operate in the short run as long as price is greater than average variable cost.

- In a *purely competitive* market structure, the tendency is toward a long-run equilibrium condition in which firms earn just normal profits, price is equal to marginal cost and average total cost, and average total cost is minimized.

- In a monopolistically competitive industry, a large number of firms sell a differentiated product. In practice, few market structures can be best analyzed in the context of the *monopolistic competition* model. Most actual market structures have greater similarities to the *purely competitive* market model or the *oligopolistic* market model.

- Advertising expenditures are optimal from a profit-maximization perspective if they are carried to the point where the marginal profit contribution from an additional unit of output is equal to the marginal cost of advertising. The optimal level of advertising intensity (the advertising expenditure per sales dollar) varies across products and industries; it is determined by the marginal profit contribution from incremental sales and by the advertising elasticity of demand.

- Exchange under incomplete information and under asymmetric information differs. *Incomplete information* refers to the uncertainty that is pervasive in practically all transactions and motivates insurance

markets. *Asymmetric information*, on the other hand, refers to private information one party possesses that the other party cannot independently verify.

- Asymmetric information in *experience-good* markets leads to *adverse selection* whereby high-price/high-quality products are driven from the market by low-quality products whose low quality is indistinguishable at the point of sale. Buyers in such *lemons markets* refuse to offer prices high enough to cover the cost of high quality because under competitive conditions suppliers will predictably commit fraud, and then perhaps move on to conduct business with unsuspecting customers under other product or company names.

- To escape adverse selection and elicit high-quality experience goods necessitates either intrusive and expensive regulation or some sort of bonding mechanism to induce *self-enforcing reliance relationships* between buyers and sellers. Warranties, independent appraisals, leases with a high residual, collateral, irrevocable money-back guarantees, contingent payments, and brand names all provide assurance to buyers that the seller will not misrepresent the product quality. Hostage mechanisms support asymmetric information exchange.

- Another way to escape adverse selection is for buyers to offer price premiums and repeat-purchase transactions to firms that resist fraudulently selling low-quality experience goods for high prices. These profits are invested by reliable sellers in *non-redeployable, highly specific assets.* Potentially *notorious firms* with redeployable assets continue to attract only customers seeking low-price/low-quality products. Under asymmetric information, at best you get what you pay for, never more.

Exercises

Answers to the exercises in blue can be found in Appendix D at the back of the book.

1. The profitability of the leading cola syrup manufacturers PepsiCo and Coca-Cola and of the bottlers in the cola business is very different. PepsiCo and Coca-Cola enjoy an 81 percent operating profit as a percentage of sales; bottlers experience only a 15 percent operating profit as a percentage of sales. Perform a Porter's Five Forces analysis that explains why one type of business is potentially so profitable relative to the other.

2. Television channel operating profits vary from as high as 45 to 55 percent at MTV and Nickelodeon down to 12 to 18 percent at NBC and ABC. Provide a Porter Five Forces analysis of each type of network. Why is MTV so profitable relative to the major networks?

3. The costs of producing steel have declined substantially from building a conventional hot-rolled steel mill down to the new minimill technology that requires only scrap metal, an electric furnace, and 300 workers rather than iron ore raw materials, enormous blast furnaces, rolling mills, reheating furnaces, and thousands of workers. What effect on the potential industry profitability would Porter's Five Forces framework suggest this new technology had? Why?

4. Ethanol is again viewed as one part of a solution to the problem of shortages of petroleum products. Ethanol is made from a blend of gasoline and alcohol derived from corn or sugarcane. What would you expect the impact of this program to be on the price of corn, soybeans, and wheat?

5. Why invest capital in purely competitive industries with equilibrium margins that are razor thin and entrants that erode quasi-profits? Suppose volume is not exceptionally large, why then?

6. Assume that a firm in a perfectly competitive industry has the following total cost schedule:

(a)

q — *the change: ML 40/5 = 8*

OUTPUT (UNITS)	TOTAL COST ($)	M.C	A.C
10	110	—	11
15	150	8	10
20	180	6	9
25	225	9	9
30	300	15	10
35	385	17	11
40	480	19	12

a. Calculate a marginal cost and an average cost schedule for the firm.
b. If the prevailing market price is $17 per unit, how many units will be produced *35* and sold? What are profits per unit? What are total profits?
c. Is the industry in long-run equilibrium at this price?

7. Royersford Knitting Mills, Ltd., sells a line of women's knit underwear. The firm now sells about 20,000 pairs a year at an average price of $10 each. Fixed costs amount to $60,000, and total variable costs equal $120,000. The production department has estimated that a 10 percent increase in output would not affect fixed costs but would reduce average variable cost by 40 cents.
The marketing department advocates a price reduction of 5 percent to increase sales, total revenues, and profits. The arc elasticity of demand with respect to prices is estimated at −2.
a. Evaluate the impact of the proposal to cut prices on (i) total revenue,
(ii) total cost, and (iii) total profits.
b. If average variable costs are assumed to remain constant over a 10 percent increase in output, evaluate the effects of the proposed price cut on total profits.

8. The Poster Bed Company believes that its industry can best be classified as monopolistically competitive. An analysis of the demand for its canopy bed has resulted in the following estimated demand function for the bed:

$$P = 1760 - 12Q$$

The cost analysis department has estimated the total cost function for the poster bed as

$$TC = \frac{1}{3}Q^3 - 15Q^2 + 5Q + 24{,}000$$

a. Calculate the level of output that should be produced to maximize short-run profits.
b. What price should be charged?
c. Compute total profits at this price-output level.
d. Compute the point price elasticity of demand at the profit-maximizing level of output.
e. What level of fixed costs is the firm experiencing on its bed production?
f. What is the impact of a $5,000 increase in the level of fixed costs on the price charged, output produced, and profit generated?

9. Jordan Enterprises has estimated the contribution margin $(P - MC)/P$ for its Air Express model of basketball shoes to be 40 percent. Based on market research and past experience, Jordan estimates the following relationship between the sales for Air Express and advertising/promotional outlays:

ADVERTISING/PROMOTIONAL OUTLAYS ($)	SALES REVENUE ($)
500,000	4,000,000
600,000	4,500,000
700,000	4,900,000
800,000	5,200,000
900,000	5,450,000
1,000,000	5,600,000

a. What is the marginal revenue from an additional dollar spent on advertising if the firm is currently spending $1,000,000 on advertising?
b. What level of advertising would you recommend to Jordan's management?

10. Which of the following products and services are likely to encounter adverse selection problems: golf shirts at traveling pro tournaments, certified gemstones from Tiffany's, graduation gift travel packages, or mail-order auto parts? Why or why not?

11. If notorious firm behavior (i.e., defrauding a buyer of high-priced experience goods by delivering low quality) becomes known throughout the marketplace only with a lag of three periods, profits on high-quality transactions remain the same, and interest rates rise slightly, are customers more likely or less likely to agree to pay high prices for an experience good? Explain.

Case Exercises

Netflix and Redbox Compete for Movie Rentals[30]

Charging $17.99 a month for an unlimited number of movie rentals (three at one time), Netflix revolutionized the movie rental business with a one-day mailing service for DVDs and acquired 12 million subscribers and $1.5 billion in revenue. However, Blockbuster, the video rental giant from the earlier $5.5 billion bricks-and-mortar movie rental business, decided to enter the mail-in delivery and online-DVD rental businesses. Blockbuster (now a division of Dish Network) drove prices down to $14.99, attracting 2 million subscribers. Netflix responded with a cut-rate service of one movie at a time for $9.99 per month, which drove the net profit right out of the business.

---

[30]"Movies to Go," *The Economist* (July 9, 2005), p. 57; and "Blockbuster Plots a Remake," *Wall Street Journal* (February 24, 2010), p. B1, and "Hollywood: The Price Is Wrong," *Wall Street Journal* (February 9, 2011), p. C14.

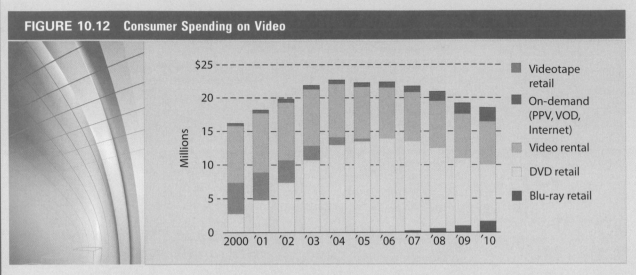

FIGURE 10.12 Consumer Spending on Video

Source: IHS Screen Digest, *Wall Street Journal* (February 9, 2011, p. B14).

Movie studios like Viacom and Time Warner also entered the market with direct-to-the-customer video on demand delivered over the web. Following two months of theatre-only releases, the studios asked $20 to $25 per showing. This fee is five times what it costs to rent a second-run or classic movie from the cable companies and 10 times Netflix's or Redbox's $1.99 or $1 fees for overnight rentals. At such exorbitant prices, the studios earn a 70 percent margin, but studies of price elasticity in home entertainment experiments suggest an eight-fold increase in volume for half-price promotions. On-demand movie rentals and Blu-ray retail sales are the only two growing segments of consumer demand for video (see Figure 10.12).

Use Porter's Five Forces model to answer the following questions:

Questions

1. What disruptive technology has threatened the bricks-and-mortar and mail-in movie rental business?
2. Does easy access to distribution channels at grocery stores for Redbox's 22,000 vending machines indicate a high- or low-entry threat in the movie rental business? Why? Why might McDonald's be an even better distribution channel than grocery stores?
3. Are there any economies of scale in the on-demand video rental business to serve as a barrier to the entry of Amazon?
4. Who are Netflix's and Redbox's suppliers? Are they in a position to appropriate much of the value in the value chain? Why or why not?
5. What factors determine the intensity of rivalry in any industry? Is the intensity of rivalry in the video rental industry high or low? Why?

Saving Sony Music

Explore the crisis that Internet file sharing of copyrighted music recordings has caused for Vivendi Universal, *Sony Music*, *EMI*, and AOL Time Warner Music, which together formerly supplied 70 percent of the global music industry.

Questions

1. How would the Internet firms Napster and Kazaa be reflected in a Porter Five Forces industry analysis?

2. Why was the Internet a disruptive technology for Sony Music? Did the new digital file transfer technology favor album-size transactions which Sony Music understood very well? Or did the new technology favor Steve Jobs's vision of an Apple iTunes Music Store focused on easily accessible 99-cent singles? What aspect of the iTunes Music Store made it more desirable that simply transferring stolen digital music files one by one?

3. What should be Sony Music's competitive strategy in response to this crisis? Include a discussion of resource-based capabilities, business opportunities, and a road map of future innovation.

4. Is your competitive strategy for Sony Music a product-differentiation strategy, a low-cost strategy, or an IT strategy? What is your strategic focus?

Price and Output Determination: Monopoly and Dominant Firms

CHAPTER PREVIEW

In this chapter we analyze how firms that operate in monopoly or near-monopoly markets make output and pricing decisions. In such markets the dominant firm does not have to accept the market price as a given. These firms base their price-cost markups on other factors such as the demand projections at various price points, indicative of the target customers' price elasticity. In this chapter we identify the reasons for single-firm dominance and analyze the components of the contribution margin and the gross margin. We introduce spreadsheet, graphical, and algebraic methods to identify profit-maximizing price and output. In addition, we look at these decisions for regulated industries: electric power, natural gas distribution, and broadcast communications. Deregulation continues to be a topic of intense debate.

MANAGERIAL CHALLENGE

Dominant Microprocessor Company Intel Adapts to Next Trend[1]

With continuous innovation, ever-faster, more-powerful chip designs, and a business plan riveted on supplying the $300 billion personal computer (PC), and tablet industries, Intel Corporation dominates the high-end market in microprocessors. After being forced out of the dynamic random access memory (DRAM) chip business by Japanese rivals in 1986, Intel reinvented itself as the lead supplier of microprocessors for PCs. Intel has an 85 percent market share in the microprocessor chips for laptops and 75 percent market share for desktops. In addition, Intel sells 90 percent of the chip sets that control the flow of data from the microprocessor to the display screens, modems, and graphical user interfaces (GUIs). Its market dominance provides it with enormous economies of scale in production and increasing returns on its marketing expenditures because of network effects. The result is high markups and margins; for example, Intel has at times earned 25 percent net profit margins on its microprocessors.

Because intellectual property is the company's most important asset, Intel protects its proprietary trade secrets about chip design and manufacture by using tight nondisclosure agreements with its customers. Some Intel chip bulk purchasers found, however, that Intel withheld vital information about technical specifications required to fully integrate the chips into new products unless it is given access to its customers' new technologies. Intergraph, a maker of high-end workstations for media applications, alleged, for example, that Intel withheld information about subtle bugs in some Intel chips until Intergraph agreed to license its GUI technology to the chip supplier.

Intel's high-end chips are designed to run Microsoft's complex software for PCs and tablets. In 2007, 261 million units were shipped on a 2.1 billion installed base of PCs. The market for digital telephones, handheld computers, video-game players, and set-top control boxes for digital televisions may be even bigger than the PC market. Such devices require inexpensive flash memory chips that quickly process data. Samsung and Advanced Micro Devices (AMD) are the leaders in this new chip segment. To break into this business, former

Cont.

©Taylor S. Kennedy/National Geographic/Getty Images

Discussion Questions

■ How large must the market share be before a firm dominates a relevant market?

■ Make a list of reasons how a single firm comes to dominate some markets.

■ What are some of the differences between operating profits and net cash flow to equity shareholders?

■ Name some other firms that you suspect earn higher-than-normal profit margins, and brainstorm about why they do so.

Intel president Andy Grove says Intel must prepare to sell lower-end chip products for under $40, despite the fact that Intel's chips previously sold for $87 to $200.

[1]Based on "Intel's Surge," *Wall Street Journal* (July 20, 2005), p. B1; "Intel Outside," *The Economist* (May 27, 2006), pp. 59–63; and *Apple Inc.*, Harvard Business School Case Publishing (2008).

MONOPOLY DEFINED

Monopoly is defined as a market structure with significant barriers to entry in which a single firm produces a highly differentiated product. Without any close substitutes for the product, the demand curve for a monopolist is often an entire relevant market demand. Just as purely competitive market structures (e.g., for AAA January wheat in Kansas City) are rare, so too pure monopoly markets are rare.

Example

The Mickey Mouse Monopoly: Disney

When it began, Disneyland in Anaheim, California, was unique. Other theme parks that were later developed, such as Six Flags, reduced Disney's monopoly power. In an attempt to restore its near-monopoly position, Disney created Disney World in Orlando, Florida, but Universal Studios, SeaWorld, and other attractions throughout the Orlando area quickly offered additional theme park experiences. Were they a complement or a substitute to Disney World? Negative cross price elasticity of demand evidence suggests that they are complements. Seventy percent of Disney World's business is repeat business; more variety inside or outside the park means more frequent returns for longer vacations. Because it anticipated these complement relationships, Disney long ago became a major commercial property developer throughout the Orlando area.

SOURCES OF MARKET POWER FOR A MONOPOLIST

Monopolists or near-monopoly dominant firms enjoy several sources of market power. First, a firm may possess a *patent* or *copyright* that prevents other firms from producing the same product. For example, Pharmacia has a patent on the product Rogaine, the hair growth stimulator for balding men.

Second, a firm may *control critical resources.* De Beers Consolidated Mines, Ltd., owns or controls most of the diamond production in South Africa and often obtains exclusive marketing agreements with other major diamond-producing countries, including the former Soviet Union. This control of raw materials has enabled De Beers to maintain high world prices for cut diamonds for nearly three-quarters of a century.

A third source of monopoly power may be a *government-authorized franchise.* In most U.S. cities, one firm is chosen to provide exclusive cable TV services to the community. The same type of monopoly power occurs when a government agency such as the FCC adopts an industry standard that favors one company over another.

Monopoly power also happens in natural monopolies because of significant *economies of scale* over a wide range of output. The first entrant firm will enjoy declining long-run average costs. Under these circumstances, one supplier of a good or service like electrical power is able to produce the output more cheaply than can a group of smaller competitors. These so-called natural monopolies are usually closely regulated by government agencies to restrict the profits of the monopolist.

Increasing Returns from Network Effects

Finally, *increasing returns in network-based businesses* can be a source of monopoly market power. When Microsoft managed to achieve a critical level of adoption for its Windows GUI, the amount of marketing and promotional expenditure required to secure the next adoption of their software actually began to fall.

Marketing and promotions are generally subject to diminishing returns. As depicted in Figure 11.1, from 0 to 30 percent market share, the marketing required to achieve

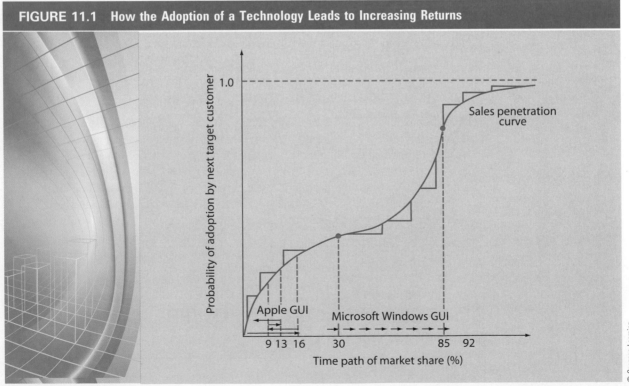

FIGURE 11.1   How the Adoption of a Technology Leads to Increasing Returns

© Cengage Learning

sales penetration curve An S-shaped curve relating current market share to the probability of adoption by the next target customer, reflecting the presence of increasing returns.

each additional share point has a diminishing effect on the probability of adoption by the next potential user (note the reduced slope of the **sales penetration curve**). Consequently, additional share points become more and more expensive over this range. When the number of other users of a network-based device reaches a 30 percent share in Figure 11.1, the next 50 or so share points became cheaper to promote. That is, beyond the 30 percent inflection point, each additional share point of users connected to Microsoft Windows, for example, increases the probability that another user would adopt. Therefore, the marketing expense required to secure another unit sale decreases. (Note the increased slope of the sales penetration curve in the middle portion of Figure 11.1.) Then beyond 85 percent, diminishing returns again set in.

These network-based effects of compatibility with other users increase the value to the potential adopter. The same thing occurs as more independent software vendors (ISVs) write applications for an operating system like Windows that has effectively become an industry standard by achieving more than 30 percent acceptance in the marketplace. The inflection points in the sales penetration curve make it likely that Microsoft will achieve monopoly control of the operating system market. Whatever customer relationships preexisted, once Microsoft achieved a 30 percent share, its increasing returns in marketing caused a network effect that displaced other competitors. Microsoft's share of the PC operating systems market did grow to 92 percent. Netscape's Internet search engine experienced similar displacement by Microsoft's Internet Explorer when Microsoft achieved a 30 percent-plus market share by bundling Internet Explorer with Windows. In effect, it gave away the search engine for free to reach the range of increasing returns on the sales penetration curve for Windows OS software.

Even with increasing returns set off by network effects, however, monopoly is seldom assured for three reasons. First, a higher price point for innovative new products can offset the cost savings from increasing returns of a competitor. This has been Apple's approach to combating Microsoft dominance on the operating systems for competitor PCs. Apple's gross margin exceeded 32 percent for 2005–2008, whereas Dell and HP averaged 18 percent and 25 percent, respectively. Similarly in smart phones segment, Apple's customers were paying $421 margins for iPhones in 2011 when Nokia and Samsung smart phones were garnering just $250 margins.

Second, network effects tend to occur in technology-based industries that have experienced falling input prices such as microprocessors in the computer chip industry. Figure 11.2 shows that between 1997 and 2009, the cost per megahertz for silicon computer chips fell from $2.00 to $0.25, hard drive storage device cost per megabyte fell from $0.40 to $0.03, and the cost per month for a T1 high-speed data transmission line fell from $475 to $300. During the same period, Corning fiber-optic cable became essentially free to anyone who would install it. In short, as these input suppliers grew to serve the expanding product markets in computer equipment and telecom devices, they encountered new productivity from learning curves and innovative design breakthroughs that drove down their costs. Because flash memory chips and telecom equipment markets tend to be highly competitive, the cost savings of input suppliers such as AMD and Corning get passed along to the final product producers, including Apple, PC-assembler Dell, cell phone manufacturer Nokia, and router manufacturer Cisco. Consequently, generally lower costs for all inputs offset in part the dominant firm advantage from increasing returns in promotion and selling expenses for network-based companies such as Microsoft and Google.

FIGURE 11.2 **How Declining Component Costs Led to Falling Product Prices in the Computer and Telecom Industries**

Silicon chips

(Graph: Cost ($ per MHz) vs. year 1997–2009, declining from $2.00 in 1997 to about $0.20 by 2009, with a spike to $1.00 around 2000.)

Hard drive storage

(Graph: Cost ($ per mgb) vs. year 1998–2009, declining from $0.40 in 1998 to about $0.03 by 2009.)

T1 line

(Graph: Cost ($ per month) vs. year 1998–2009, declining from $475 in 1998 to $300 by 2009.)

Source: "A Spoonful of Poison," *Wired* (March 2002), p. 57; and price quotes.

Example

What Went Right at Microsoft but Wrong at Apple Computer[2]

Throughout much of its history, Apple Computer, discussed in the Managerial Challenge at the beginning of Chapter 10, hovered at 7 to 10 percent market share in the U.S. personal computer market. Twice in its early history, Apple reached double-digit share points (16 percent in 1986 and 13 percent in 1993). Apple never did come close to achieving the inflection point (depicted at 30 percent in Figure 11.1). Apple therefore pursued increasing returns by attempting to become an industry standard in several personal computer submarkets such as the desktop publishing, journalism, media-based advertising, and entertainment industries.

(continued)

In addition, despite fiercely defending its GUI code for almost two decades with patent applications and trade secret infringement suits, finally in 1998–1999 Apple reversed its course and began licensing and alliance agreements with both Microsoft and IBM. Compatibility with other operating systems had been easy to achieve, but widespread adoption of Mac programming code by independent software vendors (ISVs) had not. Consequently, to obtain a critical mass of adoptions that would trigger ISVs to begin writing software applications for the Mac, Apple reversed its company policy on the closed architecture of its GUI. The GUI code at Apple was clearly technically superior to the early generation Windows products. However, the technically superior product lost out to the product that first reached increasing returns—namely, Microsoft Windows GUI running on non-Apple PCs.

The new open architecture strategy has served Apple extremely well in smart phones where value added emerges primarily through apps software provided by ISVs for little or no expense to Apple. The iPhone 5 is said to offer 300,000 applications. As a result, iPhone's market share among business customers grew from 9 to 23 percent in 2011, despite $200 higher prices than competitors' smart phones: Android from Google, Lumina from Nokia, Blackberry from RIM, or Galaxy from Samsung.

[2]Based on "Netscape to Woo Microsoft's Customers," *Reuters* (October 1, 1998); W. Brian Arthur, "Increasing Returns and the New World of Business," *Harvard Business Review* (July–August 1996); *Apple Inc.*, Harvard Business School Case Publishing (2008); "Targets Shift in Phone Wars," *Wall Street Journal*, (October 10, 2011), p. B1.

Third, technology products whose primary value lies in their intellectual property (e.g., computer software, pharmaceuticals, and telecom networks) have revenue sources that are dependent on renewals of governmental licensures and product standards. Unlike autos or steel, once R&D costs have been recouped, the marginal cost of additional copies of the software, additional doses of the medicine, or additional users on the wireless system is close to zero. Thus, every single unit sold thereafter is close to pure profit. Competitor firms that have incurred the up-front fixed costs but not succeeded in reaching the inflection point of increasing returns will rationally spend enormous sums seeking to recoup these rents through the political process and in the courts.

For example, Netscape and Sun Microsystems succeeded during Microsoft's long antitrust trial of 1997–2002 in restricting their otherwise dominant competitor. U.S. courts ordered

WHAT WENT RIGHT • WHAT WENT WRONG

Pilot Error at Palm[3]

The disappearance of PalmPilot, the once-dominant product in handheld computers, demonstrates how fragile is the position of even an industry leader in a technology-intensive business with increasing returns to promotional spending. Despite having 80 percent of the handheld operating system market and despite producing 60 percent of the handheld hardware at its peak in 2000, Palm, Inc., has now lost most of its market share to its rivals. Palm grew so fast (165 percent year-over-year sales increases) that it gave little attention to operational issues such as managing the supply of inputs and forecasting demand. In 2001, it mistimed the announcement of its m500 product

upgrades, which were delayed by supply chain bottlenecks, and Palm's customers stopped buying older models. Handspring, Sony, Hewlett-Packard, Microsoft's Pocket PC, and the popular BlackBerry drove prices lower and offered newer product features. Almost overnight, excess Palm IV and V inventories piled up on shelves, and inquiries about Apple iPods and Nokia's handheld devices shot up. Palm was forced to take a $300 million write-down on its inventory losses, and its stock price fell from $25 to $2 a share.

[3]Based on "How Palm Tumbled," *Wall Street Journal* (September 7, 2001), p. A1.

restrictions on Microsoft's installation agreements for Windows because they foreclosed competitors. And European courts have prohibited Microsoft's refusal to deal with Windows licensees who installed Google or Firefox's competing Web browser software or alternatives to Microsoft's video player software Media Player. Similarly, in pharmaceuticals Genentech's first commercial success was a multiple sclerosis drug that avoided direct challenge to a broad Schering-Plough Corporation patent by employing a special FDA exemption rule.

How do firms attempt to get around the inflection point of Figure 11.1 and achieve increasing returns? Free trials for a limited time period is one approach. Another is giving the technology away if it can be bundled with other revenue-generating product offerings. Microsoft gave away Internet Explorer (IE) for free without being charged with predatory pricing (IE's variable cost was $0.004; that is, it rounded to zero). Another approach is to undertake consolidation mergers and acquisitions; this strategy drove IBM's acquisition of a host of smaller software companies, such as Lotus, and Oracle engaged in a hostile takeover of PeopleSoft. Some companies such as Sun Microsystems (now part of Oracle) also provide JAVA and Linux programming at heavily subsidized prices to independent software vendors whose applications will provide network effects as complements to Sun's JAVA-based OS. Finally, having a product adopted as an industry standard leads to increasing returns. Sony achieved this network effect with its Blu-Ray HDTV standard.

PRICE AND OUTPUT DETERMINATION FOR A MONOPOLIST

Spreadsheet Approach:
Profit versus Revenue Maximization for Polo Golf Shirts

Table 11.1 shows the demand projections for daily sales of Polo golf shirts at a Ralph Lauren outlet store. For each style and color, the uniform price shown in column 2 is expected to elicit the number of unit sales per day listed in the first column. The third column displays the total revenue, and the fourth column shows the incremental revenue from lowering price to sell another unit—that is, the marginal revenue. For example, a uniform price reduction from $42 to $40 is required to increase unit sales from five to six shirts per day. Hence the marginal revenue at six shirts is calculated as $(6 \times \$40 = \$240) - (5 \times \$42 = \$210)$—that is, $MR = \$30$.

Sales floor personnel are typically paid a salary plus a sales commission based on the total sales revenue they sell. Such an employee wants the price at the outlet store to continue dropping as long as total sales revenue rises—that is, as long as the MR remains positive up to and including 14 shirts per day at $25.79. Any fewer shirts and total revenue ($P \times Q = \$361$) would be smaller, reducing the sales team's commission-based earnings. The store manager and Ralph Lauren, the parent company, have other motives, however. These decision makers are concerned that the 14th shirt imposes a unit operating loss of $-\$24$. That is, column 5 lists the variable cost incurred when another shirt is produced, distributed, and sold. When the marginal revenue in column 4 ($4 on the 14th shirt per day) falls below the variable cost in column 5 ($28), unit operating losses ensue. This same thing is true of the 13th, 12th, 11th shirt, and so forth.

Not until the outlet store raises its price and increases marginal revenue back to $28 will operating losses be eliminated. At this price and output ($38.31 and 7 shirts), the difference between total revenue ($268) and total variable costs (28×7) is maximized at $72 per color per day. The store manager will be charged with the objective of pursuing these maximum operating profits and finding mechanisms to motivate the sales personnel even though they would prefer maximum revenue of $361 at a $25.79 price point, imposing operating losses of $39 per day.

TABLE 11.1 RALPH LAUREN POLO GOLF SHIRTS (PER COLOR, PER STORE, PER DAY)

QUANTITY SOLD	UNIFORM PRICE	TOTAL REVENUE	MARGINAL REVENUE	VARIABLE COST	UNIT OPERATING PROFIT	CUMULATIVE PROFIT
0	$50.00	$0.00	$0.00	$28.00	$0.00	$0.00
1	$48.00	$48.00	$48.00	$28.00	$20.00	$20.00
2	$46.00	$92.00	$44.00	$28.00	$16.00	$36.00
3	$45.00	$135.00	$43.00	$28.00	$15.00	$51.00
4	$44.00	$176.00	$41.00	$28.00	$13.00	$64.00
5	$42.00	$210.00	$34.00	$28.00	$6.00	$70.00
6	$40.00	$240.00	$30.00	$28.00	$2.00	$72.00
7	$38.31	$268.17	$28.00	$28.00	$0.00	$72.00
8	$36.50	$292.00	$24.00	$28.00	($4.00)	$68.00
9	$34.50	$311.00	$19.00	$28.00	($9.00)	$59.00
10	$32.70	$327.00	$16.00	$28.00	($12.00)	$47.00
11	$30.91	$340.00	$13.00	$28.00	($15.00)	$32.00
12	$29.17	$350.00	$10.00	$28.00	($18.00)	$14.00
13	$27.46	$357.00	$7.00	$28.00	($21.00)	($15.00)
14	$25.79	$361.00	$4.00	$28.00	($24.00)	($39.00)
15	$24.07	$361.00	$0.00	$28.00	($28.00)	($67.00)
16	$22.50	$360.00	($1.00)	$28.00	($29.00)	($96.00)
17	$20.82	$356.00	($4.00)	$28.00	($32.00)	($128.00)
18	$19.28	$349.00	($7.00)	$28.00	($35.00)	($165.00)

© Cengage Learning

Example

Margins on K.P. McLahe Polo Shirts

Hand-embroidery on $155 polo shirts by K.P. McLahe is outsourced to garment workers in Vietnam for $3 per shirt. The other components of the variable cost are textile cloth ($7), buttons ($3), travel bag ($6), and contract labor at piecemeal rates of $11 per shirt. The $30 total variable cost is then marked up 116 percent to a $65 wholesale price. Thereafter, retail partners mark up the shirts another $90 to sell in men's boutiques on Fifth Avenue in New York and in International Airport shops worldwide for an M.R.S.P. (Manufacturer's Recommended Sale Price) of $155.

Graphical Approach

Figure 11.3 shows the price-output decision for a profit-maximizing monopolist. Just as in pure competition, profit is maximized at the price and output combination, where $MC = MR$. This point corresponds to a price of P_1, output of Q_1, and total profits equal to BC profit per unit times Q_1 units. For a negatively sloping demand curve, the MR function is not the same as the demand function. In fact, for any linear, negatively sloping demand function, the marginal revenue function will have the same intercept on the P axis as the demand function and a slope that is twice as steep as that of the demand curve. If, for example, the demand curve were of the form

$$P = a - bQ$$

FIGURE 11.3 **The Price and Output Determination of a Pure Monopoly**

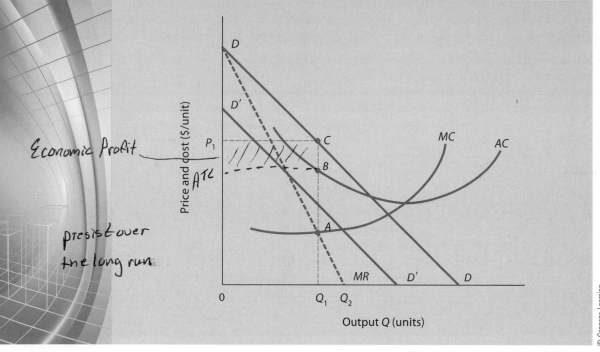

then

$$\text{Total revenue} = TR = P \cdot Q$$
$$= aQ - bQ^2$$

and

$$MR = \frac{dTR}{dQ} = a - 2bQ$$

The slope of the demand curve is $-b$, and the slope of the MR function is $-2b$.

Algebraic Approach

Example

Profit Maximization for a Theme Park Restaurant

Assume a manager is faced with the following demand curve for lunch meals in a unique theme park restaurant:

$$Q = 400 - 20P$$

and the short-run total variable cost function is

$$TC = 5Q + \frac{Q^2}{50}$$

(continued)

To maximize profits, the theme park manager would produce and sell enough lunches such that $MC = MR$, and charge the corresponding uniform price:

$$MC = \frac{dTC}{dQ} = 5 + \frac{Q}{25}$$

MR may be found by rewriting the demand curve in terms of Q:

$$P = \frac{-Q}{20} + 20$$

and then multiplying by Q to find TR:

$$TR = P \cdot Q$$

$$= -\frac{Q^2}{20} + 20Q$$

$$MR = \frac{dTR}{dQ} = -\frac{Q}{10} + 20$$

Setting $MR = MC$ yields

$$-\frac{Q^*}{10} + 20 = 5 + \frac{Q^*}{25}$$

$$Q^* = 107 \text{ units}$$

Substituting Q^* back into the demand equation, we may solve for P^*:

$$P^* = \frac{-107}{20} + 20$$

$$= \$14.65/\text{unit}$$

Hence the profit-maximizing monopolist would produce 107 meals and charge a price of \$14.65 each, which would yield a profit of

$$\pi^* = TR - TC$$

$$= (P^*Q^*) - \left(5Q^* + \frac{Q^{*2}}{50}\right)$$

$$= 14.65(107) - \left(5(107) + \frac{(107)^2}{50}\right)$$

$$= \$803.57$$

The Importance of the Price Elasticity of Demand

Recall from Chapter 3 that marginal revenue (MR), the incremental change in total revenue arising from one more unit sale, can be expressed in terms of price (P) and the price elasticity of demand (E_D), or

$$MR = P\left(1 + \frac{1}{E_D}\right) \qquad [11.1]$$

Equating MR with MC (as shown in Figure 11.3) yields the profit-maximizing relationship in terms of price and price elasticity, or

$$MC - P\left(1 + \frac{1}{E_D}\right) \qquad [11.2]$$

Hence, noncompetitive price will be greater than marginal cost. For example, if price elasticity $E_D = -2.0$, price will equal

$$MC = P\left(1 + \frac{1}{-2}\right)$$

$$MC = P(0.5)$$

$$P = 2MC$$

Note from Equation 11.2 that a monopolist will never operate in the area of the demand curve where demand is price inelastic (i.e., $|E_D| < 1$). If the absolute value of price elasticity is less than $1(|E_D| < 1)$, then the reciprocal of price elasticity $(1/E_D)$ will be less than –1, and marginal revenue $\left[P\left(1 + \frac{1}{E_D}\right)\right]$ will be negative. In Figure 11.3, the inelastic range of output is output beyond level Q_2. A negative marginal revenue means that total revenue can be increased by reducing output (through an increase in price). But we know that reducing output must also reduce total costs, resulting in an increase in profit. A dominant firm with market power over price will continue to raise prices (and reduce output) as long as the price elasticity of demand is in the inelastic range; it would be double-dumb to do otherwise. Therefore, for a monopolist, the price-output combination that maximizes profits must occur where $|E_D| \geq 1$.

Equation 11.2 also demonstrates that the more elastic the demand (suggesting the existence of better substitutes), the lower the optimal price and markup (relative to marginal cost) that any dominant firm will charge. This relationship can be illustrated with the following example.

Example

Price Elasticity and Price Levels for Monopolists

Consider a monopolist with the following total cost function:

$$TC = 10 + 5Q$$

The marginal cost (MC) function is

$$MC = dTC/dQ = 5$$

The price elasticity of demand has been estimated to be –2.0. Setting $MC = MR$ (where MR is expressed as in Equation 11.1) results in the following price rule for this profit-maximizing monopolist:

$$MC = \$5 = P(1 + 1/-2.0) = MR$$

$$P = 5/(0.5) = \$10/\text{unit}$$

If, however, demand is more price elastic, such as $E_D = -4.0$, a profit-maximizing monopolist would set the price at

$$P = \$5/(0.75) = \$6.67/\text{unit}$$

THE OPTIMAL MARKUP, CONTRIBUTION MARGIN, AND CONTRIBUTION MARGIN PERCENTAGE

Sometimes it is useful and convenient to express these relationships among optimal price, price elasticity, and variable cost as a markup percentage or contribution margin percentage. Using Equation 11.2 to solve for optimal price yields (with MC = variable cost)

$$P = \frac{E_D}{(E_D + 1)} MC = (1 + \%\text{Mark-up})MC \qquad [11.3]$$

where the multiplier term ahead of MC is 1.0 plus the markup expressed as a decimal equivalent.[4] For example, the case of $E_D = -3$ is a product with a $-3/(-3 + 1) = 1.5$ multiplier on MC—that is, a 50 percent markup. The optimal profit-maximizing price recovers the marginal cost and then marks up MC another 50 percent. If $MC = \$6$, this item would sell for $1.5 \times \$6 = \$9$ and the profit-maximizing markup is \$3, or 50 percent more than the marginal cost.

The difference between price and variable cost (i.e., the absolute dollar size of the markup) is often referred to as the *contribution margin*. With the variable cost already covered, these additional dollars are available to *contribute* to covering fixed cost and earning a profit. They are expressed as a percentage of the total price. Standard components, final assembly labor paid at piecerate rates, transportation by delivery services to the final customer, royalties paid for software licenses, and selling expenses incurred one sale at a time (such as coupons) are all illustrations of variable costs.[5] In the previous example, the \$3 markup above and beyond the \$6 marginal cost represents a 33 percent contribution to fixed cost and profit, that is, a 33 percent contribution margin on the \$9 item. Using Equation 11.3 and $E_D = -3$,

$$\frac{(P - MC)}{P} = \frac{1.5\,MC - 1.0\,MC}{1.5\,MC}$$

Contribution Margin% $= 0.5/1.5 = 33\%$

To summarize, an elasticity of -3.0 implies that the profit-maximizing markup is 50 percent, and that 50 percent markup implies a 33 percent contribution margin. Price elasticity information therefore carries pivotal implications. Combining the contribution margin percentage (33 percent) with incremental variable cost information indicates what dollar markups and product prices to announce in the marketing plan.

Again, one takeaway is that the more price elastic the demand function, the lower the optimal price that will be charged, *ceteris paribus*. In the extreme, consider the case of a firm in pure competition with a perfectly elastic (horizontal) demand curve. In this case the price elasticity of demand approaches $-\infty$; hence, 1 divided by the price elasticity approaches 0 and marginal revenue in Equation 11.1 becomes equal to price. Thus, the

---

[4]The marginal cost symbol MC refers to the accountant's narrow definition of *variable costs,* operating costs that vary with the least aggregated unit sale in the company's business plan. The term *marginal cost* is often also used in economics to refer to the last or next higher operating cost per unit when cheaper units have already been produced and sold.

[5]An overnight Boeing 747 from Shanghai assembly plants carrying laptops or iPhones to the FedEx hub in Memphis would not qualify as a variable cost because the \$50,000 per trip airfreighter expense is not incurred by Dell or Apple on a sale by sale basis. Instead, that shipping expense constitutes a direct fixed cost. Similarly, hired labor involved in manufacturing operations would not be a variable cost unless the labor expense were incurred on a piecerate basis.

profit-maximizing rule in Equation 11.2 becomes "Set price equal to marginal cost," and the profit-maximizing markup in Equation 11.3 is zero (i.e., the marginal cost multiplier equals just 1.0). Of course, this conclusion is the same price-cost solution developed in Chapter 10 in the discussion of price determination under pure competition.

Example

Markups and Contribution Margins on Chanel No. 5, Ole Musk, and Whitman's Sampler

Consider three products available at the typical drugstore counter: Chanel No. 5, Whitman's Sampler, and the private label (store brand) fragrance Ole Musk. Chanel has a loyal following of regular buyers and a price elasticity of –1.1. Whitman's has some rather close substitutes but substantial name recognition and packaging familiarity; its price elasticity measures –1.86. Finally, customers perceive many close substitutes for the generic fragrance Ole Musk, whose price elasticity measures –12.0.

Table 11.2 shows the optimal prices, markups, and contribution margins for these three products. Using Equation 11.3, the multiplier on *MC* for Chanel No. 5 is –1.1/(–1.1 + 1) = 11.0, and the optimal markup is therefore 1,000 percent (i.e., 10 times the incremental variable cost of the essences and the bottle). Because optimal price is 11.0 *MC*, the contribution margin percentage on Chanel No. 5 calculates as 10.0 *MC*/11.0 *MC* = 91%. Whitman's Sampler has a multiplier of –1.86/(–1.86 + 1) = 2.16, an optimal markup of 116 percent and a contribution margin of 1.16 *MC*/2.16 *MC* = 54%. In contrast, Ole Musk with the greatest price elasticity has a multiplier of –12/(–12 + 1) = 1.09, a markup of 9 percent, and a contribution margin percentage of 0.09 *MC*/1.09 *MC* = 8%.

So, the question remains: how does a noncompetitive firm establish a strategy to sustain higher contribution margins such as Chanel No. 5's 91 percent when other products such as private label Ole Musk achieves only 8 percent? The key ideas are laid out in the Strategy Map shown in Figure 11.4. We will illustrate with Natureview Farms (NVF) Yogurt, a Vermont-based green producer of dairy products. All effective business plans begin with a **value proposition** for the target customers. As the U.S. population became more environmentally conscious, Natureview Farms identified a younger, better-educated yogurt buyer who perceived value from *higher-quality* ingredients with longer shelf life than was typical of natural and organic ingredients. Despite the absence of chemical preservatives, NVF's yogurt remains fresh for 50 days rather than the usual 20. This additional *functionality* in combination with higher-quality ingredients *reliably exceeding customer expectations* for fresh texture and taste warranted an *enhanced price premium*. But to create financial value from these customer value drivers,

value proposition A statement of the specific source(s) of perceived value, the value driver(s), for customers in a target market.

TABLE 11.2	OPTIMAL PRICES, MARKUPS, AND MARGINS				
	E_D	PRICE	CONTRIBUTION MARGIN	MARKUP %	CONTRIBUTION MARGIN %
Chanel No. 5 ($85/¼ oz.)	–1.1	11.00 *MC*	10.00 *MC*	1,000%	91%
Whitman's Sampler ($8/lb.)	–1.86	2.16 *MC*	1.16 *MC*	116%	54%
Ole Musk ($6/4 oz.)	–12.0	1.09 *MC*	0.09 *MC*	9%	8%

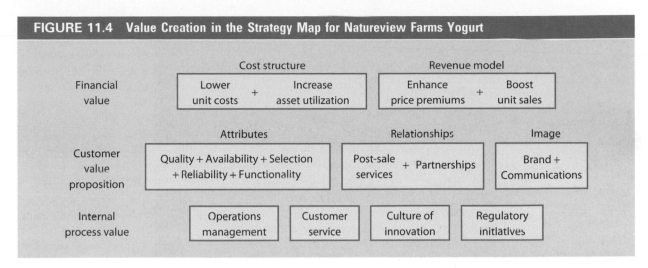

FIGURE 11.4   Value Creation in the Strategy Map for Natureview Farms Yogurt

Source: Based on "Strategy Map," *Harvard Business Review* (February 2004).

NVF found it necessary to boost *unit sales growth* and increase *asset utilization* by moving from the natural foods stores into Whole Foods and other specialty supermarkets. Handling the distribution channel issues with robust *operations management* processes and effective *marketing communications* proved critical to sustaining a high profit margin.

Gross Profit Margins

gross profit margin
Revenue minus the sum of variable cost plus direct fixed cost, also known as direct costs of goods sold in manufacturing.

Gross profit margin (or just "gross margin") is a term often used in manufacturing businesses to refer to the profit margin after subtracting from wholesale revenue both the variable manufacturing costs and any *direct* fixed costs of manufacturing traceable to the product line. For example, in a carpet plant, the gross margin would be the plant's wholesale revenue minus the sum of input costs plus machinery setup costs for the plant's production runs involving that type of carpet. A manufacturer's income statement identifies variable manufacturing costs plus direct fixed manufacturing cost as the "direct cost of goods sold" (DCGS). Thus, the gross margin is revenue minus direct cost of goods sold.[6]

Components of the Margin

Contribution margins and gross profit margins differ across industries and across firms within the same industry for a variety of reasons. First, some industries are more capital-intensive than others. Aircraft manufacturing with its large assembly plants is much more capital-intensive than software manufacturing. Boeing wide-body airframes have 72 percent gross profit margins, not because they are particularly profitable, but because airframes have high fixed costs associated with the capital investment tied up in large assembly plants. The first component of the profit margin percentage, then, is capital costs per sales dollar.

Second, differences in margins reflect differences in advertising, promotion, and selling costs. Leading brands in the ready-to-eat cereal industry have 70 percent gross

---

[6]The gross profit margin definition can be applied to retail firms but not to service firms whose direct cost of goods sold is undefined by accountants. In services, the contribution margin definition of unit profit is prevalent, and activity-based costing (ABC) determines which costs are variable to a product line or an account.

margins, but almost half of that price-cost differential (34 percent of every sales dollar) is spent on advertising and promotion. The automobile industry also spends hundreds of millions of dollars on advertising, but that amounts to only 9 percent per sales dollar. The second component of the profit margin percentage is then a company's advertising and selling expenses per sales dollar.

Third, differences in gross margins arise because of differential overhead in some businesses. The pharmaceutical industry has high gross margins, in large part because of the enormous indirect fixed cost expenditures on research and development to find new drugs. To conduct business in that product line, other pharmaceutical firms then incur patent fees and licensing costs, which raise their overhead costs and prices. Overhead costs also may differ if headquarters salaries and other general administrative expenses are high in certain firms or industries but not others.

Finally, after accounting for any differences in the indirect fixed costs of capital equipment, advertising, selling expenses, and overhead, the remaining differences in profit margins reflect differential profitability.

Example

Components of the Gross Margin at Kellogg Co.[7]

As we noted in Chapter 10, Kellogg's profit margin of 70 percent on Raisin Bran ([$4.49 Price − $1.63 DCGS]/$4.49) reflects brand loyalties built up over many years by massive and continuous advertising investments. On the leading brands, Kellogg's spends 30 percent of each sales dollar on advertising, and adds another 5 percent on couponing, slot-in shelf allowances, consumer rebates, and other promotional expenses. Capital costs entail approximately 22 percent per sales dollar. Expenditures on headquarters, general administrative, R&D, and all other overhead total 8 percent. That leaves a net profit margin of about 5 percent.

Successful restaurants have almost twice the operating profit of convenience stores on food items (60 percent versus 32 percent), and much of that differential (perhaps 25 percent) reflects net profit. The much higher net profit in a successful restaurant is a reward for bearing a higher default risk of failure. The chance of long-term success in restaurants is really quite low; three out of five lose money.

[7]Based on "Cereals," *Winston-Salem Journal* (March 8, 1995), p. A1; and "Denial in Battle Creek," *Forbes* (October 7, 1996), pp. 44–46.

Monopolists and Capacity Investments

Because monopolists do not face the discipline of strong competition, they tend to install excess capacity or, alternatively, fail to install enough capacity. A monopolist that wants to restrain entry of new competitors into the industry may install excess capacity in order to threaten to flood the market with supply and lower prices, which makes entry of new competitors less attractive.

Even in regulated monopolies such as electric utility companies, considerable evidence shows that regulation often provides incentives for a firm to overinvest or underinvest in generating capacity. Because regulated utilities have an opportunity to earn a "fair" rate of return on their assets, if the allowed return is greater (less) than the firm's true cost of capital, the company will be motivated to overinvest (underinvest) in new plant and equipment.

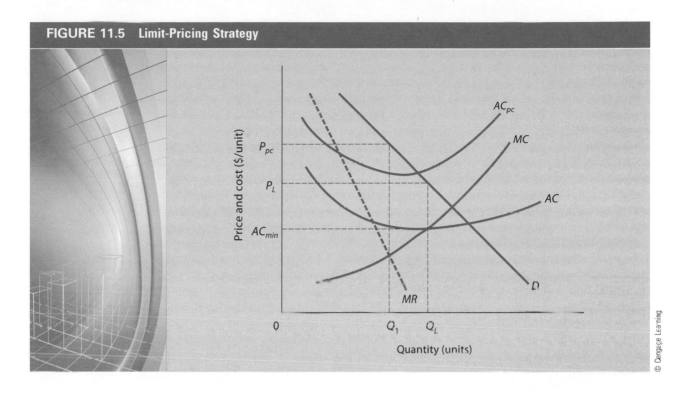

FIGURE 11.5   Limit-Pricing Strategy

Limit Pricing

Maximizing *short-run* profits by setting marginal revenue equal to marginal cost in order to yield an optimal output of Q_1 and an optimal price of P_1 may not necessarily maximize the *long-run* profits (or shareholder wealth) of the firm. By keeping prices high and earning monopoly profits, the dominant firm encourages potential competitors to commit R&D or advertising resources in an effort to obtain a share of these profits. Instead of charging the short-run profit-maximizing price, the monopolist firm may decide to engage in *limit pricing*, where it charges a lower price, such as P_L in Figure 11.5, in order to discourage entry into the industry by potential rivals. With a limit-pricing strategy, the firm forgoes some of its short-run monopoly profits in order to maintain its monopoly position in the long run. The limit price, such as P_L in Figure 11.5, was set below the minimum point on a potential competitor's average total cost curve (AC_{pc}). The appropriate limit price is a function of many different factors.[8]

The effect of the two different pricing strategies on the dominant firm's profit stream is illustrated in Figure 11.6. By charging the (higher) short-run profit-maximizing price, the firm's profits are likely to decline over time at a faster rate, as in Panel (a), than by charging a limit price as shown in Panel (b). The firm should engage in limit pricing if the present value of the profit stream from the limit-pricing strategy exceeds the present value of the profit stream associated with the short-run profit-maximization rule of $MR = MC$. Such a decision is more likely the higher the discount rate is. Choosing a high discount rate will place relatively higher weight on near-term profits in the calculation of present discounted value and relatively lower weight on profits that occur further into the future. A high discount rate is justified when the firm's long-term pricing policy,

---

[8]The limit-pricing model illustrates the importance of *potential* competition as a control device on existing firms. See D. Carlton and J. Perloff, *Modern Industrial Organization*, 3rd ed. (New York: HarperCollins, 1999), Chapter 10, for an expanded discussion of the limit-pricing concept.

FIGURE 11.6 The Effect of Pricing Strategies on Profit Streams as a Patent Expires

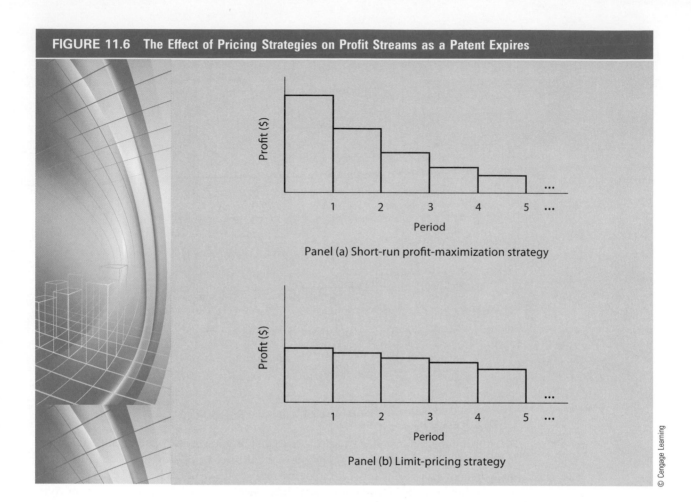

Panel (a) Short-run profit-maximization strategy

Panel (b) Limit-pricing strategy

and hence profits, are subject to a high degree of risk or uncertainty. The higher the risk, the higher is the appropriate discount rate.

Using Limit Pricing to Hamper the Sales of Generic Drugs[9]

Patent protection is the key to financial success in the pharmaceutical industry. The typical patented drug emerges from tests on 250 chemical compounds, requires 15 years of research and FDA approval processes, and accumulates total costs of entry averaging $350 million.

Capoten is Bristol-Myers Squibb's (BMS) hypertension drug for use in reducing heart-attack risk. Rather than limit pricing, BMS maintained Capoten's 57-cents-per-pill price right to the end of its 20-year patent protection in February 1996. Competition from generics selling for 3 cents per pill was swift and disastrously effective. In early 1996, BMS introduced its own generic product that cannibalized sales of the branded product still further. By the fourth quarter of 1996, Capoten sales had collapsed to $25 million from $146 million the year before. In order to restore profitability, BMS and other

[9]Based on "Too Clever by Half," *The Economist* (September 20, 1997), p. 68; "Time's Up," *Wall Street Journal* (August 12, 1997), p. A1; "Industry Merger Wave Heads to Europe," *Wall Street Journal* (November 12, 1999), p. A15; and "Wearing Off: Schering-Plough Faces a Future without Claritin," *Wall Street Journal* (March 22, 2002), p. A1.

leading pharmaceutical companies are merging in order to take advantage of economies of scale in R&D through follow-on drugs with improved efficacy or reduced side effects.

In contrast, Eli Lilly and Schering-Plough chose limit pricing and advertising for their leading medications, the antidepressant Prozac and the allergy treatment Claritin. Prozac lost patent protection in 2001, as did Claritin in 2003. One reason Schering-Plough chose a different (limit) pricing strategy is that Claritin had no improved follow-on drug available when the FDA demoted the prescription-only product to over-the-counter status at an identical dosage. As a consequence, $100-per-month-per-patient revenue was projected to decline to $9 if short-run profit maximizing prices continued. With a gross profit margin of 79 percent, Schering-Plough was facing a monumental loss of $2.1 billion in operating profits on $2.7 billion in Claritin sales. In such circumstances, smaller margins and a slower decline of market share could achieve higher profitability over a longer period.

In general, new biotechnologies have speeded up the emergence of imitation pharmaceuticals. Indeed, the first hypertension drug, Inderal, enjoyed almost a decade of pure monopoly sales before losing its exclusivity to Capoten in 1978. Prozac, on the other hand, met competition from imitators within four years of its 1988 introduction. And Recombinate, a breakthrough drug for hemophiliacs newly patented in 1992, encountered copycat products by 1994. Tactics such as limit pricing become all the more important in the presence of such quick and relatively easy imitation by fast-second competitors.

public utilities
A group of firms, mostly in the electric power, natural gas, and communications industries, that are closely regulated by one or more government agencies. The agencies control entry into the business, set prices, establish product quality standards, and influence these total profits that may be earned by the firms subject to scale economics.

Example

Pfizer Sustains Sales of Off-Patent Lipitor[10]

The cholesterol-fighting drug Lipitor once accounted for $13 billion in sales, fully one quarter of Pfizer's total revenue. In North America, once a blockbuster pharmaceutical goes off patent, the unbranded generic forms of the drug will typically take 85 percent of the market within one year. Ranbaxy, a hugely successful generic drug company from India won the right to a 180-day exclusive in selling the generic equivalent to Lipitor, atorvastatin. Through a combination of aggressive licensing and rebates, Pfizer has sustained a 33 percent market share for Lipitor. First, Pfizer reached deals with 50 health care plans that agreed to continue prescribing Lipitor at a significantly reduced price of $3.36 per daily dose rather than the generic alternative atorvastatin at $2.89. Second, Pfizer signed up 750,000 direct mail customers for whom the company offered to pay all but $4 of Lipitor's monthly co-pay relative to the typical $10 co-pay for many generic medicines. Profit is down but much less than if Pfizer had not adopted a limit pricing strategy.

---

[10]"Drugmakers: Cliffhanger," *The Economist* (December 3, 2011), p.76; "Goodbye Lipitor, *Wall Street Journal* (May 10, 2012), p. B1; "Helping Lipitor Live Longer," *Wall Street Journal* (November 21, 2011), p. B1.

REGULATED MONOPOLIES

Several important industries in the United States operate as regulated monopolies. In broad terms, the regulated monopoly sector of the U.S. economy includes **public utilities** such as electric power companies, natural gas companies, and communications companies. In the past, many of the transportation industries (airlines, trucking, railroads) also were regulated closely, but these industries have been substantially deregulated over the past 10 to 25 years.

Electric Power Companies

Electric power is made available to the consumer through a production process characterized by three distinct stages. First, the power is generated in generating plants. Next, in the transmission stage, the power is transmitted at high voltage from the generating site to the locality where it is used. Finally, in the distribution stage, the power is distributed to the individual users. The complete process may take place as part of the operations of a single firm, or the producing firm may sell power at wholesale rates to a second enterprise that carries out the distribution function. In the latter case, the distribution firm often is a department within the local municipal government or a consumer cooperative.

Investor-owned electric power companies are subject to regulation at several levels. Integrated firms that carry out all three stages of production are usually regulated by state public utility commissions. These commissions set the rates to be charged to the final consumers. The firms normally receive exclusive rights to serve individual localities through franchises granted by local governing bodies. As a consequence of their franchises, electric power companies have well-defined markets within which they are the sole provider of output. Finally, the Federal Energy Regulatory Commission (FERC) has the authority to set rates on power that crosses state lines and on wholesale power sales.

 WHAT WENT RIGHT • WHAT WENT WRONG

The Public Service Company of New Mexico

The Public Service Company of New Mexico (PNM) provides electric power service (generation and distribution) and natural gas distribution services to most of New Mexico's population. This monopoly position is regulated by the Public Service Commission of the State of New Mexico and, to a lesser extent, by the FERC. These commissions determine the rates charged to various classes of customers in order to allow a "fair return" on the capital invested.

PNM's experience in the 1990s suggests the complexity of the problems involved with rate-of-return regulation. PNM earned a 4.9 percent return on common equity during 1992, 8.0 percent on common equity during 1995, and 7.5 percent on common equity between 1997 and 1999. The industry average return on equity was 11–12 percent, according to *Value Line*. PNM earned extraordinarily low returns even though PNM is authorized by its regulatory commission to charge rates consistent with its earning a return of 12.5 percent on common equity. Why has this monopoly supplier of utility services (and many other utility companies) been unable to earn its authorized return?

PNM has experienced high growth in the demand for its services as the Sunbelt prospered and industry grew in the region. Faced with rapid growth in demand and increasing costs for its traditional fuel, natural gas, PNM's managers examined a number of alternatives, including purchasing power from nearby utilities, building

large coal-fired plants close to New Mexico's abundant coal resources, and building nuclear power plants. Given the desirability of having a diverse mix of fuel sources as a natural hedge against rising natural gas costs, PNM ultimately decided to participate with other regional utilities in the construction of several large coal-fired plants in the Four Corners region of northwest New Mexico, to build additional coal-fired plants of its own and to participate with other utilities in the construction of a five-unit nuclear power plant called Palo Verde.

The first problem PNM faced was that its load growth did not materialize as expected. Then, the state of New Mexico required that expensive pollution control devices, called scrubbers, be installed at the coal plants being constructed, thereby dramatically increasing their construction cost. Finally, the Palo Verde nuclear project was plagued by cost overruns, delays, and extensive and costly safety modifications. When the construction program was completed, PNM found itself with capacity nearly 80 percent in excess of peak demand (a 20 percent reserve margin is more normal).

The regulatory process facing utilities does not ensure that a company will earn its authorized returns. Consequently, the New Mexico state regulatory commission refused to permit PNM to recover the costs of its excess capacity. Even in the absence of regulation, PNM would probably have been unable to fully recover the costs of this excess capacity.

Some states are continuing to partially or totally deregulate the power production and transmission elements of this industry. The California crisis with deregulated electricity raises questions about the desirability of fully deregulated competition at the retail (distribution) level.[11]

Natural Gas Companies

The highly regulated natural gas industry also is a three-stage process. The first stage is the production of the gas in the field. Transportation to the consuming locality through pipelines is the second stage. Distribution to the final user makes up the third stage. The FERC historically set the field price of natural gas, but regulation at the wellhead has been effectively phased out. Today, the FERC oversees the interstate transportation of gas by approving pipeline routes and by controlling the wholesale rates charged by pipeline companies to distribution firms. The distribution function may be carried out by a private firm or by a municipal government agency. In either event, the rates charged to final users also are subject to regulatory control.

THE ECONOMIC RATIONALE FOR REGULATION

As described in the preceding section, regulated industries furnish services that are critical to the functioning of the economy. What are the justifications for imposing economic regulation on certain industries?

Natural Monopoly Argument

natural monopoly An industry in which maximum economic efficiency is obtained when the firm produces, distributes, and transmits all of the commodity or service produced in that industry. The production of natural monopolists is typically characterized by increasing returns to scale throughout the relevant range of output.

Firms operating in the regulated sector are often **natural monopolies** in which a single supplier tends to emerge because of a production process characterized by massive economics of scale. In other words, as all inputs are increased by a given percentage, the average total cost of a unit of output decreases. Consequently, the long run unit cost of output declines throughout the relevant range of output. This situation is illustrated in Figure 11.7 for a firm in long-run stable equilibrium.

Suppose that the market demand curve for output is represented by the curve DD in Figure 11.7. The socially optimal level of output would then be Q^*; at that level of output, price would be well below the average total cost per unit AC^* but equal to short-run and long-run marginal cost. A single producer is able to realize economies of scale that are unavailable to firms in the presence of competition. From a social perspective, competition would result in inefficiency in the form of higher costs such as unit cost (AC_C) for the competitive firm than the unit cost (AC_M) for the monopoly firm that is six times as large. The argument follows that production relations like those in Figure 11.7 will lead to the emergence of a single supplier. Competing firms will realize that their costs decrease as output expands. As a consequence, they will have an incentive to cut prices

---

[11]See M. Maloney, R. McCormick, and R. Sauer, *Consumer Choice, Consumer Value: An Analysis of Retail Competition in America's Electric Utility Industry* (Washington, DC: Citizens for a Sound Economy, 1996); "Electric Utility Deregulation Sparks Controversy," *Harvard Business Review* (May/June 1996); and A. Faruqui and K. Eakin, eds., *Pricing in Competitive Electricity Markets* (Boston: Kluwer, 2000).

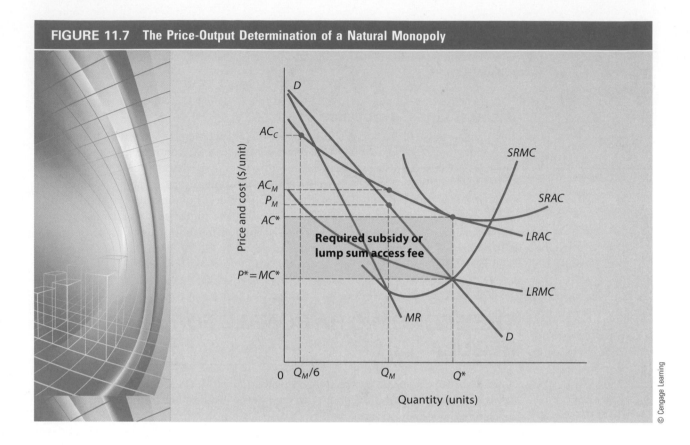

FIGURE 11.7 The Price-Output Determination of a Natural Monopoly

as long as *MR* exceeds *LRMC* to increase sales volume and spread the fixed cost. During this period, prices will be below average cost, resulting in losses for the producing firms. Unable to sustain such losses, the weaker firms gradually leave the industry, until only a single producer remains. Thus, competitive forces contribute to the emergence of the natural monopoly.

If a monopolistic position were to exist in the absence of regulation, the monopolist would maximize profit by equating marginal revenue and marginal cost at an output Q_M, leading to a higher price P_M and lower output. Thus, intervention through regulation is required to achieve the benefits of the most efficient organization of production. In its simplest form, this is the explanation of regulation based on the existence of natural monopolies.

Figure 11.7 illustrates one problem stemming from a genuine natural monopoly. Suppose that a regulatory agency succeeds in establishing the socially optimal price for output, P^*. As the cost curves indicate, this price would lead to losses for the producing firm, because price would be below the average total cost AC^*. This is obviously an unsustainable result. In this situation the regulating agency normally sets prices at average cost to make sure revenues are sufficient to cover all costs. The most efficient way to realize revenue, however, is to charge a per-unit price equal to *LRMC* and collect the shaded deficit area in Figure 11.7 as a *lump sum* access fee, perhaps divided equally among one's customers. Alternatively, with time-of-day metering, the lump sum access fees can depend on when the customer uses power—higher lump sum access fees charged at peak periods such as 4:00 P.M. to 8:00 P.M

SUMMARY

- Monopoly is a market structure with significant barriers to entry in which one firm produces a differentiated product.
- In a pure monopoly market structure, firms will generally produce a lower level of output and charge a higher price than would exist in a more competitive market structure. This conclusion assumes no significant economies of scale that might make a monopolist more efficient than a large group of smaller firms.
- The primary sources of monopoly power include patents and copyrights, control of critical resources, government "franchise" grants, economies of scale, and increasing returns in networks of users of compatible complementary products.
- Increasing returns from network effects are limited by input cost reductions among competitors, by innovative new product introductions, and by lobbying efforts.
- Monopolists will produce at that level of output where $MR = MC$ if their goal is to maximize short-run profits. Marginal cost is the variable cost incurred by last incremental output.
- The price charged by a profit-maximizing monopolist will be in that portion of the demand function where demand is elastic (or unit elastic). The greater the elasticity of demand facing a monopolist, the lesser will its price be marked up relative to marginal cost, *ceteris paribus.*
- Contribution margins are defined as dollar sales revenue per unit minus variable cost.
- *Contribution margins* and *markups* are inversely related to the price elasticity of demand.
- *Financial value* derives from lower unit cost and better asset utilization in the cost structure as well as higher price premiums and more unit sales in the revenue model.

- A *customer value proposition* derives from the attribute, relationship, and image value drivers for a target customer market.
- *Internal process value* derives from operations management processes, customer service, innovation, and regulatory initiatives.
- *Gross margins* are defined as unit revenue minus direct costs of goods sold per unit plus direct fixed cost such as set up costs, and serve to recover capital costs, selling costs, and overhead as well as earn profits.
- Limit pricing—pricing a product below the short-run profit-maximizing level—is a strategy used by some monopolists to discourage rivals from entering an industry.
- Public utilities are firms, mostly in the electric power, natural gas pipeline, and communications industries, that are closely regulated with respect to entry into the business, prices, service quality, and total profits.
- The rationales for public utility regulation are many. The *natural monopoly* argument is applied in cases where a product is characterized by increasing returns to scale. The one large firm can theoretically furnish the good or service at a lower cost than a group of smaller competitive firms. Regulators then set utility rates to prevent monopoly price gouging, ideally allowing the regulated firm to earn a return on investment just equal to its cost of capital.
- Price discrimination by utilities is often economically desirable on the basis of cost justifications and demand justifications.
- Peak-load pricing is designed to charge customers a greater amount for the services they use during periods of greater demand. Long-distance phone services typically have been priced on a peak-load basis.

Exercises

Answers to the exercises in blue can be found in Appendix D at the back of the book.

1. Information Resources, Inc. (IRI), collects data on consumer packaged goods at 32,000 scanner checkout counters and in panel surveys of 70,000 households. IRI records indicate that department store-brand pantyhose sell for a gross margin of 43 percent and a contribution margin of 29 percent, and the store inventory turns over 14 times per year.
   a. What expenses explain the difference between 43 percent and 29 percent?
   b. What percentage change in unit sales is required to increase total contributions if price is cut by 10 percent?
   c. Compare store-brand pantyhose with the products in Table 11.2. Why should Whitman's Sampler sell for a contribution margin of 54 percent when pantyhose sell for 29 percent?

in notes

2. Ajax Cleaning Products is a medium-sized firm operating in an industry dominated by one large firm—Tile King. Ajax produces a multiheaded tunnel wall scrubber that is similar to a model produced by Tile King. Ajax decides to charge the same price as Tile King to avoid the possibility of a price war. The price charged by Tile King is $20,000. Ajax has the following short-run cost curve:

$$TC = 800,000 - 5,000Q + 100Q^2$$

   a. Compute the marginal cost curve for Ajax.
   b. Given Ajax's pricing strategy, what is the marginal revenue function for Ajax?
   c. Compute the profit-maximizing level of output for Ajax.
   d. Compute Ajax's total dollar profits.

3. The Lumins Lamp Company, a producer of old-style oil lamps, estimated the following demand function for its product:

$$Q = 120,000 - 10,000P$$

   where Q is the quantity demanded per year and P is the price per lamp. The firm's fixed costs are $12,000 and variable costs are $1.50 per lamp.
   a. Write an equation for the total revenue (TR) function in terms of Q.
   b. Specify the marginal revenue function.
   c. Write an equation for the total cost (TC) function in terms of Q.
   d. Specify the marginal cost function.

$\pi = 263,625$

   e. Write an equation for total profits (π) in terms of Q. At what level of output (Q) are total profits maximized? What price will be charged? What are total profits at this output level?
   f. Check your answers in Part (e) by equating the marginal revenue and marginal cost functions, determined in Parts (b) and (d), and solving for Q.
   g. What model of market pricing behavior has been assumed in this problem?

4. Unique Creations holds a monopoly position in the production and sale of magnometers. The cost function facing Unique is estimated to be

$$TC = \$100,000 + 20Q$$

   a. What is the marginal cost for Unique?

$p = \$60$

   b. If the price elasticity of demand for Unique is currently –1.5, what price should Unique charge?
   c. What is the marginal revenue at the price computed in Part (b)?
   d. If a competitor develops a substitute for the magnometer and the price elasticity increases to –3.0, what price should Unique charge?

5. Exotic Metals, Inc., a leading manufacturer of beryllium, which is used in many electronic products, estimates the following demand schedule for its product:

PRICE ($/POUND)	QUANTITY (POUNDS/PERIOD)
$25	0
18	1,000
16	2,000
14	3,000
12	4,000
10	5,000
8	6,000
6	7,000
4	8,000
2	9,000

Fixed costs of manufacturing beryllium are $14,000 per period. The firm's variable cost schedule is as follows:

OUTPUT (POUNDS/PERIOD)	VARIABLE COST (PER POUND)
0	$0
1,000	10.00
2,000	8.50
3,000	7.33
4,000	6.25
5,000	5.40
6,000	5.00
7,000	5.14
8,000	5.88
9,000	7.00

a. Find the total revenue and marginal revenue schedules for the firm.
b. Determine the average total cost and marginal cost schedules for the firm.
c. What are Exotic Metals' profit-maximizing price and output levels for the production and sale of beryllium?
d. What is Exotic's profit (or loss) at the solution determined in Part (c)?
e. Suppose that the federal government announces it will sell beryllium, from its extensive wartime stockpile, to anyone who wants it at $6 per pound. How does this affect the solution determined in Part (c)? What is Exotic Metals' profit (or loss) under these conditions?

6. Wyandotte Chemical Company sells various chemicals to the automobile industry. Wyandotte currently sells 30,000 gallons of polyol per year at an average price of $15 per gallon. Fixed costs of manufacturing polyol are $90,000 per year and total variable costs equal $180,000. The operations research department has estimated that a 15 percent increase in output would not affect fixed costs but would reduce average variable costs by 60 cents per gallon. The marketing department has estimated the arc elasticity of demand for polyol to be –2.0.

a. How much would Wyandotte have to reduce the price of polyol to achieve a 15 percent increase in the quantity sold?
b. Evaluate the impact of such a price cut on (i) total revenue, (ii) total costs, and (iii) total profits.

7. Tennis Products, Inc., produces three models of high-quality tennis rackets. The following table contains recent information on the sales, costs, and profitability of the three models:

MODEL	AVERAGE QUANTITY SOLD (UNITS/MONTH)	CURRENT PRICE	TOTAL REVENUE	VARIABLE COST PER UNIT	CONTRIBUTION MARGIN PER UNIT	CONTRIBUTION MARGIN*
A	15,000	$30	$450,000	$15.00	$15	$225,000
B	5,000	35	175,000	18.00	17	85,000
C	10,000	45	450,000	20.00	25	250,000
Total			$1,075,000			$560,000

*Contribution to fixed costs and profits.

The company is considering lowering the price of Model A to $27 in an effort to increase the number of units sold. Based on the results of price changes that have been instituted in the past, Tennis Products' chief economist estimates the arc price elasticity of demand to be −2.5. Furthermore, she estimates the arc cross elasticity of demand between Model A and Model B to be approximately 0.5 and between Model A and Model C to be approximately 0.2. Variable costs per unit are not expected to change over the anticipated changes in volume.

a. Evaluate the impact of the price cut on the (i) total revenue and (ii) contribution margin of Model A. Based on this analysis, should the firm lower the price of Model A?

b. Evaluate the impact of the price cut on the (i) total revenue and (ii) contribution margin for the entire line of tennis rackets. Based on this analysis, should the firm lower the price of Model A?

8. The Public Service Company of the Southwest is regulated by an elected state utility commission. The firm has total assets of $500,000. The demand function for its services has been estimated as

$$P = \$250 - \$0.15Q$$

The firm faces the following total cost function:

$$TC = \$25,000 + \$10Q$$

(The total cost function does not include the firm's cost of capital.)

a. In an unregulated environment, what price would this firm charge, what output would be produced, what would total profits be, and what rate of return would the firm earn on its asset base?

b. The firm has proposed charging a price of $100 for each unit of output. If this price is charged, what will be the total profits and the rate of return earned on the firm's asset base?

c. The commission has ordered the firm to charge a price that will provide the firm with no more than a 10 percent return on its assets. What price should the firm charge, what output will be produced, and what dollar level of profits will be earned?

9. The Odessa Independent Phone Company (OIPC) is currently engaged in a rate case that will set rates for its Midland-Odessa area customer base. OIPC has total assets of $20 million. The Texas Public Utility Commission has determined that an 11 percent return on assets is fair. OIPC has estimated its annual demand function as follows:

$$P = 3,514 - 0.08Q$$

Its total cost function (not including the cost of capital) is

$$TC = 2,300,000 + 130Q$$

a. OIPC has proposed a rate of $250 per year for each customer. If this rate is approved, what return on assets will OIPC earn?

b. What rate can OIPC charge if the commission wants to limit the return on assets to 11 percent?

c. What problem of utility regulation does this exercise illustrate?

Differential Pricing of Pharmaceuticals: The HIV/AIDS Crisis[12]

The HIV/AIDS crisis has been called the worst pandemic since the fourteenth century's Black Plague. The first incident of HIV/AIDS was discovered by the U.S. Centers for Disease Control in 1981. Over the next three decades, 60 million people have become infected and 25 million have died. Most HIV/AIDS cases are reported in the developing world, where 95 percent of those with HIV live today. Beyond social welfare and humanitarian concerns, as a result of globalization and the fastest growing international business opportunities in China and India, AIDS is now everybody's business. Because the pharmaceutical industry especially relies upon governmental authority to approve formularies for reimbursement, to protect its monopoly patent rights, and to prevent importation of unauthorized, unlicensed imitation medicines, the question of how to price AIDS drugs is a public issue.

Although no one has yet developed a cure for HIV, a number of companies have patented drugs that inhibit either the virus's ability to replicate or its ability to enter host cells. Without further drug discovery, however, the best that can be done at present once a person contracts HIV is to partially and temporarily suppress the virus, thus delaying progression of the infection. The drugs that suppress HIV are called antiretrovirals, and the first, known as Retrovir (also known by its generic name zidovudine or AZT), was introduced in 1987 by Burroughs Wellcome (now GlaxoSmithKline) and was the only approved therapy available to treat HIV until 1991. Since then, several new antiretrovirals have been developed by large pharmaceutical companies such as Abbott Labs, Bristol-Myers Squibb, Merck, Roche, and smaller biotech companies such as Agouron, Gilead Sciences, Triangle Pharmaceuticals, and Trimeris. Largely as a result of these drugs, the rate of increase of AIDS-related diseases (e.g., opportunistic infections) dramatically slowed in the United States from 1992 through 1995 and actually decreased in 1996 for the first time.

Yet, even in the early days of antiretroviral drug development, HIV/AIDS drug pricing was a serious and contentious issue. The core problem is the fact that most HIV/AIDS cases are outside what the United Nations classifies as "rich countries" such as the United States. North America registered about 1.4 million cases of individuals living with HIV/AIDS and fewer than 25,000 deaths due to AIDS in 2008, but the comparative numbers for sub-Saharan Africa were 22 million cases and more than 1.9 million deaths. Similarly, the U.S. adult infection rate was estimated at slightly less than one half of a percent in 2008 versus over 5 percent in sub-Saharan Africa, where GDPs per capita often are less than $1,000 versus $30,000 in the United States. Compounding the problem is the fact that many new AIDS drugs, especially those designed to attack the growth in drug-resistant HIV, grow ever more expensive. Trimeris and Roche introduced Fuzeon in early 2003, for example, at a wholesale price of €20,245 per annum, at least three times the price of any existing HIV/AIDS drug.

The pricing decision reflects the fiscal realities of their expensive R&D-intensive business model against enlarged, global, corporate social responsibilities. A nation-state-specific pricing policy across global markets has resulted in a tenfold differential between the highest priced market, the United States, and the price charged in the poorest countries. Glaxo and Roche management teams face many serious business ethics issues in this highly charged environment. Is such a tenfold price differential sustainable?

---

[12]E. Berndt, "Pharmaceuticals in U.S. Health Care: Determinants of Quality and Price," and M. Kremer, "Pharmaceuticals and the Developing World," *Journal of Economic Perspectives* (Fall 2002), pp. 45–90.

How does one manage the resulting problem of parallel importing—that is, the unauthorized reimportation of export drugs bought at lower price points elsewhere in the world? Will abrogation of the intellectual property rights of the drug companies in the developing world threaten intellectual property protection at home? Will a public affairs backlash in high-priced markets force drug price discounts? If so, how can the massive R&D investment required for ongoing drug discovery and development be recovered? Are these companies facing such a public relations disaster that their corporate brand equity could be radically affected? What are big pharmaceutical companies' corporate responsibilities in a public health crisis? Should Glaxo (or Roche) go it alone, or instead pursue collaborative strategies with other big pharmaceutical rivals?

Questions

1. Is the monopoly on patented pharmaceuticals warranted? What barrier to entry prevents the re-importation into the United States of pharmaceuticals sold at lower prices abroad (say, in Canada)?

2. The contribution margin percentage on pharmaceuticals exceeds the 55 percent to 70 percent margins on ready-to-eat cereals. Identify three reasons why pharmaceutical margins are higher.

3. Suggest an approach to the big pharmaceutical company problem of differential pricing in the United States, Western Europe, and Japan versus the less-developed world.

Price and Output Determination: Oligopoly

CHAPTER PREVIEW

The previous two chapters analyzed price and output decisions of firms that competed in markets with either a large number of sellers (i.e., pure competition and monopolistic competition) or essentially no other sellers (i.e., monopoly). In pure competition, the firm made its price and output decisions independently of the decisions of other firms because no single firm was large enough to affect the market price. Similarly, the monopoly firm did not need to consider the pricing, output, advertising, and product actions of rival firms, because it had no competitors. This chapter, in contrast, examines interrelated decisions by firms in oligopoly market structures with a small number of competitors, where each firm's decisions are likely to evoke a response from one (or more) of these rivals. To maximize shareholder wealth, each oligopoly firm must take into account these rival responses in its own decision making. In the next chapter, game theory analysis is introduced to help you predict how your rivals will respond.

MANAGERIAL CHALLENGE

Google's Android and Apple's iPhone Displace Nokia in Smart Phones?[1]

From a stodgy Finnish industrial conglomerate selling everything from rubber boots and wire cable to toilet paper and televisions, Nokia transformed itself into a relentlessly focused technology company that dominated the handsets market. When Sweden's telecommunications-equipment giant Ericsson developed a cellular network across Scandinavia in the 1980s, Nokia provided the wireless but bulky radio telephones. Recognizing the strategic opportunity, Nokia spun off other business in the 1990s and focused its attention on the enormous market potential of digital cell phones.

Nokia grew from 22 percent market share in 1985 (half of Motorola's 45 percent) to overtake the market leader in 1998. By 2008, 39 percent of the $79 billion in cell phone sales worldwide belonged to Nokia, relative to Motorola's 14 percent, Samsung's 14 percent, Sony-Ericsson's 9 percent, and LG Electronics' 7 percent. In 2010, the 1.6 billion cell phones in service exceeded the number of land lines. With huge scale economies and a snazzy branded product, Nokia's cell phone margins, at 23 percent, were the envy of the industry. But several factors suggested Nokia's margins and market share were not sustainable.

First, high-speed worldwide wireless networks have rewritten the telecommunications landscape. 3G and 4G technologies allow the introduction of much enhanced wireless Web products such as handheld tablet computers by Apple, Samsung and Dell, game consoles from Sony-Ericsson, and most importantly, smart phones that operate as pocket audiovisual terminals, such as Apple's

Cont.

MANAGERIAL CHALLENGE *Continued*

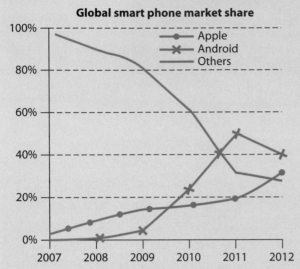

Global smart phone market share

Source: The Wall Street Journal, company websites.

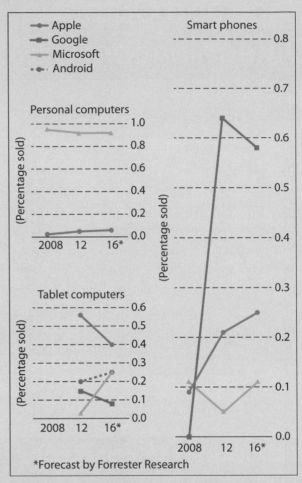

*Forecast by Forrester Research

Source: Based on Wall Street Journal (October 22, 2012).

iPhone and Android-based products from Motorola and Samsung. These two new smart phone products have taken over the global handset market (see graph displaying market shares) with product development cycle times down to six months versus two years at the start of the millennium.

Second, the most significant threat to Nokia's handset business is that smart phones create value principally through their software applications provided by third-party, independent software vendors (ISVs). And the ISVs command a significant share of the high gross margins that made Nokia so profitable. The power of these ISV suppliers was virtually nonexistent in the voice-only mobile phone business, but now the success of a smart phone is all about thousands of touch screen applications. When Apple's iPhone won important patent disputes in 2012 against Samsung's Galaxy phone and when Google purchased Motorola Mobility, the flood tide of ISVs to Apple and Google's Android operating system accelerated. Consequently, Nokia realized it badly needed an operating system partner to attract ISVs.

Third, Europe is nearly saturated with wireless handsets, which have achieved 86 percent penetration. Although Chinese cell phone demand is soaring, local vendors control distribution in that market, and price wars are commonplace. In North America, Nokia is only now starting to form alliances to stem their sliding global market share down from 50 percent in 2007 to 38 percent in 2010 to 4 percent in 2012, while Motorola's

Android-based phone has grown from 4 to 23 percent in the same period. Samsung's Android-based Galaxy phone has also been quite successful garnering 16 percent of worldwide sales. Apple's iPhone currently enjoys a 21 percent global market share, and Nokia's Lumia and RIM's Blackberry hold just 7 percent and 4 percent of the smart phone marketplace, respectively.

For decades, Microsoft has dominated software operating systems for the nearly stagnant personal computer (PC) market. It now seeks to form alliances in the fast-growing tablet and smart phone markets (see graphs of unit sales). Recently, Microsoft agreed to piggyback on Nokia by providing operating systems for the upscale Lumia smart phone by Nokia. Penetration of Microsoft's new mobile operating system Windows for Phone is expected to reach 180 million of the 1.2 billion worldwide smart phones by 2016.

Cont.

MANAGERIAL CHALLENGE *Continued*

Discussion Questions

■ Are you surprised that Nokia's Lumia smart phone has a margin of $241 on a $450 retail sale, whereas Apple makes a $459 margin on a $649 5S iPhone retail sale? Why or why not?

■ Should Nokia remain a premium cell phone supplier or instead focus on the projected growth in the low end of the camera phone market, especially in China and Latin America where China Mobile and China Unicom have 334 million subscribers and América Móvil has 117 million in Mexico compared to Vodafone's 199 million in Britain, Telefónica's 126 million in Spain, France Télécom's

and Deutsche Telekom's 98 million each in Germany and France, and AT&T's 64 million in North America?

■ Do you agree with what Nokia is doing to rekindle its smart phone business? Why or why not?

---

[1]Based on "Nokia: A Finnish Tale," *The Economist* (October 14, 2000), pp. 83–85; "Special Report: Mobile Telephones," *The Economist* (May 1, 2004), pp. 71–76; "After Legal Victory Apple, Patently Rules in Mobile Devices," *Wall Street Journal* (August 27, 2012), p. C8; "Inside Nokia's Struggle," *Wall Street Journal* (May 31, 2012), p. B4; "Nokia's Closing Window," *Wall Street Journal* (November 7, 2012), p. C16; "Apple Victory Shifts Power Balance," *Wall Street Journal* (August 27, 2012), p. B1.

OLIGOPOLISTIC MARKET STRUCTURES

An oligopoly is characterized by a relatively small number of firms offering a similar product or service. Oligopoly products may be branded, as in soft drinks, cereals, and athletic shoes, or unbranded, as in crude oil, aluminum, and cement. The main distinction of oligopoly is that the number of firms is small enough that actions by any individual firm on price, output, product style, quality, introduction of new models, and terms of sale have a perceptible impact on the sales of other firms in the industry. In this easily recognizable interdependence, each firm knows that any new price cut or large promotional campaign is likely to evoke a countermove from its rivals.

In all oligopoly markets, rival response expectations are therefore the key to firm-level analysis. If rival firms are expected to *match* price increases and price cuts as in airlines, a share-of-the-market demand curve may adequately illustrate the sales response to the pricing initiatives of one firm (such as Southwest Airlines, 20 percent share-of-the-market demand); see Figure 12.1, Panels (a) and (b). In other markets, if rival firms are slow to match price increases and cuts, oligopolists can discount to gain share and will lose share in response to price hikes. In still other markets such as I-beam steel, rivals match price cuts but ignore price increases. Consequently, Nucor Steel faces a much more price elastic demand above the going equilibrium price than the share-of-the-market demand below that price. These asymmetric rival response expectations lead to kinked oligopoly firm demand schedules discussed later in the chapter and illustrated in Figure 12.1, Panel (c).

Oligopoly in the United States: Relative Market Shares

Much of U.S. industry is best classified as oligopolistic in structure with a wide range of industry configurations. At one extreme are dominant single firms in the

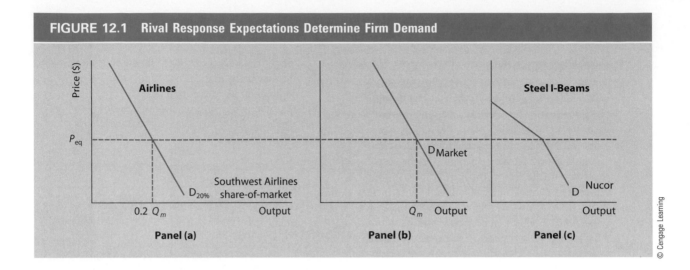

FIGURE 12.1 Rival Response Expectations Determine Firm Demand

Panel (a) — Airlines
Panel (b)
Panel (c) — Steel I-Beams

© Cengage Learning

markets for shaving razors, hand calculators, game consoles, beer, athletic shoes, microprocessors, and e-books, where Gillette (80 percent), TI (78 percent), Nintendo (65 percent), Anheuser-Busch (55 percent), Nike (43 percent), Intel (81), and Amazon (60 percent) are all several times larger than their next largest competitors (see Table 12.1).

Example

Google's Chrome Takes Share from Once Dominant Browser Internet Explorer[2]

Microsoft's web browser Internet Explorer (IE) used the increasing returns from Windows network effects throughout the 1990s to displace Netscape as the dominant Internet browser. Eventually, IE enjoyed a 93 percent market share with Netscape's descendant web browser Safari reduced to just 5 percent. Launched in 2004, Mozilla's Firefox took a 28 percent share of the web browser business by 2008, maxing out at 32 percent in 2010 and sustaining a 25 percent share in 2012. More recently, a faster browser from Google itself, Google Chrome, has over a two-year period attracted a 26 percent market share in 2012. The consequence for Microsoft's once almost monopolistic Internet Explorer has been a decline to a 40 percent market share (shown in Figure 12.2).

A quick delivery service for fulfillment of Internet shopping has been combined with Google Chrome. The subsidiary will stand alone but like Firefox it was financed by Google. Their new shipping and delivery business puts Google in direct competition with eBay. This is just one of nine major businesses in which Google is operating cloud-based computing. It is a real question whether it will prove to be synergistic to launch such a full plate of search engines: Android mobile software, airflight search, Google Maps, restaurant info from Zagat's, Chrome web browser, Google+ social networking, Ad products, YouTube, and Motorola Mobility handsets.

(continued)

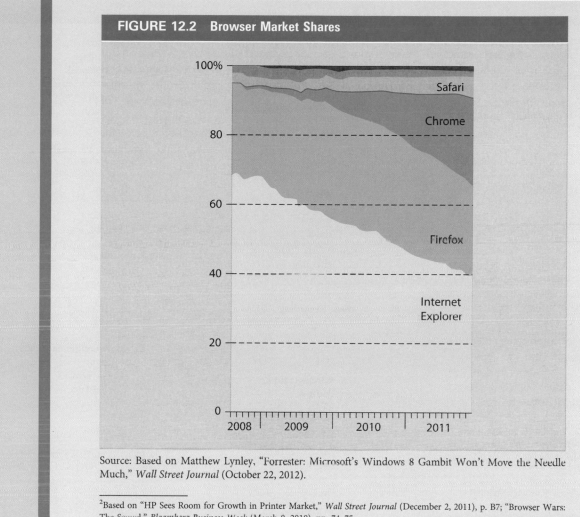

FIGURE 12.2 Browser Market Shares

Source: Based on Matthew Lynley, "Forrester: Microsoft's Windows 8 Gambit Won't Move the Needle Much," *Wall Street Journal* (October 22, 2012).

---

[2]Based on "HP Sees Room for Growth in Printer Market," *Wall Street Journal* (December 2, 2011), p. B7; "Browser Wars: The Sequel," *Bloomberg Business Week* (March 8, 2010), pp. 74–75.

In crackers, handsets, appliances, biotech, batteries, and wide-body aircraft, not one but two firms dominate (see Table 12.1). In snack foods, Nabisco's 45 percent market share and Keebler's 22 percent overshadow Pepperidge Farms' 7 percent. Similarly, Nokia and Samsung dominate the handset market, Sears and Lowe's Home Improvement dominate the home appliances market, Amgen and Roche dominate the biotech market, Duracell and Energizer dominate the battery market, and Boeing and Airbus dominate the wide-bodied aircraft market. These duopoly pairs of dominant firms often study complex tactical scenarios of moves and probable countermoves against each other. In still other cases, three firms circle warily, planning their tactical initiatives and retreats: smart phones (Google/Motorola 23 percent, Apple 21 percent, Samsung 16 percent); tea (Lipton 37 percent, Arizona 26 percent, Nestea 16 percent); rental cars (Enterprise 39 percent, Hertz Dollar Thrifty 32 percent, Avis Budget 28 percent); music recordings (Universal/Polygram 30 percent, Sony 29 percent, Warner 19 percent); U.S. Wireless (Verizon 34 percent, AT&T 32 percent, Sprint Nextel 19 percent); soft drinks (Coca-Cola 37 percent, Pepsi 30 percent, Dr. Pepper 21 percent); cereals (Kellogg 34 percent, General

TABLE 12.1 LARGEST U.S. MARKET SHARES IN OLIGOPOLISTIC INDUSTRIES

DOMINANT SINGLE FIRMS (%)

Razors and Blades (2011)
Gillette	79
Schick	18
Bic	3

Hand Calculators (2009)
Texas Instruments	78
Casio	14

Game Consoles (2008)
Nintendo	65
Sony	20
Microsoft	18

U.S. Beer (2012)
Anheuser-Busch	46
Miller-Coors	26
Heineken	6

Athletic Shoes (2008)
Nike	43
Adidas	15
Reebok	10

Microprocessors (2009)
Intel	81
AMD	19

e-Books (2012)
Amazon	60
Barnes and Noble	27
Apple	10

DUOPOLY FIRMS

Crackers (2008)
Nabisco (Kraft)	45
Keebler (Kellogg)	22
Pepperidge Farm	7

Handsets (2011)
Nokia	31
Samsung	21
Apple	5
RIM	4
Motorola	3

Appliances (2008)
Sears	32
Lowe's	20
Home Depot	9
Best Buy	7

Biotech (2008)
Amgen	21
Roche	20
Johnson & Johnson	8

Batteries (2005)
Duracell	43
Energizer	33
Rayovac	11

Wide-Body Aircraft (2010)
Boeing	50
Airbus	49

TRIOPOLY FIRMS

Smart phones (2012)
Google/Motorola	23
Apple	21
Samsung	16
Nokia	7
RIM	4

Tea (2007)
Lipton	37
Arizona	26
Nestea	16

Rental Cars (2012)
Enterprise	39
Hertz Dollar Thrifty	32
Avis Budget	28

Music Recording (2011)
Universal/Polygram	30
Sony Music	29
Warner	19
EMI	9

U.S. Wireless (2012)
Verizon	34
AT&T	32
Sprint Nextel	19
T-Mobile	13

Soft Drinks (2010)
Coca-Cola	37
Pepsi-Cola	30
Dr. Pepper	21

Cereals (2012)
Kellogg	34
General Mills	31
Post	14

Worldwide Confectionary (2012)
Mars	28
Cadbury	19
Nestlé	15
Hershey's	9
Kraft	9

LESS CONCENTRATED

U.S. (Worldwide) Autos (2012)
General Motors	17 (15)
Ford	15 (10)
Toyota	15 (15)
Fiat/Chrysler	12 (8)
Honda	11 (6)
Renault/Nissan	8 (13)
Hyundai/Kia	8 (13)
Volkswagen	5 (16)

Trucks (2007)
Freightliner	30
International	17
Mack	13
Peterbilt	12
Kenworth	11
Volvo Truck	10

Worldwide Personal Computers (2013)
HP	17
Lenovo	16
Dell	11
Apple	10
Toshiba	9

Tires (2012)
Goodyear	16
Michelin	12
Bridgestone	8
Yokohama	8
Kumho	8

Telecoms Equipment (2009)
Ericsson	23
Nokia/Siemens	18
Alcatel-Lucent	14
Huawei	13
Cisco	12
Motorola	9

Pharmaceuticals (2008)
Pfizer/Wyeth	26
GlaxoSmithKline	16
Novartis	15
Merck/Schering	15

Trade Books (2009)
Random House	18
Pearson	11
Hachette	10
HarperCollins	10
Simon & Schuster	9

Worldwide Tobacco (2010)
Philip Morris	16
British American	13
Japan Tobacco	11
Imperial Tobacco	10

Laser Printers (2011)
Hewlett-Packard	16
Canon	15
Samsung	15
Xerox	10
Ricoh	6

Source: Industry Surveys, *Net Advantage Database*, Standard & Poor's; and *Market Share Reports*, Gale Research, annual issues.

TABLE 12.2	MARKET SHARE DISTRIBUTIONS OVER TIME IN AIRLINES, CEREALS, AND WIDE-BODIED AIRCRAFT										

AIRLINES				CEREALS				WIDE-BODY AIRCRAFT			
1992		2005		1993		2011		1998		2011	
American	21%	American	19%	Kellogg	35%	Kellogg	34%	Boeing	70%	Airbus	51%
United	20	United	17	General Mills	25	General Mills	31	Airbus	30	Boeing	49
Delta	15	Delta	15	Post/Nabisco	18	Post/Ralston	13				
Northwest	14	Northwest	11	Quaker	8	Private Label	11				
Continental	11	Continental	9	Private Label	6	Quaker	6				
US Airways	9	Southwest	7	Ralston	5						

Sources: *Wall Street Journal* (December 21, 2001), p. A8; (December 27, 1996), p. A3; (October 16, 1998), p. B4; and (July 14, 2011), p. B1.

Mills 31 percent, Post 14 percent); and worldwide candy (Mars 28 percent, Cadbury 19 percent, and Nestlé 15 percent).

The market share distributions in Table 12.1 are seldom static. Instead, the dynamics of the share distribution often tell important insights. In cereals, General Mills' new product introductions continued to take marginal share points from Kellogg during 1993–2011. But it was Post that was the big loser to private-label discount cereals (e.g., Kroger Raisin Bran) (see Table 12.2). In wide-bodied aircraft, Boeing ceded market share to Airbus, and lowered its final assembly rate of production, removing bottlenecks and making itself much more profitable.

Over the 14-year period 1992–2005, the rank order of the leading airlines was largely unchanged, but every one of the major hub-and-spoke carriers lost two to three share points to the point-to-point discounters Southwest and America West (see the data in Table 12.2). By 2012, Southwest/AirTran (19%), United/Continental (19%), and Delta (19%) emerged as the largest carriers. Although no airline has a dominant market share nationally, a number of airlines have dominant positions at various airports around the country. For example, American has a 65 percent share at Dallas, Delta has an 84 percent share at Minneapolis, and US Airways/America West has an 85 percent share at Charlotte.

Example

Auto Rental and Retail Gasoline Firms Consolidate: Enterprise Rent-A-Car, and Exxon/Mobil

In auto rentals and retail gasoline, consolidation has occurred. The market shares of individual rental car companies have been very stable for the past decade, but Avis bought Budget, thereby reaching a 30 percent market share compared to Hertz's 29 percent. Then Enterprise combined with National and Alamo to achieve near parity (27 percent) with Avis and Hertz. The top three auto rental companies had 69 percent of the relevant market in 2000, whereas by 2008, the top three firms had 86 percent (see Figure 12.3). More recently, Hertz has taken over Dollar Thrifty. Massive consolidation also occurred in the retail gasoline industry, where company after company sought a large partner with whom to merge. Scale economies in exploration and development, as well as the closing of redundant gas stations, drove the trend.

Finally, Table 12.1 shows several industries in which the share distributions are less concentrated but where the strong interdependencies between leading firms remain prominent

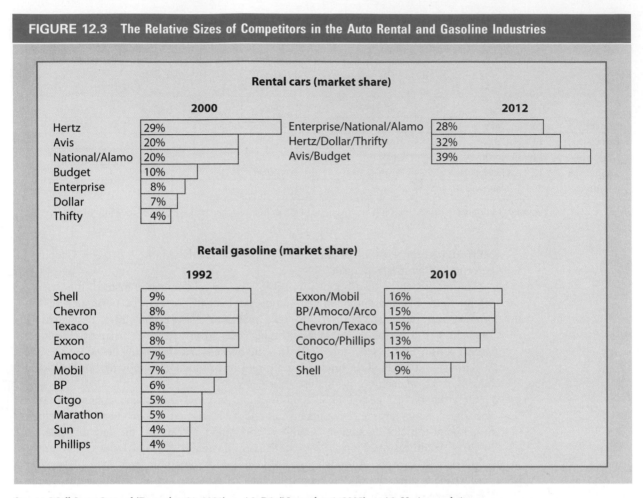

FIGURE 12.3   The Relative Sizes of Competitors in the Auto Rental and Gasoline Industries

Source: *Wall Street Journal* (December 21, 2001), p. A8, B6; (November 1, 2005), p. A2, Various websites.

in each firm's business planning. Sales in the tires, U.S. auto and truck markets are dispersed across 6–8 companies. And in three industries heavily influenced by the disruptive technology of Internet computing (namely, trade book publishing, laptop computers, and telecom equipment), the forces of competition have dispersed the shares across 5–6 firms. Similarly in telecom equipment and pharmaceuticals, market shares are more dispersed as the huge investments required to dominate the market are potentially unrecoverable.

INTERDEPENDENCIES IN OLIGOPOLISTIC INDUSTRIES

The nature of interdependencies in these oligopolistic industries can be illustrated using an airline pricing example.

The Cournot Model

One standard approach to the interdependency problem among oligopolists is merely to ignore it—that is, for a firm to assume that its competitors will act as if it does not exist.

Example

Airline Pricing: The Pittsburgh Market

Consider the case of the airline route between Pittsburgh and Dallas. One can fly this route on a number of different airlines, but only American and US Airways offer non-stop service between these cities. Initially, both airlines were charging $1,054 for a round-trip coach-class ticket. American then introduced a discounted fare for only $640, a reduction of $414. US Airways was then faced with the decision of whether to maintain its current $1,054 fare, match American's new $640 fare, or undercut American's $640 fare. American's demand function (and revenues) in the Pittsburgh-Dallas market depended on the reaction of US Airways to the fare reduction. A decision by US Airways to charge a higher fare (e.g., the current $1,054 fare) would result in additional market share for American, because many travelers would choose American's lower-priced service. A decision by US Airways to match American's new fare would result in American retaining its existing market share on the Pittsburgh-Dallas route. However, depending on the price elasticity of demand and the mix of full-fare and discounted tickets sold, the price reduction could actually increase American's revenues and profits. Finally, a decision by US Airways to undercut American's new $640 fare would lead to a lower market share and a likely further price reduction by American.

Because of the wide scope of oligopoly industry configurations in Table 12.1, several simplifying models have been used to describe oligopolists' competitive behavior regarding price, output, and other market conditions. The Cournot oligopoly model, proposed by the French economist Augustin Cournot, asserts that each firm, in determining its profit-maximizing output level, *assumes that the other firm's output will not change.*

For example, suppose that two duopolists (Firms A and B) produce identical products. If Firm A observes Firm B producing Q_B units of output in the current period, then Firm A will seek to maximize its own profits assuming that Firm B will continue producing the same Q_B units in the next period. Firm B acts in a similar manner. It attempts to maximize its own profits under the assumption that Firm A will continue producing the same amount of output in the next period as Firm A did in the current period. In the Cournot model, this pattern continues until reaching the long-run equilibrium point where output and price are stable and neither firm can increase its profits by raising or lowering output. The following example illustrates the determination of the long-run Cournot equilibrium.

Example

The Cournot Oligopoly Solution: Siemens and Alcatel-Lucent

Suppose that two European electronics companies, Siemens (Firm S) and Alcatel-Lucent (Firm T), jointly hold a patent on a component used in airport radar systems. Demand for the component is given by the following function:

$$P = 1,000 - Q_S - Q_T \qquad [12.1]$$

where Q_S and Q_T are the quantities sold by the respective firms and P is the (market) selling price. The total cost functions of manufacturing and selling the component for the respective firms are

$$TC_S = 70,000 + 5Q_S + 0.25Q_S^2 \qquad [12.2]$$

(continued)

$$TC_T = 110,000 + 5Q_T + 0.15Q_T^2 \qquad [12.3]$$

Suppose that the two firms act independently, with each firm seeking to maximize its own total profit from the sale of the component.

Siemens' total profit is equal to

$$
\begin{aligned}
\pi_S &= PQ_S - TC_S \\
&= (1,000 - Q_S - Q_T)Q_S - (70,000 + 5Q_S + 0.25Q_S^2) \\
&= -70,000 + 995Q_S - Q_TQ_S - 1.25Q_S^2 \qquad [12.4]
\end{aligned}
$$

Note that Siemens' total profit depends on the amount of output produced and sold by Alcatel-Lucent (Q_T). Taking the partial derivative of Equation 12.4 with respect to Q_S yields

$$\frac{\partial \pi_S}{\partial Q_S} = 995 - Q_T - 2.50Q_S \qquad [12.5]$$

Similarly, Alcatel-Lucent's total profit is equal to

$$
\begin{aligned}
\pi_T &= PQ_T - TC_T \\
&= (1,000 - Q_S - Q_T)Q_T - (110,000 + 5Q_T + 0.15Q_T^2) \\
&= -110,000 + 995Q_T - Q_SQ_T - 1.15Q_T^2 \qquad [12.6]
\end{aligned}
$$

Note also that Alcatel-Lucent's total profit is a function of Siemens' output level (Q_S). Taking the partial derivative of Equation 12.6 with respect to Q_T yields

$$\frac{\partial \pi_T}{\partial Q_T} = 995 - Q_S - 2.30Q_T \qquad [12.7]$$

Setting Equations 12.5 and 12.7 equal to zero yields

$$2.50Q_S + Q_T = 995 \qquad [12.8]$$

$$Q_S + 2.30Q_T = 995 \qquad [12.9]$$

Solving Equations 12.8 and 12.9 simultaneously gives the optimal levels of output for the two firms: $Q_S^* = 272.32$ units and $Q_T^* = 314.21$ units. By substituting these values into Equation 12.1, we calculate an optimal (equilibrium) selling price of $P^* = \$413.47$ per unit. The respective profits for the two firms are obtained by substituting Q_S^* and Q_T^* into Equations 12.4 and 12.6 to obtain $\pi_S^* = \$22,695.00$ and $\pi_T^* = \$3,536.17$.

CARTELS AND OTHER FORMS OF COLLUSION

cartel A formal or informal agreement among firms in an oligopolistic industry that influences such issues as prices, total industry output, market shares, and the division of profits.

Oligopolists sometimes reduce the inherent risk of being so interdependent by either formally or informally agreeing to cooperate or collude in decision making. Collusive agreements between oligopolists are called **cartels**. In general, collusive agreements are illegal in the United States and Europe; however, some important exceptions exist. For example, prices and quotas of various agricultural products (e.g., milk, oranges) are set by grower cooperatives in many parts of the country with the approval of the federal government. The International Air Transport Association (IATA) airlines flying transoceanic routes jointly set uniform prices for these flights. And ocean shipping rates are set by hundreds of collusive "conferences" on each major transoceanic route.

In addition, illegal collusive arrangements also arise from time to time. For example, cement and paving companies, as well as cardboard box manufacturers, often are indicted for price fixing. In a 2008 case, South Korean electronics giant LG Electronics paid a $400 million fine (the second-largest antitrust fine ever) for conspiring with Japanese Sharp ($129 million), Samsung Electronics Co., and Taiwanese Chunghwa Display and AU Optronics ($500 million) to fix the wholesale price from 2001 to 2006 of LCD monitors in laptops, cell phones, and televisions.[3] The six defendants controlled 80 percent of the LCD market. Two executives were sentenced to three years in jail, and these fines equal the largest ever leveled at antitrust violators in the United States. The grain-processing giant Archer Daniels Midland (ADM) pled guilty in 1996 to organizing an explicit quota and pricing system among five firms in the lysine market; lysine is an amino acid food supplement that speeds the growth of livestock. ADM paid $100 million in antitrust penalties, and ADM executives went to jail.[4] Roche and BASF, large Swiss and German industrial conglomerates in pharmaceuticals, chemicals, fragrances, and vitamins, agreed to pay $500 million and $225 million fines, respectively, to the U.S. Justice Department for their leadership of a price-fixing conspiracy in vitamin supplements. This 1999 antitrust settlement reduced Roche's profitability by 30 percent.[5] Worldwide the fines arising from the vitamin price-fixing conspiracy totaled $1.6 billion. These severe penalties indicate how serious the inefficiencies arising from cartelization of an industry can be. Businesses are wise not to ignore the prohibition against price fixing.

Example

How Ocean Shipping Conferences Have Affected Shipping Rates[6]

Since the Shipping Act of 1916, ocean freight companies have been exempt from the antitrust laws of the United States. Shipping rates on a transoceanic route are set jointly by 10 to 50 competitors acting as a "shipping conference." Two studies in 1993 and 1995 by the U.S. Agriculture Department and the Federal Trade Commission (FTC) found that rates were 18 or 19 percent lower when ocean-shipping companies broke out of these conference arrangements and negotiated as independents. Nevertheless, the conferences maintain their market power by signing exclusive-dealing contracts with large-volume customers. The enormous capacity of the shipping conferences allows more schedule frequency and greater reliability than the independents can offer. In exchange for exclusive contracts, shipping conferences have offered attractive settlement of disputed cargo claims, using speedy liquidated damage processes. In 2000, the U.S. Congress held hearings about this antitrust immunity and proposed its removal, but no legislation was passed.

---

[6]Based on "Making Waves," *Wall Street Journal* (October 7, 1997), p. A1; J. Yong, "Excluding Capacity-Constrained Entrants through Exclusive Dealing: Theory and Applications to Ocean Shipping," *Journal of Industrial Economics* 46, no. 2 (June 1996), pp. 115–129; and "Shipmates," *Wall Street Journal* (February 20, 2003), p. A1.

---

[3]"3 LCD-Makers Plead Guilty to Price Fixing," *Wall Street Journal* (July 7, 2008), p. B1; "Seoul Fines Six LCD Manufacturers in Price Fixing Case," *Wall Street Journal*, (October 31, 2011), p. B5; "Firm Fined $500 million for Price Fixing," *Wall Street Journal* (September 21, 2012), p. B2.

[4]"In ADM Saga, Executives Now on Trial," *Wall Street Journal* (July 9, 1998), p. B10.

[5]"Scandal Costs Roche," *Wall Street Journal* (May 25, 1999), p. A20.

Factors Affecting the Likelihood of Successful Collusion

The ability of oligopolistic firms to engage successfully in collusion depends on a number of factors.

Number and Size Distribution of Sellers   Effective collusion generally is less difficult as the number of oligopolistic firms involved decreases. In the 1990s, the De Beers diamond cartel in Switzerland and South Africa was effective in part because Russia agreed in 1995 to sell 95 percent of its total wholesale supply through De Beers. De Beers' central selling organization and Russia together accounted for more than 75 percent of world supply at that time.

Product Heterogeneity   Products that are alike in their characteristics are said to be homogeneous, and price is the only distinction that matters. When products are *heterogeneous* (or differentiated), cooperation is more difficult because competition is occurring over a broader array of product characteristics, such as durability, fashion timing, warranty, and after-sale policies.

Cost Structures   The more cost functions differ among competing firms, the more difficult it will be for firms to collude on pricing and output decisions. Also, successful collusion is more difficult in industries where fixed costs are a large part of total costs. A higher percentage of fixed costs implies higher contribution margins to recover those fixed costs. And, as we saw in Equation 10.2 in Chapter 10, higher margins mean a lower break-even sales change that makes discounting more attractive and restraining discounters more difficult. Therefore, breakdowns in collusively high prices often occur in industries that require highly capital-intensive production processes, such as petroleum refining, steel making, and airlines.

Size and Frequency of Orders   Successful oligopolistic cooperation also depends on the size distribution of customer orders over time. Effective collusion is more likely when orders are small, frequent, and received regularly, as in the purchase of autos. When large orders are received infrequently at irregular intervals, as in the purchase of aircraft engines, it is more difficult for firms to collude on pricing and output decisions. Hence, Pratt & Whitney, Rolls-Royce, and General Electric have never colluded on jet engine prices.

 Example

DRAM Chipmakers Pay Enormous Fines for Forming a Global Cartel[7]

The world's top four manufacturers of inexpensive random access memory (RAM) chips, a key component of all consumer electronic devices, agreed to fines and jail terms for several executives because of 1999–2002 price fixing. The criminal conspiracy raised prices 400 percent in a six-month period from $1 to $4 per 100 megabits and then orchestrated maintaining the price at $3. Dynamic random access memory (DRAM) chips are generic and easily substitutable between suppliers. As a result, a cartel agreement to limit production is necessary to maintain price above competitive levels. Samsung and Hynix, two South Korean firms that produce the majority of the chips, paid $300 million and $185 million fines, respectively. Infineon Technologies of Germany paid a $160 million fine, and four executives went to jail for several months and paid individual fines of $250,000. Micron Technology of Boise, Idaho, received immunity for cooperating with the prosecutors and complainants Dell and HP in making the case.

[7]Based on "Samsung to Pay," *Wall Street Journal* (October 14, 2005), p. A3; and "Hynix Pleads Guilty," *Wall Street Journal* (April 22, 2004), p. B6.

Threat of Retaliation An oligopolistic firm will be less tempted to grant secret price concessions to selected customers if it feels that other cartel members would detect these price reductions and then retaliate. The toilet tissue manufacturers' collusive agreement allegedly operated through public bids for institutional customers such as schools and hospitals. Sealed bids might have prevented the collusion, surprisingly.

Percentage of External Output Most cartels contain the seeds of their own destruction. Rising prices and profits attract the entry of new competitors. Any increase in supply from outside the cartel means that larger restrictions on output must be imposed on cartel members in order to sustain any given market price. At one point in 1999, De Beers had to purchase for its own inventory $3.96 billion in diamonds (in only an $8 billion market) in order to stabilize prices because so many Canadian, Australian, and Russian diamonds (external at that point to the De Beers cartel) had flooded the market.[8]

Finally, in 2000, with 37 percent of total diamond supply outside the cartel, De Beers declared the end of its 65-year cartel. Similar events ended the Organization of Petroleum Exporting Countries (OPEC) I cartel when Mexican, Venezuelan, and Norwegian oil flooded onto the market. Ocean shipping prices are breaking down today because the rate setting "conferences" now control less than 70 percent of the $85 billion North Atlantic market and less than 50 percent of the $262 billion trans-Pacific market. External suppliers reduce the likelihood of successful coordination among cartel members to maintain prices above their competitive level.

Cartel Profit Maximization and the Allocation of Restricted Output

Under both legal cartels and secret collusive agreements, firms attempt to increase prices and profits above the level that would prevail in the absence of collusion. The profit maximization solution for a two-firm cartel, E and F, is shown graphically in Figure 12.4. The *industry* demand D, marginal revenue MR, and marginal cost ΣMC curves are shown in the third panel. The industry marginal cost curve is obtained by summing horizontally across outputs the marginal cost curves of the individual firms in the first two panels: that is, $\Sigma MC = MC_E + MC_F$. Total industry profits are maximized by setting total industry output (and consequently price) at the point where industry marginal revenue equals industry marginal cost (i.e., Q^*_{Total} units of output at a price of P^* per unit).

If the cartel maximizes its total profits, the market share (or quota) for each firm should be set at a level where marginal cost of all firms is identical and the industry (summed) $MC = MR$. The optimal joint output is for Firm E to produce a quota of Q^*_E units and for Firm F to produce a quota of Q^*_F units. If Firm E were producing at a level where its marginal costs exceeded Firm F's, cartel profits could be increased by shifting output from E to F until marginal costs were equal.[9]

Cartel pricing agreements are hard to reach, but the central problem for a cartel lies in monitoring these output shares or quotas. Detecting quota violations and effectively enforcing punishment schemes are nearly impossible. Consequently, most cartels are unstable, like the price-fixing agreements among cardboard box manufacturers—these collusive agreements form approximately once a quarter and break up within a few

---

[8]Based on "De Beers to Abandon Monopoly," *Wall Street Journal* (July 13, 2000), p. A20; and "Atlantic Ocean Shipping Cartel Makes Concessions," *Wall Street Journal* (February 7, 1997), p. A2.

[9]Note that the average total costs of the two firms are not necessarily equal at the optimal (profit-maximizing) output level. Note also that Firm E is given a sizable share of the total output even though its average total costs are higher than Firm F.

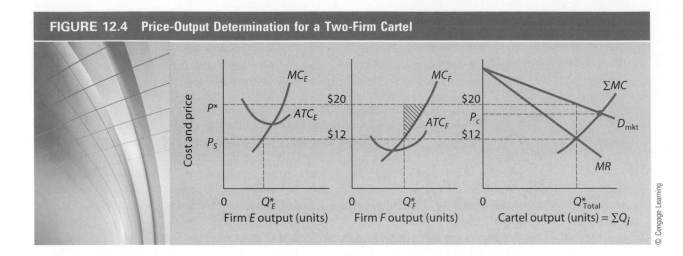

FIGURE 12.4 Price-Output Determination for a Two-Firm Cartel

© Cengage Learning

weeks. The longevity of OPEC and the De Beers diamond cartels is exceptional. Let's return to Figure 12.4 and see why.

Suppose you are Firm F facing a cartel-determined price for crude oil P^* of $20 per barrel. Your marginal costs are presently running $12 per barrel at your assigned quota of Q_F/Q_{Total}. The Aramco pipelines, which once consolidated all your throughput from the production wells to shipping terminals, have now been superseded by numerous independent shipping terminals, where the crude is relatively undifferentiated. Should you abide by your quota commitment? Is it in your best interest to do so? The answer depends on whether your additional sales beyond quota are detectable and whether your additional output will increase total supply enough to place downward pressure on the cartel price. If the answer to both questions is no, then because a 40 percent profit margin ($8) awaits your selling another barrel, a profit maximizer will be tempted to increase output and capture the hatched area of incremental profit in the middle panel of Figure 12.4.

Of course, the problem is that other cartel members may think exactly the same way. If everyone takes the cartel price as given and independently profit maximizes, then cartel supply increases to ΣMC, and the black market price must fall to the competitive level P_c of perhaps $17 just to clear the market. Enforcement of the ideal quotas Q_F and Q_E is the weak point of every cartel. In OPEC, Saudi Arabia plays a pivotal role in absorbing quota violations by other OPEC members and thereby stabilizes the cartel.

Example

Coffee Pricing Agreement Dissolves amidst Dilemma[10]

When the coffee bean harvest is larger than projected, the top Colombian and Brazilian coffee producers along with several African and Central American smaller producers often agree in principle to withhold millions of tons of coffee beans from the market in an effort to raise collapsing wholesale prices. Brazilian producers may propose to hold back 2 million bags of a projected 18-million-bag crop. Colombian producers may agree to hold back 1.3 million bags. However, both countries oppose a formal quota system that assigns production ceilings, imposes monitoring mechanisms, and penalizes violators. In 1989 and again in 1993, International Coffee Agreements collapsed over the refusal to accept assigned quotas.

(continued)

If all major coffee bean producers could rely upon one another to withhold extraordinarily large production in exceptionally good weather years, all would have higher profitability. Instead, some cartel members maximize self-interest by releasing excess supplies to the world market at just below the officially agreed-upon price. Because other cartel members think that same way, equilibrium market price then plummets. Only dupes then continue to restrain output when world market prices erode, signaling that other coffee producers are violating the agreement.

[10]"Brazil, Colombia Form Cartel for Coffee Exports," *Wall Street Journal* (September 8, 1991), p. B12.

INTERNATIONAL PERSPECTIVES

The OPEC Cartel[11]

The Organization of Petroleum Exporting Countries (OPEC) was founded in 1960 by five Persian Gulf nations who hosted ARAMCO, a joint venture set up in 1947 by the international oil companies for the exploration and development of the Middle East oil fields. ARAMCO set the price of crude oil and paid oil concession royalties used by the host nations to purchase back the ARAMCO assets. Controlling 80 percent of world petroleum output in 1973–1974, the OPEC members decided to restrain production in order to sustain a 400 percent increase in the price of crude oil from $3 to $12 per barrel. The OPEC I cartel was born. Saudi Arabia is the most influential member of this price-fixing cartel because of the tremendous size of its production capacity—almost one-half of OPEC's total output at the inception of OPEC and still 36 percent of OPEC output today.

By the early 1980s, with the price of oil at $32 to $41 ($80 in 2006 dollars), covert price cutting was rampant. Nigeria, for example, engaged in secret price cutting by reducing income taxes for the oil companies working there. Other OPEC members bartered and extended payment terms for oil purchases, thereby reducing interest expenses on the funds required to finance the purchase. During this period (often referred to as OPEC II), Saudi Arabia regularly stabilized declining oil prices by acting as a "swing producer," cutting its production to as low as 2 million barrels per day (bpd) in 1980 when its authorized quota was 4.35 million and its capacity was 10 million bpd. OPEC II ended effectively in October 1985, when Saudi Arabia reversed its policy and began increasing

its output to as much as 6 million bpd. The equilibrium market price of crude fell as low as $12.

Today OPEC controls less than 40 percent of world oil output, half of what they once did. Throughout the 1990s, production expanded in nontraditional oil-producing regions like Prudhoe Bay, Alaska; in Russia; and in the North Sea despite extraction costs three to five times higher than the $3-per-barrel exploration, development, and extraction cost in the Middle East. Venezuela has publicly challenged the role of Saudi Arabia as swing producer and price leader, especially in the western hemisphere. And Russia at 9.27 million bpd has posed the same challenge in other parts of the world.

With production breaking out all over, in 1998 and early 1999, crude oil prices collapsed to $9.96 (see Figure 12.5). To stabilize the market, OPEC members agreed in March 1999 (and again in September 2000) to a production quota system. Saudi Arabia accepted a 585,000-barrel-per-day cutback, which equaled 7 percent of its February 1999 average daily production of 8.8 million barrels. Iran, with a 12 percent share, agreed to a 264,000-barrel cutback, which also equaled a 7 percent reduction of its 3.6-million-barrel output. Venezuela accepted a 125,000-barrel-per-day cutback, which equaled a 4 percent reduction of its 3.4-million-barrel output. Crude oil prices responded almost immediately, rising more than threefold from a $10 trough to $33 per barrel in 15 months (again see Figure 12.5). The OPEC III cartel was in place, effectively restricting output to raise prices.

[11]"Why the Saudis Won't Back Down Soon," *Wall Street Journal* (April 8, 1986); and J. Griffin and W. Xiong, "The Incentive to Cheat: An Empirical Analysis of OPEC," *Journal of Law and Economics* 60, no. 2 (1997).

FIGURE 12.5   How OPEC III Production Quotas Affected Crude Oil Prices

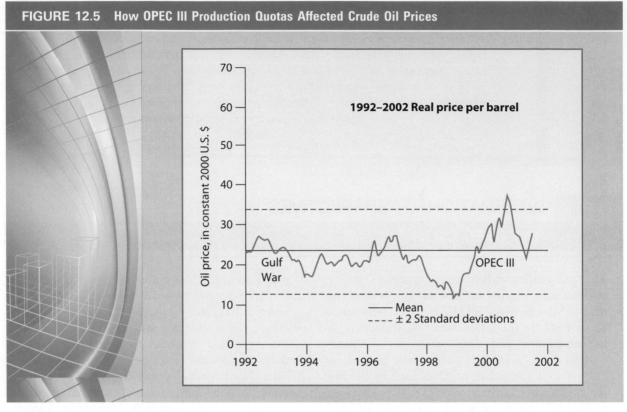

Source: Federal Reserve Bank, St. Louis, *National Economic Trends.*

Example

Exhaustible Natural Resources: Saudi Arabia Plays a Waiting Game[12]

Some resources like crude oil, coal, natural gas, and diamonds are formed over tens of thousands of years. Although limited and fixed in this geological sense, more intense exploration and development can often locate additional resources. Renewable resources such as fisheries and timberland replenish themselves if harvesting is restrained to prevent exhaustion, but the only reason for an exhaustible resource owner to not extract crude oil, or coal, or natural gas is if he or she believes that the resource price is going to rise in the future. Price changes and price change expectations are therefore the key to exhaustible resource decisions.

Define consensus expectations for future prices in time period T (P_T) as

$$P_T = P_0(1 + r)^T \qquad [12.10]$$

where r is the real rate of interest (more precisely, the inflation-adjusted risk-adjusted rate of interest). Dividing each unit of time into n subperiods and taking the limit as n goes to infinity, the compound growth version of these consensus price expectations may be written as

$$P_T = P_0[\lim_{n \to \infty}(1 + r/n)^{nT}] = P_0 e^{rT} \qquad [12.11]$$

(continued)

where e is 2.7183 ..., the base of the natural logarithms. We are now in a position to express the harvest now-or-wait decision in terms of the opportunity cost of waiting (the real rate of interest r) relative to the percentage rate of growth of resource prices:[13]

$$\frac{\Delta P_T / \Delta T}{P_T} = \frac{r P_0 e^{rT}}{P_T}$$

which reduces, using Equation 12.11, to

$$\frac{\Delta P_T / \Delta T}{P_T} = r \qquad [12.12]$$

This result states that as long as the expected rate of price increase (say, 8 percent) exceeds the interest rate (say, 4 percent), one should leave the crude oil, coal, or natural gas in the ground and harvest later. If interest rates rise above this percentage growth rate of the exhaustible resource prices, the resource should be extracted and sold now.

In 2008–2009, crude oil prices rose to $147 per barrel and then fell like a rock to $39 even though demand continued to grow. The worldwide financial crisis crushed the speculative demand, and greener hybrid-electric and all-electric vehicles were beginning to replace gasoline-engine autos. In the face of projections of flat to declining crude oil prices, Saudi Arabia decided to increase production and harvest now! From 8 million mbd in 2002, the Saudis increased production to almost 11 mbd in 2009 and 9.4 mbd in 2011 (see Figure 12.6). Although OPEC controls only 36 percent of worldwide crude oil production today (see Figure 12.7), Saudi Arabia remains a pivot point in setting world prices. As a result, gasoline remains substantially less expensive than electricity for powering cars and only about 80 percent as expensive as the full cost of hydrogen fuel for powering cars. Again, Saudi capacity expansions to 12 mbd and Saudi utilization policies of almost 11 mbd were designed to discourage the development of substitute fuels by slowing the rate of price increase for crude oil. Any other exhaustible resource owner with a 65-year supply of proven reserves would have done the same thing.

The Saudi's extraction strategy has proven successful. The price of crude oil fell steeply off its July 2008 $147 per barrel peak and within a year averaged $75 per barrel. In 2012, crude oil has averaged $85 per barrel, and the price of gasoline is again under $3.50 per gallon across most of the United States.

---

[12]Based on *OPEC Annual Statistical Bulletin*; and "Why the U.S. Is Still Hooked on Oil Imports," *Wall Street Journal* (March 18, 2003), p. A1.

[13]This step is based on the calculus result that

$$\frac{de^{rT}}{dT} = re^{rt}$$

Saudi Arabia has an enormous 264 billion barrels of known but untapped crude oil reserves that are expected to last 65 years at current rates of production (see Figure 12.7). By comparison, the United States has only 21 billion barrels and 11 years of reserves left. Therefore, the Saudis prefer to discourage the emergence of alternative fuels such as sugarcane-based ethanol in Brazil, corn-based ethanol in the United States, and natural gas for large trucks. In this sense, U.S. oil interests in Texas and Oklahoma

FIGURE 12.6 **Saudi Arabian Crude Oil Production**

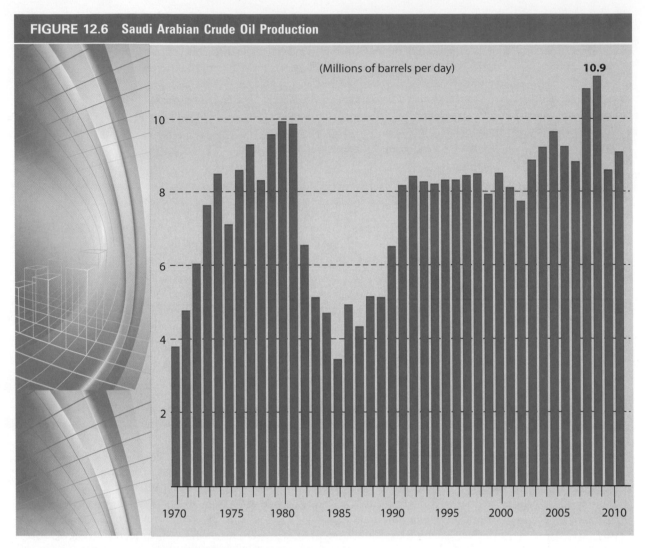

Source: U.S. Energy Information Agency.

are often at odds with Saudi Arabia. The former want policies designed to raise the oil price quickly before their reserves run out. The latter want to hold prices below levels that would trigger replacing internal combustion gasoline engines with all-electric vehicles or hydrogen fuel cells since Saudi and other OPEC oil reserves will last for nearly a century.

Example

What Drives the Price per Gallon of Gasoline Above $3.00?[14]

In recent years, the OPEC III cartel has been overshadowed by the Iraq War and by unanticipated growth of gasoline consumption in China and India. In 2006 and again in 2009, crude oil sold for $70 to $80 a barrel and gasoline prices rose above $3 per gallon. What are the component costs of this $3+ retail price of gasoline?

(continued)

One explanation might be that state and federal excise taxes or state and local sales taxes have risen, but they have remained about $0.50 to $0.60 per gallon for a decade (see Figure 12.8). Another explanation might be that retail station owners are gouging customers, but perfect competition characterizes the retail gas market, and consequently, retail margins are low and have remained unchanged at $0.15 to $0.20 for many years. Distribution bottlenecks occasionally are responsible for price spikes in a local region when pipelines break, but in general, only $0.07 of the price of gas is attributable to distribution costs. Scarcity of refining capacity is another explanation, and $0.80 of the $3.00 is attributable to refining costs that have risen somewhat in recent years.

Nevertheless, by far the largest component cost reflected in retail gas prices is crude oil (again, see Figure 12.8). Fully half of the cost of $3-per-gallon gasoline ($1.40) is attributable to the cost of crude oil itself. And it is this component that has increased enormously from $35 per barrel in 2004 to $70–$80 per barrel in 2005–2006 and again in 2009.

---

[14]Based on "Oil Nations Move Closer to a New Round of Cuts," *Wall Street Journal* (March 12, 1999), p. A3; "Crude Cuts: Will Oil Nations Stick or Stray?" *Wall Street Journal* (March 26, 1999), p. A19; "The Next Oil Shock," *The Economist* (March 6, 1999), p. 72; "Standstill Britain," *The Economist* (September 16, 2000), p. 64; and "At OPEC Some Say There's Enough Oil," *Wall Street Journal* (September 12, 2000), p. A2.

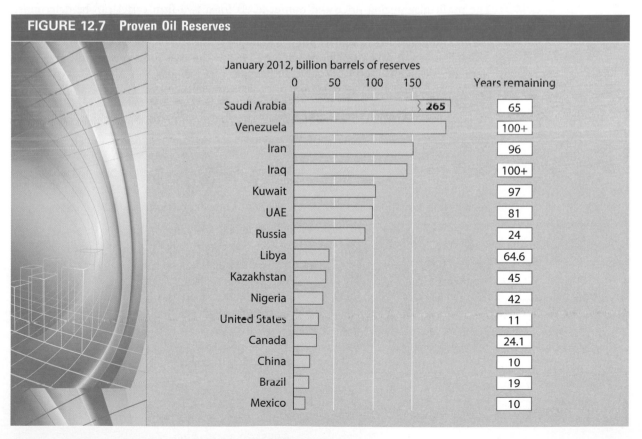

FIGURE 12.7   Proven Oil Reserves

Source: BP Statistical Review of World Energy, 2012.

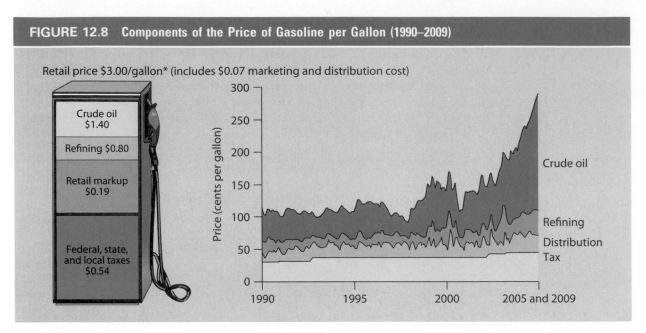

FIGURE 12.8 Components of the Price of Gasoline per Gallon (1990–2009)

Source: *Changing Gasoline Prices*, Federal Trade Commission, June, 2005.

Cartel Analysis: Algebraic Approach

The profit-maximizing price and output levels for a two-firm cartel can be determined algebraically when the demand and cost functions are given. Consider again the Siemens (Firm S) and Alcatel-Lucent (Firm T) example discussed in the previous section. The demand function was given by Equation 12.1 and the cost functions for the two firms were given by Equations 12.2 and 12.3. Suppose that Siemens and Alcatel-Lucent decide to form a cartel and act as a monopolist to maximize total profits from the production and sale of the components.

Total industry profits (π_{Total}) are equal to the sum of Siemens' and Thomson's profits and are given by the following expression:

$$\begin{aligned} \pi_{\text{Total}} &= \pi_S + \pi_T \\ &= PQ_S - TC_S + PQ_T - TC_T \end{aligned} \qquad [12.13]$$

Substituting Equations 12.1, 12.2, and 12.3 into this expression yields

$$\begin{aligned} \pi_{\text{Total}} &= (1{,}000 - Q_S - Q_T)Q_S - (70{,}000 + 5Q_S + 0.25Q_S^2) \\ &\quad + (1{,}000 - Q_S - Q_T)Q_T - (110{,}000 + 5Q_T + 0.15Q_T^2) \\ &= 1{,}000Q_S - Q_S^2 - Q_SQ_T - 70{,}000 - 5Q_S - 0.25Q_S^2 \\ &\quad + 1{,}000Q_T - Q_SQ_T - Q_T^2 - 110{,}000 - 5Q_T - 0.15Q_T^2 \\ &= -180{,}000 + 995Q_S - 1.25Q_S^2 + 995Q_T \\ &\quad - 1.15Q_T^2 - 2Q_SQ_T \end{aligned} \qquad [12.14]$$

To maximize π_{Total}, take the *partial* derivatives of Equation 12.14 with respect to Q_S and Q_T:

$$\frac{\partial \pi_{\text{Total}}}{\partial Q_S} = 995 - 2.50Q_S - 2Q_T$$

$$\frac{\partial \pi_{\text{Total}}}{\partial Q_T} = 995 - 2.30Q_T - 2Q_S$$

Setting these expressions equal to zero yields

$$2.5Q_S + 2Q_T - 995 = 0 \qquad [12.15]$$

$$2Q_S + 2.3Q_T - 995 = 0 \qquad [12.16]$$

Solving Equations 12.15 and 12.16 simultaneously gives the following optimal output levels: $Q_S^* = 170.57$ units and $Q_T^* = 284.39$ units.

Substituting these values into Equations 12.13 and 12.14 gives an optimal selling price and total profit for the cartel of $P^* = \$545.14$ per unit and $\pi_{Total}^* = \$46,291.43$, respectively. The marginal costs of the two firms at the optimal output level are equal to

$$MC_S^* = \frac{d(TC_S)}{dQ_S} = 5 + 0.50Q_S$$

$$= 5 + 0.50(170.57) = \$90.29$$

$$MC_T^* = \frac{d(TC_T)}{dQ_T} = 5 + 0.30Q_T$$

$$= 5 + 0.30(284.29) = \$90.29$$

As in the graphical solution illustrated earlier in Figure 12.2, the optimal output (or market share) for each firm in the cartel occurs where the marginal costs of the two firms are equal.

Table 12.3 summarizes the results of the Siemens and Alcatel-Lucent example: (1) where the two companies acted independently to maximize their own company profits (Cournot equilibrium), and (2) where they formed a cartel to maximize total industry profits. Several conclusions can be drawn from this comparison. First, total industry output (Q_{Total}^*) is lower and selling price (P^*) is higher when the firms collude. Also, total industry profits (π_{Total}^*) are higher when the firms set prices and output jointly than when they act independently. Finally, although it may not be true in all collusive agreements, one firm's profits (i.e., Siemens') are actually lower under the cartel solution than when it acts independently. Therefore, to get Siemens to participate in the cartel, Alcatel-Lucent probably would have to agree to share a significant part of the cartel's additional profits with Siemens.

TABLE 12.3   COMPARISON OF PRICING, OUTPUT, AND PROFITS FOR SIEMENS AND THOMSON

OPTIMAL VALUE	(1) NO COLLUSION: SIEMENS AND ALCATEL ACT INDEPENDENTLY TO MAXIMIZE THEIR OWN COMPANY'S PROFITS	(2) COLLUSION: SIEMENS AND ALCATEL FORM A CARTEL TO MAXIMIZE TOTAL INDUSTRY PROFITS
Q_S^* (Siemens' output)	272.32 units	170.57 units
Q_T^* (Alcatel-Lucent output)	314.21 units	284.29 units
$Q_{Total}^* = Q_S^* + Q_T^*$ (Total industry output)	586.53 units	454.86 units
P^* (Selling price)	\$413.47/unit	\$545.14/unit
π_S^* (Siemens' profit)	\$22,695.00	\$14,858.15
π_T^* (Alcatel-Lucent profit)	\$3,536.17	\$31,433.28
$\pi_{Total}^* = \pi_S^* + \pi_T^*$ (Total industry profit)	\$26,231.17	\$46,291.43

Revenue-Sharing in Major League Baseball[15]

Major League Baseball (MLB), a cartel of professional team owners, has been exempted from the antitrust laws since a U.S. Supreme Court decision in 1922. MLB restricts entry, approves transfers of ownership, and regulates the selection and employment of apprentice players for their first six years in professional baseball. In 1975, Curt Flood of the St. Louis Cardinals successfully challenged baseball's restrictive labor practices (the "reserve clause") for major leaguers beyond their sixth year, and a collective bargaining agreement then granted such players free agency status. Experienced players could then offer their services to the highest bidder whenever their contracts were due for renewal.

As a result, salaries skyrocketed and star players concentrated in the biggest markets (New York and Los Angeles) where owners with larger ticket revenue, higher concession sales, and bigger television contracts offered to pay more. Even the average player profited from the end of baseball's reserve clause. Average salary for major leaguers rose in inflation-adjusted dollars from $160,000 in 1972 to $1,015,000 in 1992 and $1,579,000 in 2012. Because owners spend 58 percent of team revenue on salaries and another 13 percent on the scouting system and the minor league apprentice teams, the MLB cartel intervened to restore competitive balance. MLB began a revenue-sharing system whereby the wealthiest teams are taxed 34 percent of total revenue to subsidize salaries for teams with a smaller fan base, either because of smaller markets (Minneapolis) or less success on the field (Baltimore). By 2010, subsidies totaled more than $404 million.

[15]Based on "Let the Market Rule," *Wall Street Journal* (November 10, 1998), p. A22; "Just Not Cricket," *The Economist* (May 31, 2003), p. 34; and Gerald Scully, *The Market Structure of Sports* (Chicago: Chicago University Press, 1995).

PRICE LEADERSHIP

price leadership A pricing strategy followed in many oligopolistic industries. One firm normally announces all new price changes. Either by an explicit or by an implicit agreement, other firms in the industry regularly follow the pricing moves of the industry leader.

Besides cartels, another model of price-output determination in some oligopolistic industries is **price leadership**. Many industries exhibit a pattern where one or a few firms normally set a price and others tend to follow, frequently with a time lag of a few days. In the case of basic steel products, for example, the price that prevails within a week is generally uniform from one producer to another.

Effective price leadership can only happen if price movements initiated by the leader have a high probability of being adopted and no maverick or nonconforming firms exist. The fewer the number of firms in the industry (i.e., the greater the interdependencies of decision outcomes among firms), the more effective price leadership is likely to be. Two major price leadership patterns have been observed in various industries from time to time: *barometric* and *dominant price leadership*.

Barometric Price Leadership

In barometric price leadership, one firm announces a change in price that it hopes will be accepted by others. The leader need not be the largest firm in the industry. In fact, this leader may actually change from time to time. The leader must, however, be reasonably correct in its interpretation of changing demand and cost conditions so that suggested price changes will be adopted industry-wide. In essence, the barometric price leader merely initiates a reaction to changing market conditions that other firms find in their best interest to follow. These conditions might include such things as cost increases (or decreases) and sluggish (or brisk) sales accompanied by inventory buildups (or shortages) in the industry.

Example

Barometric Price Leadership: American Airlines[16]

American Airlines (AA) has a very high proportion of business passengers out of its hub in Dallas–Fort Worth. Let's consider what happened once when AA announces that three-day advance purchase fares were no longer available on many nonstop routes. Instead, American returned to the old seven-day advance purchase require-ment to obtain a 20 percent off full coach class fare ($1,629 from Dallas to New York or $1,684 from Dallas to Miami, for example). Other much cheaper Saturday overnight fares bought 7 days or even 14 days in advance were not affected because those prices primarily target leisure travelers.

American Airlines was hoping that its major competitors, Delta, United Continen-tal, and US Airways, would take this opportunity to follow its lead and increase mar-gins. Only United Continental did so. Delta responded instead by heavily promoting a deeply discounted $198 round-trip fare on American's principal nonstop routes. Within a few days, American rescinded its pricing changes on routes where it com-peted with Delta but retained them where it had a dominant hub, as at Dallas–Fort Worth. In addition, American simultaneously announced a week of $198 fares on 10 nonstop routes from Delta's Atlanta hub and 10 nonstop routes from US Airways' Pittsburgh hub. Only United Continental's Houston hub was spared.

---

[16]Based on "Airfare Skirmish Shows Why Deals Come and Go," *Wall Street Journal* (March 19, 2002), p. B1.

Dominant Firm Price Leadership

In dominant firm price leadership, one firm establishes itself as the leader because of its larger size, customer loyalty, or lower cost structure in relation to other competing firms. The leader may then act as a monopolist in its segment of the market. What is the incen-tive for followers to accept the established price? In some cases it may be a fear of cut-throat retaliation from a low-cost dominant firm that keeps smaller firms from undercutting the prevailing price. In other cases, following a price leader may be viewed as simply a convenience.

The price-output solution for the dominant-firm model is shown in Figure 12.9. D_T shows total market demand for the product, MC_L represents the marginal cost curve for the dominant (leader) firm, and ΣMC_F constitutes the horizontal *summation* of the mar-ginal cost curves for the follower firms, each of which may well have costs higher than MC_L. In the following analysis, assume that the dominant firm sets the price knowing that follower firms will sell as much output as they wish at this price. The dominant firm then supplies the remainder of the market demand.

Given that the follower firms can sell as much output as they wish at the price P_L established by the dominant firm, they are faced with a horizontal demand curve and a perfectly competitive market situation. The follower firms view the dominant firm's price P_L as their marginal revenue and maximize profits, producing that level of output where their marginal cost equals the established price. The ΣMC_F curve therefore shows the total output that will be *supplied* at various prices by the follower firms. The dominant

FIGURE 12.9 Price-Output Determination for the Dominant Firm

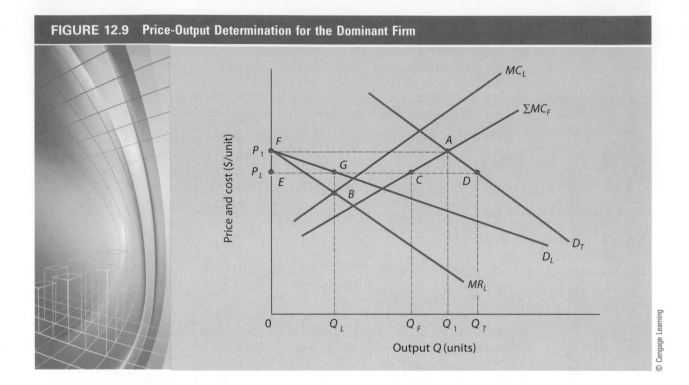

firm's residual demand curve D_L is obtained by subtracting the amount supplied by the follower firms' ΣMC_F from the total market demand D_T at each price. For example, at a price of P_L, Point G on the D_L curve is obtained by subtracting EC from ED. Other points on the D_L curve are obtained in a similar manner. At a price of P_1 the quantity supplied by the follower firms' Q_1 is equal to total market demand (Point A), and the dominant firm's residual demand is therefore zero (Point F). The dominant firm's marginal revenue curve MR_L is then obtained from its residual demand curve D_L.

The dominant firm maximizes its profits by setting price and output where marginal cost equals marginal revenue. As shown in Figure 12.9, $MR_L = MC_L$ at Point B. Therefore, the dominant firm should sell Q_L units of output at a price of P_L per unit. At a price of P_L, total demand is Q_T units, and the follower firms supply $Q_T - Q_L = Q_F$ units of output.

The following example illustrates the application of these concepts.

Example

Price Leadership: Aerotek

Aerotek and six other smaller companies produce an electronic component used in small planes. Aerotek (L) is the price leader. The other (follower [F]) firms sell the component at the same price as Aerotek. Aerotek permits the other firms to sell as many units of the component as they wish at the established price. The company supplies the remainder of the demand itself. Total demand for the component is given by the following function:

$$P = 10,000 - 10Q_T \qquad [12.17]$$

(continued)

where

$$Q_T = Q_L + Q_F \qquad [12.18]$$

that is, total output (Q_T) is the sum of the leader's (Q_L) and followers' (Q_F) output. Aerotek's marginal cost function is

$$MC_L = 100 + 3Q_L \qquad [12.19]$$

The aggregate marginal cost function for the other six producers of the component is

$$\Sigma MC_F = 50 + 2Q_F \qquad [12.20]$$

We are interested in determining the output for Aerotek and the follower firms and the selling price for the component given that the firms are interested in maximizing profits.

Aerotek's profit-maximizing output is found at the point where

$$MR_L = MC_L$$

Its marginal revenue function (MR_L) is obtained by differentiating the firm's total revenue function (TR_L) with respect to Q_L. Total revenue (TR_L) is given by the following expression:

$$TR_L = P \cdot Q_L$$

Q_L is obtained from Equation 12.18:

$$Q_L = Q_T - Q_F$$

Using Equation 12.17, one can solve for Q_T:

$$Q_T = 1,000 - 0.10P \qquad [12.21]$$

To find Q_F, we note that Aerotek lets the follower firms sell as much output (i.e., components) as they wish at the given price (P). Therefore, the follower firms are faced with a horizontal demand function. Hence

$$MR_F = P \qquad [12.22]$$

To maximize profits, the follower firms will operate where

$$MR_F = \Sigma MC_F \qquad [12.23]$$

Substituting Equations 12.22 and 12.20 into Equation 12.23 gives

$$P = 50 + 2Q_F \qquad [12.24]$$

Solving this equation for Q_F yields

$$Q_F = 0.50P - 25 \qquad [12.25]$$

Substituting Equation 12.21 for Q_T and Equation 12.25 for Q_F in Equation 12.20 gives

$$Q_L = (1,000 - 0.10P) - (0.50P - 25)$$
$$= 1,025 - 0.60P \qquad [12.26]$$

Solving Equation 12.26 for P, one obtains

$$P = 1,708.3333 - 1.6667Q_L \qquad [12.27]$$

Substituting this expression for P in defining total revenue yields

(continued)

$$TR_L = (1,708.3333 - 1.6667Q_L)Q_L$$

$$= 1,708.3333Q_L - 1.6667Q_L^2 \qquad [12.28]$$

Differentiating this expression with respect to Q_L, one obtains Aerotek's marginal revenue function:

$$MR_L = \frac{d(TR_L)}{dQ_L}$$

$$= 1,708.3333 - 3.3334Q_L \qquad [12.29]$$

Substituting Equation 12.29 for MR_L and Equation 12.16 for MC_L and equating the two gives the following optimality condition:

$$1,708.3333 - 3.3334Q_L^* = 100 + 3Q_L^* \qquad [12.30]$$

Solving this equation for Q_L^* yields

$$Q_L^* = 253.945 \text{ units}$$

or an optimal output for Aerotek of 253.9 units of the component. Substituting this value of Q_L into Equation 12.27 gives

$$P^* = 1,708.3333 - 1.6667(253.945)$$

$$= \$1,285.083$$

or an optimal selling price of $1,285.08. The optimal output for the follower firms is found by substituting this value of P into Equation 12.25,

$$Q_F^* = 0.50(1,285.083) - 25$$

$$= 617.542 \text{ units}$$

or an optimal output of 617.5 units.

THE KINKED DEMAND CURVE MODEL

Sometimes when an oligopolist cuts its prices, competitors quickly feel the decline in their sales and are forced to match the price reduction. Alternatively, if one firm raises its prices, competitors rapidly gain customers by maintaining their original prices and hence have little or no motivation to match a price increase. In this situation, the demand curve facing an individual oligopolist would be far more elastic for price increases than for price decreases. If an oligopolist *raises* its price and others do not follow, the increase in price will lead to a declining share of the market as illustrated in Figure 12.10. Demand segment KD' is the *share-of-the-market demand curve* where all rivals match price and this firm's market share remains unchanged, for example, at 21 percent. For price increases above P, however, if rival firms do not match price, the demand segment facing this firm is more elastic. For price increases, its market share declines, perhaps to 15 percent.

The oligopolist's demand curve is therefore DKD' with the prevailing price as P and output as Q. The marginal revenue curve is discontinuous because of the kink in the demand curve at K. Hence, marginal revenue is represented by the two line segments

MRX and *YMR′*. If the marginal cost curve *MC* passes through the gap *XY* in the marginal revenue curve, the most profitable alternative is to maintain the current price-output policy. The profit-maximizing level of price and output remains constant for the firm, which perceives itself to be faced with a fixed unit price, even though costs may change over a rather wide range (e.g., *MC₂* and *MC₁*). This model explains why stable prices have been observed to exist in some oligopolistic industries. But the kinked demand model is incomplete in that it offers no reason why the prevailing price level rather than some other one is chosen.

AVOIDING PRICE WARS

Knowing how to avoid a price war has become a critical success factor for many high-margin businesses in tight oligopolistic groups. Recall from our discussion of break-even sales change analysis in Chapter 10 that the higher the margin, the more tempted companies are to use price discounting to increase incremental sales. Because each additional sale incurs few additional costs, high margins encourage price discounting to gain market share. So building a business plan or adopting a strategy that reduces the power of substitutes, entrants, buyers, and suppliers, and thereby generates high profit margins, is no guarantee of success. To sustain profitability, oligopoly firms also must avoid discounting tactics in their high-margin business.

The ready-to-eat (RTE) cereal, beer, camera film, cigarette, e-book, DVD, digital music, and video game console industries have all experienced classic price wars. In some cases, the catalyst for the price war was the fast-rising market share of private labels in what had previously been a heavily branded category. In the 1990s, generic cigarettes such as "Basic" took a substantial amount of market share from premium brands Marlboro, Benson & Hedges, Winston, Merit, and Salem. The R.J. Reynolds company introduced a mid-priced "fighting brand" Doral, promoted it heavily, and grew

FIGURE 12.10 The Kinked Demand Curve Model

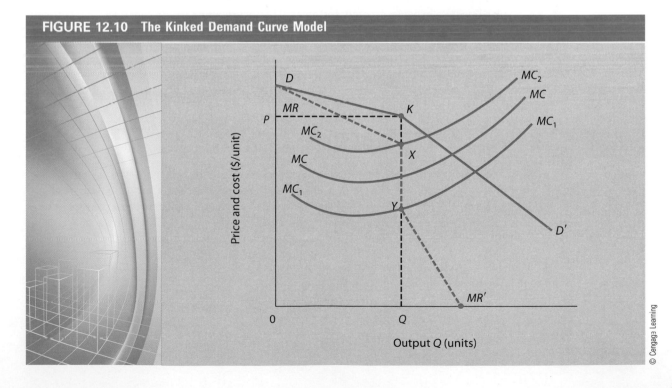

© Cengage Learning

market share quickly. Ultimately, Philip Morris (now Altria) was losing so much market share that they took 20 percent ($0.40) off the average $1.92 price of Marlboro. Similarly, a tiny cereal manufacturer, Ralston, began supplying many grocery store chains and Target with private label cereals (e.g., Kroger Raisin Bran) that sold at price points 30 percent less than the premium brands such as Kellogg's Raisin Bran. The fourth largest manufacturer, Quaker Oats, with a 7 percent market share, began selling branded cereals such as Cap'n Crunch and Life in large "value-priced" bags for $3.50 in the Target and Walmart distribution channels. The market share of these private label store brands grew rapidly, sometimes as much as 30 percent per year.

Growing the Market   One key to avoiding price wars in tight oligopolies is to recognize the ongoing nature of the pricing rivalry and attempt to mitigate the intensity of the price competition by growing the market. United-Continental Airlines cannot hope to get rid of American Airlines. Pepsi foresees a perpetual rivalry with Coke. Consequently, each rival must anticipate retaliation for aggressive discounting designed to attract away the other company's regular customers. It is better to maintain high prices and expect your rivals to do the same. Then each company can focus on opening new markets and selling more volume to established customers. Coke Classic now sells an average of six servings per day to heavy Coke drinkers. In the past five years, Coke introduced dozens of new soft drinks to countries throughout the world. As a result, the Coca-Cola concentrate syrup has never been discounted in 80 years.

Customer Segmentation with Revenue Management   Customer segmentation with differential pricing is another way to avoid price wars. If low-cost new entrants attack a major airline, one effective response that avoids initiating a price war with other major carriers involves matching prices to a targeted customer segment and then carefully controlling how much capacity is released for sale to that segment. "Fencing" restrictions such as seven-day advance-purchase requirements and Saturday night stayovers prove crucial in segmenting the price-sensitive discretionary traveler from the regular business expense account customer. The incumbent carriers can "meet the competition" in these restricted fare classes while reserving sufficient capacity for those who desire to pay for the reliability, convenience, and change order responsiveness of business-class and full-coach seats. Most importantly, established competitors can maintain high prices on unaffected departures, segments, and routes. In Chapter 14, we discuss how revenue management techniques can help accomplish these goals.

Example

Price Wars at General Mills and Post[17]

The price cut that triggered a price war in ready-to-eat (RTE) cereals was also approximately a 20 percent discount ($1.00 off the $4.80 average price for a full-size box of RTE cereal). The price war was started by Post Cereals, the distant third player in the industry with a 13 percent market share. Post had carefully analyzed the tactical situation and decided it could better maintain regular customers and compete for price-sensitive new customers if Kellogg and General Mills reduced advertising. Post believed they would do so only in response to the cash flow reductions necessitated by a massive industry-wide price cut.

General Mills was experiencing a slowly eroding 25 percent market share, while Kellogg faced a rapidly declining 35 percent market share. Every share point in the U.S. RTE cereal industry is worth $80 million in sales. In part because of a

(continued)

panic-stricken determination to arrest the erosion of their market shares, both Kellogg and General Mills quickly decided to match the Post price cut. Full-size boxes of branded products such as General Mills' Wheaties and Kellogg's Frosted Flakes were cut in price from $4.80 to $3.88. Just as Post had predicted, each of the leading firms then scaled back its advertising campaigns. Cereals such as Post Raisin Bran and Post Grape-Nuts gained share rapidly, at least for a short time until Kellogg matched the Post price cut on two thirds of its premium brands. Two years later, cereal prices in the all-important grocery store distribution channel began to return to their preprice-war levels.

Kellogg has the strongest brands in the cereals industry with 12 of the 15 top-selling cereals. Rather than match Post's price cuts, Kellogg might have poured not two but three scoops of raisins into every box of Kellogg's Raisin Bran. In the first two months after the price cuts by Post and General Mills, Kellogg lost three share points (from 35 percent to 32 percent) and Post gained four (from 16 percent to 20 percent). At $80 million per share point and 55 percent gross margins (on average across the affected brands), Kellogg's contributions on the lost sales totaled $132 million ($-3 \times \$80$ million $\times 0.55$). To retrieve that $132-million-per-year loss of operating profit, Kellogg slashed prices 19 percent on two-thirds of its brands, sacrificing more than $305 million ($-0.19 \times \$2.4$ billion sales $\times 0.66$). Market share continued to decline to 29 percent in 1999, and the capitalized value of Kellogg fell by $7 billion. Many observers wondered whether a major strategic mistake had occurred. By expending $305 million (or half that much) on advertising or product innovation or shelf space of Post or brand extensions, Kellogg would likely have accomplished more, much more.

---

[17]Based on "Denial in Battle Creek," *Forbes* (October 7, 1996); "Cereal Thriller," *The Economist* (June 15, 1996); and P. Cummins, "Cereal Firms in Cost-Price Squeeze," *Reuters News Service* (May 15, 1996).

Reference Prices and Framing Effects   In addition to segmenting the target customers into more and less price-sensitive submarkets, product line extensions can reduce gainshare price discounting by providing reference prices and framing effects that help sell the mid-range product at undiscounted prices. Consumers of unbranded products typically remember the last price they encountered on the shelf in deciding whether to purchase at the quoted price today. Branded products, however, trigger much longer reference pricing. Discounting with a major branded item such as Tide detergent tends to etch in the customer's mind a new lowball price that can be expected thereafter for many months or even years. Therefore, what one really might like to do in the face of private-label discount competition is to introduce a super-premium product offered at price points well above your traditional product. Loyal customers of the regular brand will remember these high references prices.

Because the opportunity losses in going from a mid-range Chrysler Town and Country to bargain-basement products such as a Dodge minivan (while saving $5,000, for example) tend to weigh more heavily upon consumers than the perceived satisfaction of moving upscale to super premiums such as a Mercedes-Benz M class (at an equal $5,000 higher cost), the mid-range products such as Chrysler Town and Country are expected to sell even better in the presence of the framing effect provided by super-premium products. In the 2000s, Town and Country provided 28 percent of Chrysler's sales with relatively little discounting.

WHAT WENT RIGHT • WHAT WENT WRONG

Good-Better-Best Product Strategy at Marriott Corporation and Kodak[18]

Marriott Corporation has responded to fierce price competition in the hospitality industry by introducing upscale, high-quality mid-range, and down-market product lines to its respective target customers. Ritz-Carlton, Marriott International, Marriott Marquis, Downtown Marriott, Marriott at the Airport, Courtyards by Marriott, Extended Stay, and Fairfield Inns all operate as subsidiary hotel chains under the parent Marriott Corporation but as distinct offerings.

Successful segmentation is the key to such a product strategy for avoiding ruinous price discounting. Here in hotels, length of stay, proximity to the central business district, and room type (with and without sitting areas separated from the bedroom) are characteristics that effectively segment Marriott's customer base.

In the late 1990s, Kodak pursued a similar concept with discounted Funtime Film and the Kodak disposable camera. These products were positioned for everyday use to capture the hundreds of events, posed people, and inanimate scenery that highly accessible cheap film sold through convenience store distribution channels made possible. These photos were predictably "lost" (undeveloped) in great stacks in file cabinets, desk drawers, and old shoeboxes. Although not generally used to memorialize

anything of significance, the unplanned "snapshot" accentuated the experiential event, as it happened.

"Kodak moments," in contrast, pursued a different set of value drivers. Kodak Royal Gold film provided exceptional picture resolution in many different lighting conditions. Royal Gold film was able to memorialize subtleties of expressions (of surprise, exaltation, pride in fulfilling challenging tasks, etc.). Kodak's marketing research found that many of its customers would pay a price premium to memorialize a personal emotion (such as when a woman demonstrably triumphs amidst the worst whitewater rapids in a raft filled with her brothers). Heavy advertising and event marketing further established this product image for the premier value tiers in Kodak's value map.

Similarly, Marriott has no difficulty getting a substantial price premium for hotel rooms with sitting areas in central business districts and convention hotels where customer appointments and interviews can be performed. And of course, the extended stay customer with auto transportation and several dozen trade rep appointments would prefer the cost savings of a suburban location to the short-term business traveler's convenience of a downtown or airport location.

---

[18]Based on "Film-War Spoils: A Buck a Roll?" *Wall Street Journal* (November 11, 1998), p. B1; "Eastman Kodak Company: Funtime Film," Harvard Business School Publishing (1998); and "Kodak Is Rolling Out Digital Photo Processing," *Wall Street Journal* (February 9, 1999), p. A4.

The Role of Innovation   Another way to avoid or at least reduce the effects of price wars is to differentiate through innovation. Rather than matching price cuts, a higher-priced brand can highlight conspicuous product innovations the discounters have missed. Sony's Mavica was an easy-to-use point-and-shoot digital camera that recorded images onto thumb drives or disks. The disk popped out of the camera and into any PC for easy editing, storing, and printing. While digital camera competitors Kodak and Casio were improving picture resolution to justify expensive and complicated home printer hardware peripherals using Kodak chemicals and paper, Sony simplified the process and increased customer value. As a result, the Mavica earned a premium price relative to its competitors.

Figure 12.11 analyzes an oligopolistic market with extreme brand loyalty based on innovation, customer risk avoidance, or effective brand name advertising. Kellogg's Raisin Bran faces an inverse demand segment, ($11 − Q^d) = Price, that includes the highest willingness-to-pay customers. Setting MR in this segment, $11 − $2Q^d$, equal to a marginal cost of $1, Kellogg's Raisin Bran maximizes operating profit at $Q^* = 5(000)$ and a price per box of ($11 − $5) = $6. Without as established a brand image, Post Raisin Bran must sell under $6 and accordingly faces a different segment whose inverse demand may be written as ($6 − Q^d) = Price (i.e., the line segment from $6 downward to the right along D in Figure 12.11). Setting MR at Post, $6 − $2Q^d$, equal to a higher $2 marginal cost per box yields a profit-maximizing output for Post of 2(000) at a profit-maximizing price of ($6 − $2) = $4 per box. These ($5/11 = 45$ percent) and ($2/11 = 19$ percent) market shares for Kellogg and Post, respectively, approximate their actual market shares in the RTE cereal market for raisin bran products. Additional firms with still less brand loyalty, such as Kroger Raisin Bran, would supply the remaining segments illustrated still farther downward to the right on DD′ of the raisin bran demand curve.

Example

What Went Right at Interlink Surgical Steel and Gillette?[19]

In the 1990s, Interlink sold replacement hypodermic syringes by the thousands to hospitals for 10 cents per syringe. Each time a catheter was changed, a new hypodermic syringe would be inserted into the patient's vein. A Japanese surgical steel company entered the market with an identical product for 3 cents each. Interlink promptly introduced a replacement device that only needs insertion one time; that is, any new saline or pharmaceutical drip lines can be hooked directly to an Interlink syringe device that need not be removed and replaced. This new process reduces the risk of patient infection and the inherent hazard to the nursing staff of exposure to infected patient blood. Interlink again dominates the market, and prices have stabilized at higher levels than before.

Similarly, Gillette Co. responded to a four-bladed new product introduction of Quattro by Schick-Wilkinson Sword. Quattro had stolen 3 percent of Gillette's 83 percent market share in the men's razor market. Instead of an ongoing parade of discounts, coupons, and promotions, Gillette rolled out its own innovation: a battery-powered vibrating razor called Mach3Power. M3Power improves the closeness and longevity of the shave by exciting chin hairs to push up out of their follicles. The new product costs two-thirds more than the Gillette Mach3Turbo it replaced, but the Mach3Turbo replacement cartridges are 20 percent higher-priced, and those price premiums have proven sustainable.

[19]Based on "How to Fight a Price War," *Harvard Business Review* (March–April 2000), pp. 107–116; "How to Escape a Price War," *Fortune* (June 13, 1994), pp. 82–90; and "Gillette to Launch," *Wall Street Journal* (January 16, 2004), p. A8.

FIGURE 12.11   Segmented Oligopoly with Extreme Brand Loyalty

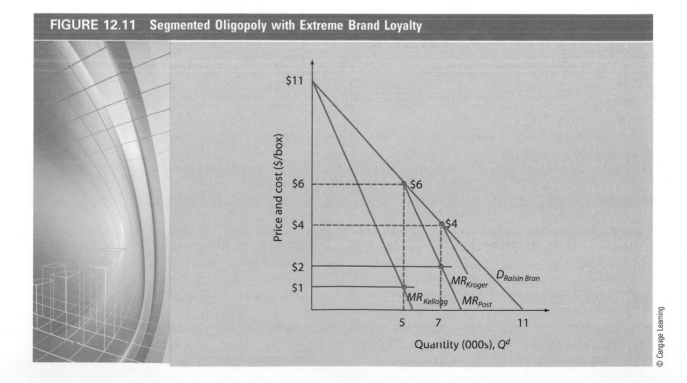

© Cengage Learning

Matching Price Cuts with Increased Advertising Perhaps the best way to avoid a price war in a small oligopolistic rivalry group is to not start one in the first place. If someone else does start a price war, often the best response is simply to match the competition and then accentuate non-price elements of the marketing mix by increasing services or advertising. When Phillip Morris cut 20 percent from the price of premium cigarettes such as Marlboro, rather than furthering the downward price spiral, Reynolds instead matched the price cut only in its premium brands, Winston and Salem, and expanded advertising. At the $2.00 per pack all-time high price before the price war, the heavy smoker had a $35 per week incentive to quit. For Marlboro, with an 82 percent contribution margin, the 20 percent price cut necessitated a 32 percent (0.82/[0.82 − 0.20] = 1.32) increase in incremental sales to achieve increased short-term profit. Instead, Marlboro market share rose only about 17 percent.

Example

Non-price Tactics in a Price War: Coors[20]

Coors implemented exactly the same non-price response in the midst of a costly price war between Anheuser-Busch and Miller Brewing. As Miller and Budweiser products reduced the category to more and more of a commodity with ever deeper discounts, Coors decided to realign their product positioning with Corona and Heineken. Amidst heavy advertising, Coors gained two share points despite prices $2-per-case higher than Miller and Budweiser.

[20]Based on "Big Brewers Find Price War Seems to Have No End," *Wall Street Journal* (July 2, 1998), p. B6.

A final key in avoiding price wars comes through the tactical insights often available from game theory analysis. Being able to identify a rival's payoffs using competitor surveillance helps predict the competitor's response to one's own price cuts. In other circumstances, cooperative high-price outcomes may arise out of mutual interest. Simply recognizing the detailed structure of the pricing "game" can be a first step in altering the competitive environment in ways that increase profitability. In the following chapter, we present game theory techniques that provide useful managerial insights for effective tactical decision making.

SUMMARY

- An *oligopoly* is an industry structure characterized by a relatively small number of firms in which recognizable *interdependencies* exist among the actions of the firms. Each firm is aware that its actions are likely to evoke countermoves from its rivals.
- In the *Cournot* model of oligopoly behavior, each of the firms, in determining its profit-maximizing output level, assumes that the other firm's output will remain constant.

- A *cartel* is a formal or informal agreement among oligopolists to cooperate or collude in determining outputs, prices, and profits. If the cartel members can enforce agreements and prevent cheating, they can act as a monopolist and maximize industry profits.
- A number of factors affect the ability of oligopolistic firms to engage successfully in some form of formal (or informal) cooperation, including the

number and size distribution of sellers, product heterogeneity, cost structures, size and frequency of orders, secrecy and retaliation, and the percentage of industry output from outside the cartel.

■ *Price leadership* is a pricing strategy in an oligopolistic industry in which one firm sets the price and, either by explicit or implicit agreement, the other firms tend to follow the decision.

■ In the *kinked demand curve* model, it is assumed that if an oligopoly firm reduces its prices, its competitors will quickly feel the decline in their sales and will be forced to match the reduction.

Alternatively, if the oligopolist raises its prices, competitors will rapidly gain customers by maintaining their original prices and will have little or no motivation to match a price increase. Hence, the demand curve for individual oligopolists is much more elastic for price increases than for price decreases and may lead oligopolists to maintain stable prices.

■ To avoid price wars, oligopoly firms can grow the market, engage in product line extensions, expand into new geographic areas, segment customers and employ differential pricing, or innovate to retain profitable customers.

Exercises

Answers to the exercises in blue can be found in Appendix D at the back of the book.

1. Assume that two companies (*C* and *D*) are duopolists that produce identical products. Demand for the products is given by the following linear demand function:

$$P = 600 - Q_C - Q_D$$

where Q_C and Q_D are the quantities sold by the respective firms and P is the selling price. Total cost functions for the two companies are

$$TC_C = 25,000 + 100Q_C$$
$$TC_D = 20,000 + 125Q_D$$

Assume that the firms act *independently* as in the Cournot model (i.e., each firm assumes that the other firm's output will not change).
   a. Determine the long-run equilibrium output and selling price for each firm.
   b. Determine the total profits for each firm at the equilibrium output found in Part (a).

2. Assume that two companies (*A* and *B*) are duopolists who produce identical products. Demand for the products is given by the following linear demand function:

$$P = 200 - Q_A - Q_B$$

where Q_A and Q_B are the quantities sold by the respective firms and P is the selling price. Total cost functions for the two companies are

$$TC_A = 1,500 + 55Q_A + Q_A^2$$
$$TC_B = 1,200 + 20Q_B + 2Q_B^2$$

Assume that the firms act *independently* as in the Cournot model (i.e., each firm assumes that the other firm's output will not change).
   a. Determine the long-run equilibrium output and selling price for each firm.
   b. Determine Firm *A*, Firm *B*, and total industry profits at the equilibrium solution found in Part (a).

3. Consider Exercise 2 again. Assume that the firms form a *cartel* to act as a monopolist and maximize total industry profits (sum of Firm *A* and Firm *B* profits).
   a. Determine the optimum output and selling price for each firm.
   b. Determine Firm *A*, Firm *B*, and total industry profits at the optimal solution found in Part (a).
   c. Show that the marginal costs of the two firms are equal at the optimal solution found in Part (a).

4. Compare the optimal solutions obtained in Exercises 2 and 3. Specifically:
   a. How much higher (lower) is the optimal selling price when the two firms form a cartel to maximize industry profits, compared to when they act independently?
   b. How much higher (lower) is total industry output?
   c. How much higher (lower) are total industry profits?
5. Alchem (L) is the price leader in the polyglue market. All 10 other manufacturers (follower [F] firms) sell polyglue at the same price as Alchem. Alchem allows the other firms to sell as much as they wish at the established price and supplies the remainder of the demand itself. Total demand for polyglue is given by the following function ($Q_T = Q_L + Q_F$):

$$P = 20{,}000 - 4Q_T$$

Alchem's marginal cost function for manufacturing and selling polyglue is

$$MC_L = 5{,}000 + 5Q_L$$

The aggregate marginal cost function for the other manufacturers of polyglue is

$$\Sigma MC_F = 2{,}000 + 4Q_F$$

   a. To maximize profits, how much polyglue should Alchem produce and what price should it charge?
   b. What is the total market demand for polyglue at the price established by Alchem in Part (a)? How much of total demand do the follower firms supply?
6. Chillman Motors, Inc., believes it faces the following segmented demand function:

$$P = \begin{cases} 150 - 0.5Q & \text{when } 0 \le Q \le 50 \\ 200 - 1.5Q & \text{for } Q > 50 \end{cases}$$

   a. Indicate both verbally and graphically why such a segmented demand function is likely to exist? What type of industry structure is indicated by this relationship?
   b. Calculate the marginal revenue functions facing Chillman. Add these to your graph from Part (a).
   c. Chillman's total cost function is

$$TC_1 = 500 + 15Q + 0.5Q^2$$

   Calculate the marginal cost function. What is Chillman's profit-maximizing price and output combination?
   d. What is Chillman's profit-maximizing price-output combination if total costs increase to

$$TC_2 = 500 + 45Q + 0.5Q^2$$

   e. If Chillman's total cost function changes to either

$$TC_3 = 500 + 15Q + 1.0Q^2$$

   or

$$TC_4 = 500 + 5Q + 0.25Q^2$$

   what price-output solution do you expect to prevail? Would your answer change if you knew that all firms in the industry witnessed similar changes in their cost functions?

7. *Library Research Project.* It was observed in the chapter that collusion among oligopolists can be facilitated in part by information sharing. As a consequence, the sharing of price information among rival oligopolists can violate U.S. antitrust laws. You can see how the U.S. Supreme Court has interpreted antitrust law as it pertains to sharing price information by reading a summary of the case of *U.S. v. U.S. Gypsum Co. et al.* (438 U.S. 422), which is available at www.stolaf.edu/people/becker/antitrust/summaries/438us422.htm. In what manner was price information shared, and why did the court find these actions to be an antitrust violation?

Case Exercises

Web-Based Satellite Phones Displace Motorola's Mobile Phone[21]

Motorola's Iridium, a go-anywhere mobile phone system that transmitted and received signals beamed down from 66 satellites, was called "the eighth wonder of the world" by Motorola CEO Chris Galvin. However, at $1,500 for a handset the size of a brick, consumers balked. Few business travelers concluded they needed the security and reliability offered in remote corners of the globe such as Kathmandu or Lagos. As a result, Motorola's 25 percent historical market share in mobile phones declined steadily to 13 percent in 2001, and Motorola stock fell 16 percent from 1997 to 2001, during a period when the S&P 500 was up 76 percent. For the business customer, RIM's Blackberry was satellite communication-based, much smaller and lighter, almost as secure, and much more mobile. For the mass market, Nokia began designing web-enabled phones that could connect to local area networks and eventually the Internet. Apple iPhones and Samsung Android phones then ushered in a new era of smart phones.

Questions

1. Characterize the product space for mobile phones when Iridium began.
2. Elaborate on the trends Nokia pursued as it designed mobile phone products in the late 1990s. (Refer to the Managerial Challenge at the beginning of this chapter.)
3. What might a more proactive Motorola have done differently had it correctly perceived the steps its rival Nokia would take?
4. Smart phones from Apple and Samsung today have imposed upon Nokia competitive pressure once associated with Motorola. What would you advise Nokia to do in light of the success of the iPhone with all its thousands of applications from independent software providers?

---

[21]Based in part on "Apple, RIM Outsmart the Phone Market," *Wall Street Journal* (July 20, 2009), p. C6.

CHAPTER 13

Best-Practice Tactics: Game Theory

CHAPTER PREVIEW

Businesses that compete against just a few rivals whose actions and reactions really matter need effective tactics for best practices decision making. Effective tactics in turn require anticipating rival response and counterresponse. Noncooperative game theory of simultaneous and sequential play was designed for just this purpose, including entry deterrence and accommodation games, bidding games, manufacturer-distributor games, product development games, research and development games, and pricing and promotion games.

All such noncooperative games between arm's-length competitors prohibit side payments and binding contracts between rivals. Instead, they depend on self-enforcing relationships to maintain strategic equilibrium. For example, each airline in a posted price game must decide whether it is in its own best interest to resist discounting to gain market share, in light of the best reply responses it anticipates from rivals. In some circumstances, mutual discounting (e.g., by Southwest Airlines and AirTran) proves to be a dominant strategy that provides protection from renegade discounters, while in other situations, mutual forbearance from discounting (e.g., by Kellogg and General Mills) leads to sustainably higher margins.

The order of play can matter in such games if credible threats and commitments influence the endgame outcomes. In this chapter we explore the role that first-mover and last-mover advantages, non-redeployable assets, credible punishment schemes, hostage mechanisms, matching price guarantees, and imperfect information can play in best-practice business tactics.

MANAGERIAL CHALLENGE

Large-Scale Entry Deterrence of Low-Cost Discounters: Southwest Airline/AirTran[1]

Since the deregulation of the U.S. airlines industry, legacy carriers such as United, American, US Airways, and Delta have faced a progression of low-cost competitors. Beginning with Southwest Airlines, continuing through People Express, Value Jet (now AirTran), Kiwi, Independence Air, JetBlue, and Spirit Airlines these firms established point-to-point operations in unserved or underserved cities and thereby created profitable business models at much lower prices. For example, from San Antonio to Los Angeles, Southwest is profitable at $300 for last-minute walk-up one-way service whereas American Airlines charges $520. From San Antonio to Philadelphia, Southwest's cost-covering fare is $280, whereas American's is $495.

Not surprisingly, one focus of the low-cost discounters has been the relentless pursuit of cost savings.

Cont.

MANAGERIAL CHALLENGE *Continued*

Point-to-point service simplifies a carrier's operations, and Southwest with 15-minute turnarounds gets 10.3 flight hours per plane per day, 46 percent more than the industry average. By increasing capacity utilization by 46 percent, Southwest lowers its indirect fixed cost per seat for interest, overhead, and time depreciation on the airframes by 31 percent $(1 - 1/1.46 = 1 - 0.69 = 0.31)$. By stripping out the first-class seats and the galley, Southwest increases its seating capacity by 33 percent from 90 to 119 seats on Boeing 737s, thereby also lowering direct fixed costs per seat it pays for flight crews, fuel, and maintenance by another 25 percent $(1 - 1/1.33 = 1 - 0.75 = 0.25)$.

In addition, the low-cost start-ups incur labor costs well below industry averages; as a result, legacy carriers have gone back time and time again to their machinist and flight crew unions seeking wage and salary concessions. In 2005, the total cost per available seat mile (ASM) varied from a high of 11.62 cents at Delta and 10.89 cents at US Airways to 7.70 cents at Southwest and 6.74 cents at JetBlue. The legacy carriers then underwent consolidation mergers (United-Continental, US Airways-America West) and bankruptcies (at United, Delta, US Airways, and American) to renegotiate labor costs downward. Today, Southwest's cost advantage has shrunk; seven major rivals incur 9.2 cents per mile versus 6.0 cents for Southwest.

In such settings, two prominent game theory questions involve the discounter's optimal capacity choice and the legacy airline's optimal pricing choice to deter or accommodate the entry. Southwest's entry strategy in any new city is to offer a uniform low-price, no-frills seat with high-frequency scheduling. By unbundling all services, adopting quick turnaround times, working longer crew shifts, and converting all first-class and galley space into additional coach-class seats, Southwest typically achieves low enough operating cost to offer 30 percent cheaper fares. Southwest's prototypical target customer is a manufacturer's trade representative who often needs to travel on short notice, but is seldom fully reimbursed through a company expense account, and who therefore often drives rather than flies.

In essence, a Southwest entry creates a new segment of the market not previously served by much more expensive and infrequently scheduled legacy carriers. These new low-willingness-to-pay customers often quickly reserve most if not all of Southwest's capacity, leaving almost none available to other air travelers. As a result, a Southwest entry may not erode the market for higher-priced incumbent airlines but rather creates a so-called Southwest effect of increased volume and load factors throughout the market, but at much lower prices. Southwest/AirTran has grown steadily to become the nation's largest airline. From 1990 to 2011, the U.S. airline industry as a whole suffered losses totaling over \$62 billion. During nine of those years, the industry was profitable but earned only \$37 billion. In such a difficult business environment, winners and losers are decided by critical success factors, such as better management decision-making about tactics.

For example, the established airlines have to decide whether to match Southwest's deeply discounted fares right away or accommodate Southwest by maintaining high fares. Southwest has to decide whether to enter with a large or small capacity. In this chapter, we will see how businesses use game-theoretic modeling to make such decisions.

Discussion Questions

■ What service characteristics not offered by Southwest might a vacationer be willing to pay for?

■ How would the answer be different for a trial lawyer traveling whenever the judge's schedule permits or for a mid-level executive traveling on an expense account?

---

[1] Based on "Rivals Invade Southwest's Air Space," *Wall Street Journal* (February 16, 2011), p. B8; "UAL Hopes Latest Cost Cuts Will Yield," *Wall Street Journal* (May 12, 2005), p. A10; "Southwest's Dallas Duel," *Wall Street Journal* (May 10, 2005), p. B1; and F. Harris, "Large Scale Entry Deterrence of Low-Cost Discounters: An Early Success of Revenue Management," *International Journal of Revenue Management* 1, no. 1 (2007), pp. 1–24.

OLIGOPOLISTIC RIVALRY AND GAME THEORY

Most oligopolistic competition takes place today in product line submarkets between a few rival incumbent firms, each with some market power over price. Consider Microsoft's Xbox, Sony's PlayStation, and Nintendo's Wii in game consoles; Bayer Aspirin, Bufferin, Excedrin in pain relievers; Pepsi and Coke in colas; Six Flags, Universal and Disney in theme parks; and Delta, US Airways, and American in air travel to Florida. Smaller competitors selling more generic products are often present in peripheral markets, but these oligopolists are notable because of some brand name or other barrier to effective entry and because of their extraordinary *interdependence*.

Recall that in a purely competitive industry, such as real estate development of tract home subdivisions, each competitor can act quite independently. Each takes price as "given," that is, determined externally in the open market, because any decision to expand or embargo his or her own supply has no appreciable effect on the enormously larger industry supply. Even if one real estate developer were to purchase many subdivisions in a community and seek to establish a brand premium, the barriers to entry are so low that any price above cost would surely attract enough new competitors to restore the competitive price-taking equilibrium.

In contrast, each firm in an oligopolistic market must pay close attention to the moves and countermoves of its rivals. Correctly anticipating entry and exit, product development initiatives, pricing changes and promotions several steps ahead of actual events and at least one step ahead of the competition are often the keys to a successful business. Despite one's best efforts, sometimes a competitor takes the lead, and then quickly adaptive behavior is preferable to reactive behavior. The best option of all is proactive behavior, and proactive behavior requires accurate and reliable predictions of rival initiatives and rival response.

game theory A theory of interdependent decision making by the participants in a conflict-of-interest or opportunity-for-collaboration situation.

The managerial purpose of game theory is to provide these predictions of rival behavior. To execute defensive strategy as well as plan strategic initiatives, each oligopolist must try to predict well in advance the actions, responses, and counter-responses of their rivals and then choose optimal strategies accordingly. Modern **game theory** was invented for precisely this purpose.

WHAT WENT RIGHT • WHAT WENT WRONG

Nintendo's Wii U[2]

Mario and Zelda remain on top but Nintendo finds its competitors closing fast, and in 2012 the half-century old public company reported its first loss (¥43 billion equal to $0.5 billion). Starting in 1974 with the first game console called Nintendo Entertainment System, Wii remains the industry leader in the United States and Japan with 40 and 12 million consoles sold respectively, since its introduction. But Sony's PlayStation is the market leader in Europe, Australia, and New Zealand with 33 million to Wii's 31 million. Microsoft's Xbox sells almost nothing in Japan but has mounted exponentially growing sales in the United States, now at 35 million with a total of 60 million sales worldwide.

With each successive generation of game consoles, prices begin high and then erode as the other two competitors arrive with new product features. In 2011, Wii descended $199 to $165 having begun at a price point of $400 in 2008. Similarly, in its third year PlayStation 3 was discounted in 2011 from $299 to $249 having begun at $600, then $399 while Xbox 3 was discounted from $249 to $199 having begun at $700, then $399, $349, and $299. With its newest offering Wii U has improved its social networking capabilities and added a fully integrated smart phone–style touch screen. Having focused on casual gamers rather than the more dedicated aficionados who tend to prefer PlayStation 3 or Xbox, Nintendo must now stem the tide to the higher tech streaming products available on smart phones and tablet computers. New PlayStation and Xbox products are due in 2013 Anticipating their competitors rival reactions will prove the key to Nintendo's success.

---

[2]"Video Games: U Turn," *The Economist* (December 1, 2012), p. 73.

A Conceptual Framework for Game Theory Analysis

A general definition of a **strategy game** is any consciously interdependent choice behavior engaged in by purposeful individuals or hierarchical groups (e.g., tribes, sports teams, or value-maximizing companies) who share a common goal. As such, strategy games have always been a part of human interactions. Some of the earliest formal analyses of strategy games involved strategic voting in the Roman senate, bargaining among Phoenician traders, and the ancient Chinese military tactics of Sun Tzu.

Consider, for example, how the private property rights to a person's belongings might evolve in a setting like the TV show *Survivor*. Table 13.1 displays the *normal form* of the strategy game in which communities of hunter-gatherers decide between agricultural pursuits combined with guarding consolidated property versus continuously hunting and marauding against targets of opportunity. History records that the private property consolidators (the Aggies) won out; let's see why.

Two competing players (Randle and Kahn) compete for resources by selecting between two actions: *Maraud*, which occasionally yields unguarded windfall treasures but leaves one's own possessions vulnerable to counterattack; or *Guard*, which frees time between defensive struggles for consolidating and multiplying the fruits of one's labors with agriculture. Kahn has a tactical advantage in marauding against anything but strongly guarded positions. However, no matter what action Kahn decides to take, an examination of the payoff matrix in Table 13.1 reveals that the specialist in agriculture Randle is always better off selecting Guard. In particular, the outcome in the NW cell (above the diagonal) is ranked first by Randle, whereas the outcome in the NE cell (again above the diagonal) is ranked fourth. Similarly, the outcome in the SW cell (above the diagonal) is ranked second by Randle, versus the outcome in the SE cell, which is ranked third. Therefore, no matter what action Kahn decides to take, Randle is always better off guarding his own consolidated property rather than marauding himself.

Guard is Randle's **dominant strategy** because his outcomes from Guard exceed the outcomes from any alternative strategy, regardless of his opponent's behavior. Knowing this fact or discovering it through trial and error, Kahn predicts his rival Randle will continue to Guard. On that presumption, Kahn then iterates back to his own choice decision and finds he prefers Guard himself. {Guard, Guard} therefore emerges as a strategic equilibrium, and the game provides a sense of how and why private property arrangements evolved as a societal institution.

TABLE 13.1 PRIVATIZATION OF PERSONAL BELONGINGS IN *SURVIVOR*: THE MARAUDER-GUARDER GAME

		Randle	
		Guard	**Maraud**
Kahn	**Guard**	Better — 1st	Worst — 4th
	Maraud	Worse — 2nd	Best — 3rd

© Cengage Learning

Note: Column-player payoffs are above the diagonal. Row-player payoffs are below the diagonal. Kahn ranks outcomes from best to worst. Randle ranks outcomes from first to fourth.

Components of a Game

The essential elements of all strategy games are present in the preceding example and include the following: players, actions, information sets, payoffs, an order of play, focal outcomes of interest, strategies, and equilibrium strategies. Let's illustrate each component in a game of service quality competition. Suppose two copier repair *players*, Ricoh Now and Sharp ER, must choose whether to offer fast-response copier repair service six or seven territories removed from their respective regional headquarters located in two different cities 100 miles apart (see Figure 13.1). Six versus seven territories of fast-response service repair are the *actions*, which must be announced simultaneously at next week's industrial trade show. The *payoffs* from the decisions are shown in Table 13.2. This payoff matrix is the **normal form of the game**, which is an appropriate way of representing any simultaneous-play (versus sequential-play) game.

normal form of the game A representation of payoffs in a simultaneous-play game.

Sharp finds that fast-response service repair in the more distant seventh territory is expensive. Cutting back to six territories reduces cost by $15 per week per customer and raises Sharp's profit from $55 to $70 per week when Ricoh also cuts back, and from $45 to $60 per week when Ricoh does not. The improved effectiveness of Sharp's service in the remaining six territories lowers the prices that rival Ricoh can charge and reduces its profit from an initial $45 down to only $30 should Ricoh continue servicing all seven territories. By cutting back to six territories itself, Ricoh can restrict its losses to just $5 ($45 now to $40 > $30). The common *information set* known to both players includes knowledge of all these payoffs.

What strategy should Ricoh adopt? First, using the concept of *dominant strategy*, it is clear that Sharp ER will discontinue service in the seventh territory. Sharp is better off cutting back to six territories independent of what Ricoh does. For Sharp, seven

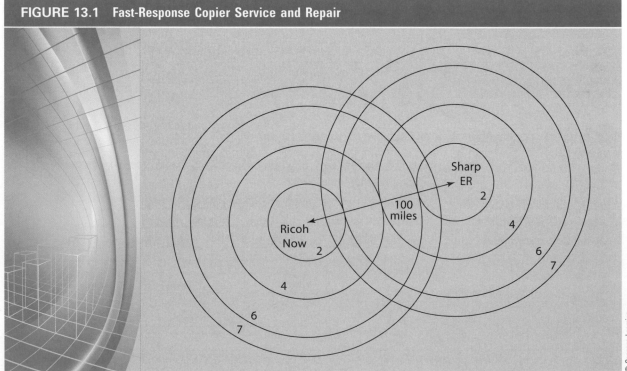

FIGURE 13.1 Fast-Response Copier Service and Repair

© Cengage Learning

TABLE 13.2	SIX OR SEVEN TERRITORIES?		

		Sharp	
		Six Territories	**Seven Territories**
Ricoh	**Six Territories**	$40 / $70	$35 / $55
	Seven Territories	$30 / $60	$45 / $45

© Cengage Learning

Note: Payoffs are profits. Sharp payoffs are above the diagonal, and Ricoh payoffs are below the diagonal.

territories is *dominated* (unambiguously less preferred than six territories). Ricoh wishes it were not so, because its most successful operation entails head-to-head, seven-territory competition against Sharp. Nevertheless, predictable reality lies elsewhere, and Ricoh must predict six-territory behavior on the part of its rival and proceed to reexamine its remaining options. Having eliminated Sharp's dominant strategy in the second column, Ricoh now has an unambiguously preferred *strategy* of providing fast-response repairs in only six territories itself. {Six, Six} is therefore the *equilibrium strategy* pair. That is, by applying the concept of a dominant strategy equilibrium to the prediction of its rival's behavior, Ricoh can iterate back to analyze its own best action. {Six, Six} is therefore referred to as an **iterated dominant strategy** equilibrium.

iterated dominant strategy An action rule that maximizes self-interest in light of the predictable dominant-strategy behavior of other players.

This concept of eliminating dominant strategies in simultaneous games and then iterating back to one's remaining choices first appeared in *The Theory of Games and Economic Behavior* by John von Neumann and Oskar Morgenstern.[3] Von Neumann and Morgenstern confined their analysis primarily to cooperative games, in which players can form coalitions, arrange side payments, and enter into binding agreements. John Nash, Reinhard Selten, and John Harsanyi won the 1994 Nobel Prize in economics for their extension of strategic equilibrium concepts to noncooperative games, sequential games, and games of imperfect information. John Nash's life was celebrated in the book *A Beautiful Mind* by Sylvia Nasar and the subsequent movie starring Russell Crowe.

Example

The Nobel Prize Goes to Three Game Theorists

Nash, Selten, and Harsanyi won the 1994 Nobel Prize in economics for their work on equilibrium strategies in sequential games ranging from chess and poker to central bank interventions, entry deterrence, research-and-development competitions, and the auctioning of the radio magnetic spectrum. Not infrequently, multiple equilibria arise in such games. Another implication is that the order of play can affect strategic decisions; moving first in a preemptive product development game can often deter a competitor's threatened entry. In other circumstances, making the last response in the endgame, as dynamic technology takes a new direction, can secure a strategic advantage. Distinguishing between these and other complex paths to the most profitable strategy is the role of equilibrium strategies in game theory.

[3]Two other useful volumes on modern game theory are A. Dixit and S. Skeath, *Games of Strategy* (New York: Norton, 2006); and Eric Rasmussen, *Games and Information*, 3rd ed. (Cambridge, MA: Basil Blackwell, 2008).

Cooperative and Noncooperative Games

cooperative game Game structures that allow coalition formation, side payments, and binding third-party enforceable agreements.

The fact that in a **cooperative game** the players can form coalitions, make side payments, and communicate to one another their private information about their own prices, profit margins, or variable costs has limited the usefulness of cooperative game theory in business settings. An illustration of a side payment in cooperative games is the mandatory compensation scheme a manufacturer might impose when one sales representative violates another's exclusive territory. Or, suppose in the previous Ricoh Now and Sharp ER example that the two firms got together to arrange a side payment to ensure a strategic equilibrium of {Six, Six}. As you may already suspect, most such cooperative game agreements between arm's-length competitors to exchange price information or arrange side payments are per se violations of the antitrust laws in the United States and Western Europe.[4] For these reasons, business strategists paid relatively little attention to game theory until *noncooperative* strategic equilibrium concepts were developed.

noncooperative games Game structures that prohibit collusion, side payments, and binding agreements enforced by third parties.

Noncooperative games prohibit collusive communication, side payments, and third-party enforceable binding agreements. Instead, such games focus on self-enforcing reliance relationships to characterize strategic equilibrium and predict rival response. One example we already encountered in Chapter 10 is the mutual reliance between buyers and sellers of high-priced experience goods, such as used cars, based on non-redeployable assets (e.g., CarFax reports and advertising by CarMax). Other examples include computer companies that build operating systems to a common standard that can communicate across PC platforms, or competing airlines that announce high fares day after day despite the quick but short-lived attraction of breaking out as a renegade discounter. Clearly, these noncooperative games differ from cooperative games in important ways that make them more applicable to business strategy.

Other Types of Games

Strategy games are also classified according to the number of players involved, the compatibility of their interests, and the number of replays of the game. We analyzed both prior games as *single-period* ("one-shot") *games*, but ongoing rivalry between the players in "Guarder-Marauder" and in "Six or Seven Territories" is highly pertinent to the strategic situation. We will turn our attention next to the distinct and somewhat paradoxical implications of so-called repeated games. In a *two-person game*, each player attempts to obtain as much as possible from the other player through different methods of cooperation, bargaining, or threatening available. *N*-person games are more difficult to analyze because subsets of players can form coalitions to impose solutions on the rest of the players. Coalitions can be of any size and can break up and re-form as the game proceeds. Parliamentary government is the classic example of an *n*-person game. Although the possibility of coalitions adds greatly to the richness of the types of situations that can be considered by game theory, coalitions add substantial complexity to the theory required to analyze such games.

two-person zero-sum game Game in which net gains for one player necessarily imply equal net losses for the other player.

In a **two-person zero-sum game**, the players have exactly opposite interests; one player's gain is the other player's loss, and vice versa. "Guarder-Marauder" serves as an intuitive example. Although a number of parlor games and some military applications can be analyzed with zero-sum games, most real-life conflict-of-interest situations do not fit within this category. In contrast, in a *two-person non-zero-sum game*, both players

---

[4]For example, the antitrust opinions in *U.S. v. National Gypsum*, 428 U.S. 422 (1978) and *U.S. v. Airline Tariff Publishing Co., et al.*, 92-52854 (1992) expressly prohibited the exchange of preannouncement price lists between competitors.

may gain or lose depending on the actions each chooses to take. "Six or Seven Territories" is a **non-zero-sum game**; limiting competition to six territories raises the total profit from the interaction to $110 rather than $90.

In all non-zero-sum games, at least one outcome is jointly preferred, and consequently, the players may be able to increase their payoffs through some form of coordination. Perhaps the most famous generic structure for such games is the "Prisoner's Dilemma." Many real-world situations, such as duopoly pricing between PepsiCo and Coca Cola, a used car sales transaction, and bargaining with channel partners in manufacturer–distributor games, can be represented as a Prisoner's Dilemma.

ANALYZING SIMULTANEOUS GAMES

The Prisoner's Dilemma

In the Prisoner's Dilemma, two suspects are accused of jointly committing a crime. To convict the suspects, however, a confession is needed from one or both of them. They are separated and no information can pass between them, making it a noncooperative game. If neither suspect confesses, the prosecutor will be unable to convict them of the crime and each suspect will receive only a short-term (one-year) prison sentence. If one suspect confesses (i.e., turns state's evidence) and the other does not, then the one confessing will receive a suspended sentence, and the other prisoner will receive a long 15-year sentence. If both suspects confess, then each will receive an intermediate six-year prison sentence. Under these unpleasant conditions, each suspect must decide, whether to confess. This conflict-of-interest situation can be represented in a game matrix such as the one shown in Table 13.3.

maximin strategy A criterion for selecting actions that minimize absolute losses.

This game can be examined by using the concept of a minimum security level that arises when players "worst case" the situation. A player employing **maximin strategy** then selects the maximum payoff when worst-case scenarios arise. For Suspect 2 (the column player), the minimum payoff from his choosing "Not Confess" is a 15-year prison sentence arising when Suspect 1 confesses (in the bottom row) and the minimum payoff from his choosing "Confess" is a six-year prison sentence arising again when Suspect 1 confesses. So, maximizing the security level would therefore motivate Suspect 2 to choose the second alternative of confessing in order to avoid the possibility of a still worse outcome from not confessing. Similar reasoning holds true for Suspect 1, and she also would

TABLE 13.3 PRISONER'S DILEMMA PAYOFF MATRIX

		Suspect 2	
		Not Confess	**Confess**
Suspect 1	**Not Confess**	1-year prison term for each suspect	Suspended sentence for Suspect 2 15-year prison term for Suspect 1
	Confess	15-year prison term for Suspect 2 Suspended sentence for Suspect 1	6-year prison term for each suspect

© Cengage Learning

be motivated to choose the alternative of confessing her guilt. Thus, the "Confess" alternative dominates the other strategy "Not Confess" and {Confess, Confess} constitutes a dominant strategy/equilibrium strategy pair and isolates the predictable solution of the players.[5]

In all such Prisoner's Dilemma games, both suspects would clearly receive a better payoff (i.e., a shorter sentence) if they both decided to choose their first alternatives ("Not Confess"). However, in seeking to maximize their predictable payoffs (or, more accurately, to maximize their security levels), the first alternative is not a rational choice for either suspect. The players could of course agree in advance to maintain their innocence. But without strong sanctions to force each other to adhere to the agreement, each would be tempted to double-cross the other by confessing his or her guilt. Remember that whichever suspect breaks the agreement first has the possibility of reducing his or her sentence from a six-year prison term to a suspended sentence.

The analogy to pricing and output decisions among firms in oligopolistic industries is striking. Suppose two cruise ship companies—Carnival Cruise and Royal Caribbean—operate only three-day Caribbean cruises from Miami. If each firm acts independently to maximize its own profits, the long-run (Cournot equilibrium) profit-maximizing price is $300 per person. If two firms act jointly to maximize total industry profits, the profit-maximizing price is $450. Assume that these two prices are the only prices under consideration.

simultaneous game A strategy game in which players must choose their actions simultaneously.

Both firms must decide their action without knowing their rival's decision, which is the essence of a **simultaneous game**. Although **sequential game** reasoning is critical to the successful conduct of many business strategies, some decisions must be made simultaneously with one's rivals. Consider offers in a silent auction, release dates for fashion clothing collections, promotional ads to meet a newspaper deadline, and posted price announcements at an electronic clearinghouse sponsored by the airline or cruise ship industry.

sequential game A game with an explicit order of play.

The payoffs to each cruise ship firm are shown in Table 13.4. The below-diagonal number in each cell is the payoff to Royal Caribbean (RC), and the above-diagonal number is the payoff to Carnival. Each firm is reluctant to choose the (jointly) more profitable $450 price. If either firm reneges and discounts to $300, then the firm that charges $450 will earn significantly lower profits than the rival. This game has a typical Prisoner's Dilemma ordering of outcomes. As we have seen, unilaterally cooperating by

TABLE 13.4 CRUISE SHIP PRICING WITH DOMINANT STRATEGY

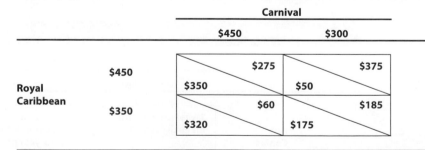

Note: Column-player payoffs (in thousands) are above the diagonal. Row-player payoffs are below the diagonal.

© Cengage Learning

---

[5]Maximin strategy will often yield actions that are not aligned with dominant strategy equilibrium if the decision maker is focused on maximizing gains or expected value of net gains rather than just minimizing absolute losses. A related strategy focuses on the minimization of opportunity losses, sometimes called minimax regret.

announcing high prices under such circumstances is foolish. For example, the payoff for Carnival from unilateral defection ($375,000) exceeds the payoff from mutual cooperation at high prices ($275,000), which itself exceeds the payoff from mutual defection at low prices ($185,000), which finally exceeds the payoff from unilateral cooperation ($60,000). Therefore, Carnival's dominant strategy is to defect.

Royal Caribbean has no such dominant strategy. Nevertheless, because RC can predict Carnival's behavior, by eliminating the prospect of Carnival's dominated $450 strategy, RC can iterate to a preferable strategy itself. Therefore, Royal Caribbean's behavior is also quite predictable, and the iterated dominant strategy equilibrium proves to be {$300, $300} or {Defect, Defect} just as in Prisoner's Dilemma. The Prisoner's Dilemma facing Royal Caribbean and Carnival is *a noncooperative positive-sum game of coordination.* In the next section we will study how to escape the dilemma by changing the structure of such games.

Dominant Strategy and Nash Equilibrium Strategy Defined

Note that a dominant strategy is not necessary for both cruise ship companies to reach an iterated dominant strategy equilibrium. The reason is that a dominant strategy requires no particular optimal or suboptimal response behavior on the part of anyone else. It is defined as an action for player i that is an optimal action $\{a_i^*\}$ in the strong sense that no matter what other players do, the payoff for player i, $\Pi_i\{a_i^*, a_{-i}\}$ exceeds the payoff for player i from any other action, $\Pi_i\{a_i, a_{-i}\}$[6]

$$\Pi_i\{a_i^*, a_{-i}\} > \Pi_i\{a_i, a_{-i}\} \qquad [13.1]$$

Consequently, one dominant strategy is quite enough to predict rival behavior and therefore identify the strategic equilibrium in any two-person one-shot simultaneous game. Once Carnival's dominant strategy (i.e., to defect and cut prices to $300) has been identified, Royal Caribbean's behavior (i.e., to also defect) is easily predictable. We have seen this outcome in "Six or Seven Territories" and in "Marauder-Guarder."

What about simultaneous games without any dominant strategy? To examine this question, we now turn to a one-shot simultaneous price announcement game between PepsiCo and Coca Cola. Each week both firms must choose whether to maintain or discount in their grocery store distribution channels. The payoffs per week per store are displayed in Table 13.5. As shown in the northeast cell, if Coca-Cola unilaterally defects to discounting, then Coca-Cola's payoff increases from $13,000 to $16,000, while Pepsi-Co's payoff declines by 25 percent from $12,000 to $9,000. Similarly, PepsiCo can turn the tables on Coca-Cola by unilaterally discounting to increase operating profits by 16 percent from $12,000 to $14,000, while Coca-Cola profits would decline from $13,000 to $10,500. Table 13.5 contains no dominant strategy. PepsiCo wants to discount when Coca-Cola maintains higher prices ($14,000 > $12,000), but just as clearly, PepsiCo wants to maintain higher prices when Coca-Cola discounts ($9,000 > $6,300). And the same contingent ambiguity is present for Coca-Cola. What criteria could possibly allow the prediction of rival behavior in this game of "Renegade Discounting?"

The answer lies in a reflexive application of the concept of **best-reply response**. If an action were the best reply to a rival's action, which in turn was the best reply to the original action, the parties would have identified an equilibrium strategy. More formally, a **Nash equilibrium strategy** is defined as an action for player i that is conditionally

best-reply response An action that maximizes self-interest from among feasible choices.

Nash equilibrium strategy An equilibrium concept for nondominant strategy games.

---

[6]A starred action refers to a maximizing choice; here, it is an action that results from maximizing profit.

TABLE 13.5 RENEGADE DISCOUNTING IN SOFT DRINKS WITH NO DOMINANT STRATEGY

		Coca-Cola	
		Maintain High Prices	**Discount Low Prices**
PepsiCo	**Maintain High Prices**	$13,000 / $12,000	$16,000 / $9,000
	Discount Low Prices	$10,500 / $14,000	$8,000 / $6,300

Note: Column-player payoffs (in thousands) are above the diagonal. Row-player payoffs are below the diagonal.

© Cengage Learning

optimal $\{a_i^*\}$ in that the payoff for player i, given best-reply responses by rivals $\Pi_i\{a_i^*, a_{-i}^*\}$, exceeds the payoff for player i from any other action $\Pi_i\{a_i, a_{-i}^*\}$ given again best-reply responses of rivals:

$$\Pi_i\{a_i^*, a_{-i}^*\} > \Pi_i\{a_i, a_{-i}^*\} \qquad [13.2]$$

In renegade discounting, the two pure Nash equilibria are $\{$Maintain$_p^*$, Discount$_c^*\}$ and $\{$Discount$_p^*$, Maintain$_c^*\}$, where the subscripts refer to PepsiCo and Coca-Cola. Recall that the order of play is not important in this game; we could have just as easily reversed these strategy pairs and listed Coca-Cola rather than PepsiCo first. The actual rivals appear to have perceived precisely this point because, for 42 weeks in 1992, they each took turns discounting on the endcaps in grocery stores across the United States.

One notable feature of these Nash equilibrium strategies is that they are nonunique. The multiple equilibria occur because the Nash equilibrium concept is less demanding (i.e., easier to satisfy) than dominant strategy equilibrium. The latter requires that an action be optimal for every possible rival response, whereas Nash equilibrium requires only that an action be optimal for a best-reply rival response. However, this knowledge does not help solve PepsiCo's problem as to what price to announce next. Remember that each bottler is announcing its price without knowing until afterward what its rival announced its own decision.

If PepsiCo believed Coca-Cola would discount half the time and maintain half the time, the expected value of PepsiCo's maintaining is $10,500 (namely, 0.5 × $12,000 + 0.5 × $9,000), whereas the expected value of PepsiCo's discounting is smaller (i.e., only $10,150). These results would seem to suggest a preference for maintaining high prices, but again, if PepsiCo kept its prices predictably high, Coca-Cola could unilaterally defect and earn $16,000, whereas PepsiCo would then realize only $9,000. So how can PepsiCo avoid tipping its hand and ending up with the $9,000 outcome rather than its own $14,000 defection outcome too often?

The answer lies in PepsiCo's randomizing the pricing process. PepsiCo must figure out what automated pricing response would make Coca-Cola indifferent between maintaining and discounting and thereby willing to randomize its own price announcement. That is, what probability of discounting by PepsiCo would make Coca-Cola indifferent by equating Coca-Cola's expected payoff from maintaining to its expected payoff from discounting? Interestingly, because the payoffs are asymmetrical, the desired probability is not 0.5. Let's see what the solution is. Using p to represent the probability that PepsiCo maintains and $(1 - p)$ if it discounts, we calculate

$$(p)\$13{,}000 + (1 - p)\$10{,}500 = (p)\$16{,}000 + (1 - p)\$8{,}000 \qquad [13.3]$$

where the Coca-Cola payoffs are arranged to correspond to the columns of Table 13.5. The solution probabilities $p = 0.454$ and $(1 - p) = 0.546$ make Coca-Cola indifferent and therefore PepsiCo less vulnerable to unilateral defection.

Note the mirror-image reflexivity associated with this Nash equilibrium solution: Coca-Cola faces a comparable payoff structure and strategy dilemma to that of PepsiCo, and would presumably want to know the probabilities of maintaining and discounting that would make PepsiCo indifferent between the two choices. Calculating as before

$$(p')\$12{,}000 + (1 - p')\$9{,}000 = (p')\$14{,}000 + (1 - p')\$6{,}300 \qquad [13.4]$$

where the PepsiCo payoffs are arranged to correspond to the rows of Table 13.5, we obtain $p' = 0.574$ and $(1 - p') = 0.426$. If randomized choice by PepsiCo is a best-reply response to Coca-Cola, and if Coca-Cola can then do no better, this renegade discounting game must have a third Nash equilibrium strategy—namely, {Maintain by PepsiCo with $p = 0.454$, Maintain by Coca-Cola with $p' = 0.574$}. This strategy pair is called a **mixed Nash equilibrium strategy**. A 0.454 probability weight on maintaining and a 0.546 probability weight on discounting by PepsiCo yields \$11,634 expected value for each of Coca-Cola's price announcement strategies. Similarly, a 0.574 probability weight on maintaining and a 0.426 probability weight on discounting by Coca Cola yields \$10,720 expected value for each of PepsiCo's price announcement strategies. The strategic equilibrium solution for this game therefore contains two pure and one mixed Nash strategy: {Maintain$_p^*$, Discount$_c^*$}, {Discount$_p^*$, Maintain$_c^*$}, and {Maintain$_p^*$ = 0.454, Maintain$_c^*$ = 0.574}.

In this tactical setting, neither firm can do better than to play these probabilities of Maintain repeatedly as the game reappears. Using a computer program that randomizes a biased (imbalanced) coin toss is one way to implement mixed Nash equilibrium strategy. In principle, however, none of these three Nash equilibrium strategies is preferable to any other. In a one-shot play of Renegade Discounting, all four cells in Table 13.5 still arise. The {\$6,300, \$8,000} outcome in the southeast cell and the {\$12,000, \$13,000} outcome in the northwest cell, as well as the two asymmetric outcomes that correspond to our two pure Nash strategies, will all sometimes arise.

In a noncooperative simultaneous one-shot game that allows no communication in advance, no side payments, and no binding agreements, players simply cannot avoid this multiplicity of possible strategic equilibria. In practice, therefore, a one-shot play of any of the three Nash strategies in the Renegade Discounting game can work out well or badly.

Of course, the {\$12,000, \$13,000} outcome is the best of all. In the next section we will see how to secure this win-win outcome by introducing repeated plays, imperfect information, and credibility mechanisms to convert this simultaneous game into a sequential game. Barry Nalebuff, professor at Yale and author of the widely read *Thinking Strategically*, calls it "changing the nature of competition" and distinguishes these tactical procedures from "collusion" between these competitors that would violate the antitrust laws.[7]

mixed Nash equilibrium strategy A strategic equilibrium concept involving randomized behavior.

---

[7]See A. Dixit and B. Nalebuff, *Thinking Strategically* (New York: Norton, 1993); and "Businessman's Dilemma," *Forbes* (October 11, 1993), p. 107.

THE ESCAPE FROM PRISONER'S DILEMMA

Multiperiod Punishment and Reward Schemes in Repeated Play Games

In this section, we relax the assumptions of single-play, complete, and perfect information games. Let's again look at the PepsiCo and Coca-Cola example with the Prisoner's Dilemma payoff structure as shown in Table 13.6. Both PepsiCo and Coca-Cola are worse off if either unilaterally defects from maintaining high prices. Each soft drink bottler would like to pursue the $12,000 payoff, but the only way to avoid the vulnerability of a unilateral defection is by defecting oneself! Dominant strategy drives both players to discount their 12-packs in the one-shot game. However, surely PepsiCo and Coca-Cola recognize they are engaged in an ongoing competitive process, not a one-shot (i.e., single-play) game. Week after week, they will encounter each other in many future replays of this pricing game at grocery and convenience stores nationwide. Consequently, tacit cooperation rather than dogmatic price cutting has a chance to evolve.

Suppose Coca-Cola begins the process by announcing a high price in Period 1. Coke's intention is to play that price continuously until PepsiCo defects and thereafter to never announce High again, which is a so-called **grim trigger strategy**. Any move by PepsiCo away from cooperative High pricing, and Coca-Cola's punishment is immediate and never-ending. Multiperiod punishment schemes are a key to inducing cooperation in Prisoner's Dilemma games, whether it is cruise ship, airline, or soft drink companies. In this case, PepsiCo compares the perpetuity opportunity loss of ($12,000 − $8,000) discounted at the interest rate r per period to the one-time gain from defection of ($17,000 − $12,000):

$$\$4,000/r > \$5,000 \quad \text{if} \quad r < 0.8 \qquad [13.5]$$

The interpretation is straightforward. At any discount rate less than 80 percent, PepsiCo's future gains from cooperatively maintaining high prices outweigh the one-time gains from defection. Thus, the dominant strategy to defect in one-shot games is no longer attractive. This calculation and conclusion reflect a generalizable **Folk theorem**, which states that for any payoff structure, a discount rate always exists that is low enough to induce cooperation in an infinitely repeated Prisoner's Dilemma. So, a grim trigger strategy can induce cooperation in an infinitely repeated Prisoner's Dilemma.[8]

grim trigger strategy A hypersensitive strategy involving infinitely long punishment schemes.

folk theorem A conclusion about cooperation in repeated Prisoner's Dilemma.

TABLE 13.6   REPEATED PRISONER'S DILEMMA IN SOFT DRINKS

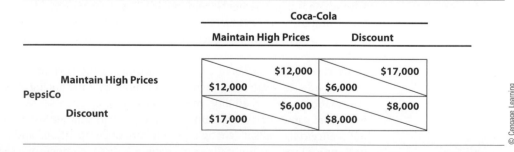

		Coca-Cola	
		Maintain High Prices	**Discount**
PepsiCo	**Maintain High Prices**	$12,000 / $12,000	$17,000 / $6,000
	Discount	$6,000 / $17,000	$8,000 / $8,000

© Cengage Learning

trembling hand trigger strategy A punishment mechanism that forgives random mistakes and miscommunications.

---

[8]Of course, one transparent disadvantage of grim trigger strategies is that cooperative outcomes cannot survive a single small mistake in reasoning or miscommunication by either player. Selten's concept of a **trembling hand trigger strategy** allows one grace period of misplay by the other party before imposing the grim punishment for defection. Of course, a wily rival who understands this strategy will take advantage of his or her opponent by claiming just as many one-period "mistakes" of defection as he or she can get away with.

However, because companies do not last forever, the Folk theorem raises an obvious question, "What about for shorter periods, say 20 weeks?" The 20-period calculation is easily done; r now must be less than 79 percent. Then what about 10 weeks, and if 10, what about for 2 weeks? Suppose it is now the beginning of week 2. We know we are out of this "cooperative" structure next week (i.e., week 3), so our remaining incentive to maintain high prices is only $\$4,000/(1 + r)$, and our incentive to defect is $\$5,000$. Now all of a sudden, for any discount rate, each player is better off defecting. This result is also generalizable. The last play of a finitely repeated Prisoner's Dilemma has the same incentives as a one-shot Prisoner's Dilemma; everybody defects. Therefore, one period away from the endgame of a finitely repeated Prisoner's Dilemma, neither party has an incentive to maintain its reputation for cooperating.

Unraveling and the Chain Store Paradox

unraveling problem A failure of cooperation in games of finite length.

The prospects of cooperation in any *finitely* repeated Prisoner's Dilemma are poor, because what is true for a 2-period game must be true by backward induction for a 3-period game. If you know in the 2-period game that it pays to defect, then in the 3-period game you must know that a certain defection is only 1 period away; therefore, you should defect now. And if that is the case for a 3-period game, then it will be the same for a 4-period game, and so on, even for a 20-period game. Reinhard Selten investigated this **unraveling problem** for finitely repeated Prisoner's Dilemmas in the context of chain store incumbents facing repeated entry threats from rivals.[9] In a Prisoner's Dilemma setting like those we've been examining, the established firm has a dominant strategy to accommodate the new entrant. But one's intuition says that in the face of enough repetitions of the chain store competition, the established firm's reputation for fighting entry can pay off. And in the extreme, this intuition is absolutely correct. In **infinitely repeated games**, the Folk theorem does apply. However, with any fewer repetitions, in even the enormous number of chain store competitions that might face a McDonald's or a Walmart, the cooperative equilibrium unravels.

infinitely repeated games A game that lasts forever.

endgame reasoning An analysis of the final decision in a sequential game.

Reinhard Selten invented the concept of **endgame reasoning** to show this paradoxical result and to emphasize the sequential nature of reputation effects. Endgame reasoning always entails looking ahead to the last play in an ordered sequence of plays, identifying the player whose decisions will control the outcome of the endgame, and then predicting that player's best-reply response. In Figure 13.2 we have a chain store incumbent (I) who accommodates or fights in response to a potential entrant (PE) who stays out or enters. Accommodation forgoes $\$20,000$ of the incumbent chain store's profit ($\$100,000 - \$80,000$) and induces future entry, but fighting the present entry to acquire a reputation for toughness in future possible entry situations entails actual losses now ($-\$10,000$). Conceive of the displayed game tree as the last three encounters of a 20-chain store competition perceived by both players from the start. Looking ahead to the endgame, it is clear that the incumbent will accommodate in the last submarket. At decision point C, the $\$100,000$ to accommodate exceeds the $\$60,000$ to fight, and the $\$80,000$ to accommodate at decision node B exceeds the $-\$10,000$ to fight. More importantly, a tough reputation gains no future payoff thereafter because it is truly the endgame. Since the potential entrant also knows it is the endgame, entry will surely take place in that last submarket.

[9]See J. Harsanyi and R. Selten, *A General Theory of Equilibrium Selection in Games* (Cambridge, MA: MIT Press, 1988); or for a less technical treatment, E. Rasmussen, *Games and Information*, 2nd ed. (Cambridge, MA: Blackwell, 1994), Chapter 5.

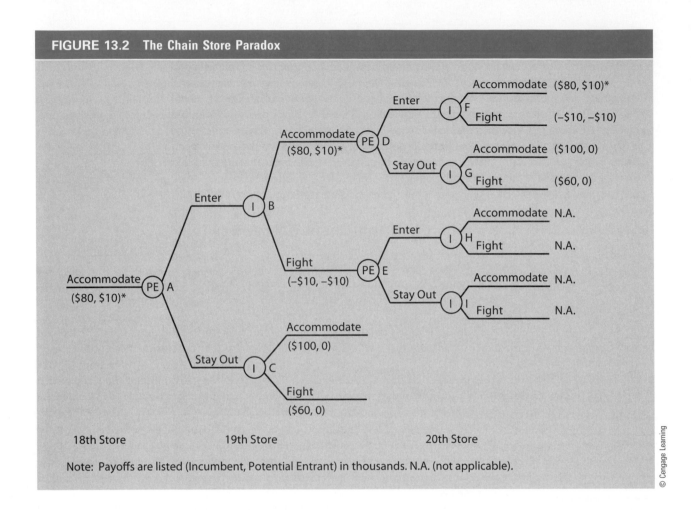

FIGURE 13.2   The Chain Store Paradox

Note: Payoffs are listed (Incumbent, Potential Entrant) in thousands. N.A. (not applicable).

Now, in looking back to the previous submarket (i.e., the 19th store), the incumbent realizes that its rival's subsequent entry in the 20th submarket is certain because both parties know that the incumbent will accommodate in that final round and therefore that, again, any attempt to acquire an enhanced reputation for fighting is useless in that 19th submarket. Accommodation is therefore the best-reply response in the proper subgame from node B onward to the endgame. Because the entrant can predict this decision as well, entry occurs in the 19th submarket at node A. But what is true of the 19th must therefore be true of the 18th, and the 17th, and so forth, right back to the start of the game.

chain store paradox A prediction of always accommodative behavior by incumbents facing entry threats.

This *backward induction reasoning* leads to the **chain store paradox**. We can calculate in submarket 1 that at reasonable rates of discount the incumbent may well have a sufficient net present value of profits from deterring future entry to justify fighting early on rather than accommodating. Yet, the predictability of its future accommodation jeopardizes the credibility of the incumbent's present fighting. This predictability of accommodation as a best-reply response of the incumbent all the way out to the endgame means the reputation effects of any present fighting unravel. Accommodation therefore occurs in every submarket or every period in the 20-submarket/20-period game just as we argued earlier it would in the 2-submarket/2-period game.

Our intuition tells us this accommodation behavior of entrant 1 is paradoxical, especially when a long line of potential entrants is waiting in the wings—hence, the term *chain store paradox*. And, as we shall now see, changing some other features of the chain store decision problem can overturn this counterintuitive result aligning the incumbent with a less passive defense of the "territory" they dominate.

Mutual Forbearance and Cooperation in Repeated Prisoner's Dilemma Games

One way to short-circuit the reasoning of the chain store paradox is to introduce an uncertain ending of the game. If the incumbent can never be sure whether future encounters beyond submarket 20 will arise, then the reputation effect of fighting in the 19th period returns. Any positive probability that the game will continue is sufficient (again, at low enough discount rates) to restore the deterrent effect of fighting in period 20. If fighting is rational in period 20, then the incumbent is willing to fight in 19, 18, and so forth, back to period 1. And if the incumbent is willing in period 1, then it may not have to fight because the other firm will not enter. The analogous implication in a finitely repeated pricing game such as repeated Prisoner's Dilemma in Soft Drinks (Table 13.6) is that the rivals will cooperate by maintaining high prices as long as the endgame is uncertain. With one period remaining, we can then write Equation 13.6 as

$$\$4,000 + \$4,000 \times \frac{1}{(1 + r)} \times p > \$5,000 \qquad [13.6]$$

where p is the probability of the game continuing beyond the next period. For $r = 0.1$, a probability as low as 0.28 is sufficient to elicit cooperation in maintaining high prices and a {\$12,000, \$12,000} northwest cell outcome in Table 13.6. Therefore, infinite repetition is not required to induce cooperation in Prisoner's Dilemma; an uncertain ending will suffice.

Example

Solving the Chain Store Paradox: Semiconductor Pricing at Intel, Motorola, and AMD[10]

These insights seem especially important in industries with fast-changing technology, such as computer chips and consumer electronics, where cost disadvantages that might end an incumbent's business are seldom permanent because the technology changes so often. One illustration is the microprocessor computer chip industry, where Intel, AMD, and Motorola compete against Japanese and Taiwanese competitors.

With each successive generation of chips (see Table 13.7), the market leaders practice life cycle pricing techniques. After a period of high target pricing and value-based pricing, Intel, with more than 70 percent of the worldwide market, limits price rather than accommodate AMD with 21 percent market share, Motorola with 5 percent, and numerous smaller competitors. That is, with a few quarters after introduction, chip prices are reduced in an attempt to deter entry by the imitators. Then, with uncertain timing, the whole process repeats itself. New chips are introduced at high prices, imitators reverse engineer the design, and limit pricing begins again. The uncertain

(continued)

TABLE 13.7 MAJOR INTEL MICROPROCESSORS AND CLOCK SPEED

YEAR	MICROPROCESSOR	MHZ
1979	8088	5
1982	286	6
1985	386	16
1989	486	25
1993	Pentium	60
1995	Pentium Pro	150
1997	Pentium II	233
1999	Pentium III	333
2002	Pentium IV	550
2004	Celeron M	1200
2005	Pentium M	1600
2006	Core2 Duo	2130
2008	Core i3	2660
2010	Core i5	3200
2012	Core i7	3600

© Cengage Learning

endpoint of these successive chip generation games leads to a non-accommodative response by the incumbent firms.

[10]Based on *Investor's Business Daily* (January 13, 1998), p. A8.

Bayesian Reputation Effects

A second ingenious escape from Prisoner's Dilemma incorporates Bayesian reputation effects about opponent type, based on the work of Nobel laureate John Harsanyi. It involves estimating the likelihood of various opponent moves based on past events. If some irrational "crazies" who do not always maximize their payoffs are known to exist in the market, a perfectly sane incumbent might end up taking actions that seem crazy. The intent of the incumbent is to secure a disreputation indistinguishable from the crazies.[11] An example would be an automobile manufacturing incumbent that "predates"—that is, prices its product below its variable cost, even though the operating losses from such a strategy may not be recoverable in excess profits later. Japanese tire manufacturers are often accused of such "dumping" in the offshore markets, especially in Europe and the United States.

Winning Strategies in Evolutionary Computer Tournaments: Tit for Tat

Robert Axelrod was intrigued by the reasons why people who are ardently pursuing their own goals often end up cooperating with competitors in long-term interactions.[12]

[11]On the asymmetric information pooling equilibrium behind this strategy, see R. Gibbons, "An Introduction to Applicable Game Theory," *Journal of Economic Perspectives* 11, no. 1 (Winter 1997), pp. 140–147; and Rasmussen, op. cit., pp. 352–356.

[12]Robert Axelrod, *The Evolution of Cooperation* (New York: Basic Books, 1984). See also "Evolutionary Economics," *Forbes* (October 11, 1993), p. 110; and Jill Neimark, "Tit for Tat: A Game of Survival," *Success* (May 1987), p. 62.

He investigated the question of optimal strategy in repeated Prisoner's Dilemma by conducting a computer simulation in which 151 strategies competed against one another 1,000 times. He discovered that those strategies that finished highest in the computer tournament had several characteristics in common. First, winning strategies are clear and simple in order to avoid triggering mistakes by one's potential cooperators. Second, winning strategies make unilateral attempts to cooperate; they never initiate defection—just the reverse—they initiate niceness. Third, as we would expect, all winning strategies are provokable—they have credible commitments to some punishment rule. Interestingly, limited-duration punishment schemes that displayed forgiveness won out over maximal-punishment grim trigger strategies that do not. The reason seemed to be that winning strategies recover from misperceptions, miscommunications, and strategic mistakes; so with tit-for-tat punishment schemes, for example, reprisals need not become self-perpetuating.

Example

Brown and Williamson's Reputation for Predating

The U.S. Supreme Court has addressed these issues and thereby set a standard for judging predatory pricing behavior by U.S. firms. In *Brooke Group Ltd. v. Brown and Williamson Tobacco Company*, 113 U.S. 2578 (1993), the Court held that pricing generic cigarettes below cost was not evidence of an undesirable predatory intent to monopolize a market because Brown and Williamson had no opportunity thereafter to earn excess profits and recoup its losses from the alleged predatory conduct. Similarly, when Kodak priced its Instamatic film camera at $11.95 despite a $28 direct manufacturing cost, it faced little prospect of later recovering the $16.05 operating loss per camera. Instead, this pricing tactic was reasonable as an attempt to clear inventory quickly before exiting the Instamatic submarket.

Whether the Court in these cases looked deeply enough into the long-term effect of deterring effective entry through disreputation effects is a hotly debated antitrust issue. Under incomplete information about opponent types, behaving like a "crazy," who predatorily prices below cost even though recovering the losses seems unlikely, may deter an opponent's entry. This disreputation effect of becoming known as a firm who might well price below cost is more valuable when the cost of new entrants is high, brand loyalty to incumbents is weak, and the number of potential entrants is large.

American Airlines discouraged the discounters Vanguard, SunJet, and Western Pacific from remaining in the Dallas–Fort Worth airline market using such tactics. In May 2001, American's indictment for predation was dismissed on the grounds that at no point did American lower price below its average variable cost. Hardnosed competitive tactics that remain within the boundaries of recovering average variable cost are legal, because antitrust law exists to protect competition (encouraging lower prices for consumers), not to protect individual competitors.

What types of actual strategies would you guess best fit these winning criteria? Surprisingly, "Tit for Tat" won the tournament! Repeating what your opponent did on the last round is simple and clearly provokable, but consistent with unilaterally initiating cooperation yourself. And perhaps most importantly, Tit for Tat is forgiving. After a single-period punishment, it reverts to cooperating as soon as the opponent/cooperator does so.

For example, one possible approach to managing competition for cruise ship companies Carnival and Royal Caribbean (RC) in Table 13.8 is to follow a Tit-for-Tat (TFT)

TABLE 13.8   CRUISE SHIP PRICING WITH PRICE MATCHING

		Carnival Pricing Policy		
		$450	**$300**	**"Match"**
Royal Caribbean Pricing Policy	**$450**	$350 \\ $275	$150 \\ $375	$350 \\ $275
	$300	$320 \\ $160	$175 \\ $185	$175 \\ $185
	"Match"	$350 \\ $275	$175 \\ $185	$350 \\ $275

Note: Column-player payoffs above the diagonal in $ thousands.

conspicuous focal point An outcome that attracts mutual cooperation.

decision rule. Royal Caribbean, who has a dominant $300 strategy, could signal a **conspicuous focal point** by promoting "staterooms" (rather than smaller, less well-appointed "cabins") as an industry standard and then choosing the $450 pricing strategy in the first period. Thereafter, RC would select the same pricing strategy in the next period as Carnival chose in the previous period. For example, if Carnival charges $450 in the current period, then RC would do likewise in the next period. On the other hand, if Carnival defects and charges $300 in the current period, then RC would retaliate by charging the same $300 price next period. Through repeated plays, the participants may learn the tit-for-tat decision rule being applied by their competitor.

Price-Matching Guarantees

How should Carnival respond to a tit-for-tat decision rule by Royal Caribbean? Let's look at the analogies between this limited duration punishment scheme and a matching price guarantee. In Table 13.8, a matching price guarantee by Royal Caribbean substantially reduces Carnival's incentive to discount down to $300 when RC has announced $450 prices. Under the heading "$300" in the second column, one sees that Carnival's $300 discounted price can no longer generate the $375,000 payoff of the first row but instead simply realizes the $185,000 payoff from a matching price policy by RC. This $185,000 payoff that arises is the same when both firms discount to $300. Because RC's customers will monitor and enforce RC's matching price guarantee by requesting rebates of ($450 − $300 =) $150 from RC whenever Carnival discounts to $300, Carnival cannot hope to gain a significant share of RC's customers by discounting. In short, the matching price guarantee has removed the possibility of gain share discounting.

To place Royal Caribbean in the same position, Carnival will likely announce a matching price guarantee as protection in those times when RC might try a sneak attack on Carnival's market share by discounting unexpectedly. Assuming, as we did earlier, that Royal Caribbean initiates play with a $450 price announcement, both cruise companies will maintain $450 prices, effectively playing "Match, Match" and escaping the Prisoner's Dilemma by realizing the {$350,000, $275,000} payoff in the far northwest and far southeast cells. Like double-the-difference price guarantees, matching price guarantees increase the expected price level and hence the profitability of all the sellers in a tight oligopoly market.

Now, how does this outcome compare to Tit for Tat (TFT)? Assume that the "Match" alternative is now unavailable in the game. Nevertheless, Carnival should see Royal Caribbean's TFT decision rule as a delayed matching price guarantee. That is, with a one-period lag, Royal Caribbean is going to match any discount that Carnival tries and subsequently match (again with a one-period lag) any return to high prices as soon as Carnival returns. These payoff paths are certain; no amount of apologizing by Carnival about mistakes and miscommunications can prevent RC's one-period punishment. Therefore, Carnival simply compares the profits from discounting unilaterally this period ($375,000 − $275,000) to a discounted opportunity loss from punishment next period ($275,000 − $160,000):

$$\$100,000 < \$115,000/(1+r) \quad \text{if} \quad r < 0.15 \qquad [13.7]$$

As long as the discount rate (r) is less than 15 percent and the continuation of this particular cruise route is certain for both firms, Carnival should not discount and thereby defect on the industry leader's pricing policy of $450.

Of course, if the probability of continuance (p) falls below 1.0, a limited duration punishment scheme such as Tit for Tat becomes much less effective immediately. For example, multiplying the future opportunity loss from punishment next period by just 10 percent less than a certainty of continuance (i.e., by 90 percent),

$$\$100,000 < \$115,000(1-0.1)/(1+r) = \$103,500/(1+r)$$
$$\$100,000 < \$103,500/(1+r) \quad \text{if} \quad r > 0.035 \qquad [13.8]$$

implies that Carnival will defect and discount to attempt to gain market share any time the interest rate is greater than 3.5 percent.[13] Tit for Tat therefore is a more effective coordination device for oligopolists that expect to encounter one another again and again, such as PepsiCo and Coca-Cola, United and Delta Airlines, Anheuser-Busch and Miller, and Carnival and Royal Caribbean.

Because the {$450, $450} actions yield $90,000 more for Royal Caribbean than the iterated dominant strategy equilibrium {$300, $300}, Royal Caribbean may well initiate cooperation and thereafter play Tit for Tat. With rational, unconfused, and well-informed competitors, communication of conspicuous focal points and multiperiod punishment schemes can induce conditional cooperation in repeated Prisoner's Dilemma. Perhaps for this reason, U.S. courts have prohibited airlines from signaling such coordination information to one another through their centralized reservation systems.

Example

Signaling a Punishment Scheme: Northwest[14]

America West (now part of US Airways) once announced a $50 fare reduction for 21-day advance purchase tickets on the busy Minneapolis–Los Angeles route dominated by Northwest Airlines (now part of Delta). Rather than cutting its own $308 fare from its Minneapolis hub to match the America West's $258 fare, Northwest responded by signaling a multiperiod punishment scheme. In particular, Northwest announced a

(continued)

---

[13]Equation 13.8 can also be written to highlight the interplay between p and r as

$$\$100,000 < \$115,000(0.9)/(1+r) = \$115,000/(1+R)$$

where R is the effective rate of interest $1/(1+R) = p/(1+r) = 0.9/(1+r)$. In the Tit for Tat example, because the probability of continuance is near 1.0, the effective rate of interest and the actual rate of interest are quite similar. For $r = 10$ percent and $p = 0.9$, $p/(1+r) = 0.9/1.1 = 0.82$, and therefore the effective rate of interest is 22 percent: $1/(1+0.22) = 0.82$. As p gets smaller, the effective and actual rates of interest diverge exponentially. For example, for an actual interest rate of 10 percent and $p = 0.55$, $p/(1+r) = 0.55/1.1 = 0.5$, and therefore the effective rate of interest is 100 percent: $1/(1+1.0) = 0.5$.

$40 reduction (from $208 to $168) for 21-day advance purchase tickets on the busy route from New York to America West's hub in Phoenix. This retaliatory fare was labeled on the Airline Tariff Publishing computer system as available for only the next two days, with possible renewal thereafter. Five days later, America West canceled its $50 discount promotion on Minneapolis to Los Angeles travel.

Antitrust law makes it illegal for companies to conspire to fix prices. **Price signaling** the particulars of a multiperiod punishment scheme in order to elicit cooperation in maintaining high prices is seen as a violation of this provision of the Robinson-Patman Act. Northwest defended its actions as "competitive initiatives and responses consistent with independent self-interest." However, the Third Circuit Appeals Court was quite clear; signaling a limited-duration punishment scheme involving prices is not legal. *U.S. v. Airline Tariff Publishing Co. et al.*, 9252854 (1992) expressly prohibited such preannouncements of price changes that might facilitate price coordination.

[14]Based on "Fare Game," *Wall Street Journal* (June 28, 1990), p. A1; "Fare Warning," *Wall Street Journal* (October 9, 1990), p. B1; and "Why Northwest Gives Competition a Bad Name," *BusinessWeek* (March 16, 1998), p. 34.

price signaling A communication of price change plans, prohibited by antitrust law.

Industry Standards as Coordination Devices

Mandatory industry standards or regulatory constraints are often another way of changing the structure of a simultaneous-play Prisoner's Dilemma into a sequential-play game. Java programming language for the Internet, the digital signal specification CDMA for cell phones, the Blu-ray specification for high-definition television, or for wireless recharging of cell phones, blenders, and power tools are examples of industry standards used in this way.[15] By restricting the flexibility of one another's responses, rivals can often secure an escape from the {Defect, Defect} dominant strategy payoffs of a simultaneous-play Prisoner's Dilemma and achieve more profitable outcomes in a sequential game.

Consider the business-to-business sale of electrical equipment illustrated in Figure 13.3. General Electric (GE) would like to manufacture and distribute a high specifications ("gold-plated") halogen recessed lighting fixture supported with full installation and after-sale service. Unfortunately, however, the GE distributor has higher payoffs from not providing full installation. Under those circumstances, GE is better off manufacturing a fixture that meets only minimal specifications. Because of the distributor's dominant strategy, the two companies earn payoffs {Worse, Better} and find themselves in a Prisoner's Dilemma. They would prefer the northwest cell {Better, Best}, but each would then be vulnerable to a defection by the other company, resulting in their Worst outcome.

By enlisting third parties (TP) such as Underwriters Laboratory in specifying an installation standard or encouraging the adoption of local building codes that require full installation, GE and its distributors can escape the Prisoner's Dilemma. A General Electric distributor would then be engaged in an illegal ("below code") sale if it provided anything less than full installation, so GE can anticipate full installation and will therefore proceed to manufacture the high specifications product. The payoffs will then improve to {Better, Best}.

[15]See "Adapt or Die," *The Economist* (March 7, 2009), pp. 20–21.

FIGURE 13.3 **Electrical Industry Standard Allows GE Distributor to Escape Prisoner's Dilemma**

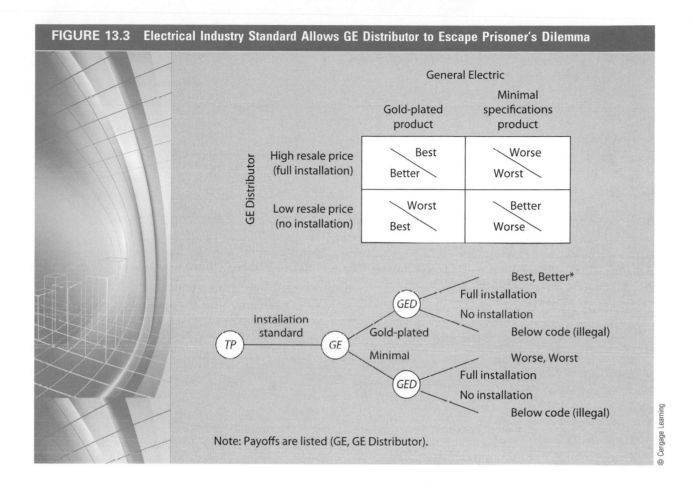

Note: Payoffs are listed (GE, GE Distributor).

ANALYZING SEQUENTIAL GAMES

To illustrate the importance of the sequential order of play in many tactical situations, consider another manufacturer–distributor coordination game that arises between heavy truck manufacturers and independent retail distributors. The payoffs for the promotion and sale of a heavy truck like those sold by Volvo-GM Truck are displayed in normal form in Table 13.9. Let's first examine the actions and payoffs in the left-hand column. The manufacturer wants their retail distributors to continue providing personal selling efforts and after-sales service, rather than discontinue these activities, and thereby increase their retail margins. In return, the manufacturer agrees to advertise the product. If full services continue and advertising occurs, the customers will tolerate higher manufacturer's suggested retail prices (MSRP). In that case, the retail distributor and the manufacturer can earn additional profits of $180,000 and $300,000, respectively. However, if retail selling effort and some after-sales services are discontinued and if MSRP increases (as in the northwest cell of Table 13.9), unit sales volume declines so sharply that the retail distributor receives only $120,000 profit while the manufacturer makes only $280,000 profit.

Independent retail distributors may feel tempted to deliver less service in many small, inconspicuous ways, especially if they suspect a lack of manufacturer-based advertising of this product will make their time and effort spent on other manufacturers' products

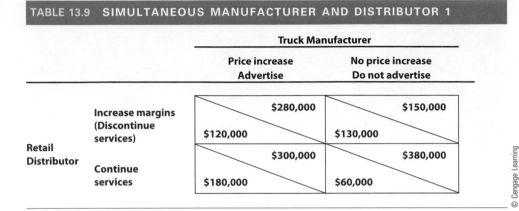

TABLE 13.9   SIMULTANEOUS MANUFACTURER AND DISTRIBUTOR 1

	Truck Manufacturer	
Retail Distributor	**Price increase** **Advertise**	**No price increase** **Do not advertise**
Increase margins (Discontinue services)	$280,000 / $120,000	$150,000 / $130,000
Continue services	$300,000 / $180,000	$380,000 / $60,000

© Cengage Learning

more valuable. Sales volume will eventually decline, but at a substantially higher margin that may well be in the retail distributor's best interests. This outcome is represented in the northeast cell of Table 13.9; with retail selling effort discontinued and no manufacturer-based advertising, both parties incur fewer expenses and realize $130,000 profit for the retailer but only $150,000 profit for the manufacturer. On the other hand, if the manufacturer does not advertise, but retailer services continue (i.e., the southeast cell), manufacturer profit skyrockets to $380,000 while the retailer only clears $60,000 because of much higher expenses.

What would you do as the retail dealer or distributor in this situation? Would you try for the increased margin by economizing on selling expenses and after-sale services? Remember that your best payoff occurs when the manufacturer anticipates your continuation of full selling effort and after-sales services, and chooses therefore to advertise and raise the customers' expectations by announcing a higher price point. And the manufacturer's best payoff occurs when you, the retailer, provide extensive dealer services, and the manufacturer economizes on advertising expenses. Note that Table 13.9 contains no pure Nash equilibrium strategies! So, how would you coordinate this on again-off again relationship?[16] Note how much additional predictability of rival behavior emerges in this coordination game if we introduce a small but pivotal change in the structure of the game: a sequential order of play.

A Sequential Coordination Game

Suppose as in Figure 13.4 the manufacturer (*M*) must commit first to the release of a product update that warrants higher pricing, and that this decision is easily observable and irreversible. Then the retail distributor (*R*) must decide whether to continue personal selling effort and after-sale services or discontinue, and finally the manufacturer will thereafter decide on whether to contribute to cooperative advertising with the retailer. It turns out that introducing this sequential order to the decision making will make it possible to predict unambiguously the optimal strategic behavior by both parties and resolve the coordination problem of the simultaneous game.

The structure of the sequential game can be represented as a **game tree** or *decision tree* as in Figure 13.4. The order of the decisions is read from left to right, and each circle represents a decision node. *Update* or *Not update* identifies possible *actions* that Player *M*

game tree A schematic diagram of a sequential game.

---

[16]We are assuming that merging the two entities into one vertically integrated firm is infeasible. In Chapter 15, we will see how these coordination problems can be resolved by, and indeed motivate, private voluntary contracting over vertical requirements between manufacturers and distributors.

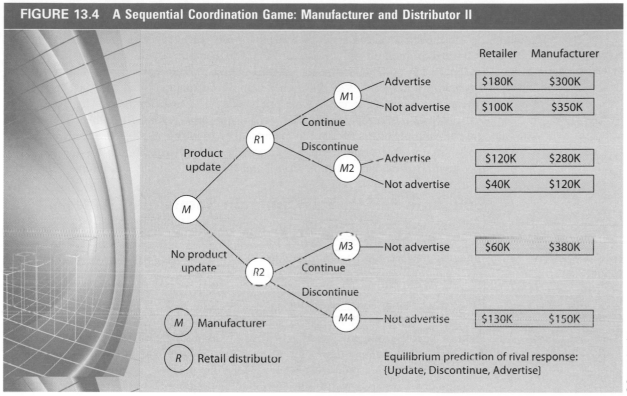

FIGURE 13.4   A Sequential Coordination Game: Manufacturer and Distributor II

	Retailer	Manufacturer
Advertise	$180K	$300K
Not advertise	$100K	$350K
Advertise	$120K	$280K
Not advertise	$40K	$120K
Not advertise	$60K	$380K
Not advertise	$130K	$150K

Equilibrium prediction of rival response:
{Update, Discontinue, Advertise}

can take at the first decision node *M. Continue* or *Discontinue* identifies possible actions of Player *R* at the second decision nodes *R*1 to *R*2, and *Advertise* or *Not advertise* identifies possible actions of the manufacturer at nodes *M*1 to *M*4. The *payoffs* for the retailer and then for the manufacturer, associated with each sequence of possible actions, are listed in the last two columns. Note that some of these payoffs mirror those in Table 13.9 while others are totally new.

The manufacturer can look ahead and foresee that an *Update* of the product will make it advantageous for the retail distributor to *Discontinue* full retail selling effort. Out of self-interest, the manufacturer commits to an update, increases MSRP prices, and then (because of best reply response analysis) follows through with advertising. That is, the manufacturer can look ahead and analyze what subsequent choices are in the retail distributor's best interest and then reason back to detect what actions are in its own (the manufacturer's) self-interest. Each party in Figure 13.4 is able to look ahead and reason back using the concept of best-reply response to predict the rival's behavior. None of this sequential reasoning was available in the simultaneous-play version of the game.

Endgame reasoning always entails looking ahead to the last play in an ordered sequence of plays, identifying the player whose decisions will control the outcome of the endgame, and then predicting that player's best-reply response. In this instance, knowing that the manufacturer controls the outcome from node *M*1 onward and that the manufacturer is better off with $350,000 from *Not advertise* forces the retail distributor to dismiss the prospect of the $180,000 outcome in the first row. That possible outcome is not consistent with best-reply response by the manufacturer who does control the endgame. Therefore, that branch should be removed ("pruned") from the game tree; the retail distributor should assume that if the product is updated and the retailer continues extensive selling effort, the manufacturer will not engage in cooperative advertising. Therefore {$100,000, $350,000} is the predictable outcome of deciding to *Continue selling effort* at node *M1*. However, the retailer's analysis is far from finished.

backward induction To reason in reverse temporal order.

The above conclusion about the endgame reasoning allows you, the retailer, to employ **backward induction** and decide for sure whether you would prefer to *Continue* or *Discontinue* at node *R1*. If the manufacturer's best-reply response from *M2* onward is to *Advertise* (which yields $280,000 rather than $120,000 for *M* and $120,000 for you), it appears that your self-interest at the prior node *R1* is to *Discontinue*. The strategy pair that provides a best-reply equilibrium for the subgame beyond *R1* is then {*Discontinue, Advertise*}, implying distributor and manufacturer payoffs of {$120,000, $280,000}, respectively. In sum, the strategy triplet that provides a Nash equilibrium for the sequential coordination game "Manufacturer–Distributor II" is then {*Update, Discontinue, Advertise*}.

Subgame Perfect Equilibrium in Sequential Games

subgame perfect equilibrium strategy An equilibrium concept for non-cooperative sequential games.

Looking ahead to the rival's best-reply responses in the endgame and then reasoning back to preferred strategy at earlier decision points is Reinhard Selten's concept of a **subgame perfect equilibrium strategy** for sequential games, a concept for which he and John Nash won the 1994 Nobel Prize in economics. Like many other pathbreaking ideas, this intuitive strategic equilibrium concept is quite deceptive in its simplicity. Recall that a Nash equilibrium strategy is a decision maker's optimal action such that the payoff, when all other players make best-reply responses, exceeds that decision maker's payoff from any other action, again assuming best-reply responses. Selten applied this Nash equilibrium concept to sequential play and invented the concept of Nash equilibrium in a proper subgame of sequential play.

Some nodes of the game tree, such as *R2* in the bottom half of Figure 13.4 and the subgames thereafter, can be eliminated from consideration because they cannot be reached by best-reply responses. Such decision points are "off the equilibrium path." Selten's idea was that only in the proper subgame nodes would the Nash equilibrium concept hold. Specifically, the $380,000 outcome in the next-to-bottom row of Figure 13.4 is the highest payoff in the entire exercise. Yet, the manufacturer should not consider this logical possibility precisely because *M3* and beyond is not a proper subgame; the payoffs {$60,000 and $380,000} cannot be reached by best-reply responses. Knowing that the manufacturer never cooperatively advertises a product that has not been updated, the retailer at *R2* rejects *Continue* in favor of a best-reply response *Discontinue*, to capture $130,000 rather than the alternative which yields only $60,000. Subgame perfect equilibrium strategy requires analyzing the outcomes associated with actions and best-reply responses at *R1* and *M2*, the only proper subgame nodes of Figure 13.4.[17] Again, {*Update, Discontinue, Advertise*} proves then to be the subgame perfect equilibrium strategy for Manufacturer–Distributor II.

Sometimes this identification of proper and improper subgames can get quite complicated when many endgames are possible. To illustrate, consider the three-way comparative advertising duel in Exercise 6 at the end of this chapter. With varying degrees of success, three firms attack one another with combative advertising in pair wise, sequential competitions until just one firm remains. It can take two complete rounds of advertising attacks and almost 20 endgames to analyze the subgame perfect equilibrium strategy for that problem.

---

[17]The reader may wonder about the relevance of *M1* if a miscommunication or strategic mistake is made by the retail distributor at node *R1*. This concern is valid because mistakes and miscommunication do happen in the reality of business rivalry. Indeed, a refinement of subgame perfect equilibrium strategy allows for just such mistakes and describes equilibrium strategy for the manufacturer in this game less uniquely as {Update and Advertise if Retailer Discontinues} but {Update and Do Not Advertise if Retailer Makes a Strategic Mistake and Continues}.

BUSINESS RIVALRY AS A SELF-ENFORCING SEQUENTIAL GAME

It is important to emphasize that the subgame perfect equilibrium concept is self-enforcing. It predicts stable rival response, not because of effective monitoring and third-party enforcement, but because each party would be worse off departing from the equilibrium strategy pair than it would be implementing it. Ultimately, it is this best-reply response idea that identifies whether a commitment is credible. And credibility can work both ways; credible commitments can also become credible threats. Let's see how.

Consider a well-established pharmaceutical manufacturer of ulcer relief medicine, who presently markets the only effective ulcer therapy, possessing no known side effects, and earns $100,000. This incumbent (let's call the firm "Pastense") faces a small potential entrant ("Potent" for short). Potent has discovered a new therapeutic process that also has the potential to cure stomach ulcers. Potent must decide whether to enter the monopoly market or stay out and license its trade secrets to any one of several interested buyers. Pastense must decide whether to maintain its present high prices, moderate its prices, or radically discount its prices. The payoffs are displayed in Figure 13.5. If the potential entrant Potent enters, and the incumbent Pastense does not moderate or discount to lower price points, suppose all the ulcer relief business goes to the new entrant and the incumbent realizes nothing. In contrast, with entry and discount prices, suppose the incumbent's product enjoys a slight cost advantage and earns a $10,000 greater payoff (i.e., $50,000 and $40,000 in the third row of Figure 13.5). Moderate incumbent prices result in a $35,000 payoff for Pastense and a $50,000 payoff for Potent.

Example

Business Gaming at Verizon[18]

Former Verizon CEO Ray Smith employed the techniques, exercises, and lessons of game theory throughout his organization. In "war games," teams of Verizon managers assumed the role of major competitors and explored tactics that could defeat Verizon's business plans. Other teams detailed future contingencies in a large game tree that allowed Verizon to map its future moves and countermoves as well as uncover the competitive effects of new technological developments (e.g., digital voice and video transmission) before they happened. In contrast to such selective scenario planning informed by game theory, traditional business planning models lock managers into assumptions the importance of which they can only gauge through sensitivity analysis. But sequential game analysis constantly reminds managers to shape the game, not just play it. It can mean reversing the order of play by recommending preemptive strikes in some circumstances (e.g., merging with Nynex) but highlighting the value of "fast-second" best-reply responses in other circumstances (e.g., in following rather than leading basic research and product development at Lucent Technologies).

In addition, Verizon has learned to recognize endgames that are unfavorable to their company and reshape the structure of the competitive rivalry in those businesses. Verizon recently redefined the scope of the telephone industry's local network strategy game by winning approval in the courts for telephone companies to own the content transmitted over their phone lines. Verizon managers are now hard at work analyzing the new larger game that includes business directories, digitized movies, and video production.

---

[18]Based on "Business as a War Game: Report from the Battlefront," *Fortune* (September 30, 1996), pp. 190–193.

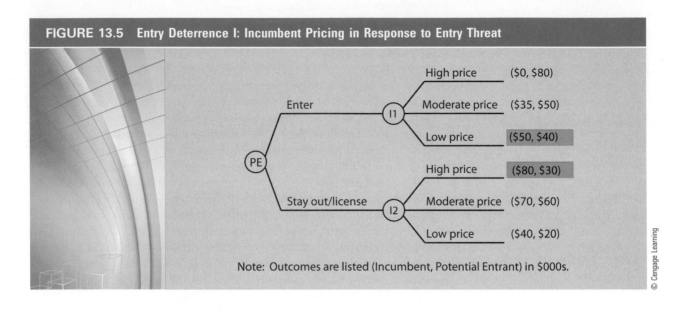

FIGURE 13.5 Entry Deterrence I: Incumbent Pricing in Response to Entry Threat

Note: Outcomes are listed (Incumbent, Potential Entrant) in $000s.

© Cengage Learning

To prevent the reduction of its profit from $100,000 as a monopolist to $50,000 post entry, Pastense itself might be a prime candidate for the purchase of Potent's trade secret. Realistically, however, it is liable to run up against antitrust constraints that restrict mergers between dominant incumbents and new entrants. Note also from node I2 in Figure 13.5 that what another established pharmaceutical manufacturer will pay to license the trade secret, with all the attendant technology transfer and marketing challenges, bears little correlation to what Potent itself could hope to earn upon entry. Potent receives its second highest payoff ($60,000) when it licenses its trade secret in a moderate price environment. Potent earns the least (namely, $20,000) when it stays out and licenses, and Pastense discounts anyway.

First-Mover and Fast-Second Advantages

As is now obvious, "Who can do what, when?" is the essence of any sequential strategy game. The order of play determines who initiates and who replies, which determines the best-reply response in the endgame, and thus the strategic equilibrium. If Potent enters, Pastense strongly prefers a Low pricing response, because $50,000 far exceeds the zero or $35,000 outcomes from either the High or Moderate alternatives. This analysis of the incumbent's best-reply response allows Potent to predict that its own $80,000 and $50,000 outcomes are infeasible. Even though each is theoretically associated with its entry, neither can be obtained if Pastense makes a best-reply response in this proper subgame.

Similarly, in the bottom endgame node I2, if Potent stays out, its royalty payoffs of $60,000 cannot be obtained, because Pastense will price High to secure $80,000 for itself rather than accept its lower $70,000 and $40,000 alternatives. Only two **focal outcomes of interest** remain for Potent in making its entry decision: the shaded payoffs of $40,000 from entering and $30,000 from staying out. Being a value-maximizing firm, Potent decides to enter, predictably, and the events of the subgame perfect strategic equilibrium {Enter, Discount} then unfold. Notice that both players could be better off with the {$70,000, $60,000} outcome in the lower node, but neither can get to that outcome. Potent cannot expect Pastense to respond with Moderate rather than High prices should Potent stay out and license.

focal outcomes of interest Payoffs involved in an analysis of equilibrium strategy.

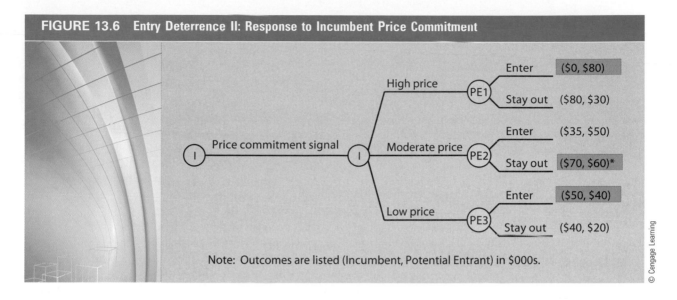

FIGURE 13.6   Entry Deterrence II: Response to Incumbent Price Commitment

Note: Outcomes are listed (Incumbent, Potential Entrant) in $000s.

© Cengage Learning

However, to illustrate the pivotal importance of the order of play, let's mix things up a bit. From the incumbent's point of view, too, the outcomes {$50,000, $40,000} are not entirely satisfactory. Given its second-mover timing, Pastense did as well as could be expected. But the incumbent may wonder whether seizing the first-mover initiative would have worked to its advantage. However, no general rule on this point exists—sometimes it will, and sometimes it will not. Each sequential game situation is in this way quite different and the analysis that "solves" a strategy game is often unique.

To analyze the question about reversing the order of play in Entry Deterrence II, we present Figure 13.6. Now, the potential entrant controls the endgame, and the incumbent must announce irreversible pricing policies in advance. Saying they are irreversible does not make it so, but more on that in the next section. Analyzing the three endgame nodes, Pastense realizes that Potent will choose to enter when high prices are precommitted, stay out when moderate prices are precommitted, and enter when discount prices are precommitted. Knowing these outcomes, Pastense announces a moderate pricing policy, and the starred {Moderate, Stay Out} strategic equilibrium is the predictable result. Not only has the potential entrant's behavior changed, but in addition, the payoff to Pastense has risen from $50,000 to $70,000. In this instance, a first-mover advantage proved to be just what the name implies.

Example

Technology Leader or Fast-Second: IBM[19]

Whether to secure first-mover advantages in the development of new computing technologies or instead engage in a pattern of quick imitation (i.e., a fast-second strategy) poses a more difficult choice than one might think. In the absence of sunk-cost investments as a barrier to entry, hit-and-run entry often proves effective. Apple Computer commercialized the graphical user interface (GUI) that Xerox invented, and Apple's breathtaking but unsuccessful Newton led the way for Palm to develop an early handheld digital device that was, in its time, very successful indeed. Microsoft made a fast-second and very successful challenge to Netscape's early dominance of Internet browsers. And Sun Microsystems appropriated successfully the reduced

(continued)

instruction-set computing (RISC) that IBM pioneered. Even in consumer perishables, Dunkin' Donuts' Coolatta is a fast second imitation of one of Starbucks' most profitable offerings, Frappuccino.

By restraining up-front investments in basic research and focusing instead on the development of products, IBM switched from a technology leader to a "first of a kind" systems problem solver for high-margin hospital, commercial developer, and information system customers. One example has been a blending of computer imaging and voice-recognition devices that allows hospital radiologists and surgeons to superimpose X-ray images and text on any personal computer (PC) throughout the local area network in a medical center. Doctors speak to one another while viewing PC-based images, and the IBM hardware and software creates a digital transcript of their diagnostic findings and expert opinions.

On the other hand, IBM Microelectronics division leveraged the company's long-standing basic R&D effort in materials science into a breakthrough in silicon chips. IBM's engineers discovered how to form copper rather than aluminum circuits and yet prevent the copper atoms from bleeding into the surface of the silicon. Copper is a more conductive material and therefore can be laid down in narrower circuits than aluminum. The more circuits etched on a square centimeter of silicon, the more powerful and cost effective the computer chip. IBM's copper on silicon circuitry patent increased computing power 40 percent for any given size chip.

Therefore sometimes first-movers have the advantage. At other times, fast second is advantageous. And sometimes it's last movers that come out on top. Each game-theoretic problem is different and must be analyzed on its own merits.

---

[19]Based on "Einstein and Eraser-Heads," *Wall Street Journal* (October 6, 1997), p. 1.

CREDIBLE THREATS AND COMMITMENTS

credible threat A conditional strategy the threat-maker is worse off ignoring than implementing.

In multiperiod games, the credibility of all threats and commitments ultimately derives from whether the threat-maker or commitment maker successfully identifies and adopts subgame perfect strategies. In Entry Deterrence I (see Figure 13.5), Pastense's threat to discount the ulcer relief medicine if Potent entered was credible precisely because discounting was, in fact, a best-reply response. Any other response would have made Pastense worse off (i.e., lowered its payoff). A **credible threat** is therefore defined as a conditional strategy that the threat-maker is worse off ignoring than implementing. By the same token, a commitment by Pastense to maintain high prices (i.e., not to discount and thereby spoil the royalty value of Potent's trade secret) if Potent would stay out of the market is a credible commitment. Again, the reason is that this action is the incumbent's best-reply response to Potent's staying out and just earning royalties from the ongoing value of its trade secret. Therefore, without any monitoring or third-party enforcement whatsoever, one can fully rely upon Pastense to honor its commitment, because it would not be in its own best interest to do otherwise.

In Figure 13.5, if Potent wanted to secure a commitment from Pastense to price at the *moderate* level in exchange for some portion of the much larger $60,000 royalties, Potent would need to employ a binding, third-party-enforceable contractual agreement. It is simply not in Pastense's best-reply-response interest to fulfill such a commitment otherwise.

You can now begin to see why purposeful individual behavior and a shared objective in groups are so critical to game theory reasoning. To predict choices of highly interdependent players, one must know what makes them tick, what true goals they seek, and what the consequence of various actions is on those goals, which is sometimes harder than it sounds. For example, performance-based incentives and takeover threats often align management objectives quite closely with stockholder value, but what motivates a closely held family-run business is sometimes difficult to fathom. Moreover, consistently transmitted signals of business strategy are often jammed by competitors or misinterpreted by the receiver. Therefore, to ensure the effective communication of credible threats and credible commitments requires some guidelines. This situation can be illustrated by returning to the "Entry Deterrence" game.

As we have seen, Pastense found the switch to first-mover status highly advantageous. By committing to maintain moderate prices rather than discount, its profits increased from $50,000 to $70,000 when Potent sold out rather than entered. The question we must now reexamine, however, is "Why did Potent believe Pastense would maintain Moderate prices?" After all, it is clear from the original game tree in Figure 13.5 that once Potent licensed its trade secret to another less capable potential entrant (let's call the new firm "Impotent"), Pastense was really better off raising its price back to the high level it had once enjoyed. Note that thereby Pastense would then receive the $80,000 payoff from high prices rather than a smaller $70,000 payoff from moderate prices. Thus, Pastense's commitment to maintain a moderate price was not a **credible commitment** because Pastense was worse off making good on the commitment than ignoring it.

One might be inclined to respond that likewise Potent can renege on its commitment to stay out of the ulcer relief business. Licensing a trade secret for royalty revenue today need not preclude Potent's potential entry tomorrow. Indeed, such royalty agreements seldom include a no-competition clause. However, the difference here is that Potent's payoff is maximized by staying out! Its commitment to staying out if the incumbent maintains moderate prices *is* in Potent's own best interest. Staying out is a best-reply response; therefore it is a credible commitment.

credible commitment
A promise that the promise-giver is worse off violating than fulfilling.

MECHANISMS FOR ESTABLISHING CREDIBILITY[20]

As second mover, Potent controls the endgame and therefore finds itself in a position to insist on the necessary assurances from Pastense. Among the alternative mechanisms for establishing credibility, Pastense might establish *a bond or contractual side payment*, which would be forfeited if Pastense raised prices. Some such contracts, referred to as *maximum resale price maintenance agreements*, do exist between retailers and their suppliers. Another possible credibility mechanism would be for Pastense to invest heavily in its moderate price strategy to establish a reputation for moderate prices. Loss of this **non-redeployable reputational asset** would discourage reneging on its commitment to maintain moderate prices. Third, Pastense could *short-circuit* or *interrupt* the repricing process by preselling its ulcer relief medicine with forward contracts. Forward sale contracts establish credible commitments because the courts generally refuse to excuse forward or futures contract breaches for any reason. Fourth, Pastense could enter into *teamwork* or *an alliance relationship* with Potent that would sufficiently dilute the

non-redeployable reputational asset A reputation whose value is lost if sold or licensed.

---

[20]This section relies heavily on A. Dixit and B. Nalebuff, *Thinking Strategically: The Competitive Edge in Business, Politics, and Everyday Life* (New York: Norton, 1993), especially Chapters 5 and 6.

rewards from reneging on its commitment, perhaps by taking an equity stake in Potent. Fifth, Pastense could change the structure of the game to require that both it and Potent only "take small steps." In the next section, we analyze leasing as a way to pursue this small-steps credibility mechanism.

And finally, the most practical response to this situation would be for Pastense to arrange an irreversible and irrevocable hostage mechanism, whereby likely future customers were granted a moderate price guarantee. Sometimes referred to as "most favored nation" clauses, these price guarantees promise double refunds if the customer discovers any lower-price Pastense transaction during the next year. As long as Potent observed at least one moderate price transaction before licensing its trade secret, it could rest assured that Pastense had now offered a credible commitment not to raise prices. The resulting double refunds, should Pastense raise prices, and the sacrifice of future transactions with its own repeat-purchase customers, should it renege on the refunds, ensure that Pastense will finally be better off honoring its commitment to moderate prices than ignoring it. And again, notice that these agreements are entirely self-enforcing; no third party needs to be relied upon to make the rival behaviors predictable; the parties themselves have every reason to ensure it.

Example

Double-the-Difference Price Guarantees: Best Buy

At times, Best Buy offers to rebate twice the differential purchase price of a DVD player to preferred customers should those customers find the same DVD player selling for less anywhere in the local area over the next three months. This double-the-difference rebate guarantee will be enforced by the courts. As in the simultaneous-play pricing game between PepsiCo and Coca-Cola, Best Buy normally would be better off discounting (maybe even steeply discounting) when competitors such as hhgregg and Sound Warehouse maintain high prices. But in the face of this double-the-difference low-price guarantee, Best Buy would lose more money on rebates than it could possibly gain from any amount of incremental business it could reasonably expect to take away from the competitors. In effect, Best Buy has given its competitors a hostage that supports a commitment to maintain high prices.

In Figure 13.7, Best Buy provides a bond of its intentions to maintain high prices by preannouncing the double-the-difference price guarantee. Sound Warehouse must then decide whether to discount or maintain high prices in light of the Best Buy rebate program. Like all good hostage mechanisms, the hostage is worth more to the hostage giver than its value in use to the recipient. That is, Sound Warehouse *could* trigger double-rebate payments at Best Buy by discounting its own price. And harming a competitor is a reasonable secondary goal, but it's only secondary. Securing your own highest payoff perhaps through legal cooperation with a competitor is the primary goal. Because Best Buy would respond to a Sound Warehouse discount by matching the lower price point, Sound Warehouse would gain no additional market share by using the hostage in this way. Indeed, for the hostage recipient such a decision would lead to the payoff labeled "Worse" in the top right-hand corner of Figure 13.7.

Knowing that Best Buy controls the endgame and that it would be in Best Buy's best interest after announcing the rebate program to match a discount price, Sound Warehouse finds itself preferring to maintain high prices. Because Best Buy is also best off by maintaining high prices, the payoff {Best*, Better} results. Thus, by introducing a price guarantee that limited its own ability to take advantage of its

(continued)

opponent's vulnerability at high prices, Best Buy secured first-best outcomes when the alternative was Worse (i.e., compare the shaded and nonshaded boxed payoffs in Figure 13.7). A **hostage mechanism** that establishes one's credible commitment to maintain high prices if the rival maintains high prices will often elicit high prices from that rival. Thus, from the point of view of both companies, double-the-difference low-price guarantees are unambiguously preferred. Of course, consumer advocates will not rejoice, but complaining about double-the-difference price guarantees attracts few sympathizers to the consumer cause.

REPLACEMENT GUARANTEES

hostage mechanism
An exchange of assets that is worth more to the hostage giver than to the hostage recipient in order to establish credibility of threats or commitments.

As we discussed in Chapter 10, all buyers rationally discount experience goods such as used cars and computer components if they cannot verify independently at the point of purchase the seller's quality claims. A replacement guarantee or a product performance repair warranty are other good examples of hostage mechanisms—in this case, hostage mechanisms that establish the credibility of a seller's commitment to deliver high-quality components in the goods it offers for sale. Should the seller violate his or her commitment, a third party (usually the courts) will impose on the seller monetary judgments that are larger than the incremental cost of upgrading from lower to higher quality inputs in the first place. Therefore, the buyer is assured of a higher quality machine

FIGURE 13.7 Double-the-Difference Price Guarantees

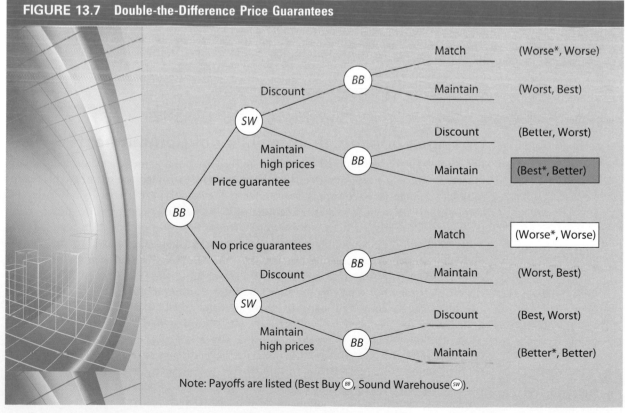

Note: Payoffs are listed (Best Buy ⒷⒷ, Sound Warehouse ⓈⓌ).

when the seller offers to include a replacement guarantee or repair warranty for the same (or a slightly higher) price. These guarantees and warranties illustrate a *credible commitment* mechanism (i.e., third-party-enforceable promises that the promise-giver would be worse off violating than keeping).

What exactly constitutes a credible replacement guarantee? Claims by Dooney & Bourke handbags, Revo sunglasses, and Sewell Cadillac for lifetime repair or replacement provide credible commitments. Why? The key is repeat customer business. Because incremental sales to established or referral customers are much less expensive than attracting new customers, the customer-for-life relationships at these companies provide a hostage mechanism. Dooney & Bourke's, Revo's, or Sewell Cadillac's normally preposterous replacement or service guarantees backed by a brand name, unique distribution channel, or other non-redeployable asset become credible because of the seller's dependence on repeat or referral business. In effect, Sewell Cadillac says, "My sunk cost investments cannot be recovered (and, by definition, cannot be liquidated at anything near their historical cost) unless I earn your repeat business."

Example

Noncredible Commitments: Burlington Industries

Classic examples of business strategies that flounder because of the absence of credible commitments include the quota "commitments" in a cartel and the "commitment" not to compete after purchasing surplus equipment in a declining industry. Burlington Industries has experienced many problems with its overseas sales of old textile looms, often acquired in mergers and then liquidated at scrap value. The foreign buyers restore the old equipment and then back ship their production into the United States despite no-competition clauses in the equipment purchase contracts. Burlington has now begun to destroy old equipment, not just dismantle it, especially in declining product lines where it wishes to pursue a niche strategy as "the last iceman." The idea is to preserve high margins by becoming the last company in one's locality to sell block ice to cruising boat owners or to wedding planners for ice sculptures. To this purpose, IBM bought up Amdahl Millennium and Hitachi Skyline mainframe computers and physically crushed them in a scrap yard.

Hostages Support the Credibility of Commitments

In Chapter 10 we encountered a noncooperative sequential games mechanism for securing cooperation in a repeated Prisoner's Dilemma game through the use of credible commitments. Potentially notorious firms selling low-quality experience goods (e.g., PC components) for high prices were identifiable in Table 10.2 as firms with entirely redeployable assets. That is, firms selling out of temporary locations, with unbranded products and no company reputation, could be reasonably expected to follow the dominant strategy of producing low quality. Consider ENow components illustrated in Figure 13.8. This company is not likely to plan on more than one transaction with any customer. It may not even plan on doing business through its present post office box or e-business site for long. Consequently, these are firms to whom no customer should offer a high price.

On the other hand, we argued that firms who asked high prices but also exhibited verifiable sunk cost investments that dissipate the rent from such prices were much better bets. Reputational advertising of nontransferable company logos (e.g., Apple Inc. or CarMax) or investment in non-redeployable assets, such as product-specific showrooms (Ethan Allen furniture) and unique retail displays (L'eggs hosiery), present a hostage to

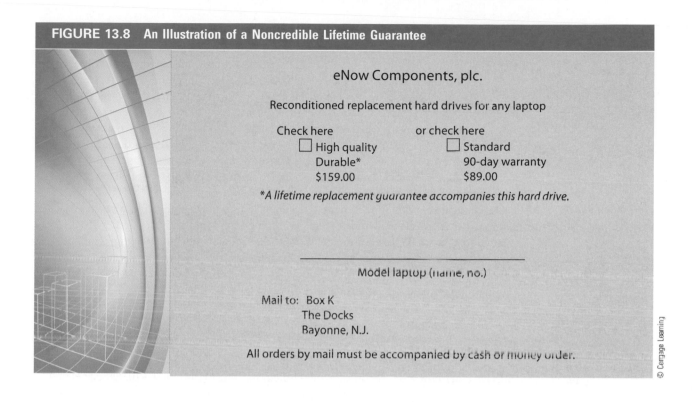

FIGURE 13.8   An Illustration of a Noncredible Lifetime Guarantee

eNow Components, plc.

Reconditioned replacement hard drives for any laptop

Check here   or check here
☐ High quality   ☐ Standard
   Durable*   90-day warranty
   $159.00 $89.00

A lifetime replacement guarantee accompanies this hard drive.

Model laptop (name, no.)

Mail to: Box K
          The Docks
          Bayonne, N.J.

All orders by mail must be accompanied by cash or money order.

© Cengage Learning

buyers. Because sellers offering hostages are worse off if they fail to deliver on the promise of high quality, a buyer can rely on these credible commitments even if unable to verify quality at the point of purchase. Although the credible commitments are noncontractual in nature, they establish reliance relationships that are as predictable as enforceable contracts.

Finally, credibility arises from cooperative game mechanisms that involve binding (third-party-enforceable) contracts such as franchise agreements, escrow bonds, and refund guarantees. These contractual mechanisms also provide hostages that support win-win exchange despite a dominant strategy that would otherwise lead players to defect. The key to the credibility of such mechanisms is the same as in noncooperative games. First, in the light of its warranty obligations, is the promise-giver better off fulfilling its promise than ignoring it? And second, can the warranty or bond *be revoked* for any reason other than just causes the promise-giver cannot control? If the answer to both questions is yes, then these contractual commitments are credible and consistent with best-reply response. If not, then they are noncredible and should not be relied upon.

Credible Commitments of Durable Goods Monopolists

What buyers will pay for a capital equipment purchase, such as a corporate jet, a mainframe computer, or a business license depends in part on how well the seller resolves some credible commitment issues. If a piece of durable equipment has a working life that will extend over several market periods, an early adopter of a new model worries about (1) obsolescence risk, (2) uncertain reliability of the new technology, and (3) the risk of falling prices subsequent to his or her purchase. How well a manufacturer addresses these three perceived risks of buying early will determine the rate of adoption and the prices paid to acquire new capital equipment.

Planned Obsolescence

The competitive advantages Cisco's newest data servers might offer an information technology user such as a direct marketer are seriously compromised whenever Cisco introduces a still newer model and makes the direct marketer's machine obsolete. In addition, other potential buyers who see somewhat less advantage in the newest server equipment will likely benefit from a Cisco price reduction at some later date. Knowing these likelihoods, the first buyers will hesitate, adopt later, and offer to pay less than they otherwise would for Cisco's new technology. To overcome this persistent problem that comes with every new generation of equipment, Cisco must somehow credibly commit to maintaining high prices and to a controlled rate of planned obsolescence that allows early buyers time to recover their investment costs.

In an industry with slow-moving technology, a dominant firm could make contractual commitments to phase in new updated equipment. At times, tractor-trailer trucks have been sold this way, and to a certain extent, the limited body style change from year to year in some automobile models (Mini Coopers, Camrys, and Accords) reflects the same idea. However, in the data server industry, Cisco cannot afford such restrictions; the competing technology simply moves too fast.

Example

Resale Value of a Mini Cooper[21]

BMW's Mini Cooper has the highest resale value after five years as a percentage of the purchase price of all autos sold in the United States ($11,800 on a $20,000 car, or 59 percent). On average, American cars are worth only 35 percent of their purchase price after five years. The giant land yacht Ford Expedition is worth the least—only 19 percent. Toyota has the highest average resale value across manufacturers after three years—52 percent—to General Motors' 43 percent.

[21]Based on "Value-Packed Vehicles," *Forbes* (November 2, 2006), pp. 51–53; and "U.S. Auto-Makers Fail to Improve Resale Value," *Wall Street Journal* (November 19, 2008), p. D3.

versioning A new product rollout strategy to encourage early adoption at higher prices.

So what alternatives remain? The buyers of durable equipment can't be expected to risk a lot of capital soon after the rollout of a new model; yet, companies such as Cisco cannot lock themselves in to delays of the future upgrades. One approach is to continuously upgrade the product at higher and higher prices, what Carl Shapiro and Hal Varian call **versioning**.[22] Microsoft adopted this continuous upgrade strategy with its Windows operating system and Apple has done the same with its iPhones. The buyer was told, in effect, not to hesitate and wait for the price to fall; the next model will be even more expensive. But of course competitive pressure may keep that from happening as technologies morph from patent-holding monopolies to fast-second imitators.

Moreover, even if no competing product appears in the marketplace, Cisco's operating systems are not consumed on the spot; they don't wear out. Like any durable goods monopolist, Cisco is perceived by the potential early adopters to be competing against itself. Similarly, Microsoft's biggest competitor for Windows 8 is Windows 7, just as the best substitute for Windows 7 was Windows XP. Another approach altogether is needed. One is to ask buyers to take small steps by leasing the equipment one market period at a time. Recall that this was one of the mechanisms we identified earlier in the chapter for establishing the credibility of commitments. Although this approach fails to slow (and

[22]See C. Shapiro and H. Varian, "Versioning: The Smart Way to Sell Information," *Harvard Business Review* (November–December 1998), pp. 106–118.

may actually quicken) the pace of new product introductions, buyers risk less up-front capital and therefore can be induced more easily to take on the new model and update their capital equipment more frequently *at higher prices.*

IBM employed exactly this approach for many years by offering only to lease its mainframe computers. Similarly, Dell Computer advertises, "How many companies will let you return your computer when it becomes obsolete?" and leases its PCs for $99 per month with the opportunity to renew for a new updated computer two years later. And BMW auto leases provide bumper-to-bumper scheduled maintenance and unexpected repairs for the lifetime of the lease. So leasing mitigates obsolescence and maintenance risk. But what about the early adopters' risk of subsequent price reductions? How does leasing address that risk?

Post-Purchase Discounting Risk

Understanding the tactical advantage of leasing requires careful analysis of the manufacturer's asymmetric information in making planned obsolescence and price discount decisions. Because the manufacturer knows the marketing plans and can estimate the pace of technology and the risk of obsolescence much better than the end-user customer, lease terms can be more favorable when the seller undertakes to absorb the risk of price promotions and planned obsolescence. That is, in a competitive marketplace for capital equipment leases (such as corporate jet leases), one would expect sellers to offer closed-end leases with guaranteed residual values.

The fixed residual offered when you return a leased corporate jet at the end of two-year lease reflects the lessor's accurate estimate of what a two-year-old corporate jet will be worth. This fixed residual value is what really establishes the credibility of the manufacturer's commitment over the lease period to refrain from discounting or introducing a new model that would render the current model obsolete. If the lessor violates his promise, the assets returned at the end of the lease would be worth less than the residual value at which the manufacturer-lessor has agreed to take them back. In effect, the manufacturer has given a hostage to the leaseholder (the lessee). By agreeing to take back the capital equipment for a preset amount and dispose of it in the resale market, the manufacturer-lessor credibly commits to a limited set of price promotions and to a limited rate of planned obsolescence.

Example

Leasing Digital Moviehouse Projectors: Hughes-JVC[23]

For the first time this century, in 2009 U.S. households spent more on movie theater admissions ($9.87 billion) than on DVD purchases or rentals. Digital cameras and projectors are clearly involved. George Lucas's *Star Wars* movies are now filmed entirely on digital movie cameras. Cinema companies such as General Cinema and AMC Entertainment much prefer digital film over the 60-pound celluloid film prints five feet in diameter. Downloading compressed-signal digital films using high-speed secure data networks will allow the movie houses much more flexibility in their scheduling. In addition, the sound and projection quality will no longer deteriorate after a few dozen showings. The movie production companies also like the new technology because a full national rollout of a celluloid movie costs approximately $7,500,000 to produce the 5,000 prints required ($1,500 per print), and it necessitates a large fleet of trucks to move the film canisters about the country.

The biggest hurdle to the fast adoption of this new technology is the $70,000 replacement cost for each of the projectors in a multiplex cinema. With the U.S.

(continued)

movie theatre industry badly overbuilt (some estimates suggest by as many as 10,000 more cinemas than are needed), General Cinema, AMC Entertainment and others are understandably hesitant to commit three-quarters of a million dollars of additional capital per ten-screen movie house.

Hughes-JVC, who manufactures one of the projectors, plans to lease the digital projectors to theatre companies using closed-end lease with fixed residuals. Hughes-JVC will therefore be credibly committed to fewer subsequent price promotions and a slower rate of planned obsolescence. In addition, with digital rather than physical distribution, leasing fees for the projectors can be tied to actual showings. This will allow cinemas in overbuilt markets to participate in earlier adoption of the new technology.

[23]Based on "Curtains for Celluloid," *The Economist* (March 27, 1999), p. 81; and "Moving Images into the Future," *The Economist* (December 6, 2008), pp. 8–10; and "Cinema Surpasses DVD Sales," *Wall Street Journal* (January 4, 2010), p. B10; "Movie Theatres Secure Financing for Digital Upgrades," *Wall Street Journal*, (February 25, 2010), p. B4.

Example

NetJets Fractional Ownership Plans for Learjet and Gulfstream Aircraft and Lexus[24]

FlexJets offers guaranteed access on four hours' notice to a fleet of Learjet and Challenger business aircraft for as little as $175,000 per year cost. NetJets, a division of Warren Buffett's Berkshire Hathaway company, offers fractional shares in "the world's largest and finest fleet of 450 Gulfstream aircraft with guaranteed availability, guaranteed costs, and guaranteed liquidity of your asset." NetJets expects to schedule more than 500,000 flights next year. A one-sixteenth share of a Citation seven-passenger jet leases for a $620,000 up-front commitment, a $7,909 monthly fee, plus $1,675 per flight hour to cover operating cost. These contractual arrangements are operating leases with fixed residuals.

To illustrate how crucial these fractional ownership-leasing arrangements are in protecting the early adopter against resale price risk, consider a $44 million Gulfstream VI. This top-of-the-line business jet typically has a book value at 24 months of $2–$28 million, but sold as a two-year-old used aircraft in late 2002 for only $18 million. Similarly, the resale value of two-year-old Lexus LS 430s and Saab 9-5s went down by 23.4 percent from $53,500 to $41,000 in 2002, compared to a 14.7 percent reduction for two-year-old models one year earlier. Again, either lessor or lessee must bear these repricing risks, but closed-end leasing with fixed residual values offers a credible commitment from manufacturers to early adopters that the seller will not flood the market at discounted prices before the early adopter's equipment needs to be replaced. Closed-end leases with a fixed residual value have therefore grown to 29 percent of all U.S. auto sales in the luxury car segment.

[24]"Prices on Private Planes Dive," *Wall Street Journal* (September 5, 2002), p. B2; and "The Bargain Jaguar," *Wall Street Journal* (March 20, 2003), p. D1.

For example, by selecting a cable television provider as a renewable license, a municipality can credibly limit the supply of the city's communication infrastructure. If the city were to insist on an outright purchase, cable entrepreneurs would be concerned that soon thereafter the city would flood the market with additional cable companies. Consequently, the amounts bid for the right to do business would decline substantially.

Licenses authorizing a business are a property right that the license holders may need to resell. Random events happen to every company, and license holders cannot assume that they will be able to operate forever. Licenses are durable capital assets, and their resale value is as much a concern as would be the value of a mainframe computer or corporate jet. Municipalities can raise more money, therefore, with renewable leases for all business licenses. What occurs in business licensing by municipal and state governments also occurs in the licensing of trade secrets and patents. Even though renewable licensing and leasing offer tactical advantages in establishing credible commitments not obtainable with outright sales, competitive market leasing will not be cheaper than buying. Any costs imposed on the seller by the credibility mechanisms (e.g., a higher residual value) will be priced into the lease. The point is simply that some credible commitments impose additional costs on the asymmetrically informed manufacturer as a lessor that are lower than the reduction in price that would be required to accomplish a comparable sale. Consequently, manufacturer profitability increases with renewable licensing and leasing, relative to the alternative profitability available from the outright sale of durable equipment, business licenses, or patents.

Lease Prices Reflect Anticipated Risks

Of course, the risk of technological developments and competitor discounts that the manufacturer cannot control still remain. The lessor and lessee have credibly committed some things and left others to chance. All such remaining risks will be priced into the terms of the residual value lease. As a result, over the lifetime of the equipment it will not be cheaper to lease rather than to buy. In other words, the buyer who chooses an extensive repair and replacement warranty contract is imposing on the seller-lessor (e.g., BMW) the risk of product failure; this risk is then fully priced into a higher lease payment for a 3 Series BMW.

closed-end leases with fixed residual values A credible commitment mechanism for limiting the depth of price promotions and the rate of planned obsolescence.

Nevertheless, manufacturers need some way of credibly committing themselves to maintaining high asking prices and a limited rate of planned obsolescence over the buyer's holding period. Only then will early adopters pay the higher prices manufacturers wish to charge in the early mature phase of an upgraded product's life cycle. **Closed-end leases with fixed residual values** offer such a credible commitment because they demonstrate and certify just what the manufacturer's best estimates of forward value truly are. Such leases therefore raise the acquisition prices early adopters of durable equipment are willing to pay.

SUMMARY

- Proactive oligopolists require accurate predictions of rival initiatives and rival response. The managerial purpose of game theory is to predict just such rival behavior. In a *game theory* analysis, each rival analyzes its competitors' optimal decision-making strategy and then chooses its own best counterstrategy.

- Business strategy games may be classified as simultaneous-play or sequential-play, one-shot or repeated, zero-sum or nonzero-sum, two-player or *n*-player, and cooperative or noncooperative.

- *Cooperative games* allow coalition formation, side payment agreements, and third-party enforceable contracts, whereas noncooperative games prohibit these characteristics.

- Simultaneous-play games occasionally arise in pricing and promotion rivalry, but the essence of business strategy is sequential reasoning.
- Dominant strategy equilibrium entails actions that maximize at least one decision maker's payoff, no matter what any other player chooses to do.
- Nash equilibrium strategy involves actions that maximize each decision maker's payoff, given best-reply responses of the other players.
- Nash equilibrium for simultaneous games identifies both pure and mixed strategies. Stability of tactical prediction arises from the fact that the players' choices reflect best-reply reactions to one another, even though no sequential timing of the actions is involved.
- Most Nash equilibrium strategies are nonunique; multiple pure Nash strategies exist.
- Mixed strategy provides an optimal rule for randomizing one's actions among multiple Nash equilibrium strategies.
- Mutual cooperation in a repeated Prisoner's Dilemma game can be secured with uncertain endgame timing, adoption of an industry standard, multiperiod punishment schemes such as Tit-for-Tat or grim trigger strategy, and strategic hostage or bonding mechanisms for establishing credible commitments and threats.
- Cooperation in noncooperative games is more likely if strategies are clear, provokable, take cooperative initiatives unilaterally, and are forgiving so as not to perpetuate mistakes. The Tit-for-Tat strategy has these characteristics.
- Playing against Tit-for-Tat strategies necessitates comparing the additional profit from unilateral defection against the discounted opportunity loss from limited-duration certain punishment next period. As the probability of continued replay declines, Tit for Tat becomes a less-effective coordination device for escaping the Prisoner's Dilemma than a matching price policy.
- The order of play matters in sequential games of coordination between manufacturers and distributors, entry deterrence and accommodation, service competition, R&D races, product development, and so on, because rivals must predict best-reply responses and counter-responses all the way out to an endgame.
- Endgame reasoning looks ahead to the last play in an ordered sequence of plays, identifies the player whose decisions control the available outcomes in the endgame, and then predicts that player's preferred action.
- Subgame perfect equilibrium strategy looks ahead to analyze endgame outcomes and then reasons back to prior best-reply responses.
- Credible threats and credible commitments are the key to endgame reasoning, and therefore credibility mechanisms are the key to subgame perfect equilibrium strategy.
- Advantages may accrue to either first-movers or fast-seconds in a business rivalry. The former can credibly threaten or credibly precommit and therefore preempt some outcomes, whereas the latter replies and can determine the best-reply response in the endgame. Which is more advantageous depends on the particulars of the tactical and strategic situation.
- A credible threat is a conditional strategy the threat-maker is worse off ignoring than implementing. A credible commitment is an obligation the commitment maker is worse off ignoring than fulfilling.
- Mechanisms for establishing credibility include establishing a bond or contractual side payment, investing in a non-redeployable reputation asset, short-circuiting or interrupting the response process, entering into a profit-sharing alliance, taking small steps, or arranging an irreversible and irrevocable hostage mechanism.
- Closed-end leases with fixed residual values are a mechanism for establishing a durable goods manufacturer's credible commitment to early adopters of new models not to discount deeply after the sale.

Exercises

Answers to the exercises in blue can be found in Appendix D at the back of the book.

1. Suppose that two Japanese companies, Hitachi and Toshiba, are the sole producers (i.e., duopolists) of a microprocessor chip used in a number of different brands of personal computers. Assume that total demand for the chips is fixed and that each firm charges the same price for the chips. Each firm's market share and profits are a function of the magnitude of the promotional campaign used to promote its version of the chip. Also assume that only two strategies are available to each firm: a

limited promotional campaign (budget) and an extensive promotional campaign (budget). If the two firms engage in a limited promotional campaign, each firm will earn a quarterly profit of $7.5 million. If the two firms undertake an extensive promotional campaign, each firm will earn a quarterly profit of $5.0 million. With this strategy combination, market share and total sales will be the same as for a limited promotional campaign, but promotional costs will be higher and hence profits will be lower. If either firm engages in a limited promotional campaign and the other firm undertakes an extensive promotional campaign, then the firm that adopts the extensive campaign will increase its market share and earn a profit of $9 million, whereas the firm that chooses the limited campaign will earn a profit of only $4 million.

   a. Develop a payoff matrix for this decision-making problem.

   b. In the absence of a binding and enforceable agreement, determine the dominant advertising strategy and minimum payoff for Hitachi.

   c. Determine the dominant advertising strategy and minimum payoff for Toshiba.

   d. Explain why the firms may choose not to play their dominant strategies whenever this game is repeated over multiple decision-making periods.

2. Consider the following payoff matrix:

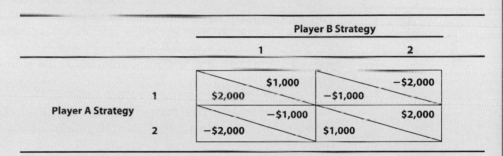

   a. Does Player A have a dominant strategy? Explain why or why not.

   b. Does Player B have a dominant strategy? Explain why or why not.

3. Suppose that two mining companies, Australian Minerals Company (AMC) and South African Mines, Inc. (SAMI), control the only sources of a rare mineral used in making certain electronic components. The companies have agreed to form a cartel to set the (profit-maximizing) price of the mineral. Each company must decide whether to *abide* by the agreement (i.e., not offer secret price cuts to customers) or *not abide* (i.e., offer secret price cuts to customers). If both companies abide by the agreement, AMC will earn an annual profit of $30 million and SAMI will earn an annual profit of $20 million from sales of the mineral. If AMC does not abide and SAMI abides by the agreement, then AMC earns $40 million and SAMI earns $5 million. If SAMI does not abide and AMC abides by the agreement, then AMC earns $10 million and SAMI earns $30 million. If both companies do not abide by the agreement, then AMC earns $15 million and SAMI earns $10 million.

   a. Develop a payoff matrix for this decision-making problem.

   b. In the absence of a binding and enforceable agreement, determine the dominant strategy for AMC.

   c. Determine the dominant strategy for SAMI.

   d. If the two firms can enter into a binding and enforceable agreement, determine the strategy that each firm should choose.

4. Two insurance companies that manage employee benefit programs are bidding for additional business in their area of expertise at a market rate of $200 per hour. The potential customers refuse to leave their current suppliers and award benefit management contracts to the new firms unless billing rates are cut by $50. Abbott, Abbott & Daughters (AA&D) decides to do just that. Your firm, Zekiel, Zekiel & Sons (ZZ&S), must decide whether to match the price cut and then allow customers to choose randomly between the two firms, or whether to lower rates still further to $100 per hour. Past experience suggests, however, that the price cutting may well not stop there. The clients will surely take their best current offer back and forth between the two firms, forcing a downward price spiral. The question therefore is, "How low will you go?" Crucially, this game has a stopping rule: At a price below the $40 cost, the additional business becomes unprofitable and must be refused. AA&D has higher costs at $66 per hour.

Again, your decision depends on an analysis of the sequence of predictable future events represented with a game tree or decision tree. Provide one. To simplify, assume that all rate cuts must be in $50 increments, that customers choose quickly between equal rate quotes using fair coin tosses (represented by capital letter N for *Nature*), that once a rate quote has been matched it cannot be lowered, and that many potential customers are present in the market. It is now your turn at node Z1 with rates at the $150-per-hour level. What should you do? Match rates or cut rates further?

5. How do the analysis and the strategic equilibrium outcome differ in Exercise 4 if the other firm enjoys a cost advantage (e.g., $35 at AA&D)? Then does the order of play (i.e., who goes first in making price cuts) matter in this bidding game with asymmetric costs?

6. Consider an ongoing sequence of pair wise marketing competitions between three companies with promotional campaigns of varying degrees of success. Each campaign involves comparative advertising belittling the target company. The company with the most loyal customers (call this firm "Most") enjoys 100 percent success when it attacks either of the others. The company with the least loyal customers ("Least") has a 30 percent success rate when it belittles either Most or "More." More experiences an 80 percent success rate. The firms each launch their advertising attacks one at a time in an arbitrary sequence. Least goes first and can attack either Most or More. More attacks second, and Most attacks third. If more than one of the opponents survives the first round of competition, the order of play repeats itself: Least, then More, then Most. Any player can skip his or her turn; that is, the three actions available to Least to initiate the game are as follows: attack More, attack Most, or do nothing and pass the turn.

Diagram the game tree and employ subgame perfect equilibrium analysis to identify the strategic equilibrium. What should the most vulnerable firm with the least loyal customers do to initiate play? What would be More's best-reply response if attacked and More survives? What if Least did nothing? What would Most do when and if its turn arose?

7. Why should the early adopters of an information technology system provided by IBM Systems Solutions be willing to pay more for a closed-end lease of the servers and other hardware required than for an outright purchase?

8. People who are regularly late often don't bother to carry watches. In response, other people tend to adjust to their tardiness by starting meetings 10 minutes after they're scheduled, coming to lunch appointments 10 minutes late, and so on. Analyze the following coordination game and explain why.

		Harry		Harry	
		Be Punctual		**Always Late**	
Tom	**Be Punctual**	100	100	50	70
	Always Late	70	50	95	95

9. Nike and Adidas face the following coordination problem in trying to decide whether to conduct heavy or light combative advertising against the other firm. What should each firm do?

		Nike		Nike	
		Light Ads		**Heavy Ads**	
Adidas	**Light Ads**	$10 M	$12 M	$4 M	$6 M
	Heavy Ads	$5 M	$4 M	$8 M	$9 M

10. The outcomes in the bottom half of the game tree describing the last (the 20th) submarket of the chain store paradox in Figure 13.2 are labeled NA (not applicable). Why? What specific equilibrium concept in sequential games rules out the applicability of these outcomes? *Hint:* How would you describe the game tree from node E onward as opposed to the game tree from node D onward?

11. The long competition between Subway and Quizno's subshops took price from $6 to $5 for selected Footlongs. Eventually, Quizno's dropped price another dollar to $4 with its Torpedo product. Market share rose for Quizno's relative to its head to head Footlong competition with Subway but margins suffered so much that Quizno's ingredient budgets had to be reduced substantially. Today, Subway specializes in upscale ingredients on six-inch $7 subs. Explain who came out ahead in this competition. How?

12. Suppose you have announced you will "meet the competition" in response to entry threats by a potential rival who has done marketing research in your target market and is offering a lower price point. What difference does it make, if any, if

technology is moving very fast in the market so that this game proves to be one-time-only simultaneous play?

13. Analyze the following sequential game and advise Kodak about whether they should introduce the new product, Picture CD.

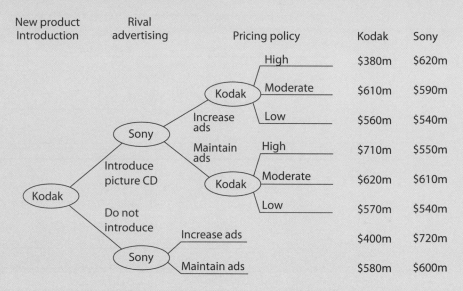

			Kodak	Sony
		High	$380m	$620m
		Moderate	$610m	$590m
		Low	$560m	$540m
		High	$710m	$550m
		Moderate	$620m	$610m
		Low	$570m	$540m
	Increase ads		$400m	$720m
	Maintain ads		$580m	$600m

14. Calculate the 8-hour-shift costs of operating a taxi with a medallion license that cost $125,000 borrowed at 10 percent interest assuming two shifts for 365 days per year, plus a $25,000 car that depreciates 50 percent in one year, plus $22 for gas and maintenance per shift per day. Would you pay $60 per shift for a taxi operator's license? Why or why not?

15. A math graduate student explains to her friend how to approach a group of smart attractive guys who have brought along famous actor Russell Crowe. What should her friend do? Ignore Russell Crowe or fixate on Russell Crowe? Explain the equilibrium reasoning underlying your answer.

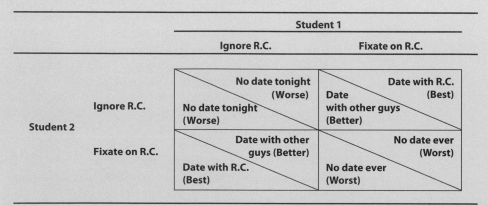

Note: Best payoff—date with R.C., Better—date with other guys, Worse—no date tonight, Worst—no date ever with any of these guys.

Case Exercises

INTERNATIONAL PERSPECTIVES

The Superjumbo Dilemma[25]

Boeing finishes assembly of wide-bodied commercial aircraft in several sizes at the rate of about one per day. Customers first pay a deposit of one-third of $84 to $127 million for a 767, one-third of $134 to $185 million for a 777, and one-third of $165 to $200 million for a 747, depending on how the planes are equipped. The second third is due after final assembly when the aircraft is painted, and the final third is due at delivery. Final assembly requires 15–25 days, the entire production schedule is 11 months long, and of course, design modifications add months to the front end of each project. The largest of the Boeing planes (the 747-400) carries 432 passengers; by comparison, the largest Airbus plane (the A380) carries 550 passengers.

As early as 1993, Boeing and Airbus entered into discussions to jointly develop a very large commercial transport (VLCT) with perhaps 1,000 seats. If each firm proceeded independently, the market for VLCTs is so small relative to the massive R&D costs that sizeable losses were assured. Either firm had superior profit available if it proceeded alone. Analyze this simultaneous play noncooperative product development game and predict what Boeing and Airbus would do and why.

In fact, both competitors decided to enter into a strategic alliance with the option to develop a superjumbo or withdraw and maintain a wide-bodied aircraft focus. Analyze Boeing's decision in light of its $45 million contribution margin on each 747 produced and sold. Net operating profit is about $15 million.

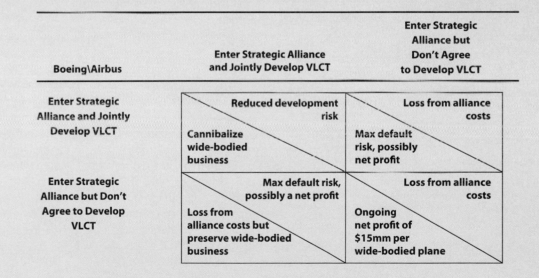

Boeing\Airbus	Enter Strategic Alliance and Jointly Develop VLCT	Enter Strategic Alliance but Don't Agree to Develop VLCT
Enter Strategic Alliance and Jointly Develop VLCT	Reduced development risk / Cannibalize wide-bodied business	Loss from alliance costs / Max default risk, possibly net profit
Enter Strategic Alliance but Don't Agree to Develop VLCT	Max default risk, possibly a net profit / Loss from alliance costs but preserve wide-bodied business	Loss from alliance costs / Ongoing net profit of $15mm per wide-bodied plane

[25]Based on M. Kretschmer, "Game Theory. The Developer's Dilemma, Boeing v Airbus," in Booz, Allen, and Hamilton, *Strategy & Business* (Second Quarter 1998); "Towards the Wild Blue Yonder," *The Economist* (April 27, 2002), p. 67; "Giving 'em Away," *BusinessWeek* (March 5, 2001), pp. 52–55; and "Global Dogfight," *Wall Street Journal* (June 1, 2005), p. A1; "The Airliner That Fell to Earth," *The Economist* (October 7, 2006), p. 69; "Carriers Oppose Plane Subsidies," *Wall Street Journal* (October 7, 2010), p. B3.

Questions

1. In light of the foregoing payoffs, why did Airbus go ahead with the A380 Super-jumbo even though its $10.7 billion development cost and rollout delays in 2010 required as many as 300 planes to break even?

2. In 2004–2006, for the first time Boeing produced fewer planes than Airbus (see Figure 13.9). If Boeing finds itself less profitable at 60 percent market share than at 45 percent, what is the likely impact on the Airbus-Boeing tactical competition?

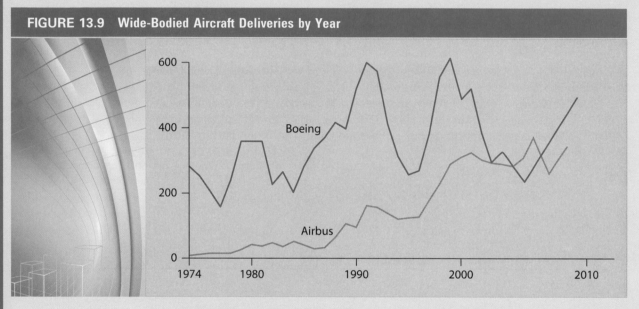

FIGURE 13.9 Wide-Bodied Aircraft Deliveries by Year

Source: *Wall Street Journal* (October 14, 2003), p. A2; and *The Economist* (August 15, 2009), p. 11.

3. The European Union claims that Boeing was given $3.2 billion in tax exemptions by the State of Washington to support the Boeing Dreamliner 787 project. The United States claims that Airbus received $6 billion in loans that do not need to be repaid to support the research, development, and launch aid for the Airbus 380 Super-jumbo. These charges and countercharges at the World Trade Organization pertain to whether either firm is "dumping" the 787s and 380s brought to the export markets. These export-credit arrangements now support almost 35 percent of Airbus and Boeing sales. What category of cost must be covered by the early penetration prices in order to avoid such predatory pricing indictments?

4. By 2010, Airbus was projecting to deliver 93 A380s. Instead, because of delays associated with installation misdesign for the electrical harnesses, Airbus delivered only 10 planes. The cost of the delay added $6 billion to the overall development costs to be recovered. That implies the break-even production run has now risen from 250 to over 300 planes. The company has produced 45 planes each of the last two years. What about the history of Boeing's 747 production run that suggests the Airbus 380 may still be a considerable success?

Entry Deterrence and Accommodation Games

In this appendix, we examine the tactical issues that arise when an incumbent firm faces an imminent threat of entry. We analyze whether to accommodate or attempt to deter the potential entrant and what capacity planning or limit pricing or sunk cost investment tactics to employ as barriers to effective entry. At the end, we characterize contestable markets as also dependent on exit barriers.

EXCESS CAPACITY AS A CREDIBLE THREAT

One type of credible threat or commitment that can markedly influence the subsequent competition is an investment in non-redeployable excess capacity. Irreversible investment in excess capacity credibly commits a high-priced incumbent to serve the price-sensitive new customers who might be attracted into the market by a potential entrant's discounting. If these and other regular customers can be expected to favor doing business with the incumbent, then excess capacity investment can substantially enhance the deterrent effect of an incumbent's threat to cut prices in response to entry.

Why exactly does excess capacity enhance the credibility of the incumbent's threat? Is it that the incumbent can thereby prevent the new entrant from acquiring a large market share? Is it that the incumbent can deny the new entrant a unique reputation for low prices? Is it that the incumbent can become more profitable than before the entry threat? The answer to all these questions is no. The sole reason any action or communication is credible is if it makes the threat-maker worse off ignoring the threat than carrying it out. In Figure 13A.1, the competitive firm that invests in excess capacity by expanding from Plant 1 to Plant 2 is worse off with unchanged output Q_1 and unit costs of \$180 at A than selling the larger output Q_2 with unit costs of \$120 at B. Lowering the price to carry out a threat thereby increases sales from Q_1 to Q_2. Ignoring the threat would leave the incumbent worse off with higher unit costs at A now that Plant 1 has been replaced by Plant 2.

PRECOMMITMENTS USING NON-REDEPLOYABLE ASSETS

To address the tactical ramifications of installing excess capacity, consider the capacity decision of a well-established hospital that faces an entry threat from an outpatient clinic specializing in obstetrics and elective plastic surgery. The hospital is constructing a new surgical wing. The hospital's business manager can build a new facility to meet the future demand projected at their currently high prices, or he or she can include some considerable excess capacity in his or her expansion plans. Suppose that the birthing rooms and type of operating theater used in obstetrics and plastic surgery are not redeployable to general surgical or other specialized uses. Instead, the excess capacity, if built, will serve

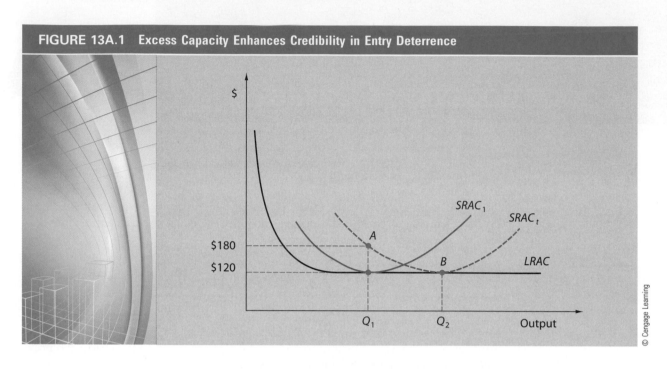

FIGURE 13A.1   Excess Capacity Enhances Credibility in Entry Deterrence

as a non-redeployable excess capacity precommitment by the hospital to compete for all the new price-sensitive business that a lower-priced outpatient surgical clinic might attract into the market.

Example

Excess Capacity in the World Car Market: Samsung and Hyundai[1]

Auto sales in the United States, Europe, and Japan plunged during the Financial Crisis of 2008–2009. Why add excess capacity in such a business environment?

Economies of scale do not seem to be involved. Even Hyundai has already reached minimum efficient scale (see Table 13A.1). Moreover, both the GM Opel-Fiat-Saab-Daewoo and Ford-Jaguar-Volvo-Land Rover-Mazda global alliances focus on designing common platforms for families so that the multimillion-dollar body-stamping machines and assembly plants can produce Opel Astra sedans one week and Fiat Zafira seven-seat minivans the next. Increasingly, up to a dozen different vehicles share the same platform and assembly line. Even with less popular vehicles, minimum efficient scale has therefore become much less difficult to achieve.

A second explanation for capacity expansions highlights the location of the new capacity, much of which is appearing in Asia, especially South Korea and Thailand. Two-thirds of the growth in new car sales between 2000 and 2010 has arisen in the developing countries of China and India. South Korean conglomerate Samsung recently opened a new robot-equipped 500,000-vehicle plant at an investment of $5 billion even though South Korean production (at 6 million vehicles) is already substantially ahead of domestic consumption (1.5 million vehicles) plus export sales (3.5 million vehicles). Predictably, local retail auto prices in South Korea collapsed as the looming overcapacity forced profit margins down to levels that no longer attract new auto industry investment.

(continued)

But that may have been exactly the idea. Incumbent manufacturers like Hyundai and Kia want to deter further entry into an economy that can easily ship to the Asian growth market. Precommitting to enough capacity that no potential entrant will doubt their threat to aggressively cut prices is a way to defend market share. If this tactical initiative works and potential entrants stay out, the incumbent firms will never have to make good on their threat.

TABLE 13A.1 2011 WORLDWIDE AUTO AND LIGHT TRUCK SALES (TOP 15)			
VW Group	13.2%	Renault	4.0%
General Motors	11.1	Suzuki	3.8
Toyota	11.0	Fiat–Chrysler	3.7
Hyundai Group	9.9	BMW	2.8
Nissan	5.8	Daimler	2.3
Peugeot Group	5.1	Mazda	1.8
Honda	4.6	Mitsubishi	1.7
Ford	4.3		

Source: International Organization of Motor Vehicle Manufacturers.

© Cengage Learning

[1]Based on Ward's Automotive *Yearbook*, "Car Making in Asia: Politics of Scale," *The Economist* (June 24, 2000), pp. 68–69; and "In Asia, GM Pins Hopes on a Delicate Web," *Wall Street Journal* (October 23, 2001), p. A23.

The structure of this game is presented in the decision tree in Figure 13A.2. The hospital chooses excess capacity or not; the outpatient surgical clinic chooses thereafter to enter or stay out, and the hospital then controls the pricing endgame. If the hospital builds excess capacity, it is more likely to cut prices in the face of entry, and the clinic is then better off staying out. If the hospital does not build excess capacity, it is more likely to accommodate the entrant by maintaining high prices, and the clinic is then better off entering. Therefore, looking ahead to predict the hospital and the clinic's best reply responses in the various proper subgames and endgames, the hospital's likely choices narrow to two strategies shaded in Figure 13A.2: {Excess capacity, Stay out, Limit pricing} and {No excess capacity, Enter, Accommodate with moderate price}.

Clearly, business as usual is no longer an option for the hospital. In particular, the previously very profitable elective surgical business with high prices, no excess capacity, and no competition in the top row of the game tree is no longer a focal outcome of interest. The entry threat may require that the incumbent hospital now maximize its remaining profit by precommitting itself to constructing some excess capacity. In that scenario, then, the clinic will consider hit-and-run entry, but probably decide instead to stay out and enter the same market in another community with less capacity present or projected.

In general, whether incumbents will choose to deter potential entrants (e.g., in the bottom half of the game tree in Figure 13A.2) by the use of excess capacity precommitments or will actually prefer to accommodate (in the top half of the game tree) by retaining their smaller capacities and lowering prices is a complex question that depends on several factors. Chapter 13 showed the answer depends in part on whether the incumbent can secure a first-mover advantage. Without it, in Entry Deterrence I, the incumbent

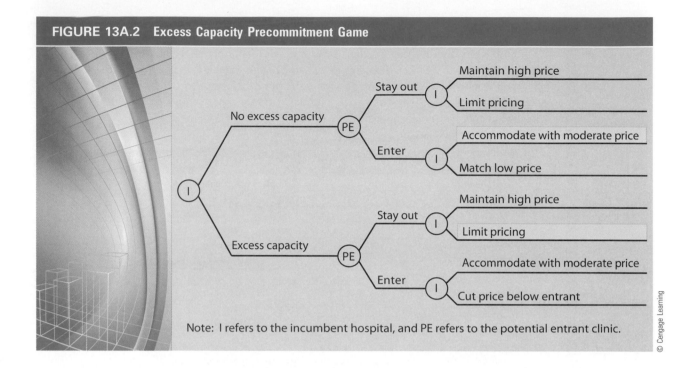

FIGURE 13A.2 **Excess Capacity Precommitment Game**

Note: I refers to the incumbent hospital, and PE refers to the potential entrant clinic.

© Cengage Learning

Pastense discounted steeply to deter entry, but with it in Entry Deterrence II, Pastense maintained moderate prices and accommodated entry.

This deterrence/accommodation decision also depends on whether the post-entry competition will be in prices among differentiated product sellers, each with some market power over price, or in quantities among homogeneous product sellers with no market power over price. Finally, the decision to deter or accommodate depends on how old and new customers in various segments of the market sort between an incumbent with excess capacity and a capacity-constrained lower-priced new entrant.

CUSTOMER SORTING RULES

brand loyalty A customer sorting rule favorable to incumbents.

efficient rationing A customer sorting rule in which high-willingness-to-pay customers absorb the capacity of low-price entrants.

If the entrant attracts only new price-sensitive customers, that's one thing. If, on the other hand, the new entrant takes away high-willingness-to-pay regular customers of the incumbent, that's something else. Not surprisingly, the former situation more typically leads to accommodation; the latter often leads to deterrence.

Probably the simplest customer sorting pattern of all is extreme **brand loyalty** to incumbents. In this case, even in the face of higher prices, customers reject the new entrant's offered capacity and instead back-order and reschedule when denied service at the incumbent. Competitive pressure from imitators normally erodes this degree of market power, but Microsoft Windows and popular local restaurants provide examples of products and services whose brand loyalty has sustained such a customer sorting pattern. At the other extreme, under **efficient rationing** of capacity, customers allocate themselves across the fixed-priced capacity of new entrant discounters in a manner that achieves maximum consumer surplus. This customer sorting rule implies that those with the highest willingness to pay will exert the effort, time, and inconvenience to seek out, queue up, and order early to secure the lowest priced capacity.

inverse intensity rationing A customer sorting rule that assures that low-willingness-to-pay customers absorb the capacity of low-price entrants.

random rationing A customer sorting rule reflecting randomized buyer behavior.

A third alternative is **inverse intensity rationing**, a much less threatening customer sorting pattern posed by new low-priced capacity in a segmented market. In this instance, the low-willingness-to-pay customers quickly absorb all the capacity of the low-priced entrant. Starting with a customer just willing to pay the entrant's low price, one proceeds conceptually up the demand curve only as far as required to stock out the new entrant. In this instance, the demand of the incumbent may be largely unaffected if the discounter's capacity remains relatively small. Finally, there is **random rationing** of the low-priced capacity. Under random rationing, all customers willing to pay the low prices—that is, both regular customers of the incumbent and the new customers attracted into the market by the entrant's discounting—have an equal chance of securing the low-priced capacity. For example, if 70 customers were present in the market at the incumbent's original high price, and 30 additional customers appear in response to the discounts, the probability of any 1 of the 100 potential customers securing service from 40 units of low-priced capacity is $40/100 = 0.4$. Conversely, the probability of not being served is $(1 - 0.4) = 0.6$, such that any customer may need to seek out higher-priced capacity with this probability. Under random rationing, therefore, the incumbent's expected demand falls as a result of the entry from 70 to $(70 \times 0.6) = 42$.

Because of the pivotal role of these customers sorting rules in predicting deterrence versus accommodation behavior, game-theoretic analysis must often be intertwined with an industry study in order to discriminate among the many possible implications. Otherwise, the rational business decisions of incumbents in these models may vary over a wide range of alternatives from the relatively passive acquisition of excess capacity all the way to the aggressive incumbent who occasionally predates by pricing below cost with no prospect of later recovering the loss. For the purpose of predicting rival behavior, this state of game-theoretic knowledge presents something of an embarrassment of riches. Hence, we reiterate the importance of doing sufficient field research to discover the particulars of the industry or firm-specific situation.

In Web Appendix D, we explore the entry deterrence and accommodation game between US Airways and People Express and between United and JetBlue. Detailed cost, price, and realized revenue data allow us to distinguish among several pricing and capacity choice implications of sequential game theory. The analysis lends support to the importance of customer sorting "rules" in explaining why People Express met with little resistance and indeed was accommodated initially by incumbents in mid-Atlantic city-pair markets. And later with a larger capacity People Express encountered effective deterrence from US Airways in the southeastern city-pair markets and was forced to exit.

A Role for Sunk Costs in Decision Making

In both theory and practice, sequential games of entry deterrence and accommodation have uncovered a very rich variety of strategic incumbent behavior in response to entry or potential entry. These include the excess capacity precommitments just discussed as well as credible price discount threats. However, they also include price discrimination and capacity allocation schemes. Such yield management or revenue management systems can provide incumbents with an effective way to deter new entrant discounters. We discuss revenue management in Chapter 14.

Finally, entry deterrence and accommodation strategy may also be expressed through advertising campaigns or other promotional investments in non-redeployable assets. As we mentioned in Chapter 13, some examples would be reputational investments in company logos (such as CarMax) or unique stand-alone retail stores such as McDonald's. Such investments precommit the incumbent to aggressively defend market share and cash flow in order to recover the cost of these non-redeployable investments.

Non-redeployable investments in specific assets are a reality in many businesses; these fixed asset expenses are said to be "sunk." Industrial machinery is often specialized to the purpose at hand and sometimes even to a particular supplier. For decades, Sara Lee Hosiery bought twisted nylon fiber for its highest quality hosiery from a sole source supplier, MacField Industries; the upstream nylon production equipment and the downstream hosiery spinning equipment were only usable as complements to this one supplier's twisted fiber input. Similarly, much of the trade secret knowledge discovered by Microsoft programmers is not easily packaged and separated out for redeployment and sale to another firm. Markets in which non-redeployable assets are common will be markets where sunk cost investments deter entry.

Perfectly Contestable Markets

contestable markets An industry with exceptionally open entry and easy exit where incumbents are slow to react.

Contestable markets are strategic industry groups in which new firms can enter and exit on short notice without anticipating losses due to sunk costs. Jet taxis provide an illustration. Even if only a few firms like Berkshire Hathaway's NetJets dominate such a market, prices seldom rise above break-even levels because of the constant "hit-and-run" tactics of the frequent entrants. Rival firms jump in and scallop off the profits whenever prices rise and then escape quickly once the profits are dissipated. This hit-and-run entry and exit pattern ensures little divergence from cost-covering competitive equilibrium.

In the perfectly contestable markets scenario, incumbents react more slowly to entry threats than their regular customers, who chase after the most inexpensive supplier of the moment. In contrast, as we have seen in Figure 13A.2, proactive incumbents can invest in excess capacity and non-redeployable assets in order to deter entry. That may sound like sunk-cost reasoning, and indeed it is. Recognizing the sequential nature of business strategy and the role of credible threats and credible commitments therein has led to a rehabilitation of the role of sunk costs in managerial decision making.

Example

Contestable Market in Bicycle Helmets: Bell Sports[2]

Bell Sports began as a motorcycle helmet manufacturer with a small side-bet business in bicycle helmets and accessories. Today, Bell has $100 million sales of bicycle helmets, 85 percent of which occur in the United States. Twenty-seven states have initiated regulations making bicycle helmets mandatory for young riders. The potential growth in Europe, where bicycle helmets have become a fashion statement, is even greater. Prices range from $30 for colorful hard-shell designs to $140 for ultra-lightweight models.

The trouble with running a fast-growing niche business is that without sunk-cost investments, Bell inevitably attracted many new entrant competitors. Bicycle helmets are easy to fabricate and quickly sell themselves. All one needs is plastic molding machines and a foam extrusion process. These technologies are easily converted from many other industries and, more importantly, can be redeployed back to those other uses upon exit. The product sells well in bike shops and in such discount stores as Kmart and Walmart without any significant sales force, point-of-sale actions, or after-sale service to differentiate one seller from another. Consequently, the bicycle helmet market is a classic case of a *contestable market*. Bell Sports is constantly subject to hit-and-run entry from other niche manufacturers—for example, Giro, Aurora, and Troxel Cycling.

The theory of contestable markets suggests that with no barriers to entry or exit and low customer costs of switching manufacturers, Bell Sports can never make

(continued)

more than a competitive profit in this business. As soon as prices rise above cost, temporary competitors enter the business, customers switch their allegiance, and Bell must lower prices. As a consequence, gross margins are low (averaging 8 percent) and fluctuate by as much as 50 percent from year to year. Bell's only alternatives are to outdo the hit-and-run entrants on new designs or to commit enough marketing investment dollars to establish a non-redeployable brand asset "Bell Helmets," like it has established in the motorcycle business. Until then, entry deterrence will prove infeasible, and entry accommodation must continue.

---

[2]Based on "Bell Sports," *Forbes* (February 13, 1995), pp. 67–68.

In fact, it is precisely because firms can do nothing about their sunk-cost investments, precisely because they are irreversible, irrevocable, and otherwise unrecoverable, that a particular threatened plan of action involving the use of these non-redeployable assets is credible. The player with sunk-cost investments has burned bridges. No better alternatives exist than to deliver on credible threats and to make credible commitments to remain in the business of serving repeat customers until the equipment becomes obsolete or wears out. Again, best-reply reasoning is the key to credibility, and credibility is the key to subgame perfect equilibrium strategy.

Brinkmanship and Wars of Attrition

Sometimes the question of tactical interest is not one of deterring or accommodating the entry of other firms but rather it is a question of how long should your own firm stay in an obviously declining business. In competing to win an exclusive license (e.g., to host the Olympics), to define an industry standard (e.g., for digital HDTV), to earn Food and Drug Administration (FDA) approval for a new class of drugs, or to capture the product loyalty of fickle customers with advertising, successive rounds of bloodletting by multiple competitors may prevent profitability until someone concedes and drops out. Hence, these entry and exit games are sometimes called "wars of attrition."

The first period of a multiperiod sequential game representing a "war of attrition" is displayed on the left-hand side of Figure 13A.3. Each period requires a $10 million "ante" at the start of the period just to remain in the game. No competitor knows his or her rivals' decision about staying when deciding whether to "hold 'em or fold 'em." It is as though auction bids were sealed and then opened simultaneously. If either firm concedes and leaves, it pays nothing, and the other firm's $10 million ante is immediately recoverable by the firm who stays.

The market payoffs come at the end of the period and are equal to $100 million if one firm concedes and $50 million if both concede. These market prizes repeat every year until the end of the game. If at the start of any period the rivals ("They") leave and concede the $100 million market to "Us," a payoff of [$100/(1 + r)] awaits—for example, at 8 percent interest rates, ($100/1.08) − $10 + $10 = $92.6 million. If "We" concede when "They" stay, $92.6 million is their payoff. If both firms concede, they immediately merge, and the market is split 50–50 with no further cost. If "They" hang tough and stay in competition, and "We" do the same, both firms lose $10 million—that is, no one wins the prize that period. Then each proceeds to make the decision as to whether to spend another $10 million ante to compete in the next period. The question is, "How long should we stay?"

Consider the three-period game. If "We" leave now, the payoff is zero when "They" stay, and $50 million when "They" concede. Let p be the probability that our opponent is

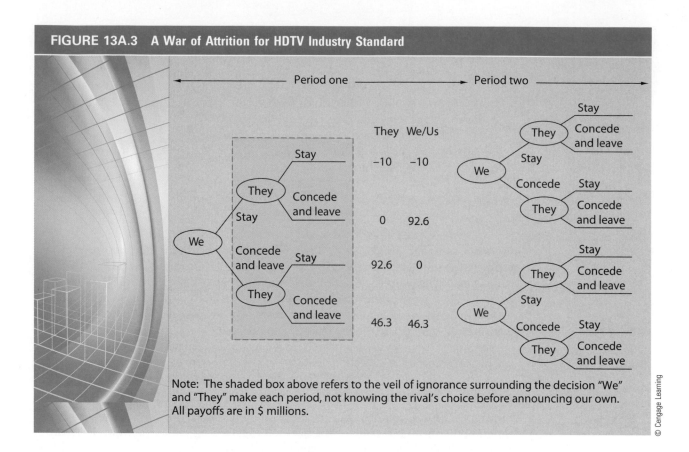

FIGURE 13A.3   A War of Attrition for HDTV Industry Standard

Note: The shaded box above refers to the veil of ignorance surrounding the decision "We" and "They" make each period, not knowing the rival's choice before announcing our own. All payoffs are in $ millions.

© Cengage Learning

a type who will concede immediately. Then the expected payoff from conceding immediately ourselves is just[3]

$$\$50p + 0(1 - p) \geq 0 \qquad [13A.1]$$

If "We" leave at the start of the second period, our expected payoff would be equal to

$$\$100p + \$50q - \$10 \geq 0 \qquad [13A.2]$$

where q is the probability that our rival ("They") will concede at the start of the second period, and $(1 - p - q)$ is the probability "They" will stay until the third period—that is, Hang Toughers never concede. If we stay to the end, our expected payoff is as follows:

$$\$200p + \$100q - \$20 \geq 0 \qquad [13A.3]$$

Setting Equation 13A.1 equal to 13A.2 and 13A.2 equal to 13A.3, then solving simultaneously, yields the values of p and q that would leave "Us" just indifferent between conceding and hanging tough. Collecting terms and simplifying, we have

$$50p + 50q = 10 \qquad [13A.4]$$

$$-100p - 50q = -10 \qquad [13A.5]$$

which together imply $p = 0$, $q = 0.2$, and $(1 - p - q) = 0.8$.

---

[3]In the discussion that follows, we ignore discounting to simplify the analysis. The payoff of $92.6 million therefore becomes $100 million.

In other words, "We" are indifferent as to conceding immediately or hanging tough and paying the $10 million ante each of the first two periods to stay until the endgame if and only if there is no less than a 20 percent chance "They" will leave in the second period and no more than an 80 percent chance "They" will stay until the endgame. "We" decide whether to stay or leave by assessing the actual situation and actual rival and then comparing these 20 percent and 80 percent derived probability break points against our subjective probability estimates of the actual situation.

TACTICAL INSIGHTS ABOUT SLIPPERY SLOPES

slippery slope A tendency for wars of attrition to generate mutual losses that worsen over time.

Note that $p = 0$ implies that neither party concedes immediately. Instead, $q = 0.2$ indicates a middle ground strategy of opponent types who test the competitive waters before conceding at the start of Period 2. This positive probability of "middle grounders" is a reflection of a **slippery slope**. Once you enter into a war of attrition and make your own first "ante" of $-$10 million (because the Bayesian probability of Hang Toughers was less than 0.8), the probability of middle grounders who will step on that slippery slope with you is NOT zero. Instead, we have seen in the simultaneous solution to Equations 13A.4 and 13A.5 that the equilibrium probability of middle grounders in this game is 0.2. That is, with the parameters assumed in this war of attrition, there is a 0.8 probability of a sequence of mutual losses, a death spiral until the less deep pocket is empty.

Hence, these so-called brinkmanship games have serious and largely uncontrollable consequences even for the player with an apparently advantaged position. If you misestimate the depth of an opponent's pocket, 80 percent of the time you will be up against Hang Toughers and stepping onto a slippery slope to financial ruin—your own financial ruin.

Example

Circuit City Driven over the Brink[4]

Consumer electronics has often been a brutally competitive business with retailers offering one price promotion after another (10 percent below the best price elsewhere, 20 percent below, 30 percent below) to try to attract business away from their rivals. In 2004, Circuit City with $4.4 billion in sales got 35 percent of its revenue from consumer electronics, 24 percent from audio products and entertainment software, and 41 percent from videos, video games, and video game equipment. Best Buy with $11.6 billion in sales in 2004 got 37 percent from consumer electronics, 19 percent from entertainment software, 6 percent from appliances, and 38 percent from home office equipment.

Best Buy and Circuit City did enter a war of attrition. DVD players launched in 1997 at an initial price of $840 were discounted to $571 by 1998, $467 by 1999, $345 by 2000, and collapsed to cost in 2001. Similarly, Blu-ray players launched in 2006 at a price of $800 were discounted to $497 by 2007, $388 by 2008, and $322 by 2009, and then collapsed to a cost of $221. Circuit City was forced into bankruptcy and exited the market.

[4]Based on "Prices No Longer Red Hot," *Wall Street Journal* (December 23, 2009), p. D9.

What is a best-reply response in the n period game? Continuing to ignore the discounting of future cash flows for the moment to simplify the analysis, if we hang tough until the rivals leave and if the rivals leave in period t, we realize the $100 million market prize for $n - t$ periods and pay $10 million for t periods. Since if we leave now, zero (i.e., $50p = 0$) is the payoff, and the expected value of all other alternatives can be no worse than this; otherwise we'll just leave now. Combining these facts

$$(n - t)\$100 - t\$10 > 0 \qquad [13A.6]$$

$$0.91n > t \qquad [13A.7]$$

where 0.91 is the ratio of the $100 million prize to the sum of (the periodic cost of $10 million plus the $100 million prize).

How should we interpret Equation 13A.7? If "We" believe the rivals will stay 91 percent of the total time or less, we should stay ourselves. If we believe "They" will stay more than 91 percent (or, with discounting, 90.25 percent) of the total time, we should concede immediately and save our $10 million ante to invest in another competitive encounter elsewhere. For the three-period case, if "We" believe the rivals will stay less than $0.9025 \times 3 = 2.71$ years, we should hang tough and stay to the end ourselves.

Obviously, these calculations apply equally to the symmetrically positioned "They" as well, so wars of attrition quickly become a matter of bluffing and signaling. The most useful insight the previous analysis offers in such entry and exit games is that each player should assess the probability of his or her rivals' leaving in light of all the available evidence and should hinge his or her own decision on the ratio of the prize to the sum of the prize plus periodic cost. Very much like playing straight draw poker, you hold rather than fold the bigger the prize and the smaller the periodic cost of hanging tough and calling your rivals' bluff.

SUMMARY

- Incumbents may seek to deter potential entrants through the use of excess capacity precommitments or credible threats of advertising campaigns and price discounts.
- Whether incumbents deter or accommodate potential entrants depends in general on the presence or absence of first-mover advantages, on the structure of competition in prices versus quantities, and on how customers sort across alternative firms when the low-priced capacity stocks out.
- Customer sorting patterns include the following: random rationing in which all customers are equally likely to obtain the low-priced capacity; efficient rationing in which the highest (then next highest) willingness-to-pay customers obtain the

low-priced capacity until it is exhausted; extreme brand loyalty in which none of the regular customers seek the low-priced capacity; and inverse intensity rationing in which the lowest (then next lowest) willingness-to-pay customers obtain the low-priced capacity until it is exhausted. With inverse intensity rationing, the customer sorting implies a segmented market and is most likely to lead to accommodation of entry.

- In wars of attrition, whether to hang tough and stay in competition for a market price or concede defeat and leave depends on the ratio of the prize to the sum of the prize plus the periodic cost of competing.

Exercises

1. Dunkin' Donuts and McDonald's McCafé have entered the specialty coffee business pioneered at Starbucks' 5,439 locations. Prices are 20 percent lower (99 cent espresso shots versus $1.45 at Starbucks), orders are simpler (Large Mocha Swirl Latte at $2.69 versus Venti Caffè Mocha at $3.35), and the wait time is under a minute versus three to five.[5] Have Starbucks Frappuccinos become an affordable luxury? Or are espresso coffee and flavored coffee going mainstream where Dunkin' Donuts and McDonald's have 17 percent and 15 percent of the fast-food outlet brewed coffee business, respectively, to Starbucks' 6 percent? Which is happening in your city? Moreover, as McCafé approaches Starbucks' market, what customer sorting rule will likely apply? Is there any reason to believe Starbucks will have a different strategy in responding to Dunkin' Donuts' 4,100 stores versus the several hundred McCafés under development? Why?

2. Sony's PlayStation 2 (PS2) dominated the game console market from 1997–2003 with 123 million units sold. Today, Nintendo's Wii has 62 percent of the market. Prices to achieve this spectacular growth have fallen continuously from $400 at launch to $250. Sony's PS3 with 20 percent market share at $1,000, then $600, and now $399 competes in a more upscale segment of the game console market against Microsoft's Xbox at 18 percent market share with prices that started at $760. Initially Xbox and PS3 tried to compete head-to-head on add-ons such as extra hand controller sets. Now, brinkmanship pricing has broken out with Xbox 360 discounted from $760 to a range of $400 to $343. Which firm is likely to blink first?

---

[5]Based on "Latte versus Latte," *Wall Street Journal* (February 10, 2004), p. B1.

CHAPTER 14

Pricing Techniques and Analysis

CHAPTER PREVIEW

This chapter builds on the price and output determination models developed in Chapters 10–13 as it considers more complex pricing issues. The first two sections examine a value-based pricing conceptual framework. Then we characterize differential pricing in segmented markets where different target market customers are charged nonuniform prices. Differential pricing is often accomplished with bundled pricing, couponing, and two-part tariffs (an access or entry fee combined with a user fee). We then discuss the concept of pricing throughout the product life cycle including target pricing, penetration pricing, pricing for organic growth, limit pricing, and niche pricing. We conclude with a section on pricing of goods and services sold over the Internet. Finally, applications of revenue management in airlines, fashion clothing, consulting firms, and baseball are explained in Appendix 14A. Together, the pricing practices presented in this chapter and its appendix provide an extensive overview of the way actual managers apply pricing techniques to maximize shareholder wealth.

Two additional pricing topics closely related to accounting (pricing of joint products and transfer pricing) are presented in web Appendix E.

MANAGERIAL CHALLENGE
Pricing the Chevy Volt[1]

Urban sprawl and flight to the suburbs have now resulted in the mean commuter trip in the United States rising to 33 miles one way. Urban traffic congestion then forces consumers to spend $115 billion burning 4 billion gallons of gasoline while waiting 34 hours per year in traffic delays. With the housing density in most American cities well below what would be required to support extensive light rail and subway lines, the typical household must find economical ways to get at least one worker from a suburban home to the central business district and back each day.

Several fuel-efficient commuter cars such as the Mini Cooper, Chevy Volt, Nissan Leaf, and Chevy Cruze have recently been introduced. The Volt and Leaf are e-REVs, extended-range electric vehicles that are recharged at the end of each 40-mile commuting trip. Each contains a small gasoline-driven internal combustion engine that runs an electric generator, but unlike hybrids such as the Ford Fusion and Toyota Prius, these e-REVs have no mechanical connection between the gasoline engine and the drivetrain. Instead, the Chevy Volt is powered by 220 lithium ion (L-ion) batteries that are plugged in for a recharging cycle of 8 hours at 110 volts (or 3 hours at 220 volts). When the battery pack falls to a 30 percent state of charge (SOC), the 69 horsepower gasoline engine comes on simply to turn the generator and maintain battery power.

Automotive engineers calculate that each mile traveled in the Chevy Volt's all-electric mode "burns" 0.26 kilowatt hours (kWh) of electricity. Therefore, the

Cont.

mean commuter trip of 33 miles requires 8.58 kWh of electricity. The price of electricity in the United States varies from a peak period in the midday and evening to a much cheaper off-peak period late at night, and from a low of $0.07 per kWh in Washington state to $0.12 in Rhode Island. On average, a representative nighttime rate is $0.10, and a representative daytime rate is $0.13. This means that each nighttime charge of a Chevy Volt will cost the household $0.86, and the comparable daytime charge downtown at work will cost $1.12 for a total operating expense of just under $2 per day. For 300 days of work, that's $600 per year.

In contrast, the gasoline-powered Mini Cooper gets 32 mpg, so at $3.24 per gallon, the Mini's operating cost is $6.68 per day or $2,000 per year. The typical commuter use of e-Rev vehicles will save $4.68 per day or $1,400 per year relative to popular fuel-efficient gasoline-powered commuter cars like the Mini Cooper and Chevy Cruze. This $1,400 cost savings represents the value-in-use of the Chevy Volt relative to its gasoline-powered near-competitors.

At an EPA-measured 93 mpg, the Chevy Volt qualifies for a $7,500 tax credit. Its L-ion battery pack which is expected to last 10 years costs an additional $12,000 (over a conventional battery). The net disposal value of a Volt after five years is expected to be $4,500. With the tax credit, these positive and negative cash flows cancel out. Hence, the value-in-use during the first five years is the source of any price premium Chevy could hope to charge over a conventional comparable commuter car. The Mini Cooper and Chevy Cruze sell for manufacturer's suggested retail price (MSRP) of $25,550. At $1,400 per year cost savings for five years with 2.5 percent financing

costs, the present discounted value of the cost savings from the Chevy Volt is $6,504. Therefore, a Chevy Volt should command a $6,504 price premium over a Mini Cooper or Chevy Cruze. That is, the value-based price of the Volt would be $25,550 + $6,504 = $32,054.

Discussion Questions

- In light of the foregoing analysis, what success do you think Chevy Volt experienced in its first two years in the U.S. market at a $41,000 MSRP?
- What part of the Volt's cost structure do you think exceeded its estimated cost enough to push the MSRP $9,000 over its value-based price?
- If the cost-covering $41,000 exceeded the value-based $32,000 price consumers were willing to pay, why didn't General Motors (GM) just introduce the car in California where the tax credit is $12,500 and the state requires each manufacturer to sell at least one pollution-free vehicle?
- Brainstorm why General Motors did not penetration price its new e-Rev technology at $25,000 to $30,000?

[1]"American Idle: On the Road," *Wall Street Journal* (February 2, 2011), p. D1; "Chevy Volt: GM's 230 MPG Moon Shot," *U.S. News and World Report* (January 7, 2010); "A New Segmentation for Electric Vehicles," McKinsey & Co., November 2009.

A CONCEPTUAL FRAMEWORK FOR PROACTIVE, SYSTEMATIC-ANALYTICAL, VALUE-BASED PRICING

In the past, pricing decisions were often treated as an afterthought. Companies either routinely marked up prices or reacted in an ad hoc fashion to a competitor's discounting. Today, systematically analyzing the customer value basis for an asking price and thereafter carefully selecting which orders to accept and which to refuse has become a critical success factor for many businesses.

Pricing decisions must always be systematic and analytical, based on hard facts instead of ad hoc hunches. In the men's aftershave business, an established incumbent recently encountered a new entrant with a penetration price 40 percent below the leading brands Skin Bracer, Old Spice, and Aqua Velva. The incumbent increased advertising but maintained its original price point and was astounded to observe a 50 percent decline in market share through its grocery store distribution channel. Only after the fact was a systematic analysis undertaken. Careful demand estimations showed that customers in the grocery store channel were price elastic and advertising inelastic.

Proactive pricing must also be tactically astute and internally consistent with a company's operations strategy. A high-cost, full-service, hub-and-spoke airline cannot slash prices dramatically even if it means 10 or 20 percent increases in market share in a high-margin segment. It must instead anticipate a matching price reaction by its lower-cost rivals, perhaps followed by still further price cuts below its own cost. Knowing these probable reaction paths in advance makes the attempt to gain market share through discounting much less attractive despite additional incremental sales at a high margin.

Most importantly, pricing should be value-based. Prestone and Zerex sell leading anticorrosive radiator fluids whose product characteristics warrant a price premium. Under apparent price pressure, Zerex often simply matches any competitor's discount as long as competing prices on generic radiator fluid cover Zerex's cost. A thorough value analysis reveals, however, that this reactive cost-based pricing fails to realize about one-third of Zerex's sustainable profit margin. Cost-based pricing has been called one of the "five deadly business sins" by Peter Drucker; what firms should do instead is "price-based costing." That is, firms should segment customers, perform an extensive customer value analysis, and then develop products whose costs allow substantial profitability in each product line the firm chooses to enter. Each firm's marketing and operations capabilities are then key to sustaining that profitability.

Costs are not irrelevant. Indeed, a key to effective pricing management is to know precisely what activity-based costs are associated with each type of order from each customer segment. Knowing these costs allows firms with optimal differential prices to identify *which orders to refuse*. This insight—that every company has orders that it should refuse—is the key to a new set of pricing techniques known as "yield management," or more generally, "revenue management (RM)." In an RM approach, costs become the consequence of a value-based pricing and product development strategy.

The appropriate conceptual framework for setting prices is the target customer's **value-in-use**. Value-in-use is the cost savings that arise from the use of your product or service relative to a next best competitor. A faster commute on a toll road or a nonstop jet to a distant city saves the $220-an-hour attorney or accountant's time value per hour. A Google ad with a documented click-through rate saves the advertising expenditure on magazine ads or TV commercials. An integrated and easy-to-use Canon digital photography system saves the casual photographer time, money, and inconvenience in image capturing, photo editing, developing, distribution, and storage.

Table 14.1 lists various tangible and psychological sources of value-in-use, including product specifications and ease of use, delivery reliability, service frequency, change order responsiveness, loyalty programs, and empathy in order processing. Many of these sources of cost savings are functional points of differentiation, but others are relationship-based. In addition, marketing communications seeks to position and brand the product through advertising, personal selling, and event marketing. Viral marketing identifies trend setters among the target customer group and seeks to place the product with those individuals, hoping that others will follow their lead. Because consumers strive to avoid psychological dissonance, products that affirm a particular lifestyle or group identity can often generate perceived value well beyond tangible cost savings. Coca-Cola and Starbucks each offers a lifestyle association and identity that would otherwise necessitate much larger clothing, travel, auto, and entertainment expenditures to achieve a similar result.

value-in-use The difference between the value customers place on functions, cost savings, and relationships attributable to a product or service and the life cycle costs of acquiring, maintaining, and disposing of the product or service.

Importantly, lowest price is seldom what triggers a purchase. Instead, a target customer's purchase is triggered by either (1) value through functions, cost savings, and relationships that exceed the product's asking price or (2) a ratio of value to asking price that is greater than a competitor's. In Table 14.1, $0.50 is not the lowest price for a digital photography print, but Nikon's offering will nevertheless trigger a purchase if the excess customer value with the Nikon digital photography system ($2.00 − $0.50) exceeds the excess value from less valuable $0.29 products—perhaps ($1.00 − $0.29).

Example

Coated Coronary Stents Reduce the Cost of Later Surgeries[2]

Each year in the United States, 1.3 million angioplasty heart surgeries are performed at an average cost of $48,399 and 448,000 coronary bypass (open heart) surgeries are performed at an average cost of $99,743. This $104 billion of cardiac surgery is very big business. In the relatively simple noninvasive angioplasty procedure, a balloon is threaded into the femoral artery along the thigh and then directed upward into a clogged coronary artery, where it is inflated to clear the blockage. Eighty percent of the time, an $800 medical device (a stent) made of coiled wire resembling the spring in a ballpoint pen is then inserted into the coronary artery to hold it open. The coronary stent market grew from introduction in the mid-1990s to $6 billion worldwide in 2006 with over a million stents sold annually in the United States and an almost equal number sold abroad. In 15 to 30 percent of these cases, however, scar tissue grows around the wire stent, reclosing the artery. That complication then necessitates $99,743 for follow-up open heart surgical procedures and additional treatments.

Recent advances by Cordis, a subsidiary of Johnson & Johnson, and by Boston Scientific, and Medtronic have coated the coronary stent with an antibiotic or a cell-killing cancer drug to stop the scar tissue from forming. In its most advanced form, hollow stents can be made to elute just the right amount of time-release pharmaceutical over a 45-day post-op period to prevent the vessel wall scarring. J&J's sirolimus-eluting stent called CYPHER eliminated the problem in routine angioplasties, reducing the incidence of re-blockage to 3 percent in various human trials. Achieving a 12 to 27 percent reduction in the likelihood of $99,743 open heart surgery saves the patient at least 0.12 × $99,743 = $11,969 in expected future medical expenses as well as avoiding the risks of the additional surgery.

Hospitals and their attending surgeons charge on average $9,700 for the overnight angioplasty procedure plus insertion of an uncoated bare metal stent (billed to patients separately at an additional $1,165) for a total cost of $10,865. The simplest coated stent is billed to patients at just under $2,000 for a total cost of $11,700 relative to the $11,969 minimum value-in-use savings it creates.

The sophisticated drug-eluting CYPHER coated stent, priced at $4,150 for a total bill of $13,850, has experienced less acceptance in the marketplace. For patients with the lowest (15 to 17 percent) chances of scar tissue closure, value-in-use is less than the asking price. Cardiologists have also begun to question whether some patients can be better treated with drugs rather than surgery. Consequently, stent sales worldwide declined to $5 billion in 2011.

---

[2]Based on "Medical Device Maker Sees Vast Market for Cardiac Stent," *Miami-Herald* (March 16, 2003), p. B1. "How Doctors Are Rethinking Drug-Coated Stents," *Wall Street Journal* (December 9, 2006), p. A1; "Use of Coated Stents on the Rise," *Wall Street Journal* (July 16, 2008), p. D2; and "Alternative Medicine Is Mainstream," *Wall Street Journal* (January 9, 2009), p. A13.

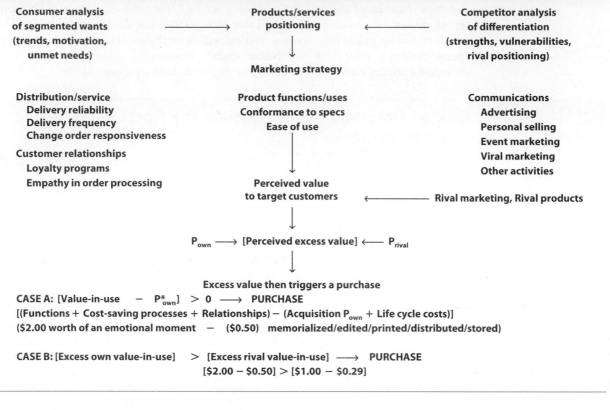

TABLE 14.1 CONCEPTUAL FRAMEWORK FOR VALUE-BASED PRICING

Consequently, firms should begin their pricing decisions by identifying the value drivers in each and every customer segment. Business air travelers, for example, value conformance to the schedule, delivery reliability, and the ability to change itineraries on short notice more than they value frequent flights, good meals, and wide seats. Because the first set of process-based value drivers is harder to imitate, sustainable price premiums are often associated with those operations processes rather than the product or service characteristics of flights, meals, and seats. Because business travelers account for only 27 percent of the traffic but 80 percent of the profitability, a critical success factor for legacy airlines is to have hub processes and route planning that sustain these hard-to-imitate processes on nonstop flights.

In sum, pricing decisions should be proactive and systematically analytical, not reactive and ad hoc. Most importantly, pricing should be value-based, not cost-based. The value-in-use conceptual framework leads naturally to a differential pricing environment in which mass-produced products or services are customized to the requirements of target customer segments.

OPTIMAL DIFFERENTIAL PRICE LEVELS

The first step in setting optimal differential prices is then to estimate demand by market segment—say, for each of two customer classes (business and nonbusiness air travelers) on the Thursday 11:00 A.M. flight from DFW to LAX. The expense account business

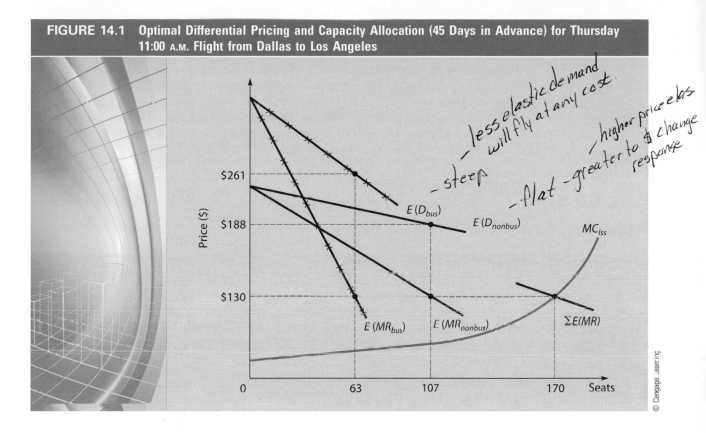

FIGURE 14.1 Optimal Differential Pricing and Capacity Allocation (45 Days in Advance) for Thursday 11:00 A.M. Flight from Dallas to Los Angeles

(handwritten annotations:)
- less elastic demand
- steep
- will fly at any cost.
- higher price elas
- flat - greater to $ change
- greater to $ change response

traveler tends to make less flexible travel plans and reserve space later and thus faces fewer close substitute alternatives than the nonbusiness traveler. Average revenue and marginal revenue schedules for business travelers therefore prove to be less price elastic than for nonbusiness travelers, as indicated in Figure 14.1.

Graphical Approach

Previously, the airline's capacity planning department will have summed all the expected marginal revenues $E(MR)$ from the various segments and determined an optimal total capacity by setting summed marginal revenue $[\Sigma E(MR)]$ equal to the marginal cost of the last seat sold (MC_{lss}).[3] The result in Figure 14.1 is that a plane with 170 seats should be scheduled for the Thursday 11:00 A.M. flight departure.

One may think of the optimal differential pricing decision as determining how this total capacity of 170 seats should be allocated across the customer segments. Because at the margin a firm forgoes revenue unless the last customer in each segment contributes a marginal revenue equal to the marginal cost of the last seat sold (MC_{lss}), the optimal allocation of seating capacity results from equating the segment-level MRs to one another:

$$MR_{bus} = (MC_{lss}) = MR_{nonbus} \qquad [14.1]$$

which in Figure 14.1 is at $MR = \$130$. Consider a case in which this condition does not hold. Suppose the 62nd seat sold in the business class contributed $160 of marginal revenue and the 108th seat sold in the nonbusiness class contributed $120. Clearly, one

---

[3]To find aggregate demand, remember that individual demands (and MRs) are horizontally summed for rival goods that cannot be shared (such as airplane seats and bite-sized candy bars), whereas demands for nonrival goods (e.g., outdoor statues, tennis courts, and national defense) are vertically summed.

could raise $40 additional revenue for unchanged costs by selling one less seat in non-business and one more in business, leaving both classes with, say, an $MR = \$130$.[4]

What prices can achieve the capacity allocation of 63 seats to the business class and 107 seats to the nonbusiness class? The answer is deceptively simple. Optimal differential prices are whatever asking prices will clear the market if the firm supplies 63 and 107 seats in these two fare classes. In Figure 14.1 the answer appears to be $261 and $188, with some effective barrier or "fencing" that prevents resale from the lower to the higher fares. The difficulty, of course, is predicting demand sufficiently well to know what prices will have this effect for the 11:00 A.M. flight next Thursday.

Algebraic Approach

Table 14.2 shows the spreadsheet data on which such a decision would be based in practice. The first three columns show the number of seats demanded, fares, and marginal

TABLE 14.2 ALLOCATING AIRLINE CAPACITY WITH DIFFERENTIAL FARES FOR LEISURE AND BUSINESS

BUSINESS CLASS			LEISURE CLASS				
EXPECTED SEAT DEMAND	FARE ($)	EXPECTED MARGINAL REVENUE ($)	EXPECTED SEAT DEMAND	FARE ($)	EXPECTED MARGINAL REVENUE ($)	TOTAL SEATS	MARGINAL COST ($)
1	1,084	1,084				1	87
2	1,032	980				2	87
3	974	858				3	87
4	907	705				4	87
5	835	550				5	87
10	613	390				10	87
			1	342	342		87
			2	331	320		95
			3	319	294		95
			4	311	288		95
20	456	280	5	305	280	25	95
			10	280	256		95
			20	260	240		95
30	381	230	30	250	230	60	100
			40	240	210		100
			50	231	194		100
40	331	180	60	222	180	100	112
			70	214	162		112
50	295	150	80	206	150	130	112
			90	198	140		120
60	268	133	100	192	133	160	125
63	261	130	107	188	130	170	130
			110	186	128		140
70	252	122	120	181	122	190	155
			130	176	115		170
80	235	110	140	173	110	220	190

© Cengage Learning

---

[4]Note that the MR of each segment is not set equal to MC. Rather, the summed MR of all segments has been set equal to MC. The individual MRs are set equal to the MC of the last unit sold (i.e., $130), and therefore equal to one another.

revenue for business-class travelers. For example, at a fare of $1,084, only one seat on the entire plane would be sold, and it would go to a business-class passenger. If the fare falls to $1,032, two seats are taken by business-class passengers. At a fare of $974, three seats are taken, and so on. Expected marginal revenue is the increase in total revenue realized from selling one more seat in the business class. For example, when a single seat is sold at $1,084, total revenue is also $1,084. When two seats are sold at a fare of $1,032, however, total revenue jumps to $2,064, and marginal revenue, which is the difference in total revenue realized from selling one more seat, is $2,064 − $1,084, or $980. Similarly, the marginal revenue associated with the third seat sold is $2,922 − $2,064, or $858.

Table 14.2 also shows corresponding information for leisure-class passengers. Note that the first leisure-class seat is sold at $342, the second at $331, and so on. The last two columns depict total seats sold and marginal cost, which is the variable cost associated with serving one additional passenger in either class.

Using this simple two-booking-class example, marginal revenue equals rising marginal cost at $130 per seat. (Marginal cost increases by steps with the addition of flight attendants needed to serve additional passengers and the additional fuel consumed because of worsening aerodynamics at high load factors.) At $MC = $130, optimal fares are obtained by equating individual marginal revenues of both segments and the marginal cost of the last seat expected to be sold (the 170th seat in this example). Business and leisure traveler marginal revenues equal $130 at 63 and 107 seats, respectively, and fares of $261 and $188 are optimal at these seat allocation levels.

Multiple-Product Pricing Decision

Figure 14.2 illustrates an analogous decision with five products; D_1 represents the demand for Product 1, D_2 for Product 2, and so on. Again, profits are maximized when the firm produces and sells quantities of the five products such that marginal revenue is equal in all markets and equal to marginal cost. The line *EMR* represents *equal marginal*

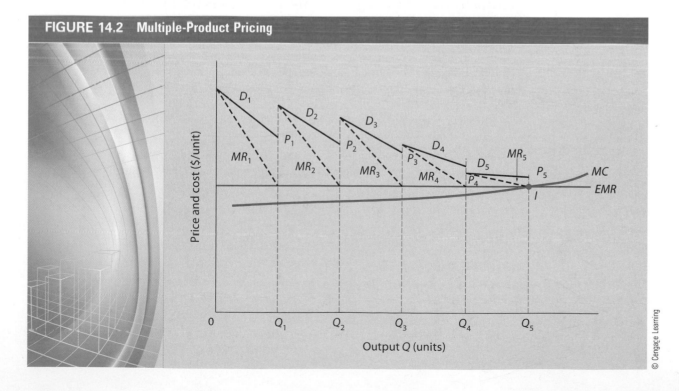

FIGURE 14.2   Multiple-Product Pricing

revenue, the firm's marginal revenue opportunity in other product lines. Because it is assumed that new product markets were entered in order of their profitability, the prices charged for the five products are arranged in declining order, from P_1 to P_5, and the elasticity of demand increases from D_1 to D_5. The height of the *EMR* line is determined by the intersection of the firm's marginal cost curve *MC* and the marginal revenue curve for the last product market that may be profitably served, MR_5 at Q_5.

The equilibrium condition in the marginal market D_5 where *P*, *MR*, and *MC* are virtually equivalent illustrates the well-known fact that nearly all firms produce some products that generate little or no incremental operating profit and are on the verge of being dropped or replaced because the contribution margin approaches zero.

Example

Supermarket Pricing

Supermarkets provide an illustration of this multiple-product pricing model. The primary resource constraint of a supermarket is shelf space, which can be allocated among a wide variety of product categories (meat, dairy products, canned goods, frozen foods, and produce). Canned goods have only a 2 percent profit margin. Generally the markups and profit margins on staple items, such as bread, milk, and soap, are lower than on nonstaple items, such as imported foods and deli items. In an effort to increase their overall profitability, many supermarkets have added higher-profit-margin categories, such as delicatessens, in-store bakeries, fresh fish, and floral departments by reallocating existing shelf space to these new categories.[5]

_____

[5]Allocation of shelf space within each product category also involves a consideration of profit margins when making decisions about stocking private label versus national brand canned goods, prepackaged versus fresh-cut meat, and so on.

Differential Pricing and the Price Elasticity of Demand

In all of the preceding examples, an inverse relationship exists between optimal price and the price elasticity of demand in separate submarkets. Recall that for profits to be maximized, marginal revenue must be equal in each of the separate submarkets. In Chapter 3, the relationship between marginal revenue (*MR*) and price (*P*) was shown to be the following (Equation 3.7):

$$MR = P\left(1 + \frac{1}{E_D}\right) \qquad [14.2]$$

where E_D is the price elasticity of demand. If P_1, P_2, E_1, and E_2 represent the prices and price elasticities in the two submarkets, we may equate marginal revenue by setting equal

$$MR_1 = P_1\left(1 + \frac{1}{E_1}\right) \text{ and } MR_2 = P_2\left(1 + \frac{1}{E_2}\right) \qquad [14.3]$$

Hence,

$$P_1\left(1 + \frac{1}{E_1}\right) = P_2\left(1 + \frac{1}{E_2}\right)$$

$$\frac{P_1}{P_2} = \frac{\left(1 + \frac{1}{E_2}\right)}{\left(1 + \frac{1}{E_1}\right)} \qquad [14.4]$$

Perhaps JetBlue Airways has determined that the price elasticity of demand for two customer segments (New York to Los Angeles unrestricted coach and for Super Saver Saturday night stay overs) is -1.25 and -2.50, respectively. To determine the relative prices (P_1/P_2) that JetBlue should charge if it is interested in maximizing profits on this route, substitute $E_1 = -1.25$ and $E_2 = -2.50$ into Equation 14.4 to yield

$$\frac{P_1}{P_2} = \frac{\left(1 + \dfrac{1}{-2.50}\right)}{\left(1 + \dfrac{1}{-1.25}\right)}$$

$$= 3.0$$

or

$$P_1 = 3.0\, P_2$$

Thus the price of an unrestricted coach seat (P_1) should be 3.0 times the price of a Super Saver coach seat (P_2).

Price elasticity is the key; the larger the number of close substitutes, the higher the price elasticity of demand, and therefore the lower the optimal markup and price-cost margin. In electricity pricing, industrial customers such as factories and hospitals can now buy their power from competing public utilities. The industrial customer has so many more close substitute alternatives that the price per kilowatt hour is less than half the price of residential or small commercial users. Again, the higher the price elasticity, the lower the optimal price, *ceteris paribus*.

The increase in profitability from engaging in differential pricing as opposed to uniform pricing across all customer segments can be illustrated with the following example.

Example

Differential Pricing at Taiwan Instrument Co.

Taiwan Instrument Company (TIC) makes computer memory chips in Formosa, which it ships to computer manufacturers in Japan (Market 1) and the United States (Market 2). Demand for the chips in the two markets is given by the following functions:

$$\text{Japan}: P_1 = 12 - Q_1 \qquad\qquad [14.5]$$

$$\text{United States}: P_2 = 8 - Q_2 \qquad\qquad [14.6]$$

where Q_1 and Q_2 are the respective quantities sold (in millions of units), and P_1 and P_2 are the respective prices (in dollars per unit) in the two markets. TIC's total cost function (in millions of dollars) for these memory chips is

$$C = 5 + 2(Q_1 + Q_2) \qquad\qquad [14.7]$$

Case I: Differential Prices TIC's total combined profit in the two markets equals

$$\pi = P_1 Q_1 + P_2 Q_2 - C \qquad\qquad [14.8]$$

$$= (12 - Q_1)Q_1 + (8 - Q_2)Q_2 - [5 + 2(Q_1 + Q_2)]$$

$$= 12Q_1 - Q_1^2 + 8Q_2 - Q_2^2 - 5 - 2Q_1 - 2Q_2$$

$$= 10Q_1 - Q_1^2 + 6Q_2 - Q_2^2 - 5 \qquad\qquad [14.9]$$

(continued)

To maximize profit with respect to Q_1 and Q_2, find the partial derivatives of Equation 14.9 with respect to Q_1 and Q_2, set them equal to zero, and solve for Q_1^* and Q_2^*:

$$\frac{\partial \pi}{\partial Q_1} = 10 - 2Q_1 = 0$$

$$Q_1^* = 5 \text{ (million) units}$$

$$\frac{\partial \pi}{\partial Q_2} = 6 - 2Q_2 = 0$$

$$Q_2^* = 3 \text{ (million) units}$$

Substituting Q_1^* and Q_2^* into the appropriate demand and profit equations yields

$$P_1^* = \$7 \text{ per unit}$$

$$P_2^* = \$5 \text{ per unit}$$

$$\pi^* = \$29 \text{ (million)}$$

This optimal solution is illustrated graphically in Figure 14.3, Panel (a).

Maximizing π with respect to Q_1 and Q_2 is equivalent to setting $MR_1 = MR_2$. The equivalence of MR_1 and MR_2 may be proved by taking the partial derivatives of the TR function with respect to Q_1 and Q_2:

$$TR = P_1 \cdot Q_1 + P_2 \cdot Q_2$$
$$= (12 - Q_1)Q_1 + (8 - Q_2)Q_2$$
$$= 12Q_1 - Q_1^2 + 8Q_2 - Q_2^2 \qquad [14.10]$$

and substituting the solution values, $Q_1^* = 5$ and $Q_2^* = 3$:

$$MR_1 = \frac{\partial TR}{\partial Q_1} = 12 - 2Q_1$$

$$MR_1^* = 12 - 2(5) = \$2 \text{ per unit}$$

$$MR_2 = \frac{\partial TR}{\partial Q_2} = 8 - 2Q_2$$

$$MR_2^* = 8 - 2(3) = \$2 \text{ per unit}$$

which equals the total marginal cost, that is, the derivative of Equation 14.7 with respect to $(Q_1 + Q_2)$.

The respective elasticities in the Japanese and U.S. markets at the optimal solution are

$$E_1 = \frac{dQ_1}{dP_1} \cdot \frac{P_1}{Q_1}$$
$$= -1\left(\frac{7}{5}\right) = -1.40$$

and

$$E_2 = \frac{dQ_2}{dP_2} \cdot \frac{P_2}{Q_2}$$
$$= -1\left(\frac{5}{3}\right) = -1.67$$

Hence we see that, as in the JetBlue Airways example, when the elasticity of demand is less (in absolute value) in Japan (Market 1) than in the United States (Market 2), the price in Japan is greater than in the United States.

(continued)

Case II: Uniform Prices Now suppose that TIC is not permitted to engage in differential pricing.

To determine the profits TIC will earn if it does not discriminate between the two markets, solve the two demand equations for Q_1 and Q_2 and add them to get a total demand function:

$$Q_1 = 12 - P_1$$

$$Q_2 = 8 - P_2$$

$$Q_T = Q_1 + Q_2$$

$$= 12 - P_1 + 8 - P_2$$

Because price discrimination is no longer possible, P_1 must equal P_2, and

$$Q_T = 20 - 2P$$

or

$$P = 10 - \frac{Q_T}{2}$$

Total profit is now

$$\pi = PQ_T - C$$

$$= 10Q_T - \frac{Q_T^2}{2} - 5 - 2Q_T$$

$$= 8Q_T - \frac{Q_T^2}{2} - 5 \qquad [14.11]$$

To find the profit-maximizing level of Q_T, differentiate Equation 14.11 with respect to Q_T, set it equal to zero, and solve for Q_T^*:

$$\frac{d\pi}{dQ_T} = 8 - Q_T = 0$$

$$Q_T^* = 8 \text{ (million) units}$$

Substituting Q_T^* into the appropriate equations yields

$$P^* = 10 - \frac{Q_T}{2} = \$6 \text{ per unit}$$

$$\pi^* = 8Q_T - \frac{Q_T^2}{2} - 5 = \$27 \text{ (million)}$$

$$Q_1^* = 12 - 6 = 6 \text{ (million) units}$$

$$Q_2^* = 8 - 6 = 2 \text{ (million) units}$$

$$MR_1^* = 12 - 2(6) = \$0 \text{ per unit}$$

$$MR_2^* = 8 - 2(2) = \$4 \text{ per unit}$$

This uniform price solution is illustrated graphically in Figure 14.3, Panel (b). As summarized in Table 14.3, note that TIC's profits are higher when it engages in differential pricing ($29 million) than when it does not ($27 million).

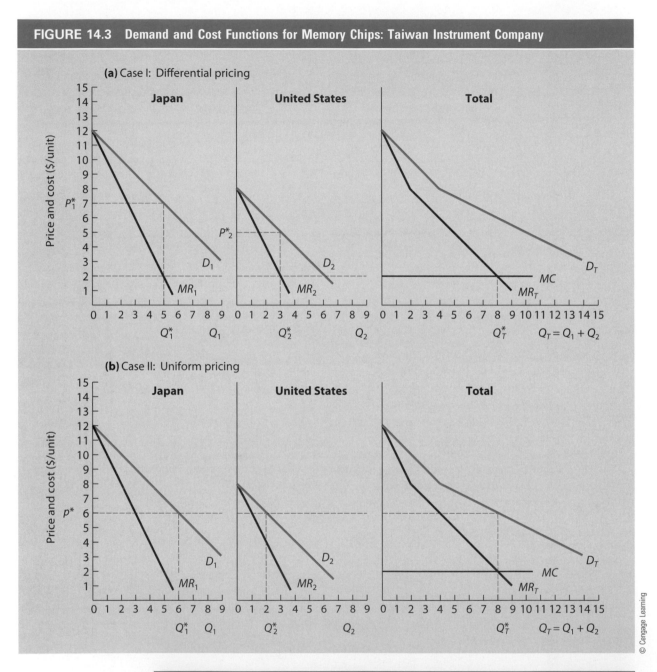

FIGURE 14.3 Demand and Cost Functions for Memory Chips: Taiwan Instrument Company

(a) Case I: Differential pricing

(b) Case II: Uniform pricing

TABLE 14.3 TAIWAN INSTRUMENT COMPANY: EFFECTS OF PRICE DISCRIMINATION

	CASE I DIFFERENTIAL PRICING		CASE II UNIFORM PRICING	
Market	1 (Japan)	2 (U.S.)	1 (Japan)	2 (U.S.)
Price P^* ($/unit)	7	5	6	6
Quantity Q^* (million units)	5	3	6	2
Marginal Revenue MR^* ($/unit)	2	2	0	4
Profit π^* ($ million)	29		27	

© Cengage Learning

DIFFERENTIAL PRICING IN TARGET MARKET SEGMENTS

After identifying the different value drivers for various segments of the target market and setting an optimal differential price, firms must prevent resale between the segments using a variety of "fences." Two of the most frequent methods of direct segmentation that prevent resale involve intertemporal pricing (1) by time-of-day or day-of-week and (2) differential pricing by delivery location.

Congestion-based pricing at peak-demand periods on roadways, bridges, and subway systems is an example of intertemporal pricing, illustrated in Figure 14.4. Peak-period drivers place demands on the Dulles toll road between 6:00 A.M. and 9:00 A.M. far in excess of its carrying capacity (Q_C). Charging commuters a toll equal to just the wear and tear imposed by their vehicle passing over the toll road pavement (i.e., an off-peak marginal cost, MC_{OP}) induces many more cars to enter the highway (Q_{PEAK}) than can be accommodated (i.e., $Q_P > Q_C$). The result is slow-downs, stoppages, and a markedly increased travel time for each commuter. As a result, beyond Q_C, the traffic volume at which this congestion begins, MC_P rises steeply, representing the incremental fuel and time delay costs imposed (by one additional car) on all the other drivers along each 10-mile stretch of congested toll road.

The advantage of a congestion toll such as $(P_P - MC_{OP}) = \$2$ is that it induces discretionary peak-period travelers to switch to other travel times and alternative modes of

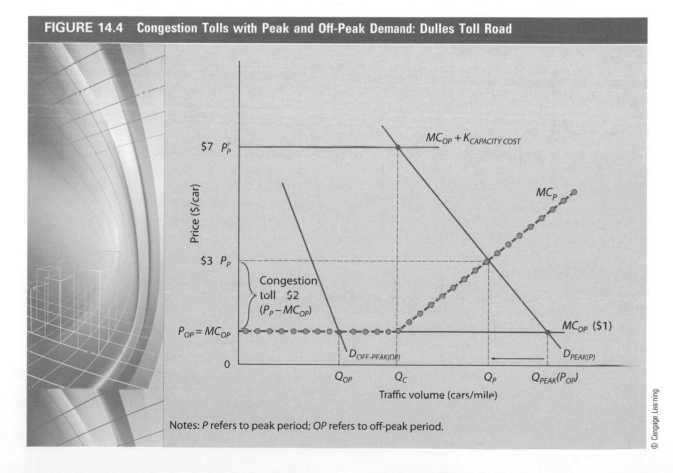

FIGURE 14.4 Congestion Tolls with Peak and Off-Peak Demand: Dulles Toll Road

Notes: *P* refers to peak period; *OP* refers to off-peak period.

transportation or routes when this specific 10-mile segment is congested. When a toll road authority sets peak-period prices of $3 just sufficient to cover this congestion cost plus the off-peak MC, traffic volume would decline from Q_{PEAK} (P_{OP}) to Q_P, and the equilibrium differential prices P_P and P_{OP} would emerge. Such **congestion pricing** reflects the true resource cost of the scarce transportation system capacity at peak travel times.

congestion pricing
A fee that reflects the true marginal cost imposed by demand in excess of capacity.

Like off-peak roadway pricing, many other examples of differential pricing entail charging differential prices for the same capacity *at different times*. Hence, such customers are not in rivalry for the same capacity. Parking meters in San Francisco can now raise price between 10:00 A.M. and 2:00 P.M. Coca-Cola has new cold drink machines that vary the price by time of day, as well as by the predicted high temperature for the day. The demanders of matinee ($5) and evening movie theaters ($9) are not in rivalry for the same theater seats. First-run movies and subsequent movie videos, hardback and later paperback editions of books, seasonal discounts in the resort and cruise ship businesses, and weekend discounts in hotels all represent effective segmentation of different target customer classes by time of purchase.

Direct Segmentation with "Fences"

Direct segmentation of target customer classes not in rivalry with one another for the same capacity can also be accomplished by selling various versions of a product customized for target segments, or by varying the price by delivery location. Customers who arrive at the suburban neighborhood rental counters of Hertz and Avis have flexibly timed, convenience-based uses for rental cars. Consequently, demand is much more price sensitive than the demand at the airport by business travelers. A recent study found that weekday rates for a midsize sedan were $43 in neighborhood rental locations versus $69 on average in airport rental locations.[6] Because round-trip taxi fares from airports to the neighborhood locations would typically far exceed the $26 price difference, Avis and Hertz customers are effectively segmented by rental location.

Another example of location-based segmentation would be fashion clothing from France's Arche or Ralph Lauren sold less expensively in discount outlets along interstate highways than in suburban storefronts or vacation resorts. Outlet mall shoppers almost never overlap with the customers these companies find in their trendy boutiques. Hence, geographic segmentation works. Outlet shoppers will also buy a less costly, less durable version of the product (e.g., a lighter-weight chemise cloth in Polo golf shirts), so in differential pricing, Ralph Lauren accomplishes more than just inventory clearance without any danger of cannibalizing full-price sales. So, total sales expand to address this new segment created by the new location.

Example

Congestion Charges on Los Angeles, San Diego, Houston, Minneapolis, Denver, and Dulles Toll Roads[7]

The typical American spent over 34 hours per year in traffic jams in 2009 due to peak-period road congestion. Los Angeles drivers spent 63 hours, equivalent to 1.5 weeks of unpaid work. Urban traffic grew by 20 percent during 1995–2005 but urban roadways increased by only 2 percent. The federal excise tax on gasoline of 18.4 cents per gallon

(continued)

---

[6]"Playing the Car-Rental Game," *Wall Street Journal* (July 31, 2002), p. D3; and "Highway Nirvana at a Price," *Wall Street Journal* (July 6, 2004), p. A15.

(which is earmarked to repair and build federal highways) has not increased since the early 1990s. But is the answer simply more highways? Communities in southern California, New Jersey, Houston, and Washington, DC, think not.

Congestion tolls that charge commuters for the incremental time loss and fuel increase their cars impose on other drivers during peak periods have been adopted on several public and private toll roads around the United States. Every day, 24,000 drivers pay a peak-period congestion toll of $3.30 per trip for a 10-mile stretch of true expressway in Orange County, California. Toll booths, which themselves cause delays, have been replaced by credit-card-size transponders mounted in dashboards from which overhead wireless receivers assess tolls as the cars speed by. Such onboard-units (OBUs) will be commonplace on all cars and trucks by 2013, and they may become the communications hub of the vehicle, offering information on road conditions ahead, directions to inexpensive gas stations, and emergency dispatch services based on the built-in global positioning satellite (GPS) device.

In Figure 14.4 the cost of additional vehicles on increased peak-period road congestion raises the peak period toll to $3 from an off-peak toll of $1. High occupancy vehicle (HOV) lanes, normally reserved for buses and carpools, can be accessed for as little as $0.25 off peak but cost $8 per trip during peak traffic volume. Adopting real-time dynamic pricing with traffic volume measured every 6 minutes, and opening HOV lanes when they are underutilized, San Diego has increased its total road capacity by 64 percent. Electronic debits for driving on inner city streets in London costs £8 per day (about $12) between 7:00 A.M. and 6:00 P.M. The congestion toll expenses of a typical commuter mount up quickly. But the effect of the tolls has been noticeable; traffic in London's designated congestion zone is down 30 percent. And time is money, so faced with the slow 25–40 mph commute on adjacent "freeways," many peak-period travelers in Los Angeles, San Diego, Houston, Minneapolis, Denver, and Washington, DC, are opting for the differential pricing of a 65 mph toll road.

---

[7]Based on "American Idle On the Road," *Wall Street Journal* (February 2, 2011), p. D1; "Transportation Infrastructure," Chapter 6, *Economic Report of the President* (Washington, DC: U.S. Government Printing Office, 2007).

Hal Varian and Carl Shapiro argued that such "versioning" is an especially good way to sell information economy items such as software.[8] A voice recognition package sells for $79 as general-purpose Voice ProPad, for $795 as Office Talk, and for $7,995 as Voice Ortho, a special-purpose medical transcriber for surgical theatres. All three versions derive from the same source code, but the more comprehensive version generates 100 times as much value to particular target customers. In contrast, when Amazon sells the *same* book or DVD at different prices to customers with different clickstreams, that degree of differential pricing for identical versions of the product often leads to adverse customer reactions. Coca-Cola is finding the same resistance to its differential time-of-day pricing in soft drink machines. As a result, many sellers adopt the techniques of *indirect segmentation* using two-part tariffs, couponing, and bundling. With indirect segmentation, the customer himself or herself selects what differential price to pay from a variety of available alternatives.

---

[8]C. Shapiro and H. Varian, "Versioning," *Harvard Business Review* (November/December 1998), pp. 106–114.

Dynamic Pricing for Electricity[9]

In principle, as experience has shown in Britain, Australia, and New Zealand, deregulation of electricity can work well if peak-load customers are asked to pay a price that reflects marginal cost. As much as 40 percent of the variation in intraday cost is attributable to extraordinary transmission line fees and old inefficient plants fired up to meet the last 5 percent of peak demand. For example, running a clothes dryer at 4:00 P.M. in July imposes wholesale costs on New England electric utilities of $0.22 per kWh, relative to approximately $0.08 per kWh at 10:00 P.M. in July, and $0.02 per kWh in April. Thirty percent of U.S. households are now connected to so-called smart meters that charge customers variable prices per hour from $0.04 per kWh to $0.17 per kWh depending on the time of day. Demand from lower-income and middle-income households appears to be quite elastic to rising electric rates during peak periods. Smart appliances can now turn off the dryer when California electricity on time-of-day meters rises in price during the 6:00 P.M. to 9:00 P.M. peak evening period.

[9]Based on "Making Meters Smarter," *BusinessWeek On-Line* (October 5, 2009); "Smart Meters Give Customers a Break," *Today* (March 21, 2007), p. 2B; "Creating a Smarter U.S. Electricity Grid," *Journal of Economic Perspectives* (Winter 2012), pp. 29–48, and P. Joskow and C. Wolfram, "Dynamic Pricing of Electricity," American Economic Review (May 2012), pp. 381–385.

Optimal Two-Part Tariffs

Two-part tariffs entail charging both a lump-sum entry fee for access to the facility or service and a per-unit user fee for each unit sale consumed. Amusement parks, nightclubs, golf and tennis clubs, copier leasing companies, cellular phone providers,

WHAT WENT RIGHT • WHAT WENT WRONG

Unlimited Data at Verizon Wireless[10]

Verizon surpassed AT&T as the nation's largest telecom carrier for smart phones. Charging $39 per month for wireless subscription and a $30 flat fee for unlimited data downloads and uploads, Verizon doubled its smart phone subscriber base from 8 to 16 million between 2009 and 2010 with all categories of its wireless customers totaling 94 million to AT&T's slightly larger 96 million subscribers. Verizon's unlimited data plan contrasted with AT&T's two-tiered limited data plans. By mid-2011, however, a marginal price of zero had generated enormous excess demand on bandwidth capacity from the heaviest data users. Streaming just three high-definition movies from Netflix requires 5 gigabytes of data. AT&T announced plans to slow the connection speed of the data users who exceeded a 3-gigabyte cap but that resulted in an enormous backlash. Regular smart phone customers streaming TV, games, and short videos from YouTube as well as occasionally accessing big databases had little interest in slower downloads even if one could save substantial money.

Instead, Verizon has segmented the market allowing customers to choose from several two-part pricing plans. Verizon's basic $30 subscription package offers just 2 gigabytes of data a month, only enough to send 1,000 e-mails, listen to 20 hours of radio, watch 2 hours of video, upload 20 Facebook photos, and surf the web. Ninety-five percent of Verizon customers fall within this range of usage but some customers use much more transmission and reception capacity. Heavier use charges beyond the flat subscription fee will now apply—5 gigabytes a month for $50, and 10 megabytes for $80. Overcharges at $10 per month per gigabyte beyond the data plan limit will also apply. Verizon decided that a differential two-part pricing solution based on a flat fee plus a user charge was far preferable to limiting service quality.

[10]"Verizon Tests Lower Unlimited Pricing," *Wall Street Journal* (November 9, 2010), p. A14; "Verizon Alters Data Pricing, *Wall Street Journal* (July 6, 2011), p. D2; "A Tangled Family Tree," *Wall Street Journal* (March 29, 2011), p. B6; "Users Rip AT&T Data Curbs," *Wall Street Journal* (March 3, 2012), p. B3.

Internet access providers, and rental car companies often employ such pricing. Their revenue per unit sale is a nonlinear function of two parts: a lump-sum monthly or daily fee that provides access to the facility, phone, computer, or rental car independent of use, and a per-hour or per-minute or per-mile fee that varies with usage. The magnitude per unit of user fees should at least cover marginal costs so that heavy demanders "pay the freight" through higher total user fees. Tying the price for a leased copier to a metering counter that effectively measures intensity of use results in a differential monthly leasing fee across customer segments plus a cheap incremental cost per copy.

Companies differ on whether to set high or low entry fees and whether to charge high or low user fees. Telecom carriers and Gillette practically give away their cell phones and razors but then charge steep prices for the calls, downloads, and blades. In contrast, iPods are pricey at the front end but iTunes thereafter are quite cheap. Similarly, most golf and tennis clubs charge substantial membership fees and annual dues, but thereafter adopt trivial user fees (e.g., $5 per court hour or $25 for greens fees).[11] As we will see, just how much above marginal cost to set the optimal user fee depends on how dissimilar are the different segments of customer demand.

Let's investigate how to analyze an optimal two-part tariff. Consider the situation depicted in Figure 14.5 for separate customer segments with relatively elastic (D_1) and relatively inelastic demand (D_2) for rental autos. These might be young couples who are renting cars for vacationing (D_1) and manufacturers' trade representatives renting cars for making sales calls (D_2). The challenge is to find a uniform daily rate (the lump-sum

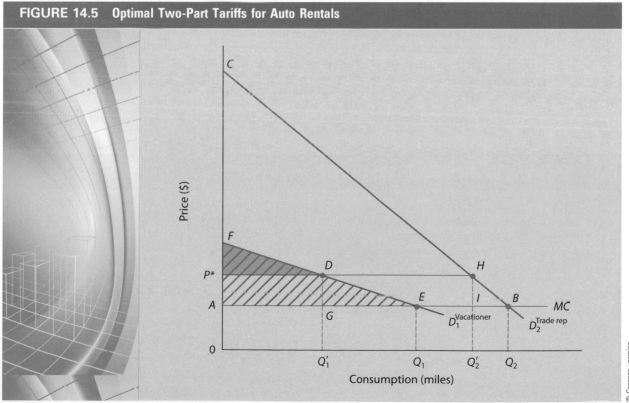

FIGURE 14.5 Optimal Two-Part Tariffs for Auto Rentals

---

[11]When the Pebble Beach golf course and the Wimbledon tennis club have $350 greens fees for a round of golf or two sets of tennis, those user fees reflect congestion-based pricing rather than optimal two-part tariffs.

access fee) and a mileage charge (the user charge) that maximize profit and keep both customer segments in the market. One alternative would be to price the mileage at its marginal cost $(MC) =$ height OA and elicit Q_1 and Q_2 usage from each segment while realizing from both the maximum daily rate that the price-sensitive vacationer along D_1 will pay (namely, hatched area AEF).

Perhaps, however, a better alternative is available. Suppose the car rental agency raises the mileage charge to P^* and reduces the daily access fee to the hatched and shaded area P^*DF. Mileage will decline in both segments (to Q_1' and Q_2', respectively), and area P^*DEA will be net revenue lost by virtue of the reduced daily access fee in both segments. However, the additional net revenue from mileage charges (P^*DGA in one segment and P^*HIA in the other segment) will more than offset the lost access fees. In particular, profits of the car rental agency will increase by the difference of area $DHIE$—area DEG. This result is generalizable to other optimal two-part tariff decisions.

Consequently, in addition to charging a positive lump-sum access fee, a price-discriminating monopolist will adopt two-part tariffs that price usage above its marginal cost. The more similar the price elasticity of demands of the target customer segments, the closer the user charge should be to marginal cost.

Couponing

Another pricing mechanism for indirectly segmenting the market and allowing the customer to select what level of consumption and total price to pay is couponing. The $49 billion spent on direct-mail marketing with accompanying rebate and coupon offers surpassed the amount spent on newspaper ($45 billion) and television ($43 billion) advertising for the first time in the United States in 2003. This direct marketing approach is made possible by successful forecasting based on consumer spending patterns. Companies have access to cash register and credit card data as well as property tax and public utility usage records. These sources allow Lowe's Home Improvement, for example, to project with more than 80 percent accuracy the month in which a particular household will buy a gas grill.

 WHAT WENT RIGHT • WHAT WENT WRONG

Two-Part Pricing at Disney World

The original studies of optimal two-part tariffs were commissioned for the Disney theme parks in California and Florida. Disney World in Orlando opened with an optimal entrance fee plus a user charge per ride. Specifically, customers purchased booklets of tickets for the rides once they were already inside the theme park, having earlier paid uniform lump-sum fees at the entrance gates. For several years this system worked quite well as first-time visitors encountered all the Disney-theme displays and venues and dispersed across the grounds taking the occasional ride. User charges per ride were sufficient to discourage persistent riding and re-riding of favorites like Space Mountain.

Before long, however, repeat-visitor demand became the key to profitable operation of the theme parks. The target customer was a couple with two children who might be on their third or fourth Disney vacation. As certain attractions and rides became the magnet that drew families back, long lines developed at the popular rides and shows. Surveys showed that customers began to feel that the tickets they purchased were not valid for rides and that entry fees to enter the park were too steep in light of the disappointing congestion inside. These negative perceptions of two-part tariffs led Disney to replace them with a menu of differential entry fees based on projected usage of the Magic Kingdom, Epcot, and Disney Studios.

More recently, Universal Studios theme parks have experimented with reducing congestion through time-stamped passes to popular rides and with preferential treatment for customers who have paid for shorter wait times.

WHAT WENT RIGHT • WHAT WENT WRONG

Price-Sensitive Customers Redeem

Pillsbury measured the price elasticity of demand for its cake mix customers who redeem coupons and found it to be −0.43, whereas that of the nonredeemers was −0.21. Similarly, Purina measured the price elasticity of coupon redeemers among its cat food customers as −1.13 and among nonredeemers as −0.49. Coupons for frozen potato dishes at Ore-Ida are redeemed by households with price elasticity of −1.33, and nonredeeming households have price elasticity of −1.97. Clearly, in all these cases, couponing is a way to segment the market and offer a discount to the more price-sensitive segment.

Such laser-like precision in targeting encourages differential pricing. If coupons worth 25 cents off the price of a box of cereal, 40 percent off the price of fashion clothing, or $50 rebates off the price of an expensive gas grill are redeemed religiously by some segments but ignored by others, Kellogg, Neiman Marcus, and Lowe's will segment the market with these direct mail promotions. The price-sensitive customers who constantly redeem coupons and file for rebates receive a lower net price, consistent with Equation 14.4.

Bundling

Bundling is another highly effective pricing mechanism that sellers use to capture profit from differential pricing across target customer segments. Have you ever wondered why Time Warner Cable offers Showtime, the channel for popular first-run movies, only in a bundled package that includes the History channel? One insight is that this paired bundle of product offerings occurs because some other Time Warner customer is a history buff who is wondering why the History channel comes with access to largely unwatched movies. That is, the operating profit to a seller from bundling negatively correlated demands is always larger than the operating profit from selling equally costly products separately. Let's see why.

reservation prices
The maximum price a customer will pay to reserve a product or service unto his or her own use.

Suppose that two sets of customers have the following **reservation prices** for two cable channels, each of which incurs variable licensing fees of $1 for a single showing to a single household. Movie buffs would pay $9 for access to first-run movies and $2 for access to historical documentaries. History buffs would pay $8 for access to the History channel and $3 for access to Showtime. If the channels are priced uniformly to both customer segments as separate products, Time Warner can realize at most $8 (or $9 − $1) on Showtime and $7 (or $8 − $1) on the History channel for a total of $15 operating profit.[12] However, note that both types of customers would pay up to $11 for the combined pair of channels rather than do without. If Time Warner made them available only as a bundled package, sales revenue would be $22 − $4 licensing fees for a total of $18 operating profit, which is greater than the $15 we previously calculated.

As long as one customer is willing to pay more for product A that another customer wants less than product B, the seller who is restricted to charging the two customers the same uniform price will always be better off bundling the two items, assuming all reservation prices exceed variable cost. Such inversely correlated demands occur in many settings. All-inclusive Caribbean resorts such as $595 per day Bitter End on Virgin Gorda or Hotel Isle de France in St. Bart's have guests who value $75 gourmet lunches and

---

[12]In this example, selling both products separately to both customer segments does not pay because of the much lower prices required. Specifically, Showtime priced separately into both segments would have to sell for as little as $3, thereby earning operating profits of $6 − $2 = $4, and the History channel would have to sell for as little as $2, earning $4 − $2 = $2. Thus, the total profit of $6 from selling all products to all customers at a uniform price would substantially diminish the potential profit of $15 from selling each product to its target market alone. If the asymmetric demands in the two segments were not so different, this result could reverse, as long as all reservation prices were greater than variable cost.

$350 per night fabulous cabanas but would not pay much for all the water sports activities and equipment, while other guests value $170 per day water sports activities but would not pay such high prices for better food or cabanas. Similarly, Elizabeth Arden's $225 all-inclusive half-day spas have clients who would not pay high-margin $50 prices for at least one of the following five services: facials, mud wraps, massage, manicures, and pedicures. Bundling all these services together always raises profitability when target customer demand is inversely correlated across the offerings as long as variable costs of the separate components are below the customers' willingness to pay for each.

Now, returning to the cable channel example, suppose the variable costs are higher at, say, $3. The History channel valued at $2 by the movie buff is no longer a profitable sale. Pure bundling includes this unprofitable sale and generates the same $22 revenue but now incurs $12 of total variable cost, yielding a profit of only $10. Forgoing the sale of the History channel to the movie buff by selling each product separately at a $9 price for Showtime and an $8 price for the History channel generates $6 (or $9 − $3) on Showtime and $5 (or $8 − $3) on the History channel, yielding a total of $11 operating profit. Quite intuitively, pure bundling will be less attractive than pricing separately when some of the bundled sales are unprofitable.

It is also easy to see why positively correlated demand across customers works against bundling. Figure 14.6 displays reservation prices along a "budget" line that our customers in the earlier example are willing to spend on the two products.[13] The y-intercept is the total willingness-to-pay constraint for the two products—namely, $P_h + P_m = \$11$. With Showtime reservation prices on the vertical axis and History channel reservation prices on the horizontal axis, each customer's mix of reservation prices lies along the line

$$P_m = \$11 - 1P_h \qquad [14.12]$$

The −1 in Equation 14.12 signifies the perfect negative correlation between the reservation prices (demand) of our movie buff and those of our history buff. But suppose Time Warner has a third type of customer whose reservation prices are positively correlated with those of the movie buffs—that is, a third type of customer who values Showtime at $8 and the History channel at $5. These reservation prices are high when the movie buff's reservation price is high and low when the movie buff's reservation price is low. Such positively correlated demand lies above the budget constraint in Figure 14.6 because the total willingness to pay on the left-hand side of Equation 14.12 is no longer $11 but rather is now $13, as shown for Point 3.

With positively correlated demands across two of the three customer types, Time Warner could sell the Showtime-History bundle to all three for $11 and earn $15 [3 × ($11 − $6)].[14] However, a better alternative is available. **Mixed bundling** sells the products both separately and as a bundle with the bundled price discounted below the sum of the two separate prices. In our three-customer-type example, Time Warner could sell Showtime for $9 and the History channel for $8, while making the Showtime-History bundle available for the package price of $13. The third type of customer would opt for the bundle, whereas each of the other types of customers would buy one product only. Revenue for this mixed bundling approach totals $30, but only four license fees are required, therefore earning $18 in profit. In general, pure bundling generates less profit than mixed bundling when positively correlated demands are involved. That's why Arden's salons sell their beauty treatments bundled for $225 or $50 each.

mixed bundling
Selling multiple products both separately and together for less than the sum of the separate prices.

---

[13]This budget line is analogous to the budget line of a household making consumption decisions, except in this case it is the firm that is constrained by the maximum expenditure the customer is willing to make on the two goods.

[14]Here we are again assuming that variable costs are at the higher level of $3 per showing.

FIGURE 14.6   Reservation Prices for Three Customer Segments

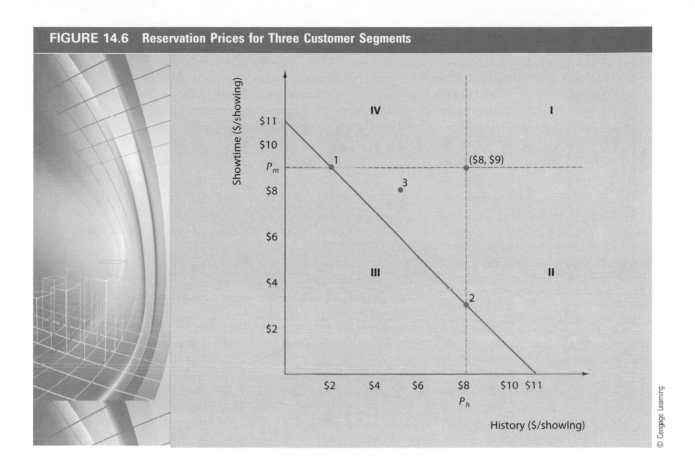

Figure 14.6 can be used to characterize the attractiveness of pure bundling for the seller. If all customers have perfectly negatively correlated demands, their reservation prices lie, as we have seen, along the $11 budget constraint. If customers have positively correlated demands, their reservation prices will lie consistently either above or below this reservation budget constraint. With separate product prices of $P_m = \$9$ and $P_h = \$8$, customers with reservation prices in Quadrant I will always buy both products rather than one of the separate products alone (Quadrants II and IV) while those in Quadrant III will never buy either product sold separately. In addition, however, we know that customers with reservation prices above the reservation budget constraint will buy the bundled package and those below will not. Optimally, Customer 3 will therefore purchase the bundle, Customer 1 will purchase Showtime alone, and Customer 2 will purchase the History channel alone. Only mixed bundling can achieve this result.

Example

McDonald's Introduces Mixed Bundles as "Extra Value Meals"

In the United States, fast food consumption skyrocketed in the last two decades as 70 percent of households became two-worker households, and families began eating out several times a week. Beer and pizza or a soft drink, burger, and fries became the standard supper for many high-time-cost households. With greater health

(continued)

consciousness, however, not everyone who wanted a burger wanted the fries. In other cases, some consumers wanted the fries but not the burger, and preferred lower fat chicken sandwiches instead. McDonald's Corporation has done its best to respond to these customer dissimilarities by introducing "Extra Value Meals" that bundled chicken sandwiches with fries and a medium soft drink.

The 2006 prices for some of McDonald's most popular menu items are listed here:

MENU ITEM	SEPARATE PRICE ($)	BUNDLED PRICE ($)	TOTAL IF PURCHASED SEPARATELY ($)
Large French Fries	1.39		
Medium Soft Drink	1.09		
McGrill Chicken Sandwich	2.69	4.29	5.17
Chicken McNuggets	2.79	4.29	5.27
McChicken Sandwich	1.00	3.39	3.48
Big and Tasty Burger	1.59	3.49	4.07
Double Cheeseburger	1.00	3.39	3.48
Big Mac	2.19	3.79	4.67
Quarter Pounder	2.19	3.79	4.67

Examining only the last two columns, we see that some bundled "Extra Value Meal" customers (McChicken Sandwich Meal and Double Cheeseburger Meal) are getting very little discount.

To summarize, two-part tariffs, couponing, and bundling are pricing mechanisms that induce customers to segment themselves indirectly. Two-part tariffs are particularly effective in capturing higher profits than uniform prices when customer segments are more nearly identical in their price elasticity of demand. Couponing works best when target segments are extraordinarily different in their price elasticity of demand. Bundling captures additional profit when segmented target customer demand is inversely correlated across multiple products.

Price Discrimination

price discrimination
The act of selling the same good or service, distributed in a single channel, at different prices to different buyers during the same period of time.

Price discrimination is defined as selling the same product or service out of the same distribution channel at different prices to different buyers during the same period of time. Examples of price discrimination include the following:

- Doctors, dentists, hospitals, lawyers, and tax preparers who charge clients who reside in wealthy zip codes more for the same service than those who reside in poorer zip codes
- Dell Inc.'s ultralight laptop, which it sells for $2,307 to small business customers, for $2,228 to health care companies, and for $2,072 to state and local governments
- Firms that sell the exact same product under two different labels at widely varying prices (Hotpoint and Kenmore appliances, Michelin and Sears Roadhandler radial tires)
- Athletic teams that sponsor family nights and ladies' nights at discount prices, while other customers pay the full price

- Hotels, restaurants, and other businesses that offer discounts to senior citizens. Differentially priced seats in coach class on a particular flight based on how far ahead you book the reservation or Saturday night stay overs
- South Korean TV manufacturers who sell products direct to the customer at a lower price in the United States than in Japan

Most differential pricing to a firm's retail customers is perfectly legal.[15] It raises profits because it transfers some of the excess customer value (the satisfaction gained from the purchase of the product) from buyer to seller relative to the excess value generated for customers who pay a lower uniform price.

If a coffee aficionado were willing to pay $4 for a large cup of fresh brewed java for which Dunkin' Donuts charges $1.95, and $5 for the same cup of fresh brewed java bundled (on request) with a shot of espresso for which Starbucks charges $3.50, the consumer's excess value would decline from $2.05 at Dunkin' Donuts to $1.50 at Starbucks. Nevertheless, in the case where this customer declines the shot of espresso, Starbucks must have offered something else of value because the customer's willingness to pay rose from $4 to $5. If this customer kept returning to Starbucks, we should assume that the lifestyle and group identity available at Starbucks attracted his or her business.

When Nationwide and GMAC auto insurance lower rates based on the reduced theft and collision risk exposure of the places you drive, that is not price discrimination. A GPS tracking device in the car confirms that the loss protection service is different.

Example

e-Business Clickstreams Allow Price Discrimination: Personify and Virtual Vineyards[16]

Personify, an Internet service company, created software that allows Web businesses to categorize buyers based on their clickstream patterns. Using this software, Virtual Vineyards, CDNow, and Amazon.com have experimented with charging different prices for the same wine, CD, or book based on the clickstream path. Let's see how this capability might work for Virtual Vineyards.

Incremental variable plus direct fixed costs in making table wines run at least $8 for the following inputs: $0.50 for the bottle itself, $0.30 for the cork, $0.20 for the label, $2 per bottle for the quickly decaying barrel used for aging, plus anywhere from $5 to $50 for the grapes. If it costs $220 to produce and stock a case of 20 bottles, and if five customers will pay $24 a bottle while another 15 customers will pay $10 a bottle, uniform pricing across all 20 customers will result in a $20 loss [($10 × 20 = $200) − $220 = −$20]. At a $10 uniform price, all 20 customers will buy but the Virtual Vineyards will stop producing this wine. Similarly, at a $24 price, only five customers will buy, and the Virtual Vineyards again discontinues this wine because of now even more substantial losses [($24 × 5 = $120) − $200 = −$100].

But suppose five customers are asked to pay $20 per bottle, while 15 more are asked to pay $9. Each group pays less than their willingness to pay and less than their proposed uniform prices of $24 and $10, yet the winery now stands to make a profit: (5 × $20) + (15 × $9) = $235 − $220 = $15. Virtual Vineyards could perhaps segment this market and prevent resale by charging $20 in the retail distribution channel and $9 for limited quantities at the winery. Alternatively, they could price

(continued)

discriminate by the clickstream of the customers visiting their Web site. New customers who first clicked through to the history of the awards won by the winery would be asked to pay $20 for the new release, whereas returning customers who renew their membership online in the frequent buyer program and whose last purchase order was a case would be asked to pay $9 for the new release.

[16]Based on "I Got It Cheaper Than You," *Forbes* (November 2, 1998), pp. 83–84; and "The Art and Science of Pricing Wine," *CNet* (July 3, 2003).

In the limiting case of *perfect price discrimination* (PPD), sometimes called *first degree* price discrimination, the seller discovers the maximum price each individual is willing to pay for each unit purchased. A PPD monopolist then charges each purchaser this maximum reservation price in order to capture the consumer's entire perceived excess value above the cost-covering price. However, because the information required for such pricing is so extensive, perfect price discrimination almost never occurs. Instead, as we have seen in studying two-part tariffs, couponing, and bundling, firms often price discriminate by allowing customers within indirectly segmented groups to determine their own price through intensity of use, redemption behavior, or selection of packages of products such as Disney World entrance fees (so-called *second degree* price discrimination). Finally, firms may attempt to price discriminate through directly segmenting classes of customers by time or location of purchase and then charging one uniform price within each customer class (so-called *third degree* price discrimination).

PRICING IN PRACTICE

To this point, the chapter discussed firms that seek to maximize short-run profits. However, pricing is an area where a longer-run life cycle view of the firm's decision making is helpful.

Product Life Cycle Framework[17]

life cycle pricing
Pricing that varies throughout the product life cycle.

In the early stages of **life cycle pricing**, the marketing, operations, and financial managers decide what the customer will value, how the firm can manage the supply chain to consistently deliver those characteristics, and how much it will cost, including the financing costs. If the value-based prices can cover this long-run full cost, the product becomes a prototype. Each proposed product or service then proceeds to marketing research, where the demand at various price points in several distribution channels usually is explored. Marketing research will identify a target price that the cross-functional product manager or the general managers will know is required on average over the product life cycle in order for the new product to provide sufficient revenue to cover fully allocated cost.

Once a product or service rollout takes place (usually at target price levels), the marketing plan often authorizes promotional discounts. In this stage of the life cycle, the firm is interested in penetrating the market. To do so requires coupons, free samples, name recognition advertising, and slot-in allowances on retail shelves. *Penetration pricing*

[17]For a discussion of the conceptual framework of value-based pricing over a product's life cycle, see T. Nagle, J. Hogan, and J. Zale, *The Strategy and Tactics of Pricing*, 5th ed. (Upper Saddle River, NJ: Prentice Hall, 2011), Chapter 7.

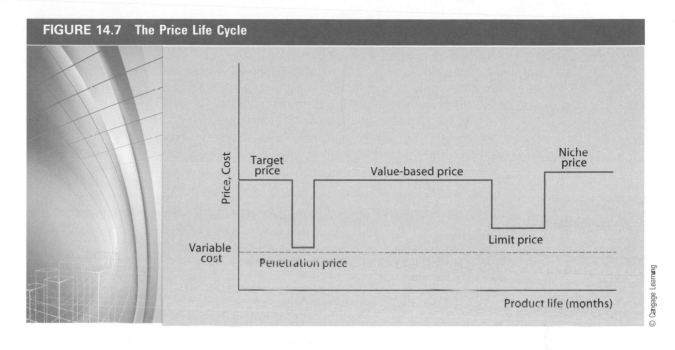

FIGURE 14.7   The Price Life Cycle

therefore characterizes this early stage of the product life cycle at which net prices to the manufacturer fall below the firm's target price, as shown in Figure 14.7.

When a new product is introduced by a firm, pricing for that product is a difficult and critical decision, especially if the product is a durable good—one that has a relatively long useful life. The difficulty of pricing the new product comes from not knowing the level of demand with confidence. If the price is initially set too low, some potential customers will be able to buy the product at a price below what they are willing to pay. These lost profits will be gone forever. This problem is accentuated when the firm initially has limited production capacity for the new product.

price skimming A new-product pricing strategy that results in a high initial product price being reduced over time as demand at the higher price is satisfied.

Under these circumstances, many firms adopt a strategy of **price skimming**, or pricing down along the demand curve. The initial price is set at a high level, even though the firm fully intends to make later price reductions. When the product is first introduced, a group of fashion-conscious or technology-conscious early adopters will pay the high price established by the firm. Once this source of demand is exhausted, the price is reduced to attract a new group of customers. Flat-screen TVs and handheld computers such as the Blackberry and Palm's Treo are excellent examples of this phenomenon. As we discussed in Chapter 13, manufacturers who engage in price skimming on industrial equipment (e.g., mainframe computers and corporate jets) need credibility mechanisms to assure early full-price customers that later discounting will be limited.

In the mature stage of the product or service life cycle, organic growth comes from focusing on product differentiation and commitment to building the brand. Marketing team initiatives will add value in both product refinements and order management processes through brand-name advertising, product updates, or increased flexibility in accepting change orders from regular customers. Each decision at this mature stage is motivated by a desire to realize the highest *value-based pricing* allowed by the competitive conditions and potential entry threats. Although at times this approach to pricing can be overwhelmed by the necessity of short-term tactics to defend market share, the product life cycle remains a planning framework to which the pricing manager often returns.

At a late mature stage of the product or service life cycle, product managers may decide to limit price, reducing it well below the value-based pricing level in order to deter entry. *Limit pricing* appears to be inconsistent with profit maximization but in fact is motivated by a long-term profitability objective.

Because competitors are constantly devising lower-cost ways of imitating leading products, limit pricing sometimes has only temporary success. If the entry threat materializes into a real live new entrant, many incumbent firms then decide to accommodate by raising prices in a particular high-price, high-margin market niche. This pricing practice is often referred to as *niche pricing*. Concluding that declining market share from entry into the mass market is inevitable, the incumbent moves upmarket and sells its experience and expertise at high prices in the top-end segments of the market, much as it did at the start of the product life cycle.

Example

Loss of Patent Protection Limits the Price of Prozac: Eli Lilly

When brand-name pharmaceuticals reach the end of their 20-year patent protection, sales may plummet unless prices are radically reduced. Some formerly patented drugs lose as much as 80 percent of their sales in the *first year* after generic substitutes are introduced. The ulcer relief medicine Zantac, which was at the time Glaxo's biggest seller, plummeted 51 percent in the first half-year after loss of patent protection. By year-end, 10 rival products were on the shelves. Zovirax, an anti-herpes medication, lost 39 percent in the first six months after generics costing only 20 percent of Zovirax' price appeared in the marketplace. And sales of Bristol-Myers Squibb's high-blood-pressure drug Capoten, at $0.57 per pill, declined 83 percent the year that a substitute generic pill at $0.03 was introduced.

In light of these disastrous experiences throughout the pharmaceutical industry, Eli Lilly limited the price of the depression treatment Prozac to variable plus direct fixed costs in order to arrest or at least slow the onslaught of imitators into its antidepressants market. We saw in Chapters 11 and 13 that such limit pricing strategies can deter entry and thereby raise the discounted present value of long-term cash flow to stockholders relative to maximizing short-run profitability.

Full-Cost Pricing versus Incremental Contribution Analysis

full-cost pricing A method of determining prices that cover overhead and other indirect fixed costs, as well as the variable and direct fixed costs.

Some inadvisable pricing practices are widely adopted: two examples are full-cost pricing and target return-on-investment pricing. **Full-cost pricing** requires that not only direct fixed costs of a particular product line such as licensing and maintenance and advertising be considered in pricing, but even indirect fixed costs of overhead and capital financing be added to variable costs to arrive at a final price. Indirect costs may be allocated among a firm's several products in a number of ways. One typical method is to estimate total indirect fixed costs assuming the firm operates at a standard level of output, such as 70 to 80 percent of capacity, and then allocate the indirect costs by volume.

Example

Niche Pricing at Pfizer[18]

Pfizer's No. 1 LDL cholesterol-reducing drug Lipitor had almost $10 billion in sales. Norvasc, Pfizer's second flagship product, had $4.34 billion in sales. Unfortunately for Pfizer, the patents on these leading cholesterol and hypertension drugs have expired.

(continued)

Pfizer estimates that three million Americans are candidates for a combined pill, Caduet (Norvasc + Lipitor), that should preserve the pricing power on Norvasc as it experiences an onslaught of generic competition. The profit potential from such combo pharmaceuticals is substantial relative to the 85 percent discounts that would otherwise be necessary to limit entry into Norvasc's stand-alone market. Another alternative niche pricing is always of limited applicability. Pfizer must expect that competitors will work hard to chip away at the appeal of one high-priced pill relative to a generic pill plus high-priced Lipitor.

[18]Based on "Drug Makers' Combo," *Wall Street Journal* (January 29, 2004), p. B1.

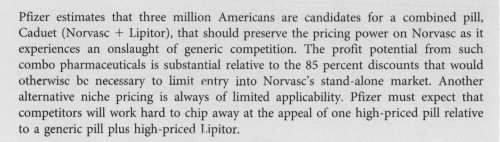

Example

Full-Cost Pricing Results in the Loss of a Big Contract at J.P. Morgan: British Telephone

Telecommunications is a fiercely competitive business. British Telephone (BT) once found that its $13 million bid to provide secure long-distance microwave business communications for the investment bank J.P. Morgan ended up $4 million higher per year than Sprint's rival bid of $9 million. When BT executives did a follow-up study to see why they had been so undercut by Sprint, they discovered that the vice president of the BT subsidiary in the United States had attempted to recover the entire annual overhead for the subsidiary headquarters from this one account. Needless to say, BT lost J.P. Morgan's business with a full-cost bid of $13 million when Sprint had offered to do essentially the same thing for $9 million. Full-cost pricing always runs the risk of such undercutting by rivals.

target return-on-investment pricing
A method of pricing in which a target profit, defined as the desired profit rate on investment × total gross operating assets, is allocated to each unit of output to arrive at a selling price.

Incremental contribution analysis
An incremental managerial decision that analyzes the change in operating profits (revenue – variable costs – direct fixed costs) available to cover indirect fixed costs.

Target return-on-investment pricing begins by selecting an acceptable profit rate on investment, usually defined as earnings before interest and taxes (EBIT) divided by total gross operating assets. This return is then prorated over the number of units expected to be produced over the planning horizon. Advocates of full-cost and target return pricing argue that it is important to allocate all fixed costs among the various products produced by the firm and that each product should be forced to bear its fair share of the fixed-cost burden.

However, each product should instead be viewed in the light of its incremental contributions to covering the business plan's fixed costs. **Incremental contribution analysis** provides a better basis for considering whether the manufacture and sale of a product should be expanded, maintained, or discontinued in favor of some higher-profit alternative. Every firm should have an effective control system in which a general manager continually monitors the overall contribution of the firm's complete product line. This person can then ensure that value-based prices contribute to both the variable cost of each product and the total fixed costs of the firm. Such target pricing is especially relevant at the launch of a product line and later at the decision to exit (see Figure 14.7).

Incremental Contribution Analysis at Continental/United Airlines

At one point Continental was filling only about 50 percent of its available seats, or about 15 percent less than the industry average. Eliminating 5 percent of its flights would have resulted in a substantial increase in this load factor but would have reduced profits as well. The airline industry is characterized by extremely high in direct fixed costs, which are incurred whether a plane flies or not: time depreciation costs on the aircraft, interest charges, and the cost of continuous pilot training, the expense of ground crews, as well as headquarters staff overhead. Consequently, Continental has found it profitable to operate a flight as long as it covers variable plus direct fixed costs of the flight.

The analysis of whether to operate a flight proceeds as follows. First, management examines the majority of scheduled flights to be certain that depreciation, overhead, and insurance expenses are met for the basic schedule. Then the possibility of scheduling additional flights is considered, based on their impact on operating profit. If revenues on a flight exceed *actual variable costs* plus direct fixed costs, the flight should be added. These relevant costs are determined by soliciting inputs from every operating department that specify exactly what extra expenses are incurred as a result of the additional flight's operation. For instance, if a ground crew that can service the additional flight is already on duty, none of the costs of this service are included in actual operating costs. If, on the other hand, overtime must be paid to service this flight, then that direct fixed cost varies with the decision to operate this flight and should be included among its costs.

Another example of such incremental contribution analysis is the case of a late-night United-Continental flight from Colorado Springs to Denver and an early morning return flight. Even though the flights often go without a passenger and little or no freight, the cost of operating them is less than an overnight hanger rental in Colorado Springs. Hence, the flights are operated, not shut down.

In performing this type of incremental contribution analysis, two important points must be stressed. First, someone in management must have coordinating authority to ensure that overall objectives are met before facing decisions based solely on incremental analysis. In the case of United-Continental, the vice president of flight planning assumed this task. Second, every reasonable attempt must be made to identify *actual* incremental costs and revenues associated with a particular decision. Once this information is determined, incremental analysis becomes a useful and powerful tool in considering a wide range of decision problems facing the firm.

Pricing on the Internet[19]

e-business offers new opportunities to cut distribution costs, reduce average retail margins, and introduce highly effective differential pricing. The office supply and home improvement industries are making use of the geographic location of the customer's IP

---

[19]An excellent survey of pricing strategy for Internet products is provided in John de Figueiredo, "Finding Sustainable Profitability in Electronic Commerce," *Sloan Management Review* (Summer 2000), pp. 41–52. See also "Getting Different Deals On-Line," *Wall Street Journal* (February 24, 2012), p. A1.

TABLE 14.4	PRICING STRATEGY FOR VARIOUS INTERNET PRODUCTS		
COMMODITY PRODUCTS	**QUASI-COMMODITY PRODUCTS**	**LOOK-AND-FEEL SEARCH GOODS**	**EXPERIENCE GOODS VARIABLE QUALITY**
Crude oil	Books	Suits	PCs
Newsprint	CDs	Homes	Produce
Sheet metal	Videos	New autos	Tires
Paper clips		Toys	Lumber
Low-cost, low-price strategy	Differentiate with reliable delivery and extra services	Employ differential pricing based on brands and time of adoption in fashion cycle	Customize and build to order with low- and high-price tiers

© Cengage Learning

address to set margins. Staples has begun reducing price by as much as 9 percent for online customers who are within 20 miles of an OfficeMax or Office Depot. Lowe's Home Improvement and Home Depot have also differentially priced by zip code. These are standard practices in gasoline and home electronics retailing but the Internet has triggered the selling of all sorts of other goods this way.

E-business also encounters several problems unique to web-based transactions. First is the anonymity of buyers and sellers who often are identified by only a web address. Offers to buy (and sell) may be reneged, receivables may never be collected, and items delivered may not be what buyers thought they had bought. The incidence of all these events is much greater in the virtual sales environment than in bricks and mortar or even mail order retail environments. As a result, offers are higher, and bids are lower, increasing the bid-ask spread to cover the cost of fraud insurance.

A second problem that the Internet accentuates is the inability to confirm product quality at the point of purchase. Internet pricing of commodity products such as crude oil, sheet metal, and newsprint paper, shown in Table 14.4, often pursues a low-cost strategy. The availability of quick resale at predictable commodity prices reassures buyers and sellers, and here Internet pricing at tight bid-ask spreads proves quite efficient. However, as one moves to the right in Table 14.4, product quality becomes harder and harder to detect at the point of sale. Firms such as Amazon and CDNow seek to substitute brand equity for the inability of customers to examine the product.

When it comes to toys, suits, homes, and new autos, consumers search for that look-and-feel for which they're willing to pay. Brands again play an important role in certifying quality, but in this case it is product branding (e.g., Game Boy, Hart Schaffner Marx, Harris Tweed) that matters, not Web site brands. Customers rely on the hostage associated with the sunk cost investment in the product brand names to establish credible quality commitments. Finally, with highly variable product quality in tires, PCs, produce, and lumber, only strong warranties, escrow accounts, and replacement guarantees or deep discounts can replace the reputation effects that help sell these experience goods in non virtual settings.

Internet sellers can add value and reduce some transaction costs in these markets by customizing and selling direct to the customer such as Dell, which provides order fulfillment but manufactures almost nothing. For this reason, services have grown quickly on the Internet; the travel industry itself accounted for 35 percent of all online sales in 2002. Table 14.5 shows that the growth rate of services far surpassed growth in consumer products online. One area of the digital consumer economy that is growing very quickly is e-books.

Amazon Pioneers e-Book Pricing[20]

From $78 million in digital book sales in 2008, e-books are expected to reach $3.6 billion in 2015. Physical book sales are dropping quickly as a result from $18 billion in 2008 to $13.8 billion projected in 2015. Print runs are down as much as 25 percent on some categories of books but publishers must maintain their legacy costs as they build e-book operations.

Amazon pioneered the new distribution channel with its Kindle e-book reader which in 2008–2009 had 90 percent of the electronic reader platform market. Bypassing the usual 100 percent retailer markup of the wholesale price set by book publishers, Amazon bought content directly from publishers and resold it to consumers for $9.99 per title. This price exceeded Amazon's variable cost but hardly covered its server farms and other capital equipment. As a result, many observers concluded that Amazon was selling books as a loss leader to drive sales of its Kindle and more recent Kindle Fire.

Steve Jobs launched the Apple iPad in January 2010 and offered publishers a totally different agency pricing model to distribute their content through iBooks. Five publishers Simon & Schuster, Hachette, Penguin, MacMillan, and HarperCollins accepted his offer to set their own final product prices while paying Apple 30 percent. Under pressure from the publishers, Amazon then adopted the new agency pricing model. As expected, the prices of e-books rose quickly from 30 to 50 percent, to $12.99 or $14.99.

Whether the new agency model facilitates price collusion is a hotly debated antitrust question.

---

[20]Based on "In Book Business: A Rewrite," *Wall Street Journal* (August 29, 2011), p. B5; "Steve Jobs, Price Fixer," *Wall Street Journal* (March 12, 2012), p. A13; "Pricing of E-Books Draws Increased Antitrust Scrutiny," *Wall Street Journal* (August 3, 2010), p. B1.

In business-to-business (B2B) transactions, pricing is more complex than in business-to-consumer transactions. In B2B, multiple attributes come into play in the price negotiation. B2B customers haggle over date of shipment, delivery costs, warranty service times and locations, delivery reliability, and replacement guarantees. These additional considerations typically mean pricing is a part of a two- or three-step process. First,

TABLE 14.5 GROWTH IN ONLINE SALES			
	INTERNET BUBBLE YEARS ($)		**COMPOUND ANNUAL GROWTH RATE (%)**
	1997	**2002**	
Consumer Services			
Travel	$654 million	$7.4 billion	83
Event Tickets	79 million	2 billion	124
Financial Services	1.2 billion	5 billion	43
Consumer Products			
Apparel	$92 million	$514 million	53
Books/CDs	156 million	1.1 billion	63
PCs	863 million	3.8 billion	45
B2B	$8 billion	$183 billion	119

Source: *BusinessWeek* (June 22, 1998), pp. 122–126, Forrester Research.

customers match their nonnegotiable requirements to the suppliers with those attributes, and those firms become the order-qualified suppliers. Then, the remaining attributes may be negotiated away against demands for a lower price point. In the heyday of the Internet bubble, B2B Internet sales grew 24-fold from $8 billion in 1997 to $183 billion in 2002; see Table 14.5.

dynamic pricing A price that varies over time based on the balance of demand and supply, often associated with Internet auctions.

Internet pricing in these B2B settings requires a matching process to qualify for an order and then a **dynamic pricing** algorithm to trade off the remaining attributes. Information technology complexity in these B2B transactions arises because customers are heterogeneous, and the attributes that qualify a firm to supply one group of customers may not match the requirements of other customers. In addition, as we shall see in Appendix 14A, delivery reliability (i.e., the probability of stockout and back order) is a continuous variable that should be optimized with a revenue management solution, not a simple on-again/off-again attribute to promise or refuse a potential customer in exchange for a somewhat larger or smaller markup.

SUMMARY

- All pricing decisions should be proactive, systematic-analytical, and value based, not reactive, ad hoc, and cost based.
- Two conditions are required for effective differential pricing:

  1. One must be able to segment the market and prevent the transfer of the product (or service) from one segment to another.
  2. Differences in the elasticity of demand at a given price between the market segments must be discernible.

- To maximize profits using differential pricing, the firm must allocate output in such a way that marginal revenue is equal in the different market segments.
- Differential pricing is often implemented through the direct segmentation of intertemporal pricing or pricing by delivery location.
- Indirect segmentation to support differential pricing is often accomplished through two-part pricing. Optimal *two-part prices* entail a lump-sum access fee and a user charge that equals or exceeds marginal cost and varies with units consumed.
- Couponing is another way to price discriminate while charging the same list prices to different customers, some of whom are highly price sensitive and will redeem coupons and others who will not.

- Bundling is a third pricing mechanism that indirectly segments customers with inversely correlated demand across multiple products.
- *Price discrimination* is the act of selling at the same time the same good or service produced by a given distribution channel at different prices to different customers.
- A good's pricing strategy varies throughout the product or service's life cycle. A frequent pattern is target pricing, followed by penetration pricing, price skimming, value-based pricing, limit pricing, and finally niche pricing.
- *Full-cost pricing* and *target pricing* are inconsistent with the marginal pricing rules of economic theory. *Incremental contribution analysis* is a widely applicable method of economic analysis that can help pricing managers achieve a more efficient and profitable level of operation.
- Pricing on the Internet suffers from anonymity and lack of reputation effects, along with search across various product qualities being especially difficult to verify prior to purchase. These complications imply distinctly different pricing approaches for commodity-like products, search goods, and experience goods.
- B2B pricing on the Internet requires a two-step process of multi-attribute matching to qualify for consideration as a supplier and then a dynamic pricing scheme to trade off additional features and functions as sources of value-in-use against lower price point alternatives.

1. The price elasticity of demand for a textbook sold in the United States is estimated to be -2, whereas the price elasticity of demand for books sold overseas is -3. The U.S. market requires hardcover books with a marginal cost of $40; the overseas market is normally served with softcover texts on newsprint, having a marginal cost of only $15. Calculate the profit-maximizing price in each market.

$$\left[Hint: \text{Remember that } MR = P\left(1 + \frac{1}{E_D}\right)\right]$$

2. The price elasticity of demand for air travel differs radically from first-class (-1.3) to unrestricted coach (-1.4) to restricted discount coach (-1.9). What do these elasticities mean for optimal prices (fares) on a cross-country trip with incremental variable costs (marginal costs) equal to $120?

3. A U.S. export-import shipping company operates a general cargo carrier service between New York and several western European ports. It hauls two major categories of freight: manufactured items and semimanufactured raw materials. The demand functions for these two classes of goods are:

$$P_1 = 100 - 2Q_1$$
$$P_2 = 80 - Q_2$$

where $Q_i = $ tons of freight moved. The total cost function for the United States is

$$TC = 20 + 4(Q_1 + Q_2)$$

   a. Determine the firm's total profit function.
   b. What are the profit-maximizing levels of price and output for the two freight categories?
   c. At these levels of output, calculate the marginal revenue in each market.
   d. What are the United States' total profits if it is effectively able to charge different prices in the two markets?
   e. If the United States is required by law to charge the same per-ton rate to all users, calculate the new profit-maximizing level of price and output. What are the profits in this situation?
   f. Explain the difference in profit levels between the differential pricing and uniform pricing cases. (*Hint:* First calculate the point price elasticity of demand under the uniform price-output solution.)

4. Sort the following products into those priced with two-part tariffs, user charges only, or lump-sum access fees only: pay-per-view movies on cable TV, pay phones, Netflix, iTunes, country club membership, soda from vending machines, laundromats, cell phones, season ticket holders with seat rights.

5. Phillips Industries manufactures a certain product that can be sold directly to retail outlets or to the Superior Company for further processing and eventual sale as a completely different product. The demand function for each of these markets is

$$\text{Retail Outlets: } P_1 = 60 - 2Q_1$$
$$\text{Superior Company: } P_2 = 40 - Q_2$$

where P_1 and P_2 are the prices charged and Q_1 and Q_2 are the quantities sold in the respective markets. Phillips' total cost function for the manufacture of this product is

$$TC = 10 + 8(Q_1 + Q_2)$$

   a. Determine Phillips' total profit function.

b. What are the profit-maximizing price and output levels for the product in the two markets?

c. At these levels of output, calculate the marginal revenue in each market.

d. What are Phillips' total profits if the firm is effectively able to charge different prices in the two markets?

e. Calculate the profit-maximizing level of price and output if Phillips is required to charge the same price per unit in each market. What are Phillips' profits under this condition?

6. In the face of stable (or declining) enrollments and increasing costs, many colleges and universities, both public and private, find themselves in progressively tighter financial dilemmas that require basic reexamination of the pricing schemes used by institutions of higher learning. One proposal advocated by the Committee for Economic Development (CED) and others has been the use of more nearly full-cost pricing of higher education, combined with the government provision of sufficient loan funds to students who would not otherwise have access to reasonable loan terms in private markets. Advocates of such proposals argue that the private rate of return to student investors is sufficiently high to stimulate socially optimal levels of demand for education, even with the higher tuition rates. Others argue against the existence of significant external benefits to undergraduate education to warrant the current high levels of public support.

As with current university pricing schemes, proponents of full-cost pricing generally argue for a standard fee (albeit higher than at present) for all students. Standard-fee proposals ignore relative cost and demand differences among activities in the university.

a. Discuss several possible rationales for charging different prices for different courses of study.

b. What are the income-distribution effects of a pricing scheme that charges the same fee to all students?

c. If universities adopted a system of full-cost (or marginal cost) pricing for various courses, what would you expect the impact on the efficiency of resource allocations within the university to be?

d. Would you complain less about large lecture sections taught by graduate students if these were priced significantly lower than small seminars taught by outstanding scholars?

e. What problems could you see arising from a university that adopted such a pricing scheme?

7. General Medical makes disposable syringes for hospitals and doctor supply companies. The company uses cost-plus pricing and currently charges 150 percent of average variable costs. General Medical learned of an opportunity to sell 300,000 syringes to the Department of Defense if they can be delivered within three months at a price not in excess of $1 each. General Medical normally sells its syringes for $1.20 each. If General Medical accepts the Defense Department order, it will have to forgo sales of 100,000 syringes to its regular customers over this time period, although this loss of sales is not expected to affect future sales.

a. Should General Medical accept the Defense Department order?

b. If sales for the balance of the year are expected to be 50,000 units less because of some lost customers who do not return, should the order be accepted? (Ignore any effects beyond one year.)

8. The Pear Computer Company just developed a totally revolutionary new personal computer. It estimates that it will take competitors at least two years to produce equivalent products. The demand function for the computer is estimated to be

$$P = 2,500 - 0.0005Q$$

The marginal (and average variable) cost of producing the computer is $900.

a. Compute the profit-maximizing price and output levels assuming Pear acts as a monopolist for its product.
b. Determine the total contribution to profits and fixed costs from the solution generated in Part (a).

Pear Computer is considering an alternative pricing strategy of price skimming. It plans to set the following schedule of prices over the coming two years:

TIME PERIOD	PRICE ($)	QUANTITY SOLD
1	2,400	200,000
2	2,200	200,000
3	2,000	200,000
4	1,800	200,000
5	1,700	200,000
6	1,600	200,000
7	1,500	200,000
8	1,400	200,000
9	1,300	200,000
10	1,200	200,000

c. Calculate the contribution to profit and overhead for each of the 10 time periods and prices.
d. Compare your results in Part (c) with your answers in Part (b).
e. Explain the major advantages and disadvantages of price skimming as a pricing strategy.

The Practice of Revenue Management[21]

Demand in excess of available capacity.

spoilage Perishable output that goes unsold.

spill Confirmed orders that cannot be filled.

Differential pricing is sometimes complicated by capacity choices that must be made before demand is known. Consider an airline, printing press operator, or elective surgery clinic, each of which must schedule capacity before the respective demands for the 11:00 A.M. flight, the press run next Thursday, or elective surgeries the next day are known. If no revenue can be realized after scheduled delivery from empty airline seats, from underutilized printing presses, or empty surgical theaters, random customer arrivals force a firm with fixed capacity to choose between underutilizing excess capacity or imposing service denials and **stockouts** on regular customers.

The **spoilage** from unsold capacity and the **spill** of high-margin repeat customers for whom no capacity remains are serious problems that may affect the firm's financial success and indeed its survival. In Figure 14A.1, a reduction in capacity from Q^{d_1} to a level

FIGURE 14A.1 Spill and Spoilage with Random Demand and Fixed Prices

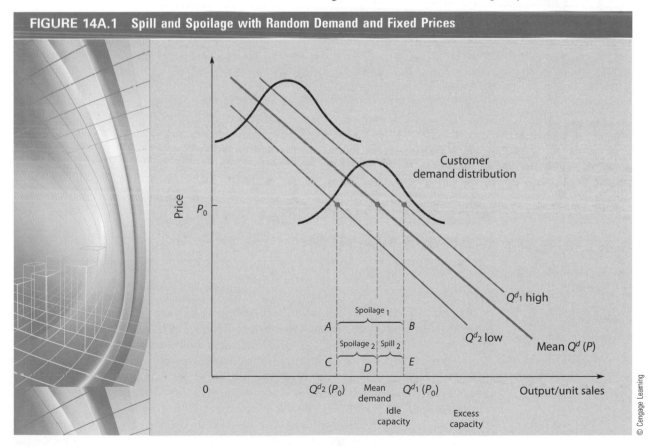

© Cengage Learning

---

[21]F. Harris and P. Peacock provide a thorough overview of yield management/revenue management techniques and potential industry applications in "Hold My Place Please: Yield Management Improves Capacity Allocation Guesswork," *Marketing Management* 4, no. 2 (Fall 1995), pp. 34–46.

just sufficient to meet mean demand at P_0 reduces the spoilage for low-demand events (Q^{d_2}) from AB to CD but introduces spill (i.e., Spill_2) for high-demand events (Q^{d_1}). Revenue or yield management (YM) is an integrated set of managerial economics techniques designed to deal with these pricing and capacity allocation problems under fixed capacity and random demand.

Example

Spill and Spoilage at Sport Obermeyer[22]

The selling season in fashion retailing is short (lasting no more than several months), and customer demand at the product-line level is fickle and hard to forecast. Consequently, buyers for retail merchants like Neiman Marcus, Bloomingdale's, Saks Fifth Avenue, Rich's, and Macy's must place orders far in advance of actual sales without really knowing which fashion trends will sell well and which will sell poorly. Sport Obermeyer faces this problem with ski clothes. In a particular winter ski season, Pandora ski parkas may become a fashion statement and quickly sell out. If Pandora parkas go on back order, creating frustrated buyers, the store will lose customers' goodwill and future sales. In addition, the lost retail contribution margin every time Sport Obermeyer "spills" one of these customers is $15.

On the other hand, Pandora's line of ski parkas may not "catch on" this season. Instead, they may end up as spoilage (i.e., a large inventory of unsold winter clothes). The merchant would then incur losses on the unsold merchandise and forgo the opportunity to sell another Champion sweatshirt that could have occupied the ski parka's shelf space. Sport Obermeyer can use the tools of yield management to balance these costs of spill and spoilage and thereby determine how many parkas to order and what shelf space to devote to parkas versus sweatshirts.

[22]Based on M. Fisher et al., "Making Supply Meet Demand in an Uncertain World," *Harvard Business Review* (May–June 1994), pp. 83–93.

A CROSS-FUNCTIONAL SYSTEMS MANAGEMENT PROCESS

Firms might respond to unanticipated demand fluctuations in the presence of capacity constraints by simply auctioning off their scarce product to the highest bidder or by holding massive clearance sales when faced with inventory overhang. Much to their detriment, department store retailers take a myopic marketing view of what markdown prices can accomplish. Fashion-conscious customers shop numerous stores to "win" the trendy items and do so with little repeat purchase loyalty. Everyone else has become habituated to wait for the inevitable and deep discount sales. The proportion of department store revenue earned through transactions at clearance sale prices rose from 8 percent in 1970 to 55 percent in 2001.[23] Even regular customers of leading department stores report buying at discount prices almost as often (46 percent) as at regular prices (54 percent). Not surprisingly, profitability in the department store retailing sector has

[23]B. P. Pashigian, "Demand Uncertainty and Sales," *American Economic Review* 78, no. 5 (December 1993), pp. 936–953; and "Priced to Move," *Wall Street Journal* (August 7, 2001), p. A6.

collapsed, and consolidation mergers have taken some of the best-known retailers out of business. What might these stores have done differently?

One alternative would be for the retail merchant's suppliers to develop flexible manufacturing systems (FMSs) so they could respond to demand fluctuations more quickly. If reorder cycles could occur several additional times within the fashion season, merchants could stockpile less inventory and yet experience fewer stockouts.

Another alternative to resolve the problems of high-margin spill is simply to acquire more capacity. Of course, no company can afford to build unlimited additional capacity. Aggregate capacity planning incorporates a careful financial analysis of the capital budgeting problem that identifies the optimal fixed capacity for any line of business. A better alternative is to reserve some of this optimal fixed capacity for late-arriving, high-margin customers. Reserving capacity as the moment of delivery approaches should not be interpreted as "excess capacity" but rather as idle capacity that presents a sustainable revenue opportunity. This insight is one that comes out of revenue management analysis.

revenue management
A cross-functional order acceptance and refusal process.

Every company has some orders that it should refuse. **Revenue management** (RM), often called yield management, is fundamentally an order acceptance and refusal process that links marketing decisions about demand creation and pricing with operations decisions about scheduling and financial decisions about capacity planning. The objective is to decide which orders to accept at particular prices and which to refuse. These relationships are depicted in Figure 14A.2 as a cross-functional triangle of account management, forecasting, and scheduling decisions. Practitioners of yield management believe that the sources of sustainable price premiums lie in these cross-functional systems management processes. In this view, innovative products and successful advertising campaigns are quickly reverse engineered and readily imitated. Advertising and product design cannot therefore provide sustainable competitive advantage. Process advantages, on the other hand, prove much more difficult for competitors to imitate.

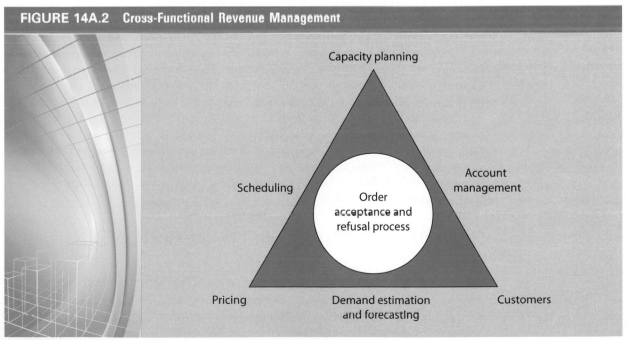

FIGURE 14A.2   Cross-Functional Revenue Management

Capacity planning

Scheduling

Account management

Order acceptance and refusal process

Pricing

Demand estimation and forecasting

Customers

© Cengage Learning

SOURCES OF SUSTAINABLE PRICE PREMIUMS

Yield management processes add conspicuous tangible value for which customers gladly pay higher prices. In most cases, the added value arises through customizing and optimizing the account and order management. In the airline industry, for example, some customers want extensive flexibility of reservations that allows frequent changes in departure and arrival times. If an airline has the operations capability and information technology to provide this service, business travelers with unconfirmed meeting schedules will offer large price premiums to secure this *change order responsiveness*. To take another example, Disney offers substantial price premiums to gift product suppliers who can deliver high quality on time as promised. When Disney order clerks submit an error-laden request that needs to be changed within the normal 30-day reorder cycle, Disney volunteers to pay even more. Such supplements to revenue go exclusively to firms that have the systems management processes that can handle extraordinary change order requests.

Firms compete on other aspects of order processing as well. Some customers want short *scheduling delays* (e.g., just-in-time retailers without warehouses). Others want high *delivery reliability* and a small probability of being denied service in the event of a stockout (e.g., business executives traveling to a stockholders' meeting). Still others value *conformance to product or service specifications*. For time-sensitive deliveries of organ transplants, for example, excellent on-time service records warrant paying high airfares. The alternative would be a much more expensive jet charter service. Manufacturers as well as service firms can establish sustainable price premiums based on these same order-processing characteristics of change order responsiveness, minimal scheduling delay, delivery reliability, and conformance to specifications.

All these sources of sustainable price premiums are prominent in airline services at "fortress hubs" where one carrier controls more than 65 percent of the seat departures. Figure 14A.3 displays the major hub airports in the continental United States and provides pricing and market share data for the top two carriers. In each of these cities, the dominant firm(s) has sufficient operating capacity and systems control to provide high-quality service. At Dallas–Fort Worth, for example, American Airlines has high schedule convenience, with departures quite close to the time preferences of a DFW-origin traveler. Similarly, at this airport American can offer high delivery reliability, schedule conformance to expectations, and change order responsiveness. Passengers, especially business travelers, will pay substantial premiums for these high-service-quality characteristics because of the additional value such flights create in their own business activities. YM systems reserve idle capacity to meet these high-value demands when the late arrival of such requests is forecasted. YM systems also "protect" fewer seats and release more capacity to deep-discount leisure segments of the market. Overall, fares per revenue passenger mile at a fortress hub such as Atlanta (where Delta has a 79 percent share) are 84 percent higher than at Orlando, where Delta again is the leading carrier but has only 32 percent of the market.

REVENUE MANAGEMENT DECISIONS, ADVANCED MATERIAL

Revenue management (RM) can be divided into three decisions: (1) a proactive pricing and aggregate capacity planning decision, (2) an inventory or capacity reallocation decision, and (3) an overbooking decision. Figure 14A.4 places these decisions in an RM

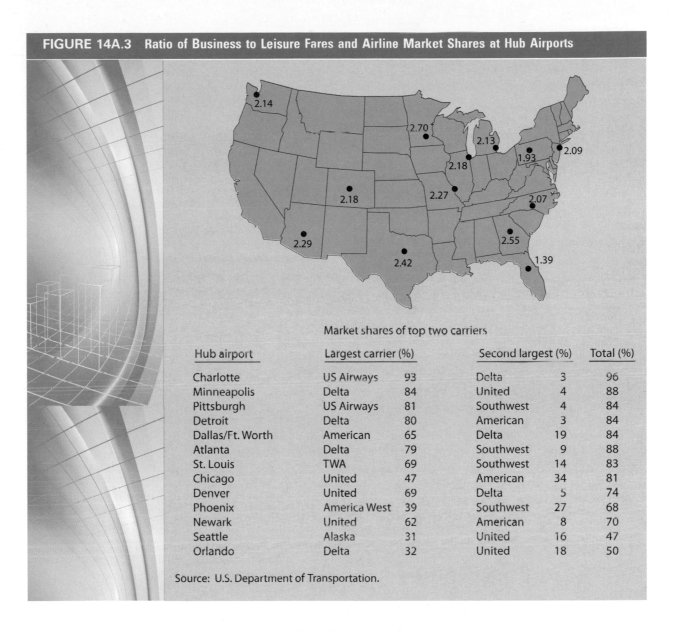

FIGURE 14A.3 Ratio of Business to Leisure Fares and Airline Market Shares at Hub Airports

Market shares of top two carriers

Hub airport	Largest carrier (%)		Second largest (%)		Total (%)
Charlotte	US Airways	93	Delta	3	96
Minneapolis	Delta	84	United	4	88
Pittsburgh	US Airways	81	Southwest	4	84
Detroit	Delta	80	American	3	84
Dallas/Ft. Worth	American	65	Delta	19	84
Atlanta	Delta	79	Southwest	9	88
St. Louis	TWA	69	Southwest	14	83
Chicago	United	47	American	34	81
Denver	United	69	Delta	5	74
Phoenix	America West	39	Southwest	27	68
Newark	United	62	American	8	70
Seattle	Alaska	31	United	16	47
Orlando	Delta	32	United	18	50

Source: U.S. Department of Transportation.

conceptual framework, showing a flowchart of the components of a revenue management process. What all three decisions have in common is a tactical focus that depends on anticipated rival responses; a systems management philosophy that integrates marketing, operations, and finance; and finally a multiproduct orientation that continuously reconfigures the firm's product offerings. We now address the managerial economics of each RM decision.

Proactive Price Discrimination

Proactive price discrimination involves maximizing profits in the light of anticipated late-arriving demand and rival firm responses. In principle, computerized decision support systems (DSS) make it possible to reauction the remaining seats on a flight or the remaining runs on the printing press each time a new customer arrives on a reservation system. Conceivably, each customer would then experience first-degree price

FIGURE 14A.4 Revenue Management Flowchart

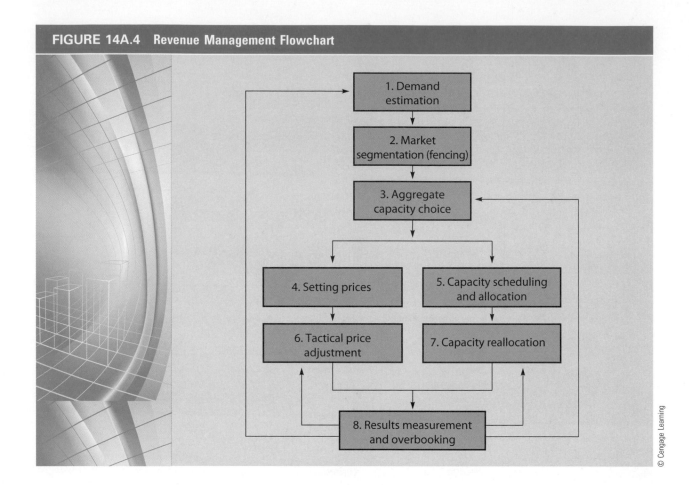

© Cengage Learning

discrimination and pay a unique price that reflects time of delivery, service costs, and price elasticity. Few RM practitioners have adopted bid price systems. Instead, most set prices and initially allocate capacity with the familiar techniques of marginal analysis that we discussed earlier in the chapter for differential fares that allocate the capacity between business and nonbusiness air travelers on the 11:00 A.M. Thursday flight DFW to LAX.

Capacity Reallocation

The second step in revenue management is to *reallocate capacity* or inventory as delivery times approach in the light of advance sales and confirmed orders. Suppose you forecasted advance sales for business class on Thursday departures from Dallas to Los Angeles in accordance with the exponential function (tickets purchased $= aB^t$) estimated in semilog form as

$$\ln(\text{tickets}) = \ln a + \ln B(t) = \alpha + \beta t \qquad [14A.1]$$

where t is a simple time trend variable. Similarly, suppose you forecasted all nonbusiness travel with a sales penetration function such as

$$\text{Tickets purchased} = e^{k_1 - k_2(1/t)} \qquad [14A.2]$$

estimated as

$$\ln(\text{tickets}) = k_1 - k_2(1/t) \qquad [14A.3]$$

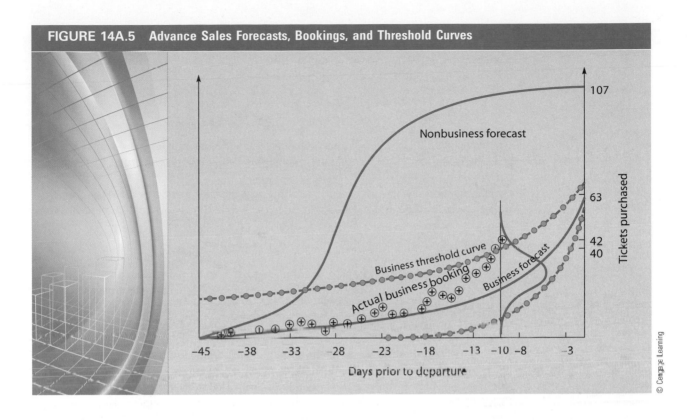

FIGURE 14A.5   Advance Sales Forecasts, Bookings, and Threshold Curves

where k_1 and k_2 are constants defining the rate of sales growth throughout the advance sales period. These forecasted business and nonbusiness "booking curves" are plotted in Figure 14A.5. Note that the curves exhibit the early- and late-arriving characteristics of demand in the nonbusiness and business markets, respectively.

The forecasted booking curves reflect new demand arrivals and cancellations and are, in that sense, net bookings. If such bookings require substantial nonrefundable deposits on advance sales, then they reflect realized revenue rather than just potential sales.[24] For the 11:00 A.M. flight to Los Angeles, the final demand target in Figure 14A.5 is 63 business and 107 nonbusiness passengers. This *initial* allocation of total capacity applies when customer reservations open 180, 120, 60, or, in our case, 45 days prior to departure. It is subject to change (and in fact often is changed) by the revenue managers.

Confidence intervals based on the different demand arrival distributions are then used to determine when actual bookings deviate a given amount, which triggers an exception report. For example, business travel appears to be greater than forecasted ticket sales at day $t - 10$ by a statistically significant amount. This violation of the **threshold sales curve** raises the question of whether to stop sales in the nonbusiness class where contribution margins ($P_{nonbus} - MC = \$188 - \$130 = \$58$) are clearly lower than in the business class segment, where $P_{bus} - MC = \$261 - \$130 = \$131$.

The answer to this capacity reallocation question lies in applied statistics and in the initial profit-maximizing capacity choice. Marginal capacity expansions are justified as long as the expected incremental revenue minus variable cost (i.e., the additional expected contribution to fixed cost) is greater than the incremental cost of additional capacity. In capacity reallocation, the cost of additional capacity in the business class is

threshold sales curve A level of advance sales that triggers reallocation of capacity.

---

[24]In the last RM decision, we consider the effects of no-shows on authorized overbookings.

an opportunity cost, or the forgone contribution from selling one less seat in the nonbusiness class. At the margin, we would reallocate capacity as long as the expected contribution margin from allocating another seat to business travelers would exceed the lost contribution margin from a boarding denial in nonbusiness. That is,

$$(P_{bus} - VC)(Prob\ Shortage_{bus}) = (P_{nonbus} - VC)$$
$$\$131(Prob\ Shortage_{bus}) = \$58$$

[14A.4]

where the *Prob Shortage*$_{bus}$ is the probability that the business class will in fact be full and, therefore, the probability that the extra business-class seat will realize its $131 marginal contribution.[25]

The preannounced prices and resulting contribution margins of $58 and $131 indicated (using Equation 14A.4) that high yield spill should occur 44.1 percent of the time:

$$(Prob\ Shortage_{bus}) = \$58/\$131 = 0.441$$

For any business-class demand distribution (e.g., normally distributed with a mean of 60 seats and a standard deviation of 20 seats), we can calculate the optimal capacity choice as

$$\mu_{seats} + z_{\alpha}\sigma_{seats} = 60 + 0.148 \times 20 = 63\ seats$$

[14A.5]

where z_{α} is the absolute value of the standard normal critical value (z value) for one-tailed alpha from Table 1 in Appendix C. These calculations correspond to the initial situation in which business-class capacity was set at 63 seats (see Figure 14.1). On this flight, 63 seats is often referred to as the **protection level** for business-class seats. Similarly, 107 seats is the **authorization level** for nonbusiness-class seats.

Now recall that at day $t - 10$ in Figure 14A.5, we received an exception report: It appears that the arrival distribution for next Thursday's flight is not normally distributed with mean 60 and standard deviation 20, that is, N(60,20). Instead, the exception report may indicate mean demand has increased to N(62,20). Again, using the fact that with prices of $261 and $188 the optimal probability of stockout in business class is 0.441, we can use Equation 14A.5 to calculate the new optimal capacity allocation at 62 seats + 0.148(20) seats = 65 seats. This result implies that a stop-sales policy of 105 seats should apply to the bookings accepted in nonbusiness travel and two seats (107 − 105) should be reallocated to business class. Continued monitoring of bookings relative to the forecast thresholds may result in a return of these seats to nonbusiness class or a still further reallocation of capacity toward business travelers.

The same questions and analyses of capacity allocation apply in assemble-to-order manufacturing when a sport apparel manufacturer or a customized paper products manufacturer must decide which orders to accept and which to refuse (i.e., how to allocate fixed total capacity). As yield management moves out of the service sector (e.g., airlines, hotels, rental cars, advertising agencies, hospitals, professional services) and into manufacturing, these managerial economics techniques become increasingly important.[26]

protection level
Capacity reserved for sale in higher margin segments.

authorization level
Capacity authorized for sale in lower margin segments.

---

[25]It is quite possible to have a positive probability of stockout on both sides of Equation 14A.4. Here, however, we assume an unlimited demand in the nonbusiness segment at the low fare of $188 for Dallas–Fort Worth–LAX. That is, the probability of stockout is assumed to be 1 on the right-hand side.

[26]See F. Harris and J. Pinder, "A Revenue Management Approach to Order Booking and Demand Management in Assemble-to-Order Manufacturing," *Journal of Operations Management* (December 1995), pp. 299–309.

Example

The Optimal Probability of a Stockout at Sport Obermeyer

Recall that Sport Obermeyer must allocate its fixed retail shelf and display rack space between Pandora parkas and Champion sweatshirts. The lost retail contribution margin every time Sport Obermeyer "spills" a Pandora parka customer is $15. The lost retail contribution margin on a Champion sweatshirt is $4. Knowing these margins and the relative sales effectiveness of particular shelf space, Sport Obermeyer can use the tools of yield management to balance the costs of spoilage and spill in order to decide the optimal incidence of stockouts in Pandora parkas. Using Equation 14A.4, Sport Obermeyer calculates that Pandora parkas should stock out 27 percent of the time: $Prob\ (Shortage_{parka}) = 0.27$. With demand distribution data, Sport Obermeyer can calculate that a probability of shortage of $4/$15 = 0.27 requires stocking 85 size 8 parkas in each of its stores.

Optimal Overbooking

optimal overbooking
A marginal analysis technique for balancing the cost of idle capacity (spoilage) against the opportunity cost of unserved demand (spill).

The third and final yield management decision is an **optimal overbooking** decision. Here the airline authorizes the reservation clerks to sell more seats than are available on each departure to combat the lost revenue from "no-shows." Of course, many tickets entail discount fares that require advance purchase, but some business-class tickets are not purchased until check-in time. This means that a confirmed sale is not realized revenue until delivery time. In some industries orders can be canceled or shipments refused. At times, air carriers experience up to 35 percent no-shows in certain city-pair markets.

The optimal overbooking decision illustrates marginal analysis in practice. Each airline seeks to minimize the summed costs of spoilage and spill. In Figure 14A.6, as expected demand of business travelers approaches planned capacity and the expected load factor approaches 100 percent, the total cost of spoilage (i.e., unsold seats × contribution$_{bus}$) declines toward zero. In contrast, as the expected load factor approaches 100 percent, the costs of high-yield spill rise for three reasons. First, oversales represent lost contributions, which might have been captured by other service offerings (e.g., later flights); that is, some customers will "balk" and go to a competitor. Second, oversales necessitate out-of-pocket expenses to compensate passengers who board the airplane and then volunteer to give up their seats. And third, oversales and the resulting stockouts sacrifice customer goodwill and brand loyalty, thereby causing lost future sales. These rising total costs of high-yield spill also are depicted in Figure 14A.6.

Total summed costs are reduced by a rising load factor as long as the rising costs of oversales are more than offset by the falling cost of spoilage. From load factors below 92 to 97 percent, the declining cost of spoilage more than offsets the rising cost of oversales for nonbusiness travel. Beyond 97 percent, the rate of spoilage cost reduction is less than the rate of oversales cost increase. This relationship is shown in the lower diagram by comparing the $MC_{\text{nonbusiness oversales}}$ to the marginal benefit of reduced spoilage, MB_{spoilage} reduction, which is the MC of unsold seats *saved* by planning a higher load factor. For the nonbusiness class, the optimal planned load factor appears to be 97 percent. In contrast, in the business class the $MC_{\text{business oversales}}$ is so much higher as load factor increases that the optimal planned load factor is associated with a higher quality 94 percent.

Both decisions are referred to as overbooking decisions because a 97 percent expected load factor for the 105 seats now allocated to nonbusiness travelers may necessitate actually booking not 0.97 × 105 = 102 seats, but rather 127 seats [(127 × (1 − 0.2) = 102] in

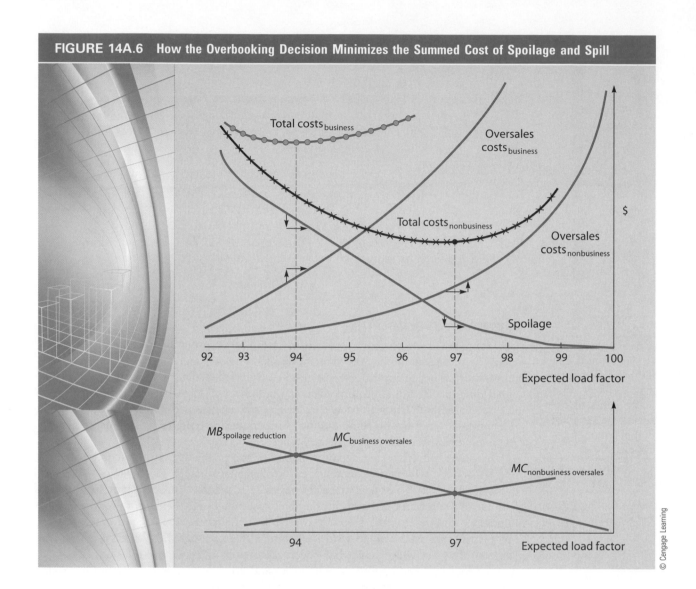

FIGURE 14A.6 How the Overbooking Decision Minimizes the Summed Cost of Spoilage and Spill

periods when no-shows are averaging 20 percent. Similarly, optimal overbooking in business may imply confirming reservations not for 61 seats in heavy (35 percent) no-show periods, but rather for 94 seats ($94 \times 0.65 = 61$). On average, 102 nonbusiness and 61 business travelers enplane for the Thursday 11:00 A.M. flight to Los Angeles. Of course, these 163 total passengers expected are only an average of actual passenger counts, which may vary on any particular departure from large spoilage to severe oversales.

Example

Pinpoint Booking Accuracy at American Airlines[27]

Price differentials on American Airlines' popular 5:30 P.M. flight from Chicago to Phoenix are huge, ranging from $238 to $1,404 round trip. American constantly adjusts the capacity allocation to each of seven fare classes as advance sales data deviate from forecast. Four weeks prior to a recent departure, American had already sold 69 of the 125 coach seats at Super Saver fares. With three weeks to departure,

(continued)

all three fare classes below $300 had reached their maximum authorization levels and were closed to further reservations. One day before departure, 130 passengers were booked on the 125-seat flight, but American was still authorizing up to five additional full coach reservations. The yield management computers predicted that cancellations and no-shows might go as high as 10. The next day, the 5:30 flight departed full with no one denied boarding. The systems management objective of yield management is "to sell the right seat to the right customer at the right price at the right time." Such outcomes of the RM system are a critical success factor for American in a period when the index of U.S. airfares has risen only 8 percent during the past 15 years.

[27]Based on "High-Tech Pricing Boosts Business Fares," *Charlotte Observer* (November 9, 1997), p. 1D; and "For U.S. Airlines, a Shakeout," *Wall Street Journal* (September 19, 2005), p. A1.

Example

Revenue Management in Baseball: The Baltimore Orioles[28]

Recent applications of revenue management have taken the techniques out of travel services and into private-pay elective surgeries, radio and television advertising, opera and symphony concerts, law firms, consulting firms, golf courses, and now baseball. Like airlines, all these businesses have fixed capacity with perishable inventory; once the last out of the fifth inning has been called, empty seats offer no realizable value. Although season ticket holders are prominent in the planning of any professional sports franchise, single-game and three-game ticket packages remain a substantial source of revenue. And unstable demand makes prediction of sales in these more immediate segments a challenging and potentially highly profitable process to do well, especially in baseball.

Most professional teams celebrate their sellouts, but some fail to realize that spare capacity (however slight) as game time approaches is a substantial revenue opportunity. Allowing discount ticket packages and promotions to displace last-minute walk-in customers often sacrifices high-margin repeat purchase business. At the same time, overall attendance in professional baseball remains below prestrike levels of the 1980s, and many games are played in ballparks only half full. The Baltimore Orioles revenue manager attempts to balance both of these errors of understocking and of overstocking. Single-game seats purchased well in advance are available at a discount.

However, a substantial capacity of well-placed seats is protected in anticipation of late-arriving, high-willingness-to-pay, game-day-only customers. Advance sales are tracked, and variances are noted relative to previous sales histories for that home stand against similar opponents. As game day approaches, authorization levels for release of discount tickets gradually adjust to reflect the probability of stockout in higher-margin segments. Ideally, on game day, perhaps 93 percent of the seats are filled with fans in a variety of different segments paying a variety of different prices, each reflecting the location, customer responsiveness, reliability, timing, and other ticketing services that particular customers prefer, thereby adding maximum value.

[28]Based on "Managing Baseball's Yield," *Barron's* (September 11, 1995), p. 50; and "Tickets with Flex," *Sports Illustrated* (February 23, 2009), p. 62.

Yield management continuously reallocates capacity and adjusts these overbooking authorizations as advance sales data roll in. The incremental revenues from effective yield management can be significant. For example, American Airlines recently calculated its additional revenue from attending to these problems at $467 million per year. Marriott International estimates that revenue management contributes as much as $200 million each year to its revenue stream. And the Canadian Broadcasting Corporation realized a $2 million revenue gain the first two weeks after it adopted revenue management techniques.[29]

SUMMARY

- Yield management (YM) or revenue management (RM) consists of pricing and capacity allocation techniques for fixed-capacity manufacturers or service firms with perishable inventory and random demand.
- Flexible manufacturing systems and production-to-order with JIT delivery can seldom fully resolve the spill and spoilage problems addressed by RM.
- RM provides an optimal order acceptance and refusal process with cross-functional resolution of account management, demand forecasting, and scheduling decisions.
- Proactive price discrimination equates the marginal revenue from different segments of the target market. It does so with differential value-based prices that reflect delivery reliability, change order

responsiveness, scheduling convenience, conformance to expectations, and the value of these service quality characteristics to the particular class of customers (i.e., third-degree price discrimination).

- RM reallocates inventory or service capacity in accordance with the condition $(P - MC)_a(Prob\ Shortage)_a = (P - MC)_b$. This procedure identifies optimal protection levels for high-margin segments, accounts, and customers and an optimal authorization level for release of capacity to lower-margin segments, accounts, and customers.
- The optimal overbooking decision equates the declining marginal cost of spoilage as load factor or capacity utilization increases with the rising marginal cost of spill (i.e., oversales).

Exercises

1. Explain the effect on capacity reallocations of advance sales data indicating mean demand of 55 rather than 60 during a slow travel week for business class, using the information in Figure 14.1, Table 14.2, and Equation 14A.4.
2. Suppose the frequent-flyer program raised the cost of high-yield spill twofold because business customers who are denied boarding now take their business to other carriers for several future trips, not just the current one. Reanalyze the overbooking decision in Figure 14A.6 under these circumstances. Will overbooking of business-class service increase or decrease?
3. An aircraft with 100 seats serves passengers through two types of fares: full ($550) and discount ($250). Extra passengers have $50 marginal cost. Demand for discount tickets is unlimited, while demand for full-fare tickets is evenly distributed between 11 and 30 seats. How many seats should be protected for full-fare passengers and not authorized for release to the discounted $250 segment?

---

[29]As cited in R. Cross, *Revenue Management: Hardcore Tactics for Market Domination* (New York: Broadway Books, 1997).

PART V

Organizational Architecture and Regulation

P art V addresses the new institutional economics of organizational architecture as well as the regulation of business. Major themes include incentive contracting, the choice of organizational form (e.g., vertically integrating to redraw the boundaries of the firm), and the regulation/deregulation debate. Chapter 15 discusses the theory of business contracting, managerial incentive contracts, the principal-agent problem, corporate governance, licensing of trade secrets, the dissolution of partnerships, and vertical integration. Appendix 15A explores optimal mechanism design in auctions and incentive compatibility for joint ventures. Chapter 16 then addresses the economic regulation of business, including antitrust, patenting, and licensing, as well as regulatory and private market approaches for controlling externalities. Chapter 17 discusses capital budgeting techniques used in acquisition, merger, and spin-off activities to change the organizational boundaries of the firm.

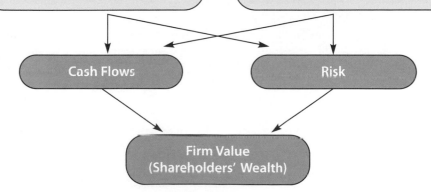

ECONOMIC ANALYSIS AND DECISIONS

1. Demand Analysis and Forecasting
2. Production and Cost Analysis
3. Pricing Analysis
4. Capital Expenditure Analysis

ECONOMIC, POLITICAL, AND SOCIAL ENVIRONMENT

1. Business Conditions (Trends, Cycles, and Seasonal Effects)
2. Factor Market Conditions (Capital, Labor, Land, and Raw Materials)
3. Competitors' Responses
4. External, Legal, and Regulatory Constraints
5. Organizational (Internal) Constraints

Cash Flows

Risk

Firm Value (Shareholders' Wealth)

© Cengage Learning

15 Contracting, Governance, and Organizational Form

CHAPTER PREVIEW

This chapter explores the coordination and control problems faced by every business organization and the institutional mechanisms designed to solve these problems in a least-cost manner. The most important organizational architecture decision is to determine the boundary of the firm (i.e., the span of hierarchical control). In dealing with external suppliers, outsource partners, internal divisions, authorized distributors, franchisees, and licensees, every firm must decide where the internal organization stops and where market transactions take over.

Contracts between business organizations provide an *ex ante* framework that defines these relationships, but all contracts are purposefully incomplete. Consequently, every firm must address the potential for post-contractual opportunistic behavior by business partners and then design governance mechanisms to reduce these contractual hazards. Should Dell make or buy subassembly components for its PCs? Should Canon license its digital camera technology for Internet distribution by Verizon, or should it invest in a strategic partnership with Verizon? Should Microsoft vertically integrate into media delivery devices by buying WebTV? Should Red Hat continue to adopt open-source architecture and allow its licensees to duplicate, modify, and redistribute its Linux-based software without charge?

We address these questions initially from the perspective of the coordination game between manufacturers and distributors using the game theory techniques of Chapter 13.

MANAGERIAL CHALLENGE

Controlling the Vertical: Ultimate TV versus Google TV[1]

Enormous business opportunities loom on the horizon for companies that operate at the intersection of Web-based Internet services and digital TV. Over the next five years, 220 million analog television sets will be replaced by $150 billion worth of Internet-enabled digital televisions.

Microsoft has invested heavily in digital entertainment programming for these smart televisions and television-enabled PCs. Its know-how and trade secret investments are largely non-redeployable and include the operating system and user interface backbone for everything from interactive museum tours to distance learning virtual courses. Now Google and Apple have both entered the business. Digital TV manufacturer Sony quickly established partnerships with Microsoft and Google in part to assess the danger to its core business and in part to take the first steps toward acquiring an equity stake in this emergent technology.

Cont.

MANAGERIAL CHALLENGE *Continued*

© Buene Vista Images/Photodisc/Getty Images

Microsoft then decided to vertically integrate and preemptively bought WebTV for $425 million (now renamed MSN TV). Microsoft intended to combine its one-way dependent and reliant digital entertainment assets with WebTV's technology to produce digital consumer products for smart phones and handheld PCs. Microsoft also sought to become a cable TV industry standard by investing more than $10 billion in equity ownership of AT&T, Telewest, Comcast, and three European cable firms.

Discussion Questions

■ Brainstorm about why Microsoft and Google, as software giants and sometime content providers, are seeking controlling interests in the technology by which their content would be delivered to end users?

■ Apple is a company that closely controls the design, manufacture, and retailing of its products. Does this imply that Apple's design and software assets are easily redeployable to many other uses than the products they offer for sale or that they are uniquely valuable in their present forms and uses?

■ What analogies can you draw between the two types of companies that have decided to vertically integrate downstream?

[1]Based on "Google Unveils Software to Join TV, Web," *Wall Street Journal* (May 21, 2010), p. B3; "Why Microsoft Is Glued to the Tube," *Business Week* (September 22, 1997), p. 96; and "Smart TV Gets Even Smarter," *Business Week* (April 16, 2001), pp. 132–133.

INTRODUCTION

Organizational form and institutional arrangements play an extensive role in eliciting efficient behavior. Incentive contracts can motivate manager-agents to pursue the interests of owner-principals. Incentive-compatible revelation mechanisms can increase the market value of joint ventures between partners such as Nokia and Siemens. On another front, allowing the freewheeling of electricity from one public utility to another or privatizing Conrail, British Telecom, Japan Air Lines, Teléfonos de México, and Société Générale can improve the incentives to maximize capitalized value in these formerly bloated public monopolies.

Institutional choices also involve the form of organization that companies adopt. For example, some manufacturers, such as Goodyear Tire, develop franchise dealerships rather than engage in the vertical requirements contracting with independent retailers preferred by other manufacturers such as Michelin. Perhaps the most important application of these concepts occurs in deciding the boundary of the firm—whether to vertically integrate throughout the supply chain like Exxon or outsource practically all manufacturing like Dell.

THE ROLE OF CONTRACTING IN COOPERATIVE GAMES

In Chapter 13, we saw that once a manufacturer commits to updating a product, distributors sometimes find that their best-reply response is to continue extensive selling efforts and post-sale services. If so, the required coordination of manufacturer and

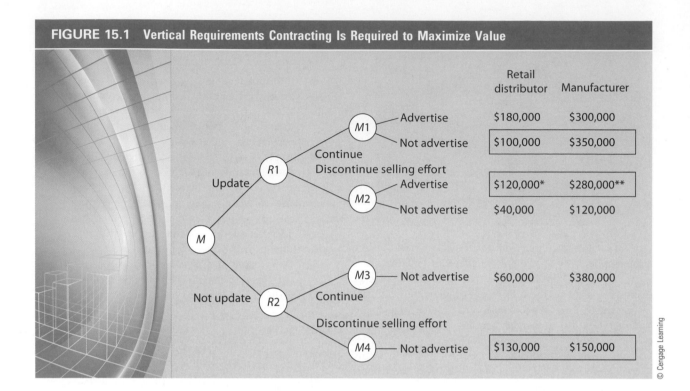

FIGURE 15.1 **Vertical Requirements Contracting Is Required to Maximize Value**

distributor actions can be achieved by a self-enforcing reliance relationship. At other times, however, the payoffs are such that coordination requires something more than the best-reply response concept we examined. Consider again the decisions in Figure 15.1. These are the same actions and payoffs we examined earlier in the Manufacturer-Distributor II game (Figure 13.4).

Recall that in the subgame perfect equilibrium {Update, Discontinue, Advertise}, the retail distributor is better off discontinuing some selling effort, knowing full well that the manufacturer's best-reply response is to advertise anyway. See the boxed and starred outcome in Figure 15.1. This odd combination of actions dominates all other sequential patterns that meet the conditions of best-reply response for each player at each proper subgame node in the decision tree. However, sales volume would decline, so the manufacturer is clearly worse off than would have been the case had the distributor continued all selling efforts. In that event, the manufacturer would realize either $300,000 or $350,000, whereas updating and advertising to prevent a sales collapse from the distributors' reduced selling effort results in a manufacturer's payoff of only $280,000.

Moreover, the institutional arrangements under which defection by the retail distributor occurs regularly are not value maximizing. The subgame perfect equilibrium strategy {Update, Discontinue, Advertise} creates total value after expenses of $120,000 + $280,000 = $400,000. {Update, Continue, Not Advertise} generates $450,000 total payoffs, and {Update, Continue, Advertise} generates $480,000 total payoffs. One might then expect some organizational form to emerge to realize this additional value. One alternative is vertical integration. By buying the distributor firm (for something slightly more than the discounted present value of the retail distributor's $120,000), the manufacturer could impose the value-maximizing actions and resolve coordination and control with internal monitoring and incentive systems within the consolidated firm.

Alternatively, manufacturers might suspend shipments to retail distributors and change distributors frequently as one after another violated the expectations of the relationship and pursued the "Discontinue" strategy. Because instability in the distribution channel imposes substantial start-up costs, the manufacturer may instead enter into a *cooperative* game of credible promises and side payments (i.e., a relational contract).

Vertical Requirements Contracts

contracts Third-party-enforceable agreements designed to facilitate deferred exchange.

Contracts are binding, third-party-enforceable agreements designed to facilitate deferred exchange. A *promisee* undertakes some costly action (perhaps making a side payment that the law terms a consideration) in exchange for and relying upon the *promisor's* pledge of a subsequent performance. Here, the manufacturer updates the product, relying upon the retail distributor to subsequently perform presale selling efforts. The manufacturer then decides about manufacturer-sponsored advertising by the retail distributor. Of course, distributors can appear to promise one thing and then deliver another, but vertical requirements contracts are one method of establishing the credibility of such promises.

vertical requirements contract A third-party enforceable agreement between stages of production in a product's value chain.

For the contracting problem in Figure 15.1, a **vertical requirements contract** might offer the distributor more than the $120,000 of the equilibrium noncooperative actions. A cooperative surplus of $480,000 (in the first row) − $400,000 (in the third row) = $80,000 is generated by retail distributors who can be induced to provide full-selling services when the manufacturer updates and advertises the product. Therefore, the manufacturer might offer the distributor's *threat point* (the $120,000 payoff from defecting) plus one-half of this increase in value from performing as promised (namely, another $40,000). Such an agreement would yield actions that increase the manufacturer's payoff from $280,000 to ($480,000 − [$120,000 + $40,000]) = $320,000. Assuming alternative distributors were available, this contract would be accepted by the present distributor, and both players would be $40,000 better off than in the subgame perfect equilibrium {Update, Discontinue, Advertise}, which made no use of third-party-enforceable contracting.[2]

Again, credible commitments are the key. Given the decision timing, the manufacturer could promise to advertise but then not do so. Because of this second possibility of post-contractual opportunism, the retail distributor may require escrow accounts for cooperative advertising, or the parties could stipulate a $51,000 damage penalty should the manufacturer breach its duty to advertise after the distributor expended full effort in attempting to sell an upgraded product. In that event, the manufacturer in Figure 15.1 would have $300,000 from advertising and $350,000 − $51,000 = $299,000 from not advertising. The retail distributor would be better off continuing its selling effort ($100,000 + $51,000) rather than discontinuing its selling effort ($120,000). We could then anticipate a value-maximizing {Update, Continue Effort, Advertise} outcome with a maximum value of $180,000 + $300,000 = $480,000 profit payoff.

Negotiating position may in the end reallocate some of the cooperative surplus back to the manufacturer in the form of franchise fees. For example, a profit-sharing franchise contract with the $51,000 stipulated penalty clause for manufacturer breach on advertising might start by asking the distributor to pay a $50,000 per period franchise fee. On

---

[2]The actual vertical requirements contract here is likely to be structured around an offer of a percentage of the profits. By acknowledging the uncertainty of the final product value, the manufacturer and distributor could agree to share this risk. In particular, a vertical requirements contract that offered to grant 33 percent of the summed profits ($160,000 of $480,000) to an authorized distributor in exchange for full-selling effort and after-sale service of an updated manufacturer-advertised product would maximize the value of this business opportunity.

net, then, the distributor would receive updated products, $180,000 in operating profits minus $50,000 in franchise fees, plus a stipulated damages agreement regarding co-op advertising funded by the manufacturer. The manufacturer would receive continued full selling effort by the distributor, $300,000 in operating profits, plus the $50,000 fee as franchisor.

The Function of Commercial Contracts

Forming such a contract provides a hostage beyond the mere reputational asset that prospective distributors might offer. In exchange for an agreed consideration, the promisee receives a credible promise. The promisor's commitment to perform is credible because the legal rules of contract interpretation and enforcement provide assurance that any expectations clearly spelled out by the parties will be met. Although courts seldom order recalcitrant contractors to perform specifically as was promised, they are quick to award **expectation damages** that leave the parties no worse off than was anticipated under the contract. Standard contract remedies therefore provide incentives for efficient precaution by the promisor and for no more than efficient reliance on the promise by the promisee.

expectation damages
A remedy for breach of contract designed to elicit efficient precaution and efficient reliance on promises.

Example

Crankshaft Delivery Delay Causes Plant Closing

The role of contract remedies as incentives is well illustrated by the historical case of *Hadley v. Baxendale*, Court of Exchequer 1854, 9 Exch 341. A mill owner ordered a replacement for a broken crankshaft from a machine shop that agreed to a standard repair and return of the mill owner's equipment. When return delivery was delayed because of poor road conditions, the mill owner sued for lost profits resulting from his extended plant closing. The court rejected this claim for extraordinary damages because the machine shop had taken the customary shipping precautions and would have been expected to do more (perhaps by arranging for an expedited delivery by express coach) only if the mill owner had stipulated the extraordinary damages that would arise from further delay.

In other words, the machine shop was entitled to expect that the mill owner would not rely excessively on the promise of a three-day repair unless informed to the contrary. If the mill owner had time-sensitive business scheduled immediately thereafter and no temporary substitute crankshaft available, it was his responsibility to disclose those potentially destructive private facts and thereby elicit a different level of precaution. Therefore, the mill owner's reliance was excessive and inefficient, not deserving of the reinforcement that would have resulted from the court awarding lost profit.[3]

[3]An excellent extended discussion of the role of contract remedies as incentives for efficient reliance and efficient precaution against nonperformance appears in R. Cooter and T. Ulen, *Law and Economics*, 5th ed. (Reading, MA: Addison-Wesley, 2008).

A stipulation procedure in the law of contract works exceptionally well for fully anticipated events. However, the rules of contract case law that have evolved (several of which are summarized in the bottom half of Table 15.1) also reduce the transaction costs of renegotiation and settlement when *unanticipated* events occur. For example, the market price that can be realized on a Volvo GM truck can change dramatically between making an investment at a manufacturing facility to design and produce an updated truck that runs only on ethanol and the subsequent promotion and sale of such trucks six months

TABLE 15.1	A SPECTRUM OF ALTERNATIVE CONTRACT ENVIRONMENTS FOR MANUFACTURERS AND DISTRIBUTORS		
	SPOT MARKET TRANSACTIONS	**VERTICAL REQUIREMENTS CONTRACT**	**RELATIONAL CONTRACT**
Timing	Instantaneous, one-time-only	Deferred exchange; promise of future performance for immediate consideration	Repeat business
Players	Anonymous buyers/sellers	Contract partners	Well-known dealers/agents
Enforcement	Barter or consideration for a consideration	Enforced by impartial third parties	Self-enforcing; best-reply responses
Information	Perfect (complete and certain) information + competition leads to efficient markets	Purposefully incomplete contracts embrace ambiguity; governance mechanisms	Reputation; signaling/bluffing games

SOME RULES OF CONTRACT LAW
Contracts facilitate deferred exchange by addressing uncertain performance outcomes (the incomplete contract problem), unobservable effort in assuring performance (the moral hazard problem), and recontracting hazards (the holdup problem).

BASIC FUNCTIONS OF CONTRACT	ILLUSTRATIVE CONTRACT RULE
1. Providing incentives for efficient precaution and efficient reliance	1. Award of expectation damages
2. Encouraging the discovery of asymmetric information	2. Required disclosure of destructive but not constructive facts
3. Providing risk-allocation mechanisms	3. Frustration of purpose doctrine
4. Reducing transaction costs	4. Nonexcusal in forward sales contracts

© Cengage Learning

later. Suppose in the meantime that the market price collapses because a competitor's new and improved hybrid-fuel truck is introduced.

If the initial truck manufacturer and distributor agreed to a fixed-price contract six months earlier, the manufacturer will get the agreed-upon revenue because the distributor took that risk. On the other hand, if changes in the regulatory environment over the six months make it illegal to sell that ethanol-based model of truck, then the **frustration of purpose doctrine** of the Uniform Commercial Code (UCC) would excuse the distributor from the contractual obligation to pay.

frustration of purpose doctrine An illustration of a default rule of contract law that can result in excusal of contract promises.

Contracts facilitate deferred exchange. The rules of contract law, as embodied primarily in the common law but also codified in statutes including the UCC, provide predictable outcomes at low transaction costs. For example, as we saw earlier, the courts almost always impose a liability for *expectation damages* on parties that breach their contract promises. Because circumstances change, expectation damages are often more efficient than forcing a promisor to fulfill the contract. In these cases, the costs of the expectations damages are often less than the costs of taking the actions specified in the contract.

In some cases, contract promises are excused altogether. These excusals fall into two categories: exceedingly rare *formation excusals* and more frequent *performance excusals*. If I sell you a damaged Learjet without disclosing the damage, you (the buyer) can ask to be excused. On the other hand, an astute buyer of a damaged jet who recognizes the potential for enhancing the value through inexpensive repair can profit from his or her asymmetric information without concern about whether the court might later set aside the sales contract and restore the plane to its original owner. Contract law supports this delicate balance of requiring the disclosure of *destructive facts* without reducing the incentive to develop asymmetric information that enhances value (i.e., *constructive facts*).

spot market transactions An instantaneous, one-time-only exchange of typically standardized goods between anonymous buyers and sellers.

Spot market transactions pose the least informational and incentive problems. For example, buying electricity off the grid at a quarter until the hour for delivery on the hour avoids pricing risk and the possibility of opportunistic behavior. Complete and certain information plus competitive entry and exit in efficient markets implies that equilibrium market prices will reflect all relevant information. This makes the current price the best forecast of future prices. However, the availability of simple commodity transactions for immediate delivery fails to solve several issues that arise in most business contracting.

Example

The Enforcement and Excusal of Contract Promises: The Extraordinary Case of 9/11[4]

In a typical *performance excuse*, contingent events like a change in regulatory constraints may frustrate the purpose of a contract. If the U.S. FDA withdraws approval for a pharmaceutical's claim to be safe and effective, Merck may obtain an excusal of its contractual agreement with the inventor to license and market the drug.

Contracts are also excused because of unforeseen natural disasters or acts of war. On the morning of September 11, 2001, Bank of New York was obligated to clear and provide cash settlements for about 84,000 government security transactions. The client firms, such as J.P. Morgan Chase & Co., had invested large sums in real-time hard-wired data feeds and sophisticated telecommunications connections to Bank of New York. Yet three of the bank's buildings in lower Manhattan were either damaged or forced to close because of the terrorist attack. At one point, Bank of New York owed Citigroup and Morgan $30 million each on settlements the bank could not authorize for final clearance because of the chaos at its business facilities.

Under other circumstances, each day said settlement was delayed would have resulted in a claim against Bank of New York for expectation damages of approximately (1/365) × 3% × $30 million = $2,465 per day. With razor-slim margins on these clearing and settlement operations, such damages would have quickly exhausted all profit. However, under the unforeseen circumstances of 9/11, an act of war had prevented performance of the settlement and clearing contract, and the Bank of New York was entitled to a performance excuse.

[4]Based in part on "Little Changes at Bank of New York," *Wall Street Journal* (March 8, 2002), p. C11.

Consider the deferred exchange of a present consideration for a promise of future forward sales. Suppose, that is, the truck manufacturer and distributor entered into a forward sales contract for diesel fuel to be used as a promotion to enhance the distributor's selling effort, and subsequently the price of diesel fuel tripled, what would happen?

forward sales contracts A consensual agreement to exchange goods delivered in the future for cash today, with no possibility of a performance excuse.

The default rule of the UCC for **forward sales contracts** is very explicit and subject to few, if any, excusals. If the truck manufacturer sold forward to the distributor 100,000 gallons of diesel at $2.33 per gallon in June 2012 for truck sales promotions at delivery in December 2012, and if the December spot market price rises to $4, the manufacturer took *that* risk of rising cost in fulfilling the contract. A manufacturer's plea that it would be ruinous financially to deliver as promised will fall on deaf ears; the manufacturer must either deliver the 100,000 gallons in December or face an immediate court judgment of ($4 − $2.33) × 100,000 = $167,000 awarded to the distributor. Every commercial contract must either stipulate the allocation of such risks or operate under the UCC default rules that are intended to increase predictability and thereby reduce the transaction costs of forward business contracting.

Table 15.1 summarizes several other characteristic differences between spot market transactions, reputation-based relationships, and vertical requirements contracts between manufacturers and distributors (that might include forward sales agreements for the diesel fuel promotion). Whether manufacturers and distributors will decide to employ spot market transactions, relational contracting, fixed profit-share franchise contracts, or vertical integration depends on the relative transaction costs of coordination and control in the various contractual settings.

Incomplete Information, Incomplete Contracting, and Post-Contractual Opportunism

incomplete information Uncertain knowledge of payoffs, choices, and other factors.

Practically all exchanges, whether for products, financial claims, or labor services, are conducted under conditions of **incomplete information**. On the one hand, decision makers often face random disturbances on the outcome of their actions. This type of incomplete information is typically handled in routine ways by risk spreading in insurance markets, which pool such casualty risks and thereby reduce the loss exposure to any individual business or household. Randomly occurring injuries at a consumer electronics assembly plant seldom coincide with injuries in a firm's delivery trucks or severe weather disruptions at a firm's shipping facility. As a result, modest insurance premiums can cover the cost of the anticipated claims involving such diversifiable risk events.

full contingent claims contract An agreement about all possible future events.

However, incomplete information as to the existence and probability of remote risks (i.e., what possible outcomes might occur) often prevent the parties at risk from writing insurance contracts. Consider the **full contingent claims contract** you and your surgeon would need to write before an organ transplant operation or two pharmaceutical companies would need before one licensed the rights to produce a pregnancy-related drug to the other. To develop all the accurate information required for an agreement about potential losses and full compensation in all possible future contingencies is simply prohibitively expensive. Consequently, few transplant patients and few business partners attempt to negotiate full contingent claims contracts. Such prohibitively expensive information costs explain why contracts are often incomplete by design.

post-contractual opportunistic behavior Actions that take advantage of a contract partner's vulnerabilities and are not specifically prohibited by the terms.

One immediate consequence of incomplete contracts is the possibility of **post-contractual opportunistic behavior** that is not specifically prohibited by the contract. Employees who receive on-the-job training (OJT) may moonlight with their new skills. Managers may reconfigure assets following a labor contract concession in ways their ongoing employees did not anticipate. Baseball players may attempt a hold out at the time of contract renewals just before a World Series. Knowing this tendency, companies provide less OJT, workers agree to fewer wage concessions, and baseball team owners develop more farm team replacement players than they otherwise would. Thus, the incompleteness of contracts results in inefficient behavior as an inescapable consequence of costly and therefore incomplete information. To reduce these inefficiencies, companies adopt governance mechanisms such as mandatory arbitration agreements to help resolve post-contractual disputes.

CORPORATE GOVERNANCE AND THE PROBLEM OF MORAL HAZARD

governance mechanisms Processes to detect, resolve, and reduce post-contractual opportunism.

Oliver Williamson, winner of the 2009 Nobel Prize in Economic Sciences, emphasizes that contracts pose the *ex ante* framework but that **governance mechanisms** provide the *ex post* implementation required to maximize value:

The parties to commercial contracts are held to be perceptive about the nature of the contractual relations of which they are a part, including an awareness of potential contractual hazards. However, because complex contracts are unavoidably incomplete—it being impossible or prohibitively costly to make provision for all possible contingencies *ex ante*—much of the relevant contractual action is borne by the *ex post* mechanisms of governance.[5]

Hence, the vertical requirements contract between the manufacturer and distributor in Figure 15.1 will be only the beginning of their agreement. In addition, the firms will need to resolve a pivotal coordination and control issue: the inherent unobservability of selling effort on the part of the retail distributor. Unobservable effort in fulfilling contract promises illustrates the post-contractual opportunistic problem of "moral hazard." After securing terms to their liking, all contract partners must be wary of the potential for shirking on the agreement in inconspicuous and hard-to-detect but potentially ruinous ways.

In the next section, we will apply the moral hazard idea to managerial contracting, but first let's consider the commercial lender's **moral hazard problem** with eliciting unobservable borrower effort in selecting safe working-capital projects. A known reliable borrower may approach a lender with a randomly occurring liquidity crisis that necessitates an extension of its bank line of credit.[6] The lender then offers terms for the loan renewal: an interest rate, principal amount, collateral requirements, and loan term. The situation is depicted in Figure 15.2. If the borrower decides to accept, a line-of-credit extension is granted. Then a random process intervenes, presenting one of

moral hazard problem A problem of post-contractual opportunism that arises from unverifiable or unobservable contract performance.

FIGURE 15.2   The Problem of Moral Hazard in Line-of-Credit Lending: A Game-Theoretic Model of Workouts

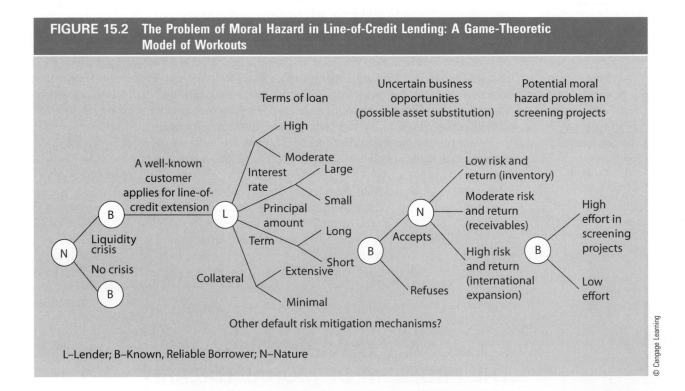

L–Lender; B–Known, Reliable Borrower; N–Nature

---

[5]Oliver Williamson, "Economics and Organization: A Primer," *California Management Review* (Winter 1996), p. 136. See also Williamson's *The Mechanisms of Governance* (New York: Oxford University Press, 1996).

[6]In the situation examined here, we abstract from the *hidden information* problem of adverse selection (by assuming that the borrowers are known customers of the lending institution) to focus attention on the *hidden action* problem of moral hazard in commercial lending.

several uncertain business opportunities to the borrower. As in earlier chapters, we signify the role of uncertainty at a node in the decision tree with a large N for a choice by Nature. The possible business opportunities are a spectrum from the relatively safe investments in inventory during periods of back order to an extension of the company's receivables policy allowing customers to pay within 90 days rather than pay cash at the point of purchase. Because product sales may be sensitive to credit terms such as "90 days same as cash," the latter use of working capital has a higher expected return but is much more risky in that uncollected customer accounts may skyrocket. Finally, borrowers may go so far as to use the new line of credit for an overseas expansion with all the attendant risk of failure and default accompanying such initiatives.

The moral hazard problem for the lender is then motivated. The commercial bank wants the borrower to exercise great care, high effort, and good business judgment in selecting projects on which to expend its newly granted working capital from the line-of-credit extension. However, banks must move carefully in setting the loan terms to elicit this largely hidden action. Remember, the bank does not know in advance what business opportunity the borrower will be facing. This is not a project financing situation where the commercial banker can take part in assessing the company's capital budgeting proposals and directly monitor its ROI and the attendant risks. Instead, this is a workout or rollover event where the bank makes the additional funds available and must then elicit subsequent borrower effort (unobservable effort) in appropriately screening projects that present themselves for possible investment.

What loan terms should the lender offer? Large loans with long repayment terms are most desired by the borrowers in order to gain the most financial flexibility in the face of their current liquidity crisis. Having more funds and more time to straighten out a business plan that has gone awry is preferable, but do these terms elicit more or less effort in screening projects so as to prevent or contain a loss? Surprisingly, higher interest rates reflective of potentially high default risk are not the answer. A high interest rate forces reliable borrowers to seek out *riskier* working-capital projects in order to secure higher expected returns and therefore be in a position to repay the loan. More moderate rates supported by extensive collateral pledges of security would seem to move the reliable borrower toward exerting more effort to find safer projects.[7]

 ## WHAT WENT RIGHT • WHAT WENT WRONG

Forecasting the Great Recession with Workouts and Rollovers

Every quarter 20 leading bank CEOs meet with the Chairman of the Federal Reserve to exchange opinions about macroeconomic indicators and business cycle forecasting. In March of 2007, almost everyone at the table reported to Chairman Ben Bernanke that loan demand was declining more steeply than any of their organizations had ever experienced. Workout and rollover requests were at an all-time high as well. The Federal Reserve ignored these leading indicators of a serious downturn in the business cycle and instead waited until August 2007 to begin loosening monetary policy and easing credit conditions. The National Bureau of Economic Research has identified the dates of the worst recession since the Great Depression from December 2007 through June 2009.

---

[7]In other circumstances, lenders would face an adverse selection problem of detecting whether unknown borrowers are from a fraudulent or reliable subpopulation of loan applicants, and the offered terms of the loan will then affect the acceptance and refusals that determine the proportion of the loan portfolio originating from each group. Moderate interest rates and high collateral are intended in that situation to allow borrowers to signal their reliable intent to repay. Outright fraud usually occurs only when collateral evaporates.

The Need for Governance Mechanisms

Perhaps the most effective way to manage the risks of loan delinquency and nonpayment may be for the lender to establish a *governance mechanism* through which it regularly reassesses a borrower's financial ratios and makes decisions about ongoing access to the extended line of credit on a real-time basis. In addition, some banks use frequent credit reporting or continuous auditing, staggered draws of the money loaned (e.g., in construction loans), or progress payments triggered by milestones in the agreement such as agreed zero-loan-balance time points in funding an inventory cycle. The more frequent, more convenient, and more audited these financial reports, the better the governance mechanism will work. In essence, the bank becomes almost a project financing partner for every major use of its funds in order to motivate the desired care, effort, and judgment from the borrower. In the end, however, direct monitoring for a project-by-project financing approval process is precluded by the definition of the problem and by the fact that bankers are not experts in all the businesses to which they lend, but the closer a governance mechanism can come to this result, the less likely a default will be.

Hiring managerial talent involves a similar moral hazard problem because managerial effort is inherently unobservable. In particular, managers are paid for their creative ingenuity in proactively solving problems; they are paid to think hard about problems that haven't happened yet. As such, managers can easily shirk their duties and instead devote their creative ingenuity to activities unrelated to their job (so-called mental moonlighting). Because of this inability to directly observe managerial effort, we mistakenly blame managers at times for poor performance attributable really to nothing more than bad luck, and we fail to acknowledge managerial merit at times because we incorrectly assume that good performance is attributable to good luck. In the next section, we will see that "incentive contracting" with a minimum salary guarantee and a performance-based bonus (e.g., a stock option or restricted stock grant) can be an efficient solution to the moral hazard problem in managerial contracting.

There is another issue with incomplete managerial contracting, however, and that one relates to contract renewals. When executives have acquired unique company-specific knowledge and skills as well as pensions and severance packages not redeployable to others, they are in a favorable position in negotiating with compensation committees of the board of directors. The executive's institutional memory is at least somewhat irreplaceable. Consequently, when it comes time to renew their contracts, senior executives often engage in "holdups."

Evidence of such holdups is plentiful: Massive executive "loans" are often forgiven, incentive-based compensation lost in the face of poor performance is often reinstated or replaced through golden parachutes triggered by a hostile takeover, and option strike prices are often reset to lower levels in down markets. Considerable effort to retain experienced senior managers is clearly value maximizing, but the compensation committee of the board must be an independent body prepared to monitor, benchmark, and whistle blow on these contract renewals if necessary. Beyond holdup, outright deception and fraud remain a frequent problem. For example, backdating option grants to dates when the strike price was in the money are clearly criminal events, and the SEC is treating them as such. Table 15.2 provides a list of the implementation mechanisms of corporate governance available to address this holdup issue.

TABLE 15.2   IMPLEMENTATION MECHANISMS OF CORPORATE GOVERNANCE

- Internal monitoring by independent board of directors committees
- Internal/external monitoring by large creditors
- Internal/external monitoring by owners of large blocks of stock
- Auditing and variance analysis
- Internal benchmarking
- Corporate culture of ethical duties
- High employee morale supportive of whistle-blowers

© Cengage Learning

WHAT WENT RIGHT • WHAT WENT WRONG

Moral Hazard and Holdup at Enron and WorldCom[8]

Misaccounting for short-term business expenses as long-term capital investments required a $3.8 billion restatement of lower operating profits at WorldCom in fiscal year 2000. Enron executives depleted pension reserve accounts while heralding the attractiveness of employee stock option plans for retirement planning. Business news of one scandal after another during the financial crisis of 2007–2009 made it abundantly clear that governance mechanisms are needed, but still the question remains, "Why, exactly?" Why don't debt contracts of bond holders, personal loan contracts that senior executives use to relocate their households, and performance-based incentive contracts aligning owner and managerial interests prevent these abuses? Is it just that too many gratuitous payments have been extracted from compensation committees, too many executive loans have been forgiven, and too many deferred stock options have been reset to lower strike prices when stock prices fell? That is, are the incentives in all this incentive contracting just misaligned? The answer is decisively "No." The more fundamental problem is that incomplete contracts invite post-contractual opportunistic behavior, requiring vigorous corporate governance mechanisms even in the presence of strong incentives.

[8]Based on "Taken for a Ride," *The Economist* (July 13, 2002), p. 64; and "WorldCom Aide Conceded Flaws," *Wall Street Journal* (June 16, 2002), p. A3.

THE PRINCIPAL-AGENT MODEL

Many types of owner-principals hire manager-agents to stand in and conduct their business affairs. Parent companies set up principal-agent relationships with subsidiaries. Manufacturer principals employ retail distributor and advertising agents. And most importantly, equity owners hire executives with managerial incentive contracts. The owners' objective in such principal-agent relationships is to offer incentives to managers to forgo alternative employment opportunities and to act in a value-maximizing manner on behalf of the owner-principals.

The Efficiency of Alternative Hiring Arrangements

Managerial hiring contracts may take on several pure or hybrid forms, including straight salary, wage rate, or profit sharing. In straight salary contracts, the manager and firm agree on a total compensation package and specific conditions of employment. In other contexts, such as consulting, the managerial consultant may receive an hourly wage rate equal to the best alternative employment opportunity in the competitive labor market for his or her type of consulting services. In Figure 15.3, the managerial consultant is hired for, say, 50 hours per week at wage rate W_a. D_l is the firm's input demand, which is the marginal revenue product of these labor services—namely, the marginal output of additional hours times the marginal revenue from selling that additional output. Because each firm is atomistic in the labor market for these management consulting services, S_l is the perfectly elastic supply facing any given employer at the going market wage. Beyond 50 hours, the declining D_l no longer exceeds the incremental input cost along S_l.

Managers also may secure employment under a pure profit-sharing contract. Like pure commission-based salespeople or manufacturer's trade representatives, the manager may accept a percentage (say 40 percent) of the receipts directly attributable to his or her efforts in lieu of wage or salary income. Think of the percentage finder's fee sometimes offered for cost-saving suggestions in big corporations or the federal government. Again in Figure 15.3, we can represent this third alternative hiring arrangement as the ray AB, wherein the manager receives 40 percent of the owner's willingness to pay for each hour of management services. Initially, this profit share will exceed the wage rate alternative. For example, during the first 22 hours of work, the profit-sharing contract will overcompensate by area ADJ (shaded area O). Thereafter the profit share falls below the manager's market wage rate per hour.

If 40 percent proves to be an equilibrium profit share, the overcompensation (shaded area ADJ, labeled O) will just equal the undercompensation for the last 28 hours of work (shaded area DCF, labeled U). This level leaves both the owners and the manager indifferent between this hiring arrangement and the alternative 50-hour-per-week wage rate contract at W_a. If the profit share were reduced to, say, 35 percent (represented by the ray IB), the dark-shaded amount of overcompensation for the first 10 hours would fail to offset the massive undercompensation for hours 10 to 50. The manager would then reject the profit-sharing contract in favor of the wage rate offer. By raising the profit share back to 40 percent, the firm appears able to restore the attractiveness of each contract, at least for certain types of workers. In reality, as we shall now see, the actual situation in hiring managerial talent is often rather different.

FIGURE 15.3 Alternative Managerial Labor Contracts

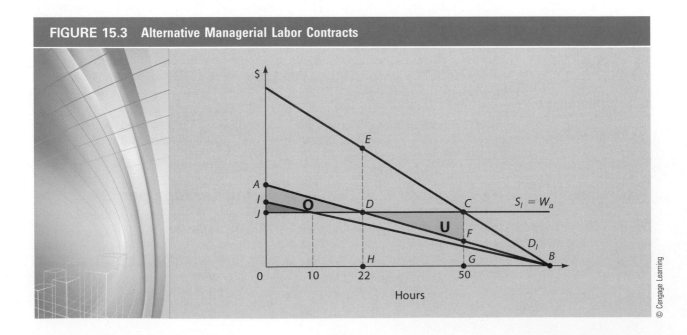

Creative Ingenuity and the Moral Hazard Problem in Managerial Contracting

Pure profit-sharing contracts contain the seeds of their own destruction. Suppose several individuals are involved in generating pharmaceutical sales, and the input that the profit sharer contributes to team production is largely unobservable. No time card can successfully monitor the input, perhaps because a measure of work effort rather than work hours is really what is required. The rational employee then considers his or her alternatives. As long as the profit-sharing compensation exceeds the alternative wage rate, he or she dedicates unobservable work effort to this job. Beyond 22 hours of work effort, however, the employee can earn more by working for someone else at the alternative wage rate W_a. Therefore, the disloyal (but rational) trade representative underworks the territory; he or she moonlights. This predictable response is another aspect of the *moral hazard problem*. Only a *moral* sense of duty to one's employer prevents this problem from becoming a real *hazard* to the business.

Predicting such behavior, the employer may decide to withdraw the offer of a pure profit-sharing contract. Let's see why. If the territory is underworked by 28 hours, the employer saves profit-sharing payments equal to area $DFGH$ in Figure 15.3 but loses output valued at the much larger $ECGH$ and therefore is out the net value $[ECGH - DFGH - ADJ$ (the overpayment area for the first 22 hours of work), all of which is equal to area $EDC]$ relative to a wage contract that just paid piece rates for 50 hours of work at an implicit wage rate of W_a per hour. The fact that work effort is largely unobservable makes the pure profit-sharing contract unattractive to the employer relative to a piece-rate contract.

This generalization is not always true. For example, in hiring attendants for parking garages, the punch-in time clock and customer complaints (e.g., horn blowing and broken parking gate barriers) monitor the required input quite well. A dismissal policy in the employment contract making time-on-task a condition of employment motivates the required input. Similar time-on-task constraints and output quotas are employed in hiring sharecroppers and retail sales clerks. In these instances, the firms and their employees have evolved effective ways to resolve the moral hazard problem. Nobel laureate Ronald Coase emphasized that private voluntary bargaining between principals and agents will often find ways to contract around such problems.[9]

The problem of moral hazard arises then only when an employee's input is directly observable only at a prohibitive cost. Consider again the pharmaceutical sales representative for whom appointment logbooks and random follow-up monitoring simply cannot detect the persuasive effort necessary to secure orders from physician customers. One could trail around after the sales representative and interview each physician after the sales calls were completed to try to detect the ingenuity and perseverance the sales rep displayed, but quite obviously, this monitoring practice would be prohibitively expensive. Instead, in the face of truly "hidden actions," the pharmaceutical company is more likely to favor some performance-based incentive contract involving benchmarking rather than the pure profit-sharing contract.

benchmarking A comparison of performance in similar jobs, firms, plants, divisions, and so forth.

During a period of **benchmarking**, the employer reassigns previously low-productivity sales territories to above-average trade representatives to see whether their effort can alter the success rate per sales call. If so, the employer concludes that lack of effort by prior sales representatives was responsible for the low sales. After several such benchmarkings, the employer is able to identify those sales representatives to be kept and

[9]See J. Farrell, "Information and the Coase Theorem," *Journal of Economic Perspectives* (Fall 1987), pp. 113–129.

those to be dismissed. Importantly, the "keepers" are then allowed to retain all the productive accounts they have developed.

For managerial jobs, however, the moral hazard problem is significantly harder to resolve. The input senior management contributes to team production is not time on task at the desk but rather what we have called *creative ingenuity*: creatively formulating and proactively solving problems that may not even have arisen as yet. Managers are paid to think, not to shuffle papers. The difficulty comes in detecting when creative ingenuity is being applied to the employer's business rather than another business for which the manager may be mentally moonlighting. Of course, eventually the difference will show up in company performance, but over how long a period and how big a difference? These questions are tough to answer satisfactorily after a senior manager has shirked his or her duties to the detriment of shareholder value.

More problematically, the shirking manager may never be let go, and the hardworking manager may never be rewarded. If random disturbances affect the company's performance, it is difficult even after the fact to separate unobservable shirking from negative random disturbances. How, then, are owners to know when to blame senior managers for downturns in company performance and when to give them credit for upturns? One governance mechanism often used to analyze these variances is the **company audit**. Managers report on the sources and uses of funds in accordance with generally accepted accounting principles (GAAP). Any period-to-period variances are then assessed and verified by independent auditors.[10] Despite dedicated efforts, auditors can seldom separate the effects of management decisions from random disturbances in company performance. That is, the moral hazard problem is much harder to solve when combined with the performance uncertainty most firms face.

> **company audit** A governance mechanism for separating random disturbances from variation in unobservable effort.

Some companies address the problem of managerial moonlighting by benchmarking one manager against another (say, in comparable plants or geographic divisions). They hope that the effects of business cycle factors and random time-series disturbances will be highly correlated across plants and divisions and that the manager's effort and creative ingenuity will therefore correspond with the plant or division's differential performance. Unfortunately, they are usually wrong. As a result, Japanese companies rely on intense loyalty-building exercises, peer pressure, and lifetime employment contracts (following some probationary period) to reduce mental moonlighting and other forms of shirking.

In isolation, neither hidden effort (unobservability) nor performance uncertainty poses any special difficulty for owner-principals hiring manager-agents. The moral hazard resulting from the unobservability of a manager's input is, by itself, resolvable by assigning the manager lagged residual income claims (e.g., deferred stock options or restricted stock). Settling up *ex post* with a manager, after all the effects of his or her effort and ingenuity have had time to influence performance, creates more effective performance-based incentives.

Example

Indexed Stock Options at Adobe Systems, Dell, and Cisco[11]

To align managerial incentives with equity owner interests, most companies regularly award deferred stock options to their managers. These performance-based bonuses entitle the holder to purchase company stock at a slight discount to its current value. If the firm's performance subsequently improves, capitalized value rises and

(continued)

---

[10]This audit mechanism is explored at greater length at the end of the chapter in the first case exercise.

both shareholders and the managers stand to gain. To exercise their options, managers often must wait three to five years, but they sometimes realize gains of 50 to 80 percent or more. In 2009, CEO compensation in *Fortune* 500 companies averaged $7 million, 71 percent of which involved deferred-stock or options-based compensation for superior performance.

To acquire the stock for these deferred compensation programs, some companies dilute equity by issuing new shares, while others repurchase shares on the open market. To reduce the cost of these "buybacks," especially in a rising market, some companies, such as Adobe Systems, Dell, and Cisco, index the exercise price for their deferred options to the average stock price of their industry. When all the related companies do well, the value of the option rises, but so does the exercise price. As a result, the managers do not exercise their options at that juncture and instead are motivated to outperform their peers in related companies in both good times and bad.

[11]Based on "Stock Options That Don't Reward Laggards," *Wall Street Journal* (March 30, 1999), p. A26; "Corporate America Faces Declining Value of Options," *Wall Street Journal* (October 16, 2000), p. A1; "The Gravy Train Just Got Derailed," *BusinessWeek* (November 19, 2001), p. 118; and "CEO Compensation Survey," *Wall Street Journal* (April 11, 2005), p. R1.

Example

P&G Pays Ad Executives Based on Their Performance

Procter & Gamble places more than $3 billion per year in advertising through Saatchi & Saatchi, Leo Burnett, and other ad agencies. Traditionally, agencies earned flat-rate fees assessed as 15 percent of the ad dollars expended for the client. In the 1990s, Ford, Colgate-Palmolive, and P&G broke out of this flat-rate system and began paying a baseline fixed fee plus a performance bonus. Now, account executives at the agencies earn a fixed salary if their creative communications are less than compelling and P&G sales stay flat. On the other hand, a hugely successful ad campaign can earn multimillion-dollar bonuses if P&G's sales growth can be attributed to the advertising. Both the clients, the ad agency owners, and the account execs now share in the risks of consumer whimsy, but a base salary provides a safety net should random misfortune occur.

Similarly, performance uncertainty taken alone creates a risk-allocation problem that may be easily resolved with insurance. Managers are somewhat less able to diversify than owners because of the specific human capital the manager often invests in a long-term relationship with his or her corporate employer. This situation results in risk averse owners and risk-averse managers frequently structuring some sort of risk-sharing agreement, such as a guaranteed baseline salary combined with a performance-based bonus.

Formalizing the Principal-Agent Problem

principal-agent problem An incentives conflict in delegating decision-making authority.

The real difficulty for managerial contracting then arises when the unobservability of management's creative ingenuity and performance uncertainty occur simultaneously. The coexistence of these problems constitutes the so-called **principal-agent problem** most firms face. Settling up *ex post facto* with management teams then no longer creates the desired incentives. Some managers get unlucky and receive blame they did not deserve, and others get lucky and receive credit they did not earn.

The principal-agent problem can be formalized as an optimization problem subject to dual constraints. The principal chooses a profit-sharing rate and a manager's salary guarantee to maximize the expected utility of the risk-averse owner-principals' profit where profit depends on the manager-agent's effort, on the cost of the managerial incentives contract, and on random disturbances. An **incentive compatibility constraint** then aligns the effort chosen by the manager in response to the share and salary offer with the effort that maximizes the expected utility of the owner-principals. That is, an incentive-compatible profit share and salary elicit the managerial effort and creative ingenuity required to maximize the owner's value. Third and finally, the **participation constraint** ensures that the manager will reject his or her next best offer of alternative employment.

In the next section, we illustrate the meaning of each of these three elements with a linear optimal incentives contract, which can solve the principal-agent problem. However, understand that an optimal managerial incentives contract is easier to describe than to attain.[12] See the second case exercise at the end of this chapter to try your hand at balancing all the competing objectives involved.

incentive compatibility constraint An assurance of incentive alignment.

participation constraint An assurance of ongoing involvement.

Screening and Sorting Managerial Talent with Optimal Incentives Contracts

Asymmetric information arises in all hiring decisions, but it often plays an especially prominent role in managerial hiring decisions. Job applicants know all the information, but potential employers have access only to the information that applicants select for their résumés. Thus, among perhaps 19 résumé facts that the personnel department might like to know, the applicant discloses only 14. Let's see how linear share contracts can be used to sort managerial talent based on one of these undisclosed characteristics— namely, a manager's risk aversion.

Suppose a large bank has two openings for which it desires managers of different risk aversion. One position is the assistant vice president for commercial construction loans in a city with overbuilt office developments and, consequently, very high vacancy rates. The other position is an assistant vice president to manage the venture capital loan portfolio, to interact with owners of new start-up businesses, and to represent the bank at the entrepreneurship club of the city. As you might suspect, the bank has two rather different people in mind as ideal candidates for these openings. In the commercial construction area, the bank seeks an instinctively cautious and safety-conscious manager who will take every opportunity to reduce the large default risk already present in this portion of the bank's business. Both jobs are simply listed as assistant vice president positions; no further details are given.

Two managers with the requisite training and experience apply for the bank positions. Their résumés are similar. However, unbeknownst to the bank, one drives an old Porsche, not insured against collision damage, and has skydiving as an undisclosed former hobby. Instead of skydiving, this individual (let's call him Dashing) now prefers bungee jumping, which he understandably decides would be inappropriate to list as a hobby on an application for a bank job. The other individual (you guessed it, Smooth)

---

[12]Even the solution we describe is limited to separable functions in effort and money income. The general principal-agent problem with risk-averse owners and managers has multiple solutions and requires *nonlinear* incentive contracts relating both salary and profit share to company performance. See J. Tirole, *The Theory of Industrial Organization* (Cambridge, MA: MIT Press, 1988), pp. 35–54; and D. Kreps, *A Course in Microeconomic Theory* (Princeton, NJ: Princeton University Press, 1990), Chapter 16.

WHAT WENT RIGHT • WHAT WENT WRONG

Why Have Restricted Stock Grants Replaced Executive Stock Options at Microsoft?[13]

In 2004, Microsoft announced that it would use approximately $30 billion of its $60 billion in cash and short-term investments to buy back stock to be used for bonuses. Between 1995 and 2005, the use of restricted stock grew from 18 percent of CEO compensation to 22 percent. But Microsoft went further. Microsoft joined numerous other companies in granting restricted stock rather than stock options as a performance-based bonus to more than 10,000 of its employees. Why change the Microsoft performance bonuses?

Several reasons are behind this change. First, restricted stock cannot be sold if an executive leaves the company. In contrast, once stock options vest, they are typically sold. During the heyday of the booming information economy in the late 1990s, Microsoft's options created literally thousands of multimillionaires among Microsoft's senior managers. Too many of these valuable human resources simply chose to retire early and move on to other pursuits. One former executive took up professional bowling. Another senior executive, Paul Allen, bought a basketball team and built a guitar museum. The change of compensation contracts to feature restricted stock is expected to enhance the retention of pivotal employees relative to granting options.

A second reason a board of directors prefers restricted stock is that senior managers are often able to negotiate option features that work against optimal incentive contracting. For example, few option exercise prices are indexed relative to the industry group or strategic competitors. So stock options reward mediocrity when all share prices in an industry rise together. Third, many senior executive options are "reloaded." As soon as the option contracts vest (in 2–5 years) and are exercised, senior managers negotiate the issue of new options with new exercise prices but the old expiration date (of typically 10 years). This clause allows executives to profit from induced volatility in their share prices. They have a powerful incentive to "swing for the fences" with high-risk projects whenever options in the money can be converted to cash at an intermediate date and then replaced with new options expiring at the original dates.

Finally, few stock option contracts restrict in any way the executive's ability to "unwind" his or her risk exposure by hedging the risks the options create. Selling short a long option position that ties the manager's wealth to that of the shareholders is hardly justifiable given that the objective of performance-based pay is the aligning of managerial incentives with shareholder interests. But the hedge fund scandal at Goldman Sachs in April 2010 suggests that such short selling of customer positions occurs on Wall Street.

Corporations should be determined to prevent the practice on Main Street. Restricted stock has none of these drawbacks.

---

[13]"Microsoft Ushers Out Era of Options," *Wall Street Journal* (July 9, 2003), p. A1; L. Bebchuk et al., "Managerial Power and Rent Extraction in the Design of Executive Compensation," *University of Chicago Law Review* 69 (2002), pp. 751–846; B. Hall and K. Murphy, "The Trouble with Stock Options," *Journal of Economic Perspectives* (Summer 2003); "Finance 2.0: An Interview with Microsoft's CFO," *The McKinsey Quarterly*, no. 1 (2005), "CEOs Get Paid," *Knowledge Wharton* (May 3, 2006), p. 3.

---

drives a dealer-serviced Land Rover on which she carries the maximum auto insurance coverage. Despite never leaving town, Smooth keeps the Rover in four-wheel drive at all times to secure the extra traction. Once while attending a formal cocktail party with a few close friends, Smooth revealed that she spent her Christmas bonus on "more insurance, of course." Thinking none of these details to be of any real significance to the bank, she too omits that information from the job application.

The bank's problem is to sort these two types of individuals, both of whom are well qualified, into the jobs appropriate for their different risk aversions. In Figure 15.4, we display the guaranteed base salary and profit-sharing rate, the two components of a **linear incentives contract**. On the horizontal axis are various percentages that represent what additions to *or subtractions from* one's pay occur as a result of the profit-sharing agreement. A greater share rate initially elicits more effort and creative ingenuity and results in greater expected profit contribution from the manager's activities. Eventually, at still higher share rates, the profit contribution actually declines. The two hill-shaped curves in Figure 15.4 represent expected profit-sharing payouts that would allow the firm to just break even on its incentive payments to the two managers. The lower

linear incentives contract A linear combination of salary and profit sharing intended to align incentives.

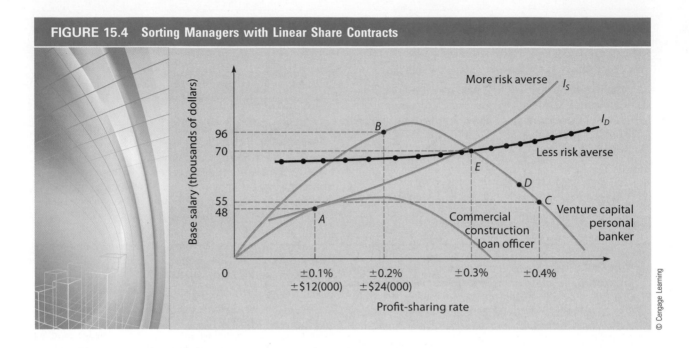

FIGURE 15.4 **Sorting Managers with Linear Share Contracts**

expected profit curve corresponds to the commercial construction loans job, and the higher curve corresponds to the venture capital loans job.

Let's suppose that the bank has expected sales of $100 million and a net cash flow from sales of 12 percent. Hence, expected profits available for distribution to owners and managers run $12 million. The bank first elicits responses to two tentative contract offers for their assistant vice president jobs. Contract *A* offers $48,000 salary plus or minus 0.1 percent of the net cash flow or $12,000, which implies a $36,000 to $60,000 possible range of income outcomes. Contract *B* offers $96,000 salary plus or minus 0.2 percent, or a $72,000 to $120,000 range. Contracts *A* and *B* are not equally attractive. One dominates the other in that minimum outcomes under Contract *B* exceed the maximum outcomes under Contract *A*. Because risk increases only modestly from 0.1 percent to 0.2 percent, both prospective employees are likely to select *B*, and therefore Contract *B* is said to result in a **pooling equilibrium**. Such an outcome is illustrated in Figure 15.4, where the indifference curves for both Smooth (I_S) and Dashing (I_D) indicate that Contract *B* would be preferred by both applicants.

To separate the two applicants according to their risk aversion, the bank withdraws Contract *B* and instead introduces a more demanding risk-return trade-off. To see how this would work, we begin by indicating on Figure 15.4 the indifference curve for the more risk-averse applicant, Smooth (I_S), that establishes a line of demarcation between contracts to the northwest, which are more preferred than *A*, and those to the southeast, which are less preferred. To induce a revelation of the risk-aversion differences between Smooth and Dashing, the bank then offers a contract pair such as *A* and *C*. Contract *C* imposes a much larger 0.4 percent profit share and offers only $55,000 expected base salary, just $7,000 above Contract *A*. Smooth finds *C* much less preferred than the original Contract *A* and immediately says so. In contrast, less risk-averse Dashing (I_D) is so close to being risk neutral (i.e., with almost flat indifference curves between expected salary and profit share), that Dashing may well prefer Contract *C*.

This **separating equilibrium** in which Smooth reveals her stronger risk aversion by rejecting *C* in favor of *A*, whereas Dashing does just the reverse, attains several of the

pooling equilibrium A decision setting that elicits indistinguishable behavior.

separating equilibrium A decision setting that elicits distinguishable behavior.

employer's objectives. First, these profit-sharing contracts are incentive-compatible contracts in that they elicit appropriate effort and creative ingenuity from both managers while maximizing the shareholders' value. Second, these profit-sharing contracts sort Dashing as the manager to head up the venture capital personal banking group and Smooth as the bank manager for the commercial construction group. The reductions in expected profit to compensate each manager would have been larger without this matching of risk aversion and job types.

However, one aspect of an optimal incentives contract remains unaddressed. The participation constraint has not yet been satisfied. An alternative employer can offer Contract *D*, which attracts Smooth with both more expected salary and lower profit risk while retaining the separating properties of the (*A*,*C*) contract pair. As long as such improvements in both risk and return are possible, Smooth will continue to resign and move. Only with contract pair (*A*,*E*) will both the incentive compatibility and participation constraints be satisfied; Dashing selects Contract *E*, while Smooth selects Contract *A*, and both remain in the bank's employ. In addition to resolving the sorting of managerial talent, if it induces the appropriate effort from both managers and prevents their being bid away to alternative employment opportunities, this linear incentives contract constitutes a solution to the principal-agent problem in managerial contracting.

CHOOSING THE EFFICIENT ORGANIZATIONAL FORM

non-redeployable, specific assets Assets whose replacement cost basis for value is substantially greater than their liquidation value.

Ultimately, the choice of organizational form (e.g., spot market transactions, relational contracting, franchise profit sharing, or vertical integration) depends upon what best suits the governance needs of the asset owners involved. Assets can be **non-redeployable, specific assets** with little or no value in second-best use, such as remote plants and work-in-process inventories, or they may be nonspecific investments that are fully redeployable, such as corporate jet aircraft, popular finished goods in inventory, and Treasury cash. In addition, some assets are dependent on unique complementary investments (e.g., specially designed computer hardware and closed-architecture software) while others are not (e.g., a flexible power plant designed to run on natural gas, coal, or biodiesel). One classic example of these asset-characteristic dichotomies is a hot-rolled-steel-making plant belonging to a company such as Republic or U.S. Steel, which requires a blast furnace, converter, reduction furnace, and rolling mill. Because melting the ore and then the metal requires substantial energy, such plants are located beside one another to avoid the reheating expense. However, the organization form question is not whether the operations will be physically integrated and in adjacent locations but rather whether they will be jointly or separately owned and managed.

At one end of the spectrum, spot market recontracting is efficient for fully redeployable durable assets not dependent upon other complementary assets. Rental cars provide a good illustration of such assets that may be allocated through spot markets with no loss of efficiency, as shown at the top left of Table 15.3. The limiting feature of this organizational form, however, is the potential for "holdup" inherent in the frequent renewal of spot market contracts. If one party has non-redeployable assets (e.g., a steel mill's blast furnace or a stadium of a sports franchise), spot market recontracting provides too many opportunities for unique engineers or star players to appropriate the surplus value in any business relationship. Owners of non-redeployable assets wish to avoid this holdup hazard by securing longer-term supply contracts.

reliant assets At least partially non-redeployable durable assets.

Reliant assets are non-redeployable durable assets that when resold must be sold in thin markets for less than their value in first-best use. These assets are highly specific to their current use because of substantial unrecoverable sunk cost investments either in acquisition, distribution, or promotion. Specialized equipment in remote locations such as a bauxite mine is the most common reliant asset. Where reliant assets are dependent on unique complements (like an aluminum plant) in order to achieve any substantial value added, one has the maximum potential for holdup in spot market recontracting. In addition to all the bargaining costs such a situation engenders, these "all-eggs-in-one-basket" ventures tend to receive underinvestment relative to what would be optimal.

Dependency relations between assets may be either one way or bilateral. Manufacturers with independent distributors are a good example of a bilateral dependent relationship involving reliant assets. Each party in a Volvo GM Heavy Truck Corporation manufacturer/distributor relationship is equally dependent on the other. In such cases, independent dealers often gravitate toward vertical requirements contracts with a fixed profit share, as shown in the bottom right corner of Table 15.3.

relational contracts Promissory agreements of coordinated performance among owners of highly interdependent assets.

When assets are dependent on unique complements but not reliant because of their substantial redeployability, the parties often adopt long-term performance-based **relational contracts**. Redeployable corporate jets and pilots provide a good illustration. Pilots need not own the planes or secure fixed profit-share contracts to operate the planes. Instead, as indicated in Table 15.3, the efficient organizational form of a jet charter company is normally one of long-term relational contracts with standby pilots who report on short notice for piecemeal assignments. This alliance works well, and both the pilots and plane owners understand that the longevity and reliability of the relationship enhances value relative to spot market recontracting.

Pepsi and Starbucks entered into an alliance to sell cold Frappuccino through soft drink machines. Starbucks' assets in this alliance are redeployable but one-way dependent on any of several companies with tens of thousands of drink machines. So, again referring to Table 15.3, a Starbucks–Pepsi alliance is the efficient organizational form. To take a related example, Genentech's biotechnology is fully redeployable but one-way dependent on marketing behemoth partners such as Pfizer or GlaxoSmithKline. As a result, Genentech has consistently entered into 10 marketing partnerships, 20 licensing agreements, and numerous product development alliances with large drug makers. In contrast, Coca-Cola and Nestlé have recently disbanded an alliance to sell Nestea and Lipton iced tea in soft-drink machines. Neither firm is one-way dependent on the other as each has numerous other partners available.

TABLE 15.3	EFFICIENT ORGANIZATIONAL FORM DEPENDS ON ASSET CHARACTERISTICS	
	FULLY REDEPLOYABLE DURABLE ASSETS	NON-REDEPLOYABLE RELIANT ASSETS
Not dependent on unique complements	Spot market recontracting	Long-term supply contracts + risk management
One-way dependent assets	Relational contracts (alliances)	Vertical integration
Bilateral dependent assets	Relational contracts (joint ventures)	Fixed profit-sharing contracts

© Cengage Learning

Example

Schwinn and Sylvania Dealers Offered Exclusive Territories[14]

The Schwinn and Sylvania companies sold their bicycles and TVs through authorized dealers who were prohibited from reselling to unauthorized bike shops and electronics stores. Although the dealers could carry other product lines, the resale restriction provided dealers with an exclusive territory. Prosecutors in the U.S. Justice Department saw this vertical territorial restriction as anticompetitive, not as a transaction cost-reducing contractual alternative to the governance mechanisms that would otherwise be necessary to protect Schwinn and Sylvania's brand-name capital.

Fortunately for Sylvania, in *Continental T.V., Inc., et al. v. GTE Sylvania Inc.*, 433 U.S. 36 (1977), the Supreme Court disagreed. In this case, the Court explicitly recognized that brand-name capital is a specialized, non-redeployable asset that would be compromised if third-party dealers were allowed to sell the Sylvania product with unauthorized marketing plans. Exclusive territories therefore became subject to a rule-of-reason analysis that recognizes a legitimate manufacturer interest in presale selling effort and post-sale services compensated by the extra retail margin attributable to the exclusive territory. Sylvania's fixed profit-sharing contracts with its dealers when combined with exclusive territories are an efficient and legal organizational form.

---

[14]See S. Dutta, J. Heide, and M. Bergen, "Vertical Territorial Restrictions and Public Policy," *Journal of Marketing* 63 (October 1999), pp. 121–134.

In contrast, consider the bilateral dependency of a relational contract between a PC assembler and a chip supplier. Without specially designed Motorola computer chips, Apple iMacs have little value, and without Apple iMacs, these Motorola chips have little value. Yet each manufacturer makes reliance investments that are specific to the other partner's design decisions. Hence, as indicated in the bottom left cell of Table 15.3, a joint venture is the efficient organizational form. The term *joint ventures* is often reserved for bilateral relationships that establish a separate corporate legal identity. Appendix 15A addresses incentive-compatible revelation mechanisms for eliciting asymmetric cost information from joint-ventures partners that remain separate arms-length companies.

Finally, when reliant assets are one-way dependent on unique complementary resources, the most efficient organizational form is vertical integration. Remote aluminum plants are one-way dependent on nearby bauxite mines. In contrast, because the bauxite can be shipped anywhere, the mine owners are not dependent on the local aluminum plant. Both assets entail substantial sunk cost investment, but only the remote aluminum plant is a non-redeployable durable asset (i.e., one with little value to other companies should the nearby bauxite source no longer be available). In this situation, upstream vertical integration by the aluminum manufacturer is required in order to prevent opportunistic holdup by the bauxite mine owners.

Sometimes capitalized value is one-way dependent on a unique *downstream* complementary firm. The huge success eBay has had in attracting sellers of one-of-a-kind items to its network of auction buyers necessitated an electronic payments platform. By 2002, PayPal had captured that market, signing up 12 million households and 3 million businesses (28,000 new users a day) who wished to authorize credit card charges with nothing more exchanged than an e-mail address and a charge amount. At one point,

WHAT WENT RIGHT • WHAT WENT WRONG

Cable Allies Refuse to Adopt Microsoft's WebTV as an Industry Standard[15]

Demand for interactive television with Internet surfing, Web shopping, interactive sports, and e-mail has grown quickly in hotel and airport lounges but slowly elsewhere. Cable companies such as AT&T and Time Warner appear most likely to trigger the adoption of these smart TVs in households through their leasing of set-top control boxes to residential customers. After acquiring WebTV (now renamed MSN TV) for $425 million in 1997, Microsoft shifted to an alliance strategy to secure the adoption of its complex software by the cable TV operators. Microsoft's interactive WebTV product known as UltimateTV was fully redeployable across competing cable service companies, and the cable companies sought to remain fully redeployable across interactive TV software providers. Because Microsoft/UltimateTV was one-way dependent on cable providers but cable had numerous other ways to generate value without Microsoft, an alliance was the efficient organizational form for these asset characteristics.

Microsoft's product offering required the cumbersome software architecture of Windows CE. Standard set-top control boxes don't have enough memory or fast enough microprocessors to support Microsoft's operating system. Consequently, Microsoft invested more than $10 billion in co-designing digital entertainment networks and new set-top control boxes with seven cable companies worldwide (AT&T: $5 billion; Telewest Comm in the United Kingdom: $2.6 billion; Comcast: $1 billion; and another $1.2 billion in Rogers, NTL, and UPC in Canada and Europe). In return, AT&T Broadband and its subsidiary TCI promised forward sales contracts for a total of 10 million set-top control boxes employing Microsoft CE software in a Motorola-built unit, the DCT5000. Today, fully 250,000 DCT5000s sit idly stacked in a Seattle warehouse. Microsoft's software was simply too complex, too costly, and too late.

The full installation costs for the Microsoft DCT5000 cable networks skyrocketed to $500 per household control box. Yet marketing research showed that cable subscribers would willingly add only $5 per month to their cable bills in order to secure these enhanced services. Ongoing delays induced Europe's largest cable company, UPC, to order set-top digital entertainment software from Liberate, a Microsoft rival. AT&T then announced that it had no plans to deploy interactive UltimateTV software and that Microsoft would build only the replacement for the scrolling online TV Guide.

Had the cable companies allowed Microsoft's Ultimate TV to become an industry standard, full-scale vertical integration would have been warranted. Microsoft's digital entertainment assets would then have been one-way dependent on cable service providers, whose assets would have been no longer redeployable. Once when Bill Gates was presenting UltimateTV as a possible industry standard, a cable company president, Brian Roberts, half-jokingly suggested that Microsoft buy the entire cable industry.

Recently, Google TV and Apple have introduced alternative channel partnerships to reach the end user. Intel has launched its own WebTV.

---

[15]Based on "Microsoft's Blank Screen," *The Economist* (September 16, 2000), p. 74; "Set-Top Setback: Microsoft Miscues," *Wall Street Journal* (June 14, 2002), "Intel to Launch WedTV," *Wall Street Journal* (February 13, 2013), p. B1.

---

61 percent of 30 million settlements on PayPal were transactions generated off eBay's 150 million postings. Consequently, in July 2002, eBay paid $1.4 billion to acquire PayPal and thereby vertically integrate downstream. PayPal had become a unique complement to non-redeployable eBay assets, and, as indicated in Table 15.3, vertical integration was the efficient organizational form.

Example

Samsung Spins Off Its Hard Drive Assembly[16]

Samsung, Hynix, and Toshiba are the kings of the direct random access and flash memory chips business with 40 percent, 30 percent, and 10 percent market shares, respectively. Samsung and Toshiba enjoy 20 percent gross margins in part because their factory yields are sky high but also because a single fabrication plant can produce 10 million chips per month and often requires as much as $1 billion in capital investment. Those barriers to entry (scale economies and capital requirements) are

(continued)

daunting given the slim net margins especially if the plants are non-redeployable to other uses.

Samsung once invested in downstream hard disk drive (HDD) assembly, a commodity business where Seagate and Western Digital earn only 4 percent gross margins and Samsung earned 7 percent. Dell frequently renegotiates its contract of supply to buy HDDs, playing each producer off against the others every three months. Recently, Samsung sold their HDD business to Seagate for $7.4 billion after failing to make a net return on investment for several years. The question is whether the asset characteristics really warranted Samsung's vertical integration into HDD assembly.

Comparing Table 15.3, Samsung fab plants for chips were non-redeployable reliant assets one-way dependent on HDD assembly factories. But the HDD assembly factories could acquire components from a variety of substitutable suppliers. Western Digital builds many of its other components for the disk drive in a fully vertically integrated supply chain. Samsung apparently found that buying all its HDD components except the requisite chips was not profitable. So, more vertical integration, not less, was what proved efficient.

---

[16]Based on S. Mumudi, "Samsung Consider Sales of Hard-Drive Unit," *MarketNotes* (April 17, 2011).

INTERNATIONAL PERSPECTIVES

Economies of Scale and International Joint Ventures in Chip Making[17]

Approximately one dozen large electronics companies in the United States, Europe, and Japan were once involved in producing memory chips. Up-front costs for each generation of chips were staggering. For example, the cost of developing the 64-megabit memory chip design and production technology was estimated to range from $600 million to $1 billion. Once developed, memory chips then required investment of an additional $600 million to $750 million in a "fab," a fabrication plant that produced up to 10 million chips a month.

Because of the asset characteristics and the massive scale economies available in such a cost structure, many of the semiconductor companies involved in these research and development efforts formed international joint ventures to share the huge fixed costs and risks involved. Some of these partnerships include the following:

U.S. COMPANY	FOREIGN PARTNER
AT&T	NEC (Japan)
Texas Instruments	Hitachi (Japan)
Motorola	Toshiba (Japan)
IBM	Siemens (Germany)

Initially these joint ventures took various forms. For example, AT&T and NEC agreed to swap basic chip-making technologies. Their redeployable trade secrets were each enhanced by unique complementary knowledge of the joint venture partner, consistent with Table 15.3. Similarly, Texas Instruments and Hitachi agreed to develop a common design and manufacturing process and then do low-volume production together, but mass production and marketing remained separate. Joint marketing was not redeployable to other companies but did require the coordination of a fixed profit-sharing agreement. Again, see Table 15.3.

Finally, a Motorola and Toshiba joint venture consolidated the production of millions of memory chips per month to realize the potential for massive scale economies in their codependent and fully redeployable outsourcing.

---

[17]Based on "The Costly Race Chipmakers Cannot Afford to Lose," *BusinessWeek* (December 10, 1990), pp. 185–187; and "Two Makers of Microchips Broaden Ties," *Wall Street Journal* (November 21, 1991), p. 84.

Prospect Theory Motivates Full-Line Forcing

At times the span of hierarchical control (i.e., the boundary of the firm) is determined by the most effective marketing. Social psychologists have long noticed that people buy both lottery tickets and disability insurance. Daniel Kahneman and Amos Tversky hypothesized that people are risk preferring at wealth levels below their current socioeconomic position and risk averse above (as in Figure 15.5). That is, their absolute value of utility losses is perceived as greater, often much greater, than an equal-dollar-valued utility gain.[18]

In a product category such as minivans, their observation is that a household contemplating a Caravan SE model with full options for $22,000 will perceive the decline in satisfaction from dropping down to a $17,000 base model Caravan as much greater than the increase in satisfaction associated with giving up another $5,000 to purchase a $27,000 Caravan LX or SXT model. The fact that perceived losses outweigh equal-value prospective gains reflects a theorem of **prospect theory** that has many implications for the optimal boundaries of the firm.

For one thing, marketers are well advised to distribute trial products ("try now, pay later") because the utility loss if the consumer contemplates returning the product and owes nothing will be greater than the utility gained by prospective additional consumption with the money saved. Second, receivables managers are well advised to ask consumers to forgo something prospective to pay for their product (i.e., a projected year-end bonus, tax refund, or frequent flyer award). Again, the payment in prospective additional consumption forgone will be perceived as less undesirable than an equivalent cash expense that means giving up other current consumption.

prospect theory
A basis for hypothesizing that the satisfaction from avoiding losses exceeds the anticipation of equal-value prospective gains.

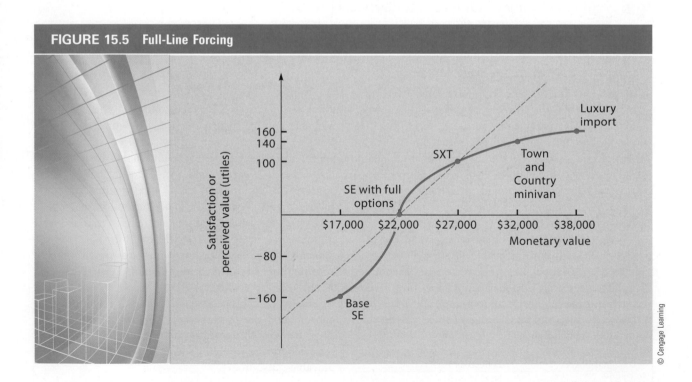

FIGURE 15.5 Full-Line Forcing

© Cengage Learning

[18]D. Kahneman and A. Tversky, "Prospect Theory: An Analysis of Decision under Risk," *Econometrica* 47, no. 2 (March 1979), pp. 263–291; and C. Camerer, "An Experimental Test of Several Generalized Utility Theories," *Journal of Risk and Uncertainty* 2, no. 1 (April 1989), pp. 61–104.

Finally, firms with good-quality house brands should encourage premium brands in the channel, and those with premium brands should encourage the introduction of super-premium brands. If no such distribution channel arrangements can be secured, the implication is that firms selling moderately priced brands should buy premium brands. If none exists, firms are advised to develop their own and force them into the channel. Hanes Hosiery pursues a "good, better, best" product strategy with private labels, L'eggs, and Hanes. Marriott developed its Fairfield Inns, Courtyard by Marriott, Marriott Resorts and International Hotels, and now Ritz Carlton. The Gap launched not only the downscale fighting brand Old Navy but also went out and acquired the upscale brand Banana Republic.

Let's return to Figure 15.5 to see exactly why full-line forcing works. Auto dealers face an especially difficult competitive environment with mobile customers, innumerable substitute makes and models, and Internet search engines comparing price discounts by competing dealers on a real-time basis. Moving their repeat-purchase "customers for life" up along a base-car-to-luxury-car product spectrum is one key to profitability in the auto dealership business. Another key is to avoid selling only base automobiles.

In Figure 15.5, stepping down from an SE model minivan with full options to a base model saves a customer $5,000 but sacrifices 50 percent of the perceived value of the minivan product line (-160 satisfaction utiles out of 320 total). Spending another $5,000 to step up to an SXT or LX luxury model garners only an additional 30 percent ($+100/320$) of the product line's perceived value. Although the unit sales of the dealership do not change, the mere presence of the LX and SXT model drives such a customer to justify spending $5,000 to avoid the greater disutility of the base model while congratulating himself or herself for avoiding spending another $5,000 for a smaller relative increase in satisfaction.

After providing high-quality (and high-margin) service and maintenance for the SE with full options over several years, the dealership then plans to see that same customer back in the showroom eyeing the SXT models. Again, full-line forcing can encourage the "upsell" to the $27,000 SXT model. Saving $5,000 by continuing to purchase SEs with options will result in a 30 percent disutility of ($-100/320$), whereas purchasing the $5,000-more-expensive Town and Country model in Figure 15.5 would increase satisfaction by only 40 utiles, 12.5 percent. Again, the careful shopper, after comparing marginal benefits and marginal costs, decides to go with the SXT, and the dealership rejoices.

Full-Line Forcing in Writing Pens, Aspirin, and Multivitamins at Walgreens and CVS

Perhaps the most amazing aspect of prospect theory is the extent to which retail market shares can be altered by the practice of full-line forcing. Walgreens and CVS fully control the distribution channel policy in their own drugstores. In-house store brands can be sold beside national brands. Suppose CVS Aspirin at $2.89 for 100 80-mg tablets secures a 30 percent market share against a generic aspirin product selling 100 80-mg tablets at $1.50. CVS can allocate additional shelf space to non-store-brand painkillers such as Bayer Aspirin at $2.70 and Tylenol at $4.29. Not surprisingly, CVS Aspirin's market share falls if the cheaper Bayer product is introduced. But what is astounding is that, in case after case, introducing the Tylenol product raises CVS Aspirin sales to a 40 percent market share, reduces generic aspirin from 70 to 40 percent, and Tylenol will attract 20 percent of the market.

(continued)

Because some people experience side effects from aspirin but not from Tylenol, a fairer comparison perhaps is to investigate the same experiment with absolutely identical multivitamins. CVS multivitamins at $3.49 per 100 tablets might again secure 30 percent of the market relative to generic multivitamins at $1.99 with 70 percent market share. Introducing One-A-Day brand multivitamins at $5.19 into the channel will actually raise the market share of CVS's product. That is, with the good-better-best product strategy, market shares might distribute as follows: 40 percent generic, 40 percent CVS, and 20 percent One-A-Day. The disutility of lost perceived consumption value outweighs equal-value utility gains. This finding arises at CVS in everything from multivitamins to writing pens.

VERTICAL INTEGRATION

Search, bargaining, and holdup costs are all reduced when internal transfers and the monitoring and incentive systems within the firm replace the spot market contracting and recontracting necessitated by operating at arm's length with outside suppliers and independent distributors. As we have seen, Nobel laureates Ronald Coase and Oliver Williamson argue that these factors explain why the firm emerged as an organizational form despite the diseconomies of ever-wider spans of managerial control.[19] Another motive for a manufacturer to vertically integrate upstream to suppliers or downstream to retail distributors involves the inefficiency of successive monopolization (i.e., the presence of market power over price at more than one stage of production). For example, the transfer of Disney Studio's downstream equity to Pixar (the upstream digital entertainment content provider) is a method of pre-commitment by Pixar to exercise upstream price restraint and not spoil the downstream market. We now illustrate these ideas further with a detailed study of vertical integration in the hosiery industry.

Consider, first, an upstream yarn supplier who operates in a competitive intermediate product market and a downstream hosiery manufacturer who enjoys the market power to mark up the wholesale price for pantyhose above its marginal cost. Figure 15.6 illustrates the situation each firm faces when the yarn inputs are combined in fixed proportions with manufacturing labor and machinery to yield hosiery output. The outside demand curve and its marginal revenue capture the hosiery manufacturer's revenue opportunities in the wholesale pantyhose product market. Given the marginal cost of hosiery production (MC_h) and the competitive price of yarn ($P_y = MC_y$), the manufacturer sets summed marginal cost of hosiery production and yarn inputs ($MC_h + MC_y$) equal to hosiery marginal revenue (MR_h) at output Q^*. This joint profit-maximizing output decision maximizes hosiery profits by setting the marginal cost of yarn equal to the net marginal revenue product of the yarn supplier. So, subtracting the downstream marginal cost (MC_h) from the downstream marginal revenues (MR_h) leaves the *net* revenue opportunity available to the upstream yarn supplier—that is, $MR_h - MC_h$. Setting this derived demand for yarn inputs equal to upstream marginal costs (MC_y) identifies Q^* as the yarn supplier's preferred throughput rate as well as the hosiery manufacturer's preferred output rate. Thus, the

---

[19]For more extensive discussion of this topic, see S. Hamilton and K. Stiegert, "Vertical Coordination," *Journal of Law and Economics* (April 2000), pp. 143–156.

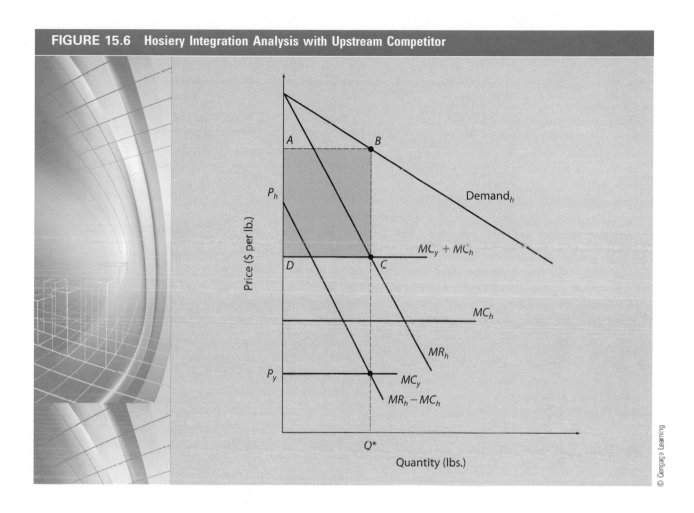

FIGURE 15.6 Hosiery Integration Analysis with Upstream Competitor

upstream supplier who prices yarn so as to just recover marginal cost imposes no throughput constraint on downstream hosiery operations.

The hosiery manufacturer in Figure 15.6 would not change the yarn input prices, nor the wholesale output prices, nor the throughput quantity if it were to vertically integrate upstream and operate the yarn supplier. Therefore, vertical integration can result only in disadvantages associated with a wider span of managerial control. For profits $ABCD$ to remain unchanged, these disadvantages would need to be offset by another factor such as reduced transaction costs. In general, in the absence of other factors, we would conclude that in Figure 15.6, the hosiery manufacturer has no profit motive for backward integration into the competitive yarn supplier's business.

In contrast, however, consider the case in which the yarn supplier has a proprietary process that is unique and therefore adds substantial value itself to the hosiery manufacturing process. In Figure 15.7, the derived demand for the yarn input is again $MR_h - MC_h$, and everything else about the hosiery operations remains the same as in Figure 15.6, except that now the upstream firm has the market power to mark up its own marginal cost (MC_y). By taking a second marginalization of the revenue, subtracting off the hosiery production cost, and setting $MMR_h - MC_h = MC_y$, the yarn supplier maximizes upstream profits $EFGH$ by choosing a price P'_y at throughput Q'. If P'_y exceeds the upstream marginal cost MC_y, the summed marginal cost facing the hosiery manufacturer is now higher, and, consequently, the desired output declines from Q^* to Q'.

Although hosiery prices rise to P'_h, the higher costs and smaller output of hosiery operations cause the profits of the downstream firm (the manufacturer) to decline (i.e., *IJKL* in Figure 15.7 < *ABCD* in Figure 15.6). That is, the presence of profit margins upstream results in a throughput constraint that unambiguously reduces downstream profitability.[20]

Backward vertical integration by the hosiery manufacturer can squeeze out the margins upstream by simply setting an internal transfer price for yarn $P_y = MC_y$. This change will return the optimal throughput to Q^*, the profit-maximizing level for the consolidated yarn and hosiery operations. That is, even after paying the upstream profits *EFGH* to secure the control rights from the yarn company, the downstream hosiery manufacturer has higher net profits (*ABCD* − *EFGH*) than its profit from independent operations *IJKL*. Consequently, we would expect these two firms to coordinate their operations either as a joint venture or as a vertically integrated hosiery manufacturer with its own retail distribution.

FIGURE 15.7 **Hosiery Integration Analysis with Upstream Market Power**

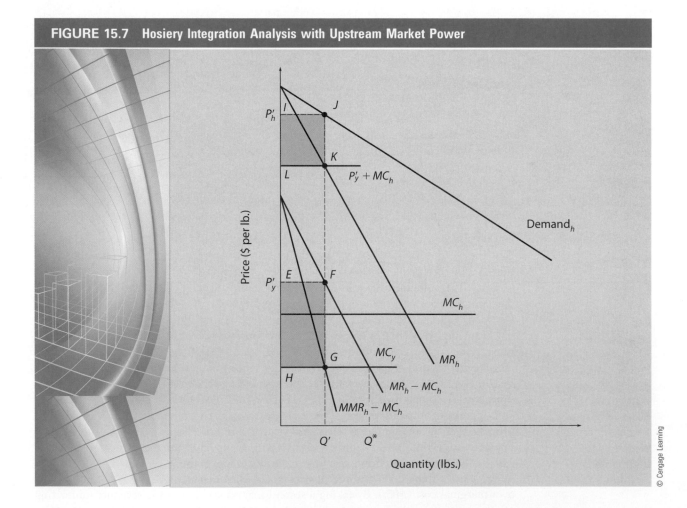

---

[20]This implication holds without qualification here because of fixed-proportions production, that is, the efficient input mix remains unchanged despite the reduction in output. Under variable proportions, vertical integration may be motivated or not, depending on the input substitutability and possible cost savings.

WHAT WENT RIGHT • WHAT WENT WRONG

Dell Replaces Vertical Integration with Virtual Integration[21]

New developments in information technology, such as the enterprise resource-planning system SAP, have widened the efficient span of hierarchical control. Rather than enabling larger vertically integrated companies, SAP enables virtual integration. Dell Inc. owns almost no PC component manufacturing operations. Instead, it outsources its requirements to several hundred supplier-partners who are tied together in a real-time monitoring, adaptation, and control system using the Internet. Its patented build-to-order business model must handle effectively an extraordinarily complex set of just-in-time component flows to support a final product assembly that ships 10,000 possible product configurations direct to a customer.

Information technology plays a key role in the governance mechanisms for this type of virtually integrated supply chain management. When this business model is successful, plant and equipment requirements decline, inventories shrink, and operating leverage rises substantially. With less fixed capital investment than a vertically integrated competitor, the return on invested capital climbs accordingly. Dell stock appreciated 300-fold in its first 15 years of operation.

---

[21]Based on "Identity Crisis," *Wall Street Journal* (October 10, 2000), p. C1; "Direct Hit," *The Economist* (January 9, 1999), pp. 55–58; and J. Margretta, "The Power of Virtual Integration," *Harvard Business Review* (March/April 1998), pp. 72–85.

The Dissolution of Assets in a Partnership

Vertical integration is the most extreme organizational form on a continuum from outsourcing with spot market transactions, through relational contracting, vertical requirements contracting, and extending to alliances and joint ventures. In Appendix 15A, we will see how subtle institutional arrangements can align the interests of partners in a joint venture. But what happens when a joint venture or partnership must be dissolved?

The optimal mechanism design for fair division necessitates sequential game analysis when the prize is decaying with the passage of time as the players negotiate. Suppose a partnership must divide $3 million in assets. The only catch is that the assets, which the two partners must agree upon dividing, decline in value by $1 million each time either party refuses the proposed division. Perhaps the assets are perishable pharmaceuticals or intellectual property that decays in value quickly. Or, alternatively, once the capital markets get wind that the partnership is fracturing, any synergistic value of the two subsets of assets quickly evaporates.

The two principals toss a coin to see who should make the first offer of how to split the $3 million. Suppose Joe wins the toss. How much should he offer to Kim to secure her acceptance of the offer and forgo her rights of first refusal? Kim gets to structure a second-round offer should this first proposed division be refused, and she will also respond to Joe's third and final offer should the second proposal be refused. Notice that the endgame to this problem happens after three rounds when the assets are gone. Think about how little Kim would be willing to accept in the third and final round. Can Kim hold out for more than this amount in the second round? What, therefore, is the maximum Joe needs to offer to trigger an acceptance in the first round? Does this game have a first-mover advantage, or is it better to play second and be the respondent in the third and final round?

These and related questions can be addressed with the sequential game techniques of Chapter 13. In Figure 15.8, Joe makes the final offer at the far right but, as you may suspect, in one sense Kim's right of refusal controls this endgame. Because $100,000 is preferable to zero, Kim's best-reply response is to accept an offer to split the final million as $900,000 for Joe and $100,000 for Kim. This analysis implies that in the preceding (second) round, Kim can offer Joe $1 million (i.e., $100,000 more

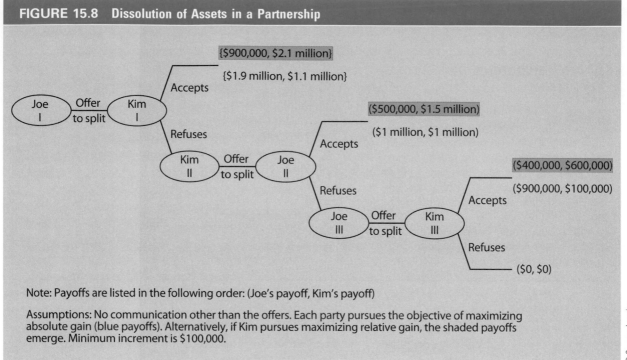

FIGURE 15.8 Dissolution of Assets in a Partnership

Note: Payoffs are listed in the following order: (Joe's payoff, Kim's payoff)

Assumptions: No communication other than the offers. Each party pursues the objective of maximizing absolute gain (blue payoffs). Alternatively, if Kim pursues maximizing relative gain, the shaded payoffs emerge. Minimum increment is $100,000.

than Joe's endgame outcome), and Joe's best-reply response is to accept. Stepping the backwards induction one more round back, this second-round analysis implies that if Joe offers Kim $1.1 million in the first round (i.e., $100,000 more than Kim's second round outcome), Kim will accept. Note that we are short-circuiting threats and modes of communication other than simply stating the offers. Also note that we assumed each party believes the other party is maximizing absolute gain without regard to the relative distribution. In such circumstances, making the first *and the last* offer appears advantageous to Joe.

Mechanism design features of this problem include the rotating offer and right of refusal, the lack of communication about objectives and credible threats, and the coin toss to decide who offers first. Any of these could be changed, and it might make quite a difference. For example, suppose Kim's reputation was that she pursued relative wealth, not absolute wealth. In that event, the outcome ($0; $0) would quite literally be preferable to the alternative of her partner Joe going $800,000 up at ($900,000; $100,000). Even splitting the last million dollars ($500,000; $500,000) would not be preferable to ($0; $0). So only an asymmetric distribution *favoring* Kim (say, $400,000; $600,000 in the shaded box) would elicit her acceptance.

In earlier rounds, Joe now knows that he must increase the unequal distribution in Kim's favor in order to secure her acceptance, and Kim knows that the same is not true of Joe. Given the $100,000 minimum increments, Kim reasons by backward induction from the ($400,000; $600,000) outcome of Round 3 that she can offer as little as ($500,000; $1.5 million) to secure Joe's acceptance in Round 2. Finally, this intermediate outcome implies by the relative-gain reasoning motivating Kim that Joe must elicit her acceptance at the start of the negotiations by offering a ($900,000; $2.1 million) split in Round 1. Comparing the blue and shaded offers in Round 1, it makes $1 million of difference whether the mechanism design allows communication of Kim's motivation to maximize relative (not absolute) gain as opposed to a mechanism design with unknown silent partners responding through intermediaries. Small changes in the institutional procedures or the organization architecture often make this large a difference in tactical encounters.

SUMMARY

- Businesses make choices about organizational form that define the span of hierarchical control from the vertically integrated oil company at one extreme to the virtual manufacturer Dell, which outsources all manufacturing and assembly to supplier-partners.

- All external and internal business relationships require a solution to the twin problems of coordination and control. External business relationships can be organized through spot market transactions, long-term contracts, or reputation effects in relational contracting. These forms of organization differ in their timing, players, enforcement, and information structure.

- Long-term vertical requirements contracts provide an *ex ante* framework for resolving coordination and control problems among manufacturers, suppliers, and distributors. Because all contracts are purposefully incomplete, *ex post* opportunistic behavior requires governance mechanisms to reduce several types of contractual hazards. The *moral hazard problem* arises because of the unobservability of effort in contract performance. The *post-contractual opportunistic behavior* called "holdup" presents another commonly occurring contractual hazard.

- Moral hazard problems can be mitigated by incentive contracting that aligns one party's interests with the other through carefully chosen terms. In lending–borrowing contracts these incentive alignment terms of the contract include collateral offered as security, the interest rate, the time period for repayment, and the size of principal. These incentive contract terms are supplemented by post-contractual monitoring and governance mechanisms including auditing, loan covenants, staggered draws and progress payments, prohibition and monitoring of specific types of balance sheet changes, and limitations on receivables policies.

- Exchange under incomplete information and under asymmetric information differs. *Incomplete information* refers to the uncertainty that is pervasive in practically all transactions and motivates insurance markets. *Asymmetric information*, on the other hand, refers to private information one party possesses that the other party cannot independently verify.

- Asymmetric information leads to the *problem of adverse selection*.

- Contracts are seldom complete because full *contingent claims contracting* is often prohibitively expensive. Intentionally incomplete contracting allows *post-contractual opportunistic behavior* and leads to holdup. Resolving the *holdup problem* in managerial contracting necessitates the use of *governance mechanisms*.

- Governance mechanisms include internal monitoring by director subcommittees and large creditors, internal/external monitoring by large block shareholders, auditing and variance analysis, benchmarking, an ethically dutiful corporate culture, and whistle-blowing.

- Managerial labor can be hired in several ways, for example, straight salary, wage rate, or profit sharing. Pure profit sharing results in moonlighting, however, because the manager's inputs (effort and creative ingenuity) are largely unobservable. Unobservable effort leads to the *moral hazard problem*, which can be resolved by setting up *ex post facto* (e.g., with deferred stock options).

- In combination, random disturbances in firm performance and unobservable managerial effort present a more difficult *principal-agent problem* to resolve. Owner-principals do not know when to blame manager-agents for weak performance or give credit for strong performance. *Optimal incentives contracts* involving some guaranteed salary and a profit-sharing bonus can, in theory, resolve the principal-agent problem.

- Linear combinations of salary and profit sharing can also be used to elicit asymmetric information about managerial preferences, sort managers by their own personal risk aversion, and prevent adverse selection in managerial hiring. Boards of directors face a holdup problem in renewing senior executive contracts, necessitating governance mechanisms.
- What form of organization to adopt (e.g., spot market transactions, long-term vertical requirements contracts, relational contracts, or vertical integration) depends on the contractual hazards that need to be avoided. What contractual hazards arise in business relationships depends on the asset characteristics, redeployability or specificity of the fixed assets, and the relative dependence of those fixed assets on unique complementary assets.
- Perceived utility losses are often larger (in absolute value) than equivalent-value utility gains, implying a hybrid utility function suggested by prospect theory.
- Prospect theory implies sellers should distribute trial products, take prospective income in payment, and full-line force.
- Vertical integration is an optimal organizational form when the assets are one-way dependent on complementary assets and are largely nonredeployable.
- Optimal mechanism design seeks to motivate value-maximizing behavior while reducing transaction costs.
- Mechanism design features such as first offer, right of first refusal, lack of communication, and credible threats in a dissolution of assets in a partnership can be analyzed as a sequential game.
- Small changes in the institutional procedures often make a large difference in the outcome and distribution of payoffs.

Exercises

Answers to the exercises in blue can be found in Appendix D at the back of the book.

1. Suppose an enhanced effectiveness of cooperative advertising occurs if the distributor shares its superior on-the-spot information about current trends in the marketplace with the manufacturer. Explain how each of the following would affect the information-sharing objective:
   a. All details of co-op advertising are agreed to up front in the franchise contract.
   b. Advertising is pursued independently by the manufacturer and the retail distributor.
   c. Cooperative advertising allowances are rebated to the distributor out of the franchise fees.
2. If contract promises were not excused because of acts of war, would the clearing and settlements clients of Bank of New York change their behavior? If so, how? What reliance behavior would be considered efficient? What reliance behavior would be considered excessive?
3. In the game-theoretic model of workouts and rollovers (Figure 15.2), identify the specific consequences of loan terms that worsen the moral hazard problem.
4. How might the lender in Figure 15.2 use knowledge of the type of asset booked by the borrower on its balance sheet to offset the liability for the loan extension? Commercial loan covenants often include a restriction on precisely this balance-sheet decision making—for example, restricting the booking of offsetting foreign assets.
5. If coal mine tonnage can be shipped elsewhere cheaply, but an adjacent coal-fired power plant is not redeployable to other uses, what organizational form would be adopted by the power plant owners? Why?
6. Would warehouse operators insist on owning their own trucking companies? Why or why not? What coordination and control problems and contractual hazards would these companies encounter?
7. What organizational form would warehouse operators and truck hauling companies adopt?

8. In benchmarking sales representatives against one another, what problems arise from continuing to reassign the above-average trade representatives to previously unproductive sales territories?

9. Explain how the optimal incentives contract would differ if the less risk-averse bank officer (Dashing in Figure 15.4) had generated the smaller expected profit (i.e., the lower hill-shaped curve).

10. In the Division of a Decaying Business game, what should you offer if the assets at the start of the game are $4 million rather than $3 million? Now is there a first-mover or second-mover advantage? Why?

11. Analyze the pure Nash equilibrium and mixed Nash equilibrium strategies in the following manufacturer–distributor coordination game. How would you recommend restructuring the game to secure higher expected profit for the manufacturer?

		Manufacturer	
		Product Update/ Higher MSRP	No Update/ Same MSRP
Distributor	Discontinue Special Selling Services	0 $1 M	$2 M $4 M
	Continue Special Selling Services	$6 M $2 M	0 0

Case Exercises

Borders Books and Amazon.com Decide to Do Business Together

Borders Books, once the leading chain of bookshop retailers, entered into an agreement with Amazon.com, the online retailer, to fulfill Internet orders from the Borders.com Web site. Using Table 15.3 and the following questions, what organizational form would you predict for this business relationship?

Questions

1. Are Amazon.com's warehouses, Web pages, and one-click sales methods fully redeployable to other products? If so, name a few such products. If not, why not?

2. Are Borders' fixed assets fully redeployable? If so, suggest how. If not, why not?

3. Is Borders dependent on Amazon as a unique complement? That is, is Amazon.com the only potential company that could process Internet-based orders for Borders?

4. Is Amazon dependent on Borders for referrals, or does it have its own Internet-based order flow?

5. Is your answer consistent with the multiyear fee-for-service contract between Borders and Amazon.com whereby Amazon processes the order, ships the book, records the sales, and pays Borders a referral fee? One Borders executive described this as a "low-risk, low-return" approach to online sales while retaining Borders's

focus on its core mission of running bookshops. This approach acknowledged the attraction of on-line book purchasing for segments of the Broders target market but failed to recognize the e-book revolution still sweeping across book retailing. Borders has declared bankruptcy and been liquidated; business strategy is not secured by efficient contracting.

Designing a Managerial Incentive Contract

Recall that in Chapter 1, Specific Electric Co. asked you to implement a pay-for-performance incentive contract for its new CEO. Using your deeper knowledge of the principal-agent problem, try it again.

The Division of Investment Banking Fees in a Syndicate

You are the lead underwriter among a syndicate of five investment banks composed of yourself, the syndicate co-manager, and syndicate members 3, 4, and 5. Your syndicate finds a deal worth $100 million in fees. You must submit a proposal as to how the fees should be divided, and the syndicate then votes by majority rule.

Your syndicate is rational and democratic in the sense that the division of fees will be decided based upon maximization of absolute gain in this single deal, and the members also have reputational reasons in future deals (where the lower-ranked members hope to achieve more influence and get a higher-ranked position) to abide by a majority decision.

If your proposal is rejected by vote of the syndicate, you are displaced as lead underwriter, removed altogether from the deal making, and replaced by the co-manager, who then makes a proposal to the remaining four. If his deal is rejected, he too is removed, and syndicate member 3 makes a proposal to the three firms remaining, and so on.

Questions

1. What should you as the lead underwriter offer and to whom? [*Hint:* Employ the methods of sequential game reasoning. Start at the endgame and work backward.]
2. Is there anything unusual about the division of these fees across the syndicate?
3. In light of surprisingly light allocation to syndicate co-managers, why would any investment bank seek out such a role?

Auction Design and Information Economics

In this appendix, we discuss optimal mechanism designs for auctions and several other institutional procedures. Priceline sells airline and concert tickets by soliciting sealed bids guaranteed by a credit card, while eBay posts ascending price offers with amendment and cancellation privileges. These are instances of alternative mechanism designs for auctions. Often the purpose of such mechanism design choices is to induce the revelation of asymmetric information that is needed to maximize shareholder value for the auction buyers or sellers.

Mechanism design can also address coordination and control problems in joint ventures and partnerships. Specifically, an incentive-compatible (IC) contract can induce partners to reveal their private proprietary information about perceived benefit or preliminary cost projections to one another. Under an IC contract, each partner will incur the net cost effects of his or her own information revelation on the other partner. Hence, the IC contract imposes a mechanism design for sharing profits that best serves the self-interest of each partner through revealing the true and complete information to the other partner. When combined with the cross-purchase of equity stakes, this IC revelation mechanism provides a powerful tool with unique capabilities for business partnerships.

OPTIMAL MECHANISM DESIGN

Queue Service Rules

optimal mechanism design An efficient procedure that creates incentives to motivate the desired behavioral outcome.

A simple business application of the concept of **optimal mechanism design** is the queue service rule for filling customer orders from those waiting to purchase. The traditional first-come, first-served procedure induces an inefficient pattern of customer arrivals at, for example, a concert site. If the box office opens at 9:00 A.M., a few potential customers arrive three hours earlier or even the night before. Others stand on queue for two hours, and many more show up to wait in line as the ticket booth opens.

What customers are willing to pay for tickets is surely affected by the inconvenience of this wait. And the subpopulation of customers who have low opportunity cost of time (and are therefore willing to arrive the earliest, wait the longest, and obtain tickets with the greatest probability) may not be the subpopulation that will pay the most for tickets. For this reason, many ticket agencies have no objection to a wealthy patron paying someone with lower opportunity cost of time to stand on queue, purchase the ticket, and transfer it at face value to the higher-willingness-to-pay customer.[1] In any case, all this waiting time is time wasted, and time is money. As a result, if other more efficient queue service rules were adopted, more of the customer's willingness to pay could be captured by the ticket sellers, concert promoters, and sports teams.

---

[1]Scalpers, of course, charge higher prices still, but note that such gray markets reveal to the ticket agency what those customers who are not willing to show up at the ticket window and wait are in fact willing to pay. This information helps the ticket agency set an optimal price.

FIRST-COME, FIRST-SERVED VERSUS LAST-COME, FIRST-SERVED

As a provisional alternative, consider last-come, first-served. Under this queue service rule, a customer has no incentive to stand on queue and wait. Indeed, any time a queue forms, all those in front of the last person to arrive have an incentive to leave and go about their other business, returning later when fewer people are likely to show up. In essence, the last-come, first-served mechanism design has removed the incentives for inefficient behavior artificially created by first-come, first-served. Customers do not inherently prefer to arrive early and peak-load their demands. Instead, it was the non-optimal queue service rule that artificially created incentives to arrive early, stand around, and wait.

With last-come first-served, in contrast, customers have an incentive to spread their arrivals throughout the ticket window's normal hours of operation. Once a more or less uniform distribution of customer arrivals throughout the day can be established, the ticket agency can adjust its capacity and set its service rate to deal with the steady stream of customers who arrive and purchase with little or no waiting.

Few ticketing operations have adopted a last-come first-served queue service rule. Why not? Under last-come first-served, recall that any customer should leave the queue whenever a later arrival preempts his or her priority ranking as the last person in line. But customers will not wish to return many times to the ticket window. Again, time is money. So, customers ahead in the queue are likely to offer side payments to later arrivals to induce *them* to leave. Predictably, those with the highest opportunity cost of time will end up bribing those with lower opportunity cost to leave and return.

Example

Containerized Shipping at Sea-Land/Maersk

Historically, ocean shipping rates have been heavily regulated based on categories of cargo (e.g., paper, film, frozen fish) and shipping lanes (e.g., Rotterdam to New York, Liverpool to Jacksonville, Seoul to San Francisco). Conferences of ocean shipping companies announced common carrier shipping rates for first-come, first-served customers. More than half the world's cargo still moves under publicly mandated ocean shipping contracts at these uniform shipping rates.

With no ability to adjust prices, salespeople maximized the volume of cargo. Because empty slots on a container ship perish as a revenue opportunity the moment the ship sails, the only good ship was a full ship. A container ship such as the *Regina Maersk* has space above decks for more than 700 containers. As a result, shippers queued up large volumes of cargo in anticipation of each ship's departure. In this mechanism design, the customers' waiting time became a substantial implicit cost totaling millions of dollars a day that otherwise might have gone to the shipper as additional revenue.

Today, deregulation is fast approaching the ocean shipping industry, and a spot market auction for space in containerized ships has emerged. The immediate consequence has been the delaying of low-priority shipments such as rolls of newsprint from one voyage to the next in favor of higher-rate cargo such as perishable pharmaceuticals. In response to this new business environment, Sea-Land/Maersk optimizes the placement of its containers around the world. Each empty container at each freight terminal is assigned a forecasted net revenue opportunity at that location and at other potential locations along the shipping route. Shippers who offer less waiting time can charge higher rates; last-come, first-served policies are being explored for certain kinds of high-margin cargo.

The problem is that this side payment system again reduces the ticket agency's receipts because in many ways it has just replaced the inefficiency of arriving early and waiting with the inefficiency of arriving often, departing, and returning. The recipients of the side payments are no worse off because they voluntarily decide to leave and return later, but those who make the side payments now turn to the window and surely offer less than they otherwise would have paid. How can the ticket agency's mechanism design deal with this subtle complication?

Stratified Lotteries for Concerts

Lotteries and online auctions may hold the key to an effective mechanism design for ticket sellers. Online sales are cheaper than phone sales because they require no operators and no toll-free line charges, as long as customers accept an Internet or faxed ticket, thereby saving the ticketing agent all mailing expense. Only 3 in 10 live entertainment tickets are distributed online today, but this channel is growing much faster than industry sales as a whole. Suppose rather than announcing in advance what position in the customer queue would be served first, the ticketing agency simply picked a position at random. In effect, that's exactly what a lottery for the right to purchase a ticket does. Any time prior to the day of sale, a customer stops by an Internet Web site to pick up a lottery number.

stratified lottery A randomized mechanism for allocating scarce capacity across demand segments.

Because customers with low willingness to pay are equally likely to get the winning lottery numbers as those with high willingness to pay, ticket agencies such as Ticketmaster often adopt a **stratified lottery** scheme. Rights to purchase high-price seats are distributed in one lottery, medium-price seats in another, and low-price seats in a third. At a designated date, the winning numbers are chosen at random and posted on the Web site and public-access TV channels. Only those customers holding the winning lottery numbers arrive to buy tickets, and because seat availability is assured, customers have no reason to arrive early, queue up, and wait. Because this lottery mechanism design reduces waiting time, the ticket agency can charge higher uniform prices for each class of seats.

Example

Online Auctions and Stratified Lotteries at Ticketmaster[2]

Holding auctions online can present a conflict of interest with Ticketmaster's traditional business of adding a $3 to $5 convenience fee for computerized ticket distribution by mail and in music stores. As the exclusive ticketing agent for 70 million venue seats annually, worth $3 billion, Ticketmaster is wary of reselling tickets above face value. The sports teams, concert halls, and promoters would then suspect Ticketmaster of underpricing the original tickets to charge convenience fees on not one but two sales. Ticketmaster could, of course, simply defer to the arenas and promoters in setting the face value prices, but a better alternative may be available.

Ticketmaster and StubHub.com have begun conducting "official" Internet auctions for various sports teams. Last year, the New York Jets earned close to $100 million in auctioned ticket sales on behalf of season ticket holders unable to attend a game. Most transactions occurred at about 30 percent over face value. The team takes approximately 10 percent of this "gate" (incremental revenue), and the rest goes to the season ticket holder. The next question then is, what type of auction should Ticketmaster design?

[2]Based on "Ticket Scalpers Find a Home on the Web," *Wall Street Journal* (February 4, 1999), p. B1; "A Winning Ticket," *The Economist* (August 22, 1998), p. 52; S. Rosen and A. Rosenfeld, "Ticket Pricing," *Journal of Law and Economics* 40, no. 2 (1997), pp. 351–377; and "Don't Scalp Us. We'll Scalp You," *BusinessWeek* (April 19, 2004), p. 44.

AUCTIONS

Types of Auctions

In recent years everything from *Monday Night Football* to mineral rights, forest land, airline tickets, used equipment, and the electromagnetic spectrum have been allocated to their highest valued use through auctions. The choices in auction design are numerous, as illustrated in Table 15A.1. Bidding can be *sequential* with rebid opportunities like eBay and most estate auctions or *simultaneous* as on Priceline. Bid prices can be *continuous* or constrained by *minimum discrete bid* improvements. For example, the New York Stock Exchange switched to continuous decimalization of its auction prices from its historical one-eighth-tick size restrictions on minimum bid improvements. Bids may be *sealed*, revealed by *open outcry*, or *posted* anonymously as on eBay. Bidding can be *one-time only* or *dynamic*, repeated in multiple rounds with cancellation and amendment of prior bids allowed (so-called *open bidding*). In addition, owners can place a minimum reservation price (the *reserve*), below which the item will not sell, or allow an auction to proceed with *no minimum*.

Perhaps the most important design differences between major types of auctions are who pays, what amount, and how the winner is determined. In some auctions *all bidders pay* (e.g., on Priceline.com where credit card information must accompany all offers). Of course, most auctions adopt the *highest-wins-and-pays* allocation rule. What the winner pays (whether it is his or her own *highest bid* or, at times, the *second-highest bid*) and how the auctioneer arrives at the winning bid can differ. **English auctions** ascend to higher and higher prices with open outcry or posted bids until the last bidder to make an offer exceeding all other offers is declared the winner.

English auctions An ascending-price auction.

Dutch auctions work in the opposite direction by identifying the first bidder to register an acceptance as the auctioneer announces a succession of descending asking prices. The wholesale flower market in the Netherlands operates in this way, hence the term *Dutch auction*. In *ascending-price auctions* the winner takes all, but in *descending-price auctions*, the winner is often given the opportunity to purchase less than the total capacity available for sale, and the auction then continues downward until supply is exhausted.

Dutch auctions A descending-price auction.

Which of these and other auction design characteristics maximize the revenue to the seller and which allocate resources to their highest-valued use are important business questions. One well-understood insight from mechanism design theory is that

TABLE 15A.1 A COMPARISON OF AUCTION MECHANISM DESIGN CHARACTERISTICS	
EBAY	**PRICELINE**
Sequential	Simultaneous
Minimum bid improvement	Continuous
Posted prices	Posted offers to buy (reverse auction)
Multiple rounds	One-time-only if seller "hits"
Open bidding	Credit card immediately authorized
Reserve	No reserve
Highest wins and pays	All accepted bids pay
First (highest) price	Whatever price was bid
English ascending price	Dutch discriminatory descending price
Consolidated feedback on seller	Seller anonymous

© Cengage Learning

asymmetric information will lead to timid bidding in ascending-price auctions because of the natural reluctance to bid more than is required to win—referred to as the *winner's curse*. To illustrate the winner's curse, consider the following auction situation:[3] You are developing a bidding strategy for an asset whose value to the seller is a random variable distributed uniformly between $0 and $100. The seller knows this value but places no minimum reservation price on the auction. He does, however, insist upon at least a small profit beyond the $1 required to cover the expenses of conducting an auction; all other offers will be refused. The asset might be a set of patent rights or a plot of commercial development land. Because of different complementary assets and skill, suppose your value is certain to be 50 percent higher than the seller's asset value. What offer should you make?

Winner's Curse in Asymmetric Information Bidding Games

If neither party knows the true value of the development land or the patent rights but only the distribution of value, an expected value of $50 plus a small premium (e.g., $55) appears initially to be a reasonable offer that will be accepted. However, if the seller knows the true value, consider what reasonable offers will be accepted and what reasonable offers will be refused. To simplify the analysis, suppose just three offers of $0, $55, and $100 and three realizations of the seller's known market value of $0, $50, or $100 are possible, as displayed in Figure 15A.1. We see that if the buyer offers $0, his bid will be refused whatever the true value of the asset. If the buyer offers $55, the seller will accept this bid only when the asset is worth $0. When the buyer offers $100, the seller will accept only when the asset is worth $0 or $50. That is, only offers that overpay for the asset will be accepted. These payoffs are shown in the shaded boxes to the right of the decision tree.

If all three outcomes $0, $50, and $100 are equally likely, then the expected value for the bidder in the middle branch of the game tree, conditional on best reply response by the seller, is $1/3(-\$55) + 1/3(\$0) + 1/3(\$0) = -\$18.33$ Similarly, in the lowest branch of the game tree, the bidder's expected value is $1/3(-\$100) + 1/3(-\$45) + 1/3(\$0) = -\$48.33$. In short, because all reasonable offers that allow the bidder as well as the seller to profit will be refused, the bidder should offer nothing at all! If you win such an auction, you are cursed with having overpaid for the asset. Welcome to the **winner's curse!**

| **winner's curse** |
| Concern about over-paying as the highest bidder in an auction. |

Table 15A.2 lists several auction price sequences for offshore oil tracts and FCC spectrum rights. The huge gap between the winning bid and the second highest bid suggest that a winner's curse was present. The winning bidder for offshore oil in the Santa Barbara channel paid $11.4 million more than the second highest bid. Similarly, Wireless Co. paid $12.2 million more than GTE bid for the cell phone spectrum license in the Dallas Metro area. Bidding sequences for star players in professional sports look similar.

Mechanism design theory reveals several insights about this asymmetric information bidding game. First, most bidders will figure out the winner's curse in an auction design such as Table 15A.2 and therefore bid timidly, if at all.[4] To induce more aggressive

---

[3]Adapted from M. Bazeman and W. Samuelson, "I Won the Auction But Don't Want the Prize," *Journal of Conflict Resolution* (December 1983), pp. 618–634. See also R. McAfee and J. McMillan, "Auctions and Bidding," *Journal of Economic Literature* (September 1987), pp. 699–738.

[4]Notice that the same conclusion applies to a continuous-bid version of the auction, though experimental evidence suggests that most first-time players misperceive the asymmetric information nature of the seller's right of refusal and incorrectly bid $50 to $75. See C. Camerer, "Progress in Behavioral Game Theory," *Journal of Economic Perspectives* 11, no. 4 (Fall 1997), pp. 167–188.

FIGURE 15A.1 **Winner's Curse in an Asymmetric Information Bidding Game**

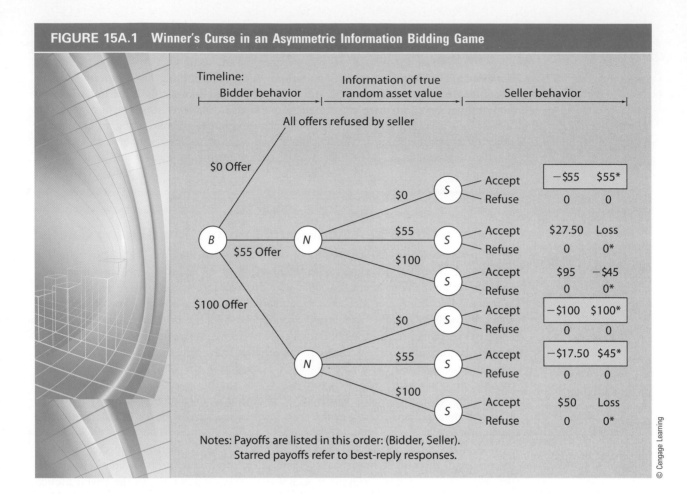

Timeline:
Bidder behavior — Information of true random asset value — Seller behavior

All offers refused by seller

$0 Offer

| | | Accept | −$55 | $55* |
| | $0 S | Refuse | 0 | 0 |

$55 Offer

| | $55 S | Accept | $27.50 | Loss |
| | | Refuse | 0 | 0* |

| | $100 S | Accept | $95 | −$45 |
| | | Refuse | 0 | 0* |

$100 Offer

| | $0 S | Accept | −$100 | $100* |
| | | Refuse | 0 | 0 |

| | $55 S | Accept | −$17.50 | $45* |
| | | Refuse | 0 | 0 |

| | $100 S | Accept | $50 | Loss |
| | | Refuse | 0 | 0* |

Notes: Payoffs are listed in this order: (Bidder, Seller).
Starred payoffs refer to best-reply responses.

© Cengage Learning

bidding in such situations, DeBeers finds it must offer additional inducements to its diamond auction participants. In repeated, multiple-round versions of such asymmetric information games, DeBeers carefully sorts its rough-cut diamonds, grading them into "sights." Reputation for reliability in grading the sights more economically than the bidders could pick, cull, and resell the rejects is what brings De Beers' buyers back, auction after auction.

Example

Winner's Curse at ESPN[5]

ABC debuted *Monday Night Football* and sold its ad slots for 30 years, but it overpaid and ended up losing approximately $150 million per year. When bids were considered for the right to televise this show for the eight years of 1998–2005 for $4 billion, NBC decided that the winner would be cursed with losses and dropped out of the bidding. ABC (a Disney company) continued bidding and eventually won the "prize" for $4.4 billion ($550 million per year). For the 2006–2011 seasons, another media division of Disney, ESPN, agreed to pay almost twice as much ($1.1 billion per year) for the next eight years. ESPN hopes to garner sufficient revenue to break even from cable subscriber fees it charges Comcast and Time Warner as well as from the traditional advertising slots.

(continued)

Viewership has tumbled 33 percent to 26 million households since the peak interest in professional football in the early 1980s. Although the new television rights do allow for more TV time-outs in which to sell commercials, $50 million per three-hour game works out to eighty-four 15-second spots (28 per hour), each costing $600,000, that will be required just to break even. By comparison, 15-second spots on the Oscars award show sell for $840,000 to reach 40 to 50 million viewers, and the Super Bowl with 90 million viewers sells for $1.25 million per slot.

[5]Based on "NFL on Monday Shifts to ESPN in Record Deal," *Wall Street Journal* (April 19, 2005), p. B3; "A Ball ESPN Couldn't Afford to Drop," *BusinessWeek* (May 2, 2005), p. 42; and "Marketers Rely on Oscar," *Wall Street Journal* (February 2, 2006), p. B3.

Second, if the asymmetric information is discoverable by appraisals, marketing research, or other similar services, another insight from auction design theory is that the seller should conduct a multiple-round auction with open bidding. Open bidding allows the bidders to react to asymmetric information revealed in prior rounds and therefore reduces the winner's curse. This idea was used by the FCC in the spectrum auctions for personal communication systems (PCSs) such as cell phones, mobile fax and data service, and voice-mail pagers.

Information Revelation in Common-Value Auctions

To illustrate this role of open bidding, consider two PCS bidders: Wireless Co., an alliance of Sprint and several large cable TV companies that spent $2.1 billion and won the rights to serve 145 million customers in 29 metropolitan service areas, and PCS PrimeCo, an alliance of three regional Bell companies that spent $1.1 billion and won the rights to serve 57 million customers in 11 metropolitan service areas. For example, in one winning bid Wireless paid $46.6 million for the Louisville, Kentucky, service area. How did Wireless decide what to bid?

TABLE 15A.2   BIDS FOR OFFSHORE OIL CONTRACTS AND FCC SPECTRUM RIGHTS

OFFSHORE OIL[a]		FCC SPECTRUM[b]		
SANTA BARBARA CHANNEL	ALASKA NORTH SLOPE	MIAMI METRO AREA	DALLAS METRO AREA	BIDDER
$43.5	$10.5	$131.7	$84.2	Wireless Co.
32.1	5.2	126.0	72.0	GTE Inc.
18.1	2.1	125.5	68.7	Wireless Co.
10.2	1.4	119.4		
6.3	0.5	119.3		
	0.4	113.8		
		113.7		
		108.4		

[a]In millions, 1969 dollars.
[b]In millions, 1995 dollars.

Source: Adapted from Tables II and IV in R. Weber, "Making More for Less," *Journal of Economics and Management Strategy* 6, no. 3 (Fall 1997), pp. 529–548.

© Cengage Learning

Suppose that both bidders know that the net present value of the rights to transmit PCS services in Louisville is a random variable uniformly distributed from $10 million to $60 million with six discrete values possible—in particular, $10 million, $20 million, $30 million, $40 million, $50 million, and $60 million. Also assume (provisionally) that both parties value the asset identically, a so-called **common-value auction**. The problem then from the bidders' point of view is to elicit sufficient information from the market environment and from the offers of other bidders to correctly identify the value and ensure a profit (i.e., not overpay for the asset). In advance, each company conducts marketing research experiments to narrow the possible outcomes and thereby better inform its own bid. Suppose Wireless Co.'s marketing research results are unable to exclude the two tails of the uniform distribution of possible values (i.e., $10 million and $60 million) but can exclude with certainty $20 million and $30 million as well as $50 million. Taken by itself, this information allows Wireless to narrow its probability assessments to $10 million, $40 million, and $60 million.

Weighting each outcome equally yields an expected value bid of $36.7 million as follows:

$$\frac{1}{3}(\$10 \text{ million}) + \frac{1}{3}(\$40 \text{ million}) + \frac{1}{3}(\$60 \text{ million}) = \$36.7 \text{ million}$$

Similarly, PCS PrimeCo conducts its own marketing research that, let's assume, excludes $10 million, $30 million, and $50 million as possible outcomes for the Louisville service area. That is, PCS PrimeCo has access to separate information that causes it to calculate a different expected value bid:[6]

$$\frac{1}{3}(\$20 \text{ million}) + \frac{1}{3}(\$40 \text{ million}) + \frac{1}{3}(\$60 \text{ million}) = \$40 \text{ million}.$$

These best estimates of the common value are based on the asymmetric information available to the two firms. Consequently, in a simultaneous sealed-bid auction, the most a seller could hope to realize is $40 million. With sealed bids, no information is conveyed to the competitor, and an optimal bidding strategy is therefore simply to shade your bid slightly below the Bayesian expected value based on your own information set. PCS PrimeCo would therefore bid something just under $40 (perhaps $39.6) million and win the spectrum rights for the Louisville service area.

Bayesian Strategy with Open Bidding Design

Notice, however, from the seller's point of view *ex post facto* (after receiving the sealed bids) that the joint information set of the two parties suggests PCS PrimeCo has underpaid. To review, the union of the two sets of marketing research outcomes excludes $10 million, $20 million, $30 million, and $50 million. Said another way, the *combined* marketing research results have narrowed the possible outcomes for the value of the

---

[6]The equally weighted probabilities of 1/3 are actually Bayesian probabilities of each possible remaining value based on a perfectly accurate forecast that $10 million, $30 million, and $50 million (the prime numbers in the set of possible asset values) have been ruled out. It is helpful if we think of the marketing research as identifying Prime and Not Prime numbers between 1 and 6 multiplied by 10 million. Then, the Bayesian probability ($20 million/Perfect Forecast of Not Prime) = (0.167 × 1.0)/[0.167 + (0.833 × 0.4)] = 0.33, where 0.167 is the prior probability before the marketing research is conducted that $20 million will be the realized asset value. The number 1.0 is the accuracy of the forecasting instrument; for example, the conditional probability that when $20 million is the true value, the conclusion from the marketing research will be that the value is Not Prime, meaning "not a prime number between 1 and 6." The number 0.833 is the prior probability that the asset value will be something other than $20 million. And finally, the number 0.4 is the probability that when something other than $20 million is the true asset value, the perfectly accurate forecasting instrument will still say Not Prime. That happens with $40 million and $60 million (i.e., twice in five possibilities).

The analysis here is easily modified to incorporate less-than-perfect forecasts from the marketing research, which is helpful because imperfect forecasts are the reality of business. See E. Rasmussen, *Games and Information*, 3rd ed. (Cambridge: Basil Blackwell, 2001), Chapter 13, Section 5.

Louisville service area to $40 million and $60 million. Neither firm has access to this much information. Each simply knows a subset of all the marketing research available. But as a seller in such a setting, the FCC wishes to elicit full revelation of *all* asymmetric information because it affects the winning bid. If $40 million and $60 million are equally likely, and the bidders can somehow discern this information, the Louisville service area is worth just under $50 million, not PCS PrimeCo's bid of just under $40 million.

One way to bring all the asymmetric information into play is to adopt a sequential open-bidding auction design in which each company is chosen at random to post its bid (in one round, then the random order of posting procedure is redone for Round 2, Round 3, etc.).[7] Then, whichever company bids first, the other company will deduce the first bidder's additional marketing research results and proceed to increase its bid in light of the more complete information available. For example, if PCS PrimeCo bids first and bids $40 million based on its own asymmetric information, Wireless Co. will then be in a position to deduce that PCS PrimeCo's marketing research excluded $10 million, $30 million, and $50 million as possible values.

That is the only information that would be consistent with a bid of $40 million in a simultaneous sealed-bid auction over an asset with a uniform distribution from $10 million to $60 million with only these six possible outcomes. Knowing from its own marketing research that $20 million, $30 million, and $50 million have also been ruled out, Wireless will immediately place a winning bid of just under $50 million:

$$\frac{1}{2}(\$40 \text{ million}) + \frac{1}{2}(\$60 \text{ million}) = \$50 \text{ million}.$$

With many more than these two bidders and other service areas in which Wireless Co. would be required to bid first and in which PCS PrimeCo had a turn playing the fast second, this sequential open-bidding auction design would work well. Winning bids would rise to the Bayesian expected asset values reflecting all available information, and highest-value users would receive the assets.

Example

Open Bidding Simultaneous Auction of PCS Spectrum Rights[8]

Thirty firms ultimately participated in the broadband spectrum auctions. The FCC specified two 30-MHz blocks for each of 51 metropolitan service areas. A special feature of these metropolitan service areas was strong interdependencies in providing service in contiguous service areas. Bidders were encouraged therefore to assemble and reassemble efficient bundles of licenses as the auction progressed. Consequently, the FCC adopted multiple-round simultaneous auctions with open bidding to allocate spectrum rights. Each bidder was told there would be several rounds of bidding, all bids in each round were announced, and each bidder was allowed to cancel or amend bids from round to round. All bids in every metro area remained open as long as any bidding activity continued in any service area. The auction lasted 112 rounds over a four-month period. Using this auction design, the FCC raised $7.7 billion. AT&T paid $49.3 million and Wireless Co. paid $46.6 million for the A block and B block spectrum rights in Louisville.

[8]Based on "Market Design and the Spectrum Auctions," A Special Issue of *Journal of Economics and Management Strategy* 6, no. 3 (Fall 1997), pp. 425ff; and "Sale of Wireless Frequencies," *Wall Street Journal* (March 25, 1998), p. A3.

---

[7]Open bidding with a nonrandom, structured sequence of role reversals on multiple auctions allows bidders to signal and punish one another (tit for tat) and therefore increases the likelihood of tacit collusion.

Strategic Underbidding in Private-Value Auctions[9]

private-value auction Auction where the bidders have different valuations even when information is complete.

One serious drawback of English open outcry auctions is the strategic reticence (tendency to underbid) that bidders exhibit. If the bidders have common information but different valuations (i.e., a so-called **private-value auction**), those with high willingness to pay have an incentive to refrain from aggressive bidding in an attempt to just exceed the bid of the player with the second highest valuation. For example, in the FCC's spectrum auctions, the cellular phone incumbents already established in a metropolitan area had higher valuation than other bidders. In the early rounds of any such open bidding auction over private values, eventual high bidders hold back. Analysis of the FCC data suggests only 53 percent of the eventual winners were the high bidders after the early rounds. Sellers worry that this strategic reticence dampens the overall level of bidding throughout the auction and may well reduce final revenue.

Suppose two bidders each value a service or asset between $0 million and $10 million. No information about the actual net present values is known. That is, no common-value information, asymmetric or otherwise, is available. In this purely private-value auction that lasts only one round, the bids are sealed, and the highest bid wins. Your valuation is $6 million. What should you bid?

With two bidders present, each must assume that the other will offer something less than his or her private value, say $k \times v$, where k is a proportion and v is the private value.[10] Any bids by Alice (P_a) that are greater than k times Bob's value (v_b) will win.

That is, any time the value to Alice $v_a = P_a/k > v_b$, Alice wins the auction and realizes a profit of $v_a - P_a$. With uniform density, the probability that Bob's value is any given number between $0 and $10 million is 1/10 million. Again, Alice wins when this value is between $0 and P_a/k dollars. Therefore, Alice's cumulative probability of winning is P_a/k events, each of which has a marginal probability of 1/10 million—that is, Alice's cumulative probability of winning is $P_a/(k \times 10$ million). Alice's expected profit from the auction may therefore be written as follows:

$$E(\text{Profit}_a) = (v_a - P_a)\frac{P_a}{k \times 10{,}000{,}000} \qquad [15A.1]$$

Differentiating Equation 15A.1 with respect to P_a and setting the derivative equal to zero, Alice's expected profit from the auction is maximized when

$$(v_a - 2P_a)\frac{1}{k \times 10{,}000{,}000} = 0 \qquad [15A.2]$$

that is, when $P_a = v_a/2$. Alice maximizes her expected profit from participating in the auction, conditional on Bob's choosing a kv_b bidding rule, by choosing to reduce her own private value by one-half. Because Alice and Bob are symmetrically situated in this bidding game, Bob too should reduce his private value by one-half. With $k = 1/2$, the players are in a Nash equilibrium. Each maximizes self-interest, conditional on the other player's bidding $v/2$, by bidding half of his or her own private value. In a two-player, simultaneous, highest-price-wins-and-pays sealed-bid auction, the magnitude of rational underbidding is fully 50 percent!

---

[9]Two excellent elaborations of this and the next topic are J. McMillan, "Bidding in Competition," *Games, Strategies, and Managers* (New York: Oxford University Press, 1992), Chapter 11; and E. Rasmussen, "Auctions," *Games and Information*, 2nd ed. (Cambridge, MA: Basil Blackwell, 1993), Chapter 12.

[10]This example relies on McMillan, *op. cit.*, pp. 138, 208–209.

FIGURE 15A.2   **Strategic Underbidding Declines and Seller Revenue Rises with Bidder Entry in Private-Value Auctions**

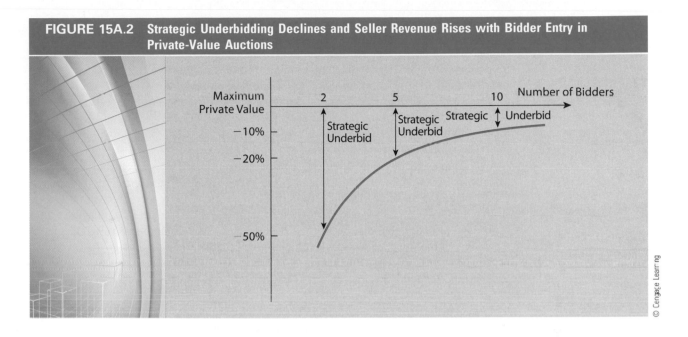

In the case of five bidders, it is easy to show that a rational bidder should reduce true private value by one-fifth, and if n bidders, by $1/n$.[11] Quite intuitively, therefore, the more bidders, the smaller is the rational underbidding. See Figure 15A.2. Sellers understand this reasoning and therefore provide sorting services (in De Beers's case) and handsome catalogs and live exhibitions (in Christie's case) to draw bidders into the auction process. Paul Klemperer of Oxford University describes how this fundamental insight determined many of the auction design decisions for the British spectrum auctions. Thirteen different companies entered the U.K. bidding, resulting in the highest per-capita revenue raised by all the European and Asian 3G auctions.

Example

Exponential Valley Inc. Auctions a Chip Patent[12]

Exponential Valley Inc., a Silicon Valley microprocessor start-up, decided to auction its portfolio of 45 issued and pending patents rather than move into production. The computer chip patents include features that would allow a competitor to match forthcoming chip products from industry leader Intel Corp. Intel regularly sues companies that make clones of its chips and has been effective in deterring entry with this strategy. The Exponential Valley patents appear to offer an opportunity to provide protection from Intel's patent infringement suits. At considerable expense, Exponential developed a large prospectus of technical and bidding information that it targeted to possible bidders: AMD, Chromatic Research Inc., and Texas Instruments. Exponential Valley did so because the larger the number of bidders, the less the strategic underbidding will be.

[12]Based on "An Auction of Chip Patents May Ignite Bidding War," *Wall Street Journal* (August 1, 1997), p. B5.

---

[11]See Rasmussen, *op. cit.*, p. 296; and P. Klemperer, "Spectrum Auctions," *European Economic Review* 46 (2002), pp. 829–845.

If sellers expend enough resources to expand the pool of bidders, in the limit the seller can realize $(n-1)/n$ of the maximum private value (v_{max}). Five bidders implies 80 percent of v_{max}. Ten bidders implies 90 percent of v_{max}. Twenty bidders implies 95 percent of v_{max}. If increasing the number of bidders from two to five results in a 30 percent increase in value, then doubling the number of bidders from five to ten results in a 10 percent increase in value, and doubling them again results in only a 5 percent increase in value. Diminishing returns to these efforts by sellers to expand the pool of bidders implies that the fundamental problem of strategic underbidding will be reduced but never eliminated.

Of course, underbidding in a private-value auction is rational only if bidders can be assured of winning in the final round. One way to reduce strategic underbidding in private-value auctions is to reduce the available information about other valuations by sealing the bids. A less extreme approach is to end the auction without warning, after several preliminary rounds, thereby in effect sealing the bids unpredictably. Of course, as we saw in the previous section, it can be in the seller's interest to induce the revelation of all asymmetric information. In fact, as noted earlier, sellers often have an incentive to preannounce expert appraisals of value (as Christie's and Sotheby's auction houses do) in order to reduce the winner's curse.

This concern is important in auction design but not always controlling. The reason is that some asymmetrically held information can, if revealed, lower the rational bid (see the first case exercise at the end of this appendix). So sealing bids is a design alternative that becomes more attractive the greater the variation in private values and the more symmetric the information pertaining to valuation among the bidders. Obviously, open bidding or pre-announcing appraisals is more attractive whenever favorable information is known to the seller. However, even when the seller is in the dark, open bidding has a positive expected value for the seller because the exchange of common-value information always reduces the winner's curse.

Second-Highest Sealed-Bid Auctions: A Revelation Mechanism

Strategic underbidding is especially troubling, of course, if the seller is collecting bid revenue from all participants in the auction. A "seller" may be attempting to assess whether buyer willingness to pay justifies investment in a new facility (e.g., a ballpark, a pool, a set of tennis courts, or a clubhouse). Each potential user is asked what he or she would pay for access if the facility were to be built. If sufficient demand exists, the facility manager then builds the facility and collects the highly divergent, discriminatory prices from each "bidder." The key to such an assessment is designing an **incentive-compatible revelation mechanism**. The same thing is true in designing a private-value auction. If, as an auction designer, one could remove the incentive to underbid and at the same time prevent a winner's curse, one could align incentives with true revelation of value. Think through the following illustration of an ingenious IC auction mechanism design that won William Vickrey the Nobel prize![13]

Vickrey suggested that rather than requiring the winning bidder to pay the high bid, what if the auction mechanism design specified in advance that the highest bid wins but that the winner would pay a reduced amount only, equal to the second-highest bid? Think through the consequences of this radical idea. By definition, under the rules of a

incentive-compatible revelation mechanism A procedure for eliciting true revelation of privately held information from agents with competing interests.

---

[13]Every game theory and mechanism design theory book describes the Vickrey auction, also known as the second-highest sealed-bid auction or the uniform price auction. Vickrey's original article is also revealing and insightful; see W. Vickrey, "Counterspeculation, Auctions, and Competitive Sealed Tenders," *Journal of Finance* 16, no. 8 (1961), p. 37.

highest pays-second-highest sealed-bid auction, the payment triggered by bidding one's true private value cannot exceed the next best alternative selling price. This use of a verifiable second opinion and exit option to shore up the bidder's protection from suffering a winner's curse was the key insight of William Vickrey's IC mechanism design. True revelation of maximum willingness to pay proves compatible, through an ingenious mechanism design, with the bidder's desire to avoid the winner's curse.

Example

Second-Highest Sealed-Bid Auction: U.S. Treasury Bills[14]

Auction design decisions in security markets select procedures that will raise the most revenue for the issuers. On this question, worldwide debate currently rages about the optimal design of Treasury bill new-issue security auctions. Denmark and Sweden adopt diametrically opposed designs. The Swedes sell government bills and bonds at discriminatory Dutch auction prices; the Danes sell in Vickrey auctions at a uniform second-highest sealed-bid price. Given this diversity of expert opinion and practice, the U.S. Federal Reserve authorized the New York Federal Reserve Bank to experiment with both designs for two-year and five-year notes. Most Treasury auctions in the United States (and indeed around the world) are discriminatory descending-price (Dutch) auctions; buyers pay whatever they bid for quantities of T-bonds along a demand schedule submitted by each bidder. If the market-clearing price implies a yield of 5.03 percent, a typical bidder may get $5 million worth of T-bonds at her highest submitted price yielding 5.00 percent, $7 million worth of T-bonds at a lower price yielding 5.02 percent, and perhaps another $10 million at the market-clearing (lowest) price yielding 5.03 percent.

Uniform price second-highest sealed-bid auctions are different. Every bidder in this Vickrey auction might pay the uniform slightly higher price associated with a yield of 5.02 percent, and the Treasury's marginal cost of raising debt capital will decline from 5.03 percent to 5.02 percent. However, some still higher-priced transactions no longer take place, and other lower-price transactions also no longer take place. Therefore, it is unclear analytically what will happen to Treasury revenue; it depends on the interest rate elasticity of T-bill demand.

This result highlights the insight that the principal advantages of second-highest sealed-bid Vickrey auctions are not to raise seller revenue but rather to minimize strategic underbidding, reveal true private valuations, and reduce bidder collusion among small numbers of bidders. In contrast, security markets are highly efficient, with numerous potential buyers willing to pay a common value for these T-bond and T-bill assets. Therefore, a second-highest sealed-bid mechanism design is more appropriate for the private placement IPO market employed in the Google IPO. Combining managerial insight about auction design with a careful analysis of the particulars of the business setting becomes crucially important.

[14]Based on "Bidding Up Debt Auctions," *BusinessWeek* (September 8, 1997), p. 26; and S. Nandi, "Treasury Auctions: What Do the Recent Models and Results Tell Us?" *Federal Reserve Bank of Atlanta Economic Review* (Fourth Quarter, 1997), pp. 4–15

Vickrey auction An incentive-compatible revelation mechanism for eliciting sealed bids equal to private value.

To sum up, no bidder in a **Vickrey auction** has any incentive to underbid. Reducing your bid below your private value has no effect on the payment due should you win. Instead, underbidding in a second-highest sealed-bid auction when you are the highest-willingness-to-pay participant simply increases the probability of losing an auction asset that it would have been possible to acquire for less than it is worth to you. And if someone else values the asset more than you, no payment is triggered by bidding up to your own private value. Therefore, for all possible cases, true revelation of private value dominates underbidding as a bidding strategy. And because bids are sealed and the auction lasts only one round, no strategic bidding, false carding, or signaling can have any effect on other participants in the auction. Therefore, No Underbidding is a dominant strategy equilibrium for all bidders.[15] Of course, realized revenue is still reduced by the full difference between the highest and second-highest valuations, but at least the seller learns the true value of the auctioned asset.

Revenue Equivalence of Alternative Auction Types[16]

Under particular circumstances, the four simplest types of auctions (English ascending price, Dutch descending uniform price, first-price sealed-bid, and highest-pays-second-highest sealed bid) yield equivalent revenue to the seller-auctioneer. For example, both first-price sealed-bid auction participants and Dutch descending uniform-price auction participants must pay whatever they bid if their bids prove to be the winning market-clearing bids. In addition, participants in both types have no access to information about bidders with lesser valuations than themselves. Consequently, the optimal bidding strategy in a Dutch uniform-price or a first-price sealed-bid auction is identical, and thus the winning bids will be identical (see Table 15A.3).

Similarly, for private-value auctions, as English auction participants learn more and more in the course of the bidding about the independent valuations of other bidders, the person with the highest valuation will ultimately offer an amount just in excess of the second-highest bidder. Second-highest sealed-bid auctions induce, as we have seen, true revelation of value from all bidders, but the winner also pays an amount just equal to the second-highest bidder. Hence, an English ascending-price auction and a second-highest sealed-bid auction yield essentially the same expected revenue to the seller in private-value auctions. Indeed, it turns out that with risk-neutral bidders and private values, all four simple auction types result in the same expected revenue (i.e., an amount just equal to the highest value minus the full difference to the next highest bid). From a seller's perspective, this revenue equivalence theorem (RET) is a depressing result; one would hope to do better.

In several instances, one auction type does raise more expected revenue than another. These optimal mechanism design differences depend upon the risk preference of the bidders and upon the common-value or private-value nature of the item being auctioned. Continuing first with the private-value auctions, if bidders are risk averse and they are operating under the lack of information of a Dutch or first-price sealed-bid design, they will seek to reduce the probability of losing the item when their valuation is highest. Consequently, relative to the situation in an English or second-highest sealed-bid auction in which the winning bidder pays essentially the second-highest bid, risk-averse Dutch or first-price sealed-bid auction participants raise their bids in order to reduce the probability of being outbid by a close second valuation. Strategic underbidding to avoid the winner's curse is still present, but it is mitigated by risk aversion. So, a seller-auctioneer can raise more revenue on average when the bidders are risk averse and the values are independent and private by conducting a Dutch or first-price sealed-bid auction. These results for private-value auctions for items such as patent licenses, sales territories, antiques, and fine art are summarized in the top section of Table 15A.3.

---

[15]The bidder's degree of risk aversion has no bearing on this result. However, more risk-averse bidders do insure against losing in winner-take-all first-price sealed-bid auctions by increasing their bid relative to the seller revenue from a second-highest sealed-bid auction. We discuss the role of risk aversion further in the next section.

[16]For a more extensive discussion of this topic, see A. Dixit, D. Reiley, and S. Skeath, *Games of Strategy*, 3rd ed. (New York: Norton, 2009), Chapter 15; and E. Rasmussen, *op. cit.*, Chapter 12.

TABLE 15A.3 SELLER EXPECTED REVENUE FROM AUCTION TYPES						
PRIVATE-VALUE AUCTIONS (PATENT LICENSE, SALES TERRITORY, ESTATE ANTIQUES)						
Risk-Neutral Bidders	Dutch = Uniform Price		First-Price = Sealed-Bid	English =		Second-Highest Sealed-Bid
Risk-Averse Bidders	Dutch = Uniform Price		First-Price > Sealed-Bid	English =		Second-Highest Sealed-Bid
COMMON-VALUE AUCTIONS (MINERAL LEASE, LOGGING RIGHTS, AIRCRAFT)						
Risk-Neutral Bidders	English >	Second-Highest > Sealed-Bid		Dutch = Uniform Price		First-Price Sealed-Bid
Risk-Averse Bidders	English >	Second-Highest $\gtrsim$ Sealed-Bid		Dutch = Uniform Price		First-Price Sealed-Bid

© Cengage Learning

As to common-value auctions for items that have thick resale markets such as crude oil, mineral leases, forest logging rights, equity and debt securities, and easily redeployable surplus equipment such as commercial delivery trucks and corporate jet aircraft, the source of uncertainty in the valuation is an estimation risk. Every bidder knows that the true value at resale is identical across all auction participants; it's just that this true value is an unknown while the oil is still in the ground, the logs still in the forest, the IPOs yet unissued, and so on. Each bidder must therefore assess this true value from his or her own forecast information in a Dutch uniform-price or first-price sealed-bid auction and from any additional information that can be gleaned from the sequence of bids in the English auction. The Bayesian updating of the initial estimates (the "priors") in the sequential process of an English auction will tend to result in a pooling of the bidders' information; therefore, winning bids in the English auction will tend toward the mean estimate of the population of forecasts. Mechanisms that facilitate the learning of this best unbiased estimate of what the harvestable common value of the resource truly is reduce strategic underbidding to avoid the winner's curse.

Hence, as shown in the bottom section of Table 15A.3, in selling common-value items, a seller-auctioneer can raise the most revenue with an English ascending-price auction. And as we saw in the previous section, second-highest sealed-bid designs can also substantially reduce the winner's curse in these common-value auctions, raising the seller's projected revenue relative to Dutch uniform-price auctions and first-price sealed-bid auctions that make it hard for the bidders to reduce their estimation risk.[17]

Example

Internet Auction Design Becomes a Big E-Business Debate: eBay versus Priceline[18]

Online auction sites now number in the thousands; eBay Inc. has grown to 150 million listings. In the information economy, online auctions are a key business model that may displace the two traditional price-setting processes: (1) one-on-one negotiation (haggling) and (2) a menu of fixed price quotes provided by the seller.

(continued)

---

[17]Risk aversion introduces the same complication into the analysis as earlier—that is, Dutch uniform-price and first-price sealed-bid participants raise their bids to reduce the probability of losing an item to a close second competitor. Still, the benefits of information pooling tend to favor English or second-highest sealed-bid designs for common-value auctions.

Business-to-business (B2B) transactions may continue to require one-on-one negotiation over the time, quality, availability, and delivery dimensions of the "deal," but in business-to-consumer transactions, auction prices themselves establish most of what is needed for a "deal."

Another very successful site, Priceline, employs an ascending-posted-price highest-wins-and-pays auction mechanism design. Bids are listed anonymously to reduce collusion and posted continuously to mitigate the strategic underbidding that accompanies any private-value auction (i.e., the winner's curse). Bid payments must be guaranteed with a credit card at the time the buyers' offers are placed; subsequently, bids cannot be cancelled and are executed automatically if the offer is accepted.

eBay has a more transparent ascending-price auction design with posted prices and highest-wins-and-pays-second-highest rules for declaring a winner. Rather than allowing sellers to remain anonymous until they decide to "hit" a Priceline buyer's posted offer, eBay consolidates feedback on the seller's past performance and hot-links it to the bidding site. Also, unlike Priceline, eBay allows open bidding (i.e., offers are repeated in multiple rounds, and prior offers may be cancelled or amended). If open bidding proves to be optimal for auctioning airline tickets, automobiles, and machinery, eBay rather than Priceline will thrive.

[18]Based on "The Heyday of the Auction," *The Economist* (July 24, 1999), pp. 67–68; "Redesigning Business: Priceline," *Harvard Business Review* (November/December 1999), pp. 19–21; "Dotty about dot.commerce?" *The Economist* (February 26, 2000), p. 24; "Going, Going, Gone, Sucker!" *BusinessWeek* (March 20, 2000), pp. 124–125; and "Inside: Is Priceline Vulnerable?" *Harvard Business Review* (December 3, 1999), pp. 19–21.

A still larger auction design issue is whether to continue the traditional ascending-price (English) auction or adopt descending-price (Dutch) auction procedures. Basement.com and OutletZoo.com start prices high and drop them in increments until all the units for sale have been demanded. Clearly, sellers can realize more revenue in discriminatory Dutch auctions by charging differentially higher prices to the early bidders than can be realized in uniform-price Dutch or English auctions that identify a market-clearing price. Of course, sophisticated institutional and industrial buyers understand this concept as well, and this segment may well prefer a traditional non-auction Web site such as Grainger.com where sellers post initial best offers and then focus on availability, delivery, installation, technical support, and other after-sale services. Establishing the value-in-use of these extras in the "total offering" may prove as critical as seller warranties and replacement guarantees to B2B customers.[19]

Contractual Approaches to Asymmetric Information in Online Auctions

In some ways, Priceline.com is like couponing without the brand-name exposure. This provides a way to price discriminate to the price-sensitive customer segments without degrading one's brand identity. Perhaps this explains why Delta Airlines took a substantial equity stake in Priceline; Delta could liquidate its inventory without cannibalizing higher fare sales. But anonymous sellers offering unverifiable product or service claims

[19]See A. Kambil and E. van Heck, *Making Markets* (Boston: HBS Press, 2002); J. Anderson and J. Narus, *Business Market Management* (New York: Prentice Hall, 1999); and R. Oliva, "Sold on Reverse Auctions," *Marketing Management* (March/April 2003), p. 45.

on Priceline must credibly commit to higher-quality products if they hope to attract anything more than rock-bottom prices. As we have seen, hostage or bonding mechanisms are the key to credible commitments.

Appraisal Mechanism   First, sellers can invest in and disseminate **appraisals** to try to distinguish their auction offerings from fraudulently advertised products. Independent certified appraisals, such as buy-back guarantees, place a floor under the value of the product offered for sale. Perhaps a tract of development land or the intellectual property in a patent lease is up for bids; the seller can pay for an appraisal about the range of values typically paid in resale markets for land or intellectual property assets with similar characteristics. Two drawbacks prevent the widespread adoption of this approach, however. Certified appraisals are expensive, and appraisals seldom establish maximum or unique asset value.

Warranty and Replacement Guarantees   The second contractual approach sellers can adopt to establish credibility for their auction claims is to signal their respective quality by offering *warranties and replacement guarantees*. These signaling features of the product offering are observable to the buyer at the point of sale and are highly correlated with the unobservable product or service quality at issue. Automobile tire manufacturers who take shortcuts vulcanizing the tire casings that embed steel wire belts in their tire treads will make shorter treadwear warranties and provide guarantees against fewer blowout hazards. The buyer can therefore pay more for tires with extensive warranties and feel confident that the tire quality is above that offered by non-warrantied suppliers. Encouraging buyers to screen alternate suppliers in this way therefore achieves a separating equilibrium of fraudulent versus reliable suppliers without the more costly extensive independent appraisal of each tire.

Closed-End Leases with Fixed Residuals   Another way for sellers to credibly commit to the delivery of a high-quality durable product is to offer to lease rather than sell the product and then to accept *lease terms with a high residual value*. This feature of leasing offers a net advantage over buying in that sellers with informational advantages will credibly commit to forward value through the take-back provisions of the lease. If one seller says you can lease with a 60 percent residual at the end of four years and another quotes a 40 percent residual at the end of four years, all other things the same, the lease payments will recover depreciation only two-thirds as great in the 60 percent residual lease. In that case, buyers may well be willing to lease a higher-quality/higher-priced product. Of course, such an approach to establishing credibility will not be adopted if sellers foresee substantial obsolescence risk. Therefore, high residuals seldom occur alone; usually other lease terms (e.g., financing charges, initial asset prices, or lease closing fees) adjust upward to "price in" the extra seller risk when residuals increase.

Contingent Payment Mechanisms   Finally, sellers can agree to accept **contingent payments**—that is, seller revenue dependent on the performance that the buyer experiences. Suppose the due diligence required to establish clear value in an asset sale is prohibitively expensive. If a tract of development land has buried fuel tanks that necessitate substantial environmental remediation but the presence of which is unknown, the land seller can agree *ex ante* to pay for the restoration of the land. Thereby, the contingent risk is insured away by a seller's credible commitment to restore the land should it prove damaged. Similarly, if timberland sales or oil field leases prove particularly productive, the buyer and seller can agree to larger money payments than if the actual harvested timber and oil pumped out prove disappointing.

These contingent payment contracts can be arranged as progress payments, so that the buyer and seller take small and continuous steps while money remains owed. Checklists of building problems that remain to be corrected often trigger the final small contingent payments between new homeowners and their builders. Sometimes corporations

appraisals An estimate of value by an independent expert.

contingent payments A fee schedule conditional on the outcome of uncertain future events.

employ contingent payments while exchanging hostages in an asset sale by requiring the seller to take a financial stake (perhaps 15 percent of the cash flow to equity owners) in the buyer's subsidiary spun off to manage the new assets. Given the low priority of an equity owner should the spin-off declare bankruptcy and need to liquidate, contingency payments increase the seller's incentives to reveal hidden features that determine the true cash flows realizable from the asset.

INCENTIVE-COMPATIBLE REVELATION MECHANISMS

Perhaps the most powerful mechanism design tool for drawing out privately held asymmetric information is William Vickrey's self-enforcing revelation mechanism. Later, Edward Clarke and Ted Groves added the idea of multiple agents in group decision making such that the mechanism design objective became demand or cost revelation in a partnership that had to be compatible with the incentives of all the parties: an incentive compatible (IC) revelation mechanism.

Example

Intel and Analog Inc. Form Partnership to Develop DSP Chip[20]

Intel Corp. has dominated the manufacture of semiconductor chips for computer microprocessors for more than a decade. With AMD and Siemens beginning to pose some threat in this traditional market and with the smart phone market growing exponentially, Intel formed a joint venture with Analog Devices Inc. to move into the chip market for communications devices such as smart phones, pagers, and wireless videophones. Intel and Analog jointly developed a new line of digital signal processor (DSP) chips. DSP chips take analog signals like voice, photo images, and videos and convert them to digital signals to be transmitted over wireless systems. New signal compression and encryption capabilities of the Intel-Analog chip competed well against rival DSP suppliers Texas Instruments (TI) and Lucent Technologies. DSP chips also appear to have application in modems and other networking devices that provide high-speed access to the Internet and in speech-recognition systems for machine-controlled automated processes in cars and factories. DSP chip sales growth has recently approached 30 percent per year, reaching total sales of $5.7 billion.

Groups of Intel and Analog engineers will collaborate on designing the core architecture of the chip, and the two companies will then separately develop and sell products based on the design. The contingent payoffs to each firm are therefore based in part on their cooperative design success and in part on their separate product development and marketing efforts. This joint venture contract provides incentives for continuing cooperation far beyond those generated by a simple profit-sharing agreement, yet it preserves each company's option to pursue some business plans privately.

---

[20]Based on Intel Corporation and Analog Design Inc. joint press releases (February 3, 1999); and "TI Lays Out DSP Plans until 2010," *Hardware Reviews and News* on the The-View.com (December 6, 1999).

Cost Revelation in Joint Ventures and Partnerships

When verification by third parties is infeasible or undesirable, companies can adopt procedures that elicit true revelation of asymmetric information pivotal to the success of the partnership. Consider a joint venture to develop several new personal computer products between a PC designer-manufacturer, such as Apple Computer and Motorola, a leading supplier of computer chips.[21] The Apple operating system depends on the capabilities of the Motorola chips, and the chips are produced in anticipation of the requirements of the operating system. The partners believe they can better sustain a competitive advantage in this fast-moving technology by jointly developing new products. After the joint venture covers development and production costs, they agree to split the profits equally.

Each partner in the joint venture has private information about cost to which the other partner does not have access. For example, as it develops the iPad, Apple discovers its operating system development costs, and Motorola discovers its computer chip design and production costs. Although neither can independently verify the other partner's asymmetric information, the success of a joint venture often depends on each partner's ability to generate enough operating profits to recover these development costs. As the partnership reaches project milestones, determining profit potential requires an accurate revelation of true costs. Let us see why and what can be done to achieve this goal.

The study of IC revelation mechanisms can provide some answers. Each partner faces random disturbances in its cost factors.[22] Sometimes software development is delayed by inconspicuous but debilitating bugs in the programming, which increase the cost from, say, $80 to $120 million. Similarly, sometimes chip development and production necessitates redesign (e.g., Intel's problems with the Pentium chip), increasing that cost from, say, $50 to $70 million. Neither partner can hope to discover and rectify all such problems in advance. However, each can detect early warning signals of cost overruns and, if need be, cancel that aspect of their joint venture.

Cost Overruns with Simple Profit-Sharing Partnerships

When both cost overruns happen simultaneously, the joint venture should shut down because the development costs of proceeding to full-scale production ($120 million + $70 million) will exceed the projected revenue available, say, $180 million. These projected operating profits and losses appear in Table 15A.4. If Apple experiences $120 million cost (the column labeled High Costs), the partnership will cancel the project whenever Motorola also experiences high cost of $70 million (the row labeled High Costs) because proceeding would result in a $10 million operating loss. By the same token, when only one partner or neither partner experiences high costs, the joint venture project should go forward and realize profits of $30 million, $10 million, and $50 million, respectively. Only with correct operate and shutdown decisions can the joint venture generate its maximum value.

The incentive problem is that initially each partner has an incentive to overstate true costs in order to be overcompensated from the joint venture revenues. For example, in Table 15A.4, if Apple reveals true costs of $80 million and Motorola claims costs of $70 million when in fact its true costs are $50 million, Motorola's joint profit share declines by $10 million from one-half of $50 million (top left cell) to one-half of $30 million (lower left cell). But with $20 million extra reimbursement from overstating its cost, Motorola ends up with (1/2) $30 million + $20 million, which exceeds one-half

[21]The general structure of this section relies on A. Dixit and B. Nalebuff, *Thinking Strategically* (New York: Norton, 1991), pp. 306–319. The illustration here is based on "Apple Wants Other PC Makers to Build Computers to Use Macintosh Software," *Wall Street Journal* (January 28, 1994), p. B5; and "IBM, Apple in PC Design Accord," *Wall Street Journal* (November 8, 1994), p. B5.

[22]Similar arguments can be made about asymmetric information regarding random disturbances in demand.

TABLE 15A.4   JOINT PROFITS (IN MILLIONS) FROM A SIMPLE PROFIT-SHARING PARTNERSHIP WITH $180 MILLION IN REVENUE

		APPLE	
		LOW COSTS ($80)	HIGH COSTS ($120)
Motorola	Low Costs ($50)	$50	$10
	High Costs ($70)	$30	−$10

of $50 million by $10 million. Similarly, if Apple overstates its costs, the Apple profit share falls from $25 million to $5 million, but this decline is more than offset by the $40 million extra reimbursement for overstating its $80 million actual cost to $120 million.

If low cost and cost overruns are equally likely at Motorola and if the probability of a cost overrun at Apple is 0.3, then expected costs are $60 million at Motorola and $92 million at Apple. With true revelation of costs, expected net profit from the joint venture is then (0.5×0.7) $50 million + (0.5×0.3) $10 million + (0.5×0.7) $30 million + (0.5×0.3) $0 = $29.5 million, or $14.75 million for each partner.[23] However, if one or both partners overstate costs, the projects with mixed costs in the southwest and northeast cells of Table 15A.4 will also be canceled, and the expected net profit from the joint venture then declines. For example, if Apple falsely reveals $120 million when low costs of $80 million are present, the joint development project is canceled whenever Motorola experiences $70 million cost. This cancellation results in the partners forgoing the $30 million profit on the mixed-cost project in the southwest cell and reduces the expected value of the joint venture to $19 million (i.e., $9.5 million per partner).[24] Value-maximizing managers facing asymmetric information seek some revelation mechanism that will provide appropriate incentives to induce the revelation of true costs, thereby preserving and capturing the full $14.75-million-per-partner expected value of both the low-cost and the mixed-cost projects.

TABLE 15A.5   INDIVIDUAL REVENUE SHARE NET OF PARTNER COST (MILLIONS)

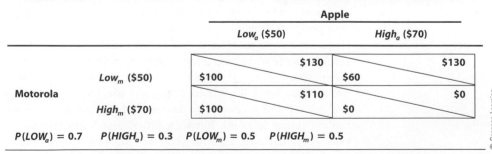

		Apple	
		Low_a ($50)	$High_a$ ($70)
Motorola	Low_m ($50)	$100 / $130	$60 / $130
	$High_m$ ($70)	$100 / $110	$0 / $0

$P(LOW_a) = 0.7$ $P(HIGH_a) = 0.3$ $P(LOW_m) = 0.5$ $P(HIGH_m) = 0.5$

Note: Column-player payoffs are above diagonal. Row-player payoffs are below diagonal.

---

[23]Note that the project in the southeast cell of Table 15A.5 is canceled because of mutual early warnings of high cost and therefore a projected operating loss.

[24]This expected value is calculated as (0.5×0.7) $50 million + (0.5×0.3) $10 million = $19 million.

Clarke-Groves Incentive-Compatible Revelation Mechanism

One such revelation mechanism is known as the IC mechanism.[25] The path-breaking idea was that to create appropriate incentives for asymmetric cost (or demand) revelation in a partnership, each party's revelation should trigger an imposition of the expected costs on (and the forgone profit opportunity losses suffered by) the other partners. In this way, the maximizing incentives of each of the asymmetrically informed partners could be made compatible. For our PC product development example, Table 15A.5 indicates the revenue shares each partner would receive under a Clarke tax mechanism. The row player Motorola gets the below-diagonal payoffs in each cell, and the column player Apple gets the above-diagonal payoffs in each cell.

After the other party's expected costs are covered, each partner's payoff is then recalculated as the residual or net revenue share from all non-canceled projects triggered by its own cost revelations. To illustrate, if Motorola reveals Low_m cost, the current project will proceed independent of Apple's cost, and Motorola will realize $88 million, which is $180 million total partnership revenue minus the $92 million expected cost of Apple:

$$\text{Expected Net Revenue Share (Low for Motorola)}$$
$$= \$180 \text{ million} - [(0.7 \times \$80 \text{ million}) + (0.3 \times \$120 \text{ million})]$$
$$= \$88 \text{ million}$$

This figure appears in the third column of Table 15A.6. However, if Motorola announces $High_m$ cost, the project is canceled whenever Apple detects early warning signs that its own cost is $High_a$. Consequently, should Motorola decide to reveal high cost when low cost is present, its net revenue would fall from $88 million to 0.7 ($180 million − $80 million) + 0.0 ($180 million − $120 million) = $70 million, also listed in the third (Net Revenue Shares) column of Table 15A.6. Motorola's net revenue share declines because of a zero probability of realizing the $60 million revenue share in the northeast cell of Table 15A.5. The false overstatement of cost by Motorola results in that project being canceled, and everyone loses. Under a Clarke tax mechanism, not just actions but information revelations themselves have consequences. And, as we shall see, building these consequences into a reimbursement system can induce the true revelation of partnership costs.

The importance of the discovery of such IC revelation mechanisms can hardly be overemphasized; they have led to many path-breaking private sector and public policy applications. Clarke first developed the concept in the context of the true demand revelations needed in consumption partnerships to finance a jointly consumed park, pool, or playground.[26] The demand revelation problem in assessing an optimal user tax share in a consumption partnership is analogous to the cost revelation problem in assessing an optimal profit share in a business partnership.

optimal incentives contract An agreement about payoffs and penalties that creates appropriate incentives.

An Optimal Incentives Contract

To organize a joint venture or partnership around a Clarke–Groves revelation mechanism usually involves the implementation of a so-called **optimal incentives contract**.

---

[25]This revelation mechanism is also referred to as the Clarke–Groves revelation mechanism after Ted Groves, who formalized the concept, thereby showing a different connection to William Vickrey's earlier work on IC auction design.

[26]To build the appropriate size urban park or swimming pool requires private information about use value and willingness to pay. However, if one asks potential demanders who assume their answer will determine their tax share, the respondents will understate their willingness to pay. See Edward Clarke, *Demand Revelation and the Provision of Public Goods* (Boston: Ballinger, 1980). For more on the applications of revelation mechanisms, see R. Cornes and T. Sandler, "Clarke's Demand-Revealing Mechanism," *Theory of Externalities, Public Goods, and Club Goods* (New York: Cambridge University Press, 1986), pp. 105–108; and Hal Varian, *Intermediate Microeconomics*, 8th ed. (New York: Norton, 2009).

TABLE 15A.6 EXPECTED NET PROFIT SHARES (MILLIONS) WITH TRUE COST REVELATION UNDER AN OPTIMAL INCENTIVES CONTRACT

	PROBABILITY	APPLE		
		NET REVENUE SHARES	PROJECTED COSTS	NET PROFIT SHARES
Low_a	0.7	$120	$80	$28
$High_a$	0.3	$ 65	$60	$ 1.5
Expected Value		$103.5	$74	$29.5

	PROBABILITY	MOTOROLA		
		NET REVENUE SHARES	PROJECTED COSTS	NET PROFIT SHARES
Low_m	0.5	$88	$50	$19
$High_m$	0.5	$70	$49	$10.5
Expected Value		$79	$49.5	$29.5

© Cengage Learning

Each party agrees in advance to a set of partnership net revenue shares associated with the expected payoffs from a revelation mechanism (see the third column of Table 15A.6). The important thing to appreciate is that the problem of independently verifying asymmetric information has not gone away. A third party attempting to enforce the contract (e.g., a U.S. district court) would still have just as much trouble verifying the claims for cost reimbursement arising under this contract as the parties had in trying to verify their own partner's cost. Entering into a partnership incentives contract does not escape the asymmetric cost information problem. Instead, the revelation mechanism creates incentives for a **self-enforcing reliance relationship** between the partners, not unlike the incentive-compatibility constraint we described in Chapter 15 as characterizing the optimal incentives contract between owner-principals and manager-agents.

self-enforcing reliance relationship A noncontractual, mutually beneficial agreement.

© nostalgie/Shutterstock

INTERNATIONAL PERSPECTIVES

Joint Venture in Memory Chips: IBM, Siemens, and Toshiba[27]

IBM once entered into an agreement with Siemens and Toshiba to co-produce computer memory chips. At the same time, AMD and Intel announced similar joint ventures to develop flash memory chips with Fujitsu and Sharp, respectively. Flash chips retain the information needed to restart computer operating systems when the power is interrupted. In all three cases, the Japanese firm will contribute its superior manufacturing capability, and the American and German firms will contribute their product design and innovative research capabilities.

The key question in such joint ventures is whether the Western companies will simply give away their technological knowledge while their Japanese partners deliver little asymmetric information in exchange. To ensure an evenly balanced partnership, the manufacturing know-how of the Japanese will be dissected, and production cost information under various market conditions will be revealed and analyzed by the joint venture partners.

[27]Based on "Pragmatism Wins as Rivals Start to Cooperate on Memory Chips," *Wall Street Journal* (July 14, 1993), p. B1.

Incredibly, the structure of incentives underlying Table 15A.6 is fully capable of inducing the partners to reveal their true costs; each would be worse off not doing so. We have already seen how Motorola would be worse off overstating its cost. Similarly, if Apple were to overstate its cost, profitable projects in the southwest cell of Table 15A.5 would be canceled. Rather than realizing 0.5 ($130 million) + 0.5 ($110 million) = $120 million from the good fortune of incurring Low_a cost, Apple would instead realize only 0.5 ($130 million) = $65 million, which fails to cover its own low-cost realization of $80 million. In addition, this false overstatement of cost and the cancellation of the profitable project in the southwest cell reduces Apple's expected receipts from the partnership to just (0.5 × 0.7) $130 million + (0.5 × 0.3) $130 million = $65 million, whereas with true revelation it realizes $103.5 million: (0.5 × 0.7) $130 million + (0.5 × 0.7) $110 million + (0.5 × 0.3) $130 million = 0.7 ($120 million) + 0.3 ($65 million) = $103.5 million. Truth-telling dominates false revelation for both partners.

We can now also explain why both Apple and Motorola would adopt an optimal incentives contract that credibly commits each partner to a true revelation of asymmetric cost information. Apple realizes an expected net profit with true revelation of $103.5 million expected receipts minus expected costs of $74 million (i.e., $29.5 million), shown in the last column of Table 15A.6. And similarly, Motorola realizes an expected net profit of $79 million expected receipts minus $49.5 million expected costs (i.e., $29.5 million). Each of these amounts equals the $29.5 million joint profits potentially available in the original simple profit-sharing contract of Table 15A.4. However, recall that each party knows in advance that the other party will have private information about cost overruns. Each could therefore predict that the simple profit-sharing partnership would lead to cost overstatement, cancellation of the mixed-cost projects, and loss of value. This proactive reasoning implies that only the mutual low-cost outcome in Table 15A.4 will escape cancellation and actually generate profit. Therefore, only a much smaller expected profit—that is, just 0.5 × 0.7 ($50 million) = $17.5 million—is assured by the simple profit-sharing contract. This smaller amount from simple profit sharing is what rational parties choosing among partnership contracts would compare to the $29.5 million expected net profit from an optimal incentives contract.

The application of IC revelation mechanisms and optimal incentives contracts has led to many exciting new types of partnership procedures. The same principles also underlie the concept of an efficient breach of contract in the economics of contract law. When one partner breaches a contractual relationship, the legal remedies take into account the opportunities forgone and expectation damage costs imposed on the partner who does not breach.[28] These concepts have become a key for achieving partnership or joint venture success in both small firms and large corporations under asymmetric information.

Implementation of IC Contracts

efficient contract breach A set of incentive-compatible procedures for awarding expectation damages in breach-of-contract suits.

IC contracts are implemented with contingent claims contracting, a standard form of instrument for sophisticated business relationships. The parties agree on the projected probabilities for the various levels of cost, the likely auditable joint operating profit for the partnership, and the unobservable reimbursable cost to each party in each contingency. These agreements form the contract expectations and define the contract damages should unforeseen events cause either party to engage in a so-called *efficient breach* of the contract.

---

[28]An excellent supplemental reading on efficient breach of contracts is R. Cooter and T. Ulen, *Law and Economics*, 5th ed. (Glenview, IL: Pearson Addison-Wesley, 2007).

The cost information revelation leads to efficient cancellation or go-ahead decisions. More generally, of course, consequences other than project cancellations can result from the information revelation of one partner. For example, the information revealed in a partnership can cause an expansion or a contraction of the R&D, prototype development, marketing research efforts, and so on, of the other partner. And any revelation of misinformation prevents what both can agree in advance would be the optimal course of action in each contingent state. It is those expected opportunity losses that the IC mechanism then deducts from joint profits to find IC contract receipts. To write such a contingent claims partnership contract presents a big challenge for the negotiating team of corporate attorneys, but the improved performance of the partnership is worth many times the legal expense.

Finally, you may have already noticed one further issue. The sum of the individual net revenue shares in every cell of Table 15A.5 when the project goes ahead is greater than $180 million, the projected operating profit from the partnership. Thus, IC revelation mechanisms generally fail to break even; instead, they "break the budget." Specifically, if both parties declare high cost, each is entitled to an IC payout ($100 million in the case of Motorola and $130 million in the case of Apple) that together break the budget. To

© nostal6ie/Shutterstock

INTERNATIONAL PERSPECTIVES

Whirlpool's Joint Venture in Appliances Improves upon Maytag's Outright Purchase of Hoover[29]

Sometimes joint ventures occur in the phasing out of a business because this may increase the value of the company's assets relative to making an outright sale. As a potential buyer of Philips's European appliance division, Whirlpool sought access to more private information than due diligence by its merger and acquisition attorneys could uncover. Philips had a consumer franchise of nine appliance brands and a pan-European network of retail dealers who were second only to Electrolux in market share. But like other intangible assets (e.g., pivotal human resources and technical know-how), brands and distribution relationships are notoriously hard to value. In a new corporate organization and culture, could the Philips brands be redeployed without Philips's extremely strong reputation in European electronics? Would the fragmented network of independent dealers remain loyal once Whirlpool's name was substituted for Philips? And most importantly, what cost savings could be realized by sourcing all of the design, procurement, and production of Whirlpool and Philips components globally to achieve economies of scale?

These questions were best answered by a joint venture in which Philips retained a 47 percent ownership stake, and Whirlpool immediately assumed management control in exchange for $381 million. After both parties shared cost and demand information for three years and fully assessed potential value, the remainder of the business was sold to Whirlpool for $610 million.

In contrast, Maytag satisfied its strategic plan to enter the European market by purchasing outright the Chicago Pacific Corporation, whose Hoover Appliance division had a substantial retail dealer network in Britain. However, Maytag knew little about the growing retail power of superstore chains near British shopping malls and still less about the marketing research on British households. Consequently, Maytag stumbled from one promotional blunder to another and eventually sold the Hoover European subsidiary at a $130 million loss. Again, with carefully designed incentives, a joint venture could have elicited the revelation of valuable asymmetric information for the greater success of Maytag's European initiative.

---

[29]Based on A.Nanda and P.Williamson, "Use Joint Ventures to Ease the Pain of Restructuring," *Harvard Business Review* (November/December 1995), pp. 119–128.

emphasize the generality of this result, the particular example Table 15A.6 has been constructed to exhibit "budget breaking" in each contingent event, except cancellation. More typically in real-world IC contracting, some cells would exhibit surplus, and others would exhibit deficit. Still, the deficit cells may arise first. What is the partnership to do? What implementation procedure can handle this deficit budgeting problem?

Recall that both partners have substantially greater net profit shares under the IC contract ($29.5 million) than the expected profit from a simple profit-sharing agreement ($17.5 million). Eliciting true information revelation really does have value, and both parties therefore would be willing to make *ex ante* commitments to cover such a deficit in the partnership. Examining the third column of Table 15A.6 shows that Apple's expected net revenue share is $103.5 million, while Motorola's is $79 million. Consequently, $182.5 million − $180 million = $2.5 million per period (perhaps $2.5 million/0.05 = $50 million as a capital sum to cover the perpetual expected deficit) must be posted as a bond to implement the IC contract procedure. Each partner would be asked to establish its credible commitment to the IC contract partnership by investing $25 million *ex ante* to achieve an increase in expected profit of ($29.5 million − $17.5 million) per period, worth perhaps $12 million/0.05 − $240 million.[30] Although the perfect alignment of incentives is then lost, these IC contracts clearly can improve partnership performance for value-maximizing managers.

SUMMARY

- First-come, first-served is a mechanism design for servicing a queue that reduces seller revenue because of predictable congestions and expected waiting time. Last-come, first-served introduces leave-and-return transaction costs and therefore also reduces seller revenue.
- Stratified lotteries and auctions can relieve congestion and reduce transaction costs in the queue, raising seller revenue.
- Auction design choices are multifaceted but at the simplest level always include who pays, what amount, and how the winner is determined. Simple auction types are English ascending-price auctions, Dutch descending-price auctions, first-price sealed-bid auctions, and second-highest sealed-bid auctions.
- Auctions also differ in the resale opportunities available to the participants. Common-value auctions have thick resale markets where the items can be easily resold at a consensual fair market value. Private-value auction items have no common

resale value and instead involve assets with differing valuations to the auction participants.
- The winner's curse implies that strategic underbidding is rational when the seller or other buyers have asymmetrically advantaged information about a common-value auction.
- Open bidding is a procedure for posting the offers in multiple rounds with cancellation and modification privileges to induce auction participants to pool their information about estimates of value. Open bidding reduces the winner's curse and raises expected auction revenue in common-value auctions.
- What simple auction types raise the greatest expected revenue for the seller-auctioneer depends upon the common-value or private-value nature of the item being auctioned and on the auction participants' risk aversion.
- Dutch auctions and first-price sealed-bid auctions have identical information structures and identical bidding strategies, and therefore they generate identical expected revenue to the seller.

---

[30]Technically, the investment to cover projected deficits will change an individual household's behavior unless we impose the restriction of quasi-linear preferences. In company settings, this assumption is plausible; see Varian, *op. cit.*, pp. 274–277.

- Relative to Dutch or first-price sealed-bid auctions, English ascending-price and second-highest sealed-bid auctions raise the seller's expected revenue in common-value auctions for items such as crude oil, forest logging rights, and aircraft because they encourage the most pooling of bidder information. In private-value auctions, bidders who are risk averse offer higher bids and therefore generate more auctioneer-seller revenue in Dutch and first-price sealed-bid auctions.

- To escape adverse selection and elicit high-quality auction goods necessitates some sort of bonding mechanism to induce self-enforcing reliance relationships between buyers and sellers. Warranties, independent appraisals, leases with a high residual, collateral, irrevocable money-back guarantees, contingent payments, and brand names all provide assurance to buyers that the seller will not misrepresent the product quality. Such hostage mechanisms support asymmetric information exchange.

- Joint ventures and partnerships face an asymmetric information problem in reimbursing each member for privately known costs that are unverifiable. In both demand revelation problems for funding public goods and cost revelation problems for partnerships, each member has an initial incentive to falsely reveal (overstate) his or her private (cost) information.

- Both understatement of demand and overstatement of cost result in the cancellation of profitable partnership projects. Yet each individual member may be better off with exaggerated cost reimbursement than with a simple profit share. Preserving the maximum value of the partnership requires an IC revelation mechanism.

- Under an IC mechanism, partners making cost revelations incur the expected costs imposed on and opportunities forgone by the other partners. Each partner agrees that not just actions but information revelations themselves have consequences for profit-share payout. Such a governance mechanism must be self-enforcing, however, because the asymmetric information problem has not disappeared. A court would have just as much trouble verifying the claims for reimbursement under this incentives contract as it would under the initial simple profit-sharing contract.

- IC revelation mechanisms do motivate partners to reveal their true projections of costs.

- IC revelation mechanisms are implemented through contingent claims contracts and often require *ex ante* posting of a bond to solve the breaking-of-the-budget problem. Quasi-linear preferences are then required to assure a unique and efficient IC revelation mechanism.

Exercises

Answers to the exercises in blue can be found in Appendix D at the back of the book.

1. What auction design features reduce the winner's curse and therefore reduce strategic underbidding?

2. Why don't airlines and hotel chains worry about self-destructive cannibalization of their own higher-priced live sales when they list seats and rooms for sale in the virtual marketplace on Priceline.com?

3. What advantage does eBay's open bidding provide to sellers? Why?

4. Which two of the following are most clearly common-value auction items: Viper sports cars, electricity, patent licenses, T-bills, antiques, or fine art?

5. If some auction participants for crude-oil field leases have estimates that the oil in the ground is worth $1.2 million, $1.3 million, or $1.5 million with certainty; other auction participants have estimates that the same oil field lease is worth $1.1 million, $1.3 million, or $1.5 million with certainty; and a third group of auction participants have estimates that the same oil field lease is worth $1.1 million, $1.2 million, or $1.3 million, and all three forecasts contain the true common value, what is that value? How would you as auctioneer-seller design an auction to reduce strategic underbidding and realize this true value?

6. Distinguish common-value and private-value auctions; provide examples of each. Distinguish descending-price (Dutch) auctions and ascending-price (English) auctions; provide examples of each.

7. You are developing a bidding strategy for an ascending-price sealed-bid auction of a crude-oil field worth between $1 million and $51 million to the seller. Because your extraction costs are lower, your value is 20 percent greater than the seller's value. The seller faces transaction costs of conducting the sale and therefore will not accept an offer unless it exceeds his or her personal value. How much should you bid?

8. How can a second-highest sealed-bid ascending-price auction design diminish the "winner's curse" and reduce the strategic underbidding that arises in highest-wins-and-pays typical ascending-price auctions with sealed bids?

9. Some newly issued T-bills are auctioned by discriminatory pricing in Dutch auctions, whereas other newly issued T-bills are auctioned by uniform-price second-highest sealed-bid ascending-price auctions. Which auction design is more like private placement of corporate newly issued bonds and IPO stock? Which auction design is more likely to increase seller revenue?

10. Fast Second and Speedo are trying to decide what to bid for a license in a cellular phone auction where the possible values of the new license are $10 million, $20 million, $30 million, $10 million, $50 million, and $60 million, each equally likely. The auction is single-round sequential, both parties have exactly the same value for the asset but neither knows its true value from the possible distribution (i.e., a so-called common-value auction), and Fast Second gets to bid after Speedo.

    Each company has invested in marketing research about the value of the license, which can come out one of two ways: possible values of $20, $30, or $50 million, or possible values of $20, $40, or $60 million. Whichever result arises is known to be 100 percent accurate (i.e., the license is worth one of the three identified amounts with certainty). Speedo proceeds with a bid of $33 million. Fast Second has marketing research saying that the value of the license is $20, $40, or $60. How much should Fast Second bid?
    Set up the Bayesian probability rule for Fast Second of BAYES PROB ($40 million value/Forecast of $33 million bid by Speedo).

11. Show that not just overstatement but also understatement of cost is dominated by truth-telling in the joint venture of Motorola and Apple.

12. What payoffs would be required under an optimal incentives contract, similar to Table 15A.6, if the cost overruns at Apple became as likely as those at Motorola?

13. In Appendix 15A, we have assumed bidder's valuations are independent, but suppose they are affiliated. That is, suppose on eBay you wish to affiliate with those who think Beatles albums are valuable, and that affects your own personal valuation. How will this change from independent to affiliated valuations affect bidding strategy on eBay? Do you observe such behavior on the site?

Case Exercises   ## Spectrum Auction

Continuing the analysis of broadband spectrum auctions from the appendix, suppose that two bidders know that the net present value of the rights to transmit PCS services in Louisville is a random variable uniformly distributed from $10 million to $60 million with six discrete values possible: $10 million, $20 million, $30 million, $40 million, $50 million, and $60 million. Also assume that both parties value the asset identically, making it a common-value auction. In advance, each company conducts marketing research experiments to narrow the possible outcomes and thereby better inform its own bid. Suppose Wireless Co.'s marketing research results exclude the two tails of the uniform distribution of possible values (i.e., $10 million and $60 million) as well as $40 million. Similarly, PCS PrimeCo conducts its own marketing research that excludes $10 million, $30 million, and $50 million as possible outcomes for the Louisville service area.

Questions

1. What should Wireless Co. bid in a single-round sealed-bid common-value auction? What should PCS PrimeCo bid in this same auction?
2. If Wireless goes first in a sequential posted-price auction with multiple rounds to follow, what should PCS PrimeCo respond in Round 2? In Round 3, will Wireless then wish to amend its earlier bid? Why or why not?
3. What auction design would be in the seller's best interest: single-round sealed-bid or multiple-round open bidding?
4. Identify other factors that could affect the optimal auction design.

Debugging Computer Software: Versioning at Intel[31]

Debugging has been a way of life in the computer industry from its inception. Indeed, the origin of the term *debugging* derives from the daily process of removing dead moths from the thousands of electronic tubes in the ENIAC, the first electronic computer. Every piece of computer hardware or software ever shipped has likely had logic faults. Indeed, most popular software programs contained thousands of known "bugs" in their first-generation products. In 1994, incomplete debugging of the floating-point division calculator in the Pentium I computer chip caused a massive product recall that cost Intel $475 million dollars. In 2010, a $700 million product recall bug was found in an access chip to Intel's Sandy Ridge Quad Core processor. In extremely data-intensive environments, the design flaw caused the chip performance to degrade over time—for example, in the digital video processing for the highest-end PCs of HP and Dell.

Why do computer component manufacturers release products with known bugs? One obvious answer is that delayed release may allow competitors to preempt the market with new technologies that render your product obsolete. Another important answer is a central insight of managerial economics that everything worth doing is not necessarily worth doing well. Computer design and manufacturing firms face a rising marginal cost of correcting thousands of bugs detected by their beta testing processes. At some point, each firm must balance the lost sales and replacement costs from product recalls against the ever-increasing cost of design perfection from more debugging.

A somewhat surprising third answer may, however, hold the key: fixing bugs in subsequent generations of software sells upgrades. Early Microsoft Windows products had a nasty bug that caused the program to crash with the finality of a hopeless error message—"unrecoverable application error." Microsoft fixed the bug and proceeded to sell millions of copies of the upgrade. Bugs in programs limit their durability, and in technology businesses the selling of upgrades is a part of the business plan. Hal Varian, chief economist of Google, calls this practice "versioning." Of course, Microsoft Windows operating system has built the ultimate powerhouse business out of selling upgrades.

Questions

1. Discuss the practice of selling upgrades as a mechanism design.
2. What dual objectives are served when a breakthrough new product is not equipped with all its known value-added features?
3. How does the versioning of products address the problems of a durable goods monopolist who must compete with his or her own discounted used products that are in good working order?

---

[31]Based on "It's Not a Bug, It's a Feature," *Forbes* (February 13, 1995), p. 192; "Intel Finds Design Flaw," *Wall Street Journal* (February 1, 2011), p. B1.

Government Regulation

CHAPTER PREVIEW

Managerial decisions designed to maximize shareholder wealth face many constraints. Some of these constraints arise from a business's moral social responsibilities. Other constraints take the form of laws or other legal obligations. A wide array of government regulations are constraining (e.g., prohibiting price fixing collusion) but in other cases enabling (e.g., protecting trade secrets). To make value-maximizing decisions, managers must fully understand the regulatory aspects of their environment. This chapter explores several types of regulatory issues: antitrust, business permitting, licensing and patents, and the cap-and-trade market-based approach to environmental regulation.

MANAGERIAL CHALLENGE
Cap and Trade, Deregulation, and the Coase Theorem

Professor Ronald Coase from the University of Chicago Law School received the Nobel Prize in Economics for his work on the relationship among property rights, transaction costs, and the role of government. Coase challenged the prevailing view that economic externalities, such as water, air, and noise pollution, could be resolved only through governmental action. Coase argued that externalities should often not be viewed as one party inflicting harm on another but rather as reciprocal imposition and receipt of side effects. For example, a steel fabrication plant might use the surrounding factory buildings to absorb noise from its production process. The owners of nearby old factories might tear them down to clear land for an amphitheater where less noise could attract more patrons.

The Coase theorem claimed that such reciprocal externalities could be resolved without government intervention if the transaction costs of arriving at a private voluntary bargaining solution were kept low. Coase argued the issue was one of the appropriate specification and assignment of property rights. For example, planes landing in Boston might need to avoid violating a sensible decibel-level entitlement assigned to property owners in Winthrop and Revere townships surrounding Logan Airport. Otherwise, tort damage claims would arise in the courts, and monetary compensation or other noise-proofing remedies would be awarded.

In air pollution control, this Coasian approach to allocating "rights to pollute" has now been adopted on nearly a worldwide basis. Under the conditions of the U.S. Clean Air Act, the Environmental Protection Agency (EPA) grants allowances for about 50 percent of the sulfur dioxide emissions from electric utility plants. Congress then gave polluters the right to trade these pollution allowances among themselves. For example, if dry cleaner already has emission levels at its plants that are within EPA bounds, it can sell its excess allowances. If Duke Power does not meet the emissions standards, it can choose either to buy the requisite pollution allowances or to install the needed pollution abatement equipment whichever is cheaper. The Chicago Board of Trade quickly created a market on which these pollution allowances are actively traded. Take a look at the auction prices for sulfur dioxide allowances (a component of acid rain) at http://www.epa.gov/airmarkets.

Interest in this so-called cap-and-trade approach, allowing market forces to operate in a constrained

MANAGERIAL CHALLENGE *Continued*

© PhotoLink/Photodisc/Getty Images

manner rather than relying on command-and-control regulation of pollution, continues to grow. After the successful U.S. development of emissions trading for sulfur dioxide in the 1990s, the European Union in 2005 introduced a carbon dioxide emissions trading system to address greenhouse gas emissions and global warming. Thin trading initially caused the market price of a ton of emissions from burning coal to rise almost as high as the cost of the coal itself. Since historically most baseline electricity comes from coal-fired plants, electricity prices rose steeply and then seesawed until regulatory institutions stabilized.

One desired consequence was that natural gas, which costs only slightly more than coal per 1,000 BTU but pollutes the environment with only half as much carbon dioxide emissions, became the fuel preferred by electricity generators. If adopted in the United States, the additional costs for a carbon dioxide emissions tax were projected by the U.S. Energy Information Administration to lower industrial output from 1 to 3 percent and GDP from 0.5 to 1 percent over the period 2012–2030.[1]

Today, with carbon emissions allowances trading for $10 per ton in California and in Europe, the optimal carbon tax has been estimated at $0.07 per gallon of $3.50 gasoline (a +2% price increase) or $3 per barrel of $80 crude oil (+4%), $0.008 per kWh of $0.12 electricity (+7%) or $14 per ton of $70 coal (+20%) and $0.41 per cubic foot of $4 natural gas (+10%). It is estimated that typical American households would pay from $226 to $726 in carbon taxes depending on their income and consumption habits.

Discussion Questions

- Contrast the United States' and the European Union's experiences with cap and trade.
- Why do electric utilities support cap-and-trade legislation?
- Why do you think the cap-and-trade bill for carbon dioxide has stalled in the U.S. House of Representatives even though electric utilities support the legislation?
- In order to reduce greenhouse gases (GHG) like carbon dioxide, would you support paying 10 percent more for electricity? 5 percent more? Why or why not? (For more on GHG, see the Case Exercises in Chapter 17.)

---

[1]"Cumulative Impact of House Cap-and-Trade Bill," *The Economist* (August 15, 2009), p. 24.

THE REGULATION OF MARKET STRUCTURE AND CONDUCT

Antitrust regulation is designed to increase competition by eliminating attempts to monopolize an industry (other than through better products or better management) as well as by attacking certain patterns of per se illegal conduct, such as price fixing and exclusionary contracts that foreclose competitor business.

Market Performance

Ultimately, what society would like is producers of goods and services who

1. allocate resources efficiently,
2. develop and quickly adopt new technologies that will result in lower costs, improved quality, or greater product diversity, and
3. operate in a manner that encourages *full employment*.

Market Conduct

A structure–conduct–performance model of the factors that influence market performance is illustrated in Figure 16.1, including the following:

1. Pricing behavior
2. Product decisions
3. Sales promotion and advertising policies
4. Research, development, and innovation strategies

Market Structure   Both market performance and market conduct depend on the structure of the particular market. The concept of market structure refers to three main characteristics:

1. The degree of *seller and buyer concentration* in the market, as well as the size distribution. Recall from Porter's 5 Forces model in Chapter 10 that seller concentration

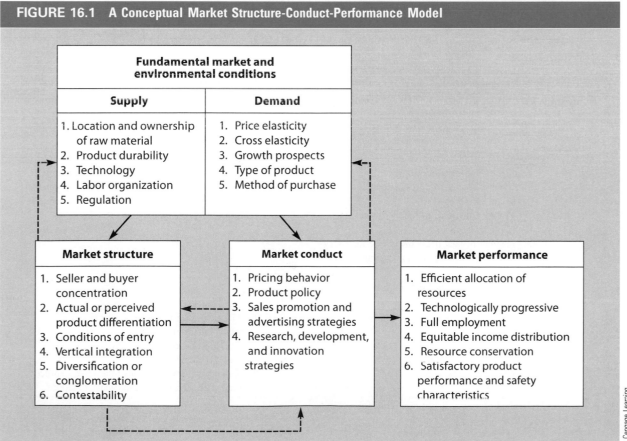

FIGURE 16.1   A Conceptual Market Structure-Conduct-Performance Model

Fundamental market and environmental conditions

Supply	Demand
1. Location and ownership of raw material 2. Product durability 3. Technology 4. Labor organization 5. Regulation	1. Price elasticity 2. Cross elasticity 3. Growth prospects 4. Type of product 5. Method of purchase

Market structure	Market conduct	Market performance
1. Seller and buyer concentration 2. Actual or perceived product differentiation 3. Conditions of entry 4. Vertical integration 5. Diversification or conglomeration 6. Contestability	1. Pricing behavior 2. Product policy 3. Sales promotion and advertising strategies 4. Research, development, and innovation strategies	1. Efficient allocation of resources 2. Technologically progressive 3. Full employment 4. Equitable income distribution 5. Resource conservation 6. Satisfactory product performance and safety characteristics

affects the intensity of rivalry, and buyer concentration affects the channel bargaining power to limit seller mark-ups.

2. *The degree of objective or perceived differentiation* between the products or services of competing producers.

3. The *conditions surrounding entry* into and exit from the market: When significant barriers to entry exist, competition may cease to become a disciplining force on existing firms. Exit barriers diminish the competitive discipline imposed by potential (as opposed to actual) competitors. Entry barriers allow established sellers to raise prices above the minimum average cost of production and distribution without motivating new sellers to enter the industry. Barriers to entry may be classified into four types: product differentiation, absolute cost advantage, economies of scale, and limited access to distribution. How these entry barriers arise, and their consequences are summarized in Table 16.1.

Contestable Markets

A perfectly contestable market is both easily accessible to potential entrants and easy to exit because capital investments are fully redeployable to alternative uses (e.g., trucks, patented inventions, information). In such markets, potential competitors continuously assess whether the incumbent's pre-entry price makes entry profitable. With freedom of

TABLE 16.1 TYPES AND CONSEQUENCES OF BARRIERS TO ENTRY	
TYPES	**CONSEQUENCES FOR NEW ENTRANTS**

A. Product differentiation barriers arise from
  1. Buyer preferences, conditioned by advertising, for established brand names.
  2. Patent control of superior product designs by existing firms.
  3. Ownership or control of favored distribution systems (e.g., exclusive auto dealerships).
	A. 1. New entrants cannot sell their products for as high a price as existing firms can.
	  2. Sales promotion costs for new entrants may be prohibitive.
	  3. New entrants may be unable to raise sufficient capital to establish a competitive distribution system.

B. Absolute cost advantages of established firm's production and distribution arise from
  1. Control of superior production techniques by patent or secrecy.
  2. Exclusive ownership of superior natural resource deposits.
  3. Inability of new firms to acquire necessary factors of production (management, labor, equipment).
  4. Superior access to financial resources at lower costs.
	B. 1. Costs of new entrants are higher than for existing firms, so even though existing firms may charge a price that results in above normal profits, new entrants may be unable to make even a normal profit at that price.

C. Economies of large-scale production and distribution (or sales promotion) arise from
  1. Capital-intensive nature of industry production processes.
  2. High initial start-up costs.
	C. 1. The entry of a new firm at a sufficient scale will result in an industry price reduction and a disappearance of the profits anticipated by the new entrants.
	  2. New firms may be unable to acquire a sufficient market share to sustain efficient operations.

D. Limited access to distribution channel	D. Closed shelf-space or Internet portals will necessitate massive slot-in investments and may prohibit certain business models.

entry and exit and fully redeployable assets, potential entrants are not worried about an incumbent's pricing reactions. If the profit disappears soon after initial entry, new entrants simply leave the industry. The ever-present possibility of profitable hit-and-run entry by potential competitors causes even a dominant incumbent firm to set prices no higher than average cost. As a result, contestable markets yield perfectly competitive market performance despite a market structure comprising just two or three firms.

Example

Why City-Pair Airlines Are Not Contestable Markets

Aircraft, of course, seem to be the classic redeployable asset subjecting air carriers to few if any barriers to exit. Put an aircraft on the resale market, and within several weeks one should be able to realize close to the full replacement value of the asset. However, several other features of the airline business do not meet the conditions of contestable markets. First, hub airport investments are sunk costs often not redeployable into other airline route structures. Second, the costs of switching from one airline to another are often raised by frequent flyer programs, flight schedules, and ticket promotions that restrict interline transfers. Finally, airline incumbents change prices two or three times a day, adjusting to competitive threats much more quickly than hit-and-run entrants can move in and out of city-pair markets. So, think of trucking (not airlines) as an example of a contestable market.

ANTITRUST STATUTES AND THEIR REGULATORY ENFORCEMENT

Federal antitrust laws in the United States were initially directed at the large stockholder trusts such as Standard Oil, American Tobacco, and several coal and railroad trusts. Under a trust agreement, the voting rights to the stock of a number of directly competitive firms were conveyed to a legal trust. The trust then managed the firms collectively, thereby maximizing profits, but high prices and restricted outputs resulted.

The Sherman Act (1890)

The Sherman Act's important provisions are brief, but they are wide ranging. It declares illegal "every contract, combination in the form of a trust or otherwise, or conspiracy in restraint of commerce among the several States, or with foreign nations ... [and] every person who shall monopolize, or attempt to monopolize, or combine or conspire with any other person or persons, to monopolize any part of the trade or commerce among the several States, or with foreign nations, shall be deemed guilty...."

The Clayton Act (1914)

The Clayton Act prohibited four anticompetitive business practices:

1. *Price discrimination* at wholesale was deemed illegal, except to the extent that it was based on differences in grade, quality, and quantity of the product sold.
2. Section 3 prohibited sellers from leasing or making "a sale or contract for the sale ... on the condition that the lessee or purchaser thereof shall not use or deal in the ...

commodity ... of a competitor." This prohibition against "*exclusive dealing* and *tying contracts*" was not absolute. It applies to the extent that the practice foreclosed customers from purchase agreements they desired to make.

3. Section 7, the *antimerger* section, barred any corporation engaged in commerce from acquiring the shares [or assets] of a competing firm or from purchasing the stocks of two or more competing firms, where substantial damage to competition results.

4. *Interlocking directorates*, defined as a case where the same person is on the board of directors of two or more firms, were declared illegal if they served to eliminate competition among parties who would otherwise compete.

Example

Why Miller Beer Is So Hard to Find in Mexico[2]

Mexico is the world's eighth largest beer market. Since the 1994 NAFTA agreement, Corona and Modelo beer exports grew fivefold to account for 11 percent of the U.S. market. Anheuser Busch owns a 50 percent non-controlling stake of the Modelo brewer. The Miller Brewing Co. has had little success in penetrating the Mexican domestic market. Modelo and FEMSA have 99 percent of the market. Some bars are paid to deal exclusively with Modelo. FEMSA owns large convenience store channels in Mexico, and Miller is not stocked on their shelves. These unreasonable restraints on trade have pricing consequences. A six-pack of Modelo Especial costs $4.60 in Mexico versus $1.80 for the best seller in Brazil and $2.20 for the best seller in Chile. Such exclusive dealing contracts that foreclose the Modelo customers from doing business with a competitor would be prohibited in the United States.

[2]Based on "Why Corona Is Big Here," *Wall Street Journal* (January 17, 2003), p. B1.

Example

Exclusionary Practices at Gore-Tex and Intel[3]

As a dominant firm with 81 percent market share in microprocessors in 2000 and 82 percent in 2010, Intel is subject to restraint on its marketing and sales practices that threaten retaliation against customers such as HP, Apple, and Dell who wish to purchase competing products from AMD. The EU fined Intel $1.45 billion in 2010, and as the FTC cannot impose fines, Intel settled in America with AMD for another $1.25 billion.

The makers of Gore-Tex with 70 percent to 90 percent of the wicking waterproof fabrics market are alleged to have threatened to withhold licensing its product to sportswear factories who bought competing fabric from Outdry Technologies (now owned by Columbia Sportswear) or eVent from General Electric. Columbia Sportswear and REI have joined other complainants in an FTC investigation of Gore's foreclosure of Columbia's wicking waterproof fabric business.

[3]Based on "Intel Slapped in Antitrust Case," *Wall Street Journal* (August 25, 2010), p. B1; "Gore-Tex Runs into Antitrust Probes," *Wall Street Journal* (June 22, 2011), p. B1.

The Robinson-Patman Act (1936)

The Robinson-Patman Act is summarized here:

1. Section 2(a) makes it illegal to discriminate in prices at wholesale when selling goods of "like grade and quality" where the effect may be to "substantially lessen

competition." A seller who is charged with price discrimination has two affirmative defenses enumerated in Section 2(b): First, the "cost defense" permits differentials in price that "make only due allowance for differences in the cost of manufacture, sale, or delivery." Second, the Act permits a lower price to be charged in one segment of the market to meet "an equally low price of a competitor."

2. Sections 2(d) and 2(e) prohibit the seller from offering secret rebates to one customer and not another. For example, Liz Claiborne cannot rebate 15 percent to the Gap without offering the same deal to department stores like Macy's.

The Hart-Scott-Rodino Antitrust Improvement Act (1976)

The Hart-Scott-Rodino Act requires companies with assets over $100 million to provide notification and information concerning any proposed merger to the Antitrust Division of the Department of Justice (DOJ) and to the Federal Trade Commission. Within 30 days, these agencies either challenge the proposed merger in federal court or allow the merger to be completed, possibly with some modifications. State attorneys general can also initiate federal antitrust suits.

Example

California's Class Action Suit against Microsoft Settled for $1.1 Billion

In January 2003, a U.S. district court in Washington found Microsoft guilty of maintaining a 92 percent monopoly of desktop operating system software by using anticompetitive practices. Two and a half years later in 2005, the defendant settled a class action lawsuit filed by the California attorney general on behalf of 13 million California individuals and businesses. Microsoft agreed to pay $5 to $29 vouchers for each California buyer who licensed either Windows 95 or Windows 98 between 1995 and 2001 as compensation for the alleged overcharges. The vouchers could be used for laptop, desktop, or tablet computers and for software from any computer company. Although the company stands to lose $1.1 billion, Microsoft in 2005 had $61 billion in cash and short-term investments.

Government agencies can use various methods to enforce the antitrust laws. Most antitrust cases are settled with *consent decrees* negotiated between the company and enforcement officials. Under a consent decree, a company agrees to take certain actions (or cease and desist from other actions) in return for the government agreeing not to seek additional penalties in the courts. In cases filed by antitrust agencies against a company, the courts may issue an *injunction* requiring (or prohibiting) certain actions by the company. The courts may also impose *fines* and, in certain instances, *prison sentences*.

In cases involving charges of monopolization, the courts may require *divestiture* of certain assets by the company. For example, in 2002 the U.S. Departments of Justice and Transportation as well as the Competition Commissioner of the European Union insisted that British Airways (BA) divest itself of 353 landing slots at London's Heathrow Airport if BA and American Airlines wished to merge. Rather than lose that many of its prized assets, BA decided to continue competing with American.

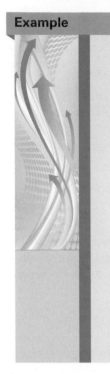

Example

Live Nation (Ticketmaster's) Acquisition of AEG Approved by Justice Department[4]

Ticketmaster, who has dominated the live music ticketing market with an 80 percent market share for 15 years, proposed in 2010 to acquire the largest concert promoter, Live Nation. Live Nation controls 142 venues worldwide including the 65,000-seat San Manuel Amphitheatre in Southern California. Concert promoter Anschutz Entertainment Group (AEG) controls 105 more venues, including the 20,000-seat Staples Center in Los Angeles and the 20,000-seat O2 Arena in London. In 2009, Live Nation launched a Paciolan ticketing system for venue owner/operators to bypass Ticketmaster and initiate their own self-ticketing.

The DOJ approved the merger between Ticketmaster and Live Nation with stipulations and a divestiture order. Ticketmaster/Live Nation was required to license its ticketing technology to AEG and refrain from selling any tickets to AEG venues after a five-year transition period. In addition, Live Nation was ordered to sell its Paciolan line of business to a third party, Comcast-Spectator. These structural remedies were taken to ensure additional ticketing competitors in live music with the reputation and credibility necessary to challenge Ticketmaster's dominance.

[4]Based on "Promoter Crowds Ticketmaster," *Wall Street Journal* (February 2, 2011) p. B1; Christine Varney, "Ticketmaster/Live Nation Merger Review and Consent Decree," Speech (March 18, 2010), Austin, TX.

ANTITRUST PROHIBITION OF SELECTED BUSINESS DECISIONS

Collusion: Price Fixing

Explicit agreements among competitors to fix prices along with other overt forms of collusion, such as market-sharing agreements, are per se illegal under the Sherman Act. That is, the courts generally declare such agreements prohibited, regardless of whether or not they cause obvious injury to competition.[5] During 2010, EMI Group, Sony BMG Music Corp., Bertelsmann Inc., Vivendi SA's Universal Music Group, and Warner Music Group Corp. were indicted for creating joint ventures (with 85 percent of the market) to conspire to inflate and maintain the price of digital music. The defendants argued that coordination was needed to deal with the double trouble presented by pirated music downloading (Napster and its successors) and Apple's wildly popular iTunes that had captured 72 percent share of the online song market. Such protestations were to no avail, and the defendants settled out of court with the Antitrust Division of the U.S. DOJ by agreeing to cease and desist as well as to pay large fines.

The EU is equally aggressive in prosecuting cartels. Between 2005 and 2011, EU Competition Commissioner Neelie Kroes levied enormous fines on 10 sets of manufacturers engaged in price-fixing conspiracies for elevators ($1.47 billion), NG switches ($1.11 billion), synthetic rubber ($768 million), flat gas ($728 million), hydrogen peroxide ($574 million), acrylic gas ($511 million), fasteners ($485 million), copper fittings ($466 million), laundry detergents ($452 million), and industrial bagging equipment ($431 million).[6]

[5]A few industries such as sugar and ocean shipping have been exempted by legislation from the antitrust laws and are legally permitted to jointly set prices and output.

[6]Based on "Europe's Antitrust Chief Defies Critics and Microsoft," *Wall Street Journal* (February 25, 2008), p. A1.

eBook Price Fixers Beware[7]

In September 2012, three book publishers (Hachette, Simon & Schuster, and Harper-Collins) settled with the Justice Department and agreed to end their restrictive pricing contracts with Apple's iBookstore. In exchange for 30 percent of the retail sales revenue, Apple had allowed the publishers to set the retail price of their titles distributed digitally as e-books. Beginning with the introduction of the iTablet in 2010, this agency pricing model for e-books displaced wholesale pricing whereby publishers sold their titles to Amazon, Barnes and Noble, Walmart, and department store chains for about half the projected retail price and then the bookstore retailer chose whatever markup they preferred.

As a result of the new pricing policies, final product prices for all e-book bestsellers rose from $9.99 to $12.99 and $14.99 or higher. The margins on e-books average $5.92/$12.99 = 46 percent versus $5.85/$26.00 = 22 percent on hardcover books (see Figure 16.2). Still, e-book sales doubled in 2011, and the industry was projecting continuing exponential growth when in April 2012 the DOJ Antitrust Division sued Apple and the five book publishers. The federal indictment alleged that Apple's contract foreclosed the publishers from selling the same title to any retail bookstore who set a lower price. Two publishers (Penguin and Macmillan) as well as Apple continue to appeal the proposed settlement, but Amazon has already begun to again discount some titles to $9.99.

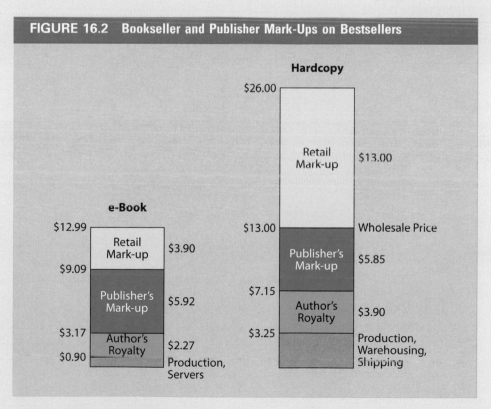

FIGURE 16.2   Bookseller and Publisher Mark-Ups on Bestsellers

Hardcopy

$26.00

Retail Mark-up — $13.00

$13.00 — Wholesale Price

Publisher's Mark-up — $5.85

$7.15

Author's Royalty — $3.90

$3.25

Production, Warehousing, Shipping

e-Book

$12.99

Retail Mark-up — $3.90

$9.09

Publisher's Mark-up — $5.92

$3.17

Author's Royalty — $2.27

$0.90

Production, Servers

Source: *Wall Street Journal*, September 12, 2011, p. B1.

---

[7]Based on "Get Ready for eBook Price Cuts in the Near Future," *Wall Street Journal* (September 10, 2012), p. B1; "Publishers Sued over eBook Price Collusion," *Financial Times* (April 12, 2012), p. A1; "U.S. Warns Apple, Publishers," *Wall Street Journal* (March 8, 2012), p. B1.

Mergers That Substantially Lessen Competition

market concentration ratio The percentage of total industry output produced by the 4, 8, 20, or 50 largest firms.

When industry sales are concentrated in a few hands, market conduct and performance are less likely to be competitive in nature. One widely used index of market concentration is the **market concentration ratio**. It may be defined as the percentage of total industry output (measured in terms of sales, employment, value added, or value of shipments) attributable to the 4, 8, 20, or 50 largest companies.

Data on market concentration ratios are regularly made available from the Census Bureau, based on the *Census of Manufacturers.*

Table 16.2 provides concentration ratios for selected industries. Some industries have become highly concentrated, such as breakfast cereals, turbine generators, aluminum, and lightbulbs. Some industries, such as hosiery, concrete block and brick, and sporting goods, are highly fragmented at the national level and are therefore expected to exhibit more competitive performance. Some industries become concentrated because of efficiencies. Consolidation mergers to reduce excess capacity occur regularly. Scale economies, learning curves, and volume discounts on components also provide possible efficiency gains from mergers. However, sizable merger premiums are often paid to target-firm shareholders. As a result, the returns to acquiring-firm shareholders are consistently negative.

Herfindahl-Hirschman Index A measure of market concentration equal to the sum of the squares of the market shares of the firms in a given industry.

Another important measure of market concentration is the **Herfindahl-Hirschman Index**, or *HHI*:

$$HHI = \sum_{i=1}^{N} S_i^2$$

where S_i is the market share of the ith firm and N is the number of firms in the industry. For example, in a relevant market consisting of just three firms, such as baby food (where Gerber has 70 percent, Beech-Nut has 16 percent, and Heinz has 14 percent

TABLE 16.2 CONCENTRATION RATIOS AND HERFINDAHL-HIRSCHMAN INDEX FOR SELECTED INDUSTRIES

SIC	INDUSTRY NAME	SHARE OF VALUE ADDED ACCOUNTED FOR BY THE 4, 8, AND 20 LARGEST COMPANIES IN EACH MANUFACTURING INDUSTRY			HERFINDAHL-HIRSCHMAN INDEX
		4-FIRM RATIO	8-FIRM RATIO	20-FIRM RATIO	
31123	Breakfast cereals	82	93	100	3,000
311511	Fluid milk	46	57	71	1012
31511	Hosiery and socks	35	45	64	318
32561	Soap and detergents	49	62	72	949
32411	Petroleum refining	47	67	92	809
32721	Flat glass	76	98	100	1,677
327331	Concrete block and brick	24	32	44	206
331315	Aluminum sheet, plate, and foil	75	89	98	2,286
333611	Turbine and turbine generator sets	88	91	96	2,403
33511	Electric lamp bulbs	90	94	98	2,848
32992	Sporting and athletic goods	24	32	46	199
33991	Jewelry and silverware	18	26	39	142

Source: *Census of Manufacturers*, U.S. Department of Commerce.

market share), the *HHI* is $70^2 + 16^2 + 14^2$, which is equal to 5,352. *HHI* has a maximum value of 10,000 and decreases as the number of firms (*N*) increases and as firm sizes become more equal. *HHI* values for selected industries are also shown in Table 16.2.[8]

Merger Guidelines (2010)

The FTC and the Antitrust Division of the DOJ in 2010 issued new merger guidelines. The *HHI* provides one factor the agencies use in deciding whether to challenge a proposed merger:

1. For markets with an *HHI* greater than 2,500, the government is likely to challenge a merger that increases the index by 100 to 200 points or more.
2. For markets with an *HHI* between 1,500 and 2,500, a merger challenge by the government is unlikely unless the index increases by 200 or more points. In practice, 87 percent of the mergers challenged by the FTC or DOJ in recent years had *HHI* over 2,400.
3. For markets with an *HHI* less than 1,500, the government is unlikely to challenge a merger.

A merger increases the *HHI* by two times the product of the market shares of the candidate firms. So, when Beech Nut (with 16 percent market share) and Heinz's baby food division (with 14 percent market share) wished to merge, the merger was challenged because the 5,352 point *HHI* changed by 448 points as follows:

$$HHI \text{ before} = S^2_{\text{Gerber}} + S^2_{\text{Beech-Nut}} + S^2_{\text{Heinz}} = 5,352$$
$$HHI \text{ after} = S^2_{\text{Gerber}} + (S_{\text{Beech-Nut}} + S_{\text{Heinz}})^2$$
$$= S^2_{\text{Gerber}} + (S^2_{\text{Beech-Nut}} + S^2_{\text{Heinz}} + 2S_{\text{Beech-Nut}}S_{\text{Heinz}})$$
$$= 70^2 \quad + (16^2 + 14^2 + 2 \cdot 16 \cdot 14)$$
$$= 5,352 + \Delta HHI$$
$$= 5,352 + 448 = 5,800$$

The 2010 merger guidelines emphasize that concentration calculations should be downplayed in favor of natural experiments and direct comparisons based on experience. Market definition is to be determined based on identifying a set of products that are reasonably interchangeable as indicated by "small but significant and non-transitory increases in price" (SSNIP) attributable to the merger. Other factors that are explicitly considered in the regulatory analysis include the likely failure of the to-be-acquired firm without the merger, the possible gains in efficiency or innovation for the (combined) firm, and the ease with which competitors have entered the industry historically.

In 2012, however, DOJ blocked a $550 million merger between Avery, the leading label maker, and 3M, the leading Post-it Notes manufacturer, even though Staples and Office Depot have recently entered both businesses with private label products.[9]

Monopolization

Companies acting alone can be charged under the Sherman Act with illegally attempting to monopolize a market or engage in monopolistic practices. However, proving such

---

[8]Not shown in the table is the most extreme case of all. Microsoft's 92 percent market share makes the *HHI* in software operating systems 8,526.

[9]"3M Drops Deal on Sticky Threat," *Wall Street Journal* (September 7, 2012), p. B1.

alleged violations of the laws often is quite difficult. Before the Microsoft case in 1998, the last large monopolization case brought by the U.S. antitrust officials resulted in the breakup of AT&T in 1984.

Example

Trustbusters Reappear: DISH Network–DIRECTV Merger Disapproved[10]

In 2007, the FTC prohibited a merger between Whole Foods Inc. and Wild Oats Markets in the premium natural and organic supermarkets, where these are the leading competitors. Similarly, in 2005 European antitrust authorities blocked the $41 billion merger of General Electric and Honeywell on market concentration grounds. The two companies dominate the market for jet engines for corporate aircraft. Again in 2011, the DOJ blocked a $39 billion proposed merger between AT&T and T-Mobile in wireless telephones.

In 2000, the FTC blocked a proposed merger between Heinz and Beech-Nut with 16 percent and 14 percent, respectively, of the baby food market. The rationale was that the *HHI* for baby foods measured 5,352, relative to the 1,800-point presumptive benchmark that causes concern. Behemoth Gerber has 70 percent of the market and is itself responsible for 4,900 of the 5,352 *HHI* points. The FTC did not accept the Heinz and Beech-Nut argument that together their two firms could realize scale economies, lower distribution and R&D costs, and thereby compete more effectively against the dominant firm.

Finally, Charlie Ergen's privately held EchoStar (DISH Network) launched a $26 billion bid for Hughes Electronics's subsidiary DIRECTV in 2007. DISH Network and DIRECTV were the top two satellite TV providers in the United States. Ergen argued that the relevant market included cable TV systems, with a combined industry share distribution as follows:

Comcast	33%
DIRECTV	17
Time Warner	17
DISH Network	13
Charter Comm.	10
Cox Comm.	10
HHI	**2,036**

The FTC and the Antitrust Division disagreed, defined the relevant market narrowly as satellite TV, and prohibited the merger.

Under the new merger guidelines in 2012, EchoStar was allowed to buy Hughes Communications. The two companies will realize cost efficiencies by removing redundant marketing and manufacturing costs. More importantly, however, even though industry concentration increases a great deal, the $1.35 billion merger will allow DISH Network to offer Internet-based programming in competition with DIRECTV who has already partnered with Time-Warner and other cable companies. The FTC now sees the proposed merger as enhancing competition in satellite-based entertainment.[11]

---

[10]Based on "Competition Policy," *The Economist* (May 3, 2007), p. 79; "Is the FTC Defending Goliath?" *BusinessWeek* (December 18, 2000), pp. 160–162; and "Murdoch Wins DIRECTV," *Wall Street Journal* (April 10, 2003), p. B1.

[11]Based on "EchoStar to Buy Hughes for $1.35 Billion," *Wall Street Journal* (February 15, 2011), p. B1.

Wholesale Price Discrimination

A large company that operates as a manufacturer or distributor in two (or more) different geographic (or product) markets and cuts wholesale prices in one market and not in the other market can be accused under the Robinson-Patman Act of engaging in illegal price discrimination. Differential pricing directly to final product customers is allowed (and often based on "what the market will bear") but not so in pricing to intermediate product resellers (wholesalers, distributors, etc.).

For example, the publisher Penguin Books paid a large judgment to independent booksellers after it was proved that Penguin offered volume discounts and other trade promotions to Barnes & Noble and Borders that were unrelated to the cost of serving those accounts. Similarly, six vending-machine companies sued Philip Morris, alleging that other distributors and retail merchants received rebates, buybacks, and promotional allowances intended to lower costs and allow the favored distributors to drive the complatants out of business. The Robinson-Patman Act was designed to prohibit precisely this kind of favoritism in wholesale trade.

Example

Potentially Anticompetitive Practices: Microsoft's Tying Arrangements[12]

Netscape alleged that software maker Microsoft used its dominant position in the market for computer operating systems to gain an anticompetitive advantage in the market for applications software such as Microsoft's Internet Explorer and Media Player. Microsoft tied its Internet access software (Microsoft Explorer) to sales of Windows 95, which provided the operating system for 92 percent of all the personal computers in the United States. Microsoft distributed Explorer free with every sale of Windows 95 to Compaq and Dell computers, priced Windows 95 without Explorer much higher, and threatened to remove the Windows 95 license if any Web browser other than Microsoft Explorer was preinstalled on the PCs that Compaq shipped.

Over four quarters in late 1996 and 1997, Microsoft's share of the Web browser market grew from 20 percent to 39 percent. By 1999, Netscape's share had fallen from a high of 84 percent to 47 percent, and Microsoft's product, accompanied by the allegedly anticompetitive practices, had resulted in a 53 percent share. Today Netscape has about 8 percent of a market that Internet Explorer dominates. Was this evidence of "substantial harm to competition" or just substantial harm to a particular competitor?

Tying arrangements that extend the monopoly power of a dominant firm in one market to another distinct product market are illegal per se. Because Microsoft's sales practices precluded Netscape from selling its Web browser, Microsoft was required under a consent decree to unbundle the two products and change its pricing practices. Nevertheless, in May 1998, the Justice Department and 20 state attorneys general filed suit, alleging illegal tying arrangements and other anticompetitive practices. Microsoft was found guilty of the alleged violations and ordered to cease and desist.

In 2004, the European Court of Justice ruled against Microsoft in a similar complaint first filed by Sun Microsystems that Microsoft illegally bundled its Media Player product with Windows. Windows software without Media Player was priced much higher. Because Microsoft has a dominant firm monopoly in PC operating systems, with market share that grew between 1997 and 2005 from 86 percent to 93 percent,

(continued)

the European Court of Justice ruled that Microsoft must unbundle its Media Player and offer the diminished-capability version of Windows more cheaply than the expanded-capability version. The Court levied a €497 million fine. In 2006, another €281 million fine was imposed for noncompliance. Finally, in 2009 Microsoft lost its final appeal and paid (with interest) €1.4 billion.

In a consent decree in late 2009, Microsoft also promised to offer until 2014 a ballot screen on PCs sold in the EU enabling the user to select Firefox or Mozilla rather than Internet Explorer as the Web browser. When 15M copies of Windows 7 shipped without said ballot screen, the EU put Microsoft on notice in 2012 of another $732 million fine. Clearly, losses of this magnitude suggest that assuring compliance with antitrust policy is an appropriate priority for shareholder wealth-maximizing managers.

[12]Based on "Browse This," *U.S. News & World Report* (December 5, 1997), p. 59; "U.S. Sues Microsoft over PC Browser," *Wall Street Journal* (October 21, 1997), p. A3; "Knowing the ABCs of the Antitrust Case against Microsoft," *Wall Street Journal* (October 30, 1997), p. B1; "Microsoft's Browser: A Bundle of Trouble," *The Economist* (October 25, 1997), p. 74; "Microsoft on Trial," *Wall Street Journal* (April 4, 2000), p. A16; "Microsoft Is Dealt Blow by EU Judge," *Wall Street Journal* (December 23, 2004), p. A3; "Europe's Antitrust Chief Defies Critics," *Wall Street Journal* (February 25, 2008), p. A1; and "Microsoft's Antitrust Fine: Sin of Omission," *The Economist* (March 9, 2012), p. 66.

Refusals to Deal

In general, a manufacturer can refuse to deal with any retail distributor who fails to follow company policies that are based on a legitimate business interest. However, this authority is subject to three limitations. First, the orders of a renegade discounter can be refused if and only if the manufacturer acts independently of compliant dealers whose sales at higher price points are suffering because of the increased competition (*United States v. GM*, 1966). Second, an explicit well-justified policy must be in place in advance; the manufacturer cannot pressure individual dealers, threaten suspension of shipments of new "hot" products, or offer to reinstate if the offending discounters agree to raise their prices (*FTC v. Stride Rite*, 1996).

Finally, manufacturers cannot "lock up" buyers of durable products by refusing to supply parts to independent service organizations (ISOs), especially if the ISO prices are far below the manufacturer's service prices. In *Eastman Kodak v. Image Technical Services* (1992), the Supreme Court argued that customers should be able to select independent service providers and nonwarranty repair from whomever they choose. Kodak's defense that ISO maintenance and repair failed to meet Kodak's quality standards was disproved by the evidence presented in Court.

Resale Price Maintenance Agreements

Manufacturers often wish to limit their distributors' flexibility to initiate price discounts. Minimum-price resale price maintenance (RPM) agreements prohibit retailers from cutting the price at which they resell the product below a manufacturer's suggested retail price (MSRP). Most such restrictions are illegal, especially when they appear motivated by the desire of competing retail dealers to reduce price competition. For example, Chevrolet dealers in Los Angeles once approached GM about using an RPM agreement to sanction the steep discounting of a "renegade" dealer in Orange County, California, who had markedly cut into their substantial profit margins. In *United States v. GM* (1966), the Supreme Court declared this anticompetitive practice illegal per se since it was motivated by an express desire to lessen price competition.

In *Leegin Creative Products, Inc. v. PSKS, Inc., DBA Kay's Kloset, 551, U.S. (2007)*, the Supreme Court reversed itself by allowing a rule of reason to apply to minimum-price

RPMs. The defendant Leegin of Dallas, Texas, makes upscale leather accessories somewhat like Coach leather goods. Kay's Kloset had a standard-form manufacturer–retailer contract to carry Leegin's products as an independent retail distributor. When Kay's Kloset persisted in discounting its leather accessories below the MSRP, Leegin cut off further shipments.

After several competing lower court decisions, for the first time ever, the U.S. Supreme Court accepted the argument that a manufacturer's business model can be so dependent on upscale positioning that a *rule of reason* should apply to minimum RPM agreements. In other words, such a manufacturer could legitimately refuse to deal with an independent retailer solely on the grounds that the retailer was in violation of the manufacturer's MSRP. Such a practice had previously been ruled a per se violation of the antitrust statutes—specifically, an anticompetitive restraint of trade. But in *Leegin* the Supreme Court ruled that third-party discounting of luxury goods could so severely damage a brand image and so completely discourage upscale services by full-price distributors that cutting off renegade discounters might in law reflect a legitimate manufacturer's interest. We discuss this landmark case further in a debate exercise at the end of the chapter.

COMMAND AND CONTROL REGULATORY CONSTRAINTS: AN ECONOMIC ANALYSIS

Federal, state, and local governments are involved in the regulation of business enterprises. Table 16.3 contains a partial listing of the federal regulatory agencies and departments. In addition to the Federal Trade Commission and Antitrust Division of the DOJ discussed earlier, many other agencies regulate business decisions. State regulations encompass a wide range of activities, including regulation of public utility companies and licensing of various businesses, such as health care facilities, and numerous professions, such as law and accounting. Local governments frequently set and enforce zoning laws and building codes. Regulatory constraints can be imposed in non-discriminatory ways on any set of similar business. For example, the European Union prohibits direct-to-consumer advertising of prescription drugs. These constraints can affect a firm's operating costs (both fixed and variable), capital costs, and revenues.

Example

Minimum Price RPM at Stride Rite and Leegin Creative Products[13]

In the late 1990s, Nintendo, New Balance Athletic, and Stride Rite all paid multimillion-dollar fines to settle charges that the manufacturers cut shipments to retail outlets that refused to charge the full MSRP. In Stride Rite's case, leading retailers were cut off if they refused to sell six styles of women's Keds at the full, undiscounted MSRP price of $45. Although Stride Rite insisted that it could suspend contracts with retailers who violated other company marketing policies and procedures, Stride Rite had refused to deal with only those particular dealers who discounted Keds. The courts ruled Stride Rite guilty of an anticompetitive business practice because the suspended dealers had been pressured to raise prices. Vertical requirements contracting between dealers and manufacturers about matters *other than resale price* is widespread and perfectly legal.

Occasionally, however, a manufacturer or distributor can demonstrate a "legitimate manufacturer's interest" in regulatory or industry standards that places a floor under

(continued)

the resale prices of its products (e.g., a rare book distributor). When one of these special exceptions is made and an RPM agreement is allowed, the new contours of antitrust policy rules are carefully examined.

Such an event occurred in June 2007. Leegin Creative Leather Products of Dallas cut off shipments of its high-end handbags, clutch purses, and key fobs to Kay's Kloset, an independent retailer who refused to stop discounting Leegin's products. Leegin argued that its business model to compete against Coach and Gucci relied upon its brand equity as an elite line of leather accessories and that this brand equity was tarnished beyond repair by discounting. On this reasoning, restrictive pricing agreements that enhance interbrand competition (between Leegin and Coach) could be allowed even though they diminish intrabrand competition (among Leegin's distributors). The U.S. Supreme Court agreed in part, ruling that RPMs should be subject to a "rule of reason" rather than being illegal per se. Leegin's policy of refusing to supply dealers who violate MSRP is now consistent with federal antitrust law but it remains illegal in several states (e.g., Kansas, New York, and California).

---

[13]Based on "StrideRite Agrees to Settle," *Wall Street Journal* (September 28, 1993), p. A5; "Retail Price Maintenance Policies," *Knowledge @ Wharton* (August 9, 2007); "Price Fixing Makes a Comeback," *Wall Street Journal* (August 18, 2008), p. B1; and *Leegin Creative Products Inc. v. PSKS Inc.*, 571 U.S. 877 (2007).

TABLE 16.3 PARTIAL LISTING OF FEDERAL GOVERNMENT REGULATORY AGENCIES

DEPARTMENT/AGENCY	PURPOSE
Environmental Protection Agency (EPA)	Regulates pollution of air, water, and land
Consumer Product Safety Commission (CPSC)	Protects against unreasonable risks of injury associated with consumer products
Equal Employment Opportunity Commission (EEOC)	Enforces laws on employment discrimination based on race, religion, and sex
Labor: Employment Standards Administration	Enforces minimum wage and overtime laws
Labor: Occupational Safety and Health Administration (OSHA)	Regulates safety and health conditions in the workplace
Labor: National Labor Relations Board (NLRB)	Regulates labor relations between employers and employees (and their unions)
Interstate Commerce Commission (ICC)	Regulates interstate surface transportation
Nuclear Regulatory Commission (NRC)	Regulates civilian use of nuclear energy
Securities and Exchange Commission (SEC)	Regulates issuance of new securities and trading of existing securities
Federal Communications Commission (FCC)	Regulates radio and television broadcasting and interstate telephone service
Federal Reserve System	Regulates commercial banks and bank holding companies
Agriculture: Food Safety and Inspection Service	Regulates meat and poultry industry for safety and accurate labeling
Health and Human Services: Food and Drug Administration (FDA)	Regulates safety of food, drugs, and cosmetics
Energy: Federal Energy Regulatory Commission (FERC)	Regulates interstate rates for transportation and sale of natural gas and transmission and sale of electricity
Transportation: Federal Aviation Administration (FAA)	Regulates safety of airplanes, airports, and airline operations
Transportation: National Highway Traffic Safety Administration (NHTSA)	Regulates safety of motor vehicles and tires
Labor: Mine Safety and Health Administration	Regulates safety and health in mines
Treasury: Office of Comptroller of the Currency	Regulates national banks
Treasury: Bureau of Alcohol, Tobacco, and Firearms (BATF)	Regulates manufacture and sale of alcoholic beverages, tobacco, explosives, and firearms

© Cengage Learning

The Deregulation Movement

Beginning in the late 1970s and continuing through the 2000s, the business environment moved toward relying less on government regulation and more on the marketplace to achieve desired economic objectives. For example, the Ocean Shipping Reform Act of 1998 deregulated freight rates for the 40-foot containers that ship apparel, consumer electronics, autos, and ores from Asia to the United States and ship computer software, forest products, and grain back to Asia. The one-way cost of $3,500 for a 6,000-garment

---

WHAT WENT RIGHT • WHAT WENT WRONG

The Need for a Regulated Clearinghouse to Control Counterparty Risk at AIG[14]

American International Group (AIG) sold $2 trillion ($2,000 billion) worth of loss protection against mortgage default risk to all the nation's commercial banks like Bank of America, Wells Fargo, and Wachovia. By referring to these financial derivative contracts as credit default *swaps* (CDSs), AIG escaped insurance industry regulation. When mortgage delinquency rates rose in 2007 from their historical average of one-half of 1 percent to 2 percent in the prime mortgage market and from 2 percent to 13 percent in the subprime mortgage market, AIG was immediately insolvent, meaning that its liabilities exceeded the present value of its future cash flows and other assets. In fact, with less than $100 billion in capital and $2,000 billion owed on its derivative positions to the banks, AIG was an insolvent counterparty of grand proportions. Only approximately 1 in 20 of the CDS contingent claim contracts under which AIG had promised to cover the mortgage losses of the nation's banks could be honored. Because of the systemic risk to the entire banking system, the Federal Reserve bailed out AIG in September 2008 and provided a guarantee that all AIG's losses would be paid.

How did such a violation of capital adequacy requirements in the regulation of banks and insurance companies ever happen? The full answer to the global financial crisis in financial derivatives from 2007 through 2009 is complex, but one key ingredient was the absence of a central clearinghouse counterparty and its associated margin calls as AIG's loss exposure worsened. In a typical derivative security transaction, investors are required to maintain escrow capital in their brokerage accounts to offset possible losses as the underlying security price on which they have written or purchased a future or an options contract moves against the position they have taken. Specifically, the clearinghouse which handles settlement of Chicago Board of Trade commodity futures on wheat and soybeans and crude oil or other exchange-traded derivatives requires these so-called margin calls in the escrow accounts of the brokers. And the brokers then in turn require additional escrow deposits from their clients. But not so in the case of AIG! Why not? One reason is that mortgage-backed derivative securities such as CDSs were not traded through a regulated exchange or settlement clearinghouse.

This crack in securities regulation happened even though at its peak the CDS market totaled $42 trillion, three times the size of the entire U.S. GDP! In 2003 the U.S. Congress took the advice of then Federal Reserve chairman Alan Greenspan to exempt mortgage-backed derivatives from these settlement and clearing procedures. Greenspan testified that such instruments could reliably transact over the counter (OTC) without the scrutiny of a regulated exchange or clearinghouse. But what was sacrificed was precisely the crucial margin requirements that the regulated clearing and settlement process would have imposed. Instead, AIG simply entered into OTC private contracts with the commercial banks that were seeking to lay off their mortgage default risk. With 20-to-1 leveraging of its capital to loss exposure, AIG became too big and too interconnected to the U.S. banking system to be allowed to fail. So, banks continued to buy AIG's mortgage default risk products even though it was perfectly obvious that if the housing market turned sour, mortgage holders would default in large numbers, thereby creating liabilities much bigger than AIG could possibly pay.

As the commercial banks' counterparty on thousands of CDS mortgage-loss-protection contracts, AIG would normally have been required to escrow additional capital as properties in California and Florida collapsed in value by 20, 30, and ultimately 45 percent. At these low asset values, mortgage borrowers found their real estate worth significantly less than their mortgage obligations, triggering massive numbers of loan defaults. In a regulated clearinghouse, AIG would then have been required to raise more capital to cover these impending losses, but instead it was allowed to simply write still more mortgage-loss-protection contracts. The Dodd-Frank Financial Reform Act of 2010 reverses the sadly mistaken 2003 decision that allowed mortgage-backed derivatives to "trade over the counter" with little regulatory supervision.

---

[14]Based on G. Gensler, "The Derivatives Debate," *Wall Street Journal* (April 21, 2010), p. A21; and L. Ausbel and P. Cramton, "Auction Design Critical for Rescue Plan," *The Economist's Voice*, Berkeley Electronic Press (September 2008).

container quickly declined to $1,500. Other consensus successes in deregulation have come in airlines, railroads, telephones, and natural gas pipelines. However, reduced regulatory supervision has at times proven problematic. Several large investment banks, commercial banks, and insurance companies (e.g., Bear Stearns, Lehman Brothers, Wachovia, and AIG) failed or were bailed out at taxpayer expense during the financial crisis of 2007–2009 when excessive leverage exposed these firms to massive default risk. Deregulation of the financial services industry in 2003 was at least partly to blame.

REGULATION OF EXTERNALITIES

In the normal course of business, every firm faces decisions that impose spillover costs upon third parties. The sharpest debate today is over air pollution, carbon footprints, and the need to reduce greenhouse gases to prevent catastrophic global warming. Both managers and the public have a keen interest in least-cost implementation of the kinds of remedies society mandates for controlling these externalities.

externality A spillover of benefits or costs from one production or utility function to another.

Externalities exist when a third party receives benefits or bears costs from consumption or production activities for which the market system does not enable it to receive full payment. Pollution by-products of trucking deliveries, for example, combine with certain atmospheric conditions and cause smog. In places such as Los Angeles, this smog may impose significant costs on asthmatic residents and some businesses such as the Pasadena Sightseeing Company. In short, externalities arise with any interdependency of household utility or firm production functions that is not reflected in market prices.

Only externalities that are not conveyed through the price system result in inefficiencies. Thus when mad cow disease causes preference for meat to shift from beef to chicken, the price of beef will fall and that of chicken will rise, making beef producers and chicken consumers worse off, and chicken producers and beef consumers better off, because of the price change. But all of these so-called **pecuniary externalities** have operated through the market price system, and they therefore pose no inefficiency.

pecuniary externality A spillover that is reflected in prices and therefore results in no inefficiency.

The legal doctrine of "coming to the nuisance" in *Spur Industries v. Del Webb Development*, S.C. Arizona, 1972 (108 Ariz. 178, 494 P.2d 700) illustrates why pecuniary externalities result in no inefficiency. If the land a developer purchases for a subdivision development is located next to a cattle feedlot, the price paid per acre will reflect the stench. The reduced price of the land internalizes the spillover effects. Later, if residents of the subdivision complain about the stench and the feedlot is declared a public nuisance, the developer may have to pay to relocate the cattle feeding business. Again, when external effects *are* reflected in prices, all affected parties directly participate in the transaction, and there is no inefficiency.

When non-pecuniary externalities are present, however, resources are likely to be misallocated. Producers or consumers are less likely to engage in an action that contributes to society's well-being if they are not fully compensated for all benefits generated. Similarly, in the case of negative externalities, a producer or consumer will likely overallocate resources to some production or consumption activity if part of the cost is shifted to others.

In general, an external cost should be reduced to the point where the marginal spillover costs saved by any further reduction just equal the marginal lost profits from the externality-generating activity. Similarly, an action that generates external benefits should be expanded to the point where the marginal benefits to all of society from such an expansion just equal the marginal costs. We illustrate the practical use of these concepts in addressing optimal taxes to reduce greenhouse gases in the next section. First, however, we explore Ronald Coase's insight that externalities are often internalized by private voluntary bargaining and subsequent contracting among a small number of affected parties.

Coasian Bargaining for Reciprocal Externalities

In many cases, externalities arise because of incompatible uses of air, land, or water resources. For example, late-night takeoffs and landings by FedEx jets may disturb sleep in houses around the airport. Feeding of thousands of animals in a small enclosed feedlot creates offensive odors in adjacent subdivisions. Agricultural land runoff of nutrient-rich water may adversely affect downstream intake by a bottled water plant. No adverse consequences would occur if either party were absent.

reciprocal externality
A spillover that results from competing incompatible uses.

Ronald Coase's famous article, "The Problem of Social Cost," illustrates a **reciprocal externality** between a spark-throwing railroad and a farmer with adjacent flammable fields. Coase's ingenious and intriguing claim was that under certain conditions involving full information and low transaction costs, the answer to the question, "Who's liable and therefore who should pay damages?" had no effect on the resource allocation decisions of these parties. In particular, if the railroad had the property right to throw sparks along its right-of-way, the trains scheduled down this track and the acreage planted along it would be exactly the same as if the railroad had the liability for all spark-induced fire damage along its tracks.

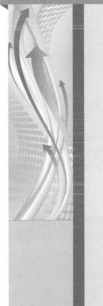

Example

Coase's Railroad

To see how this remarkable result arises through Coasian bargaining, consider the payoffs in Table 16.4. If the railroad has the property right, that is, Panel (a), the farmer incurs $600 worth of crop destruction per train per 10 acres planted along the tracks. Initially, the railroad ignores these external spillover costs and chooses an activity level of trains that maximizes its own profits, that is, two trains in the bottom row of Panel (a). The farmer would plant 10 rather than 20 acres along the tracks in order to earn $300 and avoid losing $800 (in the extreme southeast cell). If substantial impediments to bargaining were present, no further action would take place in an unregulated market environment. And yet, a mutually beneficial private voluntary bargaining opportunity would exist.

In particular, if the railroad were to cut back to one train, the farmer's profit would rise from $300 to $900, while the railroad's profit would decline by $500 (from $1,500 to $1,000). Accordingly, $501 is a minimally sufficient bribe to elicit the lower train-activity level, and $600 is the savings in fewer crops burned. Thus, Coase predicted that if the parties have few impediments to bargaining, the farmer would offer a side payment sufficient to abate the incremental (second) train and its spark hazard because the second train is worth less (to the railroad) than the incremental agricultural losses cost the farmer. Just how much the farmer will pay and how little the railroad will accept is not addressed, but one thing is clear: potential gains from trade do motivate a bargain to reduce railroad activity from two trains to one and crops acreage planted adjacent to the railroad from 20 to 10 acres.

Now, consider the case in which the railroad has the liability for spark-induced crop damages. Initially, the farmer prepares to plant 20 acres along the tracks as this activity level maximizes his or her independent profit (at $1,600). However, no trains are profitable with this much acreage in production because $600 in damages per train per 10 acres (i.e., $1,200 altogether) is owed when the railroad has $1,000 gross profit with one train, and $2,400 in damages is owed when the railroad offers to compensate the farmer for not only crop damages but also lost profit if the farmer would plant fewer acres. In particular, the railroad can offer the farmer $101 to plant 10 acres rather than 20 acres since the farmer's gross profit differs by only $100 (i.e., $1,500

(continued)

versus $1,600). If the railroad then also compensates the farmer $600 for one train's crop damage on 10 acres, the railroad owes $701 and earns a gross profit of $1,000.

Table 16.4, Panel (b), displays the gross profits before crop damages have been compensated. Shown in the middle row of Panel (b), the railroad offers the farmer compensation in excess of $100 (perhaps $101) to scale back the acreage planted from 20 acres, where farmer gross profit is $1,600, to 10 acres, where farmer gross profit is $1,500. This reallocation of activities is worth $600 in damage savings to the railroad. Again, Coasian bargaining leads the parties to agree upon one train and 10 acres.

Coase theorem A prediction about the emergence of private voluntary bargaining in reciprocal externalities with low transaction costs.

The **Coase theorem** states that reciprocal externality generators and recipients will choose efficient activity levels whatever the initial liability assignment. It makes no claim about the distributional consequences of reversing the direction of a liability assignment. Quite obviously, making the railroad liable in one instance, instead of asking the farmer to cover his or her own crop losses from burned fields in the other, results in quite different net profit outcomes. However, what the Coase theorem does assert is that in reciprocal externality settings with small numbers of affected parties, resource allocation as to the externality-generating and externality-receiving activity levels will be unchanged independent of the initial liability assignment; one train will be scheduled, and 10 acres will be planted.

Qualifications of the Coase Theorem

Some qualifications are in order, many of which Coase himself recognized. First, technical transaction costs of searching for and identifying the responsible owners and affected parties, of detecting violations of one's property rights, and of internally negotiating the side payments within a group of claimants must all remain low and be unaffected if liability assignment is reversed. Second, neither party can operate in a purely competitive

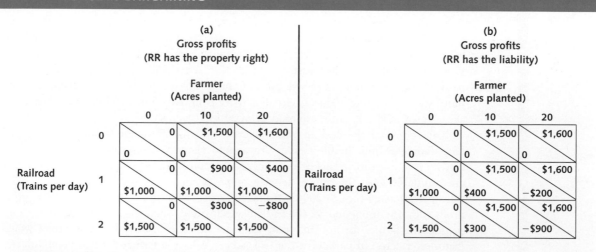

TABLE 16.4 COASIAN BARGAINING

market, for then the net profits required for side payments would be nonexistent. Third, and perhaps most important, one party quickly makes an offer the other is just willing to accept only when the information regarding the payoffs in Table 16.4, Panels (a) and (b), is complete, certain, and known to both parties.

When information is incomplete, private voluntary bargaining doesn't necessarily lead to resource allocation that is invariant to the direction of liability assignment. This qualification of the Coase theorem holds even if property rights are fully specified, completely assigned, and enforced at little or no cost. In all incompatible-use lawsuits involving asymmetrically known cost information, the precautionary actions of the plaintiff and the defendant have some bearing on the assignment of liability. For example, the parties in Coase's railroad example would avoid liability in part by employing spark arresters or land setbacks as long as the benefit in crop-loss savings exceeded the cost. However, the problem posed by asymmetric information is that some aspects of precaution are inherently unobservable or unverifiable (e.g., attentiveness to subtle signals of impending hazard) while others are observable but affect accident avoidance in a nondeterministic way (e.g., good brakes may lock up on rain-slickened roads when less effective brakes would not). Recall that unobservability and random disturbances together result in the problem of moral hazard, which we discussed in Chapter 15.

No incentive-compatible mechanism can both preserve the voluntary nature of the Coasian bargaining and also elicit true revelation of the unobservable damages. Therefore, contrary to the traditional understanding of the Coase theorem, disputants in reciprocal externality conflicts might be expected not to engage in private voluntary bargaining alone but rather to delegate the question of damage assessment and recovery to third-party court systems.[15] Civil procedural rules in an impartial court system can be seen as credible commitment mechanisms. Through these mechanisms potential disputants submit to liability assignments and wealth transfer remedies that motivate efficient accident avoidance despite frequently asymmetric information. So, the implication of the Coase theorem holds: Parties that are disputing over incompatible uses will contract their way to an efficient allocation of resources unless high transaction costs impede the required bargaining.

Impediments to Bargaining

Regulation will continue to have a role, however, because of impediments to bargaining. Several impediments are recognized in the legal system. Prohibitive notification and search costs (to identify absentee owners and notify all the affected parties) are the justification for certifying **class action suits** in the case of oil spills and other large-scale externalities affecting many claimants. Voluntary private bargaining about incompatible uses may also be impeded by the need for continuous monitoring of an unverifiable bargain, such as an agreement to restrain one's catch to the maximum sustainable rate of harvest of a deep sea fishery. Therefore, public agencies must regulate the catch.

Finally, the most significant impediment to bargaining in large-numbers externality cases is the strategic holdout or free rider. When a court grants an injunction against a polluter's operation, relief from the injunction may require that the polluter obtain a unanimous waiver from all the affected parties. If many claimants are certified as possessing such a right of waiver, each claimant has an incentive to hold out for more compensation than would be required to cover his or her damages. The predictable presence of **strategic holdouts** short-circuits Coase's private voluntary bargaining hypothesis. In such cases, the courts therefore adopt other mechanisms such as assigning liability for payment of permanent damages.

class action suits A legal procedure for reducing the search and notification costs of filing a complaint.

strategic holdout A negotiator who makes unreasonable demands at the end of a unanimous consent process.

---

[15]For more details, see F. Harris, "Economic Negligence, Moral Hazard, and the Coase Theorem," *Southern Economic Journal* 56, no. 3 (January 1990), pp. 698–704.

Example

Boomer v. Atlantic Cement Co., Inc., 26 N.Y. 2d 219

A large cement plant valued at almost $200 million spewed cement dust regularly across a neighborhood of Albany, New York. Some of the affected households were unable to continue their laundry operations; small airborne particulates required frequent washing and repainting of cars and homes. Asthmatics suffered more health problems. The Atlantic Cement plant was declared a public nuisance, and the court chose among three types of injunctions: (1) an order to cease operations until the air pollution could be abated, (2) an order to cease operations until a waiver could be obtained from each affected household, or (3) an order declaring the cement plant liable for $740,000 in permanent damages and requiring a cessation of operations until these court-specified damages were paid.

Because the first injunction hinged on undeveloped technology and the second created strategic holdouts, the New York Court of Appeals in effect licensed the ongoing nuisance to Atlantic Cement Co. for a one-time fee of $740,000 in 2006 dollars. No private voluntary bargain to reduce the cement dust could have overcome the strategic free-rider/strategic holdout problem. And, as result of having to pay court-mandated damages, the plant's owners did begin to internalize the social cost of cement production when establishing new plants.

Resolution of Externalities by Regulatory Directive

Another approach to resolving externality problems is to prohibit the action that generates the external effects. In most cases, however, this simplistic approach is suboptimal and frequently impractical. Auto emissions could be cut to zero if autos were banned, but the economic effects of such a move, at least in the short run, would be disastrous for all developed economies. Moreover, seldom does an optimal solution require that externalities be completely eliminated; a strict zero-pollution policy often entails excessive pollution-abatement costs.

Example

Mandatory Auto Inspections

Auto inspections are a good example of a solution by regulatory directive. Recognizing that significant external benefits are to be gained from reducing serious automotive accidents caused by poorly maintained equipment, no state government gives the consumer the choice of refusing regular inspection and maintenance of brakes, lights, and other safety equipment; it simply mandates inspection and repair for all vehicles. Cancer-causing lead additives in gasoline and ozone shield depleting chlorofluorocarbon (CFC) refrigeration gases have also been massively reduced by such mandatory regulatory directives (see Figure 16.3).

However, it is seldom transparently obvious exactly what regulatory directive to issue. Consider the problem of setting an overall emissions standard when multiple sources of pollution are present, as in the acidification of rain along the eastern forests from coal-fired power plants in the Midwest. Under command-and-control regulation, each of the polluting entities (each point source) must be directed as to how it should act. A simple proportionate distribution of "pollution rights" to each plant would not take into account the dramatic difference in the cost of abatement from one plant to another. Instead, optimality would equalize the marginal effectiveness of the last dollar spent on pollution abatement by each polluter. So, a low-cost point source's regulatory directive should require more abatement than a permit for a high-cost point source. Yet this sort of detailed point-source regulation is seldom achieved.

Resolution of Externalities by Taxes and Subsidies

Another potentially efficient solution to externality problems is to provide subsidies (either in the form of cash or in the form of tax relief) to those whose activities generate significant external benefits and to levy a tax on those whose activities create external costs. Such a tax and subsidy scheme, however, requires a tremendous amount of information to administer the program effectively.

Consider the analysis required for a per-unit pollution tax or greenhouse gas tax T^* in Figure 16.4. Demand per truck is the private willingness to pay (WTP) for trucking deliveries throughout the Los Angeles area. Setting marginal private cost (MPC) equal to private WTP, the trucking company will put 50,000 miles a year on its typical delivery truck. Additional delivery miles are avoided by the managers because the price additional customers are willing to pay for deliveries is less than the MPC of operating the truck. The problem is that trucking mileage generates two by-products—carbon dioxide (CO_2) and nitrous oxide (NO_2), which cause global warming and smog. To focus on the less controversial smog cost, suppose that through careful environmental science, businesses such as the Pasadena Sightseeing Co. and asthmatic citizens of Los Angeles estimate that the air pollution causes damages from lost tourist business as well as eyes, nose, and throat irritants of area BCD. Consequently, although marginal benefit (P_o) equals MPC at the private market equilibrium Point A, additional costs attributable to the NO_2

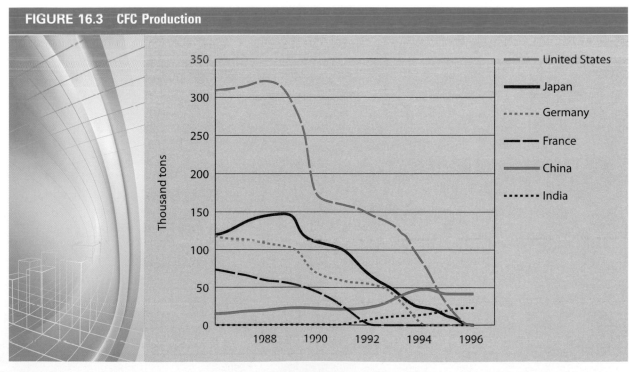

FIGURE 16.3   CFC Production

Source: *From Tomorrow's Markets, Global Trends and Their Implications for Business*, World Resources Institute (2002), p. 27. Reprinted with permission.

externality—namely, CB at 50,000 miles—suggest that full costs are substantially higher: at Point E, MPC (AB) + MExC (CB) > P_o.

When private plus external costs exceed marginal benefits to the delivery truck's customers at 50,000 miles, the joint product trucking mileage/NO_2 is produced in excess of its optimal level. Fifty thousand miles per year is too much trucking. However, the question, as always, comes down to *how much less* trucking and the associated reduction in greenhouse gases and smog pollution abatement is optimal?

In Figure 16.4, the reduction in mileage at which marginal social cost (MSC), which is the sum of MPC + MExC, just equals marginal willingness to pay for trucking is 40,000 miles at Point F. Clearly, the smog victims have damages (area GHBC) great enough to compensate the trucking company for its lost profits (area FIA) associated with a 10,000-mile reduction in mileage. And the maximum side payment smog victims would offer for the next 10,000-mile reduction from 40,000 to 25,000 (area JKHG) is smaller than the minimally sufficient bribe (area LMIF) that the trucking company would accept.

But zeroing in on 40,000 miles as the optimal mileage (not 35,000, 38,000, 42,000, or 45,000) is difficult because accurate marginal external cost information is so hard to come by. An optimal per-unit tax of T^* levied on delivery truck mileage reduces the mileage chosen from 50,000 to 40,000 through user charges in the amount $P_o + T^*$ that reflect the marginal social cost of the (trucking/NO_2) joint product. But again, T^* assumes heroically that the regulators know that 40,000 constitutes the optimal mileage.

In practice, a carbon tax or pollution emission charge would be placed on a firm's pollutants, such as pounds of particulate matter emitted from a delivery truck or power plant smokestack. A firm could continue to pollute if it pays the per-unit tax, or it could find that it is cheaper to buy pollution control equipment. If, after a reasonable period of time, a community still believes the level of particulate matter in the air is too high, the tax per pound of pollutant would be increased in a stepwise fashion until the community was satisfied with the result. The per-unit tax solution avoids the rigidity of

FIGURE 16.4 Optimal per Unit Pollution Tax

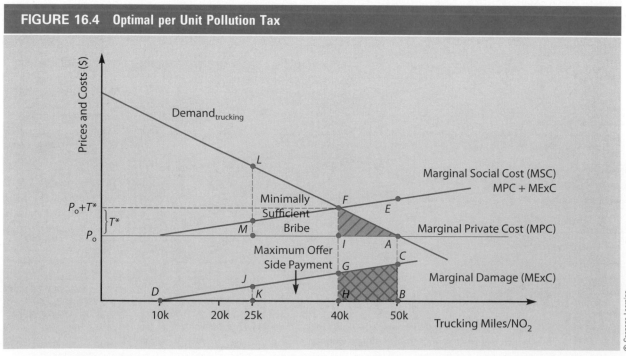

all-or-nothing regulatory directives, but the exact amount of an optimal effluent tax for water pollution, an optimal carbon tax, or an optimal emission tax for air pollution is extremely difficult to estimate.

Resolution of Externalities by Sale of Pollution Rights: Cap and Trade

As we saw in the MC, another approach to the problem of pollution is the issuance of transferable pollution rights. In effect, licenses that give the license holder a right to pollute up to some specific limit during a particular period of time are sold. This approach was adopted under the 1990 Clean Air Act. The U.S. EPA sets a maximum level of some pollutants that may be safely emitted in an area. The federal government then sells, at auction, licenses to individual firms giving them the right to pollute up to that specified amount. The licenses can be freely traded, which permits their price to vary with fluctuations in market demands and with the discovery of innovations in abatement technology. Because it is essentially market-oriented and has much lower information requirements, this cap-and-trade approach causes the appropriate levels of external costs to be internally recognized in all the price and production decisions of individual firms. Moreover, because the cap-and-trade approach creates new tradable pollution assets that are placed on the balance sheet of affected companies, many cap-and-trade initiatives enjoy the support of business and industry.

Example

Plant Expansion Requires Purchase of Open-Market Pollution Rights: Times Mirror Co.

The United States and the European Union have active markets for sulfur dioxide and nitrous oxide pollution rights. These markets allow electric utilities, trucking companies, and manufacturing firms to buy and sell pollution credits in continuous auctions. Also, a private placement market exists in which brokers, as well as some states, arrange customized contracts for pollution credits between companies that have excess rights to sell and companies that need rights to comply with environmental regulations. For example, the Times Mirror Company was able to complete a $120 million expansion of a paper-making plant near Portland, Oregon, after buying the right to emit 150 tons of additional hydrocarbons into the air annually. The pollution rights were acquired for $50,000 from the owners of two businesses that held surplus emission rights—a chemical plant that had gone out of business and a dry-cleaning firm that adopted a pollution-free cleaning fluid.

GOVERNMENTAL PROTECTION OF BUSINESS

In addition to regulating business enterprises, numerous government programs and policies protect businesses.

Licensing and Permitting

When the government requires and issues a license permitting someone to practice a particular business, profession, or trade, it is by definition restricting the entry of some other competitors into that business. Licensing is generally used to protect the public from fraud or incompetence in those cases where the potential for harm is quite large.

Nevertheless, by restricting output, government licensure raises prices by generating market power for license or permit holders.

In 2003, Mecklenburg County, North Carolina, which surrounds Charlotte, learned that its role as a ground transportation hub was threatened because the smog permits authorized by the North Carolina Environmental Commission were unavailable. North Carolina regulatory agencies foreclosed the construction of additional freight trucking terminals until some other dust-generating facility was closed. If no additional permits are authorized, those businesses with preexisting permits become more valuable.

Patents

patent A legal government grant of monopoly power that prevents others from manufacturing or selling a patented article.

Patents are by definition a governmental grant of legal monopoly power. A patent holder may prevent others from manufacturing or selling a patented product or process and may grant a license permitting others to make limited use of the patent in exchange for royalty payments. The monopoly granted by a patent is not, however, an absolute one. First, it is limited to a 17-year period, and few renewals are permitted. It is possible that a shorter patent monopoly period would provide sufficient incentives to encourage a high level of inventive activity. For example, serious proposals suggest shortening the patent period to just four years for computer software.

Second, competing firms are not prohibited from engineering around an existing patent and bringing out a closely competing, alternative design. These end-runs have triggered an arms race to acquire patent arsenals. In 2011 Google paid $12.5 billion to purchase the famous telecom engineering firm Motorola Mobility in order to better protect its Google Android smart phone from patent infringement suits by Apple, Microsoft, and Oracle. Third, many patents are successfully challenged by competitors, especially in the European Union, where patent applications are not kept secret. The U.S. Patent Office is hopelessly backlogged with 708,000 patent applications awaiting examination on a 2011 mean delay of 34 months.[16] The European Union system is much faster but, because of its transparency, less likely to secure exclusive rights.

THE OPTIMAL DEPLOYMENT DECISION: TO LICENSE OR NOT

Finally, we discuss the decision as to whether to license patents and trade secrets to competitors. Think of Apple's source code for the graphical user interface, Pfizer's automated drug discovery technology, and Disney's films and characters. Fifty years ago, 78 percent of the assets of U.S. nonfinancial corporations were tangible assets (real estate, inventories, and plant and equipment). Today, that figure is just 47 percent; intangible assets such as patents, copyrights, and goodwill have grown to nearly dominate the balance sheet.

In 2006, 10 firms passed Thomas Edison's record of 1,093 patents acquired (see Table 16.5). IBM acquired 2,972 patents, Canon acquired 1,837, and Hewlett-Packard acquired 1,801. IBM Corporation was seeking patent protection at the astounding rate of 10 patent applications per working day. AT&T was filing 7 per day with a total of 30,000 granted including patents on the first telecom transistors, first lasers, first fax machines, first satellite cell phones, the Telstar satellite, and the first picture phone.[17] In 1984 at the

---

[16]Based on "The Sputtering Invention Machine," *The Economist* (March 19, 2011), p. 69.

[17]Based on "The Knowledge Monopolies," *The Economist* (April 8, 2000), pp. 75–78; "Business Methods Patents," *Wall Street Journal* (October 3, 2000), p. B14; "Mind over Matter," *Wall Street Journal* (April 4, 2002), p. A1; and "Innovation," *Forbes* (July 5, 2004), pp. 142–146.

TABLE 16.5 TOP 10 FIRMS WITH PATENTS GRANTED IN 2006	
IBM	2,972
Canon	1,837
Hewlett-Packard	1,801
Matsushita	1,701
Samsung	1,645
Micron Technology	1,561
Intel	1,551
Hitachi	1,293
Toshiba	1,149
General Electric	906

Source: *The Economist* (May 10, 2008), p. 75.

AT&T break-up this patent portfolio was valued at $4.7 billion. By 2012, the value had risen to $31 billion.

Some of this activity is strategic patenting of technology portfolios where companies do not wish to make a new device immediately, but they can plausibly describe how they would make it, what the device is used for, and the novelty of the idea. These evidentiary requirements are required to obtain a U.S. patent.

Not just electronic devices, genetic engineering, and computer software but also business process methods are "hot" current areas of patenting activity. Patent filings for business processes exceeded 10,000 per year for the first time in 2007. Dell received a patent on the direct-to-the-consumer business model. Patent attorneys believe the ATM, frequent flyer programs, and even credit cards could be patented as business processes if they were invented today.

Financial markets are definitely capitalizing this "knowledge capital" into the equity market value of companies with patents, trade secrets, and proprietary know-how. Almost half of the $22 billion market value of Dow Chemical and more than a third of the $140 billion market value of Merck are discounted cash flow from intangible assets, mostly intellectual property. Much of Amazon.com's $11 billion market value arises from licensing fees on its business methods patents. Between 1994 and 1999, IBM boosted its annual revenues from licensing its intellectual property by more than 200 percent from $500 million to $1.6 billion. In consumer products, too, Reebok recently paid $250 million in royalties to obtain a 10-year exclusive license to market National Football League–branded uniforms, hats, and equipment and to have its trademark on the players' apparel of all NFL teams. So, substantial revenue is available from licensing, but of course licensing better enables one's competitors to attract away a firm's own regular customers.

Pros and Cons of Patent Protection and Licensure of Trade Secrets

Much debate continues about whether patent and trade secret protection motivates first-mover companies to innovate or stifles technological research by fast-second companies. Imitators often substantially advance some aspect of a new technology, but they must license the original patents or run the risk of defending themselves against patent infringement lawsuits. Jeff Bezos of Amazon.com proposed that 20-year patent protection for computer software and business methods be reduced to only 3 to 5 years. Patent protection outside the United States is already diminished. In Europe, patent applications invite legal challenge because they are publicized and because a majority of initial EU

WHAT WENT RIGHT • WHAT WENT WRONG

Delayed Release at Aventis[18]

The following list shows the top 10 patented drugs in 2000, 2006, and 2011. The instability on this list is striking. Once a drug goes off patent (e.g., Prozac in 2001 and Zocor in 2004, and Norvasac in 2008), the sales evaporate quickly. Generic drugs have become 46 percent of the U.S. prescription drug market. Generics usually enter the market at a 60–75 percent discount and eventually sell for as much as 80 percent of the original patented drug's price. Blue Cross and Blue Shield estimated this price difference to be $84 per prescription. In 2011, more than twice as many patented pharmaceuticals ($42 billion worth) were coming off patent than in any previous year.

When Eli Lilly's patent on Prozac ended, the firm lost 70 percent of its sales to generic rivals *within one month*. More typically, the loss of sales to generics for U.S. drugs coming off patent is 85 percent the first year. To prevent such disruptive shocks to the recovery of enormous fixed R&D costs, some pharmaceutical companies routinely file frivolous patent extensions that change simply the coating

BEST-SELLING PATENTED DRUGS, 2000

DRUG	PATENT OWNER	TREATMENT	DRUG	PATENT OWNER	TREATMENT
1. Losec	AstraZeneca	ulcers	6. Prozac	Eli Lilly	depression
2. Lipitor	Pfizer	cholesterol	7. Celebrex	Pfizer	arthritis
3. Zocor	Merck	cholesterol	8. Seroxat	GlaxoSmithKline	depression
4. Norvasc	Pfizer	high blood pressure	9. Claritin	Schering-Plough	allergies
5. Orgastro	Abbott Labs	ulcers	10. Zyprexa	Eli Lilly	schizophrenia

BEST-SELLING PATENTED DRUGS, 2006

DRUG	PATENT OWNER	TREATMENT	DRUG	PATENT OWNER	TREATMENT
1. Lipitor	Pfizer	cholesterol	6. Enbel	Amgen Wyeth	arthritis
2. Nexium	AstraZeneca	acid reflux	7. Effexor	Wyeth	depression
3. Plavix	Sanofi	platelet aggregation	8. Orgastro	Abbott Labs	ulcers
4. Serentide	GlaxoSmithKline	allergies	9. Zyprexa	Eli Lilly	schizophrenia
5. Norvasc	Pfizer	high blood pressure	10. Singulair	Schein	allergies

BEST-SELLING PATENTED DRUGS, 2011

DRUG	PATENT OWNER	TREATMENT	DRUG	PATENT OWNER	TREATMENT
1. Lipitor	Pfizer	cholesterol	6. Seroquel	Astra-Zeneca	depression
2. Plavix	Bristol-Myers-Squibb	platelet aggregation	7. Singulair	Merck	allergies
3. Nexium	Astra-Zeneca	acid reflux	8. Crestor	Astra-Zeneca	cholesterol
4. Abilify	Bristol-Myers-Squibb	depression	9. Cymbalta	Eli Lilly	depression
5. Advantix	GlaxoSmithKline	asthma	10. Humira	Abbott Labs	anti-inflamatory

(continued)

or the delivery system (e.g., tablet to liquid). When Prilosec, the anti-heartburn pill, went off patent in 2005, AstraZeneca introduced the copycat prescription drug Nexium. Over the next four years, 2010 through 2014, AstraZeneca lost or will lose patent protection on the $5.83 billion Seroquel antidepressant, the $3.8 billion Crestor anticholesterol, and its best-selling $6.3 billion ulcer drug Nexium. Such sums suggest why Aventis (a Franco-German drug group headquartered in Strasbourg, France) is accused of paying the American generic drug producer Andrix a $90 million bribe to delay the introduction of its cheaper generic heart attack drug.

[18]Based on "Don't Look Down," *The Economist* (January 6, 2001), p. 62; "Bloom and Blight," *The Economist* (October 26, 2002), p. 60; "Protection Racket," *The Economist* (May 19, 2001), p. 58; www.imshealth.com (accessed September 2006); "Friends for Life," *The Economist* (August 25, 2009), pp. 55–56; "Something Rotten," *The Economist* (August 8, 2009), p. 12; "Generics," *Wall Street Journal* (March 18, 2013), p. B6.

patents have been overturned. The EU has also decided not to issue patents for either computer software or business methods. In that environment, trade secrets, proprietary know-how, and internal business practices take on added importance.

Competing Business Plans at Celera Genomics and Human Genome Sciences

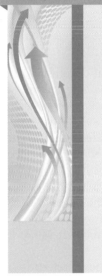

Genomics has revolutionized drug discovery and development, with some respected industry analysts predicting that "all drug discovery efforts will soon be genomics-based."[19] Celera Genomics, the company that finished reading the human genome sequence in 2000, expects to sell information (in effect to license its genome database) for as much as $90 million a year. It is hoped that comparing which genes are expressed and which remain recessive in various diseases will lead drug scientists to new blockbuster therapies and early detection of harmful side effects. However, an in-depth understanding of the biology of therapeutic mechanisms at the molecular level will also be key. Human Genome Sciences (HGS) has decided therefore to position itself as a drug maker, attempting to patent drug processes, not simply license genetic information to traditional drug companies. HGS's first product is a gene therapy that speeds the healing of wounds.

[19]*BusinessWeek* (January 8, 2001), p. 113.

Whether to "bury" one's trade secrets or to acknowledge openly their existence and license them to competitors is a significant strategic decision about the firm's contracting and governance mechanisms. No less important is the flipside decision as to whether to develop know-how in-house or to license proprietary know-how from competitors. Many executives believe that manufacturing managers and R&D experts should interact on an ongoing basis in order to develop a reservoir of non-codifiable tacit knowledge. If licensing is pursued, two-way licensing of trade secrets represents the exchange of hostages recommended by game theorists for credible long-term reliance relationships.

In Table 16.6, Motorola and Lucent Technologies (the spin-off of Bell Labs from AT&T) are trying to decide whether to develop in-house or license proprietary trade secrets in telecommunications engineering and software. Because of Lucent's long-term experience in this arena, if Motorola develops and patents the process and devices, Lucent expects to be successful as an imitator earning $9 billion. Should licensing of some proprietary know-how prove necessary, Lucent believes an inexpensive limited

WHAT WENT RIGHT • WHAT WENT WRONG

Technology Licenses Cost Palm Its Lead in PDAs[20]

In 1996, Palm single-handedly created the personal digital assistant (PDA) craze. Like Apple with its later iPhone and RIM's BlackBerry, Palm builds its own software and hardware. Initially, Palm operating systems ran three-quarters of all handheld devices that are capable of surfing the Internet. Palm's Pre and Pixi devices are $150 and $80, respectively, much cheaper than the Apple iPhone, but their applications (apps) number about 1,000 while the Apple iPhone has 300,000 apps. Palm decided to license its OS technology to competing manufacturers Handspring and Sony, the opposite of Apple's decision to have closed source software. Within two short years, Handspring surpassed Palm in manufacturing sales of PDAs by offering expansion slots and peripheral equipment such as phones and music players.

Licensing always entails such risks, but Palm really had little choice in the matter. Cell phone giant Nokia had licensed its Series 60 mobile-phone software to Siemens and Matsushita. The three firms together control 47 percent of the global cell phone manufacturing. Series 60 technology enables a cell phone to send and receive digital camera pictures and e-mail and, most importantly, to browse the Net. Palm knew that if Nokia succeeded in getting its OS adopted as an industry standard for handheld Web surfing, Nokia would set in motion a virtuous circle of increasing returns. Recently, Palm and Handspring merged into palmOne to achieve a larger installed base because worldwide Palm alone had shrunk to less than 10 percent of Nokia's market share.

[20]"Matsushita to Use Nokia's Cellphone Software," *Wall Street Journal* (December 20, 2000), p. B10; "One Palm Flapping," *The Economist* (June 2, 2001), p. 65; "As Its Phones Flop, Palm Shares the Blame," *Wall Street Journal* (February 26, 2010), p. B1.

license will be sufficient. Consequently, Motorola will be unable (in that circumstance) to recover its fully allocated research and development costs and will therefore lose money (i.e., the −$1 billion payoff in the southeast cell). In contrast, if Lucent develops and patents the needed process, its first-mover advantage would bring in substantial license fees from Motorola, who would need the proprietary knowledge gained through the trade secret license. Hence, the payoffs describing this situation are $4 billion/$3 billion in the northeast cell.

To complete the description of the payoff matrix, if neither firm develops the process, no profits accrue to either party. And if they compete head to head in a patent race, we assume the development costs will rise such that total profits fall from $7 billion to $6 billion, divided $5 to $1 between the technology leader Lucent and follower Motorola. What should Lucent do?

If Lucent could be sure Motorola was proceeding, Lucent would most prefer to wait and play "fast second." Relative to $5 billion in the northwest cell, $9 billion in the southwest cell is certainly attractive. However, Motorola can be expected to avoid the development expense and attempt itself to wait, imitate, and license as required to fill in the gaps in its own trade secrets and proprietary know-how. Indeed, Motorola has a

TABLE 16.6 TO LICENSE OR DEVELOP EXPERTISE IN-HOUSE?

		Motorola Develop/Patent	Motorola Imitate/License
Lucent	Develop/Patent	$1 billion / $5 billion	$3 billion / $4 billion
	Imitate/License	−$1 billion / $9 billion	0 / 0

© Cengage Learning

WHAT WENT RIGHT • WHAT WENT WRONG

Motorola: What They Didn't Know Hurt Them[21]

Motorola, Inc., was a pioneer in communications engineering with many of the early analog devices in radio, television, and military signal processing to its credit. More recently, Motorola developed and successfully launched the first handheld cell phones and also took the lead in satellite-based wireless communications with Iridium, a global cellular network project. Ambitious future projects include a satellite-based, high-speed, high-security videoconferencing network for corporate customers and a satellite-based transcontinental and transoceanic connection for land-based cell phone companies.

Network reliability problems began to arise, however, when Motorola insisted on slowly developing its own digital wireless proprietary know-how rather than licensing the needed trade secrets and patents from Lucent or QUALCOMM Incorporated. Motorola had little expertise in digital switches, computing equipment, and communications software. Yet proprietary knowledge in these areas proved

critical in attempting to integrate Motorola's satellite system with land-based cell phone networks. At one point, Motorola launched a cell phone system whose software essentially blocked any other user from simultaneously connecting through the same cell tower and receiving station. In effect, this device crashed the local cell network any time it was in use.

Perhaps it is not surprising that QUALCOMM and Lucent experienced less trouble adding know-how in wireless technology to their longstanding expertise in wire-based telecommunications networks than Motorola experienced trying to add know-how in digital switches and communications software to their long-standing expertise in analog wireless hardware. Motorola should have licensed the proprietary know-how rather than attempt to develop it in-house.

[21]Based on "Unsolid State: Motorola Struggles to Regain Its Footing," *Wall Street Journal* (April 22, 1998), p. A1; "How Motorola Roamed Astray," *Wall Street Journal* (October 26, 2000), p. B12.

dominant strategy to wait, imitate, and license. Consequently, Lucent anticipates that the payoff ($4 billion/$3 billion) in the northeast cell will emerge as an iterated dominant equilibrium. Recall that an iterated dominant equilibrium strategy is a self-interest-maximizing action by Lucent that is consistent with dominant-strategy responses of Motorola. At the northeast cell ($4 billion/$3 billion), neither party wishes to deviate to another action; therefore {Develop$_{Lucent}$, License$_{Motorola}$} is a Nash equilibrium strategy and the only Nash equilibrium in Table 16.6.

Although the numbers in Table 16.6 are only illustrative, thinking through the game theory analysis can often provide insight in predicting rival reaction to company moves and countermoves. In this case, an analysis such as Table 16.6 clearly indicates the advantages of the licensing alternative rather than the in-house development Motorola actually pursued.

Conclusion on Licensing

The decision to license depends in part on the availability of increasing returns and the sustainability of a company's competitive advantage from cost reductions. In Europe, where few industry standards have emerged for information technology products and where patents are often successfully challenged, first-mover firms have licensed to competitors rather than simply watch their trade secrets and proprietary know-how be steadily eroded by imitators. The result is increased competition, lower prices for consumers, and a faster rate of technological adoption. For example, in Europe prices for some digital TV components (e.g., digital video broadcasting chips) keep dropping, and the digital technology is quickly being incorporated into related products such as cell phones, pagers, and secure video business networks for corporate meetings.

In the United States, Red Hat used a general public license and open-source code programming to penetrate as quickly as possible into the operating system market with its Linux-based software that is intended to compete with Windows NT and eventually with Windows itself. Red Hat allows its suppliers and customers to copy, modify, and redistribute Red Hat software at no charge as long as they do so without charge. This open-source software strategy is an attempt to achieve the inflection point for increasing returns that Microsoft's competitors, including Apple, never reached. Apple pursued the opposite nonlicensing strategy, thereby effectively slowing the rate of adoption of Macs, and lost to IBM and Microsoft. Today, Google is pursuing Red Hat's open-source strategy with the operating system for its new smart phone offering, the Android phone.

A final tactical advantage of licensing comes from reduced re-contracting hazards. In purchasing high-end Alpha chips from Digital Equipment Corporation (now a division of Hewlett-Packard), many workstation manufacturers worry about later being subject to a "hold-up." At contract renewal, once their designs are optimized for the Alpha technology, the manufacturers are vulnerable to major price increases for these sole-source-supplied chips. Digital can credibly commit to more stable prices and thereby increase the rate of adoption for its product by licensing to both AMD and Intel. By allowing customers to dual source the Alpha chip technology, Digital credibly commits to renew its supply contracts without price gouging.

SUMMARY

- *Market performance* refers to the efficiency of resource allocation within and among firms, the technological progressiveness of firms, the tendency of firms to fully employ resources, and the impact on the equitable distribution of resources.
- *Market conduct* refers to the pricing behavior; the product policy; the sales promotion and advertising policy; the research, development, and innovation strategies; and the legal tactics employed by a firm or group of firms.
- *Market structure* refers to the degree of seller and buyer concentration in a market, the degree of actual or imagined product differentiation between products or services of competing producers, and the conditions surrounding entry into the market.
- Contestable markets are assumed to have freedom of entry and exit for potential competitors, slow-reacting incumbents, and low switching costs for consumers. In a perfectly contestable market, the resulting set of prices and outputs approaches those expected under perfect competition.

- Measures of market concentration include:
  - the market concentration ratio, defined as the percentage of total industry output attributable to the 4, 8, 20, or 50 largest companies.
  - the Herfindahl-Hirschman Index (*HHI*), which is equal to the sum of the squares of the market shares of all firms in an industry.
- A group of antitrust laws has been passed to prevent monopoly and to encourage competition in U.S. industry. The most important of these acts are the Sherman Act of 1890, the FTC and Clayton Acts of 1914, the Robinson-Patman Act of 1936, the Hart-Scott-Rodino Antitrust Improvement Act of 1976, and Merger Guidelines of 2010.
- Federal, state, and local governments all impose regulations on business enterprises. Regulatory constraints can affect a firm's operating costs (both fixed and variable), capital costs, and revenues.
- The current political and economic environment favors a significant reduction in the amount of

government regulation and interference in the operation of the private sector of the economy. Recent deregulation includes banking, transportation, natural gas pipeline, electric utility, and telecommunications industries.

■ A number of regulatory policies, such as licensing and issuing patents, are designed to restrict competition and protect business opportunities.

■ Externalities exist when a third party receives benefits or bears costs arising from an economic transaction in which he or she is not a direct participant. The impact of externalities is felt outside of (external to) the normal market pricing and resource-allocation mechanism.

■ Pecuniary externalities, in which spillover effects are reflected in the market pricing mechanism, result in no inefficiencies.

■ Ronald Coase has shown that an efficient allocation of resources can generally be achieved in the case of

small-numbers externalities by contractual bargaining between the creator and recipient of the externality.

■ Impediments to private voluntary bargaining include prohibitive search and notification costs, internal negotiation costs among large numbers of affected parties, prohibitive monitoring costs, and an absence of the surpluses required for making side payments.

■ Many possible solutions to problems of externalities exist and include solution by voluntary side payment, governmental prohibition, regulatory directive, imposition of pollution taxes or subsidies, mergers, and a sale of rights to create the externality, followed by a cap and trade market.

■ Whether to develop and license or wait and imitate is an organizational form decision about the protection afforded by patents, the relative importance of proprietary know how, the availability of industry standards, technological lock-in, value-enhancing complements, and other sources of increasing returns.

Exercises

Answers to the exercises in blue can be found in Appendix D at the back of the book.

1. If Apple iPod only played iTunes, and iTunes only could be heard on the Apple iPod, could Apple price the technologically integrated bundle any way it wanted? If other electronic music can play on an iPod, what determines whether there are any limitations on the bundled pricing of iPods and iTunes? What are those limitations?

2. An industry is composed of Firm 1, which controls 70 percent of the market, Firm 2 with 15 percent of the market, and Firm 3 with 5 percent of the market. About 20 firms of approximately equal size divide the remaining 10 percent of the market. Calculate the Herfindahl-Hirschman Index before and after the merger of Firm 2 and Firm 3 (assume that the combined market share after the merger is 20 percent). Would you view a merger of Firm 2 with Firm 3 as procompetitive or anticompetitive? Explain.

3. Suppose an industry is composed of eight firms with the following market shares:

A	30%	E	8%
B	25	F	5
C	15	G	4
D	10	H	3

Based on the (revised 2010) merger guidelines, would the Antitrust Division likely challenge a proposed merger between

a. Firms C and D (assume the combined market share is 25 percent)?

b. Firms F and G (assume the combined market share is 9 percent)? Explain your answer.

4. What are the incentives to innovate for a monopoly firm as compared with a firm in a competitive market if patent protection is not available?

5. Would you consider the fractional ownership jet taxi industry (NetJets, FlexJets, etc.) to be a contestable market? Why or why not?

6. The industry demand function for bulk plastics is represented by the following equation:

$$P = 800 - 20Q$$

where Q represents millions of pounds of plastic.

The total cost function for the industry, exclusive of a required return on invested capital, is

$$TC = 300 + 500Q + 10Q^2$$

where Q represents millions of pounds of plastic.

a. If this industry acts like a monopolist in the determination of price and output, compute the profit-maximizing level of price and output.

b. What are total profits at this price and output level?

c. Assume that this industry is composed of many (500) small firms, such that the demand function facing any individual firm is

$$P = \$620$$

Compute the profit-maximizing level of price and output under these conditions (the industry's total cost function remains unchanged).

d. What are total profits, given your answer to Part (c)?

e. Because of the risk of this industry, investors require a 15 percent rate of return on investment. Total industry investment amounts to $2 billion. If the monopoly solution prevails, as calculated in Parts (a) and (b), how would you describe the profits of the industry?

f. If the competitive solution most accurately describes the industry, is the industry operating under equilibrium conditions? Why or why not? What would you expect to happen?

g. The Clean Water Coalition proposed pollution control standards for the industry that would change the industry cost curve to the following:

$$TC = 400 + 560Q + 10Q^2$$

What is the impact of this change on price, output, and total profits under the monopoly solution?

h. Assume these standards are being proposed only in the state of Texas, which has 50 of the 500 producers. What impact would you expect the new standards to have on Texas firms? The rest of the industry?

7. Discuss the problems of aircraft noise around an airport from an externality perspective and propose a possible solution if (a) housing existed in the airport area before the airport was built and (b) housing was built adjacent to the airport after the airport was built.

8. A sheep rancher leased the mineral rights beneath her grazing land to an oil company. She fears that discharges from the oil wells will pollute her underground water resources. Consequently, the contract for the sale of mineral rights requires that the rancher and the oil company reach a mutually agreeable solution to the water contamination problem should it occur. If this bargaining fails to reach a conclusion acceptable to both sides, the mineral rights lease will be terminated automatically, and the rancher will be required to return a portion of the lease proceeds to the oil company. The portion that must be returned to the oil company is to be determined through a process of binding arbitration. Discuss likely outcomes should this problem arise.

9. Branding Iron Products, a specialty steel fabricator, operates a plant in the town of West Star, Texas. The town has grown rapidly because of recent discoveries of oil

and gas in the area. Many of the new residents have expressed concern at the amount of pollution (primarily particulate matter in the air and waste water in the town's river) emitted by Branding Iron. Three proposals have been made to remedy the problem:

a. Impose a tax on the amount of particulate matter and the amount of waste water emitted by the firm.

b. Prohibit pollution by the firm.

c. Offer tax incentives to the firm to clean up its production processes.

Evaluate each of these alternatives from the perspectives of economic efficiency, equity, and the likely long-term impact on the firm.

10. An industry produces its product, Scruffs, at a constant marginal cost of $50. The market demand for Scruffs is equal to

$$Q = 75,000 - 600P$$

a. What is the value to a monopolist who is able to develop a patented process for producing Scruffs at a cost of only $45?

b. If the industry producing Scruffs is purely competitive, what is the maximum benefit that an inventor of a process that will reduce the cost of producing Scruffs by $5 per unit can expect to receive by licensing her invention to the firms in the industry?

11. If the decision to develop and license or wait and imitate in Table 16.6 is a simultaneous-play repeated game between Lucent and Motorola for each new generation of technology, what happens if the Motorola payoff in the southwest cell is positive $2 billion? How should Motorola "play" in this modified licensing game? How should Lucent play?

Case Exercises

Do Luxury Good Manufacturers Have a Legitimate Interest in Minimum Resale Price Maintenance: *Leegin v. Kay's Kloset*?

Conduct an in-class debate on a recent antitrust case and whether it was decided correctly. The case is *Leegin Creative Products, Inc. v. PSKS, Inc., DBA Kay's Kloset*, 551, U.S. (2007). Leegin of Dallas Texas makes upscale leather accessories somewhat like Coach leather goods. Kay's Kloset had a standard-form manufacturer-retailer contract to carry Leegin's products as an independent retail distributor. When Kay's Kloset persisted in discounting its leather accessories below the suggested manufacturer's price, Leegin cut it off from further shipments. After several competing lower court decisions, for the first time ever, the U.S. Supreme Court accepted the argument that a manufacturer's business model can be so dependent on upscale positioning that a *rule of reason* should apply to minimum resale price maintenance agreements. In other words, such a manufacturer could legitimately refuse to deal with an independent retailer solely on the grounds that the retailer was in violation of the manufacturer's minimum suggested retail price. Such a practice had previously been ruled a per se violation of the antitrust statutes—specifically, an anticompetitive restraint of trade.

Debate Questions

1. Is the defendant Leegin entitled to erode and displace dominant firms such as Coach with this upscale-positioned business model supported by minimum retail pricing constraints?

Yes (here are some initial arguments to get you started): This practice causes harm to a competitor, not to competition; Leegin captured market share because it has better products, brands, management, lower cost, and good luck; this practice reduces intrabrand competition but increases interbrand competition.

No (here are some initial arguments to get you started): Minimum RPMs are an attempt at monopolization with a demonstrated intent to restrain trade; foreclosure of consumer choice is a restraint of trade.

2. Did Leegin form an illegal agreement with Kay's Kloset?

   No: Vertical restraints are appropriate in manufacturer–distributor relations; upscale positioning requires coordination throughout distribution channels; the agreement was initiated by the manufacturer, not other Leegin distributors seeking protection from price discounting by Kay's Kloset; no contractual agreement about minimum RPMs is in evidence.

   Yes: Minimum price RPMs are highly correlated with 19–27 percent price increases; independent retailers should have incentives to provide distributional efficiency, not price protection from lower-cost outlets; volume discounters like Macy's will be less able to bargain with Leegin for lower prices.

3. When defendant Leegin threatened and then refused to deal with Kay's Kloset, should that constitute a per se violation of the Sherman Act's prohibition against anticompetitive practices? ?

   No: A rule of reason should apply; legitimate manufacturer interest considers the customer target, the brand, and product positioning here for a luxury good; point-of-sale value-adding services are discouraged by renegade discounters; no motivation to high-end retail service can survive if free-riding is rampant.

   Yes: Minimum price RPMs contractually restrain retail trade; minimum price RPMs foreclosure those seeking a discount shopping experience for inventory overruns; legitimate manufacturer interest in motivating upscale retail service can be accomplished in other ways without lessening price competition; the practice will not remain isolated to luxury goods if per se prohibition is replaced by a rule of reason.

Microsoft Tying Arrangements

1. Which of the following is a violation of the antitrust laws in the United States and why? (a) Microsoft monopolizes the market in PC operating systems with a 92 percent market share; (b) Microsoft attempts to monopolize the market in Internet portals with a pattern of anticompetitive tactics (tying arrangements, refusals to deal, etc.); (c) Microsoft sells Windows plus Microsoft Internet Explorer for less than Windows without Internet Explorer installed as the default browser; (d) Microsoft gives Internet Explorer away free to individual adopters with variable cost estimated at $0.0067; (e) Microsoft threatens to delicense Compaq and Dell, who would then be unable to preinstall Windows on PCs they ship unless Compaq and Dell exclude Netscape's Internet browser from the user interface.

2. What difference does it make to the tying arrangement issues if Internet Explorer is a functionally integrated component of Windows? What if it is more like a radio in an automobile than a steering-post interlock device?

3. How should Microsoft market long-distance telephone services in the new wireless telecommunications devices that also include Internet portals?

Music Recording Industry Blocked from Consolidating

Given the following market share distributions, the U.S. Antitrust Division blocked a merger of BMG and EMI in 2001, and the European Commission blocked a merger of Time Warner's music division and EMI in 2000. Analyze these decisions and present arguments both pro and con.

U.S. MARKET SHARES (%)		WORLD MARKET SHARES (%)	
Vivendi Universal	20	Vivendi Universal	21
Sony	20	Sony	19
BMG	15	EMI	13
Time Warner	13	Time Warner	12
EMI	11	BMG	12

What else should be involved in such merger policies?

CHAPTER 7

Long-Term Investment Analysis

CHAPTER PREVIEW

Investment analysis (capital budgeting) is the process of planning for the purchases of assets whose returns (cash flows) are expected to continue beyond one year. When making capital budgeting decisions, the firm's managers commit resources to the expansion of its productive capacity, improvement of its cost efficiency, or diversification of its asset base. Each of these decisions affects future cash flows the firm expects to generate and the risk of those cash flows. Capital expenditures are a bridge between short-term price and output decisions and longer-term strategic decisions that wealth-maximizing managers must make to remain competitive. Public sector and not-for-profit managers use cost-benefit analysis and cost-effectiveness analysis, techniques also presented in this chapter, when considering many such long-term resource allocation decisions.

MANAGERIAL CHALLENGE

Industrial Renaissance in America: Insourcing of GE Appliances[1]

Several high-profile industrial companies have begun shifting production of home appliances back from China to the United States. Whirlpool is returning kitchen mixer making to Ohio, Otis is returning in-home elevators to South Carolina, and most impressively General Electric is returning the production of numerous appliances from China to Louisville, Kentucky.

In 1973, the GE Appliance Park employed 23,000 unionized timecard employees in six factory complexes turning out 60,000 appliances per week from dishwashers to ranges to water heaters. By 2010, employment was down to 1,864 with all but one factory shuttered. In the last 18 months, GE has decided to invest $800 million to bring its stateside appliance production division in Louisville back to life. CEO Jeff Immelt says he believes the capital budgeting analyses show the company can make more money manufacturing in Louisville than in China. How is that possible?

First, the trendy front-loading GE washers and dryers scheduled for a new assembly line in Factory Building 1 are like new lines of French door refrigerators; they require redesign and value-adding new features every two to three years. Product life cycles in home appliances have shortened sharply from seven years down to three. Where it was once possible to have design engineers in the States and plant managers and lead employees in China speaking different languages and flying back and forth across the Pacific making slow incremental product changes, the cycles of innovation have become feverish. Computing technology has triggered the need for breakthrough features that can capture the public's imagination in both the new-home-building and the appliance-replacement markets. Design engineers, manufacturing engineers, line workers, and marketing and sales staff all need to be in one place to realize a consultative continuous improvement manufacturing environment.

Cont.

MANAGERIAL CHALLENGE *Continued*

A GE water heater being readied for assembly in Factory Building 2 provides a good illustration. The GeoSpring water heater uses 60 percent less electricity than a typical water heater. The key is a small heat pump on the top that extracts warmth from the ambient air surrounding the appliance. In China the machine had a complex knot of tubing that necessitated difficult welds triggering numerous quality control issues. A complete redesign has reduced the assembly time from ten to two hours, cut materiel cost by 10 percent, and reduced the time from factory to Lowe's Home Improvement and Home Depot warehouses from six weeks to five days. The China-made GeoSpring water heater sold for $1,599; the Louisville-made GeoSpring retails for $1,299.

A newly adopted two-tiered wage structure with union wages starting at $13.50 rather than $21.35 per hour in the Louisville Appliance Park is clearly involved. In contrast, wages in GE's Chinese plants have risen from $0.52 in 2000 to $3 per hour today, and a less spectacular but noteworthy 18 percent wage cost increase is projected for GE capital budgeting in China. But also involved are lean manufacturing techniques precipitating design innovations and the time-to-market advantages of American production for the home appliance market.

So far, only a half million American factory jobs have returned to the United States in 2011–2012 relative to the 6 million factory jobs that were lost to outsourcing during 2000–2010. Nevertheless, net insourcing appears to be a growing trend restoring the industrial base of leading American companies. The reason why is that their capital budgeting analyses show higher net present value (NPVs) with production at home than abroad.

Discussion Questions

- What cost of capital would you apply as a discount rate for the GE Appliance Park capital spending?
- Why does GE expect wage rates in China to continue doubling every four years? At that 18 percent growth rate, will Chinese assembly line wage costs reach U.S. wage costs within a 20-year capital budgeting project?
- Explain lean manufacturing techniques? Why would this approach to production be more difficult to execute in China?
- Do you agree with GE's decision? Why or why not?

[1]Based on C. Fisherman, "The Insourcing Boom," *The Atlantic Monthly* (December 2012), pp. 1–10; "Outsourcing and Offshoring; Here, There and Everywhere," A Supplement to *The Economist* (January 17, 2013), pp. 1–22.

THE NATURE OF CAPITAL EXPENDITURE DECISIONS

capital expenditure A cash outlay designed to generate a flow of future cash benefits over a period of time extending beyond one year.

capital budgeting The process of planning for and evaluating capital expenditures.

Previous chapters were mostly concerned with analytical tools and decision models that help managers make the most efficient use of existing resources. This chapter considers decisions to replace or expand the firm's capital investment outlays. Capital outlays, by definition, have a long-range impact by determining products that will be produced, markets to be entered, the location of plants and facilities, and the type of technology (with its associated costs) to be used. Capital expenditures require careful analysis because they are costly to make and often more costly to reverse.

A **capital expenditure** is a cash outlay that is expected to generate a flow of future cash benefits lasting longer than one year. It is distinguished from a normal operating expenditure, which is expected to result in cash benefits during the coming one-year period. **Capital budgeting** is the process of planning for and evaluating capital expenditures. In addition to asset replacement and expansion decisions, other types of decisions that can be analyzed using capital budgeting techniques include research and development expenditures, investments in employee education and training, lease-versus-buy decisions, and mergers and acquisitions.

A BASIC FRAMEWORK FOR CAPITAL BUDGETING

This basic capital budgeting decision-making framework is illustrated in Figure 17.1. Suppose a company has nine investment projects under consideration, labeled *A, B, C, ... , I*. The model assumes that all projects have the same risk. This schedule of projects is often called the *investment opportunity curve*. For example, Project *A* requires an investment of $2 million and is expected to generate a 24 percent rate of return. Project *B* will cost $1 million ($3 million minus $2 million on the horizontal axis) and generate a 22 percent rate of return, and so on. Graphically, the projects are arranged in descending order by their rates of return, indicating that no firm has a limitless number of possible new projects that all generate high rates of return. As new products are produced, new markets entered, and cost-saving technologies adopted, the number of highly profitable investment opportunities tends to decline.

The *marginal cost of capital curve* represents the marginal cost of capital to the firm, that is, the cost of each additional dollar of investment capital raised in the capital markets. Using this basic model, the firm should undertake Projects *A, B, C, D,* and *E* because their returns exceed the firm's marginal cost of capital.

THE CAPITAL BUDGETING PROCESS

The process of selecting capital investment projects consists of the following important steps:

1. Generate alternative capital investment project proposals.
2. Estimate cash flows for the project proposals.

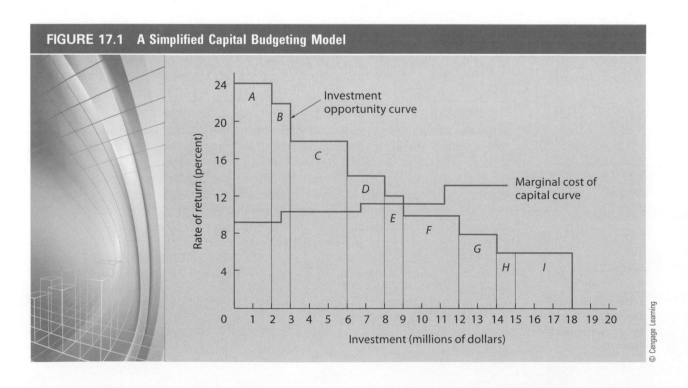

FIGURE 17.1   A Simplified Capital Budgeting Model

3. Evaluate and choose investment projects to implement.
4. Review the investment projects after they have been implemented to assure assumptions were accurate. Otherwise, one should modify assumptions as required for similar future projects.

Generating Capital Investment Projects

Ideas for new capital investments can come from many sources both inside and outside the firm. Proposals can originate at all levels in the organization, from factory workers all the way up to the board of directors. Most medium- and large-sized firms have departments whose responsibilities include searching for and analyzing capital expenditure projects. These departments include cost accounting, industrial engineering, marketing research, research and development, and corporate planning.

Example

Capital Expenditures at Chrysler: The Grand Cherokee[2]

Chrysler Corporation developed its Grand Cherokee sport utility vehicle using an unusual (for Chrysler) "platform team" approach. Seven to eight hundred engineering, marketing research, and design personnel brought the vehicle to market more quickly and at a lower cost than had been typical for other American auto companies. The Grand Cherokee was developed and a new plant built in Detroit to produce it, all for about $1.1 billion in capital outlays. Chrysler planned to sell up to 175,000 of these vehicles each year at a price point of $32,000, realizing a profit of $5,500 per unit. For almost two decades, these cash flow projections have been realized.

The Grand Cherokee capital expenditures contain elements of both demand management and cost reduction. In addition, the decision to build the Grand Cherokee in an efficient new plant in Detroit rather than in its older underutilized plant in Toledo reflected a commitment to hold costs of production at a minimum. Chrysler saw sales of its older, smaller Jeep Cherokee decline from a peak of nearly 200,000 units per year to about 125,000. Chrysler's intention was to cut the price of its old Jeep Cherokee and market it aggressively as a low-cost, sporty utility vehicle alternative. Thus, Chrysler created for itself the option either to retain the older model if it sold well at a lower price or to phase out the older model and close the Toledo plant. The evaluation process of this and many other major capital expenditure projects contains elements of cost reduction, demand management, and the creation of embedded real options.

[2]Based on "Iacocca's Last Stand at Chrysler," *Fortune* (April 20, 1992), p. 63ff.

Estimating Cash Flows

Certain basic guidelines are helpful when estimating cash flows. First, cash flows should be measured on an *incremental* basis. In other words, the cash-flow stream for the project should represent the difference between the cash-flow streams to the firm with and without acceptance of the investment project. Second, cash flows should be measured on an *after-tax* basis, using the firm's marginal tax rate. Third, all the *indirect effects* of the project throughout the firm should be included in the cash-flow calculations. If a department or division of the firm is contemplating a capital investment that will alter the revenues or costs of other departments or divisions, then these external effects should be incorporated into the cash-flow estimates. Fourth, *sunk costs* should not be considered when evaluating the project. A sunk cost is an outlay that has been made (or committed to be made). Because sunk costs cannot be avoided, they should not be considered in the decision to accept or reject a project. Fifth, the value of resources used in the project should be measured in terms of their *opportunity costs*. Recall from Chapter 8 that opportunity cost is the value of a resource in its next best alternative use.

For a typical investment project, an initial investment is made in year 0, which generates a series of yearly net cash flows over the life of the project (n). The net investment ($NINV$) of a project is defined as the initial net cash outlay in year 0. It includes the acquisition cost of any new assets plus installation and shipping costs and tax effects.[3]

The incremental, after-tax net cash flows ($NCFs$) of a particular investment project are equal to cash inflows minus cash outflows. For any year during the life of the project, these may be defined as the difference in net income after tax ($\Delta NIAT$) with and without the project plus the difference in depreciation (ΔD):

$$NCF = \Delta NIAT + \Delta D \qquad [17.1]$$

$\Delta NIAT$ is equal to the difference in net income before tax ($\Delta NIBT$) times ($1 - T$), where T is the corporate (marginal) income tax rate:

$$\Delta NIAT = \Delta NIBT(1 - T) \qquad [17.2]$$

$\Delta NIBT$ is defined as the difference in revenues (ΔR) minus the differences in operating costs (ΔC) and depreciation (ΔD):

$$\Delta NIBT = \Delta R - \Delta C - \Delta D \qquad [17.3]$$

Substituting Equation 17.3 into Equation 17.2 yields

$$\Delta NIAT = (\Delta R - \Delta C - \Delta D)(1 - T) \qquad [17.4]$$

Substituting this equation into Equation 17.1 yields the following definition of net cash flow:

$$NCF = (\Delta R - \Delta C - \Delta D)(1 - T) + \Delta D \qquad [17.5]$$

Example

Cash-Flow Estimation: Hamilton Beach/ Proctor-Silex, Inc.

To illustrate the cash-flow calculations, consider the following example. Suppose that Hamilton Beach/Proctor-Silex, a manufacturer of small electric appliances, has been offered a contract to supply a regional merchandising company with a line of food blenders to be sold under the retail company's private brand name. Hamilton Beach/Proctor-Silex's treasurer estimates that the initial investment in new equipment required to produce the blenders would be $1 million. The equipment would be depreciated (using the straight-line method)[4] over five years with a zero (0) estimated salvage value at the end of the five-year contract period. Based on the contract

(continued)

---

[3]When the new asset is replacing an existing asset, one must also include in the net investment calculation the net proceeds from the sale of the existing asset and the taxes associated with its sale. See R. Charles Moyer, James R. McGuigan, and William J. Kretlow, *Contemporary Financial Management*, 12th ed. (Cincinnati: South-Western, 2010), pp. 336–338, for a discussion of the cash-flow calculations for replacement decisions.

specifications, the treasurer estimates that incremental revenues (additional sales) would be $800,000 per year. The incremental costs if the contract is accepted will be $450,000 per year. These include cash outlays for direct labor and materials, transportation, utilities, building rent, and *additional* overhead. The firm's marginal income tax rate is 40 percent.

Based on the information, *NINV* and *NCF* can be calculated for the project. The net investment (*NINV*) is equal to the $1 million initial outlay for the new equipment. The difference in revenues (ΔR) with and without the project is equal to $800,000 per year, and the difference in operating costs (ΔC) is equal to $450,000 per year. The difference in depreciation (ΔD) is equal to the initial outlay ($1 million) divided by 5, or $200,000 per year. Substituting these values, along with T = 0.40, into Equation 17.5 yields the following:

$$NCF = (\$800{,}000 - \$450{,}000 - \$200{,}000)(1 - 0.40) + \$200{,}000$$
$$= \$290{,}000$$

Hamilton Beach/Proctor-Silex must decide whether it wants to invest $1 million now to receive $290,000 per year in net cash flows over the next five years. The next section illustrates two of the criteria used in evaluating investment proposals.

---

[4]This depreciation method is just one of several possible methods that can be used. See Moyer, McGuigan, and Kretlow, *op. cit.*, pp. 349–352, for a discussion of the various depreciation methods.

Evaluating and Choosing the Investment Projects to Implement

Once a capital expenditure project has been identified and the cash flows have been estimated, a decision to accept or reject the project is required. Acceptance of the project results in a cash flow stream to the firm—that is, a series of either cash inflows or outflows for a number of years into the future. Typically, a project will result in an initial (first-year) outflow (investment) followed by a series of cash inflows (returns) over a number of succeeding years.

Various criteria are used to assess the desirability of investment projects. This section focuses on two widely used discounted cash-flow methods:[5]

* Internal rate of return (*r*)
* Net present value (*NPV*)

internal rate of return (IRR) The discount rate that equates the present value of the stream of net cash flows from a project with the project's net investment.

Internal Rate of Return The **internal rate of return (IRR)** is defined as the discount rate that equates the present value of the net cash flows from the project with the net investment. The following equation is used to find the IRR:

$$\sum_{t=1}^{n} \frac{NCF_t}{(1+r)^t} = NINV \qquad [17.6]$$

where *n* is the life of the investment and *r* is the IRR.

---

[5]For those not familiar with discounting (present-value) techniques, Appendix A at the end of this book provides a review of these concepts.

An investment project should be accepted if the IRR is greater than or equal to the firm's required rate of return (cost of capital)—if not, the project should be rejected.

Example

Calculation of IRR: Hamilton Beach/Proctor-Silex

The IRR for the Hamilton Beach/Proctor-Silex investment project is calculated as follows:

$$\sum_{t=1}^{5} \frac{290{,}000}{(1+r)^t} = 1{,}000{,}000$$

$$\sum_{t=1}^{5} \frac{1}{(1+r)^t} = \frac{1{,}000{,}000}{290{,}000} = 3.4483$$

The term $[\sum_{t=1}^{5} 1/(1+r)^t]$ represents the present value of a \$1 annuity for five years discounted at r percent and is equal to 3.4483. The value 3.4483 in the *Period 05* row of Table A.4 in Appendix A falls between 3.5172 and 3.4331, which corresponds to discount rates of 13 and 14 percent, respectively. Interpolating between these values yields an IRR of

$$r = 0.13 + \frac{3.5172 - 3.4483}{3.5172 - 3.4331}(0.14 - 0.13)$$
$$= 0.1382$$

or 13.8 percent.

If Hamilton Beach/Proctor-Silex requires a rate of return of 12 percent on projects of this type, then the project should be accepted because the expected return (13.8 percent) exceeds the required return (12 percent). Later in this chapter we consider how to determine the required return (i.e., the firm's cost of capital).

net present value (NPV) The present value of the stream of net cash flows resulting from a project, discounted at the required rate of return (cost of capital), minus the project's net investment.

Net Present Value　The **net present value (NPV)** of an investment is defined as the present value, discounted at the firm's required rate of return (cost of capital), of the stream of net cash flows from the project minus the project's net investment. Algebraically, the NPV is equal to

$$NPV = \sum_{t=1}^{n} \frac{NCF_t}{(1+k)^t} - NINV \qquad [17.7]$$

where n is the expected life of the project and k is the firm's required rate of return (cost of capital).

An investment project should be accepted if the NPV is greater than or equal to zero and rejected if its NPV is less than zero. This is so because a positive NPV translates directly into increases in stock prices and increases in shareholder wealth.

Example

NPV Calculation: Hershey Foods

Hershey Foods is considering an investment in a new wrapping machine for its Kiss candies. The machine has an initial cost (net investment) of \$2.5 million. It is expected to produce cost savings from reduced labor and to generate additional revenues because of its increased reliability and productivity. Over its anticipated

(continued)

economic life of five years, the new Kiss wrapping machine is expected to generate the following stream of net cash flows (NCF_t).

YEAR (t)	NET CASH FLOW (NCF_t)
1	$600,000
2	800,000
3	800,000
4	600,000
5	250,000

If Hershey requires a return (k) of 15 percent on a project of this type, should it make the investment?

Hershey can solve this problem by computing the NPV of the cash flows from this project (using Equation 17.7) as follows:

YEAR (1)	CASH FLOW (2)	PRESENT VALUE INTEREST FACTOR AT 15%* (3)	PRESENT VALUE (4) = (2) × (3)
0	($2,500,000)	1.00000	($2,500,000)
1	600,000	0.86957	521,742
2	800,000	0.75614	604,912
3	800,000	0.65752	526,016
4	600,000	0.57175	343,050
5	250,000	0.49718	124,295
			($379,985)

*Appendix A, Table A.3.

Because this project has a negative NPV, it does not contribute to the goal of maximizing shareholder wealth. Therefore, it should be rejected.

NPV versus IRR   Both the net-present-value and the internal-rate-of-return methods result in identical decisions to either accept or reject individual projects. NPV is greater than (less than) zero if and only if the IRR is greater than (less than) the required rate of return k. In the case of *mutually exclusive* projects—that is, projects where the acceptance of one alternative precludes the acceptance of one or more other alternatives—the two methods may yield contradictory results; one project may have a *higher* IRR than another and, at the same time, a *lower* NPV.

Consider, for example, mutually exclusive projects X and Y shown in Table 17.1. Both require a net investment of $1,000. Based on the IRR, Project X is preferred, with a rate of 21.5 percent compared with Project Y's rate of 18.3 percent. Based on the NPV with a discount rate of 5 percent, Project Y ($270) is preferred to Project X ($240). Thus, it is necessary to determine which of the two criteria is the correct one to use in this situation. The outcome depends on what *assumptions* the decision maker chooses to make about the *implied reinvestment rate* for the net cash flows generated from each project. The net-present-value method assumes that cash flows are *reinvested at the firm's cost of capital,* whereas the internal-rate-of-return method assumes that these cash flows are

TABLE 17.1	NPV VERSUS IRR FOR MUTUALLY EXCLUSIVE INVESTMENT PROJECTS	
	PROJECT X	**PROJECT Y**
Net investment	$1,000	$1,000
Net cash flows		
Year 1	667	0
Year 2	667	1,400
NPV at 5%	$240	$270
IRR	21.5%	18.3%

© Cengage Learning

TABLE 17.2	SUMMARY OF THE CAPITAL BUDGETING DECISION CRITERIA		
CRITERION	PROJECT ACCEPTANCE DECISION RULE	BENEFITS	WEAKNESSES
Net present value (NPV) method	Accept project if project has a positive or zero NPV; that is, if the present value of net cash flows, evaluated at the firm's cost of capital, equals or exceeds the net investment required	Considers the timing of cash flows Provides an objective, return-based criterion for acceptance or rejection; most conceptually accurate approach	Difficulty in interpreting the meaning of the NPV computation
Internal rate of return (IRR) method	Accept project if IRR equals or exceeds the firm's cost of capital	Easy to interpret the meaning of IRR Considers the timing of cash flows Provides an objective, return-based criterion for acceptance or rejection	Sometimes gives decision that conflicts with NPV; multiple rates of return problem*

© Cengage Learning

*See Moyer, McGuigan, and Kretlow, *op. cit.*, p. 365, for a discussion of the multiple internal rates of return problem.

reinvested at the computed IRR. Generally, the cost of capital is considered to be a more realistic reinvestment rate than the computed IRR because it is the rate the next (marginal) investment project can be assumed to earn. In Figure 17.1, the last project invested in, Project *E*, offers a rate of return nearly equal to the firm's marginal cost of capital. Consequently, the net-present-value approach is normally superior to the IRR when choosing among mutually exclusive investments. Table 17.2 summarizes the two techniques.

ESTIMATING THE FIRM'S COST OF CAPITAL

cost of capital The cost of funds that are supplied to a firm. The cost of capital is the minimum rate of return that must be earned on new investments undertaken by a firm.

The **cost of capital** is concerned with what a firm has to pay for the capital (i.e., the debt, preferred stock, retained earnings, and common stock) it uses to finance new investments. It also can be thought of as the rate of return required by investors in the firm's securities. As such, the firm's cost of capital is determined in the capital markets and is closely related to the degree of risk associated with new investments, existing assets, and the firm's capital structure. In general, the greater the riskiness of a firm as perceived by investors, the greater the return investors will require and the greater will be the cost of capital.

The cost of capital also can be thought of as the minimum rate of return required on new investments. If a new investment earns an IRR that is greater than the cost of capital, the value of the firm increases. Correspondingly, if a new investment earns a return less than the firm's cost of capital, the firm's value decreases.

The following discussion focuses on the two major sources of funds for most firms: debt and common equity. Each of these sources of funds has a cost.

Cost of Debt Capital

The pre-tax cost of debt capital to the firm is the rate of return required by investors. For a debt issue, this rate of return k_d equates the present value of all expected future receipts—interest I and principal repayment M—with the offering price V_0 of the debt security:

$$V_0 = \sum_{t=1}^{n} \frac{I}{(1 + k_d)^t} + \frac{M}{(1 + k_d)^n}$$
[17.8]

The cost of debt k_d can be found by using the methods for finding the discount rate (i.e., yield to maturity) discussed in Appendix A.

Most *new* long-term debt (in the form of bonds) issued by companies is sold at or close to par value (normally $1,000 per bond), and the coupon interest rate is set at the rate required by investors. When debt is issued at par value, the pre-tax cost of debt, k_d, is equal to the coupon interest rate. Interest payments made to investors, however, are deductible from the firm's taxable income. Therefore, the *after-tax* cost of debt is computed by multiplying the pre-tax cost by 1 minus the firm's marginal tax rate T:

$$k_i = k_d(1 - T)$$
[17.9]

Cost of Debt Capital: AT&T

To illustrate the cost of debt computation, suppose that AT&T sells $100 million of 8.5 percent first-mortgage bonds at par. Assuming a corporate marginal tax rate of 40 percent, the after-tax cost of debt is computed as

$$k_i = k_d(1 - T)$$
$$= 8.5(1 - 0.40) = 5.1\%$$

Cost of Internal Equity Capital

Like the cost of debt capital, the cost of equity capital to the firm is the equilibrium rate of return required by the firm's common stock investors.

Firms raise equity capital in two ways: (1) *internally*, through retained earnings, and (2) *externally*, through the sale of new common stock. The cost of internal equity to the firm is less than the cost of new common stock because the sale of new stock requires the payment of flotation costs.

The concept of the cost of internal equity (or simply *equity*, as it is commonly called) can be developed using several different approaches, including the *dividend valuation model*.

Dividend Valuation Model   Recall from Chapter 1 that shareholder wealth was defined as the present value, discounted at the shareholder's required rate of return k_e, of the expected future returns generated by a firm (see Equation 1.1). For the typical firm, these future returns can take two forms: the payment of dividends to the shareholder or an increase in the market value of the firm's stock (capital gain). For the

dividend valuation model A model (or formula) stating that the value of a firm (i.e., shareholder wealth) is equal to the present value of the firm's future dividend payments, discounted at the shareholder's required rate of return. It provides one method of estimating a firm's cost of equity capital.

shareholder who plans to hold the stock indefinitely, the value of the firm (shareholder wealth, according to the **dividend valuation model**) is

$$V_0 = \sum_{t=1}^{\infty} \frac{D_t}{(1 + k_e)^t} \qquad [17.10]$$

where D_t is the dividend paid by the firm in period t.[6] If the shareholder chooses to sell the stock after n years, his or her wealth (V_0) is

$$V_0 = \sum_{t=1}^{n} \frac{D_t}{(1 + k_e)^t} + \frac{V_n}{(1 + k_e)^n} \qquad [17.11]$$

where V_n is the market value of the shareholder's holdings in period n. Equation 17.11 is identical to 17.10 because the value of the firm in period n is based on the future returns (dividends) of the firm in periods $n + 1, n + 2, ...$[7]

If the dividends of the firm are expected to grow *perpetually* at a *constant compound rate* of g per year, then the value of the firm (Equation 17.10) can be expressed as

$$V_0 = \frac{D_1}{k_e - g} \qquad [17.12]$$

where D_1 is the dividend expected to be paid in period 1 and V_0 is the market value of the firm. If D_1 is the dividend *per share* (rather than total dividends) paid in period 1, then V_0 represents the market price *per share* of common stock. Solving Equation 17.12 for k_e yields

$$k_e = \frac{D_1}{V_0} + g \qquad [17.13]$$

The following example illustrates how Equation 17.13 can be applied in estimating the cost of equity capital.

Example

Cost of Internal Equity Capital: Fresno Company

Suppose the current price of the common stock of Fresno Company (V_0) is $32. The dividend per share of the firm next year, D_1, is expected to be $2.14. Dividends have been growing at an average compound annual rate of 7 percent over the past 10 years, and this growth rate is expected to be maintained for the foreseeable future. Based on this information, the cost of equity capital is estimated as

$$k_e = \frac{2.14}{32} + 0.07 = 0.137$$

or 13.7 percent.[8]

[8]Another technique that can be used to estimate the cost of equity capital is the capital asset pricing model (CAPM). See Moyer, McGuigan, and Kretlow, *op. cit.*, Chapters 6 and 12, for a more detailed discussion of the CAPM theory and its use in calculating the cost of equity capital.

[6]A profitable firm that reinvests all its earnings and never distributes any dividends would still have a positive value to stockholders because its market value would be increasing, and shareholders could sell their stock and obtain a capital gain on their investment in the firm.

[7]The value of the firm in period n is

$$V_n = \sum_{t=(n+1)}^{\infty} \frac{D_t}{(1 + k_e)^{t-n}}$$

When this expression is substituted in Equation 17.11, Equation 17.10 is obtained.

Cost of External Equity Capital

The cost of external equity is greater than the cost of internal equity for the following reasons:

- Flotation costs associated with new shares are usually high enough that they cannot realistically be ignored.
- The selling price of the new shares to the public must be less than the market price of the stock before announcement of the new issue, or the shares may not sell. Before any announcement, the current market price of a stock usually represents an equilibrium between supply and demand. If supply is increased (all other things being equal), the new equilibrium price will be lower.

When a firm's future dividend payments are expected to grow forever at a constant per-period rate of g, the cost of external equity k_e' is defined as

$$k_e' = \frac{D_1}{V_{\text{net}}} + g \qquad [17.14]$$

where V_{net} is the net proceeds to the firm on a per-share basis.

Cost of External Equity Capital: Fresno Company

To illustrate, consider the Fresno Company example used in the cost of internal equity discussion, where $V_0 = \$32$, $D_1 = \$2.14$, $g = 0.07$, and $k_e = 13.7$ percent. Assuming that new common stock can be sold at \$31 to net the company \$30 a share after flotation costs, k_e' is calculated using Equation 17.14 as follows:

$$k_e' = \frac{2.14}{30} + 0.07$$
$$= 0.141 \text{ or } 14.1\%$$

Because of the relatively high cost of newly issued equity, many companies try to avoid this means of raising capital. The question of whether a firm should raise capital with newly issued common stock depends on the firm's investment opportunities.

Weighted Cost of Capital

Firms calculate their cost of capital to determine a discount rate to use when evaluating proposed capital expenditure projects. Recall that the purpose of capital expenditure analysis is to determine which *proposed* projects the firm should *actually* undertake. Therefore, it is logical that *the capital whose cost is measured and compared with the expected benefits from these proposed projects should be the next or marginal capital the firm raises*. Typically, companies estimate the cost of each capital component as the cost they expect to have to pay on these funds during the coming year.[9]

In addition, as a firm evaluates proposed capital expenditure projects, it normally does not specify the proportions of debt and equity financing for each individual project. Instead, each project is presumed to be financed with the same proportion of debt and equity contained in the company's target capital structure.

Thus, the appropriate cost-of-capital figure to be used in capital budgeting is not only based on the next capital to be raised but also weighted by the proportions of the capital

---

[9]Stated another way, the cost of the capital acquired by the firm in earlier periods (the *historical* cost of capital) is *not* used as the discount rate in determining next year's capital expenditures.

components in the firm's long-range target capital structure. This figure is called the *weighted*, or *overall, cost of capital.*

The general expression for calculating the weighted cost of capital k_a is as follows:

$$k_a = \begin{bmatrix} \text{equity} \\ \text{fraction} \\ \text{of capital} \\ \text{structure} \end{bmatrix} \begin{bmatrix} \text{cost} \\ \text{of} \\ \text{equity} \end{bmatrix} + \begin{bmatrix} \text{debt} \\ \text{fraction} \\ \text{of capital} \\ \text{structure} \end{bmatrix} \begin{bmatrix} \text{cost} \\ \text{of} \\ \text{debt} \end{bmatrix}$$

$$= \left[\frac{E}{D+E}\right](k_e) + \left[\frac{D}{D+E}\right](k_i) \qquad [17.15]$$

where D is the amount of debt and E the amount of equity in the target capital structure.[10]

Example

Weighted Cost of Capital: Columbia Gas Company

To illustrate, suppose that Columbia Gas has a current (and target) capital structure of 75 percent equity and 25 percent debt. (The proportions of debt and equity should be the proportions in which the firm intends to raise funds in the future.) For a firm that is not planning a change in its target capital structure, these proportions should be based on the current *market value weights* of the individual components (debt and common equity). The company plans to finance next year's budget with $75 million of retained earnings ($k_e = 12$ percent) and $25 million of long-term debt ($k_d = 8$ percent). Assume a 40 percent marginal tax rate. Using these figures, the weighted cost of capital being raised to finance next year's capital budget is calculated using Equation 17.15 as

$$k_a = 0.75 \times 12.0 + 0.25 \times 8.0 \times (1 - 0.40)$$
$$= 10.2\%$$

This discount rate should be used to evaluate projects of average risk.

---

cost-benefit analysis A resource allocation model that can be used by public and not-for-profit sector organizations to evaluate programs or investments on the basis of the magnitude of the discounted benefits and costs.

COST-BENEFIT ANALYSIS

The remainder of this chapter is devoted to some techniques of analysis that may be used to assist in public and not-for-profit sector resource-allocation decisions. The primary analytical model examined is cost-benefit analysis, although cost-effectiveness studies are also discussed.

Cost-benefit analysis is used to evaluate programs and investments based on a comparison of their benefits and costs. Cost-benefit analysis is the logical public sector counterpart to the capital budgeting techniques discussed earlier.

---

[10]If the target capital structure contains preferred stock, a preferred stock term is added to Equation 17.15. In this case, Equation 17.15 becomes

$$k_a = \left(\frac{E}{E+D+P}\right)(k_e) + \left(\frac{D}{E+D+P}\right)(k_i) + \left(\frac{P}{E+D+P}\right)(k_p)$$

where P is the amount of preferred stock in the target capital structure and k_p is the component cost of preferred stock.

Accept-Reject Decisions

Cost-benefit analysis may be used to determine whether a specific expenditure is economically justifiable. For instance, one might examine a program designed to eradicate tuberculosis considering the current costs of the disease that could be averted by a specific expenditure of funds. Benefits (averted costs) may be divided into four categories:

1. Expenditures on medical care, including physician and nurse fees, drug costs, and hospital and equipment charges
2. Loss of gross earnings during the disease
3. Reduction in gross earnings after the disease because of decreased employment opportunities resulting from the social stigma attached to the illness
4. The pain and discomfort associated with having the disease

Suppose a particular program to eradicate tuberculosis requires a one-time outlay of $250 million (Table 17.3). Assume that the total benefits (averted disease costs) of this one-year program are expected to accrue for a period of five years. If one accepts, for the moment, that an appropriate **social discount rate** is 15 percent, the program may be evaluated in the NPV analysis framework developed in the capital budgeting discussion. The decision rule is to accept the project if the (discounted) benefits are greater than or equal to the (discounted) costs. Because the program has a positive calculated net discounted benefit, in this case $81.83 million, it is an acceptable project.

Alternative decision-making criteria include the IRR and the benefit-cost ratio. According to the IRR criterion, a project is acceptable if the IRR is greater than or equal to the appropriate social discount rate. In the case of the tuberculosis eradication program, the IRR for the benefits and costs shown in Table 17.3 is 32.4 percent. Because this exceeds the social discount rate of 15 percent, the project is acceptable. According to the benefit-cost ratio criterion, a project is acceptable if the benefit-cost ratio is greater than or equal to 1.0, where the **benefit-cost ratio** is equal to the present value of the benefits (discounted at the social discount rate) divided by the present value of the costs (similarly discounted). For the tuberculosis eradication program, the benefit-cost ratio is equal to

$$\text{Benefit-cost ratio} = \frac{130.50 + 94.50 + 65.80 + 28.60 + 12.43}{250}$$
$$= 1.33$$

Because this ratio exceeds 1.0, the project is acceptable according to this criterion. All three decision criteria give identical decisions to accept or reject individual projects.

social discount rate The discount rate to be used when evaluating benefits and costs from public sector investments.

benefit-cost ratio The ratio of the present value of the benefits from a project or program (discounted at the social discount rate) to the present value of the costs (similarly discounted).

TABLE 17.3   NET COST-BENEFIT ANALYSIS

END OF YEAR	ACTUAL DOLLAR BENEFIT (COST)	PRESENT VALUE INTEREST FACTOR AT 15%*	DISCOUNTED BENEFITS AND COSTS ($ MILLION)
(1)	(2)	(3)	(4) = (2) × (3)
0	(250)	1.000	(250.00)
1	150	0.870	130.50
2	125	0.756	94.50
3	100	0.658	65.80
4	50	0.572	28.60
5	25	0.497	12.43
			Net benefits = $81.83

*Appendix B, Table 4.

© Cengage Learning

TABLE 17.4 SCHEDULE OF PROGRAM BENEFITS FOR VARIOUS COST LEVELS

PROGRAM COST ($ MILLIONS)	DISCOUNTED PROGRAM BENEFITS ($ MILLIONS)	NET PROGRAM BENEFITS ($ MILLIONS)
250	331.83	81.83
300	496.00	196.00
350	540.00	190.00
400	565.00	165.00

© Cengage Learning

TABLE 17.5 MARGINAL ANALYSIS OF BENEFITS AND COSTS

PROGRAM COST ($ MILLIONS)	MARGINAL COST ($ MILLIONS)	DISCOUNTED MARGINAL BENEFITS ($ MILLIONS)
0	—	—
250	250	331.83
300	50	164.17
350	50	44.00
400	50	25.00

© Cengage Learning

Program-Level Analysis

In addition to being used to evaluate whether an entire program is economically justifiable, cost-benefit analysis can determine whether the size of an existing program should be increased (or reduced) and, if so, by what amount. This determination may be made using traditional marginal analysis as developed earlier in the text.

Returning again to the tuberculosis control program, assume that, because of strong lobbying from the American Medical Association, a number of expenditure levels beyond the originally proposed $250 million are being considered. Table 17.4 summarizes these proposed programs and their expected benefits. An analysis that looked at only one of these proposed program expenditure levels would have concluded that any of the program levels was worthwhile because each proposal generates positive expected net program benefits.

When analyzed as a group, however, these program levels clearly show a limit to the economically justifiable expenditure of funds for tuberculosis control. The required analysis is summarized in Table 17.5. A level of expenditure of $300 million is best because it generates an additional (marginal) $164.17 million in benefits, but the marginal program cost (in comparison to the $250 million program level) is only $50 million. To increase the program to $350 million would be counterproductive, because only $44 million in benefits are generated for the additional $50 million outlay (marginal costs exceed marginal benefits).

STEPS IN COST-BENEFIT ANALYSIS

The general principles of cost-benefit analysis may be summarized by answering the following set of questions:

1. What is the objective function to be maximized?
2. What are the constraints placed on the analysis?

3. What costs and benefits are to be included, and how may they be valued?

4. What investment evaluation criterion should be used?

5. What is the appropriate discount rate?

The decision-making process in cost-benefit analysis may be traced in the flowchart presentation of Figure 17.2. Program objectives are set by the public through their political representatives. Alternatives are enumerated, explored, and revised in light of constraints that may be operative in the system. These alternatives are then compared by enumerating and evaluating program benefits and costs in a present-value framework. Discounted benefits are compared with discounted costs, and intangibles are considered so a recommendation may be made about the merits of one or more alternative programs.

FIGURE 17.2   Schematic of the Cost-Benefit Analysis Process

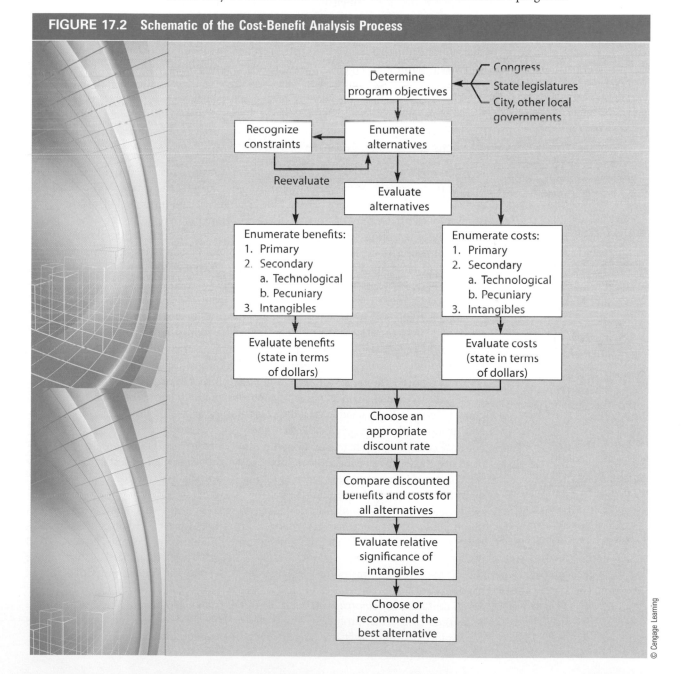

© Cengage Learning

OBJECTIVES AND CONSTRAINTS IN COST-BENEFIT ANALYSIS

Cost-benefit analysis is merely a way of evaluating alternative choices in decision making. As such, we need to examine it in light of several criteria proposed by welfare economists as important for evaluating alternatives. One such criterion is Pareto optimality. A change is said to be desirable or consistent with Pareto optimality if at least one person is made better off (in his or her own judgment) and no one is made worse off (in their own judgment).

Cost-benefit analysis is often tied to a weaker notion of social improvement, sometimes called the Kaldor-Hicks criterion, or merely the notion of a "potential" Pareto improvement. Under this criterion, a change (or an economic program) is desirable if it generates sufficient gains that, when distributed, the gains are sufficient to make all people in the community at least as well off as they were before the change. The fact that gainers may not in fact compensate losers is not a matter of direct consideration in cost-benefit analysis, but the income distributional impacts of a program are an extremely important side issue.

It is important to recognize that not all projects with benefits that exceed costs will necessarily be adopted because of the following:

1. *Physical constraints.* The type of program alternatives considered is ultimately limited by the currently available state of technology and by the production possibilities derived from the relationship between physical inputs and outputs. For example, it is not yet possible to prevent cancer; therefore, a major emphasis must be directed toward early detection and treatment.

2. *Legal constraints.* Domestic as well as international laws relating to property rights, the right of eminent domain, due process, and constitutional limits on a particular agency's activities, among others, must be considered.

3. *Administrative constraints.* Effective programs require that individuals are available or can be hired and trained to carry out the program objectives. Even the best-conceived program is worthless unless individuals with the proper mix of technical and administrative skills are available.

4. *Distributional constraints.* Programs affect different groups in different ways because gainers are rarely the same as losers. When distributional impacts are of concern, the objective of cost-benefit analysis might be presented in terms of maximizing total benefits less total costs, subject to the constraint that benefits-less-costs for a particular group reach a pre-specified level.

5. *Political constraints.* What may be optimal may not be feasible because of the slowness and inefficiency of the political process. Many times what is *best* is tempered by what is *possible*, given the existence of strong competing interest groups as well as an often cumbersome political mechanism.

6. *Financial or budget constraints.* More often than not, agencies work within the bounds of a predetermined budget. In other words, the objective function must be altered to the suboptimizing form of maximizing benefits given a fixed budget. Virtually all programs have some absolute financial ceiling above which the program may not be expanded, in spite of the magnitude of social benefits.

7. *Social and religious constraints.* It is futile to tell Indian Hindus to eat sacred cattle to solve their nutritional problems. This example is just one of the social and religious constraints that may limit the range of feasible program alternatives.

ANALYSIS AND VALUATION OF BENEFITS AND COSTS

Cost-benefit analysis is quite similar to traditional private sector profit-and-loss accounting. In the private sector, the firm is guided by the criterion that private revenues must equal or exceed private costs over the long run for the firm to survive. In contrast, in cost-benefit analysis, the economist asks whether society as a whole will be better off by the adoption or nonadoption of a specific project or by the acceptance of one project to the exclusion of alternatives.

Benefits may be measured by the market price of the outputs from a public program or by the price consumers would be *willing* to pay based on certain assumptions in the analysis. Such assumptions obviously matter, and the analyst should consider a range of plausible assumption values. Moreover, any assumptions to which the recommendations are sensitive must be reported to the decision maker. In general, *sensitivity analysis* should always accompany benefit-cost recommendations.

Direct Benefits

Benefits and costs may be categorized in a number of ways. *Primary* or *direct* benefits of a project consist of the value of goods or services produced if the project is undertaken compared to conditions without the project. The primary benefit of an irrigation project is the value of the additional crops produced on the irrigated land less the cost of seeds, labor, and equipment required to produce the crops. The primary benefits attributable to a college education might be considered as the increase in gross earnings of the graduate over what would have been earned without a college degree.

Direct Costs

Direct or *primary costs* are generally easier to measure than direct benefits. They include the capital costs necessary to undertake the project, operating and maintenance costs incurred over the life of the project, and personnel expenses. Remember that the costs being measured are opportunity costs, or the social value forgone elsewhere when factors of production in an alternate area of activity are used. If a proposed project will draw 20 percent of the required labor from the ranks of the unemployed, the market cost (wage payments) of these workers' services will overstate the true social cost. A similar conclusion applies for the use of idle land. With *no* alternative use, the opportunity cost of the use of this land is zero (for as long as no productive alternative uses exist), no matter what the government happens to actually pay its owner in compensation. Such compensation to the owner affects only the *distribution* of the benefits derived from land usage.

Indirect Costs or Benefits and Intangibles

In addition to the primary impacts of a project, government investment invariably creates *secondary* or *indirect* effects. Secondary costs and benefits may be of two types: *real* effects and *pecuniary* effects. Real secondary benefits may include reductions in necessary outlays for other government projects, for example, when an early glaucoma-detection campaign reduces the number of people who go blind, thereby reducing future government disability transfer payments. Similarly, an irrigation dam may reduce flooding and create a recreational area. These secondary benefits should be counted in a cost benefit study. The same argument applies in accounting for secondary costs. For example, the Wallisville Dam Project in Texas was alleged to cause in excess of $500,000 in damages annually to saltwater fishing because of its impacts on the tidal marshlands. This real secondary cost should have been counted in the cost-benefit analysis of the Wallisville Project.

Pecuniary benefits should generally not be included in the enumeration of "countable" benefits in a study. They generally arise in the form of lower input costs or changes in land values resulting from a project. For example, an improved highway may lead to greater business volume and profitability of gas stations, souvenir shops, and restaurants along that road, as well as higher land values and consequently higher rents to the landlords. Many of these benefits are purely distributional in nature because some business will be drawn from firms along other roads once the new road is completed.

A final group of program benefits and costs is intangibles. For these recognizable impacts of a project, it is either extremely difficult or impossible to calculate a dollar value. Intangibles may include such notions as quality of life and aesthetic contributions (or detriments). Intangibles may be analyzed by making trade-offs against tangibles in such a manner that the cost of additional increments of intangible improvement, for instance, may be compared with the forgone tangible benefits of a project.

THE APPROPRIATE RATE OF DISCOUNT

When the benefits or costs of a program extend beyond a one-year time limit, they must be discounted back to some common point in time for purposes of comparison. Most people prefer current consumption to future consumption, so the social discount rate is used to adjust for this preference.[11] As we have seen in the Managerial Challenge for this chapter, the choice of the appropriate discount rate to evaluate public investments is critical to the conclusions of any cost-benefit analysis. Projects that may appear to be justified at a low discount rate, say 5 percent, may seem to be a gross misallocation of resources at a higher rate, such as 15 percent. The choice of a discount rate is likely to have a profound impact on the type of projects to be accepted. A low rate favors investments with long lives, most of which will be of the durable "bricks and mortar" variety, whereas a high rate favors those whose benefits become available soon after the initial investment.

The discount rate performs the function of allocating resources between the public and private sectors; and an appropriate discount rate should be chosen to properly indicate when resources should be transferred from one sector to another. Simply, then, if resources can earn 10 percent in the private sector, they should not be transferred to the public sector unless they can earn something greater than 10 percent on the invested resources. The correct discount rate for the evaluation of a government project is the percentage rate of return that the resources utilized would otherwise provide in the private sector.

Example

Costs and Benefits of a Toyota Automobile Plant in Kentucky

Toyota built an assembly plant near Lexington, Kentucky, that is able to produce 200,000 automobiles annually. To get Toyota to locate the plant in Kentucky, the state agreed to invest approximately $325 million over a 20-year period. These expenditures include the following:

• Land and site preparation	$33 million
• Local highway construction	47 million

(continued)

---

[11]A review of discounting and present-value concepts is provided in Appendix A.

- Employee training center and education of workers   65 million
- Education of Japanese workers and families   5 million
- Interest on economic development bonds   167 million

The returns to the state over the 20-year period are estimated at $632 million in income, sales, and payroll taxes from Toyota, its suppliers, and related businesses.

These numbers yield an IRR of 25 percent, according to a University of Kentucky research team. Because the state's economic resources are limited, one must consider whether these resources should have been invested in other projects that would have generated even higher rates of return. However, as Brinton Milward, director of the university's Center for Business and Economic Research, explains, "Could you have put these funds into improvements in education and transportation and come up with a better benefit-cost ratio? My guess is no. Manufacturing has a pretty high multiplier" (in terms of the repeated turnover of money in the form of jobs and sales).

COST-EFFECTIVENESS ANALYSIS

Although cost-benefit analysis may be applied in a wide range of areas, in many types of government activity it is simply not feasible because of the problems of measuring the value of program outputs. For instance, program analyses in the fields of national security, health and safety, and income redistribution are more frequently conducted using the cost-effectiveness framework than the cost-benefit one. The **cost-effectiveness analysis** *begins* with the premise that some identified program outputs are useful, and it proceeds to explore (1) how these outputs may be most efficiently achieved *or* (2) what the costs are of achieving various levels of the pre-specified output.

Cost-effectiveness analysis is widely applied in Department of Defense program studies. The benefits of most defense activities may be thought of as providing levels of deterrence. For many years, for example, the strategic nuclear bomber force provided a virtually impossible-to-quantify level of deterrent benefit against first-strike nuclear attack.

cost-effectiveness analysis An analytical tool designed to assist public decision makers in their resource allocation decisions when benefits cannot be easily measured in terms of dollars but costs can be monetarily quantified.

Least-Cost Studies

The most frequent type of cost-effectiveness analysis is *least-cost studies*. As might be expected, the emphasis of these studies is to identify the least expensive way of generating some quantity of an output. For instance, a city might decide that it wishes to reduce by 20 percent the number of burglaries occurring each year within its jurisdictional limits. One approach could be to expand the size of the police force, increase the number of foot patrol officers, and increase the number of squad cars on the streets at any one time. Another possibility might be to require builders to install security bars on the windows of all new homes and to provide cash or tax incentives for current homeowners to improve their personal security systems. A third alternative might be a community drive supporting Operation Identification, where individuals place permanent identifying marks on their belongings to make "fencing" of this merchandise more difficult. Combinations of these programs are also possible. Each of these alternatives is evaluated in terms of the expenditure required to achieve the desired objective—a 20 percent reduction in burglaries.

TABLE 17.6 HYPOTHETICAL DATA RELATING TO THE COST OF ACHIEVING VARIOUS LEVELS OF AUTO EMISSION REDUCTIONS	
PERCENTAGE OF 2008 EMISSION LEVELS	**COSTS ($ MILLIONS—INCLUDING FUEL CONSUMPTION, MORE FREQUENT MAINTENANCE, AND ADDED NEW-CAR COSTS)**
90	200
70	250
40	500
20	2,500
10	7,500
5	38,000
1	140,000

© Cengage Learning

Objective-Level Studies

A second type of cost-effectiveness analysis is *objective-level studies*. These studies attempt to estimate the costs of achieving several alternative performance levels of the same objective. This approach may be illustrated with the case of reducing automobile emission levels. Table 17.6 provides some hypothetical data relating to various emission-control standards. Although these estimates in Table 17.6 may be realistic for an internal combustion reciprocating engine, they may far overstate actual costs if alternative technology like a hybrid-electric engine were assumed.

Table 17.6 *does* illustrate that as the level of objective achievement increases, the associated costs frequently increase at a much more rapid rate. This information may help the decision maker to reach more rational decisions. For example, the $2.5 billion expenditure needed to reduce emissions to 20 percent of their 2008 levels may be reasonable. What is less clear is whether an additional 19 percent (from 20 percent to 1 percent) emissions reduction is worth the required incremental expenditure of $137.5 billion ($140 billion minus $2.5 billion).

SUMMARY

- A *capital expenditure* is a current outlay of funds that is expected to provide a flow of future cash benefits.
- The capital-expenditure decision process should consist of the following steps: generating alternative investment proposals, estimating cash flows, evaluating and choosing the projects to undertake, and reviewing the projects after implementation.
- The *internal rate of return (IRR)* is the discount rate that equates the present value of the net cash flows from the project with the net investment. An investment project should be accepted

(rejected) if its IRR is greater than or equal to (less than) the firm's required rate of return (i.e., cost of capital).

- The *net present value (NPV)* of an investment is the present value of the net cash flows from the project, discounted at the firm's required rate of return (i.e., cost of capital), minus the project's net investment. An investment project should be accepted (rejected) if its NPV is greater than or equal to (less than) zero.
- The *cost of capital* is the cost of funds that are supplied to the firm. It is influenced by the riskiness of

the firm, both in terms of its capital structure and its investment strategy.

- The after-tax cost of debt (issued at par) is equal to the coupon rate multiplied by 1 minus the firm's marginal tax rate.
- The cost of equity can be estimated using a number of different approaches, including the dividend valuation model and the capital asset pricing model.
- The weighted cost of capital is calculated by weighting the costs of specific sources of funds, such as debt and equity, by the proportions of each of the capital components in the firm's long-range target capital structure.
- *Cost-benefit analysis* is the public sector counterpart of capital budgeting techniques used for resource allocation decisions.
- Cost-benefit analysis involves the following steps:

  1. Determining the program objectives
  2. Enumerating the alternative means of achieving the objectives, subject to the legal, political, technological, budgetary, and other constraints that limit the scope of action

  3. Evaluating all primary, secondary, and intangible benefits and costs associated with each alternative
  4. Discounting the benefits and costs using a social discount rate to arrive at an overall measure of the desirability of each alternative (e.g., benefit-cost ratio)
  5. Choosing (or recommending) the best alternative based on the overall measure of desirability, the relative magnitude of the unquantifiable intangibles, and sensitivity analysis.

- Because of the measurement problems arising from the intangible impacts and economic externalities of many public programs, cost-benefit analysis is most useful in comparing projects with similar objectives and similar magnitudes of intangibles and externalities.
- In cases where it is not feasible to place dollar values on final program outputs, *cost-effectiveness analysis* may be used. Cost-effectiveness analysis assumes *a priori* that the program objectives are worth achieving and focuses on the least-cost method of achieving them.

Exercises

Answers to the exercises in blue can be found in Appendix D at the back of the book.

1. A firm has the opportunity to invest in a project having an initial outlay of $20,000. Net cash inflows (before depreciation and taxes) are expected to be $5,000 per year for five years. The firm uses the straight-line depreciation method with a zero salvage value and has a (marginal) income tax rate of 40 percent. The firm's cost of capital is 12 percent.
   a. Compute the IRR and the NPV.
   b. Should the firm accept or reject the project?

2. A machine that costs $12,000 is expected to operate for 10 years. The estimated salvage value at the end of 10 years is $0. The machine is expected to save the company $2,331 per year before taxes and depreciation. The company depreciates its assets on a straight-line basis and has a marginal tax rate of 40 percent. The firm's cost of capital is 14 percent. Based on the IRR criterion, should this machine be purchased?

3. A company is planning to invest $75,000 (before taxes) in a personnel training program. The $75,000 outlay will be charged off as an expense by the firm this year (year 0). The returns estimated from the program in the form of greater productivity and a reduction in employee turnover are as follows (on an after-tax basis):

   Years 1–10: $7,500 per year

   Years 11–20: $22,500 per year

   The company has estimated its cost of capital to be 15 percent. Assume that the entire $75,000 is paid at time zero (the beginning of the project). The marginal tax rate for the firm is 40 percent.

   Based on the NPV criterion, should the firm undertake the training program?

4. Alliance Manufacturing Company is considering the purchase of a new automated drill press to replace an older one. The machine now in operation has a book value of zero and a salvage value of zero. However, it is in good working condition with an expected life of 10 additional years. The new drill press is more efficient than the existing one and, if installed, will provide an estimated cost savings (in labor, materials, and maintenance) of $6,000 per year. The new machine costs $25,000 delivered and installed. It has an estimated useful life of 10 years and a salvage value of $1,000 at the end of this period. The firm's cost of capital is 14 percent, and its marginal income tax rate is 40 percent. The firm uses the straight-line depreciation method.

    a. What is the net cash flow in year 0 (i.e., initial outlay)?

    b. What are the net cash flows after taxes in each of the next 10 years?

    c. What is the NPV of the investment?

    d. Should Alliance replace its existing drill press?

5. The Charlotte Bobcats, a professional basketball team, has been offered the opportunity to purchase the contract of an aging superstar basketball player from another team. The general manager of the Bobcats wants to analyze the offer as a capital budgeting problem. The Bobcats would have to pay the other team $800,000 to obtain the superstar. Being somewhat old, the basketball player is expected to be able to play for only four more years. The general manager figures that attendance, and hence revenues, would increase substantially if the Bobcats obtained the superstar. He estimates that *incremental* returns (additional ticket revenues less the superstar's salary) would be as follows over the four-year period:

YEAR	INCREMENTAL RETURNS ($)
1	450,000
2	350,000
3	275,000
4	200,000

The general manager has been told by the owners of the team that any capital expenditures must yield at least 12 percent after taxes. The firm's (marginal) income tax rate is 40 percent. Furthermore, a check of the tax regulations indicates that the team can depreciate the $800,000 initial expenditure over the four-year period.

    a. Calculate the IRR and the NPV to determine the desirability of this investment.

    b. Should the Bobcats sign the superstar?

6. Panhandle Industries, Inc., currently pays an annual common stock dividend of $2.20 per share. The company's dividend has grown steadily over the past 10 years at 8 percent per year; this growth trend is expected to continue for the foreseeable future. The company's present dividend payout ratio, also expected to continue, is 40 percent. In addition, the stock presently sells at eight times current earnings— that is, its "multiple" is 8.

    Calculate the company's cost of equity capital using the dividend-capitalization model approach.

7. The Gordon Company currently pays an annual common stock dividend of $4.00 per share. Its dividend payments have been growing at a steady rate of 6 percent per year, and this rate of growth is expected to continue for the foreseeable future. Gordon's common stock is currently selling for $65.25 per share. The company can

sell additional shares of common stock after flotation costs at a net price of $60.50 per share.

Based on the dividend capitalization model, determine the cost of
a. Internal equity (retained earnings)
b. External equity (new common stock)

8. The Williams Company has a present capital structure (that it considers optimal) consisting of 30 percent long-term debt and 70 percent common equity. The company plans to finance next year's capital budget with additional long-term debt and retained earnings. New debt can be issued at a coupon interest rate of 10 percent. The cost of retained earnings (internal equity) is estimated at 15 percent. The company's marginal tax rate is 40 percent.

Calculate the company's weighted cost of capital for the coming year.

9. The state of Glottamora has $100 million remaining in its budget for the current year. One alternative is to give Glottamorans a one-time tax rebate. Alternatively, two proposals have been made for state expenditures of these funds.

The first proposed project is to invest in a new power plant, costing $100 million and having an expected useful life of 20 years. Projected benefits accruing from this project are as follows:

YEARS	BENEFITS PER YEAR ($ MILLIONS)
1–5	0
6–20	20

The second alternative is to undertake a job retraining program, also costing $100 million and generating the following benefits:

YEARS	BENEFITS PER YEAR ($ MILLIONS)
1–5	20
6–10	14
11–20	4

The state Power Department argues that a 5 percent discount factor should be used in evaluating the projects because that is the government's borrowing rate. The Human Resources Department suggests using a 12 percent rate because that more nearly equals society's true opportunity rate.

a. What is implied by the various departments' desires to use different discount rates?
b. Evaluate the projects using both the 5 percent and the 12 percent rates.
c. What rate do you believe to be more appropriate?
d. Make a choice between the projects and the tax-refund alternative. Why did you choose the alternative you did?

10. The Department of Transportation wishes to choose between two alternative accident prevention programs. It has identified three benefits to be gained from such programs:

- Reduced property damage, both to the vehicles involved in an accident and to other property (e.g., real estate that may be damaged at the scene of an accident)
- Reduced injuries
- Reduced fatalities

The department's experts are willing to provide dollar estimates of property damage savings that are expected to accrue from any program, but they will estimate only the number of injuries and fatalities that may be averted.

The first program is relatively moderate in its costs and will be concentrated in a large city. It involves upgrading traffic signals, improving road markers, and repaving some potholed streets. Because of the concentration and value of property in the city, savings from reduced property damage are expected to be substantial. Likewise, a moderate number of traffic-related deaths and injuries could be avoided.

The second program is more ambitious. It involves straightening long sections of dangerous rural roads and installing improved guardrails. Although the property damage savings are expected to be small in relation to total cost, the reduction in traffic-related deaths and injuries should be substantial.

The following table summarizes the expected costs and payoffs of the two programs:

YEAR	1	2	3	4	TOTAL
Alternative #1					
Cost ($000)	200	200	100	50	550
Reduced property damage ($000)	50	100	250	100	500
Lives saved	60	40	35	25	160
Injuries prevented	500	425	300	150	1,375
Alternative #2					
Cost ($000)	700	1,800	1,100	700	4,300
Reduced property damage ($000)	150	225	475	300	1,150
Lives saved	50	75	100	125	350
Injuries prevented	800	850	900	900	3,450

Assume that a 10 percent discount rate is appropriate for evaluating government programs:

a. Calculate the net present costs of the two programs.
b. Generate any other tables that you may find useful in choosing between the programs.
c. Can you arrive at any unambiguous choice between the two alternatives? What factors are likely to weigh on the ultimate choice made?

Case Exercises | ## Industrial Development Tax Relief and Incentives

Tax-relief competition between states seeking high-paying industrial jobs threatens to overpay for any conceivable net benefits. In 1993, Alabama paid more than $300 million in highway, rail, sewer, and other infrastructure investments to obtain a $300 million Mercedes plant with 1,500 jobs. From 2006 through 2009, North Carolina built a new runway at the Triad Airport for $130 million and provided job training and tax breaks worth another $142.3 million to obtain a $300 million FedEx hub.

Questions

1. Assess the likely benefits of such a plant or hub and how one should go about analyzing them.
2. What form might a report to the Industrial Development Commission take? Outline the requisite components.

Multigenerational Effects of Ozone Depletion and Greenhouse Gases[12]

The long-term effects of ozone depletion from hydrochlorofluorocarbon (HCFC) emissions and of CO_2 and other greenhouse gases from the burning of fossil fuels are controversial. Environmental scientists insist that the release of HCFCs opened a gaping hole in the ozone shield that provides protection from the sun's ultraviolet (UV) rays. More recently, some scientists have argued that the increasing concentration of greenhouse gases has raised global temperatures. What is less controversial is that these environmental events have massive consequences for human health and wealth. Increasing incidence of skin cancers, melting polar icecaps, and rising sea levels imply tangible losses of catastrophic proportions—perhaps many billions of dollars annually. Some of these losses are immediate, but others are perhaps 100 years off.

Benefit-cost analysis normally considers projects no more than 20 to 30 years long and employs discount rates of 2 to 8 percent. How should one discount such an uncertain and distant future as is involved in ozone depletion and greenhouse gases? Assuming a constant discount rate equal to the rate of return on long-term government bonds (5.43 percent), the discount factor that should be applied to find the present value of projected benefits or losses avoided in year 100 would be $(1/1.057^{100}) = 0.003913$ or $3,913,780 present value per billion dollars of future losses avoided in year 100. Notice what happens, however, if uncertainty about the appropriate discount rate varies from 2 to 8 percent. The discount factor at 100 years would then vary from $(1/1.02^{100}) = 0.13803$ or $138,032,967 per billion dollars for 2 percent, to as little as $(1/1.08^{100}) = 0.000454$, or $454,595 per billion dollars for 8 percent.

The possibility of lower discount rates implies that more than $138 million dollars should be spent today to avoid the projected $1 billion in delayed damage 100 years from now! Of course, the higher 8 percent rate implies spending less than one-half a million to avoid the $100 billion future loss. This range of present value estimates from $138 million to $454,595 is beyond what any analyst can work with in doing sensitivity analysis. What should a benefit-cost analyst conclude? And what should businesses whose cash flows depend on "fun in the sun" recreation like golf courses and theme parks and beachside hotels or physical assets built near sea level like the New York and Shanghai business districts conclude about the justifiable capital expenditure to slow down or reverse global warming?

One insight is that it is not the 5 percent average discount rate between 2 and 8 percent that matters in such circumstances, just as the average depth of a pool does not determine the hazard to someone who cannot swim. Instead, the lowest applicable discount rate largely determines the present value of very distant cash flows because higher-discount-rate scenarios like 7 and 8 percent inevitably sum to essentially zero at 100 years.

Martin Weitzman has calculated what discount rate is implied by assuming the discount rate begins at 4 percent and then follows a random path with equiprobable higher and lower rates and a standard deviation of 3 percent. The results led him to recommend a sliding-scale discount rate of 2 percent for 25- to 75-year and 1 percent for 76- to 300-year cash flows. The fact that lower discount rates have such dramatically nonsymmetrical effects on present value when very distant benefits are involved means that the

---

[12]Based on Richard Newell and William Pizer, "Discounting the Benefits of Climate Change Mitigation," *Resources for the Future* (December 2001); Martin Weitzman, "Gamma Discounting," *American Economic Review* (March 2001); and Frederick Harris, "Alternative Energy: A Symposium," Wake Forest University (September 19, 2008); "California Sells Out of First Pollution Permits," *Wall Street Journal* (November 20, 2012), p. B2; "Europe's Dirty Little Secret: The Unwelcome Renaissance," *The Economist* (January 5, 2013), pp. 47–50.

present value of reducing CO_2 emissions and other greenhouse gases may be much higher than previously thought.

As decision makers worldwide consider the options for reducing greenhouse gases (CO_2, methane, nitrous oxide, etc.), one glaring fact surfaces quickly. The U.S. Energy Information Administration estimates that 41 percent of all the CO_2 emissions we generate in the United States come from electricity generation, and 83 percent of that comes from burning coal (see Figure 17.3). So, 34 percent (0.41×0.83) of all U.S. CO_2 emissions comes from coal-fired power plants. Not surprisingly, much interest in preventing global warming has therefore centered on alternative sources of electrical energy generation. The popular inequality RE < C refers to sources of renewable energy (RE) for powering our households and workplaces that might be less expensive than coal (C).

What exactly are the alternative sources of electrical energy? Wind power, solar power, biomass, hydro, biofuel, geothermal, and ocean tidal power all contain some attractive common features for the United States. They are renewable resources in abundant local supply with low carbon footprints. At present, only 5 percent of electrical generation comes from all these alternative energy sources rather than coal (83 percent), natural gas (15 percent), or negligible fuel oil (again see Figure 17.3). Natural gas is now much cheaper today than coal per British thermal unit (BTU), but its carbon footprint (though 80 percent cleaner than coal) is still quite substantial. Rather than spending almost $1 billion a day in net wealth transfer for foreign crude oil, Americans now perceive that natural gas is their most plentiful energy resource. Indeed, at present rates of consumption, the United States has more proven reserves of coal (100 years) and natural gas (110 years' worth) than Saudi Arabia has proven reserves of oil (85 years).

FIGURE 17.3 **Greenhouse Gas Emissions in the United States**

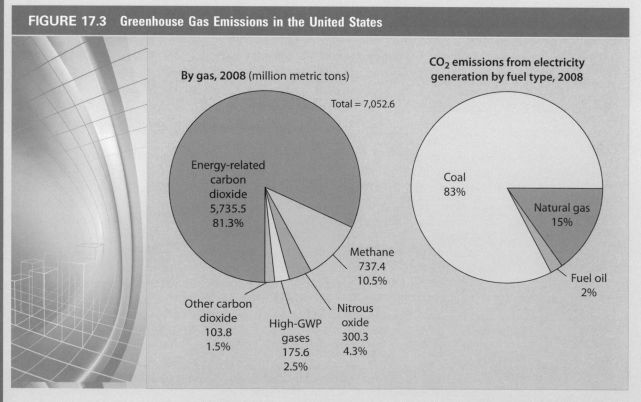

Source: U.S. Energy Information Administration, *Greenhouse Gases in the United States* (December 2009).

But 1 ton of coal generates a megawatt of electricity *plus* 1 ton of CO_2 byproduct. The marginal cost for delivered coal has varied from $45 to $82 per ton in 2007–2012, and the electricity is worth from $0.06/kWh in Washington state to $0.12/kWh in New York state. Taking the 2013 cost of coal ($88) and the weighted average value of electricity across the United States ($0.11), the electrical generation industry pays $80 per ton for coal on the spot market and produces a $110 megawatt of electricity.

The problem is that when one includes the market cost of a ton of CO_2 byproduct, using the 2013 price of the CO_2 emission trading contract in the European Union (EU) of $10,[13] a typical public utility in the United States must recover all its capital cost from the remaining tiny $12 operating profit ($110 − $88 − $10 = $12) per megawatt hour. Even a giant 500-megawatt U.S. power plant would therefore project (under a cap-and-trade carbon emissions trading regime) net cash flow of only $6,000 per hour for perhaps 20 hours a day or $120,000 per day to recover capital equipment costs and earn a profit. That sums to $42 million per year, sufficient at a 5% CoC to generate only $840 million present value of the net cash flow against the $900 million net investment of a 500-megawatt coal-fired power plant plus smokestack scrubbers, even if the cash flows last 50 years.

The way forward is natural gas (NG) production, which has exploded in the United States, resulting in an 84 percent reduction in its equilibrium price, now half the cost of coal per BTU.

Discussion Questions

1. At a 7 percent discount rate, what annual cash flow is needed to make the 500-megawatt plant profitable? What about using NG at half the cost of coal?

---

[13]California has launched the first mandated cap-and-trade carbon trading scheme in the United States; 1 ton of 2013 carbon emissions cleared for $10.09.

2. What is the effect on your analysis of CO_2 emissions trading allowances rising in price to $20 halfway back to its $39 peak price per ton reached in 2008?
3. Has the natural gas revolution in the United States made coal-fired power plants more or less profitable? Why or why not?
4. Which is more likely to be adopted a) an optimal carbon tax of 7% higher electricity cost and 2% higher gasoline costs or b) a cap and trade carbon emission trading system? Why?

The Time Value of Money

INTRODUCTION

Many economic decisions involve benefits and costs that are expected to occur at different future points in time. For example, the construction of a new office complex requires an immediate outlay of cash and results in a stream of expected cash inflows (benefits) over many future years. To determine if the expected future cash inflows are sufficient to justify the initial outlay, we must have a way to compare cash flows occurring at different points in time. Also, recall from Chapter 1 that the value of a firm is equal to the discounted (or present) value of all expected returns. These future returns are discounted at a rate of return that is consistent with the risk of the expected future returns. When future returns are more certain, the discount rate used is lower, resulting in a higher present value of the firm, *all other things being equal*. Conversely, when future returns are riskier or more uncertain, they are discounted at a higher rate, resulting in a lower present value of the firm, *all other things being equal*.

An explicit solution to the problem of comparing the benefits and costs of economic transactions that occur at different points in time requires answers to the following kinds of questions: Is $1 to be received one year from today worth less than $1 in hand today? If so, why is it worth less? How much less is it worth?

The answers to these questions depend on the alternative uses available for the dollar between today and one year from today. Suppose the dollar can be invested in a guaranteed savings account paying a 6 percent annual rate of return (interest rate). The $1 invested today will return $1(1.06) = $1.06 one year from today. To receive exactly $1 one year from today, only $1/(1.06) = $0.943 would have to be invested in the account today. Given the opportunity to invest at a 6 percent rate of return, we see that $1 to be received one year from today is indeed worth less than $1 in hand today, its worth being only $0.943. Thus, the existence of opportunities to invest the dollar at positive rates of return makes $1 to be received at any future point in time worth less than $1 in hand today.[1] This is what is meant by the *time value of money*. The investor's required rate of return is called the *discount rate*.

PRESENT VALUE OF A SINGLE PAYMENT

We can generalize this result for any future series of cash flows and any interest rate. Assume that the opportunity exists to invest at a compound rate of *r* percent per annum. Then the *present value* (*PV*) (value today) of $1 to be received at the end of year *n*, discounted at *r* percent, is

$$PV_0 = \frac{1}{(1+r)^n} \qquad [A.1]$$

---

[1] In this analysis, we are abstracting from price-level considerations. Changes in the level of prices (the value of the dollar in terms of the quantity of goods and services it will buy) can also affect the worth of the dollar. In theory, future price increases (or decreases) that are anticipated by the market will be reflected in the interest rate.

The term $1/(1 + r)^n$ is often called a present value interest factor, or $PVIF_{r,n}$. Table A.3 at the end of this Appendix contains $PVIF$ values for various interest rates, r, and periods in the future, n.

Example

Present Value

If an opportunity exists to invest at a compound rate of return of 12 percent, then the present value of $1 to be received four years ($n = 4$) from today is

$$PV_0 = \frac{1}{(1 + .12)^4} = (PVIF_{12\%,4})$$

$$= \$1(0.6355)$$

$$= \$0.6355$$

As we see in Table A.1, investing $0.6355 today at an interest rate of 12 percent per annum will give $1 at the end of four years.

Alternatively, the $PVIF$ factors from Table A.3 again could be used to find the present value of $1 expected to be received in four years ($n = 4$), assuming an interest rate of 12 percent ($r = 12\%$), as follows:

$$PV_0 = \$1(PVIF_{12\%,4})$$

$$= \$1(0.63552)$$

$$= \$0.6355$$

TABLE A.1   PRESENT VALUE OF $1 TO BE RECEIVED AT THE END OF FOUR YEARS

YEAR	RETURN RECEIVED AT END OF YEAR ($)	VALUE OF INVESTMENT AT END OF YEAR ($)	
0 (present)	—	0.6355	← Initial amount invested
1	0.6355(0.12) = 0.0762	0.6355 + 0.0762 = 0.7117	
2	0.7117(0.12) = 0.0854	0.7117 + 0.0854 = 0.7971	
3	0.7971(0.12) = 0.0957	0.7971 + 0.0957 = 0.8928	
4	0.8928(0.12) = 0.1072	0.8928 + 0.1072 = 1.000	

© Cengage Learning

Example

Present Value of a Deferred Bequest

What is the present value of an expected bequest of $2 million to your university if the expected remaining life span of the donor is eight years and the university uses an interest rate of 9 percent to evaluate gifts of this type?

$$PV_0 = \$2,000,000(PVIF_{9\%,8})$$

$$= \$2,000,000(0.50187)$$

$$= \$1,003,740$$

Your university would be indifferent between receiving $1,003,740 today or $2 million in eight years.

Solving for the Interest or Growth Rate

PVIF can also be used to solve for interest rates. For example, suppose you wish to borrow $5,000 today from an associate. The associate is willing to loan you the money if you promise to pay back $6,802 four years from today. The compound interest rate your associate is charging can be determined as follows:

$$PV_0 = \$6,802(PVIF_{r,4})$$

$$\$5,000 = \$6,802(PVIF_{r,4})$$

$$PVIF_{r,4} = \frac{\$5,000}{\$6,802}$$

$$= 0.735$$

Reading across the Period 04 row in Table A.3, 0.735 (rounded to three places for simplicity) is found in the 8 percent column. Thus, the effective interest rate on the loan is 8 percent per year, compounded annually.

Example

Calculation of Earnings Growth Rates for Hanamaker Paper

Another common application of the use of *PVIF* factors from Table A.3 is the calculation of the compound rate of growth of an earnings or dividend stream. For example, Hanamaker Paper Company had earnings per share of $2.56 in 2010. Security analysts have forecasted 2015 earnings per share to be $6.37. What is the expected compound annual rate of growth in Hanamaker Paper Company's earnings per share? We can use the *PVIF* factors from Table A.3 to solve this problem as follows:

$$\$2.56 = \$6.37(PVIF_{r,5})$$

$$PVIF_{r,5} = 0.40188$$

Looking across the Period 05 row in Table A.3 we find a *PVIF* equal to 0.40188 under the 20 percent column. Thus, the compound annual growth rate of earnings for Hanamaker Paper Company is 20 percent. (Interpolation can be used for *PVIF* values between the values found in the tables. In practice, financial calculators are normally used for these types of calculations.)

PRESENT VALUE OF A SERIES OF EQUAL PAYMENTS (ANNUITY)

The present value of a series of *equal* $1 payments to be received at the end of each of the next *n* years (an *annuity*), discounted at a rate of *r* percent, is

$$PV_0 = \frac{1}{(1+r)^1} + \frac{1}{(1+r)^2} + \cdots + \frac{1}{(1+r)^n}$$

$$PV_0 = \sum_{t=1}^{n} \frac{1}{(1+r)^t} \qquad \text{[A.2]}$$

TABLE A.2 **PRESENT VALUE OF $1 TO BE RECEIVED AT THE END OF EACH OF THE NEXT FOUR YEARS**

YEAR	RETURN RECEIVED AT END OF YEAR ($)	AMOUNT WITHDRAWN AT END OF YEAR ($)	VALUE OF INVESTMENT AT END OF YEAR ($)	
0 (present)	—	—	3.0374	← Initial amount invested
1	3.0374(0.12) = 0.3645	1.00	3.0374 + 0.3645 − 1.00 = 2.4019	
2	2.4019(0.12) = 0.2882	1.00	2.4019 + 0.2882 − 1.00 = 1.6901	
3	1.6901(0.12) = 0.2028	1.00	1.6901 + 0.2028 − 1.00 = 0.8929	
4	0.8929(0.12) = 0.1071	1.00	0.8929 + 0.1071 − 1.00 = 0.0000	

© Cengage Learning

For example, the present value of $1 to be received at the end of each of the next four years, discounted at 12 percent, is

$$PV_0 = \sum_{t=1}^{4} \frac{1}{(1+.12)^t}$$

$$= \frac{1}{(1+.12)^1} + \frac{1}{(1+.12)^2} + \frac{1}{(1+.12)^3} + \frac{1}{(1+.12)^4}$$

$$= 0.89286 + 0.79719 + 0.71178 + 0.63552 = \$3.0374$$

As shown in Table A.2, investing $3.0374 today at 12 percent will return exactly $1 at the end of each of the next four years, with nothing remaining in the account at the end of the fourth year. Again, rather than perform the present-value calculations (Equation A.2), we can use a table to look up the values we need. Table A.4 at the end of this Appendix contains the present values at various interest rates of $1 to be received at the end of each year for various periods of time. The values in Table A.4 are called present value interest factors for annuities, or $PVIFA_{r,n}$, where r is the interest rate per period and n is the number of periods (normally years).

Using the $PVIFA$ factors from Table A.4, the present value of an annuity ($PVAN_0$) can be computed as

$$PVAN_0 = PMT(PVIFA_{r,n}) \qquad [A.3]$$

where $PMT =$ the annuity amount to be received each period.

Example

Present Value of an Annuity

You have recently purchased the winning ticket in the Florida lottery and have won $30 million, to be paid in equal $3 million increments ($PMT$) at the end of each of the next 10 years. What are your winnings worth to you today using an interest rate of 8 percent? The $PVIFA$ factors from Table A.4 can be used to solve this problem as follows:

$$PVAN_0 = \$3,000,000(PVIFA_{8\%,10})$$

$$= \$3,000,000(6.7101)$$

$$= \$20,130,300$$

Thus, your $30 million winnings are worth only $20,130,300 to you today.

Solving for the Interest Rate

PVIFA factors also can be used to solve for the rate of return expected from an investment. This rate of return is often referred to as the *internal rate of return* from an investment. Suppose the Big Spring Tool Company purchases a machine for $100,000. This machine is expected to generate annual cash flows of $23,740 to the firm over the next five years. What is the expected rate of return from this investment?

Using Equation A.3, we can determine the expected rate of return in this example as follows:

$$PVAN_0 = PMT(PVIF_{r,5})$$
$$\$100{,}000 = \$23{,}740(PVIFA_{r,5})$$
$$PVIF_{r,5} = 4.2123$$

From the Period 05 row in Table A.4, we see that a *PVIFA* of 4.2123 occurs in the 6 percent column. Hence, this investment offers a 6 percent expected (internal) rate of return.

PRESENT VALUE OF A SERIES OF UNEQUAL PAYMENTS

The present value of a series of *unequal* payments (PMT_t, $t = 1,\ldots, n$) to be received at the end of each of the next n years, discounted at a rate of r percent, is

$$PV_0 = \sum_{t=1}^{n} \frac{PMT_t}{(1+r)^t}$$
$$= \sum_{t=1}^{n} PMT_t(PVIF_{r,t}) \qquad [A.4]$$

The $PVIF_{r,t}$ values are the interest factors from Table A.3. Thus, the present value of a series of unequal payments is equal to the sum of the present value of the individual payments.

Example

Project Evaluation for Intel

Intel Corporation is evaluating an investment in a new chip-manufacturing facility. The facility is expected to have a useful life of five years and yield the following cash flow stream after the initial investment outlay:

END OF YEAR t	CASH FLOW PMT_t
1	+ $1,000,000
2	+ 1,500,000
3	− 500,000
4	+ 2,000,000
5	+ 1,000,000

The negative cash flow in Year 3 arises because of the expected need to install pollution-control equipment during that year. The present value of this series of

(continued)

unequal payments can be computed using *PVIF* factors from Table A.3 and assuming a 10 percent interest (required) rate on the investment:

$$PV = \$1,000,000(PVIF_{10\%,1}) + \$1,500,000(PVIF_{10\%,2})$$
$$-\$500,000(PVIF_{10\%,3}) + \$2,000,000(PVIF_{10\%,4})$$
$$+\$1,000,000(PVIF_{10\%,5})$$
$$= \$1,000,000(0.90909) + \$1,500,000(0.82645)$$
$$-\$500,000(0.75131) + \$2,000,000(0.68301)$$
$$+\$1,000,000(0.62092)$$
$$= \$3,760,050$$

The present value of these cash flows ($3,760,050) should be compared to the required initial cash outlay to determine whether to invest in the new manufacturing facility.

TABLE A.3   PRESENT VALUE OF $1 (*PVIF*)

PERIOD	1%	2%	3%	4%	5%	6%	7%	8%	9%	10%	PERIOD
01	.99010	.98039	.97007	.96154	.95233	.94340	.93458	.92593	.91743	.90909	01
02	.98030	.96117	.94260	.92456	.90703	.89000	.87344	.85734	.84168	.82645	02
03	.97059	.94232	.91514	.88900	.86384	.83962	.81639	.79383	.77228	.75131	03
04	.96098	.92385	.88849	.85480	.82270	.79209	.76290	.73503	.70883	.68301	04
05	.95147	.90573	.86261	.82193	.78353	.74726	.71299	.68058	.64993	.62092	05
06	.94204	.88797	.83748	.79031	.74622	.70496	.66634	.63017	.59627	.56447	06
07	.93272	.87056	.81309	.75992	.71063	.66506	.62275	.58349	.54705	.51316	07
08	.92348	.85349	.78941	.73069	.67684	.62741	.58201	.54027	.50187	.46651	08
09	.91434	.83675	.76642	.70259	.64461	.59190	.54393	.50025	.46043	.42410	09
10	.90529	.82035	.74409	.67556	.61391	.55839	.50835	.46319	.42241	.38554	10
11	.89632	.80426	.72242	.64958	.58468	.52679	.47509	.42888	.38753	.35049	11
12	.88745	.78849	.70138	.62460	.55684	.49697	.44401	.39711	.35553	.31683	12
13	.87866	.77303	.68095	.60057	.53032	.46884	.41496	.36770	.32618	.28966	13
14	.86996	.75787	.66112	.57747	.50507	.44230	.38782	.34046	.29925	.26333	14
15	.86135	.74301	.64186	.55526	.48102	.41726	.36245	.31524	.27454	.23939	15
16	.85282	.72845	.62317	.53391	.45811	.39365	.33873	.29189	.25187	.21763	16
17	.84436	.71416	.60502	.51337	.43630	.37136	.31657	.27027	.23107	.19784	17
18	.83602	.70016	.58739	.49363	.41552	.35034	.29586	.25025	.21199	.17986	18
19	.82774	.68643	.57029	.47464	.39573	.33051	.27651	.23171	.19449	.16354	19
20	.81954	.67297	.55367	.45639	.37689	.31180	.25842	.21455	.17843	.14864	20
21	.81143	.65978	.53755	.44883	.35894	.29415	.24151	.19866	.16370	.13513	21
22	.80340	.64684	.52189	.42195	.34185	.27750	.22571	.18394	.15018	.12285	22
23	.79544	.63414	.50669	.40573	.32557	.26180	.21095	.17031	.13778	.11168	23
24	.78757	.62172	.49193	.39012	.31007	.24698	.19715	.15770	.12640	.10153	24
25	.77977	.60953	.47760	.37512	.29530	.23300	.18425	.14602	.11597	.09230	25

TABLE A.3	PRESENT VALUE OF $1 (*PVIF*) (CONTINUED)										
PERIOD	**11%**	**12%**	**13%**	**14%**	**15%**	**16%**	**17%**	**18%**	**19%**	**20%**	**PERIOD**
01	.90090	.89286	.88496	.87719	.86957	.86207	.85470	.84746	.84043	.83333	01
02	.81162	.79719	.78315	.76947	.75614	.74316	.73051	.71818	.70616	.69444	02
03	.73119	.71178	.69305	.67497	.65752	.64066	.62437	.60863	.59342	.57870	03
04	.65873	.63552	.61332	.59208	57175	.55229	.53365	.51579	.49867	.48225	04
05	.59345	.56743	.54276	.51937	.49718	.47611	.45611	.43711	.41905	.40188	05
06	.53464	.50663	.48032	.45559	.43233	.41044	.38984	.37043	.35214	.33490	06
07	.48166	.45235	.42506	.39964	.37594	.35383	.33320	.31392	.29592	.27908	07
08	.43393	.40388	.37616	.35056	.32690	.30503	.28478	.26604	.24867	.23257	08
09	.39092	.36061	.33288	.30751	.28426	.26295	.24340	.22546	.20897	.19381	09
10	.35218	.32197	.29459	.26974	.24718	.22668	.20804	.19106	.17560	.16151	10
11	.31728	.28748	.26070	.23662	.21494	.19542	.17781	.16192	.14756	.13459	11
12	.28584	.25667	.23071	.20756	.18691	.16846	.15197	.13722	.12400	.11216	12
13	.25751	.22917	.20416	.18207	.16253	.14523	.12989	.11629	.10420	.09346	13
14	.23199	.20462	.18068	.15971	.14133	.12520	.11102	.09855	.08757	.07789	14
15	.20900	.18270	.15989	.14010	.12289	.10793	.09489	.08352	.07359	.06491	15
16	.18829	.16312	.14150	.12289	.10686	.09304	.08110	.07073	.06184	.05409	16
17	.16963	.14564	.12522	.10780	.09293	.08021	.06932	.05998	.05196	.04507	17
18	.15282	.13004	.11081	.09456	.08080	.06914	.05925	.05083	.04367	.03756	18
19	.13768	.11611	.09806	.08295	.07026	.05961	.05064	.04308	.03669	.03130	19
20	.12403	.10367	.08678	.07276	.06110	.05139	.04328	.03651	.03084	.02608	20
21	.11174	.09256	.07680	.06383	.05313	.04430	.03699	.03094	.02591	.02174	21
22	.10067	.08264	.06796	.05599	.04620	.03819	.03162	.02622	.02178	.01811	22
23	.09069	.07379	.06014	.04911	.04017	.03292	.02702	.02222	.01830	.01509	23
24	.08170	.06588	.05322	.04308	.03493	.02838	.02310	.01883	.01538	.01258	24
25	.07361	.05882	.04710	.03779	.03038	.02447	.01974	.01596	.01292	.01048	25

TABLE A.4	PRESENT VALUE OF AN ANNUITY OF $1 (*PVIFA*)										
PERIOD	1%	2%	3%	4%	5%	6%	7%	8%	9%	10%	PERIOD
01	.9901	.9804	.9709	.9615	.9524	.9434	.9346	.9259	.9174	.9091	01
02	1.9704	1.9416	1.9135	1.8861	1.8594	1.8334	1.8080	1.7833	1.7591	1.7355	02
03	2.9410	2.8839	2.8286	2.7751	2.7233	2.6730	2.6243	2.5771	2.5313	2.4868	03
04	3.9020	3.8077	3.7171	3.6299	3.5459	3.4651	3.3872	3.3121	3.2397	3.1699	04
05	4.8535	4.7134	4.5797	4.4518	4.3295	4.2123	4.1002	3.9927	3.8896	3.7908	05
06	5.7955	5.6014	5.4172	5.2421	5.0757	4.9173	4.7665	4.6229	4.4859	4.3553	06
07	6.7282	6.4720	6.2302	6.0020	5.7863	5.5824	5.3893	5.2064	5.0329	4.8684	07
08	7.6517	7.3254	7.0196	6.7327	6.4632	6.2093	5.9713	5.7466	5.5348	5.3349	08
09	8.5661	8.1622	7.7861	7.4353	7.1078	6.8017	6.5152	6.2469	5.9852	5.7590	09
10	9.4714	8.9825	8.7302	8.1109	7.7217	7.3601	7.0236	6.7101	6.4176	6.1446	10
11	10.3677	9.7868	9.2526	8.7604	8.3064	7.8868	7.4987	7.1389	6.8052	6.4951	11
12	11.2552	10.5753	9.9589	9.3850	8.8632	8.3838	7.9427	7.5361	7.1601	6.8137	12
13	12.1338	11.3483	10.6349	9.9856	9.3935	8.8527	8.3576	7.9038	7.4869	7.1034	13
14	13.0088	12.1062	11.2960	10.5631	9.8986	9.2950	8.7454	8.2442	7.7860	7.3667	14
15	13.8651	12.8492	11.9379	11.1183	10.3796	9.7122	9.1079	8.5595	8.0607	7.6061	15
16	14.7180	13.5777	12.5610	11.6522	10.8377	10.1059	9.4466	8.8514	8.3126	7.8237	16
17	15.5624	14.2918	13.1660	12.1656	11.2740	10.4772	9.7632	9.1216	8.5435	8.0215	17
18	16.3984	14.9920	13.7534	12.6592	11.6895	10.8276	10.0591	9.3719	8.7556	8.2014	18
19	17.2201	15.2684	14.3237	13.1339	12.0853	11.1581	10.3356	9.6036	8.9501	8.3649	19
20	18.0457	16.3514	14.8774	13.5903	12.4622	11.4699	10.5940	9.8181	9.1285	8.5136	20
21	18.8571	17.0111	15.4149	14.0291	12.8211	11.7640	10.8355	10.0168	9.2922	8.6487	21
22	19.6605	17.6581	15.9368	14.4511	13.1630	12.0416	11.0612	10.2007	9.4424	8.7715	22
23	20.4559	18.2921	16.4435	14.8568	13.4885	12.3033	11.2722	10.3710	9.5802	8.8832	23
24	21.2435	18.9139	16.9355	15.2469	13.7986	12.5503	11.4693	10.5287	9.7066	8.9847	24
25	22.0233	19.5234	17.4181	15.6220	14.9039	12.7833	11.6536	10.6748	9.8226	9.0770	25

TABLE A.4 PRESENT VALUE OF AN ANNUITY OF $1 (*PVIFA*) (CONTINUED)

PERIOD	11%	12%	13%	14%	15%	16%	17%	18%	19%	20%	PERIOD
01	.9009	.8929	.8850	.8772	.8696	.8621	.8547	.8475	.8403	.8333	01
02	1.7125	1.6901	1.6681	1.6467	1.6257	1.6052	1.5852	1.5656	1.5465	1.5278	02
03	2.4437	2.4018	2.3612	2.3216	2.2832	2.2459	2.2096	2.1743	2.1399	2.1065	03
04	3.1024	3.0373	2.9745	2.9137	2.8550	2.7982	2.7432	2.6901	2.6386	2.5887	04
05	3.6959	3.6048	3.5172	3.4331	3.3522	3.2743	3.1993	3.1272	3.0576	2.9906	05
06	4.2305	4.1114	3.9976	3.8887	3.7845	3.6847	3.5892	3.4976	3.4098	3.3255	06
07	4.7122	4.5638	4.4226	4.2883	4.1604	4.0386	3.9224	3.8115	3.7057	3.6046	07
08	5.1461	4.9676	4.7988	4.6389	4.4873	4.3436	4.2072	4.0776	3.9544	3.8372	08
09	5.5370	5.3282	5.1317	4.9464	4.7716	4.6065	4.4506	4.3030	4.1633	4.0310	09
10	5.8892	5.6502	5.4262	5.2161	5.0188	4.8332	4.6586	4.4941	4.3389	4.1925	10
11	6.2065	5.9377	5.6869	5.4527	5.2337	5.0286	4.8364	4.6560	4.4865	4.3271	11
12	6.4924	6.1944	5.9176	5.6603	5.4206	5.1971	4.9884	4.7932	4.6105	4.4392	12
13	6.7499	6.4235	6.1218	5.8424	5.5831	5.3423	5.1183	4.9095	4.7147	4.5327	13
14	6.9819	6.6282	6.3025	6.0021	5.7245	5.4675	5.2293	5.0081	4.8023	4.6106	14
15	7.1909	6.8109	6.4624	6.1422	5.8474	5.5755	5.3242	5.0916	4.8759	4.6755	15
16	7.3792	6.9740	6.6039	6.2651	5.9542	5.6685	5.4053	5.1624	4.9377	4.7296	16
17	7.5488	7.1196	6.7291	6.3729	6.0472	5.7487	5.4746	5.2223	4.9897	4.7746	17
18	7.7016	7.2497	6.8389	6.4674	6.1280	5.8178	5.5339	5.2732	5.0333	4.8122	18
19	7.8393	7.3650	6.9380	6.5504	6.1982	5.8775	5.5845	5.3176	5.0700	4.8435	19
20	7.9633	7.4694	7.0248	6.6231	6.2593	5.9288	5.6278	5.3527	5.1009	4.8696	20
21	8.0751	7.5620	7.1016	6.6870	6.3125	5.9731	5.6648	5.3837	5.1268	4.8913	21
22	8.1757	7.6446	7.1695	6.7429	6.3587	6.0113	5.6964	5.4099	5.1486	4.9094	22
23	8.2664	7.7184	7.2297	6.7921	6.3988	6.0442	5.7234	5.4321	5.1668	4.9245	23
24	8.3481	7.7843	7.2829	6.8351	6.4338	6.0726	5.7465	5.4509	5.1822	4.9371	24
25	8.4217	7.8431	7.3300	6.8729	6.4641	6.0971	5.7662	5.4669	5.1951	4.9476	25

Differential Calculus Techniques in Management

Decision analysis involves determining the action that best achieves a desired goal or objective. It means finding the action that optimizes (i.e., maximizes or minimizes) the value of an objective function. For example, we may be interested in determining the output level that maximizes profits. In a production problem, the goal may be to find the combination of inputs that minimizes the cost of producing a desired level of output. In a capital budgeting problem, the objective may be to select those projects that maximize the net present value of the investments chosen. Many techniques are available for solving optimization problems such as these. This appendix focuses on the use of differential calculus.

RELATIONSHIP BETWEEN MARGINAL ANALYSIS AND DIFFERENTIAL CALCULUS

In Chapter 2, marginal analysis was introduced as one of the fundamental concepts of microeconomic decision making. In the marginal analysis framework, resource allocation decisions are made by comparing the marginal benefits of a proposed change in the level of an activity with the marginal costs of that change. The proposed change should be made as long as the marginal benefits exceed the marginal costs. By following this basic rule, resources can be allocated efficiently, and profits or shareholder wealth can be maximized.

Initially, let us assume that the objective we are seeking to optimize, Y, can be expressed algebraically as a function of *one* decision variable, X.

$$Y = f(X) \tag{B.1}$$

Recall that marginal profit is defined as the change in profit resulting from a one-unit change in output. In general, the marginal value of any variable Y, which is a function of another variable X, is defined as the change in the value of Y resulting from a one-unit change in X. The marginal value of Y, M_y, can be calculated from the change in Y, ΔY, that occurs as the result of a given change in X, ΔX:

$$M_y = \frac{\Delta Y}{\Delta X} \tag{B.2}$$

When calculated with this expression, different estimates for the amount ΔY may be obtained, depending on the size of the incremental change in X that we use in the computation. The true marginal value[1] of a function is obtained from Equation B.2 when ΔX is made as small as possible. If ΔX can be thought of as a continuous (rather than a discrete)

---

[1]For example, if X is a continuous variable measured in feet, pounds, and so on, then ΔX can, in theory, take on fractional values such as 0.5, 0.10, 0.05, 0.001, or 0.0001 feet or pounds. When X is a continuous variable, ΔX can be made as small as desired.

MANAGERIAL CHALLENGE
A Skeleton in the Stealth Bomber's Closet[2]

In 1990, the U.S. Air Force publicly unveiled its newest long-range strategic bomber, the B-2 or "Stealth" bomber. This plane is characterized by a unique flying-wing design engineered to evade detection by enemy radar. The plane has been controversial because of its high cost. However, a lesser known controversy relates to its fundamental design.

The flying-wing design originated from a secret study that concluded that a plane's maximum range could be achieved if virtually all the volume were contained in the wing. A complex mathematical appendix was attached to the study.

However, Professor of Engineering Joseph Foa discovered that a fundamental error had been made in the initial report. It turned out that the original researchers had taken the first derivative of a complex equation and found that it had two solutions. The original researchers mistakenly concluded that the all-wing design was the one that maximized range, when, in fact, it *minimized* range.

In this appendix we introduce some of the same optimization techniques applied to the Stealth bomber project. We develop tools designed to maximize profits or minimize costs. Fortunately, the mathematical functions we deal with in this chapter and throughout the book are much simpler than those that confronted the original "flying-wing" engineers. We introduce techniques that can be used to check whether a function, such as profits or costs, is being minimized or maximized at a particular level of output.

[2]Based on W. Biddle, "Skeleton Alleged in the Stealth Bomber's Closet," *Science* (May 12, 1989), pp. 650–651

---

derivative A measure of the marginal effect of a change in one variable on the value of a function. Graphically, it represents the slope of the function at a given point.

variable that can take on fractional values, then in calculating M_y by using Equation B.2, we can let ΔX approach zero.

In concept, differential calculus takes this approach. The **derivative**, or, more precisely, *first derivative*,[3] dY/dX, of a function is defined as the *limit* of the ratio $\Delta Y/\Delta X$ as ΔX approaches zero; that is,

$$\frac{dY}{dX} = \underset{\Delta X \to 0}{\text{limit}} \frac{\Delta Y}{\Delta X} \qquad [B.3]$$

Graphically, the first derivative of a function represents the *slope* of the curve at a given point on the curve. The definition of a derivative as the limit of the change in Y (i.e., ΔY) as ΔX approaches zero is illustrated in Figure B.1(a).

Suppose we are interested in the derivative of the $Y = f(X)$ function at the point X_0. The derivative dY/dX measures the slope of the tangent line ECD. An estimate of this slope, albeit a poor estimate, can be obtained by calculating the marginal value of Y over the interval X_0 to X_2. Using Equation B.2, a value of

$$M'_y = \frac{\Delta Y}{\Delta X} = \frac{Y_2 - Y_0}{X_2 - X_0}$$

is obtained for the slope of the CA line. Now let us calculate the marginal value of Y using a smaller interval, for example, X_0 to X_1. The slope of the CB line, which is equal to

$$M''_y = \frac{\Delta Y}{\Delta X} = \frac{Y_1 - Y_0}{X_1 - X_0}$$

gives a much better estimate of the true marginal value as represented by the slope of the ECD tangent line. Thus we see that the smaller the ΔX value, the better the estimate of

---

[3]It is also possible to compute second, third, fourth, and so on, derivatives. Second derivatives are discussed later in this appendix.

FIGURE B.1   First Derivative of a Function

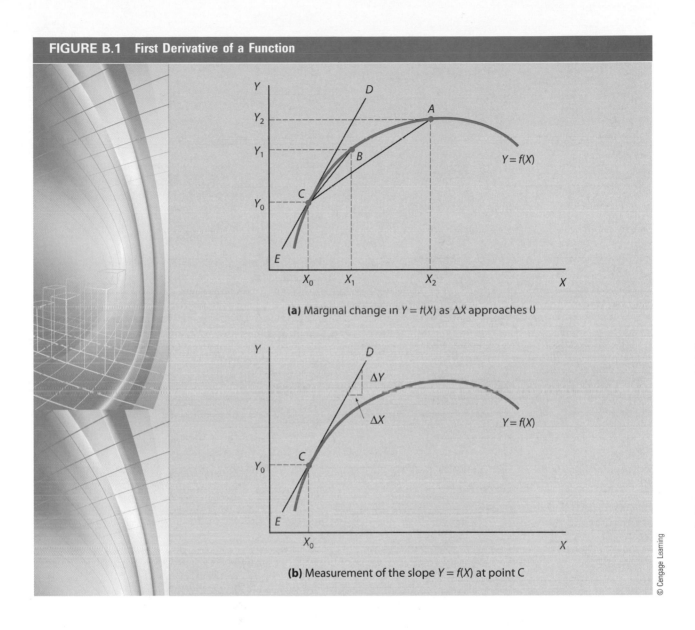

(a) Marginal change in $Y = f(X)$ as ΔX approaches 0

(b) Measurement of the slope $Y = f(X)$ at point C

the slope of the curve. Letting ΔX approach zero allows us to find the slope of the $Y = f(X)$ curve at point B. As shown in Figure B.1(b), the slope of the ECD tangent line (and the $Y = f(X)$ function at point C) is measured by the change in Y, or rise, ΔY, divided by the change in X, or run, ΔX.

Process of Differentiation

The process of differentiation—that is, finding the derivative of a function—involves determining the limiting value of the ratio $\Delta Y/\Delta X$ as ΔX approaches zero. Before offering some general rules for finding the derivative of a function, we illustrate with an example the algebraic process used to obtain the derivative without the aid of these general rules. The specific rules that simplify this process are presented in the following section.

Example

Process of Differentiation: Profit Maximization at Illinois Power

Suppose the profit, π, of Illinois Power can be represented as a function of the output level Q using the expression

$$\pi = -40 + 140Q - 10Q^2 \qquad [B.4]$$

We wish to determine $d\pi/dQ$ by first finding the marginal profit expression $\Delta\pi/\Delta Q$ and then taking the limit of this expression as ΔQ approaches zero. Let us begin by expressing the new level of profit $(\pi + \Delta\pi)$ that will result from an increase in output to $(Q + \Delta Q)$. From Equation B.4, we know that

$$\pi + \Delta\pi = -40 + 140(Q + \Delta Q) - 10(Q + \Delta Q)^2 \qquad [B.5]$$

Expanding this expression and then simplifying algebraic terms, we obtain

$$\pi + \Delta\pi = -40 + 140Q + 140\Delta Q - 10[Q^2 + 2Q\Delta Q + (\Delta Q)^2]$$
$$= -40 + 140Q - 10Q^2 + 140\Delta Q - 20Q\Delta Q - 10(\Delta Q)^2 \qquad [B.6]$$

Subtracting Equation B.4 from Equation B.6 yields

$$\Delta\pi = 140\Delta Q - 20Q\Delta Q - 10(\Delta Q)^2 \qquad [B.7]$$

Forming the marginal profit ratio $\Delta\pi/\Delta Q$ and doing some canceling, we get

$$\frac{\Delta\pi}{\Delta Q} = \frac{140\Delta Q - 20Q\Delta Q - 10(\Delta Q)^2}{\Delta Q}$$
$$= 140 - 20Q - 10\Delta Q \qquad [B.8]$$

Taking the limit of Equation B.8 as ΔQ approaches zero yields the expression for the derivative of Illinois Power's profit function (Equation B.4).

$$\frac{d\pi}{dQ} = \lim_{\Delta Q \to 0}[140 - 20Q - 10\Delta Q]$$
$$= 140 - 20Q \qquad [B.9]$$

If we are interested in the derivative of the profit function at a particular value of Q, Equation B.9 can be evaluated for this value. For example, suppose we want to know the marginal profit, or slope of the profit function, at $Q = 3$ units. Substituting $Q = 3$ in Equation B.9 yields

$$\text{Marginal profit} = \frac{d\pi}{dQ} = 140 - 20(3) = \$80 \text{ per unit}$$

Rules of Differentiation

Fortunately, we do not need to go through this lengthy process every time we want the derivative of a function. A series of general rules, derived in a manner similar to the process just described, exists for differentiating various types of functions.

Constant Functions A constant function can be expressed as

$$Y = a \qquad [B.10]$$

where a is a constant (i.e., Y is independent of X). The derivative of a constant function is equal to zero:

$$\frac{dY}{dX} = 0 \qquad \text{[B.11]}$$

For example, consider the constant function

$$Y = 4$$

which is graphed in Figure B.2(a). Recall that the first derivative of a function (dY/dX) measures the slope of the function. Because this constant function is a horizontal straight line with zero slope, its derivative (dY/dX) is therefore equal to zero.

Power Functions   A power function takes the form of

$$Y = aX^b \qquad \text{[B.12]}$$

where a and b are constants. The derivative of a power function is equal to

$$\frac{dY}{dX} = b \cdot a \cdot X^{b-1} \qquad \text{[B.13]}$$

A couple of examples are used to illustrate the application of this rule. First, consider the function

$$Y = 2X$$

which is graphed in Figure B.2(b). Note that the slope of this function is equal to 2 and is constant over the entire range of X values. Applying the power function rule to this example, where $a = 2$ and $b = 1$, yields

$$\frac{dY}{dX} = 1 \cdot 2 \cdot X^{1-1}$$
$$= 2X^0 = 2$$

Note that any variable raised to the zero power, for example, X^0, is equal to 1.

Next, consider the function

$$Y = X^2$$

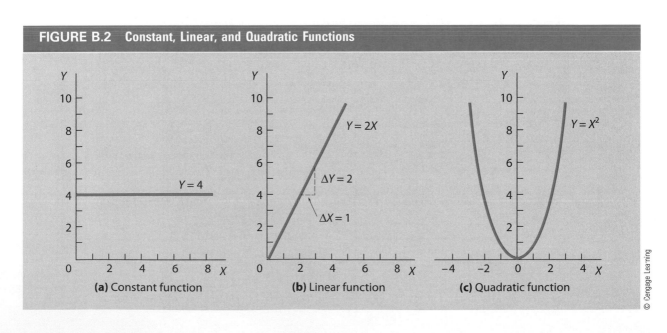

FIGURE B.2   Constant, Linear, and Quadratic Functions

(a) Constant function

(b) Linear function

(c) Quadratic function

© Cengage Learning

which is graphed in Figure B.2(c). Note that the slope of this function varies depending on the value of X. Application of the power function rule to this example yields ($a = 1, b = 2$):

$$\frac{dY}{dX} = 2 \cdot 1 \cdot X^{2-1}$$
$$= 2X$$

As we can see, this derivative (or slope) function is negative when $X < 0$, zero when $X = 0$, and positive when $X > 0$.

Sum of Functions   Suppose a function $Y = f(X)$ represents the sum of two (or more) separate functions, $f_1(X), f_2(X)$, that is,

$$Y = f_1(X) + f_2(X) \qquad [B.14]$$

The derivative of Y with respect to X is found by differentiating each of the separate functions and then adding the results:

$$\frac{dY}{dX} = \frac{df_1(X)}{dX} + \frac{df_2(X)}{dX} \qquad [B.15]$$

This result can be extended to find the derivative of the sum of any number of functions.

Example

Rules of Differentiation: Profit Maximization at Illinois Power (continued)

As an example of the application of these rules, consider again the profit function for Illinois Power, given earlier in Equation B.4:

$$\pi = -40 + 140Q - 10Q^2$$

In this example Q represents the X variable and π represents the Y variable, that is, $\pi = f(Q)$. The function $f(Q)$ is the sum of *three* separate functions: a constant function, $f_1(Q) = -40$, and two power functions, $f_2(Q) = 140Q$ and $f_3(Q) - 10Q^2$. Therefore, applying the differentiation rules yields

$$\frac{d\pi}{dQ} = \frac{df_1(Q)}{dQ} + \frac{df_2(Q)}{dQ} + \frac{df_3(Q)}{dQ}$$
$$= 0 + 1 \cdot 140 \cdot Q^{1-1} + 2 \cdot (-10) \cdot Q^{2-1}$$
$$= 140 - 20Q$$

This result is the same as obtained in Equation B.9 by the differentiation process.

Product of Two Functions   Suppose the variable Y is equal to the product of two separate functions $f_1(X)$ and $f_2(X)$:

$$Y = f_1(X) \cdot f_2(X) \qquad [B.16]$$

In this case the derivative of Y with respect to X is equal to the sum of the first function times the derivative of the second, plus the second function times the derivative of the first.

$$\frac{dY}{dX} = f_1(X) \cdot \frac{df_2(X)}{dX} + f_2(X) \cdot \frac{df_1(X)}{dX} \qquad [B.17]$$

For example, suppose we are interested in the derivative of the expression

$$Y = X^2(2X - 3)$$

Let $f_1(X) = X^2$ and $f_2(X) = (2X - 3)$. By the preceding rule (and the earlier rules for differentiating constant and power functions), we obtain

$$\frac{dY}{dX} = X^2 \cdot \frac{dY}{dX}[(2X - 3)] + (2X - 3) \cdot \frac{dY}{dX}[X^2]$$

$$= X^2 \cdot (2 - 0) + (2X - 3) \cdot (2X)$$

$$= 2X^2 + 4X^2 - 6X$$

$$= 6X^2 - 6X$$

$$= 6X(X - 1)$$

Quotient of Two Functions   Suppose the variable Y is equal to the quotient of two separate functions $f_1(X)$ and $f_2(X)$:

$$Y = \frac{f_1(X)}{f_2(X)} \tag{B.18}$$

For such a relationship the derivative of Y with respect to X is obtained as follows:

$$\frac{dY}{dX} = \frac{f_2(X) \cdot \dfrac{df_1(X)}{dX} - f_1(X) \cdot \dfrac{df_2(X)}{dX}}{[f_2(X)]^2} \tag{B.19}$$

As an example, consider the problem of finding the derivative of the expression

$$Y = \frac{10X^2}{5X - 1}$$

Letting $f_1(X) = 10X^2$ and $f_2(X) = 5X - 1$, we have

$$\frac{dY}{dX} = \frac{(5X - 1) \cdot 20X - 10X^2 \cdot 5}{(5X - 1)^2}$$

$$= \frac{100X^2 - 20X - 50X^2}{(5X - 1)^2}$$

$$= \frac{50X^2 - 20X}{(5X - 1)^2}$$

$$= \frac{10X(5X - 2)}{(5X - 1)^2}$$

Function of a Function (Chain Rule)   Suppose Y is a function of the variable Z, $Y = f_1(Z)$; and Z is in turn a function of the variable X, $Z = f_2(X)$. The derivative of Y with respect to X can be determined by first finding dY/dZ and dZ/dX and then multiplying the two expressions together:

$$\frac{dY}{dX} = \frac{dY}{dZ} \cdot \frac{dZ}{dX}$$

$$= \frac{df_1(Z)}{dZ} \cdot \frac{df_2(X)}{dX} \tag{B.20}$$

	TABLE B.1	SUMMARY OF RULES FOR DIFFERENTIATING FUNCTIONS	
	FUNCTION		**DERIVATIVE**
1.	Constant Function $Y = a$		$\dfrac{dY}{dX} = 0$
2.	Power Function $Y = aX^b$		$\dfrac{dY}{dX} = b \cdot a \cdot X^{b-1}$
3.	Sum of Functions $Y = f_1(X) + f_2(X)$		$\dfrac{dY}{dX} = \dfrac{df_1(X)}{dX} + \dfrac{df_2(X)}{dX}$
4.	Product of Two Functions $Y = f_1(X) \cdot f_2(X)$		$\dfrac{dY}{dX} = f_1(X) \cdot \dfrac{df_2(X)}{dX} + f_2(X) \cdot \dfrac{df_1(X)}{dX}$
5.	Quotient of Two Functions $Y = \dfrac{f_1(X)}{f_2 X}$		$\dfrac{dY}{dX} = \dfrac{f_2(X) \cdot \dfrac{df_1(X)}{dX} - f_1(X) \cdot \dfrac{df_2(X)}{dX}}{[f_2(X)]^2}$
6.	Function of a Function $Y = f_1(Z)$, where $Z = f_2(X)$		$\dfrac{dY}{dX} = \dfrac{dY}{dZ} \cdot \dfrac{dZ}{dX}$

© Cengage Learning

To illustrate the application of this rule, suppose we are interested in finding the derivative (with respect to X) of the function

$$Y = 10Z - 2Z^2 - 3$$

where Z is related to X in the following way:[4]

$$Z = 2X^2 - 1$$

First, we find (by the earlier differentiation rules)

$$\frac{dY}{dZ} = 10 - 4Z$$

$$\frac{dZ}{dX} = 4X$$

and then

$$\frac{dY}{dX} = (10 - 4Z) \cdot 4X$$

Substituting the expression for Z in terms of X into this equation yields

$$\begin{aligned} \frac{dY}{dX} &= [10 - 4(2X^2 - 1)] \cdot 4X \\ &= (10 - 8X^2 + 4) \cdot 4X \\ &= 40X - 32X^3 + 16X \\ &= 56X - 32X^3 \\ &= 8X(7 - 4X^2) \end{aligned}$$

These rules for differentiating functions are summarized in Table B.1.

---

[4]Alternatively, one can substitute $Z = 2X^2 - 1$ into $Y = 10Z - 2Z^2 - 3$ and differentiate Y with respect to X.

APPLICATIONS OF DIFFERENTIAL CALCULUS TO OPTIMIZATION PROBLEMS

The reason for studying the process of differentiation and the rules for differentiating functions is that these methods can be used to find optimal solutions to many kinds of maximization and minimization problems in managerial economics.

Maximization Problem

first-order condition
A test to locate one or more maximum or minimum points of an algebraic function.

As you recall from the discussion of marginal analysis, a necessary (but not sufficient) condition for finding the maximum point on a curve (e.g., maximum profits) is that the marginal value or slope of the curve at this point must be equal to zero. We can now express this condition within the framework of differential calculus. Because the derivative of a function measures the slope or marginal value at any given point, an equivalent necessary condition for finding the maximum value of a function $Y = f(X)$ is that the derivative dY/dX at this point must be equal to zero. This requirement is known as the **first-order condition** for locating one or more maximum or minimum points of an algebraic function.

Example

First-Order Condition: Profit Maximization at Illinois Power (continued)

Using the profit function (Equation B.4)

$$\pi = -40 + 140Q - 10Q^2$$

discussed earlier, we can illustrate how to find the profit-maximizing output level Q by means of this condition. Setting the first derivative of this function (which was computed previously) to zero, we obtain

$$\frac{d\pi}{dQ} = 140 - 20Q$$

$$0 = 140 - 20Q$$

Solving this equation for Q yields $Q^* = 7$ units as the profit-maximizing output level. The profit and first derivative functions and optimal solution are shown in Figure B.3. As we can see, profits are maximized at the point where the function is neither increasing nor decreasing, in other words, where the slope (or first derivative) is equal to zero.

Second Derivatives and the Second-Order Condition

second-order condition A test to determine whether a point that has been determined from the first-order condition is either a maximum point or a minimum point of the algebraic function.

Setting the derivative of a function equal to zero and solving the resulting equation for the value of the decision variable does not guarantee that the point will be obtained at which the function takes on its maximum value. (Recall the Stealth bomber example at the start of this appendix.) The slope of a U-shaped function will also be equal to zero at its low point and the function will take on its *minimum* value at the given point. In other words, setting the derivative to zero is only a *necessary* condition for finding the maximum value of a function; it is not a *sufficient* condition. Another condition, known as the **second-order condition**, is required to determine whether a point that has been

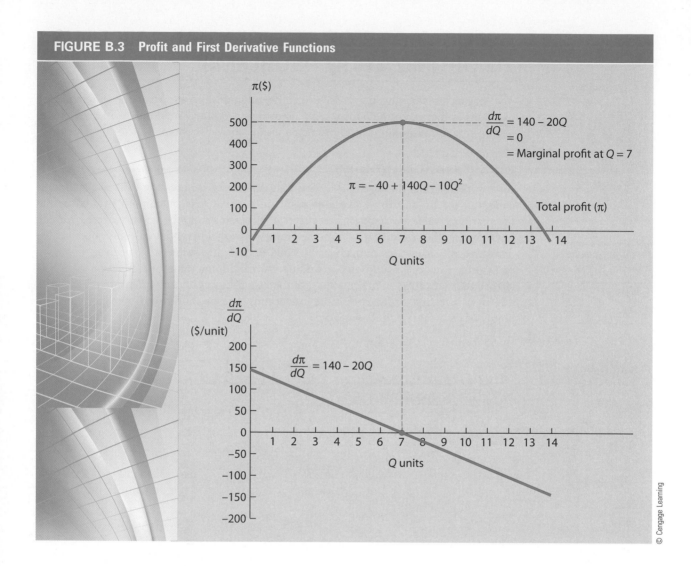

FIGURE B.3 **Profit and First Derivative Functions**

determined from the first-order condition is either a maximum point or minimum point of the algebraic function.

This situation is illustrated in Figure B.4. At both points A and B the slope of the function (first derivative, dY/dX) is zero; however, only at point B does the function take on its maximum value. We note in Figure B.4 that the marginal value (slope) is continually *decreasing* in the neighborhood of the maximum value (point B) of the $Y = f(X)$ function. First the slope is positive up to the point where $dY/dX = 0$, and thereafter the slope becomes negative. Thus we must determine whether the slope's marginal value (slope of the slope) is declining. To test whether the marginal value is decreasing, take the derivative of the marginal value and determine whether it is negative at the given point on the function. In effect, we need to find the derivative of the derivative—that is, the *second derivative* of the function—and then test whether it is less than zero. Formally, the second derivative of the function $Y = f(X)$ is written as d^2Y/dX^2 and is found by applying the previously described differentiation rules to the first derivative. A *maximum point is obtained if the second derivative is negative, that is, $d^2Y/dX^2 < 0$.*

FIGURE B.4   Maximum and Minimum Values of a Function

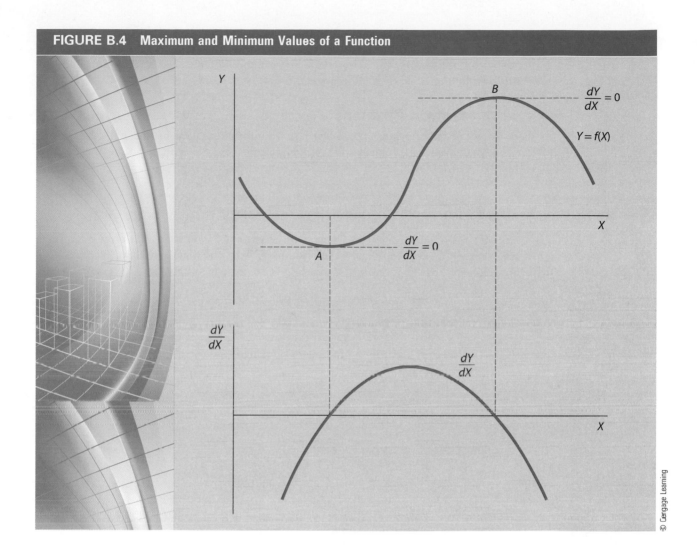

Example

Second-Order Condition: Profit Maximization at Illinois Power (continued)

In the profit-maximization example, the second derivative is obtained from the first derivative as follows:

$$\frac{d\pi}{dQ} = 140 - 20Q$$

$$\frac{d^2\pi}{dQ^2} = 0 + 1 \cdot (-20) \cdot Q^{1-1}$$

$$= -20$$

Because $d^2\pi/dQ^2 < 0$, we know that a maximum-profit point has been obtained.

An opposite condition holds for obtaining the point at which the function takes on a minimum value. Note again in Figure B.4 that the marginal value (slope) is continually *increasing* in the neighborhood of the minimum value (point *A*) of the $Y = (X)$ function. First the slope is negative up to the point where $dY/dX = 0$, and thereafter the slope becomes positive. Therefore, we test to see whether $d^2Y/dX^2 > 0$ at the given point. *A minimum point is obtained if the second derivative is positive, that is, $d^2Y/dX^2 > 0$.*

Minimization Problem

In some decision-making situations, cost minimization may be the objective. As in profit-maximization problems, differential calculus can be used to locate the optimal points.

Example

Cost Minimization: KeySpan Energy

Suppose we are interested in determining the output level that minimizes average total costs for KeySpan Energy, where the average total cost function might be approximated by the following relationship (*Q* represents output):

$$C = 15 - 0.040Q + 0.000080Q^2$$

Differentiating *C* with respect to *Q* gives

$$\frac{dC}{dQ} = -0.040 + 0.000160Q$$

Setting this derivative equal to zero and solving for *Q* yields

$$0 = 0.040 + 0.000160Q$$
$$Q^* = 250$$

Taking the second derivative, we obtain

$$\frac{d^2C}{dQ^2} = +0.000160$$

Because the second derivative is positive, the output level of $Q = 250$ is indeed the value that minimizes average total costs.

Summarizing, we see that *two* conditions are required for locating a maximum or minimum value of a function using differential calculus. The *first-order* condition determines the point(s) at which the first derivative dY/dX is equal to zero. After we obtain one or more points, a *second-order* condition is used to determine whether the function takes on a maximum or minimum value at the given point(s). The second derivative d^2Y/dX^2 indicates whether a given point is a maximum ($d^2Y/dX^2 < 0$) or a minimum ($d^2Y/dX^2 > 0$) value of the function.

PARTIAL DIFFERENTIATION AND MULTIVARIATE OPTIMIZATION

Thus far in this appendix, the analysis has been limited to a criterion variable *Y* that can be expressed as a function of *one* decision variable *X*. However, many commonly used economic relationships contain two or more decision variables. For example, a *demand function* relates sales of a product or service to such variables as price, advertising, promotion expenses, price of substitutes, and income.

Partial Derivatives

Consider a criterion variable Y that is a function of two decision variables X_1 and X_2:[5]

$$Y = f(X_1, X_2) \tag{B.21}$$

Let us now examine the change in Y that results from a given change in either X_1 or X_2. To isolate the marginal effect on Y from a given change in X_1 (i.e., $\Delta Y / \Delta X_1$), we must hold X_2 constant. Similarly, if we wish to isolate the marginal effect on Y from a given change in X_2 (i.e., $\Delta Y / \Delta X_2$), the variable X_1 must be held constant. A

partial derivative
A measure of the marginal effect of a change in one variable on the value of a multivariate function while holding constant all other variables.

measure of the marginal effect of a change in any one variable on the change in Y, holding all other variables in the relationship constant, is obtained from the **partial derivative** of the function. The partial derivative of Y with respect to X_1 is written as $\partial Y / \partial X_1$ and is found by applying the previously described differentiation rules to the $Y = f(X_1, X_2)$ function, where the variable X_2 is treated as a constant. Similarly, the partial derivative of Y with respect to X_2 is written as $\partial Y / \partial X_2$ and is found by applying the differentiation rules to the function, where the variable X_1 is treated as a constant.

Example

Partial Derivatives: Indiana Petroleum Company

To illustrate the procedure for obtaining partial derivatives, let us consider the following relationship in which the profit variable, π, is a function of the output level of two products (heating oil and gasoline) Q_1 and Q_2:

$$\pi = -60 + 140Q_1 + 100Q_2 - 10Q_1^2 - 8Q_2^2 - 6Q_1Q_2 \tag{B.22}$$

Treating Q_2 as a constant, the partial derivative of π with respect to Q_1 is obtained:

$$\frac{\partial \pi}{\partial Q_1} = 0 + 140 + 0 + 2 \cdot (-10) \cdot Q_1 - 0 - 6Q_2$$

$$= 140 - 20Q_1 - 6Q_2 \tag{B.23}$$

Similarly, with Q_1 treated as a constant, the partial derivative of π with respect to Q_2 is equal to

$$\frac{\partial \pi}{\partial Q_1} = 0 + 0 + 100 - 0 + 2 \cdot (-8) \cdot Q_2 - 6Q_1$$

$$= 100 - 16Q_2 - 6Q_1 \tag{B.24}$$

---

[5]The following analysis is not limited to two decision variables. Relationships containing any number of variables can be analyzed within this framework.

Example

Partial Derivatives: Demand Function for Shield Toothpaste

Partial derivatives can be useful in demand analysis, especially in quantitative studies. Suppose the demand for Shield toothpaste is estimated as tubes per year,

$$Q = 14.6 + 2.2P + 7.4A \qquad \text{[B.25]}$$

where Q = quantity sold, P = selling price, and A = advertising campaigns, the partial derivatives of Q with respect to P and A are

$$\frac{\partial Q}{\partial P} = -2.2 \text{ and } \frac{\partial Q}{\partial A} = 7.4$$

To take another example, for the multiplicative exponential demand function

$$Q = 3.0P^{-.50}A^{.25}$$

The partial derivative of Q with respect to P is

$$\frac{\partial Q}{\partial P} = 3.0A^{.25}(-.50P^{-.50-1})$$
$$= -1.5P^{-1.50}A^{.25}$$

Similarly, the partial derivative of Q with respect to A is

$$\frac{\partial Q}{\partial A} = 3.0P^{-.50}(.25A^{.25-1})$$
$$= .75P^{-.50}A^{-.75}$$

Maximization Problem

The partial derivatives can be used to obtain the optimal solution to a maximization or minimization problem containing two or more X variables. Analogous to the first-order conditions discussed earlier for the one-variable case, we set *each* of the partial derivatives equal to zero and solve the resulting set of simultaneous equations for the optimal X values.

Example

Profit Maximization: Indiana Petroleum Company (continued)

Suppose we are interested in determining the values of Q_1 and Q_2 that maximize the company's profits given in Equation B.22. In this case, each of the two partial derivative functions (Equations B.23 and B.24) would be set equal to zero:

$$0 = 140 - 20Q_1 - 6Q_2$$
$$0 = 100 - 16Q_2 - 6Q_1$$

This system of equations can be solved for the profit-maximizing values of Q_1 and Q_2.[6] The optimal values are $Q_1^* = 5.77$ units and $Q_2^* = 4.08$ units.[7] The optimal total profit is

$$\pi^* = -60 + 140(5.77) + 100(4.08) + 10(5.77)^2 - 8(4.08)^2 - 6(5.77)(4.08) = 548.45$$

---

[6]The second-order conditions for obtaining a maximum or minimum in the multiple-variable case are somewhat complex. A discussion of these conditions can be found in most basic calculus texts.

[7]Exercise 10 at the end of this appendix requires the determination of these optimal values.

SUMMARY

- *Marginal analysis* is useful in making decisions about the expansion or contraction of an economic activity.
- *Differential calculus*, which bears a close relationship to marginal analysis, can be applied whenever an algebraic relationship can be specified between the decision variables and the objective or criterion variable.
- The *first derivative* measures the slope or rate of change of a function at a given point and is equal to the limiting value of the marginal function as the marginal value is calculated over smaller and smaller intervals, that is, as the interval approaches zero.
- Various rules are available (see Table B.1) for finding the derivative of specific types of functions.

- A necessary, but not sufficient, condition for finding the maximum or minimum points of a function is that the first derivative be equal to zero, which is known as the *first-order condition*.
- A *second-order condition* is required to determine whether a given point is a maximum or minimum. The *second derivative* indicates that a given point is a maximum if the second derivative is less than zero or a minimum if the second derivative is greater than zero.
- The *partial derivative* of a multivariate function measures the marginal effect of a change in one variable on the value of the function, holding constant all other variables.

Exercises

1. Define Q as the level of output produced and sold, and suppose that a firm's total revenue (TR) and total cost (TC) functions can be represented in tabular form as shown here.

OUTPUT (Q)	TOTAL REVENUE (TR)	TOTAL COST (TC)	OUTPUT (Q)	TOTAL REVENUE (TR)	TOTAL COST (TC)
0	0	20	11	264	196
1	34	26	12	276	224
2	66	34	13	286	254
3	96	44	14	294	286
4	124	56	15	300	320
5	150	70	16	304	356
6	174	86	17	306	394
7	196	104	18	306	434
8	216	124	19	304	476
9	234	146	20	300	520
10	250	170			

   a. Compute the marginal revenue and average revenue functions.

   b. Compute the marginal cost and average cost functions.

   c. On a single graph, plot the total revenue, total cost, marginal revenue, and marginal cost functions.

   d. Determine the output level in the *graph* that maximizes profits (Profit = Total revenue − Total cost) by finding the point where marginal revenue equals marginal cost.

   e. Check your result in part (d) by finding the output level in the *tables* developed in parts (a) and (b) that likewise satisfies the condition that marginal revenue equals marginal cost.

2. Consider again the total revenue and total cost functions shown in tabular form in the previous problem.
   a. Compute the total, marginal, and average profit functions.
   b. On a single graph, plot the total profit and marginal profit functions.
   c. Determine the output level in the graph and table where the total profit function takes on its maximum value.
   d. How does the result in part (c) in this exercise compare with the result in part (d) of the previous exercise?
   e. Determine total profits at the profit-maximizing output level.
3. Differentiate the following functions:
   a. $TC = 50 + 100Q - 6Q^2 + .5Q^3$
   b. $ATC = 50/Q + 100 - 6Q + .5Q^2$
   c. $MC = 100 - 12Q + 1.5Q^2$
   d. $Q = 50 - .75P$
   e. $Q = .40X^{1.50}$
4. Differentiate the following functions:
   a. $Y = 2X^3/(4X^2 - 1)$
   b. $Y = 2X/(4X^2 - 1)$
   c. $Y = 8Z^2 - 4Z + 1$, where $Z = 2X^2 - 1$ (differentiate Y with respect to X)
5. Define Q to be the level of output produced and sold, and assume that the firm's cost function is given by the relationship

$$TC = 20 + 5Q + Q^2$$

Furthermore, assume that the demand for the output of the firm is a function of price P given by the relationship

$$Q = 25 - P$$

   a. Define total profit as the difference between total revenue and total cost, and express in terms of Q the total profit function for the firm. (*Note:* Total revenue equals price per unit times the number of units sold.)
   b. Determine the output level where total profits are maximized.
   c. Calculate total profits and selling price at the profit-maximizing output level.
   d. If fixed costs increase from $20 to $25 in the total cost relationship, determine the effects of such an increase on the profit-maximizing output level and total profits.
6. Use the cost and demand functions in Exercise 5 to calculate the following:
   a. Determine the marginal revenue and marginal cost functions.
   b. Show that, at the profit-maximizing output level determined in part (b) of the previous exercise, marginal revenue equals marginal cost and illustrates the economic principle that profits are maximized at the output level where marginal revenue equals marginal cost.
7. Determine the partial derivatives with respect to all of the variables in the following functions:
   a. $TC = 50 + 5Q_1 + 10Q_2 + .5Q_1Q_2$
   b. $Q = 1.5L^{.60}K^{.50}$
   c. $Q_A = 2.5P_A^{-1.30}Y^{.20}P_B^{.40}$

8. Bounds Inc. determined through regression analysis that its sales (S) are a function of the amount of advertising (measured in units) in two different media. This relationship is given by the following equation (X = newspapers, Y = magazines):

$$S(X, Y) = 200X + 100Y - 10X^2 - 20Y^2 + 20XY$$

   a. Find the level of newspaper and magazine advertising that maximizes the firm's sales.
   b. Calculate the firm's sales at the optimal values of newspaper and magazine advertising determined in part (a).

9. The Santa Fe Cookie Factory is considering an expansion of its retail piñon cookie business to other cities. The firm's owners lack the funds needed to undertake the expansion on their own. They are considering a franchise arrangement for the new outlets. The company incurs variable costs of $6 for each pound of cookies sold. The fixed costs of operating a typical retail outlet are estimated to be $300,000 per year. The demand function facing each retail outlet is estimated to be

$$P = \$50 - .001Q$$

where P is the price per pound of cookies and Q is the number of pounds of cookies sold. [*Note:* Total revenue equals price (P) times quantity (Q) sold.]
   a. What price, output, total revenue, total cost, and total profit level will each profit-maximizing franchise experience?
   b. Assume that the parent company charges each franchisee a fee equal to 5 percent of total revenues, and recompute the values in part (a).
   c. The Santa Fe Cookie Factory is considering a combined fixed/variable franchise fee structure. Under this arrangement, each franchisee would pay the parent company $25,000 plus 1 percent of total revenues. Recompute the values in part (a).
   d. What franchise fee arrangement do you recommend that the Santa Fe Cookie Factory adopt? What are the advantages and disadvantages of each plan?

10. Show that the optimal solution to the set of simultaneous equations in the Indiana Petroleum example are $Q_1^* = 5.77$ and $Q_2^* = 4.08$.

Tables

Z	0	1	2	3	4	5	6	7	8	9
TABLE C.1			**VALUES OF THE STANDARD NORMAL DISTRIBUTION FUNCTION***							
−3.0	.0013	.0010	.0007	.0005	.0003	.0002	.0002	.0001	.0001	.0000
−2.9	.0019	.0018	.0017	.0017	.0016	.0016	.0015	.0015	.0014	.0014
−2.8	.0026	.0025	.0024	.0023	.0023	.0022	.0021	.0021	.0020	.0019
−2.7	.0035	.0034	.0033	.0032	.0031	.0030	.0029	.0028	.0027	.0026
−2.6	.0047	.0045	.0044	.0043	.0041	.0040	.0039	.0038	.0037	.0036
−2.5	.0062	.0060	.0059	.0057	.0055	.0054	.0052	.0051	.0049	.0048
−2.4	.0082	.0080	.0078	.0075	.0073	.0071	.0069	.0068	.0066	.0064
−2.3	.0107	.0104	.0102	.0099	.0096	.0094	.0091	.0089	.0087	.0084
−2.2	.0139	.0136	.0132	.0129	.0126	.0122	.0119	.0116	.0113	.0110
−2.1	.0179	.0174	.0170	.0166	.0162	.0158	.0154	.0150	.0146	.0143
−2.0	.0228	.0222	.0217	.0212	.0207	.0202	.0197	.0192	.0188	.0183
−1.9	.0287	.0281	.0274	.0268	.0262	.0256	.0250	.0244	.0238	.0233
−1.8	.0359	.0352	.0344	.0336	.0329	.0322	.0314	.0307	.0300	.0294
−1.7	.0446	.0436	.0427	.0418	.0409	.0401	.0392	.0384	.0375	.0367
−1.6	.0548	.0537	.0526	.0516	.0505	.0495	.0485	.0475	.0465	.0455
−1.5	.0668	.0655	.0643	.0630	.0618	.0606	.0594	.0582	.0570	.0559
−1.4	.0808	.0793	.0778	.0764	.0749	.0735	.0722	.0708	.0694	.0681
−1.3	.0988	.0951	.0934	.0918	.0901	.0885	.0869	.0853	.0838	.0823
−1.2	.1151	.1131	.1112	.1093	.1075	.1056	.1038	.1020	.1003	.0985
−1.1	.1357	.1335	.1314	.1292	.1271	.1251	.1230	.1210	.1190	.1170
−1.0	.1587	.1562	.1539	.1515	.1492	.1469	.1446	.1423	.1401	.1379
− .9	.1841	.1814	.1788	.1762	.1736	.1711	.1685	.1660	.1635	.1611
− .8	.2119	.2090	.2061	.2033	.2005	.1977	.1949	.1922	.1894	.1867
− .7	.2420	.2389	.2358	.2327	.2297	.2266	.2236	.2206	.2177	.2148
− .6	.2743	.2709	.2676	.2643	.2611	.2578	.2546	.2514	.2483	.2451
− .5	.3085	.3050	.3015	.2981	.2946	.2912	.2877	.2843	.2810	.2776
− .4	.3446	.3409	.3372	.3336	.3300	.3264	.3228	.3192	.3156	.3121
− .3	.3821	.3783	.3745	.3707	.3669	.3632	.3594	.3557	.3520	.3483
− .2	.4207	.4168	.4129	.4090	.4052	.4013	.3974	.3936	.3897	.3859
− .1	.4602	.4562	.4522	.4483	.4443	.4404	.4364	.4325	.4286	.4247
− .0	.5000	.4960	.4920	.4880	.4840	.4801	.4761	.4721	.4681	.4641

*Note: Table values give the probability of a value occurring that is *less than z* standard deviations from the mean.

Note 1: If a random variable X is not "standard," its values must be "standardized": $z = \left(\frac{X - \mu}{\sigma}\right)$. That is:

$$P(X \leq x) = N\left(\frac{x - \mu}{\sigma}\right)$$

Note 2: For $z \leq -4$, $N(z) = 0$ to 4 decimal places; for $z \geq 4$, $N(z) = 1$ to 4 decimal places.

TABLE C.1	VALUES OF THE STANDARD NORMAL DISTRIBUTION FUNCTION (CONTINUED)								
Z	0	1	2	3	4	5	6	7	8	9
.0	.5000	.5040	.5080	.5120	.5160	.5199	.5239	.5279	.5319	.5359
.1	.5398	.5438	.5478	.5517	.5557	.5596	.5636	.5675	.5714	.5753
.2	.5793	.5832	.5871	.5910	.5948	.5987	.6026	.6064	.6103	.6141
.3	.6179	.6217	.6255	.6293	.6331	.6368	.6406	.6443	.6480	.6517
.4	.6554	.6591	.6628	.6664	.6700	.6736	.6772	.6808	.6844	.6879
.5	.6915	.6950	.6985	.7019	.7054	.7088	.7123	.7157	.7190	.7224
.6	.7257	.7291	.7324	.7357	.7389	.7422	.7454	.7486	.7517	.7549
.7	.7580	.7611	.7642	.7673	.7703	.7734	.7764	.7794	.7823	.7852
.8	.7881	.7910	.7939	.7967	.7995	.8023	.8051	.8078	.8106	.8133
.9	.8159	.8186	.8212	.8238	.8264	.8289	.8315	.8340	.8365	.8389
1.0	.8413	.8438	.8461	.8485	.8508	.8531	.8554	.8577	.8599	.8621
1.1	.8643	.8665	.8686	.8708	.8729	.8749	.8770	.8790	.8810	.8830
1.2	.8849	.8869	.8888	.8907	.8925	.8944	.8962	.8980	.8997	.9015
1.3	.9032	.9049	.9066	.9082	.9099	.9115	.9131	.9147	.9162	.9177
1.4	.9192	.9207	.9222	.9236	.9251	.9265	.9278	.9292	.9306	.9319
1.5	.9332	.9345	.9357	.9370	.9382	.9394	.9406	.9418	.9430	.9441
1.6	.9452	.9463	.9474	.9484	.9495	.9505	.9515	.9525	.9535	.9545
1.7	.9554	.9564	.9573	.9582	.9591	.9599	.9608	.9616	.9625	.9633
1.8	.9641	.9648	.9656	.9664	.9671	.9678	.9686	.9693	.9700	.9706
1.9	.9713	.9719	.9726	.9732	.9738	.9744	.9750	.9756	.9762	.9767
2.0	.9772	.9778	.9783	.9788	.9793	.9798	.9803	.9808	.9812	.9817
2.1	.9821	.9826	.9830	.9834	.9838	.9842	.9846	.9850	.9854	.9857
2.2	.9861	.9864	.9868	.9871	.9874	.9878	.9881	.9884	.9887	.9890
2.3	.9893	.9896	.9898	.9901	.9904	.9906	.9909	.9911	.9913	.9916
2.4	.9918	.9920	.9922	.9925	.9927	.9929	.9931	.9932	.9934	.9936
2.5	.9938	.9940	.9941	.9943	.9945	.9946	.9948	.9949	.9951	.9952
2.6	.9953	.9955	.9956	.9957	.9959	.9960	.9961	.9962	.9963	.9964
2.7	.9965	.9966	.9967	.9968	.9969	.9970	.9971	.9972	.9973	.9974
2.8	.9974	.9975	.9976	.9977	.9977	.9978	.9979	.9979	.9980	.9981
2.9	.9981	.9982	.9982	.9983	.9984	.9984	.9985	.9985	.9986	.9986
3.0	.9987	.9990	.9993	.9995	.9997	.9998	.9998	.9999	.9999	1.0000

Source: From CHOU, STATISTICAL ANALYSIS @, 1E. © 1969 Cengage Learning.

TABLE C.3   THE F-DISTRIBUTION—UPPER 5 PERCENT BREAKPOINTS

δ_2 \\ δ_1	1	2	3	4	5	6	7	8	9	10	12	15	20	24	30	40	60	120	∞
1	161.4	199.5	215.7	224.6	230.2	234.0	236.8	238.9	240.5	241.9	243.9	245.9	248.0	249.1	250.1	251.1	252.2	253.3	254.3
2	18.51	19.00	19.16	19.25	19.30	19.33	19.35	19.37	19.38	19.40	19.41	19.43	19.45	19.45	19.46	19.47	19.48	19.49	19.50
3	10.13	9.55	9.28	9.12	9.01	8.94	8.89	8.85	8.81	8.79	8.74	8.70	8.66	8.64	8.62	8.59	8.57	8.55	8.53
4	7.71	6.94	6.59	6.39	6.26	6.16	6.09	6.04	6.00	5.96	5.91	5.86	5.80	5.77	5.75	5.72	5.69	5.66	5.63
5	6.61	5.79	5.41	5.19	5.05	4.95	4.88	4.82	4.77	4.74	4.68	4.62	4.56	4.53	4.50	4.46	4.43	4.40	4.36
6	5.99	5.14	4.76	4.53	4.39	4.28	4.21	4.15	4.10	4.06	4.00	3.94	3.87	3.84	3.81	3.77	3.74	3.70	3.67
7	5.59	4.74	4.35	4.12	3.97	3.87	3.79	3.73	3.68	3.64	3.57	3.51	3.44	3.41	3.38	3.34	3.30	3.27	3.23
8	5.32	4.46	4.07	3.84	3.69	3.58	3.50	3.44	3.39	3.35	3.28	3.22	3.15	3.12	3.08	3.04	3.01	2.97	2.93
9	5.12	4.26	3.86	3.63	3.48	3.37	3.29	3.23	3.18	3.14	3.07	3.01	2.94	2.90	2.86	2.83	2.79	2.75	2.71
10	4.96	4.10	3.71	3.48	3.33	3.22	3.14	3.07	3.02	2.98	2.91	2.85	2.77	2.74	2.70	2.66	2.62	2.58	2.54
11	4.84	3.98	3.59	3.36	3.20	3.09	3.01	2.95	2.90	2.85	2.79	2.72	2.65	2.61	2.57	2.53	2.49	2.45	2.40
12	4.75	3.89	3.49	3.26	3.11	3.00	2.91	2.85	2.80	2.75	2.69	2.62	2.54	2.51	2.47	2.43	2.38	2.34	2.30
13	4.67	3.81	3.41	3.18	3.03	2.92	2.83	2.77	2.71	2.67	2.60	2.53	2.46	2.42	2.38	2.34	2.30	2.25	2.21
14	4.60	3.74	3.34	3.11	2.96	2.85	2.76	2.70	2.65	2.60	2.53	2.46	2.39	2.35	2.31	2.27	2.22	2.18	2.13
15	4.54	3.68	3.29	3.06	2.90	2.79	2.71	2.64	2.59	2.54	2.48	2.40	2.33	2.29	2.25	2.20	2.16	2.11	2.07
16	4.49	3.63	3.24	3.01	2.85	2.74	2.66	2.59	2.54	2.49	2.42	2.35	2.28	2.24	2.19	2.15	2.11	2.06	2.01
17	4.45	3.59	3.20	2.96	2.81	2.70	2.61	2.55	2.49	2.45	2.38	2.31	2.23	2.19	2.15	2.10	2.06	2.01	1.96
18	4.41	3.55	3.16	2.93	2.77	2.66	2.58	2.51	2.46	2.41	2.34	2.27	2.19	2.15	2.11	2.06	2.02	1.97	1.92
19	4.38	3.52	3.13	2.90	2.74	2.63	2.54	2.48	2.42	2.38	2.31	2.23	2.16	2.11	2.07	2.03	1.98	1.93	1.88
20	4.35	3.49	3.10	2.87	2.71	2.60	2.51	2.45	2.39	2.35	2.28	2.20	2.12	2.08	2.04	1.99	1.95	1.90	1.84
21	4.32	3.47	3.07	2.84	2.68	2.57	2.49	2.42	2.37	2.32	2.25	2.18	2.10	2.05	2.01	1.96	1.92	1.87	1.81
22	4.30	3.44	3.05	2.82	2.66	2.55	2.46	2.40	2.34	2.30	2.23	2.15	2.07	2.03	1.98	1.94	1.89	1.84	1.78
23	4.28	3.42	3.03	2.80	2.64	2.53	2.44	2.37	2.32	2.27	2.20	2.13	2.05	2.01	1.96	1.91	1.86	1.81	1.76
24	4.26	3.40	3.01	2.78	2.62	2.51	2.42	2.36	2.30	2.25	2.18	2.11	2.03	1.98	1.94	1.89	1.84	1.79	1.73
25	4.24	3.39	2.99	2.76	2.60	2.49	2.40	2.34	2.28	2.24	2.16	2.09	2.01	1.96	1.92	1.87	1.82	1.77	1.71
26	4.23	3.37	2.98	2.74	2.59	2.47	2.39	2.32	2.27	2.22	2.15	2.07	1.99	1.95	1.90	1.85	1.80	1.75	1.69
27	4.21	3.35	2.96	2.73	2.57	2.46	2.37	2.31	2.25	2.20	2.13	2.06	1.97	1.93	1.88	1.84	1.79	1.73	1.67
28	4.20	3.34	2.95	2.71	2.56	2.45	2.36	2.29	2.24	2.19	2.12	2.04	1.96	1.91	1.87	1.82	1.77	1.71	1.65
29	4.18	3.33	2.93	2.70	2.55	2.43	2.35	2.28	2.22	2.18	2.10	2.03	1.94	1.90	1.85	1.81	1.75	1.70	1.64
30	4.17	3.32	2.92	2.69	2.53	2.42	2.33	2.27	2.21	2.16	2.09	2.01	1.93	1.89	1.84	1.79	1.74	1.68	1.62
40	4.08	3.23	2.84	2.61	2.45	2.34	2.25	2.18	2.12	2.08	2.00	1.92	1.84	1.79	1.74	1.69	1.64	1.58	1.51
60	4.00	3.15	2.76	2.53	2.37	2.25	2.17	2.10	2.04	1.99	1.92	1.84	1.75	1.70	1.65	1.59	1.53	1.47	1.39
120	3.92	3.07	2.68	2.45	2.29	2.17	2.09	2.02	1.96	1.91	1.83	1.75	1.66	1.61	1.55	1.50	1.43	1.35	1.25
∞	3.84	3.00	2.60	2.37	2.21	2.10	2.01	1.94	1.88	1.83	1.75	1.67	1.57	1.52	1.46	1.39	1.32	1.22	1.00

(continued)

TABLE C.3   THE F-DISTRIBUTION—UPPER 1 PERCENT BREAKPOINTS (CONTINUED)

δ_1 / δ_2	1	2	3	4	5	6	7	8	9	10	12	15	20	24	30	40	60	120	∞
1	4052	4999.5	5403	5625	5764	5859	5928	5982	6022	6056	6106	6157	6209	6235	6261	6287	6313	6339	6366
2	98.50	99.00	99.17	99.25	99.30	99.33	99.36	99.37	99.39	99.40	99.42	99.43	99.45	99.46	99.47	99.47	99.48	99.49	99.50
3	34.12	30.82	29.46	28.71	28.24	27.91	27.67	27.49	27.35	27.23	27.05	26.87	26.69	26.60	26.50	26.41	26.32	26.22	26.13
4	21.20	18.00	16.69	15.98	15.52	15.21	14.98	14.80	14.66	14.55	14.37	14.20	14.02	13.93	13.84	13.75	13.65	13.56	13.46
5	16.26	13.27	12.06	11.39	10.97	10.67	10.46	10.29	10.16	10.05	9.89	9.72	9.55	9.47	9.38	9.29	9.20	9.11	9.02
6	13.75	10.92	9.78	9.15	8.75	8.47	8.26	8.10	7.98	7.87	7.72	7.56	7.40	7.31	7.23	7.14	7.06	6.97	6.88
7	12.25	9.55	8.45	7.85	7.46	7.19	6.99	6.84	6.72	6.62	6.47	6.31	6.16	6.07	5.99	5.91	5.82	5.74	5.65
8	11.26	8.65	7.59	7.01	6.63	6.37	6.18	6.03	5.91	5.81	5.67	5.52	5.36	5.28	5.20	5.12	5.03	4.95	4.86
9	10.56	8.02	6.99	6.42	6.06	5.80	5.61	5.47	5.35	5.26	5.11	4.96	4.81	4.73	4.65	4.57	4.48	4.40	4.31
10	10.04	7.56	6.55	5.99	5.64	5.39	5.20	5.06	4.94	4.85	4.71	4.56	4.41	4.33	4.25	4.17	4.08	4.00	3.91
11	9.65	7.21	6.22	5.67	5.32	5.07	4.89	4.74	4.63	4.54	4.40	4.25	4.10	4.02	3.94	3.86	3.78	3.69	3.60
12	9.33	6.93	5.95	5.41	5.06	4.82	4.64	4.50	4.39	4.30	4.16	4.01	3.86	3.78	3.70	3.62	3.54	3.45	3.36
13	9.07	6.70	5.74	5.21	4.86	4.62	4.44	4.30	4.19	4.10	3.96	3.82	3.66	3.59	3.51	3.43	3.34	3.25	3.17
14	8.86	6.51	5.56	5.04	4.69	4.46	4.28	4.14	4.03	3.94	3.80	3.66	3.51	3.43	3.35	3.27	3.18	3.09	3.00
15	8.68	6.36	5.42	4.89	4.56	4.32	4.14	4.00	3.89	3.80	3.67	3.52	3.37	3.29	3.21	3.13	3.05	2.96	2.87
16	8.53	6.23	5.29	4.77	4.44	4.20	4.03	3.89	3.78	3.69	3.55	3.41	3.26	3.18	3.10	3.02	2.93	2.84	2.75
17	8.40	6.11	5.18	4.67	4.34	4.10	3.93	3.79	3.68	3.59	3.46	3.31	3.16	3.08	3.00	2.92	2.83	2.75	2.65
18	8.29	6.01	5.09	4.58	4.25	4.01	3.84	3.71	3.60	3.51	3.37	3.23	3.08	3.00	2.92	2.84	2.75	2.66	2.57
19	8.18	5.93	5.01	4.50	4.17	3.94	3.77	3.63	3.52	3.43	3.30	3.15	3.00	2.92	2.84	2.76	2.67	2.58	2.49
20	8.10	5.85	4.94	4.43	4.10	3.87	3.70	3.56	3.46	3.37	3.23	3.09	2.94	2.86	2.78	2.69	2.61	2.52	2.42
21	8.02	5.78	4.87	4.37	4.04	3.81	3.64	3.51	3.40	3.31	3.17	3.03	2.88	2.80	2.72	2.64	2.55	2.46	2.36
22	7.95	5.72	4.82	4.31	3.99	3.76	3.59	3.45	3.35	3.26	3.12	2.98	2.83	2.75	2.67	2.58	2.50	2.40	2.31
23	7.88	5.66	4.76	4.26	3.94	3.71	3.54	3.41	3.30	3.21	3.07	2.93	2.78	2.70	2.62	2.54	2.45	2.35	2.26
24	7.82	5.61	4.72	4.22	3.90	3.67	3.50	3.36	3.26	3.17	3.03	2.89	2.74	2.66	2.58	2.49	2.40	2.31	2.21
25	7.77	5.57	4.68	4.18	3.85	3.63	3.46	3.32	3.22	3.13	2.99	2.85	2.70	2.62	2.54	2.45	2.36	2.27	2.17
26	7.72	5.53	4.64	4.14	3.82	3.59	3.42	3.29	3.18	3.09	2.96	2.81	2.66	2.58	2.50	2.42	2.33	2.23	2.13
27	7.68	5.49	4.60	4.11	3.78	3.56	3.39	3.26	3.15	3.06	2.93	2.78	2.63	2.55	2.47	2.38	2.29	2.20	2.10
28	7.64	5.45	4.57	4.07	3.75	3.53	3.36	3.23	3.12	3.03	2.90	2.75	2.60	2.52	2.44	2.35	2.26	2.17	2.06
29	7.60	5.42	4.54	4.04	3.73	3.50	3.33	3.20	3.09	3.00	2.87	2.73	2.57	2.49	2.41	2.33	2.23	2.14	2.03
30	7.56	5.39	4.51	4.02	3.70	3.47	3.30	3.17	3.07	2.98	2.84	2.70	2.55	2.47	2.39	2.30	2.21	2.11	2.01
40	7.31	5.18	4.31	3.83	3.51	3.29	3.12	2.99	2.89	2.80	2.66	2.52	2.37	2.29	2.20	2.11	2.02	1.92	1.80
60	7.08	4.98	4.13	3.65	3.34	3.12	2.95	2.82	2.72	2.63	2.50	2.35	2.20	2.12	2.03	1.94	1.84	1.73	1.60
120	6.85	4.79	3.95	3.48	3.17	2.96	2.79	2.66	2.56	2.47	2.34	2.19	2.03	1.95	1.86	1.76	1.66	1.53	1.38
∞	6.63	4.61	3.78	3.32	3.02	2.80	2.64	2.51	2.41	2.32	2.18	2.04	1.88	1.79	1.70	1.59	1.47	1.32	1.00

Source: E. S. Pearson and H. O. Hartley, *Biometrika Tables for Statisticians*, Vol. 1, Table 18.

Check Answers to Selected End-of-Chapter Exercises

Chapter 1

Case Exercise—Designing a Managerial Incentives Contract

1. $240 million
7. $167 million
8. $205 million

Chapter 2

3. Budget = $875 million
5. c. $v = 0.067$

Chapter 3

2. 44%
5. $P = \$90$
6. a. $E_D = -0.59$
8. a. $E_X = 1.34$
   Close substitutes.
9. $Q_{2006} = 5,169$
   $Q_{2007} = 3,953$

Chapter 4

3. d. $r^2 = 0.885$
9. a. $Y' = -14.7351 + 3.9214$ Size + 3.5851 Rooms − 0.1181 Age − 2.8317 Garage

Case Exercise—Soft Drink Demand Estimation

2. $E_D = -3.38$

Appendix 4A

2. a. $Y' = 1.210 + 0.838$ Selling Expenses, $r^2 = 0.93$
4. a. (i) $S' = 247.644 + 0.3926$ Advertising − 0.7339 Price
   (ii) $\text{Log}(S') = 2.4482 + 0.7296$ Log Advertising − 0.2406 Log Price

Chapter 5

3. b. Sum(Actual/Forecast)/6 = 636.6%/6 − 106.1%, thus + 6%
4. b. GNP = C + I + G = 635 + 120 + 200 = 955
7. b. $Y'_{2007} = 259.03$
8. a. December 2007 = 468

Chapter 6

1. Both increase
3. Outsource abroad and buy foreign assets
6. 15 percent decline. Relative purchasing power parity

Chapter 7

3. b. 10 or 11 men
5. c. $AP_X = 6X - 0.4X^2$
7. a. 4.88%

Case Exercise—Production Function for Wilson Company

4. $E_K = 0.415$, $E_L = 1.078$

Chapter 8

2. b. ($90,000)

Case Exercise—Cost Analysis

1. $4.55

Chapter 9

2. a. $Q^* = \$574.08$ (million)

5. a. $30,000,000

Case Exercise—Cost Functions

5. $Q^* = 1,675$

Case Exercise—Charter Airline Operating Decisions

3. Indirect Fixed Cost = $23,900

Chapter 10

8. b. $P^* = \$1,220$

9. b. $900,000 on advertising

Chapter 11

2. c. $Q^* = 125$

3. e. $\pi^* = \$263,625$

4. b. $P^* = \$60$

8. a. $ROI = 14.2\%$

9. a. $ROI = 12.98\%$

Chapter 12

2. a. $P^* = \$145$
   $Q_A^* = 30$

5. a. $P^* = \$9,666.70$, $Q^* = 666.7$

6. c. $P^* = \$125$, $Q^* = 50$

Chapter 13

3. b. Dominant strategy for AMC is to "Not Abide"

5. {$150, Match}, No

6. Least should pass. More should always attack Most, and knowing that, Most should always attack More. If they pass, Least will get a second opportunity to attack a once stronger but now weakened opponent.

8. {Late, Late} is one of two pure Nash equilibria.

Chapter 14

1. $P_{US} = \$80$, $P_{OVERSEAS} = \$22.50$

3. a. $\pi = -20 + 96Q1 + 76Q_2 - 2Q_2^1 - Q_2^2$

Appendix 14A

3. 22 seats

Chapter 15

3. High interest rates, large principal, long term, unsecured

5. Vertical integration if the power plant is dependent on this type of coal. Otherwise, long-term supply contracts.

Case Exercise—Division of Investment Banking Fees in a Syndicate

1. Lead underwriter = $97 million
   Syndicate Co-Manager = 0
   Syndicate Member 3 = $1 million
   Syndicate Member 4 = 0
   Syndicate Member 5 = $2 million

Appendix 15A

4. Electricity, T-bills

5. $1.3 million.
   Use open bidding, multiple rounds, highest-wins-and-pays.

11. Apple's expected profit is $1.5 million less from understatement.

Chapter 16

3. a. *HHI* before = 1,964. So, in general, no, although off-setting efficiency arguments may come into play as long as 1,984 is below the 2,500 standard.

6. b. $\pi^* = \$450$ million

11. Coordinate on Nash equilibrium (Lucent Imitate, Motorola Develop) in joint venture with compensation of at least $1 billion to Motorola.

Chapter 17

2. $IRR = 9.1\%$. So, No.

4. b. $NCF_{10} = \$5,560$

5. a. $IRR = 14.94\%$,
   $NPV = \$45,176$

6. $k_e = 13.4\%$

7. b. $k_e' = 13\%$

8. $k_a = 12.3\%$

9. b. Power plant:
   $NPV_{@12\%} = -\$22.71$ million,
   $NPV_{@5\%} = \$62.65$ million

Case Exercise—Cost-Benefit Analysis

1. *B/C* ratio = 1.90

Glossary

absolute cost advantage A comparison of nominal costs in two locations, companies, or economies.

adverse selection A limited choice of lower-quality alternatives attributable to asymmetric information.

agency costs Costs associated with resolving conflicts of interest among shareholders, managers, and lenders.

allocative efficiency A measure of how closely production achieves the least-cost input mix or process, given the desired level of output.

appraisals An estimate of value by an independent expert.

arbitrage Buying cheap and selling elsewhere for an immediate profit.

asset specificity The difference in value between first-best and second-best use.

asymmetric information Unequal, dissimilar knowledge.

authorization level Capacity authorized for sale in lower margin segments.

autocorrelation An econometric problem characterized by the existence of a significant pattern in the successive values of the error terms in a linear regression model.

average product The ratio of total output to the amount of the variable input used in producing the output.

backward induction To reason in reverse temporal order.

barriers to exit Economic losses resulting from non-redeployable assets or contractual constraints upon business termination.

benchmarking A comparison of performance in similar jobs, firms, plants, divisions, and so forth.

benefit-cost ratio The ratio of the present value of the benefits from a project or program (discounted at the social discount rate) to the present value of the costs (similarly discounted).

best-reply response An action that maximizes self-interest from among feasible choices.

bonding mechanism A procedure for establishing trust by pledging valuable property contingent on your nonperformance of an agreement.

brand loyalty A customer sorting rule favorable to incumbents.

break-even analysis A calculation of the output level at which total contributions cover direct plus indirect fixed costs.

break-even sales change analysis A calculation of the percentage increase in unit sales required to justify a price discount, given the contribution margin.

capital assets A durable input that depreciates with use, time, and obsolescence.

capital budgeting The process of planning for and evaluating capital expenditures.

capital expenditure A cash outlay designed to generate a flow of future cash benefits over a period of time extending beyond one year.

cartel A formal or informal agreement among firms in an oligopolistic industry that influences such issues as prices, total industry output, market shares, and the division of profits.

ceteris paribus Latin for "all other things held constant."

chain store paradox A prediction of always accommodative behavior by incumbents facing entry threats.

class action suits A legal procedure for reducing the search and notification costs of filing a complaint.

closed-end leases with fixed residual values A credible commitment mechanism for limiting the depth of price promotions and the rate of planned obsolescence.

Coase theorem A prediction about the emergence of private voluntary bargaining in reciprocal externalities with low transaction costs.

Cobb-Douglas production function A particular type of mathematical model, known as a multiplicative exponential function, used to represent the relationship between the inputs and the output.

coefficient of determination A measure of the proportion of total variation in the dependent variable that is explained by the independent variable(s).

coefficient of variation The ratio of the standard deviation to the expected value. A relative measure of risk.

cointegrated Stochastic series with a common order of integration and exhibiting an equilibrium relationship such that they do not permanently wander away from one another.

common-value auction Auction where bidders have identical valuations when information is complete.

company audit A governance mechanism for separating random disturbances from variation in unobservable effort.

complementary goods Complements in consumption whose demand decreases when the price of the focal product rises.

complementors Independent firms that enhance the focal firm's value proposition.

concentrated market A relevant market with a majority of total sales occurring in the largest four firms.

congestion pricing A fee that reflects the true marginal cost imposed by demand in excess of capacity.

consolidated A relevant market whose number of firms has declined through acquisition, merger, and buyouts.

conspicuous focal point An outcome that attracts mutual cooperation.

contestable markets An industry with exceptionally open entry and easy exit where incumbents are slow to react.

contingent payments A fee schedule conditional on the outcome of uncertain future events.

contracts Third-party-enforceable agreements designed to facilitate deferred exchange.

contribution analysis A comparison of margins earned to the direct fixed costs attributable to a decision.

contribution margin The difference between price and variable cost per unit.

cooperative game Game structures that allow coalition formation, side payments, and binding third-party enforceable agreements.

core competencies Technology-based expertise or knowledge on which a company can focus its strategy.

cost fixity A measure of fixed to total cost that is correlated with gross profit margins.

cost of capital The cost of funds that are supplied to a firm. The cost of capital is the minimum rate of return that must be earned on new investments undertaken by a firm.

cost-based strategy A business-level strategy that relies upon low-cost operations, marketing, or distribution.

cost-benefit analysis A resource allocation model that can be used by public sector and not-for-profit organizations to evaluate programs or investments on the basis of the magnitude of the discounted costs and benefits.

cost-benefit analysis A resource allocation model that can be used by public and not-for-profit sector organizations to evaluate programs or investments on the basis of the magnitude of the discounted benefits and costs.

cost-effectiveness analysis An analytical tool designed to assist public decision makers in their resource allocation decisions when benefits cannot be easily measured in terms of dollars but costs can be monetarily quantified.

credible commitment A promise that the promise-giver is worse off violating than fulfilling.

credible threat A conditional strategy the threat-maker is worse off ignoring than implementing.

cross price elasticity The ratio of the percentage change in the quantity demanded of Good A to the percentage change in the price of Good B, assuming that all other factors influencing demand remain unchanged.

cross-sectional data Series of observations taken on different observation units

(e.g., households, states, or countries) at the same point in time.

cyclical variations Major expansions and contractions in an economic series that usually are longer than a year in duration.

degree of operating leverage (DOL) The percentage change in a firm's earnings before interest and taxes (EBIT) resulting from a given percentage change in sales or output.

demand function A relationship between quantity demanded per unit of time and all the determinants of demand.

derivative A measure of the marginal effect of a change in one variable on the value of a function. Graphically, it represents the slope of the function at a given point.

diseconomies of scale Rising long-run average total costs as the level of output is increased.

dividend valuation model A model (or formula) stating that the value of a firm (i.e., shareholder wealth) is equal to the present value of the firm's future dividend payments, discounted at the shareholder's required rate of return. It provides one method of estimating a firm's cost of equity capital.

dominant strategy An action rule that maximizes the decision maker's welfare independent of the actions of other players.

durable goods Goods that yield benefits to the owner over a number of future time periods.

Dutch auctions A descending-price auction.

dynamic pricing A price that varies over time based on the balance of demand and supply, often associated with Internet auctions.

economic profit The difference between total revenue and total economic cost. Economic cost includes a "normal" rate of return on the capital contributions of the firm's partners.

economies of scope Economies that exist whenever the cost of producing two (or more) products jointly by one plant or firm is less than the cost of producing these products separately in separate plants or firms.

efficient contract breach A set of incentive-compatible procedures for awarding expectation damages in breach-of-contract suits.

efficient rationing A customer sorting rule in which high-willingness-to-pay customers absorb the capacity of low-price entrants.

endgame reasoning An analysis of the final decision in a sequential game.

engineering cost techniques A method of estimating cost functions by deriving the least-cost combination of labor, capital equipment, and raw materials required to produce various levels of output, using only industrial engineering information.

English auctions An ascending-price auction.

expectation damages A remedy for breach of contract designed to elicit efficient precaution and efficient reliance on promises.

expected value The weighted average of the possible outcomes where the weights are the probabilities of the respective outcomes.

experience goods Products and services whose quality is undetectable when purchased.

external diseconomy of scale An increase in unit costs reflecting higher input prices.

externality A spillover of benefits or costs from one production or utility function to another.

first-order condition A test to locate one or more maximum or minimum points of an algebraic function.

fixed costs The costs of inputs to the production process that are constant over the short run.

focal outcomes of interest Payoffs involved in an analysis of equilibrium strategy.

folk theorem A conclusion about cooperation in repeated Prisoner's Dilemma.

forward sales contracts A consensual agreement to exchange goods delivered in the future for cash today, with no possibility of a performance excuse.

fragmented A relevant market whose market shares are uniformly small.

free trade area A group of nations that have agreed to reduce tariffs and other trade barriers.

frustration of purpose doctrine An illustration of a default rule of contract law that can result in excusal of contract promises.

full contingent claims contract An agreement about all possible future events.

full-cost pricing A method of determining prices that cover overhead and other indirect fixed costs, as well as the variable and direct fixed costs.

game theory A theory of interdependent decision making by the participants in a conflict of interest or opportunity for collaboration situation.

game tree A schematic diagram of a sequential game.

governance mechanisms Processes to detect, resolve, and reduce post-contractual opportunism.

grim trigger strategy A hypersensitive strategy involving infinitely long punishment schemes.

gross profit margin Revenue minus the sum of variable cost plus direct fixed cost, also known as direct costs of goods sold in manufacturing.

Herfindahl-Hirschman Index A measure of market concentration equal to the sum of the squares of the market shares of the firms in a given industry.

heteroscedasticity An econometric problem characterized by the lack of a uniform variance of the error terms surrounding the regression line.

hostage mechanism An exchange of assets that is worth more to the hostage giver than to the hostage recipient in order to establish credibility of threats or commitments.

identification problem A difficulty encountered in empirically estimating a demand function by regression analysis. This problem arises from the simultaneous relationship between two functions, such as supply and demand.

incentive compatibility constraint An assurance of incentive alignment.

incentive-compatible revelation mechanism A procedure for eliciting true revelation of privately held information from agents with competing interests.

income elasticity The ratio of the percentage change in quantity demanded to the percentage change in income, assuming that all other factors influencing demand remain unchanged.

incomplete information Uncertain knowledge of payoffs, choices, and other factors.

incremental contribution analysis An incremental managerial decision that analyzes the change in operating profits (revenue—variable costs—direct fixed costs) available to cover indirect fixed costs.

industry analysis Assessment of the strengths and weaknesses of a set of competitors or line of businesses.

infinitely repeated games A game that lasts forever.

information technology strategy A business-level strategy that relies on IT capabilities.

inherent business risk The inherent variability or uncertainty of a firm's operating earnings (earnings before interest and taxes).

inputs A resource or factor of production, such as a raw material, labor skill, or a piece of equipment that is employed in a production process.

internal economies of scale Declining long-run average costs as the rate of output for a product, plant, or firm is increased.

internal hedge A balance sheet offset or foreign payables offset to fluctuations in foreign receipts attributable to exchange rate risk.

internal rate of return (IRR) The discount rate that equates the present value of the stream of net cash flows from a project with the project's net investment.

inverse intensity rationing A customer sorting rule that assures that low-willing-ness-to-pay customers absorb the capacity of low-price entrants.

iterated dominant strategy An action rule that maximizes self-interest in light of the predictable dominant strategy behavior of other players.

law of comparative advantage A principle defending free trade and specialization in accordance with lower relative cost.

learning curve effect Declining unit cost attributable to greater cumulative from longer production runs.

lemons markets Asymmetric information exchange leads to the low-quality products and services driving out the higher-quality products and services.

life cycle pricing Pricing that varies throughout the product life cycle.

linear incentives contract A linear combination of salary and profit sharing intended to align incentives.

long run The period of time in which *all* the resources employed in a production process can be varied.

maquiladora A foreign-owned assembly plant in Mexico that imports and assembles duty free components for export and allows owners to pay duty only on the "value added."

marginal analysis A basis for making various economic decisions that analyzes the additional (marginal) benefits derived from a particular decision and compares them with the additional (marginal) costs incurred.

marginal cost The incremental increase in total variable cost that results from a one-unit increase in output.

marginal factor cost (MFC$_L$) The amount that an additional unit of the variable input adds to total cost.

marginal product The incremental change in total output that can be obtained from the use of one more unit of an input in the production process (while holding constant all other inputs).

marginal rate of technical substitution (MRTS) The rate at which one input may be substituted for another input in producing a given quantity of output.

marginal revenue product (MRP$_L$) The amount that an additional unit of the variable production input adds to total revenue; also known as *marginal value added*.

marginal revenue The change in total revenue that results from a one-unit change in quantity demanded.

marginal use value The additional value of the consumption of one more unit; the greater the utilization already, the lower the use value remaining.

marginal utility The use value obtained from the last unit consumed.

marginal value added The increase in revenue added by a stage of production or service.

market concentration ratio The percentage of total industry output produced by the 4, 8, 20, or 50 largest firms.

maximin strategy A criterion for selecting actions that minimize absolute losses.

maximum sustainable yield (MSY) The largest production harvest that can be produced by the resource stock as a perpetuity.

minimum efficient scale (MES) The smallest scale at which minimum costs per unit are attained.

mixed bundling Selling multiple products both separately and together for less than the sum of the separate prices.

mixed Nash equilibrium strategy A strategic equilibrium concept involving randomized behavior.

monopolistic competition A market structure very much like pure competition, with the major distinction being the existence of a differentiated product.

monopoly A market structure characterized by one firm producing a highly differentiated product in a market with significant barriers to entry.

moral hazard problem A problem of post-contractual opportunism that arises from

unverifiable or unobservable contract performance.

multicollinearity An econometric problem characterized by a high degree of intercorrelation among explanatory variables in a regression equation.

Nash equilibrium strategy An equilibrium concept for non-dominant strategy games.

natural monopoly An industry in which maximum economic efficiency is obtained when the firm produces, distributes, and transmits all of the commodity or service produced in that industry. The production of natural monopolists is typically characterized by increasing returns to scale throughout the relevant range of output.

net present value (NPV) The present value of the stream of net cash flows resulting from a project, discounted at the required rate of return (cost of capital), minus the project's net investment.

network effects An exception to the law of diminishing marginal returns that occurs when the installed base of a network product makes the efforts to acquire new customers increasingly more productive.

noncooperative games Game structures that prohibit collusion, side payments, and binding agreements enforced by third parties.

non-redeployable assets Assets whose value in second-best use is near zero.

non-redeployable reputational asset A reputation whose value is lost if sold or licensed.

non-redeployable, specific assets Assets whose replacement cost basis for value is substantially greater than their liquidation value.

normal form of the game A representation of payoffs in a simultaneous-play game.

oligopoly A market structure in which the number of firms is so small that the actions of any one firm are likely to have noticeable impacts on the performance of other firms in the industry.

operating leverage The use of assets having fixed costs in an effort to increase expected returns.

operating risk exposure A change in cash flows from foreign or domestic sales resulting from currency fluctuations.

opportunity costs The value of a resource in its next-best alternative use.

optimal incentives contract An agreement about payoffs and penalties that creates appropriate incentives.

optimal mechanism design An efficient procedure that creates incentives to motivate the desired behavioral outcome.

optimal output for a given plant size Output rate that results in lowest average total cost for a given plant size.

optimal overbooking A marginal analysis technique for balancing the cost of idle capacity (spoilage) against the opportunity cost of unserved demand (spill).

optimal plant size for a given output rate Plant size that results in lowest average total cost for a given output.

optimal plant size Plant size that achieves minimum long-run average total cost.

overall production efficiency A measure of technical and allocative efficiency.

parallel imports The purchase of a foreign export product in one country to resell as an unauthorized import in another country.

partial derivative A measure of the marginal effect of a change in one variable on the value of a multivariate function while holding constant all other variables.

participation constraint An assurance of ongoing involvement.

patent A legal government grant of monopoly power that prevents others from manufacturing or selling a patented article.

pecuniary externality A spillover that is reflected in prices and therefore results in no inefficiency.

pooling equilibrium A decision setting that elicits indistinguishable behavior.

post-contractual opportunistic behavior Actions that take advantage of a contract partner's vulnerabilities and are not specifically prohibited by the contract terms.

present value The value today of a future amount of money or a series of future payments evaluated at the appropriate discount rate.

price discrimination The act of selling the same good or service, distributed in a single channel, at different prices to different buyers during the same period of time.

price elasticity of demand The ratio of the percentage change in quantity demanded to the percentage change in price, assuming that all other factors influencing demand remain unchanged.

price leadership A pricing strategy followed in many oligopolistic industries. One firm normally announces all new price changes. Either by an explicit or by an implicit agreement, other firms in the industry regularly follow the pricing moves of the industry leader.

price signaling A communication of price change plans, prohibited by antitrust law.

price skimming A new-product pricing strategy that results in a high initial product price being reduced over time as demand at the higher price is satisfied.

principal-agent problem An incentives conflict in delegating decision-making authority.

private-value auction Auction where the bidders have different valuations even when information is complete.

probability The percentage chance that a particular outcome will occur.

product differentiation strategy A business-level strategy that relies upon differences in products or processes affecting perceived customer value.

production function A mathematical model, a spreadsheet, or a graph that relates the maximum feasible quantity of output that can be produced from given amounts of various inputs.

production isoquant An algebraic function or a geometric curve representing all the various combinations of two inputs that can be used in producing a given level of output.

production process A fixed proportions production relationship.

prospect theory A basis for hypothesizing that the satisfaction from avoiding losses exceeds the anticipation of equal-value prospective gains.

protection level Capacity reserved for sale in higher margin segments.

public goods Goods that may be consumed by more than one person at the same time with little or no extra cost, and for which it is expensive or impossible to exclude those who do not pay.

public utilities A group of firms, mostly in the electric power, natural gas, and communications industries, that are closely regulated by one or more government agencies. The agencies control entry into the business, set prices, establish product quality standards, and influence these total profits that may be earned by the firms subject to scale economies.

pure competition A market structure characterized by a large number of buyers and sellers of a homogeneous (nondifferentiated) product. Entry and exit from the industry is costless, or nearly so. Information is freely available to all market participants, and there is no collusion among firms in the industry.

quantitative easing Expansionary monetary policy focused on longer-term bonds and mortgage backed securities.

random rationing A customer sorting rule reflecting randomized buyer behavior.

real terms of trade Comparison of relative costs of production across economies.

reciprocal externality A spillover that results from competing incompatible uses.

relational contracts Promissory agreements of coordinated performance among owners of highly interdependent assets.

relative purchasing power parity A relationship between differential inflation rates and long-term trends in exchange rates.

relevant market A group of firms belonging to the same strategic group of competitors.

reliance relationships Long-term, mutually beneficial agreements, often informal.

reliant assets At least partially non-redeployable durable assets.

reservation prices The maximum price a customer will pay to reserve a product or service unto his or her own use.

returns to scale The proportionate increase in output that results from a given proportionate increase in *all* the inputs employed in the production process.

revenue management A cross-functional order acceptance and refusal process.

risk A decision-making situation in which there is variability in the possible outcomes, and the probabilities of these outcomes can be specified by the decision maker.

sales penetration curve An S-shaped curve relating current market share to the probability of adoption by the next target customer, reflecting the presence of increasing returns.

search goods Products and services whose quality can be detected through market search.

seasonal effects Variations in a time series during a year that tend to appear regularly from year to year.

second-order condition A test to determine whether a point that has been determined from the first-order condition is either a maximum point or a minimum point of the algebraic function.

secular trends *Long-run* changes (growth or decline) in an economic time-series variable.

self-enforcing reliance relationship A non-contractual, mutually beneficial agreement.

separating equilibrium A decision setting that elicits distinguishable behavior.

sequential game A game with an explicit order of play.

shareholder wealth A measure of the value of a firm. Shareholder wealth is equal to the value of a firm's common stock, which, in turn, is equal to the present value of all future cash returns expected to be generated by the firm for the benefit of its owners.

short run The period of time in which one (or more) of the resources employed in a production process is fixed or incapable of being varied.

simultaneous game A strategy game in which players must choose their actions simultaneously.

slippery slope A tendency for wars of attrition to generate mutual losses that worsen over time.

social discount rate The discount rate to be used when evaluating benefits and costs from public sector investments.

speculation Buying cheap and selling later for a delayed profit (or loss).

spill Confirmed orders that cannot be filled.

spoilage Perishable output that goes unsold.

spot market transactions An instantaneous, one-time-only exchange of typically standardized goods between anonymous buyers and sellers.

standard deviation A statistical measure of the dispersion or variability of possible outcomes.

standard error of the estimate The standard deviation of the error term in a regression model.

sterilized interventions Central bank transactions in the foreign exchange market accompanied by equal offsetting transactions in the government bond market, in an attempt to alter short-term interest rates without affecting the exchange rate.

stockouts Demand in excess of available capacity.

strategic holdout A negotiator who makes unreasonable demands at the end of a unanimous consent process.

strategy game A decision-making situation with consciously interdependent behavior between two or more of the participants.

stratified lottery A randomized mechanism for allocating scarce capacity across demand segments.

subgame perfect equilibrium strategy An equilibrium concept for non-cooperative sequential games.

substitute goods Alternative products whose demand increases when the price of the focal product rises.

sunk cost A cost incurred regardless of the alternative action chosen in a decision-making problem.

supply curve A relationship between price and quantity supplied per unit time, holding other determinants of supply constant.

supply function A relationship between quantity supplied and all the determinants of supply.

survivor technique A method of estimating cost functions from the shares of industry output coming from each size class over time. Size classes whose shares of industry output are increasing (decreasing) over time are presumed to be relatively efficient (inefficient) and have lower (higher) average costs.

sustainable competitive advantages Difficult-to-imitate features of a company's processes or products.

target return-on-investment pricing A method of pricing in which a target profit, defined as the desired profit rate on investment × total gross operating assets, is allocated to each unit of output to arrive at a selling price.

technical efficiency A measure of how closely production achieves maximum potential output given the input mix or process.

threshold sales curve A level of advance sales that triggers reallocation of capacity.

time-series data A series of observations taken on an economic variable at various points in time.

transaction risk exposure A change in cash flows resulting from contractual commitments to pay in or receive foreign currency.

translation risk exposure An accounting adjustment in the home currency value of foreign assets or liabilities.

trembling hand trigger strategy A punishment mechanism that forgives random mistakes and miscommunications.

two-person zero-sum game Game in which net gains for one player necessarily imply equal net losses for the other player.

unraveling problem A failure of cooperation in games of finite length.

value at risk The notional value of a transaction exposed to appreciation or depreciation because of exchange rate risk.

value proposition A statement of the specific source(s) of perceived value, the value driver(s), for customers in a target market.

value-in-use The difference between the value customers place on functions, cost savings, and relationships attributable to a product or service and the life cycle costs of acquiring, maintaining, and disposing of the product or service.

variable input costs The costs of the variable inputs to the production process.

versioning A new product rollout strategy to encourage early adoption at higher prices.

vertical requirements contract A third-party enforceable agreement between stages of production in a product's value chain.

Vickrey auction An incentive-compatible revelation mechanism for eliciting sealed bids equal to private value.

volume discount Reduced variable cost attributable to larger purchase orders.

winner's curse Concern about overpaying as the highest bidder in an auction.

Index

A

ABC Network, 588
Abegglen, James, 297
Absolute cost advantage, 211
Absolute purchasing power parity, 198
Accord (automobile), 4–5, 6
Accounting costs, 281–286
  three contrasts between economic and, 282–286
  vs. economic costs, 281–286
Acquisition cost, 284
Adobe Systems, 562–563
Advanced Micro Devices (AMD), 382, 459, 593, 616
Adverse selection
  and asset specificity, 374–376
  brand-name reputations as hostages, 372–374
  and hostage or bonding mechanisms, 371–372
  and notorious firm, 368–370
  price premiums with non-redeployable assets, 374–376
  and reliance relationships, 371–372
  solutions to, 371–376
Advertising
  agencies, 365, 563
  defined, 364
  elasticity, 89–90
  intensity, 365–366
  net value, 366–367
Aerotek, 432–434
A-frame, 258
Agency conflict, 11–12
Agency costs, 15
Agency problems, 13–15
Airbus, 190, 192, 214, 216, 217, 309, 317–318, 413
Aircraft industry
  break-even analysis in, 323
  marginal costs, 309
  market share, 415

Aircraft production, 241
Airlines
  barometric price leadership, 431
  contestable markets, 615
  economies of scope in, 314
  entry deterrence, 444–445
  low-cost discounters, 444–445
  market share, 415, 539
  price signaling, 464
  pricing, 417
Allocative efficiency, 257
Allstate Insurance, 338
Alpha chip technology, 642
Altria, 436
Aluminum space-frame vehicles, 298
Amazon.com, 361, 530
AMD, 459–460
American Airlines, 28–29, 337, 431, 461, 544–545
American International Group (AIG), 627
Amgen, Inc., 16
Amoco, 225
Analog Inc., 600
Analysis of variance, 114–116, 119
Andean Group, 209
Antidumping sanctions, 213
Antitrust laws
  Clayton Act, 615–616
  Hart-Scott-Rodino Antitrust Improvement Act, 617
  Robinson-Patman Act, 616–617
  Sherman Act, 615
Antitrust prohibition
  mergers, 620–621
  monopolization, 621–622
  price fixing, 618–619
  refusals to deal, 624
  resale price maintenance agreements, 624–625
  wholesale price discrimination, 623–624

Antitrust regulations, cross price elasticities and, 90
Apple Computer, 11, 187, 199, 217, 226, 332–333, 386–387, 471, 530, 601–602, 605, 640, 642
Apple iTunes, 81
Apple stores, 11
Appraisals, 599
ARAMCO, 423
Arbitrage, 193, 202–204
Archer Daniels Midland (ADM), 419
Argentina, 209
Asian-Pacific Economic Cooperation (APEC), 210
Asking price, 30, 32–33
Assets
  dissolution of, 577–579
  specificity, 376
AstraZeneca, 343, 639
Asymmetric information, 18, 367–371, 587–589
ATC. *See* Average total cost (ATC)
Atlantic Cement Co., Inc., 632
Auctions
  asymmetric information bidding games, 587–589
  common-value, 589–590
  Dutch, 586, 596–597
  English, 586, 596–597
  first-price sealed-bid, 596–597
  incentive-compatible revelation mechanism, 594–596
  information revelation in, 589–590
  online, 585, 598–600
  open bidding design, 590–591
  optimal mechanism design, 583
  private-value, 592–594
  queue service rules, 583
  revenue equivalence of alternative types, 596–598
  second-highest sealed-bid, 594–596

Auctions (*continued*)
  types of, 586–587
  underbidding in, 592–594
  Vickrey, 594–596
  winner's curse, 587–589
Authorization level, 542
Autocorrelation, 127–129
  defined, 127
  negative, 127, 128
  positive, 127–128
Auto inspections, 632
Automobile
  assembly plants, 245–246, 258, 666–667
  dealerships, 72–73, 88, 373
  estimated demand for new, 118–119
  excess production capacity, 490–491
  rental, 69–70, 415–416, 517
Aventis, 638–639
Average cost functions, 286–290, 312.
    See also Cost functions average
  long-run and short-run, 290
Average fixed cost (AFC), 286, 289
Average product, 240, 244–246
Average profit, 44–48
  functions, 47–48
  marginal profit and, 44
  total profit and, 44
Average total cost (ATC), 286–290, 317
Avis, 415

B

Backward induction reasoning, 458
Backwards induction, 457, 468
Balance of payments, 191, 225–226
Baltimore Orioles, 545
Bananas, 214
Bank mergers, 259
Bank of Japan, 192–193
Banks, technical/allocative efficiency, 259
Bargaining, impediments to, 631
Barometric indicators. *See* Economic
    indicators
Barometric price leadership, 430–431
Barometric techniques, 156–157
  coincident indicators, 156–157
  lagging indicators, 156–157
  leading indicators, 156–157
Barriers to entry, 341–344, 614
Barriers to exit, 347
Baseball, 430, 545
Bayesian reputation effects, 460
Beautiful Mind, A (Nasar), 449
Beecham v. Europharm, 224
Beer industry, 412, 435
Beetle (automobile), 82–84
  inelastic demand, price increment and, 84
Bell Sports, 494–495
Benchmarking, 561–562
Benefit-cost ratio, 661
Bentley Clothing Store, 283
  economic profit statement of, 283

opportunity costs at, 283–284
  profitability of, 283
Berkshire Hathaway, Inc., 10, 480
Bernanke, Ben, 557
Bertelsmann Inc., 618
Best Buy, 474–475
Best-reply response, 453–454
Big Mac index, 204
Biotech stocks, 58
Birkenstocks, 198
Block booking, 375
Blockbuster, Inc., 362–363
Blue Chip Economic Indicators, 162
Bluefin tuna stocks, 271
Blu-ray digital video, 242
Boeing, 179, 180, 184, 190, 195, 214, 216,
    217, 241, 309, 317–318, 413
Bolivia, 209
Bonds, 53, 58
  corporate, 58
Boomer v. Atlantic Cement Co., Inc., 632
Boston Scientific, 503
Branch Banking and Trust (BB&T), 259
Brand loyalty, 438–439, 492
Brand names, 372–374
Brazil, 176–177, 184, 209–210, 212–214,
    222, 224
Break-even analysis
  algebraic method, 319–320
  and composition of operating costs, 323
  contribution margin, 319
  defined, 317
  graphical method, 318
  and inconsistency of planning horizon, 321
  limitations of, 321
  linear chart, 319
  and multiple products, 321
  and risk assessment, 325
  and uncertainty, 321
  vs. contribution analysis, 323–325
Break-even point, 318
Break-even sales change analysis, 346
Bristol-Myers-Squibb, 398, 526
British Petroleum, 225
  Amoco, 197
British Telephone, 527
Brooke Group Ltd. *vs.* Brown and
    Williamson Tobacco Company, 461
Brown and Williamson Tobacco Company,
    461
BTO. *See* Build to order (BTO)
Budget constraint, 69–70
Buffett, Warren E., 10
Build to order (BTO), 306
Bundling, 519–522
Bureau of Alcohol, Tobacco, and Firearms
    (BATF), 626
Bureau of Economic Analysis (Department
    of Commerce), 158, 166
Burlington industries, 476
Business cycles, 156–157

Business risk, 325
Business-to-business (B2B) transactions, 530
Business trip, consumption choices on,
    69–70
Buyers, power of, 344–345

C

Cable television industry, 313, 341, 570
Cadbury Schweppes, 349
Caduet (drug), 527
California, deregulation of electricity in,
    234–236
California Public Utility Commission, 236
Call centers, 221
Camry (automobile), 4–5, 6
Canon, 637
Capacity expansion, 4–5
Capacity reallocation, 540–542
Cap and trade, 611–612, 635
Capital assets, 282
Capital budgeting
  basic framework, 650
  defined, 649
  estimating cash flows, 651–653
  evaluating and choosing investment
    projects, 653–656
  generating capital investment projects,
    651
  marginal analysis and, 44–45
  process, 650–656
Capital elasticity, 262
Capital expenditure, 649
Capital funds, 296
Capital investment, 294
  projects, 653
Capoten (drug), 398, 526
Carburetors, 211–212
Carnival Cruise, 452
Cartels
  allocation of restricted output, 421–426
  analysis, 428–429
  collusive agreements, 418
  defined, 418
  OPEC, 423
  price-output determination, 421–422
  profit maximization, 421–426
Cash flow estimation, 652–653
"Cash for Clunkers" program, 87
Celera Genomics, 639
Cellophane, 90
Cell phones, 464
Cereal industry, 366, 415
Ceteris paribus, 393
Chain store paradox, 457–459
Chanel No. 5, 394
Chase Econometric Associates, 162
ChemChina, 180, 189
Chevron Corp, 305
Chevy Volt (automobile), 45–46, 71
  vs. Mini Cooper (automobile), marginal
    analysis, 45–46

Chicago Board of Trade, 611, 627
Chicago Pacific Corporation, 606
Chief executive officers (CEOs),
    compensation of, 13–14
China
    exports, 176–179
    foreign investments in, 187
    gross domestic product, 186, 188,
        196, 200
    gross national product, 178
    growth rate, 194
    Hangzhou region, 189–190
    imports from United States, 176–179,
        186–187
    infrastructure investments, 190
    international trade, 207–208, 212,
        221–222
    property rights, 189
    Shanghai region, 184–185, 189–190
    trading partners, 186–187, 221–222
China International Trust and Investment
    Corp., 187
China Mobile, 189
Chinese yuan, 192, 199
Chromatic Research Inc., 593
Chrysler Corp., 71, 651
Cifunsa SA, 221
Cigarette taxes, 64–66
Circuit City, 497
Cisco, 478, 562–563
Claritin (drug), 399
Clarke-Groves incentive-compatible
    revelation mechanism, 603
Class action suits, 617, 631
Clayton Act, 615–616
Clean Air Act of 1990 (CAA), 2, 611, 635
Closed-end leases with fixed residual values,
    481
Coase, Ronald, 611, 629
Coase theorem, 611–612, 630–631
Coasian bargaining, 629–630
Cobb-Douglas production function, 237,
    260–261
    empirical studies in manufacturing, 261
    returns to scale and, 260–261
Coca-Cola, 179, 217–218, 230, 344, 346, 436,
    453–456
Coefficient of determination, 114
Coefficient of variation, 56–57
Coffee
    price elasticity for, 84
    pricing agreement, 422–423
Coincident indicators, 156–157
Cointegrated stochastic series, 165
Colgate-Palmolive, 186
Collusion
    cost structures, 420
    number and size distribution of sellers,
        420
    percentage of external output, 421
    product heterogeneity, 420

size and frequency of orders, 420
    threat of retaliation, 421
Colombia, 209
Color television, 140
Comcast, 588
Common-value auctions, 589–590
Compact fluorescent light (CFL) bulbs,
    49–50
    energy savings and, 49–50
    lifetime cost savings, 51
    and net present value, 50
Company audit, 562
Compaq Computer, 335
Comparative advantage, 210–212
Competitive markets
    adverse selection, 368–370
    incomplete vs. asymmetric information,
        367
    lemons markets, 367, 370–371
    notorious firm, 368–370
    search goods vs. experience goods, 368
Competitive strategy, 334–336
Complementary goods, 34–35, 90, 112
Complementors, 341
Computer memory chips, 211
Computer price index, 360
ComputerTree, 11
Concentrated market, 339
Conference Board, 157
Congestion pricing, 514
Consensus forecasts, 162–163
Consolidated market, 339
Conspicuous focal point, 462
Constant-cost industry, 359
Constant rate of growth trends, 147–148
Consumer behavior
    and product positioning, 72
    and purchasing power effect, 68
    and substitution effect, 68–71
    surveys, 159
    targeting, 71
Consumer expenditure plans, 159
Consumer Product Safety Commission
    (CPSC), 626
Containers (shipping), 584
Contestable markets, 351, 494–495, 614–615
Continental Airlines, 528
Continental T.V., Inc., et al. v. GTE Sylvania
    Inc., 569
Contingent payments, 599–600
Contracts
    in cooperative games, 549–552
    defined, 551
    expectation damages, 552
    forward sales contracts, 554
    frustration of purpose doctrine, 553
    full contingent claims, 555
    functions of commercial, 552–555
    governance mechanisms, 555–559
    incentive-compatible, 605–607
    incentives, 564–567

incomplete information, 555
    linear incentives, 565–566
    moral hazard problem, 556–557
    optimal incentives, 603–605
    post-contractual opportunistic behavior,
        555
    promises excusals, 553
    spot market transactions, 554, 555
    vertical requirements, 551–552
Contribution analysis
    and composition of operating costs, 323
    defined, 322
    and inconsistency of planning horizon,
        321
    limitations of, 323–324
    and multiple products, 321
    and uncertainty, 321
    vs. break-even analysis, 321–322
Contribution margins, 319, 347, 364–365,
    393
Cooperative game, 450, 549–552
Coors, 440
Copper prices, 359
Copyright, 383–384
Cordis, 503
Corporate bonds, 58
Corporate governance, 555–559
    implementation mechanisms, 559
    need for, 558
Corporate restructuring, 12–13
Correlated macroeconomic shocks, 219–220
Correlation analysis, 100
Correlation coefficient, 113
    negative, 113
    positive, 113
    value of, 113
    zero, 113
Cost analysis
    depreciation cost measurement,
        282–284
    inventory valuation, 284–285
    overview, 280
    sunk cost of underutilized facilities, 285
Cost-based strategy, 337
Cost-benefit analysis
    accept-reject decisions, 661–662
    constraints, 664
    defined, 20, 660
    of direct benefits, 665
    of direct costs, 665
    of indirect costs or benefits and
        intangibles, 665–666
    objectives, 664
    program-level analysis, 662
    schematic of, 663
    steps in, 662–663
Cost-effectiveness analysis, 5
    defined, 667
    least-cost studies, 667–668
    objective-level studies, 668
Cost fixity, 345

Cost functions
  average, 286–290
  defined, 286
  long-run, 291–292
  marginal, 286–290
  short-run, 286–290
Cost functions average. *See also* Average
    cost functions
  defined, 307
  estimating, 306–317
  long-run, 311
  short-run, 310–311
Cost inflation, 197–198, 204
Cost leadership strategy, 337
Cost of capital
  debt capital, 657
  defined, 653
  external equity capital, 659
  internal equity capital, 657–658
  weighted, 659–660
Cost-output relationship
  controlling variables in, 307–308
  empirical, 308–310
  polynomial, 309
Cost overruns, 601–602
Costs. *See also* Pricing
  accounting, 281–286
  acquisition, 284
  behavior of, 286
  depreciation, 282–283
  direct, 307, 665
  economic, 8, 281–286
  explicit, 282
  fixed, 286
  indirect, 665–666
  indirect fixed, 307
  marginal, 288
  meaning, 281–286
  measurement of, 281–286, 307
  minimizing subject to output constraint,
    254–255
  opportunity, 8, 282
  output maximization subject to a cost
    constraint, 256
  overhead, 295
  overruns, 601–602
  primary, 665
  replacement, 284
  revelation, 600–601
  sunk, 285
  switching, 71
  transportation, 296
  variable, 286
  variable input, 286
Couponing, 518–519
Cournot oligopoly model, 416–418
Creative ingenuity, defined, 562
Credible commitments, 473, 476
Credible threats, 472
Credit rationing, 371
Crocs shoes, 142

Cross-functional revenue management,
    536–537
Cross price elasticity of demand
  and antitrust, 90
  combined use with demand elasticities,
    92–93
  defined, 90
  electricity use, 92
  negative, 90
  positive, 90
Cross-sectional data, 143, 261
Crude oil
  cartel, 423
  developing countries demand and, 39, 40
  input costs, 356–357
  price-output determination, 424–425
  prices, 39–43, 274–277, 356–357
  proven reserves, 427
  refineries, 249–250
  Saudi Arabian production, 41, 42,
    425–426
  Smartcar-Mini sales and, 41, 42
  speculation, 42–43
  supply market, disruptions in, 39, 40
  U.S. demand for, 41
  and U.S. trade deficit, 226
  years of proven reserves, 278
Cummins Engine Co., 36–37, 182–184,
    190–191, 195, 197, 202, 226
Current status loans, 259
Customer loyalty programs, 71
Customer segmentation, 436
Customer sorting rules
  brand loyalty, 492
  in contestable markets, 494–495
  efficient rationing, 492
  inverse intensity rationing, 493
  random rationing, 493
  sunk costs in decision making, 493–494
  wars of attrition, 495–497
CVS, 573–574
Cyclical variations, 143, 144
CYPHER stent, 503

D

Daimler-Benz, 36
Data processing jobs, 221
De Beers Consolidated Mines Ltd., 384
De Beers diamond, 375
Debt capital, cost of, 657
Debt securities, 58
Decision-making
  management responsibilities in, 5–6
  model, 5
  moral hazard in teams, 6–8
Decision tree, 466
Declining rate of growth trends, 148
Deferred stock, 12, 15
Degree of operating leverage (DOL), 323, 324
Dell Computer, 11, 332, 335, 337, 385,
    562–563, 577

Delta Airlines, 337
Demand. *See also* Supply
  combined effect of elasticities, 92
  constant elasticity, 134
  cross elasticity of, 90–92
  elastic, 73, 78
  and equilibrium market price, 29–31
  and exchange rate, 36–37
  factors and expected effect, 35
  income elasticity of, 87–90
  inelastic, 73, 78
  law of, 66
  for NFL games, 76
  price elasticity of, 64, 72–87
  and purchasing power effect, 68
  schedule, 32
  shift of, 35, 66
  speculative, 40
  and substitution effect, 68–71
  and supply, 29–31
  unit elastic, 78–79
Demand curves. *See also* Supply curves
  defined, 32
  for gasoline, 66–67
  movement along, 34, 36, 66
  in oligopoly, 434–435
  perfectly elastic, 78
  perfectly inelastic, 78
  shift in the, 34–36
Demand function
  defined, 34
  inverse, 102
  linear function, 101–102
  multiplicative exponential model,
    102–103
  statistical estimation of, 100–103
Demand schedule. *See* Demand curves
Dense wave divisional multiplexing
    (DWDM), 139
Depreciation, 307
  cost measurement, 282–284, 307
Deregulation, 611–612, 627–628
Designer jeans, 112
Deterministic trend analysis
  components of time series, 143–144
  cross-sectional data, 143
  seasonal variations, 148–150
  secular trends, 145–148
  time-series data, 143
  time-series models, 144–150
Diamonds, 375, 384
  cubic zirconium, 30
  investment in, 58
  natural, 30
Diamond-water paradox, 31–32
Diesel engines, exchange rates and, 36–37
Digital camera market, 438
Digital Equipment Corp, 642
Digital moviehouse projectors, 479–480
Digital signal processor (DSP) chips, 600
Digital TV, 548–549

Direct cost of goods sold (DCGS), 395
Direct costs, 307, 665
Direct mail coupon, targeting customers, 88
Direct segmentation, 514–515
DIRECTV, 622
Discount coupons, 69–70
Discount rate, 661, 666–667
Diseconomies of scale
    defined, 296
    effects of, 296–299
    external, 357
DISH Network, 622
Dish soap, 206–207
Disney World, 242, 383, 518
Dividend valuation model, 657–658
Doha Round, 86
DOL. *See* Degree of operating leverage
    (DOL)
Dominant firm price leadership, 431–432
Dominant strategy, 447, 452–455
Dooney & Burke, 372
Double log transformation, 134
Double-the-difference price guarantees,
    474–475
Drugs, patented, 638
Drug stores, 573
Duke Power, 3, 18
Dulles Toll Road, 513
Dummy variables, 149–150, 150–151
Dunbar Manufacturing Company, 285–286
Duopoly, 413
DuPont, 90, 184, 195, 196
Durable goods, 70–71
Durbin-Watson statistic, 128
Dutch auctions, 586, 596–597
Dynamic pricing, 516, 531
Dynamic random access memory (DRAM)
    chips, 216, 420

E
eBay, 597–598
EchoStar, 622
Econometric models
    advantages of, 159
    defined, 159
    multi-equation models, 161–162
    single-equation models, 159–161
    of U.S. economy, 161–162
Econometrics, 100
Economic costs, 8, 281–286
    accounting *vs.*, 281–286
    three contrasts between accounting and,
        282–286
Economic indicators, 156–157
    coincident, 156–157
    lagging, 156–157
    leading, 156–157
Economic profit, 8, 282
Economies of scale
    in cable industry, 313
    firm-level internal, 295–296

internal, 292
and international joint ventures, 571
learning curve effect, 292
mass customization, 293
and monopolies, 384
overall effects of, 296–299
percentage of learning, 293–294
plant-level internal, 294–295
product-level internal, 292–293
volume discounts, 292
vs. economies of scope, 314
Economies of scope
    in banking industry, 315
    controlling variables, 308
    defined, 314
    vs. economies of scale, 314
Ecuador, 209
Edison, Thomas, 49
Effective exchange rate (EER), 204–205
Efficient rationing, 492
Elastic demand, 73, 78
Electrical industry, 464–465
Electric utilities
    average cost function, 312
    deregulation, 234–236
    dynamic pricing, 516
    electricity-use elasticities, 92
    green power technologies, 234–236
    long-run cost functions, 312
    regulation of, 396
    short-run cost functions, 310–311
    sustainability, 2–4
    underutilized, 292
Electronic commerce, 338–339
Eli Lilly, 15, 225, 343, 399, 526, 638
Embedded options, 16
Embedded real options, 16, 17
Emerging market stocks, 58
Emerson Corporation, 294
EMI Group, 618
Emissions trading, 612
Employment Standards Administration, 626
Encyclopedia Britannica, 295
Endgame reasoning, 457
Engineering cost techniques, 314–315
English auctions, 586, 596–597
Enron, 559
Enterprise Rent-A-Car, 415
Entry deterrence
    customer sorting rules, 492–497
    excess capacity as credible threat, 489
    and incumbent price commitment, 471
    insights about slippery slopes, 497–498
    pre-commitment using non-redeployable
        assets, 489–492
Environmental Protection Agency (EPA), 2,
    18, 626
Epogen (drug), 16
Equal Employment Opportunity Commis-
    sion (EEOC), 626
Equal marginal revenue, 507–508

Equilibrium market price, 29–31
    of gasoline, 38–43
    and incremental costs, 32–33
    marginal utility, 32–33
Equimarginal criterion, 255
ESPN, 588
Euro, 181, 182–184, 190–192, 194, 196–197,
    218
European Commission (EC), 223
European Union (EU), 50, 176, 178, 204,
    208, 217–220
    vs. NAFTA, 222–223
Evista (drug), 343
Excess capacity, 489
Exchange rates
    and demand, 36–37
    effective, 204–205
    and import-export sales, 180–184
    operating risk exposure, 182
    transaction risk exposure, 180–181
    translation risk exposure, 181–182
Excise taxes, on cigarettes, 65–66
Executive compensation, 13–14
Executive performance pay, 14
Exhaustible natural resources, 274–279
Exide Batteries, 224
Expectation damages, 552
    liability for, 553
Expected value, 53
Experience goods, 368, 369, 370
Exponential smoothing, 153–155
    first-order, 153–154
    Walker Corporation example of, 153, 155
Exponential Valley Inc., 593
Exports, 176–179, 208–210, 222
External diseconomy of scale, 357
External equity capital, 659
Externalities
    Coase theorem, 630–631
    Coasian bargaining, 629–630
    defined, 628
    impediments to bargaining, 631
    pecuniary, 628
    reciprocal, 629–630
    resolution by regulatory directive,
        632–633
    resolution by sale of pollution rights, 635
    resolution by taxes and subsidies,
        633–635
Exxon Mobil, 12, 41, 42, 415

F
Farmlands, 58
Fast-second advantage, 470–471
FDA. *See* Food and Drug Administration
    (FDA)
Federal Aviation Administration (FAA), 626
Federal Communications Commission
    (FCC), 140, 589, 591, 626
Federal Energy Regulatory Commission
    (FERC), 626

Federal Reserve Bank of Philadelphia, 162
Federal Reserve System, 557, 626
Federal Trade Commission (FTC), 91
FEMSA, 616
Ferrero Rocher, 99
Fiber optic networks, 139–141
Firm-level internal economies of scale,
  295–296
First-come, first-served rule, 584
First-mover advantage, 470–471
First-order exponential smoothing, 153–155
Five Forces strategic model
  intensity of rivalrous tactics, 345–349
  myth of market share, 349
  power of buyers and suppliers, 344–345
  threat of entry, 341–344
  threat of substitutes, 340–341
Fixed costs, 286, 314, 320–321
Fixed input, 237–238
FlexJets, 480
Focal outcomes of interest, 470
Folk theorem, 456–457
Food and Drug Administration (FDA),
  343, 626
Food Lion, 18
Food Safety and Inspection Service, 626
Ford Explorer (sport utility vehicle), 66–67
  gasoline prices and, 67
Ford Motor Co., 38, 72–73, 83, 187, 224,
  242, 280–281, 296, 298, 365
  dealership, 88
  labor costs and, 38
Forecasting
  alternative techniques, 143
  econometric models, 159–163
  with input-output tables, 166
  sales, 159
  selecting a technique, 141–142
  significance of, 141
Forecasting techniques
  accuracy of models, 142
  alternative, 143
  barometric indicators, 156–157
  deterministic trend analysis, 143–150
  econometric models, 159–163
  forecasting with input-output tables, 166
  input-output analysis, 166
  macroeconometric models, 159–163
  selecting, 141–142
  smoothing techniques, 150–155
  stochastic time-series analysis, 163–165
  survey and opinion-polling techniques,
    157–159
Forecasts, hierarchy of, 141–142
Foreign exchange
  arbitrage, 193
  coordinated intervention, 192–193
  and government transfers, 192–193
  and import-export sales, 180–184
  and inflation, 197–198
  and interest rates, 196–197

long-term exchange rate trends, 196
managed float, 190, 199
market for U.S. dollars as, 190–193
operating risk exposure, 182, 193
and real growth rates, 194–196
risk, 180–182
short-term exchange rate fluctuations, 193
speculation in, 193
and speculative demand, 192–193
sterilized interventions, 192
and transaction demand for currency,
  190–191
transaction risk exposure, 180
translation risk exposure, 181–182
Foreign exchange risk exposures, 180–184
  operating, 182, 183–184, 194
  transaction, 180, 230
  translation, 181–182, 230
Formation excuse, 553
Fortune magazine, 158
Forward market, 17
Forward sales contracts, 554
Fountain drink, 346
Fragmented market, 339
Framing effects, 437
France, 177, 184, 193, 206, 208, 217–218,
  219, 221, 222–223
Franchise, government-authorized, 384
Free trade, 210–212
  and price elasticity of demand, 86
Free trade areas
  correlated macroeconomic shocks in,
    219–220
  defined, 218
  European Union, 217–220
  intraregional trade, 219
  mobility of labor, 219
  North American Free Trade Agreement,
    217–225
  optimal currency areas, 218–219
  value at risk, 219
Freightliner, 220
Frequent buyers, 71
Frustration of purpose doctrine, 553
Fuel surcharges, 28–29
Fuji, 339–340
Full contingent claims contract, 555
Full-cost pricing, 526–527
Full-line pricing, 572–574
Funds, historical outlay of, 282
Futures market, 17

G

Gain-share discounting, 345
Game(s)
  components of, 448–449
  cooperative, 450
  iterated dominant strategy, 449
  maximin strategy, 451
  noncooperative, 450
  normal form of, 448

repeated, 450
sequential, 452
simultaneous, 451–455
single-period, 450
strategy, 447
two-person, 450–451
Game theory
  analysis of, 447
  best-reply response, 453
  credible threats and commitments,
    472–473
  defined, 446
  dominant strategy, 447, 452–455
  managerial purpose of, 444–445
  mechanisms for establishing credibility,
    473–474
  mixed Nash equilibrium strategy, 455
  Nash equilibrium strategy, 453–454
  and oligopolistic rivalry, 446–451
  Prisoners' Dilemma, 451–453
Game tree, 466
Gasoline
  and crude oil input costs, 356–357
  demand schedule, 66–67
  equilibrium market price of, 38–43
  price components, 426–428
  price elasticity of demand for, 73–75
  resource scarcity and, 39
  taxes, 39
  U.S. household demand for, 66, 67
Gasoline prices, 356–357
  Ford Explorer (sport utility vehicle)
    and, 67
  and retail gas stations, 39
  in the U.S. (2005-2011), 38–39
Gas stations, 356
Gateway Inc., 337
Genentech, 388
General Agreement on Tariffs and Trade
  (GATT), 86
General Electric (GE), 14, 49, 297, 464, 637
General Mills, 366, 436–437
General Motors (GM), 5, 6, 83, 179, 180,
  203, 220, 258, 320–321, 478
  cost structure, 280–281
Generic drugs, 398–399
Gillette Co., 179, 439
GlaxoSmithKline, 15
Global Crossing Inc., 103, 139–141
Goldman Sachs, 280
Goods
  complementary, 34–35, 90, 112
  durable, 70–71
  experience, 368
  import-export traded, 36
  inferior, 88
  search, 368
  substitute, 34, 86, 112
Governance mechanisms, 555–559
  implementation of, 559
  need for, 558

Governmental protection of business, 635–636
Government-authorized franchise, 384
Grand Cherokee (sport utility vehicle), 651
Gray markets, 223, 225
Great Recession (2007), 557
Greenhouse gases, 673–675
Green power technologies, 234–236
Grim trigger strategy, 456
Gross domestic product (GDP), 141, 163–164, 168–169, 174, 176–179, 200, 208, 209, 225
Gross profit margin, components of, 395–396
Guttenberg, Johannes, 30
Guttenberg Bible, 30

H

Hadley v. Baxendale, 552
Hamilton Beach/Proctor-Silex, Inc., 652, 653, 654
Handbag market, 372
Hanes Corp., 347
Hangzhou, China, 189–190
Hard disk drive (HDD) assembly, 570–571
Hardwoods, 31
Harsanyi, John, 449
Hart-Scott-Rodino Antitrust Improvement Act, 617
HCFC. *See* Hydrochlorofluorocarbon (HCFC)
Health care reform, 64–66
Health maintenance organizations (HMOs), 344
Hedges
   balance sheet, 181, 230–231
   covered, 230–231
   financial, 180, 230–231
   internal, 214, 230–231
   operating, 230
Heinz Ketchup, 217–218
Herfindahl-Hirschman Index (HHI), 620
Hershey Foods, 654–655
Hertz, 415
Heteroscedasticity, 129
Hewitt Associate LLC, 185
Hewlett-Packard, 184, 188, 297, 385, 387, 636, 642
High-definition DVD, 242
Highway Safety Act of 1996, 83
Hitachi Ltd., 297, 637
HMOs. *See* Health maintenance organizations (HMOs)
Home prices, 359
Honda Motors, 4–5, 203, 212, 222, 231
Hon Industries, 349
Hostage mechanism, 371–372, 475, 476–477
Hughes-JVC, 479–480
Human Genome Sciences, 639
Hydrochlorofluorocarbon (HCFC), 673

Hynix, 420, 570
Hyundai, 490–491

I

IBM Corp., 180, 184, 186, 195, 295, 332, 335, 337, 387, 388, 471, 472, 476, 479, 604, 637
Immelt, Jeff, 14
Import controls, 212–214, 217
Import-export
   sales, 180–184
   traded goods, 36
Incentive compatibility constraint, 564
Incentive-compatible revelation mechanism
   Clarke-Groves, 603
   cost revelation, 600–601
   defined, 594, 603
Income elasticity of demand
   defined, 87
   electricity use, 92
   empirical estimates, 89
   interpreting, 88–89
   Seiko watches and, 93
   use with demand elasticities, 92–93
Income-superior products, 87, 88
Incomplete information, 367, 555
Increasing-cost industry, 359
Increasing returns, 216
   and information services, 243–244
   at Microsoft Windows, 242
   with network effects, 241–243, 384–388
   at Sony Blu-ray, 242
   and total product function, 244–246
Incremental contribution analysis, 526–528
Independent software vendors (ISVs), 387, 388
Index of Leading Economic Indicators, 158
Indirect benefits, 665–666
Indirect costs, 665–666
Indirect fixed costs, 307
Indirect segmentation, 515
Individual demand, 32–33
Industry analysis, 336
Industry standards, 464–465
Inelastic demand, 73, 78
Infant industries, 213
Inferior goods, 88
Infineon Technologies, 420
Infinitely repeated games, 457
Inflation, 197–198
Inflection point, 48, 242
Information services, 243–244
Information technology, 305–306
   strategy, 338
Ingram Book Group, 361
Inherent business risk, 325
Innovations, 438–439
Innovation theory of profit, 9
Input-output analysis, 166
Inputs
   defined, 236
   fixed, 237–238

optimal combination of, 252–255
   variable, 237–238
Insurance policies, 371
Intangibles, 665–666
Intel Corp., 186, 216, 295, 382–383, 459–460, 593, 600, 637
Intensity of rivalry, 345–349
Interest rates, 158, 163, 165, 196–197
Interlink Surgical Steel, 439
Internal economies of scale, 292
Internal equity capital, cost of, 657–658
Internal hedge, 214, 230–231
Internal rate of return (IRR)
   defined, 653–654
   vs. net present value, 654
International Monetary Fund (IMF), 177, 199
International trade
   absolute cost advantage, 211
   comparative advantage, 210–212
   free trade, 210–212
   free trade areas, 217–220
   gray markets, 223, 225
   import controls, 212–214, 217
   increasing returns, 216
   internal hedge, 214, 230–231
   knockoffs, 223–225
   network externalities, 216–217
   parallel importing, 223–225
   real terms of trade, 211
   regional trading blocs, 207–210
   shares of, 207–210
   tariffs, 209–210, 212–214, 217
   trade deficit, 225–226
Internet, 140, 528–531
Internet auctions, 585, 597–600
Internet Explorer, 242, 342, 388
Interstate Commerce Commission (ICC), 626
Intraregional trade, 219
Inventory, 151, 159
Inventory valuation, 284–285
Inverse demand function, 102
Inverse intensity rationing, 493
Investigational new drugs (INDs), 15
Investment
   net cash flow, 52
   net present value of, 48–49
Investment analysis
   capital budgeting, 650–656
   capital expenditure, 649
   cost-benefit analysis, 660–662
   cost-effectiveness analysis, 667–668
   cost of capital, 656–660
   discount rate, 666–667
   Investment opportunity curve, 650
Investment opportunity curve, 650
IRR. *See* Internal rate of return (IRR)
Isocost lines, 253–254
Iterated dominant strategy, 449
iTunes, 618

J

Japan
    bilateral trade with United States, 211
    gross domestic product, 199–200
Japanese corporations, 297
J.D. Powers, 6
JetBlue, 444, 445, 493
Jet fuel surcharges, 28–29
Jiangsu Changzhou Pharmaceutical, 225
Jobs, Steve, 11, 333
Joint ventures, 571, 600–601, 604
Jojoba beans, production cost, 31
J.P. Morgan, 527

K

Kahnemen, Daniel, 572
Kaldor-Hicks criterion, 664
Keebler's, 413
Kellogg's, 179, 366, 396, 436–437
Knockoffs, 223–225
Knowledge capital, 637
Kodak, 12, 339–340, 438, 461
Kohlberg Kravis Roberts & Co. (KKR), 12
Krispy Kreme, 16

L

Labor
    costs, 38
    mobility of, 219, 220
Labor market, perfectly competitive, 247
Lagging indicators, 156–157
La Quinta Motels, 236
Last-come, first-served rule, 584
Law of comparative advantage, 211
Law of demand, 66
Law of diminishing marginal returns,
    240–241
Leading indicators, 156–157
Learning curve effect, 292
Lease prices, 481
Least-cost studies, 667
Leegin Creative Leather Products, 626
Lee jeans, 112
Lemons markets, 367, 370–371
Leveraged buyouts (LBO), 12–13
Lewis, Michael, 262
Licensing, 635–636
Life cycle pricing, 524
Limit pricing, 397–398, 526
Lindor, 99
Linear incentives contract, 565–566
Linear model, 101–102
Linear regression model
    autocorrelation, 127–129
    heteroscedasticity, 129
    identification problem, 131–133
    multicollinearity, 131
    specification and measurement errors,
        130–131
Linear regression relation, 104

Linear trends, 146–147
Lipitor (drug), 399
Long run, 238, 357–360
Long-run average cost (LRAC), 362
Long-run cost functions
    in electricity generation, 312
    optimal capacity utilization, 291–292
    statistical estimation of, 311
Long-Term Capital Management (LTCM),
    56
    interest rate derivatives and, 56
    principal activity, 56
    return volatility, 56
Lotteries, 585
Lotus, 388
LRAC. *See* Long-run average cost (LRAC)
Lucent Technologies, 600, 639–641
Lufthansa Airfreight, 183

M

Macroeconomic forecasting, 158–159
Macroeconomic shocks, 219–220
Major league baseball, 262, 430
Managed float, 177, 190, 199
Management
    moral hazard problem and, 6–8
    responsibilities of, 5–6
Managerial contracting
    alternative hiring arrangements, 559–560
    moral hazard problem, 561–563
    optimal incentives contracts, 564–567
Managerial economics, 4
Managerial efficiency of profit, 9
Manufacturer's suggested retail price
    (MSRP), 624
Manufacturing industries
    Cobb-Douglas function, 261
    cross-sectional analysis of, 261–262
    production elasticities, 262
Maquiladora, 220
Marginal analysis
    and capital budgeting, 44–45
    defined, 43
    Mini Cooper *vs.* Chevy Volt, 45–46
    and resource allocation, 43
    Sara Lee Corp. and, 44–45
    Tenneco shipyard and, 43
Marginal cost functions, 286–290
Marginal costs, 288
    of advertising, 364
    of capital curve, 650
    defined, 32, 43
    and marginal benefits, 43–44
Marginal factor cost, 247
Marginal private cost (MPC), 633
Marginal product, 239, 244–246
Marginal profit, 44–48
    average profit and, 44
    contribution, 364–365
    functions, 47–48
    total profit and, 44

Marginal rate of technical substitution,
    250–252
Marginal return, 43
Marginal revenue, 353–354
    defined, 80
    price elasticity of demand and, 78, 80–82
    product, 247
Marginal use value, 32
Marginal utility, 32
Marginal value added, 247
Market
    barriers to entry, 614
    competitive, 367–371
    conduct, 613
    contestable, 361, 614–615
    performance, 613
    structure, 613–614
Market concentration ratio, 620
Marketing, 296
Markets, contestable, 494–495
Market share
    myth of, 349
    and oligopoly, 413–415
Market structure
    contestable markets, 361
    defined, 349
    monopolistic competition, 352
    monopoly, 351–352
    oligopoly, 352–353
    pure competition, 350–351
Market value, scarcity of resources and, 31
Marriott Corp., 438
Marshall, Alfred, 32
Mass customization, and learning
    curve, 293
Matsushita Electrical Industrial Company,
    242, 297, 637
Mavica (digital camera), 438
Maximin strategy, 451
Maximum sustainable yield (MSY), 272
Maytag, 606
McDonald's, 179, 195, 199, 204, 521–522
McGraw-Hill survey, 158–159
Measurement errors, 130–131
Medtronic, 503
Memory chips, 187, 211–212, 216, 604
Mercedes-Benz, 182–183, 190, 197
Merck, 15, 184, 224, 306
Merck vs. Primecrown, 224
MERCOSUR, 209, 210
Mergers, 620–621
    Herfindahl-Hirschman Index, 620–621
    market concentration ratio, 620
Mexico
    import-export trade, 220–221
    maquiladora, 220
    PPP-adjusted GDP in 2011, 200
    trade-weighted tariffs, 2011, 213
    as U.S. trading partner, 186, 220–221
Micron Technology, 637
Microprocessors, 382–383, 459–460

Microsoft Corp., 179, 180, 186, 195, 216–217, 220, 223, 241–242, 243, 342, 385, 386–387, 388, 471, 478, 548–549, 617, 623
  stock options at, 565
Miller Brewing Co., 616
Mine Safety and Health Administration, 626
Mini Cooper (automobile), 45–46, 478
  Chevy Volt (automobile), marginal analysis, 45–46
Mini-mills, 215
Minimum efficient scale (MES), 297
Mixed bundling, 520, 521
Mixed Nash equilibrium strategy, 455
Modelo, 616
Monday Night Football, 588
Moneyball (Lewis), 262–263
Monopolistic competition
  defined, 352
  long run, 357–361
  price-output determination under, 360–363
  short run, 361
Monopoly
  antitrust prohibition, 621–622
  capacity investments, 396
  characteristics of, 351–352
  contribution margin, 393
  control critical resources, 384
  and copyright, 383–384
  credible commitments, 477
  defined, 351, 383
  economies of scale, 384
  and government authorized franchise, 384
  gross profit margin, 395, 396
  increasing returns from network effects, 384–388
  limit pricing, 397–398
  natural, 401–402
  price and output determination in, 388–392
  regulated, 399–401
  sources of market power, 383–388
  value proposition, 394
Monopoly theory of profit, 9
Monster wafers, 295
Moral hazard problem, 556–557
  Enron and, 559
  managerial contracting and, 561–563
  WorldCom and, 559
Morgenstern, Oskar, 449
Moroney, John, 261
Motorola, 459–460, 601–602, 605, 639–641
Movie theatres, 479–480
Multicollinearity, 131
Multi-equation models, 161–162
  characteristics of, 162
  complex models of the U.S. economy, 161–162

Multiple linear regression model
  computer programs, 116
  defined, 116
  forecasting with, 116–117
  inferences about population regression coefficients, 117
  population regression coefficients, 116
Multiple-product pricing, 507–508
Multiple regression analysis, 308
Multiplicative exponential model, 102–103
Music CDs, 225
Music producers, 81

N

Nabisco, 413
Nader, Ralph, 83
Nash, John, 449, 468
Nash equilibrium strategy, 453–454
National Association of Purchasing Agents survey, 159
National Bureau of Economic Research, 156, 557
National Football League (NFL), 160
National Highway Traffic Safety Administration (NHTSA), 626
National Industrial Conference Board, 158
National Labor Relations Board (NLRB), 626
National Oceanic and Atmospheric Administration (NOAA), 273
Natural gas companies, 401
Natural monopolies, 401–402
Natureview Farms Yogurt, 394–395
NBC, 588
NCF. *See* Net cash flow (NCF)
Negative correlation, 127, 128
Negative economic profit, 284
Net cash flow (NCF), 52, 652
  from investments, 52
  probability distributions of, 52
Net income after tax (NIAT), 652
Net income before tax (NIBT), 652
NetJets, 480–481
Net present value (NPV)
  analysis, 16, 17
  barriers to entry and, 50–51
  compact fluorescent light (CFL) bulbs and, 50
  defined, 48, 654
  determining, 48–49
  need for developing, 16
  positive, sources of, 50–51
  and risk, 51
  vs. internal rate of return, 653–654
Netscape, 242, 385, 387, 623
Network effects, 241, 341, 384–388
Network externalities, 216–217
NIAT. *See* Net income after tax (NIAT)
NIBT. *See* Net income before tax (NIBT)
Niche pricing, 526–527

Nitrous oxide (NOX) emission, 2–3
Nokia, 409–410
Noncooperative game, 450
Noncredible commitments, 476
Nonlinear regression models
  double-log transformation, 134
  polynomial transformation, 135–136
  reciprocal transformation, 135
  semilogarithmic transformation, 134
Nonproduction worker elasticity, 262
Non-redeployable assets, 374–376, 489–492
Non-redeployable reputational asset, 473
Non-redeployable specific assets, 567
Non-zero-sum game, 451
Normal form of the game, 448
Normal probability distribution, 54–55
North American Free Trade Agreement (NAFTA), 38, 217–225
  and automobile asssembly, 38
  exports, 220–222
  labor cost and, 38
  members of, 210
  non tariff trade barriers, 220
  and price elasticity of demand, 86
  single currency in, 220
  vs. European Union, 222–223
Northwest Airlines, 463
Not-for-profit (NFP) organizations
  characteristics of, 19
  efficiency objective in, 20
  objectives, 20
  services, 20
Notorious firm, 368–370
NPV. *See* Net present value (NPV)
Nuclear Regulatory Commission (NRC), 626

O

Objective-level studies, 668
Objective product differentiation, 344
Objectives, establishing, 5
Occupational Safety and Health Administration (OSHA), 626
Offer price, 30, 32, 33
Office Depot, 91, 343
OfficeMax, 91, 343
Office of Comptroller of the Currency, 626
Office supply products, 91
Office supply retailers, 91, 343
Ole Musk, 394
Oligopoly
  cartels, 418–429
  collusion factors, 420–421
  Cournot model, 416–418
  defined, 352
  and extreme brand loyalty, 439
  and game theory, 446–451
  interdependencies in, 416–417
  kinked demand curve model, 434–435
  market shares, 413–415
  market structures in, 411–416

Oligopoly (*continued*)
  overview, 411
  price leadership, 430–434
  price wars, avoiding, 435–440
  relative market shares in, 411–416
  segmented, 439
  in the United States, 411–416
Olive Garden, 72
O.M. Scott & Sons, 12–13
Online auctions, 585, 598–600
Online sales, 530
OPEC, 277, 357
Opel, 203
Open bidding design, 590–591
Operating cost, composition of, 323, 324
Operating leverage, 324
Operating risk exposure, 182, 183–184, 194
Operating system, 332
Opinion-polling techniques, 157–159
  overview, 157
Opportunity cost, 8, 282, 652
Optimal capacity utilization
  optimal output for a given plant size, 291
  optimal plant size, 291
  optimal plant size for a given output
    rate, 291
Optimal differential pricing
  algebraic approach, 506–507
  demand estimation by market segment,
    504–505
  graphical approach, 505–506
  multiple-product pricing, 507–508
  and price elasticity of demand, 508–509
Optimal incentives contracts, 603–605
Optimal input level, 247–248
Optimal mechanism design, 583
Optimal overbooking, 543–546
Optimal plant size, 291
Optimal scale of operation, 311–314
Oracle Corp., 388
Ordinary least-squares (OLS), 147, 163
Organizational form, 567–574
Organization of Petroleum Exporting
  Countries (OPEC), 421, 423
Outputs, maximization of, 256
Outsourcing, 184–186
Overall production efficiency, 258
Overhead costs, 295
Oyster seedbed replenishment, 273–274
Oysters industry, 273
Ozone depletion, 673–675

P

Pacific Gas and Electric, 234
Palm, Inc., 387, 640
PalmPilot, 387
Pampers, 179, 218, 224
Panama Canal, 184–185
Paraguay, 209
Parallel imports, 223–225
Participation constraint, 564

Partnerships
  cost overruns, 601–602
  cost revelation in, 600–601
  dissolution of assets in, 577–579
Patents, 383–384, 398, 526, 636–641
  Prozac (drug), 15
PCM. *See* Price cost margin (PCM)
PCS PrimeCo., 589–591
Pecuniary benefits, 666
Pecuniary externalities, 628
Penetration pricing, 524
PeopleSoft, 388
Pepperidge Farms, 413
PepsiCo, 134, 345–346, 453–456
Perceived product differentiation, 344
Perfectly elastic demand curve, 78
Perfectly inelastic demand curve, 78
Perfect price discrimination (PPD), 524
Performance-based pay, 14
Performance excuse, 553, 554
Performing arts, 20
Performing loans, 259
Permits, 635–636
Personal communications service (PCS),
  589–590
Personal computer industry, 332, 359,
  382, 386
Personal digital assistants (PDAs), 640
Personify, 523–524
Peru, 209
PetroChina, 189
Petroleum refineries, 249–250
Pfizer, 15, 399, 526–527
Pharmaceutical industry, 15
Philip Morris, 436
Pickens, T. Boone, 41
Pillsbury, 519
Pittsburgh National, 259
Planned obsolescence, 478–479
Plant and equipment expenditure plans,
  158
Plant-level internal economies of scale,
  294–295
Pollution rights, 635
Polynomial transformation, 135–136
Pooling equilibrium, 566
Population regression coefficients, 105–107,
  110–111
Porter, Michael, 332, 336, 339
Positioning, of product, 72
Positive autocorrelation, 127–128
Post Cereals, 436
Post-contractual opportunistic behavior,
  555
Post-purchase discounting risk, 479–481
PPD. *See* Perfect price discrimination (PPD)
Pre-commitments, 489–492
Predatory pricing, 461
Premier (smokeless cigarette), 12
Present value, 49
Present value interest factor (PVIF), 48–49

Price change
  of purchasing power effect, 68
  substitution effect of, 68–71
Price competition, 345–346
Price cost margin (PCM), 347
Price discrimination, 522–524, 623
Price elasticity of demand
  in absolute values, 77
  in automobile dealerships, 72–73
  for coffee, 84
  combined use with demand elasticities,
    92–93
  defined, 64, 73
  and differential pricing, 508–512
  electricity use, 92
  empirical, 85
  factors affecting, 84–87
  free trade and, 86
  for gasoline, 73–75
  marginal revenue and, 78, 80–82
  and percentage of consumer's budget, 86
  in pizza restaurants, 72
  and positioning of income-superior
    products, 87
  and price levels for monopolists, 391–392
  and revenues, 76–77, 82–84
  Seiko watches and, 93
  and substitute goods, 86
  and time period of adjustment, 87
Price fixing, 419, 618
Price leadership
  barometric, 430–431
  defined, 430
  dominant firm, 431–432
Priceline, 597–599
Price-matching guarantees, 462–463
Price-output determination
  algebraic approach, 390–391
  graphical approach, 389–390
  for monopolist, 388–392
  under monopolistic competition, 360–363
  of natural monopoly, 402
  and price elasticity of demand, 391–392
  under pure competition, 353–360
  spreadsheet approach, 388–389
Price premiums, 374–376
Price signaling, 464
Price skimming, 525
Price variation, 217
Price wars
  avoiding, 435–440
  customer segmentation with revenue
    management, 436
  and innovation, 438–439
  and market growth, 436
  matching price cuts with increased
    advertising, 440
  nonprice tactics in, 440
  reference prices and framing effects, 437
Pricing. *See also* Costs
  bundling, 519–522

congestion, 513–515
couponing, 518–519
differential, in target market segments, 513–527
and direct segmentation, 514–515
dynamic, 516
full-cost, 525–527
incremental contribution analysis, 526–528
on the Internet, 528–531
life cycle pricing, 524–526
limit, 526–527
niche, 526–527
optimal differential, 504–512
penetration, 524
price discrimination, 512, 522–524
price skimming, 524
reservation prices, 519
target return-on-investment, 526, 527
two-part tariffs, 516–518
value-based, 500–504
value-in-use, 502
Prilosec (drug), 639
Primary benefits, 665
Primary costs, 665
Principal-agent model, alternative managerial contracts, 559–560
Principal-agent problem, 11–15, 563–564
Prisoners' Dilemma, 451–453
    Bayesian reputation effects, 460
    chain store paradox, 457–459
    endgame reasoning, 457
    Folk theorem, 456–457
    grim trigger strategy, 456
    industry standards, 464–465
    infinitely repeated games, 457
    mutual forbearance and cooperation in, 459
    price-matching guarantees, 462–463
    trembling hand trigger strategy, 456
    unraveling problem, 457
    winning strategies, 460–462
Prius (automobile), 71
Private-value auctions, 592–594
Proactive price discrimination, 539–540
Probability distributions, 52–53
    of annual net cash flows (NCF), 52
    probability, defined, 52
    risk and, 52–53
Problem, identification of, 5
Process rays, 256–257
Procter & Gamble, 224, 365, 563
Product differentiation strategy, 336–337
Production capacity, 320–321
Production function
    in automobile assembly plant, 241
    average product, 239–240
    Cobb-Douglas, 237, 260–261
    defined, 236
    determining optimal combination of inputs, 252–255

fixed input, 237–238
increasing returns with network effects, 241–243
inputs, 236
law of diminishing marginal returns, 240–241
long run, 238
for major league baseball, 262–264
marginal, 239–240
marginal rate of technical substitution, 250–252
with multiple variable inputs, 248–252
with one variable input, 239–246
production isoquants, 248–249
short run, 238
total product, 244–246
variable input, 237–238
Production isoquants, 248–249
Production process
    allocative efficiency, 257
    defined, 256
    fixed proportions, 255–257
    measuring efficiency of, 257–258
    overall production efficiency, 258
    and process rays, 256–257
    technical efficiency, 258
    technical inefficiency, 258
Production worker elasticity, 262
Product-level internal economies of scale, 292–293
Product life cycle, 524–526
Product positioning, 72
Profit
    cartels, 421–426
    and executive compensation, 13
    innovation theory of, 9
    managerial efficiency theory of, 9
    maximizing, 390–391
    monopoly theory of, 9
    risk-bearing theory of, 8–9
    temporary disequilibrium theory of, 9
    vs. revenue maximization, 388–389
Property rights, 189
Prospect theory, 572–574
Protection level, 542
Protective tariffs, 212–214, 217
Prozac (drug), 15, 225, 399, 526, 638
Public goods, 20
Public sector, 19–20
Public Service Company of New Mexico (PNM), 400
Public utilities, 399
Purchasing power effect, 68
Purchasing power parity
    absolute, 198
    Big Mac index of, 204
    qualifications of, 202
    relative, 201–202
    trade-weighted exchange rate index, 204–206
    use of, 202–204

as yardstick of comparative growth, 199–200
Pure competition
    characteristics of, 350–351
    contestable markets, 351
    long run, 357–360
    price-output determination under, 353–360
    profit maximization under, 356–357
    short run, 361
Purina, 519

Q
QUALCOMM, 641
Quanta Computer, 187
Queue service rules, 583

R
Railroads, 629–630
Random fluctuations, 143–144
Random rationing, 493
Ratio to trend method, 148–149
Rawlings Sporting Goods, 336
Razor market, 439
R&D. See Research and development (R&D)
Ready-to-eat (RTE) cereal industry, 366, 435, 436
Real options, 17
Real terms of trade, 211
Reciprocal externalities, 629–630
Reciprocal transformation, 135
Recontracting costs, 18–19
Recording companies, 81
Recreational facilities, 20
Red Hat, 642
Reference prices, 437
Refineries, 249–250
Refusals to deal, 624
Refuse collection and disposal, 295
Regression analysis, 100
Regulated monopolies, 399–401
    electric power companies, 400–401
    natural gas companies, 401
    public utilities, 399
    rationale for regulation, 401–402
Regulatory agencies, 626
Relational contracts, 568–570
Relative purchasing power parity, 201–202
Relevant market, 339
Reliance relationships, 371
Reliant assets, 568
Renewable resources, production economics of, 270–274
Rental cars, 69–70
Repeated games, 450, 457
Replacement cost, 284
Replacement guarantees
    credible commitments, 477
    defined, 475
    hostage mechanism, 475, 476–477
    lease prices and anticipated risks, 481

Replacement guarantees (*continued*)
    planned obsolescence, 478–479
    post-purchase discounting risk, 479–481
Required return, 57–58
Resale price maintenance agreements,
    624–625
Resale value, 478
Research and development (R&D), 305–306
Research In Motion, 6
Reservation prices, 519
Residual claimants, 19
Resource allocation, 11
    marginal analysis and, 43
Resources, scarcity of, 31
Restricted stock, 12, 15
Restructuring, corporate, 12–13
Retail gasoline firms, 415–416
Retail gas stations, gasoline prices and, 39
Returns to scale
    Cobb-Douglas production function and,
        260–261
    decreasing, 260
    defined, 258
    increasing, 260
    measuring, 259–260
Revenue
    maximizing, 388–389
    and price elasticity, 76–77
    and price elasticity of demand, 82–84
Revenue equivalence theorem, 596–598
Revenue management
    in baseball, 545
    capacity reallocation, 540–542
    cross-functional, 536–537
    decisions, 538–546
    defined, 537
    optimal overbooking in, 542–546
    proactive price discrimination in,
        539–540
    sources of sustainable price premiums,
        538
    spill, 535–536
    spoilage, 535–536
    stockouts, 535
Risk
    and coefficient of variation, 56–57
    defined, 52
    and expected value, 53
    measurement of, 52–57
    and net present value, 51
    and normal probability distribution,
        54–55
    premium, 57–58
    and probability distributions, 52–53
    and required return, 57–58
    and standard deviation, 54
Risk-bearing theory of profit, 8–9
Risk-free return, 57–58
Rivalry, intensity of, 345–349
R.J. Reynolds, 435
RJR Nabisco, 12

Robinson-Patman Act, 464, 616–617, 623
Root mean square error (RMSE), 142
Royal Caribbean, 452–453, 461–463
Russell Stover Candies, 99

S

Sales force polling, 159
Sales forecasting, 159
Sales penetration curve, 385
Sales promotion, 296
Sample regression line, 105–106
Samsung, 382, 419, 420, 443, 490–491,
    570–571, 637
Sara Lee Corp., 44–45
    capital budgeting decision, 44–45
    marginal analysis, 44–45
Saturn Corporation, 6
Saudi Arabia
    crude oil pricing, 276–277, 424–425
    crude oil production, 276–279, 426
Sawyer, Diane, 18
Scala S.p.A., 206–207
Scarcity of resources, market value and, 31
Schering-Plough Corp., 388, 399
Schick-Wilkinson Sword, 439
Schwinn, 569
Seagate, 571
Sea-Land/Maersk, 584
Search goods, 368
Seasonal effects, 143
    dummy variables, 149–150
    ratio to trend method, 148–149
Second-highest sealed-bid auctions,
    594–596
Secular trends
    constant rate of growth trends, 147–148
    declining rate of growth trends, 148
    defined, 143
    linear trends, 146–147
    types of, 145
Securities and Exchange Commission (SEC),
    158, 626
Seiko, 93
Self-enforcing reliance relationship, 604–605
Selling
    and optimal advertising intensity, 365–366
    optimal level of, 364–365
    and promotional expenses, 363–367
Selten, Reinhard, 449, 457, 468
Semiconductor industry, 216, 459–460, 571
Semilogarithmic transformation, 134
Sensitivity analysis, 5
Separating equilibrium, 566–567
Sequential coordination game, 466–468
Sequential game, 452
    analyzing, 465–468
    business rivalry as, 469–471, 469–472
    defined, 452
    game tree, 466
    sequential coordination game, 466–468
    subgame perfect equilibrium strategy, 468

7-Eleven Japan, 338
Sewell, Carl, 373
Sewell Cadillac, 373
Shanghai, China, 184–190
Shanghai Zhong Qi Pharmaceutical, 225
Shapiro, Carl, 478
Shareholders, and executive compensation,
    13–14
Shareholder value
    and asymmetric information, 18
    and complete markets, 17
    and recontracting costs, 18–19
    residual claimants, 19
Shareholder wealth
    defined, 10
    maximization, implications of, 15–19
    measuring, 10
    and resource allocation, 11
Sheet steel, 214–215
Shell, 41, 42
Sherman Act, 91, 615
Sherwin-Williams Company, 100–101,
    107–108
    correlation coefficients, 130
    estimated regression line, 108
    explained sum of squares (SS) for, 115
    simple regression equation of, 107
    total sum of squares (SS) for, 115
    unexplained sum of squares (SS)
        for, 115
Shipping, 584
Short run, 238, 353–356
Short-run cost functions, 286–290
    average and marginal cost functions,
        286–290
    Deep Creek Mining Company example,
        286–287
    statistical estimation of, 310–311
    variable, fixed, and total cost functions,
        288
Siemens, 428, 429, 604
Silicon wafers, 295
Simple linear regression model, 103–108
    assumptions, 104–105
Simultaneous games, 451–455, 452
Single-equation models, 159–161
Slippery slope, 497–498
Smoothing techniques
    barometric techniques, 156–157
    first-order exponential smoothing,
        153–155
    moving averages, 151–153
    overview, 150
Social discount rate, 661
Soft drink industry, 345–346, 454, 456
Sony BMG Music Corp., 618
Sony Corp., 242, 243, 355, 438
Sound Warehouse, 474
South America, 179, 209
Southern California Edison, 235
Southern Company, 2–4, 17

Southland Corp., 338
Southwest Airlines, 335, 337, 444
Specification errors, 130–131
Speculation, 193
    crude oil, 42–43
Sperm whale oil, 31
    production cost, 31
Spill, 535–536
Spoilage, 535–536
Sport Obermeyer, 536, 543
Spot market transactions, 554, 555
Spur Industries v. Del Webb Development,
    628
Standard deviation, 54
Standard error of the estimate, 108–109
Staples, 91, 343
Starbucks Corp., 17
State excise taxes, on cigarettes, 65–66
State Grid Corporation, 189
Steel, 186–187, 209, 213, 214–215, 220, 221
Steel ingot, 316
Steel production, 316
Stents, 503
Sterilized interventions, 192
Stochastic disturbance, 104
Stochastic time-series analysis, 163–165
Stock options, 14, 562–563, 565
Stockouts, 535, 542, 543
Stocks, 58
    biotech, 58
    emerging market, 58
Strategic holdout, 631
Strategic positioning, 336
Strategic trade policy, 214–215
Strategies
    cost-based, 337
    information technology, 338
Strategy game, 447
Strategy process, 334
Stratified lotteries, 585
Stride Rite, 625–626
StubHub.com, 585
Subgame perfect equilibrium strategy, 468
Subsidies, 633–635
Substitute goods, 34, 86, 90, 112, 340–341
Substitution effect, 68–71
Sulfur dioxide (SOX) emissions, 2–3, 18
Sunk cost, 285, 493–494
    at Dunbar Manufacturing Company,
        285–286
    of underutilized facilities, 285
Sun Microsystems, 195, 387, 388, 471–472,
    623
Super Bowl, 589
Supermarket pricing, 508
Superstores, 91
Suppliers, power of, 344–345
Supply. See also Demand
    change in, 38
    and demand, 29–31
    and equilibrium market price, 29–31

factors and expected effect, 37
    speculative, 40
Supply curves, 38. See also Demand curves
    movement along, 38
    shift of, 38
Supply function, 37
Survey of Current Business, 158
Surveys
    Blue Chip Economic Indicators forecaster
        surveys, 162–163
    consumer expenditure plans, 159
    of consumer intentions, 159
    inventory changes and sales expectations,
        159
    Livingston surveys, 162–163
    macroeconomic activity, 158–159
    overview, 157
    plant and equipment expenditure plans,
        158
    sales forecasting, 159
Survivor (television show), 447
Survivor technique, 316–317
Sustainability, 2
Sustainable competitive advantages, 336
Sylvania, 569

T

Taco Bell, 322–323
Taiwan Instrument Co., 509–512
Targeting, customer, 71
Target return-on-investment pricing,
    526–527
Tariffs, 212–215, 217
Taurel, Sidney, 15
Taxes, 633–635
Teamwork
    importance of, 6
    moral hazard problem in, 6–7
Technical efficiency, 258
Telecom industries, 386
Temporary disequilibrium theory
    of profit, 9
Tenneco shipyard, marginal analysis
    and, 43
Tesco, 224
Texaco-Chevron, 17
Texas Instruments (TI), 593, 600
Theme parks, 383
Theory of Games and Economic Behavior,
    The (Von Neumann/Morgenstern),
    449
Thomson, 428, 429
Threat of substitutes, 340–341
Threshold sales curve, 541
Ticketmaster, 585
Tillotson, Rex, 12
Time depreciation, 307
Time series
    components of, 143–144
    cyclical variations, 143
    data, 143–144

defined, 127
    elementary models, 144–145
    models, 144–145
    random fluctuations, 143
    seasonal effects, 143, 148–150
    secular trends, 143, 145–148
    smoothing techniques, 150–155
Times Mirror Co., 635
Time Warner, 313, 519, 588
Tobacco tax, 64–66
Toll roads, 514–515
Toshiba, 242, 570, 604, 637
Total cost, 355
Total product, 244–246
Total profit, 44–48
    average profit and, 44
    functions, 47–48
    marginal profit and, 44
Total revenue, 81, 362
Townsend-Greenspan, 162
Toyota Motors, 4–5, 179, 180, 182,
    185, 203, 212, 222, 280, 281, 478,
    666, 667
Tradable pollution allowances (TPAs),
    2–3, 18
Trade deficit, 225–226
Trade secrets, 637–641
Trade-weighted exchange rate index,
    204–206
Trading blocs, 207–210
Transaction risk exposure, 180, 230
Translation risk exposure, 181–182, 230
Transportation costs, 296
Treasury bills, 57–58, 158
    risk-free return, 57
Treasury bond, 158
Trembling hand trigger strategy, 456
Tversky, Amos, 572
Two-part tariffs, 516–518
Two-person game, 450–451
Two-person zero-sum game, 450
Tying arrangements, 623–624

U

U.K. Department of Business, Enterprise,
    and Regulatory Reform, 50
Underbidding, 592–594
United Airlines, 337
United Auto Workers (UAW), 38, 281
United-Continental Airlines, 436
United States
    bilateral trade with Japan, 211
    destination of exports, 222
    energy policy, 277
    exports, 176–179, 194–195, 207–210
    exports to China, 176–179
    gross domestic product, 176–179, 194,
        196, 209
    oil reserves, 276–279
    oligopoly in, 411–416
    trade deficit, 225–226

United States (*continued*)
  trading bloc, 207–210, 222
  trading partners, 186, 220–225
United Steel Workers (USW), 215
Unit elastic demand, 78–79
Universal Music Group, 618
Universal Studios, 383
Unraveling problem, 457
Uruguay, 209
U.S. Army Corps of Engineers, 246
U.S. Department of Commerce, 140,
  158–159, 166
U.S. Department of Energy, 39
U.S. dollar
  depreciation, 180, 191, 194–195, 206
  equilibrium price, 192
  foreign exchange market for, 190–193
U.S. Treasury bills, 57–58, 595
US Airways, 53, 348–349, 444–445, 493
UUNet, 140

V
Value at risk, 219
Value-based pricing, 501–504
Value-Mart Company, 150–151
Value proposition, 334, 394
Variable costs, 216, 217, 286
Variable identification, 100–101
Variable input
  defined, 237
  determining the optimal use of, 246–248
  long run, 238
  marginal factor cost, 247
  marginal revenue product, 247

  multiple, 248–252
  optimal input level, 247–248
  short run, 238
Variable input costs, 286
Varian, Hal, 478
Verizon, 469, 516
Versioning, 478
Vertical integration, 574–577
Vertical requirements contracts, 551–552
VF Corporation, 112
Vickrey, William, 594–595
Vickrey auction, 594–596
Virtual Vineyards, 523–524
Volkswagen (VW), 82–84
Volt, Chevy, 500–501
Volume discounts, 292
Voluntary import restraints (VIRs), 212
Volvo, 36
Von Neumann, John, 449

W
Walgreens, 573
Walker Corporation, 152–153, 155
Walmart, 91, 179, 220, 242
Warner Brothers, 242
Warner Music Group Corp., 618
Wars of attrition, 495–497
Web browsers, 342, 388, 623, 624
WebTV, 548–549, 570
Weighted cost of capital, 659–660
Western Digital, 571
Westside Plumbing and Heating Company,
  284–285
Whale oil, 31

Wharton Econometric Forecasting
  Associates, 162
Whirlpool, 606
Whitman's Sampler, 99–100, 394
  marketing mix for, 99
Whole Foods Inc., 622
Wholesale price discrimination, 623
Wide-bodied jets, 309
Wide-body aircraft, 413, 415
Wild Oats Markets, 622
Willingness to pay (WTP), 633, 634
Windows operating system, 242, 332, 478,
  617, 623
Winner's curse, 587–589
Winning strategies, 460–462
Wireless Co., 589–591
World Bank, 212
WorldCom, 103, 139–140, 559
World Trade Organization (WTO), 166,
  187, 188, 208, 210, 213–214, 216

X
Xerox, 335

Y
Yield management. *See* Revenue
  management
Yogurt, 86
You Ke (drug), 225
Young, Steve, 76

Z
Zantac (drug), 526

NOTES

NOTES

NOTES

NOTES

NOTES

NOTES

NOTES

NOTES

Example: Price Competition at the Soda Fountain:
PepsiCo Inc.   345
Example: Contribution Margins at Hanes Discourage
Discounting   347
Example: Intensity of Rivalry at US Airways   348
Example: Flat Screen Televisions Lose $126 per
Unit Sold: Sony Corporation   355
Example: Gasoline Price Rises to Record Levels Reflecting
a Spike in Crude Oil Input Costs   356
Example: Copper Price Rise by 400 Percent Contributes
to Housing Bubble   359
What Went Right/What Went Wrong: The Dynamics
of Competition at Amazon.com   361
Example: Long-Run Price and Output Determination:
Blockbuster, Inc.   362
Example: Optimal Advertising at Parkway Ford   364
Example: Ford and P&G Tie Ad Agency Pay to Sales   365
Example: Optimal Advertising Intensity at Kellogg's and
General Mills   366
Example: Credible Product Replacement Claims: Dooney &
Bourke   372
Example: Customers for Life at Sewell Cadillac   373
Example: Hostage Exchange with Efficient Uncut
Diamond Sorting at De Beers   375
Case Exercise: Netflix and Redbox Compete for Movie Rentals   379
Case Exercise: Saving Sony Music   380

Chapter 11: Price and Output Determination: Monopoly and Dominant Firms   382

Managerial Challenge: Dominant Microprocessor
Company Intel Adapts to Next Trend   382
Example: The Mickey Mouse Monopoly: Disney   383
Example: What Went Right at Microsoft but Wrong
at Apple Computer   386
What Went Right/What Went Wrong: Pilot Error at Palm   387
Example: Margins on K.P. McLahe Polo Shirts   389
Example: Profit Maximization for a Theme Park Restaurant   390
Example: Price Elasticity and Price Levels for Monopolists   392
Example: Markups and Contribution Margins on Chanel
No. 5, Ole Musk, and Whitman's Sampler   394
Example: Components of the Gross Margin at Kellogg Co.   396
Example: Pfizer Sustains Sales of Off-Patent Lipitor   399
What Went Right/What Went Wrong: The Public Service
Company of New Mexico   400
Case Exercise: Differential Pricing of Pharmaceuticals:
The HIV/AIDS Crisis   407

Chapter 12: Price and Output Determination: Oligopoly   409

Managerial Challenge: Google's Android and Apple's
iPhone Displace Nokia in Smart phones?   409
Example: Google's Chrome Takes Share from Once
Dominant Browser Internet Explorer   412
Example: Auto Rental and Retail Gasoline Firms
Consolidate: Enterprise Rent-A-Car, and Exxon/Mobil   415
Example: Airline Pricing: The Pittsburgh Market   417
Example: The Cournot Oligopoly Solution: Siemens
and Alcatel-Lucent   417
Example: How Ocean Shipping Conferences Have Affected
Shipping Rates   419
Example: DRAM Chipmakers Pay Enormous Fines
for Forming a Global Cartel   420
Example: Coffee Pricing Agreement Dissolves amidst
Dilemma   422
The OPEC Cartel   423
Example: Exhaustible Natural Resources: Saudi Arabia
Plays a Waiting Game   424

Example: What Drives the Price per Gallon of Gasoline
Above $3.00?   426
Example: Revenue-Sharing in Major League Baseball   430
Example: Barometric Price Leadership: American Airlines   431
Example: Price Leadership: Aerotek   432
Example: Price Wars at General Mills and Post   436
What Went Right/What Went Wrong: Good-Better-Best
Product Strategy at Marriott Corporation and Kodak   438
Example: What Went Right at Interlink Surgical Steel
and Gillette?   439
Example: Non-price Tactics in a Price War: Coors   440
Case Exercise: Web-Based Satellite Phones Displace
Motorola's Mobile Phone   443

Chapter 13: Best-Practice Tactics: Game Theory   444

Managerial Challenge: Large-Scale Entry Deterrence of
Low-Cost Discounters: Southwest Airline/AirTran   444
What Went Right/What Went Wrong: Nintendo's Wii U   446
Example: The Nobel Prize Goes to Three Game Theorists   449
Example: Solving the Chain Store Paradox: Semiconductor
Pricing at Intel, Motorola, and AMD   459
Example: Brown and Williamson's Reputation for Predating   461
Example: Signaling a Punishment Scheme: Northwest   463
Example: Business Gaming at Verizon   469
Example: Technology Leader or Fast-Second: IBM   471
Example: Double-the-Difference Price Guarantees: Best Buy   474
Example: Noncredible Commitments: Burlington Industries   476
Example: Resale Value of a Mini Cooper   478
Example: Leasing Digital Moviehouse Projectors: Hughes-JVC   479
Example: NetJets Fractional Ownership Plans for Learjet
and Gulfstream Aircraft and Lexus   480
Case Exercise: The Superjumbo Dilemma   487

Appendix 13A: Entry Deterrence and Accommodation Games   489

Example: Excess Capacity in the World Car Market:
Samsung and Hyundai   490
Example: Contestable Market in Bicycle Helmets:
Bell Sports   494
Example: Circuit City Driven over the Brink   497

Chapter 14: Pricing Techniques and Analysis   500

Managerial Challenge: Pricing the Chevy Volt   500
Example: Coated Coronary Stents Reduce the Cost of
Later Surgeries   503
Example: Supermarket Pricing   508
Example: Differential Pricing at Taiwan Instrument Co.   509
Example: Congestion Charges on Los Angeles, San Diego,
Houston, Minneapolis, Denver, and Dulles Toll Roads   514
Example: Dynamic Pricing for Electricity   516
What Went Right/What Went Wrong: Unlimited Data at
Verizon Wireless   516
What Went Right/What Went Wrong: Two-Part Pricing
at Disney World   518
What Went Right/What Went Wrong: Price-Sensitive
Customers Redeem   519
Example: McDonald's Introduces Mixed Bundles as
"Extra Value Meals"   521
Example: e-Business Clickstreams Allow Price
Discrimination: Personify and Virtual Vineyards   523
Example: Loss of Patent Protection Limits the Price of
Prozac: Eli Lilly   526
Example: Niche Pricing at Pfizer   526
Example: Full-Cost Pricing Results in the Loss of a Big
Contract at J.P. Morgan: British Telephone   527
Example: Incremental Contribution Analysis at
Continental/United Airlines   528
Example: Amazon Pioneers e-Book Pricing   530